The New
**Combined
Bible
Dictionary**
and
Concordance

The New Combined Bible Dictionary and Concordance

With Introduction on
How to Study the Bible
by
Charles F. Pfeiffer

MARSHALL·PICKERING

First published in the U.K. in 1990 by Marshall Pickering

Copyright © 1961 C.D. Stampley Enterprises Inc. U.S.A.

Marshall Pickering is an imprint of Collins Religious Division,
part of Collins Publishing Group, 8 Graften Street, London W1X 3LA

ISBN: 0 551 01969 7

Printed in Great Britain by Courier International, Tiptree, Essex.

Introduction to
The New Combined
Bible Dictionary and Concordance

"Study to shew thyself approved unto God, a workman that needeth not to be ashamed, rightly dividing the word of truth" (*II Tim. 2:15*), is the challenge of the Holy Bible to its readers and followers. In order to facilitate study of the Bible two basic tools are needed: a dictionary of the Bible, and a concordance of the Bible. It is the purpose of this work to provide in one convenient alphabetical listing these two basic tools, a dictionary and a concordance.

WHAT IS INCLUDED

There are over 10,000 entries in alphabetical order in *The New Combined Bible Dictionary and Concordance.* The present work is not a revision of an older work, but is a completely new and fresh approach made by a number of Biblical scholars working under the supervision of a general editor.

The Dictionary

The dictionary which is actually a one volume Bible Encyclopedia aims at: Biblical accuracy; historical reliability; universality; and, clarity, conciseness and simplicity. *Biblical Accuracy,* the facts as derived from the Bible are given and following each Biblical statement, a Scriptural reference is given where the reader can check the data for himself. *Historical Reliability,* all of the available results of Biblical archaeology and modern scholarship that help to understand the Bible have been incorporated into the dictionary. *Universality,* the dictionary is not designed for one particular church fellowship, but for every segment of modern Christianity. Concerning those topics where there are diversity of beliefs, each belief has been presented. See for example the article "Baptism." *Clarity, Conciseness, and Simplicity,* to achieve this, each article contains in a readable concise style those facts that help to make clear or illustrate the Scripture.

A Concordance

One of the most used and useful tools for Bible study is a concordance. The purpose of a concordance is to help locate quickly and accurately the exact quotation or the place of the quotation. Contained within the alphabetical listing, there is reference to every key word in the Bible. If one wanted to locate the passage:

> "Behold, a virgin shall conceive, and bear a son, and shall call his name Immanuel."

The key word in the quote is "virgin." Therefore one would look under the word "virgin." Here would be found:

> v. shall conceive, Is. 7:14

Turn to Isaiah 7:14 as indicated, and the desired quotation will be found. If one looked further, they would also find that this very same verse is also found in Matthew 1:23.

A Study Guide

To use *The New Combined Bible Dictionary and Concordance* as a study guide, turn to any topic which you wish to study. There will be found a concise article on the subject. If there is found any word within the article that is not understood or you wish further information on, turn to the place in alphabetical order where that word is treated and read. Many of the articles are written in such a way that they can be used as a study guide in preparing to teach a Bible class on a given subject. Take for example "Jesus." In addition to the Bible, thousands of volumes have been written about Him. But, when one turns to the article "Jesus Christ" here is found in a clearly outlined article the major points of the life and work of Jesus.

HOW TO USE

To use *The New Combined Bible Dictionary and Concordance* the topics are arranged in alphabetical order. First determine the topic to be studied. Secondly, find in the alphabetical listing the article. For example, under the article "Heaven." Heaven appears in capital letters and in bold face type. Following the article there are a number of concordance references which appear thusly:

> God created the *h.*, Gen. 1:1
>
> your Father . . . in *h.*, Matt. 5:16

You will note that the location in the Bible is given by book, chapter and verse.

Thus you have in your hands an extremely useful and convenient tool for the study of the Bible. Keep it within easy reach. Familiarize yourself with its wide usefulness. Use it often. The more you use it, the more you will appreciate its value as a guide to a wider and deeper knowledge of the Bible.

But, before you proceed to a use of this volume you will want to read the introductory article by Dr. Charles F. Pfeiffer, "How to Study the Bible." This will make your study of the Bible doubly profitable.

How to Study the Bible

by Charles F. Pfeiffer

Bible study can be a fascinating experience. Modern archaeological discoveries have increased our knowledge of the backgrounds of Biblical history with the result that we can now understand many Biblical events in the light of their contemporary setting. With the rapid increase in knowledge about the Bible it is well to remind ourselves that the most important source book for Biblical knowledge is still the Bible itself. Secondary sources are of value to the extent that they illuminate the Biblical text. They can profitably supplement our Bible reading, but they must not be allowed to supplant the Scriptures themselves.

Many who are convinced that Bible study is a profitable discipline never study the Bible for themselves because they fear that they will experience difficulty in understanding the text of Scripture. Feeling that the ordinary layman cannot hope to understand the Bible, they leave its interpretation to the professional theologians. The Biblical writers, themselves, addressed the men of their generation in language that was meant to be understood. We do not honor the Bible by placing it in an honored spot in our homes and thereafter neglecting it. We honor Scripture as we seek to understand its message. Although Bible students are not wholly agreed on the rules of sound interpretation, certain principles have commended themselves to most careful scholars.

I. Determine the Literal Meaning of the Text

When faced with apparent contradictions between the statements of Scripture and contemporary philosophical or scientific thought, men have resorted to numerous devices to remove their difficulties. In some instances the secular scholars have been dismissed as enemies of the faith. At other times the Scriptures have been forced into a mold designed to accommodate them to contemporary theories.

One of the earliest means of accommodating Scripture to human knowledge was the process which we term allegorizing. Its origins may be traced to the Greeks whose philosophers and historians were embarrassed at the legends of the gods whose exploits described in classical literature were most ungodlike. Sophisticated thinkers suggested that the stories should not be taken at face value, and that the student should search for deeper meanings in classical literature. In Alexandria, where Greek and Hebrew thinking met, the Jewish scholars Aristobulus and Philo applied the allegorical method of interpretation to the Old Testament Scriptures. Subsequently Origin popularized allegorical interpretation in the early Church.

The allegorist did not always deny the historicity of the Scriptural narrative, but he did insist that the Bible has a deeper meaning than the obvious historical one. In discussing the Book of Genesis, he saw Abraham's journey to Canaan as an allegory which tells the story of a Stoic philosopher who leaves Chaldea (interpreted to mean "sensual understanding") and stops for a time at Haran (interpreted to mean "holes"). The story is thus interpreted as teaching the emptiness of knowing things by the "holes," i.e. the senses. The marriage of Abraham to Sarah is the marriage of the enlightened philosopher to abstract wisdom.[1] When Jacob says, "With my staff I passed over this Jordan," the allegorizer interprets the staff as "discipline" and the Jordan as "baseness." The story is thus taken to mean that by Discipline, Jacob had risen above baseness!"[2]

Such examples of the misuse of Scripture underscore the arbitrary nature of allegory. The allegorist is not content to observe that the Bible contains parables and figures of speech which must be interpreted as such. Rather he makes all of Scripture one gigantic allegory, with no well-defined principles or laws of interpretation. The good taste of the interpreter is the only limit, and when these are missing the results may be ludicrous or tragic.

It is safe to assume that the Biblical writers usually meant what they said. When the Book of Genesis states that Abraham journeyed from Ur to Haran, we are right in concluding that the writer had a specific person and two specific places in mind. Lessons of obedience to a divine call and of a subsequent life of faithfulness can be learned from the story of Abraham. The reader should assume that the text means what it appears to mean. The first rule of interpretation must be, "Wherever possible, interpret the Bible literally."

A warning is necessary even here, however. While the literal meaning is basic to Bible interpretation, it is possible to be so literal in interpreting a passage of Scripture that idiom, literary form, figures of speech, and the history and development of language itself are overlooked. A misguided literalism degenerated into a letterism which produced meanings manifestly different from the intent of the Biblical writers. In the talmudic treatise *Sanhedrin* a scholar argued that the man who made *all* his children pass through the fire to Molech would be guilty of no sin, because Moses only said "thy seed" and not "all thy seed."[3]

To interpret the Bible correctly we must begin by reconstructing, as far as possible, the situation in which the Biblical writer, his hearers and readers moved. History, grammar, modes of thought, idiom, figures of speech, and literary forms are all pertinent. Much of this can be learned from the Bible

[1] Cf. Bernard Ramm, *Protestant Biblical Interpretation,* p. 28.
[2] F. W. Farrar, *History of Interpretation,* p. 141.
[3] F. W. Farrar, *op. cit.,* p. 54

itself as we compare Scripture with Scripture. Bible dictionaries, atlases, and other reference tools will also prove helpful.

II. Interpret the Bible According to Context

It is unfair to take a statement from any book out of its context. We do not honor the Bible when we make it a collection of texts which may be lifted from the sacred page at our pleasure and used in any way we see fit. We honor the Bible when we take it as it stands, in its entirety, and when we seek to understand the part that each passage plays in the presentation of the total message.

Everything in the Bible is not a word from God. We read the words of Satan (cf. Job 1:9-11) and the messages of Israel's enemies who are regarded as God's enemies as well. The Assyrian Rabshakeh taunted the Judaeans for their trust in God and urged them to surrender to his king, Sennacherib (Isa. 36:1-20). Such passages are written for our instruction, but we only interpret them correctly as we note the speaker and the circumstances under which the message is given.

A command or a promise of Scripture may be meaningful only in a specific context. Because of impending catastrophe, Jeremiah was commanded not to marry (Jer. 16:1-4). This cannot be quoted as a scriptural argument for celibacy, for the same prophet urged the exiles who had gone to Babylon to marry and raise families (Jer. 29:5-7). Jerusalem was soon to be destroyed, therefore Jeremiah was told to refrain from marriage. On the other hand, the Babylonian exile was to last a long time — seventy years — so that the Jews in Babylonia would have time to marry, raise families, and see their grandchildren grow to maturity in the land of their captivity. Each command was meaningful in its own context.

To the evangelist Luke, "the world" was the Roman world. When he speaks of a decree from Caesar Augustus that "all the world should be taxed" (or "enrolled") we are reminded of the vastness of the Roman Empire under Augustus, but we would not think of including India or China in that "world" in which the decree of Augustus was binding (cf. Luke 2:1).

Similarly in Genesis 41 we read of a seven year famine in the days of Joseph. The Biblical writer states that it was "severe over all the earth" (Gen. 41:57). To ask whether there was famine in Europe or America during the days of Joseph is beside the point. The "world" of the Patriarchs was the Fertile Crescent, and it was Egypt and Syria-Palestine that are relevant to the story of Joseph and his brothers. In a time of famine, Joseph's brothers who lived in Palestine had to turn to Egypt for help. It is in this context that we understand a famine "over all the earth."

III. Be Aware of Figures of Speech

Every language has its distinctive idiom. Similes, metaphors, and other figures of speech are readily recognizable in one's native tongue, but they may perplex outsiders. Palestinian Jews had no difficulty understanding the metaphor "that fox" which Jesus used of Herod (Luke 13:32).

Jesus used many metaphors in describing his relationship to his people. Frequently on his lips were such expressions as, "I am the door," "I am the vine," and "I am the good shepherd." We must not expect a mechanical consistency in the use of metaphors, however. Satan, or Christ, may be the "lion" depending on the lesson to be conveyed. The devil is "a roaring lion, walking about, seeking whom he may devour" (I Peter 5:8). Jesus, in another context, is "the lion of the tribe of Judah" (Rev. 5:5). In the first instance the lion is thought of as a ferocious animal, in the second his regal majesty is emphasized.

Examples of parables are found in both the Old and the New Testaments. In general, the parable is designed to teach a particular lesson, and background information should not be treated as allegory. In Judges 9, Jotham, a son of Gideon, tells a parable about a group of trees who wanted to choose a king for themselves. The olive tree, the fig tree, and the vine showed no interest in the job, for they all had worthwhile tasks to perform. Only the bramble (or thorn) was willing to accept the position as king. The message of the parable was clear to Jotham's audience. The person who desires to boss others is not doing anything worthwhile himself.

IV. Be Aware of the Phenomenal Nature of Biblical Language

The Bible is written in popular rather than scientific language. It was addressed to all men, not to an intellectually elite class. When Bible students call the language of Scripture "phenomenal" they mean that it is the language of appearance. The sun appears to rise and set, so the Biblical writers (as well as modern speakers and writers) speak of the rising and setting of the sun. The scientific mind might object to this terminology, but it describes phenomena as they appear to man. Even in a scientific age such terms are read and understood by intelligent people.

The earth does not have four corners, but the Biblical writers do not hesitate to speak of "the four corners of the earth." This should pose no problem to the Bible interpreter. It is equivalent in meaning to the four points of the compass.

Biblical history is written according to the principles of ancient Semetic historical literature, and it should not be judged on the basis of modern standards for historical writing. There are no quotation marks in the Bible, and no effort is made to distinguish between direct and indirect discourse. No system of documentation is used, although Biblical writers occasionally name such sources as *The Book of the Wars of the Lord* and *The Book of Jasher*. The first verse of Hebrews asserts that God had spoken "at sundry times and in divers manners".

V. Be Aware of the Literary Forms of Biblical Literature

To apply the rules for the interpretation of prose to poetry would result in confusion. Poetry generally uses archaic vocabulary and grammatical forms, and is more inclined toward the use of figures of speech than is prose. Semitic poetry characteristically uses parallelism instead of end-rhyme. Parallelism is not rigid, but the recognition of its existence often serves as an aid to interpretation. When three elements of parallel structure are known, the fourth may frequently be anticipated. In Psalm 49:1, we read:

> Hear this, all ye peoples,
> Give ear, all ye inhabitants of the earth.

The words "Hear" and "Give ear" are synonymous. Similarly the words "peoples" and "inhabitants of the earth" must refer to the same individuals. Bible scholars speak of this as an example of Synonymous Parallelism.

Sometimes a second line explains the meaning of the line that preceded it. In Psalm 29:3 we read, "The voice of the Lord is upon the waters." Without a feeling for poetic writing we might wonder what the words mean until we go on and read, "The God of glory thundereth." The Psalmist is depicting thunder as the voice of God. God is not removed from nature, for He is vitally involved in all its manifestations.

Of help in providing a basis for interpretation are those events which are described in both prose and poetry. Judges, Chapters 4 and 5, recounts the victory of the Israelites over the Canaanites in the days of Deborah and Barak. The prose account of the battle against Sisera's Canaanite army appears in Judges 4. The Canaanites were routed, and their general fled on foot, only to be slain by the valiant Jael. In the poetic account recorded in Judges 5, commonly termed the Song of Deborah, we read that the stars from their courses fought against Sisera (5:20). The poet tells us that Israel's God marshalled the forces of nature to bring about the defeat of the Canaanite foe. Both the prose and the poetic accounts are worthy of study in their own right. It is clear, however, that the prose should be read as prose, and the poetry as poetry.

VI. Be Aware of the Progressive Nature of Revelation

The opening verses of the Epistle to the Hebrews contrast the message God gave through prophetic writers of the Old Testament with God's last word in His Son. In the Old Testament as well as the New, God had spoken, but Christ is the crown and goal of all revelation. Jesus declared, "In the roll of the book it is written of me" (Heb. 10:7, quoting Ps. 40:7).

Jesus makes it clear that some things were permitted in the Mosaic Law because of the hardness of men's hearts (Mark 10:5). The fact that polygamy, divorce, and kindred ills were tolerated in Old Testament times does not justify the Christian in living according to these practices. Jesus made it clear that such customs were not in accord with God's original pattern (Mark 10:6-9). The Law was adapted to the depraved condition of the society to which it was addressed. In Christ, the Christian recognizes the fulfillment of Old Testament promise and hope.

VII. Be Aware of the Fact That Some Bible Questions Cannot Readily Be Answered

Every science has problems and scientific Bible study is no exception. The basic teachings of Scripture are clear, and the student should not allow the presence of problems to spoil his enjoyment of the Bible as a whole. Mature Christians of every age have not hesitated to plead ignorance on occasion. In discussing commentaries on the Book of Revelation, Charles H. Spurgeon professed to be confused at "these apocalyptic visions."

Our ignorance is attributable to a variety of causes. As finite beings we cannot hope for infinite knowledge. As sinful beings our minds do not function perfectly. We are removed in language, geography, and time from the world in which the events of Biblical history took place. The marvel is not that we are puzzled at so much, but that so much is clear to us. Paul said, "Now we see through a glass, darkly" (I Cor. 13:12), and, "We know in part" (I Cor. 13:9). These thoughts are applicable to our Bible study.

The Christian who approaches Scripture with a prayerful dependence on the Holy Spirit, and a will to know God's will, will find his life taking on a new dimension. Never able to boast perfection, he will nevertheless grow to spiritual maturity as he feeds on the riches of Scripture.

The New
Combined
Bible
Dictionary
and
Concordance

The New Combined Bible Dictionary and Concordance

A

A, sometimes used in the King James with a verbal noun to denote a process or a continued action (Luke 8:42, 9:42; John 21:3; Heb.11:21; I Pet. 3:20).

AARON, the first high priest of Israel: of the family of Kohath the second son of Levi, third son of Jacob. He was the brother of Moses; his parents were Amram and Jochebed (Ex. 6:20). He was an excellent speaker, and he was selected to be Moses' spokesman before Pharaoh. He later was persuaded by the people to make a molten image, for which Moses rebuked him. He died at Mount Hor about forty years after the Israelites left Egypt.
spokesman of Moses, Ex. 4:14.
son of Amram, Ex. 6:20.
had four sons, Ex. 6:23.
speaks with Pharaoh, Ex. 7:2.
works miracles, Ex. 7:10, 19.
supports Moses' hand, Ex. 17:12.
makes golden calf, Ex. 32:4.
becomes priest, Lev. 8:1–9.
murmurs with Miriam, Num. 12:2.
dies on Mount Hor, Deut. 32:50.
chosen by God, Ps. 105:26.

AARONIC, pertaining to **Aaron** and the Levitical priesthood.

AARONITES, descendants of Aaron; therefore priests. Their leader was Zadok (I Chr. 27:17).

AARON'S ROD, a staff carried by Aaron. It became a snake (Ex. 7:9–12, 15), and later budded, showing divine approval of Moses and Aaron (Num. 17:1).

AB, the fifth religious month and the eleventh civil month of the Jewish year.

Mentioned merely as the fifth month in the Scripture (Num. 33:38).

AB, the first of several Hebrew compounds, which means father. For instance, Absalom means father of peace.

ABADDON, the angel of the bottomless pit (Rev. 9:11). The word means destruction, i.e., Hades (Job 26:6; Prov. 15:11).

ABAGTHA, one of the seven chief eunuchs of Xerxes (Esther 1:10).

ABANA, one of the rivers of Damascus (II Kin. 5:12); perhaps one which Naaman would have washed in.

ABARIM, a mountain chain S.E. of the Dead Sea. Pisgah, or Mount Nebo, is a part (Deut. 3:27; 32:49).

ABASE, to make low.
everyone proud, and *a.*, Job. 40:11.
exalt low, and *a.*, Ezek. 21:26.
he is able to *a.*, Dan 4:37.

ABASED, to be made low, to be humbled.
shall be abased, Matt. 23:12.
I know how to be *a.*, Phil. 4:12.

ABATED, to be diminished, to be lacking.
waters were *a.*, Gen. 8:3, 11.
nor natural force *a.*, Deut. 34:7.

ABBA, an Aramaic word meaning "father." It is similar to our word "daddy."

ABDA, (1) father of Adoniram, Solomon's tribute officer (I Kin. 4:6). (2) The son of Shammua, and a Levite who lived in Jerusalem after the exile (Neh. 11:17).

ABDEEL, the father of Shelemaiah, who was the one appointed to apprehend Jeremiah (Jer. 36:26).

ABDI, (1) a Levite, grandfather of Ethan (I Chr. 6:44). (2) A Levite in the reign of Hezekiah (II Chr. 29:12). (3) One of the sons of Elam (Ezra 10:26).

ABDIEL, son of Guni and father of Ahi, one of the Gadites in Gilead (I Chr. 5:15).

ABDON, (1) a Levitical city in Asher (Josh. 21:30; I Chr. 6:74). (2) A son of Hillel the Pirathonite who judged Israel for eight years (Judg. 12:13). (3) The firstborn son of Gibeon, a Benjamite in Jerusalem (I Chr. 8:30). (4) A son of Shashak, a Benjamite in Jerusalem (I Chr. 8:23). (5) The son of Micah, and one of those sent by King Josiah to Huldah regarding the books found in the temple (II Chr. 34:20).

ABED-NEGO, the Babylonian name given to Azariah, one of the four princes of Judah who were carried captive in B.C. 606. He was in the fiery furnace.
named Abed-Nego, Dan. 1:7.
refused to bow, Dan. 3:13–20.
promoted by the king, Dan. 3:30.

ABEL, the second son of Adam and Eve, and brother of Cain. He brought an offering to the Lord from the best of his flock. Cain was displeased, and slew him (Gen. 4:1–8). The superiority of Abel's sacrifice is ascribed by the writer of Hebrews to faith (Heb. 11:4).
born of Eve, Gen. 4:2.
killed by Cain, Gen. 4:8.
had a better sacrifice, Heb. 11:4.

ABEL, a great stone near Beth-shemesh, where the Philistines set the ark when they brought it back to the Israelites (I Sam. 6:18). Also there is a city in Naphtali by this name (II Sam. 20:14).

ABEL-BETH-MAACHAH, a city in Manasseh or Naphtali (I Kin. 15:20; II Kin. 15:29).

ABEL-KERAMIM, a place east of the Jordan beyond Aroer (Judg. 11:33).

ABEL-MAIM, another name for Abel-beth-maachah (II Chr. 16:4).

ABEL-MEHOLAH, the birthplace of Elisha the prophet; a place in the Jordan valley (I Kin. 19:16; Judg. 7:22).

ABEL-MIZRAIM, a place probably west of the Jordan; the scene of the mourning of Egypt over Jacob (Gen. 50:11). *See* **ATAD.**

ABEL-SHITTIM, a place in the plains of Moab; the last encampment of Israel before crossing the Jordan (Num. 33:49).

ABEZ, EBEZ, a place in Issachar, in the northern part of the plain of Esdraelon (Josh. 19:20).

ABHOR, to regard with loathing and disgust.
my soul shall not *a.*, Lev. 26:11.
thou shalt utterly *a.*, Deut. 7:26.
I hate and *a.* lying, Ps. 119:163.
a. that which is evil, Rom. 12:9.
thou that *a.* idols, Rom. 2:22.

ABHORRING, an object of abhorrence.
they shall be an *a.*, Is. 66:24.

ABI, the daughter of Zachariah and the mother of Hezekiah (II Kin. 18:2).

ABI, a word meaning "father of"; the first part of many Hebrew names.

ABIA, a form of Abiah. (1) The son of Rehoboam, king of Judah (I Chr. 3:10). (2) A priest in the time of David (I Chr. 24:10).

ABIAH, another way to anglicize Abijah. (1) The second son of Samuel (I Sam. 8:2; I Chr. 6:28). (2) The wife of Hezron and mother of Ashur (I Chr. 2:24).

ABI-ALBON, one of David's mighty men (II Sam. 23:31), also called Abiel.

ABIASAPH, the last mentioned of Korah's sons (Ex. 6:24).

ABIATHAR, son of Ahimelech, son of Ahitub, priest at Nob. He was the fourth high priest in descent from Eli. He escaped slaughter by Doeg, and joined David. He became joint high priest with Zadok, but Solomon expelled him.
escapes from Doeg, I Sam. 22:20–23.
joins Adonijah, I Kin. 1:7.
son of Ahimelech, I Kin. 2:26.
expelled by Solomon, I Kin. 2:26.
appointed high priest, I Chr. 15:11

David's counsellor, I Chr. 27:34.
referred to by Christ, Mark 2:26.

ABIB, the first month of the sacred and the seventh of the civil year of the Hebrews.

ABIDA, ABIDAH, the fourth son of the five sons of Midian, the son of Abraham by Keturah (Gen. 25:4).

ABIDAN, son of Gideoni, prince of the tribe of Benjamin (Num. 1:11; 2:22).

ABIDE, to sojourn, encamp, sit down, remain.
let thy servant *a.,* Gen. 44:33.
the cloud abode, Ex. 40:35.
people *a.* in Kadesh, Num. 20:1.
we *a.* in the valley, Deut. 3:29.
a. in thy tabernacle, Ps. 61:4.
I know thy *a.,* Is. 37:28.
a. not in the truth, John 8:44.
we *a.* seven days, Acts 20:6.
a., with God, I Cor. 7:24.
now *a.* faith, I Cor. 13:13.
a. a priest, Heb. 7:3.
word of God *a.,* I John 2:14.

ABIDING, to dwell (Judg. 16:9), to hope (I Chr. 29:15), to be admitted (I Sam. 26:19).

ABIEL, means father of strength. There was a Benjamite, son of Zeror by this name (I Sam. 14:51). One of David's mighty men had this name (I Chr. 11:32).

ABIEZER, the second son of Hammoleketh, sister of Gilead and granddaughter of Manasseh (I Chr. 7:17). Also one of David's chief warriors had this name (II Sam. 23:27).

ABIEZRITE, the descendants of Abiezer (Judg. 6:11).

ABIGAIL, means father of joy. (1) Wife of Nabal and afterwards of David; noted for her beauty and wisdom (I Sam. 25:3, 14–44). (2) A sister of David, married to Jether the Ishmaelite and mother of Amasa (II Sam. 17:25).

ABIGIBEON, a descendant of Benjamin who dwelt at Gibeon (I Chr. 8:29).

ABIHAIL, (1) a Levite, father of Zuriel, chief of Merarites in the time of Moses (Num. 3:35). (2) Wife of Abishur (I Chr.

2:29). (3) Head of a family of the tribe of Gad (I Chr. 5:14). (4) Wife of Rehoboam (II Chr. 11:18). (5) Father of Esther (Esther 2:15; 9:29).

ABIHU, second son of Aaron and Elisheba; he became a priest, but was consumed, with his brother Nadab for offering strange fire to the Lord.
son of Aaron, Ex. 6:23.
went up Sinai with Moses, Ex. 24:9.
set apart for priesthood, Ex. 28:1.
died before the Lord, Lev. 10:2.

ABIHUD, one of the sons of Bela, the son of Benjamin (I Chr. 8:3).

ABIJAH, ABIJAM, ABIAH, ABIA, whose father God is. (1) A son of Jeroboam I, king of Israel; he died in his youth (I Kin. 14:1). (2) A priest in the time of David (I Chr. 24:10). (3) A son of Rehoboam (II Chr. 11:20). (4) Mother of Hezekiah, king of Judah (II Chr. 29:1). (5) One of the priests who signed the covenant made by Nehemiah and the people to serve the Lord (Neh. 10:7). (6) A priest who came from Babylon with Zerubbabel. Perhaps the same as the preceding (Neh. 12:1–4).

ABIJAM, means father of the sea; seaman. He is the son of Rehoboam; he succeeded his father as king of Judah. Another name for Abijah.
reigns after Rehoboam, I Kin. 14:31.
fought Jeroboam, I Kin. 15:7.
father of Asa, I Kin. 15:8.

ABILENE, a small district of Coele-Syria; about eighteen miles from Damascus and thirty-eight from Heliopolis or Baalbek. It was given by Claudius to Herod Agrippa, A.D. 53.
Lysanias, tetrarch of *A.,* Luke 3:1.

ABILITY, power, strength, might, fulness.
they gave after their *a.,* Ezra 2:69.
according to his *a.,* Matt. 25:15.
according to his *a.,* Acts 11:29.
a. which God giveth, I Pet. 4:11.

ABIMAEL, one of the sons of Joktan, in Arabia (Gen. 10:28). Perhaps he is the founder of the Arabian tribe of Mael.

ABIMELECH, probably a general title for royalty, as Pharaoh or Caesar. The

Philistine king of Gerar in the time of
Abraham, he took Sarah, Abraham's
wife, into his harem thinking that she
was Abraham's sister, but returned her
after a dream from the Lord. The Abimelech which Isaac met may have been
the same person, or perhaps the son of
this man. Isaac, like Abraham, told
Abimelech that his wife, Rebekah, was
his sister. Abimelech later dismissed
Isaac from his country because of the
people. Later he visited the family of
Isaac at Beersheba. They made a covenant and parted in peace.
A. took Sarah, Gen. 20:2.
A. dreams, Gen. 20:3.
God Heals A., Gen. 20:17.
a covenant at Beersheba, Gen. 21:32.
Isaac dwelt in Gerar, Gen. 26:6.
A. rebukes Isaac, Gen. 26:9.
A. dismisses Isaac, Gen. 26:16.
covenant at Beersheba, Gen. 26:33.

ABIMELECH, son of Gideon by a concubine in Shechem. At his father's death,
he revolted against his mother's family,
and destroyed Shechem. His death came
as Jotham predicted: a woman threw a
millstone upon him and crushed his skull.
son of Gideon, Judg. 8:30–31.
reigned three years, Judg. 9:22.
Shechem revolts, Judg. 9:25.
A. crushes the revolt, Judg. 9:41.
A. is slain, Judg. 9:53.

ABIMELECH, (1) father or son of Abiathar, the high priest during the time of
David (I Chr. 18:16). (2) Name in the
title of Psalms 34, apparently it is given
to Achish king of Gath (I Sam. 21:10).

ABINADAB, (1) a Levite of Kirjath-
jearim, in whose house the ark was deposited after it was returned by the
Philistines (I Sam. 7:1; II Sam. 6:3).
(2) The second of eight sons of Jesse
(I Sam. 17:13). (3) One of the four sons
of king Saul (I Chr. 9:39; 10:2). (4) The
father of one of Solomon's purveyors,
who presided over the district of Dor (I
Kin. 4:11).

ABINER, *see* **ABNER.**

ABINOAM, father of Barak, an Israelite,
who defeated the army of Jabin.
Barak son of A., Judg. 4:6.
thou son of A., Judg. 5:12.

ABIRAM, (1) one of the sons of Eliab,
a Reubenite, who with his brother Dathan conspired against Moses and Aaron,
and were destroyed by an earthquake
(Num. 16:1–33; Deut. 11:6). (2) The
oldest son of Hiel, the Bethelite, who
undertook to rebuild Jericho. He died
when the foundations were set, as Joshua
had foretold (I Kin. 16:34).

ABISHAG, a beautiful woman of the
town of Shunem in Issachar, who was
selected to be a nurse for David in his
old age (I Kin. 1:3, 4). She was his wife,
but the marriage was never consum-
mated. Later Adonijah sought her hand;
Solomon had him killed (I Kin. 2:17f.).

ABISHAI, son of David's sister Zeruiah,
brother of Joab, and one of David's chief
officers.
one of David's men, II Sam. 2:18.
assassinated Abner, II Sam. 3:30.
rescued David, II Sam. 21:16, 17.
brother of Joab, I Chr. 2:16.

ABISHALOM, a fuller form of the name
Absalom (I Kin. 15:2, 10).

ABISHUA, (1) the son of Phineas, and
fourth high priest of the Jews (I Chr.
6:4, 5, 50). (2) One of the sons of Bela,
the son of Benjamin (I Chr. 8:4).

ABISHUR, the second son of Shammai;
the husband of Abihail (I Chr. 2:28).

ABITAL, the fifth wife of David (II Sam.
3:4).

ABITUB, a son of Shaharaim, by Hushim
(I Chr. 8:11).

ABIUD, the grandson of Zerubbabel by
Shelomith (Matt. 1:3).

ABJECTS, smitten, stricken.
the *a.* gathered, Ps. 35:15.

ABLE, sufficient, strong, mighty.
Moses chose *a.* men, Ex. 18:25.
for God is *a.*, Rom. 11:23.
am persuaded he is *a.*, II Tim. 1:12.
that he may be *a.*, Titus 1:9.
a. also to bridle, James 3:2.

ABLE, be, power.
he shall be *a.* to give, Ezek. 46:5.
as he is *a.* to give, Ezek. 46:11.

ABLE, to be, to reach, to attain, to have power.
Moses was not *a.*, Ex. 40:35.
the Lord was not *a.*, Num. 14:16.
who is *a.* to stand, I Sam. 6:20.
our God, . . . is *a.*, Dan. 3:17.
believe ye I am *a.*? Matt. 9:28.
his grace, which is *a.*, Acts 20:32.
scriptures, . . . are *a.*, II Tim. 3:15.
word, which is *a.*, James 1:21.
unto him who is *a.*, Jude 24.

ABLUTION, a ceremonial washing. It might be of a person, clothing, vessels, or furniture. (1) The cleansing of an inferior condition, when one is preparing to be initiated into a higher condition (Ex. 29:4; Lev. 8:6). (2) The preparation for a special act of religious service. This was the purpose of the basin of water in Ex. 30:18–21. (3) The purification of defilement, by the eleven species of uncleanness recognized by the law of Moses (Lev. 12–15). (4) The declaration of freedom from guilt of a particular action (Deut. 21:1–9). The Pharisees abused the privilege of ablution (Matt. 23:25).

ABNER, the cousin of Saul and commander-in-chief of his army. After Saul's death he made Ishbosheth, Saul's son, king. Later he betrayed him to David. He was killed by the friends of Asahel. David mourned his death.
commanded army, I Sam. 14:50.
war with David, II Sam. 2:8f.
Ishbosheth king, II Sam. 3:7.
kills Asahel, II Sam. 2:23.
killed by Joab, II Sam. 3:27–39.

ABOARD, to go on or upon.
ship . . . we went *a.*, Acts 21:2.

ABODE, home, mansion.
come . . . make our *a.*, John 14:23.

ABOLISH, to change, to pass away.
right. shall not be *a.*, Is. 51:6.
your works may be *a.*, Ezek. 6:6.
who hath abolished, II Tim. 1:10.

ABOMINABLE, detestable, disgusting, impure.
put away *a.* idols, II Chr. 15:8.
have done *a.* works, Ps. 14:1.
broth of *a.* things, Is. 65:4.
I will cast *a.* filth, Nah. 3:6.
walked in *a.* idolatries, I Pet. 4:3.

but the *a.* shall have, Rev. 21:8.

ABOMINABLY, to do.
and he did very *a.*, I Kin. 21:26.

ABOMINATION, an impure thing, a detestable thing.
we shall sacrifice the *a.*, Ex. 8-26.
a. before the Lord, Deut. 24:4.
the *a.* of the heathen, II Kin. 21:2.
seven are an *a.*, Prov. 6:16.
delighteth in their *a.*, Is. 66:3.
overspreading of *a.*, Dan. 9:27.
an *a.* is committed, Mal. 2:11.
the *a.* of desolation, Matt. 24:15.
the *a.* of desolation, Mark. 13:14.
harlots and *a.*, Rev. 17:5.

ABOMINATION OF DESOLATION, means "desolating filthiness." The phrase in Dan. 11:31 and 12:11, doubtless refers to the removal of the worship of Jehovah, and the setting up of the idol altar on Jehovah's altar of burnt offering by Antiochus Epiphanes, who dedicated the temple to Jupiter Olympus. Jesus uses the phrase (Matt. 24:15), and seems to apply it to what the Romans were to do in Jerusalem in A.D. 70. The phrase was used even later, when Hadrian set up a boar over the Bethlehem gate, and he placed an image of himself in the most holy place.

ABOUND, to multiply, to make over and above.
faithful man shall *a.*, Prov. 28:20.
the grace of God *a.*, Rom. 5:15.
ye may *a.* in hope, Rom. 15:13.
your love may *a.*, Phil 1:9.

ABOUND, to more.
truth of God . . . *a.*, Rom. 3:7.

ABOUND, to much more.
grace did much more *a.*, Rom. 5:20.

ABOUNDING, with, to be heavy with.
no fountains *a.* with, Prov. 8:24.

ABOVE, up, upwards, more, superior to, from above.
shalt thou finish *a.*, Gen. 6:16.
God in heaven *a.*, Deut. 4:39.
a. it stood . . seraphims, Isa. 6:2.
over their heads *a.*, Ezek. 1:22.
disciple is not *a.*, Matt. 10:24.
one day *a.* another, Rom. 14:5.

ABRAHAM, means father of a multitude. His first name was Abram. Son of Terah, born in Ur of the Chaldees. His wife was Sarai, who was also his half-sister. She bore Isaac. Besides Sarai Abraham had a wife named Keturah, and also a handmaid, Hagar, whose son, Ishmael, was head of a large family. Before Isaac was born, Lot, Abraham's nephew, lived with him. They went toward Egypt together, and the Pharaoh, because of Sarai's beauty, took her into his court. After she was returned, Abram and Lot went back to Canaan, and there they separated. At this time Abram had many servants and cattle. When Abram was 99 years old, the promise which God had made him was renewed: through him all nations would be blessed. Abram's name was changed to Abraham and Sarai's name became Sarah, and the covenant of circumcision was renewed to family and servant. During this time Abraham deceived Abimelech in the same way that he did Pharaoh. Isaac was 25 when he was placed on the altar, being saved because of his father's faith. His mother died about 12 years later. Abraham died when he was about 175 years old, and was buried in the cave of Machpelah by Isaac and Ishmael.

son of Terah, Gen. 11:26.
Sarai his wife, Gen. 11:29.
sojourn in Egypt, Gen. 12:10.
Pharaoh likes Sarai, Gen. 12:17.
out of Egypt, Gen. 13:1.
Abram and Lot part, Gen. 13:12.
Ishmael is born, Gen. 16:15.
Abram's name changed, Gen. 17:5.
cov. of circumcision, Gen. 17:26.
Abimelech likes Sarah, Gen. 20:9.
Isaac is born, Gen. 21:3.
Isaac on the altar, Gen. 22:9.
Isaac saved, Gen. 22:13.
Sarah dies, Gen. 23:2.
Abraham dies, Gen. 25:8.
Covenant remembered, Ex. 2:24.
the Lord redeemed *A.*, Is. 29:22.
Jesus is the son of *A.*, Matt. 1:1.
we are *A.* seed, John 8:33.
we are *A.* children, Gal. 3:7.
Abraham's faith, Heb. 11:8.
Abraham believed God, James 2:23.

ABRAHAM'S BOSOM, a place of peace, repose, and happiness (Luke 16:22, 23).

ABRAM, Abraham's name before it was changed (Gen. 17:5).

ABROAD, outside, without, to manifest.
go *a.* out of the camp, Deut. 23:10.
scattered them *a.*, Ezek. 34:21.
name was spread *a.*, Mark 6:14.

ABRONAH, means passage. A station in the desert near Eziongeber (Num. 33:34, 35).

ABRONAS, a torrent near Cilicia, the ancient Adonis.

ABSALOM, the third son of David by Maachah. He was a handsome man. He killed his half-brother Amnon for assaulting his sister Tamar. He plotted for the throne and "stole the hearts of the people." He was killed by Joab; David mourned bitterly over his death.

son of David, II Sam. 3:3.
killed Amnon, II Sam. 13:22.
fled to Geshur, II Sam. 13:37.
sought the throne, II Sam. 15:1.
Absalom killed, II Sam. 18:14.

ABSENCE, being away from.
much more in my *a.*, Phil 2:12.

ABSENCE of,
betray him, in the *a.* of, Luke 22:6.

ABSENT, to be hidden, away from.
a. in body, but, I Cor. 5:3.
a. in the flesh, yet, Col. 2:5.

ABSTAIN, to hold off from.
a. from meats, Acts 15:29.
a. from all appearance, I Thess. 5:22.
a. from fleshly lusts, I Pet. 2:11.

ABSTINENCE, want of food.
after long *a.* Paul, Acts 27:21.

ABUNDANCE, multitude, strength, fulness, power.
a. of the rich, Eccles. 5:12.
a. of idleness, Ezek. 16:49.
a. of the heart, Luke 6:45.
a. of grace, Rom. 5:17.

ABUNDANCE, in. To make heavy, much.
giveth meat in *a.*, Job 36:31.

ABUNDANT, much, over and above.
a. in treasures, Jer. 51:13.

his *a.* mercy, I Pet. 1:3.

ABUNDANTLY, richly, exceedingly.
might have more *a.*, John 10:10.
to do exceeding *a.*, Eph. 3:20.

ABUSE, to misuse.
that I *a.* not my power, I Cor. 9:18.

ABUSERS, those who misuse themselves.
a. of themselves, I Cor. 6:9.

ABYSS, a deep gulf, a chasm (Rev. 9:11; 20:1-3.)

ACACIA, the locust tree. *See* **SHITTAH.**

ACCAD, a city in Shinar built by Nimrod (Gen. 10:10).

ACCEPT, to receive, take hold of.
the Lord also *a.* Job, Job 42:9.
God *a.* no man's person, Gal. 2:6.
not *a.* deliverance, Heb. 11:35.

ACCEPTABLE, worthy, pleasing, welcome.
a. in thy sight, Ps. 19:14.
an *a.* time: O God, Ps. 69:13.
proving what is *a.*, Eph. 5:10.
sacrifices, *a.* to God, I Pet. 2:5.

ACCEPTABLY, pleasingly.
we may serve God *a.*, Heb. 12:28.

ACCEPTANCE, good pleasure.
shall come up with *a.*, Is. 60:7.

ACCEPTATION, received fully.
and worthy of all *a.*, I Tim. 1:15.

ACCEPTED, well pleasing, receivable.
that they may be *a.*, Ex. 28:38.
he hath made us *a.*, Eph. 1:6.

ACCESS, a way.
we have *a.* by faith, Rom. 5:2.
we have boldness and *a.*, Eph. 3:12.

ACCHO, a seaport 8 miles north of Carmel, by the bay of Acre. The city of Ptolemais, in Asher. It was given to Asher by Joshua, but it was never conquered (Judges 1:31).

ACCOMPANY, to come with, follow with.
a. him into Asia, Acts 20:4.

ACCOMPLISH, to complete, finish.
hath *a.* his fury, Lam. 4:11.
all things shall be *a.*, Luke 18:31.
this must yet be *a.*, Luke 22:37.

ACCOMPLISHMENT, complete fulfillment.
to signify the *a.*, Acts 21:26.

ACCORD, of one's own accord.
of his own *a.*, II Cor. 8:17.

ACCORD, likeminded.
with one *a.*, in prayer, Acts 1:14.
daily with one *a.*, Acts 2:46.
being of one *a.*, Phil. 2:2.

ACCOUNT, reckoning, estimate, to reckon.
shall give *a.* thereof, Matt. 12:36.
shall give *a.*, Rom. 14:12.

ACCOUNTED, to be reckoned, numbered.
shall be *a.* to the Lord, Ps. 22:30.
we are *a.* as sheep, Rom. 8:36.

ACCURSED, lightly esteemed.
sinner shall be *a.*, Is. 65:20.
let him be *a.*, Gal. 1:8.

ACCUSATION, judgment.
what *a.* bring ye, John 18:29.
receive not an *a.*, I Tim. 5:19.
bring not railing *a.*, II Pet. 2:11.

ACCUSE, to judge, to bring charges against.
a. not a servant, Prov. 30:10.
the chief priests *a.*, Mark 15:3.
a. them before our God, Rev. 12:10.

ACCUSED, under accusation.
children, not *a.*, Titus 1:6.

ACCUSER, one who accuses, judges.
commanding his *a.*, Acts 24:8.
not false *a.*, not, Titus 2:3.

ACCUSTOMED, trained.
that are *a.* to do evil, Jer. 13:23.

ACELDAMA, means "field of blood." It was purchased by Judas for 30 pieces of silver (Acts 1:19).

ACHAIA, a province of Rome in Greece. Gallio was proconsul when Paul was there (Acts 18:12).

ACHAICUS, a Corinthian who visited Paul at Philippi (I Cor. 16:17).

ACHAN, ACHAR, one of the tribe of Judah who was stoned at Jericho for stealing public property (Josh. 7:1ff).

ACHAZ, a Greek form of Ahaz, one of the kings of Judah (Matt. 1:9).

ACHBOR, the father of Baal-hanan, king of Edom (Gen. 36:38). Also, Achbor was the name of the son of Michaiah, in Josiah's time (II Kin. 22:12).

ACHIM, son of Sadoc, father of Eliud, an ancestor of Joseph, Mary's husband (Matt. 1:14).

ACHIOR, a general in the army of Holofernes. Later he became a convert to the Jewish faith.

ACHISH, (1) king of Gath to whom David fled (I Sam. 21–29). (2) King of Gath who lived in Solomon's reign (I Kin. 2:39–40).

ACHMETHA, a city of Media, maybe Ecbatana (Ezra 6:2).

ACHOR, a valley near Jericho where Achan was killed (Josh. 7:24).

ACHSAH, ACHSA, daughter of Caleb and wife of Othniel (I Chr. 2:49).

ACHSHAPH, a Phoenician city, at the foot of Carmel, which was given to Asher (Josh. 11:1f.). It is modern Khaifa.

ACHZIB, a town in the western part of Judah (Josh. 15:33). Also, a city by the sea of Galilee (Josh. 19:29).

ACKNOWLEDGE, to know, to make known.
a. my transgressions, Ps. 51:3.
we a., O Lord, Jer. 14:20.
therefore a. ye them, I Cor. 16:18.

ACKNOWLEDGING, full knowledge.
the a. of the truth, Titus 1:1.

ACKNOWLEDGMENT, full knowledge.
the a. of the mystery, Col. 2:2.

ACQUAINT, make self known.

a. now thyself, Job 22:21.

ACQUAINTANCE, to know, to be known, to discern.
and mine a. are verily, Job 19:13.
forbid none of his a., Acts 24:23.

ACQUAINTED, to know, to be discerning.
and art a. with all, Ps. 139:3.
man of sorrows, and a., Is. 53:3.

ACQUIT, to declare innocent.
thou wilt not a., Job 10:14.

ACRE, an area of land.
half acre of land, I Sam. 14:14.

ACTION, acts.
by him a. are weighed, I Sam. 2:3.

ACTIVITY, workings, doings.
knowest men of a., Gen. 47:6.

ACTS, works, deeds.
all righteous a., I Sam. 12:7.
had done many a., II Sam. 23:20.
the a. of Solomon, I Kin. 11:41.
the a. of Jehu, II Kin. 10:34.
the a. of Asa, II Chr. 16:11.

THE ACTS OF THE APOSTLES, the fifth book of history in the New Testament. It was written by Luke as a continuation of the sacred history which he had already begun. It relates the actions and sufferings of the Apostles after the ascension of their Lord. It chiefly relates those of Peter, John, Paul, and Barnabas. The first part of the book tells of Peter and his sermon on Pentecost, when three thousand people were baptized and added to the Church. The book tells how the Gospel spread from Jerusalem into Samaria, and then to the "uttermost part of the earth." After the conversion of Paul, it describes three missionary journeys of the "Apostle to the Gentiles." The book ends abruptly, with Paul in prison; but it does not close before Paul preaches the Gospel of Christ to the Gentiles.

ADADAH, a city in the southern part of Judah (Josh. 15:21–22).

ADAH, (1) a wife of Lamech (Gen. 4:19). (2) One of the wives of Esau (Gen. 36:2).

ADAIAH, (1) grandfather of Josiah (II Kin. 22:1). (2) A Gershonite (I Chr. 6:41). (3) Son of Shimhi the Benjamite. (4) A descendant of Aaron in Jerusalem (I Chr. 9:10–12). (5) Of the family of Bani (Ezra 10:29). (6) A descendant of Judah by Pharez (Neh. 11:5).

ADALIA, one of Haman's ten sons who were hanged along with their father (Esther 9:8).

ADAM, the first man and "the son of God" (Luke 3:38) by special creation. He was called Adam because he was made from the ground (*adamah*). Woman was formed from his rib. When they sinned, they were punished: man to work the field in sorrow and woman to bear her children in sorrow. All men came under the sentence of death. They had three sons: Cain, Abel, and Seth. Of the other children born to them there is nothing recorded. Adam's death is stated to have been in his 930th year, but Eve's death is not given.
he named animals, Gen. 2:20.
Eve created, Gen. 2:21.
A. died, Gen. 5:5.
in *A.* all die, I Cor. 15:22.
the last *A.,* I Cor. 15:45.

ADAMAH, a city in Naphtali (Josh. 19:35, 36).

ADAMANT, stone, diamond.
as an *a.* harder than, Ezek. 3:9.

ADAMI, same as Adamah.

ADAR, ADDAR, the 12th month of the Jewish sacred year; about the time of our April.

ADAR, ADDAR, (1) a city in the southern part of Judah (Josh. 15:3). (2) The son of Bela (I Chr. 8:3).

ADBEEL, the son of Ishmael (Gen. 25:13).

ADD, to increase, to give.
ye shall *a.* forty, Num. 35:6.
ye shall not *a.,* Deut. 4:2.
can *a.* one cubit, Matt. 6:27.
Lord *a.* to the church, Acts 2:47.
anyman shall *a.,* Rev. 22:18.

ADDAN, ADDON, a place-name or a name of a person (Ezra 2:59).

ADDAR, *see* **ADAR.**

ADDED, *see* **ADD.**

ADDER, asp, viper, basilisk. Some are poisonous. The word is also used figuratively for man's treachery.
Dan shall be an *a.,* Gen. 42:17.
like the deaf *a.,* Ps. 58:4.
shalt tread upon . . *a.,* Ps. 91:13.
stingeth like an *a.,* Prov. 23:32.

ADDETH, *see* **ADD.**

ADDI, the son of Cosam and father of Melchi (Luke 3:28).

ADDICTED, to arrange in an orderly way.
they have *a.* them, I Cor. 16:15.

ADDING, *see* **ADD.**

ADDON, *see* **ADDAN.**

ADER, a son of Berah, a Benjamite (I Chr. 8:15).

ADIEL, (1) a descendant of Simeon (I Chr. 4:36). (2) A priest, the son of Jahzerah (I Chr. 9:12). (3) The father of Azmaveth (I Chr. 27:25).

ADIN, (1) the father of some who came back from Babylon with Zerubbabel (Ezra 2:15). (2) One whose descendants came with Ezra (Ezra 8:6). (3) One of those who sealed the covenant made by Nehemiah (Neh. 10:16).

ADINA, one of David's captains, a Reubenite (I Chr. 11:42).

ADINO, one of David's mighty men (II Sam. 23:8).

ADITHAIM, a place in Judah; location is unknown (Josh. 15:33–36).

ADJURE, to swear.
I *a.* thee by God, Mark 5:7.
we *a.* you by Jesus, Acts 19:13.

ADJURATION, (1) imposing of obligation upon someone (I Sam. 14:24; Josh. 6:26). (2) The expulsion of demons (Acts 19:13). (3) In the Roman Catholic Church, the use of the name of God to induce someone to do what he is obligated to do.

ADLAI, the father of Shaphat (I Chr. 27:29).

ADMAH, a city in the vale of Siddim; it was destroyed with Sodom (Gen. 19:24).

ADMATHA, one of the seven princes of Persia (Esther 1:14).

ADMINISTERED, to minister.
which is *a.* by us, II Cor. 8:19.

ADMINISTRATION, ministry.
differences of *a.*, I Cor. 12:5.

ADMIRATION, wonder and astonishment.
I wondered with *a.*, Rev. 17:6.

ADMIRED, to wonder.
and to be *a.* in all, II Thess. 1:10.

ADMONISH, to remind, to recommend.
to *a.* one another, Rom. 15:14.
teaching and *a.* one, Col. 3:16.
Moses was *a.* of God, Heb. 8:5.

ADMONITION, reminding.
written for our *a.*, I Cor. 10:11.

ADNA, (1) one of the family of Pahath-Moab (Ezra 10:30). (2) A priest in the time of Joiakim (Neh. 12:12–15).

ADNAH, (1) a captain of the tribe of Manasseh (I Chr. 12:20). (2) The chief general of the army of Jehoshaphat (II Chr. 17:14).

ADO, to be tumultuous.
make ye this *a.*, Mark. 5:39.

ADONI-BEZEK, king or lord of Bezek, a city of the Canaanites (Judges 1:5).

ADONIJAH, the fourth son of David by Haggith, born at Hebron. After the death of David, he tried to obtain the throne, but Solomon had him killed.
son of David, II Sam. 3:4.
killed by Solomon, I Kin. 2:24.

ADONIKAM, (1) one of the Israelites who came back from Babylon (Ezra 2:13). (2) One of those who came back with Ezra (Ezra 8:13).

ADONIRAM, one of Solomon's officers (I Kin. 4:6).

ADONI-ZEDEK, ADONI-ZEDEC, a king of the Canaanites in Jerusalem; slain by Joshua (Josh. 10:1).

ADOPTION, placing as a son one who was not so born. It was not practiced by the Hebrews. Paul alludes to a law of the Romans (Gal. 4:5, Eph. 1:5).

ADORAIM, a city of Judah, built by Rehoboam; now called Dura (II Chr. 11: 5–9).

ADORAM, (1) one of David's officers (II Sam. 20:24). (2) One of Solomon's officers (I Kin. 12:18).

ADORATION, it is believed that the Hebrews used all the forms of posture in their prayers as modern Arabs use. Monuments show various forms of kneeling. Kneeling is common in the Bible (I Kin. 8; Ezra 9). Prostration was also used (Acts 10:26).

ADORN, to pass over, to polish.
and as the bride *a.*, Is. 61:10.
women *a.* themselves, I Tim. 2:9.
a. the doctrine of God, Titus 2:10.

ADORNING, ornament.
whose *a.* let it not, I Pet. 3:3.

ADRAMMELECH, an idol of the Assyrians whom Shalmaneser brought to Israel; they were to colonize the land (II Kin. 17:31).

ADRAMYTTIUM, a seaport in Asia Minor, from which the boat in which Paul was wrecked originated (Acts 27:2).

ADRIA, ADRIAS, the sea on the eastern side of Italy called the Adriatic. It is mentioned in Acts 27:27.

ADRIEL, means God's flock. He was the son of Barzillai, to whom Saul gave his daughter Merab (I Sam. 18:19).

ADULLAM, (1) a royal city near Jerusalem (Josh. 12:7–15). (2) A large cave near Jerusalem (I Sam. 22:1).

ADULLAMITE, an inhabitant of Adullam.
his friend the *A.*, Gen. 38:20.

ADULTERER, one who commits adultery.
I am not as *a.*, Luke 18:11.
whoremongers and *a.*, Heb. 13:4.

ADULTERESS, one who commits adultery.
adulterer and the *a.*, Lev. 20:10.
called an *a.*, Rom. 7:3.

ADULTERIES, adulterous objects, acts.
I have seen thine *a.*, Jer. 13:27.
that was old in *a.*, Ezek. 23:43.

ADULTERY, the willful violation of the marriage contract by either of the parties, through sexual intercourse with a third party. It was forbidden by the seventh commandment. Jesus referred to the idea of their being "one flesh," that from the beginning they were made male and female (Matt. 19:4). This is also in accord with the teaching of Paul (Eph. 5: 25–33; I Cor. 7:1–13; I Tim. 3:12). Jesus even says that there can be adultery committed in heart (Matt. 5:28).
shalt not commit *a.*, Ex. 20:14.
whoso committeth *a.*, Prov. 6:32.
a. in his heart, Matt. 5:28.
woman taken in *a.*, John 8:3.
flesh manifest *a.*, Gal. 5:19.
eyes full of *a.*, II Pet. 2:14.

ADUMMIN, a ridge west of Gilgal, between Judah and Benjamin (Josh. 15:7).

ADVANCE, to increase, to make great.
the king *a.* him, Esther 10:2.
that *a.* Moses, I Sam. 12:6.

ADVANTAGE, to profit, to be useful.
what *a.* will it be, Job 35:3.
what is a man *a.*, Luke 9:25.
what *a.* then hath, Rom. 3:1.

ADVENTURE, try, attempt, set forth.
would not *a.* to set, Deut. 28:56.
not *a.* himself into, Acts 19:31.

ADVENT, THE SECOND, the second coming of Jesus Christ, which was often foretold by Jesus and often mentioned by the apostles (Matt. 24:3; I Cor. 15:23; I Thess. 2:19; Heb. 9:28). *See* **SECOND COMING.**

ADVERSARY, an enemy, a man of strife.
I will be an *a.*, Ex. 23:22.
mine *a.* had written, Job 31:35.

agree with thine *a.*, Matt. 5:25.
avenge me of mine *a.*, Luke 18:3.
your *a.* the Devil, I Pet. 5:8.

ADVERSITY, evil, held by evil.
the bread of *a.*, Is. 30:20.
which suffer *a.*, Heb. 13:3.

ADVERTISE, to counsel, to tell or to inform. Does not mean public notice.
I thought to *a.* thee, Ruth 4:4.

ADVICE, counsel.
give here your *a.*, Judg. 20:7.
herein I give *a.*, II Cor. 8:10.

ADVISE, to counsel.
a. thyself what word, I Chr. 21:12.
a. to depart thence, Acts 27:12.

ADVOCATE, the name given to the Holy Spirit by Jesus (John 14:16); and to Jesus by John (I John 2:1).

AENEAS, a paralytic of Lydda healed by Peter (Acts 9:33).

AENON, a place near Salim, at the head of the valley of Shechem, where there was much water (John 3:23).

AEON, a lifetime, an unbroken age, perpetuity of time, eternity. It is sometimes translated "forever," and sometimes with the idea of "this age."

AFAR, far off, distant.
saw the place *a.* off, Gen. 22:4.
people stood *a.* off, Ex. 20:21.
all that are *a.* off, Acts 2:39.

AFFAIR, business, matter.
a. of the king, I Chr. 26:32.
might know our *a.*, Eph. 6:22.
entangleth . . . with . . *a.*, II Tim. 2:4.

AFFECT, to influence, to have warmth of feeling for.
mine eye *a.* mine heart, Lam. 3:51.
their minds evil *a.*, Acts 14:2.
zealously *a.* you, Gal. 4:17.

AFFECTION, feeling, passion (good or bad).
with the *a.* and lust, Gal. 5:24.
set your *a.*, Col. 3:2.
being *a.*, I Thess. 2:8.

AFFINITY, to join oneself.

25

joined *a.* with Ahab, II Chr. 18:1.

AFFIRM, to maintain.
confidently *a.*, Luke 22:59.
she constantly *a.*, Acts 12:15.
nor whereof they *a.*, I Tim. 1:7.

AFFLICT, grief, distress of body and
mind.
shall *a.* your souls, Lev. 16:29.
didst *a.* the people, Ps. 44:2.
they *a.* the just, Amos 5:12.
whether we be *a.*, II Cor. 1:6.

AFFLICTED, grieved, distressed.
the cry of the *a.*, Job 34:28.
desolate and *a.*, Ps. 25:16.
mercy upon his *a.*, Is. 49:13.
being destitute, *a.*, Heb. 11:37.
be *a.*, and mourn, James 4:9.

AFFLICTION, pain, grief, distress of
body or mind.
the *a.* of my people, Ex. 3:7.
the days of *a.*, Job 30:16.
the furnace of *a.*, Is. 48:10.
in the day of *a.*, Jer. 16:19.
a. or persecution, Mark 4:17.
rather to suffer *a.*, Heb. 11:25.

AFFRIGHTED, terrified.
and they were greatly *a.*, Mark 16:5.

AFOOT, to go on foot.
ran *a.* thither, Mark 6:33.

AFORE, before, aforetime.
as I wrote *a.*, Eph. 3:3.

AFRAID, to be fearful, terrified.
shall make you *a.*, Lev. 26:6.
were ye not *a.*, Num. 12:8.
thy dread make me *a.*, Job 13:21.
what time I am *a.*, Ps. 56:3.
I will not be *a.*, Ps. 56:11.
be not *a.*, Matt. 14:27.
be not *a.* of them, Luke 12:4.
be not *a.* of their, I Pet. 3:14.
not *a.* to speak evil, II Pet. 2:10.

AFRESH, anew, again.
crucify . . . son . . . *a.*, Heb. 6:6.

AFTERWARD, later, next, at last, then.
a. he repented, Matt. 21:29.
thou shalt follow me *a.*, John 13:36.

AGABUS, a prophet in the Jerusalem
church. With others he came from Jerusalem to Antioch while Paul and Barnabas were there (Acts 11:28). Years later
this same Agabus met Paul at Caesarea,
and warned him of trouble if he went up
to Jerusalem (Acts 21:10–12).

AGAG, a title of the king of the Amale-
kites, like Pharaoh of the Egyptians, and
Caesar of the Romans (Num. 24:7; I
Sam. 15:8).

AGAGITE, of Agag; synonym for Amalekite. Used in connection with Haman,
the enemy of Mordecai (Esther 3:1, 10;
8:3, 5; 9:24).

AGAINST, near, before, beside, around.
over *a.* Jericho, Deut. 32:49.
went *a.* Israel, Josh. 8:14.
brother sin *a.* me, Matt. 18:21.
enmity *a.* God, Rom. 8:7.
lusts, which war *a.*, I Pet. 2:11.

AGAPE, a simple meal of brotherly love
celebrated daily in the apostolic times in
connection with the Lord's supper. It
was a simple feast of unity; later it was
abused (I Cor. 11:21).

AGAR, a Greek form of the name Hagar
(Gal. 4:24, 25).

AGATE, the name of one of the precious
stones in the breastplate of the high-
priest (Ex. 28:19). It is used for what
may be a ruby in Isaiah 54:12.

AGE, a word used for several Hebrew and
Greek words: generation (Job 8:8); old
age (Gen. 48:10); lifetime (Ps. 39:5);
grayheadedness (I Kin. 14:4); maturity
(Heb. 11:11); day (Gen. 18:11).

AGED, old, full.
a. men be sober, Titus 2:2.
a. women likewise, Titus 2:3.

AGEE, a Hararite, father of Shammah
(II Sam. 23:11).

AGES, generations, dispensations.
that in the *a.* to come, Eph. 2:7.
throughout all *a.*, Eph. 3:21.

AGNOSTICISM, the methodology that
holds that it can not know such things as
the existence of God or the reality of an
unseen world.

AGO, before.
these many years *a*., Ezra 5:11.

AGONE, an old form of ago.
three days *a*. I, I Sam. 30:13.

AGONY, severe mental struggles, like our anguish.
and being in an *a*., Luke 22:44.

AGRAPHA, a term applied to the sayings of the Lord not recorded in the gospels. The Bible says these actually occur (John 21:25). There is an example of one of these sayings in Acts 20:35.

AGREE, like, similar, of the same opinion, of the same mind.
a. with thine adversary, Matt. 5:25.
and to him they *a*., Acts 5:40.
when they *a*. not, Acts 28:25.

AGREEMENT, to be agreed.
your *a*. with hell, Is. 28:18.
what *a*. hath the, II Cor. 6:16.

AGRICULTURE, the cultivation of soil dates back to the time of Adam, to whom God gave the task of working the ground (Gen. 2:15). The Israelites engaged in agriculture for many years (Deut. 11:10). Each family had its stake in the soil of the land, and the occupation was held in high esteem (II Chr. 26:10).

AGRIPPA, the greatgrandson of Herod the Great. After his father was eaten of worms, Herod Agrippa succeeded him as tetrarch of Abilene. *See* **HEROD**.

AGUR, author of the sayings in Proverbs 30. Some think this is an assumed name of Solomon, such as "Koheleth," which means "preacher."

AHAB, the son of Omri, king of Israel; he reigned for 22 years. His wife was Jezebel, a woman of strong character, and an idolatress. She introduced Baal worship into Israel and had a temple built at Samaria for the worship. Elijah prophesied Ahab's doom (I Kin. 21:19).
temple to Ashteroth, I Kin. 16:29f.
death of *A*., I Kin. 21:19.
built cities, I Kin. 22:39.

AHARAH, the third son of Benjamin (I Chr. 8:1); also known as Ehi (Gen. 46: 21), Ahiram (Num. 26:38), and Aher (I Chr. 7:12).

AHARHEL, a son of Harum, a descendant of Judah (I Chr. 4:8).

AHASAI, AHZAI, a priest of the family of Immer (Neh. 11:13).

AHASBAI, a Maachathite, one of David's valiant men (II Sam. 23:34).

AHASUERUS, the title of three Median and Persian kings mentioned in the Bible. (1) The Persian king who is probably the same as Cambyses, son of Cyrus (Ezra 4:6). (2) The father of Darius the Mede (Dan. 9:1). (3) The son of Darius Hystaspis (Esther 1:1ff.).

AHAVA, the place where the Jewish exiles met on their return from Babylon to Jerusalem (Ezra 8:21).

AHAZ, the son and successor of Jotham, king of Judah. He reigned 16 years, and did not respect God.
became king, II Kin. 15:38.
an idolatrous king, II Kin. 16:8.
died dishonored, II Kin. 23:12.

AHAZIAH, (1) the son of Ahab, king of Israel. He was as completely under the control of idolatry as his father. The most important event of his life was the revolt of the Moabites (II Kin. 1:1). When he died he was succeeded by his brother Jehoram (II Kin. 1:17). (2) The son of Jehoram by Athaliah, and sixth king of Judah. He was also called Jehoahaz (II Chr. 21:17). He reigned only one year (II Kin. 8:24).

AHBAN, one of the two sons of Abishur by Abihail (I Chr. 2:29).

AHER, an ancestor of the Hushim (I Chr. 7:12).

AHI, (1) head of a family in Gad (I Chr. 5:15). (2) A descendant of Shamer, in Asher (I Chr. 7:34).

AHIAH, *see* **AHIJAH**.

AHIAM, one of David's thirty mighty men (II Sam. 23:33).

AHIAN, son of Shemidah, a Manassehite (I Chr. 7:19).

AHIEZER, (1) chief in Dan (Num. 1:12). (2) Chief of a band of bowmen with David (I Chr. 12:3).

AHIHUD, (1) chief in Asher; one of Joshua's assistants (Num. 34:27). (2) Chief in Benjamin (I Chr. 8:7).

AHIJAH, (1) son of Ahitub; grandson of Phinehas (I Sam. 14:3). He was the priest at Shiloh who cared for the ark. (2) Son of Bela (I Chr. 8:7). (3) Son of Jerahmeel. (4) One of David's 30 mighty men (I Chr. 11:36). (5) A Levite during David's reign; the treasurer of the temple (I Chr. 26:20). (6) One of the Levites who sealed the covenant with Nehemiah (Neh. 10:26).

AHIKAM, son of Shaphan the scribe (II Kin. 22:12). He was an officer in Josiah's court. He protected Jeremiah, the prophet, after he was taken out of the pit (Jer. 26:24).

AHILUD, (1) father of Jehoshaphat (II Sam. 8:16). (2) Father of Baana (I Kin. 4:12).

AHIMAAZ, (1) father of Saul's wife (I Sam. 14:50). (2) Son of Zadok, the high priest (II Sam. 15:27). (3) One of Solomon's officers (I Kin. 4:15).

AHIMAN, (1) a son of Anak, who lived in Hebron (Num. 13:22). (2) A Levite porter in the temple (I Chr. 9:17).

AHIMELECH, a greatgrandson of Eli, the priest at Nob, who gave David the shew-bread and Goliath's sword.
priest at Nob, I Sam. 21:1.
gave David bread, I Sam. 21:6.
Doeg slays priests, I Sam. 22:18.

AHIMOTH, a Kohathite in David's reign (I Chr. 6:25).

AHINADAB, one of the men who gathered supplies for Solomon (I Kin. 4:14).

AHINOAM, (1) the daughter of Ahimaaz, the wife of King Saul (I Sam. 14:50). (2) One of David's wives, a Jezreelitess (I Sam. 25:43).

AHIO, (1) son of Abinadab in whose house the ark of God remained for 20 years (II Sam. 6:3). (2) A son of Beriah, a Benjamite (I Chr. 8:14). (3) Son of Jehiel, a Benjamite (I Chr. 8:31).

AHIRA, the son of Enan, and chief of the tribe of Naphtali (Num. 2:29).

AHIRAM, a Benjamite after whom a family was named (Num. 26:38). He is Ehi of Gen. 46:21.

AHIRAMITE, a descendant of the Benjamite Ahiram (Num. 26:38).

AHISAMACH, father of Aholiab, a Danite, who worked on the temple (Ex. 31:6).

AHISHAHAR, one of the sons of Bilhan, of the tribe of Benjamin. He was a warrior (I Chr. 7:10).

AHISHAR, the steward of King Solomon (I Kin. 4:6).

AHITHOPHEL, a counselor of David, whose wisdom made him highly esteemed (II Sam. 16:23). When his counsels to Absalom were neglected for those of Hushai, he went home and hanged himself (II Sam. 17:23).

AHITUB, (1) son of Phinehas, and grandson of Eli (I Sam. 14:3). (2) Father of Zadok the high priest in the time of David (II Sam. 8:17). (3) Another priest seven generations after Zadok (I Chr. 6:11). (4) Another priest in the time of Nehemiah (Neh. 11:11).

AHLAB, a city of Asher from which the Canaanites were driven out by the Israelites (Judges 1:31).

AHLAI, (1) a daughter of Sheshan, a descendant of Judah (I Chr. 2:31). (2) Father of one of David's 30 mighty men (I Chr. 11:41).

AHOAH, son of Bela, grandson of Benjamin (I Chr. 8:4).

AHOHITE, descendant of Ahoah (II Sam. 23:28).

AHOLAH, a fictitious, or symbolic, name given to Samaria and the ten tribes (Ezek. 23:6).

AHOLIAB, a Danite, in the time of Moses (Ex. 31:6).

AHOLIBAH, means "my tent is in her." A symbolic name for Judah and Jerusalem (Ezek. 23:4).
therefore, O *A.*, Ezek. 23:22.

AHOLIBAMAH, (1) the granddaughter of Zibeon the Hivite, and one of the wives of Esau (Gen. 36:2). (2) One of the chiefs who sprang from Esau (Gen. 36:41).

AHUMAI, grandson of Shobal, son of Judah (I Chr. 4:2).

AHUZAM, one of the four sons of Ashur by Naarah, of the tribe of Judah (I Chr. 4:6).

AHUZZATH, one of the friends of Abimelech who accompanied him on his visit to Isaac (Gen. 26:26).

AHZAI, son of Meshillemoth (Neh. 11:13).

AI, HAI, (1) one of the royal cities of the Canaanites, and the place of Joshua's defeat (Joshua 10:1). (2) A town of the Ammonites, perhaps opposite Heshbon (Jeremiah 49:3).

AIAH, (1) one of the sons of Zibeon, the Horite (Gen. 36:24). (2) The father of Rizpah, Saul's concubine (II Sam. 3:7).

AIATH, AIJA, variant forms of Ai (Neh. 11:31; Is. 10:28).

AIJALON, AJALON, (1) a Levitical city of Dan (Josh. 19:42); a city of refuge (Josh. 21:24). (2) A city in Zebulun (Judges 12:12).

AIJELETH SHAHAR, AIJELETH HASH-SHAHAR, means "hind of the morning." It is supposed to be the tune to which the song was sung. It occurs only in the introduction of Ps. 22, as the name of the tune. Its actual meaning, however, is not certain.

AILETH, doth trouble.
what *a.* thee, Hagar, Gen. 21:17.
a. the people, I Sam. 11:5.
what *a.* thee, O sea, Ps. 114:5.

AIN, literally means eye. Occurs in combination with other words: En-geda, En-gannim. (1) One of the landmarks on the eastern side of Palestine, as described by Moses (Num. 34:11). (2) A city of Judah (Josh. 15:32).

AIR, particularly the lower part, the atmospheric region (Acts 22:23; I Thess. 4:17; Rev. 9:2). The devil is called "the ruler of the powers of the air" (Eph. 2:2).
to beat the *a.*, I Cor. 9:26.
to speak into the *a.*, I Cor. 14:9.
the power of the *a.*, Eph. 2:2.
the Lord in the *a.*, I Thess. 4:17.
the sun and the *a.*, Rev. 9:2.

AJAH, *see* **AIAH.**

AJALON, *see* **AIJALON.**

AKAN, *see* **JAAKAN.**

AKELDAMA, *see* **ACELDAMA.**

AKKUB, (1) one of the sons of Elioenai, a descendant of David (I Chr. 3:24). (2) One of the Levitical gatekeepers at the temple after captivity (I Chr. 9:17). (3) The head of one of the families of Nethinim that returned from Babylon (Ezra 2:45).

AKRABBIM, a place at the southern end of the Dead Sea. It was called the ascent of Akrabbim (Num. 34:4).

ALABASTER, a pink-colored gypsum named after a city in Middle Egypt, Alabastron. It. was made into cups, boxes, etc. for holding perfumes. Boxes made of other materials were also called "alabaster boxes" (Matt. 26:7; Luke 7:37).

ALAMETH, one of the nine sons of Becher, the son of Benjamin (I Chr. 7:8).

ALAMMELECH, a town in the territory of Asher (Josh. 19:26).

ALAMOTH, a musical term (I Chr. 15:20; title Ps. 46).

ALARM, the sound of the trumpet, giving the signals while on a journey or at camp (Lev. 23:24; Num. 10:5). Also, it is used for call to war, or at a public assembly (Jer. 4:19; 49:2).

ALAS, an exclamation.
a., O Lord God, Josh. 7:7.
a., my daughter, Judg. 11:35.
a for that day, Jer. 30:7.
a that great city, Rev. 18:10.

ALBEIT, an old word meaning "although it be that."
a. I do not say, Philem. 19.

ALEMETH, ALLEMETH, one of the sons of Jehoadah, the son of Ahaz (I Chr. 8:36; 9:42).

ALEPH, the first letter in the Hebrew alphabet.

ALEXANDER, (1) the son of Simon, a Cyrenian Jew who carried the cross of Christ (Mark 15:21). (2) One of the chief men who were present at the examination of Peter and John before the Sanhedrin (Acts 4:6). (3) A Jew of Ephesus; he took part in the uproar in that city. (4) A coppersmith, who, with Hymenaes and others, fell away from the faith (I Tim. 1:20).

ALEXANDRIA, a city and seaport of the land of Egypt about twelve miles from the mouth of the Nile. It was named after Alexander the Great, who founded it about B.C. 333. It was here that the Septuagint version of the Bible was made. Alexandria is not mentioned in the Old Testament, and is only mentioned incidentally in the New Testament (Acts 2:10; 6:9; 18:24; 27:6).

ALEXANDRIAN, one who is from the city of Alexandria, particularly a Jew from that city (Acts 6:9; 18:24).

ALGUM, a costly tree.
a. trees, out of Leba., II Chr. 2:8.

ALIAH, one of the dukes of Edom, descended from Esau (I Chr. 1:51).

ALIAN, one of the five sons of Shobal, a descendant of Seir (I Chr. 1:40).

ALIEN, a person born in another country, a foreigner, and so not entitled to citizenship where he lives.
a. in a strange land, Ex. 18.3.
a. in their sight, Job 19:15.
armies of the *a.,* Heb. 11:34.

ALIENATE, to change to another, to divert, to estrange.
a. the first-fruits, Ezek. 48:14.
being *a.* from, Eph. 4:18.
that were sometime *a.,* Col. 1:21.

ALIKE, just as, together.
all *a.* to all, Eccles. 9:2.
shall eat them *a.,* Deut. 12:22.

ALIVE, living, active.
killeth and maketh *a.,* I Sam. 2:6.
was dead and is *a.,* Luke 15:24.
a. to God through, Rom. 6:11.
a. without the law, Rom. 7:9.
shall all be made *a.,* I Cor. 15:22.
we who are *a.,* I Thess. 4:15.
I am *a.* forevermore, Rev. 1:18.
was dead and is *a.,* Rev. 2:8.

ALLAMMELECH, *see* **ALAMMELECH.**

ALLEGE, to adduce evidence, to quote authorities.
opening and alleging, Acts 17:3.

ALLEGORY, description of one thing under the image of another.
things are in an *a.,* Gal. 4:24.

ALLELUIA, *see* **HALLELUJAH.**

ALLIANCE, the political relations between nations by treaty. In the Bible they are known as leagues, covenants, and treaties. Abraham allied with the Canaanite princes (Gen. 14:13), and with Abimelech the Philistine king (Gen. 21:22–24). Israel, in covenant relation with God, was to hold itself aloof from other nations (Lev. 18:3). However, they were to be friends with other nations; they were not to make war on them (Deut. 2:4). Later, during the reign of the kings, many alliances were made, but the prophets denounced this practice (Ezek. 16:23; Hos. 5).

ALLON, (1) a city near Kadesh Naphtali (Josh. 19:33). (2) The head of a family in Simeon (I Chr. 4:37).

ALLON-BACHUTH, a landmark to show where Deborah, Rebekah's nurse, was buried (Gen. 35:8).

ALLOW, to let, authorize, endure, bear.
themselves also *a.,* Acts 24:15.
which I do I *a.* not, Rom. 7:15.

we were *a.* of God, I Thess. 2:4.

ALLURE, persuade, entice.
I will *a.* her, Hos. 2:14.
a. through the lusts, II Pet. 2:18.

ALMIGHTY, sufficient.
I am the *A.* God, Gen. 17:1.
I am God *A.,* Gen. 35:11.
the name of God *A.,* Ex. 6:3.
what is the *A.,* Job 21:15.
under the shadow of *A.,* Ps. 91:1.
is come to the *A.,* Rev. 1:8.
Lord God *A.,* Rev. 4:8.
the winepress . . of *A.,* Rev. 19:15.

ALMODAD, the son of Joktan, of the family of Shem (Gen. 10:26).

ALMON, one of the four sacred cities of Benjamin (Josh. 21:18). Also called Alemeth, or Allemeth (hidden), in I Chr. 6:60.

ALMOND, a nut tree, larger than a peach tree; it thrives most around the area of Syria.

ALMON-DIBLATHAIM, the 39th encampment of Israel after they left Egypt (Num. 33:46).

ALMOST, nearly, about.
a. ready to stone me, Ex. 17:4.
a. thou persuadest me, Acts 26:28.
a. all things are by, Heb. 9:22.

ALMS, a kindness, a kind act. The Hebrews had· no word for alms; they used the word righteousness for such acts. The laws of Moses made ample provision for the poor. Jesus helped the needy and the sick, giving them consolation, therefore it is his will that all in the Church show the same spirit.
rather give *a.,* Luke 11:41.
Sell . ., and give *a.,* Luke 12:33.
prayers and thine *a.,* Acts 10:4.

ALMSDEED, kindness, kind act.
was full of . . *a.,* Acts 9:36.

ALMUG, *see* ALGUM.

ALNATHAN, the Elnathan of Ezra 8:16.

ALOES, LIGN ALOES, doubtless a product of trees growing in India and China. It is mentioned four times in the Old Testament (Num. 24:6; Ps. 45:8; Prov. 7:17; Song 4:14) and once in the New Testament (John 19:39). It is highly possible that this tree could have been cultivated around the Jordan valley.

ALONE, separate, by itself, apart.
he sitteth *a.,* Lam. 3:28.
he was *a.* praying, Luke 9:18.
faith . . dead, being *a.,* James 2:17.

ALOOF, distant in interest and feeling.
my friends stand *a.,* Ps. 38:11.

ALOTH, BEALOTH, an area near Asher (I Kin. 4:16).

ALPHA, the first letter of the Greek alphabet; used with omega, the last letter, to express the beginning and the end.
I am the *A.* and Omega, Rev. 1:8.

ALPHABET, alpha and beta, the first two letters of the Greek alphabet.

ALPHAEUS, father of the lesser James (Matt. 10:3). He is called Cleopas in John 19:25.

ALTAR, the central place of worship, as a table, stones, a mount, on which a sacrifice was made to some deity. The earliest one in the Bible is that built by Noah (Gen. 8:20). The Law restricted the altars to the one in the temple. However, this was violated (Deut. 12:3). Provisions were made for two kinds of altars: (1) altar of burnt offerings (Ex. 27:8), and (2) altar of incense, the golden altar (Ex. 38:30). The latter was not strictly an altar, since no sacrifice was offered on it.

AL-TASCHITH, means "destroy not." It is found in the introduction of some Psalms (57, 58, 59, 75).

ALUSH, an encampment of Israel in the wilderness, somewhere between Sin and Sinai (Num. 33:13, 14).

ALVAH, a duke of Edom, a descendant of Esau (Gen. 36:40).

ALVAN, son of Shobal, a Horite (Gen. 36:23). Also called Alian (I Chr. 1:40).

ALWAYS, ever, continually, in all time.

I would not live *a.*, Job 7:16.
Lord *a.* before me, Ps. 16:8.
He will not *a.* chide, Ps. 103:9.
I am with you *a.*, Matt. 28:20.
rejoice in the Lord *a.*, Phil. 4:4.

AMAD, a town in Asher (Josh. 19:26).

AMAL, one of the four sons of Helem, of the tribe of Asher (I Chr. 7:35).

AMALEK, the son of Eliphaz by Timna, a concubine (Gen. 36:12). He was chief of an Idumaean tribe (Gen. 36:12). He has probably no connection with the ancient Amalekites.

AMALEKITES, an ancient race. Amalek's history is summed up by Balaam (Num. 24:20). In Abraham's time the Amalekites were found S.W. of the Dead Sea (Gen. 14:7). During Moses' time they were found at the borders of Egypt and in the Sinaitic peninsula. They were always bitter enemies of Israel. They were defeated by Saul and David, and even in the days of Hezekiah there were some to be smitten (I Chr. 4:43).

AMAM, a city in the south of Judah (Josh. 15:26).

AMANA, the northern ridge of Antilibanus (Song. 4:8).

AMARANTHINE, means "unfading." I Pet. 5:4 a similar word is used to mean "it fadeth not away."

AMARIAH, (1) a descendant of Aaron (I Chr. 6:7). (2) A later high-priest (I Chr. 6:11). (3) A Levite, a son of Hebron and grandson of Kohath (I Chr. 23:19). (4) A chief priest active in the reforms of Jehoshaphat (II Chr. 19:11). (5) A Levite appointed by Hezekiah to be over the temple dues (II Chr. 31:15). (6) Son of Bani (Ezra 10:42). (7) One of the priests that returned from Babylon with Zerubbabel (Neh. 11:4). (8) The son of Shephatiah and father of Zechariah (Neh. 11:4). (9) The great-grandfather of the prophet Zephaniah (Zeph. 1:1).

AMASA, (1) the son of Abigail, a sister of King David, by Jether, an Ishmaelite (II Sam. 17:25). He was general to Absalom, and was defeated by Joab, but pardoned by David. Joab killed him (I

Kin. 2:32). (2) A son of Hadlai and chief of Ephraim (II Chr. 28:12).

AMASAI, (1) a Levite, son of Elkanah, and father of Mahath (I Chr. 6:25). (2) One of the chief captains of Judah who joined David at Ziklag (I Chr. 12:18). (3) One of the priests who helped remove the ark from the house of Obed-edom to Jerusalem (I Chr. 15:24). (4) The father of Mahath (II Chr. 29:12).

AMASHAI, the son of Azareel, and one of the priests appointed by Nehemiah to reside at Jerusalem and do work at the temple (Neh. 11:13).

AMASIAH, the son of Zichri, Jehoshaphat's general (II Chr. 17:16).

AMAZED, troubled, astonished, awed.
were exceedingly *a.*, Matt. 19:25.
they were all *a.*, Mark 2:12.
began to be sore *a.*, Mark 14:33.

AMAZEMENT, terror, awesomeness.
with wonder and *a.*, Acts 3:10.

AMAZIAH, (1) the son and successor of Jehoash, and the ninth king of Judah. He became king at the age of twenty-five, and he reigned for twenty-nine years (II Kin. 14:1, 2). He was the first to hire men to fill his army. He conquered Edom and carried home idols for worship. He was killed by conspirators at Lachish (II Kin. 14:3–20). (2) The father of Joshah (I Chr. 4:34). (3) The son of Hilkiah and father of Hashabiah (I Chr. 6:45). (4) The priest of the golden calves at Beth-el (Amos 7:10–17).

AMBASSADOR, means "one who goes on an errand." When nations are isolated, they need men to negotiate for them. David sent ambassadors (II Sam. 10:2), Hiram sent some to Solomon (I Kin. 5:1), and Toi sent some to David (II Sam. 8:10). Their work was not that of representatives, but as heralds for the king (II Sam. 10:1–5).

AMBASSAGE, an old form of "embassy," which is a person sent on a mission (Luke 14:32).

AMBER, a reddish-yellow color.
as the color of *a.*, Ezek. 1:4.

AMBUSH, to attack by surprise.
an *a.* for the city, Josh. 8:2.
a. for the Lord, Jer. 51:12.

AMEN, a Hebrew word, usually translated verily, or sometimes not translated at all, meaning "so be it." It is used as a name for the Lord in Rev. 3:14. It is used as a response or closing of a prayer (Matt. 6:13; Rom. 11:36).

AMEND, to strengthen, to complete.
a. your ways, Jer. 26:13.
he began to *a.*, John 4:52.

AMERCE, to inflict a penalty.
they shall *a.* him, Deut. 22:19.

AMERICAN STANDARD VERSION, *see* VERSIONS.

AMETHYST, a purple or violet-colored quartz. The Greek name alludes to the belief that it would prevent intoxication if worn at feasts. It is mentioned in Ex. 28:19; 39:12; and Rev. 21:20.

AMI, *see* AMMON.

AMIABLE, beloved.
a. are thy tabernacles, Ps. 84:1.

AMINADAB, *see* AMMINADAB.

AMISS, out of place, error.
we have done *a.*, II Chr. 6:37.
hath done nothing *a.*, Luke 23:41.
ye ask *a.*, James 4:3.

AMITTAI, a native of Gath-hepher, of the tribe of Zebulun, and father of the prophet Jonah (II Kin. 14:25; Jonah 1:1).

AMMAH, the place reached by Joab and Abishai, in their pursuit of Abner (II Sam. 2:24).

AMMI, means "my people." A figurative name for the people of Israel in contrast to Lo-ammi ("not my people") of Hosea 2:1.

AMMIEL, (1) the son of Gemalli, of the tribe of Dan; one of the twelve spies sent by Moses (Num. 13:12). (2) The father of Machir of Lo-debar (II Sam. 9:4). (3) Father of Bath-sheba, wife of Uriah and afterward of David (I Chr. 3:

5). (4) One of the sons of Obed-edom (I Chr. 26:5).

AMMIHUD, AMMIHUR, (1) an Ephraimite, the father of Elishama (Num. 1:10; 2:18). (2) The father of Shemuel, who was a Simeonite chief (Num. 34:20). (3) A man of the tribe of Naphtali (Num. 34:28). (4) The father of Talmai, king of Geshur (II Sam. 13:37). (5) The son of Omri and the father of Uthai (I Chr. 9:4).

AMMINADAB, AMINADAB, (1) the son of Aram and the father of Nashon (Matt. 1:4), who was prince of the tribe of Judah at the first numbering of Israel (Num. 1:7). (2) A son of Kohath, the son of Levi (I Chr. 6:22). (3) A Levite of the sons of Uzziel (I Chr. 15:10, 11).

AMMI-NADIB, another form of Amminadab. A person whose chariots are mentioned as being swift (Song 6:12).

AMMISHADDAI, the father of Ahiezer, a chief of Dan (Num. 1:12; 2:25).

AMMIZABAD, the son and lieutenant of Benaiah (I Chr. 27:6).

AMMON, the son of Lot by his youngest daughter (Gen. 19:38). His descendants were called Ammonites (Deut. 2:20, children of Ammon (Gen. 19:38), and sometimes merely Ammon (Neh. 13:23).

AMMONITES, a nomadic race descended from Lot and Lot's daughter, as were the Moabites also. They dwelt east and north of Moab. Although Israel was forbidden to attack Ammon, the Ammonites were often in league against Israel (Deut. 23:3, 4). They were governed by a king (I Sam. 12:12). Their national deity was Molech (I Kin. 11:5). Solomon married some Moabite women (I Kin. 14:1). Doom was prophesied against Ammon (Ezek. 25:5; Zeph. 2:9). By the time of Origen (186–254 A.D.) the Ammonites merged with the Arabs.

AMON, *see* AMMON.

AMOS, (1) one of the twelve minor prophets and a native of Tekoah. He was a shepherd, and was not trained as a prophet. And yet, he was called by the

Lord to prophesy concerning Israel in the reigns of Uzziah, king of Judah, and Jeroboam, king of Israel. The times were good in both kingdoms. The prophecies were directed toward both kingdoms, but primarily to Israel. After his prophecy, he probably returned to Judah. The time and nature of his death is uncertain. (2) The ninth in the line of descent from Christ, being the son of Naum and the father of Mattathias (Luke 3:25).

AMOS, THE BOOK OF, the earliest known Old Testament prophetic book, containing poems recited by this Judean shepherd of Tekoah while visiting northern Israel about 750 B.C. In the first part of the book (1:1–2:3) he denounces the sins of the nations bordering on Israel and Judah. Next (2:4–6:14), he describes the state of those two kingdoms, especially Israel. This is followed by (7:1–9:10) his relating his visit to Bethel, and he sketches the impending punishment of Israel which he predicts to Amaziah. After this part, he rises to a more lofty height, and describes the hope of the Messiah's kingdom, when the people will be forgiven and God's blessings will be established forever.

AMOZ, the father of the prophet Isaiah (II Kin. 19:2; Isa. 1:1).

AMPHIPOLIS, a city of Macedonia through which Paul passed on his second missionary journey (Acts 17:1).

AMPLIAS, an early Christian and associate with Paul (Rom. 16:8).

AMRAM, (1) the son of Kohath who married Jochebed and was the father of Moses (Ex. 6:18, 20), (2) a descendant of Esau (I Chr. 1:41), (3) a son of Bani, who had married a foreign wife (Ezra 10:34).

AMRAMITES, descendants of Amram, the father of Moses (Num. 3:27).

AMRAPHEL, king of Shinar, who with others took Lot captive (Gen. 14:1).

AMULET, not in the King James Version but in Is. 3:20 the Revised Standard Version has "amulet" instead of "earrings". An amulet is anything worn as a protection against evil influences of a mystical kind. They often served as ornaments (Gen. 35:4).

AMZI, a Levite, the son of Bani (I Chr. 6:46); son of Zechariah (Neh. 11:12).

ANAB, a town in the southern part of Judah (Josh. 11:21).

ANAH, a descendant of Esau (Gen. 36:24).

ANAHARATH, a city about fifteen miles s.w. of the Sea of Galilee (Josh. 19:19).

ANAIAH, an associate with Ezra (Neh. 8:4).

ANAK, the father of a race of people, the Anakim (or Nephilim), who were giants (Num. 13:33).

ANAKIM, a stalwart race of people who descended from Anak and were closely associated with the Rephaim (Deut. 2:10). See ANAK.

ANAMIM, an Egyptian tribe descended from Ham (Gen. 10:13).

ANAMMELECH, a god of the Sepharvaim whose worship required child sacrifice (II Kin. 17:31).

ANAN, an associate with Nehemiah (Neh. 10:26).

ANANI, a son of Elioenai and a descendant of Solomon (I Chr. 3:24).

ANANIAH, (1) the father of Maaseiah who helped repair the wall of Jerusalem (Neh. 3:23), (2) a town of Benjamin about 3 miles north of Jerusalem toward Gibeon (Neh. 11:32).

ANANIAS, a disciple of the early church who with his wife Sapphira sold a field and gave a portion of the price to the church, pretending that it was the whole sum. He was struck dead by the Holy Spirit (Acts 5).

ANANIAS, a disciple at Damascus who was sent to Saul by God and declared to him the will of God (Acts 9:10–18; 22:12–16).

ANANIAS, a Jewish high priest before whom Paul was tried (Acts 23:2).

ANATH, father of the judge Shamgar (Judg. 3:31).

ANATHEMA, accursed, or devoted to destruction.
let him be *a.*, I Cor. 16:22.

ANATHOTH, (1) a son of Becher (I Chr. 7:8), (2) an associate with Nehemiah (Neh. 10:19), (3) a town near Jerusalem, the home of Jeremiah (Jer. 1:1; 11:21).

ANCHOR, that which keeps a ship from drifting. It is used both literally and figuratively in the New Testament.
they would have cast *a.*, Acts 27:30.
we have as an *a.*, Heb. 6-19.

ANCIENT, (1) of times past, (2) aged men (Job. 12:12), (3) men of times past (I Sam. 24:13), (4) leaders of the people (Jer. 19:1).

ANCIENT OF DAYS, an expression applied to God. This expression is applied to God because age inspires veneration and conveys the impression of majesty.
A. of days did sit, Dan. 7:9.
came to the *A.* of days, Dan. 7:13.

ANCLE, *see* ANKLE.

ANDREW, one of the twelve apostles, the brother of Peter.
Peter, and *A.*, his bro., Matt. 10:2.
A., Simon Peter's bro., John 1:40.

ANDRONICUS, a kinsman and fellow-prisoner of Paul (Rom. 16:7).

ANEM, a Levitical city of the tribe of Issachar (I Chr. 6:73).

ANER, (1) a city in the western half of the tribe of Manasseh (I Chr. 6:70), (2) one of the three men who aided Abram in the battle of the kings (Gen. 14:24).

ANETHOTHITE, an inhabitant of Anathoth (II Sam. 23:27).

ANGARY, compel, the right of a belligerent to seize property for his use. Angary does not occur in the Bible but it is an Anglicizing of the word translated "compel" (Matt. 5:41).

ANGEL, a messenger, (1) any messenger, (2) a messenger of God, (3) a messenger of the Devil. The most frequent use of angel is to denote messengers of God who portray super-human traits and sometimes perform miracles. Some are named, such as Gabriel and Michael. *See* GABRIEL and MICHAEL.
a. of the Lord said, Gen. 22:11.
the *a.* did wondrously, Judg. 13:19.
a. of his presence, Is. 63:9.
devil and his *a.*, Matt. 25:41.
the *a.* Gabriel, Luke 1:26.
face of an *a.*, Acts 6:15.
into *a.* of light, II Cor. 11:14.
as an *a.* of God, Gal. 4:14.
a. of God worship, Heb. 1:6.
God spared not the *a.*, II Pet. 2:4.
a. of the church, Rev. 2:1.

ANGELIC HYMN, the hymn Gloria in excelsis, so called because the former part of it was sung by the angels when announcing the birth of Jesus (Luke 2:14).

ANGELIC SALUTATION, the greeting extended to the Virgin Mary by the angel when he announced to her that she was to become the mother of Jesus (Luke 1:28).

ANGER, wrath, not always spoken of as sinful. God is spoken of as possessing anger; Christ displayed anger; yet Christians are warned against the possibility of sinning in anger.
fierce *a.* of the Lord, Num. 25:4.
looked on them with *a.*, Mark 3:5.
all *a.* be put away, Eph. 4:31.

ANGLE, a mediaeval English word for hook.
cast *a.* into the brooks, Is. 19:8.
all of them with the *a.*, Hab. 1:15.

ANGRY, *see* ANGER.

ANGUISH, deep distress of the emotions.
tremble, and be in *a.*, Deut. 2:25.
distress and *a.* come, Prov. 1:27.
a. as of her, Jer. 4:31.
tribulation and *a.* upon, Rom. 2:9.
much *a.* of heart, II Cor. 2:4.

ANIAM, a son of Shemidah of the tribe of Manasseh (I Chr. 7:19).

ANIM, a city in the southern part of Judah (Josh. 15:50), ten miles South West of Hebron.

ANIMALS, UNCLEAN, see **UNCLEAN ANIMALS.**

ANISE, a spice, probably the same as dill in its Biblical use.
pay tithe of mint, a., Matt. 23:23.

ANKLE, used literally in the Bible of the joint of man between the foot and the leg.
feet and a. bones, Acts 3:7.

ANKLET, ornaments of gold, silver, brass, iron or glass worn around the ankles by the women of the East (Is. 3:16).

ANNA, a prophetess who blessed Jesus when He was presented as a babe in the temple (Luke 2:36).

ANNAS, father-in-law of Caiaphas; he with Caiaphas was called high priest during the trial of Jesus. (Luke 3:2).

ANNUL. see **DISANNUL.**

ANNUNCIATION, the announcement by Gabriel to Mary that she was to bear the Christ child (Luke 1:26–30).

ANOINT, (1) to pour oil upon one in appointing him to a particular office, such as a king or priest, (2) to pour oil upon one in an act of healing.
oil and a. him, Ex. 29:7.
Zadok a. him king, I Kin. 1:34.
a. him with oil, James 5:14.

ANOINTED, used in reference usually to a king. In places such as Ps. 2:2, this term refers to Christ.
he is the Lord's a., I Sam. 24:10.
against his a., Ps. 2:2.

ANOINTING, may be literal or spiritual; to the Christians God has given an anointing to guide them.
the a. which ye have, I John 2:27.
same a. teacheth you, I John 2:27.

ANON, immediately or straightway.
and a. with joy, Matt. 13:20.
a. they tell him of her, Mark 1:30.

ANOTH, see **BETH-ANOTH.**

ANOTHER, any or some different person.
appointed me a. seed, Gen. 4:25.
one man sin against a., I Sam. 2:25.

but to love one a., Rom. 13:8.
tarry one for a., I Cor. 11:33.
exhort one a., Heb. 3:13.

ANSWER, (1) to give reply, (2) to speak with no question being asked, (3) to testify, (4) to grant a request made in prayer.
righteousness a. for me, Gen. 30:33.
for thou wilt a. me, Ps. 86:7.
a. a fool, Prov. 26:5.
Peter a. unto her, Acts 5:8.
how ye ought to a., Col. 4:6.

ANT, a wise and diligent insect often used as an example for men.
go to the a. thou, Prov. 6:6.
the a. are a people, Prov. 30:25.

ANTEDILUVIAN, the period of time before the flood.

ANTEDILUVIANS, the people who lived before the flood. For information concerning these people we are dependent upon the revelation in Gen. 4–7.

ANTELOPE, not found in the King James Version; it is called "wild ox" in Deut. 14:5 and "wild bull" in Is. 51:20.

ANTHROPOLOGY, the study of man. The Bible is not a systematic textbook about man. Nevertheless it has much teaching concerning man. Man was created by God (Gen. 1–2). Man is made up of spirit, soul and body (I Thess. 5:23). Sin entered the human race by Adam (Gen. 3; Rom. 5:12). However, man did not inherit Adam's guilt but the consequences and each man dies because of his own sins (Rom. 5:12). Man is a free moral agent and can choose to serve God and inherit eternal life (Josh. 24:15; Heb. 5:9); or disobey and be eternally lost (II Thess. 1:5–10).

ANTHROPOMORPHISM, ascribing to God human emotions and actions.
God speaks, Gen. 1:3.
God laughs, Ps. 2:4.
God has eyes, Amos 9:4.
God rides on the clouds, Hab. 3:8.

ANTHROPOPATHISM, the attributing to God of human emotions such as grief (Gen. 6:6), disgust (Lev. 20:23), jealousy (Ex. 20:5), joy (Zeph. 3:17), etc.

ANTI-CHRIST, against Christ, or instead of Christ, a word only used by the apostle John (I and II John). Generally an anti-christ is a person who is opposed to the authority of Christ as the head of the Church, and the spirit of his religion, those who deny that Jesus Christ came in the flesh. (I John 2:22; 4:3; II John 7). Later, the antichrist was considered to be one particular person who was to come. He was identified with Paul's "man of sin" (II Thess. 2:3–8) and the character described in Rev. 13:8. In the Middle Ages Pope Innocent III designated Mohammed as the antichrist; the Reformers thought it to be the papal Church. These interpretations, however, are not inherent in the text of the Bible.

ANTIOCH, in Pisidia. A town in Asia Minor, which Paul visited on his first missionary Journey (Acts 13:14).

ANTIOCH, in Syria. A city where Paul and Barnabas labored for one year. At this city the disciples were first called Christians. The church at Antioch became the starting point for the expansion of the church throughout the Roman Empire.
they were come to, *A.*, Acts 11:20.
Christians first at *A.*, Acts 11:26.
Jerusalem unto *A.*, Acts 11:27.
church that was at *A.*, Acts 13:1.

ANTIOCHUS EPIPHANES (IV), ruler of Syria B.C. 175–164. He proscribed Judaism and tried to Hellenize the Jews. His name does not appear in the Bible though he is referred to in Dan. 8:9 as the little horn. The abomination of desolation in the New Testament refers to the offering of a sow on the altar of the Temple in Jerusalem to Zeus, thus desecrating the altar (Matt. 24:15).

ANTIPAS, (1) name of the Herod who beheaded John the Baptist and before whom Jesus appeared in trial (Matt. 14:1). *See* **HEROD** (2) an early Christian martyr.
A. my faithful martyr, Rev. 2:13.

ANTIPATRIS, a town about twenty-eight miles south of Caesarea where Paul spent the night in his flight from Jerusalem to Caesarea (Acts 23:31).

ANTIQUITY, to precede in time, to be old. The word "antiquity" occurs only in Is. 23:7 in reference to the age of Tyre. Other similar expressions in the Bible are former (Ezek. 16:55) and afore (Ps. 129:6).

ANTONIA, CASTLE or TOWER OF, *see* **CASTLE, PRAETORIUM.**

ANTOTHIJAH, a son of Jeroham a descendant of Benjamin (I Chr. 8:24).

ANUB, a son of Coz and a descendant of Judah through Ashur (I Chr. 4:8).

ANVIL, the instrument of the smith for hammering on. Referred to only once in the Bible (Is. 41:7).

APACE. swiftly, a quick pace.
and he came *a.*, II Sam. 18:25.

APART, separate; used often to distinguish God's people from the world.
set *a.* unto the Lord, Ex. 13:12.
shall be put *a.* seven, Lev. 15:19.
Lord hath set *a.*, Ps. 4:3.
a desert place *a.*, Matt. 14:13.
come ye yourselves *a.*, Mark 6:31.
lay *a.* all filthiness, James 1:21.

APE, mentioned as being brought to Solomon, probably from Ceylon (I Kin. 10:22).

APELLES, a Christian in Rome, whom Paul salutes in his letter to the church in Rome (Rom. 16:10).

APHARSACHITES, or **APHARSITES** or **APHARSACITES**, a group of people living in Palestine in the time of Ezra (Ezra 4:9). Probably they were transplanted there by the Assyrians.

APHEK, name of several cities in Palestine.
a city north of Sidon, Josh. 13:4.
Aphek an Asherite city, Josh. 19:30.
a city North of Joppa, I Sam. 4:1.
a city beyond Jordan, I Kin. 20:26.

APHEKAH, a city in the hill country of Judah (Josh. 15:53).

APHIAH, father of Bechorath a son of Benjamite and ancestor of Saul (I Sam. 9:1).

APHIK, a city of Asher from which the

Canaanites were not driven (Judg. 1:31).

APHRAH, house of Aphrah, means a house of dust. (Mic. 1:10).

APHSES, the head of the eighteenth course of priests (I Chr. 24:15).

APOCALYPSE, *see* **REVELATION, BOOK OF.**

APOCRYPHA, "hidden," books supposedly hidden and found and included in the Bible. The Old Testament Apocrypha is rejected by Protestants and accepted as canonical by the Catholics. The books of the Apocrypha are: I Esdras, II Esdras, Tobit, Judith, additions to Esther, Wisdom of Solomon, Ecclesiasticus, Baruch, The Song of the Three Holy Children, The History of Susanna, Bel and the Dragon, Prayer of Manasses, I Maccabees, and II Maccabees. Most of these were written in the period between the Old and New Testaments.

APOLLONIA, a city of Macedonia through which Paul passed on his second missionary journey (Acts 17:1).

APOLLOS, a Jew from Alexandria who became a Christian. At first he knew only the baptism of John, but he was taught more perfectly by Priscilla and Aquila. He ministered in Ephesus and Corinth.
certain Jew named *A.,* Acts 18:24.
who is *A.?* I Cor. 3:5.
bring Zenas and *A.,* Titus 3:13.

APOLLYON, the name of the angel of the bottomless pit (the same as the Hebrew *Abaddon*). The name means "destroyer" in Greek.
his name is *A.,* Rev. 9:11.

APOSTLE, "one sent forth." This word refers variously to the twelve, to Matthias and Paul, and to certain others. While usually *apostle* refers to a member of the twelve, it also has the wider application to include various ones who were sent forth on a special commission.
of the twelve *a.,* Matt. 10:2.
Paul, an *a.,* I Cor. 1:1.
false *a.* deceitful, II Cor. 11:13.
the *a.* Barnabas, Acts 14:14.

APOTHECARY, one who prepares perfumes and spices.
after art of *a.,* Ex. 30:25.
ointment of the *a.,* Eccles. 10:1.

APPAIM, a son of Nadab, of the tribe of Judah (I Chr. 2:30).

APPAREL, one's garments, often by which his character is judged.
clothed in strange *a.,* Zeph. 1:8.
stood in white *a.,* Acts 1:10.
in modest *a.,* I Tim. 2:9.
gold, or putting on *a.,* I Pet. 3:3.

APPARENTLY, at present this can mean "seemingly," but in the King James Version it means "visibly," "plainly," "distinctly."
I speak even *a.,* Num. 12:8.

APPEAR, while the usual meaning is often found in the Bible, this also describes the manifestation of God or of Christ.
the Lord will *a.* to, Lev. 9:4.
Shepherd shall *a.,* I Pet. 5:4.

APPETITE, in the Bible used only to refer to the sensual element. Often it has a bad connotation.
a man given to *a.,* Prov. 23:2.
for mouth, yet *a.,* Eccles. 6:7.

APPHIA, a Christian woman in the house of Philemon (Philem. 2).

APPII FORUM, a station on the Appian Way about forty-three miles from Rome, where the Roman brethren met Paul on his journey to Rome (Acts 28:15).

APPLE, besides the usual meaning, the expression "apple of the eye" is found. It connotes something very delightful.
as the *a.* of his eye, Deut. 32:10.
like *a.* of gold, Prov. 25:11.

APPLY, usually in the Bible this refers to applying one's heart, expressing determination and purpose.
a. thine heart to, Prov. 2:2.

APPOINT, to establish, to set in an office, or to make a decree.
a. me thy wages, Gen. 30:28.
Pharaoh *a.* officers, Gen. 41:34.
a. these two ways, Ezek. 21:19.

APPOINTED, "that which has been decreed."
knoweth *a.* times, Jer. 8:7.
for at the time *a.,* Dan. 8:19.

APPREHEND, (1) to arrest—II Cor. 11:32, (2) to take possession of (Phil. 3:12, 13).

APPROACH, (1) to draw near—II Sam. 11: 20, (2) to contract a marriage (Lev. 18:6).

APPROVE, to pass favorable judgment upon.
Jesus, a man *a.,* Acts 2:22.

APRON, in the Bible a garment more for clothing than for protecting the clothes.
fig-leaves, and made *a.,* Gen. 3:7.
brought to the sick *a.,* Acts 19:12.

APT, the Bible usage implies ability more than likelihood.
a. for war, II Kin. 24:16.
be *a.* to teach, II Tim. 2:24.

AQUILA, a Jewish Christian, husband of Priscilla, who was with Paul in Corinth and accompanied him to Ephesus. He and Paul were of the same trade, tentmakers. Aquila, with his wife, taught Apollos more perfectly the way of the Lord.
certain Jew named *A.,* Acts 18:2.
A. and Priscilla, Acts 18:26.
greet *A.* and Priscilla, Rom. 16:3.

AR, a chief city of Moab, located near the eastern coast of the Dead Sea (Num. 21:28).

ARA, a son of Jether, of the tribe of Asher (I Chr. 7:38).

ARAB, a city of Judah (Josh. 15:52).

ARABAH, "burnt up." In the Hebrew this word frequently appears denoting a parched desert land. In the King James Version it appears in this form only in Josh. 18:18; here it probably refers to the desert land south of the Dead Sea.

ARABIA, this may mean where Arabia is now located, or it may include the desert region extending from Egypt and bordering Palestine on the south and east.

kings of *A.,* I Kin. 10:15.
mount Sinai in *A.,* Gal. 4:25.

ARABIANS, nomadic tribes who inhabited the desert region around Palestine. They were known as Ishmaelites and descendants of Keturah.
the *A.* brought, II Chr. 17:11.
Cretes and *A.,* Acts 2:11.

ARAD, one of the royal cities of the Canaanites. It was located near the southwestern coast of the Dead Sea (Josh. 12:14).

ARAH, a son of Ulla, of the tribe of Asher.
sons of Ullah; *A.,* I Chr. 7:39.
Shechaniah son of *A.,* Neh. 6:18.

ARAM, the name of at least three different people in the Bible. Also a term designating the country lying northeast of Palestine.
father of *A.,* Gen. 22:21.
sons of Shamer; *A.,* I Chr. 7:34.
Esrom begat *A.,* Matt. 1:3.

ARAMEANS, inhabitants of Aram. *See* SYRIANS.

ARAMAIC, referring to the Arameans, particularly to their language. Portions of Daniel and Ezra are written in Aramaic. In Is. 36:11 it is called the Syrian language.

ARAMITESS, a female inhabitant of Aram (1 Chr. 7:14).

ARAM-GESHUR, *see* GESHUR.

ARAM-MAACAH, an independent Aramaean kingdom not mentioned by name in the Bible, but referred to in II Sam. 8:6. *See* MAACAH.

ARAM-NAHARAIM, "Aram of the two rivers." This is found in the title to Ps. 60. It is translated "Mesopotamia" (Gen. 24:10).

ARAM-REHOB, *see* REHOB.

ARAM-ZOBAH, *see* ZOBA.

ARAN, son of Dishan, a descendant of Esau (Gen. 36:28).

ARARAT, a mountainous district between Asia Minor and the Caspian Sea.
the mountains of *A.*, Gen. 8:4.
the kingdoms of *A.*, Jer. 51:27.

ARAUNAH, a Jebusite who sold a threshing-floor to David. It later was the site of Solomon's temple.
threshing-place of, II Sam. 24:16.

ARBA, ancestor of the Anakim, a race of giants (Josh. 15:13).

ARBAH, a city south of Jerusalem. It is also called Kirjath-Arba and Hebron. (Gen. 35:27).

ARBATHITE, probably an inhabitant of Beth-arabah. Abi-albon, one of David's mighty men was an Arbathite (II Sam. 23:31).

ARBITE, a man from Arba. Paarai, one of David's mighty men was an Arbite (II Sam. 23:35).

ARCH, an architectural term used to describe a structure in Ezekiel's temple.
likewise to the *a.*, Ezek. 40:16.
windows and their *a.*, Ezek. 40:22.
a. round about, Ezek. 40:30.

ARCHAEOLOGY, the scientific study of the material remains of past human life and activities. Biblical archeology deals with the excavation, decipherment and critical evaluation of such remains that touch directly or indirectly upon life in Biblical times. This field of study has been very fruitful in: (1) Illustrating and explaining Biblical historical statements; (2) Showing the Bible to be historically trustworthy where it has been possible to check; and (3) Supplementing the Biblical history which is often brief, being incidental to the message of redemption. The present dictionary takes into full account proven archeological results.

ARCHANGEL, an angel of high rank. Michael is called an archangel (Jude 9).

ARCHELAUS, son of Herod the Great. He reigned over a part of his father's kingdom after Herod's death (Matt. 2·22).

ARCHERS, those who used the bow. *See* ARCHERY, BOWMAN.

a. have sorely grieved, Gen. 49:23.
noise of the *a.*, Judg. 5:11.
men of valour, *a.*, I Chr. 8:40.
a. shot at king, II Chr. 35:23.

ARCHERY, the bow and arrow was for hunting (Gen. 21:20) and for battle (I Sam. 31:3).

ARCHEVITE, inhabitants of Erech in Babylon, one of the four cities originally built by Nimrod (Gen. 10:10). Later one of the tribes which Osnappar transplanted to Samaria (Ezra 4:9).

ARCHI, a city or district in the neighborhood of Bethel near the border of Ephraim (Josh. 16:2). See ARCHITE.

ARCHIPPUS, a Christian servant in the church at Colosse.
say to *A.* take heed, Col. 4:17.
A. our fellowsoldier, Philem. 2.

ARCHITE, a family whose possessions were upon the southern boundary of the tribe of Ephraim (Josh. 16:2).

ARCHITECTURE, the art of building in Palestine was mainly evolved from a single type, the rectangular, flat-roofed house of stone or brick. The most magnificent architectural structures in the Bible are the successive temples (I Kin. 6; II Chr. 3; Ezek. 40–44).

ARCTURUS, a part of the constellation Bootes and one of the three most brilliant stars of the Southern Hemisphere (Job 9·9; 38:32).

ARD, named as a son of Benjamin (Gen. 46:21), and as a son of Bela (Num. 26:40) and a grandson of Benjamin. He is called Addar (I Chr. 8:3).

ARDITE, a descendant of Addar, or Ard the son or grandson of Benjamin. *See* ARD.

ARDON, a son of Caleb (I Chr. 2:18).

ARELI, one of the seven sons of Gad, and founder of the family of Arelites (Gen. 46:16; Num. 26:17).

ARELITES, the descendants of Areli (Num. 26:17).

AREOPAGITE, a member of the Areopagus court at Athens.
was Dionysius the *A.*, Acts 17:34.

AREOPAGUS, another name for Mar's Hill. Areopagus is its Latin form. It was called Mar's Hill because Mars, the god of war, was said to have been tried there for the murder of the son of Poseidon. It was situated on a high and rocky place at Athens, just west of the Acropolis. There was an ancient court which sat here. The Court of the Areopagus, consisted of life members (Areopagites). Religion (they were considered the ministers of the furies) and education of the youth was under their control. Its political powers were never clearly defined. Paul was brought before this court in A.D. 51 (Acts. 17:19).

ARETAS, a name common to many of the kings of Arabia Petraea. Aretas IV is the king mentioned by Paul as being king of Damascus (II Cor. 11:32).

ARGOB, a region in Bashan and part of the conquered territory of Og assigned to Manasseh (Deut. 3:4).

ARGOB, a prince slain by Pekah when he murdered Pekahiah the king of Israel (II Kin. 15:25).

ARGUING, a form of discussion or reasoning.
doth your *a.* reprove?, Job 6:25.
fill my mouth with *a.*, Job 23:4.

ARIDAI, one of the ten sons of Haman, hanged by the Jews in Babylonia (Esther 9:9).

ARIDATHA, the sixth son of Haman, hanged by the Jews (Esther 9:9).

ARIEH, an associate with Argob (II Kin. 15:25)

ARISTOBULUS, a Christian in Rome whose household Paul saluted.
them which are of *A.*, Rom. 16:10.

ARK, NOAH'S, *see* **NOAH.**

ARK OF THE COVENANT, the chest in the Most Holy Place of the tabernacle which contained a golden pot of manna, Aaron's rod that budded, and the tables of the covenant. It was oblong and made of shittim (acacia) wood. It was overlaid without and within with gold. On the upper lid the mercy-seat was placed. On each end of the ark was one of the two cherubim of gold, whose wings overshadowed the mercy-seat. In the tabernacle worship this was the symbol of God's presence. On one day of the year, the Day of Atonement, the high priest appeared before the ark, as the symbol of God's presence, to make atonement for the sins of the people.
they shall make an *a.*, Ex. 25:10.
mercy seat, upon the *a.*, Lev. 16:2.
the *a.* went before them, Num. 10:33.
when ye see the *a.*, Josh. 3:3.
the *a.* of the covenant, Jer. 3:16.
the *a.* overlaid round, Heb. 9:4.

ARK OF MOSES, the little basket which Moses' mother made for baby Moses and in which she set him adrift. The daughter of Pharaoh found the ark and cared for Moses.
she took for him an *a.*, Ex. 2:3.
when she saw the *a.*, Ex. 2:5.

ARKITE, a family of the Canaanites (Gen. 10:17; I Chr. 1:15).

ARM, may mean either part of the body (Job 31:22) or strength (Is. 51:9).

ARM, to put on armor (I Sam. 17:38).

ARMAGEDDON, "hill of Megiddo," the scene of the great battle between the forces of good and evil. For Old Testament occurrences, *see* **MEGIDDO.**
in the Hebrew tongue *A.*, Rev. 16:16.

ARMED, *see* **ARM.**

ARMENIA, the same as Ararat. Three districts of Armenia are mentioned in the Bible: (1) Ararat (Is. 37:38), (2) Minni (Jer. 51:27), (3) Togarmah (Ezek. 27:14; 38:6).
into the land of *A.*, II Kin. 19:37.

ARMENIAN, pertaining to Armenia.

ARM HOLE, the armpit (Jer. 38:12; Ezek. 13:18).

ARMIES, in I Sam. 17:23 meaning the battleline or ranks.

ARMLET, an ornament to be worn on the arms, especially by women. The word does not appear in the King James Version, but it is implied in II Sam. 1:10.

ARMONI, son of Saul by Rizpah (II Sam. 21:8).

ARMOR, ARMOUR, arms or weapons. The main offensive weapons were the sword, spear, bow and arrows, sling, and battle-axe. The defensive armor consisted of the breastplate, the habergeon, the helmet, greaves (for the feet), and shields.
he put his *a.,* I Sam. 17:54.
they washed his *a.,* I Kin. 22:38 .
house of his *a.,* Is. 39:2.
taketh from him his *a.,* Luke 11:22.
a. of righteousness, II Cor. 6:7.
whole *a.* of God, Eph. 6:11.

ARMOUR-BEARER, one who carries the armour, usually for another (Judg. 9:54).

ARMOURY, (1) a treasury (Jer. 50:25), (2) thing joined together (Neh. 3:19), (3) heap of swords (Song. 4:4).

ARMY, in the Old Testament generally this refers to the Jewish army and the armies of Israel's foes (II Chr. 25:9; Ex. 14:9). In the New Testament the reference is usually to the Roman army, of which Cornelius was a member (Acts 10:1).

ARNAN, a descendant of David (I Chr. 3:21).

ARNI, does not occur in the King James Version, but in the Revised Version it is used in Luke 3:33 for Aram.

ARNON, a river forming the northern boundary of Moab (Num. 21:13).

AROD, ARODI, a son of Gad in Num. 26:17. (In Gen. 46:16 he is called Arodi.)

ARODITES, descendants of Arod (Num. 26:17).

AROER, (1) a city near Rabbath Ammon (Num. 32:24), (2) an Amorite city on the river Arnon (Deut. 3:12), (3) a city in southern Judah (I Sam. 30:28), (4) perhaps a city different from and farther north than the other three (Is. 17:2).

AROERITE, an inhabitant of Aroer (I Chr. 11:44).

ARPACHSHAD, *see* **ARPHAXAD.**

ARPAD, a city near Hamath, north of Damascus (II Kings 18:34).

ARPHAXAD, (1) a son of Shem (Gen. 10:22), (2) in the apocrypha a king "who reigned over the Medes in Ecbatana" (Judith 1:1–4).

ARRAY, (1) to put on, as clothes (Esther 6:9), (2) to prepare for battle (Jer. 50: 42).

ARROGANCY, pride (Prov. 8:13).

ARROW, (1) the weapon used with the bow, (2) any cutting word or judgment.
Jonathan shot an *a.,* I Sam. 20:36.
a. of the Almighty, Job 6:4.

ARTAXERXES, a king of Persia. Probably he is the same as Longimanus, the son of Xerxes, who reigned B.C. 464–425.
in the days of *A.,* Ezra 4:7.
twentieth year of *A.,* Neh. 2:1.

ARTEMAS, a companion of Paul (Titus 3:12).

ARTIFICER, a skilled craftsman (I Chr. 29:5; Isa. 3:3).

ARTILLERY, weapons. In its only occurrence in the Bible (I Sam. 20:40), it refers to bow and arrows.

ARUBOTH, ARUBBOTH, a district of Palestine under the reign of Solomon (I Kin. 4:10). It lay to the southwest of Jerusalem.

ARUMAH, a place near Shechem. It was the residence of Abimelech (Judg. 9:41).

ARVAD, an island two or three miles off the Phoenician coast. In Ezek. 27:8, II its inhabitants are associated with Tyre.

ARVADITE, an inhabitant of Arvad (Gen. 10:18).

ARZA, steward of the house at Tirzah to Elah, king of Israel (I Kin. 16:9).

ASA, (1) the third king of Judah. He instituted many reforms in an attempt to restore pure religion. (I Kin. 15:11, 14). (2) a Levite, an ancestor of Berechiah (I Chr. 9:16).

ASAHEL, (1) a nephew of David, known for being a fast runner. Being pursued by Asahel, Abner killed him in self defense (II Sam. 2:21ff.). (2) A Levite who went throughout the cities of Judah teaching the law to the people (II Chr. 17:8). (3) One who was over the tithes and offerings in the time of Hezekiah (II Chr. 31:13). (4) The father of Jonathan in the time of Ezra (Ezra 10:15).

ASAHIAH, ASAIAH, a servant of King Josiah who enquired of Huldah the prophetess concerning the book of the law which was found in the temple (II Kin. 22:14). He is called Asaiah in II Chr. 34:20.

ASAIAH, (1) another name for Asahiah, (2) a descendant of Simeon (I Chr. 4: 36), (3) a Levite of the family of Merari (I Chr. 6:30); he was among those who helped bring the ark from Obed-edom (I Chr. 15:11), (4) a Shilonite (I Chr. 9:5); he could be the same as the Maaseiah of Neh. 11:5.

ASAPH, (1) a Levite in the time of David who was an outstanding musician. Psalms 50 and 73–83 are attributed to him. He is also called a seer (II Chr. 29: 30). (2) An ancestor of Joah the recorder; he could be the same as the other one (II Kin. 18:18). (3) The keeper of the king's forest under Artaxerxes (Neh. 2: 8).

ASAPH, SONS OF, a title used to refer to musical guilds (I Chr. 25:1).

ASAREEL, a son of Jehaleleel, of the tribe of Judah (I Chr. 4:16).

ASARELAH, one of the sons of Asaph (I Chr. 25:2).

ASCEND, (1) to climb up, as a mountain (Josh. 6:5), (2) to go up into heaven (Eph. 4:9).

ASCENSION, although the word itself is not found in the Bible, the ascension of Jesus is a fundamental doctrine in the New Testament. It is briefly mentioned in Mark 16:19 and Luke 24:51; A more detailed account is given in Acts 1:9–11. Upon the fact of the ascension rests the belief in Christ's resurrection, the faith that Christ is now in heaven as our intercessor, and the assurance that He will come "in like manner as ye have seen him go into heaven." (Acts 1:11).

ASCRIBE, to impute to.
a. . . ye greatness, Deut. 32:3.
a. righteousness, Job 36:3.
a. ye strength, Ps. 68:34.

ASENATH, daughter of Potipherah, priest of On; wife of Joseph (Gen. 41:50).

ASER, *see* **ASHER.**

ASH, a tree mentioned in Is. 44:14. Without doubt this is not the true ash but possibly a kind of cedar, pine or fir tree.

ASHAMED, confounded or put to shame.
wife were not *a.,* Gen. 2:25.
not *a.* of the gospel, Rom. 1:16.

ASHAN, a town in the low country of Judah belonging to Simeon (Josh. 19:7).

ASHARELAH, also Asarelah; one of the sons of Asaph. (I Chr. 25:2).

ASHBEA, the expression "house of Ashbea" occurs in I Chr. 4:21. It is uncertain whether it is the name of a place or a man; it is probably a man.

ASHBEL, a son of Benjamin (Gen. 46: 21).

ASHBELITES, descendants of Benjamin (Num. 26:38).

ASHCHENAZ, a son of Gomer, a descendant of Japheth (I Chr. 1:6).

ASHDOD, one of the five chief cities of the Philistines.
brought the ark to *A.,* I Sam. 5:1.
in the speech of *A.,* Neh. 13:24.
fought against *A.,* Is. 20:1.
inhabitant from *A.,* Amos 1:8.

ASHDODITES, ASHDOTHITES, inhabitants of Ashdod (Neh. 4:7; Josh. 13:3).

ASHDOTHPISGAH, a valley or fountain near Mt. Pisgah (Deut. 3:17).

ASHER, ASER, the eighth son of Jacob, and the second by Zilpah, Leah's handmaid (Gen. 30:13). Also the name of town east of Shechem (Josh. 17:7).

ASHERA, a Canaanite goddess frequently associated with Baal and worshiped by poles or trees. Often *Ashera* refers to these symbols instead of the goddess herself. Hence in the King James Version *Ashera* is often translated "groves." (Judg. 3:7; 6:25).

ASHERITE, a member of the tribe of Asher (Judg. 1:32).

ASHES, they were put on the head as a sign of mourning (Esther 4:1). In the priestly rituals they were used to purify the unclean (Num. 19; Heb. 9:13).

ASHHUR, *see* ASHUR.

ASHIMA, a god about whom very little is known. The men of Hamath who settled in Samaria made this god (II Kin. 17:30).

ASHKELON, one of the five chief cities of the Philistines (Judg. 14:19). It is also written *Askelon*.

ASHKENAZ, *see* ASHCHENAZ.

ASHNAH, a city (1) between Zoreah and Zanoah, northwest of Jerusalem (Josh. 15:33), (2) between Jiptah and Nezib, southwest of Jerusalem (Josh. 15:43). The location of these towns is very uncertain.

ASHPENAZ, the chief of Nebuchadnezzar's eunuchs (Dan. 1:3).

ASHRIEL, *see* ASRIEL.

ASHTAROTH, ASTAROTH, the city where Og, king of Bashan, lived (Deut. 1:4).

ASHTERATHITE, an inhabitant of Ashtaroth (I Chr. 11:44).

ASHTEROTH KARNAIM, the place where Chedorlaomer smote the Rephaim (Gen. 14:5).

ASHTORETH, the chief female divinity of the Phoenicians. Solomon is mentioned as worshiping her (I Kin. 11:5).

ASHUR, the son of Abiah and Hezron of the descendants of Judah. He was the father of Tekoa (I Chr. 2:24).

ASHURITES, a group of people over which Abner made Ishbosheth ruler (II Sam. 2:9). Their origin is very uncertain.

ASHVATH, a son of Japhlet, of the tribe of Asher (I Chr. 7:33).

ASIA, in the Bible this does not refer to the continent of Asia, but to a province in the western part of Asia Minor. Ephesus was its capital.
preach the word in *A*., Acts 6:9.
that dwelt in *A*., Acts 19:10.
seven churches in *A*., Rev. 1:11.

ASIARCHS, men chosen annually by the people of Asia to oversee the games and spectacles. In the King James Version they are called "certain of the chief of Asia" (Acts 19:31).

ASIEL, an ancestor of Jehu, of the tribe of Simeon (I Chr. 4:35).

ASK, in the Bible it may mean (1) inquire (Mark 9:32), (2) demand (Dan. 2:10), (3) pray (James 1:6), (4) seek counsel (Is. 30:2), (5) expect (Luke 12:48).

ASKELON, *see* ASHKELON.

ASKETH, ASKING, ASKED, *see* ASK.

ASLEEP, this word may mean (1) resting in sleep, or (2) dead.
Jonah was fast *a*., Jonah 1:5.
he fell *a*., Acts 7:60.
the fathers fell *a*., II Pet. 3:4.

ASNAH, the children of Asnah were among the Nethinim who returned from captivity with Zerubbabel (Ezra 2:50).

ASNAPPER, a king who set certain nations in Samaria after the captivity of Israel (Ezra 4:10). Most authorities think he is Assurbanipal.

ASP, a poisonous snake, possibly the Egyptian cobra. In Ps. 58:4; 91:13 it is translated *adder*.
cruel venom of the *a*., Deut. 32:33.

44

the hole of the *a.*, Is. 11:8.

ASPATHA, one of the sons of Haman, whom the Jews slew (Esther 9:7).

ASRIEL, one of the sons of Gilead of the tribe of Manasseh (Num. 26:31).

ASRIELITES, descendants of Asriel, (Num. 26:31).

ASS, there are five different words in the Old Testament denoting the various species of the ass. To the Hebrews the ass was a symbol of meekness, intelligence and patience; it was an animal of peace, while the horse was an animal of war. The most honorable among the Jews rode upon asses.
Issachar a strong *a.*, Gen. 49:14.
a. said to Balaam, Num. 22:30.
jaw-bone of an *a.*, Judg. 15:16.
riding on an *a.*, Zech. 9:9.
find an *a.* tied, Matt. 21:2.

ASSHUR, a son of Shem (Gen. 10:22).

ASSHUR, *see* **ASSYRIA.**

ASSHURIM, a tribe of people who descended from Dedan, a son of Abraham (Gen. 25:3).

ASSIR, (1) a son of Korah, a Levite (Ex. 6:24), (2) another descendant of Korah and ancestor of Samuel (1 Chr. 6:23), (3) a son of Jeconiah, a descendant of Solomon (I Chr. 3:17).

ASSOS, a seaport in the district of Mysia in the province of Asia; the place where Paul met and joined Luke and others of his company on the third missionary journey (Acts 20:14).

ASSUR, *see* **ASSYRIA.**

ASSURANCE, a guarantee; in Is. 32:17 the American Standard Version translates this word *confidence.*
none *a.* of thy life, Deut. 28:66.
of righteousness *a.*, Is. 32:17.
the full *a.* of hope, Heb. 6:11.

ASSWAGE, to grow less, subside; an old spelling of *assuage.*

ASSYRIA, ASSHUR, ASSUR, a once powerful country on the Tigris River; its

capital was Nineveh, which was built by Nimrod (Gen. 10:11). Records of the existence of this country date from as early as B.C. 2000. In the Bible the later Assyrian empire is mainly referred to. This empire flourished around the eighth century B.C. Some of its outstanding kings are Tiglathpileser, Shalmaneser, and Sargon. In B.C. 722 Assyria carried captive the ten northern tribes of Israel. The prophecies of Nahum and Jonah are directed mainly to Assyria.
the east of *A.*, Gen. 2:14.
carried captive to *A.*, II Kin. 17:6.
unclean things in *A.*, Hos. 9:3.
will destroy *A.*, Zeph. 2:13.

ASSYRIAN, of or from Assyria (Is. 10:5).

ASTAROTH, *see* **ASHTAROTH.**

ASTONISHED, ASTONIED, amazed, put to confusion. Astonied is an old spelling of astonished.
enemies shall be *a.*, Lev. 26:32.
and sat down *a.*, Ezra 9:3.
the people were *a.*, Matt. 7:28.
trembling and *a.*, Acts 9:6.

ASTRAY, lost, errant.
ox go *a.*, Deut. 22:1.
like sheep have gone *a.*, Is. 53:6.
went *a.* after idols, Ezek. 44:10.

ASTROLOGERS, (1) those described by the term today (Is. 47:13), (2) any kind of magician or enchanter (Dan. 4:7).

ASUPPIM, HOUSE OF, literally "house of the gatherings." The exact meaning of this is uncertain; perhaps it refers to certain store-rooms (I Chr. 26:15, 17).

ASYNCRITUS, a Christian in Rome whom Paul saluted (Rom. 16:14).

ATAD, the threshing-floor of Atad was where the children of Jacob mourned the passing of their father (Gen. 50:10). It was also called Abel-mizraim (Gen. 50:11). It is spoken of as being "beyond the Jordan"; thus it was on the west side of the Jordan River.

ATARAH, the wife of Jerahmeel and the mother of Onam (I Chr. 2:26).

ATAROTH, (1) a town in Gilead which

the tribe of Gad possessed because it was good for cattle (Num. 32:3), (2) a city on the border of Ephraim (Josh. 16:2), (3) another town on the border of Ephraim (Josh. 16:7), (4) a place or person mentioned in the list of the descendants of Judah (I Chr. 2:54).

ATAROTH-ADAR, a town on the border of Benjamin (Josh. 16:5).

ATER, the children of Ater were among the children of the porters (Ezra 2:42). Ninety-eight of the children of Ater of Hezekiah returned with Zerubbabel (Ezra 2:16).

ATHACH, a city in Judah to which David sent the spoil of his enemies (I Sam. 30: 30). It is possibly the same as Ether.

ATHAIAH, the son of Uzziah. He was among those of the tribe of Judah who dwelt in Jerusalem (Neh. 11:4).

ATHALIAH, the daughter of Ahab and Jezebel, who lived about B.C. 890. She usurped the throne of Judah and attempted to destroy all the royal seed. One infant, Joash, escaped this effort. He was later produced as the rightful king, and Athaliah was slain (II Kin. 11).

ATHARIM, in the King James Version the "way of the Atharim" is translated the "way of the spies" in Num. 21:1. Some claim it means "the way of tracks" or a caravan road.

ATHEISM, literally, a belief that there is no God.

ATHENIAN, one who lives in Athens (Acts 17:21).

ATHENS, the chief seat of Grecian learning and civilization during the period of the New Testament. It is located about five miles from the coast in the ancient province of Attica. It is named from the goddess Athena. Outstanding features of the city are: the *Acropolis* (one of the major hills on which the city was built), the *Areopagus* or Mars' Hill from where Paul delivered his sermon in Acts 17, and the Parthenon (the most perfect production of Grecian architecture. On his second missionary journey Paul preached in Athens and left behind several converts.

There is no record of a church established there in the apostolic times.
brought Paul to *A.*, Acts 17:15.
ye men of *A.*, Acts 17:22.
Paul departed from *A.*, Acts 18:1.
to be left at *A.*, I Thess. 3:1.

ATHIRST, very thirsty.
saw we thee *a.*, Matt. 25:44.
to him that is *a.*, Rev. 21:6.
let him that is *a.*, Rev. 22:17.

ATHLAI, a son of Bebai. He was among those who put away foreign wives (Ezra 10:28).

ATONEMENT, reconciliation, the process by which God and man can once again become "at-one."
make an *a.* for sin, Ex. 32:30.
make *a.*, for thyself, Lev. 9:7.
now received *a.*, Rom. 5:11.

ATONEMENT, DAY OF, the day that atonement was made for the sins of Israel. It was observed on the tenth day of Tisri, which corresponds to the first part of October. It is sometimes referred to by the Hebrew name *Yom Kippur.* On this day the high priest would bathe himself and offer a bullock as an offering for himself and his family which he bought, and two goats and a ram which were paid for by the public treasury. He then cast lots on two goats. One he would kill (the one called *For Jehovah*) and enter within the Holy of Holies to appear before God with its blood and to sprinkle its blood upon the mercy-seat of the ark. Upon the other (the one called *For Azazel*) he would confess the sins of the people and then drive it into the wilderness; this became known as the scapegoat. The manner of observing this day is set forth in Lev. 16.
be a day of *a.*, Lev. 23:27.
in the day of *a.*, Lev. 25:9.

ATROTH, *see* ATROTH-SHOPHAN.

ATROTH-BETH-JOAB, the name of a family in I Chr. 2:54. In the King James Version it is translated "Ataroth the house of Joab."

ATROTH-SHOPHAN, a town built by the children of Gad (Num. 32:35). In the King James Version Ataroth and Shophan are considered two separate towns.

ATTAI, (1) the son of Jarha and father of Nathan of the tribe of Judah (I Chr. 2:35,36), (2) a man from the tribe of Gad who joined David at Ziklag (I Chr. 12:11), (3) a son of Rehoboam (II Chr. 11:20).

ATTAIN, is used in its literal sense in Acts 27:12, where it means to reach a place. Elsewhere it is used in its still prevalent figurative sense.
they *a.* to innocency, Hos. 8:5.
might *a.* to Phenice, Acts 27:12.
a. to the resurrection, Phil. 3:11.

ATTALIA, a seaport town in Pamphylia in Asia Minor. Paul and Barnabas left from Attalia to sail home to Antioch on their first missionary journey (Acts 14:25).

ATTEND, (1) to care for (Esther 4:5), (2) to give attention to (Prov. 7:24).

AUGUSTUS, Augustus Caesar, born B.C. 63, was the first Roman emperor. He ruled from B.C. 23 to A.D. 14. At the time of Jesus' birth he sent forth a decree that all the world should be taxed (Luke 2:1). The name *Augustus* also appears in Acts 25:21,25; here it does not refer to the forementioned ruler, but it would best be rendered "emperor" or "His Majesty."

AUGUSTUS' BAND, the army of the emperor (Acts 27:1).

AUTHOR, the originator and leader.
God is not the *a.*, I Cor. 14:33.
the *a.* of eternal, Heb. 5:9.
the *a.* and finisher, Heb. 12:2.

AUTHORITY, (1) power or dignity, (2) a command.
as one having *a.*, Matt. 7:29.
by what *a.* doest thou, Matt. 21:23.
gave them *a.*, Luke 9:1.
woman to usurp *a.*, I Tim. 2:12.

AUTHORIZED VERSION, *see* **VERSIONS.**

AVA, AVVA, a place from which the king of Assyria brought inhabitants to live in Samaria (II Kin. 17:24). It is possibly the same as Ivah.

AVAIL, to accomplish.

this *a.* me nothing, Esther 5:13.
circumcision *a.* not, Gal. 5:6.
righteous man *a.* much, James 5:16.

AVEN, (1) a place in Syria (Amos 1:5), (2) an abbreviation for Beth-Aver, or Bethel (Hos. 10:8), (3) a city in Egypt, probably Heliopolis or On (Ezek. 30:17).

AVENGE, to take vengeance.
thou shalt not *a.*, Lev. 19:18.
a. the blood of, Deut. 32:43.
shall not God *a.*, Luke 18:7.
a. not yourselves, Rom. 12:19.

AVENGER OF BLOOD, under the Mosaic law if one were killed, the nearest of kin could kill the one who slew him; he was known as the avenger of blood. The one pursued by the avenger of blood could flee to one of the cities of refuge. If he was judged innocent, he could dwell safely in the city of refuge until the death of the priest. After that he could dwell in the land without fear. These laws are described in Num. 35.

AVIM, AVVIM, AVIMS, AVITES, AVVITES, (1) some early inhabitants of Palestine (Deut. 2:23), (2) inhabitants of Ava (II Kin. 17:31).

AVITH, the city of Hadad the son of Bedad, an Edomite (Gen. 36:35).

AVOID, to go away, withdraw, shun.
a. it, pass not, Prov. 4:15.
divisions, and *a.*, Rom. 16:17.
to *a.* fornication, I Cor. 7:2.
unlearned quest. *a.*, II Tim. 2:23.
a. foolish quest., Titus 3:9.

AVOUCH, acknowledge openly.
this day *a.* the Lord, Deut. 26:17.
Lord hath *a.* thee, Deut. 26:18.

AVVA, *see* **AVA.**

AVVIM, AVVITES, *see* **AVIM.**

AWAKE, (1) come out of natural sleep (Luke 9:32), (2) come out of spiritual sleep (Eph. 5:14), (3) raise from the dead (John 11:11).

AWE, reverential fear.
stand in *a.*, Ps. 4:4.
world stand in *a.*, Ps. 33:8.
heart standeth in *a.*, Ps. 119:161.

AWL, a sharp pointed tool used to bore the ear of a slave who wished to remain with his master (Ex. 21:6; Deut. 15:17).

AXE, (1) an instrument similar to the modern ax (II Kin. 6:5), (2) any instrument for inflicting judgment (Isa. 10:15).

AXLE-TREE, a part of a chariot, probably the axle (I Kin. 7:32).

AZAL, an unidentified place near Jerusalem (Zech. 14:5).

AZALIAH, the son of Meshullam and father of Shaphan the scribe (II Kin. 22:3).

AZANIAH, the father of Jeshua, a Levite (Neh. 10:9).

AZARAEL, a Levite musician (Neh. 12: 36).

AZAREEL, AZAREL, (1) a Korhite who was with David at Ziklag (I Chr. 12:6), (2) a son of Heman, a musician in the time of David (I Chr. 25:18); he is called Uzziel in I Chr. 25:4, (3) the son of Jeroham of the tribe of Dan (I Chr. 27: 22), (4) one of the sons of Bani who put away a foreign wife (Ezra 10:41), (5) father of Amashai and son of Ahasai (Neh. 11:13).

AZARIAH, twenty-three men bear this name in the Bible.
Son of Nathan, I Kin. 4:5.
Same as Uzziah, II Kin. 14:21.
Son of Ethan, I Chr. 2:8.
Son of Jehu, I Chr. 2:38.
Son of Ahimaaz, I Chr. 6:9.
Son of Johanan, I Chr. 6:10.
Son of Hilkiah, I Chr. 6:13, 14.
Son of Zephaniah, I Chr. 6:36.
Son of Oded, II Chr. 15:1.
Son of Jehoshaphat, II Chr. 21:2.
Same as Ahaziah, II Chr. 22:6.
Son of Jeroham, II Chr. 23:1.
A high priest, II Chr. 26:17.
Son of Johanan, II Chr. 28:12.
Father of Joel, II Chr. 29:12.
Son of Jehalelel, II Chr. 29:12.
A high priest, II Chr. 31:10, 13.
Son of Maaseiah, Neh. 3:23, 24.
A leader of the Jews, Neh. 7:7.
A Levite with Ezra, Neh. 8:7.
A priest with Nehemiah, Neh. 10:2.
Same as Jezaniah, Jer. 43:2.

Same as Abed-nego, Dan. 1:6.

AZAZ, father of Bela and son of Shema (I Chr. 5:8).

AZAZEL, the meaning is uncertain; it refers to the scape-goat upon which the high priest laid his hands and confessed the sins of the people; he then drove the goat into the wilderness. This was a part of the ritual on the Day of Atonement (Lev. 16:26). The King James Version translates this word *scape-goat*.

AZAZIAH, (1) a Levite musician in the time of David (I Chr. 15:21), (2) the father of Hoshea (I Chr. 27:20), (3) a Levite in the reign of Hezekiah (II Chr. 31:13).

AZBUK, the son of Nehemiah (Neh. 3:16).

AZEKAH, a town of Judah in a rich agricultural district. It is defined as being near Shochoh, but it has not yet been found (I Sam. 17:1).

AZEL, the son of Eleasah, a Benjamite of the family Saul through Jonathan (I Chr. 8:37f., 9:43f).

AZEM, a city assigned to Simeon in the South of Judah. It is also spelled Ezem (Josh. 15:29; I Chr. 4:29).

AZGAD, an Israelite whose family returned from exile with Zerubbabel and Ezra (Ezra 2:12, 8:12).

AZIEL, a Levite who was a musician of the tabernacle during the time the ark was brought up from the house of Obededom (I Chr. 15:20).

AZIZA, an Israelite of the family of Zattu who had taken a strange wife (Ezra 10:27).

AZMAVETH, (1) one of David's thirty mighty men (II Sam. 23:31), (2) a descendant from Jonathan, the son of Saul (I Chr. 9:42), (3) the father of certain followers of David (I Chr. 12:3, (4) a village also called Bethazmaveth (Ezra 2:24), (5) one of the officers of David's treasury (I Chr. 27:25).

AZMON, a place on the southern border

of Canaan, between Hazaradar and "the river of Egypt" (Num. 34:4, 5; Josh. 15:4).

AZNOTH-TABOR, a place probably near Mt. Tabor in the West of Naphtali composed of two hills (Josh. 19:34).

AZOR, one of the ancestors of Christ, son of Eliakim (Matt. 1:13, 14).

AZOTUS, the Greek form of Ashdod where Philip was found after having baptized the Ethiopian eunuch (Acts 8:40).

AZRIEL, (1) a man of valor who was one of the chiefs of the half tribe of Manasseh beyond the Jordan (I Chr. 5:24), (2) Jerimoth's father who came to rule the tribe of Naphtali (I Chr. 27:19), (3) the father of Seraiah, an officer of Jehoiakim who was sent to take Baruch, the scribe (Jer. 36:26).

AZRIKAM, (1) a descendant of David, son of Neariah (I Chr. 3:23), (2) a descendant of Saul, the son of Azel (I Chr. 8:38), (3) a descendant of Merari who was a Levite (Neh. 11:15), (4) an officer of the house of Ahaz (II Chr. 28:7).

AZUBAH, (1) the mother of King Jehoshaphat (I Kin. 22:42), (2) the wife of Caleb, Hezron's son (I Chr. 2:18, 19).

AZUR, or **AZZUR,** (1) the father of Hananiah of Gibeon who deceitfully encouraged Zedekiah against the Babylonians (Jer. 28:1), (2) the father of Jaazaniah, whom Ezekiel saw in a vision (Ezek. 11:1).

AZZAH, another form of the more commonly used "Gaza" (Deut. 2:23, I Kin. 4:24, Jer. 25:20). *See* GAZA.

AZZAN, the father of Paltiel, who was a prince of Issachar and was commissioned to the apportioning of the land West of the Jordan (Num. 34:26).

B

BAAL, a Canaanitish god thought to inhabit special localities. Worship to Baal was often accompanied by fornication, self-mutilation and child sacrifice.

high places of *B.,* Num. 22:41.
but if *B.* be God., I Kin. 18:21.
name of *B.* saying, I Kin. 18:26.
not bowed to *B.,* I Kin. 19:18.
burn incense to *B.,* Jer. 7:9.

BAAL, a descendant of Reuben (I Chr. 5:5). (2) A descendant of Benjamin. The son of Jehiel and uncle to Saul, the king (I Chr. 8:30).

BAAL, a town marking the boundary of the tribe of Simeon (I Chr. 4:33).

BAALAH, another name for Kirjath-Jearim, a town in Benjamin north-west of Jerusalem (Josh. 15:9).

BAALATH, a town which fell to Dan in the allotment of Canaan (Josh. 19:44).

BAALATH-BEER, a town marking the boundary of the tribe of Simeon (Josh. 19:8).

BAAL-BERITH, one of the Baalim worshiped at Shechem (Judg. 8:33; 9:46).

BAALE, identified with Baalah or Kirjath-Jearim. A town of Judah from which David carried the ark (II Sam. 6:2).

BAAL-GAD, a place in the valley of Lebanon near Mt. Hermon (Josh. 11:17; 12:7; 13:5).

BAAL-HAMON, a place where Solomon had a vineyard (Song 8:11).

BAAL-HANAN, (1) an Edomite king (Gen. 36:38). (2) A Gederite who tended David's olive trees and sycamore trees. (I Chr. 27:28).

BAAL-HAZOR, a place near Bethel in Ephraim where Absolom slew Amnon (II Sam. 13:23).

BAAL-HERMON, a place to the east of the Jordan on the northern border of Manasseh. Perhaps another name for Mt. Hermon. (Judg. 3:3; I Chr. 5:23).

BAALI, Baal with first person possessive suffix, "My Baal, my Lord" (Hos. 2:16).

BAALIM, plural of Baal.

BAALIS, a king of the Ammonites about the time of the fall of Jerusalem in B.C. 586 (Jer. 40:14).

BAAL-MEON, a city of the Amorites given to the tribe of Reuben and rebuilt by them (Num. 32:38). It was later called Beth-meon (Jer. 48:23; Josh. 13:17).

BAAL-PEOR, a god of the Moabites whose worship was accompanied by fornication. (Num. 25:1–9).

BAAL-PERAZIM, a place near the valley of Rephaim where David defeated the Philistines (II Sam. 5:18–20).

BAAL-SHALISHA, the man bringing the barley loaves and corn to Elisha was from this town (II Kin. 4:42–44).

BAAL-TAMAR, a place near Gibeah where the Israelites prepared to attack Gibeah, a Benjaminite town, (Judg. 20:33).

BAAL-ZEBUB, the god of Ekron (II Kin. 1). *See* **BEEL-ZEBUB.**

BAAL-ZEPHON, a place in the land of Goshen near which the children of Israel encamped before crossing the sea (Ex. 14:2, 9).

BAANA, (1) two of the officers in charge of providing food for Solomon and his household (I Kin. 4:12, 16). (2) A son of Zadok, who helped repair the walls of Jerusalem (Neh. 3:4).

BAANAH, (1) one of two Benjaminite brothers who slew Ishbosheth (II Sam. 4: 1–12). (2) A Netophathite and father of one of David's valiant men (I Chr. 11: 30). (3) Officer in charge of Solomon's food supply stationed at Asher (I Kin. 4:10). (4) An exile returning with Zerubbabel (Ezra 2:2; Neh. 7:7).

BAARA, one of the two wives of Shaharaim of the tribe of Benjamin (I Chr. 8:8).

BAASEIAH, a descendant of Levi through Gershom (I Chr. 6:40).

BAASHA, third king of the Kingdom of Israel and founder of its second dynasty after he slew Nadab (I Kin. 15:27).

BABBLER, (1) "master of the tongue" (Eccles. 10:11). (2) An idle talker (Acts 17:18).

BABBLING, empty sound, vain talking.
who hath *b*.?, Prov. 23:29.
shun vain *b*., II Tim. 2:16.

BABE, new born or unborn human offspring; youth.

BABEL, other name for Babylon (Gen. 10:10).

BABEL, TOWER, OF, a great tower made of bricks constructed in a plain in the land of Shinar (Chaldea) for the purpose of making a name for the people and to prevent their being scattered abroad (Gen. 11:1–9).

BABYLON, the capital of Babylonia, laid on both sides of the Euphrates. Here was the beginning of the kingdom of Nimrod (Gen. 10:10), and here the tower of Babel was erected. Historically this city was unimportant until about 1830 B.C. when its first dynasty was established. This city reached its greatest heights in the reigns of Hammurabi (1800 B.C.) and Nebuchadrezzar (605–562 B.C.) who conquered Judah and carried the Jews into captivity. At this time Babylon was the most splendrous city of the world, but in 539 B.C. it fell to Cyrus of Persia and afterward rapidly decayed to the point that it was only a desert village in the Christian era. Figuratively, Babylon is used for Rome in the Book of Revelation (Rev. 17:18; 18:2, 21). The reference in I Pet. 5:13 is uncertain.

BABYLONIA, a region of Western Asia, also called Shinar (Gen. 10:10, 11:2) and Chaldea (Jer. 24:5). It is bordered on the north by Assyria, on the east by Elam, on the south by the Persian Gulf and on the west by the Arabian Desert. Ancient cities were Ur, Nippur, Erech, Lagash and others. The area known as Babylonia, including these cities, was brought together under the dominion of Hammurabi about 1800 after which the Old Babylonian Kingdom continued until about 1550 after which the area fell under the sway of outside rulers, the Kassites from the east (1550–1169 B.C.) and later the Assyrians. Under Nabopolassar the

Neo-Chaldean Empire replaced Assyria as world ruler by conquering Assyria, destroying Nineveh, the capital of Assyria, in 612 B.C. Nebuchadnezzar, son and successor of Nabopolassar, defeated Egypt at Carchemish in 605 B.C. and began his long and brilliant reign, which brought Babylon and Babylonia to their greatest heights. After Nebuchadnezzar Babylonia gradually declined.

BABYLONIANS, inhabitants of Babylon or Babylonia. They were of Shemite origin.

BABYLONISH GARMENT, "robe of Shinar," a heavily ornamented robe such as was worn by kings (Josh. 7:21).

BACA, a valley mentioned in Ps. 84:6; but perhaps should be translated "weeping" as in the ASV.

BACHRITES, descendants of Becher, a descendant of Ephraim (Num. 26:35).

BACKBITE, to speak against, slander.
b. not with tongue, Ps. 15:3.
b., haters of God, Rom. 1:30.

BACKBITER, one who backbites, one who speaks against.
b., haters of God, Rom. 1:30.

BACKBITING, talking against.
countenance a b., Prov. 25:23.
wraths, strifes, b., II Cor. 12:20.

BACKBONE, spine, firm part.
hard by the b., Lev. 3:9.

BACKSIDE, behind, back part.
flock to the b., Ex. 3:1.
hang over the b., Ex. 26:12.
within and on the b., Rev. 5:1.

BACKSLIDER, one who goes back or turns back.
the b., in heart, Prov. 14:14.

BACKSLIDING, turning back, turning away.
b., shall reprove thee, Jer. 2:19.
our b., are many, Jer. 14:7.
I will heal their b., Hos. 14:4.

BACKWARD, to the back parts, rearward.
rider shall fall b., Gen. 49:17.

shadow return b., II Kin. 20:10.
went b., and fell, John 18:16.

BAD, base, evil, rotten.
a b., for a good, Gen. 24:50.
whether good or b., Num. 13:19.
they were so b., Jer. 24:2.
cast the b., away, Matt. 13:48.

BADGER, ROCK, see **CONEY.**

BADGER SKINS, used for the outer covering of the tabernacle (Ex. 25:5), and for sandals (Ezek. 16:10). However, these skins seem unsuitable for these types of uses. The Revised Version has rendered the Hebrew original by "seal," with a marginal of "porpoise." The skins of these animals would suit the requirements of the case, and it is not unlikely that the term is to be understood in the broad sense of such marine creatures.

BAG, purse, sachel, sack, or pouch.
have in thy b., Deut. 25:13.
in a shepherd's b., I Sam. 17:40.
a b. of money, Prov. 7:20.
gold out of a b., Is. 46:6.
provide yourselves b., Luke 12:33.
and had the b., John 12:6.

BAHARUMITE, a person from Bahurim (II Sam. 23:31; I Chr. 11:33).

BAHURIM, a place near the road leading from Jerusalem to the Jordan (II Sam. 16:5; I Kin. 2:8).

BAJITH, the temple of the gods of Moab (Is. 15:2).

BAKBAKKAR, a Levite of the line of Asaph (I Chr. 9:15).

BAKBUK, head of one of the families of the Nethinims that returned from the exile with Zerubbabel (Ezra 2:50; Neh. 7:53).

BAKBUKIAH, a Levite and a chief person in time of Nehemiah (Neh. 11:17).

BAKE, to cook. Also **Baked, Baking.**
Lot did b., Gen. 19:3.
flour and b. twelve, Lev. 24:5.
ten women shall b., Lev. 26:26.
b. it with man's, Ezek. 4:12.

BAKE MEATS, food, a baker's product (Gen. 40:17).

BAKER, one in charge of the public ovens (Hos. 7:6), or in charge of a king's ovens (I Sam. 8:13; Gen. 40:1).

BAKING, see **BAKE**.

BALAAM, a prophet from Pethor, a city on the Euphrates river. He was engaged by Balak, king of Moab, to curse the Israelites (Num. 24:1-9).

BALAC, see **BALAK** (Rev. 2:14).

BALADAN, father of Berodach-baladan the king of Babylon in the time of Hezekiah (II Kin. 20:12).

BALAH, one of the cities falling to Simeon in the allotment of Canaan (Josh. 19:2).

BALAK, the king of Moab during the immigration of the Israelites into Canaan (Num. 22-24).

BALANCES, instrument used to weigh objects, esp. gold and silver. It consisted of crossbeam which turned on a pin at the top of an upright pole.
just *b* Lev. 19:36 .
b. to weigh, Ezek. 5:1 .
weighed in the *b*., Dan. 5:27 .
a pair of *b*., Rev. 6:5 .

BALANCING, poising (Job 37:16).

BALD, without hair (Lev. 13:40; Jer. 48:37).

BALD HEAD, (2 Kin. 2:23).

BALD LOCUST, a small insect which could be eaten (Lev. 11:20); a grasshopper. See **LOCUST**.

BALDNESS is considered in Scripture a defect marring personal beauty. Baldness had points of contact with leprosy, but was differentiated from that disease (Lev. 13:40-44). Artificial baldness signified mourning (Jer. 16:6), and was inflicted upon captives (Deut. 21:12). It was forbidden to the priests (Lev. 21:5, 17-20) and, perhaps for a different cause, to all Israelites (Deut. 14:1, 2). An exception was the Nazarite (Num. 6:9, 18).
shall not make *b*., Lev. 21:5.
nor make any *b*., Deut. 14:1.
well set hair, *b*., Is. 3:24.
b. is come upon Gaza, Jer. 47:5.

BALL, any round object (Is. 22:18).

BALM, a healing salve made from the storax tree; a medicine for which Gilead was famous.
bearing spicery and *b*., Gen. 37:25 .
no *b*. in Gilead? Jer. 8:22 .
Gilead, and take *b*., Jer. 46:11.
take *b*. for her pain, Jer. 51:8.

BAMAH, the high place, where heathen deities were worshiped in Canaan (Ezek. 20:29).

BAMOTH, one of the sites of the encampments of the Israel east of the Jordan (Num. 20:19, 20).

BAMOTH-BAAL, one of the cities given to Reuben in the allotment of the territory east of the Jordan (Josh. 13:17).

BAND, a bond, a fetter. (Judg. 15:14; Dan. 4:15).

BAND, a troop of men (1 Kin. 11:24).

BANI, (1) a Gadite, and one of David's mighty men (II Sam. 23:36). (2) A descendant of Judah who dwelt in Jerusalem (I Chron. 9:4). (3) A family of exiles returning with Zerubbabel (Ezra 2:10; Neh. 10:14). (4) A descendant of Levi through Merari (I Chr. 6:46). (5) A Levite among the exiles returned (Neh. 3:17). Father of Uzzi, an overseer at Jerusalem after the return of the exiles (Neh. 11:22).

BANISH, to drive or force away
home again his *b*., II Sam. 14:13.
b. be not expelled, II Sam. 14:14.

BANISHMENT, driving away; being driven away.
unto death, or to *b*., Ezra 7:26.
causes of *b*., Lam. 2:14.

BANK, while loaning money was not viewed favorably by the Hebrews (Ex. 22:25; Lev. 25:37), money lending was practiced in New Testament times. (Matt. 25:27). In Luke 19:23 the word means a moneychanger's table. See **MONEYCHANGER, LOAN**.

BANK, (1) a mound for siege (II Sam. 20:15; II Kin. 19:32); (2) a river's edge (Gen. 41:17; II Kin. 2:13).

BAPTISM, this vital subject has seen a variety of conflicting interpretations among professed disciples of Christ. This article attempts a brief notice of the different positions held.

I. **The Baptism of John.** Baptism first appears in the New Testament in connection with the work of John the Baptist who demanded baptism of the Jews in calling them to repentance in anticipation of the Messiah's coming (Matt. 3:1–6, 11; Mark 1:3–5). A probable background to the practice is seen in Jewish proselyte baptism and ceremonial washings (Mark 7:2–4).

II. **The Baptism of Jesus.** Jesus himself was baptized by John, not for remission of sins, but "to fulfill all righteousness" (Matt. 3:15; Mark 1:9). A heavenly voice approved this act of our Lord's induction into his public ministry (Matt. 3:17).

III. **Christian Baptism.** Jesus baptized through the agency of his disciples (John 3:22; 4:1, 2). Some hold that there was basically no difference between Christian baptism and that of John, but most accept Acts 19:1–5 as strong evidence that Christ's baptism superseded that of John. Among Christ's last words on earth was His command to make disciples, baptizing them (Matt. 28:18–20). This Great Commission began to be carried out on the day of Pentecost (Acts 2:38, 41). Baptism is mentioned in each case of conversion in Acts (8:12, 38; 9:18; 16:15, 33; 18:8; 22:16) and is often referred to in the Epistles. Faith in Christ as God's Son, repentance, and baptism for remission of sins thus go hand-in-hand in the New Testament.

IV. **The Significance of Baptism.** Baptism is a symbolic act whereby the believer portrays the death, burial and resurrection of Jesus and also the believer's own death to sin and resurrection to a new life in the Spirit (Rom. 6:1–4). The imperative question about this act of faith is whether it is essential to salvation. Many believe that it is, contending that the New Testament makes baptism the act of entrance into the body of the faithful (I Cor. 12:13), into the state of forgiveness of sins (Acts 2:38; 22:16), and into union with Christ (Gal. 3:27). I Peter 3:21 ("The like figure whereunto even baptism doth also now save us . . .") is seen as an emphatic affirmation of the necessity of baptism. The connection between salvation by grace and salvation by faithful obedience is believed demonstrated in Titus 3:5, where baptism is mentioned as the "washing of regeneration." The water itself is not believed to contain saving power; this power is in the blood of Christ. But the blood is appropriated to the individual in his faithful obedience (I Pet. 3:21). Many, however, oppose the view that baptism is essential to salvation. Paul's reply to the jailer (Acts 16:31) and his statement, "Christ sent me not to baptize, but to preach the gospel" (I Cor. 1:14–17) are relied upon to indicate that baptism, while symbolic, is non-essential. Baptism is considered a sign and seal of conversion which has already taken place. That baptism saves is rejected as a doctrine of works (Eph. 2:8–9), but baptism is considered necessary to the Christian's perfect obedience and to entrance into the visible church.

V. **Modes of Baptism.** (A) *The Immersionist View.* That baptism is performed correctly only by a complete dipping of the candidate is argued from the following: (1) *Baptizo,* the Greek verb translated "baptize" is defined by the Greek-English lexicons of Liddell and Scott, and Thayer as "to dip, dip under," and "to dip, to immerse, submerge," respectively; (2) The Greek Orthodox Church (which should know Greek) has always practiced only immersion; (3) Only immersion fits the symbolism of a burial used in Rom. 6:3–5 and Col. 2:12; (4) That New Testament examples of baptism were immersions is indicated by the language used in such passages as Mark 1:9–10 and Acts 8:38.

(B) *The Non-Immersionist View.* A number of churches insist that emphasis upon immersion attaches too much importance to ceremonial detail. These also argue: (1) In some cases *baptizo* probably means only "washing" (Luke 11:38; Mark 7:4; Heb. 9:10); (2) Insufficient water for immersion is felt to be the case on Pentecost (Acts 2) and in the deserted area of Acts 8:26–39. (3) While historians hold that immersion was the prevailing type of baptism in the first century, sprinkling or pouring began to be practiced in early centuries. Thus, it is felt that sprinkling, pouring or immersion are equally valid as baptism.

VI. **The Subjects of Baptism.** (A) *Believers.* Immersionists usually contend that believers are the only fit subjects for baptism, since Scripture requires faith and repentance before baptism (Mark 16:16; Acts 2:38; 8:36; 19:4, 5). New Testament preachers baptized those who gladly received (believed) the Gospel (Acts 2:41; 8:12). Infants, who cannot believe, are thus considered excluded by Scripture as fit subjects for baptism. (B) *Infants.* Many Protestant churches and the Roman Catholic Church practice infant baptism. This is felt to be necessary for the removal of sins inherited from parents and justified by the analogy of infant membership in the Old Covenant (Gen. 17:12; Lev. 12:3). Col. 2:11 is appealed to as evidence that, just as male babies were circumcised, so all infants of Christian parents should be baptized (sprinkled).

VII. **Other Baptisms.** (A) *Baptism of the Holy Spirit* was received by the apostles (Acts 2:1–4), as promised (Mark 1:8; Acts 1:5), and by Cornelius (Acts 10:44). Eph. 4:5 allows for only one continuing baptism, which would be the water baptism commanded by Christ (Matt. 28:18–20) and practiced generally by the early church. (B) *Baptism for the Dead* (I Cor. 15:29). This may refer to Christian baptism which pictures resurrection from the dead, or it may be an *ad hominem* argument against a false practice. Vicarious baptism is eliminated by the Scriptural doctrine of individual responsibility. (C) *Baptism of Fire* (Matt. 3:9–12; Luke 3:16–17) is also problematical and perhaps refers to Pentecost (Acts 2:3) or to judgment or punishment. (D) *Baptism is used also as a metaphor for suffering* (Matt. 20:22; Luke 12:50). Doubtless, complete inundation in agony or sorrow is the idea.

Pharisees come to his *b.*, Matt. 3:7.
baptized with *b.*, Matt. 20:22..
b. of John, whence, Matt. 21:25.
I have a *b.* to be, Luke 12:50.
beginning from the *b.*, Acts 1:22.
after the *b.* which John, Acts 10:37.
b. of repentance, Acts 13:24.
knowing only the *b.*, Acts 18:25.
unto John's *b.*, Acts 19:3.
John baptized with *b.*, Acts 19:4.
buried with him by *b.*, Rom. 6:4.
one faith, one *b.*, Eph. 4:5.
buried with him in *b.*, Col. 2:12.
of doctrine of *b.*, Heb. 6:2.
whereunto, even *b.*, I Pet. 3:21.

BAPTIST, JOHN THE, *see* **JOHN THE BAPTIST**

BAPTIZE, to perform the rite of baptism. *See* **BAPTISM.**
I *b.* you with water, Matt. 3:11.
believeth and is *b.*, Mark 16:16.
repent, and be *b.*, Acts 2:38.
Eunuch and he *b.* him, Acts 8:38.
be *b.* and wash, Acts 22:16.
been *b.* into Christ, Gal. 3:27.

BAR, (1) a bolt for a door or gate (Ps. 107:16); (2) a pole (Num. 4:10).

BAR-, a prefix to proper names, meaning, son of—. Comparable to the Scottish Mac—.

BARABBAS, a thief, murderer and insurrectionist whom Pilate released at the Passover instead of Jesus on the demand of the priests (Matt. 27:16–26).

BARACHEL, father of Elihu, the Buzite (Job 32:2, 6).

BARACHIAH, BARACHIAS, father of Zachariah the prophet (Matt. 23:35).

BARAK, an Israelite from Kadesh-naphtali who, under the influence of Deborah rallied the Israelites against Jabin king of Canaan and defeated him (Judg. 4:1–5:12).

BARBARIAN, anyone who was not a Greek or who did not speak the Greek language. The term was not entirely derogatory and simply meant a foreigner.
b. saw the venomous, Acts 28:4.
to the Greeks and *b.*, Rom. 1:14.
a *b.* and he a *b.* to me, I Cor. 14:11.
Greek nor Jew, *b.*, Col. 3:11.

BARBAROUS, foreign, alien.
the *b.* people showed us, Acts 28:2.

BARBASAS, JOSEPH, *see* **JOSEPH.**

BARBASAS, JUDAS, *see* **JUDAS.**

BARBED IRONS, a pointed weapon, dart.
skin with *b.* irons, Job 41:7.

BARBER, one who cares for the hair and beard.

take thee a *b*. razor, Ezek. 5:1.

BARE, uncovered, naked.
his head *b*., Lev. 13:45.
thou was naked and *b*. Ezek. 16:7.
b. grain, it may, I Cor. 15:37.

BAREFOOT, unshod, without shoes on.
he went *b*., II Sam. 15:30.
walking naked and *b*., Is. 20:2.
walked naked and *b*., Is. 20:3.
Ethiopians . . naked and *b*., Is. 20:4.

BARHUMITE, another form of Baharumite.

BARIAH, a descendant of David through Solomon (I Chr. 3:22)

BAR-JESUS, *see* ELYMAS.

BAR-JONA, Peter's surname, meaning "son of Jona" (Matt. 16:17; John 1:42). *See* PETER.

BARKOS, a head of one of the families of the Nethinims who returned from the exile with Zerubbabel (Ezra 2:53).

BARLEY, a cereal grain of Palestine which was made into bread.
flax and the *b*. was, Ex. 9:31.
twenty loaves of *b*., II Kin. 4:42.
hath five *b*. loaves, John 6:9.
three measures of *b*., Rev. 6:6.

BARN, an open threshing floor; a place for collecting or for putting away.
gather into thy *b*., Job 39:12.
seed yet in the *b*., Hag. 2:19.
nor gather into *b*., Matt. 6:26.
pull down my *b*., Luke 12:18.
storehouse nor *b*., Luke 12:24.

BARNABAS, one of the early Christians. He sold his property and laid the money at the apostles feet (Acts 4:36, 37); introduced Paul to the Christians in Jerusalem (Acts 9:27); went to Antioch to preach (Acts 11:19–24) and secured the assistance of Paul for the work there (Acts 11: 22–26). He accompanied Paul on his first missionary journey (Acts 13:1ff) and to the conference at Jerusalem (Acts 15:1ff). His name means "son of exhortation."

BARNABAS, JOSEPH, *see* JOSES.

BARNFLOOR, an open threshing floor.

out of the *b*., II Kin. 6:27.

BARREL, an earthen jar used for keeping flour, water, etc. This was similar to a close-mouthed pitcher (I Kin. 17:12; 18: 33).

BARREN, unfruitful. Used of persons, it means childless. *See* BARRENNESS.
but Sarai was *b*., Gen. 11:30.
Rachel was *b*., Gen. 29:31.
because Elizabeth was *b*., Luke 1:7.
that ye be neither *b*., II Pet. 1:8.

BARRENNESS, sterility. In the Old Testament failure to produce fruit was a reproach. Sometimes barrenness was considered as a punishment from God (I Sam. 1:6; Ps. 107:34). Certain marriage relationships which were forbidden by Moses were visited with barrenness (Lev. 20:20–1).
a fruitful land into *b*., Ps. 107:34.

BARSABAS, a surname meaning "son of Sabas." In Revised Standard Version, Barsabbas. (1) Joseph Barsabas was a disciple nominated along with Matthias to succeed Judas Iscariot (Acts 1:23). (2) Judas Barsabas was a disciple sent to Antioch with Paul and Barnabas (Acts 15:22).
Joseph called *B*., Acts 1:23.
Judas *B*., Acts 15:22.

BARTHOLOMEW, (son of Tolmai), one of the twelve apostles Jesus chose. He is supposed by many to have been the same man who in John is called Nathanael. *See* Matt. 10:3; Mark 3:18; Luke 6:14 and Acts 1:13 for lists of the apostles. *See* APOSTLE.

BARTIMAEUS, (son of Timaeus, or son of honor), a blind beggar of Jericho whom Jesus healed as He went out of the city on His last journey to Jerusalem (Mark 10:46–52).

BARUCH, (the name means "blessed"). (1) Son of Neriah and brother of Seraiah, King Zedekiah's chamberlain (Jer. 51:59) Baruch was Jeremiah's faithful scribe; He wrote down the prophet's words and read them to the people and to the angry king Jehoiakim (chs. 32, 36 and 45 of Jer). (2) A son of Zabbai who aided Nehemiah in repairing the walls of Jerusalem (Neh. 3:20). (3) One of the leaders who signed the covenant with Nehemiah

(Neh. 10:6). (4) Son of Colhozeh, a descendant of Perez, the son of Judah (Neh. 11:5).

BARZILLAI, (son of iron), (1) a wealthy and aged Gileadite of Rogelim who brought provisions to David when David fled from his son Absalom (II Sam. 17: 27–9). David remembered this kindness and later befriended the sons of Barzillai (II Sam. 19:31–9; I Kin. 2:7). (2) Barzillai the Meholathite, whose son Adriel was married to one of Saul's daughters (II Sam. 21:8; I Sam. 18:19). (3) A priest who married a descendant of Barzillai the Gileadite and assumed the same name. His genealogy became confused and because of this his descendants in Ezra's time were deemed unfit for the priesthood (Ezra 2:61; Neh. 7:63).

BASE, the bottom of anything, considered as its support; a foundation. This word is used in the descriptions of the building of the tabernacle and temple and the furnishings of these (I Kin. 7:27–43).

BASE, lowly in place or position. In Acts 17:5 a rabble group is spoken of as "lewd fellows of the baser sort."
they were children of *b.*, Job 30:8..
kingdom might be *b.*, Ezek. 17:14..
b. things of this world, I Cor. 1:28.
who in presence am *b.*, II Cor. 10:1.

BASEMATH, BASHEMATH, BASMATH, (1) a wife of Esau, she was a daughter of Elon, the Hittite (Gen. 26: 34), thus probably identical with or a sister of Adah (Gen. 36:2). (2) Another wife of Esau, a daughter of Ishmael and sister of Nebaioth (Gen. 36:3). Also called Mahalath (Gen. 28:9). Esau married her because his father was not pleased with his Canaanite wives. (3) A daughter of Solomon and wife of Ahimaaz, a commissary officer in Solomon's service (I Kin. 4:15).

BASHAN, a region East of Jordan extending from Mt. Hermon on the North to Gilead in the South, Bashan was noted in the Old Testament period for its productiveness (Jer. 50:19) and for its fine breed of cattle (Ps. 22:12; Deut. 32:14). Prominent cities in Bashan include Edrei (Deut. 3:10), Ashtaroth (Deut. 1:4) and Golan, a city of refuge (Josh. 20:8).

Moses describes the cities of Bashan in Deut. 3:5.

BASHAN, HILL OF, Ps. 68:15 says, "The hill of God is as the hill of Bashan;" this figure does not fit the long, level tableland, but it does fit the summits of Hermon or the volcanic cones scattered across Bashan.

BASHAN-HAVOTH-JAIR, (the Bashan of the villages of Jair), the name Jair gave to the places he had conquered in Bashan (Deut. 3:14; Josh. 13:30).

BASHEMATH, *see* **BASEMATH.**

BASIN, a container or bowl. (1) A large basin was part of the furnishing of the Tabernacle and the Temple (Num. 4:14; Zech. 14:20). (2) A smaller basin was used for washing (John 13:5) and for drinking (Is. 22:24).
blood that is in the *b.*, Ex. 12:22.
by weight for every *b.*, I Chr. 28:17.
b. and fire-pans the, Jer. 52:19.
poureth water into a *b.*, John 13:5.

BASKET, a vessel made of willow, rush, palm-leaf, etc. and used for various household and agricultural purposes. Baskets differed greatly in size and shape, some hampers being even large enough to contain a man (Acts 9:25).
in the *b.* all manner of, Gen. 40:17.
the bread in the *b.* of, Lev. 8:31.
a *b.* of summer fruit, Amos 8:1.
wall in a *b.*, Acts 9:25.
took up twelve *b.*, Matt. 14:20.

BASMATH, *see* **BASEMATH.**

BASON, *see* **BASIN.**

BASTARD, an illegitimate child. Jewish tradition applies the term to the offspring of any marriage prohibited by the Law. Among the Jews the bastard had no claim to an inheritance or to proper treatment as a child; this is the background of the reference in Heb. 12:8.
a *b.* shall not enter, Deut. 23:2.
b. shall dwell in Ashdod, Zech. 9:6.
chastisement, then are *b.*, Heb. 12:8.

BAT, this flying mammal is numerous in Palestine with nearly twenty different types having been found. Bats inhabit dark and deserted places (Is. 2:20). The fruit-eating bat is a pest, but the insect-eating bat is beneficial. The bat was forbidden as food in the Law (Lev. 11:19; Deut. 14:18).

BATH, a liquid measure equal to about 8 gallons, the bath is the largest Jewish liquid measure. It is equal to the ephah, or one/tenth homer (Ezek. 45:10).
two thousand *b.*, I Kin. 7:26.
an hundred *b.* of wine, Ezra 7:22.
vineyard shall yield one *b.*, Is. 5:10.
tenth part of a *b.*, Ezek. 45:14.

BATH, a washing. Also Bathed, Bathing. (1) Ordinary bathing. The hot, dusty climate of Palestine and the open footwear of the people made necessary frequent washing of the feet (Gen. 24:32; 43:24; John 13:5). Ordinary bathing of the whole body is mentioned in Ex. 2:5 and II Sam. 11:2. (2) Special bathing was done before visiting a superior (Ruth 3:3) and after mourning (II Sam. 12:20). (3) Religious baths were practiced before a service (Ex. 19:10) to appear clean before God. The high priest bathed at his inauguration (Lev. 8:6) and on the day of atonement (Lev. 16:4, 24). Here and elsewhere physical cleanliness is associated with purity. *See* ABLUTION, PURIFICATION.
shall *b.* himself, Lev. 15:5, 8.
nor *b.* his flesh, Lev. 17:16.
sword shall be *b.* in, Is. 34:5.

BATH-RABBIM, (daughter of many), the gate of Heshbon near which were the pools compared to the eyes of the beloved in Song 7:4.

BATHSHEBA, (daughter of the oath), daughter of Eliam (II Sam. 11:3) or Ammiel (I Chr. 3:5), and wife of Uriah, Bathsheba committed adultery with David while her husband was away at war. Unable to arrange for it to appear that Uriah was father of the coming, illicit child, David contrived the death of Uriah and, after Bathsheba's mourning, married her (II Sam. 11:3–27). She bore David four sons, among them Solomon (II Sam. 5:14) who succeeded David as king.
Sin of *B.* with David, II Sam. 11:4.
The illicit child dies, II Sam. 12:14.
B. aids Solomon, I Kin. 1:11–31.
B's request refused, I Kin. 2:24.

BATH-SHUA, (daughter of riches), another name for Bathsheba (I Chr. 3:5).

BATTERING-RAM, a large beam with a head of iron, the battering-ram was propelled against the wall of a fort or city under siege in order to break down or through the wall (Ezek 4:2).
set *b.* rams against it, Ezek. 4:2.
appoint *b.* rams against, Ezek. 21:22.

BATTLE, armed conflict. *See* WARFARE
they joined *b.*, Gen. 14:8.
before the Lord to *b.*, Num. 32:27.
the Lord mighty in *b.*, Ps. 24:8.
b. of the great day, Rev. 16:14.

BATTLE-AX, an ax-like club used as a weapon of war.
Thou art my *b.*, Jer. 51:20.

BATTLE-BOW, a bow used as a weapon of war, and made of tough wood, metal (Ps. 18:34) or two straight horns joined together.
The *b.* shall be cut off, Zech. 9:10.
came forth the *b.*, Zech. 10:4.

BATTLEMENT, (1) a breastwork around the flat wall of a house, required for protection from accidents (Deut. 22:8); (2) the parapet of a city wall from which the defenders of a city fought the enemy (Jer. 5:10).

BAVAI, BAVVAI, a son of Henadad who repaired part of the wall of Jerusalem (Neh. 3:18).

BAY, an inlet of a sea (Josh. 15:5; 18:19).

BAY, the color of a horse in Zech. 6:3. The bay horse was powerful.

BAY TREE, the word means literally "a tree in its native soil," (Ps. 37:35).

BAZLITH, the head of one of the families of Nethinim that returned to Jerusalem from the exile (Neh. 7:54; Ezra 2:52).

BAZLUTH, another name for Bazlith.

BDELLIUM, a precious substance, most likely a fragrant gum, but perhaps a mineral. Bdellium was a product of Havilah (Gen. 2:12) and to it manna is compared (Num. 11:7).

BEACON, a directing signal (Is. 30:17).

BEALIAH, (whose Lord is master), a Benjamite hero who joined David at Ziklag (I Chr. 12:5).

BEALOTH, a town in South Judah (Josh. 15:24).

BEAM, (1) the main shaft of a weaver's frame (I Sam. 17:7; II Sam. 21:19); (2) a large, dressed timber used for building purposes. Contrasting a beam with a mote (twig), Jesus showed the hypocrisy of those who with great sin reprove the lesser faults of others (Matt. 7:3–5).

BEANS, a common agricultural product of Palestine (II Sam. 17:28). During famine beans were mixed with ground grain to form a coarse bread (Ezek. 4:9).

BEAR, the Biblical bear is the Syrian bear, a local variety of the European and Asiatic brown bear still found in Lebanon and East of the Jordan. David killed a lion and a bear to protect his flock (I Sam. 17:34–37). Two bears tore forty-two children who mocked Elisha (II Kin. 2:24). Bears used figuratively represent a nation or empire (Dan. 7:5) or a ferocious destroyer (II Sam. 17:8; Hos. 13:8; Amos 5:19).

BEAR, to give birth to (Gen. 17:17; Is. 7:14; Luke 1:13), to yield (James 3:12).

BEAR, to carry or endure.
greater than I can *b.*, Gen. 4:13.
let me *b.* the blame, Gen. 43:9.
they shall *b.* thee up, Ps. 91:12.
doth not *b.* his cross, Luke 14:27.
b. infirmities of weak, Rom. 15:1.
b. in my body marks of, Gal. 6:17.

BEARD, The Jews cherished the beard as the badge of the dignity of manhood. In one case neglect of the beard is set down as madness (I Sam. 21:13). The *b.* was shaved or plucked out in time of mourning (Is. 15:2; Jer. 41:5). Mutilation of another's beard was a great indignity (II Sam. 10:4; Is. 50:6).
mar the corners of *b.*, Lev. 19:27.
down on *b.*, Aaron's *b.*, Ps. 133:2.
razor to pass on *b.*, Ezek. 5:1.

BEARETH, BEARING, BEARS, *see* BEAR.

BEAST, an animal. In the Bible this word usually denotes a mammal in distinction from a man, a bird, or a fish. The word is often used figuratively and usually refers to the sensuous nature of animals (Ps. 73:22) or, more often, to their ferocious, brutal nature (Dan. 7:3; Jer. 12:9; Ezek. 34:28). Thus, wild beasts, in figurative settings, may symbolize selfish, tyrannical monarchies.
let earth bring forth *b.*, Gen. 1:24.
ask now the *b.*, Job 12:7.
like the *b.* that perish, Ps. 49:12.
I fought with *b.*, I Cor. 15:32.
kind of *b.* is tamed, James 3:7.
as natural brute *b.*, II Pet. 2:12.

BEATING, a type of punishment widely used (Prov. 22:15; Lev. 19:20; Deut. 22: 18). The number of blows was to be limited to forty (Deut. 25:3), and usually the corrector stopped one short to keep from going over the number (II Cor. 11:24).

BEATITUDE, blessedness, the name given to any of the pronouncements of blessings given by Jesus in Matt. 5:3–12, the beginning of the Sermon on the Mount.

BEAUTIFUL, having beauty. *See* BEAUTY.
Rachel was *b.*, Gen. 29:17.
b. are the feet, Is. 52:7.
b. house is burned up, Is. 64:11.
gate called *b.*, Acts 3:2.

BEAUTIFY, to make beautiful.

BEAUTY, physical, moral, or spiritual loveliness.
praise *b.* of holiness, II Chr. 20:21.
behold *b.* of the Lord, Ps. 27:4.
b. of old men, Prov. 20:29.
b. is vain, Prov. 31:30.
burning instead of *b.*, Is. 3:24.

BEAUTY and BANDS, the name given to two symbolic staves in Zech. 11:7–14. The breaking of these symbolizes the breaking of the covenant and the union between Judah and Israel.

BEBAI, (1) the head of one of the families returning from Babylon with Zerrubbabel (Ezra 2:11; Neh. 7:16); (2) the name of one who sealed the covenant with Nehemiah (Neh. 10:15).

BECHER, (young camel), (1) the second son of Benjamin (Gen. 46:21; I Chr. 7:6). Becher is omitted in the list in I Chr. 8:1. (2) A son of Ephraim, called also Bered (I Chr. 7:20). His descendants were called Bachrites (Num. 26:35).

BECHORATH, son of Aphiah, an ancestor of Saul (I Sam. 9:1).

BECOMETH, is suitable or fitting for.
holiness *b.* thy house, Ps. 93:5.
excellent speech *b.* not, Prov. 17:7.
thus it *b.* us, Matt. 3:15.
be as *b.* the gospel, Phil. 1:27.

BECORATH, *see* BECHORATH.

BED, a common article of household furniture. The bed for the poor was the ground (Gen. 28:11; Ex. 22:26), for others a mat (Matt. 9:6), but for the rich perhaps an ivory couch with ornate coverings (Amos 3:12; 6:4).

BEDAD, father of Hadad, a king in Edom (Gen. 36:35; I Chr. 1:46).

BEDAN, (1) a deliverer of Israel (I Sam. 12:11) not listed in Judges. Some suppose him to be the judge Abdon. (2) the son of Ulam of the house of Manasseh (I Chr. 7:17).

BEDEIAH, a son of Bani, who divorced his Gentile wife on the return from Babylon (Ezra 10:35).

BEDSTEAD, *see* BED. The giant bed of King Og was a curiosity (Deut. 3:11) being 6x13½ feet.

BEE, Palestine abounded in bees, for it was a land "flowing with milk and honey" (Deut. 32:13). Only once does the word bee occur in connection with honey (Judg. 14:8); other, figurative references allude to the swarming and stinging of bees. (Deut. 1:44; Ps. 118:12; Is. 7:18).

BEELIADA, a son of David (I Chr. 14:7), also called Eliada (II Sam. 5:16).

BEELZEBUB, in Christ's day this was the current name for the chief of demons, identified with Satan (Matt. 10:25; 12:24; Mark 3:22; Luke 11:15–19). Baalzebub, (lord of flies), the Philistine god worshipped at Ekron (II Kin. 1:2) was likely considered by the Jews a demon and referred to in these passages. Beelzebul, the reading sometimes found, means "lord of dung" or "lord of the house" and may be conscious perversion of Beelzebub.
If I by *B.* cast, Matt. 12:27.
but by *B.,* prince, Mark 3:22.

BEER, (a well), (1) a desert place on the march of the Israelites; here God gave them water (Num. 21:16); (2) a town in Judah to which Jotham fled in fear of Abimelech (Judg. 9:21).

BEERA, a son of Zophah and descendant of Asher (I Chr. 7:37).

BEERAH, a prince of the house of Reuben carried into captivity by the Assyrian Tiglath-pileser (I Chr. 5:6).

BEER-ELIM, (well of heroes), a spot on the border of Moab (Is. 15:8), perhaps the same as **Beer** (1).

BEERI, (1) a Hittite, and father of Judith, a wife of Esau (Gen. 26:34). (2) The father of the prophet Hosea (Hos. 1:1).

BEER-LAHAI-ROI, (well of the Living One who sees me), the fountain in the Negeb between Kadesh and Bered, where the angel found Hagar (Gen. 16:7, 14).

BEEROTH, (1) a city of the Hivites who made a league with Joshua (Josh. 9:17), it was allotted to Benjamin (Josh. 18:25; II Sam. 4:2). (2) Beeroth of the sons of Jaakan was a desert place through which the Israelites twice passed (Num. 33:31; Deut. 10:6).

BEEROTHITE, an inhabitant of Beeroth of Benjamin (II Sam. 4:2; 23:37).

BEERSHEBA, (a well of an oath, or well of seven), a city in the southernmost part of Palestine, Beersheba received its name from the well dug and the pact made by Abraham and Abimelech (Gen. 21:31). Beersheba was a residence of Isaac (Gen. 26:33). Beersheba is often mentioned as a boundary of Israel (II Sam. 17:11). In Amos' day Beersheba was a center of false worship (Amos 8:14).

BEESHTERAH, a Levitical city allotted to the Gershonites (Josh. 21:27). It is the same as Ashtaroth (I Chr. 6:71).

BEETLE, (Lev. 11:22), *see* **LOCUST.**

BEEVES, cattle (Lev. 22:21).

BEFALL, to come upon; to occur to. Also Befallen, Befalleth, Befell.
lest mischief *b.* him, Gen. 42:4.
troubles shall *b.* them, Deut. 31:17.
shall no evil *b.* thee, Ps. 91:10.
things that shall *b.* me, Acts 20:22.

BEFORE, (1) in sight of (Gen. 43:14); (2) Rather than (II Sam. 6:21); (3) First in time (Is. 43:13) or place (Luke 22:47).
come *b.* the Lord, Mic. 6:6.
I have told you *b.*, Matt. 24:25.
he seeing this *b.* spake, Acts 2:31.
to things that are *b.*, Phil. 3:13.
was *b.* a blasphemer, I Tim. 1:13.

BEG, BEGGAR, BEGGING, because the poor among the Hebrews were given certain privileges (Lev. 19:10; 25:5; Deut. 24:19), professional begging as done today was rare in the Old Testament. Begging is predicted for the posterity of the wicked (Ps. 109:10). In the New Testament the afflicted alms-seeker is found (Mark 10:46; Luke 16:20; Acts 3:2).
shall the sluggard *b.*, Prov. 20:4.
to *b.* I am ashamed, Luke 16:3.
b. the body of Jesus, Luke 23:52.
again to *b.* elements, Gal. 4:9.

BEGIN, start, commence.
this they *b.* to do, Gen. 11:6.
and *b.* at my sanctuary, Ezek. 9:6.
shall he *b.* to say, Luke 13:26.
do we *b.* again to, II Cor. 3:1.
if it first *b.* at us, I Pet. 4:17.

BEGINNING, the commencement, the start.
In the *b.* God created, Gen. 1:1.
latter more than *b.*, Job 42:12.
fear of Lord *b.*, Ps. 111:10.
these are *b.* of sorrows, Matt. 24:8.
In the *b.* was the Word, John 1:1.
the *b.*, the first born, Col. 1:18.

BEGINS, *see* **BEGIN.**

BEGOTTEN, procreated, generated.
have I *b.* them, Num. 11:12.
this day have I *b.* thee, Ps. 2:7.
have *b.* strange children, Hos. 5:7.
glory as of the only *b.*, John 1:14.
he gave his only *b.* Son, John 3:16.
bringeth in first *b.*, Heb. 1:6.

who hath *b.* us again, I Pet. 1:3.
loveth him that is *b.*, I John 5:1.
he that is *b.* of God, I John 5:18.
Jesus who is the first *b.*, Rev. 1:5.

BEGUILE, deceive, delude. Also Beguiled.
serpent *b.* me, Gen. 3:13.
lest as the serpent *b.*, II Cor. 11:3.
lest any *b.* you with words, Col. 2:4.
cease from sin, *b.*, II Pet. 2:14.

BEGUN, started. *See* **BEGIN.**

BEHALF, benefit, interest, defense.
statute on *b.* of Israel, Ex. 27:21.
to speak on God's *b.*, Job 36:2.
glad on your *b.*, Rom. 16:19.
to glory on our *b.*, II Cor. 5:12.
in *b.* of Christ, Phil. 1:29.
glorify God on this *b.*, I Pet. 4:16.

BEHAVE, conduct oneself, act properly. Also Behaved, Behaveth.
I will *b.* wisely, Ps. 101:2.
think he *b.* uncomely, I Cor. 7:36.
charity doth not *b.*, I Cor. 13:5.
how thou oughtest to *b.*, I Tim. 3:15.

BEHAVIOR, deportment, conduct.
David changed his *b.*, I Sam. 21:13.
bishop must be of good *b.*, I Tim. 3:2.
women in *b.* becometh, Titus 2:3.

BEHEADED, cut off head of, decapitated.
slew him, and *b.* him, II Sam. 4:7.
b. John, Matt. 14:10.
them that were *b.*, Rev. 20:4.

BEHELD, *see* **OBSERVE.**
I *b.* transgressors, Ps. 119:158.
b. the work of God, Eccles. 8:17.
b. Satan as lightning, Luke 10:18.
we *b.* his glory, John 1:14.
I passed by and *b.*, Acts 17:23.

BEHEMOTH, a Hebrew word designating a class of tame or wild beasts. The Behemoth in Job 40:15–24 is probably a hippopotamus.

BEHIND, back or after in place or time.
those left *b.* stayed, I Sam. 30:9.
cast me *b.* thy back, I Kin. 14:9.
cast all my sins *b.*, Is. 38:17.
forgetting things *b.*, Phil. 3:13.

BEHOLD, to observe or see. Also Beholdest, Beholdeth, Beholding.

b. this heap, *b*. this, Gen. 31:51.
b. he smote the rock, Ps. 78:20.
b. a virgin, Is. 7:14.
b. my hands and my feet, Luke 24:39.
to *b*. my glory, John 17:24.
b. I stand and knock, Rev. 3:20.

BEHOVED, behooved, was necessary for.
it *b*. Christ to suffer, Luke 24:46.
b. him to be made like, Heb. 2:17.

BEING, (1) existing; (2) existence; (3) one that exists.
freed from *b*. bondsmen, Josh. 9:23.
cut them off from *b*., Ps. 83:4.
in him move and have *b*., Acts 17:28.
who *b*. in form of God, Phil. 2:6.

BEKA, BEKAH, an early Jewish weight, being half a shekel (Ex. 38:26).

BEL, the national god of Babylon, also known as Marduk or Merodach (Is. 46:1; Jer. 50:2; 51:44).

BELA, BELAH (1) a king of Edom (Gen. 36:32; I Chr. 1:43), perhaps contemporary with Moses. (2) the eldest son of Benjamin (Gen. 46:21) and the ancestral head of the Belaites (Num. 26:38). (3) a son of Azaz, a Reubenite (I Chr. 5:8). (4) another name for the city of Zoar (Gen. 14:2, 8).

BELAITES, the descendants of Bela (Num. 26:38).

BEL AND THE DRAGON, a book of the Apocrypha; it argues the foolishness of false gods.

BELIAL, (worthlessness, wickedness). A "son" or "man of Belial" is simply a wicked, worthless man (Deut. 13:13; Judg. 19:22; II Sam. 16:7). In II Cor. 6:15 the word refers to Satan as the personification of all evil.

BELIEVE, to accept as true; to have faith or confidence; to commit oneself (John 20:30–1). *See* **FAITH**.
that they may *b*., Ex. 4:5.
b. in the Lord God, *b*., II Chr. 20:20.
if ye will not *b*., Is. 7:9.
which ye will not *b*., Hab. 1:5.
b. ye that I am able, Matt. 9:28.
Lord, I *b*. help mine, Mark 9:24.
men through him might *b*., John 1:7.
if ye *b*. not, John 8:24.

I *b*. thou art Christ, John 11:27.
b. on the Lord Jesus, Acts 16:31.
b. in thy heart that God, Rom. 10:9.
the devils also *b*., James 2:19.
to you that *b*., I John 3:23.
b. not every spirit, I John 4:1.

BELIEVED, accepted, had faith.
who hath *b*. our report, Is. 53:1.
which are surely *b*., Luke 1:1.
they *b*. the scripture, John 2:22.
when they *b*. Philip, Acts 8:12.
then Simon himself *b*., Acts 8:13.
many of Corinthians *b*., Acts 18:8.
in whom they have not *b*., Rom. 10:14.
damned who *b*. not, II Thess. 2:12.

BELIEVEST, accepts, has faith.
I saw thee, *b*. thou, John 1:50.
shall never die, *b*., John 11:26.
b. thou? I know thou *b*., Acts 26:27.
b. there is one God, James 2:19.

BELIEVETH, accepteth, hath faith.
simple *b*. every word, Prov. 14:15.
possible to him that *b*., Mark 9:23.
b. and is baptized, Mark 16:16.
b. in him not perish, John 3:16.
that *b*. not is condemned, John 3:18.
to every one that *b*., Rom. 1:16.
whoso *b*. Jesus is Christ, I John 5:1.

BELIEVING, accepting, having faith (John 20:27).
ask in prayer, *b*., Matt. 21:22.
b., ye might have life, John 20:31.
rejoiced, *b*. in God, Acts 16:34.
joy and peace in *b*., Rom. 15:13.
yet *b*. ye rejoice with, I Pet. 1:8.

BELL, (1) small golden bells hung from the high priest's robe (Ex. 28:33–5). Women in Isaiah's day wore little bells (Is. 3:16–18). (2) "Bells of the horses" in Zech. 14:20 were probably concave brass ornaments in the horse's rigging.

BELLOWS, an instrument for blowing, used for fanning a fire (Jer. 6:29). This passage refers to purifying metals by fire, a figure for purifying men.

BELLY, among the Hebrews the belly was regarded as the seat of carnal desires (Titus 1:12; Phil. 3:19; Rom. 16:18). The word is used figuratively as the word "heart" is used today (Prov. 18:8; 20:27; 26:22).

BELONG, to be connected with, or to be the property of. Also **Belonged, Belongest, Belonging.**
interpretations *b.* to God, Gen. 40:8.
these things *b.* to wise, Prov. 24:23.
my name, because ye *b.*, Mark 9:41.
careth for things *b.*, I Cor. 7:32.

BELOVED, dearly loved, a term of endearment.
b. of the Lord, Deut. 33:12.
drink abundantly, O *b.*, Song 5:1.
go, love a woman *b.*, Hos. 3:1.
in Rome, *b.* of God, Rom. 1:7.
accepted in the *b.*, Eph. 1:6.
elect, holy and *b.*, Col. 3:12.

BELSHAZZAR, (name means "may Bel protect the king"), the eldest son and co-regent of Nabonidus. The Nabonidus Chronicle found by archeologists indicates that Nabonidus entrusted the kingship to his son Belshazzar when he went on an expedition to Tema. Belshazzar was thus regally "son of Nebuchadnezzar" (Dan. 5:2, 22; 7:1; 8:1).

BELTESHAZZAR, (Bel protect his life), the Babylonian name given to the prophet Daniel (Dan. 1:7).

BEMOAN, to lament; to express grief.
they *b.* Job, comforted, Job 42:11.
who shall *b.* thee, Jer. 15:5.
I have heard Ephraim *b.*, Jer. 31:18.
who will *b.*, Nahum 3:7.

BEN, (1) a prefix to Hebrew names which means "son of." (2) A Levite porter appointed by David to the service of the ark (I Chr. 15:18).

BEN-ABINADAB, an officer of Solomon who provided for the king's household for a month each year (I Kin. 4:11).

BENAIAH, "built by Jehovah." Twelve men bear this name in the Bible.
a man of Pirathon, II Sam. 23:30.
a prince of Simenon, I Chr. 4:36.
a Levite, I Chr. 15:18.
a priest of the temple, I Chr. 15:24.
a son of Jehoiada, I Chr. 27:5.
a son of Asaph, II Chr. 20:14.
another Levite, II Chr. 31:13.
a son of Parosh, Ezra 10:25.
a son of Pahath-moab, Ezra 10:30.
a son of Bani, Ezra 10:35.
a son of Nebo, Ezra 10:43.

father of Pelatiah, Ezek. 11:1.

BEN-AMMI, son of Lot by his youngest daughter. He was progenitor of the Ammonites (Gen. 19:38).

BEND, to crook, to draw taut.
wicked *b.* their bow, Ps. 11:2.
b. their tongue, Jer. 9:3.
all ye that *b.*, bow, Jer. 50:14.
vine did *b.* roots, Ezek. 17:7.

BEN-DEKER, One of the twelve officers who provided victuals for King Solomon and his household (I Kin. 4:9).

BENEATH, under.
in the earth *b.*, Ex. 20:4.
depart from hell *b.*, Prov. 15:24.
ye are from *b.*, I am, John 8:23.

BENE-BERAK, (sons of lightning), one of the cities of Dan (Josh. 19:45).

BENEDICTION, a statement of blessing. Num. 6:24–6 is a beautiful benediction.

BENEFACTOR, one who confers benefits. A title given to worldly rulers, but reserved by Jesus for true servants (Luke 22:25).

BENEFITS, favors, kindnesses.
forget not all his *b.*, Ps. 103:2.
partakers of the *b.*, I Tim. 6:2.
b. should not be of, Philem. 14.

BENE-JAAKAN, (sons of Jaakan), a halting place enroute to Canaan (Num. 33:31).

BENEVOLENCE, kindness. In I Cor. 7:3 the word indicates marital consideration.

BEN-GEBER, one of Solomon's commissary officers (I Kin. 4:13).

BENHADAD, (son of the god Hadad), title of the king of Syria (Amos 1:4; Jer. 49:27). Two, and perhaps three, Syrian kings with this name are discussed in the Bible: (1) Benhadad I, who aided Asa against Baasha (I Kin. 15:20–2). He is probably the same Benhadad who sought Elisha (II Kin. 6:8) and was murdered by Hazael (II Kin. 8:15). If not, this latter figure would be Benhadad II. (2) Benhadad II (or III) son of Hazael, who was defeated by Jehoahaz (II Kin. 13:25).

BEN-HAIL, (son of strength), a prince sent by Jehoshaphat to Judah (II Chr. 17:7).

BEN-HANAN, (son of grace), a son of Shimon of the house of Judah (I Chr. 4:20).

BEN-HESED, (son of Hesed), a commissary officer for Solomon (I Kin. 4:10).

BEN-HUR, (son of Hur), a commissary officer for Solomon (I Kin. 4:8).

BENINU, a Levite who with Nehemiah sealed the covenant (Neh. 10:13).

BENJAMIN, (1) the youngest son of Jacob and the second by Rachel (Gen. 35:18), who died in bearing him. He was loved by his father and brothers (Gen. 42:4; 43:34; 45:14). His descendants made up the tribe of Benjamin. (2) The tribe. It inherited land between Judah and Ephraim (Josh. 18:11), which was a key position in defending the country. Benjamin fought under Deborah (Judg. 5:14) against Sisera. Ehud the Judge (Judg. 3:15), King Saul (I Sam. 10:20), and the Apostle Paul (Phil. 3:5) were from this tribe. Benjamin eventually became closely connected with Judah (I Kin. 12:20–1). (3) A great-grandson of Benjamin, son of Jacob (I Chr. 7:10). (4) One of those who had married a strange wife (Ezra 10:32, and probably also Neh. 3:23 and 12:34).

BENJAMIN, GATE OF, a gate in the wall of Jerusalem, also called the High Gate (Jer. 20:2; 37:13; 38:7; Zech. 14:10).

BENJAMITE, a descendant of the patriarch Benjamin (I Sam. 9:21; 22:7).

BENO, a son of Jaaziah of the house of Levi (I Chr. 24:26, 27).

BENONI, (son of my pain), the name the dying Rachel gave to her youngest son. Jacob changed it to Benjamin (Gen. 35:18).

BEN-ZOHETH, a son of Ishi of the house of Judah (I Chr. 4:20).

BEON, (Num. 32:3). This place is elsewhere called Baal-Meon. *See* BAAL-MEON.

BEOR, (1) father of Bela, a king of Edom (Gen. 36:32; I Chr. 1:43). (2) Father of the seer Balaam (Num. 22:5). He is called Bosor in II Pet. 2:15.

BERA, a king of Sodom who was subdued by Chedorlaomer (Gen. 14:2, 10).

BERACAH, BERACHAH, (blessing), (1) a Benjamite warrior who joined David at Ziklag (I Chr. 12:3). (2) A valley between Bethlehem and Hebron, where the victorious group under Jehoshaphat blessed the Lord (II Chr. 20:26).

BERACHIAH, *see* BERECHIAH (2).

BERAIAH, (God has created). A son of Shimei of the house of Benjamin (I Chr. 8:21).

BEREA, a Macedonian city which was the residence of many Jews, whom Paul commended for their careful study of the Scriptures (Acts 17:10–13). Berea is now known as Verria.

BEREAN, a person from Berea.

BEREAVE, to deprive, to make destitute. Also **Bereaved, Bereaveth.**
I will *b.* them, Jer. 15:7.
children, will I *b.*, Hos. 9:12.

BERECHIAH, BERACHIAH, BARACHIAS, BARACHIAH, (blessed by God), (1) a son (or brother) of Zerubbabel (I Chr. 3:20). (2) Son of Shimea and father of Asaph (I Chr. 6:39; 15:17), he was a doorkeeper for the ark (I Chr. 15:23). (3) A former inhabitant of Jerusalem, a Levite (I Chr. 9:16). (4) A chief of the tribe of Ephraim (II Chr. 28:12). (5) Father of Meshullam the builder (Neh. 3:4, 30; 6:18). (6) Father of the prophet Zechariah (Zech. 1:1, 7).

BERED, (1) a grandson of Ephraim (I Chr. 7:20), perhaps identical with Becher (Num. 26:35). (2) An important town in the Negeb mentioned in the story of Hagar (Gen. 16:14).

BERI, a son of Zophah, and a mighty warrior of Asher (I Chr. 7:36).

BERIAH, (1) a son of Asher, and father of Heber and Malchiel (Gen. 46:17; I

Chr. 7:30). His descendants were called Beriites (Num. 26:44). (2) A son of Ephraim, called Beriah because of family misfortune (I Chr. 7:23). (3) A descendant of Benjamin (I Chr. 8:13). (4) A Levite in the line of Gershon (I Chr. 23:10).

BERITES, a people mentioned only in II Sam. 20:14. They probably lived in northern Palestine, perhaps in Beroth.

BERITH, a Hebrew word meaning "covenant." In Judges 9:46 a false god is called Berith, short for **Baal-Berith.**

BERNICE, eldest daughter of Agrippa I. After the death of her husband Herod, king of Chalcis, she lived, perhaps incestuously, with her brother, Agrippa II. Paul defended himself before these two (Acts 25:23; 26:30).

BERODACH-BALADAN, see **MERODACH-BALADAN.**

BEROTHAH, BEROTHAI, a place mentioned by Ezekiel as part of the northern limit of the restored promised land he envisioned (Ezek. 47:16). Now identified with Bereitan 35 miles North of Damascus.

BEROTHAI (II Sam. 8:8), see **BEROTHAH.**

BEROTHITE (I Chr. 11:39), see **BEEROTHITE.**

BERYL, a precious stone, probably golden yellow in color. The Hebrew word thus translated was "tarshish" and probably alluded to the place of origin. The stone mentioned in Rev. 21:20 is related to the emerald in class.
b. in the breastplate, Ex. 28:20.
hands as ring with *b.*, Song 5:14.
wheels of color of *b.*, Ezek. 1:16.
body was like the *b.*, Dan. 10:6.

BESAI, a head of the Nethinim, whose descendants returned from Babylon (Ezra 2:49; Neh. 7:52).

BESEECH, to entreat, to beg.
I *b.* thee shew me thy, Ex. 33:18.
Lord, I *b.* thee, Ps. 116:4.
obey, I *b.* thee, Jer. 38:20.

I *b.* thee, torment, Luke 8:28.
prisoner of the Lord *b.*, Eph. 4:1.
for love's sake I *b.*, Philem. 9.

BESET, to harass, to hem in.
thou hast *b.* me behind, Ps. 139:5.
sin which doth *b.*, Heb. 12:1.

BESIDE, by the side of, near by; other than or in addition to. To be beside oneself is to be crazy.
leadeth me *b.* still, Ps. 23:2.
b. all this, today is, Luke 24:21.
Paul, thou art *b.*, Acts 26:24.

BESIEGE, to surround with armed forces in order to compel surrender.
shall *b.* thee in gates, Deut. 28:52.
go, O Elam, *b.* O Media, Is. 21:2.

BESODEIAH, father of Meshullam, the builder (Neh. 3:6).

BESOM, a broom. To sweep away as with a broom is a destruction figure (Is. 14:23).

BESOR, THE BROOK, a stream flowing into the Mediterranean South of Gaza (I Sam. 30:9, 10, 11).

BESOUGHT, asked earnestly, begged.
so the devils *b.* him, Luke 8:31.
Jairus *b.* him greatly, Luke 8:41.
b. Pilate that he might, John 19:38.
I *b.* Lord, II Cor. 12:8.

BEST, most excellent.
take of the *b.* fruits, Gen. 43:11.
every man at *b.* state, Ps. 39:5.
bring forth the *b.* robe, Luke 15:22..
covet the *b.* gifts, I Cor. 12:31.

BESTEAD, situated.
hardly *b.* and hungry, Is. 8:21.

BESTIALITY, the act of having sexual relations with an animal. Bestiality is severely condemned in Scrpiture (Ex. 22:19; Lev. 18:23; 20:16).

BESTOW, to give, to impart.
he may *b.* a blessing, Ex. 32:29.
they did *b.* on Baalim, II Chr. 24:7.
b. all my fruits, Luke 12:17.
though I *b.* all goods, I Cor. 13:3.

BETAH, (confidence), called Tibhath (I

Chr. 18:8), a city of Syria-Zobah captured by David (II Sam. 8:8).

BETEN, (belly, hollow), a city on the border of Asher (Josh. 19:25).

BETH, the second letter of the Hebrew alphabet, corresponding to our B. The word "Beth" means house (Gen. 24:32; I Sam. 1:7). It came to be used also in the sense of a family.

BETHABARA, (house of the ford), a place on the Jordan where John baptized (John 1:28). Some of the oldest manuscripts read here "Bethany."

BETHANATH, (house of Anath), a city in the region of Naphtali from which city the Canaanites were not expelled (Josh. 19:38; Judg. 1:33).

BETHANOTH, a town in the mountains of Judah (Josh. 15:59).

BETHANY, (house of unripe figs). (1) A village on Mount Olivet about two miles from Jerusalem (John 11:18). It was the home of Simon the leper (Mark 14:3) and Mary, Martha and Lazarus (John 11:18). Jesus made Bethany his Judean home (Matt. 21:17; Mark 11:11). Near here Christ ascended (Luke 24:50). (2) A name given instead of Bethabara in some ancient manuscripts (John 1:28).

BETH-ARABAH, one of the six cities of Judah "in the wilderness" (Josh. 15:61); it is on the North end of the Dead Sea. A city of Benjamin, perhaps Bethabara, is also called by this name (Josh. 18:22).

BETH-ARAM, *see* **BETH-HARAN.**

BETH-ARBEL, scene of a disaster inflicted on the people by Shalman (Hos. 10:14). The town is probably the present-day Irbid, near Tiberias.

BETH-AVEN, (house of nothingness), a place in the mountains of Benjamin (Josh. 7:2; I Sam. 13:5). Hosea seems to use the name in mockery for idolatrous Bethel (Hosea 4:15; 10:5; see Amos 5:5).

BETH-AZMAVETH, a village of Benjamin. Forty-two from here returned with Zerubbabel (Neh. 7:28; 12:29; Ezra 2:24).

BETH-BAAL-MEON, a place assigned to Reuben in the plains East of Jordan (Josh. 13:17). Also called **Baal-Meon** (Num. 32:38) and **Beon** (Num. 32:3).

BETH-BARAH, a main ford on the Jordan (Judg. 7:24).

BETH-BIREI, a site in the Negeb belonging to Simeon (I Chr. 4:31).

BETH-CAR, a place marking the limit of an Israelite pursuit of Philistines (I Sam. 7:6-12).

BETH-DAGON, (house of Dagon), (1) a town near the Southeast border of Asher (Josh. 19:27). (2) A city in the low country of Judah, near Lydda (Josh. 15:41).

BETH-DIBLATHAIM, (house of two fig-cakes), a city of Moab denounced by Jeremiah (Jer. 48:22); called **Almondiblathaim** (Num. 33:46) and **Diblath** (Ezek. 6:14).

BETHEL, (house of God). (1) A town in Simeon (I Sam. 30:27), better known as Bethul (Josh. 19:4) or Bethuel (I Chr. 4:30). (2) A town about twelve miles North of Jerusalem, so named because of Jacob's vision there (Gen. 28:11, 19).
Abraham camped at *B.*, Gen. 13:3.
Originally called Luz, Gen. 28:19.
Assigned to Benjamin, Josh. 18:22.
Idolatry at *B.*, I Kin. 12:28-33.
Josiah cleanses *B.*, II Kin. 23:15.
Hosea condemns *B.*, Hos. 4:15.
Amos condemns *B.*, Amos 5:5.

BETHELITE, a native of Bethel (I Kin. 16:34).

BETH-EMEK, (house of the valley), a valley town of Zebulun (Josh. 19:27).

BETHER, a range of mountains (Song 2:17), perhaps the same as the mountains of spice (Song 8:14).

BETHESDA, (house of grace), a spring-fed pool in Jerusalem, thought to have healing powers. Here Jesus healed a man lame thirty-eight years (John 5:2-9).

BETH-EZEL, a town in South Judah (Mic. 1:11).

BETH-GADER, a place in Judah (I Chr. 2:51), probably the same as Gedor (Josh. 15:58).

BETH-GAMUL, (house of recompense), a city of Moab (Jer. 48:23).

BETH-GILGAL, (house of Gilgal). The Gilgal in the plain East of Jericho (Neh. 12:29). *See* GILGAL.

BETH-HACCEREM, BETH-HACCHEREM, (house of the vineyard). A Judean town on a height (Neh. 3:14). It was used as a signaling station (Jer. 6:1).

BETH-HARAN, BETH-ARAM, an Amorite city taken and fortified by the Gadites (Josh. 13:27; Num. 32:36).

BETH-HOGLA, BETH-HOGLAH, (house of a partridge), a place in Benjamin, near Jericho (Josh. 15:6; 18:19).

BETH-HORON, (house of the hollow), the name of two towns, Beth-Horon the Upper (Josh. 16:5) and the Lower (Josh. 16:3). These were built by Sherah (I Chr. 7:24); assigned to Ephraim, and given to the Kohathites (Josh. 21:22; I Chr. 6:68). They were strategically located near Gibeah on the road from the coast, and thus were often fortified (I Kin. 9:17). This place figured in Joshua's famous, divinely aided victory over the Amorites (Josh. 10:10).

BETHINK, to think, to consider (I Kin. 8:47; II Chr. 6:37).

BETH-JESHIMOTH, BETH-JESIMOTH, a town in Moab, near the mouth of the Jordan (Num. 33:49; Josh. 12:3; Ezek. 25:9).

BETH-LE-APHRAH, (house of dust), rendering in Revised Version of Mic. 1:10. Site unknown, perhaps in Philistian Plain.

BETH-LEBAOTH, (house of lionesses), a town in Simeon (Josh. 15:32; 19:6).

BETHLEHEM, (house of bread). (1) A town in Judah, about five miles South of Jerusalem, noted as the birthplace of the Messiah (Mic. 5:2; Matt. 2:1). It is also called Bethlehem Ephratah, Bethlehem Judah, and the city of David who was also born at Bethlehem (I Sam. 16:1). Bethlehem is the setting for most of the Book of Ruth (Ruth 1:1; 2:1). The city overlooks the main highway to Hebron and Egypt. Micah's prophecy of this town as the birthplace of the Messiah (Mic. 5:2) and its fulfillment (Matt. 2:1) are impressive. (2) A town of Zebulun, seven miles East of Nazareth (Josh. 19:15).

BETHLEHEMITE, an inhabitant of Bethlehem in Judah (I Sam. 16:1; 17:58).

BETHLEHEM JUDAH, Bethlehem in Judah (Judg. 17:7; 19:1; I Sam. 17:12).

BETH-MAACHAH, (house of Maachah), a city in Naphtali, where Joab besieged Sheba (II Sam. 20:14-5). Also called **Abel-Beth-Maachah** (I Kin. 15:20; II Kin. 15:29).

BETH-MARCABOTH, (place of chariots), a town in Simeon, where dwelt descendants of Shimei (Josh. 19:5; I Chr. 4:31). The exact site is uncertain.

BETH-MEON, (Jer. 48:23), *see* BETH-BAAL-MEON.

BETH-NIMRAH, (house of the leopard), a fortified city in Gad (Num. 32:36).

BETH-PALET, (house of escape), a town assigned to Simeon (Josh. 15:27), and inhabited after the captivity (Neh. 11:26). Exact location uncertain now.

BETH-PAZZEZ, (house of dispersion), a city of Issachar (Josh. 19:21).

BETH-PELET, *see* BETH-PALET.

BETH-PEOR, (house of Peor), a place in Moab East of Jordan, abominable for its idolatry. It was given to Reuben (Josh. 13:20). Near here occurred Moses' final reading of the law to Israel and his burial (Deut. 4:44-6; 34:6).

BETHPHAGE, (house of unripe figs), a town near Bethany on the Mount of Olives (Matt. 21:1; Mark 11:1; Luke 19:29). No trace of it now remains.

BETH-PHELET, *see* BETH-PALET.

BETH-RAPHA, a descendant of Judah, and son of Eshton (I Chr. 4:12).

BETH-REHOB, (house of the street), an Aramean town near Laish-Dan (Judg. 18:28). Mercenary soldiers from Bethrehob aided the Ammonites against David (II Sam. 10:6). Most likely Rehob (Num. 13:21) is Beth-Rehob.

BETHSAIDA, (house of fishing), (1) a city on the West coast of the Sea of Galilee. It was the home of Peter, Andrew and Philip (John 1:44; 12:21), and Jesus often visited it. Bethsaida was rebuked by Jesus for refusing to hear Him (Luke 10:13). Bethsaida probably adjoined Capernaum (Matt. 8:14; Mark 1:29). (2) A city East of the Jordan, where Jesus miraculously fed a multitude (Luke 9:10-17). Most likely the healing in Mark 8: 22-26 occurred at this Bethsaida. Philip the Tetrarch built up this town and called it Julias, in honor of Julia, the daughter of Augustus.

BETH-SHEAN, BETH-SHAN, (house of security, or house of Shahan), a city in Issachar assigned to Manesseh, from which the Canaanites were not driven (Josh. 17:11; Judg. 1:27). This ancient fortress strategically overlooked the Valley of Esdraelon. At this place the Philistines desecrated the bones of Saul (I Sam. 31:10-13). The site of this ancient town has yielded many archeological remains.

BETH-SHEMESH, (house of the sun), (1) a city near the northern part of the western border of Judah (Josh. 15:10; I Sam. 6:9-19); this was a Levitical city (Josh. 21:16). (2) A city near the southern border of Issachar (Josh. 19:22). (3) A city in Naphtali from which the Canaanites were not driven (Josh. 19:38; Judg. 1:33). (4) A city in Egypt upon which Jeremiah pronounced doom (Jer. 43:13). This is almost certainly the city usually called Heliopolis.

BETH-SHEMITE, an inhabitant of Bethshemesh in Judah (I Sam 6:14).

BETH-SHITTAH, a town near the Jordan where the Midianites fled from Gideon (Judg. 7:22).

BETH-TAPPUAH, (house of apples), a

town about five miles West of Hebron (Josh. 15:53), probably the modern Taffuh.

BETHUEL, (1) a city of southern Judah, also called Bethul (I Chr. 4:30; Josh. 19: 4) and once Bethel (I Sam. 30:27). (2) Son of Nahor by Milcah; the nephew of Abraham, and father of Rebekah (Gen. 22:22; 24:15, 24, 47).

BETHUL, contraction for **Bethuel** (1).

BETH-ZUR, a strategic elevated fortress between Hebron and Bethlehem (II Chr. 11:7; Neh. 3:16), prominent in the intertestamental period.

BETIMES, (1) early (Gen. 26:31; (2) in proper time (Prov. 13:24); (3) diligently (Job 8:5).

BETONIM, a town East of Jordan in Gad's territory (Josh. 13:26).

BETRAY, to deliver to an enemy by treachery; to hand over.
if ye come to *b.*, I Chr. 12:17.
shall *b.* one another, Matt. 24:10.
sought to *b.* him, Luke 22:6.
one of you shall *b.*, Mark 14:18.
Jesus knew who *b.*, John 6:64.
into heart of Judas *b.*, John 13:2.

BETRAYED, delivered in treachery.
Judas who *b.* him, Matt. 10:4.
sinned, in that I *b.*, Matt. 27:4.
woe to man by whom *b.*, Mark 14:21.
night he was *b.* he, I Cor. 11:23.

BETROTH, to engage or promise in marriage. In Bible times a betrothal was considered binding, and there were formal ceremonies to celebrate it. Also **Betrothed.**
shall *b.* a wife, Deut. 28:30.
will *b.* thee to me, Hos. 2:19.
b. thee to me, Hos. 2:20.

BETTER, (1) having good qualities in greater degree (II Kin. 5:12). (2) Preferable in use, fitness, rank, etc.
b. for us to have served, Ex. 14:12.
please the Lord *b.*, Ps. 69:31.
two are *b.* than one, Eccles. 4:9.
are you not much *b.*, Matt. 6:26.
were *b.* that a millstone, Mark 9:42.
are we *b.* than they, Rom. 3:9.
being made so much *b.*, Heb. 1:4.

Mediator of a *b*. covenant, Heb. 8:6.

BETTING, gambling. Samson's riddle is an example of betting (Judg. 14:12-9).

BETWEEN, (1) in the space or interval that separates. Also **Betwixt.** (2) Joining (Gen. 9:16).
enmity *b*. thy seed, Gen. 3:15.
how long halt ye *b*., I Kin. 18:21.
her adulteries from *b*., Hos. 2:2.
no difference *b*. Jew and, Rom. 10:12.
one Mediator *b*. God, I Tim. 2:5.

BEULAH, (married), a figurative name (Is. 62:4) describing Israel restored to God's blessing. The marriage figure is commonly used after Hosea

BEVERAGE, a liquid for drinking. Water was most common drink, although milk was also used much. A sour drink was a thirst-quencher (Ruth 2:14). *See* **DRINK.**

BEWAIL, to express deep sorrow; lament, often accompanied by striking breast.
I may go and *b*., Judg. 11:37.
I will *b*. with weeping, Is. 16:9.
that I shall *b*., II Cor. 12:21.
shall *b*. her, Rev. 18:9.

BEWARE, to be on one's guard (against).
b. lest thou forget, Deut. 6:12.
b. of false prophets, Matt. 7:15.
b. of the leaven of, Mark 8:15.
b. of dogs, *b*. of evil, Phil. 3:2.
b. lest any man spoil, Col. 2:8.
b. lest ye also, II Pet. 3:17.

BEWITCH, (1) to deceive by sorcery (Acts 8:9). (2) To charm or fascinate (Gal. 3:1).

BEWRAY, (Prov. 29:24; Is. 16:3), *see* **BETRAY.**

BEYOND, (1) on the farther side of (Gen. 50:10). (2) Over and above (Mark 6:51) "Beyond Jordan" is usually figured from the position of the writer.

BEZAI, (1) a chief who with Nehemiah sealed the covenant (Neh. 10:18). (2) Descendants of Bezai returned with Zerubbabel to Jerusalem (Ezra 2:17; Neh. 7:23).

BEZALEL, BEZALEEL, (in the shadow or protection of God), (1) the workman

to whom was intrusted the construction of the tabernacle; he was chosen and aided by God in his task (Ex. 31:1-11; 35:30; 38:22). (2) An Israelite of Ezra's time who divorced his foreign wife (Ezra 10:30).

BEZEK, (1) the residence of Adoni-bezek taken by Judah and Simeon (Judg. 1:4), in the territory allotted to Judah. (2) The place where Saul marshaled his army before going to aid Jabesh-gilead (I Sam. 11:8).

BEZER, (1) a son of Zophah of the house of Asher (I Chr. 7:37). (2) A Reubenite city of refuge and Levitical city East of Jordan (Deut. 4:23; Josh. 20:8; 21:36).

BIBLE, the Word of God, the Scriptures, composed of the Old Testament (39 books) and the New Testament (27 books). The Old Testament was written mainly in Hebrew (with a small portion in Aramaic), and the New Testament in Greek. The Jews commonly divided the Old Testament into 3 parts—law, prophets and psalms (Luke 24:44). Both of the Testaments contain elements of law, history and prophecy. Modern writers usually divide each Testament into four sections. The Old Testament thus contains: 5 books of law; 12 books of history; 5 books of poetry; and 17 books of prophecy. The New contains: 4 books of biography of Christ; Acts, a history of the early church; 21 letters containing doctrine; and the prophecy of Revelation.

BICHRI, a Benjamite, whose son Sheba revolted against David (II Sam. 20:1, 2, 6, 7, 10).

BID, to command, summon, invite.
the day I *b*. you shout, Josh. 6:10.
b. me come to thee, Matt. 14:28.
they *b*. you observe, Matt. 23:3.
they also *b*. thee again, Luke 14:12.
receive him not, nor *b*., II John 10.

BIDKAR, the captain of Jehu, who cast the dead body of Jehoram into the field of Naboth (II Kin. 9:25).

BIER, the funeral coffin.
followed the *b*., II Sam. 3:31.
and touched the *b*., Luke 7:14.

BIGAMY, the act of being married to

more than one person at the same time. Lamech was the first bigamist (Gen. 4:19).

BIGTHA, one of Xerxes seven chamberlains who were commanded to fetch Queen Vashti (Esther 1:10).

BIGTHAN, BIGTHANA, one of the chamberlains of Xerxes who was caught in conspiring against the king and was hanged (Esther 2:21, 6:2).

BIGVAI, (1) one of the chiefs who came up from Babylon with Zerubbabel (Ezra 2:2), (2) one of the heads of Israel who subscribed with Nehemiah to the covenant (Neh. 10:16), (3) the ancestor of a certain man who came up with Ezra (Ezra 8:14).

BILDAD, a Shuhite, who was one of Job's three friends who disputed with him in his suffering. (Job 2:11).

BILEAM, a Levitical city in the western half of Manasseh (I Chr. 6:70).

BILGAH, a Temple priest of the fifteenth course as set by David (I Chr. 24:14). Also a certain priest who came up with Zerubbabel (Neh. 12:5).

BILGAI, thought to be the same as Bilgah (Neh. 10:8).

BILHAH, the handmaid of Rachel, Jacob's wife, and mother of Dan and Naphtali.
gave to Rachel . . . *b*., Gen. 29:29.
B. conceived, and bare, Gen. 30:5.
the sons of *B*., Gen. 37:2.

BILHAN, (1) the son of Ezer who was a Horite chief (Gen. 36:27), (2) a son of Jedial, a Benjamite (I Chr. 7:10).

BILL, a book or anything written.
b. of divorcement, Deut. 24:1.
Take thy *b*., and sit, Luke 16:6.

BILLOW, a heaped wave or breaker.
waves and thy *b*., Ps. 42:7.
thy *b*. and thy waves, Jonah 2:3.

BILSHAN, a Jewish prince who returned with Zerubbabel (Ezra 2:2; Neh. 7:7).

BIMHAL, a son of Japhlet and a descendant of Asher (I Chr. 7:33).

BIND, to gird, fetter, yoke.
they shall *b*. the breast, Ex. 28:28.
shalt *b*. them for a sign, Deut. 6:8.
b. the tares in, Matt. 13:30.
no man could *b*. him, Mark 5:3.

BINDING, obliging (Num. 30:13), and an edge (Ex. 28:32).

BINEA, a Benjamite who was the son of Moza and the father of Rapha (I Chr. 8:37).

BINNUI, (1) a Levite whose son was appointed to assist in the weighing of the gold and silver vessels brought up from Babylon (Ezra 8:33), (2) a son of Pahath-moab (Ezra 10:30), (3) an Israelite of the family of Bani (Ezra 10:38), (4) a son of Henadad who was a Levite and who returned with Zerubbabel (Neh. 12:8).

BIRD, about thirty species of birds are peculiar to Palestine, but as many as 348 types have been found in the area. The Law of Moses distinguished between clean and unclean birds (Lev. 11:13–19; Deut. 14:11–20). Doves and pigeons were used for sacrifice (Luke 2:24), and quails, partridges, etc. were eaten.
every *b*. of every sort, Gen. 7:14.
fly away like a *b*., Hos. 9:11.
into an image like to *b*., Rom. 1:23.
and hateful *b*., Rev. 18:2.

BIRD, SPECKLED, *see* **SPECKLED BIRD.**

BIRSHA, a king of Gomorrah during the time of Abraham (Gen. 14:2).

BIRTH, to bear, bring forth.
children come to *b*., II Kin. 19:3.
b. of Jesus Christ, Matt. 1:18.
whom I travail in *b*., Gal. 4:19.
travailing in *b*., Rev. 12:2.

BIRTHDAY, the day of one's birth which from ancient times has been celebrated by various peoples.
Pharaoh's *b*., Gen. 40:20.
Herod's *b*. was kept, Matt. 14:6.
Herod, on his *b*., Mark 6:21.

BIRTH, NEW, *see* **NEW BIRTH.**

BIRTHRIGHT, the advantages accruing to the eldest son. These included great respect in the household, a "double portion" of his father's property (Deut. 21: 15–17), and succession to the father's official authority (II Chr. 21:3). Esau gave up his privileges of birth for a little food (Gen. 25:33).

BIRZAVITH, a grandson of Beriah (I Chr. 7:31).

BISHLAM, one of the officers of King Artaxerxes who wrote against the Jews who were rebuilding the temple at the time of Zerubbabel (Ezra 4:7).

BISHOP, an officer in the New Testament church, called also an elder (Titus 1:5–7; I Tim. 3:1–7) and a shepherd or pastor (I Peter 5:1–4; Acts 20:28). New Testament congregations had each a plurality of bishops (Phil. 1:1).

BISHOPRIC, an office of oversight (Acts 1:20).

BIT, a bridle, including the curb, used on horses (Ps. 32:9); sometimes it is used of a muzzle which prevented an animal from biting (Ps. 39:1).

BITE, to seize with the teeth.
Dan, an adder, that *b.*, Gen. 49:17.
serpent shall *b.* him, Eccles. 10:8.
prophets that *b.* with, Mic. 3:5.
if ye *b.* and devour, Gal. 5:15.

BITHIAH, a descendant of Judah, the wife of Mered and the daughter of Pharaoh (I Chr. 4:18).

BITHRON, a district in the Jordan valley on the East side through which Abner passed following the death of Asahel (II Sam. 2:29).

BITHYNIA, the North West province of Asia Minor. It was evangelized fairly early (I Pet. 1:1) although Paul was not permitted to go there (Acts 16:7).

BITTER, not only is it used in a literal sense but also in a symbolical describing affliction (Exod. 1:14), evil (Jer. 4:18), etc.
Esau cried with a *b.* cry, Gen. 27:34.
affliction of Israel *b.*, II Kin. 14:26.
b. as wormwood, Prov. 5:4.
be not *b.*, Col. 3:19.

if ye have *b.* envying, James 3:14.

BITTERLY
Almighty hath dealt *b.*, Ruth 1:20.
Peter wept *b.*, Matt. 26:75.

BITTERN, a kind of bird or animal, perhaps a porcupine (Is. 14:23, 34:11).

BITTERNESS, the state of being bitter.
Hannah was in *b.* of, I Sam. 1:10.
surely the *b.* of death, I Sam. 15:32.
in the gall of *b.*, Acts 8:23.
b. be put away, Eph. 4:31.
root of *b.* springing, Heb. 12:15.

BITUMEN, a pitch which was used to seal objects against moisture. It was used in the building of Noah's ark (Gen. 6:14). It also seems to have been used in preparing the chest in which the baby Moses was placed (Ex. 2:3).

BIZJOTHJAH, one of the towns which fell to Judah near Beersheba (Josh. 15: 28).

BIZTHA, one of the seven eunuchs of King Xerxes who were instructed to bring in Vashti (Esther 1:10).

BLACK, the darkest of colors.
there is no *b.* hair in, Lev. 13:31.
my skin is *b.*, Job 30:30.
hair white or *b.*, Matt. 5:36.
lo a *b.* horse, Rev. 6:5.
sun became *b.* as, Rev. 6:12.

BLACKISH, covered with darkness.
Which are *b.* by, Job 6:16.

BLACKNESS, darkness, bitterness.
let *b.* of the day, Job 3:5.
heavens with *b.*, Is. 50:3.
not come to *b.*, Heb. 12:18.
is reserved *b.* of, Jude 13.

BLADE, (1) a weapon (Judg. 3:22), (2) stalk (Matt. 13:26; Mark 4:28).

BLAINS, a type of boil or swollen pimple (Ex. 9:9).

BLAME, to accuse.
let me bear *b.*, Gen. 43:9.
no man should *b.* us, II Cor. 8:20.
he was to be *b.*, Gal. 2:11.
holy and without *b.*, Eph. 1:4.

BLAMELESS, to be without blame.
ye shall be *b.*, Gen. 44:10.
be *b.* in the day, I Cor. 1:8.
righteousness of law *b.*, Phil. 3:6.
soul, body, *b.*, I Thess. 5:23.
bishop must be *b.*, I Tim. 3:2.
a deacon, found *b.*, I Tim. 3:10.
b. the husband of, Titus 1:6.

BLASPHEME, to slander or speak evil
against. To blaspheme against the Holy
Spirit as the Jews did (Mark 3:22), was to
accredit the power of the miracles of
Jesus to devils.
b. God and the king, I Kin. 21:10.
b. against Holy Ghost, Mark 3:29.
may learn not to *b.*, I Tim. 1:20.
b. the God of, Rev. 16:11.

BLASPHEMER, one who speaks injuriously.
nor *b.* of your goddess, Acts 19:37.
who was before a *b.*, I Tim. 1:13.
men shall be *b.*, II Tim. 3:2.

BLASPHEMOUS, speaking injuriously
(Acts 6:11, 13).

BLASPHEMY, words slanderously
spoken.
this day of *b.*, II Kin. 19:3.
manner of *b.* forgiven, Matt. 12:31.
out of heart proceed *b.*, Mark 7:22.
put off malice, *b.*, Col. 3:8.
the name of *b.*, Rev. 13:1.
opened his mouth in *b.*, Rev. 13:6.

BLAST, a violent wind.
with *b.* of thy nostrils, Ex. 15:8.
by *b.* of God they, Job 4:9.
the *b.* of the terrible, Is. 25:4.

BLASTED, having been subject to blast.
seven thin ears *b.*, Gen. 41:6.
and *b.* before it be, II Kin. 19:26.

BLASTING, a disease of grain caused by
the wind.
and with *b.*, and, Deut. 28:22.
pestilence, *b.*, mildew, I Kin. 8:37.
you with *b.* and, Amos 4:9.

BLASTUS, one of the chamberlains of
King Herod Agrippa with whom the men
of Tyre and Sidon negotiated to acquire an audience with the king (Acts
12:20).

BLAZE, to speak a matter abroad (Mark
1:45).

BLEATING, the voice of sheep.
to hear the *b.*, Judg. 5:16.
this *b.* of the sheep, I Sam. 15:14.

BLEMISH, a defect whether physical,
mental, or spiritual.
lamb without *b.*, Ex. 12:5.
two rams without *b.*, Lev. 5:15, 18.
holy and without *b.*, Eph. 5:27.
a lamb without *b.*, I Pet. 1:19.
spots they are and *b.*, II Pet. 2:13.

BLESS, to pronounce blessed or happy.
God blesses by giving prosperity both
temporal or spiritual or by sanctifying
something (Gen. 30:25; Ps. 29:11; Eph.
1:3; Gen. 2:3). Man blesses God when he
praises or thanks Him for His goodness
(Ps. 104:1; Ps. 103:1). Men bless other
men by praying for God's blessings upon
them (Num. 6:23; II Sam. 6:18).
I will *b.* thee, Gen. 12:2.
blessing I will *b.* thee, Gen. 22:17.
the Lord *b.* thee, Ruth 2:4.
sent him to *b.* you, Acts 3:26.
b. and curse not, Rom. 12:14.
being reviled we *b.*, I Cor. 4:12.
cup of blessing we *b.*, I Cor. 10:16.

BLESSED, to be or declare happy or
fortunate.
b. are they that dwell, Ps. 84:4.
b. are they that keep, Ps. 119:2.
b. are they that mourn, Matt. 5:4.
b. are they that do His, Rev. 22:14.

BLESSEDNESS, happiness.
describeth the *b.* of, Rom. 4:6.
is then the *b.* ye spake, Gal. 4:15.

BLESSING, a gift or act of one who
blesses.
thou shalt be a *b.*, Gen. 12:2.
the *b.* of Abraham, Gal. 3:14.
us with spiritual *b.*, Eph. 1:3.
receive honour glory, *b.*, Rev. 5:12.

BLIND, closed or contracted eyes unable
to see.
maketh the seeing *b.*, Ex. 4:11.
take away the *b.* and, II Sam. 5:6.
two *b.* men followed, Matt. 9:27.
b. receive their sight, Matt. 11:5.
b. Bartimaeus sat by, Mark 10:46.
a guide to the *b.*, Rom. 2:19.
that lacketh these is *b.*, II Pet. 1:9

BLINDFOLD, to cover one's eyes. It was employed as one of the mockeries through which Jesus went (Luke 22:64).

BLINDNESS, the inability to see; also used in reference to spiritual hardness (Eph. 4:18).
at the door with *b.*, Gen. 19:11.
Smite people with *b.*, II Kin. 6:18.
b. in part is happened, Rom. 11:25.

BLOOD, the life-fluid which flows in the body. It is used figuratively at times to represent life (Gen. 9:6), race (Acts 17:26), or even a great slaughter (Is.34:3). It has a kind of sacredness attached to it because of its close relation to life itself (Gen. 9:4). Thus it was used as a sacrifice in substitute for its offerer (Lev. 17:11).
thy brother's *b.* crieth, Gen. 4:10.
take *b.* of bullock, Ex. 29:12.
shall purge the *b.* of, Is. 4:4.
His *b.* be on us, Matt. 27:25.
purchased with His *b.*, Acts 20:28.
guilty of body and *b.*, I Cor. 11:27.
His own *b.* He entered, Heb. 9:12.
b. of Christ cleanseth, I John 1:7.

BLOODGUILTINESS, guilty of murder (Ps. 51:14).

BLOODY, containing the nature of blood.
a *b.* husband art thou, Ex. 4:25.
Lord abhor *b.* man, Ps. 5:6.
lay sick of a *b.* flux, Acts 28:8.

BLOOM, to sprout or blossom forth. (Num. 17:8).

BLOSSOM, a flower or sprout.
b. shot forth, Gen. 40:10.
and bloomed *b.*, Num. 17:8.
b. shall go up as dust, Is. 5:24.

BLOSSOM, to flower or sprout forth.
man's rod shall *b.*, Num. 17:5.
Israel shall *b.* and bud, Is. 27:6.
rejoice, and *b.* as the, Is. 35:1.
the rod hath *b.*, pride, Ezek. 7:10.

BLOT, to rub off or wipe away. For man to have his sins blotted out is for God to completely forgive him (Is. 44:22). For man to be blotted out of the book of God is to loose His providence and care (Ex. 32:32).
not, *b.* me out of Thy, Ex. 32:32.
b. out the remembrance, Deut. 25:19.

your sins may be *b.* out, Acts 3:19.
b. out the hand-writing, Col. 2:14.

BLOT, a stain or spot.
if any *b.* hath cleaved to, Job 31:7.

BLOW, a smiting or sounding.
didst *b.* with thy wind, Ex. 15:10.
when I *b.*, then *b.* ye, Judg. 7:18.
wind *b.* where it listeth, John 3:8.
that wind should not *b.*, Rev. 7:1.

BLUE, a color the dye of which was made from a species of shellfish. Princes, nobles, few idols were clothed in this color (Ezek. 23:6; Jer. 10:9).
robe of the ephod of *b.* Ex. 28:31.
b. purple, Ex. 25:4.
Mordecai in apparel of *b.*, Esther 8:15.
b. and purple is their, Jer. 10:9.

BLUNT, to be weak, dull (Eccles. 10:10).

BLUSH, to feel and show shame.
I am ashamed and *b.*, Ezra 9:6.
neither could they *b.*, Jer. 8:12.

BOANERGES, a name which the Lord gave James and John. Mark defines it as the "Sons of Thunder" (Mark 3:17).

BOAR, male swine, pig (Ps. 80:13).

BOARD, a plank or piece of wood used for building purposes.
overlay *b.* with gold, Ex. 26:29.
hollow with *b.* make, Ex. 27:8.
the rest, some on *b.*, Acts 27:44.

BOAST, to praise or exalt oneself.
heart lifteth to *b.*, II Chr. 25:19.
Jew, and makest thy *b.*, Rom. 2:17.
for which I *b.*, II Cor. 9:2.
not of works lest any *b.*, Eph. 2:9.

BOAT, water craft. The references to them in the Holy Land are few. There were ferry boats across Jordan (II Sam. 19:18); there were fishing boats on the Sea of Galilee (Mark 4:36); and Paul's great voyage to Rome was on a boat (Acts 27).

BOAZ, a rich man of Bethlehem, a kinsman to the husband of Naomi, Elimelech (See Ruth 2:1, 19; 3:2, 7; 4:1, 18).

BOCHERU, son of Azel who was a Benjamite of Saul's family through Jonathan (I Chr. 8:38; 9:44).

BOCHIM, a place just above Gilgal to the West of the Jordan. There the Israelites were corrected by an angel (Judg. 2: 1, 5).

BODILY, corporeal, material.
descended in *b*. shape, Luke 3:22.
his *b*. presence is weak, II Cor. 10:10.
fulness of Godhead *b*., Col. 2:9.
b. exercise profiteth, I Tim. 4:8.

BODY, the material part of man in contrast with the soul and spirit (Eccles. 12:7; I Thess. 5:23). Sometimes the body is directed to evil by a sinful heart (Rom. 6:6; 7:24; Mark 7:21), but the Christian strives to allow the Spirit to control his mind and body (I Cor. 6:19). Figuratively, the church is presented as the Body of Christ (Eph. 1:22-3; Col. 1:18). This figure, drawn from the analogy of the human body, emphasizes the unity of the church under the headship of Jesus (I Cor. 12:12–26).
took the *b*. of Saul, I Sam. 31:12.
whole *b*. be cast into, Matt. 5:29, 30.
I keep under my *b*., I Cor. 9:27.
one *b*. Eph 4:4.

BOHAN, a Reubenite, after whose name a stone was called. The stone was later used as a boundary between Judah and Benjamin (See Josh. 15:6; 18:17).

BOIL, (1) to bubble up (See Lev. 8:31; I Kin. 19:21). (2) An inflamed pimple which at times brings much suffering (See Job 2:7, 8).

BOISTEROUS, strong and loud.
saw the wind *b*., Matt. 14:30.

BOLD, BOLDNESS, to be confident and daring.
b. as a lion, Prov., 28:1.
Barnabas waxed *b*., Acts 13:46.
he preached *b*., Acts 9:27.
in whom we have *b*., Eph. 3:12.
more *b*. to speak, Phil. 1:14.
with all *b*., Phil. 1:20.
having *b*. to enter, Heb. 10:19.

BOLLED, the calix of flowers.
the flax . . . bolled, Ex. 9:31.

BOLSTER, the place at the head, some-

times just a pillow (See I Sam. 19:13, 16; 26:7).

BOND, a fetter or chain.
bind herself by a *b*., Num. 30:3.
loosed from his *b*., Luke 13:16.
the *b*. of iniquity, Acts 8:23.
in *b*. of peace, Eph. 4:3.
put on charity, the *b*. of, Col. 3:14.

BONDAGE, servitude, slavery.
brought us out of *b*., Ex. 13:14.
not received spirit of *b*., Rom. 8:15.
or sister not under *b*., I Cor. 7:15.
is he brought into *b*., II Pet. 2:19.

BOND MAID, a handmaid or young female slave.
whoso lieth with a *b*., Lev. 19:20.
one by a *b*. the other, Gal. 4:22.

BOND MAN, a male slave.
instead of lad a *b*., Gen. 44:33.
b. the Lord redeemed, Deut. 15:15.
every *b*. hid themselves, Rev. 6:15.

BOND SERVANT, one who is the slave of another.
compel to serve a *b*. *s*., Lev. 25:39.

BOND WOMAN, a female slave.
cast out this *b*., Gen. 21:10.
son of the *b*. was born., Gal. 4:23.
not children of the *b*., Gal. 4:31.

BONE, in addition to literal references, this word is used in various simple figures: (1) In keeping with Hebrew practice of expressing emotional disturbance by physical terms, various conditions of the bones express envy (Prov. 12:4), fear (Job 4:14), grief (Job 30:30), ill health (Prov. 17:22), etc. (2) "Bone of my bones" (Gen. 2:23) indicates sameness of nature and nearness of relationship (II Sam. 5:1; Eph. 5:30).
break a *b*., Ex. 12:46.
the *b*. of Joseph, Josh. 24:32.
thou not of my *b*., II Sam. 19:13.
b. came together, Ezek. 37:7.
full of dead men's *b*., Matt. 23:27.
flesh and of his *b*., Eph. 5:30.

BONNET, a turban or hat.
thou shalt make *b*., Ex. 28:40.
Lord will take away *b*., Is. 3:20.
shall have linen *b*., Ezek. 44:18.

BOOK, in Biblical times it seems to have

been used to refer to anything written, such as a purchase (Jer. 32:12) or a bill of divorce (Deut. 24:1).
a memorial in a *b.*, Ex. 17:14.
not in *b.* of law, Deut. 28:61.
are written in *b.* of life, Phil. 4:3.
prophecy of this *b.*, Rev. 22:10.

BOOTH, a tent-like structure made from branches of trees and shrubs (Gen. 33 17). It was used for the shelter of both men and beasts (Job 27:18).

BOOTY, prey, spoil.
b. the rest of the prey, Num. 31:32.
their camels shall be *b.*, Jer. 49:32.
thou shalt be for *b.*, Hab. 2:7.

BOOZ, the Bethlehemite Boaz. Booz is the Greek form (Matt. 1:5).

BORDER, the line marking an enclosed place.
Zebulun his *b.* shall, Gen. 49:13.
Lord shall enlarge *b.*, Deut. 12:20.
enlarge the *b.* of, Matt. 23:5.
and touched *b.*, Luke 8:44.

BORE, to pierce or puncture.
master shall *b.* his ear, Ex. 21:6.
Jehoiada took chest *b.*, II Kin. 12:9.
canst thou *b.* his jaw, Job 41:2.

BORN, brought forth in birth.
a child *b.* to him, Gen. 17:17.
b. in his kingdom, Eccles. 4:14.
b. of a woman, Matt. 11:11.
can a man be *b.*?, John 3:4.
to this end was I *b.*, John 18:37.
I was free *b.*, Acts 22:28.
as new *b.* babes desire, I Pet. 2:2.
sin, because *b.* of God, I John 3:9.

BORN AGAIN, *see* **NEW BIRTH.**

BORNE, to bear, carry, or to be lifted up.
ark may be *b.* with, Ex. 25:14.
which have *b.* burden, Matt. 20:12.
grievous to be *b.*, Matt. 23:4.
sick of palsy, was *b.* of, Mark 2:3.

BORROW, to receive a loan.
every woman shall *b.* of, Ex. 3:22.
him that would *b.* of, Matt. 5:42.
they *b.* of Egyptians, Ex. 12:35.

BORROWER, one who borrows.
and the *b.* is servant to, Prov. 22:7.
with the lender, so with *b.*, Is. 24:2.

BOSCATH, *see* **BOZKATH.**

BOSOM, the front part of the body which is between the arms. It may also refer to the part of the dress which was used for a bag to carry grain, etc. (II Kin. 4:39).
thy hand into thy *b.*, Ex. 4:6.
lay in his *b.*, II Sam. 12:3.
angels into Abraham's *b.*, Luke 16:22.
in the *b.* of the Father, John 1:18.
leaning on Jesus' *b.*, John 13:23.

BOSOR, the Greek form of Beor, the father of Balaam (II Pet. 2:15).

BOSS, the curved ornaments of a shield Job 15:26).

BOTCH, a type of inflammation of the body (Deut. 28:27, 35).

BOTH, two together.
were *b.* naked, Gen. 2:25.
and Miriam, *b.* came, Num. 12:5.
b. shall fall, Matt. 15:14.
reconcile *b.* unto God, Eph. 2:16.

BOTTLE, containers for liquids were made from various materials. Animal skins were sewn into bag form and slowly dried (Gen. 21:14; Josh. 9:4). Heat and fermentation, of course, affected such skins (Matt. 9:17). Earthenware bottles were also widely used (Jer. 19:10, 11), and pottery remains have been very helpful to archeologists in studying and dating ancient ruins. Metal, and perhaps even glass, may have been rarely used for bottles.

BOTTOM, the lower part, foundation,
they sank into the *b.* as, Ex. 15:5.
I went down to the *b.* of, Jonah 2:6.
top to *b.*, Matt. 27:51.

BOTTOMLESS, very deep, depthless. The bottomless pit seems to refer to the prison-house of demons (Rev. 9:1, 2).
angel of the *b.* pit, Rev. 9:11.
and cast him into the *b.* pit, Rev. 20:3.

BOUGH, twig or branch.
Joseph is a fruitful *b.*, Gen. 49:22.
be as a forsaken *b.*, Is. 17:9.
made their nests in *b.*, Dan. 4:12.

BOUGHT, to purchase, gain.
Jacob *b.* a field, Gen. 33:19.
them that sold and *b.*, Matt. 21:12.

b. five yoke of oxen, Luke 14:19.
b. with a price, I Cor. 6:20.

BOUND, held fast, girded.
where Joseph was *b.*, Gen. 40:3.
be *b.* in heaven, Matt. 16:19.
Peter *b.* with chains, Acts 12:6.
b. by law of husband, Rom. 7:2.

BOUNDS, appointed limits.
thou shalt set *b.* to the, Ex. 19:12.
I have removed the *b.*, Is. 10:13.
hast determined the *b.*, Acts 17:26.

BOUNTIFUL, rich, good, and plentiful.
he that hath a *b.* eye, Prov. 22:9.
churl be said to be *b.*, Is. 32:5.

BOUNTIFULLY, abundantly.
the Lord hath dealt *b.*, Ps. 116:7.
deal *b.* with servant, Ps. 119:17.
soweth *b.* shall reap *b.*, II Cor. 9·6.

BOUNTIFULNESS, the state of abundance.
enriched to all *b.*, II Cor. 9:11.

BOUNTY, power, blessing.
gave of his royal *b.*, I Kin. 10:13.
make up your *b.*, II Cor. 9:5.

BOW, the principal weapon of offence in ancient Palestine. It is used also to signify military power (Gen. 49:24). It is also a symbol of God's power and wrath (Ps. 7:12). It is the name given to what we call the rainbow (Gen. 9:13).
man drew a *b.* and smote, I Kin. 22:34.
my *b.* was renewed, Job 29:20.
a deceitful *b.*, Ps. 78:57.
on the horse had a *b.*, Rev. 6:2.

BOW, to bend or incline.
I *b.* myself in house, II Kin. 5:18.
Jesus *b.* His head and, John 19:30.
every knee shall *b.*, Rom. 14:11.

BOWELS, the internal parts of a man. It is also used to refer to the seat of feelings such as pity and compassion (Gen. 43:30, etc.).
of thine own *b.* shall, Gen. 15:4.
burst, and all his *b.*, Acts 1:18.
put on *b.* of mercies, Col. 3:12.
shutteth up his *b.*, I John 3:17.

BOWL, a basin or dish made of wood, shells of nuts, etc. and were used for

pottage and various liquids (II Kin. 4:40).
golden *b.* be broken, Eccles. 12:6.
that drink wine in *b.*, Amos 6:6.
shall be filled like *b.*, Zech. 9:15.

BOWMAN, one who used a bow.
from the noise of the *b.*, Jer. 4:29.

BOWSHOT, the distance a bow may shoot.
him as it were a *b.*, Gen. 21:16.

BOX, (1) a flask used for holding oil and perfume (Matt. 26:7). (2) A type of tree in Palestine (Is. 41:19).

BOXTREE, (Is. 41:19; 60:13), a tree of uncertain identity, which was once common in the forests of Lebanon. Some think the boxtree was the cypress.

BOY, a male youth.
the *b.* grew, and Esau, Gen. 25:27.
they have given a *b.*, Joel 3:3.
streets shall be full of *b.*, Zech. 8:5.

BOZEZ, a high rock near the pass of Michmash (I Sam. 14:4).

BOZKATH, a town in Judah (II Kin. 22:1 Boscath; Josh. 15:39).

BOZRAH, a city in Edom and the capital (Gen. 36:33). It was also a city in Moab (Jer. 48:24).

BRACELET, a circle of string or jewelry worn around the wrists, often to suspend a seal-ring. (Gen. 38:18, 35)
b. on his arm, II Sam. 1:10.
take away the chains, *b.*, Is. 3:19.

BRAIDED, *see* **BROIDERED.**

BRAKE, past tense of the verb, break. (1) to snap, divide, destroy, (2) to divide (*see* **LORD'S SUPPER**), (3) to disobey, as a covenant.
the hail *b.* every tree, Ex. 9:25.
whose covenant he *b.*, Ezek. 17:16.
soldiers *b.* the legs of, John 19:32.

BRAKE BREAD, *see* **LORD'S SUPPER,**
to divide, distribute, eat, partake.
blessed and *b.* and gave, Matt. 14:19.
I *b.* the five loaves, Mark 8:19.
came together to *b.* bread, Acts 20:7.

BRAMBLE, one of many types of thorny

bushes common in Palestine, usually considered valueless (Luke 6:44). Also used figuratively for a worthless person or class of persons (Judg. 9:14).

BRANCH, a figure of speech referring to Jesus Christ.
and a *b.* shall grow out, Is. 11:1.
to David a righteous *b.,* Jer. 23:5.
forth my servant the *b.,* Zech. 3:8.
whose name is the *B.,* Zech. 6:12.

BRANCH, (1) the part of a tree or vine bearing the leaves and fruit and connecting them to the trunk or vine. (Matt. 24:31), (2) used figuratively for Christians in referring to their relationship with Christ, the true vine, (John 15:5).

BRANDISH, to display fearsomely, to wave or swing a weapon as if to cause awe or fear (Ezek. 32:10).

BRASEN, *see* **BRAZEN.**

BRASEN SEA, *see* **MOLTEN SEA.**

BRASEN SERPENT, *see* **BRAZEN SERPENT.**

BRASS, more properly copper or bronze (copper and tin) since modern-day brass was unknown in Bible times.
take gold, silver, and *b.,* Ex. 25:3.
and thighs were of *b.,* Dan. 2:32.
sounding *b.* or cymbal, I Cor. 13:1.

BRAVERY, fearless, of great courage. Found only in the King James version (Is. 3:18).

BRAWLER, one guilty of wrangling, or of being quarrelsome.
a bishop must be no *b.,* I Tim. 3:3.
to be no *b.,* Titus 3:2.

BRAY, (1) the loud, harsh cry of an ass. Used in Job 6:5 and figuratively of the cry of a person when hungry (Job 30:7), (2) to crush as in mortar. Probably a type of punishment (Prov. 27:22).

BRAZEN, to be made of brass.
make *b.* rings, Ex. 27:4.
b. vessels. Mark 7:4.

BRAZEN SEA, *see* **MOLTEN SEA.**

BRAZEN SERPENT, a figure of a ser-

pent, made by Moses of brass (Num. 21:8) in obedience to God's command.
in pieces the *b. s.,* II Kin. 18:4.......318

BREACH, a gap, separation, rupture, or a breaking apart. Used literally, as in a wall (Ezek. 26:10), and figuratively, as in a separation from God (Prov. 15:4).

BREAD, *see* **SHEWBREAD,** (1) the food made from flour (Gen. 3:19), (2) all things necessary for life (Matt. 6:11), (3) the food that God fed to the children of Israel in the wilderness (John 6:31), and (4) used figuratively for Jesus Christ (John 6:35).
fetch a morsel of *b.,* Gen. 18:5.
not eaten *b.* neither, Deut. 29:6.
gave them *b.* out of, John 6:31.
I am the *b.* of life, John 6:35.
b. which came down out, John 6:41.
came together to break *b.,* Acts 20:7.
b. we break, is it not, I Cor. 10:16.
was betrayed, took *b.,* I Cor. 11:23.

BREAK, to separate into parts, to divide into fragments, and figuratively, to renounce (as a covenant).
thou shalt *b.* his yoke, Gen. 27:40.
b. down their images, Ex. 23:24..
I will never *b.* my cov., Judg. 2:1.
b. in pieces and bruise, Dan. 2:44.
thieves *b.* through and, Matt. 6:19.

BREAKER, *see* **COVENANT BREAKER,** one who or that which breaks, disrupts, or destroys another person or thing. Used in this way in Mic. 2:13.

BREAKEST, to break, snap, divide.
thou *b.* ships of Tarshish, Ps. 48:7.

BREAST, (1) the upper portion of the thorax, body, or trunk, (2) the mammary glands of the human female, (3) used figuratively for parents or motherhood, and (4) the heart.
blessings of the *b.* and, Gen. 49:25.
the *b.* of the ram, Ex. 29:26.
pluck fatherless from *b.,* Job 24:9.
thy *b.* to clusters of, Song 7:8.
upon their *b.,* Nahum 2:7.
publican smote upon *b.,* Luke 18:13.

BREASTPLATE, (1) a piece of embroidery which the high priest wore over his breast, (2) defensive armor for the breast, (3) used figuratively for faith and love.

make a *b*. and an ephod, Ex. 28:4.
he put in the *b*. the, Lev. 8:8.
having on the *b*. of, Eph. 6:14.
b. as it were *b*. of iron, Rev. 9:9.

BREATH, the inhaling or exhaling of air.
nostrils the *b*. of life, Gen. 2:7.
whose hand *b*. is, Dan. 5:23.
to all life and *b*., Acts 17:25.

BREATHE, to inhale and exhale air in respirating (Josh. 11:11), and used figuratively, to threaten, (Ps. 27:12).

BRED, past tense of Breed, used only in Ex. 16:20, to be the cause of birth.

BREECHES, trousers, garment for the high priest (Ex. 28:42; Lev. 6:10).

BREED, to multiply, reproduce after its kind (Gen. 8:17).

BRETHREN, (1) the sons of one father and one mother or of either of them, (2) neighbors or kinsmen who are closely bound together, and (3) those who have professed the same faith.
strife, we be *b*., Gen. 13:8.
no man hath left *b*. for, Mark 10:29.
and children, and *b*., Luke 14:26.
now, *b*. I know that, Acts 3:17.
moreover these six *b*., Acts 11:12.
salute the *b*. with a, Rom. 16:14.

BRETHREN OF THE LORD, James, Joses, Simon, and Judas are given in the Gospels as the brethren of Jesus (Matt. 13:55; Mark 6:3). These are mentioned in connection with Mary (Matt. 12:47-50; Mark 3:31-35; Luke 8:19-21). They were at Capernaum shortly after Jesus began his public ministry (John 2:12). It was only after the resurrection that they believed that he was the Messiah (John 7:5). The epistles of James and Jude may very well be by Jesus' brothers, and the former became the head of the Jerusalem Church (Acts 21:18; Gal. 1:19).

BRIBE, a price, reward, gift, or favor bestowed upon one to obtain unfair advantage or pervert justice.
have I received *b*., I Sam. 12:3.
from holding of *b*., Is. 33:15.

BRIBERY, the act of giving or offering a bribe, the solicitation of a bribe.
the tabernacles of *b*., Job 15:34.

BRICK, a molded construction material, made of earth (clay or mud, usually mixed with straw) hardened by fire or the sun.
let us make *b*., and burn, Gen. 11:3.
they had *b*. for stone, Gen. 11:3.
incense upon altars of *b*., Is. 65:3.

BRICK KILN, domed oven made of brick in which the molded material was put to heat by fire to make brick.
them pass through *b*., II Sam. 12:31.
make strong the *b*., Nahum 3:14.

BRIDE, a woman newly married or about to be married. Figuratively used for the Church as the bride of Christ.
as a *b*. adorneth herself, Is. 61:10.
a *b*. forget her attire?, Jer. 2:32.
hath the *b*. is the, John 3:29.
as a *b*. adorned for her, Rev. 21:2.
Spirit and the *b*. say, Rev. 22:17.

BRIDE AND BRIDEGROOM, the relationship of husband to wife. Figuratively for Christ and the Church (Rev. 21:2). Paul refers to this figure in Eph. 5:22-33.

BRIDECHAMBER, the place to which the newly married withdrew after the public ceremony of marriage (Judg. 15:1).

BRIDEGROOM, a man newly married or about to be married. He was exempt from military service from betrothal to one year after marriage (Deut. 20:7, 24:5). The word is also used figuratively for Christ as husband of the church (John 3:29; Rev. 21:9). The figure of the church as the bride of Christ emphasizes the purity which much characterize the church (II Cor. 11:2; Eph. 5:27). In the Old Testament Israel was portrayed as the unfaithful wife of Jehovah (Hos. 2:2, 14-23).

BRIDLE, a device used to harness, control, or handle animals. Figuratively, to restrain one, as in the use of the tongue or lips.
put my *b*. in thy lips, II Kin. 19:28.
a *b*. for the ass, Prov. 26:3.
seem religious and *b*., James 1:26.
to *b*. the whole body, James 3:2 .
even unto horse *b*., Rev. 14:20.

BRIEFLY, in short time, quickly.
it is *b*. comprehended, Rom. 13:9.

I have written *b*., I Pet. 5:12.

BRIER, *see* **BRAMBLE, THISTLE, THORN,** any of numerous low-lying vines or bushes, usually with thorns which abounded in Palestine in Bible times and even today (Is. 55:13).

BRIGANDINE, armor or coat of mail (Jer. 46:4). *See* **HABERGEONS.**

BRIGHT, reflecting light, shining, opposed to dark.
scattered his *b*. cloud, Job 37:11.
stood before me in *b*., Acts 10:30.

BRIGHTNESS, radiating light, shining. Used figuratively of Jesus Christ in Heb. 1:3.
great image, whose *b*., Dan. 2:31.
from Heaven above *b*., Acts 26:13.
b. of his glory, Heb. 1:3.

BRIM, brink, edge, lip, top.
b. like *b*. of a cup, I Kin. 7:26.

BRIMSTONE, particularly refers to sulphur and to any inflammable substance.
the whole land is *b*., Deut. 29:23.
burning with *b*., Rev. 19:20.

BRING, to add, gather, cause to come.
what shall we *b*. the man?, I Sam. 9:7.
I will *b*. them, and, Zech. 8:8.
b. forth fruit meet, Matt. 3:8.
b. them up in the nurture, Eph. 6:4.

BROAD, wide, expanded, spacious.
long, and five cubits *b*., Ex. 27:1.
make them *b*. plates for, Num. 16:38.
b. is the way that, Matt. 7:13.

BROIDERED, braided (as hair), plaited, checker work.
a *b*. coat, a mitre, Ex. 28:4.
not with *b*. hair, or gold, I Tim. 2:9.

BROILED, past tense of broil, to cook by direct exposure to heat (Luke 24:42).

BROKE, BROKEN, the result of a breaking, snapping, parting, dividing, shattering, bruising, or destroying.
b. my covenant, Gen. 17:14.
vessel shall be *b*., Lev. 6:28.
that which is . . . *b*., Lev. 22:24.
slay the *b*. in heart, Ps. 109:16.
that stone shall be *b*., Luke 20:18.
was not the net *b*., John 21:11.

BROKEN FOOTED, deformed, breach of the foot (or hand), crooked, not perfect. (Lev. 21:19). Absence of this fault was required for priests of Israel.

BROKEN HANDED, *see* **BROKEN FOOTED.**

BROKEN HEARTED, sorrowful, distraught, downcast, those without hope.
me to heal the *b*., Luke 4:18.

BROOD, to hover over, as the Spirit of God hovered (brooded) upon the face of the waters (Gen. 1:2).

BROOD, flock as of chickens, those belonging to a hen (Luke 13:34).

BROOK, a torrent, small stream, freshet, or the bed of the watercourse when dry. Used figuratively of friends who fail to be steadfast (Job 6:15).
stones out of the *b*., I Sam. 17:40.
disciples over the *b*., John 18:1.

BROOM, a tree, probably the juniper. (Job 30:4), not found in the King James version.

BROTH, a soup made with meat (Judg. 6:19). Used figuratively in Is. 65:4 to mean a mixture of abominable things.

BROTHER, *see* **BRETHREN.**

BROTHERHOOD, the association of brothers, particularly brothers of like faith (I Pet. 2:17).

BROTHERLY, in an attitude characterized as a brother, as one would treat his brother in the flesh. This term signifies a very close relationship. *See* **BROTHERLY LOVE.**
remembered not the *b*., Amos 1:9.

BROTHERLY LOVE, the love of one as if to a brother; a love indicating the closest fellowship of man to man. Found only in the New Testament.
another with *b*., Rom. 12:10.
as touching *b*., I Thes. 4:9.
let *b*. love continue, Heb. 13:1.
to godliness, *b*., II Pet. 1:7.

BROUGHT, past tense of bring, led, gathered, taken, transported, drawn near, or became.

shall not be *b.*, Ex. 9:19.
ye shall be *b.*, Josh. 7:14.
shall be *b.* before, Matt. 10:18.
were scattered and *b.*, Acts 5:36.

BROW, forehead, top of the face (as of a cliff).
and thy *b.* brass, Is. 48:4.
the *b.* of the hill, Luke 4:29.

BROWN, dusky, dark-colored, scorched.
Gen. 30:32–40 contain all these words of the Bible.

BRUISE, to damage, injure, afflict, or otherwise harm. It is used figuratively as to hamper or restrain or to show weakness or inability.
b. thy head, . . shalt *b.*, Gen. 3:15.
staff of this *b.*, II Kin. 18:21.
nor will he *b.* it with, Is. 28:28.
shall it break and *b.*, Dan. 2:40.

BRUIT, hearing or report.
noise of the *b.* is come, Jer. 10:22.
hear the *b.* of thee, Nahum 3:19.

BRUTISH, to be like an animal, speechless, irrational.
b. man knoweth not, Ps. 92:6.
is *b.* in knowledge, Jer. 51:17.

BUCK, *see* ROEBUCK.

BUCKET, a skin vessel with which to draw water (Is. 40:15). Used figuratively in Num. 24:7 for abundance of water.

BUCKLER, a small shield of the soldier's armor, used in hand to hand fighting. It was about one-half the size of the large, protective shield (I Kin. 10:16).
men able to bear *b.*, I Chr. 5:18.
b. and shields, that, II Chr. 23:9.

BUD, (1) the sprout, blossom, shoot as in Num. 17:8, (2) a verb meaning to cause to break forth, to sprout, to break forth, as in Heb. 9:4.

BUFFET, to hit with the fist, a rude maltreatment in derision, affliction, opposition and punishment.
face, and to *b.* him, Mark 14:65.
of Satan to *b.* me, II Cor. 12:7.
ye be *b.* for your faults, I Pet. 2:20.

BUILD, to construct, cause to arise (as a family), to add to, to prepare.

two did *b.* the house, Ruth 4:11.
will *b.* thee a house, II Sam. 7:27.
which *b.* his house, Matt. 7:24.
I should *b.* upon another, Rom. 15:20.
I *b.* again the things, Gal. 2:18.

BUILD, BUILT, past tense of build, to have completed constructing, adding to, preparing.
Jerusalem is *b.* as a city, Ps. 122:3.
wastes shall be *b.*, Ezek. 36:10.

BUILDER, he who builds, constructs, adds to or prepares.
Solomon's *b.* and Hiram's, I Kin. 5:18.
when the *b.* laid the, Ezra 3:10.
which the *b.* rejected, Luke 20:17.
stone which the *b.*, I Pet. 2:7.

BUILDING, (1) a constructed, permanent edifice useable for a dwelling or for worship, and (2) the constructing of such a structure.
the *b.*, with the walls, Ezek. 41:13.
the *b.* of the temple, Matt. 24:1.
and six years … . in *b.*, John 2:20.

BUKKI, son of Abishua and father of Uzzi the fifth from Aaron in the line of the high priests (I Chr. 6:5).

BUKKIAH, a Kohathite Levite, of the sons of Heman, the leader of the sixth band, in the temple music service. (I Chr. 25:4).

BUL, the eighth religious month of the Jewish year (I Kin. 6:38).

BULLOCK, bull, ox, steer, a sacrificial animal of the Israelites.
every altar a *b.*, Num. 23:4.
they sacrifice *b.* in, Hos. 12:11.

BULLS, male of cattle.
Their *b.* gendereth, and, Job 21:10.
eat the flesh of *b.*, Ps. 50:13.
If the blood of *b.* and, Heb. 9:13.
the blood of *b.* . . . . should, Heb. 10:4.

BULRUSH, a swamp plant of the reed, flag and rushes.
for him an ark of *b.*, Ex. 2:3.
in vessels of *b.*, Is. 18:2.

BULWARKS, a bastion or tower along the walls of a city from which the defenders hurled stones (Deut. 20:20).

BUNAH, son of Jerahmeel of the family of Pharez (I Chr. 2:25).

BUNCH, translated also **Bundle**, a small amount which can be carried by a man.
take a *b.* of hyssop, Ex. 12:22.
100 *b.* of raisins, II Sam. 16:1.
treasures upon *b.*, Is. 30:6.
bind them in *b.* to burn, Matt. 13:30.
gathered a *b.* of, Acts 28:3.

BUNNI, a Levite who helped Ezra teach the people the law of Moses (Neh. 9:14), and a Levite, an ancestor of Shemaiah (Neh. 11:15), and also a family of Jews that, with Nehemiah, sealed the covenant (Neh. 10:15).

BURDEN, (1) a load (Ex. 23:5), used figuratively for sins (Ps. 38:4), heavy taxes (Hos. 8:10), etc. (2) An oracle from God (Is. 13:1; Zech 9:1).
to unlade her *b.*, Acts 21:3.
I did not *b.* you, II Cor. 12:16.
ye one another's *b.*, Gal. 6:2.
bear his own *b.*, Gal. 6:5.

BURDENSOME, to become a burden, a load, or a weight.
myself from being *b.*, II Cor. 11:9.
might have been *b.*, I Thess. 2:6.

BURIAL, burial in Bible times followed soon after death (Gen. 23:1–20). The body was washed (Acts 9:37) and bound loosely with cloth (Matt. 27:59). The more prosperous anointed their dead (John 12:7; 19:39). Then the body was carried on a simple bier to the tomb, usually a rock cave (Gen. 25:9; Matt. 27:60), and interned. *See* SEPULCHRE, MOURNERS.
joined with them in *b.*, Is. 14:20.
buried with the *b.* of an, Jer. 22:19.
did . . . for my *b.*, Matt. 26:12.

BURIED, past tense of bury, *see* BURIAL.
and was *b.* in Shamir, Judg. 10:2.
was *b.* with his fathers, I Kin. 14:31.
we are *b.* with him by, Rom. 6:4.
b. with him in baptism, Col. 2:12.

BURN, to consume, kindle, or heat as with fire, to flame up, to radiate light or heat and his anger *b.* in, Esther 1:12.
musing the fire *b.*, Ps. 39:3.
b. and shining light, John 5:35.
woman, *b.* in their, Rom. 1:27.
to marry than *b.*, I Cor. 7:9.

lake which *b.* with fire, Rev. 21:8 . . . . **219**

BURNING BUSH, the bush which Moses saw, kindled by God, but not consumed at which time God commanded Moses to deliver the children of Israel (Ex. 3:2).

BURNISHED, refined by fire, purified of impurities (as metals). Also, the results of such refinement (Ezek. 1:7).

BURNT, past tense of burn, to be consumed (as with fire), to consume (as with passion), to flame up, radiate (Deut. 32:24).

BURNT OFFERING, voluntary offerings of the children of Israel which were governed by the rules of offering in Lev. 1, 2, and 3. They were not sin or trespass offerings. It was entirely consumed by the fire as a sign of the offerer's entire surrender to God. Regular burnt offerings were offered (1) every morning and evening (Ex. 29:18), (2) every Sabbath (Num. 28:9), (3) and at the new moon, the three great festivals, the Day of Atonement, and the Feast of Trumpets (Num. 28:11). Sometimes incorrectly called **Burnt Sacrifices**.
took the wood of the *b.*, Gen. 22:6.
upon the head of the *b.*, Lev. 1:4.
knowledge . . . more than *b.*, Hos. 6:6.
more than all whole *b.*, Mark 12:33.
offerings and *b.*, Heb. 10:8.

BURNT SACRIFICE, *see* **BURNT OFFERING**.

BURST, to break, rend, tear, disrupt suddenly, as in an explosion.
thy presses shall *b.* out, Prov. 3:10.
thy yoke . . . *b.* thy bonds, Jer. 2:20.
new wine doth *b.*, the, Mark 2:22.
he *b.* asunder in the, Acts 1:18.

BURY, to intern, entomb, deposit in a grave or sepulchre.
that I may *b.* my dead. Gen. 23:4.
shalt in any wise *b.*, Deut. 21:23.
of Jews is to *b.* John 19:40.

BURYING PLACE, sepulchre or grave for burying. The field in which the sepulchre or grave was located.
possession of a *b.*, Gen. 23:4.
bury me in their *b.*, Gen. 47:30.

BUSH, *see* **BRAMBLE**, a term often

meaning bramble (as in Luke 6:44) and referring to any of many small plants as thorn bushes, brambles and the like. The plant that was not consumed by fire (Ex. 3:2). *See* BURNING BUSH.

BUSH, BURNING BUSH, that particular bush not consumed by fire from which God called Moses to lead the children of Israel from Egypt (Ex. 3:2; Acts 7:30).

BUSHEL, a dry measure of four pecks. It is slightly more than the ephah, which contains three pecks and three pints (Ex. 16:36). Used only in the New Testament in a figurative sense, it is doubtful if the Jews used it as a measure.
and put it under a *b.*, Matt. 5:15.
putteth it under a *b.*, Luke 11:33.

BUSHES, plural of Bush, found only in Job 30:4; Job 30:7, and Is. 7:19.

BUSIED, to make oneself busy, to be actively engaged in an undertaking.
servant was *b.* here and, I Kin. 20:40.
sons of Aaron *b.* in, II Chr. 35:14.

BUSINESS, activity, undertaking, plan, or proposed work.
charged with any *b.*, Deut. 24:5.
utter this our *b.*, we, Josh. 2:20.
about my Father's *b.*, Luke 2:49.
may appoint over *b.*, Acts 6:3.

BUSYBODY, a meddlesome person, one active in another man's affairs.
but some of you are *b.*, I Tim. 5:13.
suffer as a *b.*, I Pet. 4:15.

BUT, except, nevertheless, and other like uses of a conjunction.
b. the name of that, Gen. 28:19.
b. the ark of God had, II Chr. 1:4.
had not known sin *b.* by, Rom. 7:7.
the law, *b.* by faith, Gal. 2:16.
Who is a liar *b.* he, I John 2:22.

BUTLER, an official of the king of Egypt mentioned only in chapters 40 and 41 of Genesis. His exact duties are not definite but they included filling and bearing the drinking vessel to the King. *See* CUP-BEARER. Compare Neh. 1:11.

BUTLERSHIP, the office of the Butler (Gen. 40:21).

BUTTER, curdled milk, cream, or cheese.

It is thought that modern-type butter was unknown in Biblical times.
Abraham took *b.* and milk, Gen. 18:8.
b. and honey shall be, Is. 7:15.

BUTTOCKS, hip, seat, bottom.
garments . . . to their *b.*, II Sam. 10:4.258
even with . . . *b.* uncovered, Is. 20:4..527

BUY, to purchase, obtain in exchange for money, acquire, get.
we might *b.* corn, because, Neh. 5:3.
b. me thy field that is, Jer. 32:7.
year, and *b.* and sell, James 4:13.

BUYER, he who purchases, gets, obtains, exchanges for money, acquires.
naught, saith the *b.*, Prov. 20:14.
as with the *b.*, so with, Is. 24:2.

BUZ, a name meaning "contempt" used for two persons, (1) the second son of Nahor, brother of Abraham (Gen. 22:21). and (2) the father of Jahdo (I Chr. 5:14).

BUZITE, an inhabitant of a region called Buz (Jer. 25:23; Job 32:2).

BUZZI, an Aaronite, father of Ezekiel, the prophet (Ezek. 1:3).

BYWAYS, secondary roads or paths, crooked ways (Judg. 5:6).

BYWORD, a proverb or saying, a nickname indicating a type, often in derision or scorn.
thou shalt become a *b.*, Deut. 28:37.
Israel shall be a *b.*, I Kin. 9:7.
thou makest us a *b.*, Ps. 44:14.

C

CAB, KAB, a unit of dry measure. Its capacity was approximately three pints.
c. of dove's dung, II Kin. 6:25.

CABBON, a town in the low country of Judah. It is perhaps the same as Machbenah (I Chr. 2:49).

CABINS, cells inside a dungeon.
Jeremiah kept in them, Jer. 37:16.

CABUL, a city in southeastern Asher a few miles southeast of Acre (Josh. 19:27).

It was later on used to designate a region of Galilee.
and goeth out to *C.*, Josh. 19:27.
the land of *C.*, I Kin. 9:13.

CAESAR, the name of the members of the Julian family. Augustus adopted it as title for the Roman emperor, a practice which lasted two centuries. Eleven Roman Caesars ruled during New Testament times, but only four are named in the scriptures. Augustus (Luke 2:1) gave the world taxation decree. John the Baptist began his work (Luke 3:1) in the fifteenth year of Tiberius' reign. The famine predicted by Agabus happened during the reign of Claudius. Claudius also was the one who ordered all Jews to leave Rome (Acts 18:2). It was to Nero that Paul made his great appeal (Acts 25:1–13).
tribute unto *C.*, Matt. 22:17.
a decree from *C.*, Luke 2:1.
no king but *C.*, John 19:15.
I appeal unto *C.*, Acts 25:11.
be brought before *C.*, Acts 27:24.
of *C.*, household, Phil. 4:22.

CAESAREA, a seaport town about fifty miles from Jerusalem. It was built by Herod the Great and named in honor of Caesar Augustus. It was the Roman capital of Palestine. It was the home of Philip the Evangelist and Cornelius, the first Gentile convert to Christ (Acts 10:1, 24). Paul was a prisoner there for two years. The death of Herod Agrippa took place there (Acts 12:19, 23).
home of Cornelius, Acts 10:1.
the disciples of *C.*, Acts 21:16.
they came to *C.*, Acts 23:33.
Paul was kept there, Acts 25:4.
Bernice came unto *C.*, Acts 25:13.

CAESAREA PHILIPPI, a city in the extreme north of Palestine. It is near one of the two main sources of the Jordan River. It was the scene of Christ's declaration to His disciples that He would build His church (Matt. 16:18). Christ's transfiguration took place here (Matt. 17:1–13).

CAGE, a box in which birds were kept, taken to market or caught (Jer. 5:27).
c. full of birds, Jer. 5:27.
Babylon is become a *c.*, Rev. 18:2.

CAIAPHAS, the son-in-law of and high priest with Annas (John 18:13) between

A.D. 18 and 36. He was a Sadducee. His long term seems to indicate he was a man of some renown. It was he who condemned Jesus, saying He was guilty of blasphemy (Matt. 26:57–66). He also participated in the trial of Peter and John (Acts 4:5–7).
the palace of *C.*, Matt. 26:3.
Jesus was taken to him, Matt. 26:57.
high priest with Annas, Luke 3:2.
son-in-law of Annas, John 18:13.
gave Jews counsel, John 18:14.

CAIN, the eldest son of Adam and Eve. He killed his brother, Abel, in a fit of anger and then denied it to God. He was exiled from his home by God for his sin. He went to the land of Nod, married a member of the Adamic family, and settled there permanently. He built a city which he named after Enoch, his son, and became the father of a race distinctive along mechanical lines (Gen. 4:1–25). A city of Judah a few miles southeast of Hebron is also called Cain (Josh. 15:57).
Eve bore *C.*, Gen. 4:1.
a tiller of ground, Gen. 4:2.
he slew his brother, Gen. 4:8.
Lord put mark on him, Gen. 4:15.
town in south Judah, Josh. 15:57.
made inferior sacrifice, Heb. 11:4.
gone in the way of *C.*, Jude 11.

CAINAN, KENAN, the son of Enos. He was also the great-grandson of Adam. He was the father of Mahalaleel and died at the age of 910 (Gen. 5:14). Cainan was also the name of the son of Arphaxad in the line of the Messiah (Luke 3:36).
Enos begat *C.*, Gen. 5:9.
the days of *C.*, Gen. 5:14.
which was .. of *C.*, Luke 3:36.

CAKE, a term which generally refers to bread (Judg. 7:13). A cake was usually baked on hot stones. *See* **BREAD.**
tempered with oil, Ex. 29:2.
unleavened *c.*, Lev. 8:26.
c. of flour and oil, Num. 6:15.
a *c.* not turned, Hos. 7:8.

CALAH, one of the oldest cities known in Assyria, having been built by Asshur (Gen. 10:11). It was the capital of the empire (B. C. 930–720). The site is now marked by the Nimrod ruins, which has furnished a large portion of the Assyrian remains now in Britain.

CALAMITY, an accident or misfortune.
the day of their *c.*, Deut. 32:35.
laugh at your *c.*, Prov. 1:26.
c. come suddenly, Prov. 6:15.

CALAMUS, a sweet plant (Song 4:14)
which was used in making the anointing
oil (Ex. 30:23). It was brought from Asia
Minor to Tyre (Ezek. 27:19).

CALCOL, CHALCOL, a son of Zerah,
son of Judah by his daughter-in-law
Tamar (I Chr. 2:6).

CALDRON, a pot used for cooking flesh
(Ezek. 11:7). The figure of the seething
pot was used by the prophets to predict
coming destruction for the nation of Judah (Jer. 1:13; Ezek. 11:3).
a seething pot or *c.*, Job 41:20.
c. and pans, and bowls, Jer. 52:19.
this city is the *c.*, Ezek. 11:3.
flesh within the *c.*, Mic. 3:3.

CALEB, means bold or impetuous. He
was the only man besides Joshua, of
those Hebrews who left Egypt with
Moses, who was allowed to enter the
land of promise. The son of Jephunneh,
he was among the twelve spies sent from
Kadesh to spy out the land of Canaan.
Upon his return he urged the people of
Israel to press on and take the land before them. For this attitude he was allowed to enter the promised land (Num.
14:24), representing the tribe of Judah
in its division (Num. 34:19). He also received the city of Hebron for an inheritance (Josh. 14:13). Caleb was also the
name of the son of Hezron (I Chr. 2:18)
and the son of Hur (I Chr. 2:50).
my servant *C.*, Num. 14:24.
C. to enter the land, Num. 14:30.
C. given Hebron, Josh. 14:13.
brother to Othneil, Judg. 3:9.
C. the son of Hezron, I Chr. 2:18.
C. the son of Hur, I Chr. 2:50.

CALEB-EPHRATAH, a place near Bethlehem which is believed to have been
named after Caleb and his wife Ephratah.
Hezron was dead in *C.*, I Chr. 2:24.

CALEBITE, a descendant of Caleb.

CALF, a young cow or bullock which was
used by the Jews for food (Gen. 18:7)
and for sacrificial purposes (Heb. 9:12,
19). It was the object of worship in
Egyptian religion and was probably
transmitted to the Hebrews when they
were in Egypt (Ex. 32:4). Apis was the
sacred bull worshipped in Egypt.
made it a molten *c.*, Ex. 32:4.
a sin-offering, Lev. 9:8.
sacrificing to the *c.*, I Kin. 12:32.
c. is worshipped, Ps. 106:19.
c. at peace with lion, Is. 11:6.
killed the fatted *c.*, Luke 15:27.
second beast like a *c.*, Rev. 4:7.

CALF, GOLDEN, following the example
learned in Egypt, the Israelites made and
worshipped a calf image at Sinai (Ex.
32:4). When Jeroboam founded the
northern kingdom, he set up two such
calves, one at Bethel and one at Dan (I
Kin. 12:29). *See* **CALF.**

CALKER, one who seals the seams in a
ship. One who is given to repairing.
wise men were *c.*, Ezek. 27:9.
c. fall into ... sea, Ezek. 27:27.

CALL, a verb with several shades of
meaning. It can mean to label something
or someone (Is. 5:20; Gen. 1:5; 3:20;
4:25). In some passages it means to summon or beckon (Esther 5:10). In certain
other passages it seems to mean to lay
out in order, to collect, and to say (Matt.
19:17, Luke 20:37).
c. the light day, Gen. 1:5.
Adam *c.* wife Eve, Gen. 5:20.
I *c.* upon the Lord, II Sam. 22:7.
c. evil good, Is. 5:20.
c. upon thy God, Jonah 1:6.
I *c.* my son, Matt. 2:15.
not to *c.* the righteous, Mark 2:17.
c. his own sheep, John 10:3.
c. us to glory, II Pet. 1:3.

CALLED, shows that one has been given
an invitation. In the New Testament the
called are the same as the elect. Both are
names applied to the body of believers,
the Christians.
many are *c.*, Matt. 20:16.
the *c.* of Jesus Christ, Rom. 1:6.
c. to be saints, I Cor. 1:2.

CALLING, a vocation or profession.
the gifts and *c.* of God, Rom. 11:29.
ye see your *c.*, I Cor. 1:26.
hope of his *c.*, Eph. 1:18.
high *c.* of God, Phil. 3:14.
worthy of this *c.*, II Thess. 1:11.
an holy *c.*, II Tim. 1:9.

make your *c* . . . sure, II Pet. 1:10. . . . **199**

CALM, a dumbness or stillness.
makes the storm a *c.*, Ps. 107:29.
there was a great *c.*, Matt. 8:26.

CALM, to cease or be quiet.
so shall the sea be *c.*, Jonah 1:12.

CALNEH, a city about sixty miles south-east of Babylon, on the left bank of the Euphrates. In the 8th century it was captured by the Assyrians, and never really regained its power.
C. in land of Shinar, Gen. 10:10.
pass ye unto *C.* and see, Amos 6:2.

CALNO, a city in Syria which was unsuccessful in withstanding the onrush of Assyria (Is. 10:9). It is perhaps identical with Calneh.

CALVARY, the name of the place of the crucifixion of Jesus Christ. It is not a proper name at all, but was brought about when translators adopted the word Calvaria (i.e., "bare skull"), the Latin word chosen to render the Greek word. The expression "Mount Calvary" can hardly be justified since it is only eighteen feet in height. It is known as Golgotha, the place of the skull (Matt. 27:33).

CALVE, CALVES, a verb with several shades of meaning. It can mean to be in pain or travail (Job 39:1) or it may mean to yield or bear (Jer. 14:5). In another connection it may mean to allow to escape (Job 21:10).
their cow *c.* Job 21:10.
the hinds do *c.*, Job 39:1.
c. in the field, Jer. 14:5.

CAMEL, an animal which was unclean to the Jews (Lev. 11:4) because it parted not the hoof. Even though he had humps on his back he was very useful in the ancient days. He was known early to the Egyptians (Gen. 12:16). He may be called a desert ship because of his endurance. The camel is generally obedient, but not sweet in disposition. Camels were used by Abraham, Jacob and Joseph (Gen. 12:16, 30:43, 37:25).
give thy *c.* drink, Gen. 12:16.
he stood by the *c.*, Gen. 24:30.
room for the *c.*, Gen. 24:31.
she lighted off the *c.*, Gen. 24:64.
it was an unclean animal, Lev. 11:4.

raiment of *c.* hair, Matt. 3:4.
c. through needle's eye, Matt. 19:24.
swallow a *c.*, Matt. 23:24.

CAMON, a town supposedly in Gilead (Judg. 10:5) where Jair was buried.

CAMP, an encampment or stopping-place for a traveling group of people. It is especially characteristic of an army (II Sam. 1:2; II Kin. 19:35). The Hebrews, on the move from Egypt to Canaan with Moses and Aaron leading the way, were called a camp of people (Ex. 14:20).
noise of war in the *c.*, Ex. 32:17.
the gate of the *c.*, Ex. 32:26.
come into the *c.*, Lev. 14:8.
without the *c.*, Lev. 16:27.
the midst of the *c.*, Num. 2:17.
put out of the *c.*, Num. 5:2.
stranger . . in thy *c.*, Deut. 29:11.
great shout in the *c.*, I Sam. 4:5.
the *c.* of Saul, II Sam. 1:2.
c. of the Assyrians, II Kin. 19:35.

CAMP, to recline or settle down.
c. before the mount, Ex. 19:2.
I will *c.* against thee, Is. 29:3.
grasshoppers, . . *c.*, Nahum 3:17.

CAMPHIRE, the ancient form of camphor. It was a shrub like privet.
as a cluster of *c.*, Song 1:14.
pleasant fruits; *c.*, Song 4:13.

CAN, a verb which shows potential or ability. It is used as an auxiliary to other verbs.
c. number the dust, Gen. 13:16.
No man *c.* serve, Matt. 6:24.
Who then *c.* be saved, Matt. 19:25.
who *c.* forgive sins, Mark 2:7.
How *c.* a man be born again, John 3:4.
how *c.* he love God, I John 4:20.

CANA, a village in Galilee which is famous as the place in which Jesus performed His first public miracle (John 2:1–11). He later healed the nobleman's son there also (John 4:46–54). It was the home place of Nathaniel, one of the original twelve apostles (John 21:2).

CANAAN, a son of Ham and grandson of Noah (Gen. 9:22). Zidon, his oldest son, founded the city which bears his own name in Phoenicia and began that famous nation. The other sons of Canaan were fathers of the tribes in Syria and Palestine (Gen. 10:15–19; I Chr. 1:13–

16). Canaan also became the name used for the country of Palestine. At first, however, it probably only signified the coastal region of the land (Num. 13:29; Josh. 11:3). When the land was promised to Abraham and to his race it was called the land which flowed with milk and honey. The land was the home of a multitude of pagan tribes.

Ham, the father of *C.*, Gen. 9:22.
was a servant of servants, Gen. 9:25.
and *C.* begat Zidon, Gen. 10:15.
dwelt in the land of *C.*, Gen. 13:12.
I will give unto thee . . *C.*, Gen. 17:8.
the daughters of *C.*, Gen. 28:8.
borders of the land of *C.*, Ex. 16:35.
over Jordan into . . *C.*, Num. 35:10.
thee will I give . . *C.*, I Chr. 16:18.
speak the language of *C.*, Is. 19:18.
a woman of *C.*, Matt. 15:22.

CANAANITES, descendants of Canaan, the son of Ham, the son of Noah. The word came to be used in two different senses. In one sense, the Canaanites were the people who lived in the area of the Mediterranean coast and the Jordan Valley (Gen. 10:18–20; Josh. 11:3). In the broader, more general sense the word signifies all the dwellers in Palestine which were not the seed of Abraham (Gen. 12:6; Num. 21:3). They were put into servitude by King Solomon (I Kin. 9:20,21).

the *C.* was then in land, Gen. 12:6.
Jews not to marry them, Gen. 24:37.
drive out the *C.*, Ex. 33:2.
the *C.* dwell by the sea, Num. 13:29.
C. dwell in the valley, Num. 14:25.
fight against the *C.*, Judg. 1:3.
Simon the *C.*, Matt. 10:4.

CANAANITESS, a woman of Canaan.

CANAANITISH, pertaining to Canaan.

CANAANEAN, CANAANITE, a member of a Jewish patriotic party, meaning the same as the Greek Zealot (Matt. 10:4).

CANDACE, a queen of Ethiopia who is mentioned but once in the New Testament (Acts 8:27). Her name is not a proper one, but is the name of a dynasty of Ethiopian queens. A prominent eunuch of her court was preached to by Philip the evangelist and was baptized by the same as he was on his way home (Acts 8:38).

CANDLE, a lamp or light.
the *c.* of the wicked, Job 21:17.
c. shines upon my head, Job 29:3.
spirit of man is the *c.*, Prov. 20:27.
search Jerusalem with *c.*s, Zeph. 1:12.
men do not light *c.*, Matt. 5:15.
they need no candle, Rev. 22:5.

CANDLESTICK, a place of light. The candlestick of the tabernacle, and afterwards of the temple, had six branches. It was one of the articles of the holy place (Lev. 24:2–4) and was the only light of the tabernacle and the temple. The fuel used was pure olive oil and the light was kept burning from evening until morning (Ex. 27:20,21; I Sam. 3:3).

it had six branches, Ex. 25:35.
three branches of the *c.*, Ex. 37:18.
in *c.*, four bowls, Ex. 37:20.
seven lamps against *c.*, Num. 8:2.
c. of pure gold, I Kin. 7:49.
the *c.* of silver, I Chr. 28:15.
meant to hold a candle, Matt. 5:15.
seven golden *c.*, Rev. 1:12.
remove thy *c.*, Rev. 2:5.

CANE, a sweet-smelling reed which was valued for its perfume (Is. 43:24).

CANKER, a consumption, corrosion, or gangrene.
word will eat as . . a *c.*, II Tim. 2:17.

CANKERWORM, a winged insect which moves about in a swarm like the locust. It is very destructive to vegetation (Nahum 3:16). It is rendered caterpillar in Jer. 51:27.

ate what the locust left, Joel 1:4.
eat thee up as the *c.*, Nahum 3:15.
the *c.* spoils, Nahum 3:16.

CANKERED, to be rusted or corroded.
gold and silver is *c.*, James 5:3.

CANNEH, a place probably in the south coast of Arabia, now called Canne. It is perhaps the same as Calneh.
Haran, and *C.*, and Eden, Ezek. 27:23.632

CANON OF SCRIPTURE, the word canon signifies a straight rod or stick used in measuring. A canon, therefore, is anything which may be used as a standard or criteria. The Bible is considered the standard of faith and practice. The books which belong in the Bible are called canonical, i.e. authoritative. Uncanonical books, such as the Apocrypha, are books which are not to be considered as inspired and thus are not entitled to a place in the Bible. Since the books of the Bible were written over a long period of time, the Canon of Scripture was established over an extended period. As for the Old Testament, the Jews first accepted the 5 books of Law, then the writings of the prophets (including the books of history), and finally the other writings. These same books Christians accepted as canonical (Luke 24:44; John 10:35) and added 27 other inspired books, the New Testament. In the historical formation of the canon, only those books which were definitely authoritative were accepted. One has only to read the books which were rejected to see the vast difference between them and the canonical, inspired books of Scripture.

CANTICLES, another name for the Song of Solomon.

CAPERNAUM, a town on the northwestern side of the Sea of Galilee. It was in the land of Gennesaret, on the rich, busy plain. Jesus did some mighty works there, and castigated the people because they had not turned to God in repentance when they saw the great works done (Matt. 11:23).
C., . . exalted unto heaven, Matt. 11:23.
Jesus abode there, Mark 2:1.
C. a city of Galilee, Luke 4:31.
Jesus taught there, John 6:59.

CAPHTOR, a place three times mentioned as the origin of the Philistines (Deut. 2:23; Jer. 47:4; Amos 9:7). It is believed to be the same as the isle of Crete.

CAPHTORIM, CAPHTHORIM, the people of Caphtor.
came Philistim, and C., Gen. 10:14.
came forth out of C., Deut. 2:23.

CAPPADOCIA, a province in Asia Minor, surrounded by Pontus, Cilicia, Syria, Lycaonia and Galatia. Jews from this place were in Jerusalem to hear the great sermon by Peter on the day of Pentecost (Acts 2:9) and some Christians from there were among the readers of Peter's first epistle (I Pet. 1:1).

CAPTAIN, this term is broadly used in

Scripture to represent: (1) The Hebrew commander of a division (Judg. 4:2; II Sam. 10:16); (2) An officer over a certain number (Num. 31:14); (3) The Roman commander of a garrison (Acts 21:31; 28:16); (4) Various civil officers (I Sam. 9:16; Jer. 51:23). Heb. 2:10 pictures Jesus as author and pioneer of salvation.
c. of . . guard, Gen. 37:36.
c. over thousands, Deut. 1:15.
c. over fifties, Deut. 1:15.
Sisera, the c., Judg. 4:7.
c. of the host, II Kin. 9:5.
with chief priests and c. Luke 22:4.
c. of the temple, Luke 22:52.
the c. of the temple, Acts 4:1.
eat the flesh of . . c., Rev. 19:18.

CAPTIVE, one that is taken prisoner, exiled, or removed from his homeland. The Jews which were carried away into Babylonian exile were called captives (Ezek. 1:1). In the New Testament, those under the power of the devil are said to be captives (II Tim. 2:26).
my daughters . . c., Gen. 31:26.
first born of the c., Ex. 12:29.
the lawful c., Is. 49:24.
sons are taken c., Jer. 48:46.
deliverance to the c., Luke 4:18.
be led away c., Luke 21:24.
lead c. silly women, II Tim. 3:6.

CAPTIVITY, a term used to show the removal of a people into another land. In a sense, the bondage in Egypt of the Hebrews could be called captivity, however, the term is generally applied to the Assyrian captivity of the northern kingdom in 722 B.C. and the Babylonian captivity of Judah in March, 597 B.C. (II Kin. 17:5,6; Ezek. 1:1). The actual captivity of Judah began in 606 B.C. and ended in 536 B.C. when Babylon fell and Cyrus released the Hebrews. The captivity lasted about seventy years. The termination of the Assyrian captivity is not known.
into c. from Jerusalem, II Kin. 24:15.
until the c., I Chr. 5:22.
went up out of the c., Ezra 2:1.
the children of the c., Ezra 6:20.
those of the c., Jer. 29:31.
king shall go into c., Jer. 49:3.
Judah . . went into c., Ezek. 25:3.
he led c. captive, Eph. 4:8.

CARBUNCLE, a bright, glittering stone,

perhaps the same as an emerald, which was quite precious.
gates of *c.*, Is. 54:12.
the emerald . . the *c.*, Ezek. 28:13.

CARCAS, the seventh chamberlain who served King Ahasuerus (Esther 1:10).

CARCASE, CARCASS, a dead body of a beast (Judg. 14:8) or a human being (Josh. 8:29). According to the law of Moses, a place was unclean which housed a dead carcase. Anyone touching the carcase was unclean until evening (Lev. 11:39).
c. of an unclean beast, Lev. 5:2.
c. shall ye not touch, Lev. 11:8.
c. was cast in the way, I Kin. 13:24.
lion . . stood by the *c.*, I Kin. 13:24.
c. . . fall as dung, Jer. 9:22.
c. fell in . . wilderness, Heb. 3:17.

CARCHEMISH, CHARCHEMISH, a very important city in the western Euphrates region. It was captured by Sargon in 717 B.C. (Is. 10:9) and later was the scene of one of the most important battles in ancient history. It was in 605 B.C. that Nebuchadnezzar and the Babylonians defeated Pharaoh-necho and the Egyptians in the famous battle of Carchemish. After this battle the Babylonians were established as the number one power in the eastern Mediterranean area. Necho fought there, II Chr. 35:20.
Is not Calno as *C.*, Is. 10:9.
the river Euphrates in *C.*, Jer. 46:2.

CARE, a word which can denote anxiety, trembling, fear, division or distraction.
the *c.* of the asses, I Sam. 10:2.
with all this *c.*, II Kin. 4:13.
the *c.* of this world, Matt. 13:22.
the *c.* of this world, Mark 4:19.
choked with *c.* and riches, Luke 8:14.
c. of all the churches, II Cor. 11:28.
Casting . . *c.* upon him, I Pet. 5:7.

CARE, to be an object of care or to become distracted. Also Cared.
c. thou for any man, Matt. 22:16.
c. thou not . . we perish, Mark 4:38.
dost thou not *c.*, Luke 10:40.
an hireling . . *c.* not, John 10:13.
he *c.* for the poor, John 12:6.
Gallio *c.* for none, Acts 18:17.
he *c.* for you, I Pet. 5:7.

CAREAH, KAREAH, the father of Jo-

hanan, the governor of Judah during the time of Gedeliah, Babylon's puppet (II Kin. 25:23).

CAREFUL, (1) anxious, worried (Luke 10:41; Phil. 4:6); (2) attentive, diligent (Phil. 4:10; Tit. 3:8).
thou hast been *c.*, II Kin. 4:13.
not be *c.* in year, Jer. 17:8.
we are not *c.*, Dan. 3:16.

CARITES, (ones ready), a body of troops mentioned in II Kin. 11:4. The King James Version renders "captains."

CARMEL, a mountain in Palestine, directly east of the Sea of Galilee, pushing into the Mediterranean Sea. It was the scene of the contest between the prophet Elijah and the prophets of Baal (I Kin. 18:17–40). It is also the name of a town in the hill country of Judah (Josh. 15:55) where Nabal had his possessions (I Sam. 25:2–40).
Saul came to *C.*, I Sam. 15:12.
Nabal was there, I Sam. 25:5.
Elijah went up to . . *C.*, I Kin. 18:42.
the excellency of *C.*, Is. 35:2.
the forest of his *C.*, Is. 37:24.
C. by the sea, Jer. 46:18.
he shall feed on *C.*, Jer. 50:19.
and the top of *C.*, Amos 1:2.
in the midst of *C.*, Mic. 7:14.

CARMELITE, CARMELITESS, an inhabitant of Carmel, in the mountains of Judah (I Sam. 27:3; I Chr. 11:37).

CARMI, means vinedresser. He was the son of Reuben, the eldest son of Jacob. Carmi was also the name of the father of Achan (Josh. 7:1).
son of Reuben, Gen. 46:9.
brother of Hezron, Ex. 6:14.
father of Achan, Josh. 7:1.
a son of Judah, I Chr. 4:1.

CARMITES, a Reubenite clan which descended from Carmi (Num. 26:6).

CARNAL, pertaining to the flesh. In the Old Testament the word has neither a good nor a sinister denotation, but in the New Testament, especially in the letters of Paul, it takes on a sinister meaning (Rom. 7:14; I Cor. 3:3).
but I am *c.*, Rom. 7:14.
ye are yet *c.*, I Cor. 3:3.
are ye not *c.*, I Cor. 3:4.

weapons .. are not *c.*, II Cor. 10:4.
law of a *c.* command, Heb. 7:16.
and *c.* ordinances, Heb. 9:10.

CARNALLY, an adverb answering the question "how." It describes anything which is fleshly. In the New Testament it is opposite to any spiritual activity or connection (Rom. 8:6).
thou shalt not lie *c.*, Lev. 18:20.
shows sexual activity, Lev. 19:20.
man lie with her *c.*, Num. 5:13.
to be *c.* minded is death, Rom. 8:6.

CARPENTER, as a specific profession, carpentry is first mentioned in the scriptures in connection with the building of David's house (II Sam. 5:11). Carpenters from Tyre came to Jerusalem. Carpenters had such tools as the hammer, nail, saw and ax (Jer. 10:4; Is. 10:15), and plane, compass, line (Is. 44:13). Carpentry was the occupation of Jesus (Mark 6:3).
c. and masons, II Sam. 5:11.
laid it out to the *c.*, II Kin. 12:11.
hired masons and *c.*, II Chr. 24:12.
Lord showed .. four *c.*, Zech. 1:20.
the *c.* son, Matt. 13:55.
Is not this the *c.*, Mark 6:3.

CARPUS, a man in Troas with whom Paul left a cloak.
cloak ... left ... with *C.*, II Tim. 4:13.. **181**

CARRIAGE, a word which means baggage in the King James Version.
left his *c.*, I Sam. 17:22.
laid up his *c.*, Is. 10:28.
c. were .. loaden, Is. 46:1.

CARRY, to cause to come or go. Also Carried, Carries, Carrying.
c. corn for the famine, Gen. 42:19.
bound him .. and *c.*, II Kin. 25:7.
c. them to Babylon, Jer. 20:5.
c. captives into Egypt, Dan. 11:8.
c. about in beds, Mark 6:55.
shall gird thee; and *c.*, John 21:18.
men *c.* Stephen, Acts 8:2.
c. me away in the spirit, Rev. 17:3.

CARSHENA, a prince of Persia and Media during the reign of Ahasuerus, B.C. 520 (Esther 1:14).

CART, a two-wheeled cattle-drawn vehicle which was made of wood (I Sam. 6:14). It was not the same as the chariot. Sometimes the carts were covered and

sometimes uncovered (Num. 7:3). They were used in carrying persons, burdens, or produce (Gen. 45:19; I Sam. 6:7; Amos 2:13)₎
tie the kine to the *c.*, I Sam. 6:7.
one carried the ark, I Sam. 6:8.
c. came into the field, I Sam. 6:14.
drave the new *c.*, II Sam. 6:3.
the wheel of his *c.*, Is. 28:28.
c. .. full of sheaves, Amos 2:13.

CARVE, to cut in or engrave.
the *c.* image, Judg. 18:18.
c. work with gold, I Kin. 6:35.
he set a *c.* image, II Chr. 33:7.
decked bed with *c.* works, Prov. 7:16.

CARVING, an art in woodwork. It may be artificer work (Ex. 31:5) or it may be sculptured work (I Kin. 6:32).
in *c.* of timber, Ex. 31:5.
c. of cherubim, I Kin. 6:32.

CASE, a word, cause or matter.
the *c.* of the slayer, Deut. 19:4.
thou shalt in any *c.*, Deut. 22:1.
in such a *c.*, Ps. 144:15.
shall in no *c.* enter, Matt. 5:20.

CASEMENT, a part of a window operated by a hinge which allows it to be opened (Prov. 7:6). The Hebrew word is rendered lattice in Judges 5:28.

CASIPHIA, a place located on the road from Jerusalem to Babylon. It was the abode of the Levites in the Persian Empire (Ezra 8:17).

CASLUHIM, a tribe which descended from Mizraim, the son of Ham. The tribe settled in upper Egypt it is believed (Gen. 10:14; I Chr. 1:12). Mizraim, in Hebrew, means Egypt.

CASSIA, a choice perfume, it was one of the principal spices in the composition of the anointing oil (Ex. 30:24). It was among the precious merchandise of Tyre (Ezek. 27:19).

CAST, to throw or pour out.
c. child under .. shrubs, Gen. 21:15..
every son .. *c.* into .. river, Ex. 1:22.
c. it beside the altar, Lev. 1:16.
and *c.* a cloth, II Sam. 20:12.
c. his mantle, I Kin. 19:19.
c. ... body into the graves, Jer. 26:23.
is .. *c.* into the fire, Matt. 3:10.

c. them into prison, Acts 16:23.
Hath God *c.* away, Rom. 11:1.
c. down imaginations, II Cor. 10:5.
c. into lake of fire, Rev. 20:10.

CASTAWAY, something or someone who
is not approved. It is disposed of.
I .. should be a *c.*, I Cor. 9:27.

CASTLE, a well fortified structure which
can be used for defensive purposes. The
castle of the Jebusites was captured by
David (I Chr. 11:5, 7). Castles were built
in the cities and forests of Judah (II Chr.
17:12; 27:4).
their names .. by *c.*, Gen. 25:16.
burnt .. all .. goodly *c.*, Num. 31:10.
built in Judah *c.*, II Chr. 17:12.
like the bars of a *c.*, Prov. 18:19.
Paul .. led into the *c.*, Acts 21:37.
be brought into the *c.*, Acts 22:24.
entered into the *c.*, Acts 23:16.

CASTLE, PRAETORIUM, *see* **PRAE-
TORIUM CASTLE.**

CASTOR AND POLLUX, the sons of
Jupiter, king of the gods, and Leda. It
was the name of the vessel in which Paul
sailed from Malta to Rome (Acts 28:11).

CATCH, to lay or keep hold on.
pursued, .. and *c.* him, Judg. 1:6.
wives .. whom they *c.*, Judg. 21:23.
c. him by the feet, II Kin. 4:27.
c. him and kissed him, Prov. 7:13.
c. them in .. net, Hab. 1:15.
the wolf *c.* them, John 10:12.
c. Paul and Silas, Acts 16:19.

CATERPILLAR, a devourer. *See* **LO-
CUST.** It seems at times to be the same
as the cankerworm (Ps. 105:34).
a dearth :. or *c.*, II Chr. 6:28.
gave .. increase .. unto *c.*, Ps. 78:46.
cankerworm, and the *c.*, Joel 1:4.

CATTLE, in the Old Testament this word
can refer to any of the domestic animals,
horses, goats, sheep, camels, and oxen.
sheep .. oxen .. fat *c.*, I Kin. 1:9.
great and small *c.*, Eccles. 2:7.
treading of lesser *c.*, Is. 7:25.
not brought .. small *c.*, Is. 43:23.
plowing or feeding *c.*, Luke 17:7.

CAUL, (1) the diaphragm or midriff located above the liver. Along with the
kidneys and other fats it was burned as

an offering (Ex. 29:13, 22; Lev. 3:4). (2)
The thin membrane around the heart
(pericardium) is also called the caul
(Hos. 13:8). (3) A headdress worn by
women for ornament was also called a
caul (Is. 3:18).
the *c.* that is above; Ex. 29:13.
the *c.* .. with the kidneys, Lev. 4:9.
used as sin offering, Lev. 9:10.
take away .. their *c.*, Is. 3:18.
the *c.* of their heart, Hos. 13:8.

CAUSE, may denote a reason (II Sam.
13:16), a word or matter (Deut. 1:17), a
plea (Jer. 5:28), a judgment (II Sam.
15:4), or a controversy (Ex. 23:2).
c. brought .. Moses, Ex. 18:26.
c. that is too hard, Deut. 1:17.
Lord will maintain .. *c.*, Ps. 140:12.
put away .. for every *c.*, Matt. 19:3.
no *c.* of death in him, Luke 23:22.
For the same *c.*, Phil. 2:18.

CAUSE, the reason for some activity or
state of being. Also **Causes, Causeth.**
if a man *c.* a blemish, Lev. 24:19.
the Lord shall *c.*, Deut. 28:7.
c. to multiply, Ezek. 16:7.
c. great joy, Acts 15:3.
them which *c.* divisions, Rom. 16:17.
c. that it be read, Col. 4:16.

CAUSEWAY, a raised path or a cast up
road.
c. of the going up, I Chr. 26:16.
four at the *c.*, I Chr. 26:18.

CAVE, a hole, an exposed place or an
opening in the ground. A great cave near
Allepo will hold 3000 soldiers. Maun-
drell described caves near Sidon which
contain 200 rooms. Lot was the first one
recorded as having lived in a cave (Gen.
19:30). The cave of Machpelah (Gen.
23:9) was used as a burial site for the
family of Abraham.
the *c.* of Machpelah, Gen. 23:9.
Sarah buried in one, Gen. 23:19.
a hiding-place, Josh. 10:16.
in the *c.* mouth, Josh. 10:27.
the sides of the *c.*, I Sam. 24:3.
a place of refuge, Ezek. 33:27.
It was a *c.*, John 11:38.
in dens and *c.*, Heb. 11:38.

CEASE, to come to an end.
and the manna *c.*, Josh. 5:12
the strife *c.*, Prov. 26:20.
the wind *c.*, Matt. 14:32.

tongues .. shall *c.*, I Cor. 13:8.

CEDAR, a wood which is grown especially in Lebanon (Is. 2:13). The Hebrew word, *erez*, can also mean the pine, cyprus, fir, and juniper. Some think that all the land in Lebanon which is 3000 to 7000 feet altitude was once completely covered with cedars.
priest shall take *c.*, Num. 19:6.
and devour the *c.*, Judg. 9:15.
Tyre sent .. *c.* trees, II Sam. 5:11.
gave Solomon *c.* trees, I Kin. 5:10.
c. .. from Lebanon, Ezra 3:7.
the height of the *c.*, Amos 2:9.
fire may devour .. *c.*, Zech. 11:1.

CEDRON, *see* **KIDRON.**

CELEBRATE, to praise or to keep a festival (Lev. 23:41) or sabbath (Lev. 23:32).
ye *c.* your sabbath, Lev. 23:32.
c. the seventh month, Lev. 23:41.
death can not *c.*, Is. 38:18.

CELESTIAL, upon, over or above the heavens, heavenly.
also .. *c.* bodies, I Cor. 15:40.
glory of the *c.* one, I Cor. 15:40.

CELLAR, the treasure or treasury. It was generally a place of storage for wine or other important things.
for the wine *c.*, I Chr. 27:27.
the *c.* of oil, I Chr. 27:28.

CENCHREA, CENCHREAE, a Corinthian harbor which was located about ten miles east of Corinth. The church there was visited by Paul (Acts 18:18). It was the home of Phebe, the deaconess (Rom. 16:1).
Paul shaved head there, Acts 18:18.
the church which is at *C.*, Rom. 16:1.

CENSER, an instrument which was used in the burning of incense (Lev. 16:12, 13). It was portable, made of metal and was fitted to contain burning coals (II Chr. 26:18; Luke 1:9).
c. full of burning, Lev. 16:12.
every man his *c.*, Num. 16:17.
priest took .. brazen *c.*, Num. 16:39.
c. of pure gold, I Kin. 7:50.
had the golden *c.*, Heb. 9:4.
angel took the *c.*, Rev. 8:5.

CENSUS, a system of numbering the amount of population. The Jews did this by registering by tribe, family and house (Num. 1:18). A specific census of Israel was taken three times, the first at Sinai after the departure from Egypt (Num. 1). The number of adult males amounted to 603,550. The second census was taken after the years of wandering and amounted to a little less than the first (Num. 26: 1–51). The third census was taken by David and it revealed that he had 1,300,000 fighting men (II Sam. 24:1–9; I Chr. 21:1–6). Just before the birth of Jesus, Augustus ordered an enrollment of the people for the purpose of taxation (Luke 2:1).

CENTURION, a title given to the military officer who was over one hundred men (Acts 21:32; 22:26). Cornelius, the first gentile convert to Christ was a centurion (Acts 10:1). Four centurions are mentioned in the New Testament (Acts 27:1, 3, 43; Matt. 8:5–13; 27:54).
one came to Jesus, Matt. 8:5.
the *c.* sent friends, Luke 7:6.
took soldiers and *c.*, Acts 21:32.
Paul said unto the *c.*, Acts 22:25.
called one of the *c.*, Acts 23:17.
c. found a ship, Acts 27:6.
c. delivered .. prisoners, Acts 28:16.

CEPHAS, a surname which was given Simon Peter by Jesus. Cephas is the Aramaic for stone (John 1:42; I Cor. 1:12; 3: 22). *See* **PETER.**

CEREMONIES, the particular details of a rite (Num. 9:3).

CERTAIN, a definite or specific person, thing or matter.
there were *c.* men, Num. 9:6.
c. of the elders, Jer. 26:17.
c. Chaldeans came near, Dan. 3:8.
c. strange things, Acts 17:20.
c. we can carry, I Tim. 6:7.

CERTAINLY, surely or definitely.
c. this is the day, Lam. 2:16.
c. .. was .. son of God, Luke 23:47.

CERTAINTY, that which is already established.
Know for a *c.*, Josh. 23:13.
come with the *c.*, I Sam. 23:23.
have known the *c.*, Acts 22:30.

CERTIFY, to make known.
Esther *c.* the king, Esther 2:22.

I c. you, brethren, Gal. 1:11.

CHAFED, signifies bitterness.
they be c. in . . minds, II Sam. 17:8.

CHAFF, the straw which is separated from the grain in the winnowing process. The grain, with the straw, was trodden, picked up with a fork, and tossed in the wind. The grain came down into the grain pile, but the chaff was blown away. It had no real value (Job 21:18; Ps. 1:4; Is. 17:13; Zeph. 2:2). Chaff is used figuratively to denote the presence of false doctrine (Is. 33:11; Matt. 3:12).
carried by storm, Job 21:18.
as c. before the wind, Ps. 35:5.
chased as the c., Is. 17:13.
the day pass as the c., Zeph. 2:2.
burned with fire, Matt. 3:12.

CHAIN, a metallic bracelet made of gold, iron or brass which was used as ornaments (Gen. 41:42) or as fetters for prisoners (II Sam. 3:34; Acts 28:20; Eph. 6:20; II Tim. 1:16).
made of pure gold, Ex. 28:14.
bound him in c., Jer. 52:11.
with fetters and c., Mark 5:4.
c. fell of . . his hands, Acts 12:7.
not ashamed of . . c., II Tim. 1:16.
angel . . having . . c., Rev. 20:1.

CHALCEDONY, a word appearing in Rev. 21:19 as one of the precious stones in the wall of the New Jerusalem. It is a specie of quartz found near Constantinople. It was probably a greenish stone, silicate of copper.

CHALCOL, CALCOL, the son or descendant of Zerah (I Chr. 2:6). He and his offsprings were noted for their wisdom (I Kin. 4:31).

CHALDEA, a region which originally was the southern portion of Babylonia, but later was applied to the entire country of Babylonia. The cities of Ur (Abraham's home) and Erech were in the south and Babylon, Cutha and Sippara were in the north. It is believed that the earliest era of civilization sprang up around Chaldea.
C. shall be a spoil, Jer. 50:10.
the inhabitants of C., Jer. 51:24.
in a vision . . into C., Ezek. 11:24.
the Babylonians of C., Ezek. 23:15

CHALDEANS, CHALDEES, natives of Chaldea. In the early days they settled near the Persian Gulf. In the eighth century B.C. they consolidated Babylonia under the leadership of Merodach-baladan, but were put down by Sennacherib, the Assyrian king, as they sought to become a great world power. The New Babylonian empire started about 625 B.C., under Nabopolassar the Chaldean, and reached its zenith under king Nebuchadnezzar. God called Abraham, the head of the messianic nation (Gen. 11:31; 12:1), from Ur of the Chaldees.
bands of the C., II Kin. 24:2.
king of Babylon, the C., Ezra 5:12.
the land of the C., Is. 23:13.
and falleth to the C., Jer. 21:9.
Fear not to serve . . C., Jer. 40:9.
sword is upon the C., Jer. 50:35.
the tongue of the C., Dan. 1:4.
I raise up the C., Hab. 1:6.

CHALKSTONE, very brittle limestone.
stones of . . altar as c., Is. 27:9.

CHALLENGE, to affirm or say to be so. It usually denotes controversy (Ex. 22:9).

CHAMBER, any place in a house which may be used for sleeping, lodging, privacy or any special occasion.
a place for weeping, Gen. 43:30.
place of eating, II Sam. 13:10.
c. of the south, Job 9:9.
used by a bridegroom, Joel 2:16.
in the secret c., Matt. 24:26.
laid her in . . upper c., Acts 9:37.

CHAMBERLAIN, an officer of the royal chambers. Blastus was the chamberlain of Herod (Acts 12:20). Erastus was the chamberlain and treasurer of the city of Corinth (Rom. 16:23). In some passages they seemed to be eunuch officers (Esther 1:10).
seven c. that served, Esther 1:10.
Hege the king's c., Esther 2:3.
some belonged to Esther, Esther 4:4.
Herod had one, Acts 12:20.
Corinth had one, Rom. 16:23.

CHAMELEON, a kind of lizard. It was noted for its ability to change its color to match its surroundings. It was an unclean animal in Jewish law (Lev. 11:30).

CHAMOIS, species of wild goat found in

Arabia (Deut. 14:5). The Hebrews were allowed to eat its flesh.

CHAMPAIGN, open country. It may be a plain, a wasteland or a desert. (Deut. 11:30).

CHAMPION, a mighty one or one that rises to meet a grave situation (I Sam. 17:51). Goliath, the giant, was called a champion out of the camp of the Philistines (I Sam. 17:4).
there went out a c., I Sam. 17:4.
there came up the c., I Sam. 17:23.
Philistines saw c., I Sam. 17:51.

CHANAAN, see CANAAN.

CHANCE, an occurrence or accident.
a c. that happened, I Sam. 6:9.
but time and c., Eccles. 9:11.
by c. there came, Luke 10:31.

CHANCE, to happen unexpectedly.
nest c. to be before, Deut. 22:6.
I happened by c., II Sam. 1:6.
it may c. of wheat, I Cor. 15:37.

CHANCELLOR, a master of counsel, taste, or reason. He seems to be an advisory official.
Rehum the c., Ezra 4:8.
Then wrote Rehum the c., Ezra 4:9.
unto Rehum the c., Ezra 4:17.

CHANGE, an exchange.
gave .. c. of raiment, Gen. 45:22.
thirty c. of raiment, Judg. 14:12.
two c. of garments, II Kin. 5:23.
c. and war .. against me, Job 10:17.
wait, till my c. comes, Job 14:14.
made of necessity a c., Heb. 7:12.

CHANGE, to make different; alter in condition or appearance.
c. beast for beast, Lev. 27:10.
c. their glory, Ps. 106:20.
I will c. their glory, Hos. 4:7.
shall c. the customs, Acts 6:14.
we shall all be c., I Cor. 15:51.
priesthood being c., Heb. 7:12.

CHANGER, see MONEYCHANGER.

CHANNEL, a path which usually is associated with a body of water (Ps. 18:15).
c. of the sea, II Sam. 22:16.
c. of waters were seen, Ps. 18:15.

CHANT, to part, separate, sing aloud. This is a method of singing which was characteristic of the class of leisure during the days of the prophet Amos (Amos 6:5).

CHAPEL, a holy place, sanctuary. In I Macc. 1:47 it was an idol's temple. Bethel is called the king's chapel in Amos 7:13.

CHAPITER, the upper part of a pillar (Ex. 38:17). The tops of the pillars of the temple are called chapiters (Jer. 52:22). A word which means the same is "capital".
overlaid .. c. with gold, Ex. 36:38.
made of molten brass, I Kin. 7:16.
c. upon the two pillars, I Kin. 7:20.
bowls of the c., I Kin. 7:41.
pommels of the c., II Chr. 4:12.

CHAPMAN, a travelling merchant, also called a peddler.
c. and merchants, II Chr. 9:14.

CHAPT, to be parched or dried out.
the ground is c. .. no rain, Jer. 14:4.

CHARASHIM, a place at the back of the plain of Sharon which was founded by Joab, a man of Judah and of the family of Othniel. It was reinhabited by the Benjamites after the exile (Neh. 11:35).

CHARCHEMISH, see CARCHEMISH.

CHARGE, may signify hand (Num. 31:49), a thing to be watched (Gen. 26:5; Deut. 11:1), a judgment (I Kin. 4:28), a burden (I Kin. 11:28), a provision (I Cor. 9:7) or a private or extra special message (Acts 16:24).
and kept my c., Gen. 26:5.
the c. of the Lord, Lev. 8:35.
c. of the tabernacle, Num. 1:53.
ruler over .. the c., I Kin. 11:28.
Levites to their c., II Chr. 8:14.
the c. of the altar, Ezek. 40:46.
at his own c., I Cor. 9:7.
c. I commit unto thee, I Tim. 1:18.

CHARGE, to put a load or burden on. It may mean to accuse (Job 1:22) or to command (Ex. 1:22).
c. all his people, Gen. 26:11.
a command of Pharaoh, Ex. 1:22.
c. the young men, Ruth 2:9.
c. the messenger, II Sam. 11:19.
c. he his disciples, Matt. 16:20.

he *c.* them straitly, Mark 5:43.
I *c.* thee before God, I Tim. 5:21.
c. them that are rich, I Tim. 6:17.

CHARGEABLE, to be heavy, to make heavy, or to put a burden upon. It strongly denotes responsibility to a task.
lest we be *c.*, II Sam. 13:25.
governors . . were *c.*, Neh. 5:15.
I was *c.* to no man, II Cor. 11:9.
not be *c.* unto any. I Thess. 2:9.

CHARGER, a tray, the platter upon which the head of John the Baptist was brought to Salome, Herodias' daughter (Matt. 14:8). The silver dishes used at the dedication of the altar were called chargers (Num. 7:13).
offering . . one silver *c.*, Num. 7:13.
twelve *c.* of silver, Num. 7:84.
head in a *c.*, Matt. 14:8.
give me . . in a *c.*, Mark 6:25.

CHARIOT, a two-wheeled vehicle which was used for peaceful purposes or in war. It rested on an axle and was open at the back. Horses pulled it. The first one mentioned in the Bible is in connection with Joseph who is said to have been placed in Pharaoh's chariot (Gen. 41:43). When used in war the strength of a nation was determined by the amount of chariots she had (Ex. 14:7). The Hebrews did not generally use them because the hills of Palestine were not adapted for them. At one time the Philistines had 30,000 (I Sam. 13:5).
Joseph made ready his *c.*, Gen. 46:29.
took off . . *c.* wheels, Ex. 14:25.
used in Egypt, Ex. 15:4.
Absalom used them, II Sam. 15:1.
stalls for horses and *c.*, II Chr. 9:25.
bind *c.* to swift beast, Mic. 1:13.
used for journeying, Acts 8:28.
join thyself to *c.*, Acts 8:29.
c. of many horses, Rev. 9:9.
sheep . . horses . . *c.*, Rev. 18:13.

CHARITABLY, according to love. An adverb telling how something may be done.
walkest thou not *c.*, Rom. 14:15.

CHARITY, a translation of the Greek word *agape*, which properly means love (I Cor. 8:1,13; Rom. 5:5,8). It is said to be even greater than faith and hope (I Cor. 13:13).
but *c.* edifieth, I Cor. 8:1.
c. suffers long, I Cor. 13:4.

c. never faileth, I Cor. 13:8.
put on *c.*, Col. 3:14.
it fulfills the law, I Tim. 1:5.
in your feasts of *c.*, Jude 12.

CHARMED, the state of impotence caused by a charm or a type of hypnosis.
which will not be *c.*, Jer. 8:17.

CHARMER, one who is put in the same category with idols, those possessing familiar spirits and wizards. They were consulted for advice (Is. 19:3).
a *c.*, or a consulter, Deut. 18:11.
the voice of the *c.*, Ps. 58:5.
the idols, and . . *c.*, Is. 19:3.

CHARRAN, a form of Haran (Acts 7:2, 4).

CHASE, to drive away or to pursue.
ye shall *c.* . . enemies, Lev. 26:7.
one *c.* a thousand, Deut. 32:30.
c. them unto . . Zidon, Josh. 11:8.
c. out of the world, Job 18:18.

CHASTE, clean, pure and consecrated. It is characteristic of a virgin (II Cor. 11:2).
c., keepers at home, Titus 2:5.
your *c.* conversation, I Pet. 3:2.

CHASTEN, to instruct, convict or discipline. The fathers chasten the sons (Deut. 8:5) and God, treating men as His children, chastens them (Heb. 12:6).
a man *c.* his son, Deut. 8:5.
God does this to man, Deut. 8:5.
neither *c.* . . in . . displeasure, Ps. 6:1.
Lord . . *c.* me sore, Ps. 118:18.
c. son . . there is hope, Prov. 19:18.
c. of the Lord, I Cor. 11:32.
As many as I love, I *c.*, Rev. 3:19.

CHASTISE, to correct or punish for the purpose of refining or purifying.
will *c.* . . . seven times, Lev. 26:28.
done by the elders, Deut. 22:18.
done with whips, I Kin. 12:11.
c. him, and release, Luke 23:16.

CHASTISEMENT, the act of instructing, disciplining and correcting.
the *c.* of our peace, Is. 53:5.
the *c.* of a cruel one, Jer. 30:14.
if ye be without *c.*, Heb. 12:8.

CHATTER, to chirp as a bird. Speech which is unintelligible (Is. 38:14).

CHEBAR, a river of Chaldea where the prophet Ezekiel first received his visions from God (Ezek. 3:15).
captives by the river *C.*, Ezek. 1:1.
was in land of Chaldea, Ezek. 1:3.
Ezekiel had vision there, Ezek. 43:3.

CHECK, an instruction or chastisement.
the *c.* of my reproach, Job 20:3.

CHECKER, lattice work done on windows.
nets of *c.* work, I Kin. 7:17.

CHEDORLAOMER, the king of Elam with great power in western Asia during the days of Abraham. He took Lot from Sodom and Abraham rescued him (Gen. 14:1–16).

CHEEK, the jaw or side of the face.
the *c.* bone, Ps. 3:7.
thy *c.* are comely, Song 1:10.
tears on her *c.*, Lam. 1:2.
smite upon the *c.*, Mic. 5:1.
smite on thy right *c.*, Matt. 5:39.

CHEER, well minded or disposed.
be of good *c.*, Matt. 9:2.
unto them, be of good *c.*, Mark 6:50.

CHEER, to lift the countenance and make glad.
shall *c.* up his wife, Deut. 24:5.
which *c.* God and man, Judg. 9:13.
thy heart *c.* thee, Eccles. 11:9.

CHEERFUL, good, glad, full of joy.
c. feasts, Zech. 8:19.
God loves a *c.* giver, II Cor. 9:7.

CHEESE, a curdled milk product which is mentioned three times in the Bible. It is impossible to know whether or not it was like the product on the modern market.
carry these ten *c.*, I Sam. 17:18.
and *c.* of kine, II Sam. 17:29.
curled me like *c.*, Job 10:10.

CHELAL, the son of Pahath-moab. He married a foreign wife while in Babylonian captivity but divorced her upon his return to Palestine (Ezra 10:30).

CHELLUH, the son of Bani who married a foreign wife in exile in Babylon. He divorced her upon his return to his home during the days of Ezra (Ezra 10:35).

CHELUB, (1) the brother of Shuah and the father of Mehir of the tribe of Judah (I Chr. 4:11). (2) This was also the name of the father of Ezri, the officer which David appointed head over his gardeners (I Chr. 27:26).

CHELUBAI, a son of Hezron (I Chr. 2: 9). He is also called Caleb (I Chr. 2:18, 42). *See* CALEB.

CHELUHI, *see* CHELLUH.

CHEMARIM, an ascetic; one who goes about dressed in black (Zeph. 1:4). This was the name given to idolatrous priests who officiated at Beth-el (II Kin. 23:5; Hos. 10:5) and in Judah (Zeph. 1:4).

CHEMOSH, the national idol of the Moabites and Ammonites. It is not, however, identical with Molech, the god of human sacrifice. Human sacrifices were offered to Chemosh (II Kin. 3:27). In the days of Solomon a high place was built for Chemosh, but Josiah later tore it down (I Kin. 11:7; II Kin. 23:13).
O people of *C.*, Num. 21:29.
Solomon built an altar, I Kin. 11:7.
god of the Moabites, I Kin. 11:33.
C. . . into captivity, Jer. 48:7.
be ashamed of *C.*, Jer. 48:13.

CHENAANAH, (1) the fourth son of Bilhan. He was a soldier in the days of David (I Chr. 7:10). (2) The name of the father of Zedekiah, the false prophet, who hit Micaiah when he foretold of Ahab's destruction (I Kin. 22:11; II Chr. 18:10).

CHENANI, the Levite who conducted the devotion of the Jews after Ezra read to them from the book of the law (Neh. 9:4).

CHENANIAH, a chief Levite of the house of Izhar who had charge of the musical services when David removed the ark from the house of Obed-edom (I Chr. 15: 27). He and his sons were officials of the sanctuary (I Chr. 26:29).

CHEPHAR-HAAMMONAI, a city of Benjamin which once was a home of the Ammonites (Josh. 18:24).

CHEPHIRAH, a city of the Gibeonites which was given to the tribe of Benjamin (Josh. 9:17; 18:26). It was once again inhabited after the return from captivity (Ezra 2:25; Neh. 7:29).

CHERAN, the son of Dishon, the Horite (Gen. 36:26; I Chr. 1:41).

CHERETHITES, men of Philistia who served in David's bodyguard (II Sam. 8: 18; 15:18; I Kin. 1:38, 44). This name also applies to a Philistine tribe in the south of Canaan which came from Crete.
C. passed on before, II Sam. 15:18.
Benaiah . . over the C., I Chr. 18:17.
I will cut off the C., Ezek. 25:16.
the nation of the C., Zeph. 2:5.

CHERISH, to hold or treat. It denotes tender care and nourishment.
let her c. him, I Kin. 1:2.
and c. the king, I Kin. 1:4.
nourisheth and c. it, Eph. 5:29.
nurse c. her children, I Thess. 2:7.

CHERITH, the stream where Elijah hid himself during the great drought (I Kin. 17:3, 5). It was east of Jordan.

CHERUB, CHERUBIM, flying creatures which seem to have been used as guards in the Old Testament. After Adam and Eve were expelled from the Garden of Eden, they were placed as guards of the tree of life (Gen. 3:24). Golden cherubims faced each other, in a kneeling position, in the Holy of Holies. They symbolized Jehovah's presence in the midst of the people (Ex. 25:18–20; 37:7-9; Num. 7: 89; Ps. 80:1). They were fifteen feet high and were overlaid with gold in the Solomonic temple (I Kin. 6:22–28). Cherubim played roles in both the visions of Ezekiel and John when God displayed His glory to them (Ezek. 10: 1–22; Rev. 4:6–9).
were guards of Eden, Gen. 3:24.
make two c. of gold, Ex. 25:18.
placed at mercy seat, Ex. 37:8.
they had wings, I Kin. 6:27.
c. covered the ark, II Chr. 5:8.
dwellest between the c., Ps. 80:1.
above head of the c., Ezek. 10:1.
coals of fire between c., Ezek. 10:2.
sound of the c. wings, Ezek. 10:5.
four wheels by the c., Ezek. 10:9.
c. lift their wings, Ezek. 11:22.
the c. of glory, Heb. 9:5.

CHESALON, a town on the northern boundary of Judah (Josh. 15:10), ap-

proximately ten miles west of Jerusalem on Mount Jearim.

CHESED, the fourth son of Nahor, and Nephew of Abraham (Gen. 22:22).

CHESIL, a place in the south of Judah (Josh. 15:30).

CHESTNUT, a plane tree.
the hazel and c. tree, Gen. 30:37.
c. trees not like . . branches, Ezek. 31:8.

CHEST, a container or ark which holds money (II Kin. 12:10) or clothes (Ezek. 27:24).
the priest took a c., II Kin. 12:9.
much money in the c., II Kin. 12:10.
cast into the c., II Chr. 24:10.
the c. was brought, II Chr. 24:11.
c. of rich apparel, Ezek. 27:24.

CHESULLOTH, a town which seems to have derived its name from its situation on the slope of a mountain (Josh. 19:18). It was located between Jezreel and Shunem.

CHEW, to crush or grind with the teeth.
not eat of them that c., Lev. 11:4.
he c. not the cud, Lev. 11:7.
c. cud . . among . . beasts, Deut. 14:6.
for they c. the cud, Deut. 14:7.

CHEZIB, a town of the Canaanites which later belonged to Judah. It is probably identical with Achzib.
and he was at C., Gen. 38:5.

CHICKEN, young of a fowl. This term appears only in Matt. 23:37.
as a hen gathereth . . c., Matt. 23:37.

CHIDE, to strive or contend with.
and c. with Laban, Gen. 31:36.
people did c. with Moses, Ex. 17:2.
Why c. ye with me, Ex. 17:2.
c. with him sharply, Judg. 8:1.

CHIDON, the scene of the death of Uzzah who was killed when he placed his hand upon the ark to steady it (I Chr. 13:9). It was somewhere near Jerusalem but its exact location can not be plotted on the map.

CHIEF, a leader, a head, a mighty one, the one in the front or a prince.
prince of a c. house, Num. 25:14.

and the *c.* fathers, Num. 31:26.
the *c.* of your tribes, Deut. 1:15.
So Joab .. was *c.*, I Chr. 11:6.
whosoever would be *c.*, Matt. 20:27.
the *c.* of the people, Luke 19:47.
sinners .. I am *c.*, I Tim. 1:15.

CHIEFLY, most of all or first of all.
c. of Caesar's household, Phil. 4:22.
c. them after the flesh, II Pet. 2:10.

CHILD, an offspring. In the Bible a child
is looked on as a gift from God (I Sam.
1:11). Jewish parents were admonished
to teach the children and raise them to be
true members of the covenant (Deut.
6:7; 11:19). The child was expected to
reverence his parents and very severe
penalties were given for his misconduct
(Lev. 19:3; Ex. 21:15,17; Deut. 27:16).
The oldest sons received a double portion of the inheritance. The child might
be sold for a debt owed by the parents
(II Kin. 4:1; Neh. 5:5). The word child
also may mean a person noted for certain
qualities, as "children of the world"—
selfish; "children of light" having true
religion; "child of song," a good singer.
And the *c.* grew, Gen. 21:8.
a *c.* of his old age, Gen. 44:20.
she may nurse the *c.*, Ex. 2:7.
that the *c.* died, II Sam. 12:18.
stretched .. upon the *c.*, I Kin. 17:21.
when the *c.* was grown, II Kin. 4:18.
a poor and a wise *c.*, Eccles. 4:13.
unto us a *c.* is born, Is. 9:6.
Ephraim .. a pleasant *c.*, Jer. 31:20.
to circumcise the *c.*, Luke 1:59.
shall receive this *c.*, Luke 9:48.
I understood as a *c.*, I Cor. 13:11.
that from a *c.* known, II Tim. 3:15.

CHILDBIRTH, at childbirth women
were helped by nurses, midwives, even in
the time of the patriarchs (Gen. 35:17;
Ex. 1:15), even though women in the
East often gave birth so easily as not to
need this special help. The newborn
baby was bathed in water, rubbed with
salt, and wrapped in swaddling clothes
(Ezek. 16:4; Luke 2:7). It was usually
tended by the mother herself (Gen. 21:7;
I Sam. 1:23). After eight days the boys
were circumcised, and were named (Gen.
25:25). Forty days after the birth of a
boy and eighty after the birth of a girl,
the mother had to offer a purification
sacrifice in the temple (Lev. 12:1-8).
Weaning sometimes did not occur until

two or three years (II Macc. 7:27), and
was celebrated with a festival (Gen.
21:8).

CHILDLESS, barren or empty of children.
seeing I go *c.*, Gen. 15:2.
they shall die *c.*, Lev. 20:20.
Write ye this man *c.*, Jer. 22:30.
and he died *c.*, Luke 20:30.

CHILDREN, plural of child.

CHILDREN OF THE EAST, the people
who dwelt between Canaan and the Euphrates.
the people of the east, Gen. 29:1.
and the *c.* gathered, Judg. 6:33.
c. lay along, Judg. 7:12.

CHILDREN OF EDEN, the people who
dwelt in Adiabene in Mesopotamia, near
Gozan, Haren and Reseph. (Is. 37:12).

CHILDREN, SONG OF THE THREE,
a book of the Apocrypha.

CHILEAB, a son of David which was
born to Abigail (II Sam. 3.3). He is
called Daniel in I Chr. 3.1.

CHILION, the younger of two sons of
Naomi who died in Moab (Ruth 1:2,5).
He was a brother-in-law tc Ruth and
husband to Orpah.

CHILMAD, a region probably between
Assyria and Arabia which traded with
Tyre. It is spoken of in connection with
Sheba and Asshur (Ezek. 27:23).

CHIMHAM, the son of Barzillai, the
Gileadite, who was sent to David in the
place of his father (II Sam. 19:37, 38).

CHIMHAM, GERUTH, *see* **GERUTH
CHIMHAM.**

CHIMNEY, an outlet for smoke.
smoke out of the *c.*, Hos. 13:3.

**CHINNERETH, CHINNEROTH, CIN-
NEROTH,** a city of Naphtali (Josh.
19:35). It is also the name of an inland
sea that is better known as Lake Gennesaret (Josh. 13:27) and Sea of Galilee
(John 6:1).
reach unto sea of *C.*, Num. 34:11.
the plain south of *C.*, Josh. 11:2.

of the sea of *C.*, Josh. 13:27.
Ben-hadad against *C.*, I Kin. 15:20.

CHIOS, an island which was named by
Paul in his account of his voyage from
Troas to Caesarea (Acts 20:15). It is
located in the Greek Archipelago, north
of Samos. It claims to be the birthplace
of the poet Homer.

CHISLEU, CHISLEV, the third month of
the secular and ninth of the sacred Jewish
year. It corresponds to a part of December and January (Neh. 1:1; Zech. 7:1).

CHISLON, the father of Elidad, the
prince of Benjamin, who played a role in
the division of land of Canaan west of
the Jordan (Num. 34:21).

CHISLOTH-TABOR, a place near Mount
Tabor in Zebulum (Josh. 19:12). *See*
CHESULLOTH.

CHITLISH, KITHLISH, a village in the
lowland of Judah (Josh. 15:40).

CHITTIM, KITTIM, descendants of
Javan, the son of Japheth, the son of
Noah (Gen. 10:4; I Chr. 1:7). They
dwelt in Cyprus. Balaam predicted that
a fleet would leave from Chittim and
assault Assyria (Num. 24:24). In Is. 23:1
it seems to be a resort for the ships of
Tyre.
from the coast of *C.*, Num. 24:24.
pass over to *C.*, Is. 23:12.
over the isles of *C.*, Jer. 2:10.
out of the isles of *C.*, Ezek. 27:6.
the ships of *C.*, Dan. 11:30.

CHIUN, a name used for Kaiwan, the
planet Saturn.

CHOICE, a selection from among more
than one alternative.
c. of our sepulchres, Gen. 23:6.
all your *c.* vows, Deut. 12:11.
thy *c.* valleys, Is. 22:7.
thy *c.* cedars, Jer. 22:7.
God made *c.*, Acts 15:7.

CHOKE, to suffocate, strangle, crowd
out, or cut off the breath. This word
plays a leading role in a parable of Jesus
(Matt. 13:7).
the thorns . . *c.* them, Matt. 13:7.
herd ran . . and were *c.*, Mark 5:13.
c. with cares and riches, Luke 8:14.

into the lake, and were *c.*, Luke 8:33.

CHOLER, to be moved with—to become
or show oneself to be bitter.
moved with *c.*, Dan. 8:7.
king moved with *c.*, Dan. 11:11.

CHOOSE, make choice of, to pick out
what is the more useful and fitting.
wives . . which they *c.*, Gen. 6:2.
Moses *c.* able men, Ex. 18:25.
ye have *c.* . . . the Lord, Josh. 24:22.
c. you one bullock, I Kin. 18:25.
c. thee to build, I Chr. 28:10.
hath *c.* that good part, Luke 10:42.
c. you out of the world, John 15:19.
God *c.* Christians, I Pet. 2:9.
ye are a *c.* generation, I Pet. 2:9.

CHOP, to cut with quick, heavy blows.
c. them into pieces, Mic. 3:3.

CHORASHAN, a town in Judah which
may be the same as Ashan (Josh. 15:42).
It was given to the tribe of Simeon in the
land division.

CHORAZIN, a city just north of the Sea
of Galilee. Jesus severely denounced it
(Matt. 11:21; Luke 10:13).

CHOZEBA, COZEBA, a town in Judah
which is thought to have been the same as
Chezib (Gen. 38:5), and Achzib (Josh.
15:44).

CHRIST, one who has been anointed.
See **JESUS CHRIST.** The word signifies
that one has had oil rubbed upon him.
The rubbing of oil on one signified that
the receiver of the anointing had been
chosen for a certain honor. Jesus was
called the Christ because he was the
chosen one of the Father in heaven. In
the New Testament the word is used as
the Greek substitute for the Hebrew
word *Messiah.* The Christ was a term
which showed that the Messiah of the
Old Testament prophecies was meant
(Matt. 16:16; Mark 8:29; John 1:41).
Jesus, the personal name given to Christ
at birth, is often used with Christ—Jesus
Christ—so that Christ is practically a
part of the proper name of Jesus (John
1:17; Acts 11:17; Rom. 5:1). It has been
suggested that the word denotes Jesus'
kingly authority and mediatorial position
as the "Servant of the Lord."
where *C.* should be born, Matt. 2:4.

he was Jesus the *C.*, Matt. 16:20.
saying, I am the *C.*, Matt. 24:5.
thou art the *C.*, Mark 8:29.
because ye belong to *C.*, Mark 9:41.
Savior, which is *C.*, Luke 2:11.
whether he were the *C.*, Luke 3:15.
Ought not *C.* . . suffered, Luke 24:26.
C. . . the seed of David, John 7:42.
God . . raise up *C.*, Acts 2:30.
Philip . . preached *C.*, Acts 8:5.
the gospel of *C.*, Rom. 1:16.
C. pleased not himself, Rom. 15:3.
The churches of *C.*, Rom. 16:16.
and I of *C.*, I Cor. 1:12.
the cross of *C.*, I Cor. 1:17.
the members of *C.*, I Cor. 6:15.
the law of *C.*, I Cor. 9:21.
ye are the body of *C.*, I Cor. 12:27.
crucified with *C.*, Gal. 2:20.
baptized into *C.*, Gal. 3:27.
C. . . in your hearts, Eph. 3:17.
the doctrine of *C.*, Heb. 6:1.
the Spirit of *C.*, I Pet. 1:11.
denieth . . Jesus is . . *C.*, I John 2:22.
reigned with *C.*, Rev. 20:4.
shall be priests . . of *C.*, Rev. 20:6.

CHRISTS, FALSE, lying Christs or anointed ones. They are not really Christs, but only claim to be. *See* **ANTI-CHRISTS.**
shall arise false *C.*, Matt. 24:24.
false *C.* . . and prophets, Mark 13:22.

CHRISTIAN, the word which signifies a follower of Christ. The name was first given to the followers of Jesus at Antioch of Syria (Acts 11:26). Some say the disciples began calling themselves by this name and some say the enemies began calling them by the name. Agrippa used the word while speaking to Paul (Acts 26:28). The word appears but three times in the New Testament.
called *C.* first . . Antioch, Acts 11:26.
persuadest me to be a *C.*, Acts 26:28.
suffer as a *C.*, I Pet. 4:16.

CHRISTIANITY, a word which does not appear in the Bible. The popular definition of the word is "the whole of the religion of Christ." It is used especially when distinguishing it from other world religions.

CHRISTMAS, that day celebrated as the Lord's birthday. The date of Jesus' birth is not known but most of Christendom now accepts December 25 as the date of birth. The New Testament does not state the date, nor does it state that Christ's birthday should be celebrated.

CHRONICLES, records of events in the proper order of time. Public annals were kept in most ancient kingdoms (I Kin. 14:19; I Chr. 27:24).
c. of king David, I Chr. 27:24.
c. before the king, Esther 2:23.
records of the *c.*, Esther 6:1.

CHRONICLES, BOOKS OF, these books cover nearly the same period as the Books of Kings, but are written from a different viewpoint, the author of Chronicles being primarily interested in moral and spiritual instruction. Thus, Chronicles (originally one book instead of two) seems to emphasize the religious and priestly aspects of the history. Therefore, it is perhaps not sufficient to consider these books as merely supplementary to the fuller history of Samuel and Kings. Jewish tradition constantly named Ezra as the inspired compiler of Chronicles. These books may be outlined as follows: (I) Genealogies from Adam to Christ (I Chr. 1:1–9:44); (II) David's History (I Chron. 10:1–29:30); (III) Solomon's History (II Chron. 1:1–9:31); (IV) History of the Judahite Kings (II Chron. 10:1–36:23).

CHRYSOLITE, a precious, golden stone which is in the foundation of the New Jerusalem (Rev. 21:20).

CHRYSOPRASUS, a golden-green stone whose color is produced by nickel oxide. In John's vision of the New Jerusalem the tenth foundation of the city consisted of this stone (Rev. 21:20).

CHUB, the name of a people who were in alliance with Egypt against Nebuchadnezzar around 610 B.C.
mingled people, and *C.*, Ezek. 30:5.

CHUN, a town on the way to the Euphrates which was plundered by David (I Chr. 18:8).

CHURCH, the Greek word *ekklesia* which is translated "church" means "the called out" and originally signified a group of people assembled for a civil purpose (See Acts 19:32 where the word is rendered "assembly"). This word was used in the New Testament to denote the body of the faithful in Christ. In this connection the word suggests the following ideas:

(1) The Church Universal includes all those who have believed and obeyed the Gospel (Acts 2:47; Eph. 5:25). This group which Christ bought with His blood (Acts 20:28) is also called the spiritual Body of Christ (Eph. 1:23; Col. 1:18), the Kingdom of God (*see* KINGDOM), the Family (House) of God (I Tim. 3:15) and the Bride of Christ (Eph. 5:25; Rev. 21:2). The church shows God's eternal wisdom (Eph. 3:10). Prophesied by Christ (Matt. 16:18), the church was established on Pentecost (Acts 2:1–47).

(2) The Church Local. "Church" is also used to designate a local congregation of Christians (I Cor. 1:2; I Thess. 1:1). In this geographical sense the word is often used in the plural, "churches" (Rom. 16:16; Gal. 1:2; Rev. 1:4). The officers of each fully developed local church were elders (also called bishops or pastors) and deacons (Acts 6:3; 14:23; Phil. 1:1; I Tim. 3:1–8; Titus 1:5–9). The elders were directing overseers in the churches (I Pet. 5:1).

(3) The Assembled Local Congregation (I Cor. 11:18). Today, it is customary to refer to the building where the church assembles as "the church." This is not Biblical usage. The New Testament church is a group of people, not a building.

I will build my *c.*, Matt. 16:18.
Lord added to the *c.*, Acts 2:47.
it was persecuted, Acts 8:1.
feed the *c.* of God, Acts 20:28.
a servant of the *c.*, Rom. 16:1.
the *c.* of the Gentiles, Rom. 16:4.
c. of Christ salute, Rom. 16:16.
c. which is at Corinth, I Cor. 1:2.
in every *c.*, I Cor. 4:17.
edifying of the *c.*, I Cor. 14:12.
I persecuted the *c.*, I Cor. 15:9.
The *c.* in Asia, I Cor. 16:19.
care of all the *c.*, II Cor. 11:28.
Christ is . . head of . . *c.*, Eph. 5:23.
the body, the *c.*, Col. 1:18.
c. of the living God, I Tim. 3:15.
the *c.* in thy house, Philem. 2.
casteth out of the *c.*, III John 10.

angels of the . . *c.*, Rev. 1:20.
Spirit saith unto the *c.*, Rev. 2:7.

CHURCH SLEEPER, Eutychus fell asleep during one of Paul's long sermons and fell to his death (Acts 20:9). Paul restored him to life.

CHURL, a rustic, surly, ill-bred man.
called liberal, nor the *c.*, Is. 32:5.
instruments . . of the *c.*, Is. 32:7.

CHURNING, the method of applying pressure to milk to make butter (Prov. 30:33).

CHUSHAN-RISHATHAIM, the Mesopotamian king who oppressed Israel eight years but was defeated by Othneil (Judg. 3:10).

CHUZA, the stewart of Herod Antipas. His wife, Joanna, gave service to Jesus (Luke 8:3).

CIEL, to cover over or overlay.
he *c.* with fir tree, II Chr. 3:5.
it is *c.* with cedar, Jer. 22:14.
dwell in . . *c.* houses, Hag. 1:4.

CIELING, the overhead interior lining of a room.
the walls of the *c.*, I Kin. 6:15.

CILICIA, a province in southeast Asia Minor just north of the Mediterranean. Its chief town, Tarsus, was the home of Saul, later called Paul (Acts 21:39; 23:34). Paul labored in this place (Acts 9:30; Gal. 1:21).
of them of *C.*, Acts 6:9.
through Syria and *C.*, Acts 15:41.
Paul's home, Acts 21:39.
he (Paul) was of *C.*, Acts 23:34.
the sea of *C.*, Acts 27:5.
regions of Syria and *C.*, Gal. 1:21.

CINNAMON, a fragrant substance used by the Jews in the anointing oil (Ex. 30:23). It was also used to perfume beds (Prov. 7:17). It is the bark of the cinnamon tree. Oil is taken from the bark.

CINNEROTH, *see* **CHINNERETH.**

CIRCLE, an arch, a vault or a compass. A perfect circle has 360 degrees.
the *c.* of the earth, Is. 40:22.

99

CIRCUIT, a roundabout journey; travelling in a circle.

And he went . . in *c.*, I Sam. 7:16.
in the *c.* of heaven, Job 22:14.
c. unto the ends of it, Ps. 19:6.

CIRCUMCISE, to cut off, away, or around. *See* CIRCUMCISION.

c. . . flesh . . of foreskin, Gen. 17:23.
Abraham *c.* . . son, Gen. 21:4.
will *c.* thine heart, Deut. 30:6.
Jesus received it, Luke 1:59.
done on the sabbath day, John 7:22.
Timothy received it, Acts 16:3.
Paul received it, Phil. 3:5.

CIRCUMCISION, the act of cutting around or away. The rite of cutting the foreskin of males did not begin with the Hebrews. It was practiced in Egypt as early as 3000 B.C. The practice is now done by the Moslems also, but not for the same reason which the Hebrews do. To the Jew circumcision is the seal of Jehovah's covenant with them (Gen. 17:1-14). It was performed on the male child when he was eight days old (Lev. 12:3). When a foreigner wanted to enter the commonwealth of Israel he was required to submit to circumcision (Gen. 34:14-17, 22; Ex. 12:48). The term "the circumcision" as used in the New Testament denotes those of the loyal Jewish religion (Gal. 2:8; Col. 4:11). It is spiritualized in the New Testament, signifying the putting off of sins (Col. 2:11).

because of the *c.*, Ex. 4:26.
Moses . . gave . . *c.*, John 7:22.
the covenant of *c.*, Acts 7:8.
they of the *c.*, Acts 10:45.
c. . . profiteth, if, Rom. 2:25.
be counted for *c.*, Rom. 2:26.
c. . . of the heart, Rom. 2:29.
what profit . . of *c.*, Rom. 3:1.
the sign of *c.*, Rom. 4:11.
minister of the *c.*, Rom. 15:8.
C. is nothing, I Cor. 7:19.
gospel of the *c.*, Gal. 2:7.
neither *c.* availeth, Gal. 5:6.
For we are the *c.*, Phil. 3:3.
c. made without hands, Col. 2:11.
they of the *c.*, Titus 1:10.

CIRCUMSPECT, to be watchful in order to insure being accurate.
said unto you be *c.*, Ex. 23:13.

CIS, the same as Kish. It is the Greek form of Kish, the father of Saul.

Saul, the son of *C.*, Acts 13:21.

CISTERN, a well or pit used to catch and hold rain water (II Kin. 18:31; Jer. 2:13). Springs are scarce in Palestine and summers are dry so it was necessary for the Jews to have cisterns. They were placed out in the open, on top of towers of the wall, and in courtyards (II Sam. 17:18; Jer. 38:6). When empty they were sometimes used as dungeons (Gen. 37:22).

the waters of . . *c.*, II Kin. 18:31.
out of thine . . *c.*, Prov. 5:15.
wheel broken at . . *c.*, Eccles. 12:6.
the waters of his . . *c.*, Is. 36:16.
and hewed . . *c.*, Jer. 2:13.

CITIES, plural of city. *See* CITY.

CITIES OF REFUGE. Six Levitical cities were appointed for the protection of those who had accidentally caused another's death. These were Bezer, Ramoth-gilead and Golan east of Jordan, and Kedesh, Shechem and Hebron west of Jordan. Those who fled to these cities were guaranteed a fair trial, and, if innocent, were allowed to stay protected in the city (Num. 35:12, 24, 25). *See* AVENGER OF BLOOD.

CITIES OF THE PLAIN, five cities: Sodom, Gomorrah, Admah, Zeboiim, and Bela or Zoar (Gen. 13:12; 19:29). It can not be firmly established just where they were located.
Lot dwelt there, Gen. 13:12.
God destroyed them, Gen. 19:29.

CITIZEN, a person who belongs to a city or state and enjoys certain rights and privileges, as well as responsibilities, which being a citizen entails.
joined . . to a *c.*, Luke 15:15.
his *c.* hated him, Luke 19:14.
a *c.* of no mean city, Acts 21:39.
fellow *c.* with . . saints, Eph. 2:19.

CITY, a large assemblage of dwellings, surrounded by a protecting wall which was usually very thick (Gen. 18:26; Josh. 10:39; Luke 23:51). Many cities were built by the sea or upon hills for greater security. A watchman was stationed in a tower on the wall to give warning of attack (II Sam. 18:24). The gate of a Hebrew city was the center

for business and legal matters (Ruth 4:1, 10).
the men of the *c.*, Gen. 19:4.
without the *c.*, Gen. 19:16.
in the walled *c.*, Lev. 25:30.
inhabitants of . . *c.*, Deut. 13:13.
the elders of the *c.*, Deut. 21:19.
c. . . the Lord . . chosen, II Chr. 12:13.
the judges of the *c.*, II Chr. 19:5.
into the strong *c.*, Ps. 60:9.
a defenced *c.*, Jer. 1:18.
the daughters of my *c.*, Lam. 3:51.
c. called Nazareth, Matt. 2:23.
came into his own *c.*, Matt. 9:1.
the *c.* of Samaria, Acts 8:5.
street of . . *c.* . . pure gold, Rev. 21:21.

CITY, FENCED, *see* **FENCED CITY.**

CITY OF CONFUSION, a symbolic name for Jerusalem in time of danger (Is. 24:10).

CITY OF DAVID, the stronghold of Zion which David took from the Jebusites (II Sam. 5:6–9; I Chr. 11:5, 7). David and Solomon were buried there (I Kin. 2:10; 11:43). It was also the title of Bethlehem, the birthplace of David (Luke 2:4, 11) and Jesus Christ.
Zion: . . the *c. o. D.*, II Sam. 5:7.
David buried there, I Kin. 2:10.
houses in the *c. o. D.*, I Chr. 15:1.
of the *c. o. D.*, II Chr. 32:30.
breaches of the *c. o. D.*, Is. 22:9.

CITY OF DESTRUCTION, the prophetic name given to a city of Egypt which was inhabited by Jews (Is. 19:18).

CITY OF SALT, *see* **SALT, CITY OF.**

CLAD, to cover, wrap or clothe.
c. . . with a new garment, I Kin. 11:29.
and was *c.* with zeal, Is. 59:17.

CLAMOROUS, loud and uncouth.
foolish woman is *c.*, Prov. 9:13.

CLAMOUR, uncultivated noise.
anger, and *c.*, Eph. 4:31.

CLAP, to smite the hands together.
c. . . hands among us, Job 34:37.
all the tree . . shall *c.*, Is. 55:12.
Because thou hast *c.*, Ezek. 25:6.

CLAUDA, CAUDA, a small island located southwest of Crete (Acts 27:16).

CLAUDIA, a Christian lady in Rome (II Tim. 4:21).

CLAUDIUS, the successor of Caligula as Roman emperor. He reigned between A.D. 41–54. It was he who expelled the Jews from Rome (Acts 18:2). *See* CAESAR.
in the days of *C.*, Acts 11:28.
C. had commanded, Acts 18:2.

CLAUDIUS LYSIAS, the Roman officer in Jerusalem who protected Paul from the Jewish mob. When he learned that Paul was a Roman citizen he unbound him and sent him by night to Caesarea (Acts 22:24, 23:35).

CLAW, a cloven or parted hoof. Animals which had feet that were cloven into two claws were declared good for food (Deut. 14:6).
the cleft into two *c.*, Deut. 14:6.
tear their *c.*, Zech. 11:16. . .

CLAY, dirt used in the making of bricks and pottery (Is. 45:9; Jer. 18:4). It was also used in sealing jars and sepulchres (Jer. 32:14; Matt. 27:66). It was very early used for tablets upon which records were kept (Ezek. 4:1).
in houses of *c.*, Job 4:19.
formed out of the *c.*, Job 33:6.
c. was marred, Jer. 18:4.
c. . . in . . potter's hand, Jer. 18:6.
his feet part . . of *c.*, Dan. 2:33.
Jesus made *c.*, John 9:11.

CLEAN, pure and unblemished; unsoiled or untarnished. In the Old Testament it generally denotes two ideas. One is that of innocence (Job 11:4; Prov. 16:2) and the other is that of purity or acceptability (Gen. 7:2; Lev. 10:14; Num. 5:28). Certain animals were declared pure and some impure (clean and unclean). The clean animals were good for food, but the unclean animal was not. Animals which parted the hoof, or clovenfooted, and chewed the cud were valid for food. In the New Testament one was called clean when he had become pure through the power of God working through His son Jesus (John 15:3; II Pet. 2:18).
Of every *c.* beast, Gen. 7:2.
unto a *c.* place, Lev. 6:11.
a healed person is *c.*, Lev. 13:13.
unclean fowls and *c.*, Lev. 20:25.
the unclean and the *c.*, Deut. 12:22.

Create . . a *c.* heart, Ps. 51:10.
c. through the word, John 15:3.
those that were *c.,* II Pet. 2:18.

CLEAN, to be purified; become pure. In the Old Testament it may denote purity of person (II Kin. 5:10) or ritual cleansing (Lev. 14:8; 17:15). It sometimes also may denote purity of heart (Prov. 20:19; Is. 1:16). In the New Testament it denotes the healing of a leper by Jesus (Matt. 8:2).
washed . . and . . be *c.,* Lev. 13:58.
I have made my heart *c.,* Prov. 20:9.
Wash . . make . . *c.,* Is. 1:16.
sprinkle . . water . . be *c.,* Ezek. 36:25.
thou canst make me *c.,* Matt. 8:2.
be thou *c.,* Matt. 8:3.

CLEAN AND UNCLEAN, in the Old Testament these words generally designate ceremonial distinctions. The contrast between clean and unclean was limited by Moses to three particulars— food, contact with the dead, and bodily conditions. (1) Food. Things strangled, dead of themselves, or killed by animals of prey were forbidden, as were certain classes of beasts, birds and fish which are discussed in detail in Lev. 11 and Deut. 14. (2) Contact with Death rendered one unclean and made cleansing necessary (Num. 19; Lev. 11). (3) Bodily Conditions. Leprosy (Lev. 13, 14), Sexual Discharge, Flow of blood (Num. 5:2), and even childbirth rendered unclean (Lev. 15:5-24). *See* **LEPROSY, PURIFICATION.**

CLEANSE, to purify, to make clean, or to remove a defect. In both the Old and New Testament the word often refers to the cleansing of one's sins (Ps. 19:12; 51:2; II Cor. 7:1; I John 1:7). *See* **UNCLEAN ANIMALS.**
c. the altar, Ex. 29:36.
c. Judah and Jerusalem, II Chr. 34:5.
c. . . from secret faults, Ps. 19:12.
c. me from my sin, Ps. 51:2.
his leprosy was *c.,* Matt. 8:3.
c. . . from all filthiness, II Cor. 7:1.
c. . . hands . . sinners, James 4:8.

CLEAR, light, shining, luminous.
c. as the sun, Song 6:10.
like a *c.* heat, Is. 18:4.
approved . . to be *c.,* II Cor. 7:11.
c. as crystal, Rev. 22:1.

CLEAVE, a verb with two entirely different meanings. In one sense it denotes a cutting, splitting or rending apart. Abraham clave the wood which was to be used in sacrificing Isaac (Gen. 22:3). On the other hand, the word may denote a joining to someone or something because of certain natural or acquired tastes or ties (Gen. 2:24; Dan. 11:34; Acts 17:34).
c. unto his wife, Gen. 2:24.
soul *c.* unto Dinah, Gen. 34:3.
but Ruth *c.* unto her, Ruth 1:14.
c. the wood of the cart, I Sam. 6:14.
Solomon *c.* . . in love, I Kin. 11:2.
bone *c.* to my skin, Job 19:20.
soul *c.* unto the dust, Ps. 119:25.
cutteth and *c.* wood, Ps. 141:7.
he *c.* the rock also, Is. 48:21.
c. to his wife, Matt. 19:5.
certain men *c.* unto him, Acts 17:34.
c. to that which is good, Rom. 12:9.

CLEFT, a rent, hollow place or fissure.
the *c.* into two claws, Deut. 14:6.
the *c.* of the rocks, Is. 2:21.
smite . . house with *c.,* Amos 6:11.

CLEMENCY, a mildness of temper as shown by a superior to an inferior.
hear us of thy *c.,* Acts 24:4.

CLEMENT, a fellow worker with Paul at Philippi (Phil. 4:3).

CLEOPAS, one of the disciples on the way to Emmaus when the risen Christ appeared to them (Luke 24:18).

CLEOPHAS, the husband of one of the Marys (John 19:25). It is likely that he is the same person as Alphaeus (Matt. 27:56; Mark 3:18; Luke 6:15).

CLERK, an officer of Ephesus who had enough power and authority to halt a city uproar which involved Paul and some Ephesian craftsmen and merchants. He was probably a town scribe and recorder (Acts 19:35).

CLIFF, anciently called Clift (Is. 57:5). It is a steep, accented rock which has been split off by violence.
come up by the *c.,* II Chr. 20:16.
the *c.* of the valleys, Job 30:6.

CLIMB, to mount or ascend.
c. . . upon the rocks, Jer. 4:29.

they shall c. the wall, Joel 2:7.
c. . . upon the houses, Joel 2:9.
c. . . a sycamore tree, Luke 19:4.

CLIP, to diminish by cutting off, as with shears (Jer. 48:37).

CLOAK, CLOKE, an over covering, an outer garment or a tunic. Symbolically, it may mean a pretext (John 15:22). *See* **CLOTHING.**
let him have thy c., Matt. 5:40.
now they have no c., John 15:22.
c. left at Troas, II Tim. 4:13.

CLOD, a lump of earth or clay.
flesh . . clothed with . . c., Job 7:5.
The c. of the valley, Job 21:33.
seed is rotten under . . c., Joel 1:17.

CLOPAS, *see* **CLEOPHAS.**

CLOSE, very near; impending.
they sailed c. by, Acts 27:13.

CLOSE, to shut in or surround from all sides; enclose; cover in.
c. up all the wombs, Gen. 20:18.
earth c. upon them, Num. 16:33.
Lord . . hath c. your eyes, Is. 29:10.
he c. the book, Luke 4:20.

CLOSET, a storage room or an inner chamber. It may be a dressing room (Joel 2:16) or may be a secret place of prayer (Matt. 6:6).
the bride out of her c., Joel 2:16.
thou prayest, enter c., Matt. 6:6.
ye have spoken . . in c., Luke 12:3.

CLOTH, a fabric fashioned by weaving or felting. It was used for garments and for religious rites (Ex. 31:10). *See* **CLOTH-ING.**
The c. of service, Ex. 35:19.
spread a c. of blue, Num. 4:7.
spread a purple c., Num. 4:13.
he took a thick c., II Kin. 8:15.
a piece of new c., Matt. 9:16.

CLOTHE, to provide with clothing or a covering. The clothing does not have to refer to bodily garments (Rev. 18:16).
be c. with salvation, II Chr. 6:41.
be c. with shame, Ps. 35:26.
be c. with desolation, Ezek. 7:27.
c. with linen garments, Ezek. 44:17.
c. with camel's hair, Mark 1:6.
c. in white raiment, Rev. 3:5.

CLOTHES, garments for the body. *See* **CLOTHING.** The tearing or rending of clothes among the Jewish people was a sign of distress and consternation.
Reuben . . rent his c., Gen. 37:29.
shall wash his c., Lev. 14:8.
stripped off his c., I Sam. 19:24.
covered him with c., I Kin. 1:1.
put off our c., Neh. 4:23.
strip thee . . of thy c., Ezek. 23:26.
high priest rent . . c., Matt. 26:65.
put . . c. on him, Matt. Mark 15:20.
bound . . with grave c., John 11:44.

CLOTHING, the first Biblical mention of dress is the clothing made from fig leaves by Adam and Eve; this was replaced by skins (Gen. 3:7,21). Clothing was made later from wool (Lev. 13:47), linen (Ex. 9:31) and flax (Luke 16:19). Hebrew men wore inner and outer tunics, which were loose fitting robes often made from a single piece of cloth with holes for the head and arms. A mantle or cloak was used for an outer wrap in keeping with weather conditions (I Kin. 11:30). A leather or cloth girdle tied the tunic at the loins and supplied its fold as a pocket. Men of high position wore more and finer garments, of course, and often wore ornamental headdress (Is. 3:20). The difference between the dress of men and women was small, but obvious with the women wearing longer clothing made from finer materials. Veils were worn in the presence of strangers (Gen. 24:65). Moses' Law forbade men to wear women's clothes, and vice versa (Deut. 22:5).
naked of their c., Job 22:6.
her c. is silk, Prov. 31:22.
blue and purple is . . c., Jer. 10:9.
come . . in sheep's c., Matt. 7:15.
weareth the gay c., James 2:3.

CLOUD, a visible collection of particles of water suspended in the air. The morning cloud was noted for its temporary, unreliable nature (Hos. 6:4). In the days of Moses the glory of the Lord appeared in a cloud (Ex. 16:10). A cloud had a part in the baptizing of the Hebrews unto Moses (I Cor. 10:2).
my bow in the c., Gen. 9:13.
glory of the Lord . . in . . c., Ex. 16:10.
the c. of the incense, Lev. 16:13.
c. covered . . tabernacle, Num. 9:15.
the c. is consumed, Job 7:9.
blotted as a c. thy sins, Is. 44:22.

c. in the day of rain, Ezek. 1:28.
cover . . sun with a *c.*, Ezek. 32:7.
goodness . . as a morning *c.*, Hos. 6:4.
a voice out of the *c.*, Matt. 17:5.
baptized . . in the *c.*, I Cor. 10:2.
he cometh with *c.*, Rev. 1:7.

CLOUD, PILLAR OF, a miraculous
cloud guided the wandering Israelites by
day, while a pillar of fire led them at
night (Ex. 13:21,22). In the pillar of
cloud God revealed his presence during
the Exodus (Num. 12:5; Deut. 31:15).

CLOVEN, split or divided throughout. In
the scriptures the word is used in connection with hooves (Deut. 14:7), tongues
(Acts 2:3), and feet (Lev. 11:3).
that divide the *c.* hoof, Deut. 14:7.
there appeared . . *c.* tongues, Acts 2:3.

CLUSTER, a number of things of the
same kind; a cluster of grapes (Num.
13:23).
a branch with one *c.*, Num. 13:23.
the *c.* of grapes, Num. 13:24.
their *c.* are bitter, Deut. 32:32.
c. of raisins, I Sam. 25:18.
no *c.* to eat, Mic. 7:1.

CNIDUS, a city of Caria on the southwest
coast of Asia Minor which Paul passed
en route to Rome (Acts 27:7).

COAL, there is no evidence that the Jews
used coal, the mineral, but rather charcoal, coal made by burning wood (Is.
47:14; John 18:18; 21:9).
censer . . of burning *c.*, Lev. 16:12.
having a live *c.*, Is. 6:6.
used to bake bread, Is. 44:19.
a *c.* to warm at, Is. 47:14.
c. of fire on . . head, Rom. 12:20.

COAST, a border, bound (Ex. 10:4;
10:19).
locusts into thy *c.*, Ex. 10:4 52
in the utmost *c.*, Num. 22:36 132
shall be your south *c.*, Josh. 15:4 188
c. of the Amorites, Judg. 1:36 199
inhabitants of the sea *c.*, Zeph. 2:5 . . . 692
depart out of . . *c.*, Matt. 8:34 7
the *c.* of Judea, Mark 10:1 38
expelled . . out of . . *c.*, Acts 13:50 . . . 113
the *c.* of Asia, Acts 27:2 126

COAT, a garment which reached nearly to
the knees. It usually had short sleeves
though it might have sleeves of full

length. It was a kind of overcoat. A coat
of nail was a kind of breast plate (I
Sam. 17:5).
c. of many colours, Gen. 37:3.
a broidered *c.*, Ex. 28:4.
c. of fine linen, Ex. 39:27.
the collar of my *c.*, Job 30:18.
take away thy *c.*, Matt. 5:40.
journey, neither two *c.*, Matt. 10:10.
girt his fisher's *c.*, John 21:7.

COCK, the male of the domestic fowl.
The crowing of the cock indicated
the third watch of the night (Mark
13:35).
before the *c.* crow, Matt. 26:34.
and . . the *c.* crew, John 18:27.

COCKATRICE, a creature of the imagination. It is said to have been hatched
by a serpent from the egg of a cock. It is
called an adder in Prov. 23:32.
come forth a *c.*, Is. 14:29.
They hatch *c.* eggs, Is. 59:5.
I will send . . *c.*, Jer. 8:17.

COCKLE, a stinkweed found among
grain (Job 31:40).

CODOMANNUS, DARIUS, *see* DARI-
US.

COFFER, a box or chest hanging from
the side of a cart (I Sam. 6:8,11,15;
It was used for carrying jewels and
other valuables.
put . . jewels . . in a *c.*, I Sam. 6:8.
c. with . . mice of gold, I Sam. 6:11.

COGITATION, melancholy thinking;
meditation in earnest. It denotes a problem being mulled over.
my *c.* . . . troubled me, Dan. 7:28.

COLD, having a relatively low temperature; having little or no warmth.
it is opposite of heat, Gen. 8:22.
As the *c.* of snow, Prov. 25:13.
the *c.* flowing waters, Jer. 18:14.
a cup of *c.* water, Matt. 10:42.
would thou were hot or *c.*, Rev. 3:15.

COLHOZEH, the son of Hazaiah and
father of Baruch (Neh. 11:5) who took
part in repairing part of the wall of
Jerusalem (Neh. 3:15).

COLLAR, the mouth of a coat.
as the *c.* of my coat, Job 30:18.

COLLECTION, a gathering in the form of taxes or tribute (II Chr. 24:6,9) and freewill contributions (I Cor. 16:1).
to bring in . . the c., II Chr. 24:6.
Now concerning the c., I Cor. 16:1.

COLLEGE, a quarter of the city of Jerusalem. It is a poor translation of *mishneh* in II Kin. 22:14.
in Jerusalem in the c., II Kin. 22:14.
she dwelt . . in the c., II Chr. 34:22.

COLLOPS, rolls of flesh on a body. It denotes fatness (Job 15:27).

COLONY, a settlement in a place conquered by Rome. Roman citizens would settle a place and it would be declared, by the senate, a Roman colony. Philippi became a colony under Augustus (Acts 16:12). Other colonies of Rome were Antioch of Pisidia, Alexandria, and Troas.

COLOSSE, a city of Phrygia in Asia Minor. A church was probably established there by Epaphras, an associate of Paul, and Archippus (Col. 1:2,7; 4:17; Philem. 2). Philemon and Onesimus were members of this local church (Col. 4:9). Paul wrote an epistle to them. *See* COLOSSIANS, EPISTLE TO.

COLOSSIAN, an inhabitant of Colossae.

COLOSSIANS, EPISTLE TO THE, the Apostle Paul wrote to the Christians at Colossae to exhort them to resist false teaching and to remain true to the teaching of Christ, their head. The false teaching prevalent in Colossae seems to have had both Jewish legalism and pagan asceticism and philosophy as elements (Col. 2:16–23). This false doctrine is met by stressing the pre-eminence of Christ (Col. 1:13–23) whom Paul had before declared to the Colossians (Col. 1:23–29). The Colossians are encouraged to refuse to be led away from Christ, the Head (Col. 2:1–23), but, instead, to live as those who are risen with Christ should live (Col. 3:1–4:6). Colossians emphasizes the truth that Christ is Head of His body, the church (Col. 1:18), and thus presents the corollary to the emphasis of Ephesians that the church is the spiritual body of Christ (Eph. 1:22–23).

COLOUR, the evaluation of the quality of light by the use of the eyes. In certain passages, it may mean complexion (Lev. 13:55).
a coat of many c., Gen. 37:3.
not changed his c., Lev. 13:55.
lay . . stones with fair c., Is. 54:11.
as the c. of amber, Ezek. 1:27.

COLT, the young of the camel, ass or other animals of the horse kind. Jesus rode on the colt of an ass into Jerusalem in his great entrance into the city (John 12:15).
camels with their c., Gen. 32:15.
rode on thirty ass c., Judg. 10:4.
brought . . c. to Jesus, Mark 11:7.
King . . on an ass's c., John 12:15.

COME, to arrive by movement or in course of progress. The expression "and it *came* to pass" meant "now it happened."
c. into the ark, Gen. 6:18.
The Lord c. to Sinai, Deut. 33:2.
David c. to Saul, I Sam. 16:21.
tidings c. to Joab, I Kin. 2:28.
cry c. before him, Ps. 18:6.
shall c. against thee, Ezek. 23:24.
the kingdom shall c., Mic. 4:8.
when the evening was c., Matt. 14:23.
there c. a voice, Mark 1:11.
fear c. on all, Luke 1:65.
when he was c. to years, Heb. 11:24.
Now is c. salvation, Rev. 12:10.
Therefore shall . . plagues c., Rev. 18:8.

COMING, approach; arrival; advent. The word is used by the New Testament writers in telling of the return of Christ to claim His people (Matt. 24:3; I Thess. 3:13; James 5:8).
trembled at his c., I Sam. 16:4.
the sign of thy c., Matt. 24:3.
the c. of . . Just One, Acts 7:52.
much hindered from c., Rom. 15:22.
the c. of our Lord, I Cor. 1:7.
c. of . . Jesus Christ, I Thess. 3:13.
c. of . . Lord . . nigh, James 5:8.
not be ashamed . . at . . c., I John 2:28.

COMELY, grace, graceful, fair or becoming.
it is . . c. . . to eat, Eccles. 5:18.
Thy cheeks are c., Song 1:10.
that which is c., I Cor. 7:35.
c. that a woman pray, I Cor. 11:13.
our c. parts, I Cor. 12:24.

COMFORT, a soothing, solace or consolation.

kindness be for my *c.*, Ps. 119:76.
c. of the Holy Ghost, Acts 9:31.
the God of all *c.*, II Cor. 1:3.
I am filled with *c.*, II Cor. 7:4.
if any *c.* of love, Phil. 2:1.

COMFORT, to give soothing solace or consolation.
thou hast *c.* me, Ruth 2:13.
David *c.* Bath-sheba, II Sam. 12:24.
My bed shall *c.* me, Job 7:13.
When wilt thou *c.* me, Ps. 119:82.
to *c.* all that mourn, Is. 61:2.
might *c.* your hearts, Eph. 6:22.
c. the feeble minded, I Thess. 5:14.

COMFORTED, consoled.
Isaac was *c.* after his, Gen. 24:67.
were not a little *c.*, Acts 20:12.
hearts might be *c.*, Col. 2:2.
we were *c.* over you, I Thess. 3:7.

COMFORTER, one who gives consolation.
sent *c.* unto thee, II Sam. 10:3.
miserable *c.* are ye all, Job 16:2.
I looked for *c.* but, Ps. 69:20.
whence shall I seek *c.*, Nah. 3:7.

COMFORTER, THE, this expression is used by Jesus to refer to the Holy Spirit whom the Father sends to work in the lives of Christians (John 14:16, 26; 15:26; 16:7). *See* **HOLY SPIRIT.**

COMFORTLESS, without consolation.
I will not leave you *c.*, John 14:18.

COMMAND, to order or direct with authority. Also **Commanded, Commanding.**
Hezekiah *c.* to offer, II Chr. 29:27.
the king *c.* to call, Dan. 2:2.
Why did Moses . . *c.*, Matt. 19:7.
he *c.* even the winds, Luke 8:25.
The chief captain *c.*, Acts 22:24.
These things *c.* and teach, I Tim. 4:11.
that which was *c.*, Heb. 12:20.

COMMANDER, one who directs with authority.
given him for a . . *c.*, Is. 55:4.

COMMANDMENT, a command or mandate. There were ten commandments given to Moses and Israel by Jehovah on Mount Sinai (Ex. 20). Kings also gave commandments (II Chr. 31:13; Dan. 3:22). Jesus gave commandments to His

followers (John 13:34; 14:15; 14:21; 15:10).
thy *c.* are faithful, Ps. 119:86.
thy *c.* are my delights, Ps. 119:143.
the *c.* is a lamp, Prov. 6:23.
doctrines *c.* of men, Matt. 15:9.
which is the great *c.*, Matt. 22:36.
A new *c.* I give, John 13:34.
If ye keep my *c.*, John 15:10.
the law of *c.*, Eph. 2:15.
no new *c.*, I John 2:7.
This is the *c.*, II John 6.

COMMANDMENTS, TEN, *see* **TEN COMMANDMENTS.**

COMMEND, to mention as worthy of confidence, notice, kindness, etc.; to deliver with confidence (Luke 23:46).
I *c.* mirth, Eccles. 8:15.
I *c.* my spirit, Luke 23:46.
I *c.* you to God, Acts 20:32.
But God *c.* his love, Rom. 5:8.
We *c.* not ourselves, II Cor. 5:12.

COMMERCE AND TRADE, exchange of products among men has existed from very early times. Babylonia, Phoenicia and Egypt were all early merchant nations (Gen. 39:1; Is. 23:8; Ezek. 27). At first the Hebrews were almost totally an agricultural people, but Solomon developed extensive commercial enterprises (I Kin. 9:26–8; 10:22–29), even building small cities for storage (II Chr. 8:4–6). After Solomon, trade declined, but Judah continued to furnish oil and other commodities to Egypt and Phoenicia (Ezek. 27:17; Hos. 12:1).

COMMISSION, what is turned over to one; a charge.
the king's *c.*, Ezra 8:36.
with authority and *c.*, Acts 26:12.

COMMISSION, GREAT, *see* **GREAT COMMISSION.**

COMMIT, a verb with two main ideas. It may mean to give in charge or trust (Ps. 37:5; Luke 16:11), or it may mean to do, perform or perpetrate (Deut. 21:22; II Cor. 12:21).
he hath *c.* all, Gen. 39:8.
c. that wicked thing, Deut. 17:5.
shalt not *c.* . . . lewdness, Ezek. 16:43.
they *c.* falsehood, Hos. 7:1.
which *c.* such things, Rom. 1:32.
keep that which is *c.*, I Tim. 6:20.

COMMODIUS, convenient or satisfactory for a purpose (Acts 27:12).

COMMON, that which is plain or ordinary. Food which the Jews refused to eat was called common (Acts 11:8) and people counted as unimportant were called common (Acts 10:28). A common language is the language of the majority.
one of the *c.* people, Lev. 4:27.
into the graves of the *c.*, Jer. 26:23.
men of the *c.* sort, Ezek. 23:42.
they had all things *c.*, Acts 4:32.
put .. in the *c.* prison, Acts 5:18.
nothing *c.* or unclean, Acts 11:8.

COMMONWEALTH, a polity or community. The commonwealth of Israel (Eph. 2:12) refers to the religious, social Jewish society as a whole.

COMMOTION, noisy confusion or chaos generally associated with war (Luke 21:9).
great *c.* out of the north, Jer. 10:22.
hear of wars and *c.*, Luke 21:9.

COMMUNE, to converse; talk together; exchange thoughts and feelings.
I will *c.* with thee, Ex. 25:22.
David .. *c.* with Abigail, I Sam. 25:39.
the king *c.* with them, Dan. 1:19.
c. one with another, Luke 6:11.
sent for .. and *c.* with, Acts 24:26.

COMMUNICATE, to share as common to those concerned.
I .. *c.* unto them, Gal. 2:2.
him that is taught .. *c.*, Gal. 6:6.
no church *c.* with me, Phil. 4:15.
willing to *c.*, I Tim. 6:18.

COMMUNICATION, the passing of ideas from one person or persons to another. In certain passages it seems to signify the speech used to transport ideas (Eph. 4:29). It may signify those with whom communication is made (I Cor. 15:33).
Abner had *c.*, II Sam. 3:17.
let your *c.* be, Matt. 5:37.
evil *c.* corrupt, I Cor. 15:33.
Let no corrupt *c.*, Eph. 4:29.
the *c.* of thy faith, Philem. 6.

COMMUNION, the act of using a thing in common, fellowship.
the *c.* of the blood, I Cor. 10:16.

the *c.* of the body, I Cor. 10:16.
what *c.* ... light with, II Cor. 6:14..

COMPACT, to be joined or fitted together closely.
a city that is *c.*, Ps. 122:3.

COMPANIES, groups of persons in units.
sit down by *c.*, Mark 6:39.

COMPANION, one who accompanies or associates with another. Gaius and Aristarchus were Paul's companions in travel (Acts 19:29).
a *c.* of riotous men, Prov. 28:7.
c. hearken to thy voice, Song 8:13.
Paul's *c.* in travel, Acts 19:29.
c. in labour, Phil. 2:25.
your brother, and *c.*, Rev. 1:9.

COMPANY, a number of persons assembled or associated together; a group of people. It may refer to a group of religious leaders (Hos. 6:9), rebels (Num. 16:40) or soldiers (Judg. 7:20).
a *c.* of nations, Gen. 35:11.
Korah, and .. his *c.*, Num. 16:40.
he and all his *c.*, II Kin. 5:15..
Paul and his *c.*, Acts 13:13.
innumerable *c.* of angels, Heb. 12:22.

COMPARE, to bring together for the purpose of noting likenesses and differences.
who .. can be *c.* unto, Ps. 89:6.
things .. not to be *c.*, Prov. 8:11.
c. ourselves with some, II Cor. 10:12.

COMPARISON, the act of comparing.
What have I done .. in *c.*, Judg. 8:2.
with what *c.*, Mark 4:30.

COMPASS, to surround or encircle.
sorrows of death *c.* me, Ps. 18:4.
A woman shall *c.* a man, Jer. 31:22.
c. me about with lies, Hos. 11:12.
ye *c.* sea and land, Matt. 23:15.
shall see Jerusalem *c.*, Luke 21:20.

COMPASSION, a feeling of pity or sorrow for another's suffering. It is one of God's characteristics (II Kin. 13:23; Rom. 9:15), and is also characteristic of Christians (I Pet. 3:8).
Lord .. will .. have *c.*, Deut. 30:3.
Jesus had *c.* on them, Matt. 20:34.
on whom I will have *c.*, Rom. 9:15.
having *c.* one .. another, I Pet. 3:8.

COMPEL, to force or drive, esp. to a course of action. *See* ANGARY.
But his servants . .*c.* him, I Sam.. 28:23.
they *c.* one Simon, Mark 15:21.
c. to be circumcised, Gal. 2:3.

COMPLAIN, to express pain or dissatisfaction. It may denote strife (Judg. 21:22).
when the people *c.*, Num. 11:1.
brethren came . . to *c.*, Judg. 21:22.

COMPLETE, to fill up; conclude; finish.
ye are *c.* in him, Col. 2:10.
that ye may stand . . *c.*, Col. 4:12.

COMPREHEND, to be acquainted with, to understand, to contain or to sum up. It denotes a mental process.
c. . . dust of . . earth, Is. 40:12.
darkness *c.* it not, John 1:5.
is briefly *c.*, Rom. 13:9.

CONANIAH, a chief Levite in the time of Josiah. He was generous in contributing to the offerings (II Chr. 35:9).

CONCEAL, to cover or hide in order to keep silent.
will not *c.* his parts, Job 41:12.
c. thy loving kindness, Ps. 40:10.
Declare . . and *c.* not, Jer. 50:2.

CONCEIT, an exaggerated estimate of one's own importance. "In his own conceit" means "in his own eyes."
high wall in . . own *c.*, Prov. 18:11.
wise in . . own *c.*, Prov. 26:5.
Christians warned of it, Rom. 11:25.

CONCEIVE, to become with child. Sometimes it may mean to think or devise or reckon (Jer. 49:30).
Leah *c.* and bare, Gen. 29:32.
and shall *c.* seed, Num. 5:28.
that which is *c.* in her, Matt. 1:20.

CONCERN, that which relates or pertains to one's business.
things which *c.* . . Lord, Acts 28:31.
which *c.* infirmities, II Cor. 11:30.

CONCERNING, with reference to a matter; regarding that which is important.
Daniel *c.* the kingdom, Dan. 6:4.
give . . angels charge *c.*, Matt. 4:6.
C. . . Son Jesus Christ, Rom. 1:3.

CONCISION, (cut down) a term used by Paul of those who insisted upon circumcision.
beware of . . *c.*, Phil. 3:2.

CONCLUDE, to bring to a decision or settlement. It denotes finality.
have written and *c.*, Acts 21:25.
c. . . man . . justified . . faith, Rom. 3:28.
God . . *c.* . . all in unbelief, Rom. 11:32.

CONCORD, a sounding together; agreement.
what *c.* . . Christ with, II Cor. 6:15.

CONCUBINE, a common law wife of lower rank, ordinarily taken from among slaves or captives (Gen. 16:2; 29:29). A man could put his concubine away easily (Gen. 21:10–14), but she had some rights (Ex. 21:7–11; Deut. 21:10–14). Solomon had three hundred concubines (I Kin. 11:3).
Saul had a *c.*, II Sam. 3:7.
three hundred *c.*, I Kin. 11:3.
the sons of the *c.*, I Chr. 3:9.
wives, and his *c.*, Dan. 5:2.

CONCUPISCENCE, same as lust; illicit desire; sensual appetite.
all manner of *c.*, Rom. 7:8.
the lust of *c.*, I Thess. 4:5.

CONDEMN, to make judgment against or express strong disapproval of.
Lord will not . . *c.* him, Ps. 37:33.
have *c.* the guiltless, Matt. 12:7.
believeth not is *c.*, John 3:18.
c. sin in the flesh, Rom. 8:3.
I speak not . . to *c.*, II Cor. 7:3.

CONDEMNATION, act of condemning or state of being condemned. In the New Testament, one who is without faith in Christ is seen in a state of condemnation (Rom. 5:18).
in the same *c.*, Luke 23:40.
shall not come into *c.*, John 5:24.
lest ye fall into *c.*, James 5:12.
ordained to this *c.*, Jude 4.

CONDESCEND, to assume equality with an inferior; to abase self.
c. to men of lower estate, Rom. 12:16.

CONEY, same as the rock badger (Ps. 104:18).
c. . . he cheweth the cud, Lev. 11:5.
the rocks for the *c.*, Ps. 104:18.

CONFECTION, perfume made by an apothecary (Ex. 30:35, 37).

CONFECTIONARY, a lady perfumer (I Sam. 8:13).

CONFESS, may mean to admit something, such as a sin (Lev. 5:5), or to agree on a point or a principle (Rom. 10:9).
c. . . sins of . . Israel, Neh. 1:6.
I will *c.* . . transgressions, Ps. 32:5.
c. with thy mouth, Rom. 10:9.
every tongue shall *c.*, Rom. 14:11.
c. . . name before . . Father, Rev. 3:5.

CONFESSION, admission of a wrong (Dan. 9:4) or agreement with a fact (Rom. 10:10).
make *c.* unto the Lord, Ezra 10:11.
c. . . unto salvation, Rom. 10:10.
witnessed a good *c.*, I Tim. 6:13.

CONFIDENCE, full trust; belief in the reliability of a person or thing.
in quietness and . . *c.*, Is. 30:15.
access with *c.*, Eph. 3:12.
we hold fast the *c.*, Heb. 3:6.
beginning of our *c.*, Heb. 3:14.
this is the *c.* . . we have, I John 5:14.

CONFIDENT, to have trust; be persuaded.
fool rageth, and is *c.*, Prov. 14:16.
We are *c.*, II Cor. 5:8.
Being *c.* of this . . thing, Phil. 1:6.

CONFIRM, to make certain or sure; establish firmly; make valid.
Lord had *c.* him king, I Chr. 14:2.
he shall *c.* the covenant, Dan. 9:27.
C. . . souls of . . disciples, Acts 14:22.
c. the promises made, Rom. 15:8.
ye would *c.* your love, II Cor. 2:8.

CONFLICT, a battle, struggle or contro versy; a collision of interests.
Having the same *c.*, Phil. 1:30.
knew what great *c.*, Col. 2:1.

CONFORMED, to be fashioned the same way. The same form.
to be *c.* to the image, Rom. 8:29.
not *c.* to this world, Rom. 12:2.

CONFOUND, to confuse; to mix; to put to shame; to overthrow.
Lord . . *c.* the language, Gen. 11:9.
lest I *c.* thee, Jer. 1:17.
c. the Jews, Acts 9:22.
he . . shall not be *c.*, I Pet. 2:6.

CONFUSION, embarrassment; perplexity; bewilderment.
My *c.* is . . before me, Ps. 44:15.
their everlasting *c.*, Jer. 20:11.
The city of *c.*, Is. 24:10.
city . . filled with *c.*, Acts 19:29.
God . . not . . author of *c.*, I Cor. 14:33.

CONGREGATION, in the Old Testament this term signifies the Hebrew people collectively as a community bound by religious rather than political bonds (Num. 15:15). Sometimes the term includes foreign settlers (Ex. 12:19). The congregation is considered present in an assembly of its authorized representatives (Ex. 12:3 and 12:21), who thus make necessary group decisions (Judg. 20:1; Josh. 9:15–21). In the New Testament the Christian congregation is the church. *See* CHURCH.
c. of children of Israel, Ex. 16:1.
whole *c.* of Israel, Lev. 4:13.
the *c.* bade stone them, Num. 14:10.
the *c.* of the Lord, Num. 27:17.
the princes of the *c.*, Josh. 22:30.
the *c.* was broken up, Acts 13:43.

CONGREGATION, MOUNT OF, *see* MOUNT OF CONGREGATION.

CONIAH, a name given to king Jehoiachin, king of Judah, who was carried away to Babylon in 597 B.C. *See* JEHOIACHIN.
was the son of Jehoiakim, Jer. 22:24.
called a broken idol, Jer. 22:28.

CONONIAH, an overseer among the Levites in the days of Hezekiah, king of Judah. He had charge of the tithes (II Chr. 31:12, 13).

CONQUER, to have or win the victory.
went forth . . to *c.*, Rev. 6:2.

CONQUER, one who gains the victory by struggle.
we are more than *c.*, Rom. 8:37.

CONSCIENCE, the mental faculty which decides upon the moral quality of one's thoughts and actions. The Scriptures speak of a good, pure and seared conscience (Acts 23:1; I Tim. 3:9; I Cor. 8:7).
being convicted by . . *c.*, John 8:9.
c. also bearing witness, Rom. 2:15.
their *c.* being weak, I Cor. 8:7.

and for *c.* sake, I Cor. 10:28.
I serve .. with pure *c.*, II Tim. 1:3.

CONSECRATE, to devote to or set apart
for some definite purpose.
I will *c.* .. unto the Lord, Mic. 4:13.
Son, who is *c.*, Heb. 7:28.
living way, .. he .. *c.*, Heb. 10:20.

CONSENT, to be willing, to be inclined
to, to assent.
Hearken not .. nor *c.*, I Kin. 20:8.
he *c.* .. in this matter, Dan. 1:14.
I *c.* unto the law, Rom. 7:16.

CONSIDER, to view attentively, or
scrutinize.
the priest shall *c.*, Lev. 13:13.
When I *c.* thy heavens, Ps. 8:3.
c. mine enemies, Ps. 25:19.
I *c.* all the living, Eccles. 4:15.
he *c.*, and turneth, Ezek. 18:28.
but *c.* not the beam, Matt. 7:3.
let us *c.* one another, Heb. 10:24.

CONSIST, to be made up or composed
of. Also **Consisted, Consisting, Consists.**
a man's life *c.*, Luke 12:15.
and by him all things *c.*, Col. 1:17.

CONSOLATION, solace and comfort
given to the stricken and oppressed ones.
"The consolation of Israel" (Luke 2:25)
probably refers to the coming of the
Messiah.
the *c.* of Israel, Luke 2:25.
The son of *c.*, Acts 4:36.
your *c.* and salvation, II Cor. 1:6.
If there be .. any *c.*, Phil. 2:1.

CONSPIRE, to plot something evil or
unlawful. It denotes deceitfulness.
they *c.* .. to slay him, Gen. 37:18.
all .. *c.* against me, I Sam. 22:8.
I *c.* against .. master, II Kin. 10:9.

CONSPIRACY, a combination of persons for an evil purpose.
Absalom's *c.* was, II Sam. 15:12.
a *c.* of her prophets, Ezek. 22:25.
forty who made this *c.*, Acts 23:13.

CONSTANTLY, steadfastly (Titus 3:8).

CONSTRAIN, to press or urge diligently.
she *c.* him to eat bread, II Kin. 4:8.
Jesus *c.* his disciples, Matt. 14:22.
c. you to be circumcised, Gal. 6:12.
love of Christ *c.* us, II Cor. 5:14.

CONSULT, to seek counsel or advice
from; inquire of; take counsel.
David *c.* with .. captains, I Chr. 13:1.
I *c.* with myself, Neh. 5:7.
chief priests *c.*, John 12:10.

CONSUME, to devour, use up or destroy.
famine shall *c.* the land, Gen. 41:30.
the fire hath *c.*, Lev. 6:10.
and heat *c.* the snow, Job 24:19.
a razor .. *c.* the beard, Is. 7:20.
take heed that ye be not *c.*, Gal. 5:15.
God is a *c.* fire, Heb. 12:29.
may *c.* it upon .. lusts, James 4:3.

CONTAIN, to have within itself; hold
within limits.
laver *c.* forty baths, I Kin. 7:38.
bath may *c.* the tenth part, Ezek. 45:11.
c. two or three firkins, John 2:6.
is *c.* in the Scripture, I Pet. 2:6.

CONTEMN, to hate, loathe, or despise.
It denotes disregard and irreverence.
c. the rod of my son, Ezek. 21:10.
a vile person is *c.*, Ps. 15:4.

CONTEMPT, loathing, despising or abhorrence. It denotes disrespect.
He poureth *c.*, Job 12:21.
Remove from me .. *c.*, Ps. 119:22.
some to .. everlasting *c.*, Dan. 12:2.

CONTEMPTIBLE, despicable.
say, table of Lord is *c.*, Mal. 1:7.
his speech *c.*, II Cor. 10:10.

CONTEND, to struggle in opposition; to
compete. To contend for the faith (Jude
3) means "stand up for the faith."
may he *c.* with him, Eccles. 6:10.
canst thou *c.* with horses, Jer. 12:5.
c. .. before the mountains, Mic. 6:1.
c. for the faith, Jude 3.

CONTENT, to be pleased or satisfied
with present conditions or state of being.
Moses was *c.* to dwell, Ex. 2:21.
Moses heard .. was *c.*, Lev. 10:20.
be *c.* with your wages, Luke 3:14.
whatsoever state .. be *c.*, Phil. 4:11.

CONTENTION, a striving in rivalry.
a man of *c.*, Jer. 15:10.
raise .. strife and *c.*, Hab. 1:3.
c. was so sharp, Acts 15:39.
avoid .. *c.*, Titus 3:9.

CONTENTIOUS, quarrelsome.
fire, so is a *c.*, Prov. 26:21.
if any seem to be *c.*, I Cor. 11:16.

CONTENTMENT, a state of satisfaction
godliness with *c.* is gain, I Tim. 6:6.

CONTINUAL, without cessation or in-
termission, to the end.
a *c.* burnt offering, Ex. 29:42.
for the *c.* shewbread, II Chr. 2:4.
lest by her *c.* coming, Luke 18:5.
c. sorrow in heart, Rom. 9:2.

CONTINUALLY, with continuance or
continuity.
for a memorial .. *c.*, Ex. 28:29.
the lamps to burn *c.*, Lev. 24:2.
c. upon thine heart, Prov. 6:21.
sacrifice of praise .. *c.*, Heb. 13:15.

CONTINUANCE, holding, indefinite
time.
in *c.* were fashioned, Ps. 139:16.
who by patient *c.*, Rom. 2:7.

CONTINUE, to go forward or onward in
any course of action; keep on. It often
means to remain (John 2:12).
if he *c.* a day or two, Ex. 21:21.
c. three years without, I Kin. 22:1.
c. in .. work of .. wall, Neh. 5:16.
that *c.* until night, Is. 5:11.
if they *c.* in faith, I Tim. 2:15.
shall *c.* in the Son, I John 2:24.

CONTRADICT, speak against.
spoken by Paul *c.*, Acts 13:45.

CONTRADICTION, speaking against
without all *c.*, less, Heb. 7:7.

CONTRARIWISE, on the contrary.
c. ye ought rather, II Cor. 2:7.
but *c.*, when they saw, Gal. 2:7.
c. blessing, knowing, I Pet. 3:9.

CONTRARY, opposite in nature or
character.
but will walk *c.*, Lev. 26:23.
the *c.* is in thee, Ezek. 16:34.
the wind was *c.*, Mark 6:48.
that is of the *c.* part, Titus 2:8.

CONTRIBUTION, that which is given
out of liberality. It was that which was
given the poor saints of Jerusalem by
those in Macedonia (Rom. 15:26).

CONTRITE, broken in spirit by a sense of
guilt. It induces humility.
a broken and *c.* heart, Ps. 51:17.
of the *c.* ones, Is. 57:15.
and of a *c.* heart, Is. 66:2.

CONTROVERSY, disputation concerning a matter at hand.
matters of *c.*, Deut. 17:8.
the Lord hath a *c.*, Hos. 4:1.
without *c.* great .. mystery, I Tim. 3:16.

CONVENIENT, suitable or appropriate
for a need or situation.
with food *c.* for me, Prov. 30:8.
it seemeth good and *c.*, Jer. 40:4.
a *c.* day was come, Mark 6:21.
things which are not *c.*, Rom. 1:28.

CONVERSATION, an archaic rendering
of several Greek and Hebrew words. It
means citizenship in Phil. 3:20. In other
passages it means conduct (Eph. 4:22;
Heb. 13:5; I Pet. 1:15).
be of upright *c.*, Ps. 37:14.
concerning the former *c.*, Eph. 4:22.
our *c.* is in heaven, Phil. 3:20.
Having your *c.* honest, I Pet. 2:12.
with the filthy *c.*, II Pet. 2:7.

CONVERSION, a turning about, or upon. *See* REGENERATION.
c. of the Gentiles, Acts 15:3.

CONVERT, to turn.
The law of .. Lord .. *c.*, Ps. 19:7.
they .. should be *c.*, Matt. 13:15.
Repent .. and be *c.*, Acts 3:19.
he which *c.* ... sinner, James 5:20.

CONVINCE, to make manifest. In certain places it means to convict (Jude
15).
Which .. *c.* me of sin, John 8:46.
he .. *c.* the Jews, Acts 18:28.

CONVOCATION, a time in which all
Jews were called together and refrained
from any work. An example was the
Sabbath (Lev. 23:1–3), Pentecost (Lev.
23:15–21) and the Day of Atonement
(Lev. 23:24–28).
shall be a holy *c.*, Ex. 12:16.
eighth day shall be .. *c.*, Lev. 23:36.
first day shall be .. *c.*, Num. 28:18.

COOL, wind.
in the *c.* of the day, Gen. 3:8.

COOL, to make cool.

and *c.* my tongue, Luke 16:24.

COOS, a small island in the Aegean Sea (Acts 21:1). It was formerly called Meropis, and was the birthplace of Hippocrates. Paul spent the night there when on his voyage to Judea from Miletus.

COPING, the projecting stones on which the ends of timbers are laid (I Kin. 7:9).

COPPER, a metal abundantly familiar to the Hebrews. Wherever brass, iron and steel are mentioned copper is the metal meant in the original.
vessels of fine *c.*, Ezra 8:27.

COPPERSMITH, brazier.
Alexander the *c.*, II Tim. 4:14.

COPY, a second, double, transcript.
a *c.* of this law, Deut. 17:18.
the *c.* of the letter, Ezra 4:11.
the *c.* . . . was read, Ezra 4:23.

COR, a dry and liquid measure.
bath out of the *c.*, Ezek. 45:14.

CORAL, the skeletons of sea animals used for making jewelry (Job 28:18; Ezek. 27:16).

CORBAN, the term in general use to denote sacrifice (Num. 7:12-17). Jesus censured its abuse (Mark 7:11), calling it men's tradition.
it is *c.*, Mark 7:11.

CORD, rope, twine, string.
bound him with . . *c.*, Judg. 15:13.
c. of affliction, Job 36:8.
c. of his sins, Prov. 5:22.
scourge of a small *c.*, John 2:15.

CORE, the Greek form of Korah. *See* KORAH.
in the gainsaying of *C.*, Jude 11.

CORIANDER, an aromatic plant found in Egypt, Persia, and India, mentioned twice in Scripture (Ex. 16:31; Num. 11:7).

CORINTH, a Grecian city situated upon an isthmus connecting the Peloponnesus and the mainland, forty miles west of Athens. It had two harbors, Cenchrea on the east and Lechaeum on the west.

These made Corinth a center of trade. Cenchrea was mentioned in connection with Paul and Phebe (Acts 18:18; Rom. 16:1). Corinth had a mixed population of Romans, Greeks, and Jews. It was wealthy and immoral. Paul's epistles to the Corinthians form an index of the moral character of the people. It was destroyed by the Romans, B.C. 146, and after 100 years of desolation the new city visited by Paul was built by Julius Caesar, and peopled with freedmen from Rome. Paul lived here for eighteen months, and became acquainted with Aquila and Priscilla. Paul's visit is narrated in Acts 18.
Paul . . came to *C.*, Acts 18:1.
Apollos was at *C.*, Acts 19:1.
I came not . . unto *C.*, II Cor. 1:23.
Erastus abode at *C.*, II Tim. 4:20.

CORINTHIAN, an inhabitant of Corinth.
and many of the *C.*, Acts 18:8.

CORINTHIANS, EPISTLES TO THE, the first letter to the Corinthians was written by Paul at Ephesus about A.D. 55. His purpose in writing was to correct abuses of conduct which was threatening to disrupt the church at that place. When Paul received a letter concerning the problems there (I Cor. 7:1), he proceeded to answer them one by one. Paul's discussion of these problems is meaningful for the churches of all times, because he is concerned with the permanent principles underlying these problems. He discusses the problems related to party rivalries (1:10-4:21), moral disorders (5:1-6:20), marriage and celibacy (7:1-40), idol offerings (8:1-11:1), religious gatherings (11:2-34), spiritual gifts (12:1-14:40), and the resurrection of the dead (15:1-58).
In the second epistle Paul was concerned about a report that Titus had brought to him. He heard that the church was in the main correcting its abuses. But, on the other hand, there were some Judaizers who claimed that they came with a "higher authority." Paul then proceeds to give them a personal defense of himself and his actions (1:12-7:16). By way of encouragement, he mentions the collection for the poor Christians in Jerusalem (8:1-9:15). In the last part, he defends himself against his adversaries (10:1-13:10).

CORMORANT, a pelican, a ceremonially

unclean bird (Lev. 11:17). It is also the name of a plunging bird with a great appetite (Is. 34:11; Zeph. 2:14).
pelican, .. and the *c.*, Deut. 14:17....158
the *c.* and the bittern, Zeph. 2:14....693

CORN, any kind of grain is designated by this word (Gen. 27:28; Deut. 7:13; 8:8).
lay up *c.*, Gen. 41:35.
the offering of the *c.*, Neh. 10:39.
disciples plucked .. *c.*, Luke 6:1.
there was *c.* in Egypt, Acts 7:12.

CORNELIUS, a Roman centurion (commander of 100 men) at Caesarea who worshipped God. He seems to have been worshipping the true God before his conversion (Acts 10:2), and not the pagan deities. He and his household were the first Gentile converts to Christ (Acts 10:1–48), and were received by Peter.
angel appeared to him, Acts 10:3.
sent men to Peter, Acts 10:17.
God heard his prayer, Acts 10:31.

CORNER, wing, angle.
smite *c.* of Moab, Num. 24:17.
c. of sea, Josh. 18:14.
precious *c.* stone, Is. 28:16.
pray, stand in *c.*, Matt. 6:5.
is become head of *c.*, Luke 20:17.
angels .. on four *c.*, Rev. 7:1.

CORNET, a wind instrument made from a ram's horn (Ps. 98:6; Hos. 5:8). The Hebrew word rendered "cornet" is also rendered "trumpet" (Lev. 25:9). Its first mention in the Bible is in connection with the giving of the Law (Ex. 19:16). It was also used on certain special feast days (Lev. 25:9).
they sware .. with *c.*, II Chr. 15:14.
with trumpets and .. *c.*, Ps. 98:6.
the sound of the *c.*, Dan. 3:5.

CORPSE, dead body.
were all dead *c.*, II Kin. 19:35.
end of their *c.*, Nahum 3:3.

CORRECT, to reason with, to instruct.
happy the man God *c.*, Job 5:17.
shall not he *c.*? Ps. 94:10.
Lord loveth he *c.*, Prov. 3:12.
wicked shall *c.* thee, Jer. 2:19.
had fathers .. which *c.*, Heb. 12:9.

CORRECTION, reproof, instruction.

whether for *c.* or, Job 37:13.
as fool to *c.*, Prov. 7:22.
they received no *c.*, Jer. 2:30.
she receiveth not *c.*, Zeph. 3:2.
is profitable for *c.*, II Tim. 3:16.

CORRUPT, bad, polluted, rotten.
my breath is *c.*, Job 17:1.
to your *c.* doings, Ezek. 20:44.
hast *c.* thy wisdom, Ezek. 28:17.
lying and *c.* words, Dan. 2:9.
have *c.* the covenant, Mal. 2:8.
moth and rust doth *c.*, Matt. 6:19.
doth *c.* bring, Luke 6:43.
c. communications, Eph. 4:29.
your riches are *c.*, James 5:2.
did *c.* the earth, Rev. 19:2.

CORRUPTIBLE, pervertible.
made like *c.* man, Rom. 1:23.
to obtain *c.* crown, I Cor. 9:25.
not of *c.* seed, I Pet. 1:23.

CORRUPTION, wasting, depravity, decay.
their *c.* is in them, Lev. 22:25.
I have said to *c.*, Job 17:14.
from pit of *c.*, Is. 38:17.
brought .. life from *c.*, Jonah 2:6.
it is sown in *c.*, I Cor. 15:42.
of the flesh reap *c.*, Gal. 6:8.

CORRUPTION, MOUNT OF, a hill near Jerusalem, where Solomon established high places for the worship of Ashtoreth, Chemosh, and Milcom, which were afterward thrown down by Josiah (II Kin. 23:13). It was probably located just south of the Mount of Olives.

COSAM, the son of Elmodam. He is named in the genealogy of Jesus (Luke 3:28).

COSMETICS, these were used much among the Hebrew women. The painting of the face and eyes is mentioned in II Kin. 9:30 and Ezek. 23:40. It was probably done for the purpose of accenting the eyes (Jer. 4:30). An ocher-red substance, camphire, henna, obtained from a shrub (Song 1:14; 4:13) was used as a nail stain and hair dye.

COST, expense, outlay.
which *c.* me nothing, II Sam. 24:24.
offer .. without *c.*, I Chr. 21:24.
and counteth the *c.*, Luke 14:28.

COTE, an enclosure for flocks (II Chr. 32:28).

COULTER, an agricultural instrument.
the *c.*, and .. forks, I Sam. 13:21.

COUNCIL, a word which usually signifies the Jewish Sanhedrin, a legislative body of 71 members and headed by the high priest. It could condemn to death but could not execute (Matt. 26:3,57). This was done by the Romans alone. Jesus (Matt. 26:59), Peter and John (Acts 4), Stephen (Acts 6:12) and Paul (Acts 22:30) were tried before it.
in danger of the *c.*, Matt. 5:22.
deliver you up to *c.*, Mark 13:9.
called the *c.* together, Acts 5:21.
all that sat in the *c.*, Acts 6:15.
chief priests .. *c.*, Acts 22:30.
Paul .. in the *c.*, Acts 23:6.
I stood before the *c.*, Acts 24:20.

COUNSEL, wisdom or prudence given to one by another.
the *c.* of the princes, Ezra 10:8.
provoked .. with .. *c.*, Ps. 106:43.
Pharisees .. rejected .. *c.*, Luke 7:30.
the *c.* of the heart, I Cor. 4:5.

COUNTENANCE, the appearance of the face.
why is thy *c.* fallen, Gen. 4:6.
Lord lifted .. his *c.*, Num. 6:26.
maketh a cheerful *c.*, Prov. 15:13.
c. was like lightning, Matt. 28:3.

COUNTRY, land, domain.
their *c.* and nations, Gen. 10:20.
in *c.* of Moab, Num. 21:20.
in the plain *c.*, Deut. 4:43.
all the *c.* wept, II Sam. 15:23.
come from far *c.*, II Chr. 6:32.
your *c.* is desolate, Is. 1:7.
in same *c.* shepherds, Luke 2:8.
c. was nourished, Acts 12:20.
they seek a *c.*, Heb. 11:14.

COUNTRY, EAST, *see* **EAST COUNTRY.**

COURAGE, strength, fortitude.
be strong, good *c.*, Deut. 31:6.
good *c.*, play the men, II Sam. 10:12.
wait, be of good *c.*, Ps. 27:14.
his power and his *c.*, Dan. 11:25.
God and took *c.*, Acts 28:15.

COURSE, race, way.

stars in their *c.*, Judg. 5:20.
finish *c.* with joy, Acts 20:24.
c. of this world, Eph. 2:2.
have free *c.*, II Thess. 3:1.
finished my *c.*, II Tim. 4:7.
on fire *c.* of nature, James 3:6.

COURSE OF PRIESTS AND LEVITES, David divided the priests and Levites into 24 orders or courses (I Chr. 24:1-18; 27:1-15). Each course had its own organization and its cycle of one week to perform. On the three great annual festivals, all 24 orders officiated. Zacharias, the father of John the Baptist, belonged to the course of Abia (Luke 1:5).

COURT, an open enclosure connected with a building. There were courts around the temple (I Kin. 6:36; II Kin. 21:5).
the *c.* of the tabernacle, Ex. 27:9.
side of the *c.* gate, Ex. 38:15.
stoned him .. in the *c.*, II Chr. 24:21.
pavement .. for the *c.*, Ezek. 40:17.
c. .. without the temple, Rev. 11:2.

COVENANT, an agreement, compact or league (Gen. 21:27,32; I Sam. 18:3). God's first covenant was with Adam and Eve (Gen. 2:16,17), promising favor for obedience. The second was with Noah (Gen. 9:12-16), promising that the world would never again be destroyed by a flood. Other divine covenants were with Abraham (Gen. 13:17; 17:2,4,7,11,13,14), Israel (Ex. 31:16), the Levites (Mal. 2:4,8), Phineas (Num. 25:12,13) and David (II Sam. 7:15,16). God also gave the new covenant (Jer. 31:31) which was designed for all peoples, not just for Israel. Christ is the mediator of the new covenant (Heb. 8:6-13; 9:1; 12:24) and the Holy Spirit the administrator of it (John 7:39; II Cor. 3:6-9).
I establish my *c.*, Gen. 9:9.
the Lord made a *c.*, Gen. 15:18.
for an everlasting *c.*, Gen. 17:7.
the ark of the *c.*, Num. 10:33.
and kept thy *c.*, Deut. 33:9.
transgressed my *c.*, Josh. 7:11.
make a *c.* with .. God, Ezra 10:3.
I .. make a new *c.*, Jer. 31:31.
Zedekiah .. made a *c.*, Jer. 34:8.
the brotherly *c.*, Amos 1:9.
his holy *c.*, Luke 1:72.
Mediator of a better *c.*, Heb. 8:6.
the blood of the *c.*, Heb. 10:29.

COVENANT, THE ARK OF, it was called "the ark of the covenant" (Num. 10:33; Deut. 31:26; Heb. 9:4), because in it were deposited the two tables of stone, upon which were written the ten commandments. It was also called "the ark of testimony" (Ex. 25:16) and "the ark of God" (I Sam. 3:3; 4:11). The ark was carried by the priests in advance of the hosts (Num. 10:33). The surrounding nations looked upon the ark as the god of Israel (I Sam. 4:6,7). It was captured by the Philistines for a time (I Sam. 4:3-11), but it finally found rest in the temple, when it was completed (I Kin. 8:6-9). It was probably destroyed by the Babylonians (II Esdras 10:21, 22).

COVERT, a covered place which may be used for shelter (Is. 4:6) or for a place of hiding (Job 38:40).
the c. of thy wings, Ps. 61:4.
a c. from storm, Is. 4:6.
He hath forsaken his c., Jer. 25:38.

COVET, to desire inordinately and without regard to rights of others.
Thou shalt not c., Ex. 20:17.
c. fields, and take them, Mic. 2:2.
I c. no man's silver, Acts 20:33.
while some c. after, I Tim. 6:10.

COVETOUS, eagerly desirous.
Pharisees who were c., Luke 16:14.
c. of extortioners, I Cor. 5:10.
lovers of self, c., II Tim. 3:2.
with c. practices, II Pet. 2:14.

COVETOUSNESS, avariciousness.
truth, hating c., Ex. 18:21.
my heart to c., Ps. 119:36.
he that hateth c., Prov. 28:16.
eyes but for c., Jer. 22:17.
beware of c., Luke 12:15.
c. which is idolatry, Col. 3:5.
nor a cloke of c., I Thess. 2:5.
conversation without c., Heb. 13:5.

COW, a full-grown female of the bovine variety of cattle. Cows are mentioned in connection with Levitical laws (Lev. 22:28) and the coming messianic kingdom (Is. 11:7).

COZ, see HAKKOZ.

COZBI, a Midianitess who was slain by Phineas (Num. 25:6-8).

COZEBA, see CHOZEBA.

CRACKNELS, a kind of bread which crumbled easily (I Kin. 14:3).

CRAFT, deceit, work, occupation.
cause c. to prosper, Dan. 8:25.
take him by c., Mark 14:1.
our c. is in danger, Acts 19:27.
of whatsoever c., Rev. 18:22.

CRAFTINESS, cunning.
wise in own c., Job 5:13.
perceived their c., Luke 20:23.
not walking in c., II Cor. 4:2.
cunning c., whereby, Eph. 4:14.

CRAFTY, subtle.
devices of c., Job 5:12.
tongues of c., Job 15:5.
c. counsel against, Ps. 83:3.

CRANE, a wader, migratory, utters a twittering cry, and goes in vast flocks (Is. 38:14; Jer. 8:7).

CREATE, to make, to produce.
c. in me a clean, Ps. 51:10.
the Lord will c., Is. 4:5.
c. fruit of lips, Is. 57:19.
c. new heavens, Is. 65:17.

CREATED, formed, made.
God c. heaven and, Gen. 1:1.
rested .. from c., Gen. 2:3.
day God c. man, Deut. 4:32.
holy one hath c., Is. 41:20.
Lord that c. thee, Is. 43:1.
Lord c. new thing, Jer. 31:22.
c. in righteousness, Eph. 4:24.
meats, God c. to, I Tim. 4:3.
hast c. all things, Rev. 4:11.

CREATION, the Bible begins with the account of God speaking the world into existence (Gen. 1:1-2:3). The things created were the heavens and earth, all forms of life, the heavenly bodies, and the elements (Gen. 1; Ps. 51:10; 148:5; Is. 40:26; Amos 4:13). The New Testament sheds light upon the creation by showing the creative power of Christ, the Word (John 1:1-3).
the beginning of the c., Mark 10:6.
from the c., Rom. 1:20.
the whole c. groaneth, Rom. 8:22.

CREATOR, one who creates. See CREATION.
remember thy c. in, Eccles. 12:1.
Lord, the c. of the, Is. 40:28.

as to a faithful c., I Pet. 4:19.

CREATURE, (1) a created object (Rom. 8:39); (2) humanity individually or collectively (Mark 16:15; Rom. 8:20); (3) an animal (Gen. 1:21,24).
he is a new c., II Cor. 5:17.
nor is there any c., Heb. 4:13.
third part of the c. in, Rev. 8:9.

CREDITOR, one to whom money is owed.
every c. that lendeth, Deut. 15:2.
was a certain c., Luke 7:41.

CREEP, crawl. Also **Creepeth, Creeping.**
among all that c., Lev. 11:31.
c. things praise, Ps. 148:10.
Peter saw c. things, Acts 10:12.
sort are they who c., II Tim. 3:6.

CRESCENS, an assistant of Paul, who left Rome for Galatia (II Tim. 4:10).

CRETANS, inhabitants of **Crete.**

CRETE, a large mountainous island in the Mediterranean midway between Syria and Malta. It was the home of a great civilization in ancient times. Later, Cretans became noted for their military skill and their untruthfulness (Tit. 1:12). Paul sent Titus to Crete to aid in organizing the church there (Titus 1:5,12,14).

CRETES, CRETIANS, inhabitants of **Crete.**

CRIB, see **MANGER.**

CRICKET, see **LOCUST.**

CRIED, screamed, shouted, wept.
Esau c. with a great, Gen. 27:34.
Peter c. saying, Lord, Matt. 14:30.
Jesus c. if any man, John 7:37.
they c. with loud voice, Rev. 6:10.

CRIETH, CRIEST, screams, shouts, weeps.
thy brother's blood c., Gen. 4:10.
send her away, she c., Matt. 15:23.
hire of labourers c., James 5:4.

CRIME, a violation of law.
this is an heinous c., Job 31:11.
answer concerning c., Acts 25:16.

CRIMSON, deep red in color.

your sins be red like c., Is. 1:18.
clothe self with c., Jer. 4:30.

CRIPPLE, a disabled person (Acts 14:8).

CRISPUS, ruler of the Jewish synagogue at Corinth, who was converted by Paul to Christ (Acts 18:8, I Cor. 1:14).

CROCODILE, see **LEVIATHAN.**

CROOKED, (1) bent; (2) false, dishonest.
and c. generation, Deut. 32:5.
which is c. cannot, Eccles. 1:15.
midst of a c. nation, Phil. 2:15.

CROSS, a structure for death by crucifixion. It consisted of two beams attached to one another at right-angles. To the upper part of the cross, over the victim's head, appeared his name (Matt. 27:37). In the preaching of the apostles which followed the resurrection of Jesus the cross symbolized the suffering Jesus underwent for the purpose of saving man (Gal. 6:14; Eph. 2:16). The cross, before Jesus' death, meant *burden of life.* See **CRUCIFIXION.**
let him . . take . . c., Matt. 16:24.
come down from the c., Matt. 27:40.
he bearing the c., John 19:17.
in one body by the c., Eph. 2:16.
the blood of his c., Col. 1:20.

CROWN, a headdress worn for ornamentation or to show high position (Ex. 29:6; Ezek. 21:26). A royal crown was worn by the king (Ps. 21:3; II Sam. 12:30). Jesus wore a crown of thorns at his death (Matt. 27:29) because the people were making fun of his kingship. Christ is described as having been crowned with glory and honor (Heb. 2:9). The Christian, Paul told Timothy, has a crown of righteousness (II Tim. 4:8).
a c. of gold, Ex. 25:11.
their king's c., II Sam. 12:30.
The c. of pride, Is. 28:3.
a c. of thorns, Matt. 27:29.
obtain a corruptible c., I Cor. 9:25.
a c. of righteousness, II Tim. 4:8.
a c. of life, Rev. 2:10.

CRUCIFIED, put to death upon a cross. See **CRUCIFIXION.**
betrayed to be c., Matt. 26:2.
where Jesus was c., John 19:20.
old man is c. with, Rom. 6:6.
we preach Christ c., I Cor. 1:23.

I am *c*. with Christ, Gal. 2:20.

CRUCIFY, to put to death upon a cross. *See* **CRUCIFIXION**.
ye shall kill and *c*., Matt. 23:34.
led him away to *c*., Matt. 27:31.
cried out again, *c*., Mark 15:13.
they *c*. two thieves, Mark 15:27.
cried, *c*. him, *c*. him, Luke 23:21.
they *c*. to themselves, Heb. 6:6.

CRUEL, merciless.
wine as *c*. venom, Deut. 32:33.
jealousy is *c*., Song 8:6.
trial of *c*. mockings, Heb. 11:36.

CRUELTY, barbarous, inhuman treatment.
instruments of *c*. are, Gen. 49:5.
such as breathe out *c*., Ps. 27:12.

CRUMBS, tiny fragments of bread, etc.
dogs eat of the *c*., Mark 7:28.
be fed with *c*., Luke 16:21.

CRUSE, a small vessel for holding water (I Sam. 26:11), oil (I Kin. 17:12), or ointment (Matt. 26:7).

CRUCIFIXION, an ancient method of capital punishment in which the victim was bound alive to a cross. This form of capital punishment was in use among many nations, including the Greeks and the Romans. While stoning was the common Jewish method of execution, the Jews insisted that the Romans crucify Jesus (Matt. 27:22), doubtless because crucifixion was a horrible and accursed death (Deut. 21:23). The cross was designed for slaves and the worse type of malefactors. Jesus was scourged (Matt. 27:26) and then compelled to carry his cross to the place of execution (John 19:17). Crucifixion was slow and painful, death usually being hastened by breaking the victim's legs (John 19:31–33). A cup of vinegar with gall was sometimes given to deaden pain, but Jesus refused this (Matt. 27:34).

CRUSH, compress violently. Also **Crushed**.
not offer what is *c*., Lev. 22:24.
Nebuchadnezzar hath *c*., Jer. 51:34.
kine of Bashan which *c*., Amos 4:1.

CRY, a loud call; an appeal for help.
according to the *c*., Gen. 18:21.

their *c*. is come up, I Sam. 9:16.
when he heard their *c*., Ps. 106:44.
the *c*. of Jerusalem is, Jer. 14:2.
there shall be a *c*., Zeph. 1:10.
at midnight a *c*. made, Matt. 25:6.

CRY, to call loudly, to appeal.
and they *c*. unto me, Ex. 22:23..
I will *c*. to God, Ps. 57:2.
not hear when they *c*., Ezek. 8:18.
avenge elect, who *c*., Luke 18:7.
Spirit, whereby we *c*., Rom. 8:15.
break forth and *c*., Gal. 4:27.

CRYING, calling loudly, appealing.
heard noise of the *c*., I Sam. 4:14.
of one *c*. in wilderness, Matt. 3:3.
prayers with strong *c*., Heb. 5:7.
no more death nor *c*., Rev. 21:4.

CRYSTAL, clear, transparent substance which may be glass (Job 28:17), ice (Ezek. 1:22) or quartz (Rev. 4:6; 22:1).

CUB, (Ezek. 30:5). *See* **CHUB**.

CUBIT, a word derived from the Latin word *cubitum*, denoting the length of the arm to the elbow. An Egyptian cubit was a little more than twenty and a half inches, the Babylonian cubit a little longer, and the Hebrew eighteen inches.
ark .. three hundred *c*., Gen. 6:15.
Goliath .. six *c*., I Sam. 17:4.
the other wing .. five *c*., II Chr. 3:11.
Which .. can add one *c*., Matt. 6:27.

CUCKOW, an unclean bird (Lev. 11:16) of the sea bird variety.
the *c*., and the hawk, Deut. 14:15.

CUCUMBER, there are two kinds of cucumbers in the East, the kind ordinarily known and a tougher, more dry, and less flavorful variety. It was known by the ancient Egyptians and the Hebrews. The Israelites regretted not having this watery vegetable on their thirsty journey through the wilderness (Num. 11:5). In Is. 1:8 a garden of cucumbers is mentioned. The vegetable was so well liked that a lodge was built for the watchman, in order to make certain that the tempting vegetable would eventually get to its rightful owner.

CUD, chewed food. It signifies the food which has returned from the stomach to

be chewed again. Animals that chewed the cud were clean animals (Lev. 11:3).
camel . . cheweth the *c*., Lev. 11:4.
hare . . cheweth the *c*., Lev. 11:6.
swine . . cheweth not the *c*., Lev. 11:7

CUMMIN, an herb cultivated in Palestine for its seeds which are used as seasoning (Matt. 23:23).

CUN, *see* BEROTHAI.

CUNNING, skillful, expert.
Esau was a *c*. hunter, Gen. 25:27.
devise *c*. works in gold, Ex. 31:4.
who is a *c*. player, I Sam. 16:16.
about by *c*. craftiness, Eph. 4:14.

CUP, a vessel for drinking, made in Biblical times from common metals, precious metals, or earthenware (Gen. 44:2; Jer. 19). Figuratively, the word may designate: (1) the contents of a cup (Matt. 26:39); (2) something portioned out, of which one must partake (Ps. 11:6), either suffering (Matt. 20:23) or blessedness (Ps. 16:5; 23:5).
Pharaoh's *c*. was in, Gen. 40:11.
c. of cold water only, Mark 9:41.
let this *c*. pass from, Luke 22:42.

CUPBEARER, a household officer who poured wine for the king (Gen. 41:9; II Kin. 18:17; II Chr. 9:4; Neh. 1:11). Only very reliable men were chosen to avoid danger of poisoning. The position was influential in the court.

CURSE, an invocation for harm to come upon another (Gen. 9:25); evil that comes in response to such a prayer.
put the *c*. upon, Deut. 11:29.
are cursed with a *c*., Mal. 3:9.
themselves under *c*., Acts 23:12.
of law, are under the *c*., Gal. 3:10.

CURSE, (1) to pray for injury upon another (Deut. 23:4); (2) to bring evil upon (Gen. 12:3); (3) to utter profanity or blasphemy (Matt. 26:74).
shall not *c*. ruler of, Ex. 22:28.
bless them that *c*., Luke 6:28.
bless and *c*. not, Rom. 12:14.
therewith *c*. we men, James 3:9.

CURSED, (1) did curse; (2) being under a curse (Gen. 3:17); (3) deserving of a curse (II Pet. 2:14). *See* CURSE.
Shimei who *c*. me with, I Kin. 2:8.

sons have sinned and *c*., Job 1:5.
c. be the man that, Jer. 17:5.
depart from me, ye *c*., Matt. 25:41.

CURSER, one who curses. *See* CURSE.

CUSH, (1) a son of Ham and his descendants (Gen. 10:6–8; I Chr. 1:8–10). (2) The land of the Cushites is undoubtedly Ethiopia and is often called that (II Kin. 19:9; Ezek. 29:10). (3) A Benjamite who was an enemy of David was called Cush (Ps. 7, title).

CUSHAN, the section of Arabia settled by the Cushites (Hab. 3:7). Some have suggested that the name stands for Cushan-rishathaim.

CUSHAN-RISHATHAIM, *see* CHUSHAN-RISHATHAIM.

CUSHI, the father of Zephaniah (Zeph. 1:1). It was also the name of one of the men who informed David of the defeat of Absalom (II Sam. 18:21–23,31,32). Still another with this name was an ancestor of Jehudi (Jer. 36:14).

CUSHITE, a descendant of Cush.

CUSTOM, (1) a toll or tax (Luke 5:27); (2) manner or habit (Luke 4:16); (3) tradition (John 18:39).
pay toll, tribute and *c*., Ezra 4:13.
according to *c*. of, Luke 1:9.
we have no such *c*., I Cor. 11:16.

CUT, sever. To cut off a person from the people was to excommunicate him (Ex. 30:33). Unnatural cutting of the flesh was widely practiced by idolaters (I Kin. 18:28) and mourners of ancient times, but was forbidden by Moses (Lev. 19:28; 21:5). Matt. 5:30 figuratively teaches that Christ and eternal life should be dearest to us. Jesus taught that the heart, not the hand, is source of evil (Mark 7:21).
nor lament, nor *c*., Jer. 16:6.
they were *c*. to heart, Acts 5:33.
thou shalt be *c*. off, Rom. 11:22.
would they were *c*. off, Gal. 5:12.

CUTH, CUTHAH, a city on the Euphrates from which Shalmanezer brought colonists to Samaria (II Kin. 17:24,30).

CYMBAL, a musical instrument of plates of brass which gave a clanging sound (II Sam. 6:5; I Cor. 13:1).
to sound with *c.*, I Chr. 15:19.
with trumpets and . . *c.*, I Chr. 15:28.
the loud *c.*, Ps. 150:5.
a tinkling *c.*, I Cor. 13:1.

CYPRESS, a tree mentioned in Is. 44:14.

CYPRUS, an island in the Mediterranean about forty miles from Cilicia. Its area is slightly under 4000 square miles. It was the native home of Barnabas (Acts 4:36). It was visited by Paul on his first missionary journey (Acts 13:4) and later by Barnabas and John Mark (Acts 15:39).
home of Barnabas, Acts 4:36.
they sailed to *C.*, Acts 13:4.
we sailed under *C.*, Acts 27:4.

CYRENE, a city of northern Africa. A citizen of Cyrene, Simon, was forced to carry Jesus' cross (Matt. 27:32). Cyrenians had a synagogue in Jerusalem (Acts 6:9). Lucius of Antioch was a Cyrenian (Acts 13:1).

CYRENIAN, a native of Cyrene (Mark 15:21; Luke 23:24). The Cyrenians had a Synagogue in Jerusalem (Acts 6:9).

CYRENIUS, *see* QUIRINIUS.

CYRUS, the father of the Persian empire. He released the Jews from captivity in Babylon in 536 B.C. and allowed them to return to their home, an act which Isaiah had foretold over 150 years before (Is. 44:28; 45:1-14). He restored the sacred vessels of the Temple which had been taken to Babylon by Nebuchadnezzar (Ezra 1:1-11; 5:13,14; 6:3).
the first year of *C.*, II Chr. 36:22.
the spirit of *C.*, Ezra 1:1.
C. king of Persia, Ezra 1:8.
called Jehovah's shepherd, Is. 44:28.

D

DABAREH, *see* DABERATH.

DABBASHETH, a town on the border of Zebulum and Issachar (Josh. 19:11).

DABERATH, DABAREH, a Levitical

Damage

town of Issachar (Josh. 19:12; 21; 28; I Chr. 6:72).

DAGGER, a sharp weapon used by Ehud to slay Eglon of Moab (Judg. 3:16-22).

DAGON, the national god of the Philistines (Judg. 16:23) with famous temples at Gaza and Ashdod; thought to have been the face and hands of a man and tail of a fish. The ark of God was taken from Israel by the Philistines and brought to the house of Dagon (I Sam. 5:2-7).

DAILY, day by day, each day.
gathering manna *d.*, Ex. 16:5.
the *d.* burnt offering, Num. 29:6.
give us our *d.* bread, Matt. 6:11.
added to the church *d.*, Acts 2:47.
d. in the temple, Acts 5:42.
searched Scriptures *d.*, Acts 17:11.
Christ needeth not *d.*, Heb. 7:27.

DAINTIES, costly, delicate, and rare luxuries.
Asher yield *d.*, Gen. 49:20.
abhorreth *d.* meat, Job 33:20.
be not desirous of *d.*, Prov. 23:3.
d. are departed, Rev. 18:14.

DALAIAH, a descendant of Judah (I Chr. 3:24). *See* DELAIAH.

DALE, KING'S, name of a valley near Jerusalem (Gen. 14:17; II Sam. 18:18).

DALETH, fourth letter of the Hebrew alphabet.

DALMANUTHA, a town on the west side of the Sea of Galilee (Mark 8:10).

DALMATIA, a Roman province east of the Adriatic Sea (II Tim. 4:10).

DALPHON, second of the ten sons of Haman (Esther 9:7).

DAM, mother.
seven days with *d.*, Ex. 22:30.
not take *d.* with you, Deut. 22:6.

DAMAGE, suffering of loss.
why should *d.* grow, Ezra 4:22.
and drinketh *d.*, Prov. 26:6.
should have no *d.*, Dan. 6:2.
will be with *d.*, Acts 27:10.
d. by us in nothing, II Cor. 7:9.

DAMARIS, a woman of Athens converted by the apostle Paul (Acts 17:34).

DAMASCENES, people of the city of Damascus (II Cor. 11:32).

DAMASCUS, an ancient and most important city of Syria, north of Palestine.
reigned in *D.*, I Kin. 11:24.
Hezion dwelt at *D.*, I Kin. 15:18.
rivers of *D.*, II Kin. 5:12 .
Elisha came to *D.*, II Kin. 8:7ff.
he recovered *D.*, II Kin. 14:28.
King Ahaz at *D.*, II Kin. 16:10–12.
Syrians of *D.*, I Chr. 18:5.
gods of *D.*, II Chr. 28:23.
head of Syria, Is. 7:8.
Samaria as *D.*, Is. 10:9 .
burden of *D.*, Is. 17:1ff.
concerning *D.*, Jer. 49:23ff.
oracle against *D.*, Amos 1:3–5.
Paul converted at *D.*, Acts 9:1–18.
in *D.* the governor, II Cor. 11:32.

DAMNABLE, destructive (II Pet. 2:1).

DAMNATION, judgment, condemnation.
receive greater *d.*, Matt. 23:14.
danger of eternal *d.*, Mark 3:29.
resurrection of *d.*, John 5:29.
whose *d.* is just, Rom. 3:8.
eateth and drink. *d.*, I Cor. 11:29.
having *d.* because, I Tim. 5:12.
d. slumbereth not, II Pet. 2:3.

DAMNED, to be judged, condemned.
believeth not be *d.*, Mark 16:16.
doubteth is *d.*, Rom. 14:23.
d. who believed not, II Thess. 2:12.

DAMSEL, a girl or a young woman.
Rebekah called a *d.*, Gen. 24:14–61 .
laws concerning *d.*, Deut. 22:15–29.
Jesus healed a *d.*, Mark 5:39–41.

DAN, the son of Bilhah, Rachel's maid (Gen. 30:5,6). By the blessing of Jacob on his deathbed it was settled that Dan and his other sons by handmaids should be legally entitled to a portion of the family inheritance. It is stated that Dan shall judge his people but that he shall be a "serpent in the way," an allusion to his craftiness (Gen. 49:16, 17). Of the patriarch himself there are no details of his life.
children of *D.*, Num. 1:38.
camp of *D.*, Num. 2:25.
sons of *D.*, Num. 26:42.

families of *D.*, Num. 26:42.
D. a lion's whelp, Deut. 33:22.
D. remain in ships, Judg. 5:17.

DAN, CITY OF, a city in the north (originally Laish) which was captured by the Danites and given a new name (Judg. 18:29). It was at the northern extremity of the land of Israel as is evidenced by the adage, "from Dan to Beer-sheba." Jeroboam set up a golden calf in Dan (I Kin. 12:28–30). The city was finally destroyed by Benhadad (I Kin. 15:20). It is also mentioned in Jer. 4:15, 8:16. The reference to Dan in Ezek. 27:19 is probably referring to "Vedan" which is thought to be Aden in Arabia.

DAN, TRIBE OF, at the exodus the tribe of Dan numbered sixty-two thousand seven hundred warriors (Num. 1:39). Their position on the journey was on the north of the tabernacle. One of the prominent Danites was Aholiab (Ex. 31:6). Samson was also a Danite (Judg. 13:2). Dan was the last to receive his portion of land in Canaan. It was on the seacoast, and included the cities of Joppa, Lydda, and Ekron. The Danites probably became fishermen (Judg. 5:17). Under the pressure of the Philistines, the Danites moved north into the mountains (Judg. 18:14–29).

DANCE, DANCES, DANCING, a form of rejoicing by twisting and turning with the use of rhythm. The dancing of the Hebrews was primarily a religious exercise. It was generally accompanied by music and song. It was engaged in by both sexes (Ps. 68:25), although mostly by women. Seldom did opposite sexes intermingle. There were occasions when men testified to their joy by dancing (II Sam. 6:5, 14). The dances probably consisted only in circular movements with artless steps, the women beating cymbals and triangles (Judg. 11:34). At the national festivities other instruments were played (Ps. 68:25; 150:4). There is no trace of the public female dancer, as is found in modern days, found in the Bible. The dancing of Herodias's daughter was introduced by the Greeks (Matt. 14:6; Mark 6:22).
timbrels and *d.*, Ex. 15:20.
d. over victories, Judg. 11:34.
singing and *d.*, I Sam. 18:6.

drinking and *d.*, I Sam. 30:16.
their children *d.*, Job 21:11.
mourning turned to *d.*, Ps. 30:11.
praise His name in *d.*, Ps. 149:3.
a time to *d.*, Eccles. 3:4.
virgin rejoice in *d.*, Jer. 31:13.
d. turned to mourning, Lam. 5:15.
ye have not *d.*, Matt. 11:17.
daughter of Herodias *d.*, Matt. 14:6.
music and *d.*, Luke 15:25.

DANCED, DANCING, *see* DANCE.

DANDLED, to play with or to delight in (Is. 66:12).

DANGER, a perilous situation.
in *d.* of judgment, Matt. 5:21.
in *d.* of eternal dam., Mark 3:29.
only craft is in *d.*, Acts 19:27.
d. to be called in, Acts 19:40.

DANGEROUS, to be insecure, perilous (Acts 27:9).

DANIEL, (1) the second son of David by Abigail (I Chr. 3:1); (2) a Levite and descendant of Ithamar associated with Ezra (Ezra 8:2; Neh. 10:6).

DANIEL, a prophet of the Babylonian exile who lived into the Persian period (Dan. 1:21). He entered the service of the royal court with his three companions and received the Chaldean name Belteshazzar (Dan. 1:7). He was a man of God, observing the Law of Moses even when it was opposed to the king's laws; and because of his defiance of the king's decree, he was cast into a lions' den. However God closed the lions' mouths and saved His servant (Dan. 6:16–23). Darius appointed Daniel the first of three presidents over the one hundred and twenty provinces (Dan. 6:1, 2).

DANIEL, BOOK OF, one of the prophetical books of the Old Testament describing the work and visions of Daniel, who lived during the Babylonian exile. The first six chapters deal with his visions during the time of Nebuchadnezzar and the personal history of the prophet to the time of Cyrus. Chapters seven onward deal with Daniel's great prophetic visions.

DANITES, the descendants of Dan, the son of Jacob. These are those belong-

ing to the tribe of Dan (Judg. 13:2; 18:1, 11; I Chr. 12:35).

DAN-JAAN, Dan playing the pipe is the literal meaning of this place between Gilead and Zidon and near Dan (II Sam. 24:6).

DANNAH, a city belonging to the tribe of Judah, located about eight miles from Hebron in the mountains (Josh. 15:49).

DARA, the son of Zerah, son of Judah by Tamar (I Chr. 2:6); the name means bearer or holder.

DARDA, one of four great wise men but inferior in wisdom to Solomon (I Kin. 4:31).

DARE, to have daring, also rendered as durst.
d. ask Him questions, Mark 12:34.
d. no man join, Acts 5:13.
some even would *d.*, Rom. 5:7.
d. any of you, I Cor. 6:1.
d. not bring, Jude 9.

DARIC, a gold coin of Persia, which was in Palestine after the captivity (Ezra 2:69; Neh. 7:70). The name may be derived from "dara," the Persian name for king, or from "Darius, the king" (Darius Hystaspis), who may have coined it. It was worth about five dollars. This rendering also appears for dram in some passages in the Revised Version (I Chr. 29:7; Ezra 2:69; Neh. 7:70). The daric is the first coined money mentioned in the Bible.

DARIUS, the name of three personages in the Old Testament. (1) Darius Hystaspis, called the Great (521–486 B.C.), the restorer of the Persian empire founded by Cyrus the Great. Darius continued the policy of kindness which Cyrus began (Ezra 4:5, 24; Hag. 1:1; Zech. 1:1, 7). (2) Darius the Persian, the last king of Persia (336–330 B.C.), whose empire was destroyed by Alexander the Great. He was probably the same as Darius Codomannus. He is mentioned in Neh. 12:22. (3) Darius the Mede (Dan. 11:1). In Dan. 9:1 he is described as the son of Ahasuerus, and a Persian. He is also described as succeeding Belshazzar (Dan. 5:30, 31).

DARK, signifying the absence of light.
when it was *d.*, Gen. 15:17.
plague be *d.*, Lev. 13:6.
gates began to be *d.*, Neh. 13:19.
having no part *d.*, Luke 11:36.
and it was not *d.*, John 6:17.
Mary came when yet *d.*, John 20:1.
shineth in a *d.* place, II Pet. 1:19.

DARKEN, to be or become dark.
so that land was *d.*, Ex. 10:15.
light is *d.* in heavens, Is. 5:30.
d. earth in clear day, Amos 8:9.
sun be *d.*, Matt. 24:29.
foolish heart was *d.*, Rom. 1:21.
third part was *d.*, Rev. 8:12.

DARKLY, dimly (I Cor. 13:12).

DARKNESS, state of being without
light.
d. His secret place, Ps. 18:11.
such as sit in *d.*, Ps. 107:10.
fool walketh in *d.*, Eccles. 2:14..
a land of *d.*, Jer. 2:31.
a day of *d.*, Joel 2:2.
sun turned into *d.*, Joel 2:31.
not walk in *d.*, John 8:12.
works of *d.*, Eph. 5:11.
called out of *d.*, I Pet. 2:9.
in Him is no *d.*, I John 1:5.

DARKON, a servant of Solomon, whose
descendants returned from the exile in
Babylon with Zerubbabel (Ezra 2:56;
Neh. 7:58).

DARLING, means only, lonely, singly,
united; hence beloved and occurs in
Ps. 22:20; 35:17.

DART, an arrow, light spear, or point.
Joab took three *d.*, II Sam. 18:14.
Hezekiah made *d.*, II Chr. 32:5.
nor the *d.*, cannot hold, Job 41:26.
to quench fiery *d.*, Eph. 6:16.
thrust thro' with a *d.*, Heb. 12:20.

DASH, DASHED, to smite, beat, crush.
right hand, *d.*, Ex. 15:6.
wilt *d.* their children, II Kin. 8:12.
shall *d.* young men, Is. 13:18.
was *d.* on child, Hos. 10:14.

DATHAN, a Reubenite who joined with
Korah, Abiram, and On in a conspiracy
against Moses and Aaron in the wilderness and was swallowed up by the earth

(Num. 16:1–27; 26:9; Deut. 11:6; Ps.
106:17).

DAUB, to plaster or overlay.
she *d.* ark with slime, Ex. 2:3.
d. it with untempered, Ezek. 13:10.
her prophets *d.* them, Ezek. 22:28.

DAUGHTER, is the feminine counter-
part of a son, yet may also designate
a stepsister, niece, or any feminine descendant (Gen. 20:12; 24:48; Num.
25:1; Deut. 23:17). It is also used in
reference to the feminine portions of
communities (Num. 25:1; II Sam. 1:20;
Luke 1:5).
the *d.* of Bethuel, Gen. 24:24.
laws concerning *d.*, Lev. 18:9ff.
d. and inheritances, Num. 36:8.
mount of *d.* of Zion, Is. 10:32.
virgin *d.* of my people, Jer. 14:17 .
married the *d.* of, Mal. 2:11.
my *d.* is even now dead, Matt. 9:18.
d. of Herodias danced, Matt. 14:6.
the *d.* of Zion, Matt. 21:5.
son of Pharaoh's *d.*, Heb. 11:24.

DAUGHTER-IN-LAW, a son's wife.
Sarah his *d.*, Gen. 11:31.
Judah to Tamar his *d.*, Gen. 38:11.
arose with her *d.*, Ruth 1:6.
d. against her mother, Mic. 7:6.
d. against her mother, Matt. 10:35.
mother-in-law against, Luke 12:53.

DAUGHTERS, *see* **DAUGHTER.**
begat sons and *d.*, Gen. 5:4.
sons of God saw *d.*, Gen. 6:2.
turn again, my *d.*, Ruth 1:11.
d. shall prophesy, Joel 2:28.
D. of Jerusalem, Luke 23:28.
d. shall prophesy, Acts 2:17.
God's sons and *d.*, II Cor. 6:18.
whose *d.* are ye, I Pet. 3:6.

DAVID, the second king of Israel, the first
of the tribe of Judah, and in the line of
the Messiah (Matt. 1:6). His birthplace
was Bethlehem (I Sam. 16:1; Luke 2:4).
Besides him there were seven older
brothers and two sisters born to his
father Jesse (I Sam. 16:10). He was also a
descendant of Ruth the Moabitess by
Boaz (Ruth 4:21, 22). David is described
as being ruddy and good looking (I Sam.
16:12). He was a shepherd of the flocks (I
Sam. 16:11). He defended his flock by
killing a lion and a bear and by the help
of God delivered the Israelites from the

Philistines by killing Goliath the giant (I Sam. 17:34–36, 49–51). He soothed King Saul by his playing and was anointed by Samuel to replace Saul as king (I Sam. 16:13, 23). After Saul's death David became king of Judah at Hebron and after seven years became king over all Israel (II Sam. 2:4; 5:5). He conquered Jerusalem (II Sam. 5:7), made it his capital, subdued many surrounding nations, and ruled over all the land God had promised His people from the River of Egypt to the River Euphrates. He died at the age of seventy (II Sam. 5:4).

anointed by Samuel, I Sam. 16:13.
Saul's musician, I Sam. 16:14ff.
marries Michal, I Sam. 18:20ff.
escapes from Saul, I Sam. 19.
covenant with Jon., I Sam. 20:16.
spares Saul's life, I Sam. 26:7ff.
king over Judah, II Sam. 2:4.
takes Jerusalem, II Sam. 5:7.
brings ark to Zion, II Sam. 6:12.
plans to build Temple, II Sam. 7.
episode with Bathsheba, II Sam. 11.
Nathan's parable, II Sam. 12:1ff.
Absalom's rebellion, II Sam. 15.
revolt of Sheba, II Sam. 20.
numbers the people, II Sam. 24:1ff.
Joseph, son of D., Matt. 1:20.
lineage of D., Luke 2:4.

DAVID, CITY OF, an expression for both Bethlehem of Judah, the birthplace and family home of David (Luke 2:4, 11), and the city of Jerusalem (II Sam. 5: 6–8).

DAWN, the break of day.
rose about d. of day, Josh. 6:15.
came woman in d., Judg. 19:26.
I prevented the d., Ps. 119:147.
as it began to d., Matt. 28:1.
till the day d. and the, II Pet. 1:19.

DAY, may designate either the time it takes the earth to make one revolution on its axis or the daylight period between two nights.
God called the light d., Gen. 1:5.
each d. for a year, Num. 14:34.
rebellious from d. I knew, Deut. 9:24.
was no d. like that, Josh. 10:14.
do I wait all the d., Ps. 25:5.
third d. He will raise us, Hos. 6:2.
be raised the third d., Matt. 16:21.
He rose again third d., I Cor. 15:4.

DAY OF ATONEMENT, see ATONEMENT, DAY OF.

DAY OF JUDGMENT, that day at the end of time in which God will judge the world.
tolerable in d. of j., Matt. 10:15.
and Sidon at d. of j., Matt. 11:22.
boldness in d. of j., I John 4:17.

DAY OF THE LORD, (1) that day when Christ shall return to reward His servants and punish the wicked (I Cor. 5:5; I Thess. 5:2,3), (2) a day mentioned in the Old Testament which appears to represent the time God will punish a nation (Amos 5:18; Zeph. 2:2).

DAYSMAN, an umpire or arbitrator (Job 9:33).

DEACON, a word which means servant but which is also used in the New Testament to designate an office in the church. It is first used in Phil. 1:1 in connection with the bishops or elders of the Philippian church. In the New Testament each congregation was organized with elders (also called bishops, shepherds, overseers, or presbyters), who had the qualifications set forth in I Tim. 3 and Titus 1, and with the deacons. The elders were responsible for the oversight of each congregation and the deacons seemingly helped them discharge the business of caring for widows and serving tables (cf. Acts 6: 1ff). The deacons also had qualifications to fill before they could serve (I Tim. 3:8–13).

DEAD, to be without life in this world. The Hebrew word for soul is rendered in some places as dead (Lev. 19:28; 21:1; 22:4). In other places a word meaning the shades (of the dead) is used (Job 26:5; Ps. 88:10; Prov. 2:18). In Judg. 5:27 it is said of a man who fell down dead (destroyed). The English word dead is further the rendering of other words meaning to put to sleep (I Cor. 7:39), and to end (life) (Matt. 2:19; 9:18; Acts 2:29).
bury my d., Gen. 23:4.
cuttings for the d., Lev. 19:28.
be as one d., Num. 12:12.
laid he d. child, I Kin. 3:20.
the d., praise not, Ps. 115:17.
Son of man be risen, Matt. 17:9.
God of the d., Matt. 22:32.
Lazarus raised, John 12:1.

quickeneth the *d.*, Rom. 4:17.
first born from *d.*; Col. 1:18.
I saw the *d.*, Rev. 20:12.

DEADLY, mortal, causing death as deadly enemies (Ps. 17:9), deadly destruction (I Sam. 5:11), deadly poison (James 3:8), deadly wound (Rev. 13:3, 12) or any deadly thing (Mark 16:18).

DEADNESS, state of being dead (Rom. 4:19).

DEAD SEA, a more modern name for what the Bible calls the salt sea (Num. 34:3, 12; Deut. 3:17), the east sea (Ezek. 47:18; Joel 2:20), the former sea (Zech. 14:8), and the sea of the plain (Deut. 3:17; II Kin. 14:25). The name Dead Sea seems to date from about two hundred years after Christ or the second century A.D. It has also been called the Asphalt Sea by some early writers. This sea lies in the southern extremity of the Jordan valley, separating Canaan from Moab. It is fifty-three miles long and an average of nine to ten miles wide. It is the lowest lying sea or lake in the world, being twelve hundred and ninety feet below sea level. It is estimated to be thirteen hundred feet deep in some places. Since it has no outlet, it is very salty and thus was properly called the "salt" sea.

DEAD SEA SCROLLS, those scrolls found in caves south of Jericho in the Dead Sea area and containing Biblical and inter-testamental materials. There are two scrolls of Isaiah, one being complete, most of the first two chapters of Habakkuk, and fragments of all the Old Testament books with the exception of Esther. These findings by archaeology contribute to our possession of some of the oldest texts of the Old Testament, to our understanding of inter-testamental times, and to a better understanding of Hebrew and Aramaic.

DEAF, silent, dull, or incapable of hearing.
who maketh the *d.*, Ex. 4:11.
as a *d.* man, Ps. 38:13.
d. hear words, Is. 29:18.
the *d.* hear, Matt. 11:5.
to Him one *d.*, Mark 7:32.
thou *d.* spirit come out, Mark 9:25.

DEAL, to do or divide.

d. kindly and truly, Gen. 24:49.
shall *d.* with her, Ex. 21:9.
d. thus with me, Num. 11:15.
d. kindly with you, Ruth 1:8.
d. in fury, Ezek. 8:18.
d. subtilly with our, Acts 7:19.
Jews have *d.* with, Acts 25:24.
God *d.* with you, Heb. 12:7.

DEALINGS, association, traffic (John 4:9).

DEAR, carries the meaning of precious (Jer. 31:20), love (Col. 1:13), loved or beloved (Eph. 5:1; Col. 1:7), prized (Acts 20:24), and much prized (Luke 7:2).

DEARTH, famine, scarcity of food.
d. was in all lands, Gen. 41:54.
was a *d.* in land, II Kin. 4:38.
corn because of *d.*, Neh. 5:3.
came a *d.* over all, Acts 7:11.
be a great *d.*, Acts 11:28.

DEATH, the loss of life. *See* **DEAD.**
the *d.* of Abraham, Gen. 25:11.
the common *d.*, Lev. 16:1.
after *d.* of Moses, Josh. 1:1.
after *d.* of Joshua, Judg. 1:1.
gates of *d.*, Job 38:17.
terrors of *d.*, Ps. 55:4.
messengers of *d.*, Prov. 16:14.
redeem them from *d.*, Hos. 13:14.
not taste of *d.*, Matt. 16:28.
no cause of *d.*, Luke 23:22.
loosed the pains of, Acts 2:24.
baptism into his *d.*, Rom. 6:4.
neither *d.* nor life, Rom. 8:38.
d. is swallowed up, I Cor. 15:54.

DEBASE, to make low or to humble (Is. 57:9).

DEBATE, (1) discussion or disagreement; (2) quarrel, strife (Rom. 1:29).
d. cause with neigh., Prov. 25:9.
in measure wilt *d.*, Is. 27:8.
full of envy, *d.*, Rom. 1:29.
lest there be *d.*, II Cor. 12:20.

DEBIR, (1) an Amorite king slain by Joshua (Josh. 10:3), (2) a city of Judah near Hebron and the same as Kirjath-sepher and Kirjath-sannah (Josh. 10:38, 39; 11:21; 12:13), (3) a boundary of the tribe of Gad and called the border of Debir (Josh. 13:26).

DEBORAH, (1) Rebekah's nurse (Gen. 35:8), (2) the only woman judge of Israel. Her story is found in Judg. 4, 5.

DEBT, that which is owed. The Mosaic law emphasized the aiding of the poor (Deut. 15:7), but all loans to fellow Israelites were to be without interest (Deut. 15:2). Usury was looked upon with contempt (Prov. 28:8; Ezek.18:8). Even without interest the creditor was to have great consideration for the debtor. A creditor could not enter a debtor's house and take what he wanted, but he had to wait without (Deut. 24: 10, 11). A debt could not be exacted during the Sabbatic year (Deut. 15:1–15). At other times the hereditary land of the debtor could be taken until the year of Jubilee. Also a debtor's wife and children could be sold as hired servants until the Jubilee year (Lev. 25: 39–41). Debts in the New Testament are pictured as normal (Matt. 25:27).
pay thy *d.*, II Kin. 4:7.
sureties for *d.*, Prov. 22:26.
forgive . . our *d.*, Matt. 6:12.
forgave him the *d.*, Matt. 18:27.
not . . grace, but . . *d.*, Rom. 4:4.

DEBTOR, one who owes something.
restored to *d.* pledge, Ezek. 18:7.
as we forgive our *d.*, Matt. 6:12.
creditor had two *d.*, Luke 7:41.
I am *d.* to the Greeks, Rom. 1:14.
d. to do the whole law, Gal. 5:3.

DECALOGUE, a word made from two Greek words meaning "ten" and "word," therefore meaning the ten words. This term was used by the early Christian Greek writers to designate the ten commandments of the law of Moses.

DECAPOLIS, a district containing ten cities in the northeastern part of Galilee (Matt. 4:25; Mark 5:20; 7:31). The cities were Scythopolis, Hippos, Gadara, Pella, Philadelphia, Gerasa, Dion, Canatha, Raphana, and Damascus. They were first built by the followers of Alexander the Great, and they were rebuilt by the Romans in 65 B.C.

DECAY, has reference to that which is dried up (Job 14:11; Is. 44:26), to that brought low (Eccles. 10:18), to that

made old (Heb. 8:13). See also Lev. 25: 35; Neh. 4:10.

DECEASE, DECEASED, death.
d. they shall not rise, Is. 26:14.
when he married, *d.*, Matt. 22:25.
and spake of his *d.*, Luke 9:31.
after my *d.* in rem., II Pet. 1:15.

DECEIT, guile, deception, or sometimes falsehood.
his mouth is full of, Ps. 10:7.
imagine *d.*, Ps. 38:12.
counsels of the wicked, Prov. 12:5.
no *d.* in his mouth, Is. 53:9 .
balances of *d.*, Hos. 12:7.
full of envy, *d.*, Rom. 1:29.
have used *d.*, Rom. 3:13.
philosophy and vain *d.*, Col. 2:8.

DECEITFUL, full of guile, crookedness, falsehood.
devise *d.* matters, Ps. 35:20.
a *d.* tongue, Ps. 120:2.
the heart is *d.*, Jer. 17:9.
bag of *d.* weights, Mic. 6:11.
false apostles, *d.*, II Cor. 11:13.
the *d.* lusts, Eph. 4:22.

DECEITFULLY, to deal with guile.
sons of Jacob answered, Gen. 34:13.
let not Pharaoh deal *d.*, Ex. 8:29.
thing *d.* gotten, Lev. 6:4.
work of the Lord *d.*, Jer. 48:10.
handling the word of, II Cor. 4:2.

DECEITFULNESS, state of being deceitful.
the *d.* of riches choke, Matt. 13:22.
hardened thro' *d.* of sin, Heb. 3:13.

DECEIVABLENESS, (II Thess. 2:10). Ability to deceive. *See* **DECEIVE.**

DECEIVE, DECEIVED, to mock, lead astray, lie, oppress, entice, or to reason amiss.
your father hath *d.*, Gen. 31:7.
the man that *d.*, Prov. 26:19.
let not Hezekiah *d.*, Is. 36:14.
let not prophets *d.*, Jer. 29:8.
are ye also *d.*, John 7:47.
d. you with vain words, Eph. 5:6.
d. your own selves, James 1:22.
we *d.* ourselves, I John 1:8.
Satan, which *d.*, Rev. 12:9.
he should *d.*, Rev. 20:3.
go out to *d.*, Rev. 20:8.

DECEIVER, one who causes another to err or go astray.
to my father as a *d.*, Gen. 27:12.
deceived and *d.* are his, Job 12:16.
we rem. that *d.* said, Matt. 27:63.
is a *d.* and antichrist, II John 7.

DECENTLY, becoming (I Cor. 14:40).

DECIDE, to determine (I Kin. 20:40).

DECISION, VALLEY OF, the name Joel applies to the Valley of Jehoshaphat (Joel 3:14).

DECK, to beautify or adorn.
d. thyself with majesty, Job 40:10.
I have *d.* my bed, Prov. 7:16.
she *d.* with earrings, Hos. 2:13.
was *d.* with gold, Rev. 17:4.
city that was *d.*, Rev. 18:16.

DECLARATION, a showing, explanation, or exposition (Esther 10:2; Job 13:17; Luke 1:1).

DECLARE, to speak or make known.
my name may be *d.*, Ex. 9:16.
d. to you his covenant, Deut. 4:13.
fishes shall *d.*, Job 12:8.
d. parable of tares, Matt. 13:36.
d. to be the Son, Rom. 1:4.
the day shall *d.* it, I Cor. 3:13.
d. plainly they seek, Heb. 11:14.
have seen *d.* we to, I John 1:3.
message we *d.* unto you, I John 1:5.

DECLINE, to incline or turn aside.
to *d.* after many, Ex. 23:2.
nor *d.* from sentence, Deut. 17:11.
nor have our steps *d.*, Ps. 44:18.
let not heart *d.* to her, Prov. 7:25.

DECREASE, to lessen (Gen. 8:5; Ps. 107:38; John 3:30).

DECREE, the rendering of several Biblical words meaning a bond, law, or statute. These words are sometimes translated law or edict. When a king made a decree, it was published for all to know.
established a *d.*, II Chr. 30:5.
a *d.* for the rain, Job 28:26.
hath made a *d.*, Ps. 148:6.
unrighteous *d.*, Is. 10:1.
by a perpetual *d.*, Jer. 5:22.
d. be far removed, Mic. 7:11.
a *d.* from Caesar, Luke 2:1.

the *d.* of Caesar, Acts 17:7.
d. in his heart, I Cor. 7:37.

DEDAN, (1) a grandson of Cush, the son of Ham, the son of Noah (Gen. 10:7; I Chr. 1:9), (2) a son of Jokshan, son of Abraham by Keturah (Gen. 25:3; I Chr. 1:32), (3) name of the location of the land of the descendants of Dedan, which land probably was that between the Dead Sea and the Persian Gulf (Jer. 25:23; 49:8; Ezek. 25:13; 27:15, 20).

DEDANIM, Dedanites descendants of Raamah, grandson of Ham (Is. 21:13).

DEDICATE, to separate, hallow, or make anew.
spoils did they *d.*, I Chr. 26:27.
I build to *d.* it to, II Chr. 2:4.

DEDICATED, separated or devoted.
a new house, not *d.*, Deut. 20:5.
d. the house, I Kin. 8:63.
nor *d.* without blood, Heb. 9:18.

DEDICATION, the act of dedicating.
at *d.* of this house, Ezra 6:17
at Jerus. feast of *d.*, John 10:22.

DEDICATION, FEAST OF, this festival was instituted by Judas Maccabaeus in 165 or 164 B.C. In I Macc. 4:52-59 it is called "the dedication of the altar." It was a joyous festival, and commemorated the purifying of the temple, the removal of the polluted altar, and the restoration of the worship of Jehovah. It began on the 25th of Chislev, and lasted eight days. The Jews sang the "Hallel," and there was a great illumination of the temple and the houses. The feast was also called the "feast of lights." The rival schools of Jewish thought headed by Hillel and Shammai differed as to the order of the burning of the candles. Shammai taught that eight candles should be used the first night, seven the second night, and so on until there was only one the last night. Hillel chose exactly the opposite order. Our Lord, with doubt, attended this festival at Jerusalem (John 10:22). It is still observed by the Jews.

DEED, an act or work.
done *d.* ought not to, Gen. 20:9.
very *d.* for this cause, Ex. 9:16.
who was mighty in *d*, Luke 24:19.
by *d.* of law no flesh, Rom. 3:20.

hath done this *d.*, I Cor. 5:2.
in word, but in *d.*, I John 3:18.

DEEM, to suspect (Acts 27:27).

DEEP, having great depth.
darkness on face of *d.*, Gen. 1:2.
fountains of *d.* were stop., Gen. 8:2.
dried waters of *d.*, Is. 51:10.
make their waters *d.*, Ezek. 32:14.
I was in a *d.* sleep, Dan. 8:18.
who descend into *d.*, Rom. 10:7.
search *d.* things, I Cor. 2:10.
night and day in *d.*, II Cor. 11:25.

DEEPER, to a greater depth.
it is *d.* than hell, Job 11:8.
a people of *d.* speech, Is. 33:19.

DEEPLY, characterized by depth.
Israel have *d.* revolted, Is. 31:6.
they have *d.* corrupted, Hos. 9:9.
Jesus sighed *d.*, Mark 8:12.

DEEPNESS, the state of being deep (Matt. 13:5).

DEER, FALLOW, *see* **FALLOW DEER.**

DEFAME, to speak injuriously (I Cor. 4:13).

DEFEAT, to break, frustrate, or make void (II Sam. 15:34; 17:14).

DEFENCE, a fortress, apology, or covering.
cities for *d.*, II Chr. 11:5.
Almighty shall make thy *d.*, Job 22:25.
the Lord is our *d.*, Ps. 89:18.
brooks of *d.*, Is. 19:6.
made his *d.*, Acts 19:33.
hear ye my *d.*, Acts 22:1.
d. and confirmation, Phil. 1:7.
d. of the gospel, Phil. 1:17.

DEFENCED, to be fenced off (Is. 25:2; 27:10; Jer. 1:18; 4:5).

DEFEND, to hedge about, save, deliver.
arose to *d.* Israel, Judg. 10:1.
I will *d.* this city, II Kin. 19:34.
Lord shall *d.* them, Zech. 9:15.
he *d.* him, and, Acts 7:24.

DEFER, to prolong, tarry, or be behind.
hope *d.* maketh sick, Prov. 13:12.
discretion *d.* anger, Prov. 19:11.
vowest *d.* not to, Eccles. 5:4.

d. not, for own sake, Dan. 9:19.
Felix *d.* them, Acts 24:22.

DEFILE, to pollute, make profane, render unclean, or corrupt.
he had *d.* Dinah, Gen. 34:5.
neither shall ye *d.*, Lev. 11:44.
d. my sanctuaries, Ezek. 28:18.
lest they should be *d.*, John 18:28.
conscience is *d.*, I Cor. 8:7.
dreamers *d.* the flesh, Jude 8.

DEFILED, unclean, polluted.
he shall be *d.*, Lev. 13:46.
d. by the dead, Num. 5:2.
Israel is *d.*, Hos. 5:3.
eat with *d.* hands, Mark 7:2.

DEFRAUD, to deprive, cheat.
shalt not *d.* neighbor, Lev. 19:13.
d. not, Mark 10:19.
rather suffer to be *d.*, I Cor. 6:7.
d. not, except with, I Cor. 7:5.
we have *d.* no man, II Cor. 7:2.
no man *d.* his brother, I Thess. 4:6.

DEFY, to be indignant; to reproach.
curse me Jacob, *d.*, Num. 23:7.
I *d.* armies of Israel, I Sam. 17:10.
that he should *d.* armies, I Sam. 17:26.
God whom hast *d.*, I Sam. 17:45.
when they *d.* Philistines, II Sam. 23:9.

DEGENERATE, degraded (Jer. 2:21).

DEGREE, a going up; rank; a unit.
low *d.* vanity, high *d.*, Ps. 62:9.
back ten *d.*, Is. 38:8.
them of low *d.*, Luke 1:52.
purchase a good *d.*, I Tim. 3:13.
brother of low *d.*, James 1:9.

DEGREES, SONG OF, a title given to Psalms 120 through 134 meaning the song of steps. Cf. Ps. 121 for a good illustration of the step style.

DEHAVITES, DEHAITES, a people whom the king of Assyria transported to Samaria at the captivity of Israel (Ezra 4:9).

DEKAR, DEKER, the father of one of Solomon's officers (I Kin. 4:9).

DELAIAH, (1) a priest under the rule of David (I Chr. 24:18), (2) the head of a family (Ezra 2:60; Neh. 7:62); one who sought to dishearten Nehemiah (Neh.

6:10); a prince in Judah during Jehoiakim's reign (Jer. 36:12, 25).

DELAY, to keep back; linger.
not *d.* to offer, Ex. 22:29.
Moses *d.* to come down, Ex. 32:1.
d. not to keep, Ps. 119:60.
Lord *d.*, Matt. 24:48.
not *d.* to come to them, Acts 9:38.
without *d.* morrow I sat, Acts 25:17.

DELECTABLE, delightful (Is. 44:9).

DELICACY, wantonness (Rev. 18:3).

DELICATE, dainty or luxurious.
the *d.* man or, Deut. 28:54.
no more be called *d.*, Is. 47:1.
likened Zion to *d.*, Jer. 6:2.
bald for thy *d.*, Mic. 1:16.

DELICATELY, an adverb meaning dainty in I Sam. 15:32; Lam. 4:5 and pleasure in Luke 7:25.

DELICIOUSLY, wantonly (Rev. 18:7).

DELIGHT, (1) pleasure; (2) take pleasure.
no *d.* in a wife, Deut. 21:14.
his *d.* is in the law of, Ps. 1:2.
they *d.* in lies, Ps. 62:4.
scorners *d.* in their, Prov. 1:22 .
upright are his *d.*, Prov. 11:20.
call the sabbath a *d.*, Is. 58:13.
d. in the law of God, Rom. 7:22.

DELILAH, a woman of Philistia in whom Samson delighted. She betrayed him to the Philistines (Judg. 16:4–18), by discovering the source of his strength.

DELIVER, to free, redeem, save.
I will *d.* the inhabit., Ex. 23:31.
I will *d.* this multi., I Kin. 20:13.
none can *d.* out, Job 10:7.
d. soul from going into, Job 33:28.
d. my soul, Ps. 6:4.
residue will I *d.*, Jer. 15:9.
to *d.* any man to die, Acts 25:16.
d. such a one to Satan, I Cor. 5:5.
death, and doth *d.*, II Cor. 1:10.
Lord know how to *d.*, II Pet. 2:9.

DELIVERANCE, the act of delivering.
to save by a great *d.*, Gen. 45:7.
saved by a great *d.*, I Chr. 11:14.
to preach *d.* to, Luke 4:18.

not accepting *d.*, Heb. 11:35.

DELIVERER, one who delivers.
raised up *d.* to, Judg. 3:9.
thou art my *d.*, Ps. 40:17.
my fortress and my *d.*, Ps. 144:2.
did God send to be a *d.*, Acts 7:35.
come out of Sion *d.*, Rom. 11:26.

DELIVERY, bearing. (Is. 26:17).

DELUGE, *see* FLOOD.

DELUSION, vexations (Is. 66:4) or error (II Thess. 2:11).

DEMAND, request strongly.
d. of thee, Job 38:3.
Soldi. *d.* what shall, Luke 3:14.
when he was *d.* of, Luke 17:20.
d. who he was, Acts 21:33.

DEMAS, a worker with Paul who later forsook him (II Tim. 4:10).
Demas, greet you, Col. 4:14.
Demas, Lucas, my, Philem. 24.

DEMETRIUS, (1) an Ephesian silversmith who bitterly opposed Paul (Acts 19:24, 38), (2) a Christian of good report among all (III John 12).

DEMONS, from the Greek *daimon.* It is used once in the New Testament (Acts 17:18) for deity, but is usually used for inferior spiritual beings, angels who sinned (Matt. 25:41; Rev. 12:7). They are the ministers of the devil in Luke 4:35; 9:1; John 10:21. Satan is called the "prince of devils" (Matt. 9:34; Mark 3:22; Luke 11:15). Demons had the power to afflict men with disease. They recognized Jesus as the Son of God (Matt. 8:29). According to Jewish opinion, which passed over to the Christians, the gods of the nations were demons. The demons are represented as reserved in chains until the judgment (Jude 6; II Pet. 2:4).

DEMONIAC, the word means to be under the power of a demon, and it is frequently used in the New Testament but commonly rendered "possessed with a devil."

DEMONSTRATION, a showing or pointing out (I Cor. 2:4).

DEN, a hole, cave, or pit.

Daniel in the lions' *d.*, Dan. 6:7f.
a *d.* of robbers, Jer. 7:11.
Judah a *d.* of dragons, Jer. 10:22.
a young lion cry out, Amos 3:4.
a *d.* of thieves, Mark 11:17.
d. and caves, Heb. 11:38.
in the *d.* and rocks, Rev. 6:15.

DENARIUS, a pence or penny. It was a Roman silver coin used in the time of Christ.

DENOUNCE, to put before (Deut. 30:18).

DENY, to disown or withhold.
lest ye *d.* your God, Josh. 24:27.
I be full and *d.*, Prov. 30:9.
him will I *d.*, Matt. 10:33.
let him *d.* himself, Matt. 16:24.
d. me thrice, Matt. 26:34.
he cannot *d.* himself, II Tim. 2:13.
in works they *d.* him, Titus 1:16.

DEPART, to go, leave, withdraw.
sceptre shall not *d.*, Gen. 49:10.
book of the law, Josh. 1:8.
d. from evil, and do, Ps. 34:14.
my words shall not *d.*, Is. 59:21.
the diseases *d.*, Acts 19:12.
having a desire to *d.*, Phil. 1:23.
d. from iniquity, II Tim. 2:19.
d. for a season, Philem. 1:15.

DEPARTURE, leaving (Ezek. 26:18; II Tim. 4:6).

DEPOSED, to be put down (Dan. 5:20).

DEPRAVITY, a theological word which denotes man's sinful nature, usually in connection with the doctrine of original sin.

DEPRIVE, to forget, be lacking, or bereaved (Gen. 27:45; Job 39:17).

DEPTH, deep place; abyss.
d. have covered them, Ex. 15:5.
the *d.* were troubled, Ps. 77:16.
in the *d.* of hell, Prov. 9:18.
d. of the riches, Rom. 11:33.
length, and *d.*, Eph. 3:18.
the *d.* of Satan, Rev. 2:24.

DEPUTY, a governor or pro-consul.
a *d.* was king, I Kin. 22:47.
to turn *d.*, Acts 13:8.
Gallio *d.* of Achaia, Acts 18:12.

DERBE, a city of Lycaonia in Asia Minor which Paul visited on his first missionary tour (Acts 14:6, 20), to which he later returned (Acts 16:1), and also the home of Gaius (Acts 20:4).

DERIDE, to laugh at (Hab. 1:10) or to turn up the nose at (Luke 16:14; 23:35).

DERISION, scorn.
a *d.* to them, Ps. 44:13.
in *d.* daily, Jer. 20:7.
a *d.* to all my people, Lam. 3:14.
be their *d.* in Egypt, Hos. 7:16.

DESCEND, to come down.
angels of God, Gen. 28:12.
d. from the mountain, Josh. 2:23.
up into heaven, or *d.*, Prov. 30:4.
Spirit of God *d.*, Matt. 3:16.
angel of the Lord *d.*, Matt. 28:2.
see the Spirit *d.*, John 1:33.
d. into the deep, Rom. 10:7.
Lord himself shall, I Thess. 4:16.

DESCENT, (1) a coming down (Luke 19:37), (2) genealogy (Heb. 7:3, 6).

DESCRIBE, to write or say; explain.
land and *d.* it, Josh. 18:4.
d. to him the princes, Judg. 8:14.
d. the blessedness, Rom. 4:6.
d. righteousness of law, Rom. 10:5.

DESCRY, to spy out (Judg. 1:23).

DESERT, recompense or judgment (Ps. 28:4; Ezek. 7:27).

DESERT, either a dry or uninhabited place, a plain, or a wilderness.
three days' journey into *d.*, Ex. 5:3.
grieve him in *d.*, Ps. 78:40.
Chaldea shall be a *d.*, Jer. 50:12.
behold, he is in *d.*, Matt. 24:26.
departed into a *d.* place, Mark 6:32.
they wandered in *d.*, Heb. 11:38.

DESERT OF THE SEA, an unknown part of Arabia (Is. 21:1).

DESERVING, a recompense according to deeds (Judg. 9:16).

DESIRABLE, pleasing (Ezek. 23:6).

DESIRE, to delight in or long for.
thy *d.* to thy husband, Gen. 3:16.

all the *d*. of thy, I Sam. 23:20.
d. to fear thy name, Neh. 1:11.
the *d*. of thine heart, Ps. 37:4.
d. of the righteous, Prov. 11:23.
Lazarus *d*. the crumbs, Luke 16:21.
d. to find a tabernacle, Acts 7:46.
my heart's *d*. and, Rom. 10:1.
d. the office of a, I Tim. 3:1.
shall *d*. to die, Rev. 9:6.

DESIROUS, governed by desire.
not *d*. of his dainties, Prov. 23:3.
was *d*. to see him, Luke 23:8.
d. to apprehend me, II Cor. 11:32.
not be *d*. of, Gal. 5:26.
affectionately *d*. of you, I Thess. 2:8.

DESOLATE, waste, lonely.
whole land shall be *d*., Jer. 4:27.
mountain of Zion is *d*., Lam. 5:18.
land of Egypt shall be, Ezek. 29:9.
Samaria shall become, Hos. 13:16.
Edom shall be a *d*., Joel 3:19.
his habitation be *d*., Acts 1:20.
the *d*. hath many more, Gal. 4:27.
a widow and *d*., I Tim. 5:5.
make her *d*. and, Rev. 17:16.
in one hour she is, Rev. 18:19.

DESOLATION, a waste.
your sanctuaries unto *d*., Lev. 26:31f.
what *d*. he hath made, Ps. 46:8.
shall become a *d*., Jer. 22:5.
in Babylon become a, Jer. 50:23.
Nineveh a *d*., Zeph. 2:13.
abomination of *d*., Matt. 24:15.
know that the *d*., Luke 21:20.

DESPAIR, to be hopeless.
Saul *d*. of me, I Sam. 27:1.
to cause my heart to *d*., Eccles. 2:20.
we *d*. even of life, II Cor. 1:8.
perplexed, not in *d*., II Cor. 4:8.

DESPERATE, despairing, rash. (Job 6:
26; Is. 17:11; Jer. 17:9).

DESPISE, to hold in contempt, esteem
lightly, dishonor, push aside.
her mistress was *d*., Gen. 16:4.
d. my statutes, Lev. 26:15.
she *d*. him in her, II Sam. 6:16.
whoso *d*. the word, Prov. 13:13.

ye *d*. this word, Is. 30:12.
and *d*. the other, Matt. 6:24.
he therefore that *d*., I Thess. 4:8.
d. the shame, Heb. 12:2.
d. dominion, and speak, Jude 8.

DESPISER, one who thinks down upon
another.
behold ye *d*., Acts 13:41.
d. of those that, II Tim. 3:3.

DESPISETH, *see* **DESPISE.**

DESPITE, spite, malice.
d. against Israel, Ezek. 25:6.
d. unto Spirit, Heb. 10:29.

DESPITEFUL, spiteful.
with *d*. heart, Ezek. 25:15.
d., proud, boasters, Rom. 1:30.

DESPITEFULLY, malignantly.
them which *d*. use, Matt. 5:44.
use them *d*., and to, Acts 14:5.

DESTITUTE, devoid, lacking, in want,
forsaken.
prayer of the *d*., Ps. 102:17.
minds, *d*. of truth, I Tim. 6:5.
being *d*., afflicted, Heb. 11:37.
d. of daily food, Jas. 2:15.

DESTROY, to cut off, consume or make
desolate.
I will *d*. man, Gen. 6:7.
be a flood to *d*., Gen. 9:11ff.
shall utterly *d*. all, Deut. 12:2f.
Jews slew and *d*., Esther 9:6ff.
d. them that speak, Ps. 5:6.
ask Barabbas, and *d*., Matt. 27:20.
will *d*. the wisdom, I Cor. 1:19.
d. the first born, Heb. 11:28.

DESTROYED, *see* **DESTROY.**
Egypt is *d*., Ex. 10:7.
d. for lack of knowledge, Hos. 4:6.
d. of the destroyer, I Cor. 10:10.
to be taken and *d*., II Pet. 2:12.

DESTROYER, one who corrupts, or tears
down.
d. come into houses, Ex. 12:23.
the *d*. of our country, Judg. 16:24.
in prosperity *d*. come, Job 15:21.
is companion of a *d*., Prov. 28:24.
d. of Gentiles is, Jer. 4:7.
were destroyed of *d*., I Cor. 10:10.

DESTROYING, Is. 28:2; Jer. 51:25.

DESTRUCTION, demolition, ruin.
d. and death say, Job 28:22.
d. of the poor, Prov. 10:15.
pride goeth before *d*., Prov. 16:18.
Hell and *d*. are never, Prov. 27:20.

a cry of *d.*, Is. 15:5.
vessels of wrath fitted, Rom. 9:22.
whose end is *d.*, Phil. 3:19.
bring swift *d.*, II Pet. 2:1.
their own *d.*, II Pet. 3:16.

DETAIN, to restrain or keep in.
d. me I will not eat, Judg. 13:16.
d. was that day *d.*, I Sam. 21:7.

DETERMINATE, definite (Acts 2:23).

DETERMINATION, decision (Zeph. 3:8).

DETERMINE, resolve.
Solomon *d.* to build, II Chr. 2:1.
his days are *d.*, Job 14:5.
seventy weeks are *d.*, Dan. 9:24.
when he was *d.*, Acts 3:13.
hath *d.* the times, Acts 17:26.
d. not to know any, I Cor. 2:2.

DETEST, to hold as abominable (Deut. 7:26).

DETESTABLE, abominable.
shall take away *d.*, Ezek. 11:18.
heart walk after their *d.*, Ezek. 11:21.
no more defile with *d.*, Ezek. 37:23.

DEUEL, the father of Eliasaph, the captain of the tribe of Gad at the numbering of the people at Sinai (Num. 1:14; 2:14; 7:42, 47).

DEUTERONOMY, BOOK OF, the name of this book comes from *deuteros,* meaning second, and *nomos,* meaning law. The content shows that it is a repetition of the civil and moral law, which was a second time delivered to Moses, with some additions and explanations. In Deuteronomy Moses delivers three addresses and brings the story of his own life to a close. Another writer evidently fills in the details of the death of Moses. In the "plains of Moab" the children of Israel stood before Moses and heard these last words from his lips. The book mentions several events which took place between Egypt and their reaching the plains of Moab; it also gives exhortation for obedience in the future. Moses himself was not permitted to cross over into the "promised land," for he had failed to sanctify the Lord at Meribah-Kadesh.

The Messiah is explicitly foretold in this book (Deut. 18:15). Christ and the Apostles quoted very extensively from this book. All Christ's answers to Satan's tempting are from this book; and the voice from heaven, directing the Apostles to hearken to Him, refers to a prophecy of Him in Deut. 18:15. It was this prophecy which was recalled when Philip told Nathanael about Jesus (John 1:45), and it was referred to when Peter preached on Solomon's porch (Acts 3:12). The Shema (Deut. 6:4–9) is repeated every day by the Jews all over the world. It was this passage that Jesus quoted as the greatest commandment of the Law (Matt. 22:36–38). The book of Deuteronomy is profitable reading for the Christian who desires to study the Law.

DEVICE, thought, plan, or counsel.
d. which ye wrongfully, Job 21:27.
maketh the *d.* of, Ps. 33:10.
no work, nor *d.*, Eccles. 9:10.
shall forecast his *d.*, Dan. 11:24f.
art and man's *d.*, Acts 17:29.
not ignorant of his, II Cor. 2:11.

DEVIL, the rendering of several Hebrew and Greek words for an evil spiritual being. It is found in both the singular and plural, for the greatest of all fallen beings and for devils in general. The word used for devils in Lev. 17:7 and II Chr. 11:15 means hairy, a kid, or a goat. In Deut. 32:17 and Ps. 106:37 another word is used with the meaning of spoiler or destroyer. A number of New Testament references for devil (or devils) are the renderings of words that mean shade, defiled spirit, or accuser.
tempted of the *d.*, Matt. 4:1ff.
have cast out *d.*, Matt. 7:22.
the prince of the *d.*, Matt. 9:34.
sowed them is the *d.*, Matt. 13:39.
d. out of her daughter, Mark 7:26.
driven of the *d.*, Luke 8:29.
can a *d.* open, John 10:21.
give place to the *d.*, Eph. 4:27.
the *d.* also believe, James 2:19.
contending with the *d.*, Jude 9.
should not worship *d.*, Rev. 9:20.
old servant, called the, Rev. 12:9.
d. that deceived, Rev. 20:10.

DEVILISH. (James 3:15), Satanic, wicked.

DEVISE, to think, design, or purpose.
to *d.* cunning works, Ex. 31:4.

d. not evil against, Prov. 3:29.
do they not err that, Prov. 14:22.
he that *d.* to do, Prov. 24:8.
Lord hath both *d.*, Jer. 51:12.
woe to them that *d.*, Mic. 2:1.
cunningly *d.* fables, II Pet. 1:16.

DEVOTE, to vow, to set apart, to consecrate. Also **Devoted.**
as a field *d.*, Lev. 27:21.
d. thing is holy, Lev. 27:28.
everything *d.* in Israel, Num. 18:14.

DEVOTION, the object of worship of the Athenians (Acts 17:23).

DEVOUR, to eat, consume.
seven thin ears *d.*, Gen. 41:7.
d. the strength of the, Job 18:13.
to *d.* the poor, Prov. 30:14.
d. the palaces of, Jer. 17:27.
fowls of the air *d.*, Luke 8:5.
seeking whom he may *d.*, I Pet. 5:8.
to *d.* her child, Rev. 12:4.

DEVOUT, reverential.
was just and *d.*, Luke 2:25.
d. men car. Steph. to, Acts 8:2.
Cornelius, Acts 10:2.
stirred up *d.* women, Acts 13:50.
Ananias a *d.* man, Acts. 22:12.

DEW, early morning moisture.
morning the *d.* lay, Ex. 16:13.
his heavens shall drop *d.*, Deut. 33:28.
d. lay on my branch, Job 29:19.
clouds drop down *d.*, Prov. 3:20.
early *d.* it goeth, Hos. 6:4.
heaven stayed from *d.*, Hag. 1:10.
heavens give their *d.*, Zech. 8:12.

DIADEM, the rendering of several Biblical words which refers to something about the head (Job 29:14; Is. 62:3), a royal tiara (Is. 28:5), or to perhaps the tiara of the high priest (Ezek. 21:26).

DIAL, SUN DIAL, an instrument for the measurement of time. The Bible mentions one built by Ahaz (II Kin. 20:11; Is. 38:8). It is also called the "steps of Ahaz" and probably consisted of an obelisk at the foot of about twenty steps, so constructed that the shadow fell on the highest step at noon and on the lowest step on either side in the morning and evening.

DIAMOND, a precious stone more frequently called adamant in the Bible. The word adamant means invincible and is the source of our word diamond. A diamond point was also used for writing on hard materials.
second row a *d.*, Ex. 28:18.
written with point of *d.*, Jer. 17:1.
the *d.* the beryl, Ezek. 28:13.

DIANA OF THE EPHESIANS, a Greek goddess more commonly called Artemis. She was the mother-goddess, an emblem of fertility. Her chief temple, located in Ephesus, was one of the seven wonders of the ancient world. There was an idol of her in this temple probably carved out of a meteorite. Smaller idols were used in her worship by individuals and thus furnished a good business for silversmiths.
silver shrines for *D.*, Acts 19:24.
great is *D.*, of the, Acts 19:28.

DIBLAH, *see* **DIBLATH.**

DIBLIAM, the name of the father of Gomer, the wife of Hosea (Hos. 1:3).

DIBLATH, DIBLAH, a place mentioned only in Ezek. 6:14. It is described as being located in the northern extremity of Palestine. The correct reading is probably Riblah.

DIBON, DIBON-GAD, a Moabite town on the east side of the Jordan which was taken over and rebuilt by the children of Gad. Later, in the time of Isaiah and Jeremiah, it was repossessed by Moab. The Moabite Stone was found here in 1868.
perished even to *D.*, Num. 21:30.
children of Gad built *D.*, Num. 32:34.

DIBRI, a Danite, father of Shelomith, a woman whose son was stoned to death for blasphemy (Lev. 24:11).

DIDYMUS, *see* **THOMAS.**

DIE, to expire, to lose life. The Bible views the death of a man as the time when the soul is separated from the body (James 2:26).
in earth shall *d.*, Gen. 6:17.
shall *d.* in sins, John 8:24.
to men once to *d.*, Heb. 9:27.

DIED, the state of having lost life.

all flesh *d.*, Gen. 7:21.
due time Christ *d.*, Rom. 5:6.

DIET, the food and drink regularly consumed (Jer. 52:34).

DIETH, *see* **DIE.**

DIFFER, to be unlike, to disagree.
maketh thee to *d.*, I Cor. 4:7.

DIFFERENCE, the state of unlikeness.
Lord out a *d.* between, Ex. 11:7.
put no *d.* between, Acts 15:9.

DIG, DIGGED, to excavate, to unearth.
witness that I have *d.*, Gen. 21:30.
if a man *d.* a pit, Ex. 21:33.
d. in the earth, Matt. 25:18.

DIGNITIES, in Greek it is the plural of glories. A person higher in honor.
speak evil of *d.*, II Pet. 2:10.

DIGNITY, exalted in character.
art excellency of *d.*, Gen. 49:3
folly is set in *d.*, Eccles. 10:6..
d. shall proceed of, Hab. 1:7.

DIKLAH, the name of a son of Joktan. (Gen. 10:27; I Chr. 1:21).

DILEAN, a town in the low country of Judah (Josh. 15:38).

DILIGENCE, quality of being diligent.
thy heart with all *d.*, Prov. 4:23.
giving all *d.* to add, II Pet. 1:5.

DILIGENT, giving persevering attention, industrious, busy.
now much more *d.*, II Cor. 8:22.
d. that ye be found, II Pet. 3:14..

DILIGENTLY, done in a diligent manner.
wilt *d.* hearken to Ex. 15:26.
taught *d.* the things, Acts 18:25.
the prophets sought *d.*, I Pet. 1:10.

DILL, *see* **ANISE.**

DIM, not bright or distinct, weak.
eyes of Israel were *d.*, Gen. 48:10.
is gold become *d.*, Lam. 4:1.

DIMINISH, to make less, to degrade.
you shall not *d.* ought, Ex. 5:8.
will I also *d.* thee, Ezek. 5:11.

DIMNAH, a Levitical city in Zebulun (Josh. 21:35). It is also called Rimmon (I Chron. 6:77).

DIMON, a place east of the Dead Sea in Moab which was denounced by Isaiah (Is. 15:9). The place may be the same as Dibon.

DIMONAH, a city in the south of Judah (Josh. 15:22). It may be the same as the Dibon of Neh. 11:25.

DINAH, the daughter of Jacob by Leah, a full sister of Simeon and Levi (Gen. 30: 21). Genesis tells of her being seduced by Shechem, a Hivite prince, and of the consequent destruction of the Shechemites by Simeon and Levi (Gen. 34).

DINAITES, a people settled in Samaria after it was taken by the Assyrians (Ezra 4:9).

DINE, to take dinner.
these men shall *d.*, Gen. 43:16.
besought him to *d.*, Luke 11:37.

DINHABAH, the capital city of king Bela of Edom. (Gen. 36:32; I Chron. 1:43). Its location is uncertain.

DINNER, the principal meal of the day.
have prepared my *d.*, Matt. 22:4.
first washed before *d.*, Luke 11:38.

DIONYSIUS, a prominent Athenian converted to Christianity by the preaching of Paul on Mars Hill (Acts 17:19–34). In later church history some writings were attributed to him but these are now known to be spurious and are called the Pseudo-Dionysian works.

DIOTREPHES, a person condemned by the apostle John in his third epistle. He was one who desired pre-eminence and thus refused John's authority and was inhospitable to visiting brethren (III John 9, 10).

DIP, to immerse, also signified to dye from the type of action in dyeing. "To baptize" is taken from this root.
d. it in the blood, Ex. 12:22.

Lazarus that he may *d.*, Luke 16:24.

DIPHATH, *see* **RIPHATH.**

DIPPED, DIPPING, *see* **DIP.**

DIRECT, to make straight, to guide.
sent Judah to *d.* his, Gen. 46:28.
shall *d.* thy paths, Prov. 3:6.
Lord *d.* your hearts, II Thess. 3:5.

DIRECTLY, in a direct manner, without
anything intervening, immediately.
sprinkle blood *d.* before, Num. 19:4.
the way *d.* before, Ezek. 42:12.

DISALLOW, to disapprove and thus to
reject.
because her father *d.*, Num. 30:5.
d. indeed of men, but, I Pet. 2:4.

DISANNUL, DISANNULLED, to put as
of no value, to deprive of authority, to
make void.
with death shall be *d.*, Is. 28:18.
covenant law cannot *d.*, Gal. 3:17.

DISAPPOINT, to deprive of hope, to fail
to come up to expectation.
O Lord *d.* him, Ps. 17:13.

DISCERN, (1) to distinguish between, or
to determine worth or significance, (2)
to see by eye of understanding.
d. thou what is thine, Gen. 31:32.
unworthily, not *d.*, I Cor. 11:29.
senses exercised to *d.*, Heb. 5:14.

DISCERNING OF SPIRITS, a spiritual
gift employed by certain men in the
apostolic age which enabled them to
judge from what spirits a message
proceeded, whether the Holy Spirit,
human or demoniac spirits. In this way
the truth of the doctrine was preserved
(I Cor. 12:10; cf. I Cor. 14:29).

DISCHARGE, to release, to send away.
cause them to be *d.*, I Kin. 5:9.
no *d.* in that war, Eccles. 8:8.

DISCIPLE, literally a learner, one who
follows one's teaching. Jesus required of
His disciples that they continue in His
word (John 8:31). From the disciples
Jesus selected the twelve apostles for
special service. Members of the New
Testament church are called disciples in
the Acts.

d. not above master, Matt. 10:24.
cross, cannot be my *d.*, Luke 14:27.
d. called Christians, Acts 11:26.
first day of week *d.*, Acts 20:7.

DISCIPLINE, calling to soundness of
mind or self-control.
also their ears to *d.*, Job 36:10.

DISCOMFIT, DISCOMFITED, to scatter in fight, to frustrate plans.
Joshua *d.* Amalek and, Ex. 17:13.
young men shall be *d.*, Is. 31:8.

DISCONTENTED, dissatisfied, uneasy in
mind.
every one that was *d.*, I Sam. 22:2.

DISCORD, lack of agreement, dissension.
him that soweth *d.*, Prov. 6:19.

DISCOURAGE, DISCOURAGED, to
depress, to lessen in courage.
why *d.* ye hearts, Num. 32:7.
children lest they be *d.*, Col. 3:21.

DISCOVER, (1) to reveal or to disclose.
(2) to detect for the first time.
we will *d.* ourselves, I Sam. 14:8.
I will *d.* her lewdness, Hos. 2:10.
they *d.* a certain creek, Acts 27:39.

DISCREET, DISCREETLY, from the
word for discipline, hence of sound mind;
to have or to show good judgment.
look out a man *d.* and, Gen. 41:33.
that he answered *d.*, Mark 12:34.
young women to be *d.*, Titus 2:5.

DISCRETION, the act or quality of
being discreet.
d. shall preserve thee, Prov. 2:11.
out heavens by his *d.*, Jer. 10:12.

DISDAINED, to think unworthy, a feeling of contempt.
saw David, he *d.* him, I Sam. 17:42.
d. to set with dogs, Job 30:1.

DISEASE, lacking strength, a weakness
or infirmity. A fault in the body or mind
which would produce these characteristics is a disease. The more prevalent
diseases in Palestine are: ague (fevers of
various kinds), blains and boils, canker
(our modern cancer), leprosy, and palsy.
The Jews were not very advanced in treatment of diseases.
I shall recover of *d.*, II Kin. 1:2.

with a loathsome *d.*, Ps. 38:7.
all that were *d.*, Matt. 14:35.
d. departed from them, Acts 19:12.

DISFIGURE, to make unsightly.
they *d.* their faces, Matt. 6:16.

DISGRACE, (1) condition of being out of favor or dishonored, (2) cause of shame or dishonor, (3) verb: to bring shame or reproach.
do not *d.* the throne, Jer. 14:21.

DISGUISE, to change the dress or the appearance of, to conceal identity.
Saul *d.* himself, I Sam. 28:8.
Josiah *d.* himself, II Chron. 35:22.

DISH, several words are translated dish, one meaning a shallow bowl (II Kin. 21:13) and others meaning a deep bowl (Ex. 25:29; Matt. 26:23).
make *d.* thereof, Ex. 25:29.
butter in a lordly *d.*, Judg. 5:25.
with me in the *d.*, Matt. 26:23.

DISHAN, the youngest son of Seir, the Horite, and head of an Idumean tribe. (Gen. 36:21, 28; I Chron. 1:38, 42).

DISHON, the name of two descendants of Seir, the Horite. (1) Seir's fifth son (Gen. 36:21). (2) Seir's grandson (Gen. 36:25).

DISHONEST, DISHONESTY, (1) lacking integrity, not to be trusted. Dishonest always appears with gain in the Bible. (2) Dishonesty has the primary significance of shame.
at they *d.* gain, Ezek. 22:13.
hidden things of *d.*, II Cor. 4:2.

DISHONOUR, DISHONOURETH, disgrace, shame, reproach.
us to see king's *d.*, Ezra 4:14.
d. their own bodies, Rom. 1:24.
woman *d.* her head, I Cor. 11:5.

DISINHERIT, to cut off from or to deprive of an inheritance.
will *d.* them and make, Num. 14:12.

DISMAYED, troubled or perplexed.
fear not, nor be *d.*, Deut. 31:8.
wise men are *d.*, Jer. 8:9.

DISMISSED, sent away, discharged.
spoken, he *d.* assembly, Acts 19:41.

DISOBEDIENCE, (1) condition of being unable to persuade, obstinate rejection; (2) sometimes denotes a refusal to hear (Rom. 5:19; Jer. 11:10); (3) almost synonymous with unbelief (John 3:36; Heb. 3:18–19).
by one man's *d.* many, Rom. 5:19.
d. received a just, Heb. 2:2.

DISOBEDIENT, failure to obey.
was *d.* to the word, I Kin. 13:26.
boasters, *d.* to parents, Rom. 1:30.
were sometime *d.*, I Pet. 3:20.

DISORDERLY, comes from a military term meaning not keeping rank. It denotes insubordination to authority, slackness, undisciplined.
them that are *d.*, I Thess. 5:14.
walk among you *d.*, II Thess. 3:11.

DISPATCH, to send off, to put to death.
d. them with swords, Ezek. 23:47.

DISPENSATION, (1) the primary meaning of the word refers to the management of a household. (2) A job or property entrusted to someone, a stewardship. (3) An arrangement or administration by God.
d. of the gospel is, I Cor. 9:17.
the *d.* of the fulness, Eph. 1:10.
heard of the *d.* of grace, Eph. 3:2.

DISPERSE, to break up, to scatter abroad.
Saul said, *d.*, I Sam. 14:34.
scatter them and *d.*, Ezek. 12:15.
obeyed him were *d.*, Acts 5:37.

DISPERSION, (1) the term is used in Jer. 25:34 to refer to the sin of the shepherds (kings) of Judah in allowing their flock to scatter. (2) Dispersion came to be a technical term referring to the Jews who were scattered abroad from Palestine. In the King James version the Greek word *diaspora* is translated "dispersed" (John 7:35) and "scattered abroad" (James 1:1; I Pet. 1:1). The causes of the dispersion were: (1) captivity by the Assyrians in 722 (II Kin. 15:29), (2) the Babylonian captivity in 586 B.C. (II Kin. 24:12–16), (3) voluntary emigration to chief towns for trade purposes. The number and location of the Jewish synagogues in Acts tells of the extent of the dispersion.

DISPLAYED, to show or to reveal.

banner that it may be *d.*, Ps. 60:4 .

DISPLEASE, DISPLEASED, (1) to incur disapproval and anger, (2) to be very grieved, to be wroth.
if it *d.* thee, Num. 22:34.
it *d.* Jonah exceedingly, Jonah 4:1.
he was much *d.*, Mark 10:14.

DISPLEASURE, feeling of one who is displeased, discomfort, anger.
afraid of the hot *d.*, Deut. 9:19.
vex them in his sore *d.*, Ps. 2:5.

DISPOSED, DISPOSING, minded, ordering.
hath *d.* whole world, Job 34:13.
the whole *d.* thereof, Prov. 16:33.
he was *d.* to pass, Acts 18:27.

DISPOSITION, act or power of disposing or managing, an ordinance.
received the law by *d.*, Acts 7:53.

DISPOSSESS, to put out of possession.
d. the inhabitants of, Num. 33:53.
how can I *d.* them, Deut. 7:17.

DISPUTATION, act of disputing, a debate or questioning.
had no small *d.*, Acts 15:2.
not to doubtful *d.*, Rom. 14:1.

DISPUTE, DISPUTED, debate, controversy.
had been much *d.*, Acts 15:7.
Paul *d.* in synagogue, Acts 17:17.
Michael *d.* about body of, Jude 9.

DISQUIET, DISQUIETED, to deprive of peace and rest, to be uneasy.
why art thou *d.* within, Ps. 42:5.
and *d.* inhabitants of, Jer. 50:34.

DISSEMBLED, to hide under a false semblance, to pretend or disguise.
stolen and *d.* also, Josh. 7:11.
Jews *d.* likewise, Gal. 2:13.

DISSENSION, disagreement in opinion.
had no small *d.*, Acts 15:2.
there arose a great *d.*, Acts 23:10.

DISSIMULATION, a pretension, hypocrisy.
love be without *d.*, Rom. 12:9.
away with their *d.*, Gal. 2:13.

DISSOLVE, DISSOLVED, to separate

into parts, to destroy or bring to an end by dispersal.
thou canst *d.* doubts, Dan. 5:16.
tabernacle were *d.*, II Cor. 5:1.
things shall be *d.*, II Pet. 3:11.

DISTAFF, the staff for holding the flax or wool in spinning.
her hands hold the *d.*, Prov. 31:19.

DISTIL, to drop, to obtain as if by distilling.
speech shall *d.* as dew, Deut. 32:2.
clouds *d.* on man, Job 36:28.

DISTINCTION, difference.
except they give a *d.*, I Cor. 14:7.

DISTINCTLY, evidently, clearly.
of the law of God *d.*, Neh. 8:8.

DISTRACTED, bewildered.
thy terrors I am *d.*, Ps. 88:15.

DISTRACTION, loss of attention.
attend Lord without *d.*, I Cor. 7:35.

DISTRESS, to trouble.
me in day of my *d.*, Gen. 35:3.
in my *d.* I called, II Sam. 22:7.
pleasure in *d.*, II Cor. 12:10.
our affliction and *d.*, I Thess. 3:7.

DISTRESS, DISTRESSED, to afflict or harass.
greatly afraid and *d.*, Gen. 32:7.
will *d.* the inhabitants, Jer. 10:18.

DISTRIBUTE, to divide among several.
Moses did *d.* for, Josh. 13:32.
rich to be ready to *d.*, I Tim. 6:18.

DISTRIBUTION, that which is distributed.
d. was made to every one, Acts 4:35.
your liberal *d.* to, II Cor. 9:13.

DITCH, any kind of deep hole or pit.
fallen into the *d.*, Ps. 7:15.
both shall fall into *d.*, Luke 6:39.

DIVERS, DIVERSE, different in kind, several.
cattle gender with *d.* Lev. 19:19.
sick people with *d.* Matt. 4:24.
in *d.* manners spake, Heb. 1:1.

DIVERSITIES, differences, variety.
d. of gifts, I Cor. 12:4.

set in the church *d.*, I Cor. 12:28.

DIVES, this word does not appear in the English Bible. It is the Latin word for "the rich man" and is the term often applied to the rich man in the story of the rich man and Lazarus (Luke 16:19–31).

DIVIDE, to sever, to separate.
d. living child in two, I Kin. 3:25.
lights to *d.* day from, Gen. 1:14.
and *d.* it among, Luke 22:17.

DIVINATION, the art of obtaining secret knowledge, usually of the future, in a way other than genuine prophecy by the Spirit of God. The Bible recognizes that such knowledge could be gained by demon power (I Sam. 28:7–14; II Thess. 2:10–12), but it strongly condemns this practice and forbids the people of God from consorting with such (Deut. 18: 10–12).
with the rewards of *d.*, Num. 22:7.
prophesy visions and *d.*, Jer. 14:14.
with spirit of *d.*, Acts 16:16.

DIVINE, DIVINING, to use or practice divination, to foretell by divination.
such a man as I can *d.*, Gen. 44:15.
prophets that *d.* lies, Ezek. 13:9.

DIVINE, an adjective meaning of or pertaining to God; Godlike or heavenly.
a *d.* sentence is in, Prov. 16:10.
his *d.* power hath, II Pet. 1:3.

DIVORCE, DIVORCEMENT, a legal separation of man and wife. The law of Moses permitted divorce when some uncleanness or "unseemly thing" is found in a woman (Deut. 24:1–4). Jewish teachers differed on what was meant by "unseemly thing." The vagueness of the phrase promoted much abuse among the Jews. A writing of a "bill of divorcement" (Is. 50:1; Jer. 3:8) in ancient times required Levitical approval. This tended to check the actions of a rash husband. Also, to guard against rashness, a man was forbidden to remarry his divorced wife if she marries another.
    Jesus taught that the liberty to put away one's wife was given because of the hardness of Jewish heart (Deut. 24:1). He taught that he who divorces his wife except for fornication, and marries another, commits adultery (Matt. 19:9).

Also he who marries a divorced woman commits adultery (Luke 16:18). Some believe that divorce is completely forbidden on the bases of the following passages: Mark 10:2–12; Luke 16:18; I Cor. 7:10, 39.

DIVORCED, DIVORCING, *see* DIVORCE.

DIZAHAB, a town east of the Jordan of Moab which was near the encampment of Israel when Moses spoke the words of Deuteronomy (Deut. 1:1). The exact site is unknown.

DO, to produce, to perform.
d. to her as it pleaseth, Gen. 16:6.
d. all thy work, Ex. 20:9.
what shall we *d.* Acts 2:37.
d. all in the name, Col. 3:17.

DOCTOR, learned-man, teacher.
in the midst of *d.*, Luke 2:46.
stood up Gamaliel a *d.*, Acts 5:34.

DOCTRINE, teaching. In the New Testament "the doctrine" is the teaching of Jesus Christ—the gospel.
astonished at his *d.*, Matt. 7:28.
in the apostle's *d.*, Acts 2:42.
teach no other *d.*, I Tim. 1:3.
abideth not in the *d.*, II John 9.

DODIA, *see* DODO.

DODANIM, a family or race descendant from Javan, the son of Japheth (Gen. 10:4).

DODOVAH, a man of Mareshah in Judah and father of the Eliezer who foretold the destruction of Jehoshaphat's fleet (II Chron. 20:37).

DODO, (1) a descendant of Issachar and grandfather of the judge Tola (Judg. 10: 1), (2) an Ahohite, father of Eleazar, one of David's three mighty men (II Sam. 23: 9). He may be the Dodai mentioned in I Chron. 27:4 as a commander of David's troops, (3) a Beth-lehemite, father of Elhanan, one of David's thirty heroes (II Sam. 23:24; I Chron. 11:26).

DOE, the female ibex (wild goat). Mentioned in Prov. 5:19 as a roe.

DOEG, an Edomite and chief of king

Saul's herdsmen. He was at Nob when David was assisted in his flight from Saul by Ahimelech the priest. He informed Saul of this and at the order of Saul slew Ahimelech and his priests (I Sam. 21:7; 22:9–19).

DOES, DOEST, DOETH, *see* **DO.**

DOG, a humble friend of man, even from ancient times. He has been sculptured on monuments of ancient Assyria and Egypt. They were mentioned as shepherd dogs by Job (30:1). Isaiah compared the vile rulers of Israel to dogs (56:10). The dog is a lowly animal in the East. They are not treated as pets, and they eat anything that comes in their way. Since it was an unclean and despised animal, the word "dog" became a term of reproach.
moreover the *d.* came, Luke 16:21.
beware of *d.*, Phil. 3:2.
d., and sorcerers, and, Rev. 22:15.

DOING, working, doing.
wickedness of thy *d.*, Deut. 28:20.
man . . evil in his *d.*, I Sam. 25:3.
this is . . Lord's *d.*, Matt. 21:42.
not . . weary in well *d.*, Gal. 6:9.
d. this . . shalt live, I Tim. 4:16.

DOLEFUL, wailing, howling.
full of *d.* creatures, Is. 13:21.
lament . . with *d.*, Mic. 2:4.

DOMINION, power, rule.
shalt have the *d.*, Gen. 27:40.
upright shall have *d.*, Ps. 49:14.
kingdoms of his *d.*, Jer. 34:1.
death hath no more *d.*, Rom. 6:9.
d. over your faith, II Cor. 1:24.
glory, and *d.* forever, Rev. 1:6.

DONE, *see* **DO.**

DOOR, an opening. It is sometimes used figuratively to mean an opportunity (Hos. 2:15; I Cor. 16:9).
sin lieth at the *d.*, Gen. 4:7.
ye everlasting *d.*, Ps. 24:7.
Achor for a *d.* of hope, Hos. 2:15.
the *d.* of thy mouth, Mic. 7:5.
shut the *d.*, pray, Matt. 6:6.
a great *d.* . . is opened, I Cor. 16:9.
God would open . . a *d.*, Col. 4:3.

DOORKEEPER, one who keeps a post at the door, to guard the place from intruders. Doorkeepers were appointed to guard

the door of the tabernacle (1 Chr. 15:23, 24). Persons were sometimes appointed to guard the street door of the houses (John 18:16).

DOORPOST, a threshold. Moses told the Israelites that they should write the divine commands "upon the posts of thy house and thy gates" (Deut. 6:9). The practice of putting inscriptions on the door was an ancient Egyptian custom, and was evidently followed by the Israelites at an early time.

DOPHKAH, one of the encampments of Israel in the desert (Num. 33:12, 13).

DOR, an ancient city of the Canaanites (Josh. 11:2). They were once a tributary to Solomon (Judg. 1:27).

DORCAS, a kindly Christian woman from Joppa, whom Peter raised from the dead (Acts 9:36–41). She was also called Tabitha, which was probably the way that the Jews knew her.

DOST, DOTH, *see* **DO.**

DOTE, to be foolish.
and they shall *d.*, Jer. 50:36.
but *d.* about questions, I Tim. 6:4

DOTHAN, a plain about 14 miles north of Shechem (Gen. 37:17), and famous for its pasturage. It was there that Joseph was sold by his brethren to the Egyptians (Gen. 37:25). It was also the scene of Elisha's vision of the mountain full of horses and chariots (II Kin. 6:13).

DOUAY VERSION, *see* **VERSIONS.**

DOUBLE, twofold.
giving . . a *d.* portion, Deut. 21:17.
with a *d.* heart speak, Ps. 12:2.
counted worthy of *d.*, I Tim. 5:17.
d. minded . . unstable, James 1:8.

DOUBLE, to make double.
dream was *d.* unto, Gen. 41:32.
d. the sixth curtain, Ex. 26:9.
let . . sword be *d.*, Ezek. 21:14.

DOUBLE-MINDED, the state of mind which is in opposition to that which is simple, unequivocal, and sincere (James 1:8, 4:8).

DOUBT, an uncertainty due to contradictory conclusions.
dissolving of *d.*, Dan. 5:12.
amazed, and were in *d.*, Acts 2:12.
I stand in *d.* of you, Gal. 4:20.

DOUBT, to question.
not *d.* in his heart, Mark 11:23.
go . . , *d.* nothing, Acts 10:20.
he that *d.* is damned, Rom. 14:23.

DOUBTFUL, wavering, questioning.
neither be . . of *d.* mind, Luke 12:29.
not to *d.* disputation, Rom. 14:1.

DOUBTING, *see* DOUBT.

DOUBTLESS, at least, certainly.
shall *d.* come again, Ps. 126:6.
yet *d.* I am to you, I Cor. 9:2.
d., and I count all, Phil. 3:8.

DOUGH, a swelling from fermentation.
firstfruits of our *d.*, Neh. 10:37.
women knead their *d.*, Jer. 7:18.
he hath kneaded the *d.*, Hos. 7:4.

DOVE, PIGEON, a bird mentioned often in the Scriptures. They make their nest in the clefts and holes of the rocks (Song 2:14; Jer. 48:28). They are timid (Hos. 11:11) and gentle (Song 1:15); and therefore they are suitable for sacrifice (Gen. 15:9; Luke 2:24). Their earliest mention is in connection with Noah and the Ark. Because of its gentleness, it was used to describe the descent of the Holy Spirit on Jesus Christ (Matt. 3:16). Wild doves are very numerous in the Holy Land. Being acceptable for sacrifices, they were also clean, and used for food.
he sent forth a *d.*, Gen. 8:8.
did mourn as a *d.*, Is. 38:14.
Ephraim . . like a silly *d.*, Hos. 7:11.
descended like a *d.*, Matt. 3:16.

DOVE'S DUNG, there are three explanations given for this expression: (1) that it is a kind of plant; (2) that it was in reality dung, but it was used for fertilizer; and (3) that the people, in a time of famine, actually ate this repulsive material. It is possible that it is an article of food in II Kin. 6:25, for there is evidence of similar occurrence throughout history.

DOWN, beneath, below.
cast thyself *d.*, Matt. 4:6.
herd ran violently *d.*, Mark 5:13.

fell *d.* from . . loft, Acts 20:9.

DOWNWARD, beneath, low.
beast that goeth *d.*, Eccles. 3:21.
shall take root *d.*, Is. 37:31.

DOWRY, the price paid for a wife. The suitor gave the bride a betrothal or bridal gift, as well as presents for her parents and brothers. The average amount for the dowry was apparently fifty shekels of silver (Deut. 22:28). It was sometimes paid in service (Gen. 29:25–28). Saul required the foreskins of the enemy for the dowry of his daughter (I Sam. 18:25). In the modern sense of the word, as something given to the daughter by the father, there are few cases (Judg. 1:15; I Kin. 9:16).

DRAFT, a special selection of men for a particular duty. In ancient Israel all men over twenty years of age were liable to military service. All the men were registered (Num. 1:3, 18); and some were exempted. Those who had received no return on certain business investments (new houses, or vineyards) were exempt (Deut. 20:5, 6). Betrothed and newly married men were exempt from military service for a year (Deut. 20:7; 24:5). "Fearful and fainthearted" men were discharged (Deut. 20:8; Judg. 7:3).

DRAG, to net, to drag.
came . . , *d.* the net, John 21:8.

DRAGON, (1) with reference to some of the desert animals, it is best translated as wolf (Is. 13:22). (2) It is used for sea monsters (Ps. 74:13). (3) It is used for serpents, even the smaller ones (Deut. 32:33). (4) It is a crocodile in Ezek. 29:3. (5) In the New Testament, it is used to refer to Satan and the Devil (Rev. 12:3, 4, 7, 9, 13, 16, 17; 20:2).
shall slay the *d.*, Is. 27:1.
Pharaoh . . the great *d.*, Ezek. 29:3.
wailing like a *d.*, Mic. 1:8.
d. having seven heads, Rev. 12:3.

DRAGON WELL, fountain of jackals.
went before the *d.*, Neh. 2:13.

DRAMS, darics (persian coins).
and ten thousand *d.*, I Chr. 29:7.

DRANK, *see* DRINK.

DRAUGHT, catch, haul.
let down .. nets for *d.*, Luke 5:4.

DRAUGHT, privy, cess-pool.
made it a *d.* house, II Kin. 10:27.
cast out into the *d.*, Matt. 15:17.

DRAVE, *see* **DRIVE.**

DRAW, DRAWETH, DRAWING, to
pull, to move, to come.
come out to *d.* water, Gen. 24:13.
d. near the place, Judg. 19:13.
d. out the staves, I Kin. 8:8.
d. thy sword, I Chr. 10:4.
d. nigh to .. house, Luke 15:25.
Father .. *d.* him, John 6:44.
d. nigh to God, James 4:8.

DRAWER, one who draws.
the *d.* of thy water, Deut. 29:11.

DRAWN, pulled, carried, marked.
shalt be *d.* away, Deut. 30:17.
one *d.* unto death, Prov. 24:11.
d. away of .. own lust, James 1:14.

DREAD, fear, terror.
fear and *d.* shall fall, Ex. 15:16.
let him be your *d.*, Is. 8:13.
d. not, neither be, Deut. 1:29.
good courage, *d.* not, I Chr. 22:13.

DREADFUL, to be feared, reverenced.
how *d.* is this place, Gen. 28:17.
beast *d.* and terrible, Dan. 7:7.
my name is *d.*, Mal. 1:14.

DREAM, images, thoughts, or emotions
occurring during sleep. There is much
significance attached to dreams in the
Bible (Gen. 37:6, 9; Judg. 7:13; Dan.
2:28; Matt. 1:20; 2:12). They are sometimes regarded as communications with
God (Job 33:14–17; Jer. 23:28). There
are such things as lying dreams and false
dreams (Jer. 23:25; Zech. 10:2). The interpretation of dreams belongs to God
(40:8).
God came .. in a *d.*, Gen. 20:3.
a dreamer of *d.*, Deut. 13:1.
d. of a night vision, Is. 29:7.
old men .. dream *d.*, Joel 2:28.
appeared .. in a *d.*, Matt. 1:20.
old men .. *d.* dreams, Acts 2:17.

DREGS, lees, grounds.
hast drunken the *d.*, Is. 51:17.

DRESS, a garment. Men and women were
forbidden to wear each others garments
(Deut. 22:5). Oriental dress has preserved
a peculiar uniformity in all ages, from
Abraham to the modern Bedouin. *See*
CLOTHING.

DRESS, to make good, till.
when he *d.* the lamps, Ex. 30:7.
plant .. and *d.*, Deut. 28: 39.

DRESS, to do, to make.
he hasted to *d.* it, Gen. 18:7.
d. in the frying pan, Lev. 7:9.
that I may .. *d.* it, I Kin. 17:12.

DREW, *see* **DRAW.**

DRIED, DRIEDST, DRIETH, *see* **DRY**

DRINK, water took first place as their
drink, although milk was used very much,
but was considered as a food. Milk was
commonly served with meals (Gen. 18:8;
Deut. 32:14; Judg. 4:19). For the better
quenching of thirst the common people
used a sour drink (Ruth 2:14), a sort of
vinegar mixed with oil. The well-to-do
drank wine, probably mixed with water,
and often mixed with spice. They also
used a stronger intoxicating drink.
meat, *d.*, and oil, Ezra 3:7.
gave *d.* to my people, Is. 43:20.
their *d.* is sour, Hos. 4:18.
and ye gave me *d.*, Matt. 25:35.
if .. thirst, give him *d.*, Rom. 12:20.

DRINK, to drink, to banquet.
do not *d.* wine, Lev. 10:9.
d. the blood of goats, Ps. 50:13.
eat and *d.* and enjoy, Eccles. 2:24.
give us .. water to *d.*, Dan. 1:12.
d. but are not filled, Hag. 1:6.
give me to *d.*, John 4:7.
earth .. *d.* in rain, Heb. 6:7.
d. of the wine of, Rev. 14:10.

DRINK OFFERING, *see* **OFFERING
and SACRIFICE.**

DRINK, STRONG, *see* **STRONG DRINK.**

DRIVE, to cause to flee, to cast out, to
compel, to guide.
he *d.* out the man, Gen. 3:24.
the wicked is *d.* away, Prov. 14:32.
I will *d.* them out, Hos. 9:15.
d. asunder the nations, Hab. 3:6.
d. of the devil, Luke 8:29.

d. of fierce winds, James 3:4.

DRIVER, a charioteer.
d. of his chariot, I Kin. 22:34.

DRIVING, impelling, leading on.
is like .. *d.* of Jehu, II Kin. 9:20.

DROMEDARY, the one-humped Camel. In Is. 60:6 and Jer. 2:23, the word indicates a swift camel. In I Kin. 4:28 and Esther 8:10, it is probably used for "horse."
straw for *d.*, I Kin. 4:28.
a swift *d.* traversing, Jer. 2:23.

DROP, a liquid globule, a drop.
maketh small the *d.*, Job 36:27.
behold nations as a *d.*, Is. 40:15.
sweat .. as *d.* of blood, Luke 22:44.

DROP, to drop, to distil. Also **Dropped, Dropping.**
behold, the honey *d.*, I Sam. 14:26.
clouds *d.* . . the dew, Prov. 3:20.
d. down, ye heavens, Is. 45:8.

DROPSY, a symptom of a number of different diseases, mostly of the heart, liver, kidneys, and brain. It causes collections of water in the cavities of the body, or on its surface, or in the limbs. Jesus healed one with the dropsy (Luke 14:2).
man .. which had a *d.*, Luke 14:2.

DROSS, refuse, waste material.
silver is become *d.*, Is. 1:22.
Israel is become *d.*, Ezek. 22:18.

DROUGHT, dearth, thirst.
and scorpions, and *d.*, Deut. 8:15.
d. and heat consume, Job 24:19.
through the land of *d.*, Jer. 2:6.

DROVE, *see* **DRIVE.**

DROVE, flock, herd.
all this *d.* which I, Gen. 33:8.

DROWN, to overflow, to sink, to swallow up. Also **Drowned.**
neither can floods *d.*, Song 8:7.
d. in the depths, Matt. 18:6.
Egyptians .. were *d.*, Heb. 11:29.

DROWSINESS, sleepiness.
d. will clothe a man, Prov. 23:21.

DRUNKARD, one who drinks to excess.

our son, a *d.*, Deut. 21:20.
d. and glutton, Prov. 23:21.
woe to the *d.* of, Is. 28:1.
a railer, or a *d.*, I Cor. 5:11.
nor *d.* inherit, I Cor. 6:10.

DRUNKEN, to be softened with drink, to be intoxicated.
as a *d.* man staggers, Is. 19:14.
am like a *d.* man, Jer. 23:9.
drink with the *d.*, Matt. 24:49.
d. with the blood, Rev. 17:6.

DRUNKENNESS, the state of intoxication. It is first mentioned in the Bible in connection with Noah (Gen. 9:21). The use of strong drink is warned against frequently in the Bible (Lev. 10:9; Prov. 23:29–32). Drunkenness is a reproach (Rom. 13:13; Gal. 5:21; Eph. 5:18; I Thess. 5:7). Drunkards are excluded from Christian fellowship and the Kingdom of Heaven (I Cor. 5:11; 6:10). Figuratively men are represented as being drunk with sorrow (Is. 63:6; Jer. 51:57). Drunkenness sometimes denotes abundance, satiety (Deut. 32:42; Is. 49:26).

DRUSILLA, the youngest daughter of Herod Agrippa I, by his wife Cypros. She was early promised in marriage to Epiphanes, son of Antiochus, but the match was broken off in consequence of his refusing to perform his promise of conforming to the Jewish religion. She married Azizus, king of Edessa, but later became the wife of Felix, procurator of Judea. In Acts 24:24 she is mentioned in such a manner that she may be naturally supposed to have been present when Paul preached before Felix in A.D. 57.

DRY, withered, without water, dry.
d. upon the earth, Judg. 6:37.
make the rivers *d.*, Ezek. 30:12.
make Ninevah *d.*, Zeph. 2:13.
shake .. the *d.* land, Hag. 2:6.
sea as by *d.* land, Heb. 11:29.

DRY, to wither, to parch.
d. up mighty rivers, Ps. 74:15.
d. up all their herbs, Is. 42:15.
water thereof was *d.*, Rev. 16:12.

DUE, matter, portion, judgment.
rain .. in .. *d.* season, Deut. 11:14.
pay all that was *d.*, Matt. 18:34.
receive the *d.* award, Luke 23:41.

render to all their *d.*, Rom. 13:7.

DUKE, leader, ruler, anointed, prince.
d. of Esau, Gen. 36:15–43.
the *d.* of Edom shall, Ex. 15:15.
d. Timnah, *d.* Aliah, I Chr. 1:51.

DULCIMER, a musical instrument mentioned in Dan. 3:5, 15. It was probably similar to our modern dulcimer, a box strung with about 50 wires, played with two small hammers, held in the hand.

DULL, slothful, stupid.
ye are *d.* of hearing, Heb. 5:11.

DUMAH, the son of Ishmael, founder of the tribe of Ishmaelites. They lived near Edom (Gen. 25:15; Is. 21:11) and called the area where they lived Dumah (Gen. 25:14). There is also a town in Judah, near Hebron, with the name Dumah (Josh. 15:52).

DUMB, unable to speak, blunted.
I was *d.* with silence, Ps. 39:2.
thou shalt be *d.*, Ezek. 3:26.
maketh the *d.* to speak, Mark 7:37.
devil, and it was *d.*, Luke 11:14.
d. before . . shearers, Acts 8:32.

DUNG, used for both manure and fuel. To prepare it for fuel, they carefully dried it. Many poor people would have to spread it outside their houses to dry (Ezek. 4:12). The word dung is omitted in II Kin. 10:27, where the phrase "draught house" is substituted.

DUNGEON, pit chamber. *See* **PRISON**.
put me into the *d.*, Gen. 40:15.
entered into *d.*, Jer. 37:16.

DUNG GATE, a gate of ancient Jerusalem, located at the southwest part of Mount Zion. It was no doubt called this because it was used for a place to dump garbage. It is used in Neh. 2:13; 3:13; 12:31.

DUNG HILL, (1) a heap of manure (Is. 25:10; Luke 14:35). (2) A privy (II Kin. 10:27). To sit upon the dung heap denoted the deepest kind of degradation (I Sam. 2:8).

DURA, a plain in the province of Babylon in which Nebuchadnezzar set up a golden image (Dan. 3:1). A mound in that area

has been recently identified with that territory.

DURABLE, lasting.
and for *d.* clothing, Is. 23:18.

DURETH, consist, remain.
but *d.* for awhile, Matt. 13:21.

DURST, *see* **DARE**.

DUST, an image of what is low, mean and impure. Abraham calls himself but dust and ashes (Gen. 18:27). The dust of the desert was sometimes carried by whirlwinds to great distances, leaving only desolation. Among the punishments against the Hebrews, when they forsook Jehovah, was that dust and ashes, instead of rain, would come from heaven (Deut. 28:24).
God formed man of *d.*, Gen. 2:7.
d. upon their heads, Josh. 7:6.
pant after the *d.*, Amos 2:7.
shake off the *d.*, Matt. 10:14.
d. on their heads, Rev. 18:19.

DUTY, obligation, owing.
her *d.* of marriage, Ex. 21:10.
d. is . . to minister, Rom. 15:27.

DWARF, small, lean.
crook-backed, or a *d.*, Lev. 21:20.

DWELL, sojourn, live.
d. in the land of, Ex. 2:15.
the Canaanites that *d.*, Judg. 1:9.
d. in the midst of, Is. 6:5.
where no man *d.*, Jer. 2:6.
Judah shall *d.* forever, Joel 3:20.
his spirit that *d.*, Rom. 8:11.
spirit of God *d.*, I Cor. 3:16.
Holy Ghost that *d.*, II Tim. 1:14.
d. the love of God, I John 3:17.
where Satan *d.*, Rev. 2:13.

DWELLING, home, habitation.
in heaven thy *d.*, I Kin. 8:30.
the *d.* of the wise, Prov. 21:20.
d. shall be with beasts, Dan. 4:25.
d. among the tombs, Mark 5:3.

DYE, *see* **COLOURS**.

DYING, expiring.
and she lay a *d.*, Luke 8:42.
the *d.* of the Lord, II Cor. 4:10.
Jacob, when he was *d.*, Heb. 11:21.

DYSENTERY, the rendering in the Revised Version for bloody flux, a malignant intestinal disease (Acts 28: 8).

E

EACH, two or more considered separately or one by one.
took *e.* man his sword, Gen. 34:25.
e. prince on his day, Num. 7:11.
doth not *e.* one of you, Luke 13:15.
and it sat upon *e.*, Acts 2:3.

EAGLE, a bird of the family *falconidae* Sometimes the word may refer to vultures. The distinction can be made by noticing the word "flock" because eagles do not flock. An example of this is Mic. 1:16 where the reference must be to the griffon vulture.
I bear you on *e.* wings, Ex. 19:4.
were swifter than *e.*, II Sam. 1:23.
the *e.* that hasteth to, Job 9:26.
the *e.* be gathered, Matt. 24:28.
was like a flying *e.*, Rev. 4:7.
two wings of a great *e.*, Rev. 12:14.

EAR, the organ of hearing. Blood was put upon the right ear of the priest at their consecration (Ex. 29:20); also blood was put on the healed leper in his cleansing (Lev. 14:14). The women adorned their ears with earrings (Ex. 32:2). When a servant refused to leave their masters, they were fastened to the door by their ear as a mark of perpetual service (Ex. 21:6; Deut. 15:17).
proclaim in the *e.* of, Judg. 7:3.
he that hath *e.*, Matt. 11:15.
sink down into your *e.* Luke 9:44.
into the *e.* of the Lord, James 5:4.

EARLY, the word usually refers to an hour about dawn (Luke 24:22), but may refer to the beginning of a season (James 5:7).
shall rise up *e.*, and, Gen. 19:2.
up *e.* in the morning, I Sam. 29:10.
the week, very *e.* in, Luke 24:1.
e. in the morning he came, John 8:2.
the temple *e.* in the, Acts 5:21.

EARN, to receive for work or service (Hag. 1:6).

EARNEST, a pledge or token given as the assurance of the fulfilment of a bargain or promise.

given us the *e.* of, II Cor. 1:22.
the *e.* of the Spirit, II Cor. 5:5.
e. of our inheritance, Eph. 1:14.

EARNEST, sincerely zealous.
he prayed more *e.*, Luke 22:44.
put the same *e.* care, II Cor. 8:16.
prayed *e.* that it might, James 5:17.
ye should *e.* contend for, Jude 3.

EARNESTLY, fervently.
he prayed more *e.*, Luke 22:44.
e. looked upon him, Luke 22:56.
why look ye so *e.*, Acts 3:12.
covet *e.* best gifts, I Cor. 12:31.
prayed *e.* not rain, James 5:17.
e. contend for faith, Jude 3.

EAR OF GRAIN, the grain of Bible lands was not corn as used in America, but barley, rye, or wheat. The "ears" spoken of are, therefore, the heads containing the grain.
seven *e.* of corn came up, Gen. 41:5.
pluck the *e.* of corn, Matt. 12:1.
went, to pluck the *e.* of, Mark 2:23.
the blade, then the *e.*, Mark 4:28..

EARRING, an ornamental pendant hung from the ears. In the oriental lands worn by both sexes in Bible times.
man took a golden *e.*, Gen. 24:22.
all their *e.* which, Gen. 35:4.
e. of his prey, Judg. 8:24.
every one an *e.* of gold, Job 42:11.

EARTH, land and water, the whole visible surface of the globe. The Hebrews may have thought of the earth as being held up by pillars (Job 9:6; Ps. 75:3) which was on a foundation (Job 38:4; Ps. 104:5). Beneath the earth was the place of the dead (Deut. 32:22; Job 11:8). Man was created from the earth (Gen. 2:7). The term "earth" can also apply to "the inhabitants of the earth" (Gen. 6:11; 11:1). In John 3:31 it is used in contrast to heaven, to denote the carnal.
the heaven and the *e.*, Gen. 1:1.
the *e.* open her mouth, Num. 16:30.
off the face of the *e.*, Deut. 6:15.
rain upon the *e.*, I Kin. 17:14.
hangeth the *e.* upon, Job 26:7.
made heaven and *e.*, Ps. 115:15.
glory is above the *e.*, Ps. 148:13.
cut off from the *e.*, Prov. 2:22.
kingdoms of the *e.* may, Is. 37:20.
e., so are my ways higher, Is. 55:9.

new heavens and a new *e*., Is. 65:17.
uttermost part of the *e*., Acts 1:8.
and *e*. my footstool, Acts 7:49.
heaven and *e*. is named, Eph. 3:15.
and *e*. which are now, II Pet. 3:7.
that bear witness in *e*., I John 5:8.

EARTHEN, made of clay or earth.
But the *e*. vessel, Lev. 6:28.
and basons, and *e*., II Sam. 17:28..
a potter's *e*. bottle, Jer. 19:1.
treasure in *e*. vessels, II Cor. 4:7.

EARTHLY, mundane; existing upon earth; of the material of the earth.
of the earth is *e*., and, John 3:31.
that if our *e*. house, II Cor. 5:1.
who mind *e*. things, Phil. 3:19.
but is *e*., sensual, James 3:15.

EARTHQUAKE, a tremulous motion or shaking of the earth caused by violent action of subterraneous heat and vapors. There can be no doubt that Palestine was subject to occasional earthquakes. Among the few recorded, the most remarkable occurred in the reign of Uzziah (Amos 1:1; Zech. 14:5). Josephus interprets this quake as divine punishment upon Uzziah. Of the particular details of this quake, we know absolutely nothing. Earthquakes are mentioned in connection with the crucifixion (Matt. 27:51–54), the resurrection (Matt. 28:2), and the imprisonment of Paul and Silas (Acts 16:26). These seem to have been of a miraculous origin.

EARTHY, made of earth or soil.
is of the earth, *e*., I Cor. 15:47.
As is the *e*., I Cor. 15:48.
the image of the *e*., I Cor. 15:49.

EASE, taking or causing to take rest.
now therefore *e*. thou, II Chr. 10:4.
shall *e*. my complaint, Job 7:13.
I will *e*. me of mine, Is. 1:24.

EASE, relaxation: signifies rest from endurance and suffering; carelessness or indifference with reference to moral or religious interests.
Moab hath been at *e*., Jer. 48:11.
at *e*. in Zion, Amos 6:1.
heathen that are at *e*., Zech. 1:15.
take thine *e*., Luke 12:19.

EASIER, less burdensome or laborious.
for whether is *e*., Matt. 9:5.

it is *e*. for a camel, Matt. 19:24.
whether is it *e*. to say, Mark 2:9.
and it is *e*. for heaven, Luke 16:17.

EASILY,
charity is not *e*., I Cor. 13:5.
sin doth so *e*. beset., Heb. 12:1.

EAST, EASTWARD, the direction toward the sunrise; the determining point of compass for the Hebrews.
planted a garden *e*. in, Gen. 2:8.
Canaanite on the *e*., Josh. 11:3.
looking toward the *e*., I Kin. 7:25.
wise men from the *e*., Matt. 2:1.
shall come from the *e*., Luke 13:29.

EAST, CHILDREN OF THE, MEN OF THE, PEOPLE OF THE, a designation of the inhabitants of the country east of Palestine. Some, if not all, of these people were regarded as descending from the concubines of Abraham (Gen. 25:6).
the people of the *e*., Gen. 29:1.
the children of the *e*., Judg. 6:3.
all the men of the *e*., Job 1:3.
spoil the men of the *e*., Jer. 49:28.
to the men of the *e*., Ezek. 25:4.

EAST COUNTRY, the region lying east of Palestine, especially the Arabian and Syrian deserts.
unto the *e*. country, Gen. 25:6.
from the *e*. country, Zech. 8:7.

EASTER, originally the spring festival in honor of Eastra or Ostara a Teutonic goddess. This name was transferred to the paschal feast sometime after the close of the New Testament canon. The word occurs in the Bible in the King James Version one time (Acts 12:4). It is a mistranslation. The proper translation is "passover."

EAST SEA or **EASTERN SEA,** *see* **DEAD SEA.**

EAST WIND, a wind blowing from the east which is hot and sultry in Egypt and Palestine.
blasted with the *e*. wind, Gen. 41:6.
with the *e*. wind, Job 15:2.
He causes an *e*. wind to, Ps. 78:26.
day of the *e*. wind, Is. 27:8.

EASY, not hard; not burdensome.
knowledge is *e*. to him, Prov. 14:6.
my yoke is *e*. my burden, Matt. 11:30

ye utter words *e.*, I Cor. 14:9.

EAT, taste; devour; to take food.
thou mayest freely *e.*, Gen. 2:16.
Lord, saying, *e.* no, I Kin. 13:9.
the swine did *e.*, Luke 15:16.
That ye may *e.*, Luke 22:30.
did *e.* their meat, Acts 2:46.
as often as ye *e.*, I Cor. 11:26.
should he *e.*, II Thess. 3:10.
no right to *e.* which, Heb. 13:10.
shall *e.* your flesh, James 5:3.

EBAL, (1) another reading for Obal (I
Chr. 1:22). (2) One of the sons of Shobal,
son of Seir, the Horite, of Idumea (Gen.
36:23). (3) One of the two mountains
separated by the valley of Shechem. It is
two thousand six hundred feet above the
sea. The modern name is Sitti Salamigah,
so named after a Mohammedan female
saint. Ebal is where the blessings of
Israel were pronounced (Deut. 11:29;
Josh. 8:30–35), while the curses were
pronounced from Gerizim.
curse upon mount *E.*, Deut. 11:29.
in mount *E.*, Deut. 27:4.
stand upon mount *E.*, Deut. 27:13.
of Israel in mount *E.*, Josh. 8:30.
over against mount *E.*, Josh. 8:33.

EBED, (servant, slave); (1) father of Gaal
(Judg. 9:28). (2) a companion of Ezra's
at his return (Ezra 8:6).

EBED-MELECH, an Ethiopian eunuch in
the service of Zedekiah, through whose
interference Jeremiah was released from
a dungeon (Jer. 38:7ff.). God through
Jeremiah promised him safety when Jerusalem was captured (Jer. 39:15ff.).
when *E.* the Ethiopian, Jer. 38:7.
E. went forth out of, Jer. 38:8.
king commanded *E.*, Jer. 38:10.
Go and speak to *E.*, Jer. 39:16.

EBEN-EZER, (stone of help); (1) place
where Israel was defeated by the Philistines (I Sam. 4:1, 2); probably where the
ark was taken (I Sam. 4:3–11). (2) A stone
set up by Samuel as a memorial of the
divine help in overcoming the Philistines
(I Sam. 7:12).

EBER, HEBER, (1) a descendant of Shem
through Arpachshad (Gen. 10:22, 24);
the progenitor of a group of peoples
(Gen. 10:21). The word means "the other
side" and denotes the people who came

"from the other side of the river," from
Haran (Gen. 11:31), from where Abraham and his dependents migrated to
Canaan. (2) A Gadite (I Chr. 5:13). (3) A
son of Elpaal (I Chr. 8:12). (4) A son of
Shashak (I Chr. 8:22, 25). (5) A priest of
the family of Amok (Neh. 12:20).

EBEZ, ABEZ, the meaning is not known.
One of the sixteen cities in Issachar (Josh.
19:20).

EBIASAPH, a descendant of Korah (I
Chr. 6:23). *See* ABIASAPH.

EBIONITES, a sect of heretics often mentioned by the church Fathers. To them
Jesus was merely a man. They rejected
the Virgin Birth, and insisted that the
Holy Spirit descended upon Jesus for the
first time at His baptism.

EBONY, valuable wood used for inlaying
and ornamental turnery (Ezek. 27:15).

EBRON, a town of Asher (Josh. 19:28),
perhaps the same as Abdon. *See* HE-
BRON.

EBRONAH, *see* ABRONAH (Num. 33:
34, 35).

ECBATANA, a city in the province of the
Medes. *See* ACHMETHA.

ECCLESIASTES, one who sits and speaks
in an assembly or church; a preacher.
The name, Ecclesiastes, is borrowed from
the Septuagint version of the Old Testament. The Hebrew title "Koheleth" conveys nearly the same idea. The book has
generally been ascribed to Solomon as
the author. Ecclesiastes is an inquiry into
the chief good of man, and can be divided into four discourses. The first (1–2)
describes the vanity of theoretical wisdom
and practical wisdom. The second (3–5)
describes man's dependence on a higher
providence, and shows that there can be
no higher good than self-enjoyment,
which is not easy to attain (4). The third
(6–8) shows the vanity of grasping at
riches (6), and describes practical wisdom
in spite of the incongruities of life (8:15).
The fourth brings us to the conclusion of
the whole matter, "to fear God and keep
his commandments" (Eccles. 12:13). It
was the author's purpose to argue from
lower principles at first, in order to show

the weakness of these principles. We are told that it was one of the "scrolls" read by the Jews at the feast of the tabernacles.

ECCLESIASTICUS, one of the books of the Apocrypha, also called "The Wisdom of Jesus the Son of Sirach." It is believed to have been written in Hebrew, and within the land of Palestine. It is an exhortation to cheerfulness in the time of trouble. It probably belongs to a time before the Maccabean period.

ED, (a witness); the name of the altar erected by the two and one half tribes of Israel east of the Jordan to show that they were of common descent (Josh. 22:34).

EDAR, *see* **EDER.**

EDEN, (1) the earliest home of man; the dwelling place of our first parents. The actual location of the place is a matter of conjecture (Gen. 2:8; 3:23, 24). There is a similar tradition in all nations, it being the "golden age" of the Greeks. Its location in the Bible is "eastward," probably somewhere along the course of the rivers Tigris and Euphrates. It was perhaps here that Adam and Eve were tempted and ate of the tree of knowledge and were expelled from the garden (Gen. 3:4–6, 23). (2) One of the markets that supplied Tyre with richly embroidered stuffs (Is. 37:12; Ezek. 27:23). It was called the "house of Eden." (3) A Levite, son of Joah (II Chr. 29:12).
garden eastward in *E.*, Gen. 2:8.
from the garden of *E.*, Gen. 3:23.
children of *E.*, II Kin. 19:12.
children of *E.*, Is. 37:12.
wilderness like *E.*, Is. 51:3.
and *E.*, the merchants, Ezek. 27:23.
E. the garden of God, Ezek. 28:13.
the garden of *E.*, Joel 2:3.
from the house of *E.*, Amos 1:5.

EDER, (1) a town in the south part of Judah (Josh. 15:21). The exact location is unknown. (2) a son of Mushi (I Chr. 23:23; 24:30).

EDGE, the end of something; the cutting part of a sharp instrument.
e. of the sword, Gen. 34:26.
e. of the one curtain, Ex. 26:4.
people with the *e.*, I Sam. 15:8.
fall by the *e.*, Luke 21:24.

e. of the sword, Heb. 11:34.

EDIFY, to build up; promoting the spiritual growth and development. Also **Edification** and **Edifying.**
and were *e.*, Acts 9:31.
but charity *e.*, I Cor. 8:1.
e. the church, I Cor. 14:4.
church may receive *e.*, I Cor. 14:5.
given us for *e.*, II Cor. 10:8.
and *e.* one another, I Thess. 5:11.

EDOM, (1) means "red." This name was given to Esau after he sold his birthright to his brother for a mess of "red" pottage (Gen. 25:30). (2) The country south of Palestine which was settled by the descendants of Esau. Edom, or Idumea, lay along the route pursued by the Israelites from Sinai to Kadeshbarnea, along the east side of the great valley of Arabah. On the north of Edom lay the land of Moab. Edom was rich and fertile and lay on the caravan route to the East. Today it is rocky and barren, and the caravans have ceased to travel the old road, as prophesied in Is. 34:10.

EDOMITES, the descendants of Esau, and therefore of the seed of Abraham. They expelled the original inhabitants of land, the Horites (Deut. 2:12). They had a king long before Israel did (Gen. 36:31), and the kings were probably elective. The princes of the Edomites are named in Gen. 36:40–43, and were probably petty chiefs of their several clans. Esau's bitter hatred to his brother Jacob was continued by posterity. They refused to let Israelites pass through their land (Num. 20:18–21). They were defeated by Saul (I Sam. 14:47). Joab, in the time of David, destroyed nearly their whole male population (I Kin. 11:15). When Nebuchadnezzar attacked Jerusalem the Edomites joined him, and helped plunder the city (Ps. 137:7). Because of this they were denounced by the later prophets (Is. 34:5–8; Jer. 49:17; Amos 1:11; Obad. 8, 10). They were overcome by John Hyrcanus (135–105 B.C.) and were made to adopt circumcision. Herod the Great and his father, Antipater, were Idumeans, and hated the Jews. 20,000 Idumeans helped Titus destroy Jerusalem (70 A.D.).

EDREI, a city of Og where the kingdom of Og was defeated by the Israelites.
the battle at *E.*, Num. 21:33.

at Astaroth in *E*., Deut. 1:4.
Salchah and *E*., Deut. 3:10.
Ashtaroth and at *E*., Josh. 12:4.

EDUCATION, discipline of mind or character through study or instruction. Similar to "chasten" as used in the Bible. *See* SCHOOL.

EFFECT, consequence, result, conclusion.
God of none *e*., Matt. 15:6.
God without *e*., Rom. 3:3.
made of none *e*., Rom. 4:14.
promise of none *e*., Gal. 3:17.

EFFECTUAL, EFFECTUALLY, powerful in action, to put forth power, to work.
door and *e*. is opened, I Cor. 16:9.
which is *e*. in the, II Cor. 1:6.
wrought *e*. in Peter, Gal. 2:8.
which *e*. worketh, I Thess. 2:13.

EFFEMINATE, soft; soft to the touch; luxurious and dainty. Used of persons guilty of addiction to sins of the flesh (I Cor. 6:9).

EGG, Deut. 22:6 prohibits taking a sitting bird from its eggs. Job asks, in the midst of his afflictions, "is there any taste in the white of an egg"? (6:6) Suffering, to Job, was not to be enjoyed like the sampling of a delicate food. An egg is contrasted with a scorpion as an article of food (Luke 11:12).
young ones, or *e*., Deut. 22:6.
white of an *e*., Job 6:6.
hatch cockatrice's *e*., Is. 59:5.
shall ask an *e*., Luke 11:12.

EGLAH, wife of David and mother of Ithream (II Sam. 3:5).

EGLAIM, a city of Moab. The location is unknown (Is. 15:8).

EGLATH-SHELISHIYAH, a place in Moab (Jer. 48:34 ASV).

EGLON, (1) a king of Moab, an enemy of Israel who was assassinated by Ehud (Judg. 3:12ff.). (2) A city in Judah about 16 miles northeast of Gaza. (Josh. 15:39).
Debir king of *E*., Josh. 10:3.
The king of *E*., Josh. 12:12.
Bozkath, and *E*., Josh. 15:39.
Lord strengthened *E*., Judg. 3:12.

EGYPT, a country in the northeastern angle of Africa. The common name of Egypt in the Bible is "Mizraim." The dual ending of this word could have reference to the natural division of the country into an upper and a lower region. The singular, "Mazor," also occurs, and may refer to one of the regions. Egypt is also called "the land of Ham" (Ps. 105:23). Egypt lies within the Sahara desert, and has been the home of civilization because of the Nile river, which deposits a rich layer of black soil. This is probably why Egypt is known by the natives as "Qemet," which means "black." Apart from the wide delta region, Egypt was a territory about ten to twenty miles wide, and extending about five hundred miles south into the desert. The huge limestone cliffs were a great help to the Egyptians in their growth. From these the great pyramids were built.

It is impossible to trace out the origins of these people. About 3000 B.C. this ancient culture had risen to a point of high civilization. What is known as the Old Kingdom lasted until about 2200 B.C. during which most of the great pyramids were built. The Middle Kingdom lasted approximately from 2000 to 1800 B.C. This was a period of great literary and political achievement. Following this, the land was invaded by the Hyksos. In the sixteenth century B.C. they were expelled from the land, and the Egyptian Empire arose. Egypt now attained its summit of power. Their territory was from the Euphrates in Syria to the fourth cataract of the Nile in central Africa.

It was in Egypt that the Israelites grew into clans and tribes. It was "out of Egypt" that God called his people (Hos. 14:1). Egypt played a large part in the growth of Israel as a nation.
Abram went down to *E*., Gen. 12:10.
out of the land of *E*., Gen. 21:21.
go not down into *E*., Gen. 26:2.
with thee into *E*., Gen. 46:4.
a new king over *E*., Ex. 1:8.
people which are in *E*., Ex. 3:7.
brethren which are in *E*., Ex. 4:18.
hand upon *E*., Ex. 7:4.
out of the land of *E*., Ex. 29:46.
land of *E*., wherein ye, Lev. 18:3.
in the land of *E*., Num. 3:13.
we did eat in *E*., Num. 11:5.
died in the land of *E*., Num. 14:2.
he did for you in *E*., Deut. 1:30.
out of the land of *E*., Deut. 5:6.

came out of *E.*, Josh. 2:10.
in *E.* in Pharaoh's, I Sam. 2:27.
Israel out of *E.*, II Sam. 7:6.
Pharaoh king of *E.*, I Kin. 3:1.
brought out of *E.*, II Chr. 1:16.
terror unto *E.*, Is. 19:17.
and flee into *E.*, Matt. 2:13.
out of *E.* by Moses, Heb. 3:16.
the treasures in *E.*, Heb. 11:26.
he forsook *E.*, Heb. 11:27.

EGYPT, BROOK OF, *see* **EGYPT, RIVER OF.**

EGYPT, RIVER OF, a little desert stream that perhaps formed the dividing line between Canaan and Egypt.
from the river of *E.*, Gen. 15:18.
unto the river of *E.*, Num. 34:5.
unto the river of *E.*, Josh. 15:4.
unto the river of *E.*, I Kin. 8:65.

EGYPTIAN(S), the inhabitants of Egypt.
the *E.* shall see, Gen. 12:12.
and the *E.* mourned, Gen. 50:3.
spied an *E.* smiting, Ex. 2:11.
in the sight of the *E.*, Ex. 3:21.
E. said, Let us flee, Ex. 14:25.

EHI, a son of Benjamin (Gen. 46:21).

EHUD, (1) a son of Bilham and great-grandson of Benjamin (I Chr. 7:10). (2) A son of Gera, of the tribe of Benjamin, and second judge of the Israelites (Judg. 3:15).

EITHER, one or the other of two; each of two; in place of.
E. three years', I Chr. 21:12.
e. he will hate, Matt. 6:24.
E. how canst thou, Luke 6:42.
on *e.* side one, John 19:18.

EKER, a man of Judah, a son of Ram, of the house of Jerahmeel (I Chr. 2:27).

EKRON, the most northerly of the five chief Philistine cities (Josh. 13:3). It was assigned to Judah then to Dan. The ark of God was sent to Ekron by the Philistines and from there was returned to Israel. Also **Ekronites.**
unto the borders of *E.*, Josh. 13:3.
coast thereof, and *E.*, Judg. 1:18.
ark of God to *E.*, I Sam. 5:10.
the god of *E.*, II Kin. 1:2.

EKRONITE, an inhabitant of the Philis-

tine city of Ekron (Josh. 13:3; I Sam. 5:10).

ELADAH, a descendant of Ephraim (I Chr. 7:20).

ELAH, (1) the son and successor of Baasha, king of Israel (I Kin. 16:8f.). He had reigned for a little more than a year when he was killed by Zimri. (2) Father of Hoshea, the last king of Israel (II Kin. 15:30). (3) A duke of Edom (Gen. 36:41). (4) a son of Caleb (I Chr. 4:15). (5) A Benjamite, son of Uzzi (I Chr. 9:8).

ELAH, VALLEY OF, a valley in which the Israelites were camped when David killed Goliath (I Sam. 17:2, 19).

ELAM, (1) a son of Shem (Gen. 10:22). (2) A Benjamite (I Chr. 8:24). (3) A Korahite (I Chr. 26:3). (4) Heads of families in the return from exile (Ezra 2:7; 2:31; 8:7). (5) A chief of the people (Neh. 10:14). (6) A priest (Neh. 12:42).

ELAM, the name of a country inhabited by the descendants of Shem (Gen. 14:1–9; Is. 11:11). Its capital was Shushan, one of the powerful cities of antiquity. In the time of Abram, the king of Elam was one of the most powerful kings in Asia (Jer. 49:34–39). There is a reference to the Elamites in the book of Acts (2:9), their being at the Pentecostal feast.

ELAMITES, the original inhabitants of Elam (Gen. 10:22; Ezra 4:9).

ELASAH, (1) an Israelite who had married a foreign wife (Ezra 10:22). (2) A son of Shaphan, by whom, with Gemariah, king Zedekiah sent a message to Babylon (Jer. 29:3).

ELATH, ELOTH, a town on the gulf of Akaba, on the eastern border of the wilderness of Paran.
the plain from *E.*, Deut. 2:8.
He built *E.*, II Kin. 14:22.
recovered *E.* to Syria, II Kin. 16:6.

EL-BERITH, *see* **BAAL-BERITH.**

EL-BETH-EL, (God of Bethel), the name which Jacob gave to the place where God appeared to him when fleeing from Esau (Gen. 35:7).

ELDAAH, a son of Midian (Gen. 25:4; I Chr. 1:33).

ELDAD, one of the seventy elders chosen by Moses to help bear the burden of government (Num. 11:26).

ELDER, the title designates high officials generally (Gen. 50:7). The term was usually applied to older men who exercised authority over the people (Deut. 27:1; Ezra 10:8), and represented the nation in affairs of state (Ex. 3:18), and in religious acts (Lev. 4:15). It seems that each city had its elders (Deut. 19:12) as well as the nation.

In the church founded by Christ and the apostles; elder, presbyter, bishop, or overseer were interchangeable designations (Acts 20:17, 28; Titus 1:5, 7), though not strictly synonymous. The distinction between elder and bishop, as two offices, dates from the second century. From very early we find a plurality of elders in each congregation where there were qualified men (Acts 9:30; 14:23; I Tim. 3:1ff.). Elders had the spiritual oversight of the local churches (Acts 20:28), exercised rule and gave instruction (I Tim. 5:17; Titus 1:9).

e. of his house, Gen. 50:7.
gather the *e.* of Israel, Ex. 3:16.
seventy men of the *e.*, Num. 11:16.
the *e.* of his city, Deut. 19:12.
ten men of the *e.*, Ruth 4:2.
called all the *e.* of, I Kin. 20:7.
and the *e.* sat with, II Kin. 6:32.
princes and the *e.*, Ezra 10:8.
assembly of the *e.*, Ps. 107:32.
certain of the *e.*, Jer. 26:17.
tradition of the *e.*, Mark 7:3.
e. of the Jews, Luke 7:3.
sent it to the *e.*, Acts 11:30.
ordained them *e.*, Acts 14:23.
Rebuke not an *e.*, I Tim. 5:1.
ordain *e.* in every, Titus 1:5.
for the *e.* of the, James 5:14.
The *e.* which are, I Pet. 5:1.
The *e.* unto the, II John 1.
and twenty *e.* sitting, Rev. 4:4.

ELEAD, a descendant of Ephraim who was killed by the people of Gath while he attempted to carry away their cattle (I Chr. 7:21).

ELEADAH, *see* ELADAH (I Chr. 7:20).

ELEALEH, a place on the east of Jordan in the country given to Reuben.

Heshbon, and *E.*, Num. 32:3.
built Heshbon, and *E.*, Num. 32:37.
shall cry, and *E.*, Is. 15:4.
even unto *E.*, Jer. 48:34.

ELEASAH, (1) a descendant of Judah (I Chr. 2:39). (2) A descendant of Saul and Jonathan (I Chr. 8:37; 9:43).

ELEAZAR, (1) third son of Aaron by Elisheba (Ex. 6:23). Later became chief of the Levites (Num. 3:32), and succeeded his father as high priest (Num. 20:28; Deut. 10:6). (2) A son of Abinadab, sanctified to keep the ark of the Lord (I Sam. 7:1). (3) One of David's mighty men, a son of Dodo (II Sam. 23:9). (4) A Levite, a son of Mahli, a Merarite (I Chr. 23:21). (5) A priest who accompanied Ezra from Babylon (Ezra 8:33). (6) A priest who took part in the dedication of the wall of Jerusalem (Neh. 12:42). (7) An ancestor of Jesus (Matt. 1:15).

ELECT, chosen; selected.
mine *e.* in whom, Is. 42:1.
for the *e.* sake, Matt. 24:22.
together his *e.* from, Mark 13:27.
charge of God's *e.*, Rom. 8:33.

ELECTION, a choice, a picking out. The idea of election in the Bible applies to three things: (1) the choice of nations, (2) the choice of individuals to a particular work, and (3) the choice of individuals to be the children of God. In regard to the third sense there has been much controversy in theological thought. There are two main positions in this controversy, that held by John Calvin and that held by Jacob Arminius. For the Calvinists individual election is absolute, unconditional, and based upon the eternal decree of God. The Arminians hold that election is conditional upon repentance and faith, that the choice of the individual is somehow involved in receiving God's grace. One of the main differences in the two views is their ideas concerning the number of the elect. In Calvinism the number is limited, and in Arminianism the benefits of the atonement wrought by Christ are universal.

EL-ELOHE-ISRAEL, (God, the God of Israel), the name given by Jacob to an altar which he erected near Shechem (Gen. 33:20).

EL ELYON, a name of God to show that He is the "Exalted one" (Gen. 14:18). *See* **GOD, NAMES OF.**

ELEMENT(S), (1) the constituent parts of the physical universe (II Pet. 3:10). (2) The rudimentary principles of religion (Gal. 4:3,9).

ELEPH, a village of Benjamin (Josh. 18: 28).

ELEPHANT, a native of the near east. In 1468 there was a great Elephant hunt at the Euphrates by which Thutmose III celebrated his conquest over Syria and Palestine. Assyrian reliefs picture elephants. The ivory from their tusks were used widely in art objects. Ivory is mentioned twice in the Bible, I Kin. 10:22; II Chr. 9:21. The elephant is mentioned in the book of Maccabees.

ELHANAN, (1) a son of Jaareoregim who killed the brother of Goliath of Gath (II Sam. 21:19). (2) A son of Dodo, and one of David's thirty heroes (II Sam. 23:24).

ELI, a descendant of Aaron through Ithamar (Lev. 10:1, 2, 12), because Eli's son, Ahimelech, is said to be one of "the sons of Ithamar" (I Chr. 24:3). Eli was the chief priest during part of the eleventh century. He also acted as judge (I Sam. 7:6, 15–17). His sons were Hophni and Phineas. These boys were exciting disgust in the people because of their misconduct (I Sam. 2:12–17), and Eli was aware of their actions, for he mildly rebuked them. God's denunciation of the house of Eli came through Samuel and an unnamed prophet (I Sam. 2:27–36). His sons carried the ark of the covenant into the battlefield, and they were slain, the ark being captured by the Philistines. When Eli heard this, he fell backward from his seat, broke his neck, and died. He was nearly one hundred years old. As a high priest, he was a man of faith. As a judge, he seems to be careful and just, except in the partiality shown toward his sons. As a father, Eli let his love for his sons overshadow his better judgment.

ELIAB, (1) a son of Helon and the captain of the tribe of Zebulun who helped Moses number the people (Num. 1:9; 2:7). (2) A Reubenite, son of Pallu (Num. 16:1; 26:8; Deut. 11:6). (3) The eldest brother of David (I Chr. 2:13) and the first of the sons of Jesse who was presented to Samuel when he came to Bethlehem to anoint a king (I Sam. 16:6). (4) An ancestor of Samuel the prophet, and the son of Nahath and father of Jeroham (I Chr. 6:27). (5) A Gadite who joined David in the wilderness (I Chr. 12:9). (6) A Levite, who was appointed to conduct music in the sanctuary in the time of David (I Chr. 15:18).

ELIADA, (1) one of David's sons (II Sam. 5:16). (2) A descendant of Benjamin and a captain in the army of Jehoshaphat (II Chr. 17:17).

ELIADAH, father of Rezon of Zobah (I Kin. 11:23).

ELIAH, *see* **ELIJAH.**

ELIAHBA, one of David's mighty men (II Sam. 23:32).

ELIAKIM, (1) a son of Hilkiah; master of Hezekiah's household (II Kin. 18:18). (2) Original name of king Jehoiakim (II Kin. 23:34). (3) An ancestor of Christ (Luke 3:30).
came out to them *E.,* II Kin. 18:18.
he sent *E.,* II Kin. 19:2.
call my servant *E.,* Is. 22:20.
forth unto him *E.,* Is. 36:3.

ELIAM, (1) father of Bath-sheba (II Sam. 9:3). (2) One of David's mighty men (II Sam. 23:34).

ELIAS, *see* **ELIJAH.**

ELIASAPH, (1) son of Deuel and head of the tribe of Gad at the census in the wilderness (Num. 1:14). (2) Son of Lael and prince of the Gershonites (Num. 3:24).

ELIASHIB, (1) a descendant of David (I Chr. 3:24). (2) Head of the eleventh course of priests (I Chr. 24:12). (3) The high priest at the time of the rebuilding of the wall under Nehemiah (Neh. 3:1).

ELIATHAH, a son of Heman appointed for the service of song (I Chr. 25:4, 27).

ELIDAD, a chief of Benjamin in the division of Canaan (Num. 34:21).

ELIEHOENAI, ELIHOENAI, head of a family in the return from exile (Ezra 8:4).

ELIEL, (1) an ancestor of Samuel (I Chr. 6:34). (2) A chief of Manasseh, east of Jordan (I Chr. 5:24). (3) A Levite in the time of Hezekiah (II Chr. 31:13).

ELI, ELI, LAMA SABACHTHANI, "my God, my God, why hast thou forsaken me"? One of the phrases spoken by Jesus on the cross (Matt. 27:46). It is identical with the opening words in Aramaic of Ps. 22.

ELIENAI, a son of Shimhi, a Benjamite (I Chr. 8:20).

ELIEZER, (1) "Eliezer of Damascus" mentioned in Gen. 15:2, 3, apparently as a steward of Abraham. It is held that he was adopted as an heir, and meanwhile was Abraham's chief servant. (2) The second of the two sons of Moses and Zipporah. His father gave him this name because God had helped him and delivered him from the sword of Pharaoh. Eliezer means "God of help." Eliezer had one son, Rehabiah, from whom sprang a numerous posterity (I Chr. 23:17; 26:25). (3) Son of Becher and grandson of Benjamin (I Chr. 7:8). (4) One of the men who blew with trumpets before the ark when it was brought to Jerusalem (I Chr. 15:24). (5) Son of Zichri, and ruler of the Reubenites in the reign of David (I Chr. 27:16). (6) Son of Dodavah, and a prophet in the time of Jehoshaphat (II Chr. 20:37). (7) A chief of the Jews during the exile (Ezra 8:16). (8), (9), (10) A priest, a Levite, and an Israelite who divorced their Gentile wives after the exile (Ezra 10:18, 23, 31). (11) Son of Jorim and father of Jose (Luke 3:29).

ELIHOREPH, one of Solomon's scribes (I Kin. 4:3).

ELIHU, (1) an Ephraimite, son of Tohu and an ancestor of Samuel (I Sam. 1:1). (2) A Manassite captain who joined David on his way to Ziklag (I Chr. 12:20). (3) A friend of Job's, the son of Barachel (Job 32–37).

ELIJAH, ELIAS, ELIAH, one of the greatest of the prophets. He was a Tishbite but lived in Gilead (I Kin. 17:1). He wore a garment of skin or of coarse camel-hair, which was girt about his loins with a leather girdle (II Kin. 1:8). He suddenly appeared when Ahab, influenced by his wife Jezebel, had given himself to the worship of Baal. He told the king of a drought which was a penalty for the rejection of Jehovah. This drought lasted three and a half years (James 5:17). During the great famine Elijah was fed by ravens (I Kin. 17:6), then by a widow of the city Zarephath who was blessed because she shared her last food (I Kin. 17:12f.). In the third year of the drought Elijah challenged the prophets of Baal to prove Baal. There followed the scene on mount Carmel (I Kin. 18:21ff.). Soon after this event the rain came (I Kin. 18:45). Jezebel was angry and promised to slay Elijah (I Kin. 19:2) but he fled to mount Horeb. He was divinely sustained for forty days and nights (I Kin. 19:8). Jehovah rebuked Elijah and sent him back to duty. After a number of divinely guided conflicts with the Baal worshippers, Elijah was carried into heaven without dying (II Kin. 2:1ff.). The last book of the Old Testament predicts that God will send Elijah before the coming of the great and dreadful day of the Lord (Mal. 4:5, 6). The New Testament explains that this reference is to John the Baptist, who was like the prophet in humble dress and appearance (Mark 1:6), in fidelity and in work (Matt. 11:14; Mark 9:13; Luke 1:17).

and *E.* the Tishbite, I Kin. 17:1 .
the Lord came to *E.*, I Kin. 18:1.
E. mocked them, I Kin. 18:27.
Jezebel all that *E.*, I Kin. 19:1.
dost thou here, *E.*, I Kin. 19:13.
E. passed by him, I Kin. 19:19 .
Ahab said to *E.*, I Kin. 21:20.
and *E.* departed, II Kin. 1:4 .
his knees before *E.*, II Kin. 1:13 .
would take up *E.*, II Kin. 2:1.
E. went with Elisha, II Kin. 2:1.
E. took his mantle, II Kin. 2:8 .
E. went up by a, II Kin. 2:11.
the mantle of *E.*, II Kin. 2:13.
to him from *E.*, II Chr. 21:12.
I will send you *E.*, Mal. 4:5 .
this is *E.*, which, Matt. 11:14.
them Moses and *E.*, Matt. 17:3.
scribes that *E.* must, Mark 9:11.
in the days of *E.*, Luke 4:25.
Scripture saith of *E.*, Rom. 11:2.

E. was a man subject, James 5:17.

ELIKA, a Harodite, one of David's mighty men (II Sam. 23:25).

ELIM, the second encampment of the Israelites after crossing the Red Sea (Ex. 15:27).

ELIMELECH, a man of Bethlehem of Judah, the husband of Naomi (Ruth 1:1, 5).

ELIOENAI, (1) a descendant of Simeon (I Chr. 4:36). (2) A Benjamite of the family of Becher (I Chr. 7:8). (3) Two men who had married foreign wives (Ezra 10:22, 27).

ELIPHAL, a son of Ur and one of David's mighty men (I Chr. 11:35).

ELIPHALET, ELIPHELET, (1) a son of David born in Jerusalem (I Chr. 3:6). (2) The last of David's sons by his wives (II Sam. 5:16). (3) One of David's mighty men (II Sam. 23:34).

ELIPHAZ, (1) a son of Esau (Gen. 36:4). (2) One of Job's friends (Job 2:11ff.).

ELIPHELEH, a Levite set over the choral service when the ark was brought up from the house of Obed-edom (I Chr. 15:18, 21).

ELIPHELET, *see* **ELIPHALET.**

ELISABETH, ELIZABETH, the wife of Zacharias and mother of John the Baptist. She was of a priestly family and related to Mary the mother of Jesus.
and her name was *E.,* Luke 1:5.
no child, because *E.,* Luke 1:7.
thy wife *E.* shall bear, Luke 1:13.
wife *E.* conceived, Luke 1:24.

ELISHA, ELISEUS, (God is salvation), son of Shaphat, and a native of Abel-Meholah, where Elijah found him. He became Elijah's pupil and successor for several years (I Kin. 19:16). He was with Elijah when he divided the Jordan, and was carried away on a chariot of fire. Elisha's work was to show the people that the God of Israel could be the salvation of the people. Upon receiving his call as a prophet, he slew one yoke of oxen. boiled its flesh, and gave a feast for all his relatives and friends, and then followed Elijah (I Kin. 19:16). His first act was to heal the bitter waters of Jericho. He then anathematized the young lads who mocked God's prophet, he multiplied the widow's pot of oil, restored the Shunamite's son, cured the poisoned pottage, cured Naaman's leprosy, and he restored the ax lost in the Jordan. He struck blind the whole Assyrian army, he predicts plenty and the death of the king, he anoints Jehu king over Israel, and predicts the death of Benhadad. He resembled Christ in his miracles and in his character. He had no successor.
and *E.* the son of, I Kin. 19:16.
and found *E.* the son, I Kin. 19:19.
Elijah went with *E.,* II Kin. 2:1.
E. said unto him, II Kin. 2:2.
doth rest on *E.,* II Kin. 2:15.
and *E.* said unto her, II Kin. 4:2.
and when *E.* was, II Kin. 4:32.
the house of *E.,* II Kin. 5:9.
but *E.* the prophet, II Kin. 6:12.
E. said, Lord, open, II Kin. 6:20.
the time of *E.,* Luke 4:27.

ELISHAH, a son of Javan (Gen. 10:4); also a people who produced blue and purple dye (Ezek. 27:7).

ELISHAMA, (1) the son of Ammihud, and "captain" of the tribe of Ephraim at the Exodus (Num. 1:10; 2:18; 7:48). (2) The second of nine sons of David born at Jerusalem (I Chr. 3:6). (3) The seventh of the same series of sons (I Chr. 3:8; 14:7). (4) An Israelite of the family of David, father of Nethaniah, and grandfather of Ishmael, who slew Gedaliah (II Kin. 25:25). (5) An Israelite of the tribe of Judah and son of Jekamiah (I Chr. 2:41). (6) One of the two priests sent with the Levites by Jehoshaphat to teach the law through the cities of Judah (II Chr. 17:8). (7) A scribe or secretary to Jehoiakim (Jer. 36:12, 20, 21).

ELISHAPHAT, one of the captains of hundreds who supported Jehoiada in the revolt against Athaliah (II Chr. 23:1).

ELISHEBA, the wife of Aaron and mother of Nadab, Abihu, Eleazar and Ithamar (Ex. 6:23).

ELISHUA, a son of David, born at Jerusalem (II Sam. 5:15).

ELIUD, son of Achim, and father of Eleazar, in the ancestry of Christ (Matt. 1:14, 15).

ELIZAPHAN, ELZAPHAN, (1) a son of Uzziel, and chief of the Kohathites in the wilderness (Ex. 6:22; Num. 3:30). (2) Prince of the tribe of Zebulun in the wilderness (Num. 34:25).

ELIZUR, prince of Reubenites in the wilderness (Num. 1:5; 2:10).

ELKANAH, (God has possessed), the name of several men, all apparently Levites. (1) The second son of Korah and the brother of Assir and Abiasaph (Ex. 6: 24). (2) Son of Shaul, or Joel, being the father of Amasai, and ninth in descent from Kohath (I Chr. 6:25; 36). (3) Son of Ahimoth, and great-grandson of one of the above (I Chr. 6:26, 35). (4) Son of Jeroham and father of Samuel (I Chr. 6:27, 28, 33, 34). He had two wives, Hannah and Peninnah. Hannah was childless until she prayed to God, after which Samuel was born. Elkanah was a pious man, going up yearly to Shiloh to sacrifice (I Sam. 1:3). (5) The father of Asa (I Chr. 9:16). (6) One of the men who joined David at Ziklag (I Chr. 12:6). (7) A chief officer in the court of Ahaz of Judah (II Chr. 28:7).

ELKOSHITE, a citizen of Elkosh (Naham 1:1). The location is unknown.

ELLASAR, a city in or near Babylonia (Gen. 14:9).

ELM, (terebinth); a small tree (Hos. 4:13).

ELMODAM, an ancestor of Christ (Luke 3:28).

ELNAAM, the father of certain valiant men in David's army (I Chr. 11:46).

ELNATHAN, (1) the father of Nehushta, who was mother of Jehoiachin, king of Judah (II Kin. 24:8). He is perhaps the same as the son of Achbor sent by Jehoiakim to bring the prophet Urijah from Egypt (Jer. 26:22). (2) (3) (4) Three of the Israelites of position and understanding sent by Ezra to invite the priests and Levites to accompany him to Jerusalem (Ezra 8:16).

ELOHIM, a term used in the ordinary sense of gods, whether true or false (Ex. 12:12; 35:2). There is a prevalent idea that Jehovah is used to refer to God in his special revelation to his people, and Elohim is used to represent God in his relation to the world, as Creator. Elohim is the word used when speaking to the Gentiles, unless Jehovah is in question. Elohim is also used when God is contrasted with men or things. Also **Eloah.**

ELOI, ELOI, LAMA SABACHTHANI, "my God, my God, why hast thou forsaken me"? The words of Jesus on the cross as recorded in Mark 15:34. As recorded in Matt. 27:46 the first two words are in Hebrew, "Eli, Eli, lama sabachthani."

ELON, (1) the mother of one of Esau's wives (Gen. 26:34). (2) A Zebulonite who judged Israel (Judg. 12:11). (3) A village of Dan (Josh. 19:43). *See* **BASEMATH.**

ELON-BETH-HANAN, a town in Dan and perhaps the same as Elon (I Kin. 4:9).

ELONITES, descendants of Elon (Num. 26:26).

ELOQUENT, learned; skilled in literature and the arts; a man of words.
I am not *e.*, Ex. 4:10.
artificer, and the *e.*, Is. 3:3.
an *e* man, and, Acts 18:24.

ELOTH, *see* **ELATH.**

ELPAAL, the name of a descendant of Benjamin (I Chr. 8:11).

ELPALET, a son of David (I Chr. 14:5), perhaps the same as Eliphalet (I Chr. 3:6).

EL-PARAN, a place in the south of Canaan and west of Edom, where the Horites dwelt in Seir (Gen. 14:6).

ELPELET, *see* **ELPALET.**

EL-SHADDAI, *see* **GOD, NAMES OF.**

ELTEKEH, a town of Dan assigned to the Levites (Josh. 19:44; 21:23).

EKTEKON, a village in the hill country of Judah (Josh. 15:59).

ELTOLAD, a city in southern Judah (Josh. 15:30), assigned to the Simeonites (Josh. 19:4).

ELUL, the sixth month of the Hebrew year, corresponding to August-September.

ELUZAI, one of David's heroes (I Chr. 12:5).

ELYMAS, a false prophet who withstood Saul and Barnabas at Paphos in Cyprus (Acts 13:8).

ELZABAD, (1) one of the valiant Gadites who came to David (I Chr. 12:12). (2) A Levite and son of Shemaiah (I Chr. 26:7).

ELZAPHAN, *see* **ELIZAPHAN.**

EMBALM, EMBALMING, the process of treating a dead body in such a manner as to prevent it from decaying. The people of Egypt embalmed in order to keep the body fit for the return of the soul after death. Contrary to popular belief, the method of embalming is no secret. After the bodies were cleaned and spiced, according to their social standing, of the family, they were then placed in a salt solution for a given number of days. The embalming of the dead took place after the Egyptian fashion in the case of Joseph and Jacob (Gen. 50:2, 26). The method was only imitated by the Hebrews to the extent that they anointed the body with oil (John 12:7) and wound the body with linen (John 12:39).

EMBOLDEN, to make powerful, bold or brave (Job 16:3; I Cor. 8:10).

EMBRACE, clasp; cleave to, salute.
thou shalt *e.* a son, II Kin. 4:16.
thou dost *e.* her, Prov. 4:8.
disciples, and *e.* them, Acts 20:1.
them, and *e.* them, Heb. 11:13.

EMBROIDERY and **NEEDLEWORK,** not plain sewing, but ornamental work (Ex. 26: Judg. 5:30; Ps. 45:14). The work required creativity and skill in designing patterns. The Israelites probably learned the art in Egypt, and it appears that some had attained distinction, especially in the tribe of Dan and Judah (Ex. 35:30; I Chr. 4:21). Parts of the Tabernacle and

the girdle of the high priest were embroidered (Ex. 26:36; 27:16; 28:39).

EMEK-KEZIZ, a town of Benjamin evidently near Jericho. In King James Version translated Keziz (Josh. 18:21).

EMERALD, a precious stone of light green color.
shall be an *e.,* Ex. 28:18.
second row, an *e.,* Ex. 39:11.
thy fairs with *e.,* Ezek. 27:16.
like unto an *e.,* Rev. 4:3.

EMERODS, rounded eminences or swellings; tumors; boils.
and with the *e.,* Deut. 28:27.
smote them with *e.,* I Sam. 5:6.
Five golden *e.,* I Sam. 6:4.
are the golden *e.,* I Sam. 6:17.

EMIMS, early inhabitants of Moab (Deut. 2:10).

EMINENT, physical elevation; lofty; heaped up (Ezek. 16:24, 31ff.).

EMMANUEL, *see* **IMMANUEL.**

EMMAUS, a town seven and a half miles from Jerusalem, the scene of Christ's revelation of himself to two of his disciples after his resurrection (Luke 24:13). The exact location, however, is disputed.

EMMOR, the father of Sychem (Acts 7: 16). *See* **HAMOR.**

EMPIRE, kingdom (Esther 1:20).

EMPLOY, to go in from before (Deut. 20:19).

EMPTY, vain; to be free; unoccupied.
the pit was *e.,* Gen. 37:24.
ye shall not go *e.,* Ex. 3:21.
he findeth it *e.,* Matt. 12:44.
sent him away *e.,* Luke 20:10.

EMPTY, to draw out; expose; pour out.
and *e.* her pitcher, Gen. 24:20.
they *e.* their sacks, Gen. 42:35.
shall *e.* his vessels, Jer. 48:12.
therefore *e.* their net, Hab. 1:17.

EMULATION, (1) signifies the stirring up of jealousy or envy in others, because of what we are, or have, or profess (Gal.

5:20). (2) To make one zealous in a good sense (Rom. 11:14).

ENABLE, endue with strength (I Tim. 1:12).

ENAM, a village in the lowlands of Judah (Josh. 15:34).

ENAN, father of Ahira, prince of the tribe of Naphtali (Num. 1:15).

ENCAMP, to form a camp; a place where temporary structures are erected for accommodation.
and e. in Etham, Ex. 13:20.
shall ye e. by the sea, Ex. 14:2.
shall e. round about, Num. 1:50.
and e. in Gilgal, Josh. 4:19.

ENCAMPMENT, *see* **CAMP.**

ENCHANTERS, magicians who used incantations to conjure up the spirits to liberate those tormented by evil spirits. They sought the aid of the evil ones that they might produce certain supernatural happenings (Ex. 7:11).
an e., or a witch, Deut. 18:10.
nor to your e., Jer. 27:9.

ENCHANTMENT, sorcery, witchcraft, soothsaying, charms, and all kinds of magic art.
did so with their e., Ex. 7:22.
neither shall ye use e., Lev. 19:26.
times and used e., II Kin. 21:6.
will bite without e., Eccles. 10:11.

ENCOUNTER, to meet face to face (Acts 17:18).

ENCOURAGE, to urge forward; persuade; to strengthen.
e. him: for he shall, Deut. 1:38.
They e. themselves, Ps. 64:5.
the carpenter e. the, Is. 41:7.

END, final object or purpose; termination; completion; hinder part; extremity.
even unto the e. of, Deut. 11:12.
glean unto the e., Ruth 2:23.
endureth to the e., Matt. 10:22.
and the e. everlasting, Rom. 6:22.
Whose e. is destruction, Phil. 3:19.

END, a bringing to completion together; marking the completion or consumma-

tion of the various parts of a scheme. Also **Ended** and **Ending.**
when Jesus had e., Matt. 7:28.
days were almost e., Acts 21:27.
in the e. of the, Heb. 9:26.

ENDAMAGE, to cause loss (Ezra 4:13).

ENDANGER, forfeit: cause to owe; expose to loss (Dan. 1:10).

ENDEAVOUR, to be zealous; make haste; to seek after.
immediately we e. to, Acts 16:10.
E. to keep the unity, Eph. 4:3.
heart, e. the more, I Thess. 2:17.
I will e. that, II Pet. 1:15.

ENDED, ENDING, *see* **END.**

ENDLESS, indissoluble (Heb. 7:16); something to which no limit can be set (I Tim. 1:4).

EN-DOR, a town belonging to the tribe of Manasseh (Josh. 17:11).

ENDUE, ENDUED, to know; to be clothed with.
God hath e. me, Gen. 30:20.
e. with prudence, II Chr. 2:12.
until ye he e. with, Luke 24:49.

ENDURE, to abide; to bear up under suffering.
I could not e., Job 31:23.
clean, e. for ever, Ps. 19:9.
the man that e., James 1:12.
of the Lord e., I Pet. 1:25.

ENEAS, a man of Lydda healed by Peter (Acts 9:33). *See* **AENEAS.**

EN-EGLAIM, a place near the Dead Sea (Ezek. 47:10).

ENEMY, one who is hostile; an adversary; an opponent.
I will be an e., Ex. 23:22.
delivered all their e., Josh. 21:44.
Love your e., Matt. 5:44.
world is the e. of God, James 4:4.

ENGAGED, to pledge (Jer. 30:21).

EN-GANNIM, (1) a village of Judah (Josh. 15:34). (2) A town on the border line of Issachar (Josh. 19:21), assigned to the Gershonite Levites (Josh. 21:29).

ENGEDI, a town on the western shore of the Dead Sea (Ezek. 47:10), in Judah (Josh. 15:62).

ENGLISH VERSIONS, *see* **VERSIONS.**

ENGRAFTED, to plant in (James 1:21).

ENGRAVE, to carve or cut in. Also **Engraved, Engraving.**
shalt thou *e.* the, Ex. 28:11.
written and *e.* in, II Cor. 3:7.

EN-HADDAH, a city of Issachar (Josh. 19:21).

EN-HAKKORE, a spring in Lehi which burst forth when Samson cried to the Lord (Judg. 15:19).

ENHAZOR, a fenced city of Naphtali (Josh. 19:37).

ENJOIN, to charge; command.
who hath *e.* him, Job 36:23.
to *e.* thee that, Philem. 8.
which God hath *e.*, Heb. 9:20.

ENJOY, to have pleasure. Also **Enjoyed.**
possession, and *e.* it, Josh. 1:15.
by thee we *e.* great, Acts 24:2.
than to *e.* the, Heb. 11:25.

ENLARGE, to extend; to make great; to spread out. Also **Enlarged, Enlarging.**
Thou hast *e.* my steps, Ps. 18:36.
they might *e.* their, Amos 1:13.
e. the borders of, Matt. 23:5.
our heart is *e.*, II Cor. 6:11.

ENLIGHTEN, to give light; to illumine.
Lord is pure, *e.*, Ps. 19:8.
understanding being *e.*, Eph. 1:18.
who were once *e.*, Heb. 6:4.

EN-MISHPAT, a place called Kadesh in Paran (Gen. 14:7).

ENMITY, hate; animosity; hostility.
I will put *e.* between, Gen. 3:15.
carnal mind is *e.*, Rom. 8:7.
in his flesh the *e.*, Eph. 2:15.
world is *e.* with God, James 4:4.

ENOCH, (1) the oldest son of Cain (Gen. 4:17). (2) A city built by Cain and called

after his son (Gen. 4:17). (3) A descendant of Jared and progenitor of Methuselah (Gen. 5:21). He lived 365 years and God took him (Gen. 5:18ff.), and he did not see death (Heb. 11:5).

ENOCH, BOOKS OF, three apocalyptic books written about a seer and a hero named Enoch. The main body of what must be the original Enoch tells of Enoch's travels through the heavens, various astronomical matter, two visions, and a section of exhortations.

ENOS, the son of Seth and the grandson of Adam (Gen. 5:6–11; Luke 3:38). He lived to be nine hundred and five years old, and is interesting because of a singular expression used after his name in Gen. 4:26, "Then began men to call upon the name of the Lord." In I Chr. 1:1 the name is Anglicized Enosh.

ENOUGH, sufficient; abundant; fullness.
goat's milk *e.* for, Prov. 27:27.
say not, It is *e.*, Prov. 30:15.
It is *e.* for the, Matt. 10:25.
unto them, It is *e.*, Luke 22:38.

ENQUIRE, to ask; to seek; to examine.
and David *e.* of, II Sam. 21:1.
E., I pray thee, I Kin. 22:5.
dost not *e.* wisely, Eccles. 7:10.
if ye *e.* any thing, Acts 19:39.

ENRICH, to make rich.
king will *e.* him, I Sam. 17:25.
didst *e.* the kings, Ezek. 27:33.
thing ye are *e.* by, I Cor. 1:5.
Being *e.* in, II Cor. 9:11.

EN-RIMMON, a town of Judah (Neh. 11:29).

EN-ROGEL, a fountain just outside Jerusalem (II Sam. 17:17).

ENSAMPLE, an image; a pattern.
unto them for *e.*, I Cor. 10:11.
have us for an *e.*, Phil. 3:17.
ye were *e.* to all, I Thess. 1:7.
but being *e.* to the, I Pet. 5:3.

EN-SHEMESH, a spring forming an important landmark between Judah and Benjamin (Josh. 15:7).

ENSIGN, banner; token; signal.
with the *e.* of, Num. 2:2.

set up their *e.* for, Ps. 74:4.
lift up an *e.* to, Is. 5:26.

ENSNARED, trapped; entangled; snared (Job 34:30).

ENSUE, to pursue; to follow after (I Pet. 3:11).

ENTANGLE, to entrap; to ensnare.
they might *e.*, Matt. 22:15.
are again *e.* therein, II Pet. 2:20.

EN-TAPPUAH, a spring probably in the land of Tappuah which belonged to Manasseh (Josh. 17:7).

ENTER, to go in; to come in. Also Entered, Entereth, Enters.
selfsame day *e.* Noah, Gen. 7:13.
wisdom *e.* into, Prov. 2:10.
cannot *e.* into the, John 3:5.
e. into a ship of, Acts 27:2.
not *e.* in because, Heb. 3:19.

ENTERING, opening; going in; entrance.
at the *e.* of the gate, Josh. 8:29.
stood in the *e.* of, Judg. 9:35.
manner of *e.* in, I Thess. 1:9.

ENTERTAIN, to receive as guest (Heb. 13:2).

ENTICE, to seduce; to persuade; to lure with bait.
if sinners *e.* thee, Prov. 1:10.
violent man *e.* his, Prov. 16:29.
not with *e.* words, I Cor. 2:4.
own lust, and *e.*, James 1:14.

ENTIRE, complete; whole in every part (James 1:4).

ENTRANCE, opening; way in.
place in the *e.* of, I Kin. 22:10.
that kept the *e.*, II Chr. 12:10.
of Nimrod in the *e.*, Mic. 5:6.

ENTREAT, ask; desire; beseech.
and *e.* them spitefully, Luke 18:32.
e. evil 400 years, Acts 7:6.
courteously *e.* Paul, Acts 27:3.
we were shamefully *e.*, I Thess. 2:2.

ENTRY, opening; entrance; going in.
king's *e.* without, II Kin. 16:18.
keepers of the *e.*, I Chr. 9:19.

which is by the *e.*, Jer. 19:2.

ENVIEST, *see* ENVY.

ENVIOUS, to be jealous; to be zealous.
neither be thou *e.*, Ps. 37:1.
not thou *e.* against, Prov. 24:1.

ENVIRON, to surround; to encompass; to encircle (Josh. 7:9).

ENVY, jealousy or zeal.
and *e.* slayeth, Job 5:2.
The *e.* also of, Is. 11:13.
were filled with *e.*, Acts 13:45.
charity *e.* not, I Cor. 13:4.

ENVY, a feeling of displeasure produced by learning of the advantages of others; covetous.
he knew that for *e.*, Matt. 27:18.
full of *e.*, murder, Rom. 1:29.
whereof cometh *e.*, I Tim. 6:4.
in us lusteth to *e.*, James 4:5.

EPAENETUS, one of the first converts of Achaia to Christianity (Rom. 16:5).

EPAPHRAS, a christian of Asia Minor who established the Church at Colossae. He was a "fellow-servant" with Paul.
learned of *E.* our, Col. 1:7.
E., who is one of, Col. 4:12.
salute thee *E.*, Philem. 23.

EPAPHRODITUS, a messenger of the Church at Philippi to Paul during his two years in prison in Rome.
to send to you *E.*, Phil. 2:25.
received of *E.* the, Phil. 4:18.

EPHAH, (1) a branch of the Midianites (Gen. 25:4). (2) A concubine of Caleb (I Chr. 2:46). (3) A son of Jahdai of Judah (I Chr. 2:47).

EPHAH, a measure containing ten omers (Ex. 16:36), which is about 1½ bushels.
tenth part of an *e.*, Num. 5:15.
about an *e.* of, Ruth 2:17.
making the *e.* small, Amos 8:5.
an *e.* that goeth, Zech. 5:6.

EPHAI, the father of some of the forces left in Judah after the carrying away to Babylon (Jer. 40:8).

EPHER, (1) a branch of the Midianites (Gen. 25:4). (2) A man of Judah and son of Ezra (I Chr. 4:17). (3) A chief man in the half-tribe of Manasseh (I Chr. 5:24).

EPHES-DAMMIM, a place between Shochoh and Azekah (I Sam. 17:1).

EPHESIAN, belonging to Ephesus; a native of Ephesus.
Diana of the *E.* Acts, 19:28.
city of the *E.* is, Acts 19:35.

EPHESIANS, DIANA OF THE, a deity of Asiatic origin, the mother goddess of the earth, whose seat of worship was the temple in Ephesus, the capital of the Roman province of Asia (Acts 19). *See* **DIANA OF THE EPHESIANS.**

EPHESIANS, EPISTLE TO THE, was written by the apostle Paul during his first captivity at Rome, apparently immediately after he had written the letter to the Colossians and during that period (probably early in A. D. 62) when his imprisonment had not assumed the severer character which seems to have marked its close. This letter was addressed to the saints at Ephesus and the faithful in Christ Jesus. The theme is to show that God's scheme of redemption is fulfilled in the church.

EPHESUS, the capital city of the Roman province of Asia and an illustrious city in the district of Ionia, nearly opposite the island of Samos. With an artificial harbor accessible to the largest ships, and rivaling the harbor at Miletus, standing at the entrance of the valley which reaches far into the interior of Asia Minor, and connected by roads with the chief cities of the province, Ephesus was the most easily accessible city in Asia, both by land and sea. Conspicuous at the head of the harbor of Ephesus was the great temple of Diana or Artemis, the tutelary divinity of the city. This temple was a store house for the best statuary and the most beautiful paintings. It was also a refuge for criminals.

Paul visited this city on his second journey (Acts 18:19ff.) and again on the third (19:8ff.). He stayed there for more than two years (19:8, 10). While in Ephesus, Paul was strongly opposed by the worshippers of Diana (Acts 19:23ff.). Yet, a church was started and the gospel was spread into all of Asia from this point (19:10).

EPHLAL, a man of Judah of the family of Jerahmeel (I Chr. 2:37).

EPHOD, father of Hanniel, prince of Manasseh in the time of Moses (Num. 34:23).

EPHOD, the official garment of the high priest, which was later worn by the ordinary priests (I Sam. 22:18). Samuel wore such a garment even as a boy, because of his being set apart for life-long service (I Sam. 2:18).

EPHPHATHA, the words spoken by Jesus when he healed a deaf mute (Mark 7:34). The words mean "be thou opened."

EPHRAIM, (1) the second son of Joseph by Asenath, the daughter of Poti-pherah (Gen. 46:20). Upon him was conferred the birthright blessing (Gen. 48:17–19). He is the traditional ancestor for the tribe of Ephraim. (2) The tribe of Ephraim. They were one of the smaller tribes, ranking tenth at the time of the census at Sinai (Num. 1:32; 2:19). During their march in the wilderness, they were encamped on the west side of the tabernacle (Num. 2:18–24). The boundaries of Ephraim are given in Josh. 16, and it was somewhere in the center of Palestine. The tabernacle was set up in Ephraim at Shiloh (Josh. 18:1). After this the power of Ephraim increased, and it eventually became the main support of the northern kingdom, which came to be designated by its name. The reunion of Judah and Ephraim was the hope of the prophets as the fulfillment of Israel's glory (Is. 7:2; Ezek. 37:15–22). After the captivity there were "children of Ephraim" living in Jerusalem (I Chr. 9:3). (3) A city to which Jesus withdrew to escape the plots of the Jews (John 11:54). (4) One of the gates of Jerusalem, on the north side of the city (II Kin. 14:13; II Chr. 25:23). (5) A part of a mountain range in central Palestine within the boundaries of Ephraim. Samuel's parents were of Mount Ephraim (I Sam. 1:1). (6) The Forest of Ephraim, the scene of Absalom's defeat and death (II Sam. 18:6–9). This probably took place near Mahanaim, on the east of the Jordan.

EPHRAIMITES, the descendants of Ephraim (Judg. 12:4).

EPHRAIN, a city of Benjamin near Jerusalem (II Chr. 13:19).

EPHRATAH, (1) an ancient name of Bethlehem in Judaea (Ruth 4:11). (2) A wife of Caleb (I Chr. 2:19). (3) The territory of Ephraim (Ps. 132:6).

EPHRATH, (1) a city of Judah; the same as Ephratah (Gen. 35:16). (2) Caleb's second wife; the same as Ephratah (I Chr. 2:19).

EPHRATHITE, an inhabitant of Bethlehem-Judah (Ruth 1:2).

EPHRON, (1) a resident of Hebron and owner of the cave of Machpelah which he sold to Abraham (Gen. 25:9). (2) A city which was taken from Jeroboam by Abijah (II Chr. 13:19).

EPICUREANS, one of the leading philosophic sects of Greece and Rome. It derived its name and its existence from the great philosopher Epicurus. He was pure in life so that some thought he was destitute of passions. He desired that one pursue the pleasure derived from the exercise of the intellect and the moral faculty. They rejected Paul's preaching in Athens but did not riot against him. (Acts 17:18–20).

EPISTLE, the term used to designate twenty-one of the twenty-seven writings of the New Testament. There are also letters mentioned in the Old Testament (II Sam. 11:14; Jer. 29:1; Ezra 4:6; Neh. 2:7). There are fourteen epistles of Paul (if we include Hebrews). He usually dictated to an amanuensis. The epistles to Timothy and Titus are called "pastoral epistles" because of the pastoral content. The "catholic" or "general epistles" were so called because they are not addressed to any particular church or individual, but to Christians in general. These are the epistles of John and Peter, James and Jude.

EQUAL, the same in size, number, or quality.
made them e. unto, Matt. 20:12.
making himself e., John 5:18.
robbery to be e. with, Phil. 2:6.

which is just and e., Col. 4:1.

EQUITY, uprightness.
strike princes for e., Prov. 17:26.
knowledge, and in e., Eccles. 2:21.
reprove with e., Is. 11:4.
in peace and e., Mal. 2:6.

ER, (1) eldest son of Judah by the daughter of Shua the Canaanite (Gen. 38:3). (2) A son of Shelah (I Chr. 4:21). (3) An ancestor of Jesus (Luke 3:28).

ERAN, a descendant of Ephraim (Num. 26:36).

ERANITES, descendants of Eran (Num. 26:36).

ERASTUS, (1) one of those ministering to Paul (Acts 19:22) who was sent on in advance from Ephesus to Macedonia. (2) The "treasurer" of the city, probably Corinth, especially if this Erastus is the same as Paul's companion mentioned in II Tim. 4:20 who remained in Corinth.

ERE, before; not yet.
are delivered e. the, Ex. 1:19.
be e. they be quiet, Jer. 47:6.
come down e. my, John 4:49.

ERECH, one of the cities of Nimrod's kingdom (Gen. 10:10).

ERECTED, to set up (Gen. 33:20).

ERI, a son of Gad (Gen. 46:16).

ERITES, the descendants of Eri, son of Gad (Num. 26:16).

ERR, to go astray; to wander off; to miss the mark; to fail.
if ye have e., Num. 15:22.
wherein I have e., Job 6:24.
after, they have e., I Tim. 6:10.
you do e. from, James 5:19.

ERRAND, a word or message to deliver.
I have told mine e., Gen. 24:33.
a secret e. unto thee, Judg. 3:19.
I have an e. to, II Kin. 9:5.

ERROR, mistake; wandering; sin.
mine e. remaineth, Job 19:4.
that it was an e., Eccles. 5:6.
sinner from the e., James 5:20.
them who live in e., II Pet. 2:18.

ESAIAS, the Greek form of Isaiah used in the New Testament. *See* **ISAIAH.**
the prophecy of *E.*, Matt. 13:14.
hath *E.* prophesied, Mark 7:6.
read the prophet *E.*, Acts 8:30.
E. saith, Lord, Rom. 10:16.

ESARHADDON, a son and successor of King Sennacherib (705-681 B.C.) on the throne of Assyria. As soon as he became king, he rebuilt Babylon, which his father had destroyed. He spread his empire all the way to Memphis by 670 B.C. He died on his way to put down a revolt in Egypt in 688 B.C. Esarhaddon's reign is mentioned in II Kin. 19:37; Is. 37:38.

ESAU, the oldest son of Isaac and twin brother of Jacob. Esau was so named because he was hairy (Gen. 25:24-26). He became a skillful hunter. On one occasion he came home from hunting very hungry and tired. He asked for some food which Jacob had just prepared. Jacob asked for, and received, Esau's birthright in exchange for the food. From this desire for food Esau was called Edom (Gen. 25:30) Esau's descendants increased into the Edomite nation (Gen. 36:9). They lived in the mount Seir (Deut. 2:4).
called his name *E.*, Gen. 25:25.
he called *E.* his eldest, Gen. 27:1.
from the hand of *E.*, Gen. 32:11.
Thus dwelt *E.* in, Gen. 36:8.
unto Isaac Jacob and *E.*, Josh. 24:4.
Isaac; *E.* and, I Chr. 1:34.
Was not *E.* Jacob's, Mal. 1:2.
I hated *E.*, and, Mal. 1:3.

ESCAPE, to flee; a way out; to go out.
and *e.* that night, I Sam. 19:10.
worthy to *e.*, Luke 21:36.
but he *e.* out of, John 10:39.
how shall we *e.*, Heb. 2:3.
they have *e.* the, II Pet. 2:20.

ESCHEW, to turn aside; avoid.
God, and *e.* evil, Job 1:1.
let him *e.* evil, I Pet. 3:11.

ESDRAELON, PLAIN OF, a plain which joined the Jordan valley with the maritime plain, by the Mediterranean, and which separated the mountains of Samaria from those of Galilee. It is a Greek form of the Hebrew Jezreel.

ESDRAS, THE BOOKS OF, Esdras is the Greek name for Ezra. The books which carry the Greek form of his name are found in the Apocrypha. I Esdras is a combination of different authors, of narratives relating to Zerubbabel. II Esdras is probably of Egyptian origin. It is on God's providence and the signs of the last age.

ESEK, a well dug by Isaac in the valley of Gerar, which the Philistine herdmen claimed (Gen. 26:20).

ESHAN, ESHEAN, a village in the mountains of Judah (Josh. 15:52).

ESHBAAL, fourth son of Saul (I Chr. 8:33). *See* **ISH-BOSHETH.**

ESHBAN, a son of Dishon, son of Seir (Gen. 36:26).

ESHCOL, (1) an Amorite chieftain, who, with his brothers, Abner and Mamre, allied with Abraham in the recovery of Lot from the hands of Chedorlaomer (Gen. 14:13, 24). (2) The valley in the area of Hebron, in which the spies found large grapes (Num. 13:23, 24).

ESHEAN, *see* **ESHAN.**

ESHEK, a descendant of Saul through Jonathan (I Chr. 8:39).

ESHKALONITES, the inhabitants of Eshkelon (Josh. 13:3).

ESHTAOL, a town in the lowland of Judah (Josh. 15:33).

ESHTAULITE, an inhabitant of Eshtaol (I Chr. 2:53).

ESHTEMOA, ESHTEMOH, (1) a Levitical town in the mountains of Judah. (2) A Maachathite, a descendant of Ezra (I Chr. 4:17).
and Anab, and *E.*, Josh. 15:50.
and *E.* with her, Josh. 21:14.
them which were in *E.*, I Sam. 30:28.

ESHTON, a descendant of Chelub, reckoned in the genealogy of Judah (I Chr. 4:12).

ESLI, an ancestor of Christ who lived after the captivity (Luke 3:25).

ESPECIALLY, most; most of all; above all.

but *e.* among my, Ps. 31:11.
e. unto them who, Gal. 6:10.
e. they who labour, I Tim. 5:17.
but *e.* the parchments, II Tim. 4:13.

ESPOUSALS, the engagement period and early days of marriage.
the day of his *e.*, Song. 3:11.
love of thine *e.*, Jer. 2:2.

ESPOUSE, to betroth; promise in marriage. Also **Espoused.**
which I *e.* to me, II Sam. 3:14.
mother Mary was *e.*, Matt. 1:18.
virgin *e.* to a man, Luke 1:27.
for I have *e.* you, II Cor. 11:2.

ESPY, to see; to spy out; to search.
he *e.* his money, Gen. 42:27.
by the way, and *e.*, Jer. 48:19.
that I had *e.* for, Ezek. 20:6.

ESROM, son of Phares in the genealogy of Jesus (Matt. 1:3).

ESSENES, a Jewish sect in the time of Christ. They lived apart from other people and practiced a more or less ascetic life. Each colony had its own synagogue, a common hall for meals and assemblies, and provision for daily bathing in running water. Whoever became a member of the sect gave up all of his possessions to it. They read the law of Moses each morning and evening, and endeavored to live by it in every detail. They were industrious and their lives were simple. They did not deny the fitness of marriage; but they abstained from wedlock, except one party among them.

ESTABLISH, to fix; make fast.
earth which he hath *e.*, Ps. 78:69.
so were the churches *e.*, Acts 16:5.
ye may be *e.*, Rom. 1:11.
yea, we *e.* the law, Rom. 3:31.
he may *e.* the second, Heb. 10:9.

ESTATE, condition; position.
concerning the *e.* of, Eccles. 3:18.
stand up in his *e.*, Dan. 11:7.
might know your *e.*, Col. 4:8.

ESTEEM, ESTEEMED, to judge; consider; suppose.
and we *e.* him, Is. 53:3.
man *e.* one day, Rom. 14:5.
each *e.* other, Phil. 2:3.
e. the reproach, Heb. 11:26.

ESTHER, the daughter of Abihail, and probably of the tribe of Benjamin. She was a very beautiful Jewish maiden. She was an orphan, and had been brought up by Mordecai who held an office in the household of Ahasuerus, king of Persia, and dwelt at "Shushan the palace." When Vashti was dismissed as queen and all the fairest virgins of the kingdom were brought before the king for a successor, he chose Esther. The king did not know that she was of the Jewish race, so when Haman suggested that the Jews were a pernicious race, he gave him authority to kill all of them and to take their property. Esther interceded for her people and they were saved. The details are found in the book of Esther.

ESTHER, THE BOOK OF, is an episode from the reign of Ahasuerus (Xerxes), king of Persia (485–464 B.C.). The book tells how Esther, a Jewish maiden, became Xerxes' queen; how she delivered her people from the destruction planned by Haman, the king's favorite; and how the feast of Purim was instituted in commemoration of this deliverance. The book gives no claim to date or authorship for itself. The statement, "Mordecai wrote these things" (9:20), refers to the letter that follows, not to the book. The chief personages of the book are Vashti, Haman, Esther, and Mordecai. The story relates to the royal feast of Ahasuerus, and the divorce of Vashti (ch. 1). Haman attempts to carry out a plan of destruction of the Jews. But his plot is defeated, through the help of Esther, and honor was paid to Mordecai (chs. 2–4). The institution of the feast of Purim, in commemoration of this deliverance, and Mordecai's advancement (chs. 5–10). Though the name of God is not found in the book, his providential hand can be seen, defeating and overruling evil to the greater good of the Jews, and even to the heathen (1:2, 4–10).

The name "Purim" means "Lots." The festival, which lasted two days, was so called because Haman cast lots to determine the time which would be most conducive for his plans (Esther 3:7). And at the festival, when the book of Esther is read, the people curse Haman everytime his name is read. At the end they unite in blessing Esther and Mordecai.

ESTIMATE, ESTIMATION, to set in order valuation.

with thy *e.* by, Lev. 5:15.
the Lord by thy *e.,* Lev. 27:2.
priest shall *e.* it, Lev. 27:14.

ESTRANGE, to make unknown (Jer. 19:4).

ESTRANGED, to be strange; separate; turn aside.
are verily *e.* from me, Job 19:13.
wicked are *e.* from, Ps. 58:3.
were not *e.* from, Ps. 78:30.
they are all *e.* from, Ezek. 14:5.

ETAM, (1) a village of the tribe of Simeon (I Chr. 4:32). (2) A place in Judah rebuilt by Rehoboam (II Chr. 11:6).

ETAM, ROCK OF, place where Samson retired after his slaughter of the Philistines (Judg. 15:8, 11).

ETERNAL, age lasting; perpetual.
e. God is thy, Deut. 33:27.
may have *e.* life, Matt. 19:16.
danger of *e.* damnation, Mark 3:29.
author of *e.* salvation, Heb. 5:9.

ETERNITY, duration; continuity (Is. 57:15).

ETHAM, the second station of Israel after leaving Egypt (Is. 13:20).

ETHAN, (1) a descendant of Judah (I Chr. 2:6). (2) A Levite, of the family of Gershom, house of Libni (I Chr. 6:42). (3) A descendant of Merari the son of Levi (I Chr. 6:44). (4) An Ezrahite renowned for his wisdom (I Kin. 4:31).

ETHANIM, the seventh month of the Hebrew year (I Kin. 8:2). Corresponds to September-October.

ETHBAAL, a king of the Tyrians and Sidonians, and father of Jezebel (I Kin. 16:31).

ETHER, a city in the lowlands of Judah (Josh. 15:42), but allotted to the tribe of Simeon (19:7).

ETHIOPIA, a country called in the Hebrew language Cush, which is continually mentioned in connection with Egypt and sometimes with Libya, and most certainly have been in eastern Africa. Also used to denote the people of Cush.

the whole land of *E.,* Gen. 2:13.
India even unto *E.,* Esther 1:1.
behold, a man of *E.,* Acts 8:27.

ETHIOPIAN(S), the name generally given to the descendants of Cush son of Ham.
because of the *E.* woman, Num. 12:1.
and the *E.* captives, Is. 20:4.
Can the *E.* change, Jer. 13:23.
queen of the *E.,* Acts 8:27.

ETH-KAZIN, a town on the eastern side of Zebulun (Josh. 19:13).

ETHNAN, a man of Judah, son of Helah (I Chr. 4:7).

ETHNI, a Gershonite Levite (I Chr. 6:41).

EUBULUS, a Christian perhaps of Rome (II Tim. 4:21).

EUCHARIST, a term used to denote the Lord's Supper, based on the Greek Eucharistein "to give thanks" (Luke 22:19; Matt. 26:27; Mark 14:23). After the Lord had taken the bread and the cup, he gave thanks. *See* **LORD'S SUPPER.**

EUNICE, mother of Timothy (II Tim. 1: 5). She was a Jewess who was probably converted on Paul's first missionary journey.

EUNUCH, an emasculated person. They were commonly employed in Oriental courts as a measure of safety against possible intrigues with those in the harems. The Hebrew word has a double meaning, it also signifies chamberlain (Gen. 37: 36). Pharaoh's eunuch was married (Gen. 39:1). The use in Matt. 19:12 does not concern the physical feature of the case, but has to do with renouncing the married state for the sake of service.
two or three *e.,* II Kin. 9:32.
there are some *e.,* Matt. 19:12.
the *e.* said, See, here, Acts 8:36.
both Philip and the *e.,* Acts 8:38.

EUODIAS, a Christian woman at Philippi blemished by bickering with Syntyche (Phil. 4:2).

EUPHRATES, is probably a word of Aryan origin, signifying "the good and

162

abounding river." It is most frequently denoted in the Bible by the term "the river." The Euphrates is the largest, the longest and by far the most important river of Western Asia. It rises in the Armenian mountains and flows into the Persian Gulf. The entire course is about 1780 miles, and more than two-thirds is navigable for boats.

fourth river is *E.*, Gen. 2:14.
border at the river *E.*, II Sam. 8:3.
unto the river *E.*, II Kin. 24:7.
in the great river *E.*, Rev. 9:14.

EUROCLYDON, a tempestuous northeast wind which blows over the Mediterranean Sea (Acts 27:14).

EUTYCHUS, a young man of Troas restored to life by Paul (Acts 20:9).

EVANGELIST, one who announces good tidings; a function in the early church distinct from apostles, prophets, pastors, and teachers (Eph. 4:11); a preacher of the gospel.

of Philip the *e.*, Acts 21:8.
the work of an *e.*, II Tim. 4:5 .

EVE, (live; life-giving), the name given to the first woman.

his wife's name *E.*, Gen. 3:20.
Adam know *E.* his, Gen. 4:1.
beguiled *E.* through, II Cor. 11:3.
formed, then *E.*, I Tim. 2:13.

EVEN, evening; late evening.
morning unto *e.*, Ex. 18:14.
the *e.* was come, Matt. 8:16.
when *e.* was come, Mark 11:19.
when *e.* was now, John 6:16.

EVEN, only; till; during; and; but.
e. the first day, Ex. 12:15 .
E. unto the morrow, Lev. 23:16.
not *e.* the publicans, Matt. 5:46.
possible, *e.* the elect, Mark 13:22.

EVENING, before the Exile the Hebrews divided the day into evening, morning, and midday. Evening, in the counting, consisted of the hours between sundown and sunrise. The Hebrew day extended from evening to evening (Gen. 1:5, 8, 13, 19). The Babylonian day was from morning to morning. Sometimes the word "evening" is used in the Hebrew to denote the interval between twilight and complete darkness (Prov. 7:9).

it was *e.* his, Matt. 14:15.
it is toward *e.*, Luke 24:29.

EVENT, result; outcome; occurrence.
one *e.* happeneth, Eccles. 2:14.
one *e.* to the, Eccles. 9:2.
is one *e.* unto all, Eccles. 9:3.

EVER, continuous; age-lasting.
and live for *e.*, Gen. 3:22.
after thee for *e.*, Deut. 12:28.
he continueth *e.*, Heb. 7:24.
he *e.* liveth to, Heb. 7:25.
glory for ever and *e.*, Heb. 13:21.
for ever and *e.*, I Pet. 4:11.

EVERLASTING, duration; age-lasting; eternal.
for an *e.* possession, Gen. 17:8.
an *e.* covenant, II Sam. 23:5.
into *e.* punishment, Matt. 25:46.
may have *e.*, John 6:40.
unworthy of *e.* life, Acts 13:46.

EVERMORE, continual; always.
glorify thy name for *e.*, Ps. 86:12.
Lord, *e.* give us, John 6:34.
is blessed for *e.*, II Cor. 11:31.
Rejoice *e.*, I Thess. 5:16.

EVERY, each one.
gospel to *e.* creature, Mark 16:15.
be baptized *e.* one, Acts 2:38.
salvation to *e.* one, Rom. 1:16.
For *e.* man shall, Gal. 6:5.

EVI, one of the five kings of Midian, allies or vassals of Sihon, slain in the war waged by Moses against the Midianites because they seduced the Israelites to licentious idolatry (Num. 31:8; Josh. 13:21).

EVIDENCE, conviction; proof; test.
subscribed the *e.*, Jer. 32:10.
took the *e.* of, Jer. 32:11.
the *e.* of things, Heb. 11:1.

EVIDENT, clear; manifest; open.
for it is *e.* unto, Job 6:28.
of God, it is *e.*, Gal. 3:11.
it is *e.* that, Heb. 7:14.
it is far more *e.*, Heb. 7:15.

EVIL, iniquity; bad; malignant; useless; injurious.
knowledge of good and *e.*, Gen. 2:9.
to no man *e.* for, Rom. 12:17.
the days are *e.*, Eph. 5:16.
tempted with *e.*, James 1:13.

Not rendering *e*. for, I Pet. 3:9.
own works were *e*., I John 3:12.
doeth *e*. hath not, III John 11.

EVIL-MERODACH, means "man of Marduk." He was the son and successor of the great Nebuchadnezzar on the throne of Babylon, 562 B.C. He released Jehoiachin, king of Judah, who had been imprisoned 37 years (II Kin. 25:27:30; Jer. 52:31). He was so unrestrained in law and in decency that the priestly party induced his brother-in-law, Neriglissar, to slay him, and seize the throne (560 B.C.).

EVIL-SPIRIT, *see* DEMON.

EVOLUTION, a scientific and philosophical theory designed to explain the origin and course of all things in the universe. Often the term is used to cover absolute origin but a moment's reflection will make it clear that such a view can never secure a place in the realm of pure science. Many scientists assume evolution to be true.

EWE, a female sheep.
thy *e*. and thy, Gen. 31:38.
two hundred *e*., Gen. 32:14.
whether it be cow or *e*., Lev. 22:28.

EWE LAMB, young female sheep.
set seven *e*. lambs, Gen. 21:28.
one *e*. lamb of, Lev. 14:10.
one little *e*. lamb, II Sam. 12:3.

EXACT, to get money from; to demand interest or taxes.
shall not *e*. it of, Deut. 15:2.
he *e*. the silver and, II Kin. 23:35.
Ye *e*. usury, Neh. 5:7.
E. no more than, Luke 3:13.

EXACTION, a demand for money lent on pledge (Neh. 10:31).

EXALT, to lift up; to elevate.
Righteousness *e*. a, Prov. 14:34.
he that *e*. his gate, Prov. 17:19.
shall *e*. himself, Matt. 23:12.
hand of God *e*., Acts 2:33.

EXALTED, to be lifted up.
shall be *e*. above the, Is. 2:2.
their heart was *e*., Hos. 13:6.
I should be *e*., II Cor. 12:7.
rejoice in that he is *e*., James 1:9.

EXAMINE, investigate; try; prove; test.
E. me, O Lord, Ps. 26:2.
having *e*. him before, Luke 23:14.
let a man *e*. himself, I Cor. 11:28.
E. yourselves, II Cor. 13:5.

EXAMPLE, a specimen; a copy; a type.
things were our *e*., I Cor. 10:6.
fall after the same *e*., Heb. 4:11.
for an *e*. of suffering, James 5:10.
leaving us an *e*., I Pet. 2:21.

EXCEED, surpass; excel; abound.
until David *e*., I Sam. 20:41.
Solomon *e*. all the, I Kin. 10:23.
righteousness shall *e*., Matt. 5:20.
righteousness *e*. in, II Cor. 3:9.

EXCEEDING, abundant; above; great.
must be *e*. magnifical, I Chr. 22:5.
e. in dyed attire, Ezek. 23:15.
rejoiced with *e*. great, Matt. 2:10.
is able to do *e*., Eph. 3:20.

EXCEEDINGLY, abundant; extraordinary.
waters prevailed *e*., Gen. 7:19.
magnified Solomon *E*., I Chr. 29:25.
being *e*. mad against, Acts 26:11.
and *e*. the more, II Cor. 7:13.

EXCEL, surpass; exceed; mighty.
thou shalt not *e*., Gen. 49:4.
Solomon's wisdom *e*., I Kin. 4:30.
that ye may *e*. to, I Cor. 14:12.
the glory that *e*., II Cor. 3:10.

EXCELLENCY, surpassing; pre-eminence.
strength, the *e*. of, Gen. 49:3.
with majesty and *e*., Job 40:10.
with *e*. of speech or, I Cor. 2:1.
the *e*. of the knowledge, Phil. 3:8.

EXCELLENT, surpassing; great.
how *e*. is thy, Ps. 8:1.
e. as the cedars, Song 5:15.
and *e*. in working, Is. 28:29.
him from the *e*., II Pet. 1:17.

EXCELLETH,EXCELLING,see**EXCEL.**

EXCEPT, unless; besides; to omit.
e. our youngest, Gen. 44:26.
together, *e*. they be, Amos 3:3.
E. a man be born, John 3:5.
e. some man, Acts 8:31.

EXCESS, incontinence; lack of self-control; overflow.

of extortion and *e.*, Matt. 23:25.
wine, wherein is *e.*, Eph. 5:18.
lusts, *e.* of wine, I Pet. 4:3.
to the same *e.*, I Pet. 4:4.

EXCHANGE, trade; barter.
it and the *e.* thereof, Lev. 27:10.
neither *e.*, nor, Ezek. 48:14.
man give in *e.*, Matt. 16:26.
give in *e.* for his, Mark 8:37.

EXCHANGER, one who exchanges money
for profit (Matt. 25:27). *See* **MONEY CHANGERS.**

EXCLUDE, shut out.
then? It is *e.*, Rom. 3:27.
they would *e.* you, Gal. 4:17.

EXCUSE, beg off; plead for self.
began to make *e.*, Luke 14:18.
have me *e.*, Luke 14:19.
else *e.* one another, Rom. 2:15.
think ye that we *e.*, II Cor. 12:19.

EXECRATION, a curse.
shall be an *e.*, Jer. 42:18.
shall be an *e.*, Jer. 44:12.

EXECUTE, to do; to judge; to make.
I will *e.* judgment, Ex. 12:12.
E. true judgment, Zech. 7:9.
him authority to *e.*, John 5:27.
to *e.* judgment, Jude 15.

EXECUTIONER, a looker-out; spy; scout;
one of the guard (Mark 6:27).

EXEMPTED, free; acquitted (I Kin. 15:22).

EXERCISE, to use; train up; to work up.
Lord which *e.* loving, Jer. 9:24.
herein do I *e.*, Acts 24:16.
e. thyself rather unto, I Tim. 4:7.
e. to discern both, Heb. 5:14.

EXHORT, to admonish; entreat; warn;
urge.
he testify and *e.*, Acts 2:40.
e. and to convince, Titus 1:9.
But *e.* one another, Heb. 3:13.
e. you that ye, Jude 3.

EXHORTATION, an appeal; encouragement.
any word of *e.* for, Acts 13:15.
edification, and *e.*, I Cor. 14:3.
to reading, to *e.*, I Tim. 4:13.

forgotten the *e.*, Heb. 12:5.

EXHORTED, -ETH, -ING, *see* **EX-
HORT.**

EXILE, to remove. *See* **CAPTIVITY.**
and also an *e.*, II Sam. 15:19.
captive *e.* hasteneth, Is. 51:14.

EXODUS, the departure of the Israelites
from Egypt under the leadership of Moses. They numbered six hundred thousand men, and they departed with a
mixed multitude, and flocks and herds,
and much cattle. The death of the firstborn of Egypt, the destruction of Pharaoh's army, the careful listing of halting
places, the journey to Sinai, the giving of
the Law, and the building of the Tabernacle are dramatically narrated in the
book of Exodus.

EXODUS, BOOK OF, Exodus tells of the
departure of the Israelites from Egypt.
The story of Genesis is continued, and
Exodus relates the history of the Israelites from the death of Joseph to the construction of the Tabernacle at Sinai. The
family mentioned in Genesis has become
a great nation, with its consolidation in
view of the promises, its sanctions, its
priesthood, and its leadership under Moses. The nation is looking forward to
something even more substantial. The
central event in the book is the giving of
the Law to Moses, a Law written by the
finger of God. While Moses was receiving
the tables of stone on which the commandments were written, the people were
building an idol. When Moses saw this,
he broke the stones, and prayed to the
Lord on behalf of his people. God answered Moses' prayer and renewed the
tables. The book also has a prophetical
element in it. It establishes in the Passover
a type of Christ's sacrifice (I Cor. 5:7).
And Aaron is recognized as a type of
Jesus Christ, the great high priest of the
New Testament (Heb. 9:11).

EXORCIST, one who professes to cast
out demons (Acts 19:13).

EXPECT, to wait for; look for.
e. to receive, Acts 3:5.
e. till his enemies, Heb. 10:13.

EXPECTATION, hope; looking for; eager
longing.

e. of the wicked, Prov. 10:28.
such is our *e.*, Is. 20:6.
people were in *e.*, Luke 3:15.
my earnest *e.*, Phil. 1:20.

EXPEDIENT, profitable; advantageous.
it is *e.* for us, John 11:50.
It is *e.* for you, John 16:7.
things are not *e.*, I Cor. 6:12.
this is *e.* for, II Cor. 8:10.

EXPEL, to cast out.
he shall *e.* them, Josh. 23:5.
e. me out of my, Judg. 11:7.
be not *e.* from, II Sam. 14:14.
and *e.* them out, Acts 13:50.

EXPENSES, expenditure.
let the *e.* be given, Ezra 6:4.
e. be given unto, Ezra 6:8.

EXPERIENCE, test; skill; try.
have learned by *e.*, Gen. 30:27.
great *e.* of wisdom, Eccles. 1:16.
and patience *e.*, Rom. 5:4.

EXPERIMENT, the process of proving (II Cor. 9:13).

EXPERT, one who knows; to be taught.
being *e.* in war, Song 3:8.
a mighty *e.* man, Jer. 50:9.
e. in all customs, Acts 26:3.

EXPIRE, to fulfil; to finish.
forty years were *e.*, Acts 7:30.
years are *e.*, Rev. 20:7.

EXPOUND, to set out; to expose; explain. Also **Expounded.**
three days *e.* the, Judg. 14:14.
he *e.* all things, Mark 4:34.
e. unto them, Luke 24:27.
e. unto him the way, Acts 18:26.

EXPRESS, exactly resembling the original (Heb. 1:3).

EXPRESSLY, in stated terms.
If I *e.* say unto, I Sam. 20:21.
Spirit speaketh *e.*, I Tim. 4:1.

EXTEND, to draw out; to stretch out.
hath *e.* mercy unto, Ezra 7:28.
be none to *e.* mercy, Ps. 109:12.
I will *e.* peace, Is. 66:12.

EXTINCT, extinguished.
my days are *e.*, Job 17:1.

they are *e.*, they, Is. 43:17.

EXTOL, to exalt; raise up; exalt. Also **Extolled.**
I will *e.* thee, Ps. 30:1.
e. him that rideth, Ps. 68:4.
and *e.* and honour, Dan. 4:37.

EXTORTION, robbery; plundering.
neighbours by *e.*, Ezek. 22:12.
they are full of *e.*, Matt. 23:25.

EXTORTIONER, to wring out; one that snatches away.
the *e.* is at an, Is. 16:4.
other men are, *e.*, Luke 18:11.
covetous, or *e.*, I Cor. 5:10.
nor *e.*, shall, I Cor. 6:10.

EXTREMITY, the utmost; last end (Job 35:15).

EYE, the physical organ; may be used to represent the whole person.
then your *e.* shall, Gen. 3:5.
and put out his *e.*, Judg. 16:21.
grace in thine *e.*, Ruth 2:10.
in thine own *e.*, Matt. 7:4.
Is thine *e.* evil, Matt. 20:15.
blinded their *e.*, John 12:40.
E. hath not seen, I Cor. 2:9.
e. of your understanding, Eph. 1:18.
unto the *e.* of him, Heb. 4:13.
Having *e.* full of, II Pet. 2:14.

EYEBROWS, there were regulations regarding the shaving and plucking of eyebrows (Lev. 14:9; Deut. 14:1).

EYELIDS, that part of movable skin with which an animal covers or uncovers the eyeball.
and on my *e.* is, Job 16:16.
his *e.* try, the, Ps. 11:4.
let thine *e.* look, Prov. 4:25.
and our *e.* gush, Jer. 9:18.

EYESALVE, an eye medicine used by oculists in the famous medical school at Laodicea (Rev. 3:18).

EYESERVICE, service performed only under the master's eye.
Not with *e.*, Eph. 6:6.
e., as men pleasers, Col. 3:22.

EYEWITNESS, seeing with one's eyes; a looker on.
beginning were *e.*, Luke 1:2.

but were *e.* of his, II Pet. 1:16.

EZAR, *see* **EZER.**

EZBAI, the father of one of David's mighty men (I Chr. 11:37).

EZBON, (1) a son of Gad (Gen. 46:16). (2) The head of a father's house, family of Bela, tribe of Benjamin (I Chr. 7:7).

EZEKIAS, the Greek form of **HEZE-KIAH.**
and Achaz begat *E.*, Matt. 1:9.
E. begat Manasses, Matt. 1:10.

EZEKIEL, one of the four great prophets. He was a priest and the son of Buzi (Ezek. 1:3). He was taken captive with Jehoiachin about eleven years before the destruction of Jerusalem (II Kin. 24:10–16). His prophetic career began about five years after being captured. His only reference to himself informs us that he was married and had a house (Ezek. 3:24, 8:1, 24:18). His wife was lost by a sudden and unforeseen stroke. He is said to have been murdered in Babylon by some Jewish prince whom he had convicted of idolatry, and to have been buried in the tomb of Shem and Arphaxad, on the banks of the Euphrates.

EZEKIEL, BOOK OF, was written by the prophet himself. His task was to impress upon the exiles the fact that calamity had come because of their own sinfulness. "The soul that sinneth, it shall die" (Ezek. 18:4). Thus, the prophecy inculcates the great doctrine of personal responsibility. Even the theocracy must end in its outward form if the people continue to sin. But, God does not delight in the death of the wicked. He cries, "Turn ye, turn ye from your evil ways; for why will ye die, O house of Israel?" (Ezek. 33:11). The sinful nation must be destroyed, but God will not forsake His own.

EZEL, the place where David hid until Jonathan could inform him of Saul's disposition toward him (I Sam. 20:19).

EZEM, a city of Simeon (I Chr. 4:29). *See* AZEM.

EZER, (1) the father of Hushah, one of the descendants of Hur, of the tribe of

Judah (I Chr. 4:4). (2) A son of Ephraim (I Chr. 7:21). (3) One of the Gadite champions who went to David at Ziklag (I Chr. 12:9). (4) The son of Jeshua, a ruler of Mizpah, who repaired part of the city walls near the armory (Neh. 3:19). (5) One of the priests who assisted in the dedication of the walls of Jerusalem under Nehemiah (Neh. 12:42). (6) One of the sons of Seir, and native princes of Mount Hor (Gen. 36:21; I Chr. 1:42).

EZION-GEBER, a town on the Red Sea where the Israelites stopped as they journeyed in the wilderness. Also **Ezion-Gaber.**
and encamped at *E.*, Num. 33:35.
Elath, and from *E.*, Deut. 2:8.
navy of ships in *E.*, I Kin. 9:26.
went Solomon to *E.*, II Chr. 8:17.

EZNITE, one of David's worthies (II Sam. 23:8).

EZRA, (1) a descendant of Hilkiah the high priest in Josiah's reign. All that is really known of Ezra is contained in the last four chapters of the book of Ezra and in Nehemiah chapters eight and twelve. (2) A descendant of Judah through Caleb (I Chr. 4:17). (3) The head of one of the twenty-two courses of priests that came up from exile with Zerubbabel (Neh. 12:1).

EZRA, BOOK OF, consists of two main parts. First, the account of the return from Babylon of the Jews under Zerubbabel, the erection of the temple and the restoration of divine service. Second, an account of another body of Jews from the exile, this group being led by Ezra and his reformations. One purpose of the book is to give an account of the restoration of the nation to its land from the priestly point of view.

EZRAH, a Judahite (I Chr. 4:17).

EZRAHITE, a descendant of Zerah, belonging to the tribe of Judah, as Ethan and Heman (I Kin. 4:31).

EZRI, one of David's agricultural superintendents (I Chr. 27:26).

F

FABLE, a fictitious story employed for

the purpose of enforcing some truth or principle. Of the fable, as distinguished from the parable, there are but two instances in the Bible: that of the trees choosing their king (Judg. 9:8–15); and that of the Cedar of Lebanon and the thistle (II Kin. 14:9). Using it in a different sense, the New Testament identifies fable with invention or falsehood.
nor give heed to *f.*, I Tim. 1:4.
but refuse old wives' *f.*, I Tim. 4:7.
shall be turned into *f.*, II Tim. 4:4.
not giving heed to *f.*, Titus 1:14.
cunningly devised *f.*, II Pet. 1:16.

FACE, the front part of a man's head or his countenance. When it is applied to God, it denotes His presence, suggesting either His anger or His favor (Ps. 44:3; Gen. 16:6, 8).
in sweat of *f.*, Gen. 3:19.
Moses fled *f.* of Pharaoh, Ex. 2:15.
skin of *f.* shone, Ex. 34:29.
will curse thee to *f.*, Job 1:11.
anoint head, wash *f.*, Matt. 6:17.
f. bound with napkin, John 11:44.
withstood him to the *f.*, Gal. 2:11.
beast had *f.* as man, Rev. 4:7.

FACES, BREAD OF, is the literal rendering of the term "showbread," which was always in the presence of God.

FADE, to wither or pass away.
strangers shall *f.* away, Ps. 18:45.
and we all *f.* as a leaf, Is. 64:6.
inheritance *f.* not away, I Pet. 1:4.
glory that *f.* not, I Pet. 5:4.

FAIL, to be lacking, to perish.
cattle, if money *f.*, Gen. 47:16.
no man's heart *f.*, I Sam. 17:32.
of the law to *f.*, Luke 16:17.
prophecies they *f.*, I Cor. 13:8.
time would *f.* me, Heb. 11:32.
any man *f.* of grace, Heb. 12:15.

FAIN, to fix the mind or desire on.
f. flee out of hand, Job 27:22.
f. filled belly, Luke 15:16.

FAINT, to be weary, become weak.
and he was *f.*, Gen. 25:29.
when thou wast *f.*, Deut. 25:18.
inhabitants of land *f.*, Josh. 2:9.
their soul *f.* in them, Ps. 107:5.
fasting, lest they *f.*, Matt. 15:32.
to pray, not to *f.*, Luke 18:1.
reap, if we *f.* not, Gal. 6:9.

f. not at my, Eph. 3:13.
and *f.* in your minds, Heb. 12:3.
nor *f.* when rebuked, Heb. 12:5.
labored, and hast not *f.*, Rev. 2:3.

FAIR, clean, pure, good, beautiful.
daugh. of men were *f.*, Gen. 6:2.
Tamar was *f.*, II Sam. 13:1.
houses great and *f.*, Is. 5:9.
leaves were *f.*, Dan. 4:12.
will be *f.* weather, Matt. 16:2.
Moses was exceeding *f.*, Acts 7:20.
make *f.* show in flesh, Gal. 6:12.

FAIR HAVENS, a harbor in the island of Crete (Acts 27:8).

FAIR SPEECH, easy discourse, persuasive words (Prov. 7:21; Rom. 16:18).

FAIRER, FAIREST, comparative and superlative of fair.
younger sister *f.* than, Judg. 15:2.
f. than child. of men, Ps. 45:2.
countenances app. *f.*, Dan. 1:15.

FAIRS, wares or anything for sale (Ezek. 27:12, 27).

FAITH, it is true that in the Old Testament the Hebrew word for faith usually has reference to faithfulness, steadfastness, or trustworthiness. The one exception seems to be Hab. 2:4, however, where the word is contrasted to the one whose soul is lifted up which is in reality self-trust. The opposite, of course, would be trust or confidence (in someone or something else). This is exactly the use Paul makes of this passage in Rom. 1:17. When the closeness of the two meanings are seen the difficulty of the transition made in Hab. 2:4 is done away. There is implied in steadfastness a confidence in a certain object upon which when the believer lays hold he himself becomes reliable and faithful. Or it might be said, to believe is to hold firmly onto something with confidence and conviction. In the New Testament the word is used in the passive since in Rom. 3:3 where it speaks of the faith (faithfulness) of God. But the common use is active, meaning to believe something or in someone. In the Synoptic Gospels Christ is summoning men to a conviction that God, through the Messiah, is able to fulfill prophesy. The Gospel of John always avoids the use of the noun "faith" and uses the verb

"to believe" as if to say that faith in Christ is a working active process or way of life. Though James says that faith without works is dead (James 2:17), he is not saying that man is justified by faith plus works of merit, but by a faith that expresses itself through works of love and obedience. Paul has a profound use of faith meaning trust and confidence. To be justified by faith is to reach that status completely without works of merit (Rom. 3:28; 11:6). By works of merit Paul does not mean obedience for he certainly holds to that (Rom. 6:17; II Thess. 1:8); he means works by which one actually earns his salvation. Faith is a putting on of Christ and a complete confidence in His blood for justification (Gal. 3:26, 27; Rom. 3:25). *See* BELIEF.
in whom is no *f*., Deut. 32:20.
shall live by *f*., Hab. 2:4.
Lord increase our *f*., Luke 17:5.
a man full of *f*., Acts 6:5.
obedience to *f*., Rom. 1:5.
being not weak in *f*., Rom. 4:19.
one *f*. one baptism, Eph. 4:5.
work of *f*., I Thess. 1:3.
finisher of our *f*., Heb. 12:2.
earnestly contend for *f*., Jude 3.

FAITH, RULE OF, the expression is not found in the Bible, but the thought behind it is. Christians correctly speak of the Bible as the only rule of faith, by which they mean that the Sacred Scriptures are the only source of religious authority (II Tim. 3:16–17).

FAITHFUL, FAITHFULNESS, (1) as applied to God, the terms suggest God as being worthy of love and confidence from man, and that He will keep His promises with respect both to rewards and punishments (Ps. 36:5; Is. 11:15), (2) as applied to man, the term suggests trustworthiness (Neh. 7:2).
render to man his *f*., I Sam. 26:23.
no *f*. in their mouth, Ps. 5:9.
make known thy *f*., Ps. 89:1.
ye have judged me *f*., Acts 16:15.
God is *f*., I Cor. 1:9.
Onesimus, a *f*. brother, Col. 4:9.
He is *f*. to forgive, I John 1:9.
be *f*. unto death, Rev. 2:10.
words are true and *f*., Rev. 21:5.

FAITHFULLY, with faithfulness, with stability.

for they dealt *f*., II Kin. 12:15.
f. and with perfect, II Chr. 19:9.
doest *f*. whatsoever, III John 5.

FAITHLESS, unsteadfast, the opposite of faithful.
O *f*. generation, Matt. 17:17.
not *f*. but believing, John 20:27.

FALCON, a bird or birds included in the hawk family called also a kite (Lev. 11:14; Deut. 14:13), and vulture (Job 28:7).

FALL, to descend or stumble.
deep sleep to *f*. on, Gen. 2:21.
f. when none pursue, Lev. 26:36.
hair of head *f*. ground, I Sam. 14:45.
his dread *f*. on you, Job 13:11.
spirit before *f*., Prov. 16:18.
great was the *f*. of it, Matt. 7:27.
to mountains *f*. on us, Luke 23:30.
f. in brother's way, Rom. 14:13.
lest any *f*. after same, Heb. 4:11.
a star *f*. from heaven, Rev. 9:1.

FALL OF MAN, this is the result of the sin of Adam and Eve in the Garden of Eden recorded in Gen. 3. Following their transgression they were driven from their home (Gen. 3:23), the man to till the ground by the sweat of his face and the woman to bring forth children in sorrow (Gen. 3:19, 16), the climax of their punishment being death (Gen. 2:17; 3:19). From that day onward death has passed to all men (Rom. 5:12). It seems that all men sinned representatively in Adam and therefore all die (I Cor. 15: 22).

FALLING AWAY, THE, an event mentioned in II Thess. 2:3 which Paul said must take place before the second coming of Christ. In connection with it the man of sin is to be revealed. The author is possibly speaking of emperor worship for which the Christians were greatly oppressed or perhaps the apostasy of the church with the coming of any great evil power.

FALLOW DEER, so called from the animal's reddish-brown color (Deut. 14:5; I Kin. 4:23).

FALLOW GROUND, a field that has been plowed left for the seeding. Summer fallow, if used correctly, was a sure way of killing weeds (Jer. 4:3; Hos. 10:12).

FALLS, *see* **FALL.**

FALSE, deceitful, untrue.
not raise *f.* report, Ex. 23:1.
done thee, *f.* tongue, Ps. 120:3.
giveth heed to *f.* lips, Prov. 17:4.
have told *f.* dreams, Zech. 10:2.
any thing by *f.*, Luke 19:8.
such are *f.* apostles, II Cor. 11:13.
because of *f.* brethren, Gal. 2:4.
be *f.* teachers, II Pet. 2:1.

FALSE CHRISTS, those who falsely claim to be the Christ. Jesus prophesied that such would arise (Matt. 24:24; Mark 13:22). The first definite fulfilment of the prediction seems to have been Bar Chocaba who lived in the first half of the second century A.D.

FALSE PROPHETS, those who teach false doctrine.
f. p. in sheep's, Matt. 7:15.
many *f. p.* shall rise, Matt. 24:11.
there were *f. p.*, II Pet. 2:1.
f. p. gone out, I John 4:1.

FALSEHOOD, lying, deceit.
have wrong. *f.*, II Sam. 18:13.
brought forth *f.*, Ps. 7:14.
they commit *f.*, Hos. 7:1.
walking in spirit and *f.*, Micah 2:11.

FALSELY, in a lying way, deceitfully.
not deal *f.* with me, Gen. 21:23.
he hath sworn *f.*, Lev. 6:5.
testified *f.* against, Deut. 19:18.
they swear *f.*, Jer. 5:2.
evil against you *f.*, Matt. 5:11.
science *f.* so called, I Tim. 6:20.

FALSE WITNESS, one who lies.
thou bear *f. w.*, Deut. 5:20.
that beareth *f. w.*, Prov. 25:18.
and set up *f. w.*, Acts 6:13.

FAME, ones reputation.
f. was heard in, Gen. 45:16.
heard *f.* of thee, Num. 14:15.
we have heard *f.*, Job 28:22.
f. thereof went abroad, Matt. 9:26.
they spread abroad his *f.* Matt. 9:31..
Herod heard of *f.* of Jesus, Matt. 14:1.

FAMILIAR, closely acquainted, intimate.
my *f.* friends have, Job 19:14.
my *f.* friend lift up heel, Ps. 41:9.

FAMILIAR SPIRIT, a diving demon

present in the physical body of the conjurer.
not have *f. s.*, Lev. 20:27.
that hath *f. s.*, I Sam. 28:7.
Man, dealt with *f. s.*, II Chr. 33:6.
seek *f. s.*, Is. 8:19.

FAMILY, the institution of God lying at the foundation of all human society. It is monogamous in nature: "For this cause shall a man leave his father and mother, and cleave to his wife" (Matt. 19:5). Wives are to be subject to their husbands (Eph. 5:21), and husbands are to love their wives (Eph. 5:25). Parents are to care for their own (I Tim. 5:8), and are not to provoke their children to wrath (Eph. 6:4). The filial obligations are obedience (Luke 2:51; Eph. 6:1), reverence (Ex. 20:12), and grateful requital (I Tim. 5:4).
every man to his *f.*, Lev. 20:5.
f. of father's tribe, Num. 36:6.
man and all his *f.*, Judg. 1:25.
selleth *f.*, Nah. 3:4.
f. in heaven and earth, Eph. 3:15....

FAMINE, hunger, want of food. It is mentioned as one of the scourges which God sent to chastise men for their wickedness (Lev. 26:21). Having a variety of causes, and often lasting for long periods of time, famines are mentioned as occurring in the days of Abraham (Gen. 12:10), of Isaac (Gen. 26:1), of Joseph (Gen. 41:53–56), of the Judges (Ruth 1:1), of David (II Sam. 21:1), of Ahab (I Kin. 17:1), of Elisha (II Kin. 4:38). Agabus prophesied of a famine in Judea during the reign of Claudius (Acts 11: 28, 29).
f. in land, besides first, Gen. 26:1.
fainted by reason of *f.*, Gen. 47:13.
Lord call. for a *f.*, II Kin. 8:1.
great *f.* through land, Luke 4:25.
mighty *f.* in that land, Luke 15:14.
in one day, death, *f.*, Rev. 18:8.

FAMISH, to make lean, to be hungry.
all land of Egypt *f.*, Gen. 41:55.
not suffer right. to *f.*, Prov. 10:3.
their honor. men are *f.*, Is. 5:13.
will *f.* gods of earth, Zeph. 2:11.

FAMOUS, honourable, noteworthy.
f. in congregation, Num. 16:2.
be thou *f.* in, Ruth 4:11.
may be *f.* in Israel, Ruth 4:14.
become *f.*, Ezek. 23:10.
daughters of *f.* nations, Ezek. 32:18.

FAN, a winnowing-shovel, with which grain, was thrown up against the wind to be cleansed from the chaff and straw.
winnowed with *f.*, Is. 30:24.
a dry wind not to *f.*, Jer. 4:11.
will fan with *f.*, Jer. 15:7.
f. is in hand, Matt. 3:12.

FANNERS, strangers (Jer. 51:2).

FAR, distant, remote.
f. from thee to slay, Gen. 18:25.
stranger from *f.* land, Deut. 29:22.
Lord *f.* from wicked, Prov. 15:29.
be it *f.* from thee, Matt. 16:22.
not *f.* from land, John 21:8.
up *f.*; above all, Eph. 4:10.

FARE, prosperity, hire, or making merry
look how thy br. *f.*, I Sam. 17:18.
paid the *f.* thereof, Jonah 1:3.
rich man *f.*, Luke 16:19.

FAREWELL, a greeting or good-bye.
bid them *f.* at home, Luke 9:61.
well, *f.*, Acts 15:29.
finally brethren *f.*, II Cor. 13:11.

FARM, a field used for cultivation. The owner usually lived in a village and went out to his land as the need arose (Matt. 22:5).

FARTHER SIDE, the other side, beyond (Mark 10:1).

FARTHING, the name of two New Testament coins: (1) *Quadrans*, equivalent to three-eighths of a cent (Matt. 5:26; Mark 12:42), (2) *Assarion*, equal to one cent and a half (Matt. 10:29; Luke 12:6).

FASHION, to make a shape or pattern of a thing.
never saw it on this *f.*, Mark 2:12.
make tabernacle to *f.*, Acts 7:44.
f. world pass. away, I Cor. 7:31.
found in *f.* as man, Phil. 2:8.
f. like to his body, Phil. 3:21.
the grace of *f.*, James 1:11.
not *f.* to former lusts, I Pet. 1:14.

FAST, securely attached, firmly fixed.
we will bind thee *f.*, Judg. 15:13.
strength set *f.* moun., Ps. 65:6.
f. hold of instruction, Prov. 4:13.
lay in ship. *f.* asleep, Jonah 1:5.

FASTS, FASTING, the Mosaic law ap-
pointed a fast on the Day of Atonement. There is no mention of any other periodical fast in the Old Testament except in Zech. 7:1–7; 8:19. Public fasts were occasionally proclaimed to express national humiliation and to supplicate divine favor (I Sam. 7:6; II Chr. 20:3). Private fasts, frequently observed under the influence of grief, vexation, or anxiety, are recognized once in the law (Num. 30:13). In the New Testament the only references to the Jewish fasts are the mention of "the fast" in Acts 27:9 and the allusions to the weekly fasts (Matt. 9:14; Acts 10:30). The Jewish fasts were observed with varying degrees of strictness. Sometimes there was entire abstinences from food (cf. Esther 4:16). On other occasions there appears to have been only a restriction to a very plain diet (Dan. 10:3). The New Testament contains no command for Christians to fast.
child dead, why *f.*, II Sam. 12:23.
when *f.* I will not hear, Jer. 14:12.
ye at all *f.* unto me, Zech. 7:5.
ye *f.* be not sad, Matt. 6:16.
f. laid hands on them, Acts 13:3.
and had prayed with *f.*, Acts 14:23.
give yourselves to *f.*, I Cor. 7:5.
f. often, II Cor. 11:27.

FASTEN, to attach.
f. nail into ground, Judg. 4:21.
f. head in temple, I Chr. 10:10.
nails *f.* by masters, Eccles. 12:11.
eyes of all *f.* on him, Luke 4:20.
Peter *f.* his eyes on him, Acts 3:4.
when I had *f.* eyes, Acts 11:6.
a viper *f.* on his hand, Acts 28:3.

FASTEST, *see* FAST.

FASTING, not eating, abstaining.
among Jews *f.*, Esther 4:3.
passed the night *f.*, Dan. 6:18.
not send them away *f.*, Matt. 15:32
served God with *f.*, Luke 2:37.
had prayed with *f.*, Acts 14:23.
labours, watchings, *f.*, II Cor. 6:5.

FAT, the layer of subcutaneous fat and the suet around the viscera which was forbidden as food in the Law of Moses (Lev. 3:17). It was to be burnt upon the altar in sacrifice to God (Lev. 3:16).
Able brought *f.* of flock, Gen. 4:4.

all the *f.* is the Lord's, Lev. 3:16.
ye eat *f.* and clothe, Ezek. 34:3.
shall eat flesh of *f.*, Zech. 11:16.

FAT, "vat," the word used to translate the Hebrew term in Joel 2:24; 3:13. The "vats" or "winepresses" appear to have been excavated out of the native rock of the hills on which the vineyards lay.

FATHER, a word which means "protector," and has several meanings. It can mean an ancestor (I Kin. 15:11; II Kin. 14:3), a founder (Gen. 10:21; 17:4, 5; 19:37), a benefactor (Job 29:16), a teacher (I Sam. 10:12), or an intimate relationship (Job 17:14). The position of the father as the head of the family finds its root in the patriarchal government (Gen. 3:16; I Cor. 11:3). God is designated as Father of Jesus Christ (Eph. 1:17; I Cor. 8:6), "the Father of lights" (James 1:17), "the Father of spirits" (Heb. 12:9), and the Father of man (Acts 17:26; Luke 3:8).
be *f.* of many nations, Gen. 17:4.
f. was an Egyptian, Lev. 24:10.
correcteth, as *f.* son, Prov. 3:12.
f. where mine honor, Mal. 1:6.
loveth *f.* more than me, Matt. 10:37.
leave *f.* and cleave to, Matt. 19:5.
baptizing in name of *f.*, Matt. 28:19.
Abba, *f.* all, Mark 14:36.
son ask bread of *f.*, Luke 11:11.
only begotten of *F.*, John 1:14.
F. loveth the Son, John 3:35.
F. hath life in Himself, John 5:26.
F. beareth witness of me, John 8:18.
be *f.* of them believe, Rom. 4:11.
whereby we cry, Abba, *F.*, Rom. 8:15
is Lord, to glory of *F.*, Phil. 2:11.
Melchizedek without *f.*, Heb. 7:3.
an advocate with the *F.*, I John 2:1.
sanctified by God the *F.*, Jude 1.

FATHER-IN-LAW, one giving a daughter in marriage (Ex. 3:1); one related by affinity (Gen. 38:25); a wife's father (John 18:13).

FATHERLESS, orphan.
not afflict *f.* child, Ex. 22:22.
ye overwhelm the *f.*, Job 6:27.
are helper of *f.*, Ps. 10:14.
leave thy *f.* children, Jer. 49:11.
in thee *f.* findeth, Hos. 14:3.
religion to visit *f.*, James 1:27.

FATHER'S BROTHER, strictly one beloved, an uncle.
married unto *f. b.*'s sons, Num. 36:11.145
made his *f. b.* king, II Kin. 24:17.

FATHER'S HOUSE, the name given to families among the Israelites (Josh. 22: 14).

FATHOM, the length of the arms outstretched or 4 cubits (6 ft.) (Acts 27:28).

FATLING, (1) an animal put up to be fatted for slaughter (II Sam. 6:13), (2) a choice sheep (Ps. 66:15).
Saul spared best of *f.*, I Sam. 15:9.
burnt sacrifices of *f.*, Ps. 66:15.
lion, and the *f.* together, Is. 11:6.
all of them *f.*, Ezek. 39:18.
oxen and *f.* are killed, Matt. 22:4.

FATNESS, richness, goodness.
give thee of the *f.*, Gen. 27:28.
should I leave my *f.*, Judg. 9:9.
f. of his flesh wax, Is. 17:4.
sword of Lord fat with *f.*, Is. 34:6.
soul of priests with *f.*, Jer. 31:14.
of *f.* of olive, Rom. 11:17.

FATTED FOWL, are mentioned among the daily provisions for the table of Solomon (I Kin. 4:23). Probably the "lark-heeled cuckoo" is meant.

FAULT, error, failure, sin.
I remember *f.* this day, Gen. 41:9.
found no *f.* in him, I Sam. 29:3.
I find no *f.* in this man, Luke 23:4.
f. one to another, James 5:16.
when buffeted for *f.*, I Pet. 2:20.

FAULTLESS, free from fault.
if first had been *f.*, Heb. 8:7.
able to present you *f.*, Jude 24.

FAULTY, characterized with fault.
king spake as one *f.*, II Sam. 14:13.
shall they be found *f.*, Hos. 10:2.

FAVOUR, grace, kindness, pleasure.
gave Jos. *f.* in sight, Gen. 39:21.
not show *f.* to young, Deut. 28:50.
might have no *f.*, Josh. 11:20.
David hath found *f.*, I Sam. 16:22..
findeth me shall obtain *f.*, Prov. 8:35
Jesus increased in *f.*, Luke 2:52.
f. with all the people, Acts 2:47.
high-priest desired *f.*, Acts 25:3.

FAVOURABLE, characterized with favor.
be *f.* for our sakes, Judg. 21:22.
God will be *f.* unto him, Job 33:26.
be *f.* no more, Ps. 77:7.
hast been *f.* to thy land, Ps. 85:1.

FAVOURED,FAVOURING,FAVOURS,
see FAVOURS.

FEAR, reverence, terror, carefulness, trembling.
f. of you be on beast, Gen. 9:2.
Jacob sware by *f.* of Isaac, Gen. 31:53.
provide such as *f.* god, Ex. 18:21.
shalt *f.* thy God., Lev. 19:14.
f. of thee on nations, Deut. 2:25.
one that *f.* God, Job 2:3.
in thy *f.* will I, Ps. 5:7.
f. God, give audience, Acts 13:16.
f. to whom *f.* is due, Rom. 13:7.
through *f.* of death, Heb. 2:15.
with meekness and *f.*, I Pet. 3:15.

FEARFUL, characterized with fear.
like thee, *f.* in praises, Ex. 15:11.
f. let return, Deut. 20:8.
f. O ye of little, Matt. 8:26.
f. sights in, Luke 21:11.
f. have part in the lake, Rev. 21:8.

FEARFULNESS, state of being fearful.
f. and trembling, Ps. 55:5.
f. affrighted me, Is. 21:4.
f. surprised the hypocrites, Is. 33:14.

FEARING, *see* FEAR.

FEAST, *see* FESTIVALS.

FEASTING, banqueting, drinking.
day of *f.* and, Esther 9:17.
days of their *f.* were, Job 1:5.
than to the house of *f.*, Eccles. 7:2.
go into house of *f.*, Jer. 16:8.

FEAST, LOVE, *see* AGAPE.

FEATHER, the plumage of a fowl.
gavest *f.* to ostrich, Job 39:13.
f. with gold, Ps. 68:13.
shall cover thee with *f.*, Ps. 91:4.
an eagle full of *f.*, Ezek. 17:3.
hairs like eagles' *f.*, Dan. 4:33.

FED, to have nourished, supplied food.
who *f.* me all my, Gen. 48:15.
f. them with bread, I Kin. 18:4.
f. to the full, Jer. 5:7.
hunger and *f.* thee, Matt. 25:37.

f. swine, Mark 5:14.
have *f.* you with milk, I Cor. 3:2.

FEEBLE, weak, trembly.
Amalekite smote *f.*, Deut. 25:18.
conies are *f.* folk, Prov. 30:26.
our hands waxed *f.*, Jer. 6:24.
to be more *f.*, I Cor. 12:22.
the *f.* minded, I Thess. 5:14.
lift up the *f.* knees, Heb. 12:12.

FEEBLENESS, state of being feeble (Jer. 47:3).

FEED, to nourish, supply with food.
f. their father's flock, Gen. 37:12.
f. in another's field, Ex. 22:5.
f. after their manner, Is. 5:17.
f. you with, Jer. 3:15.
Lord will *f.* them, Hos. 4:16.
sent him to *f.* swine, Luke 15:15.
hunger *f.* him, Rom. 12:20.
give all to *f.* poor, I Cor. 13:3.

FEEL, to handle or know.
that I may *f.* thee, Gen. 27:21.
I may *f.* the pillars, Judg. 16:26.
if haply might *f.* after, Acts 17:27.
who being past *f.*, Eph. 4:19.
f. of our infirmities, Heb. 4:15.

FEET, the terminal part of the legs.
gathered up his *f.* in bed, Gen. 49:33.
f. of priests in Jordan, Josh. 3:15.
pierced hands and *f.*, Ps. 22:16.
my *f.* in a large room, Ps. 31:8.
off the dust of *f.*, Matt. 10:14.
his *f.* received strength, Acts 3:7.
Agabus bound his own *f.*, Acts 21:11.

FEIGN, pretend, deceive.
f. himself mad, 1 Sam. 21:13.
f. thyself a mourner, II Sam. 14:2.
prayer not out *f.*, Ps. 17:1.
f., them. just men, Luke 20:20.
with *f.* words, II Pet. 2:3.

FELIX, a cruel Roman procurator of Judaea, appointed by the emperor Claudius to office 52 A.D., whose freedman he was (Acts 23:24; Acts 24:3ff). It was Paul who reasoned with Felix concerning "righteousness, and self-control, and the judgment to come." Although terrified by the gospel's message, Felix answered, "Go thy way for this time; and when I have a convenient season, I will call thee unto me."

FELL, to cause to fall, to have fallen.
his countenance *f.*, Gen. 4:5.
wall *f.* down flat, Josh. 6:20.
f. a voice from, Dan. 4:31.
he *f.* asleep, Luke 8:23.

FELLOES, the curved pieces which united together form the rim of the wheel (I Kin. 7:33).

FELLER, a person.
no *f.* is come up, Is. 14:8..

FELLOW, a man, companion, partner.
this *f.* came in to, Gen. 19:9.
why smit. thou thy *f.*, Ex. 2:13.
why came this mad *f.*, II Kin. 9:11.
f. also, Matt. 26:71..
away with such a *f.*, Acts 22:22.
this man a pestil. *f.*, Acts 24:5.

FELLOW-CITIZENS, citizens together.
f.-c. with saints, Eph. 2:19.

FELLOW-HEIRS, joint inheritors.
Gentiles be *f.-h.*, Eph. 3:6.

FELLOW-HELPER, one helping another.
Titus my *f.-h.*, II Cor. 8:23.

FELLOW-LABORER, one who works with another.
with other *f.-l.*, Phil. 4:3.
sent Tim. our *f.-l.*, I Thess. 3:2.
Paul to Phile. our *f.-l.*, Philem 1.

FELLOW-SERVANT, one who serves with another.
f.-s. who owed him, Matt. 18:28.
f.-s. fell down at feet, Matt. 18:29.
f.-s. should be fulfilled, Rev. 6:11.

FELLOW-SOLDIER, one who serves as a soldier with another.
Epaphroditus my *f.-s.*, Phil. 2:25.
Paul to Archippus, *f.-s.*, Philem. 2.

FELLOW-WORKERS, those who labour together.
these only are my *f.-w.*, Col. 4:11.

FELLOWSHIP, companionship, familiar intercourse. Christians have it not only with one another (Acts 2:42), but also with God and Christ (I John 1:3), and the Holy Spirit (II Cor. 13:14).
to keep, or in *f.*, Lev. 6:2.
called to *f.* of his Son, I Cor. 1:9.

the right hand of *f.*, Gal. 2:9.
have *f.* with us, I John 1:3.
we have *f.* with, I John 1:6.

FELT, to feel.
Isaac, who *f.* him, Gen. 27:22.
felt in her body, Mark 5:29.

FEMALE, a woman, wife.
male and *f.* created, Gen. 1:27.
went in male and *f.*, Gen. 7:16.
likeness of male or *f.*, Deut. 4:16.
in Christ male nor *f.*, Gal. 3:28.

FEN, mire, swamp.
the covert and fens, Job 40:21.

FENCE, walls which were made of unmortared stones, to secure cultivated lands, sheepfolds, etc. In the crevices of such fences, snakes delighted to hide (Eccles. 10:8).
f. me with bones, Job 10:11.
as a tottering *f.*, Ps. 62:3.
a vineyard, and he *f.* it, Is. 5:2.

FENCED CITY, usually translated "stronghold" or "fort" (II Chr. 11:11; Is. 29:3). The wall was one of the distinctions between a city and a village. The city had walls; the village sometimes only had a tower to warn the people of danger. We learn that very early castles and fortresses were built outside the walled towns to protect the cattle (Deut. 3:5; II Chr. 26:10). The Israelites found many walled cities when they entered Canaan (Num. 13:28; Josh. 11:12; Judg. 1:27–33).

FERRET, GECKO, one of the unclean animals listed in Lev. 11:30. It is a lizard, and is named "Gecko" because of the sound it makes. It is not to be connected with the ferret, which is a weasel-like animal.
the *f.* unclean, Lev. 11:30.

FERRY BOAT, a vessel used for crossing a stream (II Sam. 19:18).

FERVENT, to boil, to be hot, fervid.
Apollos. *f.* in spirit, Acts 18:25.
f. in spirit, Rom. 12:11.
your *f.* mind, II Cor. 7:7.
melt with *f.* heat, II Pet. 3:10.

FERVENTLY, outstretched, extended.
f. in prayers, Col. 4:12..

with pure heart *f.*, I Pet. 1:22.

FESTIVAL, MACCABEAN, *see* **DEDICATION, FEAST OF.**

FESTIVALS, Jewish. (1) Septenary Festivals, or Cycles of Sabbaths. These included the Weekly Sabbath (Ex. 20: 8–11), Seventh New Moon or Feast of Trumpets (Num. 28:11–15), Sabbatic Year (Ex. 23:10–11); Year of Jubilee (Lev. 25:8–16); New Moon (Num. 10: 10). (2) Yearly Festivals. These included the Feast of Passover and Unleavened Bread (Ex. 12:1–28); Pentecost, or Feast of Weeks (Ex. 34:22); Day of Atonement (Lev. 16:1–34); Feast of Tabernacles (Lev. 16:34–42). (3) Post-Exilic Festivals. They included the Feast of Purim (Esther 9:24–32); Feast of Dedication (I Macc. 4:52. John 10:22).

FESTUS, PORCIUS, the Roman governor who was appointed by Nero to succeed Felix about A.D. 60 (Acts 24:27). He was present with King Agrippa when Paul made his defence before him (Acts 26).

FETCH, to gather, take, receive.
will *f.* morsel of bread, Gen. 18:5.
thence will *f.* thee, Deut. 30:4..
king doth not *f.*, II Sam. 14:13.
f. me a little water, I Kin. 17:10.
f. my knowl. from, Job 36:3.
come, and *f.* us out, Acts 16:37.

FETTER, a chain or shackle used for binding prisoners either by the wrists or ankles.
bound Samson with *f.*, Judg. 16:21.
feet put in *f.*, II Sam. 3:34.
Jehoiakim bound with *f.*, II Chr. 36:6.
often with *f.*, Mark 5:4.

FEVER, the translation in the Revised Version for *Ague.* This is doubtless a general term for the fevers of the land (Deut. 28:22; Lev. 26:16). It may have been malarial fever.
smite thee with a *f.*, Deut. 28:22.
Peter's wife's mother *f.*, Matt. 8:14.
hour *f.* left him, John 4:52.
father of Pub. sick *f.*, Acts 28:8.

FEW, little in number.
I being *f.*, will slay, Gen. 34:30.
are not my days *f.*, Job 10:20.
f. days be destroyed, Dan. 11:20.
faithful in *f.* things, Matt. 25:21.

hear *f.* words, Acts 24:4.
for *f.* days chastened, Heb. 12:10.
f. names even in Sardis, Rev. 3:4.

FIDELITY, faith, steadfastness.
showing good *f.*, Titus 2:10.

FIELD, any cultivated ground.
f. and cave made sure, Gen. 23:20.
cause a *f.* to be eaten, Ex. 22:5.
Joab's *f.* is near, II Sam. 14:30.
good seed in his *f.*, Matt. 13:24.
bought the potter's *f.*, Matt. 27:7.
this man purchased a *f.*, Acts 1:18.
which reaped your *f.*, James 5:4.

FIERCE, inspiring terror.
anger, for it was *f.*, Gen. 49:7.
voice of *f.* lion, Job 4:10.
devils, exceeding *f.*, Matt. 8:28.
they were more *f.*, Luke 23:5.
driven of *f.* winds, James 3:4.

FIERCENESS, state of being fierce.
swallow ground with *f.*, Job 39:24.
land desolate *f.* of, Jer. 25:38.

FIERY, characterized with fire.
sent *f.* serpents, Num. 21:6.
make thee a *f.* serpent, Num. 21:8.
midst of *f.* furnace, Dan. 3:6.
able to quench *f.* darts, Eph. 6:16.
judgment and *f.*, Heb. 10:27.

FIFTH, pertaining to number five.
smote A. under *f.* rib, II Sam. 2:23.
smote Ama. under *f.* rib, II Sam. 20:10.
when he opened *f.* seal, Rev. 6:9.
the *f.* angel sounded, Rev. 9:1.
f. angel poured out, Rev. 16:10.

FIFTEEN.
Bethany *f.* furl. off, John 11:18.
found it *f.* fathoms, Acts 27:28.
I abode with P. *f.* days, Gal. 1:18.

FIFTY.
even to *f.*, Num. 4:3.
age of *f.* serve no more, Num. 8:25.
hid them by *f.* in cave, I Kin. 18:4.
down quickly, write *f.*, Luke 16:6.
art not yet *f.* years old, John 8:57.

FIFTIETH, pertaining to fifty.
shall hallow *f.* year, Lev. 25:10.
jubilee shall that *f.* year, Lev. 25:11.

FIG, the fruit of a fig tree. *See* **FIG-TREE**.
f. leaves for aprons, Gen. 3:7.
Egyptian cake of *f.*, I Sam. 30:12.
fall *f.* from, Is. 34:4.
them like vile *f.*, Jer. 29:17.
do men gather *f.* of, Matt. 7:16.
or vine *f*, James 3:12.

FIG TREE, a famous tree of the East, the fruit of which is one of the favorite articles of food (I Sam. 25:18). It is also an important article of commerce. If the trees did not produce, the whole nation suffered. When they produced, it was a sign of divine favor. The tree concealed its fruit with its leaves. The tree was a hypocrite if on approaching it, one found no fruit (Mark 11:13). Mention is made that it was also used for medicine (II Kin. 20:7; Is. 38:21).
trees said to *f.-t.*, Judg. 9:10.
keepeth *f.-t.*, Prov. 27:18.
he saw *f.-t.* in way, Matt. 21:19.
f.-t. withered, Matt. 21:20.
behold the *f.-t.*, Luke 21:29.
f.-t. I saw thee, John 1:48.

FIGHT, a contest, struggle.
will go up and *f.*, Deut. 1:41.
host was going to *f.*, I Sam. 17:20.
my fingers to *f.*, Ps. 144:1.
men forborne to *f.*, Jer. 51:30.
then would my ser. *f.*, John 18:36.
f. I not as beateth, I Cor. 9:26.
I have fought a good *f.*, II Tim. 4:7.
ye kill, ye *f.* and war, James 4:2.

FIGHTINGS, fights.
without *f.* within fears, II Cor. 7:5.
come wars and *f.*, James 4:1.

FIGURE, (1) a form, a building (Is. 44:13), (2) an antitype (Heb. 9:24), (3) a parable (Heb. 9:9; 11:19), (4) a type (Acts 7:43).
similitude of any *f.*, Deut. 4:16.
with carved *f.* of, I Kin. 6:29.
f. ye made to, Acts 7:43.
f. of him that was, Rom. 5:14.
which was a *f.* of, Heb. 9:9.
like *f.* even baptism, I Pet. 3:21.

FILE, this word is incorrectly translated "file" in the Authorized Version and the Revised Version. Archaeology has now shown that the word, *pim*, means a weight of about 7.6 grams. The text should read: "the charge was a pim for the plowshares and for the mattocks, and a third of a shekel for sharpening the axes and for setting the goads" (I Sam. 13:21) as in the Revised Standard Version.

FILL, to pour full, make complete. Also **Filled**.
f. waters in the seas, Gen. 1:22.
locusts shall *f.* houses, Ex. 10:6.
f. mouth with laughing, Job 8:21.
f. breadth of thy land, Is. 8:8.
f. courts with slain, Ezek. 9:7.
is put in to *f.* it, Matt. 9:16.
f. water-pots with, John 2:7.
God of hope *f.* you, Rom. 15:13.
f. up what is behind, Col. 1:24.
cup *f.*, *f.* double, Rev. 18:6.

FILLET, the rods which united together the tops of the pillars round the court of the Tabernacle and from which the curtain was hung.
their *f.* shall be of, Ex. 27:10.
overlaid chapiters and *f.*, Ex. 36:38.
f. of twelve cubits, Jer. 52:21.

FILLETED, to bind with or as with a fillet.
be *f.* with silver, Ex. 27:17.
overlaid chapiters and *f.*, Ex. 38:28.

FILTH, foul matter, anything that soils or defiles.
when washed *f.* of, Is. 4:4.
will cast abominable *f.*, Nah. 3:6.
as the *f.* of world, I Cor. 4:13.
not put away *f.* of flesh, I Pet. 3:21.

FILTHINESS, state of being filthy.
carry *f.* out of holy, II Chr. 29:5.
unclean with *f.* of people, Ezra 9:11.
full of vomit and *f.*, Is. 28:8.
nor let *f.* be named, Eph. 5:4.
lay apart all *f.*, James 1:21.
full of abominations and *f.*, Rev. 17:4.

FILTHY, characterized with filth.
much more *f.* is man, Job 15:16.
all our right. as *f.* rags, Is. 64:6.
you put off *f.*, Col. 3:8.
not given to *f.* lucre, Titus 1:7.
f. dreamers defile, Jude 8.
f. let him be *f.* still, Rev. 22:11.

FIN, part of a fish.
whatsoever hath *f.*, Lev. 11:9.
whatsoever hath not *f.*, Deut. 14:10.

FINALLY, adverb meaning the end.

f. brethren, farewell, II Cor. 13:11.
f. my brethren, rejoice, Phil. 3:1.
f., brethren, pray, II Thess. 3:1.

FIND, to locate, discover.
sin shall *f.* you out, Num. 32:23.
grant ye may *f.* rest, Ruth 1:9.
wicked till *f.* none, Ps. 10:15.
few there be that *f.*, Matt. 7:14.
if haply he might *f.*, Mark 11:13.
doth he yet *f.* fault, Rom. 9:19.
f. mercy of Lord, II Tim. 1:18.

FINE, of superior quality.
three measures of *f.* meal, Gen. 18:6.
offering be of *f.* flour, Lev. 2:1.
that work in *f.* flax, Is. 19:9.
most *f.* gold changed, Lam. 4:1.
bought *f.* linen, Mark 15:46.
man in *f.* linen, Luke 16:19.
merchandise of *f.* flour, Rev. 18:13.

FINING POT, melting pot.
f. p. if for, Prov. 17:3.
f. p. for silver, Prov. 27:21.

FINGER, the five terminating members
of one's hand. Figuratively it is used to
denote the special and immediate agency
of a person.
magicians said the finger of, Ex. 8:19.
written with *f.* of God, Ex. 31:18.
putting forth of the *f.*, Is. 58:9.
with *f.* of God cast out, Luke 11:20.
with *f.* wrote on, John 8:6.
reach hither thy *f.*, and, John 20:27.

FINISH, to complete doing.
f. it above, Gen. 6:16.
all work *f.*, Ex. 39:32.
sufficient to *f.*, Luke 14:28.
is not able to *f.* it, Luke 14:29.
I might *f.* my course, Acts 20:24.
he will *f.* the work, Rom. 9:28.
would also *f.* in you, II Cor. 8:6.

FINISHER, one who finishes.
author and *f.* of faith, Heb. 12:2.

FIR, a tree whose wood was used to make
musical instruments (II Sam. 6:5). It
was also used in the construction of
Solomon's Temple and in shipbuilding
(I Kin. 6:34; II Chr. 3:5; Ezek. 27:5). It
may have been the juniper or the cypress.
f. trees rejoice at thee, Is. 14:8.
f. trees of Senir, Ezek. 27:5.

FIRE, the principle of combustion. We
do not know when man first learned to
use fire. It seems to be implied in the
sacrifices of Cain and Abel (Gen. 4:3).
It also symbolized the presence of the
Lord. It was used for heating and cooking. Each house had a hearth (Is. 30:14);
fire pans, or braziers (Jer. 36:22), were
used to carry hot coals to other rooms.
Figuratively it was used to depict calamity or judgment, and it also expressed
the possession of divine inspiration.
took *f.* in hand, Gen. 22:6.
f. was on tabernacle, Ex. 40:38.
mount. burnt with *f.*, Deut. 4:11.
the *f.* of God is fallen, Job 1:16.
have cast *f.* into sanctu., Ps. 74:7.
burning and fuel of *f.*, Is. 9:5.
fruit is cast into *f.*, Matt. 3:10.
wilt thou that we *f.*, Luke 9:54.
in flaming *f.* taking, II Thess. 1:8.
buy gold tried in *f.*, Rev. 3:18.

FIREBRAND, (1) a bent stick for stirring
fire (Amos 4:11; Is. 7:4). (2) A torch
made of a stick (Judg. 15:4, 5). (3)
Sparks, brands (Prov. 26:18). (4) A burning mass (Ps. 102:3).
took *f.* put, Judg. 15:4.
madman casteth *f.*, Prov. 26:18.
two tails of these smoke *f.*, Is. 7:4.
f. plucked out of bur, Amos 4:11.

FIREPAN, one of the vessels of the Temple service.
make basons and *f.*, Ex. 27:3.
he made the *f.* of brass, Ex. 38:3.

FIRKIN, a unit of liquid measure (John
2:6). It appears to be equivalent to an
ephah or bath, therefore about eight or
nine gallons.
containing two or three *f.* John 2:6.

FIRM, stationary.
stood *f.* on, Josh. 3:17.
his heart is as *f.* as, Job 41:24.
consulted to make *f.*, Dan. 6:7.
of hope *f.* to end, Heb. 3:6.

FIRMAMENT, the pure expanse which
envelops the earth. God created the
firmament on the second day of creation,
for the purpose of separating the sea
from the clouds. Some argue that the
Hebrews meant a solid support when
they used firmament. The firmament is
compared to a curtain stretched (Ps. 140:
2; Is. 40:22). The language used is highly

figurative. The firmament. separated the waters above and below (Gen. 1:6, 7).
f. in midst of waters, Gen. 1:6.
called the *f.* Heaven, Gen. 1:8.
f. showeth handiwork, Ps. 19:1.
shine as bright. of *f.*, Dan. 12:3.

FIRST, at the beginning.
f. came out red, Gen. 25:25.
f. of fruits bring, Ex. 23:19.
glory of the *f.* house, Ezra 3:12.
f. be reconciled to, Matt. 5:24.
seek ye *f.* kingdom, Matt. 6:33.
worse than *f.*, Matt. 12:45.
faith dwelt *f.* in grand., II Tim. 1:5.
f. heaven and *f.* earth, Rev. 21:1.

FIRSTBORN, applied to animals and human beings; the eldest child or the firstling of the flock. The firstborn of both were dedicated to the Lord (Ex. 12:12). The firstborn son was the one who succeeded the father in inheritance or throne. Figuratively, the firstborn stands for the most excellent. It is a perfect description of Christ (Heb. 12:23). Christ is said to be the first-born from the dead (Col. 1:18).

FIRST DAY OF THE WEEK, Sunday, the Lord's Day.
upon the *f. d.* very early, Luke 24:1.
upon *f. d.* of the week, Acts 20:7.

FIRST-FRUITS, like the firstborn of man and beast, the first fruits were sacred to the Lord, who is king of the soil (Ex. 23:19; Deut. 18:4). In general, first-fruits included those in the raw state (as grain and fruit), those prepared for use as food (wine, oil, flour, and dough), including even wool (Ex. 22:29; Deut. 18:4).

FIRSTLING, first born.
Able brought *f.* of flock, Gen. 4:4.
f. of ass thou shalt, Ex. 13:13.
f. of uncl. beasts, Num. 18:15.
f. males sanctify, Deut. 15:19.

FISH, the Hebrews recognized fish as one of the great divisions of the animal kingdom (Gen. 1:26, 28). The Mosaic Law (Lev. 11:9, 10) pronounced unclean such fish as were devoid of fins and scales; these were and are regarded as unwholesome in Egypt.
over *f.*, of sea, Gen. 1:26.
liken. of any *f.*, Deut. 4:18.

ask *f.* will he give, Matt. 7:10.
take up *f.* that first, Matt. 17:27.
they saw *f.* laid, John 21:9.

FISH GATE, the name of one of the gates of Jerusalem (II Chr. 33:14; Neh. 3:3). It probably took its name from the fact of fish being brought in on the way to the city, or from the fish market being located close by.

FISHING, this has always been an industry pursued by a large number of people in Palestine. The Sea of Galilee was and still is remarkably well stored with fish. Jerusalem derived its supply chiefly from the Mediterranean (Ezek. 47:10). The methods of taking fish in the Bible are: Angling with a hook (Is. 19:8), spearing (Job 41:7), and netting (Ezek. 26:5).

FISHER, one who fishes.
f. also shall mourn, Is. 19:8.
send for many *f.*, Jer. 16:16.
f. shall stand upon it, Ezek. 47:10.
they were *f.*, Matt. 4:18.
f. of men, Matt. 4:19.
Peter girt *f.* coat to, John 21:7.

FIST, one's hand closed tightly.
one smite . . . with *f.*, Ex. 21:18.
hath gath. wind in *f.*, Prov. 30:4.
smite with *f.* of wicked, Is. 58:4.

FIT, timely, appropriate.
by hand of a *f.* man, Lev. 16:21.
f. to say king, Job 34:18.
made *f.* for no work, Ezek. 15:5.
f. for kingdom of, Luke 9:62.
not *f.* for the land, Luke 14:35.

FITCHES, (1) vetches, an herbaceous annual plant belonging to the natural order, that grows in south Europe and north Africa. Its black seeds are used like pepper, and have almost as pungent a flavor. The Syrians sprinkled these seeds over the flat cakes before baking them (Is. 28:25). (2)

FITLY, properly, suitably.
word *f.* spoken, Prov. 25:11.
building *f.* framed, Eph. 2:21.
body *f.* joined, Eph. 4:16.

FIVE, the fifth number.
four kings with *f.*, Gen. 14:9.
f. lords of, Josh. 13:3.

are not *f.* sold, Luke, 12:6.
hast had *f.* husbands, John 4:18.
f. times forty strips, II Cor. 11:24.

FIXED, something made stationary.
heart is *f.*, Ps. 57:7.
heart *f.* trusting in Lord, Ps. 112:7.
us is a gulf *f.*, Luke 16:26.

FLAG, (1) any green and coarse herbage, such as rushes or reeds, that grow in marshy locations (Gen. 41:2, 18), (2) weeds of any nature (Ex. 2:3, 5; Is. 19:6).

FLAGON, (1) probably a cake of pressed raisins (II Sam. 6:19; I Chr. 16:3; Song 2:5). Raisin cakes were delicacies (Hos. 3:1), and figuratively represented idolatrous worship which appealed to senses. (2) A bottle or pitcher made of earthenware (Is. 22:24). The word is sometimes used for a kind of musical instrument.

FLAKE, the dewlaps or flabby portion of the crocodile's neck (Job 41:23), which was firmly attached to the body.

FLAME, fire.
in *f.* of fire, Ex. 3:2.
f. dry up branches, Job 15:30.
f. burnt up the wicked, Ps. 106:18.
tormented in this *f.*, Luke 16:24.
make ministers *f.* of fire, Heb. 1:7.
as *f.* of fire, Rev. 1:14.

FLAMING, to be burning.
at garden of Eden *f.*, Gen. 3:24.
f. flame not be, Ezek. 20:47.
chariots be *f.*, Nah. 2:3.

FLANK, the internal muscles of the loins close to the kidneys, onto which fat adheres (Lev. 3:4, 10); therefore the viscera in general.

FLASH, the appearance of a bright light.
appear. of *f.* of lightn., Ezek. 1:14.

FLAT, spread out smooth.
that hath *f.* nose, Lev. 21:18.
Baalam fell *f.* on face, Num. 22:31.
wall of city fall *f.*, Josh. 6:5.

FLATTER, to make smooth, shatter praise and attention upon, often times for ulterior motives.
they *f.* with their tongue, Ps. 5:9.
did *f.* him with mouth, Ps. 78:36.

favor than he that *f.*, Prov. 28:23.
man that *f.*, Prov. 29:5.

FLATTERY, the result of one who flatters.
speaketh *f.* to friends, Job 17:5.
f. of strange woman, Prov. 6:24.
shall he corrupt by *f.*, Dan. 11:32.
many shall cleave with *f.*, Dan. 11:34.

FLAX, a well-known plant used in making cloth. The fibers are twisted, bleached, and woven into linen. The growing stalks grow two or three feet. They are then dried on the house-tops (Josh. 2:6). The failure of the crop meant that the judgment of God was upon them (Hos. 2:9).
f. was smitten, Ex. 9:31.
she hid with *f.*, Josh. 2:6.
seeks wool and *f.*, Prov. 31:13.
lovers that give me *f.*, Hos. 2:5.

FLAY, a type of punishment.
blood, the Levites *f.*, II Chr. 35:11.
f. their skins, Mic. 3:3.

FLEA, an insect.
come after *f.*, I Sam. 24:14.
to seek a flea, I Sam. 26:20.

FLED, to run away.
left garment and *f.*, Gen. 39:12.
fowl and beast *f.*, Jer. 9:10.
f. before earthquake, Zech. 14:5.
disciples *f.*, Matt. 26:56.
f. from sepulchre, Mark 16:8.
f. for refuge, Heb. 6:18.
heaven and earth *f.*, Rev. 20:11.

FLEE, to escape, run away.
near to *f.* unto, Gen. 19:20.
fain *f.* out of hand, Job 27:22.
will ye *f.* for help, Is. 10:3.
f. fornication, I Cor. 6:18.
man of God *f.*, I Tim. 6:11.
devil, he will *f.*, James 4:7.
death shall *f.* from them, Rev. 9:6.

FLEECE, the wool of sheep, whether on the animal or shorn off.
first of *f.* give, Deut. 18:4.
f. of wool in, Judg. 6:37.
warm. with *f.* of sheep, Job 31:20.

FLESH, (1) the whole creation (Gen. 6: 13, 17), (2) the body as distinguished from the spirit (Job 14:22), (3) human nature (Gen. 2:23), (4) the sensuous nature of man (John 1:13).

God closed up *f.*, Gen. 2:21.
f. burn with fire, Ex. 29:14.
what *f.* can do, Ps. 56:4.
no *f.* be justified, Rom. 3:20.
that no *f.* should, I Cor. 1:29.
fathers of *f.* who, Heb. 12:9.
filthy dream. defile *f.*, Jude 8.
fowls were filled with *f.*, Rev. 19:21.

FLESH HOOK, an instrument used in sacrificial ceremonies (Ex. 27:3). It was probably a fork, with fins bent back to draw away the flesh (I Sam. 2:13, 14).

FLESHLY, fleshlike, unspiritual.
not with *f.* wisdom, II Cor. 1:12.
puffed by *f.* mind, Col. 2:18.
abstain from *f.* lusts, I Pet. 2:10.

FLESH POT, probably a vessel of bronze with three legs utilized for culinary purposes by the Egyptians (Ex. 16:3).

FLIES, an insect.
send swarms of *f.*, Ex. 8:21.
sent divers sorts of *f.*, Ps. 78:45.
sorts of *f.*, Ps. 105:31.
dead *f.* cause ointment, Eccles. 10:1.

FLIGHT, a fleeing away.
f. be not in winter, Matt. 24:20.
turned to *f.* armies, Heb. 11:34.

FLINT, a hard rock, properly a variety of quartz. In the Revised Version it was used for knives (Ex. 4:25; Josh. 5:2). Figuratively it means an unbending attitude.
water out of rock of, Deut. 8:15.
turning *f.* into, Ps. 114:8.
set my face like *f.*, Is. 50:7.
harder than *f.*, Ezek. 3:9.

FLOATS, a type of raft used on the water.
I will conv. by sea in *f.*, I Kin. 5:9.
to thee in floats by sea, II Chr. 2:16.

FLOCK, a herd of sheep. Figuratively it is used of God's people (Is. 40:11, Matt. 26:31).
was feeding *f.* with, Gen. 37:2.
took lamb out of *f.*, I Sam. 17:34.
keeping watch over *f.*, Luke 2:8.
take heed to all the *f.*, Acts 20:28.
wolves not sparing *f.*, Acts 20:29.
who feedeth a *f.*, I Cor. 9:7.
feed *f.* of God. I Pet. 5:2..
being ensamples to the *f.*, I Pet. 5:3.

FLOOD, the great world-engulfing event as told in Gen. 6–9. It was caused by man's wickedness (Gen. 6:5–7, 11–13). Noah built the ark, and he, his family, and the animals were saved from the flood because of his righteousness. During the time of Noah, who was tenth from Adam, man grew wicked. Every thought of man was continuously wicked (Gen. 6:5). Because of the promise that all nations would be blessed through Abraham, God chose Noah. Now Noah was a "just man and perfect" and he "walked with God." Through one of Noah's three sons, Shem, God preserved the Messianic line. Isaiah refers to the flood as "the waters of Noah (59:4). Jesus speaks of the flood as if it were actual history (Matt. 24:37; Luke 17:26). Peter speaks of God's long suffering "which waited in the days of Noah while the ark was preparing wherein few, that is eight souls, were saved by water" (I Pet. 3:20). He also cites it as God's righteous judgment (II Pet. 2:5).

FLOOR, a level, or open place.
furnish out of *f.*, Deut. 15:14.
a fleece of wool in *f.*, Judg. 6:37.
overlaid *f.* of house, I Kin. 6:30.
upon every corn *f.*, Hos. 9:1.
f. shall be full of, Joel 2:24.
purge *f.*, Matt. 3:12.

FLOUR, ground grain for making bread, the support of life in the world of antiquity. At the first only barley was ground, but later wheat was used and barley was kept for the poor. Fine flour was presented in connection with sacrifice in general, and by poor people as a sin offering (Lev. 5:11–13).
wheat *f.* thou make, Ex. 29:2.
handful of the *f.*, Lev. 2:2.
ephah of *f.*, Judg. 6:19.
took *f.* and kneaded, I Sam. 28:24.
f. parched corn, II Sam. 17:28.

FLOURISH, to thrive, grow abundantly.
in his days right. *f.*, Ps. 72:7.
righteous shall *f.*, Ps. 92:12.
of upright shall *f.*, Prov. 14:11.
your bones shall *f.*, Is. 66:14.
I was at rest, and *f.*, Dan. 4:4.

FLOW, to be full or to go by as a stream.
his goods shall *f.*, Job 20:28.
nations shall *f.* unto it, Is. 2:2.

f. to goodness of, Jer. 31:12.
hills shall *f.* with milk, Joel 3:18.
out of belly *f.*, John. 7:38.

FLOWER, the term applied to the flower ornaments of the golden candlestick (Ex. 25:31; 37:17), and also the imitation lily ornaments round the edge of the great laver (I Kin. 7:26). They are used to represent the brevity of human life because of their speedy decay (Job 14:2; Ps. 103:15); the quick downfall of the Israelite kingdom (Is. 28:1); and the sudden departure of the rich (James 1:10, 11).
f. in one branch, Ex. 25:33.
forth as *f.* is cut, Job 14:2.
as *f.* of field, Ps. 103:15.
goodliness is as *f.*, Is. 40:6.
she pass *f.* of age, I Cor. 7:36.

FLOWING, FLOWS, *see* **FLOW.**

FLUTE, or pipe is a musical instrument listed among others (Dan. 3:5, 7, 10, 15) used at the worship of the golden image of Nebuchadnezzar. It resembled the modern flute, and was made of reeds, copper, and other material. It was used as the principal wind-instrument.

FLUTTERETH, to flap the wings quickly without flying (Deut. 32:11).

FLUX, the same as our dysentery, which in the East is generally epidemic and infectious (Acts 28:8).

FLY, the translation of two insect pests of Palestine. One is probably the ordinary housefly, called *Zebhubh* (Is. 7:18; Eccles. 10:1). The other, *arobh*, is probably the dog-fly (Ex. 8:21–31), or, as is translated more recently, gnats.

FLY, to go through the air like a bird.
didst *f.* on the spoil, I Sam. 15:19.
did *f.* on wings of, II Sam. 22:11.
all cattle and *f.* fowl, Ps. 148:10.
riches *f.* away, Prov. 23:5.
they shall *f.* as eagle, Hab. 1:8.
beast like a *f.* eagle, Rev. 4:7.
that *f.* midst of heaven, Rev. 19:17.

FOAL, an ass's colt.
took twenty asses, ten *f.*, Gen. 32:15.
binding his *f.* to the vine, Gen. 49:11.
colt *f.* of ass, Zech. 9:9.

FOAM, the original word is rendered "foam" in Hos. 10:7. Actually, it means a broken branch, a fagot, or splinter. The Revised Standard Version translates it as "chip."

FOAMETH, FOAMING, to froth.
f. and gnasheth with, Mark 9:18.
on ground and wallowed, *f.*, Mark 9:20
waves *f.* out own, Jude 13.

FODDER, a mixture which ir rendered "corn" in Job 24:6 and "provender" in (Is. 30:24; Job 6:5).

FOE, enemy.
destroyed before *f.*, I Chr. 21:12.
mine enemies and *f.*, Ps. 27:2.
man's *f.* be of house, Matt. 10:36.
I make *f.* footstool, Acts 2:35.

FOLD, (1) hedged or fenced places (Num. 32:16), (2) pasture land (Mic. 2:12), (3) in a spiritual sense (John 10:16).
maketh their *f.*, Is. 13:20.
Sharon shall be *f.*, Is. 65:10.
some thirty *f.*, Matt. 13:8.
one *f.* and one shepherd, John 10:16.

FOLD, to clasp or interweave, also **Folding.**
f. of hands, Prov. 6:10.
f. his hands together, Eccles. 4:5.
they be *f.* together, Nah. 1:10.

FOLK, nation people.
conies but feeble *f.*, Prov. 30:26.
f. shall labor in fire, Jer. 51:58.
hands on few sick *f.*, Mark 6:5.
multitude of impotent *f.*, John 5:3.
bringing sick *f.*, Acts 5:16.

FOLLOW, to go after.
not willing to *f.*, Gen. 24:8.
companions *f.* her, Ps. 45:14.
we *f.* on to know, Hos. 6:3.
f. Me, Matt. 4:19.
sheep hear *f.* me, John 10:27.
f. after charity, I Cor. 14:1.
man of God *f.*, I Tim. 6:11.
f. peace with all, Heb. 12:14.
they that *f.* the Lamb, Rev. 14:4.

FOLLOWER, one who follows someone or something.
f. of me, I Cor. 4:16.
be ye *f.* of God, Eph. 5:1.

181

f. of us and of, I Thess. 1:6.
f. of them who, Heb. 6:12.
be *f.* of that is good, I Pet. 3:13.

FOLLOWETH,FOLLOWING, *see* **FOLLOW.**

FOLLY, vanity, silliness.
wrought *f.* in Israel, Gen. 34:7.
do not this *f.*, Judg. 19:23.
layeth not *f.* to them, Job 24:12.
know wisdom and *f.*, Eccles. 1:17.
bear with me in my *f.*, II Cor. 11:1.
f. be made manifest, II Tim. 3:9.

FOOD, the diet of eastern nations has been in all ages light and simple, vegetables being the principal food. Bread and preparations of corn were common items on their tables. Milk held a conspicuous place as affording substantial nourishment. Of the vegetables those that received the most notice were lentils, beans, leeks, onions, and garlic (cf. Num. 11:5). The meat mostly used was that of calves, lambs, oxen not above three years, harts, roebucks, hallow deer and birds of various kinds. Fish, with the exception of such as were without scales and fins were also consumed.
every tree good for *f.*, Gen. 2:9.
tree was good for *f.*, Gen. 3:6.
did eat angels' *f.*, Ps. 78:25.
much *f.* in tillage, Prov. 13:23.
fill. our hearts with *f.*, Acts 14:17.
minister bread for *f.*, II Cor. 9:10.
f. and raiment, I Tim. 6:8.
destitute of daily *f.*, James 2:15.

FOOL, one who is rash, unreasonable; the term often refers to one who is not mentally retarded but who is lacking in moral qualities.
have played the *f.*, I Sam. 26:21.
prating *f.*, Prov. 10:8.
f. mouth is destruction, Prov. 18:7.
f. walketh in darkness, Eccles. 2:14.
his end be a *f.*, Jer. 17:11.
shall say, Thou *f.*, Matt. 5:22.
f. this night thy soul, Luke 12:20.
no man think me a *f.*, II Cor. 11:16.
I shall not be a *f.*, II Cor. 12:6.

FOOLISH, to act as a fool.
f. nation, Deut. 32:21.
f. not stand in thy sight, Ps. 5:5.
likened to a *f.* man, Matt. 7:26.
f. heart was darkened, Rom. 1:21.

nor *f.* talking, Eph. 5:4.

FOOLISHNESS, the state of being foolish.
because of my *f.*, Ps. 38:5.
heart of fools pro. *f.*, Prov. 12:23.
know wickedness of *f.*, Eccles. 7:25.
f. come from within, Mark 7:22.
by *f.* of preaching save, I Cor. 1:21.
wisdom of world is *f.*, I Cor. 3:19.

FOOT, the terminal part of the leg. the term "feet" is a delicate way of explaining the performance of the necessities of nature (I Sam. 24:3; Judg. 3:24).
no man shall lift up foot, Gen. 41:44.
nor did thy *f.* swell, Deut. 8:4.
Barak was sent on *f.*, Judg. 5:15.
keep thy *f.* when goest, Eccles. 5:1.
Lord trodden under *f.*, Lam. 1:15.
salt trodden under *f.*, Matt. 5:13.
bound hand and *f.*, John 11:44.
so much as to set his *f.*, Acts 7:5.
trodden under *f.* the, Heb. 10:29.
clothed with garm. to *f.*, Rev. 1:13.
city shall tread under *f.*, Rev. 11:2.

FOOTMAN, (1) generally a fighting man who traveled on foot in distinction from those who went on horseback or in chariots, (2) a group of runners in attendance to the king (I Sam. 22:17).
to the *f.* Saly priests, I Sam. 22:17.
thou hast run with *f.*, Jer. 12:5.

FOOTSTEPS, a footfall or tread.
that my *f.* slip not, Ps. 17:5.
thy *f.* are not known, Ps. 77:19.
f. of anointed, Ps. 89:51.

FOOTSTOOL, a piece of furniture, which was used in supporting the feet when sitting (II Chr. 9:18). The footstool of God is the earth (Ps. 110:1).
house for *f.* of God, I Chr. 28:2.
worship at his *f.*, Ps. 99:5.
it is his *f.*, Matt. 5:35.
earth is my *f.*, Acts 7:49.
till enemies be *f.*, Heb. 10:13.
sit here under my *f.*, James 2:3.

FORBAD, did forbid.
whatsoever Lord *f.*, Deut. 2:37.
John *f.* him saying, Matt. 3:14.
f. madness of prophet, II Pet. 2:16.

FORBARE, to refrain.
Saul *f.* to go forth, I Sam. 23:13.

Ishmael *f.* and slew not, Jer. 41:8.

FORBEAR, to refrain.
f. to vow it, Deut. 23:22.
f. why be smitten, II Chr. 25:16.
will hear, or *f.*, Ezek. 2:5.
power to *f.* working, I Cor. 9:6.
f. in love, Eph. 4:2.
could no longer *f.*, I Thess. 3:1.

FORBEARANCE, a refraining, holding back.
riches of *f.*, Rom. 2:4.
remission of sins thro' *f.*, Rom. 3:25.

FORBID, to prohibit.
my lord *f.* them, Num. 11:28.
f. him not, Mark 9:39.
f. not to take coat also, Luke 6:29.
can any man *f.* water, Acts 10:47.
f. not, I Cor. 14:39.

FORCE, power, strength.
his natural *f.* abated, Deut. 34:7.
their *f.* is not right, Jer. 23:10.
with *f.* ye ruled them, Ezek. 34:4.
not strengthen *f.*, Amos 2:14.
violent take it by force, Matt. 11:12.
to take Paul by *f.*, Acts 23:10.
testament is of *f.* after, Heb. 9:17.

FORCE, to overpower, overcome.
if the man *f.* her, Deut. 22:25.
concubine have they *f.*, Judg. 20:5.
I *f.* myself, I Sam. 13:12.
with flat. she *f.* him, Prov. 7:21.

FORCES, the strength of someone or some nation such as its army or fortifications.
will not esteem the *f.* Job 36:19.
f. of Gentiles shall, Is. 60:5.
assemble multi. of *f.*, Dan. 11:10.
honor the God of *f.*, Dan. 11:38.

FORCIBLE, characterized by strength.
how *f.* are right words. Job 6:25.

FORD, a crossing place in a river or stream which was usually rather shallow (Gen. 32:22; Josh. 2:7).

FORECAST, to scheme ahead of time.
f. his devices, Dan. 11:24.

FOREFATHERS, ancestors.

turn. to iniquities of *f.*, Jer. 11:10.
whom I served from *f.*, II Tim. 1:3.

FOREFRONT, the front part or place.
Uriah in *f.* of battle, II Sam. 11:15.
Jehoshaphat in *f.*, II Chr. 20:27.

FOREHEAD, the upper front part of the head.
stone sunk in his *f.*, I Sam. 17:49.
Uzziah leprous in *f.*, II Chr. 26:20.
strong against their *f.*, Ezek. 3:8.
mark of beast in his *f.*, Rev. 14:9.
his name be in their *f.*, Rev. 22:4.

FOREIGNER, one who sojourns in a foreign country. The Jews looked upon the Gentiles as foreigners. *See* STRANGERS.
f. not eat thereof, Ex. 12:45.
of a *f.* exact it again, Deut. 15:3.
ye are no more *f.*, Eph. 2:19.

FOREKNOW, to know beforehand.
whom he did *f.*, Rom. 8:29.
not cast away people he *f.*, Rom. 11:2.

FOREKNOWLEDGE, a knowing beforehand.
delivered by *f.* of God, Acts 2:23.
according to *f.* of God, I Pet. 1:2.

FOREMOST, first, chief.
he commanded the *f.*, Gen. 32:17.
running of the *f.*, II Sam. 18:27.

FOREORDAIN, to appoint or set in order beforehand.
who verily was *f.*, I Pet. 1:20.

FOREPART, the front part.
f. of ship stuck fast, Acts 27:41.

FORERUNNER, when an ancient king prepared to travel, he would send someone before him to prepare the highway. The one sent was a forerunner. John the Baptist was the forerunner of Christ (Matt. 11:10; Mark 1:2; Luke 7:27). Also Christ is our forerunner, because he has entered heaven on our behalf, that we might follow (Heb. 6:20).
wither *f.* is for us, Heb. 6:20.

FORESEE, to see beforehand. Also **Foreseeth.**
man *f.* the evil, Prov. 22:3.
f. Lord always before, Acts. 2:25.
the Scripture *f.* that God, Gal. 3:8.

FORESHIP, a ship's prow.

183

anchors out of the *f.*, Acts 27:30.

FORESKIN, the loose skin on the sex organ of a male which was cut off in circumcision. Since this Jewish act was a figure of purification, the foreskin represented corruption; because of this we have the phrase, "foreskin of the heart" (Deut. 10:16). The skin at times was returned as a trophy of killed Gentiles (I Sam. 18:25).
flesh of *f.*, Gen. 17:11.
flesh of his *f.*, Lev. 12:3.
circumcise *f.* of heart, Deut. 10:16.
away the *f.* of heart, Jer. 4:4.
let thy *f.* be uncovered, Hab. 2:16.

FORESKINS, HILL OF, a location close to Gilgal perhaps, which was so-called because after the nation had been circumcised Israelites were buried there (Josh. 5:3).

FOREST, a wooded area.
will enter into *f.* of, II Kin. 19:23.
beast of the *f.* mine, Ps. 50:10.
lion out of *f.*, Jer. 5:6.
cut any out of *f.*, Ezek. 39:10.
f. of vintage is come, Zech. 11:2.

FORETELL, to tell beforehand.
I have *f.* you, Mark 13:23.
f. of these days, Acts 3:24.
I *f.* you as if present, II Cor. 13:2.

FOREWARN, to warn beforehand.
f. whom ye shall fear, Luke 12:5.
we also have *f.* you, I Thess. 4:6.

FORFEIT, to give over.
substance should be *f.*, Ezra 10:8.

FORGAT, did forget.
thou *f.* iniquity, Gen. 40:23.
they *f.* the Lord, I Sam. 12:9.
f. God their saviour, Ps. 106:21.
I *f.* prosperity, Lam. 3:17.

FORGE, to stitch or sew on.
proud have *f.* a lie, Ps. 119:69.

FORGER, one who forges.
ye are *f.* of lies, Job 13:4.

FORGET, to not remember.
till thy brother *f.*, Gen. 27:45.
covenant shall not *f.*, II Kin. 17:38.
can a woman *f.* child, Is. 49:15.

dost *f.* us for ever, Lam. 5:20.
never *f.* any of works, Amos 8:7.
to communicate *f.* not, Heb. 13:16.

FORGETFUL, FORGETFULNESS, characterized by forgetting.
known in land of *f.*, Ps. 83:12.
not *f.* to entertain, Heb. 13:2.
a *f.* hearer, but a doer, James 1:25.

FORGIVE, to excuse, pardon.
f. trespass of brethren, Gen. 50:17.
pray *f.* the trespass, I Sam. 25:28.
f. sin of servant, I Kin. 8:36.
f. not their iniquity, Jer. 18:23.
f. us as we *f.*, Matt. 6:12.
can *f.* sins, Mark 2:7.
thought of heart be *f.*, Acts 8:22.
ought rather to *f.*, II Cor. 2:7.
to whom ye *f.*, II Cor. 2:10.
for Christ's sake *f.* you, Eph. 4:32.
having *f.* all trespasses, Col. 2:13.
sins they be *f.*, James 5:15.
to *f.* us our sins, I John 1:9.
your sins are *f.*, I John 2:12.

FORGIVEN, lifted away, absolved.
transgression is *f.*, Ps. 32:1.
thy sins *f.* thee, Matt. 9:2.
whom little is *f.*, Luke 7:47.
f. all your trespasses, Col. 2:13.

FORGIVENESS, the state of pardon.
there is *f.* with thee, Ps. 130:4.
our God belong *f.*, Dan. 9:9.
f. but in danger, Mark 3:29.
to give *f.*, Acts 5:31.
him is preached *f.*, Acts 13:38.
they may receive *f.* of, Acts 26:18.
have *f.* of sins, Eph. 1:7.

FORGOTTEN, cease to remember.
plenty shall be *f.*, Gen. 41:30.
shall not be *f.*, Ps. 9:18.
were *f.* in the city, Eccles. 8:10.
Tyre shall be *f.*, Is. 23:15.
shall never be *f.*, Jer. 20:11.
sabbaths to be *f.*, Lam. 2:6.

FORK, an instrument for handling hay, (I Sam. 13:21).

FORM, an appearance, figure, shape.
earth was without *f.*, Gen. 1:2.
this *f.* of speech, II Sam. 14:20.
appeared *f.* of a hand, Ezek. 10:8.
f. of fourth like, Dan. 3:25.
in another *f.*, Mark 16:12.
hast *f.* of knowledge, Rom. 2:20.

f. of doctrine, Rom. 6:17.
being in *f.* of God, Phil. 2:6.
f. of sound words, II Tim. 1:13.
a *f.* of godliness, II Tim. 3:5.

FORM, to shape, make.
God *f.* man of dust, Gen. 2:7.
forgot. God that *f.* thee, Deut. 32:18.
am *f.* out of clay, Job 33:6.
f. thee from the womb, Is. 44:2.
f. the light, Is. 45:7.
before I *f.* thee in, Jer. 1:5.
f. say to him *f.* it, Rom. 9:20.
till Christ be *f.*, in you, Gal. 4:19.
Adam first *f.* then, I Tim. 2:13.

FORMER, first, before.
do after *f.* manner, II Kin. 17:34.
f. loving-kindnesses, Ps. 89:49.
show *f.* things, Is. 41:22.
remember *f.* things of old, Is. 46:9.
f. treatise have I made, Acts 1:1.
according to *f.* lusts, I Pet. 1:14.
f. things passed away, Rev. 21:4.

FORNICATION, in general it refers to
illicit sexual intercourse (Acts 15:29;
Rom. 1:29). When distinguished from
adultery (Matt. 15:19) it seems to have
reference to a married man having intercourse with an unmarried woman,
whereas adultery is the man having intercourse with a married or promised-in-
marriage woman.
f. in Canaan, Ezek. 16:29.
saving for *f.*, Matt. 5:32.
we be not born of *f.*, John 8:41.
works of the flesh, *f.*, Gal. 5:19.
mortify therefore *f.*, Col. 3:5.
should abstain *f.*, I Thess. 4:3.
to repent of her *f.*, Rev. 2:21.
nor repent of their *f.*, Rev. 9:21.
wine of wrath of *f.*, Rev. 14:8.

FORNICATOR, one who commits fornication.
not to company with *f.*, I Cor. 5:9.
with *f.* of world, I Cor. 5:10.
a brother be a *f.*, I Cor. 5:11.
nor shall *f.* inherit, I Cor. 6:9.
lest there be any *f.*, Heb. 12:16.

FORSAKE, to abandon, leave.
this people will *f.* me, Deut. 31:16.
I *f.* my sweetness, Judg. 9:11.
and truth *f.*, Prov. 3:3.
teachest to *f.* Moses, Acts 21:21.
Demas hath *f.*, me, II Tim. 4:10.

not *f.* the assembling, Heb. 10:25.
by faith Moses *f.*, Heb. 11:27.

FORSAKEN, deserted, left.
God hath *f.* him, Ps. 71:11.
be as *f.* bough, Is. 17:9.
f. fountain of, Jer. 17:13.
f. the covenant, Jer. 22:9.
persecuted, not *f.*, II Cor. 4:9.
Demas hath *f.* me, II Tim. 4:10.
f. the right way, II Pet. 2:15.

FORSOOK, did forsake.
they *f.* the Lord, Judg. 2:12.
he *f.* counsel, I Kin. 12:8.
f. all, followed, Luke 5:11.
all men *f.* me, II Tim. 4:16.

FORSWEAR, to commit perjury.
thou not *f.* thyself, Matt. 5:33.

FORT, the ancient cities were often fortified with wall as a means of protection
and battle.
David dwelt in the *f.*, II Sam. 5:9.
f. of walls bring down, Is. 25:12.
building *f.* cut off many, Ezek. 17:17.
they in the *f.* shall die, Ezek. 33:27.
f. of own land, Dan. 11:19.

FORTH, forward, beyond.
blessed be Lord, time *f.*, Ps. 113:2.
be driven out right *f.*, Jer. 49:5.
that time *f.* began, Matt. 16:21.
that day *f.* ask, Matt. 22:46.
that day *f.*, John 11:53.

FORTHWITH, immediately.
and *f.* they sprung up. Matt. 13:5.
and *f.* sent him away, Mark 1:43.
f. came out blood and, John 19:34.
f. the angel departed, Acts 12:10.

FORTIFY, to make stronger, make fortifications.
f. city against thee, Judg. 9:31 .
Jews *f.* themselves, Neh. 4:2.
come from *f.* cities, Mic. 7:12.
f. thy power mightily, Nahum 2:1.
f. thy strongholds, Nahum 3:14 .

FORTRESS, stronghold.
my *f.*, II Sam. 22:2.
f. shall he bring down, Is. 25:12.
O Lord, my *f.*, Jer. 16:19.
thy *f.* shall be, Hos. 10:14.

FORTUNATUS, a certain disciple at

Corinth who visited the Apostle Paul at Ephesus and returned with the letter of I Corinthians (I Cor. 16:17).

FORTY, a number.
f. stripes he may give, Deut. 25:3.
walked *f.* years in, Josh. 5:6.
f. years long grieved, Ps. 95:10.
I led you *f.* years, Amos 2:10.
above *f.* years old, Acts 4:22.
saw works *f.* years, Heb. 3:9.
with whom grieved *f.* years, Heb. 3:17.

FORUM, perhaps a market (Acts 28:15).

FORWARD, ahead.
and they went not *f.*, Jer. 7:24.
f. the affliction, Zech. 1:15.
more *f.* of his own, II Cor. 8:17.
I also was *f.* to do, Gal. 2:10.
if bring *f.* on journey, III John 6.

FOUGHT, did fight.
f. me without cause, Ps. 109:3.
have *f.* with beasts, I Cor. 15:32.
f. a good fight, II Tim. 4:7.
Michael *f.* dragon, Rev. 12:7.

FOUL, unclean.
my face is *f.* Job 16:16.
it will be *f.* weather, Matt. 16:3.
rebuked the *f.* spirit, Mark 9:25.

FOUND, to have located, discovered.
the dove *f.* no rest, Gen. 8:9.
servants *f.* well, Gen. 26:19.
pursuers *f.* them not, Josh. 2:22.
not *f.* aught in hand, I Sam. 12:5.
when they had *f.* him, Mark 1:37.
came in, and *f.* her, Acts 5:10.

FOUNDATION, the base on which a building rests. It may mean also the origin of something (Job 4:19), or the beginning (Matt. 13:35).
not been in Eg. since *f.*, Ex. 9:18.
f. is in mountains, Ps. 87:1.
discovering *f.* to neck, Hab. 3:13.
laid the *f.* on rock, Luke 6:48.
f. can no man lay, I Cor. 3:11.
laid *f.* of the earth, Heb. 1:10.

FOUNDED, to make, create, locate.
he hath *f.* it on seas, Ps. 24:2.
place thou *f.* for them, Ps. 104:8.
f. his troop in earth, Amos 9:6.
it fell not, *f.*, Matt. 7:25.
it was *f.* on a rock, Luke 6:48.

FOUNDER, one who founds, or finds.
gave them to the *f.*, Judg. 17:4.
the *f.* melteth in vain, Jer. 6:29.
of the hands of the *f.*, Jer. 10:9.

FOUNTAIN, a spring of water.
found Hagar by a *f.*, Gen. 16:7.
a *f.* wherein is water, Lev. 11:36.
with thee is the *f.*, Ps. 36:9.
f. of living, Jer. 2:13.
f. of her blood, Mark 5:29.
f. send forth, James 3:11.
no *f.* can yield salt, James 3:12.

FOUR, a number.
river became *f.* heads, Gen. 2:10.
f. parts be own, Gen. 47:24.
over them *f.* kinds, Jer. 15:3.
and behold *f.* horns, Zech. 1:18.
yet *f.* months, harvest, John 4:35.
f. days ago was first, Acts 10:30.
round throne *f.* beasts, Rev. 4:6.

FOURFOLD, four times.
restore the lamb *f.*, II Sam. 12:6.
anything, I restore *f.*, Luke 19:8.

FORESCORE, eighty.
Moses was *f.* years old, Ex. 7:7.
land had rest *f.* years, Judg. 3:30.
and if they be *f.* years, Ps. 90:10.
f. and four years, Luke 2:37.
thy bill and write *f.*, Luke 16:7.

FOURSQUARE, four cornered, each side being the same in length.
the city lieth *f.*, Rev. 21:16.

FOURTEEN.
serv. *f.* years for, Gen. 31:41.
man above *f.* years, II Cor. 12:2.
f. years after I went up, Gal. 2:1.

FOURTH, pertaining to the number four.
in *f.* gen. come hither, Gen. 15:16.
in *f.* year fruit holy, Lev. 19:24.
came in *f.* watch, Matt. 14:25.
f. beast like flying, Rev. 4:7.
the *f.* angel sounded, Rev. 8:12.

FOWL, a bird.
dominion over *f.*, Gen. 1:26.
f. of heaven was, Gen. 7:23.
of clean *f.* may eat, Deut. 14:20.
are ye better than *f.*, Luke 12:24.
wherein were *f.*, Acts 10:12.
angel cried to all *f.*, Rev. 19:17.

f. filled with flesh, Rev. 19:21.

FOWLER, one who catches birds.
from the snare of the *f.*, Ps. 91:3.
soul out of the snare of *f.*, Ps. 124:7.
as a bird from the *f.*, Prov. 6:5.
prophet is a snare of *f.*, Hos. 9:8.

FOX, the translation of a Greek word
which means a true fox, and the translation of a Hebrew word meaning a true
fox or a jackal, a wild dog. The latter
roved in packs. The 300 foxes caught by
Samson were probably Jackals (Judg.
15:4). The one referred to as capable of
breaking down Nehemiah's stone wall
was probably a true fox.
Samson caught *f.*, Judg. 15:4.
f. shall break stone, Neh. 4:3.
are like *f.*, Ezek. 13:4.
f. have holes, Matt. 8:20.
go tell *f.* I cast out, Luke 13:32.

FRAGMENTS, pieces left over.
took up the *f.*, Matt. 14:20.
many baskets of *f.*, Mark 8:19.
gather up the *f.*, John 6:12.

FRAIL, weak, fragile.
may know how *f.* I am, Ps. 39:4.

FRAME, structure, building.
he knoweth our *f.*, Ps. 103:14.
was as the *f.* of city, Ezek. 40:2.

FRAME, to construct, make.
not *f.* to pronounce it, Judg. 12:6.
thy tongue *f.* deceit, Ps. 50:19.
I *f.* evil against you, Jer. 18:11.
in whom the build. *f.*, Eph. 2:21.
worlds *f.* by word, Heb. 11:3.

FRANKINCENSE, a gum resin with a
pungent balsamic odor (Ex. 30:34). It
was taken from a tree akin to the terebinth. It had a bitter taste. It was associated with Myrrh, and used for gifts
(Lev. 2:1; Matt. 2:11). In the Authorized Version it is incorrectly translated "incense" (Is. 43:23; 60:6; Jer.
6:20).
spices with pure *f.*, Ex. 30:34.
priest burn oil with *f.*, Lev. 2:16.
they presented to him *f.*, Matt. 2:11.
no man buy their *f.*, Rev. 18:13.

FRANKLY, freely, readily.
f. forgave them both, Luke 7:42.

FRAUD, deceit, trickery.

his mouth is full of *f.*, Ps. 10:7.
hire kept back by *f.*, James 5:4.

FRAY, to frighten away.
f. them, Deut. 28:26.
these are come to *f.*, Zech. 1:21.

FREE, to be at liberty, unbound.
I will not go out *f.*, Ex. 21:5.
be *f.* from bitter wat., Num. 5:19.
servant *f.* from master, Job 3:19.
then are children *f.*, Matt. 17:26.
truth shall make you *f.*, John 8:32.
but I was *f.* born, Acts 22:28.
f. gift is of many, Rom. 5:16.
made *f.* from sin, Rom. 6:18.
am I not *f.*, I Cor. 9:1.
bond or *f.*, Eph. 6:8.
as *f.* not using, I Pet. 2:16.
f. and bond to receive, Rev. 13:16.

FREEDOM, the state of being free.
not *f.* given her, Lev. 19:20.
great sum this *f.*, Acts 22:28.

FREELY, liberally, without cost.
of every tree *f.* eat, Gen. 2:16.
if people eaten *f.*, I Sam. 14:30.
let me *f.* speak, Acts 2:29.
of fountain of life *f.*, Rev. 21:6.

FREEMAN, one who is free.
called, is the Lord's *f.*, I Cor. 7:22.

FREEWILL, voluntary.
his *f.* offerings, Lev. 22:18.
accept *f.* offerings, Ps. 119:108.

FREEWILL, to offer willingly.
all his *f.* offerings, Lev. 22:18.
offered a *f.* offering, Ezra 3:5.
the *f.* offerings of my, Ps. 119:108.

FREQUENT, often.
in prisons more *f.*, II Cor. 11:23.

FRESH, new, vigorous.
taste of manna as *f.*, Num. 11:8.
my glory was *f.* in me, Job 29:20.
be *f.* than a child's, Job 33:25.
anointed with *f.* oil, Ps. 92:10.
yield salt water and *f.*, James 3:12.

FRET, to be sad, downhearted.
is a *f.* leprosy, Lev. 13:51.
to make her *f.*, I Sam. 1:6.
his heart *f.* against, Prov. 19:3.
when hungry they *f.*, Is. 8:21.

f. me in these things, Ezek. 16:43.

FRIED, a type of cooking.
of fine flour, *f.*, Lev. 7:12.
for that which is *f.*, I Chr. 23:29.

FRIEND, a person with whom one has a
close pleasant relationship.
God spake as man to *f.*, Ex. 33:11.
pity be showed from *f.*, Job 6:14.
f. closer than brother, Prov. 18:24.
neighbor and his *f.*, Jer. 6:21.
shall have a *f.*, Luke 11:5.
our *f.* Lazarus sleepeth, John 11:11.
made Blastus their *f.*, Acts 12:20.
Abraham call. *f.* of, James 2:23.
f. of world, is enemy of, James 4:4.

FRIENDLY, characterized with friendship.
to speak *f.* to her, Judg. 19:3.
spoken *f.* to handm., Ruth 2:13.
show himself *f.*, Prov. 18:24.

FRIENDSHIP, the state of being
friends.
no *f.* with angry man, Prov. 22:24.
f. of world is enmity, James 4:4.

FRINGE, a twisted thread or tassel. They
were sewn on the hem of the garment to
remind the Jew of God's commandments (Num. 15:38, 39).
make *f.* put on *f.*, Num. 15:38.
make thee *f.*, Deut. 22:12.

FROG, an amphibian which is mentioned
in two connections in the Bible. They
were a part of the plagues in Egypt (Ex.
8:2–14; Ps. 78:45), and they were unclean spirits (Rev. 16:13–14). Both the
edible frogs and the green tree-frogs are
found in Palestine.
all thy borders with *f.*, Ex. 8:2.
the magicians brought up *f.*, Ex. 8:7.
he sent *f.* which, Ps. 78:45.
the land brought forth *f.*, Ps. 105:30.
unclean spirits like *f.*, Rev. 16:13.

FRONT, the part before.
f. of battle, II Sam. 10:9.

FRONTIER, an advanced region or
settlement (Ezek. 25:9).

FRONTLETS, ornaments and phylacteries which were worn on the forehead and on the arms. *See* **PHYLAC-
TERY.**

be for *f.* between eyes, Ex. 13:16.
shall be as *f.*, Deut. 6:8.

FROST, frozen dew.
f. consumed by night, Gen. 31:40.
as small as the hoar *f.*, Ex. 16:14.
f. of heaven, Job 38:29.
body cast out to *f.*, Jer. 36:30.

FROWARD, perverse, crooked.
a very *f.* generation, Deut. 32:20.
counsel of *f.* carried, Job 5:13.
f. abomination to Lord, Prov. 3:32.
be subject to *f.*, I Pet. 2:18.

FROWARDNESS, perverseness.
delight in *f.* of wicked, Prov. 2:14.
f. is in his heart, Prov. 6:14.
of wicked speak. *f.*, Prov. 10:32.

FROZEN, to be solidified because of cold
temperature.
face of the deep is *f.*, Job 38:30.

FRUIT, the offspring of living things.
every tree wherein is *f.*, Gen. 1:29.
Cain brought of the *f.*, Gen. 4:3.
I forsake my *f.*, Judg. 9:11.
f. of their doings, Is. 3:10.
and his *f.* good, Matt. 12:33.
sought *f.* and found none, Luke 13:6.
f. of Spirit is love, Gal. 5:22.
this is *f.* of labor, Phil. 1:22.
offer *f.* of our lips, Heb. 13:15.
waiteth for precious *f.*, James 5:7.
f. withereth, without *f.*, Jude 12.

FRUITFUL, bearing fruit.
be *f.*, Gen. 1:22.
make thee exceed. *f.*, Gen. 17:6.
children of Israel were *f.*, Ex. 1:7.
hath vineyard in *f.* hill, Is. 5:1.
gave rain and *f.*, Acts 14:17.
f. in every good work, Col. 1:10.

FRUSTRATE, to make void, bring to
nothing.
hired to *f.* purpose, Ezra 4:5.
f. tokens of the liars, Is. 44:25.
I do not *f.* grace of, Gal. 2:21.

FRYING PAN, a utensil used for boiling
meat, etc.
meat-off. baken in *f.-p.*, Lev. 2:7.
in *f.-p.* be priest's, Lev. 7:9.

FUEL, material used for burning. In the
East wood is scarce and must be substituted with withered stalks (Matt. 6:30),

thorns (Ps. 58:9), and animal excrements (Is. 9:5).
and *f.* of fire, Is. 9:5.
people be as *f.* of fire, Is. 9:19.
into fire for *f.*, Ezek. 15:4.
be for *f.* to fire, Ezek. 21:32.

FUGITIVE, a deserter, refugee.
ye Gileadites are *f.*, Judg. 12:4.
f. that fell to king, II Kin. 25:11.
his *f.* flee to Zoar, Is. 15:5.
all his *f.* fall by, Ezek. 17:21.

FULFILL, to complete. Also **Fulfilled.**
f. her week, and we, Gen. 29:27.
he might *f.* word of, I Kin. 2:27.
to *f.* all righteousness, Matt. 3:15.
shall *f.* all my will, Acts 13:22.
to *f.* the lust thereof, Rom. 13:14.
not *f.* lust of flesh, Gal. 5:16.
to *f.* the word of God, Col. 1:25.
ye *f.* the royal law, James 2:8.
hearts to *f.* his will, Rev. 17:17.

FULL, to be complete, filled.
old, and *f.* of years, Gen. 25:8.
in *f.* tale to king, II Sam. 18:27.
house *f.* of sacrifices, Prov. 17:1.
f. of light, Matt. 6:22.
Jesus being *f.* of Holy, Luke 4:1.
f. of envy, murder, Rom. 1:29.
to them of *f.* age, Heb. 5:14.
four beasts *f.* of eyes, Rev. 4:6.

FULLER, one who cleans or whitens clothes (Mark 9:3). The fuller dipped the clothes in an alkaline solution, which bleached them. Soda, lye, urine, and chalk were rubbed into the cloth, or made into a solution. Nitre and soap are mentioned in the scripture (Prov. 25:20; Jer. 2:22; Mal. 3:2). The clothes were then hung out to dry in a field, which came to be known as a fuller's field. The whiteness of Jesus' garment was contrasted with the whiteness of the fuller's art (Mark 9:3).

FULLER'S FIELD, a field used for drying the bleached clothes of the fuller's art. One such field, outside the city, was the scene of Rabshakeh's interview with Hezekiah's men (II Kin. 18:17). The offensive odours connected with the fuller's trade no doubt made it imperative that he practice outside the city.

FULLY, completely.

that followed me *f.*, Num. 14:24.
as stubble *f.* dry, Nah. 1:10.
day was *f.* come, Acts 2:1.
grapes *f.*, Rev. 14:18.

FULLNESS, the state of being full.
sea roar and *f.* thereof, I Chr. 16:32.
world mine, and *f.*, Ps. 50:12.
much more their *f.*, Rom. 11:12.
f. of time was come, Gal. 4:4.
in *f.* of times, Eph. 1:10.
with all *f.* of God, Eph. 3:19.
in him all *f.* dwell, Col. 1:19.
in him dwelleth *f.* of God, Col. 2:9.

FUNERAL, ancient funerals among the Israelites were performed by the deceased's own kinsmen (Gen. 25:9, Judg. 16:31). Later, however, this custom was changed and the arrangements were left in the charge of others (Amos 5:16). The body was washed (Acts 9:37) and wrapped in cloth (Matt. 27:59). After the burial the ceremonies were concluded by a meal (II Sam. 3:35; Jer. 16:5).

FURBISH, to burnish, renovate.
f. spears, put on, Jer. 46:4.
sword sharpened. *f.*, Ezek. 21:9.
given to be *f.*, Ezek. 21:11.

FURIOUS, filled with rage.
with *f.* man not go, Prov. 22:24.
f. man aboundeth in, Prov. 29:22.
was very *f.*, Dan. 2:12.
Lord revengeth and is *f.*, Nah. 1:2.

FURLONG, an equivalent of one tenth English mile.
Emmaus from J. sixty *f.*, Luke 24:13.
about twenty-five *f.*, John 6:19.
twelve thousand *f.*, Rev. 21:16.

FURNACE, a place where fire is heated
smoking *f.* burning, Gen. 15:17.
hath taken out of *f.*, Deut. 4:20.
f. for gold, Prov. 17:3.
midst of fiery *f.*, Dan. 3:6.
cast into *f.* of fire, Matt. 13:42.
feet as burned in *f.*, Rev. 1:15.

FURNISH, to supply, provide.
thou shalt *f.* him, Deut. 15:14.
f. table in wilder., Ps. 78:19.
f. to go into captivity, Jer. 46:19.

FURNITURE, living accommodations

Rachel put in *f.*, Gen. 31:34.
and his *f.*, Ex. 31:7.
candlestick and his *f.*, Ex. 35:14.
end of all pleasant *f.*, Nah. 2:9.

FURROW, a trench in the ground.
or *f.* thereof complain, Job 31:38.
unicorn in *f.*, Job 39:10.
might water it by *f.*, Ezek. 17:7.
hemlock in *f.* of field, Hos. 10:4.
altars as heaps in *f.*, Hos. 12:11.

FURTHER, forward, farther.
come, but no *f.*, Job 38:11.
what *f.* need of, Matt. 26:65.
he would gone *f.*, Luke 24:28.
shall proceed no *f.*, II Tim. 3:9.
what *f.* need, Heb. 7:11.

FURTHERANCE, progress.
rather to *f.* of gospel, Phil. 1:12.

FURY, tense anger.
thy brother's *f.* turn, Gen. 27:44.
where is *f.* of oppressor, Is. 51:13.
trample them in my *f.*, Is. 63:3.
ran unto him in *f.*, Dan. 8:6.
let thy *f.*, be turned, Dan. 9:16.
zealous with great *f.*, Zech. 8:2.

G

GAAL, son of Ebed who aided the She-chemites in their rebellion against Abim-elech (Judg. 9:26–41).

GAASH, more accurately Mount Gaash in the region of Mount Ephraim. Here Joshua was buried. The "brooks" or "valleys of Gaash" were probably at the foot of the hill (II Sam. 23:30).

GABA, *see* **GEBA.**

GABBAI, a chief among the Benjamites after the exile in Babylon.
after him G., Sallai, Neh. 11:8.

GABBATHA, place from which Pilate sentenced Jesus. Also called "The Pave-ment." Possibly connected with Herod's palace.
pavement, in Hebrew, *G.*, John 19:13.

GABRIEL, the word used to designate the heavenly messenger, sent to explain to Daniel the visions which he saw (Dan. 8:16; 9:21). In the New Testament

he announced the birth of John the Baptist (Luke 1:11), and the birth of the Messiah (Luke 1:26).

GAD, (1) Jacob's seventh son, firstborn of Zilpah (Gen. 30:11–13). (2) Gad "the seer," or "the king's seer." He advised David to enter the land of Judah (I Sam. 22:5). At his direction an altar was erect-ed for burnt offerings and peace offerings (II Sam. 24:11–25). (3) Gad, the tribe of. As one of the sons of Jacob, Gad became the father of a tribe in Israel. Seven sons are ascribed to him at the entry into Egypt (Gen. 46:16). In the wandering in the wilderness the tribe was in the camp of Reuben on the south side of the taber-nacle (Num. 1:14, 2:10–16). In the time of David the Gadites assisted him in vari-ous ways (I Chr. 12:8; II Sam. 17:24, 27–29). In the division Gad went with the kingdom of the north. Later Tiglathpi-leser carried the tribe of Gad, and the neighboring tribes, into Assyrian captiv-ity (II Kin. 15:29; I Chr. 5:26). (4) A valley mentioned in II Sam. 24:5.

GAD, a Canaanite god whose name ap-pears in various place names, as Baal-gad, Migdal-gad, Gaddai, Gaddiel.

GADARA, Josephus states this city was the metropolis, capital city, of Perea. It was southeast of the southern extremity of the Sea of Galilee, about six miles from the Sea (Luke 8:26–27). *See* **GER-ASENES, GERGESA.**

GADARENES, GERASENES, GERGE-SENES, the inhabitants of Gadara. The American Standard Version has Gera-senes in Mark 5:1; Luke 8:26, 37.

GADDI, son of Susi, a spy from the tribe of Manasseh. He was sent by Moses to assist in exploring the land of Canaan (Num. 13:11).

GADDIEL, son of Sodi, a chief of Zebu-lon sent with others to spy out Canaan (Num. 13:10).

GADI, father of Menahem, a king of Is-rael (II Kin. 15:14, 17).

GADITE, the descendants of Gad.

GAHAM, son of Nahor by his concubine Reumah (Gen. 22:24).

GAHAR, one of the Nethinim whose sons came up with Zerubbabel from captivity to Jerusalem (Ezra 2:47; Neh. 7:49).

GAI, a place name in the Revised Version for the valley (I Sam. 17:52).

GAIN, to obtain, to acquire.
ye would *g.*, Dan. 2:8.
g. the whole world, Matt. 16:26.
g. besides them, Matt. 25:20.
to have *g.* this harm, Acts 27:21.
I might *g.* the Jews, I Cor. 9:20.
g. the weak, I Cor. 9:22.

GAINSAY, to speak against, contradict.
not be able to *g.*, Luke 21:15.
convince the *g.*, Titus 1:9.
perish in the *g.*, Jude 11.

GAIUS, (1) native of Macedonia, companion of Paul, seized by mob at Ephesus (Acts 19:29). (2) Native of Derbe, companion of Paul on return from Macedonia into Asia (Acts 20:4). (3) Corinthian whom Paul baptized, at whose home Christians assembled (Rom. 16:23; I Cor. 1:14). (4) Person to whom John wrote his third epistle (3 John 1).

GALAL, (1) one of the sons of Asaph (I Chr. 9:15). (2) Descendant of Jeduthun, father of Shemaiah (I Chr. 9:16; Neh. 11:17).

GALATIA, the land of the Galli, Gauls. Two possible explanations have been given for the locality designated by the term "Galatia". (1) Geographically the term referred to a country in northern Asia Minor. (2) Politically the term designated a province of the Roman empire. The problem has been to determine the exact area intended by references (I Cor. 16:1; Gal. 1:2, etc.) made to the country. W. M. Ramsay has urged the political identification with great ability, but on the basis of the Greek construction in Acts 16:6,7, and other relevant considerations some scholars have been reluctant to completely accept the view.

GALATIANS, inhabitants of Galatia.

GALATIANS, EPISTLE TO, the letter was written to combat certain Judaistic teachers. Paul's apostleship was challenged, the doctrine of salvation by the grace of God as revealed in the gospel was being obscured. Paul had founded the churches in the area, probably on his first tour. On the second tour Paul returned to visit the churches again (Acts 16:6). A third visit was made during the third tour (Acts 18:23). After this visit Paul went to Ephesus, Macedonia, and Greece (Acts 19:1, 20:1,2). In the absence of Paul the Judaistic teachers had become insistent in their claims, and some of the Galatians were led into error. Paul writes to correct the situation. The date is about A.D. 55–56, the place of composition Macedonia or Greece.

GALBANUM, a resinous gum of a brownish yellow color, strong of odor, obtained possibly from Persia (Ex. 30:34), was to be used in the preparation of the sacred incense.

GALEED, the name given by Jacob to a heap of stones erected by Jacob and his brethren as a witness of a covenant he had made with Laban (Gen. 31:43–53).

GALILEANS, inhabitants of Galilee, the northern province of Palestine (Mark 14:70; Luke 13:1; John 4:45).

GALILEE, a district or province of Palestine. In ancient times it referred to a district in the land of Naphtali in which were centered the twenty towns given by Solomon to Hiram of Tyre in payment for his work in providing timbers for the construction of the temple (Josh. 20:7; I Kin. 9:11). In the time of Christ the term was used of one of the three provinces into which Palestine was divided: Judea, Samaria, and Galilee. Two large divisions of the country were upper and lower Galilee. Upper Galilee included the mountain range between the upper Jordan and Phoenicia. Lower Galilee included the plain of Esdraelon and the hill country adjoining it on the north to the foothills of the mountains beyond. Because of the large percentage of Gentiles in the area, it was called Galilee of the Gentiles. The busy traffic, the large population, the less obstinate disposition of the people no doubt contributed to the more extensive work of Christ in this area.

GALILEE, SEA OF, *see also,* **SEA.** This

name occurs five times in the New Testament (Matt. 4:18; 15:29; Mark 1:16; 7:31; John 6:1). Elsewhere it is called "the sea of Tiberias" (John 21:1); "the lake of Gennesaret" (Luke 5:1); "the sea" (John 6:16). The Old Testament names were "sea of Chinnereth" (Num. 34:11); "sea of Chinneroth" (Josh. 12:3). The Sea is a pear-shaped body of water in the trough of the Jordan valley, almost due E. of the bay of Acre. The surface of the water is about 680 feet below the Mediterranean Sea. The depth varies from 130 to 148 feet. The greatest length is about 13 miles, the greatest breadth is more than 7 miles. The Sea was a busy center of boatbuilding, fishing, and fish curing in the time of Christ. Nine large cities bordered the Sea. Located about sixty miles from Jerusalem, the Sea was the scene of many events in the life of Christ.

GALL, bitter, whether used of animal secretions or vegetable extracts. Some have suggested the poppy plant as the chief source of gall. If so, the drink offered to Christ may have been designed to reduce pain (Matt. 27:34).
water of *g.*, Jer. 8:14.
wormwood and the *g.*, Lam. 3:19.
judgment into *g.*, Amos 6:12.
vinegar . . . with *g.*, Matt. 27:34.
in the *g.* of bitterness, Acts 8:23.

GALLERY, an architectural term, signifying a projection of a story or porch, a terrace (Ezek. 41:15; 42:3). It is used in Song 1:17, perhaps as a panel work or fretted ceiling. It is used in the description of Ezekiel's Temple (Ezek. 41:15).

GALLEY, a large ship which is propelled by oars operated by a battery of men (Is. 33:21).

GALLIM, a city of uncertain location, mentioned in connection with Palti, to whom Michal, David's wife, was given; and in connection with the catalogue of cities terrified by the approach of Sennacharib (I Sam. 25:44; Is. 10:30).

GALLIO, proconsul of Asia before whom Paul was brought for trial. An inscription found at Delphi shows that he was proconsul at Corinth in 52 A.D. Gallio's decision recorded in Acts is important because it implies that Paul's teachings were classified along with Jewish teachings, and therefore were lawful (Acts 18: 12-17).

GALLOWS, a tree or stake for impaling the victim. It could be lowered for this purpose, then raised to attract public attention. (Esther 5:14, 6:4; 7:9, 10; 8:7; 9:13, 25).

GAMALIEL, (1) the son of Pedahzur, and the captain of the tribe of Manasseh (Num. 7:54; 10:23). (2) A Pharisee and doctor of the law, grandson of the great Jewish teacher Hillel, and the teacher of Paul. His influence was great among the Jews. Traditions say he became a Christian, but this is unlikely in view of the great respect in which later Jewish writers held him (Acts 5:34; 22:3).

GAMES, the word "game" does not occur in the Bible. However, allusions in the Old Testament and the New Testament make it certain that various games were known and enjoyed among the people. Ancient gaming boards, dice, toys, marbles, miniature houses and animals, dolls, boomerangs, whistles, fish-hooks, and other gaming devices have been found by archaeologists.

In the Old Testament allusion is made to the keeping of birds (Job 41:5), conversation and joking (Jer. 15:17; Prov. 26:19), and to various military activities which may be considered to have elements of amusement. These include especially the use of the bow and the sling (I Sam. 20:20, 35–40; Judg. 20:16; I Chr. 12:2). In later years the Hebrews looked upon the Grecian games, and especially the *gymnasium*, as honoring heathen practices.

In the New Testament allusion is often made to various Grecian games by Paul. The rules, preparations, and rewards so familiar to the people are given spiritual content by their use in illustrating the life and destiny of Christians (I Cor. 4:9; 9:24–27; 15:32; Phil. 3:14; Col. 3:15; II Tim. 2:5; 4:7, 8; Heb. 10:33; 12:1).

GAMMADIM, occurs only in Ezek. 27: 11. Some think the term describes the valour of the troops of Tyre.

GAMUL, a priest who was chief of the

twenty-second of the twenty-four courses of priests (I Chr. 24:17).

GAP, an opening in a wall (Ezek. 13:5; 22:30).

GARDEN, the term is used of various types of cultivated areas. Flowers, spices, fruit, and household vegetables would be grown therein. These were surrounded by a wall or hedge, watered by a fountain or stream, and when possible protected by a guard.
g. eastward in Eden, Gen. 2:8.
tree of the g., Gen. 3:1.
a g. of herbs, Deut. 11:10.
a g. inclosed, Song 4:12.
into my g., Song 5:1.
cast into his g., Luke 13:19.
where was a g., John 18:1.

GARDEN OF EDEN, see EDEN.

GAREB, (1) one of the heroes in David's army (II Sam. 23:38; I Chr. 11:40). (2) Hill in the vicinity of Jerusalem (Jer. 31:39).

GARLIC, an edible plant with a disagreeable, penetrating odor (Num. 11:5).

GARMENT, see CLOTHING.

GARMITE, name applied to Keilah (I Chr. 4:19).

GARNER, a place where goods are stored (Ps. 144:13; Matt. 3:11; Luke 3:17).

GARNISH, to overlay, to make brilliant.
hath g. the heavens, Job 26:13.
g. the sepulchres, Matt. 23:29.
g. with all manner, Rev. 21:19.

GARRISON, a military post, a fortified area for war. The word might also be used of columns erected in a conquered country (I Sam. 10:5; 13:23; 14:1; II Sam. 23:14; Ezek. 26:11; II Cor. 11:32).

GASHMU, variation of the name Geshem (Neh. 6:6).

GATAM, fourth son of Eliphaz (Gen. 36:11, 16; I Chr. 1:36).

GATE, passageway or structure to close passageway, door. Often made of wood

or metal, the gate or door served an important part in defense of a city. The entrance into the city served as (1) a place of public gathering (Gen. 19:1; 23:10; 34:20, 24; I Sam. 4:18); (2) a place for public deliberation, or audience for important visitors (Deut. 16:18; 21:19; 25:7; Josh. 20:4; Judg. 9:35); (3) public markets (II Kin. 7:1).

GATH, one of the five chief cities of the Philistines, and the native home of Goliath (Josh. 13:3; I Sam. 6:17; 17:4, 23). It was located on the border of Judah and Philistia (I Sam. 21:10; I Chr. 18:1), though the exact site is unknown. Because of its strategic location it was sought after by many opposing forces (II Kin. 12:17; II Chr. 11:8; 26:6; Amos 6:2). Here David abode for a time in flight from Saul (I Sam. 21:10–15).

GATHER, to gather together, to heap up.
be a sacred g., Lev. 23:35.
I will g. you, Is. 43:5.
who does not g., Matt. 12:30.
where all Jews g., John 18:20.
g. . . of church, I Cor. 14:23.

GATHERED, assembled.
community had g., Lev. 8:4.
g. in Egypt, Hos. 9:6.
large crowds g., Luke 5:15.

GATH-HEPHER, a town on the border of Zebulon, about 3 miles from Nazareth (II Kin. 14:25). It is called Gittar-Hepher (Josh. 19:13).

GATH-RIMMON, a levitical city in Dan, near Joppa, in the plain of Philistia (Josh. 19:45; 21:24; I Chr. 6:69). Also, another city was so named, situated in the land of the half-tribe of Manasseh (I Chr. 6:70).

GAVE, bestowed. See GIVE.
g. an inheritance, Josh. 19:49.
g. the Levites, II Chr. 35:9.
we g. up and let, Acts 27:15.

GAY, fine.
a g. city, now, Jer. 49:25.
weareth the g. clothing, James 2:3.

GAZA, one of the chief cities of the Philistines (Josh. 10:41; 11:22; 13:3). Assigned to Judah, this tribe subdued it, but not for long (Judg. 1:18; 3:3; 13:1). It was the site of Samson's humiliation (Judg. 16:1–3).

GAZATHITES, inhabitants of Gaza (Josh. 13:3).

GAZE, see, look, behold.
intruding to g., Ex. 19:21.
g. up to heaven, Is. 8:21.
g. on misery, Hab. 1:3.

GAZELLE, the smallest of the antelopes in the Holy Land. It is the roebuck.
a g. or a hart, Deut. 12:15.

GAZER, (II Sam. 5:25), see **GEZER.**

GAZEZ, a name which occurs twice in I Chr. 2:46. First it refers to a son of Caleb by Ephah, second to a son of Haran.

GAZITE, GAZATHITE, an inhabitant of Gaza (Judg. 16:2).

GAZZAM, the sons of Gazzam (Ezra 2:48; Neh. 7:51).

GEBA, GABA, a city of Benjamin, the suburbs of which were allotted to the priests (Josh. 21:17; I Chr. 6:60). In Joshua 18:24 the name is given as **Gaba.**

GEBAL, (1) a mountain area in the land of Edom, extending south from the Dead Sea (Ps. 83:7). (2) A city of the Gibbites (Ezek. 27:9).

GEBER, (1) father of one who had charge of various cities in Solomon's kingdom (I Kin. 4:13). (2) Son of Uri.(I Kin. 4 :19).

GEBIM, city in Benjamin (Isa. 10:31).

GECKO, see **FERRET.**

GEDALIAH, (1) Son of Juduthun and second assistant in the singers selected by David for the temple service (I Chr. 25:3, 9). (2) Descendant of Jeshua and one of the priests who put away their strange (foreign) wives after the captivity (Ezra 10:18, 19). (3) Son of Pashur and one of the Jewish princes who conspired to accuse and imprison Jeremiah (Jer. 38:1ff). (4) Son of Ahikam and governor for a time of Judea after the departure of Nebuchadnezzar. In an act of betrayal

Gedaliah was killed by Ishmael and his helpers. A feast was celebrated in memory of Gedaliah (II Kin. 25:22–25; Jer. 39–41; Zech. 7:5; 8:19).

GEDEON, form of Gideon (Heb. 11:32).

GEDER, a Canaanite city captured by Joshua (Josh. 12:13).

GEDERAH, a town in the lowlands of Judah (Josh. 15:36).

GEDERATHITE, inhabitant of Gederah (I Chr. 12:4).

GEDERITE, epithet given to Baal-hanan (I Chr. 27:28).

GEDEROTH, town in Judah (Josh. 15: 41; II Chr. 28:18).

GEDEROTHAIM, one of the valley towns of Judah (Josh. 15:36).

GEDOR, (1) a chief of the Benjamites, a resident of Jerusalem (I Chr. 8:31; 9:37). (2) Town in the mountains of Judah, some of whose residents joined David at Ziklag (Josh. 15:58; I Chr. 12:7). (3) A town mentioned in I Chr. 4:39. (4) A family in Judah (I Chr. 4:4). (5) An ancestor of Saul (I Chr. 8:31).

GEHAZI, servant of Elisha. He reminded Elisha of a way to reward the Shunamite woman (II Kin. 4:12ff.), had a part in the raising of the dead child (II Kin. 4:25–36), and for his sin in the events following the healing of Naaman he was smitten with leprosy (II Kin. 5:20–27). Later he appeared in the court of King Joram (II Kin. 8:1–6).

GEHENNA, transliterated Greek word translated "Hell" in the New Testament. According to the common view, a valley outside of Jerusalem, possibly to the south (exact site uncertain), used in ancient times as the place of worship to Moloch, idol-god of the Ammonites. The abhorrence of the Jews for the place was shown by the casting there of all manner of refuse, dead animals, and unburied criminals. Fires were kept burning to consume the refuse and reduce the odor. Thus it came to be called the Gehenna of fire. In the New Testament the term is transferred to the place of final punishment of the wicked. In the following passage the Greek word is translated "Hell": Matt. 5:22, 29, 30; 10:28; 18:9; 23:15, 33; Mark 9:43, 45, 47; Luke 12:5; James 3:6. *See* HELL.

GELILOTH, place on the boundary of Judah and Benjamin (Josh. 18:17).

GEMALLI, father of Ammiel, the Danite spy (Num. 13:12).

GEMARIAH, (1) son of Hilkiah, who, with Elasah, went to Babylon as an ambassador (Jer. 29:3ff). (2) Son of Shaphan the scribe, and father of Michaiah (Jer. 36:10–25).

GENEALOGY, race accounts or family registers showing family or tribal descent. These were especially important to the Jewish people because of the lines of family and tribal inheritance (I Chr. 1–9; Ezra 2:61, 62; Neh. 7:63, 64). Difficulties obtained in the comparison of the genealogies are due to lack of comparative material, possible loss or corruption by copyists, and occasional omissions (Matt. 1:1–17; Luke 3:23–38).

GENERATION, (1) production of offspring (Gen. 5:1). (2) A period of time, the extent of which has been variously estimated (Gen. 15:16). (3) The persons constituting a generation at a specific time (Matt. 11:16).
from *g.* to *g.*, Lev. 6:18..
till all the *g.*, Num. 32:13.
to the tenth *g.*, Deut. 23:3.
present evil *g.*, Matt. 12:45.
mercy is on *g.*, Luke 1:50.

GENESIS, the first book of the Old Testament. It is called "Genesis," because it gives an account of the "Generations" of man (Gen. 2:4). It may be divided into two parts: the history of the world to the call of Abraham; and the history of four patriarchs. The author was Moses, and the book reveals the origin of the world, traces the beginning of the Hebrew nation in Abraham, traces the history of the chosen people through the generations of Abraham, Isaac, Jacob, and the sons of Jacob, especially Joseph, until the entrance into Egypt. The book ends with the death of Joseph, but should be read continuously through to the next book also.

GENNESARET, (1) name given to a fertile, crescent shaped plain on the western shore of the Sea of Galilee. It is about 2½ miles long, one mile wide. It was visited by Jesus. See Matt. 14:34; Mark 6:53. (2) For the Lake of Gennesaret *see* GALILEE, SEA OF.

GENTILE, a term applied to non-Jews. All persons not descendants of Abraham were so designated. In ancient times, with the exception of several tribes in Canaan, the Jews accepted Gentiles with kindness. In fact, some Gentiles attained places of importance in the Jewish nation (II Sam. 11; 18; Deut. 10:19). But, by New Testament times the term had become one of reproach and contempt. Allusions are made to this contempt (Eph. 2:11–22; Col. 3:11). However, by the system of proselyting Gentiles could be permitted to participate in some parts of the Jewish ritual. The attitude of the Jews was one of rejection of the gospel, that of the Gentiles largely that of acceptance (Acts 13:44–49). *See* HEATHEN.

GENTLE, GENTLENESS, condescension, mildness, kindness.
g. hath made me, II Sam. 22:36.
I beseech ... by the *g.*, II Cor. 10:1.
of the Spirit is *g.*, Gal. 5:22.
we were *g.* among you, I Thess. 2:7.
must be *g.*, II Tim. 2:24.

GENUBATH, son of Hadad (I Kin. 11:20).

GERA, (1) son of Bela, grandson of Benjamin (Gen. 46:21; I Chr. 8:3). (2) Father (or ancestor) of Ehud the judge (Judg. 3:15). (3) Father of Shemei (II Sam. 16:5; 19:16, 18; I Kin. 2:8).

GERAH, as a measure of weight about 1/20th of a shekel; as a measure of money about $.03.

GERAR, a Philistine city south of Gaza where both Abraham and Isaac lived for a time, and where they came into contact with Abimelech (Gen. 10; 20; 26; II Chr. 14).

GERASA, GERGESA, *see* GADARA.

GERGESENE, *see* GADARA, GERASA.

GERIZIM, a mountain situated opposite Mt. Ebal, over the valley of Shechem. Here occurred the reading of blessings and curses as Moses had directed (Deut. 11:29; 27:12; Josh. 8:33ff.). Here also Jotham gave his parable of the trees and brambles (Judg. 9:7ff.). Tradition has associated many Old Testament events with this mountain. The Samaritans built a temple here after the captivity.

GERSHOM, (1) the first-born son of Moses and Zipporah (Ex. 2:22; 18:3). (I Chr. 23:15, 16: 26:24). (2) The oldest son of Levi (I Chr. 6:16, 17, 20). (3) The son of Manasseh, and father of Jonathan (Judg. 18:30). (4) A descendant of Phinehas, who went up with Ezra from Babylon (Ezra 8:2).

GERSHON, the eldest son of Levi (Gen. 46:11; Ex. 6:16; Num. 3:17). He was also called Gershom.

GERSHONITES, the descendants of Gershon, and one of the three great divisions of the Levites. Even though they were descended from the eldest son, the Kohathites were given first place. In the wilderness their position was behind the tabernacle westward (Num. 3:23). Their official functions were carrying the curtains, hangings, coverings, instruments of service and other things of use in the tabernacle (Num. 3:25). Thirteen of the Levitical cities were apportioned to the Gershonites (Josh. 21:6, 27–33).

GERUTH-CHIMHAM, "the habitation of Chimham" (Jer. 41:17).

GERZITE, *see* **GIRZITE.**

GESHAM, son of Jahdai (I Chr. 2:47).

GESHEM, GASHMU, an Arabian mentioned in Neh. 2:19; 6:1, 2, 6. He was also called Gashmu.

GESHUR, a small principality of Syria, northeast of Bashan (Deut. 3:13, 14; Josh. 12:5). It was ruled by Talmai, whose daughter David married (II Sam. 3:3). Absolom fled thither after murdering Amnon (II Sam. 13:37, 38). Joab returned him thence to Jerusalem (II Sam. 14:23).

GESHURI, GESHURITES, (1) inhabitants of Geshur (Deut. 3:14; Josh. 13:2; 12:2; 13:11, 13; I Sam. 27:8). (2) A desert tribe in Arabia (Josh. 13:2; I Sam. 27:8).

GETHER, third son of Aram (Gen. 10: 23).

GETHSEMANE, an olive yard at the foot of the Mount of Olives. Jesus was accustomed to come to this secluded spot, often with his disciples (Luke 22:39). Here Jesus prayed in agony just prior to his betrayal (Mark 14:32; Luke 22:44; John 18:1).

GEUEL, son of Machi, of the tribe of Gad, sent as a spy by Moses to search out the land of Canaan (Num. 13:15).

GEZER, ancient city of Canaan, N.W. of Jerusalem. Horam or Elam, king of the city was killed by Joshua (Josh. 10:33; 12:12). It formed one of the southern boundaries of Ephraim (Josh. 16:3).

GEZRITES, GIRZITES, name given in connection with the Geshurites and Amalekites in I Sam. 27:8.

GIAH, unidentified place on the route followed by Abner in his flight from Joab (II Sam. 2:24).

GIANT, men of extraordinary size or height. (1) The Nephilim are first mentioned in Gen. 6:4. They were apparently called Nephilim because they "fell" upon the people and oppressed them. (2) The Rephaim were a race which settled on the eastern side of the Jordan. Og, king of Bashan, was said to have had a bed of iron which was nine cubits long and four cubits wide. He is said to have been of a race of giants (Josh. 12:4). (3) The Anakim were the giants reported by the spies in Num. 13:33. (4) The Emim were a race who dwelt in the country of the Moabites (Gen. 14:5), and were described as "tall, as the Anakim" (Deut. 2:11). (5) Zamzummims were from the land of Ammon (Deut. 2:20). Goliath, of the Philistines (I Sam. 17:4) was of a remnant of the Anakim. Ishbi-benob was also born of the giants (II Sam. 21:16–22).

GIBBAR, father of some who came back to Palestine from Babylon under Zerubbabel (Ezra 2:20).

GIBBETHON, a Philistine city allotted to Dan, later given to the Kohathites (Josh. 19:44; 21:23; I Kin. 15:27; 16:15).

GIBEA, a name mentioned in connection with Caleb, Sheva, and Machbenah (I Chr. 2:49).

GIBEAH, (1) Gibeah-haaraloth, the hill of the foreskins (Josh. 5:3, margin). (2) Gibeah of Judah, city in the land belonging to Judah, S.W. of Jerusalem (Josh. 15:57). (3) Gibeah of Benjamin (Judg. 19:12ff.); birthplace of Saul and his residence after he became king (I Sam. 10:26; 11:4; 15:33; etc.). Here the Gibeonites hung Saul's descendants (II Sam. 21:6). (4) Gibeah in Kirjath-Jearim, probably a hill in that city, and the resting place of the ark from the time of its return by the Philistines until the removal by David (II Sam. 6:3, 4; see also I Sam. 7:1, 2).

GIBEATH, probably the same place as Gibeah of Benjamin (Josh. 18:28).

GIBEATHITE, native of Gibeah (I Chr. 12:3).

GIBEON, one of the cities of the Hivites, the inhabitants of which tricked Joshua in the making of a league (Josh. 9:3–17). Later allotted to Benjamin, it became a Levitical town (Josh. 18:25; 21:17). The tabernacle was later placed there (I Chr. 16:39; I Kin. 3:4, 5; II Chr. 1:3ff.).

GIBEONITES, inhabitants of Gibeon.

GIBLITES, the inhabitants of Gebal.

GIDDALTI, son of Heman (I Chr. 25:4, 29).

GIDDEL, (1) children of Giddel were among the Nethinim who returned with Zerubbabel from captivity (Ezra 2:47; Neh. 7:49). (2) children of Giddel were among the "children of Solomon's servants" who returned with Zerubbabel from the captivity (Ezra 2:56; Neh. 7:58).

GIDEON, youngest son of Joash, resident of Ophrah, fifth recorded judge of Israel. In the oppression of Israel by the Midianites Gideon was called to serve. His army was reduced to 300 men. A brilliant midnight attack brought the rout and slaughter of the Midianites. This victory meant the success of Gideon for many years.
called by angel, Judg. 6:11.
sign of the fleece, Judg. 6:36.
refuses kingship, Judg. 8:22.
father of 70 sons, Judg. 8:30.
buried in Ophrah, Judg. 8:32.

GIDEONI, a Benjamite (Num. 1:11; 7:60, 65; 10:24).

GIDOM, place east of Gibeah, exact locality uncertain (Judg. 20:45).

GIER-EAGLE, an unclean bird, probably the Egyptian vulture (Lev. 11:18; Deut. 14:17).

GIFT, there are at least fifteen expressions used for gifts in the Hebrew language. The New Testament emphasizes that gifts should be given without thought of reward; that it is more blessed to give than to receive. The word "gifts" receives a spiritual meaning in the New Testament. Salvation is a gift from God (Eph. 2:8). Eternal life is a gift (Rom. 6:23). The Holy Spirit is received by believers as a gift (Acts 2:38).
God's *g.* come, Ps. 127:2.
keep your *g.*, Dan. 5:17.
offer me your *g.*, Amos 5:22.
free *g.* of God, John 4:10.
about spiritual *g.*, I Cor. 12:1.
g. to the poor, II Cor. 9:9.
but God's *g.*, Eph. 2:8.

GIHON, (1) the second river of Paradise, (Gen. 2:13). (2) A place near Jerusalem, memorable as the scene of the anointing and proclamation of Solomon as king (I Kin. 1:33, 38, 45).

GILALAI, one of the priests' sons at the consecration of the rebuilt wall of Jerusalem (Neh. 12:36).

GILBOA, a mountain range on the eastern edge of the plain of Esdraelon. The mountains rise not more than 1,696 ft. above sea level. In the Bible the area is associated with the last conflict between Saul and the Philistines and the subsequent defeat and death of Saul and Jonathan (I Sam. 28:4; 31:1, 8; II Sam. 1:6, 21; 21:12; I Chr. 10:1, 8).

GILEAD, (1) a mountain region east of the Jordan River, extending from the Sea of Galilee to the upper end of the Dead Sea. The area, about 60 miles long and 20 wide, was bounded by Bashan, Moab, and Ammon (Gen. 31:21; Deut. 3: 12–17). (2) A city named in Hos. 6:8; 12: 11. Possibly it is identified with Gilead near Mizpah (Judg. 10:17). (3) A mountain mentioned in Judges 7:3, connected with the activities of Gideon. (4) Son of Machir, grandson of Manasseh (Num. 26:29, 30). (5) Father of Jephthah (Judg. 11:1, 2). (6) Son of Michael and father of Jaroah, of the tribe of Gad (I Chr. 5:14).
a son of Machir, Num. 26:29.
refuge for Hebrews, I Sam. 13:7.
land of Elijah, I Kin. 17:1.
smitten by Hazael, II Kin. 10:32.
no balm in Gilead? Jer. 8:22.

GILEAD, BALM OF, *see* **BALM.**

GILEADITES, (1) the inhabitants of Gilead (Judg. 12:4). (2) A branch of the tribe of Manasseh, descendants of Gilead (Num. 26:29; Judg. 10:3).

GILGAL, (1) the first camp of Israel after the crossing of the Jordan (Deut. 11:30; Josh. 4:19; 5:9, 10; 9:6; 10:7; 14:6; 15:7). Samuel judged at this place (I Sam. 7:16); it was used as a place of sacrifice (I Sam. 10:8; 13:8–10); Agag was killed here by Samuel (I Sam. 15:33); strangely, it was the site of the crowning and rejection of Saul as the first king (I Sam. 11: 14, 15). (2) A place visited by Elisha and Elijah, not the same as (1) above (II Kin. 2:1, 2; 4:38). (3) A place mentioned in Joshua 12:23.

GILOH, a town in the mountains of Judah (Josh. 15:51); birthplace and scene of the suicide of Ahithophel (II Sam. 15:12; 23:34).

GILONITE, a native of Giloh (II Sam. 15:12; 23:34).

GIMEL, the third letter of the Hebrew alphabet, used to designate the third division of the 119th Psalm.

GIMZO, a town captured by the Philistines in the reign of Ahaz (II Chr. 28:18).

GIN, a noose or trap of wire or hair for snaring birds.

g. shalt take him, Job 18:9.
set *g.* for me, Ps. 140:5.
for a *g.* and snare, Is. 8:14.
fall where no *g.*, Amos 3:5.

GINATH, father of Tibni, the rival of Omri (I Kin. 16:21, 22).

GINNETHON, a priest who sealed the covenant with Nehemiah (Neh. 10:6).

GIRD, to bind around, to gird.
your loins *g.*, Ex. 12:11.
g. his sword, I Sam. 17:39.
God *g.* me with, Ps. 18:32.
g. thyself, and bind, Acts 12:8.
breasts *g.* with, Rev. 15:6.

GIRDLE, a piece of clothing worn by both men and women in the East. Its use was to support the hip joints, hold up the clothing, and carry various objects. Most of them were made of leather or cord (II Kin. 1:8; Matt. 3:4). More elaborate ones were made of linen (Jer. 13:1; Ezek. 16:10), and were sometimes decorated heavily (Dan. 10:5; Rev. 1:13; 15:6). Behind it the scribes put their inkhorns, and the military men tucked their swords (II Sam. 20:8; Ps. 45:3). They made excellent gifts because of their being highly decorated (I Sam. 18:4; II Sam. 18:11). The girdle of the high priest was a kind of blue, purple, and scarlet sash (Ex. 28:39). The idea is used figuratively in the New Testament. To "gird up the loins" was a common expression for putting one's self in readiness (Luke 12:35).
g. of ephod, Ex. 28:8.
g. wherewith he is, Ps. 109:19.
g. of loins loosed, Is. 5:27.
a leathern *g.*, Matt. 3:4.
took Paul's *g.*, Acts 21:11.
with a golden *g.*, Rev. 1:13.

GIRGASITE, GIRGASHITE, one of the nations who possessed the land of Canaan east of the Sea of Galilee (Gen. 10:16; 15:21; Deut. 7:1; Josh. 3:10; 24: 11; Neh. 9:8).

GIRL, lass, female child.
sold *g.* for wine, Joel 3:3.
g. playing in . . streets, Zech. 8:5.

GIRT, *see* **GIRD.**

GIRZITE, the translation in the Revised Version for Gezrites.

GISPA, GISHPA, one of the overseers of the Nethinim (Neh. 11:21).

GITAH-HEPHER, *see* **GATH-HEPHER.**

GITTAIM, the place to which the Beerothites fled (II Sam. 4:3).

GITTITE, inhabitant of the Philistine city of Gath (Josh. 13:3). Six hundred of the inhabitants became the body-guard of David (II Sam. 15:18, 19).

GITTITH, a musical term in the title of Ps. 8, 81, 84. It probably refers to a musical instrument used by the people of Gath.

GIVE, to give.
g. the Levites, Num. 3:9.
land which I *g.*, Josh. 1:2.
g. him reward, II Sam. 4:10.
g. my heart, Eccles. 1:13.
g. her bill of, Jer. 3:8.
g. glory unto, Mal. 2:2.
Lord God shall *g.*, Luke 1:32.
law .. *g.* by Moses, John 1:17.
g. glory to God, Rom. 4:20.
God .. that *g.* all, James 1:5.

GIVER, one who gives.
g. of usury to him, Is. 24:2.
loveth a cheerful *g.*, II Cor. 9:7.

GIZONITE, occurs in I Chr. 11:34 in connection with the guard of David, some of whom were "sons of Hashem the Gizonite."

GLAD, pleased, cheerful, joyful.
g. in his heart, Ex. 4:14.
maketh a *g.* father, Prov. 10:1.
heard and .. were *g.*, Mark 14:11.
I am *g.*, therefore, Rom. 16:19.
let us be *g.*, Rev. 19:7.

GLADLY, joyfully.
Herod heard him *g.*, Mark 6:20.
g. received his word, Acts 2:41.
ye suffer fools *g.*, II Cor. 11:19.

GLADNESS, joy, rejoicing, mirth.
day of your *g.*, Num. 10:10.
with *g.* of heart, Deut. 28:47.
praises with *g.*, II Chr. 29:30.
g. is taken away, Is. 16:10.
receive it with *g.*, Mark 4:16.
eat meat with *g.*, Acts 2:46.
Lord with all *g.*, Phil. 2:11.
with the oil of *g.*, Heb. 1:9.

GLASS, was made by the Egyptians and the Phoenicians, and was known by dwellers in the Nile valley as far back as the end of the third millennium B.C. In Phoenician excavations exquisite jewelry made of glass has been found. The Romans developed the art of glass-making to a high degree. Alexandria and Corinth were leaders in such manufacturing. The Old Testament references (Ex. 38:8; Isa. 3:23) probably refer to mirrors of polished metal rather than to actual glass articles. In the New Testament two different words are found in the original language. One word refers to a mirror, made of polished metal, not of glass (I Cor. 13:12; James 1:23); the other refers to a stone which is transparent and to glass itself. In the latter sense the word is to be understood in Rev. 4:6; 15:2; 21:18, 21.

GLEAN, GLEANING, to gather what has been left by a reaper. Strict laws were given by Moses concerning the care of the poor in the harvest times. The corners were not to be wholly reaped, ears left upon the field were not to be gathered, and fallen fruit was to be left for the distressed and the foreigner. Especially beautiful are the scenes of gleaning in the book of Ruth.
thou shalt not *g.* vineyard, Lev. 19:10.
she came and *g.*, Ruth 2:3.
g. grapes shall be left, Isa. 17:6.

GLEDE, a member of the hawk family, one of the abominations in Deut. 14:13. The kite is mentioned in Lev. 11:14.

GLISTERING, in the Old Testament, to be brilliant in color, possibly reddish in hue (I Chr. 29:2); in the New Testament to be radiant, to shine, to flash out as lightning (Luke 9:29), explained in Mark 9:3 as shining, exceeding white as snow.

GLITTER, GLITTERING, from a term referring to lightning, used of the glitter of swords and spears, flashing in the sun.
whet my *g.* sword, Deut. 32:41.
g. sword cometh, Job 20:25.
g. spear and shield, Job 39:23.
thy *g.* spear, Hab. 3:11.

GLOOMINESS, thick darkness, time of sadness (Joel 2:2; Zeph. 1:15).

GLORIFIED, beautified, honored.

I will be *g.*, Lev. 10:3.
Lord, thou art *g.*, Is. 26:15.
g. in midst of, Ezek. 28:22.
Son of man *g.*, John 13:31.
may be *g.* together, Rom. 8:17.
shall come to be *g.*, II Thess. 1:10.

GLORIFY, beautify, honor, magnify.
hast thou not *g.*, Dan. 5:23.
g. ye the Lord, Is. 24:15.
g. your Father, Matt. 5:16.
Jesus . . not yet *g.*, John 7:39.
g. God in your body, I Cor. 6:20.
g. God in day of, I Pet. 2:12.

GLORIOUS, honorable, exalted.
praise thy *g.* name, I Chr. 29:13.
of his *g.* kingdom, Esther 1:4.
make his praise *g.*, Ps. 66:2.
stand in *g.* land, Dan. 11:16.
light of *g.* gospel, II Cor. 4:4.
a *g.* church, Eph. 5:27.
looking for *g.* appearing, Titus 2:13.

GLORY, praise, honour, splendor.
he gotten all this *g.*, Gen. 31:1.
Lord must be of *g.*, I Chr. 22:5.
King of *g.* shall come in, Ps. 24:7.
given thee power and *g.*, Dan. 2:37.
their *g.* is spoiled, Zech. 11:3.
g. of his Father, Matt. 16:27.
G. to God in the highest, Luke 2:14.
God of *g.* appeared, Acts 7:2.
to whom be *g.*, Rom. 11:36.
crucified the Lord of *g.*, I Cor. 2:8.
the *g.* of this mystery, Col. 1:27.
many sons to *g.*, Heb. 2:10.
joy . . . full of *g.*, I Pet. 1:8.
Spirit of *g.* and of God, I Pet. 4:14.
give *g.* to him, Rev. 14:7.

GLORY, to boast, to exult.
g. in his holy name, I Chr. 16:10.
g. ye in his . . name, Ps. 105:3.
him shall they *g.*, Jer. 4:2.
let not the rich *g.*, Jer. 9:23.
we *g.* in tribulation, Rom. 5:3.
g. in your flesh, Gal. 6:13.
g. not, and lie not, James 3:14.

GLORYING, boasting, exulting.
your *g.* is not good, I Cor. 5:6.
great is my *g.* of you, II Cor. 7:4.

GLUTTON, GLUTTONOUS, a riotous
liver, a prodigal.
our son, is a *g.*, Deut. 21:20.
drunkard and *g.*, Prov. 23:21.

behold a man *g.*, Matt. 11:19.

GNASH, to grind, to bite.
he *g.* upon me, Job 16:9.
they *g.* upon me, Ps. 35:16.
he shall *g.*, Ps. 112:10.
enemies hiss and *g.*, Lam. 2:16.
they *g.* on him, Acts 7:54.

GNAT, the wine-gnat or midge which
breeds in fermenting or evaporating wine
(Matt. 23:24). Straining the wines was
because of the prohibition to eat certain
creeping, flying things (Lev. 11:22, 23).
The saying of the Lord about straining
out the gnat (Matt. 23:34) is no doubt
taken from this idea.

GNAW, chew, tear, scrape.
they *g.* not the bones, Zeph. 3:3.
g. their tongues, Rev. 16:10.

GO, to move, to proceed.
belly shalt thou *g.*, Gen. 3:14.
I will not *g.*, Num. 10:30.
g. in peace, I Sam. 1:17.
g., enquire of Baal, II Kin. 1:2.
g. unto Jerusalem, Ezra 8:31.
g. not forth hastily, Prov. 25:8.
as light that *g.*, Hos. 6:5.
let bridegroom *g.*, Joel 2:16.
ye shall *g.* forth, Mal. 4:2.
I *g.* to Jerusalem, Rom. 15:25.
g. in way of Cain, Jude 11.
he shall *g.* no more, Rev. 3:12.

GOAD, PRICK the implement now used
in the Syrian plains is usually a straight
oak stick about eight feet long. One
end is sharpened or connected to a
pointed piece of iron; the other has a
flat, chisel-shaped iron. The former is
used to prod the oxen while plowing, the
other is used to scrape the ploughshare.
Probably the ancient goad was similar.
Such a tool might be used most successfully in fighting if one were well trained.
See Judg. 3:31; I Sam. 13:21; Eccles.
12:11.

GOAH, *see* **GOATH.**

GOAT, an animal often associated with
sheep, and used together often, once in
sharp contrast (Matt. 25:32, 33). The
disposition of the goat was less lovely
than the sheep, and so it was less chosen
for sacrifices. However, it was allowed
(Lev. 3:12; 4:24; 9:15; Num. 15:27).

Goats were the second in importance to sheep. In Matt. 25:32, 33, sheep and goats are used to represent the righteous and wicked respectively. The flesh of the kid is good for food. Also the milk is very valuable. The skin is used for bottles. The hair was used for cloth, for cloaks, or tents (Song 1:5; Ex. 36:14), or pillows (I Sam. 19:13).

g. for sin offering, Num. 7:16.
pillow of g.'s hair, I Sam. 19:13.
he g. before the, Jer. 50:8.
I punished the g., Zech. 10:3.
divideth sheep from g., Matt. 25:32.

GOATH, GOAH, a place near Jerusalem (Jer. 31: 39).

GOB, scene of two encounters between the warriors of David and the Philistines (II Sam. 21:18, 19).

GOD, the Bible being God's revelation to man. God speaks from the very first page. The Bible does not seek to prove the existence of God by abstract reasoning, but begins with the very act of Creation.

The Names of God. Two of the most important names in the Old Testament are Jehovah and Elohim. In the Authorized Version the first name is translated "LORD" and the second is translated "God." Some have made the distinction that Jehovah means God's special revelation to his people Israel, while Elohim means God in his relationship to the world at large, as its Creator and Ruler. Elohim is used when the gentiles are spoken to, or about, concerning God. Elohim is the plural form of Eloah. El is sometimes used as a shortened form of Eloah. El-Shaddai, or God Almighty, was a name used by the Patriarchs (Gen. 17:1; Ex. 6:3). God told Moses, when he spoke to him in the burning bush, that his name was "I AM THAT I AM" (Ex. 3:14), a statement that only affirms that God is present to his people. Another name for God is Adonai, usually translated "Lord."

The Unity of God. The Jews repeated daily that their God was one (Deut. 6:4). There is none other God, but the Lord (I Kin. 8:60; Is. 44:6).

The Natural Qualities of God. He is self-existent (Ex. 3:14), eternal (I Tim. 1:17), omnipresent (Acts 17:27), omniscient (I John 3:20), omnipotent (Gen. 17:1), and infinite (Is. 9:6).

The Moral Perfection of God. He is holy (Josh. 24:19; Hos. 11:9), just (Gen. 18:25), merciful (Heb. 4:16), and he is love (I John 4:8).

The Triune God. The Godhead is revealed in three distinct persons in the Bible. The Father praised the Son in Matt. 3:16, 17; Mark 1:10; and Luke 3: 21, 22. The Father is God (Matt. 11:25; John 6:27; Rom. 15:6; I Cor. 8:6; Eph. 4:6; James 1:27. The Son is God (John 1:1, 18; Rom. 9:5; Phil. 2:6; Col. 2:9; Heb. 1:8). The Spirit is God (Acts 5:3; I Cor. 2:10; Eph. 2:22). That each is distinct and has a different work is implied in the above passages.

GODDESS, this term occurs in I Kin. 11: 5, 33. It refers to Ashtoreth, the female idol of the Zidonians. In the New Testament the term is applied to Diana, goddess of the Ephesians (Acts 19:27, 35, 37).

GODHEAD, this term occurs in three verses: Acts 17:29; Rom. 1:20; Col. 2:9. Accordingly the term "Godhead" indicates that the Being to whom this word is applied possesses all the qualities and attributes which belong to God.

GODLINESS, reverent conduct.
quiet life in all g., I Tim. 2:2.
women professing g., I Tim. 2:10.
g. is profitable, I Tim. 4:7.
g. with contentment, I Tim. 6:6.
form of g., II Tim. 3:5.
add to patience g., II Pet. 1:6, 7.

GODLY, kind, pious, reverential.
seek a g. seed, Mal. 2:15.
live g. in Jesus, II Tim. 3:12.
righteously, and g., Titus 2:12.
after g. sort, II John 6.

GOG, (1) son of Joel, descendant of the tribe of Reuben (I Chr. 5:4). (2) Prince of Meshech, Rosh, and Tubal (Ezek. 38–39). (3) The name connected with Magog to indicate the area to be brought under the influence of Satan after his loosing (Rev. 20:8). *See* MAGOG.

GOIIM, the translation in the Revised Version for the kingdom of Tidal; it is translated "of nations" in the Authorized Version (Gen. 14:1, 9).

GOLAN, a city in the territory of Manasseh in Bashan, on the eastern side of the Jordan (Josh. 20:8; 21:27).

GOLD, a precious metal widely used in the Old and New Testament periods. In ancient times it was obtained from Havilah (Gen. 2:11); Sheba (I Kin. 10:22); and Ophir (I Kin. 9:28). Gold was chiefly used for ornamentation and the production of furniture in the ancient times.

g. about his neck, Gen. 41:42.
neither gods of g., Ex. 20:23.
lay up g. as dust, Job 22:24.
made g. my hope, Job 31:24.
more desired than g., Ps. 19:10.
the g. become dim, Lam. 4:1.
swear by g., Matt. 23:16.
g. have I none, Acts 3:6.
man with a g. ring, James 2:2.
city pure g., Rev. 21:18.

GOLDEN CALF, see **CALF, GOLDEN.**

GOLDEN RULE, the rule given by Jesus according to which one does to others as he would wish others would do unto him (Matt. 7:12; Luke 6:31).

GOLGOTHA, the Hebrew name for the spot where Jesus was crucified (Matt. 27:33; Mark 15:22; John 19:17). The name is interpreted by these writers as meaning "the place of a skull," supposedly from the shape of the hill so designated, or possibly from the human skulls there as the place of execution. The most probable site is that northeast of the modern Damascus Gate.

GOLIATH, (1) the giant of Gath and the champion of the Philistine army (I Sam. 17:4–23; 21:9; 22:10; II Sam. 21:19; I Chr. 20:5ff.). (2) The Goliath of II Sam. 21:19 is another person, probably a son or brother of the first Goliath.

GOMER, (1) son of Japheth (Gen. 10: 2ff; I Chr. 1:5). The name afterward occurs as that of a tribe, probably one of the northern nations (Ezek. 38:6). (2) The daughter of Diblaim, the wife of Hosea. In response to the appointment of God Hosea married this harlot (Hos. 1:3).

GOMORRAH, GOMORRHA, one of the cities which joined with four others in rebellion against Chedolaomer and his allies (Gen. 14:1–11). The battle was followed by the capture of Lot (Gen. 14:

12–16). Gomorrah, along with the others, was destroyed. However, Zoar was spared at the request of Lot (Gen. 19: 18–25).

GOOD, kind, beneficial, good.
the light was g., Gen. 1:4.
I will do you g., Gen. 32:9.
be g. toward David, I Sam. 20:12.
say a g. word, I Kin. 22:13.
the Eternal g. to me, Ps. 27:13.
Eternal, he is g., Ps. 135:3.
not a single g. man, Eccles. 7:20.
who call g. evil, Is. 5:20.
one alone is g., Matt. 19:17.
no one is g., Luke 18:19.
rich in g. works, I Tim. 6:18.

GOODLINESS, kindliness.
g. . . is as flower, Is. 40:6.

GOODLY, beautiful, agreeable.
he was a g. child, Ex. 2:2. .
g. are thy tents, Num. 24:5.
g. wings unto the, Job 39:13.
as his g. horse, Zech. 10:3.
seeking g. pearls, Matt. 13:45.
man . . in g. apparel, James 2:2.

GOODNESS, kindness.
rejoiced for all g., Ex. 18:9.
Lord God abundant in g., Ex. 34:6.
g. and mercy shall follow, Ps. 23:6.
tremble for all the g., Jer. 33:9.
how great is his g., Zech. 9:17.
g. of God leadeth thee, Rom. 2:4.
g. and severity of God, Rom. 11:22.
fruit of the Spirit is g., Gal. 5:22.
pleasure of his g., II Thess. 1:11.

GOODS, substance, possessions.
g. . . in his hand, Gen. 24:10.
houses full of g., Neh. 9:25.
when g. increase, Eccles. 5:11.
and spoil his g., Mark 3:27.
g. to feed poor, I Cor. 13:3.
spoiling of your g., Heb. 10:34.

GOPHER, the type of wood of which the ark was made (Gen. 6:14).

GOSHEN, (1) the land in the northeast section of the Egyptian delta which was given to the Jewish nation under Jacob during the "prime-ministership" of Joseph. The section thus located was very fertile, excellent for grazing and farming, though less desirable to the

Pharaoh's because of great distance from the Nile (Gen. 46:34). (2) A district of southern Palestine, between Gaza and Gibeon (Josh. 10:41; 11:16). (3) A town in the mountains of Judah, mentioned along with Debir, Socoh, and others (Josh. 15:51).

GOSPEL, good news. Various aspects of the message may be combined to produce such expressions as: gospel of our Lord Jesus Christ; gospel of the grace of God; gospel of God; etc.
g. of Jesus Christ, Mark 1:1.
repent and believe the g., Mark 1:15.
for the g. sake, I Cor. 9:23.
the truth of the g., Gal. 2:5.
fellowship in the g., Phil. 1:5.
faith of the g., Phil. 1:27.
truth of the g., Col. 1:5.
hope of the g., Col. 1:23.
obey not the g., II Thess. 1:8.
bonds of the g., Philem. 13.
the everlasting g., Rev. 14:6.

GOURD, (1) one Hebrew term occurs in Jonah 4:6–10. The exact plant involved is a matter of disagreement. Some contend for what is called the "castor oil plant," others for the "bottle gourd," a plant with a creeping, vinelike appearance. Still others have suggested a variety of pumpkin. (2) The wild gourds of II Kings 4:39.

GOVERN, to exercise rule.
g. the kingdom of, I Kin. 21:7.
he that hateth . . g., Job 34:17.
g. nations upon earth, Ps. 67:4.

GOVERNMENT, rule, authority, power.
g. shall be on his, Is. 9:6.
helps, g., diversities, I Cor. 12:28.
them that despise g., II Pet. 2:10.

GOVERNOR, one who rules by authority delegated from a superior to whom he is responsible. Old Testament terms suggest a leader (Zech. 9:7; 12:5, 6); a ruler (Gen. 45:26; II Chr. 23:20); a prince (II Chr. 1:2); a captain or viceroy (I Kin. 10:15; II Chr. 9:14; Ezra 8:36; Neh. 2:7, 9; 5:14, 15, 18; Hag. 1:1; Mal. 1:8); an overseer (Jer. 20:1); and a chief (I Kin. 22:26; II Kin. 23:8). New Testament words suggest an ethnarch or ruler of people (II Cor. 11:32); one who guides

in a straight course (James 3:4); a leader (Matt. 2:6; Acts 7:10); a house manager (Gal. 4:2); and a guide (Matt. 10:18). The Roman officer who administered the affairs of a province by the authority of the Emperor was called a governor (Matt. 10:18; Mark 13:9; Luke 21:12; I Pet. 2:14). The Roman official often called the procurator was also called the governor. This officer had charge of imperial revenue, and in smaller provinces served as the judicial administrator. The offices of Pilate, Felix, and Festus are thus to be understood (Matt. 27:2–27; Acts 23:24–34; 24:1, 10; 26:30).

GOZAN, a city and district of Mesopotamia, on or near the middle of the Euphrates River. Through it the River Chabur flowed, thither some of the exiled Israelites were brought by Pul, Tiglath-pileser, and Shalmaneser, possibly Sargon (II Kin. 17:6; 18:11; 19:12; I Chr. 5:25; Isa. 37:12).

GRACE, the kindness by which God bestows favors and blessings upon the ill-deserving, grants to sinners the pardon of their offences.
Esther obtained g., Esther 2:17.
the Spirit of g., Zech. 12:10.
g. and truth came by Jesus, John 1:17.
word of his g., Acts 14:3.
believed through g., Acts 18:27.
g. and peace to you, Rom. 1:7.
that g. may abound, Rom. 6:1.
election of g., Rom. 11:5.
g. might redound, II Cor. 4:15.
g. is sufficient, II Cor. 12:9.
called you to g., Gal. 1:6.
glory of his g., Eph. 1:6.
by g. are ye saved, Eph. 2:8.
justified by his g., Titus 3:7.
throne of g., Heb. 4:16.
g. to serve God, Heb. 12:28.
heirs of g., I Pet. 3:7.
grow in g., II Pet. 3:18.
g. of Lord Jesus Christ, Rev. 22:21.

GRACIOUS, abounding in grace.
God be g., Gen. 43:29.
and be g., Num. 6:25.
be g. to us, Isa. 33:2.
how g. when pangs, Jer. 22:23.
Lord will be g., Amos 5:15.
thou art a g. God, Jonah 4:2.
wondered at g. words, Luke 4:22.
the Lord is g., I Pet. 2:3.

GRAFF, GRAFT, the process of inserting a portion of one plant (as a cultivated olive tree) into another (as a wild olive tree).
wild olive were *g.*, Rom. 11:17.

GRAIN, the term occurs once in the Old Testament (Amos 9:9), and suggests a grain of wheat involved in winnowing. The New Testament word indicates a kernel, grain, or seed (Matt. 13:31; 17:20; Mark 4:31; Luke 13:19; 17:6; I Cor. 15:37).

GRANT, to give permission, to allow.
g. thy petition, I Sam. 1:17.
God would *g.* me, Job 6:8.
g. us salvation, Ps. 85:7.
g. my two sons, Matt. 20:21.
g. he find mercy, II Tim. 1:18.
g. to sit with me, Rev. 3:21.

GRAPE, fruit of the grapevine. *See* **VINE.**
blood of the *g.*, Deut. 32:14.
unripe *g.*, Job 15:33.
tender *g.*, Song 2:13.
clusters of *g.*, Song 7:7.
the *g.* gleanings, Mic. 7:1.
gather *g.* of thorns, Matt. 7:16.
gather they *g.*, Luke 6:44.

GRASS, tender grass, hay, green herbs.
earth bring forth *g.*, Gen. 1:11.
showers upon the *g.*, Deut. 32:2.
g. of the fields, II Kin. 19:26.
rain upon mown *g.*, Ps. 72:6.
dew upon the *g.*, Prov. 19:12.
all flesh is *g.*, Isa. 40:6.
give every one *g.*, Zech. 10:1.
God so clothe the *g.*, Matt. 6:30.
flower of the *g.*, James 1:10.
withereth the *g.*, James 1:11.
flesh is as grass, I Pet. 1:24.

GRASSHOPPER, *see* **LOCUST.**

GRAVE, burial place, tomb. *See* **TOMB.**
pillar of Rachel's *g.*, Gen. 35:20.
with sorrow to *g.*, Gen. 42:38.
down to the *g.*, I Sam. 2:6.
at Abner's *g.*, II Sam. 3:32.
the *g.* is my house, Job 17:13.
soul . . . near to the *g.*, Job 33:22.
silent in the *g.*, Ps. 31:17.
lain in the *g.*, John 11:17.
out of his *g.*, John 12:17.
g. where is thy victory, I Cor. 15:55.

GRAVEL, small stones.
be filled with *g.*, Prov. 20:17.
bowels like *g.*, Isa. 48:19.
broken my teeth with *g.*, Lam. 3:16.

GRAVEN IMAGE, an image which is carved with a sharp instrument in contrast to one which is molded. The images were usually made out of stone, clay, wood, or metal (Is. 30:22, 45:20; Dan. 2:31–33). The making of graven images was forbidden by the second of the Ten Commandments (Ex. 20:4; Deut. 5:8). *See* **IMAGE.**
melteth *g. i.*, Is. 40:19.
confounded by *g. i.*, Jer. 10:14.
g. i. will I cut out, Mic. 5:13.

GRAVITY, being sober. grave.
with all *g.*, I Tim. 3:4.
in doctrine showing *g.*, Titus 2:7.

GRAY, GRAYHEADED, used of old age.
bring down my *g.* hairs, Gen. 42:38.
man of *g.* hairs, Deut. 32:25.
old and *g.* headed, I Sam. 12:2.
beauty . . . is the *g.* hairs, Prov. 20:29.

GREAT, large, numerous, mighty, much.
make thee *g.* nation, Gen. 12:2.
made thee *g.* name, II Sam. 7:9.
g., O Lord, II Sam. 7:22.
were in *g.* fear, Ps. 14:5.
is *g.* reward, Ps. 19:11.
how *g.* thy works, Ps. 92:5.
called *g.* in kingdom, Matt. 5:19.
pearl of *g.* price, Matt. 13:46.
and *g.* commandment, Matt. 22:38.
g. is Diana of the, Acts 19:28.
this is a *g.* mystery, Eph. 5:32.
g. white throne, Rev. 20:11.

GREAT COMMISSION, Jesus' last charge to his disciples while on the earth (Matt. 28:19; Mark 16:15–18).

GREATER, larger, superior.
Lord *g.* than all, Ex. 18:11.
g. than Solomon is, Matt. 12:42.
thou shalt see *g.*, John 1:50.
servant not *g.* than, John 13:16.
swear by no *g.*, Heb. 6:13.
God is *g.* than, I John 3:20.

GREATEST, foremost, most important.
know least unto *g.*, Jer. 31:34.
g. among herbs, Matt. 13:32.
who *g.* in kingdom, Matt. 18:1.
who should be *g.*, Mark 9:34.

the *g.* is charity, I Cor. 13:13.

GREATLY, in a great degree.
g. multiply sorrow, Gen. 3:16.
anger kindled *g.*, Num. 11:10.
people mourned *g.*, Num. 14:39.
g. to be praised, Ps. 48:1.
we are *g.* confounded, Jer. 9:19.
governor marvelled *g.*, Matt. 27:14.
ye do *g.* err, Mark 12:27.

GREATNESS, increase, abundance.
g. of mercy, Num. 14:19.
thine is the *g.*, I Chr. 29:11.
his excellent *g.*, Ps. 150:2.
g. of his folly, Prov. 5:23.
g. of his strength, Is. 63:1.
exceeding *g.* of power, Eph. 1:19.

GREAT SEA, the Mediterranean (Num. 34:6; Josh. 15:12, 47; Ezek. 47:19. 20).

GREAVES, *see* **ARMOUR.**

GRECIA, *see* **GREECE.**

GRECIAN, GRECIANS, the Old Testament uses the term apparently for the inhabitants of the country of Greece and the islands surrounding it. The term in the New Testament refers to Greek-speaking Jews who had been born in foreign lands and who spoke the Greek tongue while continuing as Jews.
sold unto the *G.*, Joel 3:6.
murmuring of the *G.*, Acts 6:1.
against the *G.*, Acts 9:29.
spake unto the *G.*, Acts 11:20.

GREECE, a country in southern Europe lying east of Italy and west of Asia Minor. The country was populated by a brave people. In the centuries before the coming of Jesus Christ Greece had been supreme in the affairs of the world. In the time of Christ Greece was subject to the powers of Rome. However, through its language and culture, Greece continued to exercise great influence in the ancient world.
thy sons, O *G.*, Zech. 9:13.
came to *G.*, Acts 20:2.

GREED, GREEDINESS, GREEDY, base desires.
lion that is *g.*, Ps. 17:12.
every one that is *g.*, Prov. 1:19.
he coveted *g.* all day, Prov. 21:26.

hast *g.* gained, Ezek. 22:12.
uncleanness with *g.*, Eph. 4:19.
not *g.* of filthy lucre, I Tim. 3:3.
ran *g.* after error, Jude 11.

GREEK, *see* **GRECIANS.**
debtor . . . to the *G.*, Rom. 1:14.
also to the *G.*, Rom. 1:16.
G. seek after wisdom, I Cor. 1:22.
unto the *G.* foolishness, I Cor. 1:23.
being a *G.*, Gal. 2:3.
neither *G.* nor Jew, Col. 3:11.

GREYHOUND, this word occurs in Prov. 30:31. The stag, zebra, eagle, war-horse, or even a man in armor have been suggested.

GRIEF, sorrow, sadness, bitterness.
g. unto Isaac, Gen. 26:35.
know own *g.*, II Chr. 6:29.
life spent with *g.*, Ps. 31:10.
in much wisdom is *g.*, Eccles. 1:18.
hath borne our *g.*, Is. 53:4.
added *g.* to sorrow, Jer. 45:3.
with joy, not *g.*, Heb. 13:17.

GRIEVE, to distress.
g. him at his heart, Gen. 6:6.
g. for the hardness, Mark 3:5.
and went away *g.*, Mark 10:22.
Peter was *g.* because, John 21:17.
he hath not *g.* me, II Cor. 2:5.
g. not the Holy Spirit, Eph. 4:30.

GRIEVOUS, painful, offensive.
their sin is *g.*, Gen. 18:20.
famine be very *g.*, Gen. 41:31.
g. swarm of flies, Ex. 8:24.
cursed with *g.* curse, I Kin. 2:8.
g. things proudly, Ps. 31:18.
g. vision declared, Is. 21:2.
my wound is *g.*, Jer. 10:19.
g. wolves enter, Acts 20:29.
no chastening but *g.*, Heb. 12:11.
commandments not *g.*, I John 5:3.

GRIND, crush, mill, oppress.
did *g.* in prison, Judg. 16:21.
g. faces of the, Is. 3:15.
g. him to powder, Matt. 21:44.

GRINDERS, GRINDING. Those who grind at the mill. The grinders of Eccles. 12:3, 4 are women working at the mill.

GROAN, a sound of pain or grief.
men *g.* out of city, Job 24:12.
he *g.* in spirit, John 11:33.

whole creation *g.*, Rom. 8:22.
g. cannot be uttered, Rom. 8:26.
we *g.*, desiring, II Cor. 5:2.

GROUND, soil, earth, place, field, dust.
cursed is the *g.* for, Gen. 3:17.
place is holy *g.*, Ex. 3:5.
break up fallow *g.*, Jer. 4:3.
fell into good *g.*, Matt. 13:8.
cast seed into *g.*, Mark 4:26.
g. of certain rich man, Luke 12:16.
Jesus wrote on *g.*, John 8:6.

GROUNDED, founded, settled.
rooted and *g.* in love, Eph. 3:17.
continue in faith *g.*, Col. 1:23.

GROUND, FALLOW, *see* **FALLOW GROUND.**

GROVE, GROVES, (1) in Gen. 21:23 the term refers to the tamarisk tree, a tree of long life, hard wood, and ever-green leaves. (2) The term *asherah* or grove refers probably to an idol or image near a temple or sacred area.

GROW, increase, to be fruitful.
g. like a cedar, Ps. 92:12.
g. up as a tender, Is. 53:2.
Branch, he shall *g.*, Zech. 6:12.
g. up as calves, Mal. 4:2.
lilies, how they *g.*, Luke 12:27.
g. unto holy temple, Eph. 2:21.
faith *g.* exceedingly, II Thess. 1:3.
milk, that ye *g.*, I Pet. 2:2.
g. in grace and, II Pet. 3:18.

GRUDGE, give with ill will.
not *g.* or of necessity, II Cor. 9:7.
g. not one against, James 5:9.
hospitality without *g.*, I Pet. 4:9.

GUARD, an English word usually used to mean a bodyguard, a group of chosen men. One of the offices which was considered high was that of Captain of the guard (Gen. 37:36; II Kin. 10:25). Another use was with reference to a runner who ran before the chariot of the ruler (I Sam. 22:17). David's guard consisted of foreign mercenaries, the Cherethites and the Pelethites, commanded by Benaiah (II Sam. 20:23; 23:22). The famed Praetorian Guard is mentioned in the Revised Version (Phil. 1:13) and is alluded to in the Authorized Version (Acts 28:16).

GUDHODAH, fortieth station of the Israelites after the exodus from Egypt, Deut. 10:7.

GUEST, Old Testament word meaning "called" (I Kin. 1:41, 49; Prov. 9:18; Zeph. 1:7). In the New Testament it means "those reclining" (Matt. 22:10, 11) and "gone in to lodge" (Luke 19:7).

GUESTS, visitors.
her *g.* in depths, Prov. 9:18.
he hath bid his *g.*, Zeph. 1:7.
furnished with *g.*, Matt. 22:10.
g. with a sinner, Luke 19:7.

GUIDE, leader, chief, captain, ruler.
meek *g.* in judgment, Ps. 25:9.
g. me with counsel, Ps. 73:24.
no *g.*, overseer, Prov. 6:7.
Lord shall *g.* thee, Is. 58:11.
g. our feet into way, Luke 1:79.
g. you into all truth, John 16:13.
except someone *g.* me, Acts 8:31.

GUILE, deceit, craftiness.
slay with *g.*, Ex. 21:14.
caught . . . with *g.*, II Cor. 12:16.

GUILTLESS, innocent.
Lord not hold him *g.*, Ex. 20:7.
then man be *g.*, Num. 5:31.
hold him not *g.*, I Kin. 2:9.
not condemned *g.*, Matt. 12:7.

GUILT, GUILTY, wicked, ill-deserving.
be unclean and *g.*, Lev. 5:2.
be found *g.*, Prov. 30:10.
g. of death, Matt. 26:66.
may become *g.*, Rom. 3:19.
g. of the body, I Cor. 11:27.

GULF, a great pit or chasm.
a great *g.* fixed, Luke 16:26.

GUNI, (1) one of the sons of Naphtali, Gen. 46:24; Num. 26:48; I Chr. 7:13. (2) Father of Abdiel and grandfather of Ahi, I Chr. 5:15.

GUNITES, general name for the descendants of Guni (Num. 26:48).

GUR, name for an ascent near Ibleam, on the road from Jezreel to Beth-haggan (II Kin. 9:27).

GURBAAL, place in Arabia captured by Uzziah (II Chr. 26:7).

GUSH, GUSHED, flow, pour out.
till the blood *g.*, I Kin. 18:28.
rock . . waters *g.* out, Is. 48:21.
eyelids *g.* with water, Jer. 9:18.

GUTTER, a water shaft or drinking trough.
set rods in the *g.*, Gen. 30:38.
laid rods in the *g.*, Gen. 30:41.

H

HAAHASHTARI, a descendant of Judah (I Chr. 4:6).

HABAIAH, a priest whose descendants returned from Babylon with Zerubbabel (Ezra 2:61, Neh. 7:63).

HABAKKUK, eighth in the list of twelve minor prophets. Nothing certain known about his life. Simply referred to as a prophet (Hab. 1:1, 3:1).

HABAKKUK, BOOK OF, as this book deals with the invasion of Palestine by the Chaldeans (1:6) its appearance may be dated some time in the reign of Jehoiachim—about 600 B.C. The prophet complains of God's silence before the wickedness of Israel. God answers that he is raising the Chaldeans against Israel. But this raises the question, Why let the "wicked swallow up the man more righteous than he?" But the Chaldeans will also be punished. Chapter 3 is a psalm of praise to God.

HABAZINIAH, HABAZZINIAH, a Rechabite (Jer. 35:3) who lived about 607 B.C. and was tested by the prophet Jeremiah.

HABERGEON, breastplate.
the dart, nor the *h.*, Job 41:26.
and the bows, and the *h.*, Neh. 4:16.

HABITABLE, *see* HABITATION (Prov. 8:31).

HABITATION, translates several Hebrew and Greek words, and used in sense of a place to dwell (Ps. 69:25, Acts 1:20, etc.). Used figuratively of God as the "habitation of his people," etc. (Ps. 71:3, 91:9). Jerusalem, the temple, etc. are referred to as God's habitation (Ps. 132:5, Eph. 2:22).

prepare him an *h.*, Ex. 15:2.
unto thy holy *h.*, Ex. 15:13.
let *h.* be desolate, Ps. 69:25.
go to a city of *h.*, Ps. 107:7.
Jerusalem a quiet *h.*, Isa. 33:20.
angels left own *h.*, Jude 6.

HABOR, a river of Mesopotamia, tributary of Euphrates. Some of the deported Israelites placed there (I Chr. 5:26).

HACHALIAH, in Revised Version father of Nehemiah (Neh. 1:1, 10:1).

HACHILAH, the hiding place of David when an attempt was made to betray him to Saul (I Sam. 23:19, 26:1, 3).

HACHMONI, a man known as the father or ancestor of Jashobean, the chief of David's soldiers (I Chr. 11:11), and of Jehiel, in the royal house (I Chr. 27:32).

HACHMONITE, a descendant of Hachmoni (I Chr. 11:11).

HADAD, HADAR, name of an Aramean god, and probably an official title like Pharaoh. Applied to several men: (1) one of Ishmael's sons (Gen. 25:15); (2) an Edomite king who defeated the Midianites (Gen. 36:35); (3) another Edomite king, King James Version has Hadar (Gen. 36:39); (4) Prince of royal house of Edom who escaped from Joab and fled to Egypt (I Kin. 11:14ff).

HADADEZER, HADARAZER, an Aramean king of Zorah, near Damascus. Defeated by Israelites under Joab (II Sam. 8:3, 10:7ff.) and later at Helam by David (II Sam. 8:4, 10:18).

HADADRIMMON, a place in the valley of Megiddo, named after two Syrian deities. King Josiah lost his life there (II Chr. 35:22–25).

HADAR, *see* HADAD.

HADARAZER, *see* HADADEZER.

HADASHAH, city in valley of Judah toward Philistine border (Josh. 15:37).

HADASSAH, the earlier Jewish name of Esther (Esther 2:7).

Hadattah

HADATTAH, an extreme southern town of Judah (Josh. 15:25).

HADES, *see* **HELL, GEHENNAH.**

HADID, a place in Benjamin, many of whose inhabitants returned from captivity (Ezra 2:33).

HADLAI, father of Amasa, an Ephraimite (II Chr. 28:12).

HADORAM, (1) a son of Joktan (Gen. 10:27, I Chr. 1:21. (2) Son of Toi (Tou), king of Hamath, sent by his father with valuable presents to David upon his victory over their common enemy, Hadadezer, king of Syria (I Chr. 18:10). Also called Joram (II Sam. 8). (3) Tribute collector under Rehoboam, stoned to death by people of the ten tribes (II Chr. 10:18).

HADRACH, name of a country (Zech. 9:1) on Orontes River near Damascus.

HAGAB, one of the Nethinim whose descendants returned from Babylon under Zerubbabel (Ezra 2:46).

HAGABA, HAGABAH, *see* **HAGAB** (Ez. 2:45).

HAGAR, AGAR, means "wanderer" or "to flee." She was an Egyptian, handmaid of Sarah, taken as Abraham's wife; mother of Ishmael (Gen. 16:1, 21:9–10). In Gal. 4:24ff. Paul uses the story of Hagar as an allegory; Hagar represents the bondage of the Law; Sarah represents the freedom of the Gospel.

HAGARENES, HAGARITE, HAGRITE, a nation east of Jordan dispossessed by Reuben, Gad, and Manasseh in the days of Saul (I Chr. 5:10). Later they, like the Moabites, were again hostile (Ps. 83:6). They are assumed to be descendants of Hagar.

HAGERITE, a designation of Jaziz, overseer of David's flocks (I Chr. 27:31). *See* **HAGARITE.**

HAGGAI, festal. Tenth in order of the twelve minor prophets, and the first of the three, who after the Babylonian captivity, prophesied in Palestine. Nothing is known of the place or time of his origin, or of his ancestry. With Zechariah he urged the renewal of the building of the Temple, secured the permission and assistance of the king, and his example and zeal led to its completion about 516 B.C.

HAGGAI, BOOK OF, the prophet Haggai (see above) was an older contemporary of Zechariah and together they urged the returned exiles to finish the Temple (begun 536 and completed 516 B.C.). Haggai preached four messages in the second year of the Persian king Darius (520 B.C.), and parts of these sermons compose the book (1:1–15, 2:1–9, 2:10–19, 2:20–23). These consist of a plan to finish the Temple, with predictions of success for Israel and doom for her enemies. Haggai is generally thought to have been the author.

HAGGERI, a Hagerite. One of the valiant men of David's guards (I Chr. 11:38).

HAGGI, one of the sons of Gad (Gen. 46:16), father of the family of Haggites (Num. 26:15).

HAGGIAH, a descendant of Levi through Merari (I Chr. 6:30).

HAGGITES, descendants of Haggai.

HAGGITH, wife of David, mother of Adonijah (II Sam. 3:4, I Kin. 1:5, 11, 2:13, etc.).

HAGRITE, *see* **HAGHRITE.**

HAI, another form of Ai (Gen. 12:8, 13:3). In Josh. 7 the men of Ai defeated Israel for the first time.

HAIL, (1) a greeting expressing a desire for the welfare of the person addressed. (2) As frozen rain, hail was sometimes miraculous in origin (Josh. 10:11, Ex. 9:24) and figured in Israel's deliverance. (3) Used figuratively, it symbolizes God's judgment on His enemies and those of His people (Is. 28:2, 17, Hag. 2:17).

HAILSTONE, *see* **HAIL** (Josh. 10:11).

HAIR, the Hebrews considered long hair on the head and chin to be a mark of true manliness. It was Absalom's abundance of hair which made people think he was handsome (II Sam. 14:25), while another was insulted because of his baldness (II Kin. 2:23). One of the terms of the Nazerite vow was not to cut their hair (Num. 6:5). Women always wore their hair long (Song 4:1; Luke 7:38), and black hair was especially prized (Song 5:11). The women curled their hair (Is. 3:24), and in New Testament times even men began to do so (Josephus, *Ant.*, xiv, 9, 4). The New Testament tells us that every hair of our head is numbered (Matt. 10:30). Women's hair generally exceeded in length that of the men.

bring my gray *h.*, Gen. 42:38.
h. in plague white, Lev. 13:3.
sling at *h.* breadth, Judg. 20:16.
not an *h.* fall, I Kin. 1:52.
h. of my flesh stood, Job 4:15.
more than the *h.* of, Ps. 40:12.
instead of *h.* baldness, Isa. 3:24.
hoar *h.* carry you, Isa. 46:4.
that plucked off *h.*, Isa. 50:6.
cut *h.* O Jerusalem, Jer. 7:29.
h. like Eagle's feathers, Dan. 4:33.
raiment of camel's *h.*, Matt. 3:4.
not make one *h.* white, Matt. 5:36.
h. of head numbered, Matt. 10:30.
wipe them with *h.*, Luke 7:38.
wiped feet with *h.*, John 11:2.
long *h.* a glory, I Cor., 11:15.
not broided *h.*, I Tim. 2:9.
not plaiting *h.*, I Pet. 3:3.
h. white like wool, Rev. 1:14.

HAKKATAN, (Katan), the little one, father of Johanan (Ezra 8:12).

HAKKOZ, KOZ, COZ, (1) head of a family of Judah, I Chr. 4:8 (King James Version has Coz). (2) Ancestral head of the seventh course of priests (I Chr. 24:10, Ezra 2:61).

HAKUPHA, one of the Nethinim who returned from Babylon with Zerubbabel (Ezra 2:51, Neh. 7:53).

HALAH, the area in Assyria where some of the captive Israelites were taken by Sargon. Location uncertain (II Kin. 17:6, 18:11).

HALAK, the "smooth" or "bare" mountain. In Josh. 11:17, 12:7 it is given as the southern limit of Joshua's conquest.

HALE, to draw or dràg along.
h. thee to the judge, Luke 12:58.
h. men and women, Acts 8:3.

HALHUL, a town in the hill country of Judah (Josh. 15:58). Gad, the seer, was buried there. Preserved about four miles north of Hebron.

HALI, a town assigned to Asher (Josh. 19:25), of unknown location.

HALLELUJAH, literally, "praise ye Jah" or "praise Jehovah." A frequent worshipful expression, found especially in the latter part of Psalms. Many begin and end with it (Ps. 106, 111, 113, 117, 135). In the New Testament it occurs in Rev. 19:1–6 in a song of praise to God.

HALLOHESH, HALOHESH, the ancestral head of a postexilic family, who covenanted with Nehemiah (Neh. 3:12, 10:24).

HALLOW, HALLOWED, the Hebrew and Greek words mean to set apart, dedicate, consecrate, for a holy purpose. "Things" are hallowed or set apart (Ex. 29:36, 20:8); Christians are sanctified or hallowed. (Acts 20:32, I Cor. 1:2, 6:11); God's name is to be hallowed (Matt. 6:9).

HALOHESH, a variant form of **HALLO-HESH.**

HALT, lame, crippled.
enter into life *h.*, Matt 18:8.
multitude of blind, *h.*, John 5:3.

HALT, to leap, pass over, halt.
and he *h.* upon his, Gen. 32:31.
how long *h.* ye, 1 Kin. 18:21.

HAM, the derivation of the term is uncertain but "hot" rather than "dark" or "black" seems to be preferred. Youngest son of Noah (Gen. 5:32) and was saved from the flood (Gen. 7:13). Later incurred Noah's wrath (Gen.9:21ff.). His descendants listed in Gen. 10:6–18. Later his name was given to a country (Gen. 14:5) and poetically refers to Egypt (Ps. 105:23, 27, 106:22).

HAMAN, son of Hammedatha, and prime minister of Ahasuerus, king of Persia (Esther 3:1). His plot against Mordecai and the Jews, and his execution, are all contained in the book of Esther.

HAMATH, HEMETH, fortress. A city state in Syria, north of Israel. Fought with Israel against Assyria but fell, and like Israel her people were dispersed (Gen. 10:18, II Kin. 18:34).

HAMATHITE, founder of Hamath (Gen. 10:18; I Chr. 1:16). *See* **HAMATH.**

HAMATH-ZOBAH, probably refers to the city of Hamath, although some distinguish it, on the Orontes (II Chr. 8:3).

HAMITE, HAMITIC, of or pertaining to Ham.

HAMMATH, hot spring. (1) Father of the house of Rechab (I Chr. 2:55). (2) A town given to Naphtali (Josh. 19:35).

HAMMEAH, *see* **MEAH.**

HAMMEDATHA, father of the notorious Haman, usually referred to as the "Agagite," a title of the kings of the Amalekites. Esther 3:1, 10, 8:5.

HAMMELECH, the king. Father of Jerahmeel who was commanded by Jehoiakim to arrest Jeremiah and Baruch (Jer. 36:26, 38:6).

HAMMER, the rendering of several Hebrew words. (1) Refers to the tool of the carpenter or stone mason (I Kin. 6:7, Jer. 10:4) or the mallet used to drive tent pins (Judg. 4:21). Used figuratively of Babylon (Jer. 50:23).

HAMMOLEKETH, the queen. A woman listed in the genealogies of Manasseh, daughter of Machir and sister of Gilead (I Chr. 7:17–18). One of her children was Abiezer, ancestor of Gideon.

HAMMON, (1) a town in Asher's territory (Josh. 19:28). Present site unknown. (2) A Levitical city of Naphtali, given to the Gershonites (I Chr. 6:76). Probably same as Hammath and Hammoth-dor, a city of refuge.

HAMMOTH-DOR, *see* **HAMMON.**

HAMMUEL, *see* **HAMUEL.**

HAMMURABI, *see* **AMRAPHEL.**

HAMONAH, multitude. The place where the multitudes of Gog are to be buried (Ezek. 39:16).

HAMONGOG, multitude of Gog. The name given by Ezekiel to the valley in which the slaughtered army of Gog are to be buried (Ezek. 39:11).

HAMOR, a Hivite, from whom Jacob purchased the ground in which Joseph was buried (Gen. 33:19, Josh. 24:32). Also found as Emmor (Acts 7:16).

HAMRAN, form of Hemdan (I Chr. 1:41).

HAMUEL, a son of Mishma, a Simeonite, of the family of Shaul (I Chr. 4:26).

HAMUL, second of two sons of Pharez, son of Judah, by Tamar (I Chr. 2:5).

HAMULITES, descendants of Hamul (Num. 26:21).

HAMUTAL, a daughter of Jeremiah of Libnah, one of King Josiah's wives, and mother of Jehoahaz and Mattaniah or Zedekiah (II Kin. 23:31).

HANAMEEL, son of Shalkum and cousin of Jeremiah, to whom he sold a field in Anathoth while Jerusalem was besieged (Jer. 32:6–12).

HANAN, (1) a descendant of Shashak, one of the chief men of Benjamin (I Chr. 8:23). (2) Last named of the six sons of Azel the Benjamite (I Chr. 8:38). (3) Son of Maachah, and one of David's mighty men (I Chr. 11:43). (4) A Nethinim whose posterity returned from the captivity with Zerubbabel (Ezra 2:46, Neh. 7:49). (5) A Levite who helped Ezra read the Law to the people (Neh. 8:7). (6) A chief of the people who subscribed to Nehemiah's covenant (Neh. 10:22). (7) Son of Igdaliah and an officer about the Lord's house (Jer. 35:4).

HANANEEL, TOWER OF, a tower that formed a part of the wall of Jerusalem (Neh. 3:1, 12:39).

HANANI, (1) one of the sons of Heman, chosen by lot, for the service of song in the sanctuary (I Chr. 25:4, 25). (2) A prophet who rebuked Asa, king of Judah, for seeking help from Syria against Israel. Later imprisoned (II Chr. 16:7–10). (3) A descendant of Immer who took a "strange wife" in the captivity (Ezra 10:20). (4) A brother of Nehemiah who went from Jerusalem to Shushan and afterwards was made governor of Jerusalem under Nehemiah (Neh. 1:2, 7:2). (5) A priest and musician who assisted in the ceremonial purification of the walls of Jerusalem (Neh. 12:36).

HANANIAH, (1) A son of Zerubbabel, of the family of David (I Chr. 3:19). (2) A son of Shishak and a chief in Benjamin (I Chr. 8:24). (3) A son of Heman, appointed by David to take charge of one group of musicians (I Chr. 25:4, 23). (4) A captain in Uzzah's army (II Chr. 26:11). (5) An Israelite who renounced his Gentile wife after the captivity (Ezra 10:28). (6) An apothecary and priest (Neh. 3:8). (7) A priest who helped repair the wall (Neh. 3:30). (8) A "ruler of the palace" and one associated with Nehemiah's brother, Hanani, in charge of the gates of Jerusalem (Neh. 7:2). (9) One of the "chief of the people" who sealed the covenant made by Nehemiah and the people to serve God (Neh. 10:23). (10) A false prophet in days of Zedekiah, king of Judah (Jer. 28:1–17). (11) Grandfather of Irijah, captain of the guard at the gate of Benjamin, who arrested Jeremiah (Jer. 37:13). (12) Original name of Shadrach, one of the three Hebrew children (Dan. 1:6, 7, 11, 2:17).

HAND, the hand and the arm are sometimes used symbolically in the Scriptures in many ways to indicate power, support, submission, protection, etc.
h. offend thee, Matt. 5:30.
water and washed his *h.*, Matt. 27:24.
pluck them out of my *h.*, John 10:28.
h. and his side, John 20:20.
on of apostles' *h.*, Acts 8:18.
worshipped with men's *h.*, Acts 17:25
angels in the *h.*, Gal. 3:19.
cleanse your *h.*, James 4:8.

HAND, AT, near, close by.
day of the Lord is at *h.*, Is. 13:6.
kingdom of heaven is at *h.*, Matt. 3:2.
the day is at *h.*, I Pet. 4:7.

HANDBREADTH, width of the palm of the hand.
It was an *h.* thick, I Kin. 7:26.
made my days as an *h.*, Ps. 39:5.

HANDFUL, HANDFULS.
brought forth by *h.*, Gen. 41:47.
some of the *h.*, Ruth 2:16.
h. with quietness, Eccles. 4:6.

HANDKERCHIEF, NAPKIN, a cloth used for wiping away sweat. The one talent man used one to wrap his lord's money (Luke 19:20). It was also used to wrap the head of the dead (John 11:44; 20:7).
brought unto sick *h.*, Acts 19:12.

HANDLE, use hands, touch.
upon the *h.* of, Song 5:5.

HANDLE, to touch, use. Also **Handled, Handleth, Handling.**
as *h.* the harp and organ, Gen. 4:21.
h. spear and shield, II Chr. 25:5.
h. me, for a spirit, Luke 24:39.
h. the word of God, II Cor. 4:2.
taste not, *h.* not, Col. 2:21.

HANDMAID, a maidservant, female slave or servant.
had an *h.*, an Egyptian, Gen. 16:1.
I am Ruth thy *h.*, Ruth 3:9.
the affliction of thy *h.*, I Sam. 1:11.
the servants and the *h.*, Joel 2:29.
the *h.* of the Lord, Luke 1:38.

HANDS, TO LAY ON, occurs in patriarchal usage (Gen. 48:14) and Jesus with the children (Matt. 19:15). Used in the Old Testament as part of the appointment and consecration of persons to office (Num. 27:18–20). In the New Testament, used in bestowing supernatural gifts of the Holy Spirit, healing the sick, etc. (Mark 5:23, 41, 6:5, 16:18, Acts 8:15–18, 19:6). Also seems to have been used in appointing men to a work (Acts 14:3, I Tim. 4:14). *See* **LAYING ON OF HANDS.**

HANDSTAFF, a javelin (Ezek. 39:9).

HAND WRITING, *see* **WRITING.**

HANES, an Egyptian city mentioned only in Is. 30:4.

HANG, TO, HANG UP, among the Jews, hanging was generally spoken of as following death by some other means to aggravate capital punishment (Num. 25:4, Deut. 21:22, II Sam. 21:6, 9). The person hanged should not be left overnight (Deut. 21:23).
Pharaoh shall *h.*, Gen. 40:19.
h. them on five trees, Josh. 10:26.
the king to *h.* Mordecai, Esther 6:4.
He *h.* the earth, Job 26:7.
a millstone were *h.*, Matt. 18:6.
malefactors which was *h.*, Luke 23:39.
that *h.* on a tree, Gal. 3:13.

HANGING, used in the Old Testament for the suspending of inanimate objects such as gates, doors, curtains, and corpses. It refers to a form of capital punishment (Esther 5:14, 6:4, 7:9, 10, Gen. 40:22). Corpses of those executed (by stoning) were often hanged on a tree as an exhibition of their shame. They had to be removed before evening (Gen. 40:19; Deut. 21:22; Josh. 8:29, 10:26; Esther 2:23). Sometimes victims were hanged by being impaled on a stake.

HANIEL, a less correct form of Hanniel. (1) A son of Ephod, prince of Manasseh (Num. 34:23). (2) A son of Ulla, prince of Asher (I Chr. 7:39).

HANNAH, one of Elkanah's two wives, mother of Samuel, a prophetess herself (I Sam. 1:2, 2:21). In her song is the first occurrence of "anointed" or Messiah (I Sam. 2:10).

HANNATHON, a city of Zebulon, on the northern border (Josh. 19:14).

HANNIEL, *see* **HANIEL.**

HANOCH, HENOCH, (1) third son of Midian and grandson of Abraham and Keturah (Gen. 25:4, I Chr. 1:33). (2) Oldest son of Reuben from whom came the Hanochites (Gen. 46:9, Ex. 6:14, Num. 26:5).

HANOCHITES, descendants of Hanoch (Num. 26:5).

HANUN, (1) son and successor of Nahash, king of Ammonites (II Sam. 10:1, I Chr. 19:2-6). (2) A Jew who helped repair the valley gate of Jerusalem after the captivity (Neh. 3:13). (3) Sixth son of Zaloph who repaired parts of the wall of Jerusalem (Neh. 3:30).

HAPHRAIM, a town on the border of Issachar (Josh. 19:19).

HAPLY, perchance, perhaps.
if *h.* the people, I Sam. 14:30.
if *h.* he might, Mark 11:13.
lest *h.* ye be, Acts 5:39.

HAPPEN, occur, take place.
no evil *h.* to just, Prov. 12:21.
time and chance *h.*, Eccles. 9:11.
shew us what shall *h.*, Isa. 41:22.
what things should *h.*, Mark 10:32.

HAPPIZZEZ, ancestral head of the 18th course of priests (I Chr. 24:15). *See* **APHSES.**

HAPPY, contented; fortunate, favored.
h. art thou, O Israel, Deut. 33:29.
h. is the man whom God, Job 5:17.
h. shalt thou be, Ps. 128:2.
h. is he that hath God, Ps. 146:5.
h. is he that hath mercy, Prov. 14:21.
h. man that feareth, Prov. 28:14.
keepeth the law, *h.*, Prov. 29:18.
I think myself *h.*, Acts 26:2.
we count them *h.*, James 5:11.
name of Christ *h.* are, I Pet. 4:14.

HARA, a section of Assyria to which the Israelites of Samaria were deported (I Chr. 5:26).

HARADAH, a station on the wilderness route from Sinai to Kadesh (Num. 33:24).

HARAN, (1) one of Terah's three sons and Abraham's brother, father of Lot (Gen. 11:26ff.). (2) Son of Ephoh, a concubine of Caleb (I Chr. 2:46). (3) One of the sons of Shimai, a Gershonite, appointed by David to superintend the offices of the tabernacle (I Chr. 23:9).

HARAN, CITY OF, (King James Version in New Testament has Harran), an important ancient commercial city in northern Mesopotamia. A stopping place on Abraham's journey from Ur to Palestine. His father died there (Gen. 11:31, 32).

HARARITE, mountaineer. Thought to designate a native of the hill country of Judah or Ephraim. A designation of three of David's guards, Agee, Shammah, and Sharar (II Sam. 23:33).

HARBONA, HARBONAH, one of the chamberlains of King Ahasuerus who suggested the hanging of Haman (Esther 1:10, 7:9).

HARD, difficult, severe.
too *h.* for the Lord? Gen. 18:14.
h. causes brought Moses, Ex. 18:26.
way transgressor is *h.*, Prov. 13:15.
that thou art an *h.* man, Matt. 25:24.
h. for thee to kick, Acts 9:5.

HARDEN, to make hard.
h. Pharaoh's heart, Ex. 7:13.
and *h.* their necks, Neh. 9:16.
hath *h.* their heart, John 12:40.
Whom He will He *h.*, Rom. 9:18.
h. not your heart, Heb. 3:8.
h. through the deceitfulness, Heb. 3:13.

HARDLY, scarcely, barely, harshly.
Sarai dealt *h.*, Gen. 16:6.
Pharaoh would *h.*, Ex. 13:15.
rich man shall *h.*, Matt. 19:23.

HARDNESS.
dust groweth into *h.*, Job 38:38.
h. as a good soldier, II Tim. 2:3.

HARDNESS OF HEART, make callous.
h. of your hearts, Matt. 19:8.
h. of their hearts, Mark 3:5.
after thy *h.* and impenitent heart, Rom. 2:5.

HARE, a long eared, swift, timid, rodent which is declared unclean because it chews the cud but does not part the hoof. (Lev. 11:6; Deut. 14:7). Four species of this rodent may be found in Palestine.
h., because he cheweth, Lev. 11:6.
the *h.*, and the coney, Deut. 14:7.

HAREPH, father of Bethgader and son of Caleb by one of his wives (I Chr. 2:51). *See* **HERETH.**

HARETH, HERETH, the place in the mountain where David fled from Saul (I Sam. 22:5).

HARHAIAH, father of Uzziel, who repaired part of the walls after the captivity (Neh. 3:8).

HARHAS, HASRAH, grandfather of Shallum, husband of Huldah the prophetess (II Kin. 22:14. Hasrah in II Chr. 34:22).

HARHUR, a Nethinim whose descendants returned from Babylon with Zerubbabel (Ezra 2:51, Neh. 7:53).

HARIM, (1) ancestral name of a large postexilic family (Ezra 2:32, 10:31). (2) Ancestral head of the third course of priests as set up by David (I Chr. 24:8, Ezra 2:39, 10:21). (3) An individual belonging to 1. or 2. (Neh. 12:15).

HARIPH, a man whose family returned from the exile with Zerubbabel (Neh. 7:24). One of those who signed the covenant (Neh. 10:19).

HARLOT, used in the Bible to designate a person of either sex who is lewd and licentious, but is used most frequently of a woman who practices sexual indulgence for gain. A prostitute. This profession dates back into patriarchal times (Gen. 38:15). Harlots in Canaan at the time of the conquest seem to have been innkeepers (Josh. 2:1). They often sat alongside of the roads and sang songs (Gen. 38:14; Isa. 23:16). The frequent use of the term "strange women" indicates that a large number of harlots in Palestine were foreign women (Judg. 11:2; Prov. 2:16; 5:10, 17, 20). The term is applied figuratively to Israel to describe her unfaithfulness to Jehovah (Jer. 2:20, 3:1; Ezek. 23:5).
our sister as with *h.*, Gen. 34:31.
took her to be an *h.*, Gen. 38:15.
Rahab the *h.*, Josh. 6:17.
Samson saw an *h.*, Judg. 16:1.
city become an *h.*, Isa. 1:21.
mother hath played *h.*, Hos. 2:5.
a boy for an *h.*, Joel 3:3.
wife shall be an *h.*, Amos 7:17.
members of an *h.*, I Cor. 6:15.
faith the *h.* Rahab, Heb. 11:31.
Rahab the *h.* justified, James 2:25.

HARM, injury, evil.
make amends for *h.*, Lev. 5:16.
no *h.* in pot, II Kin. 4:41.
prophets no *h.*, I Chr. 16:22.

Do him no *h.*, Jer. 39:12.
Do thyself no *h.*, Acts 16:28.
who will *h.* you, I Pet. 3:13.

HAR-MAGEDON, *see* **ARMAGED-DON.**

HARMLESS, incapable of injury or evil; unoffending.
h. as doves, Matt. 10:16.
h., the sons of God, Phil. 2:15.
holy, *h.*, undefiled, Heb. 7:26.

HARNEPHER, one of the sons of Zophah, in the tribe of Asher (I Chr. 7:36).

HARNESS, HARNESSED, act of fastening animals to a cart or vehicle (I Sam. 6:7, 10; Jer. 46:4). A part of armor (I Kin. 22:34). *See* **ARMOR.**

HAROD, the spring at which the test of drinking was applied before the battle with the Midianites (Judg. 7).

HARODITE, two of David's captains were so called, Shammah and Elika (II Sam. 23:25). Harorite in I Chr. 11:27.

HAROEH, the name of a small clan or perhaps a place in the genealogy of the Calebites, descended from Hur (I Chr. 2:52). *See* **REAIAH.**

HARORITE, an epithet for one of David's valiant men (I Chr. 11:27). Probably the same as Harodite.

HAROSHETH, a city in the north of Palestine, home of Sisera (Judg. 4:2, 13, 16).

HARP, a popular musical instrument used by the Hebrews. It was invented long before the flood (Gen. 4:21), and remained in use throughout Hebrew history. David played it with his hand (I Sam. 16:23); later Josephus described it as being played with a plectrum. When it was not in use, it was hung on the wall (Ps. 137:2). It was used for the accompaniment of vocal music, was used in the temple service, and is mentioned often in the Psalms.
the *h.* and the organ, Gen. 4:21.
took an *h.*, and played, I Sam. 16:23.
the psaltery and the *h.*, Ps. 150:3.
whether pipe or *h.*, I Cor. 14:7.
harping with their *h.*, Rev. 14:2.

HARPER, one who plays on a harp (Rev. 14:2, 18:22).

HARROW, the word so rendered in II Sam. 12:31, I Chr. 20:3, is probably a threshing machine; the verb refers to the "breaking of clods" (Job 39:10, Is. 28:24, Hos. 10:11).

HARSHA, a Nethinim whose descendants returned from Babylon with Zerubbabel (Ezra 2:52; Neh. 7:45).

HART, an animal which may have been abundant in Palestine in the time of King Solomon (I Kin. 4:23) but which is now very rare in this region. It is declared clean in the Bible (Deut. 12:15, 22, 15:22).
the roebuck and the *h.*, Deut. 12:22.
oxen, besides *h.*, I Kin. 4:23.
as the *h.* panteth after, Ps. 42:1.
a roe or a young *h.*, Song 2:9.
lame man leap as an *h.*, Is. 35:6.
princes become like *h.*, Lam. 1:6.

HARUM, the ancestral head of a family of Judah (I Chr. 4:8).

HARUMAPH, father of Jedaiah, which latter was one of the priests who repaired part of the walls of Jerusalem (Neh. 3:10).

HARUPHITE, a name applied to Shephatiah (I Chr. 12:5) indicating one descended from Haruph or a native of Hariph.

HARUZ, father of Meshullemath, wife of King Manasseh (II Kin. 21:19).

HARVEST, cutting. Began with the barley at the Passover (Lev. 23:9–14, II Sam. 21:9) and ended with the wheat and Pentecost (Gen. 30:14, Ex. 23:16). About seven weeks in duration, lasting from the middle of April to the first of June. Figuratively it is used for judgment (Jer. 51:33, Hos. 6:11); an ingathering of souls (Matt. 9:37, 38, John 4:35); and the end of the world (Matt. 13:39).
while earth remaineth, *h.*, Gen. 8:22.
when ye reap *h.*, Lev. 19:9.
beginning of barley *h.*, Ruth 1:22.
h. the hungry eateth, Job 5:5.
he that sleepeth in *h.*, Prov. 10:5.
in the heat of *h.*, Isa. 18:4.
three months to *h.*, Amos 4:7.
h. is plenteous, Matt. 9:37.
together until *h.*, Matt. 13:30.

214

time is come, the *h.*, Rev. 14:15.

HARVEST, FEAST OF, *see* PENTE-
COST.

HASADIAH, a son of Zerubbabel (I Chr.
3:20).

HASENUAH, a Benjamite, whose descendants dwelt in Jerusalem after the
captivity (I Chr. 9:7).

HASHABIAH, (1) two Levites of the sons
of Merari (I Chr. 6:45, 9:14). (2) A son of
Jeduthum (I Chr. 25:3, 19). (3) a Hebron-
ite (I Chr. 26:30). (4) a ruler of the
Levites (I Chr. 27:17). (5) A Chief Levite
under King Josiah (II Chr. 35:9). (6) A
Levite who returned with Ezra (Ezra
8:19). (7) One of the twelve priests entrusted with the holy vessels (Ezra 8:24,
Neh. 12:24). (8) A chief of the Levites
who repaired part of the walls and subscribed the covenant to Jehovah (Neh.
3:17, 10:11).

HASHABNAH, probably same as Hashabiah, one of the chiefs who subscribed
Nehemiah's covenant (Neh. 10:25).

HASHABNIAH, (1) father of Hattuck
(Neh. 3:10). (2) A Levite (Neh. 9:5).

HASHBADANA, a scribe or priest who
stood with Ezra while he read the law to
the people (Neh. 8:4).

HASHEM, the sons of Hashem, the Gizonite, are named as among David's guard
(I Chr. 11:34). Joshem in II Sam. 23:32.

HASHMONAH, a station of Israel in the
wilderness near Mt. Hor. (Num. 33:29, 30).

HASHUB, (1) the name of two persons
who helped in rebuilding the wall of
Jerusalem (Neh. 3:11, 23, 10:23). (2) A
Levite and father of Shemaiah, who had
general oversight of the temple (Neh.
11:15, I Chr. 9:14).

HASHUBAH, one of the five sons of
Zerubbabel, but some identify him as a
descendant of David (I Chr. 3:20).

HASHUM, (1) ancestral head of a large
postexilic family. Perhaps also the home
of the family (Ezra 2:19, 10:33). (2) A
priest or a scribe (Neh. 8:4).

HASHSHUPHA, HASUPHA, one of the
Nethinim whose descendants returned
from Babylon with Zerubbabel (Ezra
2:43, Neh. 7:46).

HASRAH, *see* HARHAS.

HASSENAAH, a Jew whose sons rebuilt
the fish gate in the repair of the walls
of Jerusalem (Neh. 3:3).

HASSEUNAH, *see* HASEUNAH.

HASSHUB, *see* HASHUB.

HASSOPHERETH, Sophereth (as rendered in the Revised Version) (Ezra 2:55).

HASTE, speed, hurry; to hurry.
h., escape thither, Gen. 19:22.
shall eat it in *h.*, Ex. 12:11.
h. with feet sinneth, Prov. 19:2.
I the Lord will *h.*, Isa. 60:22.
brought Daniel in *h.*, Dan. 2:25.
h. unto the coming, II Pet. 3:12.

HASTILY, with haste, hurriedly, speedily.
inheritance gotten *h.*, Prov. 20:21.
forth *h.* to strive, Prov. 25:8.
rose up *h.*, John 11:31.

HASTY, speedy; without due caution,
rash.
h. exalteth folly, Prov. 14:29.
h. only to want, Prov. 21:5.
be not *h.* in spirit, Eccles. 7:9 .
why is decree so *h.*, Dan. 2:15.
better and *h.* nation, Hab. 1:6.

HASUPHA, *see* HASHUPHA.

HAT, an article of clothing worn by the
Hebrew Children when cast into the
fiery furnace (Dan. 3:21).

HATACH, HATHACH, a eunuch in the
palace of Xerxes, appointed to wait on
Esther (Esther 4:5, 9, 10).

HATE, abhor, love less.
Esau *h.* Jacob, Gen. 27:41.
husband *h.* her and write, Deut. 24:3.
I *h.* him for he does, I Kin. 22:8.
that *h.* the righteous, Ps. 34:21 .
the Lord *h.*, yea seven, Prov. 6:16.
lest he *h.* thee, Prov. 9:8 .
spareth his rod *h.*, Prov. 13:24.
a time to *h.*, Ecc. 3:8.

h. thine enemy, Matt. 5:43.
when men shall *h.* you, Luke 6:22.
world *h.* you, John 15:18.
no man ever yet *h.* Eph. 5:29.
h. his brother is a murderer, I John 3:15.

HATEFUL, full of hate; hated, detestable, repugnant
iniquity be found *h.*, Ps. 36:2.
h. and hating, Titus 3:3.
unclean and *h.* bird, Rev. 18:2.

HATER, one who hates.
h. of Lord should, Ps. 81:15.
backbiters, *h.* of God, Rom. 1:30.

HATEST, HATETH, *see* **HATE.**

HATHACH, variant spelling of **Hatach.**

HATHATH, son of Othniel and grandson of Kenaz, of the tribe of Judah (I Chr. 4:13).

HATING, *see* **HATE.**

HATIPHA, a Nethinim whose descendants returned from exile with Zerubbabel (Ezra 2:54, Neh. 7:56).

HATITA, the ancestral head of one of the subdivisions of porters or doorkeepers, of the second temple (Ezra 2:42, Neh. 7:45).

HATTIL, ancestral head of one of the subdivisions of Solomon's servants (Ezra 2:57, Neh. 7:59).

HATTUSH, (1) descendant of David who accompanied Ezra to Jerusalem (Ezra 8:2). (2) Son of Shemaiah, ancestor of Zerubbabel (I Chr. 3:22). (3) Son of Hashabniah who helped rebuild Jerusalem (Neh. 3:10). (4) A priest who united in the covenant with Nehemiah. (Neh. 10:4).

HAUGHTY, HAUGHTINESS, proud, arrogant.
h. spirit before a fall, Prov. 16:18.
the *h.* of men, Is. 2:11.
daughters of Zion are *h.*, Is. 3:16.
no more be *h.*, Zeph. 3:11.

HAUNT, foot, to sit down or still, to go habitually up and down.
where his *h.* is, I Sam. 23:22.
men were wont to *h.*, I Sam. 30:31.

HAURAN, hollow land; a fertile basin about 50 miles square and about 2000 foot elevation, southeast of Mt. Hermon (Ezek. 47:16, 18).

HAVEN, shore, beach, harbor.
dwell at the *h.* of the sea, Gen. 49:13.
their desired *h.*, Ps. 107:30.
h. was not commodious, Acts 27:12.

HAVENS, FAIR, a haven at the south of Cape Salmone in Crete (Acts 27:8). *See* **FAIR HAVENS.**

HAVILAH, (1) a region near the Pison branch of the river in Eden (Gen. 2:11–12). (2) A district in Arabia whose people were nomads (Ishmaelites) (Gen. 25:18). (3) Second son of Cush (Gen. 10:7, I Chr. 1:9). (4) Twelfth son of Joktan (Gen. 10:29, I Chr. 1:23).

HAVOTH-JAIR, village of Jair. Villages in Bashan, east of Jordan (Num. 32:41, Deut. 3:14, Judg. 10:4).

HAWK, a bird declared unclean by the Law of Moses (Lev. 11:16; Deut. 14:15). Eighteen species have been found, ranging from the tiny sparrow hawk to the buzzard.

HAY, the terms so translated are very general and indicate grass or early blade of grains (Prov. 27:25, Is. 15:6, I Cor. 3:12).

HAZAEL, (God beholds), an officer of the Syrian king Benhadad, whom Elijah was directed to anoint to be king in his stead (I Kin. 19:15). Hazael killed Benhadad after returning from hearing Elijah predict Benhadad's death and Hazael's evil (II Kin. 8:7–13, 15). Hazael fought strongly against the Israelite kings Jehu and Jehoahaz (II Kin. 10:32–3; 13:1–9, 22). For a while he successfully resisted Shalmaneser III.

HAZAIAH, head of a postexilic family (Neh. 11:5).

HAZAR-ADDAR, Hazar means enclosure and is a term often prefixed to geographical names to show their dependence on some other place. Hazar-Addar was a place in the southern desert part of Palestine (Num. 34:4, Josh. 15:3).

HAZAR-ENAN, a town listed on the northern border of Israel, probably near Dan (Num. 34:9ff, Ezek. 47:17).

HAZAR-GADDAH, a city in the south of Judah (Josh. 15:27).

HAZAR-HATTICON, named in Ezekiel's prophecy as the ultimate boundaries of the land (Ezek. 47:16).

HAZARMAVETH, an Arabian clan, descended from Joktan (Gen. 10:26, I Chr. 1:20).

HAZAR-SHUAL, identity unknown, but it was a town on the south border of Judah; later included in Simeon's territory (Josh. 15:28, Neh. 11:27, Josh. 19:3).

HAZAR-SUSAH, a town in southwest Judah, later occupied by Simeonites (Josh. 19:5, I Chr. 4:31).

HAZAZON-TAMAR, (Hazezon-Tamar), probably the ancient name of Engedi (Gen. 14:7, II Chr. 20:2).

HAZEL, a type of tree, better translated "almond" (Gen. 30:37).

HAZELELPONI, sister of Jotham and descendant of Judah (I Chr. 4:3).

HAZER-HATTICON, *see* **HAZAR-HATTICON.**

HAZERIM, a term referring to the original inhabitants of the coast region west of Judah, expelled by the Philistines (Deut. 2:23).

HAZEROTH, Israel's second stop after leaving Sinai (Num. 11:35, 12:16). Here occurred Miriam and Aaron's sedition.

HAZGZON-TAMAR, *see* **HAZAZON-TAMAR.**

HAZIEL, a Levite in the family of Shimei in time of David (I Chr. 23:9).

HAZO, one of the sons of Nahor by Milcah (Gen. 22:22).

HAZOR, (1) an important city in northern Palestine (Josh. 11:1ff, 19:36, Judg.

4:2). Home of Jabin, a Canaanitish king. (2) A town in the south of Judah (Josh. 15:23). (3) A city occupied by Benjamites after the captivity (Neh. 11:33).

HAZOR-HADATTAH, new Hazor. A place in the south of Judah (Josh. 15:25).

HAZZELELPONI, *see* **HAZELELPONI.**

HEAD, used in many ways in the Bible, generally easily understood except certain figurative uses. Sometimes put for the whole person (Gen. 49:26, Prov. 10:6); sometimes for life itself (Dan. 1:10, I Sam. 28:2). Used of God (I Cor. 11:3), of Christ (Eph. 1:22), of rulers, chief men, etc. (I Sam. 15:17, Is. 9:14–15). (1) "Heads" of houses indicate chieftains, princes, elders, etc. (2) "Blood upon the head" indicates responsibility for the death of someone (Josh. 2:19, II Sam. 1:16). (3) "Lift up the head" indicates elevation in either pride or power (Judg. 8:28, Gen. 40:20).
h. of the corner, Acts 4:11.
coals of fire on his *h.,* Rom. 12:20.
h. of every man is Christ, I Cor. 11:3.
h. over all things, Eph. 1:22.
the *h.* of the wife, Eph. 5:23.

HEADBAND, an article of female dress, most likely a girdle (Is. 3:20). It is rendered "attire" in Jer. 2:32.

HEADY, falling forward. A form of wickedness, rash, reckless (II Tim. 3:4).

HEAL, HEALED, make whole.
I am the Lord that *h.* Ex. 15:26.
the Lord will *h.* me, II Kin. 20:8.
who *h.* all thy diseases, Ps. 103:3.
h. the broken in heart, Ps. 147:3.
his stripes we are *h.,* Is. 53:5.
h. all manner of sickness, Matt. 4:23.
h. the broken-hearted, Luke 4:18.
pray that ye be *h.,* James 5:16.
stripes ye were *h.,* I Pet. 2:24.

HEALING, curing, making whole or well.
there is no *h.* for, Jer. 14:19.
h. in his wings, Mal. 4:2.
h. all manner of, Matt. 4:23.
h. all oppressed of, Acts 10:38.
gifts of *h.,* I Cor. 12:9.

HEALTH, soundness of body.
the *h.* of my countenance, Ps. 42:11.
h. to all their flesh, Prov. 4:22.
I will restore *h.*, Jer. 30:17.
this is for your *h.*, Acts 27:34.
prosper and be in *h.*, III John 2.

HEAP, a pile; a mass.
this *h.* be witness, Gen. 31:52.
into ruinous *h.*, II Kin. 19:25.
stones out of *h.*, Neh. 4:2.
Jerusalem on *h.*, Ps. 79:1.
make Jerusalem *h.*, Jer. 9:11.
Babylon become *h.*, Jer. 51:37.
Samaria as an *h.*, Mic. 1:6.

HEAP, to amass; to pile.
h. up words, Job 16:4.
h. up silver as dust, Job 27:16.
h. coals of fire, Prov. 25:22.
thou shalt *h.* coals of fire, Rom. 12:20.
shall they *h.* to themselves, II Tim. 4:3.
h. treasure together, James 5:3.

HEAR, perceive sound.
ears but they *h.* not, Ps. 135:17.
his ear from *h.* the law, Prov. 28:9.
be more ready to *h.* than, Ecc. 5:1.
by *h.* ye shall *h.*, Matt. 13:14.
God *h.* not sinners, John 9:31.
ears are dull of *h.*, Acts 28:27.
Faith cometh by *h.*, Rom. 10:17.
ye are dull of *h.*, Heb. 5:11.
not a forgetful *h.*, James 1:25.

HEARD, perceived sound.
because Lord hath *h.*, Gen. 16:11.
God *h.* their groaning, Ex. 2:24.
the joy of Jerusalem *h.*, Neh. 12:43.
when he cried the *h.*, Ps. 22:24.
weeping no more *h.*, Isa. 65:19.
congregation hath *h.*, Hos. 7:12.
ye have *h.* it was, Matt. 5:21.
hear, and have not *h.*, Matt. 13:17.
thy prayer is *h.*, Luke 1:13.
h. this, were pricked, Acts 2:37.
have they not *h.*?, Rom. 10:18.
ye *h.* that antichrist, I John 2:18.

HEARERS, those who hear.
a *h.* of the word, James 1:23.
not a forgetful *h.*, James 1:25.

HEAREST, HEARETH, *see* **HEAR.**
h. thou men's words, I Sam. 24:9.
said unto him, *h.*, Matt. 21:16.
bloweth, and thou *h.*, John 3:8.
the world *h.* them, I John 4:5.

HEARING, perceiving of sound.
read law in *h.*, Deut. 31:11.
by *h.* of ear, Job 42:5.
h. they hear not, Matt. 13:13.
faith cometh by *h.*, Rom. 10:17.
the *h.* of faith, Gal. 3:5.
are dull of *h.*, Heb. 5:11.

HEARKEN, hear, listen. Also **Hearkened.**
wives, *h.* unto my, Gen. 4:23.
h., O Israel, unto, Deut. 4:1.
h. unto voice of, Deut. 15:5.
so will we *h.*, Josh. 1:17.
better to *h.*, I Sam. 15:22.
h. unto counsel, Prov. 12:15.
h. unto father, Prov. 23:22.
h., ye that follow, Is. 51:1.
will *h.* and turn, Jer. 26:3.
h., earth, and all, Mic. 1:2.
h. every one of, Mark 7:14.
men of Judea, *h.*, Acts 2:14.
damsel came to *h.*, Acts 12:13.
men and brethren, *h.*, Acts 15:13.

HEART, there are several meanings for
this word in the Bible. (1) It is the center
of the physical workings of the body,
that on which life depends (Judg. 4:12;
I Kin. 21:7; Acts 14:17). (2) It is spoken
of as the seat of the emotions, such as joy
and sorrow (Is. 65:14), fear (Ps. 143:4),
hate (Lev. 19:17), and love (I Tim. 1:5).
When a person turns away from God, it
is his heart that is hardened (Is. 63:17).
If one opens his heart to Christ, it can
be the dwelling place of Christ (Eph.
3:17) and the Holy Spirit (II Cor.
1:22).
Lord looketh on the *h.*, I Sam. 16:7.
h. with all diligence, Prov. 4:23.
h. is deceitful above all, Jer. 17:9.
there will your *h.* be, Matt. 6:21.
the abundance of the *h.*, Matt. 12:34.
God with all thy *h.*, Matt. 22:37.
not your *h.* be troubled, John 14:1.
the *h.* man believeth, Rom. 10:10.
love with a pure *h.*, I Pet. 1:22..

HEARTILY, zeal or zest.
do it *h.* as to the Lord, Col. 3:23.

HEARTH, refers to hot stoves (Gen. 18:6)
or a pan or brazier (Jer. 36:23).

HEAT, inflame, grow hot.
h., summer and winter, Gen. 8:22.
tent door in the *h.*, Gen. 18:1.
devoured with burning *h.*, Deut. 32:24.

bones are burnt with *h.*, Job 30:30.
melt with fervent *h.*, II Pet. 3:10.

HEATH, not a true heath in Palestine but probably a desert scrub or a dwarf juniper (Jer. 17:6, 48:6).

HEATHEN, a word meaning "nations" and later the Jews were distinguished from the other "nations" or "heathen". They were forbidden to intermarry (Josh. 23:12), worship their gods, etc. In the New Testament it refers to unbelievers and Gentiles (Gal. 3:8).
in sight of the *h.*, Lev. 26:45.
in statutes of *h.*, II Kin. 17:8.
why do the *h.* rage? Ps. 2:1.
be as a *h.* man, Matt. 18:17.
God would justify the *h.*, Gal. 3:8.

HEATING, *see* **HEAT.**

HEAVEN, the English translation of several Hebrew and Greek words. The emphasis in some of these is "height; hence, heaven is something above. The term is applied to the firmament, which is spread out like an arch above the earth. Sometimes, it is used with "earth" to denote the whole universe (Gen. 1:1); also it is used to denote the "sky", the place where the sun, moon and stars dwell (Ezek. 32:7, Matt. 24:29, 16:1); it is also used of the regions above the sky, the location of things eternal and perfect, where God and other heavenly beings dwell (Matt. 5:34, 23:22). This is probably what Paul referred to as the "third heaven" (II Cor. 12:2). Scripture does not specifically describe the first and second heavens; some view the first as the atmosphere, the second as the spaces where supernatural beings dwell, and the third is the abode of God. It is a place (II Cor. 12:2, John 14:1-3) of glory and beauty (Rev. 21:1-22:7).
God created the *h.*, Gen. 1:1.
as stars of *h.*, Deut. 1:10.
fire come from *h.*, II Kin. 1:10.
Lord God of *h.*, Ezra 1:2.
Lord's throne is in *h.*, Ps. 11:4.
for God is in *h.*, Eccles. 5:2.
windows of *h.*, Mal. 3:10.
kingdom of *h.* is at hand, Matt. 3:2.
your Father .. in *h.*, Matt. 5:16.
h. and earth shall, Matt. 24:35.
a sign from *h.*, Mark 8:11.
reward .. great in *h.*, Luke 6:23.
h. is my throne, Acts 7:49.

wrath .. revealed from *h.*, Rom. 1:18.
up to third *h.*, II Cor. 12:2.
or angel from *h.*, Gal. 1:8.
conversation is in *h.*, Phil. 3:20.
hope .. for you in *h.*, Col. 1:5.
inheritance .. in *h.*, I Pet. 1:4.
voice came from *h.*, II Pet. 1:18.
door was opened in *h.*, Rev. 4:1.

HEAVENLY, (1) divine; (2) celestial.
h. Father will forgive, Matt. 6:14.
plant my *h.* Father, Matt. 15:13.
if I tell you of *h.*, John 3:12.
not disobedient to *h.*, Acts 26:19.
bear image of the *h.*, I Cor. 15:49.
tasted of the *h.* gift, Heb. 6:4.
an *h.* country, Heb. 11:16.

HEAVE OFFERING, a religious gift offered up by the Israelites (Lev. 7:14; Num. 15:19). Most likely, "heave" (lifted up) simply means the goods were separated from other possessions and presented to the Lord. These offerings could only be used by priests and their children (Num. 18:19; Lev. 22:10).

HEAVINESS, sorrow, depression.
I rose from my *h.*, Ezra 9:5.
foolish son is *h.* of, Prov. 10:1.
there shall be *h.* and, Is. 29:2.
I have great *h.* and, Rom. 9:2.
joy be turned into *h.*, James 4:9.

HEAVY, weighty, burdensome.
Moses' hands were *h.*, Ex. 17:12.
father's *h.* yoke, I Kin. 12:4.
ye that are *h.* laden, Matt. 11:28.
they bind *h.* burdens, Matt. 23:4.
eyes were very *h.*, Mark 14:40.

HEBER, of the other side, immigrant. (1) Last named of seven chiefs of the Gadites (I Chr. 5:13). (2) A chief in the tribe of Benjamin (I Chr. 8:17). (3) Grandson of Asher and father of the Heberites (Num. 26:45). (4) Husband of Jael who slew Sisera (Judg. 4:17ff).

HEBERITES, (Num. 26:45), descendants of Heber of the tribe of Asher.

HEBREW, *see* **HEBREWS.**

HEBREWESS, a Hebrew girl or woman. *See* **HEBREW.**

HEBREW LANGUAGE, the language of the Old Testament with the exception of a few chapters written in Aramaic. It is referred to as the "language of Canaan" (Is. 19:18) or the "Jewish language" (II King. 18:26, 28). It is a Semitic language.

Spoken and written Hebrew was already in use before Moses and the Israelites came up out of Egypt. It originated from the old Phoenician alphabet and probably had a Canaanite origin. By New Testament times it had been replaced by Aramaic.

HEBREWS, the origin of the term "Hebrew" is not quite certain. Abram was the first one so-called (Gen. 14:13). His descendants were later called by that name (Gen. 40:15, 43:32, Ex. 2:11). The name may be derived from Eber, Abram's ancestor (Gen. 10:21–22). Or it may be the idea of Abram who "crossed over", that is, the river Euphrates (Josh. 24:2–3). Other possibilities of origin are presented by various scholars. His descendants preferred the name Israel (Gen. 32:28) and after the captivity they were known as Jews (from Judah).

HEBREWS, BOOK OF, the dominant aim of this doctrinally important New Testament book is to show the superiority and the finality of God's revelation to men through Christ (1:1–2, 8:6) as over against Judaism or any other previous revelation of God.

The authorship cannot be definitely established, because neither the internal nor external evidence (in tradition) is conclusive. A strong tradition is that Paul wrote it, but the author does not identify himself and many question that Paul is the author. Generally it has been viewed as having been written to Jewish Christians but some (e.g. Moffatt) do not feel that is true. It is probably better, though, to view it as written to Jewish Christians to strengthen their faith and to prevent their lapse into Judaism (2:1–4, 6:4–8, 10:26–31).

The author accomplishes his purpose primarily by showing the superiority of Christ over the angels, Moses, and the Old Testament priesthood and ritual as well as that of the whole "new covenant" or gospel system over the Judaistic system.

HEBRON, (1) a town in the mountains of Judah, about 2800 feet in elevation, between Beersheba and Jerusalem. Was named Kirjath-arba (Gen. 23:2, Josh. 14:15, 15:13) Mamre (Gen. 13:18). Inhabited by the Canaanites and Anakim, Abraham (Gen. 13:18), Isaac and Jacob (Gen. 35:27); Sarah was buried there (Gen. 23:17–20), and David made it the center of the kingdom for a while (II Sam. 2:1–4, 5:5). (2) Son of Kohoth, and grandson of Levi, and uncle to Moses and Aaron (Ex. 6:18, Num. 3:19). 3. Son of Mareshah and descendant of Judah (I Chr. 2:42, 43).

HEBRONITES, descendants of Hebron (see above). (Ex. 6:18, I Chr. 26:23, 30, 31).

HEDGE, a translation of several Hebrew and Greek words with the basic idea of to surround or inclose; whether a stone wall, vineyard hedge or other materials (Num. 22:24, Prov. 24:31).
hast thou not made *h.*, Job 1:10.
I will take away *h.*, Is. 5:5.
I will *h.* up thy way, Hos. 2:6.
h. about it digged, Mark 12:1.

HEED, give attention.
take ye therefore good *h.*, Deut. 4:15.
wicked doer giveth *h.*, Prov. 17:4.
h., watch and pray, Mark 13:33.
take *h.* how he buildeth, I Cor. 3:10.
take *h.* lest by any means, I Cor. 8:9.
standeth take *h.*, I Cor. 10:12.
Take *h.* unto thyself, I Tim. 4:16.

HEEL,
thou shalt bruise his *h.*, Gen. 3:15.
he hath lifted up his *h.*, Ps. 41:9.
his *h.* against me, John 13:18.

HEGAI, HEGE, the eunuch in charge of Xerxes' harem (Esther 2:3, 8, 15).

HEIFER, the heifer was not used for plowing but only for treading out the grain. The word is used figuratively to represent nations as being rebellious, or young and strong, etc. (Hos. 4:16, 10:11, Is. 15:5).
plowed with my *h.*, Judg. 14:18.
Egypt is like *h.*, Jer. 46:20.
Ashes of an *h.*, Heb. 9:13.

HEIGHT, elevation; measure of stature.
h. of the ark shall, Gen. 6:15.

nor *h.* nor depth shall, Rom. 8:39.
what is *h.* of love, Eph. 3:18.
breadth and *h.* of city, Rev. 21:16.

HEIR, eldest son became head of a tribe
or family with largest share of the estate
(Gen. 21:10, 14, 24:36, Judg. 11:12).
shall not be thine *h.*, Gen. 15:4.
this is the *h.*, Matt. 21:38.
if children, then *h.*, Rom. 8:17.
an *h.* of God through Christ, Gal. 4:7.
h. together, I Pet. 3:7.

HELAH, one of the wives of Ashur,
father of Tekoah (I Chr. 4:5, 7).

HELAM, the place where David defeated
the Syrians under Hadadezer (II Sam.
10:16–17).

HELBAH, a town of Asher, not far from
Sidon, from which the Canaanites were
not expelled (Judg. 1:31).

HELBON, mentioned only in Ezek. 27:18
in connection with the "wine of Helbon."

HELDAI, (1) a descendant of Othniel of
David's forces (I Chron. 27:15). Also
called Heleb and Heled (I Chron. 11:30,
II Sam. 23:9). (2) One returned from the
captivity, associated with Zechaniah
(Zech. 6:10, 14-called Helem).

HELEB, (II Sam. 23:29), a warrior of
David better known as Heldai.

HELED, (I Chr. 11:30), a warrior of David
better known as Heldai. *See* HELDAI.

HELEK, son of Gilead, of the tribe of
Manasseh, whose descendants were
called "Helekites" (Num. 26:30, Josh.
17:2).

HELEKITES, descendants from Helek
(Num. 26:30).

HELEM, (1) head of an Asherite clan (I
Chr. 7:35), probably same as Hotham
(v. 32). (2) *See* HELDAI.

HELEPH, a city at the northwest border
of Naphtali (Josh. 19:33).

HELEZ, (1) one of David's mighty men
(II Sam. 23:26, I Chr. 27:10). (2) Son
of Azariah, of the tribe of Judah (I Chr.
2:39).

HELI, father-in-law of Joseph the husband
of Mary who bore the Christ (Luke 3:23).

HELKAI, probably a form of Hilkiah, a
chief priest in the time of the high priest
Joiakim (Neh. 12:15).

HELKATH, a Levitical city (Josh. 21:31)
assigned on the east border of Asher
(Josh. 19:25).

HELKATH-HUROK, (I Chr. 6:75), a
corrupted name for Helkath.

HELL, with one exception (II Pet. 2:4)
the word "hell" translates three different
words: "sheol" in the Old Testament
and "hades" and "gehenna" in the New
Testament. The idea of a place of suffering and punishment for the wicked is of
course found in other words than these.
  "Sheol" occurs 65 times in the Old
Testament and in the King James Version
it is "grave" 31 times, "hell" 31 times,
and "pit" three times. The general idea is
"place of the dead". This does not mean
that the "grave" is all that is involved in
the word "sheol". Abraham, Moses, Jacob, and Aaron are buried in graves far
from the sepulchres of their ancestors, yet
are said to be "gathered to their fathers"
an expression for "sheol."
  "Hades" is the New Testament equivalent of sheol. It occurs 11 times in the
New Testament and, except in I Cor.
15:55, it is rendered "hell" by the King
James Version. The Revised Version does
not translate it and leaves it as hades.
In some passages this intermediate state
between death and the resurrection is
associated with judgment and suffering
(Matt. 11:23, Luke 16:23).
  "Gehenna," or the valley of Hinnom,
was the place where the Jews apostatized
and worshipped Moloch (I Kin. 11:7). It
was later converted by Josiah to a place
of abomination where dead bodies were
burned (II Kin. 23:13–14). It thus became a symbol and was used by the Lord
to indicate burning and suffering. It occurs 12 times in the New Testament and
denotes the eternal state of the lost after
the resurrection. *See* GEHENNA.
burn to lowest *h.*, Deut. 32:22.
h. is naked before him, Job. 26:6.
not leave soul in *h.*, Ps. 16:10.
if I make my bed in *h.*, Ps. 139:8.
house is the way to *h.*, Prov. 7:27.

h. hath enlarged, Is. 5:14.
be brought down to *h*., Is. 14:15.
though they dig into *h*., Amos 9:2.
out of belly of *h*., Jonah 2:2.
in danger of *h*., Matt. 5:22.
escape damnation of *h*., Matt. 23:33.
set on fire of *h*., James 3:6.
I have keys of *h*., Rev. 1:18.
death and *h*. were cast, Rev. 20:14.

HELLENIST, a Greek-speaking Jew (Acts 6:1, 9:29, 11:20).

HELMET, armor for the head. *See* **ARMOUR.**
had a *h*. of brass, I Sam. 17:5.
hanged shield and *h*., Ezek. 27:10.
take *h*. of salvation, Eph. 6:17.
for *h*. the hope of, I Thess. 5:8.

HELON, father of Eliab, prince of Zebulun during the Exodus (Num. 1:9, 2:7, 10:16).

HELP, assist, aid. Also **Helped.**
h. meet for him, Gen. 2:18.
our *h*. and shield, Ps. 33:20.
God is a very present *h*., Ps. 46:1.
Macedonia and *h*. us, Acts 16:9.
grace to *h*. in time of need, Heb. 4:16.
the Lord is my *h*., Heb. 13:6.

HELPER, one who helps.
Lord, be thou my *h*., Ps. 30:10.
God is my *h*., Ps. 54:4.
salute Urbane, our *h*., Rom. 16:9.
Lord is my *h*., Heb. 13:6.

HELPETH, aids, helps. *See* **HELP.**
thy God *h*. thee, I Chr. 12:18.
Spirit also *h*. our, Rom. 8:26.

HELVE, the handle or wooden part of an axe (Deut. 19:5).

HEM, the extremity or outer border of the garment, on which the Pharisees later laid so much stress (Ex. 28:33, Matt. 23:5, Num. 15:38–39).
the *h*. of his garment, Matt. 9:20.
touch the *h*. of his garment, Matt. 14:36.

HEMAM, son of Lotan, son of Seir. Same as Hamam (Gen. 36:22).

HEMAN, (1) one of four persons celebrated for their wisdom (I Kin. 4:31). Probably the grandson of Judah (I Chr.

2:6). (2) Son of Joel and grandson of Samuel (I Chr. 6:33).

HEMANITE, descendants of Heman.

HEMATH, (1) a Kenite, ancestor of Rechabites (I Chr. 2:55). (2) Erroneous form of Hamath (I Chr. 13:5).

HEMDAN, a son of Dishon, son of Seir (Gen. 36:26).

HEMLOCK, a rendering of several Hebrew words, but evidently referring to a noxious, poisonous weed (Hos. 10:4, Deut. 29:17, Amos 6:12).

HEN, son of Zephaniah, probably refers to Josiah in Zech. 6:10, 14).

HEN, a female fowl.
h. gathereth her chicks, Matt. 23:37.

HENA, a city overthrown by Sennacherib before he invaded Judea (II Kin. 18:34, 19:13).

HENADAD, a Levite whose sons were active after the captivity (Ezra 3:9, Neh. 3:18, 24).

HENCEFORTH, from this time forward.
ground not *h*. yield, Gen. 4:12.
shall not see me *h*., Matt. 23:39.
h. be no more children, Eph. 4:14.
h. there is laid up, II Tim. 4:8.

HENOCH, same as **ENOCH** and **HANOCH** (I Chr. 1:3, 33).

HEPHER, (1) ancestor of a Manassite clan of Gilead, the Hepherites (Num. 26: 32, 27:1). (2) One of David's heroes (I Chr. 11:36). (3) A district in south Judah (I Kin. 4:10). (4) A Canaanite city (Josh. 12:17).

HEPHERITE, a descendant of Hepher (Num. 26:32).

HEPHZIBAH, (1) queen of Hezekiah and mother of Manasseh (II Kin. 21:1). (2) Symbolical name given to Zion by Isaiah (Is. 62:4).

HERB, HERBS, BITTER, the Israelites were commanded to eat "bitter herbs" with the Passover bread (Ex. 12:8, Num.

9:11) to remember the bitterness of their afflictions in Egypt.
a dinner of *h*., Prov. 15:17.
greater than all *h*., Mark 4:32.
all manner of *h*., Luke 11:42.
who is weak, eateth *h*., Rom. 14:2.

HERD, Cattle.
had flocks, and *h*., Gen. 13:5.
flocks and all the *h*., I Sam. 30:20.
look well to thy *h*., Prov. 27:23.
into the *h*. of swine, Matt. 8:31.

HERES, a city of Dan, near Aijalon, which the Ammonites continued to hold, (Judg. 1:35).

HERESH, a Levite who returned from the captivity (I Chr. 9:15).

HERESY, the Greek word refers to parties or types of religious thought in New Testament times. Thus it was applied to the Sadducees, Pharisees, and to Christians as a group (Acts 24:5, 14, 28:22). In the Epistles it is used of divisions, strifes, and factions, not necessarily doctrinal in origin (I Cor. 11:19, Gal. 5:20, II Pet. 2:1).

HERETH, HARETH, a forest where David hid from Saul (I Sam. 22:5).

HERITAGE, inheritance.
give it you for an *h*., Ex. 6:8.
children are an *h*., Ps. 127:3.
lords over God's *h*., I Pet. 5:3.

HERMAS, a person whom Paul greets in Rom. 16:14.

HERMES, a disciple Paul greets in Rom. 16:14.

HERMOGENES, a disciple in Asia Minor who had deserted Paul, along with Phygellus (II Tim. 1:15).

HERMON, a mountain which formed the northern boundary of the country beyond the Jordan (Josh. 11:17, 12:1), conquered from the Amorites (Deut. 3:8). It is about 40 miles northeast of the Sea of Galilee, and rises over 9000 feet above sea level. Its melting snows form the main source of the Jordan River. It is probably the mount on which Jesus was transfigured (Matt. 17).

HEROD, several individuals in the Scriptures are referred to by this family title or surname. This has led to some confusion.

(1) **Herod the Great** (37–4 B.C.) is the first of the New Testament Herods. His father was Antipater, and he was an Idumean. These were Edomites, descendants of Esau, and were proselytes to Judaism. Herod was made king over Palestine but could not assert his rights until he captured Jerusalem in 37 B.C. Herod was cruel and ruthless. His rebuilding of the Temple begun in 20 B.C. was largely to placate the Jews. It was he who sought to slay Jesus by slaying all the male children (Matt. 2:13, 16).

(2) **Herod Archaelaus,** the oldest of three sons of Herod the Great. Ruled for a while as ethnarch over half of his father's kingdom but after ten years the revolts were so severe he was banished to Gaul (Matt. 2:22).

(3) **Herod Antipas** (4 B.C.–39 A.D.). A wily, cunning king ("that fox," Luke 13:32), tetrarch of Galilee and Perea. He married Herodias, wife of his half-brother Philip I and granddaughter of Herod the Great. He put John the Baptist to death (Mark 6). Was later deposed by Caligula and banished to Gaul.

(4) **Herod Philip II** (4 B.C.–34 A.D.), a tetrarch and very worthy ruler. Built Caesarea Philippi (Matt. 16:13) (Luke 3:1).

(5) **Herod Agrippa I** (37–44 A.D.), a grandson of Herod the Great, son of Aristobulus (Acts 12:1, 6, 11, 19–21). His death is recorded in Acts 12:22–23.

(6) **Herod Agrippa II** (53–70 A.D.), son of Herod Agrippa I, and king of the northeastern one third of Palestine (Acts 25:22, 23, 26–28, 32). He is the one before whom Paul appeared.

HERODIANS, a religious-political party of the Jews of the apostolic age, strongly opposed to Jesus (Matt. 22:16, Mark 3:6, 12:13). Not much is known of their beliefs. The party was probably formed under Herod the Great, and was loyal to the Herod dynasty.

HERODIAS, feminine of Herod. Daughter of Aristobulus, son of Herod the Great and the sister of Herod Agrippa I. Her unholy relation with Herod Antipas brought forth John the Baptist's rebuke; so Herod had him beheaded (Mark 6:17-18).

HERODION, a Christian at Rome, kinsman of Paul (Rom. 16:11).

HEROD PHILIP, see **HEROD.**

HEROD'S TEMPLE, see **TEMPLE.**

HEROD THE GREAT, see **HEROD.**

HERON, a bird. At least six different species have been identified in Palestine. It was counted unclean according to the Law (Lev. 11:19; Deut. 14:18).

HESED, the father of Ben-hesed, an officer of Solomon's in Aruboth and Hepher (I Kin. 4:10).

HESHBON, a town east of the Jordan, originally a Moabitish town, but at the time of Moses it was ruled over by Sihon, king of the Amorites and king of Heshbon (Josh. 21:23-26, 39, I Chr. 6:81).

HESHMON, a town in southern Judah (Josh. 15:27), perhaps the same as Agmon in verse 4.

HETH, in Gen. 10 and I Chr. 1 Heth is listed as a son of Canaan, but he was the forefather of the Hittites, who are referred to as "sons and daughters of Heth" (Gen. 23:3, 5, 7, 10, 16, 18, 25:10, 27:46). The Hittite empire held sway in Palestine several centuries before Israel entered the region from Egypt, see **HITTITES.**

HETHLON, the name of a place in northern Palestine marking the boundary (Ezra 47:15, 48:1). Its actual location is not absolutely certain.

HEW, HEWER, HEWING, the "hewers of wood" seem to have been among the lowest classes of the people (Josh. 9:27 Deut. 29:11). Solomon had 80,000 hewers in the mountains (I Kin. 5:15).
h. thee two tables of stone, Ex. 34:1.
h. of thy wood, Deut. 29:11.
good fruit is *h.* down, Matt. 3:10.
h. out in the rock, Matt. 27:60.

HEXATEUCH, six, the first six books of the Old Testament.

HEZEKI, a son of Elpael, and descendant of Benjamin (I Chr. 8:17). Some translations have Hizki.

HEZEKIAH, SON OF AHAZ, (II Kin. 18:1, 2) and king of Judah (715-682 B.C.). In spite of his idolatrous father, Hezekiah was a good king, and his first act was to repair the Temple and root out the Canaanite worship. Brought about a great reformation (II Chr. 29:1-36). Warred successfully against the Philistines. The Assyrians besieged Jerusalem but could not take it. Hezekiah was seriously ill and having no heir he prayed that his life be spared and he was given a 15-year extension (II Kin. 20:1, II Chr. 32:24).

HEZEKIAH, other than the famous king of Judah three men in the Bible have this name. (1) A son of Neariah of Judah (I Chr. 3:23). (2) The head of a family of returnees from exile (Ezra 2:16; Neh. 7:21). (3) An ancestor of the prophet Zephaniah (Zeph. 1:1).

HEZION, father of Tabrimon and grandfather of Benhadad I, to whom Asa sent treasures to get aid against Baasa (I Kin. 15:18). Probably same as Rezon (I Kin. 11:23).

HEZIR, (1) head of seventeenth course of priests as established by David (I Chr. 24:15). (2) One of the heads of the people who sealed the covenant with Nehemiah (Neh. 10:20).

HEZRAI, same as Hezro (II Sam. 23:35).

HEZRO, a Carmelite and one of David's mighty men (I Chr. 11:37).

HEZRON, (1) third son of Reuben (Gen. 46:9, Ex. 6:14). His descendants were called Hezronites. (2) Grandson of Judah and the elder of Pharez's sons (Gen. 46:12, Ruth 4:18-19). (3) A place on the southern boundary of Judah (Josh. 15:3, 25).

HEZRONITE, descendants of **Hezron.**

HID, HIDDEN, conceal, concealed.
it was *h* in his tent, Josh. 7:22.
five kings are found *h.,* Josh. 10:17.

nothing *h.* from Solomon, II Chr. 9:2.
my sins are not *h.* Ps. 69:5.
iniquity *h.* from my eyes, Jer. 16:17.
h. that shall not be, Matt. 10:26.
are *h.* from him, Acts 26:26.
have renounced the *h.*, II Cor. 4:2.
h. man of the heart, I Pet. 3:4.

HIDDAI, one of David's heroes, from near Mt. Gaash (II Sam. 23:30), called Hurai in I Chr. 11:32.

HIDDEKEL, the ancient name of the Tigris River (Gen. 2:14, Dan. 10:4). On its banks were located Nineveh and Ashur.

HIDDEN, *see* **HIDE.**

HIDE, secrete, conceal, withhold.
Adam and his wife *h.*, Gen. 3:8.
she *h.* him, Ex. 2:2.
slew the Egyptians and *h.* Ex. 2:12.
wheat, to *h.* it from, Judg. 6:11.
h. under the shadow, Ps. 17:8.
trouble he shall *h.* me, Ps. 27:5.
darkness *h.* not from thee, Ps. 139:12.
h. things from the wise, Matt. 11:25.
gospel be *h.* it is *h.* II Cor. 4:3.
hath been *h.* in God, Eph. 3:9.
life is *h.* with Christ, Col. 3:3.

HIEL, a, Bethelite who rebuilt Jericho (I Kin. 16:34) and suffered the curse pronounced by Joshua (Josh. 6:26).

HIERAPOLIS, referred to in Col. 4:13; was situated near Colossae and Laodicea in the Lycus River valley.

HIGGAION, a word that occurs, perhaps, as a musical direction (Ps. 9:16, 19:14, 92:3). It indicates a murmuring or muttering.

HIGH, lifted up; elevated.
with an *h.* arm brought, Acts 13:17.
mind not *h.* things, Rom. 12:16.
it is *h.* time, Rom. 13:11.
for the prize of *h.*, Phil. 3:14.
wall, great and *h.*, Rev. 21:12.

HIGHER, more elevated, more advanced.
king shall be *h.*, Num. 24:7.
my ways *h.* than your, Is. 55:9.
Friend, go up *h.*, Luke 14:10.
subject to *h.* powers, Rom. 13:1.

HIGHEST, most elevated, exalted.
H. himself shall, Ps. 87:5.
Hosanna in the *h.*, Matt. 21:9.
glory to God in the *h.*, Luke 2:14.
love the *h.* seats, Luke 20:46.

HIGHLY, greatly.
thou art *h.*, Luke 1:28.
think of self more *h.*, Rom. 12:3.
God also hath *h.*, Phil. 2:9.
esteem them very *h.*, I Thess. 5:13.

HIGH PLACE, localities chosen as places of worship of God or of idols (Gen. 12:7; 31:54). They were features of the Canaanite religion and the Israelites had been instructed to destroy them (Num. 33:52, Deut. 33:29). These places were often connected with immorality (Hos. 4:11–14, Jer. 3:2). The prophets denounced them (Ezek. 6:3); Hezekiah and Josiah tore them down (II Kin. 18:4, 22, 23:5, 8, 13).

HIGH PRIEST, the first to fill this, the highest office in Israel's hierarchy, was Aaron, followed by his son Eleazar. The distinct function of the high priest was to make a sin offering for himself (Lev. 4:3) and the congregation (Lev. 4:13ff.) on occasion and to make the sacrifice on the Day of Atonement (Lev. 16). Also he consulted the Lord by the means of Urim and Thummim, on matters affecting Israel (Num. 27:21, I Sam. 30:7). *See* PRIEST.
to Caiaphas the *h. p.*, Matt. 26:58.
servant of the *h.p.*, Luke 22:50.
merciful and faithful *h.p.*, Heb. 2:17.
a *h.p.* which cannot, Heb. 4:15.
h.p. forever after the order, Heb. 6:20.
second went the *h.p.* alone, Heb. 9:7.

HIGHWAY, public road.
"We will go by the *h.*," Num. 20:19.
h. of the fuller's field, Is. 7:3.
an *h.* for the remnant, Is. 11:16.
h. shall be there and a way, Is. 35:8.
a *h.* for our God, Is. 40:3.
the *h.* and the hedges, Luke 14:23.

HILEN, *see* **HOLON** (I Chr. 6:58).

HILKIAH, (1) a son of Hosah, a Levite in the reign of David (I Chr. 26:11). (2) Father of Eliakim, steward of Hezekiah (II Kin. 18:18). (3) A son of Shalkum (I Chr. 6:13) and high priest during

Josiah's reign. He discovered the Book of the Law which helped bring on the reformation (I Kin. 22:4ff). (4) A Merarite Levite (I Chr. 6:45). (5) A priest and father of Jeremiah the prophet (Jer. 1:1). (6) A priest, contemporary with Ezra and Nehemiah (Neh. 8:4, 11:11).

HILL, a rounded natural land elevation. High hills were used as places of heathen worship (Jer. 2:20; 17:2).
built altar under the *h.*, Ex. 24:4.
city set on an *h.*, Matt. 5:14.
and evèry *h.* shall be, Luke 3:5.
to say to the *h.*, Luke 23:30.
midst of Mars' *h.*, Acts 17:22..

HILLEL, father of the judge Abdon (Judg. 12:13, 15).

HIN, a Hebrew liquid measure equalling about six pints (Ex. 29:40; 30:24).

HIND, kind of deer.
Naphtali is a *h.*, Gen. 49:21.
my feet like *h.* feet, Ps. 18:33.
h. and pleasant roe, Prov. 5:19.

HINDER, obstruct, prevent.
h. me not, seeing, Gen. 24:56.
what doth *h.* me to be?, Acts 8:36.
should *h.* the gospel, I Cor. 9:12.
who did *h.* you, that?, Gal. 5:7.

HINDER, rear.
smote him with *h.* end, II Sam. 2:23.
toward the *h.* sea, Zech. 14:8.
Jesus was in *h.* part, Mark 4:38.

HINGE, doors in the East turned rather on pivot pins fitting into pivot sockets. These were sometimes made of metal (I Kin. 7:50), but more often of the same material as the door. Such became hard to open (Prov. 26:14).

HINNON, VALLEY OF, a person unknown whose name was given to the Valley of Hinnom (Josh. 18:16, Neh. 11:30). Called the "valley of the son of Hinnon." or the "children of Hinnon." A deep ravine, south and west of Jerusalem. The earliest mention is Josh. 15:18, 18:16. Here Solomon erected high places for Molech (I Kin. 11:7) and infant sacrifice to the fire gods was practiced here. Later the rubbish, etc. of the city was burned here. This name, Gehenna,

thus came to denote eternal torment. *See* Hell, GEHENNA.

HIP AND THIGH, a proverbial expression for a great slaughter (Judg. 15:8).

HIRAH, an Adullamite and friend of Judah (Gen. 38:1, 12).

HIRAM, HURAM, HIROM, I Kin. 5:10, 18). A common Phoenician royal name. (1) King of Tyre, who sent an embassy to David after he had taken the stronghold of Zion. He helped David build his house (II Sam. 5:11) and Solomon build the Temple (I Kin. 5:1ff). (2) Son of a widow of the tribe of Naphtali, and of a Tyrian father. Sent by King Hiram to work in the Temple (I Kin. 7: 13, 14, 40).

HIRE, wages.
God hath given my *h.*, Gen. 30:18.
her *h.* shall be holiness, Is. 23:18.
the *h.* of an harlot, Mic. 1:7.
labourer worthy of *h.*, Luke 10:7.

HIRE, to employ. Also **Hired.**
h. counsellors against, Ezra 4:5.
h. a goldsmith, Is. 46:6.
went out to *h.*, Matt. 20:1.
dwelt in own *h.* house, Acts 28:30.

HIRELING, a mercenary.
those that oppress *h.*, Mal. 3:5.
he that is an *h.*, John 10:12.

HISS, a term usually of insult and contempt (Job 27:23, I Kin. 9:8, II Chr. 29:8). Also used of enticing or alluring, as a bee keeper (Is. 5:26, 7:18).

HISTORY OF SUSANNA, a book of the Apocrypha which tells an imaginative story about Daniel.

HITHER, here.
that ye sold me *h.*, Gen. 45:5.
bring him *h.* to me, Matt. 17:17.
bring *h.* fatted calf, Luke 15:23.
call *h.* Simon, whose, Acts 10:32.

HITHERTO. until now; to this place.
my Father worketh *h.*, John 5:17.
h. have ye asked, John 16:24.
but was let *h.*, Rom. 1:13.
for *h.* ye were not able, I Cor. 3:2.

HITTITES, referred to frequently in the Old Testament by their own name, also as descendants of Heth (Gen. 10:15). In Abraham's day some were located near Hebron (Gen. 23:1-20). Esau married Hittite wives (Gen. 26:34-35). They were in Canaan in the time of Joshua (Num. 13:29, Josh. 9:1-2, 11:3). The Hittites are now known to have had a great empire that centered in Asia Minor.

HIVITES, one of the seven nations of Canaan who were to be destroyed by Israel (Deut. 7:1). They seem to have been especially in the north, towards Hermon (Josh. 11:3, Judg. 3:3). Some connect them with the Horites.

HIZKI, see HEZEKI (I Chr. 8:17).

HIZKIAH, an ancestor of Zephaniah (Zeph. 1:1).

HIZKIJAH, HIZKIAH, a postexilic descendant of David (I Chr. 3:23). See Neh. 10:17.

HOAR, HOARY FROST, white or gray.
the *h.*, on the ground, Ex. 16:14.
rise up before the *h.*, Lev. 19:32.

HOAR, HOARY HEAD, white, white head.
rise up before the *h.*, Lev. 19:32.
h. go down to the grave, I Kin. 2:6.
h. is a crown of glory, Prov. 16:31.

HOBAB, a man Moses used to guide Israel through the wilderness (Num. 10:29-32). His relation to Moses was probably that of a brother-in-law (Judg. 4:11, Num. 10:29).

HOBAH, the place north of Damascus to which Abraham pursued Chedorlaomer and his allies (Gen. 14:15).

HOBAIAH, see HABAIAH (Neh. 7:63).

HOD, a son of Zophah, of the tribe of Asher (I Chr. 7:37).

HODAVIAH, HODAIAH, HODEVAH, (1) name of a clan of Manasseh (I Chr. 5:24). (2) A son of Elioenai (I Chr. 3:24). (3) A son of Hasennah and father of Meshullam, in Benjamin (I Chr. 9:7). (4) A Levite whose descendants returned with Zerubbabel (Ezra 2:40). Same as Hodevah (Neh. 7:43).

HODESH, one of the wives of Shaharaim of Judah whose children are listed in I Chr. 8:8-9.

HODEVAH, see HODAVIAH.

HODIAH, one of the two wives of Mered (I Chr. 4:19) and mother of Jered and Heber.

HODIJAH, (1) a Levite who helped Nehemiah teach the law (Neh. 8:7, 9:5). (2) A Levite who signed the covenant with Nehemiah (Neh. 10:13). (3) An Israelite who was a party to this covenant (Neh. 10:18).

HOGLAH, the third of five daughters of Zelophehad, who in the absence of male heirs, received inheritance (Num. 26:33, 27:1, Josh. 17:3).

HOHAM, king of Hebron who joined the league against Gibeon, but defeated and slain by Joshua (Josh. 10:3).

HOLD, a term translated as fortress, especially used to indicate the lurking places of David (I Sam. 22:4, 5, 24:22). Used also of places of confinement (Acts 4:3).
hand *h.* a weapon, Neh. 4:17.
right hand shall *h.* me, Ps. 139:10.
that can *h.* no water, Jer. 2:13.
h. the tradition, Mark 7:3.
h. fast that which is good, I Thess. 5:21.
h. faith and a good, I Tim. 1:19.
h. our confidence, Heb. 3:14.

HOLE, an opening, hollow place, or pit.
Jehoiada bored an *h.*, II Kin. 12:9.
child play on *h.* of, Is. 11:8.
hide it there in a *h.*, Jer. 13:4.
The foxes have *h.*, Luke 9:58.

HOLIER, (Is. 65:5) more holy. See HOLY.

HOLIEST, most holy. See HOLY.
which is called the *h.*, Heb. 9:3.
way into the *h.* was, Heb. 9:8.
enter into the *h.* by, Heb. 10:19.

HOLINESS, the Hebrew and Greek words indicate a separation, a setting apart. These words thus involve the general ideas of sanctity; separation from all that is sinful. It is used of persons, places, things. The idea is also involved in the words sanctify, sanctified, etc. Holiness as a quality in man is enjoined on the basis of God's holiness (I Sam. 2:2, Rev. 15:4). It is both the ground (I Pet. 1:16) and the standard of man's holiness (Matt. 5:48). Places and things are holy in the sense of being dedicated to a purpose, or ceremonially consecrated (Ex. 3:5, Josh. 5:15, Hab. 2:20, Is. 11:9).

like thee glorious in *h.*, Ex. 15:11.
h. to the Lord, Ex. 28:36.
throne of his *h.*, Ps. 47:8.
Israel was *h.* to Lord, Jer. 2:3.
sworn by his *h.*, Amos 4:2.
to Spirit of *h.*, Rom. 1:4.
unblameable, in *h.*, I Thess. 3:13.
partakers of his *h.*, Heb. 12:10.

HOLLOW, not solid; having a cavity.
h. of his thigh. Gen. 32:25.
make altar *h.* with, Ex. 27:8.
God clave *h.* place, Judg. 15:19.
measured waters in *h.*, Is. 40:12.

HOLM-TREE, (Is. 44:14), a type of oak, incorrectly called "cypress" in the King James Version. This is one of the finest trees of Bible lands.

HOLON, HILEN, (1) a town in the mountains of Judah (Josh. 15:51, 21:15). (2) City in the plains of Moab on which judgment was pronounced by Jeremiah (Jer. 48:21).

HOLY, (1) sacred; (2) hallowed, set apart to the worship of God.
thou standest is *h.*, Ex. 3:5.
to me a *h.* nation, Ex. 19:6.
sabbath to keep it *h.*, Ex. 20:8.
Lord your God am *h.*, Lev. 19:2.
Levites *h.* to Lord, II Chr. 35:3.
by mouth of *h.* prophets, Luke 1:70.
against thy *h.* child, Acts 4:27.
with a *h.* kiss, Rom. 16:16.
to present you *h.*, Col. 1:22.
a *h.* priesthood, I Pet. 2:5.
H. h. h. Lord God, Rev. 4:8.
let him be *h.* still, Rev. 22:11.

HOLY DAY, in Ps. 42:4 the Hebrew word means to celebrate as a religious festival. In Col. 2:16 it is better understood as a feast day.

HOLY GHOST, HOLY SPIRIT, variously called "the Spirit" (I Tim. 4:1) or the "Spirit of God" or the "Spirit of Christ", etc. The doctrine of the Holy Spirit, as part of the doctrine of the Trinity is in part at least beyond human comprehension, and we are limited to the statements of the Scriptures. The Scriptures present the Holy Spirit as a distinct personality and as part of the Godhead or Trinity (Matt. 3:16–17, 28:19, John 14:16–17, 15:26), and personal pronouns are used (John 16:13–14, Acts 13:2). His deity is likewise emphasized by giving to him names that belong to God (Acts 5:3–4, Is. 6:9, Heb. 10:15) and divine attributes are stated as belonging to him (I Cor. 2:11, 12:11, Heb. 9:14).

The work of the Holy Spirit is of the utmost importance to men. He is the immediate source of life (Ps. 104:29, Job 32:8, Num. 11:17); he played a part in the coming of Christ (Luke 1:35, John 1:32, 3:34); and he is the revealer of divine truth and thus the source of the inspired Scriptures (John 14:26, 16:13, I Cor. 2:10–13, II Tim. 3:16). This means the Holy Spirit is active in conversions and in the edification of the believer by the Word of which he is the author (Eph. 6:17, John 16:8—cf. Acts 2:37—Acts 20:32). As part of this the Holy Spirit is said to dwell in us (Rom. 8:9, I Cor. 6:19–20, Eph. 4:30, Eph. 5:18, etc.).

HOLY WEEK, this is a modern term used to refer to the week of the Crucifixion and the Resurrection. It is commemorated during the week before Easter.

HOMAN, a son of Lotan, grandson of Seir (I Chr. 1:39). Also called Hemam (Gen. 36:22).

HOME, place of residence. Biblical use of "house" to mean "family," and "home" to mean "residence" is the opposite of modern distinctions between these terms.
man goeth to long *h.*, Eccles. 12:5.
neither keepeth at *h.*, Hab. 2:5.
go *h.* to thy friends, Mark 5:19.
he cometh *h.* he calleth, Luke 15:6.
took her to his own *h.*, John 19:27.
let him eat at *h.*, I Cor. 11:34.
at *h.* in the body, II Cor. 5:6.
chaste, keepers at *h.*, Titus 2:5.

HOMER, a Hebrew measure of capacity equalling ten ephahs (Ezek. 45:11).

HONEST, sincere, earnest.
h. and good heart, Luke 8:15.
provide things *h.*, Rom. 12:17.
whatsoever things are *h.*, Phil. 4:8.
in godliness and *h.*, I Tim. 2:2.
h. among the Gentiles, I Pet. 2:12.

HONESTLY, honorably, uprightly.
walk *h.* as in day, Rom. 13:13.
may walk *h.* toward, I Thess. 4:12.

HONEY, a choice article of food. The wandering Israelites described the appealing land of Canaan as the land "flowing with milk and honey" (Ex. 3:8, 17). Bees were abundant even in the remote crevices of the desert rocks. The principle word for honey also means grape honey, which the Israelites made. This is what Jacob sent Joseph (Gen. 43:11). Honey was used with pastry (Ex. 16:31) and mingled with the drink as well as eaten alone. The wild honey which John the Baptist ate (Matt. 3:4) could have been either vegetable honey or honey of wild bees. Josephus mentions honey made from grapes.
floweth with milk and *h.*, Josh. 5:6.
bees and *h.* in the carcase Judg. 14:8.
h. and the honeycomb, Ps. 19:10.
locusts and wild *h.*, Matt. 3:4.
thy mouth as sweet as *h.*, Rev. 10:9.

HONEYCOMB.
lips drop as a *h.*, Prov. 5:3.
pleasant words an *h.*, Prov. 16:24.
soul loatheth an *h.*, Prov. 27:7.
broiled fish and of an *h.*, Luke 24:42.

HONOUR, HONOR, respect paid to God (I Chr. 16:27, Ps. 66:2, 96:6); to parents, kings, etc. (Ex. 20:12, I Pet. 2:17); to the wise, good, etc. (Prov. 15:33, 29:23). Also used of the reward, status, etc. given to subjects (Num. 22:17, 37, II Chr. 1:11–12) and finally to the righteous (John 5:44, Heb. 2:7, II Pet. 1:17).
will get me *h.*, Ex. 14:17.
full of riches and *h.*, I Chr. 29:28.
prophet not without *h.*, Matt. 13:57.
seek for glory and *h.*, Rom. 2:7.
worthy of double *h.*, I Tim. 5:17.
builded, hath more *h.*, Heb. 3:3.
receive glory and *h.*, Rev. 5:12.

HONOUR, to show honour to. *See* HONOUR above.
h. father and mother, Ex. 20:12.
they *h.* God and man, Judg. 9:9.
and *h.* not his father, Matt. 15:6.
h. widows that are, I Tim. 5:3.
h. all men, fear God, I Pet. 2:17.

HONOURABLE, deserving honor, noble.
of Arimathaea, an *h.*, Mark 15:43.
also of *h.* women not a, Acts 17:12.
marriage is *h.* in all, Heb. 13:4.

HONOURETH, *see* HONOUR.

HOOD, a type of headdress composed of twisted cloths of various colors (Is. 3:23).

HOOF, horny part of an animal's foot.
h. be left behind, Ex. 10:26.
parteth the *h.*, Lev. 11:3.
I will make thy *h.* brass, Mic. 4:13.

HOOK, (1) a ring, placed in the nose of animals or captives, to lead them (II Kin. 19:28, Is. 37:29, II Chr. 33:11). (2) A vinedresser's pruning hook (Is. 2:4, 18:5, Joel 3:10). (3) A fleshhook for taking meat out of the pot (Ex. 27:3, I Sam. 2:13–14).

HOOPOE, lapwing (Lev. 11:19; Deut. 14:18).

HOPE, the Biblical idea embraces both the expectation and the desire for the thing expected. Sometimes the term refers to the expectation itself, and sometimes to the thing expected (Col. 1:5). The non-Christian has "no hope" (Eph. 2:12); or the hope of the wicked shall come to naught (Prov. 11:23, 24: 20); but the hope of the righteous is not in vain (Ps. 9:18, 37:4–5, 40:4).
set their *h.* in God, Ps. 78:7.
the *h.* of his people, Joel 3:16.
rejoice in *h.*, Rom. 5:2.
we are saved by *h.*, Rom. 8:24.
faith, *h.*, and love, I Cor. 13:13.
which have no *h.*, I Thess. 4:13.
a *h.* that is in you, I Pet. 3:15.

HOPE, to desire.
that I should *h.*, Job 6:11.
I *h.* in thy word, Ps. 119:81.
promise our tribes *h.*, Acts 26:7.
why doth he *h.* for, Rom. 8:24.
I *h.* to send presently, Phil. 2:23.
be sober, and *h.*, I Pet. 1:13.

HOPHNI, one of Eli's two sons, and a wicked priest (I Sam. 2:12, 27–36, 3:11). Perished in the battle of Aphek (I Sam. 4:11ff).

HOR, MOUNT, the mountain. (1) The mountain on which Aaron died (Num. 20:25–27). It was at the edge of Edom (Num. 33:37). (2) A mountain named only in Num. 34:7–8 as a mark of the northern boundary of Israel. Probably refers to the Lebanon range. *See* **MOUNT HOR.**

HORAM, king of Gezer, overthrown by Joshua (Josh. 10:33).

HOREB, used interchange⸱ ⸱ly with Sinai as the place where the law was given (Ex. 3:1, 17:6, 33:6, I Kin. 8:9). Some consider it a lower part or peak of Mt. Sinai, others the name of a whole mountain of which Sinai was a peak. *See* **SINAI.**

HOREM, a "fenced city" of Naphtali (Josh. 19:38).

HOR-HAGIDGAD, a station of Israel in the wilderness (Num. 33:32–33).

HORI, (1) a son of Lotan, grandson of Seir (Gen. 36:22, I Chr. 1:39). (2) A Simeonite whose son, Shaphat, was sent by Moses to explore Canaan (Num. 13:5).

HORIM, Deut. 2:12, 22. *See* **HORITE.**

HORITE, several references to an obscure people, the Horites or Horim (see above). They were defeated by Chedorlaomer (Gen. 14:6) and destroyed by Esau's descendants (Deut. 2:12, 22). Today they have been identified as Hurrians.

HORMAH, principal town of a Canaanitish king in southern Palestine (Josh. 12:14) where the Israelites were defeated when trying to go into Canaan against God's will (Num. 14:45, 21:1–3, Deut. 1:44, Josh. 15:30, 19:4).

HORN, several uses of the word in Scripture. (1) Trumpets or horns to blow. At first they were just horns, perforated at the tip; later they were made of metal, as the silver trumpets of the priests (Num. 10:1ff). (2) Vessels, flasks, etc. made of horn and used for drinking, etc. (I Sam.

16:1, 13). (3) The projections of the altar of burnt offering (Ex. 27:2, 30:2) were called "horns" (I Kin. 1:50). (4) Peak or summit of a hill (Is. 5:1).
push with his *h.*, Ex. 21:29.
Samuel took *h.* of oil, I Sam. 16:13.
came forth a little *h.*, Dan. 8:9.
raised up an *h.* of, Luke 1:69.

HORNET, named as a pest through which God would drive out Israel's enemies from the land of promise (Ex. 23:28, Deut. 7:20, Josh. 24:12).

HORONAIM, a city in southern Moab (Jer. 48:3, 34, Is. 15:5) near Zoar.

HORONITE, a title given to Sanballat, who opposed Nehemiah (Neh. 2:10, 19, 13:28), since he was from Bethhoron.

HORRIBLE, dreadful, terrifying.
up also out of a *h.* pit, Ps. 40:2.
h. thing is committed, Jer. 5:30.
seen in the prophets *h.*, Jer. 23:14.
have seen a *h.* thing, Hos. 6:10.

HORSE, horses were used much by the Egyptians (Gen. 47:17; Ex. 9:3; 14:9; 15:19). Solomon imported many horses from Egypt, and after his time they became common in Palestine for warfare (I Kin. 22:4; II Kin. 3:7; 9:18; 9:33). Before their introduction into Egypt horses had been domesticated by Indo-European nomads east of the Black Sea. Hebrews were at first forbidden to retain captured horses (Deut. 17:16; Josh. 11:4–9), but they soon ceased to regard this restriction. Riding a horse was usually a sign of military rank, but many high functionaries rode other animals (Zech. 9:9).

HORSEGATE, a gate in the old wall of Jerusalem at the west end of the bridge leading from Zion to the Temple (Neh. 3:28, Jer. 31:40).

HORSELEACH, the term (Prov. 30:15) is of uncertain meaning, but it may be "sucker." There are a variety of leaches or bloodsuckers in the east, bothersome to man and beast.

HORSES, *see* **HORSE.**

HOSAH, hopeful. (1) a city of Asher, on the boundary line from Tyre to Achzib (Josh. 19:29). (2) A Levite of the family of Meran who was appointed doorkeeper to the ark after it arrived in Jerusalem (I Chr. 16:38).

HOSANNA, the exclamation of the people during Christ's triumphal entry into Jerusalem (Matt. 21:9, 15, Mark 11:9–10). It is taken from Ps. 118:25 and means "Save, we pray!" It also occurs in II Kin. 19:19.

HOSEA, the name is identical with Joshua and Hoshea in derivation and meaning. Hosea, son of Beeri, is the first of the minor prophets in the Hebrew canon. He prophesied in the reign of Uzziah, Jotham, Ahaz, and Hezekiah in Judah or Jeroboam II in Israel (Hos. 1:1). The exact length of his activity is unknown, but it probably would run through most of the last half of the eighth century, B.C. (c.748–700). This being true, Hosea lived through the last days of Israel, the northern kingdom. Israel was the scene of his prophetic activity (5:1, 6:8–9), and his time and relation to Israel were similar to those of Jeremiah with Judah and its fall, over a century later. Various views have been taken about his marriage to Gomer, an impure woman, evidently by God's command (1:2–9). Some believe there were two marriages, the first in chap. 1–2 and the second in chapter 3. Both of these women and these marriages represented Israel and God's relation to her. Others (e.g. Keil) view it as an, "internal event" or "spiritual intuition". Another view is that "wife of whoredom" (1:2) is not a prostitute but a woman who violated her marriage vows and in continuing with her and receiving her back. Hosea both feels and illustrates God's love for unfaithful Israel.

HOSEA, BOOK OF, the facts about the author are given above. The prophecy concerns Israel, but some think the book itself was composed in Judah after the fall of Israel. This book is the prophecy of God's unchanging love for Israel. A fourfold theme: Israel's idolatry, wickedness, captivity, and restoration. Hosea's three children and their names help portray God and Israel's relation: Jezreel (God sows seed), Lo-ruhamah (not shown mercy), and Lo-ammi (not my people). The book has two main

parts: chapters 1–3 in narrative form give Hosea's domestic experience. Chapters 4–14 are a series of denunciations, pleas, and exhortations. The theme is 4:1, "There is no truth, no mercy, no knowledge of God in the land." Yet even then, God holds out hope of repentance and restoration (chapter 14).

HOSEN, an article of clothing like a coat or tunic (Dan. 3:21).

HOSHAIAH, (1) a man who assisted in the dedication of the wall of Jerusalem after Nehemiah rebuilt it (Neh. 12:32). (2) Father of Jezaniah or Azariah, one of the men who urged Jeremiah to allow the Jews to flee from Nebuchadnezzar into Egypt (Jer. 42:1, 43:2).

HOSHAMA, a son of King Johoiathin, born during his captivity (I Chr. 3:18).

HOSHEA, Hebrew for Hosea. (1) Original name of Joshua, sometimes written Oshea (Deut. 32:44, Num. 13:8, 16). (2) Son of Elah and last king of Israel. Slew his predecessor Pekah (II Kin. 15:30). Successive invasions by Assyria led to fall of Samaria in 721 B.C. (II Kin. 17:5–6, 18:9–12). Hoshea's ultimate fate is unknown. (3) Son of Azaziah and prince of Ephraim in the time of David (I Chr. 27:20). (4) A chief of Israel who joined in the covenant with Nehemiah (Neh. 10:23).

HOSPITALITY, a solemn duty among the Orientals, including the Hebrews (Lev. 19:34). There are many Old Testament illustrations (Gen. 18:1–8, 19:1–3, 24:25). The same principle applies in the New Testament (Luke 14:12–14, Tit. 1:8, I Pet. 4:9, Heb. 13:2). The basic idea of the Greek word is "love of strangers".
given to *h.*, Rom. 12:13.
given to *h.*, I Tim. 3:2.
use *h.* one to another, I Pet. 4:9.

HOST, (1) used of one who receives and entertains hospitably (Rom. 16:23). (2) One who receives "all," or an innkeeper (Luke 10:35). (3) Used of armies (Ex. 14:28, 15:4, II Sam. 24:4).
earth finished and all *h.*, Gen. 2:1.
the *h.* of Issachar, Num. 10:14.
and *h.* in Red Sea, Ps. 136:15.

prince of the *h.*, Dan. 8:11.
multitude of heavenly *h.*, Luke 2:13.

HOSTS, LORD OF, *see* **LORD OF HOSTS.**

HOSTAGE, one delivered over to another as security for some future act. A common practice in ancient warfare to capture and bargain with hostages (II Kin. 14:14, II Chr. 25:24).

HOT, fiery, violent.
h., and he cast the, Ex. 32:19.
bread we took *h.*, Josh. 9:12.
Lord waxed *h.* Judg. 2:14, 20.
furnace exceeding *h.*, Dan. 3:22.
seared with a *h.* iron, I Tim. 4:2.
neither cold nor *h.*, Rev. 3:16.

HOTHAM, one of the sons of Heber, and grandson of Asher (I Chr. 7:32). Probably same as Helem (vs. 35–37).

HOTHAN, an Aroerite, father of Shama and Jehiel, two of David's men (I Chr. 11:44).

HOTHIR, son of Heman, who with his kinsmen had charge of a group of the Levitical singers (I Chr. 25:4, 28).

HOUGH, a method of "hamstringing" or rendering useless the horses of Israel's enemies by cutting the tendons of the hind legs (Josh. 11:6, II Sam. 8:4, I Chr. 18:4).

HOUR, period of time.
in the selfsame *h.*, Matt. 8:13.
in that same *h.*, Matt. 10:19.
of that day and *h.*, Matt. 24:36.
watch with me one *h.*, Matt. 26:40.
h. is coming in, John 5:28.
third *h.* of the day, Acts 2:15.
temple at the *h.* of prayer, Acts 3:1.
same *h.* of the night, Acts 16:33.
the *h.* of temptation. Rev. 3:10.

HOURS, more than one hour. *See* **HOUR.**
are there not twelve *h.*, John 11:9.
about two *h.*, Great, Acts 19:34.

HOUSE, the formerly nomadic Israelites lived in houses first in Egypt and later, of course, in Palestine. Building materials varied with locale and the builder's prosperity. The poor used mud, brick, lime and sandstone; the rich used hewn stone (I Kin. 7:9). While houses of the poor

had only one story (and often one room) those of the rich often had two, and were built around a courtyard (II Sam. 17:18). The upper chamber was used for group activities because necessary pillars made lower rooms small (I Kin. 17:19; II Kin. 4:10; Mark 14:15; Acts 1:13). The flat roofs were used for various purposes (Josh. 2:6; I Sam. 9:25; Acts 10:9), and outside stairs to the roof were common (Matt. 24:17). The word "house" is often used in Scripture in the sense of "household" or "family."
father's *h.*, unto a land, Gen. 12:1.
h., we will serve, Josh. 24:15.
an *h.* as he promised, I Kin. 2:24.
mountain of the Lord's *h.*, Is. 2:2.
all that are in the *h.*, Matt. 5:15.
wise man which built his *h.*, Matt. 7:24.
ye devour widow's *h.*, Matt. 23:14.
Solomon built an *h.*, Acts 7:47.
feared God with all his *h.*, Acts 10:2.
be saved and thy *h.*, Acts 16:31.
the church in their *h.*, Rom. 16:5.
h. of this tabernacle, II Cor. 5:1.
the *h.* of faith, Gal. 6:10.
ruleth well his own *h.*, I Tim. 3:4.
in the *h.* of God, I Tim. 3:15.
is builded by some man, Heb. 3:4.

HOUSEHOLD, family.
will command his *h.*, Gen. 18:19.
call them of his *h.*, Matt. 10:25.
was baptized and her *h.*, Acts 16:15.
are of Aristobulus' *h.*, Rom. 16:10.
of the *h.* of God, Eph. 2:19.
are of Caesar's *h.*, Phil. 4:22.

HOUSEHOLDER, head of a family.
servants of the *h.*, Matt. 13:27.
a certain *h.* planted, Matt. 21:33.

HOUSETOP, flat roof of a house.
grass on the *h.t.*, Is. 37:27.
preach ye upon the *h.t.*, Matt. 10:27.
on the *h.t.* not come, Matt. 24:17.
the *h.t.* to pray, Acts 10:9.

HOWL, cry, wail.
h. ye for day of Lord, Is. 13:6.
h. for Babylon, Jer. 51:8.
I will wail and *h.*, Micah 1:8.
rich men, weep and *h.*, James 5:1.

HOZAI, this is perhaps a proper name the author of a history of Manasseh (II Chr. 33:19). The King James Version renders "sayings of the seers."

HUKKOK, a city on the southern border of Naphtali (Josh. 19:34). Another city of that name is mentioned in I Chr. 6:75. (Helkath in Josh. 21:31).

HUKOK, see HUKKOK.

HUL, son of Aram, grandson of Shem (Gen. 10:23, I Chr. 1:17).

HULDAH, a prophetess, wife of Shallum, who lived in Jerusalem in the reign of Josiah, who sent Hilkiah to her. She prophesied concerning Josiah and the destruction of Jerusalem (II Kin. 22:14–20, II Chr. 34:22–28).

HUMBLE, to be meek, not proud.
to *h.* thee, Deut. 8:2.
people shall *h.,* II Chr. 7:14.
a man shall be *h.,* Is. 2:11.
shall *h.* himself, Matt. 18:4.
h. himself shall be exalted, Luke 18:14.
he *h.* himself, Phil. 2:8.
h. yourselves, James 4:10.
h. yourselves under the, I Pet. 5:6.

HUMBLY, in meekness.
I *h.* beseech thee, II Sam. 16:4.
love mercy and walk *h.,* Mic. 6:8.

HUMIAH, a city of Judah, near Hebron (Josh. 15:54).

HUMILITY, HUMILIATION, lowliness, meek.
before honour is *h.,* Prov. 15:33.
h. his judgment was taken, Acts 8:33.
the Lord with all *h.* of mind, Acts 20:19.
voluntary *h.* and worshipping, Col. 2:18.
clothed with *h.,* I Pet. 5:5.

HUNDRED, HUNDREDS, one of the groups into which Moses divided the people (Ex. 18:21).
have an *h.* sheep, and one, Matt. 18:12.
shall receive an *h.,* Matt. 19:29.
some sixty, and some an *h.,* Mark. 4:8.
about an *h.* and twenty, Acts 1:15.
above five *h.* brethren, I Cor. 15:6.
was four *h.* and thirty, Gal. 3:17.
an *h.* and forty, Rev. 7:4.

HUNGER, to want food.
they which *h.* and thirst, Matt. 5:6.
h. with good things Luke 1:53.
shall never *h.,* John 6:35.
enemy *h.,* feed him, Rom. 12:20.

full and to be *h.,* Phil. 4:12.
with sword and with *h.,* Rev. 6:8.

HUNGRY, feeling hunger. See HUNGER.
h. and thirsty, soul, Ps. 107:5.
bread to the *h.,* Ezek. 18:7.
hath filled the *h.* with, Luke 1:53.
Peter became very *h.,* Acts 10:10.
be full and to be *h.,* Phil. 4:12.

HUNT, to pursue for capture or killing.
Esau went to field to *h.,* Gen. 27:5.
evil *h.* violent man, Ps. 140:11.
h. them from every, Jer. 16:16.
h. every man his brother, Mic. 7:2.

HUNTER, one who hunts. See HUNT.
mighty *h.* before Lord, Gen. 10:9.
Esau was a cunning *h.,* Gen. 25:27.
from hand of the *h.,* Prov. 6:5.

HUNTEST, hunts. See HUNT.
yet thou *h.* my soul, I Sam. 24:11.
h. me as a fierce lion, Job 10:16.

HUNTING, inscriptions from Egypt and Babylon show the popularity of this sport among ancient kings. First mentioned Biblically in Gen. 10:9, hunting was done by farmers and shepherds to secure food (Gen. 27:3) or to defend flocks from beasts of prey (I Sam. 17:34). Equipment included bows (Gen. 27:31), slings (I Sam. 17:40), net, snares and pits (Is. 51:20; II Sam. 23:20). Moses gave laws about the blood of game (Lev. 17:13) and about birds (Deut. 22:6).

HUPHAM, see HUPPIM.

HUPHAMITES, descendants of Hupham (Num. 26:39).

HUPPAH, a priest of David's time, in charge of the thirteenth class of priests (I Chr. 24:13).

HUPPIM, (Gen. 46:21; I Chr. 7:12), supposedly same as Hupham, but the latter passage above seems to make Huppim grandson of Benjamin, not a son.

HUR, (1) a man connected with Moses and Aaron at the defeat of the Amalekites (Ex. 17:10, 12, 24:14). (2) Grandfather of Bezaleel, a workman in the tabernacle (Ex. 31:2, 35:30). (3) One of five kings of Midian killed with Balaam by the Israelites (Num. 31:8). (4) Father of Ben-Hur,.

HURAI, a native of the valleys of Mt. Gaash (I Chr. 11:32, II Sam. 23:30).

HURAM, *see* **HIRAM.**

HURI, a descendant of Gad, (I Chr. 5:14).

HURT, damage.
sweareth to his *h.*, Ps. 15:4.
they devise my *h.*, Ps. 41:7.
healed *h.* of my people, Jer. 6:14.
voyage will be with *h.*, Acts 27:10.

HURT, (1) to cause pain; (2) to damage.
suffer him not to *h.*, Gen. 31:7.
not *h.* nor destroy in, Is. 11:9.
it shall not *h.* them, Mark 16:18.

HURTFUL, damaging.
city is *h.* to kings, Ezra 4:15.
David from the *h.* sword, Ps. 144:10.
fall into *h.* lusts, I Tim. 6:9.

HUSBAND, the man to whom a woman is married is her husband.
wife gave Hagar to *h.*, Gen. 16:3.
neither am I her *h.*, Hos. 2:2.
if her *h.* be dead, she, Rom. 7:3.
reconciled to her *h.*, I Cor. 7:11.
she reverence her *h.*, Eph. 5:33.
bride adorned for *h.*, Rev. 21:2.

HUSBANDMAN, a farmer or other worker of the soil (Gen. 9:20, 26:12, 37:7).

HUSHAH, a descendant of Hur in the tribe of Judah (I Chr. 4:4, II Sam. 21:18).

HUSHAI, a friend and companion of David (II Sam. 15:32ff, 16:16ff).

HUSHAM, a Temanite and native prince of Mt. Seir (Gen. 36:34–35, I Chr. 1:45, 46).

HUSHATHITE, of David's men (Sibbechai), probably indicating he was from Hushah (II Sam. 21:18, I Chr. 11:29).

HUSHIM, (1) son of Dan (Gen. 46:23). (2) A name given as that of the "sons of Asher," (I Chr. 7:12, 8:1). (3) A wife of Shaharaim, (I Chr. 8:8, 11).

HUSKS, (1) outer covering of corn (Num. 6:4; II Kin. 4:42); (2) Pods of the carob tree (Luke 15:16).

HUZ, UZ, son of Nahor and Milcah (Gen. 22:1).

HUZZAB, (Nahum 2:7) is established.

HYACINTH, *see* **JACINTH.**

HYENA, a carnivorous mammal (I Sam. 13:18).

HYMENAEUS, a person in Ephesus who with Alexander (I Tim. 1:20) and Philetus (II Tim. 2:17) had departed from the truth and made "shipwreck of the faith."

HYMN, a song of praise (Eph. 5:19; Col. 3:16). Jesus and His Apostles sang a hymn after the Last Supper (Matt. 26:30; Mark 14:26).

HYPOCRISY, originally an actor; then it came to be applied to one, especially in religion, who pretended to be what he was not. This term is most frequently used by Christ in his denunciation of the Pharisees (Matt. 23:13–14ff).

HYPOCRITE, a false pretender.
h.'s hope shall perish, Job. 8:13.
thou *h.*, first cast, Matt. 7:5.
scribes, Pharisees, *h.*, Luke 11:44.
thou *h.*, doth not each, Luke 13:15.

HYPOCRITICAL, feigning, pretending.
with *h.* mockers, Ps. 35:16.
against an *h.* nation, Is. 10:6.

HYSSOP, a plant described in I Kin. 4:33 as one "that springeth out of the wall." A bunch of hyssop was used to sprinkle blood in various sacrificial and purification ceremonies of the Jews (Ex. 12:22, Lev. 14:6, 49, Ps. 51:7, Heb. 9:19).

HYSTASPIS, DARIUS, *see* **DARIUS.**

I

I AM, literally, He Who Is, a title for God (Ex. 3:14).

IBHAR, one of the sons of David, born in Jerusalem (I Chr. 3:6).

IBLEAM, a city with surrounding villages of Asher, assigned to Manasseh (Josh. 17:11).

IBENEIAH, son of Jehoram, a Benjamite (I Chr. 9:8).

IBRI, a Merarite Levite in the time of David (I Chr. 24:27).

IBZAN, the tenth "judge of Israel" (Judg. 12:8–10).

ICHABOD, the son of Phineas and grandson of Eli (I Sam. 4:21).

ICONIUM, a city of Paul's First Missionary Journey (Acts 14:1–6), capital of Lyaconia, center of carpet making and leather working. It was on the Roman road from Ephesus to the Euphrates Valley, 120 miles north of the Mediterranean Sea.

IDALAH, one of the cities of the tribe of Zebulon (Josh. 19:15).

IDBASH, a man of Judah (I Chr. 4:3).

IDDO, (1) the father of Abinadab (I Kin. 4:14), (2) a Gershonite Levite, father of Zerah (I Chr. 6:21), (3) son of Zechariah and ruler of the half-tribe of Manasseh, East (I Chr. 27:21), (4) a seer whose "visions" against Jereboam contained some of the acts of Solomon (II Chr. 9:29). (5) The grandfather of the prophet, Zechariah (Zech. 1:1), and (6) the chief of the Jews established at Casiphia. It was to him that Ezra sent for Levites and Nethinim to join his company (Ezra 8-17–20).

IDLE, (1) one who is slothful or lazy (Ex. 5:8), (2) one unemployed (Matt. 20:3), (3) an unprofitable person or word (Matt. 12:36).

IDOL, see IMAGE. (Col. 3:5).
turn ye not unto *i*, Lev. 19:4.
served groves and *i*, II Chr. 24:18.
sacrificed unto the *i*, Ps. 106:38.
that abhorest *i*, Rom. 2:22.
not worship devils, and *i*, Rev. 2:14.

IDOLATRY, the worship of idols or gods supposedly dwelling in images or represented by them. This ancient practice existed among the ancestors of the Israelites (Josh. 24:2; Gen. 31:30) and in all the nations that had contact with Israel, except Persia. God commanded the destruction of all idols (Num. 33:52; Deut. 7:5; 29:17). Solomon allowed his foreign wives to practice idolatry. After revolting and establishing the northern kingdom, Jeroboam set up images unto God. Later Kings Ahab and Manasseh encouraged Baalism (I Kin. 16:31; II Kin. 21:2). Paul denounces idolatry in Acts 15:29; 17:24–30 and I Cor. 8:1–8. The Christian must guard against idols of the heart (Col. 3:5; I John 5:21).
beloved, flee from *i*, I Cor. 10:14.
covetousness, which is *i*, Col. 3:5.

IDUMEA, Greek form of Edom.
in the land of *I*, Is. 34:6.
mount Seir, and all *I*, Ezek. 35:15.
I, and beyond Jordan, Mark 3:8.

IDUMEAN, one of Idumea.

IEZER, *see* ABIEZER.

IEZERITE, *see* ABI-EZRITE.

IGAL, (1) the son of Joseph and agent from Issachar to spy out the land of Canaan (Num. 13:7), (2) the son of Nathan and one of David's mighty warriors (II Sam. 23:36), and (3) same as Igeal (I Chr. 3:22).

IGDALIAH, father of Hanan (Jer. 35:4).

IGEAL, *see* IGAL.

IGNORANCE, lack of knowledge.
shall sin through *i*, Lev. 4:2.
through *i* you did it, Acts 3:17.
compassion on the *i*, Heb. 5:2.
willingly are *i* of, II Pet. 3:5.

IGNORANT, unlearned, uninformed.
they were *i*. men, Acts 4:13.
not have you *i*., Rom. 1:13.
let him be *i*., I Cor. 14:38.
i. of Satan's devices, II Cor. 2:11.
they are willingly *i*., II Pet. 3:5.

IGNORANTLY, without knowledge.
soul that sinneth *i*., Num. 15:28.
ye *i*. worship, declare, Acts 17:23.
because I did it *i*. in, I Tim. 1:13.

IIM, IYIM, a city in the extreme south of Judah (Josh. 15:29).

IJEABARIM, IYEABARIM, station of the Israelites in the wilderness (Num. 33:44).

IJON, a town of Naphtali in North Palestine (I Kin. 15:20).

IKKESH, father of Ira the Tekoite (II Sam. 23:26).

ILAI, also called Zalmon, one of David's heroes (I Chr. 11:29; II Sam. 23:28).

ILLUMINATED, given light, spoken of. Christians who had a saving knowledge of the Gospel (Heb. 10:32).

ILLYRICUM, used only once in Scripture in II Tim. 4:10, referring to the area immediately North of present-day Greece.

IMAGE, *see* **IDOLATRY,** a likeness, similarity.
man in our *i*, Gen. 1:26.
and behold a great *i*, Dan. 2:31.
whose *i* and super-, Luke 20:24.
Christ, who is the *i*, II Cor. 4:4.
not the very *i* of the, Heb. 10:1.

IMAGINE, to meditate, devise, purpose.
which they have *i*. to, Gen. 11:6.
people *i*. a vain thing?, Ps. 2:1.
do you *i*. against, Nahum 1:9.
you *i*. evil against his, Zech. 8:17.

IMLA, IMLAH, father of the prophet, Micaiah (II Chr. 18:7).

IMMANUEL, *see* **EMMANUEL,** (God is with us). Symbolic name of the child whose birth Isaiah promised as a sign of deliverance to King Ahaz (Is. 7:14; 8:8) when Judah was direly threatened by Syrian-Ephraimic forces. Matthew 1:23 applies the prediction also to the Messiah.

IMMEDIATELY, from that very time, soon, promptly, instantly, straightway.
i. the man was made, John 5:9.
I. therefore I sent to, Acts 10:33.

IMMER, (1) father of Meshillemith (I Chr. 9:12) whose descendants returned from Babylon with Zerubbabel (Ezra 2:37), (2) a priest in the time of David (I Chr. 24:14), (3) one who accompanied Zerubbabel from Babylon (Ezra 2:59),

(4) the father of Zadok (Neh. 3:29), and (5) the father of Pashur (Jer. 20:1).

IMMORTAL, without mortality, a characteristic of God listed in I Tim. 1:17.

IMMORTALITY, unending existence. The question of life after death vexed the Hebrews (Job 14:14) and, while individual immortality was only glimpsed by the Old Testament people (Heb. 11:13–16), the doctrine is asserted (Job 19:25–27; Ps. 49:15; 16:10; 73:24; Dan. 12:2). Vagueness and uncertainty, however, led the Hebrews to cherish most temporal promises as reward for obedience. Pharisees and Sadducees in Jesus' day were split on the immortality issue (Luke 20:27–38). Jesus illuminated the truth of immortality (II Tim. 1:10), and, thus, the New Testament confidently affirms it (Matt. 13:43; 25:31–46; John 3:16; 14:1–3; I Cor. 15:19–58; I Thess. 4:13–18).
them who seek for *i*, Rom. 2:7.
mortal must put on *i*, I Cor. 15:53.
shall have put on *i*, I Cor. 15:54.
only hath *i*. dwelling, I Tim. 6:16.
brought *i*. to light, II Tim. 1:10.

IMMUTABILITY, IMMUTABLE, unchangeable. (Heb. 6:17, 18).

IMNA, a son of Helem (I Chr. 7:35).

IMNAH, JIMNA, JIMNAH, (1) the first named of the sons of Asher (I Chr. 7:30) and (2) the father of Kore (II Chr. 31:14).

IMNITES, descendants of Imnah (Num. 26:44).

IMPART, to apportion, give a share of.
neither hath he *i*. to, Job 39:17.
let him *i*. to him that, Luke 3:11.
that I may *i*. unto you, Rom. 1:11.

IMPEDIMENT, hindrance, fault.
one that had *i*. in, Mark 7:32.

IMPLACABLE, not ready to forgive or placate.
natural affection, *i*., Rom. 1:31.

IMPORTUNITY, shamelessly.
of his *i*. he will rise, Luke 11:8.

IMPOSE, lay upon.
not lawful to *i* toll, Ezra 7:24.
ordinances, *i.* on, Heb. 9:10.

IMPOSSIBLE, powerless, weak.
with men this is *i.*, Matt. 19:26.
i. for those who were, Heb. 6:4.
without faith it is *i.*, Heb. 11:6.

IMPOTENT, without power or strength.
deed done to the *i.*, Acts 4:9.
man at Lystra, *i.*, Acts 14:8.

IMPOVERISHED, made poor, weak.
so *i.* that he hath, Is. 40:20.
saith, we are greatly *i.*, Mal. 1:4.

IMPRISONMENT, put in prison.
goods, or to *i.*, Ezra 7:26.
mockings, bonds, *i.*, Heb. 11:36.

IMPUDENT, headstrong, stubborn.
i. children, and stiff, Ezek. 2:4.

IMPUTE, to charge or credit another.
nor shall it be *i.*, Lev. 7:18.
but sin is not *i*, Rom. 4:8.
righteousness might be *i.*, Rom. 4:11.
i. to him for righteous-, James 2:23.

IMRAH, a chief of the tribe of Asher
(I Chr. 7:36).

IMRI, (1) the father of Omri of Judah,
(I Chr. 9:4) and (2) the father of Zaccur
(Neh. 3:2).

INCARNATION, not a Biblical term but
one which refers to the coming of God
(Matt. 1:23) in the flesh, including His
miraculous conception and birth (John
1:1–14; Rom. 1:2–5; Phil. 2:6–11; I
John 1–3). *See* JESUS CHRIST.

INCENSE, an aromatic compound which
gives forth its perfume in burning. Instructions for incense for the Jewish altar
are found in Ex. 30:22–38. The gold plated
altar of incense in the Holy Place was
used twice daily (Ex. 30:1–9). On the
annual day of atonement the high priest
burnt incense in the Holy of Holies
(Lev. 16:12, 13).
censer, and put *i.*, Lev. 10:1.
i. is an abomination, Is. 1:13.
praying at time of *i.*, Luke 1:10.
given to him much *i.*, Rev. 8:3.

INCLINE, to lean toward, bend forward.

i. your hearts to Lord, Josh. 24:23.
i. your ears to the words, Ps. 78:1.
but ye have not *i.*, Jer. 25:4.

INCLOSE, compass, surround, encircle.
are *i.* in their own fat: Ps. 17:10.
the wicked have *i.*, Ps. 22:16.
i. a great multitude of, Luke 5:6.

INCONTINENT, without strength or re-
straint.
false accusers, *i.*, II Tim. 3:3.

INCORRUPTIBLE, cannot be corrupted,
marred, made defective.
shall be raised, *i*, I Cor. 15:52.
seed, but of *i.*, I Pet. 1:23.

INCREASE, abundance, produce, fruit.
yield you the *i.*, Lev. 19:25.
but God gave the *i.*, I Cor. 3:6.
increaseth with *i.* of, Col. 2:19.

INCREASE, to add to, intensify, grow.
i. thy army and come, Judg. 9:29.
they shall *i.* as they, Zech. 10:8.
he must *i*, but I must, John 3:30.
they will *i.* to more, II Tim. 2:16.

INCREDIBLE, not believable.
thought *i.* God should, Acts 26:8.

INCURABLE, not capable of healing.
and my wound *i.*, Jer. 15:18.
for her wound is *i.*, Mic. 1:9.

INDEED, verily, surely, truly, certainly.
yet *i.* she is my sister, Gen. 20:12.
ye shall be free *i.*, John 8:36.
law, neither *i.* can it, Rom. 8:7.
that are widows *i.*, I Tim. 5:3.

INDIA, the country which was the eastern
boundary of the empire of King Ahasuerus (Esther 1:1).

INDIGNATION, insolence, wrath, rage.
he was full of *i.*, Esther 5:9.
pour out thine *i.* upon, Ps. 69:24.
were filled with *i.*, Acts 5:17.

INDITING, bring forth (Ps. 45:1).

INDUSTRIOUS, active, zealous, worker.
and that he was *i.*, I Kin. 11:28.

INEXCUSABLE, without excuse.
therefore thou art *i.*, Rom. 2:1.

INFALLIBLE, without possibility of error (Acts 1:3).

INFANT, suckling, babe.
as *i.* which never saw, Job. 3:16.
no more thence an *i.*, Is. 65:20.

INFIDEL, unbeliever. In modern conversation, this word is practically synonymous with "atheist"; however, the term in II Cor. 6:14–17, an infidel is classified with darkness, unbelievers, and unrighteous, signifying those who reject God's Way, His plan, and His Son.

INFINITE, without end, number, or limit.
his understanding is *i.*, Ps. 147:5.
and it was *i.*, Nahum 3:9.

INFIRMITY, sickness, disease, weakness.
separation for her *i.*, Lev. 12:2.
himself took our *i.*, Matt. 8:17.
which had an *i.* thirty, John 5:5.
of the *i.* of your flesh, Rom. 6:19.
ought to bear the *i.* of, Rom. 15:1.
the feeling of our *i.*, Heb. 4:15.

INFLUENCES, chains, ties, fastenings.
the sweet *i.* of Pleades, Job 38:31.

INGATHERING, FEAST OF, also called the Feast of Tabernacles (II Chr. 8:13) because the Israelites were commanded to live in booths and the Festival of Jehovah (or the Festival) (I Kin. 8:2; II Chr. 5:3) because it was the most important or well known. It was ordered by Moses (Ex. 23:16) to celebrate the ingathering of the labor of the fields, the fruit of the earth (Lev. 23:39), and the ingathering of the threshing floor and the winepress (Deut. 16:13). The dwelling in booths were to be matters of joy in Israel (Lev. 23:41) and was to be a reminder to them of God's fatherly care to them during their wilderness wanderings. The other two great annual feasts were Passover and Pentecost. *See* **TABERNACLE, FEAST OF.**
feast of the *i*, in the, Ex. 23:16.
feast of *i.* at the year, Ex. 34:22.

INHABIT, to dwell, sit down, occupy.
land which ye shall *i.*, Num. 35:34.
shall build houses and *i*, Is. 65:21.
houses, but not *i.*, Zeph. 1:13.

INHABITANT, dweller, occupant.
when the *i.* of the, Gen. 50:11.

all the *i.* of the earth, Ps. 33:14.
the *i.* of the earth have, Rev. 17:2.

INHERIT, heir, possess.
thou mayest *i.* the land, Gen. 28:4.
i. the kingdom pre-, Matt. 25:34.
things shall not *i.*, Gal. 5:21.
faith and patience *i.*, Heb. 6:12.

INHERITANCE, portion, possession, thing occupied. Among the Jews, the land that God gave them was distributed to the next of kin by a rigidly enforced system. Ordinarily the birthright could not be denied the heir but it might be taken away by a trespass against the father (Gen. 49:4). Personal property might be distributed at the will of the owner. This was the property requested by the son in Luke 15:12. *See* **HEIR.**
any portion or *i.* for, Gen. 31:14.
divide the land by *i.*, Num. 34:18.
mar mine own *i.*, Ruth 4:6.
seize on his *i.*, Matt. 21:38.
the earnest of our *i.*, Eph. 1:14.
promise of eternal *i.*, Heb. 9:15.

INIQUITY, INIQUITIES, perversity, injustice, errors, deviating from the true.
not beheld *i.* in Jacob, Num. 23:21.
sins, and for the *i.*, Dan. 9:16.
all ye workers of *i.*, Luke 13:27.
with the reward of *i.*, Acts 1:18.
the bond of *i.* and the, Acts 8:23.
fire, a world of *i.*, James 3:6.

INJURED, to do injustice, to wrong.
ye have not *i.* me at, Gal. 4:12.

INJURIOUS, despiteful, insulting.
who was before . . . *i.*, I Tim. 1:13.

INJUSTICE, violence, injury, wrong.
not for *i.* in my hands, Job 16:17.

INK, any writing substance made of powdered charcoal, lampblack, or soot, mixed with water.
wrote them with *i.*, Jer. 36:18.
would not write with *i.*, II John 12.

INKHORN, (Ezek. 9:2), a long tube for holding pens, sometimes made of wood, but usually of metal. The writer carried the inkhorn in his girdle.

INN, in the Old Testament this word indicates merely a place where one spent

the night, either under a tent or in a cave (Gen. 42:27; Ex. 4:24; Jer. 9:2). Such stops were located near some water supply. Religious observance of hospitality made commercial inns unnecessary (Judg. 19:15-21). "Inns" in a more modern sense are seen in the New Testament (Luke 2:7; 10:34).
for them in the *i.*, Luke 2:7.
brought him to an *i.*, Luke 10:34.

INNER, the one enclosed, innermost.
king into the *i.* court, Esther 4:11.
into the *i.* prison, Acts 16:24.
might in the *i.* man, Eph. 3:16.

INNOCENCY, innocent, pure.
i. of my hands have I, Gen. 20:5.
before him *i.* was found. Dan. 6:22.

INNOCENT, *see* INNOCENCY.

INNUMERABLE, without number.
i. evils have compassed, Ps. 40:12.
i. multitude gathered, Luke 12:1.
is by the sea shore *i.*, Heb. 11:12.
an *i.* company of angels, Heb. 12:22.

INORDINATE, unrestrained, excessive.
corrupt in her *i.* love. Ezek. 23:11.
fornication, *i.* affection, Col. 3:5.

INQUISITION, a seeking out.
shall make diligent *i.*, Deut. 19:18.
when *i.* was made of, Esther 2:23.
maketh *i.* for blood, Ps. 9:12.

INSCRIPTION, writing or engraving.
an altar with this *i.*, Acts 17:23.

INSPIRATION, a supernatural influence by which the writings of God's spokesmen are given Divine trustworthiness. Holy men spake as moved by God (I Pet. 1:20, 21). Jeremiah (13:1), Ezek. (1:3), and the Apostle Paul (Eph. 3:1-10) all claimed to speak by direct revelation. Jesus states that the Old Testament Scriptures were inviolable and Paul also stated that "all scripture" is inspired of God (II Tim. 3:16, 17). Thus, the Scriptures are man's source of information and authority. He may not determine a private interpretation (I Peter 1:20, 21) since God's Word gives man all things that pertain unto life and Godliness (II Pet. 1:3). This faith was once for all delivered to the Saints (Jude 3) and is prof-

itable for all needs; doctrine, reproof, correction, instruction in righteousness that man may be perfect, thoroughly furnished unto every good work (II Tim. 3:16). *See* REVELATION.

INSTANT, urgent, short time.
yea, it shall be an *i.*, Is. 29:5.
coming in that *i.*, Luke 2:38.
patient, continuing *i.*, Rom. 12:12.
the word, be *i.* in, II Tim. 4:2.

INSTRUCT, to teach, nurture.
that he might *i.* thee, Deut. 4:36.
I will *i.* thee and teach, Ps. 32:8.
man was *i.* in the way, Acts 18:25.
meekness *i.* them that, II Tim. 2:25.

INSTRUCTION, chastisement, teaching.
thou hatest *i.*, and, Ps. 50:17.
for *i.* in righteous-, II Tim. 3:16.

INSTRUMENT, tool, weapon.
i. of cruelty are in, Gen. 49:5.
pattern of all the *i.*, Ex. 25:9.
players on *i.* shall be, Ps. 87:7.
thee *i.* of a foolish, Zech. 11:15.
members as *i.* of unright-, Rom. 6:13.

INTEGRITY, perfection, sincerity.
the *i.* of my heart, have, Gen. 20:5.
holdeth fast his *i.*, Job 2:3.
the *i.* of the upright, Prov. 11:3.

INTENT, to purpose.
to the *i.* that the liv-, Dan. 4:17.
for what *i.* he spake, John 13:28.
to the *i.* we should not, I Cor. 10:6.
thoughts and *i.* of the, Heb. 4:12.

INTERCESSION, to go between.
Spirit maketh *i.* for, Rom. 8:26.
that prayers and *i.* be, I Tim. 2:1.
liveth to make *i.* for, Heb. 7:25.

INTERCESSOR, mediator, a go-between.
that there was no *i.*, Is. 59:16.

INTERMEDDLE, entangled, mixed.
a stranger doth not *i.*, Prov. 14:10...494

INTERPRET, explain fully, clarify.
none that could *i.* them, Gen. 41:8.
do all *i.*? I Cor. 12:30.
pray that he may *i.*, I Cor. 14:13.

INTERPRETATION, explanation.

the *i.* of his dream. Gen. 40:5.
Cephas, which is by *i.*, John 1:42.
to another the *i.* of, I Cor. 12:10.
is of private *i.*, II Pet. 1:20.

INTREAT, entreat, plead, ask, beg, request.
I. for me to Ephron, the, Gen. 23:8.
Lord,....shall he *i.* Is. 19:22.
I *i.* thee also true yoke-, Phil. 4:3.
easy to be *i.*, full of, James 3:17.

INTRUDING, treading upon.
i. into things he hath, Col. 2:18.

INVADE, to assault, go in, enter, wage war, attack.
not let Israel *i.*, II Chr. 20:10.
Philistines had *i.*, II Chr. 28:18.
will *i.* them with troops, Hab. 3:16.

INVENT, INVENTED, to devise.
engines, *i.* by cunn-, II Chr. 26:15.
i. instruments of music, Amos 6:5.

INVENTIONS, things devised, planned.
vengeance of their *i.*, Ps. 99:8.
knowledge of witty *i.*, Prov. 8:12.

INVISIBLE, unseen.
the *i.* things of him from, Rom. 1:20.
visible and *i.*, whether, Col. 1:16.
seeing him who is *i.*, Heb. 11:27.

INWARD, inside, toward the inside, inner, secret, within, concealed.
i. part is very wicked-, Ps. 5:9.
i. thought is, that their, Ps. 49:11.
law in their *i.* parts, Jer. 31:33.
law of God after *i.*, Rom. 7:22.
the *i.* man is renewed, II Cor. 4:16.

IOB, a variant rendering for Job.

IPHEDEIAH, a son of Shashak, a Benjamite, mentioned in I Chr. 8:25.

IPHTAH, JIPHTAH, a town in Judah (Josh. 15:43).

IPHTAH-EL, JIPHTHAH-EL, a valley on Zebulun's north border (Josh. 19:14).

IR, a Benjamite, the father of Machir, mentioned in I Chr. 7:12.

IRA, there are three men by this name in the Bible; (1) a priest to David (II Sam.

20:26), (2) the Ithrite, one of David's guards (II Sam. 23:38), and (3) another of David's guards (I Chr. 11:40).

IRAD, son of Enoch and grandson of Cain. Mentioned only in Gen. 4:18.

IRAM, a duke of Edom of the family of Esau (Gen. 36:43).

IRI, a son of Bela (I Chr. 7:7).

IRIJAH, a captain of the guard at Jerusalem (Jer. 37:13).

IRNAHASH, a descendant of Chelub from Judah (I Chr. 4:12).

IRON, (1) the first mention of iron in Scripture refers to Tubal-cain as the first iron-worker (Gen. 4:22). Even before it became common in the Iron Age (1200–300 B.C.), iron was known to the civilized nations of antiquity. It was used mostly for military weapons (I Sam. 17:7), chariots (Josh. 17:16), tools (I Kin. 6:7) and farming implements (II Sam. 12:31; Amos 1:3). The word figuratively designates strength (Deut. 33:25; Mic. 4:13). (2) A fenced city of Naphtali (Josh. 19:38).
an instrument of *i.*, Num. 35:16.
a bedstead of *i.*, Deut. 3:11.
his legs of *i.*, feet, Dan. 2:41.
seared with a hot *i.*, I Tim. 4:2.
them with a rod of *i.*, Rev. 2:27.

IRPEEI, a city of Benjamin, west of Jerusalem (Josh. 18:27).

IRSHEMESH, a city of Dan, possibly identical with Bethshemesh (Josh. 19:41).

IRU, eldest son of Caleb (I Chr. 4:15).

ISAAC, the son of promise to Abraham and Sarah (Gen. 17:19) who was born to them when his father was 100 years old. His wife was Rebekah, a cousin, whom he married when he was forty years of age. His sons were Jacob and Esau, from whom the Israelites and the Edomites were descended. He died at Hebron at the age of 180. He is often referred to in the phrase, Abraham, Isaac, and Jacob, as one of the Jewish fathers.
shalt call his name, *I.*, Gen. 17:19.
bound *I.* his son, and, Gen. 22:9.
I. digged again the well, Gen. 26:18.

Abraham, *I.*, and Israel, Ex. 6:8.
of Abraham, and of *I.*, Acts 3:13.
but, in *I.* shall thy, Rom. 9:7.
by faith, *I.* blessed, Heb. 11:20.

ISAIAH, ESAIAS, a prophet of God during the reigns of Uzziah, Jotham, Ahaz, and Hezekiah, kings of Judah. He was the son of Amoz (1:1), but his tribe is unknown. His prophecies covered about sixty years preaching, at first, repentance but when the people would not listen, he preached the coming captivity.
Hezekiah came to *I.*, II Kin. 19:5.
acts of Uzziah. did *I.*, II Chr. 26:22.

ISAIAH, BOOK OF, Isaiah, considered by many the "Prince of Old Testament Prophets," pled with Judah to turn from idolatry and apostasy in order to escape punishment. The futility of his work Isaiah knew from the moment of his divine call (Is. 6:9–12). Isaiah's message to Judah was: Your nation is deeply corrupted; you must repent. Because you will not repent, God will punish you with captivity, from which only a tiny righteous remnant will return to be restored to the land (Is. 40–48). Through this remnant God will bring the Messiah (Is. 9:6; 53:1–12). The book also contains oracles against foreign nations (Is. 13–23) and record of events in Hezekiah's reign (Is. 36–39). Isaiah was a statesman as well as a prophet. His Messianic emphasis has given him the name "Messianic Prophet."

ISCAH, daughter of Haran and sister to Milcah and Lot (Gen. 11:29).

ISCARIOT, *see* **Judas.**

ISCARIOT, SIMON, *see* **SIMON.**

ISHBAH, father of Eshtemoa in the line of Judah (I Chr. 4:17).

ISHBAK, son of Abraham and Keturah (Gen. 25:2).

ISHBIBENOB, a warrior of the Rephaims, slain by Abishai (II Sam. 21:16).

ISHBOSHETH, the youngest of Saul's sons, (II Sam. 2:8; I Chr. 8:33).

ISHHOD, *see* **ISHOD.**

ISHI, (1) the father of Sheshan and descendant of Judah (I Chr. 2:31), (2) another descendant of Judah (I Chr. 4:20), (3) a Simeonite whose sons invaded the Amelekites (I Chr. 4:42), and (4) one of the mighty men of valor of Manasseh (I Chr. 5:24), (5) a symbolic name which God's people were to give to Him when they returned to Him (Hos. 2:16).

ISHIAH, *see* **ISSHAH.**

ISHIJAH, ISSHIJAH, a man who married a foreign wife (Ezra 10:31).

ISHMA, a descendant of Caleb, the spy (I Chr. 4:3).

ISHMAEL, son of Abraham and Hagar, his wife's handmaid, born when Abraham was 86 years old (Gen. 21:5). He was cast out with his mother by Sarah, miraculously preserved by God, and was present with Isaac at his father's burial (Gen. 25:9). Esau married his daughter (Gen. 28:9). His death is recorded in Gen. 25:17, 18. He is generally regarded as the father of the modern-day Arabians. Others by this name are: (1) son of Azel, descendant of Saul (I Chr. 8:38), (2) father of Zebadiah, ruler of the house of Judah under Jehoshaphat (II Chr. 19:11), (3) son of Jehohanan who assisted Jehoiada in restoring Josiah to the throne (II Chr. 23:1), (4) one of the sons of Pashur (Ezra 10:22) and (5) the murderer of Gedaliah who was superintendent of the province of Judah, in Babylon. He was of royal seed. (Jer. 41:1; II Kin. 25:25).

ISHMAEELITES, *see* **ISHMAELITE.**

ISHMAELITE, ISHMEELITES, a descendant of Ishmael. In Gen. 37:25, the term is applied to a band of travelers and in I Chr. 2:17 it is applied to Jether.

ISHMAIAH, a prince of Zebulun in David's reign (I Chr. 27:19).

ISHMERAI, a descendant of Benjamin (I Chr. 8:18).

ISHOD, ISH-HOD, one of the tribe of Manasseh, east of the Jordan (I Chr. 7-18).

ISHPAH, *see* **ISPAH.**

ISHPAN, one of the sons of Shashak, residing at Jerusalem (I Chr. 8:22).

ISHTOB, *see* **TOB**.

ISHUAH, *see* **ISHVAH**.

ISHUAI, ISHUI, ISUI, JESUI, (1) the third son of Asher (Gen. 46:17), (2) son of Saul and Ahinoam (I Sam. 14:49).

ISHVAH, ISHUAN, ISUAH, the second son of Asher (Gen. 46:17; I Chr. 7:30).

ISLAND, ISLE, (1) any habitable place (Is. 42:15), and (2) actual islands, completely surrounded by water, as Crete (Jer. 47:4).
i. of the Gentiles. Gen. 10:5.
from the *i.* of, Is. 11:11.
through the *i.* to Paphos, Acts 13:6.
in the *i.* that is, Rev. 1:9.

ISMACHIAH, one of the Levites under Hezekiah in charge of the sacred offerings (II Chr. 31:13).

ISMAIAH, a Gibeonite warrior who joined David at Ziklag (I Chr. 12:4).

ISPAH, a son of Beriah. (I Chr. 8:16).

ISRAEL, (1) the new name of Jacob after he wrestled with the angel at Peniel (Gen. 32:28, 30). (2) The collective name for the twelve tribes (Ex. 3:16, 18).

ISRAEL, KINGDOM OF, after the division of the kingdom, the northern part came to be known as the kingdom of Israel in contrast to the kingdom of Judah. This kingdom of Israel was formed when Rehoboam would not reduce the taxes which Solomon had imposed (I Kin. 12:9–17). Jeroboam I set up rival centers of worship in Bethel and Dan, introducing the golden calf into the sanctuary (II Kin. 10:29).
Ahab, their most outstanding king, allowed Jezebel to bring in Baal worship (I Kin. 16:30–33). Some other kings were Jeroboam II, Jehu, Jehoash, and Pekah. The northern kingdom ended with the Fall of Samaria (722 B.C.).

ISRAELITE, one belonging to Israel.
I. was slain, Zimri, Num. 25:14.
who are *I.* to whom, Rom. 9:4.
also am an *I.* of the, Rom. 11:1.

ISRAELITES, JOURNEYS OF THE, *see* **WILDERNESS OF THE WANDERING.**

ISRAELITISH, pertaining to Israel.

ISSACHAR, the ninth son of Jacob and the fifth by Leah, almost always referred to as the name of the tribe.
called his name *I.*, Gen. 30:18.
of the children of *I.*, Num. 1:28.
lot came out to *I.*, Josh. 19:17.
of the tribe of *I.*, Rev. 7:7.

ISSACHARITE, one who belongs to the tribe of Issachar.

ISSHIAH, ISHIAH, JESIAH, (1) a greatgrandson of Moses (I Chr. 24:21); (2) an Issacharite (I Chr. 7:3); (3) son Uzziel (I Chr. 23:20; 24:25); (4) one who allied himself with David at Ziklag (I Chr. 12:6).

ISSHIJAH, *see* **ISHIJAH**.

ISSUE, to flow, go out of, go forth, run.
that hath an issue, Num. 5:2.
waters *i.* out from under, Ezek. 47:1.
a fiery stream *i.* and, Dan. 7:10.
an *i.* of blood twelve, Matt. 9:20.

ISSUE OF BLOOD, a disease characterized by hemorrhage (Matt. 9:20; Luke 8:43).

ISUAH, *see* **ISHVAH**.

ISUI, *see* **ISHVI**.

ITALIAN, of Italy, from Italy (Acts 10:1).

ITALY, the country of Europe stretching from the Alps to the Straits of Messina, with Rome as the capital, the seat of government of the Roman conquerors of the Israelites.
lately come from *I.*, Acts 18:2.
should sail into *I.*, Acts 27:1.
They of *I.* salute you. Heb. 13:24.

ITCHING, continued discomfort, requiring continued attention. In II Tim. 4:3 it refers to those whose ears need constant attention, always interested in hearing some new thing, wanting something different.

ITHAI, one of David's thirty valiant men (I Chr. 11:31).

ITHAMAR, youngest son of Aaron. hand of *I.*, son of, Ex. 38:21. *I.* ministered in the, Num. 3:4. of the sons of *I.*, I Chr. 24:3.

ITHIEL, (1) a Benjamite, the son of Jessiah, (Neh. 11:7) and (2) one of the two persons to whom Agur delivered his discourse (Prov. 30:1).

ITHMAH, a Moabite of David's bodyguard (I Chr. 11:46).

ITHNAN, a city of South Judah on the edge of the desert (Josh. 15:23).

ITHRA, an Ishmaelite, the father of A-masa (I Kin. 2:5; II Sam. 17:25).

ITHRAN, (1) a son of Dishon (I Chr. 1:41) and (2) a son of Zophah an Ashorite (I Chr. 7:37).

ITHREAM, sixth son of David, born at Hebron of Milcah, (II Sam. 3:5).

ITHRITE, descendants of Jether. Ira and Gaer were Ithrites. (II Sam. 23:38).

ITTAH-KAZIN, a landmark of the boundary of Zebulun, near Gath-hepher (Josh. 19:13).

ITTAI, ITHAI, (1) the Gittite, a Philistine in David's army who stayed with David even when David requested him to return to his own country. (II Sam. 15:21), (2) a son of Ribai (I Chr. 11:31).

ITURAEA, a small province at the base of Mount Hermon under the tetrarchy of Philip (Luke 3:1).

ITURAEANS, belonging to Ituraea.

IVAH, IVVAH, one of the cities of the Assyrians from which they brought colonists to repeople Samaria (II Kin. 18:34).

IVORY, a product of the elephant's tusk which was imported into Tyre by "men of Dedan" (Ezek. 27:15) and "ships of Tarshish" (I Kin. 10:22). It was used for ornamenting houses, constructing furniture, etc. Tusks of ivory are called "horns" in Ezek. 27:15.

IVVAH, *see* **IVAH**.

IYE-ABARIM, *see* **IJE-ABARIM**.

IYIM, *see* **IIM**.

IZCHAR, a son of Kohath and grandson of Levi (Ex. 6:18).

IZEHAR, *see* **IZHAR**.

IZEHARITES, *see* **IZHARITES**.

IZHAR, IZEHAR, (1) son of Kohath and father of Korah (Ex. 6:18; Num. 3:19; I Chr. 6:2). (2) Son of Ashur of the family of Hezron (I Chr. 4:7), rendered Jezoar in the King James Version.

IZHARITES, persons of the family of Izhar and his descendants (Num. 3:27).

IZLIAH, *see* **JERZIAH**.

IZRAHIAH, a grandson of Tola son of Issachar (I Chr. 7:3).

IZRAHITE, the family and descendants of Shamhuth, one of David's thirty valiant men (I Chr. 27:8).

IZRI, ZERI, a Levite set over the service of song by David (I Chr. 25:12).

IZZIAH, *see* **JEZIAH**.

J

JAAKAN, the son of Ezer and the ancestor of Benejaakan, whose well was chosen as a camp-site by the Israelites on two occasions (I Chr. 1:42; Num. 33:30–32; Deut. 10:6). The name is given as Jakan in I Chr. 1:42 and as Akan in Gen. 36:27.

JAAKOBAH, one of the descendants of Simeon (I Chr. 4:36).

JAALA, JAALAH, one of the servants of Solomon (Ezra 2:56; Neh. 7:58).

JAALAM, JALAM, son of Esau by Aholibamah (Gen. 36:5, 14; I Chr. 1:35).

JAANAI, JANAI, one of the chief Gadites that lived in Bashan (I Chr. 5:12).

JAAREOREGIM, the father of Elhanan (II Sam. 21:19).

JAARESHIAH, *see* **JARESIAH**.

JAASAU, JAASU, an Israelite who had married a foreign wife (Ezra 10:37).

JAASIEL, JASIEL, (1) one of the mighty men of David (I Chr. 11:47), (2) the son of Abner (I Chr. 27:21).

JAAZANIAH, (1) a captain, who was a Maacathite, (II Kin. 25:23), (2) a chief of the Rechabites, (Jer. 35:3), (3) son of Shaphan, (Ezek. 8:11), (4) a wicked prince of Judah (Ezek. 11:1).

JAAZER, JAZER, a town on the East of Jordan near Gilead (Num. 32:1, 3).

JAAZIAH, a Levite who descended from Merari (I Chr. 24:26, 27).

JAAZIEL, AZIEL, a Levitical musician in the time of David (I Chr. 15:18).

JABAL, the son of Lamech by Adah.

JABBOK, a small brook which lies East of Jordan.
and passed over ford *J.*, Gen. 32:22.
unto any place of river *J.*, Deut. 2:37.
Sihon ruled unto river *J.*, Josh. 12:2.
even unto *J.*, Judg. 11:13, 22.

JABESH, (1) the father of Shallum, (II King. 15:10, 13, 14), (2) a shortened form of Jabesh-Gilead (I Chr. 10:12).

JABESH-GILEAD, a city of Gilead near to Bethshan (I Sam. 31:11). At the death of Saul and his sons it was the men of Jabesh who buried them and received a blessing from David (I Sam. 31:8; II Sam. 2:5).

JABEZ, (1) a wealthy head of a family of Judah (I Chr. 4:9ff), (2) a city, inhabited by scribes (I Chr. 2:55).

JABIN, (1) king of Hazor who was overthrown by Joshua (Josh. 11:1–14), (2) another king of Hazor, possibly of the same line, who was overthrown by Barak (Judg. 4:2ff).

JABNEEL, (1) a city in northern Judah (Josh. 15:11), (2) a city on the border of Naphtali (Josh. 19:33).

JABNEH, (II Chr. 26:6).

JACHAN, JACAN, one of the chiefs of the Gadites (I Chr. 5:13).

JACHIN, (1) one of the sons of Simeon (Gen. 46:10), (2) a priest who lived in Jerusalem after the captivity (I Chr. 9:10; Neh. 11:10), (3) chief of the twenty-first course of priests during the time of David (I Chr. 24:17), (4) one of the brazed pillars in the porch of Solomon's temple (I Kin. 7:15–22).

JACHINITE, one of the clans of Simeon founded by Jachin (Num. 26:12).

JACINTH, HYACINTH, LIGURE, a stone perhaps equal to our sapphire (Rev. 9:17, 21:20).

JACKAL, though this word is not found in the King James Version of the Bible it should have been used at times in places where "dragon" appears (Job 30: 29; Ps. 44:19; Is. 13:22; 34:13; 35:7; 43: 20; Jer. 9:11; 10:22; 14:6; 49:33; 51:37). The Jackal is a small dog-like animal with a slightly bushy tail and a peculiar howl. It is a coward and roams abroad at night.

JACOB, the son of Isaac by Rebekah and the twin brother to Esau. His name was later changed to "Israel" (Gen. 32:28). He became the father of the twelve sons of Jacob who became the fathers of the twelve tribes of the nation of Israel.
he was called *J.*, Gen. 25:26.
the voice is *J.*'s., Gen. 27:22.
J. saw Rachel, Gen. 29:10.
J. looked, behold, Esau, Gen. 33:1.
sons of *J.*, Gen. 34:7, 13, 25.
J., called Bethel, Gen. 35:6.
a star out of *J.*, Num. 24:17.
J. shall rejoice, Ps. 14:7.
J. sojourned in land, Ps. 105:23.
the Holy One of *J.*, Is. 29:23.
with Abraham, Isaac, *J.*, Matt. 8:11.
J.'s well was there, John 4:6.
J. have I loved, but, Rom. 9:13.
away ungodliness from *J.*, Rom. 11:26.

JADA, the last named of Onam's sons (I Chr. 2:28, 32).

JADAU, one of the sons of Nebo who had married a foreign wife (Ezra 10:43).

JADDUA, one of the heads of the people who sealed the covenant made by Nehmiah (Neh. 10:21).

JADDUA, the last high priest the Old Testament mentions (Neh. 12:11, 22).

JADON, one of those who aided in rebuilding the walls of Jerusalem after the exile of Babylon (Neh. 3:7).

JAEL, the wife of the Kenite, Heber. She slew Sisera with one of the wooden pins of the tent (Judg. 4:17-22).

JAGUR, a town in southern Judah near Edom (Josh. 15:21).

JAH, a form for Jehovah (Ps. 68:4).

JAHATH, (1) a clan of Judah which lived near Kiriath-jearim (I Chr. 4:2), (2) a descendant of Levi through Gershom (I Chr. 23:10), (3) a descendant of Kohath (I Chr. 24:22), (4) a Merarite Levite who helped oversee the temple repairs during the reform of Josiah (II Chr. 34:12).

JAHAZ, JAHAZA, JAHAZAH, a city of the Amorite nation where Sihon was overcome by Israel (Num. 21:23; Deut. 2:32).

JAHAZIAH, JAHZEIAH, son of Tikvah, who also aided Ezra in determining those who had married foreign wives (Ezra 10:15).

JAHAZIEL, (1) one of the men who joined David at Ziglag (I Chr. 12:4), (2) one of the priests who was also a trumpeter before the ark during the reign of David (I Chr. 16:6), (3) a Kohathite, the son of Hebron, the grandson of Levi (I Chr. 23:19, 24:23), (4) son of Zechariah, a Levite who prophesied victory to Jehoshaphat (II Chr. 20: 14), (5) Jahaziel's son, a Jew of the captivity returned with Ezra (Ezra 8:5).

JAHDAI, a descendant of Caleb whose sons' names are given (I Chr. 2:47).

JAHDIEL, one of the mighty men of the tribe of Manasseh (I Chr. 5:24).

JAHDO, son of Buz the Gadite who was also the father of Jeshishai (I Chr. 5:14).

JAHLEEL, one of the three sons of Zebulun (Gen. 46:14; Num. 26:26).

JAHLEELITES, the descendants of Jahleel (Num. 26:26).

JAHMAI, the grandson of Issachar through Tola (I Chr. 7:2).

JAHWEH, JAHWEH TSEBAOTH, *see* GOD.

JAHZAH, *see* JAHAZ.

JAHZIEL, JAZEEL, one of the sons of Naphtali (Gen. 46:24). The name is also given Gahziel (I Chr. 7:13).

JAHZEELITES, the descendants of the above Jahzeel (Num. 26:48).

JAHZEIAH, *see* JAHAZIAH.

JAHZERAH, a priest who was the son of Meshullum and probably the same as Azareel (I Chr. 9:12; Neh. 11:13).

JAHZIEL, *see* JAHZEEL.

JAILOR, the keeper of a prison (Acts 16:23).

JAIR, (1) a descendant of Manasseh (Num. 32:41; Deut. 3:14), (2) the eighth judge of Israel (Judg. 10:3-5), (3) the father of Elhanan (I Chr. 20:5), (4) the father of Mordecai (Esth. 2:5).

JAIRITE, a descendant of Jair, Ira (II Sam. 20:26).

JAIRUS, a synagogue ruler whose only daughter was restored to life by Jesus (Mark 5:22; Luke 8:41).

JAKAN, *see* JAAKAN.

JAKEH, the father of Agur (Prov. 30:1).

JAKIM, (1) a son of Shimhi(I Chr. 8: 19), (2) the head of the twelfth course of the priest as appointed by David (I Chr. 24:12).

JALAM, *see* JAAKAN.

JALON, a descendant of Caleb who was also the son of Ezra (I Chr. 4:17).

JAMBRES, *see* **JANNES AND JAMBRES.**

JAMES, THE SON OF ZEBEDEE, (Matt. 4:21), and the brother of John (Mark 5:37). The Lord called these two the "sons of thunder" (Mark 3:17). James suffered martyrdom under Herod Agrippa (Acts 12:2). He was one of the twelve.

JAMES, THE LESS, another one of the twelve apostles. He is called the son of Alphaeus (Matt. 10:3) and Mary, the sister of Mary the mother of the Lord (Matt. 27:56).

JAMES, THE BROTHER OF THE LORD, it appears that James and his brothers and sisters were actual brothers and sisters of Jesus (Matt. 13:55; Mark 6:3). He was not one of the original twelve, though later he was called an apostle (Gal. 1:19), and at first did not even believe in Jesus (John 7:5). He later became an important figure in the church of Jerusalem (Acts 15:13; Gal. 2:9).

JAMES, EPISTLE OF, a writing to predominantly Jewish Christians, the brother of the Lord in this letter exhorts and admonishes them and us to be fortified against persecution or trials (James 1:1–18; 5:7–11) and, most important, to be "doers of the word" (1:21–27) who manifest faith through obedience in life (2:14–26). Thus, James stresses that inactive faith is like a dead corpse (2:17, 24). James speaks not of meritorious human works without God (Rom. 3:27–28; Eph. 2:9), but instead speaks of faith working in life (Gal. 5:6; Eph. 2:10).

JAMIN, (1) one of the sons of Simeon (Gen. 46:10), (2) a son of Ram (I Chr. 2:27), (3) one of the priests whose duty was to explain the law to the people when it was read by Ezra (Neh. 8:7).

JAMINITES, the descendants of Jamin, (Num. 26:12).

JAMLECH, one of the heads of the tribe of Simeon (I Chr. 4:34).

JANAI, *see* **JANUM.**

JANGLING, vain talking (Titus 1:6, 10).

JANNA, JANNAI, son of Joseph and also the father of Melchi (Luke 3:24).

JANNES AND JAMBRES, according to tradition they opposed Moses (II Tim. 3:8).

JANOAH, a town of Naphtali overran by Tiglath-pileser in 734 B.C. (II Kin. 15:29).

JANOHAH, a border town of Ephraim (Josh. 16:6, 7).

JANUM, JANIM, a town of Judah evidently not far from Hebron (Josh. 15:53).

JAPHETH, one of the three sons of Noah who was saved in the ark with his wife (Gen. 5:32; 7:7; I Pet. 3:20). He was the father of seven sons (Gen. 10:2) and his prosperity inhabited the "isles of the Gentiles" (Gen. 10:5).

JAPHIA, (1) a Lachish king who was destroyed by Joshua (Josh. 10:3), (2) a son of David (II Sam. 5:15), (3) a border town of Zebulun (Josh. 19:12).

JAPHLET, the great-grandson of Asher and the son of Heber (I Chr. 7:32, 33).

JAPHLETI, a landmark on the southern boundary of Ephraim (Josh. 16:3).

JAPHLETITES, an unidentified tribe of people mentioned in Josh. 16:3.

JAPHO, the Hebraic form for Joppa (Josh. 19:46).

JARAH, a son of Ahaz (I Chr. 9:42).

JAREB, either a name or description of the King of Assyria (Hos. 5:13, 10:6).

JARED, one of the patriarchs who was the fifth from Adam. (Gen. 5:15–20; I Chr. 1:2).

JARESIAH, JAARESHIAH, a son of Jehoram (I Chr. 8:27).

JARHA, an Egyptian slave who married the daughter of Sheshan, his master. Jarha (I Chr. 2:34–41).

JARIB, (1) a son of Simeon (I Chr. 4:24),

(2) one of Ezra's chief men (Ezra 8:16), (3) a priest who had married a foreign wife but divorced her after the captivity (Ezra 10:18).

JARMUTH, (1) a Canaanite royal city which was taken and given to Judah (Josh. 10:3f; 15:35), (2) a Levitical city of Issachar (Josh. 21:29).

JAROAH, one of the chiefs of Gad who lived at Bashan (I Chr. 5:14).

JASHAR, see JASHER.

JASHEN, a man whose sons were listed among David's heroes (II Sam. 23:32).

JASHER, JASHAR, THE BOOK OF, a book the composition of which appears to have been a collection of poetical praise to certain heroes of Israel (Josh. 10:13; II Sam. 1:17).

JASHOBEAM, (1) the chief of the thirty heroes of David (I Chr. 11:11; 12:6; 27:2), (2) a Korhite who was with those who joined David at Ziklag (I Chr. 12:6).

JASHUB, (1) one of the sons of Issachar and also the ancestral head of the Jashubites (Num. 26:24; I Chr. 7:1), (2) a son of Bani who divorced his foreign wife (Ezra 10:29).

JASHUBILEHEM, either a person or place among the descendants of Shelah, a son of Judah (I Chr. 4:22).

JASHUBITES, the family whose ancestral head was Jashub (Num. 26:24).

JASIEL, see JAASIEL.

JASON, the host of Paul and Silas at Thessalonica. When a mob, which came to take Paul, did not find him, they dragged Jason before the ruler who finally released him (Acts 17:5-9).

JASPER, a precious stone, the identity of which is uncertain (Ex. 28:20; 39:13; Rev. 4:3; 21:11).

JATHNIEL, a son of Meshelemiah, who was a Levite (I Chr. 26:2).

JATTIR, a city of Judah the outskirts of which were assigned to the priests (Josh. 24:14; I Chr. 6:57).

JAVAN, (1) a son of Japheth (Gen. 10:2, 4; I Chr. 1:5, 7). (2) The name given to certain Gentile lands (cf. Is. 66:19; Ezek. 27:13.

JAVEH, see GOD.

JAVELIN, a spear-like offensive weapon (Num. 25:7; I Sam. 18:10, 11; 19:9; 20:33).

JAW.
bore his *j*. through, Job 41:2.
their *j*. teeth knives, Prov. 30:14.
put hooks in thy *j*., Ezek. 29:4.
the yoke on their *j*., Hos. 11:4.

JAZER, see JAAZER.

JAZIZ, a shepherd of David's flocks who was also a Hagarite (I Chr. 27:31).

JEALOUS, intolerant of rivalry.
God am a *j*. God, Ex. 20:5.
j. of his wife, Num. 5:14, 30.
j. for Jerusalem, Zech. 1:14.
I am *j*. over you, II Cor. 11:2.

JEALOUSY, state of being jealous.
the spirit of *j*. come, Num. 5:14.
they provoked Him to *j*., Deut. 32:16.
provoke you to *j*. by, Rom. 10:19.
to provoke to *j*. Rom. 11:11.

JEARIM, a mountain on the northern boundary of Judah (Josh. 15:10).

JEATERAI, a Levite of the linage of Gershom (I Chr. 6:21).

JEBERECHIAH, the father of a Zechariah who was not the prophet (Is. 8:2).

JEBUS, JEBUSI, before it was taken from Jebusite control this city went by this name. It was later changed to the famous Jerusalem (Josh. 15:8; Judg. 19: 10). In Josh. 18:16, 28 it was also called Jebusi.

JEBUSITE, the descendants of Ham by his son Canaan. They had control of Jerusalem until the time of David.
Canaan begat the *J*., Gen. 10:16.

drive out the *J.*, Ex. 33:2.
of Araunah the *J.*, II Sam. 24:16.
and Ekron as a *J.*, Zech. 9:7.

JECAMIAH, *see* **JEKOMIAH.**

JECHOILIAH, *see* **JECHOLIAH.**

JECHOLIAH, JECHOILIAH, wife of King Amaziah and mother of Azariah (II Kin. 15:2). In II Chr. 26:3 the name is given as Jecoliah.

JECHONIAS, the Greek form for Jechoniah (Matt. 1:11, 12).

JECOLIAH, *see* **JECHOLIAH.**

JECONIAH, another form of Jehoiachin (I Chr. 3:16; Esther 2:6; Jer. 24:1, 27:20, 28:4, 29:2).

JEDAIAH, (1) the son of Shimri (I Chr. 4:37), (2) one who aided in rebuilding the walls of Jerusalem (Neh. 3:10), (3) the head of the second division of priests as appointed by David (I Chr. 24:7), (4) a priest who returned to Jerusalem with Zerubbabel (Neh. 12:7, 21).

JEDIAEL, (1) the ancestral head of many families of Benjamin (I Chr. 7:6), (2) the son of Shimri and one of the mighty men of David (I Chr. 11:45), (3) the son of Meshelemiah (I Chr. 26:2).

JEDIDAH, the mother of Josiah who was king of Judah (II Kin. 22:1).

JEDIDIAH, a name that God gave to Solomon (II Sam. 12:25).

JEDUTHUN, one of David's masters of sacred music (I Chr. 16:38). Once he is called the "king's seer." (II Chr. 35:15). (I Chr. 25:1, 3; 16:42).

JEEZER, the son of Gilead of Manasseh (Num. 26:30).

JEEZERITES, the offspring of Jeezer (Num. 26:30).

JAGAR-SAHADUTHA, the Aramaic name which Laben gave to the pile of stones he set up as a memorial of the covenant between Jacob and himself (Gen. 31:47).

JEHALELEEL, JEHALELEEI, one of the descendants of Judah. Sons of his are listed in I Chr. 4:16.

JEHALELEL, a Levite, the son of whom, Azariah, aided in restoring the temple during the reign of Hezekiah (II Chr. 29:12).

JEHDEIAH, (1) a Levite, who was a family head of Shubael (I Chr. 24:20), (2) a Meronothite who was one of the officers of David charged with the royal asses (I Chr. 27:30).

JEHEZEKEL, JEHEZKEL, a priest under David who was the head of the twentieth course (I Chr. 24:16).

JEHIAH, the keeper of the ark associated with Obed-edom at the time David brought it to Jerusalem (I Chr. 15:24).

JEHIEL, JEHUEL, (1) a Benjamite who evidently founded Gibeon. Some of his sons are listed in I Chr. 9:35, (2) one of the mighty men of David (I Chr. 11:44), (3) a Levite musician appointed to play when David brought up the ark (I Chr. 15:18, 20), (4) the son of Hachmoni who seemed to be a tutor to the "king's sons" (I Chr. 27:32), (5) one of the sons of King Jehoshaphat (II Chr. 21:2), (6) one of the descendants of Heman who also aided in the temple cleaning during the reign of Hezekiah (II Chr. 29:14, cf 31:13), (7) one of the three rulers of the temple during the reign of Josiah (II Chr. 35:8), (8) the father of Obadiah who also returned with Ezra from Babylon (Ezra 8:9), (9) the son of Harim who was also a priest that divorced his foreign wife after the exile (Ezra 10:21), (10) the son of Elam who also divorced his Gentile wife following the exile (Ezra 10:26).

JEHIELI, a Levite whose sons had charge of the treasures of the Lord (I Chr. 26:21, 22).

JEHIZKIAH, the son of Shallum, a chief of Ephraim, who with Obed opposed the enslavement of the captives of Judah (II Chr. 28:12).

JEHOADAH, JEHOADOAH, son of Ahaz, a descendant of King Saul (I Chr.

8:36). He is called Jarah in I Chr. 9:42.

JEHOADDAN, JEHOADDIN, the mother of Amaziah, king of Judah (II Kin. 14:2; II Chr. 25:1).

JEHOAHAZ, (1) the son of Jehu who succeeded his father as king of Israel (II Kin. 10:35), (2) the son of Josiah and one who reigned over Judah for three months (I Chr. 3:15; II Kin. 23:31, 36), (3) the son of Jehoram, king of Judah (II Chr. 21:17; 25:23). He is also called Ahaziah.

JEHOASH, (1) the son of Ahaziah who became the eighth king of Judah (II Kin. 11:12). He is among the three kings whose names are omitted in Christ's genealogy (Matt. 1:8), (2) the son of Jehoahaz and his successor as king of Israel (II Kin. 13: 10, 11; 14:8–16).

JEHOASH, a variant form of Joash.

JEHOHANAN, (1) son of Meshelemiah who was a Korhite (I Chr. 26:3), (2) one of the captains of King Jehoshaphat's army (II Chr. 17:15, cf. also II Chr. 23:1), (3) a descendant of Bebai who put away his foreign wife following the exile (Ezra 10:28), (4) a priest who was head of the family of Amariah (Neh. 12:13), (5) a priest who was present during the dedication of the walls of Jerusalem (Neh. 12: 42).

JEHOIACHIN, JECONIAH, CONIAH, the son of Jehoiakim and who succeeded his father as king of Judah (II Kin. 24:8; II Chr. 36:9). After a reign of three months he was carried to Babylon by Nebuchadnezzar where, after many years, he died (Jer. 24:1, 29; II Kin. 25: 27–30; Jer. 52:31–34).

JEHOIADA, (1) one of the chief warriors of David, and the father of Benaiah (II Sam. 8:18; 20:23), (2) the high priest during the time of Ahaziah, the Queen Athaliah, and Jehoash, king of Judah (II Kin. 11:4–12:16; II Chr. 23:1–24:14), (3) a son of Paseah, (Neh. 3:6), (4) a priest left at the time of the captivity (Jer. 29:26).

JEHOIAKIM, the son of Josiah by Zebudah (II Kin. 23:36). He was made

vassal king over Judah by Pharaoh-necoh in the place of his brother Jehoahaz (II Kin. 23:33–35; II Chr. 36:3, 4).

JEHOIARIB, the head of one of the twenty-four courses of priest as they were set in order by David (I Chr. 24:7).

JEHONADAB, the son of Shimeah and the nephew of David (II Sam. 13).

JEHONADAB, the son of Rechab who was the founder of the Rechabites (Jer. 35:19; II Kin. 10:23).

JEHONATHAN, (1) the same as Johathan, the son of King Saul, (2) the son of Uzziah and who was an official over some of the storehouses of David (I Chr. 27:25), (3) a Levite commissioned by Jehoshaphat to teach the law in the cities of Judah (II Chr. 17:8), (4) a priest and the head of the family of Shemaiah in the time of Joiakim (Neh. 12:6, 18).

JEHORAM, a king of Israel, son of Ahab and Jezebel (II Kin. 1:17, 3:1).

JEHORAM, a king of Judah who was the son and successor of Jehoshaphat (II Kin. 8:16; II Chr. 21:1–6).

JEHOSHABEATH, the wife of the high priest, Jehoiada (II Chr. 22:11).

JEHOSHAPHAT, JOSAPHAT, (1) the son of Ahilud, who held an office in the courts of David and Solomon (II Sam. 8:16; 20:24; I Kin. 4:3), (2) the son of Paruah and an overseer of the district of Issachar (I Kin. 4:17), (3) the son of Asa and the fourth king of Judah. (I Kin. 15: 24; II Kin. 8:16; II Chr. 17:1–21:3), (4) the son of Nimshi and the father of Jehu (II Kin. 9:2, 14), (5) one of the trumpeters at the time the ark was moved from the house of Obededom to Jerusalem (I Chr. 15:24).

JEHOSHAPHAT, VALLEY OF, the name of the valley between Jerusalem and the Mount of Olives. It was here that Jehoshaphat defeated the enemies of Israel (II Chr. 20:22). It is used of Divine judgment in Joel 3:2, 12.

JEHOSHEBA, see **JEHOSHABEATH.**

JEHOSHUA, JEHOSHUAH, the same as Joshua (Num. 13:16; I Chr. 7:27).

JEHOVAH, in the American Standard Version of the Bible the Hebrew sign for God YHWH is rendered Jehovah by inserting the vowels in the Hebrew word for "lord." The King James Version and the Revised Standard Version use "LORD" to translate this term. The Hebrew word may connote the idea of independent and underived existence, the "I am that I am" of Ex. 3:14. God revealed himself as YHWH first to Moses (Ex. 6:3). *See* GOD.

JEHOVAH-JIREH, the name that Abraham gave to the mountain upon which he almost offered his son Isaac in sacrifice (Gen. 22:14).

JEHOVAH-NISSI, the name which Moses gave to the altar on the mount where he held up his hands during the battle with the Amalekites (Ex. 17:15).

JEHOVAH, SERVANT OF, *see* SERVANT OF JEHOVAH.

JEHOVAH-SHALOM, an altar which Gideon erected in Ophrah to the Lord as the God of peace (Judg. 6:24).

JEHOVAH-SHAMMAH, the name given by the prophet Ezekiel to the new Jerusalem as seen in the vision (Ezek. 48:35).

JEHOZABAD, (1) the son of Shomer and one of the servants of Jehoash who were responsible for his death (II Kin. 12:21; II Chr. 24:26), (2) the son of Obed-edom who was one of the doorkeepers of the temple (I Chr. 26:4, 15), (3) one of the officers under King Jehoshaphat (II Chr. 17:18).

JEHOZADAK, the son of Seraiah the high priest (I Chr. 6:14, 15). He was taken into exile by Nebuchadnezzar (I Chr. 6: 15). Joshua, his son, was high priest after the captivity (Hag. 1:1, 12, 14; Zech. 6: 11; Ezra 3:2, 8; Neh. 12:26).

JEHU, (1) a prophet, the son of Hanani (I Kin. 16:1, 7; II Chr. 19:2, 3; 20:34), (2) the son of Jehoshaphat and became the eleventh king of Israel (II Kin. 9:1–13), (3) the son of Obed (I Chr. 2:38),

(4) son of Josibiah (I Chr. 4:35–41), (5) an Antothite who joined himself to David at Ziklag (I Chr. 12:3).

JEHUBBAH, son of Shamer, a man of the tribe of Asher (I Chr. 7:34).

JEHUCAL, JUCAL, the son of Shelemiah who was commissioned by Hezekiah to go with Zephaniah to Jeremiah requesting the prophet to pray for the nation (Jer. 37:3; 38:4).

JEHUD, a town of Dan situated between Baalath and Beneberak (Josh. 19:45).

JEHUDI, the son of Nethaniah commissioned by the court of Jehoiakim to fetch Baruch and also charged by the king to bring the denunciation of Jeremiah and to read it (Jer. 36:14, 21, 23).

JEHUDIJAH, probably the wife of Mered (I Chr. 4:18).

JEHUEL, *see* JEHIEL.

JEHUSH, the son of Eshek, somehow related to Saul (I Chr. 8:39).

JEHUSH, *see* JEUSH.

JEIEL, (1) a descendant of Ruben (I Chr. 5:7), (2) one of the Levites who aided in bringing the ark to Jerusalem in the time of David (I Chr. 16:5; 15:18, 21), (3) a Levite who pronounced that Jehoshaphat would be successful against the Ammonites and Moabites (II Chr. 20:14), (4) a scribe who lived in the time of Uzziah (II Chr. 26:11), (5) the son of Elizaphan who aided in restoring the temple at the time of Hezekiah (II Chr. 29:13), (6) an important Levite who shared in the rites of the great Passover during the reign of Josiah (II Chr. 35:9), (7) the son of Adonikam who accompanied the caravan of Ezra to Jerusalem (Ezra 8:13), (8) the son of Nebe who put away his foreign wife (Ezra 10:43).

JEKABZEEL, a town of Judah (Neh. 11: 25).

JEKAMIAH, JECAMIAH, (1) the son of Shallum and a descendant of Sheshan of Judah (I Chr. 2:41), (2) the son of Jeconiah.

JEKUTHIEL, a descendant of Judah (I Chr. 4:18).

JEMIMA, JEMINAH, the daughter of Job (Job. 42:14).

JEMUEL, the son of Simeon (Gen. 46:10; Ex. 6:15).

JEPHTHAE, the Greek form for Jephthah (Heb. 11:32).

JEPHTHAH, one of the judges of Israel and who was the illegitimate son of Gilead (Judg. 11, 12).

JEPHUNNEH, (1) the father of Caleb who was a faithful Israelite and companion of Joshua (Num. 13:6; 26:65; Josh. 14:6; I Chr. 4:15; 6:56), (2) the son of Jether, (I Chr. 7:38).

JERAH, the son of Joktan (Gen. 10:26; I Chr. 1:20).

JERAHMEEL, (1) the son of Hezron and the ancestral head of the Jerahmeelites (I Chr. 2:9), (2) the son of Kish and a Merarite Levite (I Chr. 24:29), (3) the son of Hammelech (Jer. 36:26).

JERAHMEELITE, the descendants of Jerahmeel, (I Sam. 27:10; 30:29).

JERED, JARED, (1) a patriarch who lived before the flood (Gen. 5:15–20; I Chr. 1:2), (2) a son, perhaps, of Ezra of the tribe of Judah (I Chr. 4:18).

JEREMAI, the son of Hashum who put away his foreign wife after the captivity (Ezra 10:33).

JEREMIAH, (1) the father of Hamutal who was the mother of Jehoahaz and Zedekiah (II Kin. 23:31; 24:18; Jer. 52: 1), (2) a chief man of the east tribe of Manasseh who lived, it seems, at the time of the Assyrian exile (I Chr. 5:24), (3) a man of Benjamin who joined himself to David at Ziklag (I Chr. 12:4), (4) a Gadite who joined himself to David's men (I Chr. 12:10), (5) a Gadite who joined himself to David's men (I Chr. 12:13), (6) a priest at the time of Nehemiah (Neh. 10: 2; perhaps also 12:34), (7) a certain priest who came with Zerubbabel to Jerusalem (Neh. 12:1), (8) the son of Habazaniah (Jer. 35:3).

JEREMIAH, the son of Hilkiah and one of the great prophets of the Old Testament (Jer. 1:1). He prophesied during the reign of Josiah, Jehoiakim, and Zedekiah all kings of Judah, "unto the carrying away of Jerusalem captive in the fifth month" (Jer. 1:2, 3).

JEREMIAH, BOOK OF, this book contains the collected prophecies of Jeremiah which were penned by his scribe Baruch about 604 B.C. A first copy was burned by King Jehoiakim (Jer. 36:32). Jeremiah sternly warned Judah and Jerusalem, its capital, to turn back from the ruinous idolatry and apostasy that brought on Babylonian captivity. When the nation refused to heed, he warned of the futility of resistance and the certainty of captivity. Jeremiah also prophesied against various nations. His book contains also glimpses of a better day after captivity and predictions of the coming Messiah.

JEREMIAS, the Greek form for Jeremiah (Matt. 16:14).

JEREMOTH, (1) a chief man of Benjamin from the house of Beriah and Elpaal (I Chr. 8:14), (2) the son of Mushi (I Chr. 23:23). His name is Jerimoth in I Chr. 24:30, (3) the son of Heman and the head of one of the courses of musicians (I Chr. 25:22), (4) the son of Elam who divorced his foreign wife following the captivity (Ezra 10:26), (5) the son of Zattu who put away his foreign wife after the Babylonian Captivity (Ezra 10:27).

JEREMY, the same as Jeremiah the prophet (Matt. 2:17; 27:9).

JERIAH, JERIJAH, a Kohathite Levite who was a head man of the house of Hebron (I Chr. 23:19; 24:23). His name is written as Jerijah in I Chr. 26:31.

JERIBAI, the son of Elnaam who served as a bodyguard of David (I Chr. 11:46).

JERICHO, an old city in the plain between the mountains of Moab and the precipices of the west. When the nation of Israel entered the promised land Joshua sent spies to investigate the city. These spies were hidden by Rahab the harlot who was saved from the destruction because of her service to them (Josh. 2:1–21; 6:25). The city was finally taken when

God caused the walls to fall down after the tribes had marched around them a prescribed number of times (Josh. 6:1–27).

JERIEL, a descendant of Issachar (I Chr. 7:2).

JERIJAH, the same as Jeriah (I Chr. 26: 31).

JERIMOTH, (1) the son of Bela who was of the tribe of Benjamin (I Chr. 7:7), (2) the son of Becher and the head of a certain house of Benjamin (I Chr. 7:8), (3) a man of Benjamin who joined himself to David at Ziklag (I Chr. 12:5), (4) the son of Mushi and is also called Jeremoth (I Chr. 24:30), (5) the son of Heman and a chief of the musicians (I Chr. 25:4). In verse 22 he is called Jeremoth, (6) the son of Azriel, chief of Naphtali in the time of David (I Chr. 27:19), (7) the son of King David, (II Chr. 11:18), (8) a Levite superintendent of temple offerings (II Chr. 31:13).

JERIOTH, seems to be a wife of Caleb, the son of Hezron (I Chr. 2:18).

JEROBOAM, the son of Nebat who became the first king of Israel after the division of the kingdom (I Kin. 11:26; 12: 1–20. In order to keep his people from going to Jerusalem to worship, he set up high places with altars for them to worship at home (I Kin. 12:26–33).

JEROBOAM, II, the son of Joash and the fourteenth king of Israel who reigned forty-one years (II Kin. 14:23). He condoned the high places also and yet was successful in war. He broke the bondage of Syria, took the cities of Damascus and Hamath, and restored Israel from Lebanon to the Dead Sea (II Kin. 13:4; 14:25, 27; 14:28; Amos 1:3–5; II Kin. 14: 25). In spite of the apparent success the nation internally had fallen into grave corruption (Amos 2:6–8; 4:1, 6:6; Hos. 4:12–14; 1:2; 13:6). Hosea condemned the nation and Amos predicted the fall of the house of the king (Hos. 1:2; Amos 7:9, 17).

JEROHAM, (1) the son of Elihu and the grandfather of Samuel (I Sam. 1:1; I Chr. 6:27, 34), (2) the father of some chief men of Benjamin at Jerusalem (I Chr. 8:

27), (3) the father of Ibneiah, who was also a chief man of Benjamin at Jerusalem (I Chr. 9:8), (4) a certain priest (I Chr. 9:12), (5) a man of Gedor whose sons, Joelah and Zebadiah, joined themselves to David at Ziklag (I Chr. 12:7), (6) a man of Dan (I Chr. 27:22), (7) the father of Azariah (II Chr. 23:1).

JERUBBAAL, a name given to Gideon (Judg. 6:32; 7:1; I Sam. 12:11).

JERUBBESHETH, the same as Jerubbal with Baal changed to bosheth (II Sam. 11:21).

JERUEL, a wilderness around the Dead Sea which Jahaziel mentioned in his prophecy concerning the battle between Jehoshaphat and the Moabites and Ammonites (II Chr. 20:16).

JERUSALEM, the most important city of Palestine and one important in both Old and New Testament. This city was known as Salem in Abraham's time (Gen. 14:18; Ps. 76:2) and as Jebus during its occupation by Jebusites (Judg. 19:10, 11). Jerusalem is located fourteen miles west of the Dead Sea and thirty-three miles east of the Mediterranean. Situated on a high rocky plateau, this city is not on a main waterway or highway. Its central location, however made it ideal as the capital of the united kingdom of Israel in the time of David and Solomon and as the capital of Judah later. The city's altitude of 2,550 ft., coupled with the fact that its eastern, western and southern borders are steep valleys, made the site militarily defensible (II Sam. 5:6). Jerusalem is over four thousand years old. Present day Jerusalem consists of two parts, the old mile-square walled city with its Armenian, Jewish, Moslem and Christian quarters, and the new modern city.
Jebus, which is *J.*, Judg. 19:10.
Goliath's head to *J.*, I Sam. 17:54.
so I came to *J.* Neh. 2:11.
windows open toward *J.*, Dan. 6:10.
J. with iniquity, Mic. 3:10.
the offering of *J.*, Mal. 3:4.
went out to him *J.*, Matt. 3:5.
parents brought Him to *J.*, Luke 2:22
should not depart from *J.*, Acts 1:4.
you liberality unto *J.*, I Cor. 16:3.
the new *J.*, Rev. 3:12.

JERUSHA, the daughter of Zadok, mother of Jotham (II Kin. 15:33).

JERUSHAH, the same as Jerusha (II Chr. 27:1).

JESAIAH, the same as Jeshaiah (I Chr. 3:21; Neh. 11:7).

JESHAIAH, (1) the son of Hananiah and the grandson of Zerubbabel (I Chr. 3: 21), (2) the son of Jeduthun and one of the heads of the Levitical Musicians (I Chr. 25:3, 15), (3) the son of Rehabiah and a descendant of Eliezer (I Chr. 26: 25). In I Chr. 24:21 he is called Isshiah, (4) the son of Athaliah and head of the family of Elam who returned from Babylon (Ezra 8:7), (5) a Merarite Levite who met Ezra at Ahava (Ezra 8:19), (6) a certain Benjamite (Neh. 11:7 the same as Jesaiah).

JESHANAH, an Israelite city which was captured by Abijah (II Chr. 13: 19).

JESHARELAH, the son of Asaph and one of the heads of the musicians (I Chr. 25:14). He is called Asarelah in I Chr. 25:2.

JESHEBEAB, one of the heads of the priests (I Chr. 24:13).

JESHER, the son of Caleb (I Chr. 2:18).

JESHIMON, the territory north of the Dead Sea (Num. 21:20; 23:28; I Sam. 23:19).

JESHISHAI, the son of Jahdo (I Chr. 5:14).

JESHOHAIAH, the head of the Simeonites (I Chr. 4:36).

JESHUAH, (1) a priest at the time of David (I Chr. 24:11; see also Ezra 2:36; Neh. 7:39), (2) a certain Levite commissioned by Hezekiah to distribute offerings to the people (II Chr. 31:15), (3) the son of Jehozadak who returned with Zerubbabel from the Babylonian captivity (Ezra 2:2, Neh. 7:7; 12:1, 7, 10), (4) one whose descendants returned from the Babylonian captivity (Ezra 2:6; Neh. 7: 11), (5) a certain Levite whose descend-

ants returned from the Babylonian captivity (Ezra 2:40; Neh. 7:43), (6) the father of a certain Jozabad who was commissioned by Ezra to receive the offering of the service (Ezra 8:33), (7) the father of a certain Ezer who aided in the repairing of the wall at the time of Nehemiah (Neh. 3:19), (8) a Levite who aided in expounding the law to the people at the time of Ezra (Neh. 8:7; 9:4, 5; 12:8), (9) in Neh. 8:17 he is the same as Joshua, the son of Nun, (10) the son of Kadmiel (Neh. 12:24), (11) a city of the kingdom of Judah (Neh. 11:26).

JESHUAH, see JESHUA, (1).

JESHURUN, JESURUN, the name given to the people of Israel (Deut. 32:15; 33:5, 26; Isa. 44:2).

JESIAH, see ISSHIAH.

JESIMIEL, a Simeonite prince who along with others went to the valley of Gedor at the time of Hezekiah (I Chr. 4:36).

JESSE, the son of Boaz and Ruth (Ruth 4:17, 22; Matt. 1:5, 6; Luke 3:32) and the father of King David (I Sam. 17:12; 16: 11; 17:34, 35).

JESTING, light talk (Eph. 5:4).

JESUI, see ISHUI, (Num. 26:44).

JESUITES, the descendants of Ishui (Num. 26:44).

JESURUN, see JESHURUN (Is. 44:2).

JESUS CHRIST, the Son of God.
　Name. The divinely given personal name "Jesus" is the equivalent of the Hebrew "Joshua" and means "God is salvation" (Matt. 1:21). The official title "Christ" and its Hebrew parallel "Messiah" mean "anointed" (Matt. 16:18; John 1:41).
　Date. Jesus was born about 4 B.C. (The calendar is based on erroneous calculations by Exiguus who renumbered 754 of the Roman table to A.D. 1, but whose sixth century figures were four years in error.)
　Political Situation. After the exile Palestine was ruled successively by the Persians, Greeks, Egyptians and Syrians.

The Maccabees brought independence for almost a century, but midway in the first century B.C. the country became part of the Roman province of Syria. The Jews were much divided concerning Roman rule. Sadducees submitted and collaborated, while Pharisees avoided politics. Herodians favored administration by the Herods. Zealots opposed foreign rule fanatically. Jesus met political questions adroitly (Matt. 22:17-21; John 18:33-8).

Religious Situation. Jewish spirituality in Jesus' day was generally low. The powerful Pharisees and Sadducees dominated formal religion. The more influential Pharisees stressed formalism and hair-splitting legalistic theology, voiding truth by traditions (Matt. 15: 1-9) and forgetting foundation principles (Matt. 23:23). Sadducees were politically inclined, but they controlled the Sanhedrin and the office of High Priest. Both John the Baptist and Jesus denounced these groups (Matt. 3:7; 16:6; 23).

Early Life. The story of Jesus' birth is well-known (Matt. 1, 2; Luke 1:26:35; 2:1-39). The Messiah is traced to Abraham in Matthew and to Adam in Luke. Only a glimpse of Jesus' youth is given (Luke 2:41-52); his development was well-balanced (2:52). He was trained in carpentry (Mark 6:3).

His Baptism. About A.D. 26 John the Baptist began to preach repentance and baptism in view of the coming Messiah and kingdom. Jesus came and was baptized, not for forgiveness, but "to fulfill all righteousness." (Matt. 3:1-17; Mark 1:4-11).

His Temptation. After the baptism Jesus was led into the wilderness where he fasted forty days. Satan then came and tempted the Son three times, but each time Jesus resisted with appeal to Scripture (Matt. 4:1-11; Luke 4:1-13).

Duration of Jesus' Public Ministry. Ministry is considered by most to have been about three years. Although the first three Gospels give little information for dating, John's references to yearly feasts have significance for dating. John mentions three Passovers (2:13; 6:4; 11: 55). If John 5:1 also refers to a Passover (which is doubtful), the ministry exceeded three years.

Early Judean Ministry. After calling some disciples and working a miracle in Galilee (John 1:35-47; 2:1-11), Jesus went to Jerusalem where occurred a cleansing of the temple and the Nicodemus interview. Enroute to Galilee he spoke to the woman at the well (John 2:13-4:26).

Early Galilean Ministry. Knowledge of his acts in Judah preceded Jesus into Galilee (John 4:43-5). Although the Nazareth synagogue rejected him as he declared his mission, many of the people received him (Luke 4:16-30). Moving his residence to Capernaum, Jesus called other disciples and performed miracles (Matt. 4:13-22; 9:2-9; John 4:46-54). On a visit to Jerusalem He aroused Pharisee opposition by acts on the Sabbath (John 5:1-16; Matt. 12:1-14). The twelve apostles were sent out to proclaim the coming kingdom to the Jews (Matt. 10; Luke 6:13-6). Important messages of this period include the Sermon on the Mount (Matt. 5-7) and many parables (Matt. 13). Quieting the storm, healing the Gadarene demoniac, raising Jairus' daughter, feeding 5,000, and walking on water were outstanding miracles of this period (Matt. 8:23-34; 9:23-6; 14:15-33). At this time Jesus received the news of the beheading of John the Baptist (Matt. 14:1-13).

Later Galilean Ministry. In northern Galilee and in Decapolis Jesus taught about six months, preparing his followers for his coming death. (Matt. 16:21). Here occurred Peter's confession (Matt. 16:16) and the Transfiguration (Matt. 17), and here Jesus taught the lessons recorded in Matt. 18 and John 8:12-51. Working of miracles to produce faith continued (Matt. 15:21-38; 17:14-27).

The Perean Ministry. It seems that during this period Jesus alternated between Judea and Perea. At this time Jesus sketched some of his most famous parables (Luke 10:30-37; 15:1-16:31), denounced Phariseeism, taught much about prayer, and proclaimed the coming kingdom (Luke 11:1-13; 37-54; 17:20-37). He pitied the rich young ruler and rebuked the self-seeking James and John (Matt. 19:16-26; 20:20-8). He amazed men by raising the dead Lazarus (John 11).

Later Judean Ministry. Six days before Passover Jesus went to Bethany where the anointing with costly ointment occurred (John 12:1-8). On the next day he made triumphal entry into Jerusalem (Matt. 21:1-11; John 12:12-19) and returned to Bethany. On *Monday* he entered Jerusalem, purged the temple and symbolically cursed a barren tree (Mark 11:11–26). Returning to Jerusalem *Tuesday*, he met the verbal challenges of his foes (Matt. 21:23–7; 22:15–46) and condemned their hypocrisy (Matt. 23), while commending the poor widow's sacrifice (Mark 12:41–4). He predicted the temple's end and taught about the last judgment (Matt. 24–25). On this day Judas conspired against him (Matt. 26:14–16). *Wednesday* Jesus remained at Bethany. *Thursday* he kept Passover, instituted the Lord's Supper, and gave discourses (Matt. 26:17–30; John 13:1–17:26). On *Friday*, after anguish in Gethsemane, our Lord was betrayed and arrested (Luke 22:39–54; John 18:1–14). The Jews tried him hastily, then arranged trial before Pilate, who, knowing his innocence, pacified the angry Jews with the crucifixion sentence (John 18:29–19:22).

Death, Burial and Resurrection. *See* CRUCIFIXION. After Jesus' agonizing death, Joseph of Arimathaea, a secret disciple who was a Sanhedrin member was granted the body for burial, and Nicodemus, another Sanhedrin member, aided in the burial. With other faithful disciples these prepared and bound the body, and laid it in a new, rock-hewn tomb (Matt. 27:26–66; Mark 15:16–47; Luke 23:32–56; John 19:23–42). The Romans sealed the tomb's stone cover and set a watch. Jesus triumphantly arose on the third day (Matt. 28:1–7). *See* RESURRECTION, ASCENSION.

Some Elements of Jesus' Teaching. The Son of God always pointed men to the Father (John 1:14–18). Jesus taught entrance by the new birth (John 3:3–5) into His coming spiritual kingdom (Matt. 13; 16:18–19; John 18:33–37). *See* KINGDOM OF GOD.

JESUS JUSTUS, a friend of the Apostle Paul (Col. 4:11).

JETHER, (1) the same as Jethro, Moses' father-in-law (Ex. 4:18), (2) the son of Gideon slain by Abimelech (Judg. 9:18, 20), (3) the father of Amasa who was general of the army of Absalom (I Kin. 2:5, 32). (4) the son of Jada and a descendant of Hezron (I Chr. 2:32), (5) the son of Ezra (I Chr. 4:17), (6) the head of a certain family of Asher and the father of Jephunneh (I Chr. 7:38).

JETHETH, one of the dukes of Esau (Gen. 36:40; I Chr. 1:51).

JETHLAH, ITHLAH, a city located on the border of Dan (Josh. 19:42).

JETHRO, a priest of Midian and the father-in-law of Moses, (Ex. 3:1, 4:18). While Israel was in the wilderness, it was under the advice of Jethro that certain men were chosen to share in the responsibility of the government with Moses (Ex. 18:8–27).

JETUR, the son of Ishmael the descendants of whom are the Ituraeans (Gen. 25:15; I Chr. 1:31; 5:19; Luke 3:1).

JEUEL, a descendant of Zerah, who lived in Jerusalem after the Babylonian captivity (I Chr. 9:6).

JEUSH, (1) the son of Esau who became a sheik of Edom (Gen. 36:5, 14, 18; I Chr. 1:35), (2) the son of Bilhan and the grandson of Benjamin (I Chr. 7: 10), (3) the son of Shimei and who was also a Levite (I Chr. 23:10, 11), (4) the son of Rehoboam (II Chr. 11:19).

JEUZ, the son of Shaharaim and the chief of a house of Benjamin (I Chr. 8:10).

JEW, the name used to designate the kingdom of Judah (II Kin. 16:6; 25: 25; Jer. 32:12; 38:19; 40:11; 41:3) and later came to be used for all the Israelites (John 4:9; Acts 18:2, 24).

JEWEL, JEWELRY, translation of various Hebrew words for different trinkets or ornaments, often made of silver or gold (Num. 31:50; I Sam. 6:8, 15; Ezek. 16:12; Hos. 2:13). *See* NOSE JEWEL.
j. of silver and gold, Ex. 11:2.
j. of gold, Num. 31:50.
adorneth with her *j.*, Isa. 61:10.
take thy fair *j.*, Ezek. 16:39.

JEWESS, a Hebrew woman (Acts 16:1; 24:24; II Tim. 3:15).

JEWISH, belonging or pertaining to the Jews (Tit. 1:14).

JEWRY, perhaps equal to Judah in Dan. 5:13 and to Judaea in Luke 23:5.

JEZANIAH, *see* JAAZANIAH.

JEZEBEL, the daughter of Ethbaal who was king of Tyre and Sidon, (I Kin. 16: 31). She influenced the worship of heathen gods in the court of Ahab (I Kin. 16:31, 32; 18:19). When her husband was disappointed at not getting the vineyard of Naboth, she arranged to have him slain (I Kin. 21). She was finally killed by the order of Jehu by being cast down from an upper window (II Kin. 9:33).

JEZER, the son of Naphtali and ancestor of the Jezerites (Gen. 46:24; Num. 26: 49; I Chr. 7:13).

JEZERITES, the descendants of Jezer (Num. 26:49).

JEZIAH, IZZIAH, the son of Parosh who put away his foreign wife after the Babylonian captivity (Ezra 10:25).

JEZIEL, the son of Azmaveth who joined himself to David at Ziklag (I Chr. 12:3).

JEZLIAH, IZLIAH, the son of Elpaal who appears to have been a chief man of Benjamin (I Chr. 8:18).

JEZOAR, the son of Helah (I Chr. 4:7).

JEZRAHIAH, an official over the singers at the dedication of the Jerusalem walls following the exile of Babylon (Neh. 12:42).

JEZREEL, (1) a descendant of Etam of the tribe of Judah (I Chr. 4:3), (2) the son of the prophet Hosea (Hos. 1:4, 5), (3) a city in Issachar some fifty-five miles north of Jerusalem (Josh. 19:18). (4) a town of Judah (Josh. 15:56; I Sam. 25:43; 27:3).

JEZREEL, VALLEY OF, the valley which lies on the northern side of the city of Issachar. The name was later used in reference to the entire plain of Esdraelon (Josh. 17:16; Judg. 6:33; Hos. 1:5).

JEZREELITE, one who lives in Jezreel of Issachar (I Kin. 21:1, II Kin. 9:21, 25).

JEZREELITESS, a woman of Jezreel of Judah (I Sam. 27:3; 30:5; II Sam. 2:2; 3:2; I Chr. 3:1).

JIBSAM, the son of Tola and the same as Ibsam (I Chr. 7:2).

JIDLAPH, the son of Nahor and the nephew of Abraham (Gen. 22:22).

JIMNA, JIMNAH, *See* **IMNAH** (Num. 26:44; Gen. 46:17).

JIMNITES, the descendants of Jimna (Num. 26:44).

JIPHTAH, a city of Judah (Josh. 15:43).

JIPHTHAHEL, a valley between Asher and Naphtali (Josh. 19:14, 27).

JOAB, (1) the son of Zeruiah, David's sister (II Sam. 2:13), (2) the son of Seraiah and ancestor of those that dwell at Charashim (I Chr. 4:14), (3) one whose descendants returned from the Babylonian exile with Ezra (Ezra 2:6; Neh. 7:11).

JOAH, (1) the son of Asaph and the recorder under Hezekiah the king (II Kin. 18:18, 26, 37; Isa. 36:3, 22), (2) the son of Zimnah and a Levite who was perhaps the one who aided Hezekiah in reforming the worship of the temple (I (Chr. 6:21; II Chr. 29:12), (3) the son of Obed-edom (I Chr. 26:4), (4) the son of Joahaz (II Chr. 34:8).

JOAHAZ, the father of Joah (II Chr. 34:8).

JOANAN, ancestor of Mary's husband (Luke 3:27).

JOANNA, (1) the son of Rhesa and the grandson of Zerubbabel (Luke 3:27), (2) the wife of Chuza to whom the Lord appeared after His resurrection (Luke 8:3; 24:10).

JOASH, JEHDASH, (1) the father of Gideon (Judg. 6:11, 29–31; 7:14; 8:13, 29–32), (2) one who was commissioned by King Ahab to throw Micaiah the prophet into prison (I Kin. 22:26; II Chr. 18:25), (3) one of the kings of Judah (II Kin. 11:2; 12:19, 20; 13:1, 10; etc.), (4) one of the kings of Israel (II Kin. 13:9, 12, 13, 14, etc.). *See* JEHOASH, (5) a descendant of·Shelah (I Chr. 4:22), (6) the son of Shemah who joined himself to David at Ziklag (I Chr. 12:3).

JOASH, (1) the son of Becher and a head man in his family (I Chr. 7:8), (2) one who supervised the cellars of oil in the reigns of David and Solomon (I Chr. 27:28).

JOATHAM, the son of Uzziah (Matt. 1:9).

JOB, the son of Issachar (Gen. 46:13) and called Jashub in Num. 26:24; I Chr. 7:1).

JOB, THE BOOK OF, one of the great books of the Old Testament which takes its name from its chief character. The story begins with a contest between God and Satan to see whether Job would remain faithful to the Lord even though his material blessings were taken away (Job. 1:–2:). Finally Job is stricken with boils and then there is a lengthy discussion between him and his three friends, Eliphaz, Bildad and Zophar, concerning the reason of his suffering. They contend that Job is paying for his sins, but Job is firm in upholding his righteousness. Of course the answer of the Lord at the close of the Book is one which neither Job nor his friends have considered. They have been talking on a subject about which they know nothing. The thing to do is to just rely upon the powerful hand of God and let Him work things the way He will regardless of His motive.

JOBAB, (1) the son of Joktan (Gen. 10: 29; I Chr. 1:23), (2) the son of Zerah and a king of Edom (Gen. 36: 33, 34; I Chr. 1:44, 45), (3) the king of Madon ·who was overrun by Joshua (Josh. 11:1), (4) the son of Shaharaim (I Chr. 8:9), (5) the son of Elpaal (I Chr. 8:18).

JOCHEBED, the mother of Moses, Aaron, and Miriam (Num. 26:59).

JODA, JUDA, an ancestor of Jesus (Luke 3:26).

JOED, the son of Pedaiah, whose descendant, Sallu, lived in Jerusalem following the captivity (Neh. 11:7).

JOEL, (1) the son of Samuel and who was commissioned to be a judge in Beersheba (I Sam. 8:2; I Chr. 6:33; 15:17). (2) one of the descendants of Simeon whose family went to the valley of Gedor (I Chr. 4:35), (3) one of the descendants of Reuben (I Chr. 5:4, 8), (4) one of the chief men of the Gadites who lived in Bashan (I Chr. 5:12), (5) the son of Azariah and a Levite who aided Hezekiah in restoring the services of the temple (I Chr. 6:36; II Chr. 29:12), (6) the son of Izrahiah and a chief man of Issachar at the time of David (I Chr. 7:3), (7) one of the mighty men of David (I Chr. 11:38). (8) a Levitical chief of the family of Gershom whom David commissioned to aid in removing the ark (I Chr. 15:7, 11). (9) the son of Pediah and a chief of Manasseh west at the time of David (I Chr. 27:20), (10) the son of Nebo who put away his heathen wife following the captivity (Ezra 10:43), (11) the son of Zichri (Neh. 11:9), (12) the son of Pethuel and one of the twelve prophets. (Joel 1:1; Acts 2:16).

JOEL, THE BOOK OF, one of the books of the Old Testament which takes its name from its author. The book begins with a description of a plague of locust and a command to repent. He also mentions the coming day of the Lord in which an enemy will come into the city (Joel 1:1–2:27). Joel then takes up a brighter side and prophesies of the Messianic age in which the Spirit of God will be poured out upon all flesh (2:28–32; cf. Acts 2:17). He then tells of the time when Judah will be returned from captivity and the nations will be brought into judgment (3:1–21).

JOELAH, the son of Jeroham who joined himself to David at Ziklag (I Chr. 12:7).

JOEZER, a Korhite who joined himself to David at Ziklag (I Chr. 12:6).

JOGBEHAH, a city built again by the Gadites (Num. 32:35; Judg. 8:11).

JOGLI, the father of a certain Bukki who was commissioned to divide the promised land (Num. 34:22).

JOHA, (1) the son of Beriah and a chief of Benjamin (I Chr. 8:16), (2) a Tizite and one of the mighty men of David (I Chr. 11:45).

JOHANAN, (1) the son of Careah who was among those who carried Jeremiah to Egypt (Jer. 43:1–7; 40:13–16; 41:11–16; II Kin. 25:23), (2) the son of Josiah the king (I Chr. 3:15), (3) the son of Elioenai and a descendant of Zerubbabel (I Chr. 3:24), (4) the son of Azariah and possibly the same as Jehoiada (I Chr. 6:9, 10; II Chr. 24: 15), (5) one of those who joined himself to David at Ziklan (I Chr. 12:4), (6) one of the Gadite warriors (I Chr. 12:12), (7) the father of the Azariah (II Chr. 28:12), (8) the son of Hakkatan who was among those that came with Ezra from Babylon (Ezra 8:12), (9) the son of Eliashib and possibly the same as Johanan mentioned in Neh. 12:22, 23 (Ezra 10:6), (10) the son of Tobiah an Ammonite (Neh. 6:18).

JOHN, (1) a certain priest on the council before whom Peter and John were brought following the cure of the lame man (Acts 4:6), (2) the Hebrew name for Mark (Acts 12:12, 25; 13:5; 15:37).

JOHN, THE APOSTLE, the son of Zebedee and Salome (Mark 1:20; Luke 5:10; Mark 15:40; Matt. 27:56). Jesus called John at the same time with his brother James and with Simon (Peter) and Andrew (Mark 1:19–20; Luke 5:10). Later John was chosen to be one of the twelve apostles (Mark 3:13–19). The books of the New Testament generally accredited to his authorship are: The Gospel According to John, I John, II John, III John, and the Book of Revelation.

JOHN, THE BAPTIST, the forerunner of the Lord Jesus as foretold in Isa. 40:3 and Mal. 3:1. The name Baptist simply means "one who baptizes." John was the son of Zacharias, a priest in the course of Abia (Luke 1:5). His ministry began shortly before that of Jesus when he preached in the wilderness of Judah to "repent ye; for the kingdom of heaven is at hand" (Matt. 3:2). He announced that Christ would come after him and would be mightier than he (Matt. 3:11). It was this Herod, who had John beheaded (Mark 6:23–29).

JOHN, FIRST EPISTLE OF, one of the New Testament books apparently written by the apostle somewhere around 90 A.D. The purpose of the book seems to be to correct the false teachings of Gnosticism which held that Jesus did not really come in the flesh. John says that they had heard Him and seen Him with their eyes and they had handled Him with their hands (I John 1:1).

JOHN, GOSPEL OF THE, the book written by the apostle and located as the fourth book in the New Testament. It seems that the main purpose of the book is to demonstrate what real faith in Jesus Christ is. For this reason the noun "faith" never occurs. On the other hand the verb "to believe" is very frequent. John's point is that only that faith which is active and working is justifying. Perhaps his strongest example is John 12:42, 43 where it is stated that certain of the rulers believed in Him but would not confess Him. The self-righteous Jews had only a verbal relationship to God rather than one which was living and working. Real faith is that relationship to God which causes one to rely upon through trust and to submit by obedience to the will of God.

JOHN, SECOND EPISTLE OF, a very short letter written by one who calls himself the "elder" to "the elect lady and her children" (II John 1). He speaks of the commandment love (II John 5) and mentions the false teaching of the Gnostics that Jesus Christ comes not in the flesh (II John 7).

JOHN, THIRD EPISTLE OF, a very short letter written by the "elder" to "Gaius the beloved" (III John 1). The writer wishes to correct the man Diotrephes who "loveth to have the preeminence" (III John 9).

JOIADA, the son of Eliashib who became high priest (Neh. 12:10, 11, 22).

JOIAKIM, the son of Jeshua and who was a high priest (Neh. 12:10).

JOIARIB, (1) a wise man with whom Ezra sought advice (Ezra 8:16–20), (2) the son of Zechariah of the tribe of Judah (Neh. 11:5), (3) the head of one of the courses of priests (Neh. 11:10), (4) one of the priests who returned to Jerusalem with Zerubbabel (Neh. 12:6).

JOIN, to connect or fasten together.

all these kings were *j.*, Gen. 14:3.
lest then *j.* enemies, Ex. 1:10.
j. himself to citizen, Luke 15:15.
whole body fitly *j.*, Eph. 4:16.

JOINT, junction, union.
j. of harness, I Kin. 22:34.
like foot out of *j.*, Prov. 25:19.
every *j.* supplieth, Eph. 4:16.
of *j.* and marrow, Heb. 4:12.

JOKDEAM, a city in Judah (Josh. 15:56).

JOKIM, a descendant of Judah through Shelah (I Chr. 4:22).

JOKMEAM, a place in the Jordan Valley given to the Levites (I Chr. 6:68).

JOKNEAM, a city of Palestine on the edge of Zebulun (Josh. 12:22, 19:11; 21:34; I Kin. 4:12).

JOKSHAN, the son of Abraham by Keturah (Gen. 25:2, 3; I Chr. 1:32).

JOKTAN, the son of Eber and the brother of Peleg (Gen. 10:25, I Chr. 1:19, 23).

JOKTHEEL, (1) a city of Judah (Josh. 15:38), (2) a name given to Selah by Amaziah (II Kin. 14:7; see II Chr. 25:11–13).

JONA, the same as Jonas.

JONADAB, JEHONADAB, (1) the son of Shimeah and the nephew of David (II Sam. 13:3, (2) a Rechabite (Jer. 35:6, 8).

JONAH, the son of Amittai and one of the minor prophets. He was of the tribe of Zebulun (II Kin. 14:25).

JONAH, THE BOOK OF, the fifth in order of the minor prophets of the Old Testament. The book gives the biographical account of the prophet's ministry to the wicked city of Nineveh. He was commissioned by the Lord to go and preach repentance to the people. Instead he fled toward Tarshish by way of Joppa where he caught a ship. The Lord sent a great wind on the sea and finally the sailors cast Jonah over the side as a measure to save the ship. The prophet was then swallowed by a large fish (Jonah 1). Chapter two records a prayer of Jonah which he

prayed while in the fish's belly and the fact that the prophet was vomited up on dry land. Chapter three tells of the second charge given by the Lord to go preach to Nineveh. This time Jonah obeyed and the city was brought to repentance. In chapter four God teaches displeased Jonah the lesson of the gourd.

JONAN, JANAM, the son of Eliakim an ancestor of Jesus (Luke 3:30).

JONAS, (1) same as the prophet Jonah (Matt. 12:39, 40, 41; 16:4; Luke 11:29, 30, 32), (2) the father of Peter the apostle (John 21:15–17).

JONATHAN, (1) the son of Gershom (Judg. 18:1–30), (2) the son of King Saul (I Sam. 14:1) and the close friend of David (I Sam. 18:1), (3) the son of Abiathar, a high priest (II Sam. 15:27, 36), (4) the son of Shimeah (II Sam. 21:21; I Chr. 20:7), (5) the son of Shage and an important warrior of David (II Sam. 23:32; I Chr. 11:34), (6) the son of Jada (I Chr. 2:32, 33), (7) one whose son Ebed returned from Babylon with Ezra (Ezra 8:6), (8) the son of Asahel who aided in separating the men from their foreign wives (Ezra 10:15), (9) the son of Joiada (Neh. 12:11). (10) a certain priest at the time of Joiakim (Neh. 12:14), (11) the son of Shemaiah and the father of Zechariah (Neh. 12:35), (12) a certain scribe in whose house Jeremiah was set in prison (Jer. 37:15, 20; 38:26), (13) the son of Kareah who was among the number who held conference with Gedaliah (Jer. 40:8).

JONATH-ELEM-REHOKIM, JONATH-ELEM-RECHOKIM, (Ps. 56), a musical term, probably denoting the tune of the psalm.

JOPPA, JAPHO, a city on the Mediterranean that was assigned to Dan (Josh. 19:43).

JORAH, a man after whose name a number of people returned from Babylonian exile (Ezra 2:18).

JORAI, a Gadite chieftain (I Chr. 5:13).

JORAM, JEHORAM, (1) the son of Toi, the king of Hamath (II Sam. 8:9, 10),

(2) a descendant of Eliezer (I Chr. 26: 25).

JORDAN, (the descender), this famous Palestinian river begins in the lower slopes of Mt. Hermon and flows almost directly South to the Dead Sea, dropping from about sea level at Lake Huleh to 700 feet below the Mediterranean level at the Sea of Galilee and 1,292 feet below sea level at the Dead Sea. Its only important tributaries are the Yarmuk and the Jabbok from the East. Although normally small, the Jordan can become torrential in the rainy season, as it was when the Israelites crossed miraculously as they entered Canaan (Josh. 3:14–17). Ordinarily, the river was crossed at one of several fords. Jordan has always been an important political boundary.

Lot chose plain of *J.*, Gen. 13:11.
inherit beyond *j.*, Josh. 13:8.
in *J.*, Matt. 3:6, Mark 1:5, 9.
Bethabara beyond *J.*, John 1:28.

JORIM, the son of Matthat and one of the ancestors of Jesus Christ (Luke 3:29).

JORKEAM, JORKOAM, the son of Raham and a descendant of Caleb; (I Chr. 2:44).

JOSABAD, the same as Jozabad (1).

JOSAPHAT, the Greek form for the name Jehoshaphat (Matt. 1:8).

JOSE, an ancestor of Jesus (Luke 3:29).

JOSEDECH, the son of Seraiah and another form of Jehozadak and Jozadak (Hag. 1:1, 12, 14, 2:2, 4; Zech. 6:11).

JOSEPH, the son of Jacob and Rachel and the brother of Benjamin (Gen. 30: 22–24; 35:16–18). The elder brothers of Joseph disliked him very much for the dreams he had and for the favor showed him by his father (Gen. 37:3–11). One day the lad came seeking his brothers in the field, they conspired to kill him; but being reasoned with by Reuben, they put him in a pit and later sold him to a caravan going down to Egypt (Gen. 37: 22–28). Jacob was deceived into believing that a wild beast had slain the boy (Gen. 37:29–33). In Egypt, Joseph had fortune and then trouble in the house of his master, Potiphar. He was cast into prison (Gen. 39:1–20). There he made friends by interpreting dreams and later when Pharaoh had a dream, he was summoned from his imprisonment and was made to be second in power throughout the land of Egypt, after having revealed that a great famine would come upon the land (Gen. 41). When the famine did come, Jacob sent his sons to Egypt to buy food (Gen. 42:1–3). The rest of the account tells how Joseph brought all of his father's house to Egypt and fed them during the years of famine (Gen. 42:4–50). Upon the request of Joseph, his bones were carried out of Egypt at the exodus of the children of Israel (Gen. 50:25; Ex. 13:19).

JOSEPH, (1) the father of Igal, who later was commissioned by Moses to be a spy from Issachar (Num. 13:7), (2) the son of Asaph (I Chr. 25:2, 9), (3) an Israelite who put away his heathen wife following the Babylonian captivity (Ezra 10:42), (4) the son of Shebaniah and a chief priest following the exile (Neh. 12:14), (5) the husband of Mary, the mother of Jesus (Matt. 1:18–25), (6) the son of Mattathias and one of the ancestors of Jesus (Luke 3:24), (7) the son of Judah and one of the ancestors of Jesus (Luke 3:26), (8) the son of Jonan and one of the ancestors of Jesus (Luke 3:30), (9) a man of Arimathaea who aided in the burial of the body of Jesus (John 19:38–42; Matt. 27:58–60; Mark 15:43–46; Luke 23:50), (10) one of the names of Barsabas, who after the death of Judas, was a candidate for the office of apostle (Acts 1:23–25).

JOSEPHUS, a Jewish historian, public official and general about A.D. 37-100. He is not mentioned in the Bible.

JOSES, (1) one of the brothers of the Lord (Matt. 13:55; Mark 6:3), (2) a certain Levite of Cyprus (Acts 4:36), (3) the son of Mary (Matt. 27:56; Mark 15:40, 47).

JOSHAH, the son of Amaziah and a prince of Simeon (I Chr. 4:34).

JOSHAPHAT, one of the mighty men of David the king (I Chr. 11:43).

JOSHAVIAH, the son of Elnaam and

was connected with David's bodyguard (I Chr. 11:46).

JOSHBEKASHAH, the son of Heman and a leader of the temple musicians (I Chr. 25:4, 24).

JOSHEB-BASSEBET, a Tachmonite and a chief of the three heroes of David (II Sam. 23:8). He is the same as Joshabeam in I Chr. 11:11.

JOSHIBIAH, JOSIBIAH, of the family of Asiel, a Simeon (I Chr. 4:35).

JOSHUA, JEHOSHUA, JEHOSHUAH, OSHEA, the son of Nun and who succeeded Moses as leader of the children of Israel (Ex. 33:11; Deut. 31:23).

JOSHUA, (1) a man of Beth-shemesh into whose field the ark came as it was returned to Israel (I Sam. 6:14, 18), (2) the Jerusalem governor during the Josiah reformation (II Kin. 23:8), (3) the son of Josedech and the high priest at the time of Haggai and Zechariah (Hag. 1:1, 12, 14; Zech. 3:1–10).

JOSHUA, THE BOOK OF, the fifth in order of the books of the Old Testament. It gives the account of the crossing of the Jordan and the conquest of the land of Palestine (Josh. 1:1–12:24); the distribution of the land to the Israelites (Josh. 13:1–22:34); the final address of Joshua and his death (Josh. 23:1–24–33).

JOSIAH, (1) the son of Amon and Jedidah and the sixteenth king of Judah (II Kin. 21:26; 22:1; II Chr. 34:1). He did that which was right in the sight of the Lord (II Kin. 22:2). During his reign he carried out various reforms throughout the land (II Kin. 23), (2) the son of Zephaniah who lived at Jerusalem following the exile (Zech. 6:10).

JOSIAS, the Greek form of Josiah (Matt. 1:10, 11).

JOSIBIAH, the son of Seriah and who was the father of Jehu who moved to Gedor (I Chr. 4:35).

JOSIPHIAH, one whose son led a number of men to Jerusalem under Ezra (Ezra 8:10).

JOT, a word used at times to express a very small particle and probably has reference to the Greek Iota which corresponds to the English i (Matt. 5:18).

JOTBAH, the city of Haruz (II Kin. 21:19).

JOTBATH, *see* **JOTBATHAH.**

JOTBATHAH, an encampment of Israel (Num. 33:33, 34). It is called Jotbath in Deut. 10:7).

JOTHAM, (1) the son of Gideon who escaped the massacre of Abimelech (Judg. 9:5), (2) the son of Uzziah and Jerusha who became the eleventh king of Judah (II Kin. 15:5, 32, 33; II Chr. 27:1), (3) the son of Jahdai (I Chr. 2:47).

JOURNEY, to travel, take a trip.
made *j.* prosperous, Gen. 24:21.
pursued seven day's *j.*, Gen. 31:23 .
from Jerusalem a day's *j.*, Acts 1:12.
to see you in my *j.*, Rom. 15:24.
in *j.* often, in perils, II Cor. 11:26.

JOURNEYS OF THE ISRAELITES, *see* **WILDERNESS OF THE WANDERING.**

JOY, happiness, gladness, delight.
people rejoiced with *j.*, I Kin. 1:40 .
give them oil of *j.*, Isa. 61:3 .
babe leaped for *j.*, Luke 1:44.
kingdom of God is *j.*, Rom. 14:17.
making request with *j.*, Phil. 1:4 .
count it *j.* when, James 1:2.

JOYFUL, full of joy, exceedingly glad.
went to their tents *j.*, I Kin. 8:66.
no *j.* voice come therein, Job 3:7.
make *j.* noise to rock of, Ps. 95:1 .

JOZABAD, (1) a man of Benjamin who joined himself to David at Ziklag (I Chr. 12:4, the same as Josabad), (2) a captain of Manasseh who joined himself to David (I Chr. 12:20), (3) another captain of Manasseh who joined David (I Chr. 12:20), (4) an overseer during the time of Hezekiah (II Chr. 31:13), (5) a Levitical prince who made offerings in the time of Josiah (II Chr. 35:9), (6) a certain Levite commissioned by Ezra to weigh the gold and silver brought to the sanctuary (Ezra 8:33), (7) the son of Pashur (Ezra 10:22), (8) a certain Levite who put away his Gentile wife after the exile (Ezra 10:23), (9) a certain Levite who aided Ezra in giving the law to the people (Neh. 8:7).

JOZACHAR, JOZACAR, the son of Shimeath and one of the servants of Joash who killed the king at Millo (II Kin. 12:21; II Chr. 24:25).

JOZADAK, JEHOZADAK, see Johoza-dak (Ezra 3:2, 8; 5:2, 10:18; Neh. 12:26).

JUBAL, the son of Lamech who invented the harp and organ (Gen. 4:21).

JUBILEE, one of the feast of the Jews which was to be celebrated once every fifty years. All real property would revert back to its original holder. It was to be a year in which there would be no reaping, but the people were instructed to live on what the land might produce of itself (Lev. 25:9; 10:54; 27:17; Num. 36:4).

JUCAL, a shortened form of Jehucal (Jer. 38:1).

JUDA, the same as Judas or Judah. (1) the son of Jacob (Luke 3:33; Heb. 7:14; Rev. 5:5; 7:5), (2) one of the Lord's brothers (Mark 6:3), (3) one of the ancestors of the Lord (Luke 3:26), (4) one of the ancestors of the Lord (Luke 3:30).

JUDAEA, see **JUDEA.**

JUDAH, the son of Jacob and Leah (Gen. 29:35). It was through the blood line of this patriarch that Christ was born (Matt. 1:2).

JUDAH, (1) a certain Levite who came to Jerusalem with Zerubbabel (Neh. 12:8), (2) the son of Senuah (Neh. 11:9), (3) one who followed the princes around part of the wall of Jerusalem after it had been rebuilt (Neh. 12:34).

JUDAH, THE KINGDOM OF, after the death of Solomon, the kingdom was divided into two separate kingdoms, the northern one called Israel, and the southern Judah. Solomon's son, Rehoboam became king of Judah with Jeroboam as king of Israel (I Kin. 11:43–12).

JUDAHITE, inhabitant of Judah or member of the tribe of Judah. See **JUDAH.**

JUDAISM, the religion of the Jews.

JUDAIZER, one who conforms or teaches others to conform to Judaism.

JUDAIZING, conforming to the religious teachings of the Jews.

JUDAS, the Greek form of the Hebrew name Judah, which was a common name among the Jews (Matt. 10:4; 13:55; Luke 16:16).
(1) The translation in the King James Version for Judah, son of Jacob (Matt. 1:2, 3).
(2) An ancestor of Jesus through Joseph (Luke 3:30).
(3) Judas of Galilee, who, with Sadduk, instigated a revolt against Rome (Acts 5:37).
(4) Judas Iscariot, one of the twelve apostles, betrayer of Jesus. His surname evidently means "man of Kerioth." It may be the same as the modern Karjetan, south of Hebron, or Kuriut, on the northeastern border of Judea. He was made steward of the disciples, and must have been trusted. The betrayal of Jesus and the subsequent suicide of Judas are narrated (Matt. 26:14–16; 47–56; 27:3–8; Acts 1:16–19).
(5) One of the twelve apostles, not Iscariot (John 14:22), also called Lebbaeus and Thaddaeus (Matt. 10:3; Mark 3:18). He was the son or brother of James (Luke 6:16).
(6) One of the sons of Mary (Matt. 13:55), and possibly the author of the epistle of Jude. See **BRETHREN OF THE LORD.**
(7) A man of Damascus with whom Paul lodged (Acts 9:11).
(8) Judas Barsabas, a leader of the church in Jerusalem. He and Silas were chosen to accompany Paul and Barnabas to Antioch (Acts 15:22–33).

JUDE, the brother of James and perhaps the brother of the Lord (Jude 1:1).

JUDE, EPISTLE OF, most likely written about A.D. 75 by the Jude who was a brother of Jesus, this letter denounces certain false teachers who opposed authority, practiced licentiousness, and denied Christ (Jude 3–6). Jude pictures the evil of such views and exhorts

Christians to faithfulness and defense of the truth (Jude 3, 20–23).

JUDEA, the name given to the southern division of the country of Palestine in the time of the Romans. The northern boundary was Samaria and the southern the desert.
went into prov. of *J.*, Ezra 5:8.
them which be in *J.* flee, Matt. 24:16.
in all *J.* ye shall be, Acts 1:8.
do not believe in *J.*, Rom. 15:31.
churches which in *J.*, I Thess. 2:14.

JUDEAN, of Judah, pertaining to Judea.

JUDGE, to try, decide, *see* **JUDGES.**
J. of all the earth, Gen. 18:25.
j. betwixt us both, Gen. 31:37.
j. over us, Ex. 2:14.
the Lord was with *j.*, Judg. 2:18.
j. fatherless and oppressed, Ps. 10:18.
j. not that ye be not *j.*, Matt. 7:1.
j. after flesh, John 8:15.
sittest thou to *j.* me, Acts 23:3.
j. quick and dead, II Tim. 4:1.
be *j.* according to men, I Pet. 4:6.
j. every man according to, Rev. 20:13.

JUDGES, those officers who ruled over the children between the time of Joshua and the crowning of Saul. When the Hebrews took possession of the land of Palestine there were still heathen neighbors who corrupted them with idolatry and often oppressed them. In their distress they would cry to God and He would raise up a judge to deliver His people. After the judge died the people would revert back to their wickedness and the cycle would begin again (Judg. 2:16–19). These judges produced justice in the land not only through warfare but also by enacting the laws of the Lord. The chronology of the judges might be stated thus: Othniel (Judg. 3:9–12), Ehud (Judg. 3:15–30), Shamgar (Judg. 3:31), Deborah (Judg. 4:4–5:31), Gideon (Judg. 6:2–8:38), Tola (Judg. 10:1, 2), Jair (Judg. 10:3), Jephthah (Judg. 11: 1–12:7), Ibzan (Judg. 12:8–10), Elon (Judg. 12:11, 12), Abdon (Judg. 12: 13–15), Samson (Judg. 15:20, 16:31), Eli (I Sam. 4:18), Samuel (I Sam. 7:9).

JUDGES, THE BOOK OF, the seventh book in order of the Old Testament. It gives the history of the Children of Is-

rael from the time of Joshua to that of Samuel. The book reveals how when the people turned their backs upon the law of God they were oppressed by the nations around them; but when they restored their loyalty to the Lord their prosperity was also restored (Judg. 2: 16–19).

JUDGMENT, the result of trying, judging, and or condemning. The Judgment Day is a day in which the Lord will judge the world in righteousness (Acts 17:31; Matt. 25:31–46).
after many, to wrest *j.*, Ex. 23:2.
doth God pervert *j.*, Job 8:3.
prepared His throne for *j.*, Ps. 9:7.
in danger of the *j.*, Matt. 5:21.
send forth *j.* unto, Matt. 12:20.
committed all *j.* to Son, John 5:22.
reprove the world of *j.*, John 16:8.
reasoned of *J.* Felix, Acts 24:25.
knowing the *j.* of God, Rom. 1:32.
token of the *j.* of God, II Thess. 1:5.
after this the *j.*, Heb. 9:27.
j. begin at house of God, I Pet. 4:17.
hour of *j.* is come Rev. 14:7.

JUDGMENT HALL, *see* **PRAETORI-UM.**

JUDITH, the daughter of Beeri and the wife of Esau (Gen. 26:34).

JULIA, a woman who was a disciple at the city of Rome (Rom. 16:15).

JULIUS, the centurion commissioned to take the apostle Paul to Rome (Acts 27: 1, 3, 43).

JUNIA, JUNIAS, a certain disciple at the city of Rome (Rom. 16:7).

JUNIPER, an almost leafless desert shrub. It furnishes poor shade (I Kin. 19:4), but its roots make good fuel (Ps. 120:4). The Hebrew word is more correctly rendered "broom tree."

JUPITER, the sky god who is supreme among the Romans and equal to the Greek Zeus (Acts 14:12; 19:35).

JUSHAB-HESED, either the son of Pedaiah or of Zerubbabel (I Chr. 3:19, 20).

JUST, right, righteous.

Noah was *j*. man, Gen. 6:9.
man be more *j*. than God, Job 4:17.
bless. habitation of *j*., Prov. 3:33.
to punish the *j*. is, Prov. 17:26.
Joseph, being a *j*. man, Matt. 1:19.
innocent of blood of *j*., Matt. 27:24.
ye denied the *J*., Acts 3:14.
the commandment holy, *j*., Rom. 7:12.
bishop must be *j*. holy, Tit. 1:8.
the *j*. for the unjust, I Pet. 3:18.
He is *j*. to forgive sins, I John 1:9.

JUSTICE, that which is right.
execute the *j*. of, Deut. 33:21.
David executed *j*., II Sam. 8:15.
and *j*. take hold on thee, Job 36:17.
seest perverting of *j*., Eccles. 5:8.
and do *j*. for my salvation, Isa. 56:1.
O princes, execute *j*., Ezek. 45:9.

JUSTIFICATION, with the Greeks justice was cold meaning strict adherence to the law. With the Hebrews, however, the qualities of mercy and pity were involved so that for one to meet the state of justification meant not to be perfect but to have received mercy from the Lord after having submitted to His will. This same idea pervades the New Testament. For one to be just in God's sight is not living to perfection (which no man can do) but receiving mercy and forgiveness of sins by having faith in Christ (Rom. 3:28). This faith, however, is not merely mental acceptance that there is a God but the complete submission, reliance, and commitment to the will of God.
raised again for our *j*., Rom. 4:25.
gift of many offences to *j*., Rom. 5:16.
free gift on all to *j*., Rom. 5:18.

JUSTIFIED, to be made just.
by works man is *j*., James 2:24.

JUSTIFY, make just, vindicate.
will not *j*. wicked, Ex. 23:7.
if I *j*. myself, Job 9:20.
righteous servant *j*., Is. 53:11.
willing to *j*. himself, Luke 10:29
that God would *j*., Gal. 3:8.

JUSTLY, in a just way.
Lord require to do *j*., Mic. 6:8.
indeed *j*. we receive, Luke 23:41
holily and *j*., I Thess. 2:10.

JUSTUS, (1) Barsabas who was one of the candidates to fill the vacant apostleship of Judas Iscariot (Acts 1:23), (2) a certain disciple at Corinth in whose house Paul preached (Acts 18:7), (3) also called Jesus, a fellow-worker of Paul (Col. 4:11).

JUTAH, JUTTAH, a certain Levitical city in Judah (Josh. 15:55; 21:16).

K

KAB, *see* **CAB.**

KABZEEL, a city in South Judah, (Josh. 15:21).

KADESH, KADESH-BARNEA, a region where the Israelites twice camped while journeying from Egypt to Canaan; it is about seventy miles South of Hebron. From this place Moses sent out the spies (Num. 13:2) and at this place the people rebelled (Num. 14:4). Because of the rebellion the people were punished, and thus Kadesh (sanctuary) became En-Mishpat (Fountain of Judgment). Here Miriam died (Num. 20:1), and here Moses sinned in striking the rock (Num. 20:2–11).

KADMIEL, (1) a Levite who returned from Babylon with Zerubbabel (Ezra 2:40; Neh. 7:43; 12:8). (2) A Levite who led devotions of the people after Ezra taught them the Law (Neh. 9:4; 10:9).

KADMONITES, a tribe mentioned only in Gen. 15:19 as one of the nations to be conquered by Israel.

KAIN, a town in the hill country of Judah (Josh. 15:57).

KALLAI, a priest who returned with Zerubbabel (Neh. 12:1, 20).

KAMON, CAMON, the place where Jair was buried (Judg. 10:3–5).

KANAH, (1) a stream serving as boundary between Ephraim and Manasseh (Josh. 16:8, 17:19, (2) a town in northern Asher (Josh. 19:28).

KAPH, 11th letter of the Hebrew alphabet, used as heading in Ps. 119:81.

KAREAH, CAREAH, father of Johanan and Jonathan (Jer. 40:8; 41:11; 43:2).

KARKA, KARKAA, place in Judah, between the Mediterranean and the Dead Sea (Josh. 15:3).

KARKOR, a place East of Jordan where Gideon's army overtook Zebah and Zalmunna (Judg. 8:10).

KARTAH, a Levitical town in the territory of Zebulun (Josh. 21:34).

KARTAN, *see* **KIRJATHAIM.**

KATTATH, a town of Zebulun (Josh. 19:15), perhaps same as Kitron.

KEDAR, (1) second son of Ishmael, and father of the tribe of Kedar (Gen. 25:13; I Chr. 1:29). (2) A nomadic tribe of Ishmaelites (Is. 60:7).

KEDEMAH, (eastward), the last named son of Ishmael, and probably head of the tribe Kedemah (Gen. 25:15; I Chr. 1:31).

KEDEMOTH, a Levitical city in Reuben (Josh. 13:18; 21:37).

KEDESH, (1) a city in extreme southern Judah, perhaps identical with Kadesh-barnea (Josh. 15:23). (2) A Levitical city in Issachar (I Chr. 6:72), also called Kishion (Josh. 19:20) and Kishon (Josh. 21:28). (3) A city of refuge in Naphtali (Josh. 19:37; 20:7).

KEDESH-NAPHTALI, *see* **KEDESH (3).**

KEEP, hold fast, protect, perform.
garden of Eden to *k.*, Gen. 2:15.
k. it a feast to Lord, Ex. 12:14.
k. back thy servant, Ps. 19:13.
k. thy judgments, Ps. 119:106.
k. sound wisdom, Prov. 3:21.
k. mercy and judgment, Hos. 12:6.
k. your own tradition, Mark 7:9.
if ye *k.* in memory, I Cor. 15:2.
k. yourselves in the love, Jude 21.
I will *k.* thee from, Rev. 3:10.

KEEPER, one who watches.
Abel was *k.* of sheep, Gen. 4:2.
am I my brother's *k.*?, Gen. 4:9.
k. of prison awaking, Acts 16:27.

KEHELATHAH, a desert camp of the Israelites (Num. 33:22).

KEILAH, a city in the Judean lowlands, which David saved from a Philistine siege and was repaid by treachery (I Sam. 23:1–13).

KELAIAH, (Ezra 10:23), *see* **KELITA.**

KELITA, a Levite who divorced his Gentile wife after the captivity (Ezra 10:23).

KEMUEL, (1) a son of Abraham's brother Nahor (Gen. 22:21). (2) Son of Shiphtan (Num. 34:24). (3) Father of Hasbabiah (I Chr. 27:17).

KENAN, (I Chr. 1:2), *see* **CAINAN.**

KENATH, a city in Gilead taken from the Canaanites by Nobah and called by his name (Num. 34:42).

KENAZ, (1) a son of Eliphaz, the firstborn of Esau. He became chief of an Edomite tribe (Gen. 36:11; I Chr. 1:36). (2) A brother of Caleb, and father of Othniel (Josh. 15:17; Judg. 1:13). (3) A grandson of Caleb (I Chr. 4:15).

KENEZITE, KENIZZITE, the clan whose name-father was Kenaz. Their land was promised to Abraham (Gen. 15:19).

KENITE, a group of skilled metal smiths who settled along the southwest shore of the Dead Sea (Judg. 1:16).

KENIZZITE, *see* **KENEZITE.**

KERCHIEF, (1) Ezek. 13:18–21 refers to some kind of divination. (2) In the New Testament the kerchief was used: as a money wrapper (Luke 19:20); as a head binding for the dead (John 11:44); and as an article of dress (Acts 19:12).

KEREN-HAPPUCH, name given to Job's youngest daughter (Job 42:14).

KERIOTH, KIRIOTH, (1) a city in southern Judah (Josh. 15:25). (2) A Moabite city containing a sanctuary to the false god Chemosh; Condemned in Jer. 48:24 and Amos 2:2.

KERIOTH-HEZRON, *see* **KERIOTH** and **HAZOR.**

KEROS, one of the Nethinim whose de

scendants returned with Zerubbabel (Ezra 2:44; Neh. 7:47).

KETTLE, a pot (I Sam. 2:14).

KETURAH, the second wife of Abraham (Gen. 25:1).

KEY, often used figuratively for power or authority (Matt. 16:19; Rev. 1:18; 3:7).
k. of house of David, Is. 22:22.
give the k. of kingdom, Matt. 16:19.
k. of bottomless pit, Rev. 9:1.

KEZIA, KEZIAH, Job's second daughter after his adversity (Job 42:14).

KEZIZ, a city of Benjamin (Josh 18:21).

KIBROTH-HATTAAVAH, a desert camp of the Israelites a day's journey from Sinai. (Num. 11:34; 33:16; Deut. 9:22).

KIBZAIM, a Levitical city in Ephraim (Josh. 21:22), also called Jokmeam (I Chr. 6:68).

KICK, to strike with the foot.
wherefore k. ye at my, I Sam. 2:29.
hard to k. against pricks, Acts 9:5.

KID, a young goat.
fetch me two k., Gen. 27:9.
k. for sin offering, Lev. 5:6.
never gavest me a k., Luke 15:29.

KIDNAPPING, this crime was punishable by death in Hebrew law (Ex. 21:16; Deut. 24:7).

KIDNEYS, internal organs of the body. (1) Animal kidneys were a choice part of the burnt offering (Ex. 29:13; Lev. 3:4; 4:9). (2) Used figuratively for the inner seat of desire, the word is usually rendered "reins" (Job 16:13; Ps. 73:21; Prov. 23:16; Jer. 12:2).

KIDRON, CEDRON, a sporadic stream that flows through the Valley of Jehoshaphat, it was called the "brook that flowed through the midst of the land" (II Chr. 32:4). David crossed it in fleeing from Absalom (II Sam. 15:23). In times of reform idols were burnt and thrown into the Kidron (I Kin. 15:13; II Kin. 23:4–6; II Chr. 29:16; 30:14). Over this stream Jesus passed into the garden to pray (John 18:1).

KILL, to deprive of life, to slay.
Cain, should k. him, Gen. 4:15.
I k. and I make alive, Deut. 32:39.
swearing, lying, k., Hos. 4:2.
fear not them which k., Matt. 10:28.
and shall k. you, Matt. 24:9.
ye seek to k. me, John 8:37.
took counsel to k. Paul, Acts 9:23.
Rise, Peter, k. and, Acts 10:13.
letter k., but Spirit, II Cor. 3:6.
do not k., James 2:11.

KINAH, a town in the extreme south of Judah toward Edom (Josh. 15:22).

KIND, specie, class, or type.
yielding fruit after k., Gen. 1:11.
this k. goeth not out, Mark 9:29.
one k. of flesh, I Cor. 15:39.

KIND, gracious, considerate.
God is k. to unthankful, Luke 6:35.
charity is k., I Cor. 13:4.
be k. one to another, Eph. 4:32.

KINDLE, to set on fire; to excite.
wrath is k. against thee, Job 42:7.
if it be already k., Luke 12:49.
a matter a fire k., James 3:5.

KINDLY, considerately.
Lord deal k. with you, Ruth 1:8.
be k. affectioned one, Rom. 12:10.

KINDNESS, grace, favour.
Lord, show k. to, Gen. 24:12.
I have showed you k., Josh. 2:12.
his marvellous k., Ps. 31:21.
for his merciful k., Ps. 117:2.
by long suffering, k., II Cor. 6:6.
put on k. humbleness, Col. 3:12.
brotherly k.; to k., II Pet. 1:7.

KINDRED, family to which one belongs.
Abram to leave k., Gen. 12:1.
out of every k., Rev. 5:9.
to preach to every k., Rev. 14:6.

KINE, (Gen. 41:2; Amos 4:1).

KING, a monarchial ruler. This term is applied in the Bible to rulers of towns as well as rulers of larger areas (Gen. 14:2). Among the Hebrews the title was applied to the supreme head of the nation, beginning with Saul (I Sam. 9:19; 10:24). The manner of ancient kings is pictured in I Sam. 9:10–18. Because the word suggests one with authority and dominion, it is

applied figuratively to: God, as the real
sovereign ruler of the universe (Prov.
8:15; I Tim. 1:17); to Christ as the sole
head and governor of the Church, His
Kingdom (I Tim. 6:15; Matt. 27:11; John
18:36-7; Col. 1:13); to the people of God
(Luke 22:29; Rev. 1:6); to Death as
"king of terrors" (Job 18:14); and to
leviathan as king over the children of
pride (Job 41:34).
Melchizedek *k.* of Salem, Gen. 14:18.
I have made a *k.* over, I Sam. 12:1.
eyes have seen the *K.*, Is. 6:5.
Lord is our *k.*, he will, Is. 33:22.
many days without *k.*, Hos. 3:4.
K. that cometh in name, Luke 19:38.
to the *k.* as supreme, I Pet. 2:13.
fear God, honor the *k.*, I Pet. 2:17.
K. of kings, Rev. 17:14.

KINGDOM, a monarchy; a state in which
the head is a king. (1) **The United Kingdom** Israel was first a theocracy (with
God as king), but later a monarchy with
Saul the first king (I Sam. 9:7, 19; 10:24).
The establishment of such a kingdom had
been prophesied by Moses (Deut. 17:14–
20). Saul was followed by David, who
was a better king and one more faithful
to God than Saul. Under David regal
succession became hereditary (II Sam.
7:12) with the eldest son following his
father on the throne (II Chr. 21:3) with
some exceptions (II Chr. 11:22; II Kin.
23:34). If the regent was a minor provisions were made (I Kin. 15:13; II Kin.
12:2). Solomon succeeded David and
was the last ruler of the United Kingdom. (2) **The Divided Kingdom.** The accession of Solomon's son Rehoboam
brought the division of Israel into two
kingdoms, Judah and Israel (I Kin.
12:19), about 933 B.C. The Northern
Kingdom, Israel, lasted until 722 B.C. and
had 19 kings, all of them bad; the Southern Kingdom, Judah, lasted until the Babylonian conquest was completed in 586
B.C. and had about the same number of
kings, some of whom were good kings. *See*
SAUL, DAVID, SOLOMON, ISRAEL,
JUDAH; ISRAEL, KINGDOM OF.

KINGDOM OF GOD, the reign of God
in the hearts of men. The spirit of this
reign is realized in the Church. The Bible
often speaks of the Kingdom of God,
Heaven, and the Church. (1) Both are
spoken of in the Gospels as near (Mark
9:1; Matt. 16:18; 18:17) and after Pente-

cost (Acts 2) as being in existence (Acts
2:47; Col. 1:13; Rev. 1:6; 9); (2) The
same people are in both (Col. 1:13; Rev.
1:6; 9); (3) Both are characterized by
gradual growth (Matt. 13:31–3). Thus,
the Church is God's spiritual kingdom
(John 18:36) where God's will is done.
Heaven is sometimes referred to as God's
eternal Kingdom (Matt. 25:31–4; 13:43;
I Cor. 6:9; Gal. 5:21; Eph. 5:5; II Tim.
4:1; II Pet. 1:11).

KINGS, BOOKS OF, these two books of
the Old Testament are named from the
opening Hebrew words of I Kings, which
read when translated, "and the king."
These two books were originally a single
volume. The Books of Kings carry on the
historical narrative where II Samuel
leaves off, just prior to David's death.
The history is continued to the thirty-
seventh year of King Jehoiachin's captivity in Babylon (II Kin. 25:27). Thus,
these books record: (1) Solomon's reign
(I Kin. 1:1–11:43); (2) The contempora-
neous reigns of the kings of Israel and Judah (I Kin. 12:1–II Kin. 17:41); and (3)
The reigns of the kings of Judah to the
fall of Judah (II Kin. 18:1–25:30). The
time span covered is from 972 to 560 B.C.

KINGS DALE, *see* DALE, KINGS.

KIR, the place where Tiglathpileser led
captive the people of Damascus (II Kin
16:9; Amos 1:5).

**KIR-HARESETH, KIR-HARASETH,
KIR-HERES, KIR-HARESH,** probably
identical with Kir of Moab (Is. 15:1).
This city was taken by Joram, king of
Israel, from Mesha, king of Moab (II
Kin. 3:21–27; Jer. 48:31).

KIRIATH, *see* **KIRJATH.**

KIRIATHAIM, *see* **KIRJATHAIM.**

KIRIATH-ARBA, *see* **KIRJATH-ARBA.**

KIRIATH-ARIM, *see* **KIRJATH-ARIM.**

KIRIATH-BAAL, *see* **KIRJATH-BAAL.**

KIRIATH-HUZOTH, *see* **KIRJATH-
HUZOTH.**

KIRIATH-JEARIM, *see* **KIRJATH-
JEARIM.**

KIRIATH-SANNAH, see **KIRJATH-SANNAH.**

KIRIATH-SEPHER, see **KIRJATH-SEPHER.**

KIRIOTH, see **KERIOTH.**

KIRJATH, KIRIATH, a town in Benjamin, perhaps the same as Kirjath-jearim (Josh. 18:28).

KIRJATHAIM, KIRIATHAIM, (1) a city of refuge in Naphtali, also called Kartan (I Chr. 6:76; Josh. 21:32); (2) an ancient town East of Jordan (Gen. 14:5; Num. 32:37; Josh. 13:19; Jer. 48:1).

KIRJATH-ARBA, KIRIATH-ARBA, a city in the hills of Judah, named for Arba the Anakite (Gen. 23:2; Josh. 15:54; Judg. 1:10). It is better known as Hebron.

KIRJATH-ARIM, KIRIATH-ARIM, (Ezra 2:25), another name for **Kirjath-Jearim.**

KIRJATH-BAAL, another name for **Kirjath-Jearim** (Josh. 15:60).

KIRJATH-HUZOTH, KIRIATH-HU-ZOTH, a Moabite city, to which Balak took Balaam to offer up sacrifice (Num. 22:39–41).

KIRJATH-JEARIM, KIRIATH-JEA-RIM, (city of forests), a Gibeonite town (Josh. 9:17) first assigned to Judah (Josh. 15:60), but later to Benjamin (Josh. 18:28); called also Baalah and Kirjath-baal (Josh. 15:9, 60).

KIRJATH-SANNAH, KIRIATH-SAN-NAH, a city in the hill country of South Judah, later called Debir (Josh. 15:7, 15; 21:15). See **DEBIR.**

KIRJATH-SEPHER, KIRIATH-SE-PHER, another name for **Kirjath-sannah** or **Debir** (Judg. 1:11–12).

KIR OF MOAB, a fortified Moabite city (Is. 15:1). See **KIR-HARASETH.**

KISH, (1) father of King Saul (I Sam. 9:3). (2) A son of Jehiel the Gibeonite (I Chr. 8:30). (3) A son of Mahli, Levi's grandson (I Chr. 23:21; 24:29). (4) Son of Abdi the Levite. (II Chr. 29:12). (5) Great-grandfather of Mordecai (Esther 2:5). (6) A city in Mesopotamia near Babylon.

KISHI, (I Chr. 6:44), see **KUSHAIAH.**

KISHION, a Levitical city and city of refuge in Issachar (Josh. 19:20; 21:28).

KISHON, a winter stream in Central Palestine, called also the waters of Magiddo (Judg. 5:19–21).

KISON, (Ps. 83:9), form for **Kishon.**

KISS, in the Old Testament kissing the lips was a form of salutation for relatives (Gen. 29:11; Song 8:1), and kissing the cheek was a salutation for friends. In the Church the "holy kiss" was a customary friendly salutation symbolical of brotherhood ties (Rom. 16:16; I Cor. 16:20; II Cor. 13:21; I Thess. 5:26; I Pet. 5:14). Kissing the ground or the feet was a Hebrew sign of submission (Gen. 41:40; I Sam. 24:8; Ps. 72:9). Kissing in adoration of idols is mentioned in I Kin. 19:18; Hos. 13:2).

KITE, a rapacious bird of prey belonging to the hawk family. It was forbidden for food in the Law (Lev. 11:14; Deut. 14:13).

KITHLISH, a town in the lowland of Judah (Josh. 15:40).

KITRON, a town in Zebulun, from which the Canaanites were not driven (Judg. 1:30).

KITTIM, (Gen. 10:4), see **CHITTIM.**

KNEAD, to prepare dough (Gen. 18:6; I Sam. 28:24; Hos. 7:4).

KNEELING, act of bending the knee (Gen. 24:11) or worship (Ps. 95:6; Luke 22:41).

KNEES, the middle joints of the legs.
bow the *k.*, Gen. 41:43.
they bowed the *k.*, Matt. 27:29.
every *k.* shall bow, Rom. 14:11.

KNEW, realized, perceived.
Adam and Eve *k.*, Gen. 3:7.
prophet whom Lord *k.*, Deut. 34:10.
I never *k.* you, Matt. 7:23.

for he *k*. man, John 2:25.
be sin, who *k*. no sin, II Cor. 5:21.

KNIFE, early knives were made of stone, later ones of iron. They were used little for eating, but were used for killing animals (Lev. 7:33; 8:15), for sharpening pens (Jer. 36:23) and probably as razors (Num. 6:5, 9, 19).

KNIT, tied together, as knotted cords.
Israel were *k*., Judg. 20:11.
my heart shall be *k*., I Chr. 12:17.

KNOCK, rap.
k. and shall be opened, Luke 11:9.
stand at door and *k*., Rev. 3:20.

KNOP, a decorative ornament shaped like a flower bud (Ex. 25:31; 37:17).

KNOW, to perceive, realize. This word is also used for sexual intercourse (Gen. 4:1; Matt. 1:25).
God does *k*. that, Gen. 3:5.
k. that I am God, Ps. 46:10.
k. that God shall, Eccles. 11:9.
thou shalt *k*. the Lord, Hos. 2:20.
shall *k*. them by fruits, Matt. 7:16.
I *k*. that Messias, John 4:25.
k. ye not that so, Rom. 6:3.
may *k*. ye have eternal, I John 5:13.

KNOWLEDGE, power of knowing.
tree of *k*. of good, Gen. 2:9, 17.
night unto night shows *k*., Ps. 19:2.
he that increaseth *k*., Eccles. 1:18.
God gave them *k*., Dan. 1:17.
retain God in their *k*., Rom. 1:28.
whether there be *k*., I Cor. 13:8.
increasing in the *k*., Col. 1:10.
man renewed in *k*., Col. 3:10.
add to virtue *k*., II Pet. 1:5.
grow in grace and *k*., II Pet. 3:18.

KNOWN, realized, perceived.
this thing is *k*., Ex. 2:14.
thy way may be *k*., Ps. 67:2.
thou hast *k*. my reproach, Ps. 69:19.
tree is *k*. by fruits, Luke 6:44.
this *k*. to you, Acts 2:14.
we have *k*. Christ, II Cor. 5:16.
might be *k*. by church, Eph. 3:10.
we have *k*., I John 4:16.

KOA, (Ezek. 23:23), probably the Kuti, who lived north of Babylon.

KOHATH, the second of Levi's three sons from whom the three Levitical families derive their origin (Gen. 46:11; Ex. 6:16–20).

KOHATHITES, the descendants of Kohath. (Num. 4:15).

KOLAIAH, (1) Benjamite ancestor of the returnee Sallu (Neh. 11:7); (2) father of Ahab, which later Jeremiah denounced (Jer. 29:21).

KOPH, *see* **KAPH.**

KORAH, (1) third son of Esau by Aholibamah, he became chief of a small Edomite tribe (Gen. 36:5, 18). (2) Co-conspirator with Dathan and Abiram against Moses (Num. 16:1–49; Jude 11). (3) Eldest of Hebron's four sons (I Chr. 2:43).

KORAHITES, Levites who were descended from Korah (I Chr. 9:19, 31).

KORE, (1) father of the Levite Shallum, the doorkeeper of the tabernacle (I Chr. 9:19; 26:1). (2) Mistranslation for Korahites in I Chr. 26:19. (3) A Levite (II Chr. 31:14).

KORHITES, *see* **KORAHITES.**

KOZ, *see* **HAKKOZ.**

KUSHAIAH, KISHI, father of Ethan the Merarite appointed by David as a temple musician (I Chr. 15:17; 6:44).

L

LAADAH, a member of the Judahite family of Shelah (I Chr. 4:21).

LAADAN, *see* **LADAN.**

LABAN, son of Bethuel and grandson of Nahor (Gen. 24:10; 28:5). Laban received the fleeing Jacob (Gen. 29:13), and later Jacob married Leah and Rachel, Laban's daughters (Gen. 29:16–28).
Meets Abraham's Servant, Gen. 24:29.
Forbids Jacob to leave, Gen. 30:25.
Flocks divided, Gen. 30:31–43.
Laban overtakes Jacob, Gen. 31:23.
A Covenant made, Gen. 31:43–55.

LABAN, an unidentified desert place (Deut 1:1), perhaps same as **Libnah.**

LABOR, LABOUR, toil, work.
work, that they may *l.*, Ex. 5:9.
days shalt thou *l.*, Deut. 5:13.
land he did not *l.*, Josh. 7:3.
wicked, why then *l.*, Job 9:29.
they *l.* in vain, Ps. 127:1.
reward for their *l.*, Eccles. 4:9.
come to me all that *l.*, Matt. 11:28.
l. not for meat that, John 6:27.
but rather *l.*, working, Eph. 4:28.
I know thy *l.*, Rev. 2:2.

LABOURER, worker.
harvest plenteous, but *l.*, Luke 10:2.
l. worthy of his hire, Luke 10:7.
we are *l.* together, I Cor. 3:9.
l. worthy of reward, I Tim. 5:18.

LABOURING, working.
l. ye ought to support, Acts 20:35.
l. for you in prayer, Col. 4:2.

LABOUR TROUBLE, the dispute over wages with the manager, the householder, in the parable of Jesus in Matthew 20:10–13; 21:33–36 suggests that labour-management problems are of ancient origin.

LABOUR UNION, in the Graeco-Roman world of Bible times labour guilds were common. When Paul preached in Ephesus, Demetrius, the leader of the guild of silversmiths who made shrines of Diana, brought charge against Paul that his preaching was injurious to the guild (Acts 19:23–39).

LACHISH, a royal city of Canaan and one of the main fortified cities in Judah, Lachish was situated thirty miles southwest of Jerusalem.
Joshua conquers *L.*, Josh. 10:31–35.
Amaziah killed at *L.*, II Kin. 14:19.
Resists Sennacherib, II Kin. 18:13.
Nebuchadrezzar destroys, II Kin. 24.
Fortified by Rehoboam, II Chr. 11:9.
Reoccupied after exile, Neh. 11:30.

LACK, to be deficient; need.
shall *l.* five of, Gen. 18:28.
gathered had no *l.*, Ex. 16:18.
young lions do *l.*, Ps. 34:10.
what *l.* I yet, Matt. 19:20.
life to supply *l.*, Phil. 2:30.

LADAN, *see* **LAADAN.**

LADDER, (Gen. 28:12), a device for climbing; a set of stairs.

LADE, load.
l. beasts and go, Gen. 45:17.
ye *l.* men with, Luke 11:46.
women *l.* with sins, II Tim. 3:6.

LADIES AID SOCIETY, the example of Dorcas (Acts 9:36) commends good works. Dorcas was noted for her "good works and almsdeeds." Many modern day societies are called Dorcas Societies.

LADY, a woman with dignity.
wise *l.* answered her, Judg. 5:29.
elder to the elect *l.*, II John 1.

LAEL, (belonging to God) father of the Gershonite chief Eliasaph (Num. 3:24).

LAHAD, son of Jahath (I Chr. 4:2).

LAHAI-ROI, *see* **BEER-LAHAI-ROI.**

LAHMAM, a city in the plain of Judah (Josh. 15:40).

LAHMI, Goliath's brother (I Chr. 20:5).

LAID, placed, set.
ax is *l.* to root, Matt. 3:10.
where they have *l.* him, John 20:2.
nothing *l.* to charge, Acts 23:29.
necessity is *l.* upon, I Cor. 9:16.

LAISH, (a lion), (1) a Benjamite to whose son Saul gave Michal (I Sam. 25:44). (2) A place in northern Palestine, taken by the Danites (Josh. 19:47; Judg. 18:7), called also Leshem and Dan. (3) A place named in Is. 10:30, probably near Jerusalem.

LAKKUM, LAKUM, a place in northeast Naphtali (Josh. 19:33).

LAMA, *see* **ELOI, ELOI, LAMA SABACHTHANI.**

LAMB, a young sheep. Lambs formed an important part of almost every Old Testament sacrifice (Num. 6:14; Lev. 4:32; Ex. 29:38–41). A non-resisting sacrificial lamb symbolized the promised Messiah (Is. 53:7), and John calls Jesus "Lamb of God" (John 1:29). This symbolism occurs also in Revelation (5:12; 7:9; 19:7; 22:1). Christ is called

the Christian's passover in I Cor. 5:7.
where is the *l*.?, Gen. 22:7.
took poor man's *l*., II Sam. 12:4.
as a *l*. without blemish, I Pet. 1:19.
white in blood of *l*., Rev. 7:14.
they that follow *l*., Rev. 14:4.
l. is the light, Rev. 21:23.
written in *l*.'s book, Rev. 21:27.

LAME, crippled, physically disabled.
shall the *l*. leap, Is. 35:6.
the *l*. walk, Matt. 11:5.
call poor, the *l*. and, Luke 14:13.
man *l*. from womb, Acts 3:2.

LAMECH, (1) descendant of Cain, Lamech the first polygamist (Gen. 4:18–24).
(2) Noah's father (Gen. 5:25–31).

LAMED, twelfth letter of Hebrew alphabet, (Ps. 119: 89).

LAMENT, to wail, mourn.
Israel went to *l*., Judg. 11:40.
for this *l*. and howl, Jer. 4:8.
ye shall *l*. and weep, John 16:20.

LAMENTATION, mourning.
mourned with sore *l*., Gen. 50:10.
in Ramah *l*. and, Matt. 2:18.
great *l* over Stephen, Acts 8:2.

LAMENTATIONS, BOOK OF, the
theme of the book is the mourning of a
devout Israelite over the capture and
destruction of Jerusalem and the temple
by the Babylonians. The whole tone is
one of deep tragedy. Lamentations consists of five chapters, each of which is
an elegiac poem. The first four poems are
alphabetic, with each verse (in the third
chapter, each group of three verses) beginning with a new letter of the Hebrew
alphabet. The final Babylonian destruction of Jerusalem occurred in 587 B.C.,
and Lamentations was thus probably
written early in the Exile.

LAMP, ancient lamps were ordinarily
made of clay in the shape of a covered
saucer. The light-bearing parts of the
golden candlesticks of the tabernacle
were called lamps (Ex. 25:37, I Kin. 7:49;
II Chr. 4:20). The King James Version
uses "lamp" sometimes to refer to a
torch (Judg. 7:16; Is. 62:1; Dan. 10:6).
Oil lamps in marriage processions is
alluded to in Matt. 25:1. *See* **LIGHT.**

LANCET, *see* **SPEAR.**

LAND, (1) earth, ground; (2) country.
let dry *l*. appear, Gen. 1:9.
the *l*. was corrupted, Ex. 8:24.
come to a large *l*., Judg. 18:10.
famine in that *l*., Luke 15:14.
having *l*. sold it, Acts 4:37.

LAND OF PROMISE, *see* **PROMISED
LAND.**

LANGUAGE, *see* **TONGUE, HEBREW
LANGUAGE.**
earth was of one *l*., Gen. 11:1.
a people of strange *l*., Ps. 114:1.
a nation, whose *l*., Jer. 5:15.
them speak in his own *l*., Acts 2:6.

LANGUISH, to become weak, to lose
vitality. Also Languisheth, Languishing.
for fields of Hebron *l*., Is. 16:8.
haughty people do *l*., Is 24:4.

LANTERN, (John 18:3). *See* **LAMP.**

LAODICEA, a city in Asia Minor, near
Colossae, it was named for Laodice,
wife of Antiochus II (261–246 B.C.). At
Laodicea a church of Christ was established early (Col. 2:1; 4:16) and it was
one of the seven churches of Asia
addressed in Revelation (Rev. 1:11;
3:14–22). The church in Laodicea was a
poor-rich church, being composed of
people materially wealthy, but spiritually poor. This characteristic accounts
for the indifference condemned in Rev.
3:15–16. Laodicea produced a famous
eyesalve, but the people needed spiritual
eyesalve (Rev. 3:18).'

LAODICEAN, an inhabitant of **Laodicea.**

LAPPIDOTH, LAPIDOTH, husband of
the prophetess Deborah (Judg. 4:4).

LAPWING, HOOPOE, a bird of Palestine, it is about the size of a thrush and
is brightly colored. It is filthy in its feeding and breeding habits. In ancient
Egypt it was considered sacred. This
bird was forbidden as food by the Law
(Lev. 11:19; Deut. 14:18).

LASCIVIOUSNESS, licentiousness; that
which tends to incite lewd emotions.
heart proceed *l*., Mark 7:22.
l. a work of the flesh, Gal. 5:19.
given over to *l*., Eph. 4:19.
turned grace into *l*., Jude 4.

LASEA, a city of Crete, near Fair Havens (Acts 27:8).

LASHA, a place which marked a border of the Canaanites (Gen. 10:19), identified by some as Calirrhoe, a Dead Sea resort.

LASSHARON, LASHARON, a Canaanite town west of Jordan, taken by Joshua (Josh. 12:18).

LAST, final.
shall overcome at *l.*, Gen. 49:19.
these be the *l.* words, II Sam. 23:1.
l. state worse than, Matt. 12:45.
in *l.* days scoffers, II Pet. 3:3.
mockers in *l.* time, Jude 18.

LAST SUPPER, *see* **LORD'S SUPPER.**

LATCHET, the thong fastening the sandal to the foot (Is. 5:27; Mark 1:7; Luke 3:16; John 1:27). Handling the sandals of their masters was the work of the lowliest slaves.

LATIN, (Luke 23:38), the vernacular language of the Romans. Most of them also spoke Greek in the time of Christ.

LATTER, last; second of two things.
first rain and *l.* rain, Deut. 11:14.
glory of *l.* house, Hag. 2:9.
in the *l.* times, I Tim. 4:1.

LATTICE, a type of screen for a window (Judg. 5:28; Prov. 7:6; Song 2:9).

LAUGH, to express mirth, or derision.
wherefore did Sarah *l.*?, Gen. 18:13.
they that see *l.* me, Ps. 22:7.
and a time to *l.*, Eccles. 3:4.
they *l.* him to scorn, Matt. 9:24.
ye that weep, shall *l.*, Luke 6:21.

LAUGHTER, in Scripture this usually shows joy (Gen. 21:6; Ps. 126:2), but at times mockery (Gen. 18:13) or security (Job 5:22). Used of God it shows disregard (Ps. 2:4; Prov. 1:26).

LAVER, a basin for washing. In the tabernacle a brass laver was used for the priests to wash before offering sacrifice (Ex. 30:18–21; 38:8). Solomon's temple had ten lavers for the washing of animals for burnt offerings (I Kin. 7:27, 39; II Chr. 4:6).

LAW, the Hebrew word "torah" which is translated "law" signifies instruction received from a superior authority and which serves as a rule of conduct. It is used for human instruction (Prov. 1:8; 3:1), but more extensively of divine teaching. Usually the term indicates the Law of God given to Moses, which is contained in the Pentateuch (Ex. 20:1–31:18; Lev.; Num.; Deut.). This legislation is called "the Law" (Josh. 8:34; Matt. 12:5), "the Law of Moses" (Josh. 8:31; Luke 2:22), "the Law of the Lord" (Ezra 7:10; Luke 2:23–4), and other similar expressions. Because the Law formed the framework for the whole Jewish system, the title is sometimes used to refer to the whole of the Old Testament (John 10:34; 15:25; I Cor. 14:21). This Mosaic system, including the Ten Commandments as a way of life, ended with the death of Christ (John 1:17; Gal. 3:24; Col. 2:14). The Book of Hebrews emphasizes the superiority of the New Covenant in Christ, which, it should be noted, incorporates and deepens the principles of the Ten Commandments, with the sole exception of the one regarding the seventh day. "Law" is also used of: (1) Human law (I Cor. 6:1); (2) Natural law (Rom. 2:14–15); (3) The way of Christ (Rom. 8:2; James 1:25).
Joseph made it a *l.*, Gen. 47:26.
heart to study the *l.*, Ezra 7:10.
read from the *l.*, Neh. 8:8.
to *l.* and the testimony, Is. 8:20.
thou hast forgotten *l.*, Hos. 4:6.
no wise pass from *l.*, Matt. 5:18.
great command in *l.*, Matt. 22:36.
a doctor of the *l.*, Acts 5:34.
change of the *l.*, Heb. 7:12.
l. had shadow of good, Heb. 10:1.
transgression of *l.*, I John 3:4.

LAWFUL, allowed by law, right.
do what is not *l.*, Matt. 12:2.
l. to heal on sabbath, Matt. 12:10.
l. to put away wife?, Mark 10:2.
l. to give tribute to?, Luke 20:22.
l. to scourge a Roman?, Acts 22:25.

LAWLESS, unruly (I Tim. 1:9).

LAWYER, one conversant with the law.
l. rejected the counsel, Luke 7:30.
a *l.* asked him, Luke 10:25.
woe unto you, *l.* Luke 11:46.
Jesus spake to *l.*, Luke 14:3.

LAY, to place, to set upon something.
bricks ye shall *l.*, Ex. 5:8.
them that *l.* field, Is. 5:8.
l. them on hearts, Matt. 23:4.
I *l.* in Zion a chief, I Pet. 2:6.

LAY, did lie.
a woman *l.* at his, Ruth 3:8.
nowhere to *l.* his head, Luke 9:58.
l. impotent folks, John 5:3.

LAYING ON OF HANDS, a symbolic act expressing blessing (Gen. 48:14), dedication (Ex. 29:10) or the imparting of spiritual authority (Acts 13:3), including miraculous power (Acts 8:18).

LAZARUS, (God has helped), (1) Lazarus of Bethany, the brother of Martha and Mary (John 11:1). He is famous because Jesus miraculously raised him from the dead. (2) Name of a poor man in the parable of Luke 16:19–31.

LEAD, this common metal was early known to the Hebrews, being found in abundance in the Sinai Peninsula and elsewhere. It was one of the heaviest metals known (Ex. 15:10) and was used in engraving upon rocks (Job 19:23) and in purifying gold (Jer. 6:29; Ezek. 22:18–22).

LEAD, to conduct, guide, direct.
pillar of cloud to *l.*, Ex. 13:21.
l. me, O Lord in, Ps. 5:8.
l. me in thy truth, Ps. 25:5.
l. in way everlasting, Ps. 139:24.
little child shall *l.*, Is. 11:6.
l. not into temptation, Matt. 6:13.
if blind *l.* blind, Matt. 15:14.
we not power to *l.*, I Cor. 9:5.
to *l.* them out of land, Heb. 8:9.

LEAF, (1) a tree leaf (Gen. 8:11); (2) a sliding part of a door (Is. 45:1); (3) a page or column (Jer. 36:23). Leaves are used figuratively for life which is prosperous (Ps. 1:3; Jer. 17:8) or adverse (Job 13:25; Is. 64:6).

LEAGUE, alliance, tract, covenant.
no *l.* with inhabitants, Judg. 2:2.
l. between me and, I Kin. 15:19.
l. with the stones Job 5:23.

LEAH, eldest daughter of Laban. She became Jacob's wife by deceit (Gen. 29:16–23). She bore to him Reuben, Sim-

eon, Levi, Judah, Issachar, and Zebulun and Dinah (Gen. 29:32–5; 30: 17–21).

LEAN, to bend; to rely for support.
will *l.* on the Lord, Mic. 3:11.
who *l.* on his breast, John 21:20.
Jacob worshipped, *l.*, Heb. 11:21.

LEANNESS, lack of Spiritual quality (Ps. 106:15).

LEAP, to jump or spring.
all rams which *l.*, Gen. 31:12.
then shall the lame *l.*, Is. 35:6.
and *l.* for joy, Luke 6:23.
and he *l.* up stood, Acts 3:8.

LEARN, to gain knowledge.
they may *l.* to fear me, Deut. 4:10.
might *l.* thy statutes, Ps. 119:71.
go and *l.* what that, Matt. 9:13.
l. of me, for I am, Matt. 11:29.
l. parable of the fig, Mark 13:28.
every man that hath *l.*, John 6:45.
doctrine ye have *l.*, Rom. 16:17.
let woman *l.* in, I Tim. 2:11.
no man could *l.* song, Rev. 14:3.

LEASING, (Ps. 4:2; 5:6) old English word for lying or falsehood.

LEAST, smallest, most unimportant.
l. in father's house, Judg. 6:15.
my family, the *l.* of, I Sam. 9:21.
art not *l.* of princes, Matt. 2:6.
of these *l.* commands, Matt. 5:19.
he that is *l.* among, Luke 9:48.
I am *l.* of apostles, I Cor. 15:9.

LEATHER, curing of skins was a special skill in Egypt, and probably from that land the Israelites learned leather-making. Dyeing is mentioned in Ex. 25:5, and leather girdles are mentioned in II Kin. 1:8 and Matt. 3:4. Although some were tanners (Acts 9:43; 10:6), this was considered by many Jews an undersirable occupation.

LEAVE, (1) permission (Num. 22:13; Mark 5:13); (2) to depart from (John 16:28). Also **Leaves, Leaveth, Leaving;** (3) Farewell (Acts 18:18).
l. father and mother, Gen. 2:24.
Entreat me not to *l.*, Ruth 1:16.
l. there thy gift, Matt. 5:24.
peace I *l.* with you, John 14:27.
I will never *l.* thee, Heb. 13:5.

LEAVEN, substance added to dough to

cause it to rise, like yeast. It was usually a small portion of old (fermented) dough (Ex 12:15; 13:7; Deut. 16:14). Because leaven exerts a decaying influence in dough, the word came to symbolize corruption, and thus was forbidden in the Passover (Ex. 12:15). However, leaven was allowed in the wave and praise offerings (Lev. 7:13; 23:17). Figuratively, leaven is used to suggest evil influence (Matt. 16:12; Mark 8:15; I Cor. 5:6–8) and, in another case, to illustrate the influential growth of the Kingdom (Matt. 13:33).

shall be made with *l.*, Lev. 2:11.
thanksgiving with *l.*, Amos 4:5.
l. of the Pharisees, Matt. 16:6.
l. leaveneth whole lump, I Cor. 5:6.
purge out the old *l.*, I Cor. 5:7.

LEAVENETH, *see* **LEAVEN.**

LEAVES, *see* **LEAF** or **LEAVE.**

LEAVETH, LEAVING, *see* **LEAVE.**

LEBANA, LEBANAH, (white), one of the Nethinim whose descendants returned with Zerubbabel (Ezra 2:45).

LEBANON, (white), a snow-capped mountain range of Syria which forms the northern boundary of Palestine (Deut. 1:7; Josh. 1:4). This range forks into two ranges: the Lebanon group West of Jordan, and the Anti-Lebanon group East of Jordan. Lebanon is remarkable for its scenic grandeur, and thus supplied Old Testament writers with many expressive figures (Ps. 72:16; 104:16; Song 4:15; Is. 2:13; 35:2; 60:13; Hos. 14:5). Lebanon was noted especially for its magnificent cedars (Ps. 29:5; Song 5:15), and also for its wines (Hos. 14:7) and its cool waters (Jer. 18:14).

LEBAOTH, (Josh. 15:32), *see* **BETH-LEBAOTH.**

LEBBAEUS, *see* **JUDAS.**

LEBONAH, a town near Shiloh (Judg. 21:19).

LECAH, (I Chr. 4:21), a place in Judah founded by Er.

LED, guided, conducted.

thou in mercy hast *l.*, Ex. 15:13.
shall be *l.* captive, Amos 7:11.
Jesus *l.* of the Spirit, Luke 4:1.
l. as a sheep to, Acts 8:32.
as many as are *l.* by, Rom. 8:14.

LEEK, an onion-like vegetable (Num. 11:5).

LEES, sediment from wine or liquor. "Wines on the lees" are wines left on the sediment for thorough fermentation. Filtering then gives strong clear wine (Is. 25:6). Left too long the wine became syrupy; this condition symbolizes slothful indifference (Jer. 48:11; Zeph. 1:12).

LEFT, departed.
they *l.* their ships, Matt. 4:22.
l. all and followed, Mark 10:28.
l. not without witness, Acts 14:17.

LEFT-HANDED MEN, left-handed warriors were rare, but the Benjamites had a select and skillful group of 700 of them (Judg. 20:16). The judge Ehud was also left-handed (Judg. 3:15).

LEGION, a Roman army regiment comprised of from three thousand to six thousand men. The word came to mean simply a great number (Matt. 26:53; Mark 5:9).

LEGS, the legs of crucified persons were broken to hasten death (John 19:31).

LEHABIM, a people of Midianitish stock (Gen. 10:13; I Chr. 1:11), probably the same as the Libyans.

LEHI, (cheek, jawbone), the place in Judah where Samson killed Philistines with a jawbone (Judg. 15:9–16).

LEMUEL, an unknown king to whom the maxims in Prov. 31:2–9 are addressed.

LEND, to allow temporary use of.
if thou *l.* money to, Ex. 22:25.
shalt *l.* to many, Deut. 15:6.
I have not *l.* on usury, Jer. 15:10.
do good and *l.*, Luke 6:35.

LENTIL, LENTILE, a vegetable bearing seeds like small beans. Lentils were and are considered very tasty for food (Gen. 25:34).

LEOPARD, a wily, ferocious beast (Is. 11:6; Jer. 5:6; Dan. 7:6; Hab. 1:8) with a beautiful spotted skin (Jer. 13:23). The leopard is used to describe in part the beast in Rev. 13:2.

LEPER, one who has **Leprosy.**

LEPROSY, much unlike modern leprosy, the Biblical disease translated by "leprosy" was a whiteness (Ex. 4:6) which disfigured the victim without disabling him. Naaman was active, though leprous (II Kin. 5:1). Sometimes the leper developed boils (Lev. 13:18–28). A leper was ceremonially unclean only as long as the disease was partial. If the whole body became covered, the leper was clean, and could go into the temple (Lev. 13:12–17). The reason for the uncleanness of leprosy thus seems to be the spotty, mottled appearance of partial leprosy, not the contagion of the disease. Mildew spots on cloth and fungous growths on walls were thus ceremonially unclean and were called "leprosy" (Lev. 13:47–59; 14:33–53). Jesus miraculously cured some lepers (Matt. 10:8; 11:15; Luke 7:22; 17:14), and these cures are called "cleansings" instead of "healings." The stigma of leprosy was its ugly appearance and the fact that it rendered its victim unfit for normal association (Lev. 13:1–17, 29–46).

LESHEM, *see* **LAISH.**

LESS, a smaller part of.
when sown it is *l.*, Mark 4:31.
members we think *l.*, I Cor. 12:23.
l. than least of all, Eph. 3:8.

LET, (1) allow; (2) rent; (3) hinder.
why do you *l.* people, Ex. 5:4.
Joshua *l.* the people, Josh. 24:28.
was *l.* hitherto, Rom. 1:13.

LETTER, a written message.
how large a *l.*, Gal. 6:11.
have written a *l.*, Heb. 13:22.

LETUSHIM, (hammered), second son of Dedan and great-grandson of Abraham (Gen. 25:3).

LEUMMIM, (peoples), third son of Dedan, Abraham's great-grandson (Gen. 25:3).

LEVI, (1) Jacob's third son by Leah (Gen. 29:34). He was the ancestral father of the **Levites.** (2) Son of Melchi in the lineage of Jesus (Luke 3:24). (3) Son of Simeon in the lineage of Jesus (Luke 3:29). (4) One of the apostles, also called **Matthew.**

LEVIATHAN, a writhing mythological animal. The word is used of a crocodile (Job 41:1; Ps. 74:14), a serpent (Is. 27:1) and a sea monster (Ps. 104:26). Leviathan probably symbolizes evil, as "dragon" is used to refer to Satan.

LEVITES, the descendants of Levi (Ex. 6:25; Josh. 21:3), especially those of the tribe who were appointed for the service of the sanctuary (Num. 3:5; Ezra 2:70). Their duties according to families is given in Num. 3:21–39. Cities were assigned to them out of the other tribes (Num. 35:1–8). The priests were taken out of this tribe (Deut. 31:9). The Levites who were not priests assisted in religious work and service (Num. 18:4; II Chr. 17:8–10).

LEVITICAL, LEVITICALLY, pertaining to the **Levites.**

LEVITICUS, written by Moses, this third book of the Bible is called Leviticus because it relates the duties of the Levites and priests, and the laws of priestly ceremony. Leviticus teaches: (1) Laws of Sacrifice (chs. 1–7); (2) Laws of Consecration of Priests (chs. 8–10); (3) Laws of Uncleanness and the Law of Atonement (11–16); (4) Laws of Holiness and Fellowship with God (chs. 17–27). The book may be justly termed the "Book of the Priesthood." Leviticus breathes the concepts of the majesty and holiness of God and the holiness demanded of His people. The Levitical priestly system is superseded in the New Testament by the priesthood of Christ (Heb. 7:11–8:13).

LEWDNESS, shameful wickedness.
she hath wrought *l.*, Jer. 11:15.
they commit *l.*, Hos. 6:9.
matter of wicked *l.*, Acts 18:14.

LIAR, one who speaks untruth knowingly.
he is a *l.* and father, John 8:44.
and every man a *l.*, Rom. 3:4.
Cretians are always *l.*, Titus 1:12.

we make him a *l.*, I John 1:10.

LIBERAL, generous.
your *l.* to Jerusalem, I Cor. 16:3.
for *l.* distribution, II Cor. 9:13.
who giveth to all *l.*, James 1:5.

LIBERTINES, a group mentioned only in Acts 6:9, probably composed of freed Roman or Jewish slaves.

LIBERTY, freedom from bondage (Lev. 25:10; Is. 61:1).
ye shall proclaim *l.*, Lev. 25:10.
sent me to proclaim *l.*, Is. 61:1.
l. for the bruised, Luke 4:18.
into the law of *l.*, James 1:25.

LIBNAH, (1) a wilderness station of Israel (Num. 33:20). (2) A Canaanite city near Lachish, captured by Joshua (Josh. 10:32), made a Levitical city (Josh. 21:13), and later fortified (II Kin. 19:8, 9, 35).

LIBNI, (white) (1) first son of Gershon (Ex. 6:17) and grandson of Levi. (2) Son of Mahli (I Chr. 6:29).

LIBNITE, a descendant of Libni.

LIBYA, the country of the Lubim (Dan. 11:43), it lay between Egypt and Carthage (Ezek. 30:5; Acts 2:10). Cyrene was one of its cities. *See* LUBIM.

LIBYAN, an inhabitant of **Libya.**

LICE, a class of parasitic insects (Ex. 8:16–18; Ps. 105:31).

LIE, intentional falsehood.
trust in a *l.*, Jer. 28:15.
truth into a *l.*, Rom. 1:25.
God, that cannot *l.*, Titus 1:2.
ye know that no *l.*, I John 2:21.

LIE, recline. Sometimes used of sexual intercourse.
he shall *l.* with thee, Gen. 30:15.
Come, *l.* with me, Gen. 39:7.
maketh me to *l.* down, Ps. 23:2.
they *l.* in wait, Eph. 4:14.

LIEUTENANT, *see* SATRAP.

LIFE, (1) natural Life (Gen. 2:7; 6:17; Ps. 17:14; James 4:14); (2) eternal life in communion with God (Luke 18:30; John 3:16; 17:3; Rom. 2:7); (3) absolute life. God in Christ is the Source of all

life (John 14:6; Col. 3:4; I John 1:1, 2).
creature that hath *l.*, Gen. 1:20.
give *l.* for *l.*, Deut. 19:21.
thou hast granted *l.*, Job 10:12.
show me path of *l.*, Ps. 16:11.
is tree of life, Prov. 11:30.
therefore I hated *l.*, Eccles. 2:17.
the way of *l.*, Jer. 21:8.
covenant of *l.* and peace, Mal. 2:5.
no thought for *l.*, Matt. 6:25.
enter into *l.* halt, Matt. 18:8.
l. consisteth not in, Luke 12:15.
in him was *l.* and, John 1:4.
neither death nor *l.*, Rom. 8:38.
l. I now live, Gal. 2:20.
right to tree of *l.*, Rev. 22:14.

LIFT, raise, elevate.
l. up her voice, Gen. 21:16.
l. up his spear, II Sam. 23:18.
will *l.* up an ensign, Is. 5:26.
l. up the hands, Heb. 12:12.
he shall *l.* you up, James 4:10.

LIGHT, light came into existence by the speaking of God (Gen. 1:3). Later, natural lights were created (Gen. 1:14). Figuratively, God is connected with light (I John 1:5; I Tim. 6:16). Light also expresses the spiritual illumination of knowledge (Ps. 119:105; Rom. 13:12), and thus Christ is the "light of men" (John 1:4) and disciples who reflect His light are lights in the world (Matt. 5:14; Phil. 2:15).
Lord is my *l.* and. Ps. 27:1.
l. sown for righteous, Ps. 97:11.
raiment white as *l.*, Matt. 17:2.
l. to lighten Gentiles, Luke 2:32.
called for a *l.*, Acts 16:29.
Lamb is the *l.*, Rev. 21:23.

LIGHTNING, atmospheric flash of light.
divided way for the *l.*, Job 38:25.
as *l.* cometh out of, Matt. 24:27.
Satan as *l.* fall, Luke 10:18.

LIGHTS, FEAST OF, *see* DEDICATION, FEAST OF.

LIGN-ALOES, *see* ALOES.

LIGURE, *see* JACINTH.

LIKE, (1) similar to; (2) be pleased by.
who *l.* unto thee, Ex. 15:11.
one *l.* Son of Man, Dan. 7:13.
tempted *l.* as we are, Heb. 4:15.

LIKENESS, resemblance, similitude.
make man after our *l.*, Gen. 1:26.
l. will ye compare him?, Is. 40:18.
l. of glory of Lord, Ezek. 1:28.
l. of his death, Rom. 6:5.
his Son in *l.* of men, Rom. 8:3.

LIKHI, third son of Shemidah (I Chr. 7:19).

LILY, a class of brightly colored flowers which abounds in Palestine (Matt. 6:28).

LIME, substance obtained from limestone by heat. It was used in mortar mix. (Is. 33:12; Amos 2:1).

LIMIT, LIMITED, LIMITETH, (1) boundary (Ezek. 43:12); (2) provoke (Ps. 78:41); (3) define (Heb. 4:7).

LINE, cord, boundary, portion.
this *l.* of scarlet, Josh. 2:18.
l. fallen in pleasant, Ps. 16:6.
l. is gone out, Ps. 19:4.

LINEN, cloth made from flax. Egypt was famous for its linen (Prov. 7:16), but some linen was made in Palestine (Josh. 2:6; Prov. 31:24). Linen was one of the finest of ancient fabrics, and was used for the best clothing (Ex. 28:6; Gen. 41:42; Luke 16:19), for quality curtaining (Ex. 26:1), and for burials of the rich (Matt. 27:59).
garment of *l.* and wool, Lev. 19:19.
get a *l.* girdle, put, Jer. 13:1.
city clothed in fine *l.*, Rev. 18:16.

LINGER, tarry, hesitate.
while Lot *l.* the men, Gen. 19:16.
whose judgment *l.* not, II Pet. 2:3.

LINTEL, beam which forms the upper framework of a door (Ex. 12:22).

LINUS, a Roman Christian known to Paul and Timothy (II Tim. 4:21).

LION, not now extant in Palestine, this powerful, daring beast was once dreaded by Hebrew shepherds (I Sam. 17:34; Is. 31:4) and even city-dwellers (II Kin. 17:25; I Kin. 13:24). Lions were used for execution (Dan. 6:7). Figuratively, the lion symbolized: Majesty (Gen. 49:9; Rev. 5:5); Wrath (Is. 31:4; 38:13); Bold-

ness (Prov. 28:1); Bravery (II Sam. 1:23); and Fearful Power (I Pet. 5:8).
stronger than a *l.*?, Judg. 14:18.
l. hath roared, who?, Amos 3:8.
devil as a roaring *l.*, I Pet. 5:8.
l. of tribe of Judah, Rev. 5:5.

LIPS, external organs of the mouth.
l. of a strange woman, Prov. 5:3.
l. of a fool, Eccles. 10:12.
man of unclean *l.*, Is. 6:5.
honoreth me with *l.*, Matt. 15:8.
other *l.* will I speak, I Cor. 14:21.
fruit of our *l.* giving, Heb. 13:15.
his *l.* that they speak, I Pet. 3:10.

LITTLE, small.
l. water, I pray you, Gen. 18:4.
l. sleep, *l.* slumber, Prov. 6:10.
O ye of *l.* faith, Matt. 14:31.
fear not, *l.* flock, Luke 12:32.
exercise profits *l.*, I Tim. 4:8.
made *l.* lower than angels, Heb. 2:9.
tongue is *l.* member, James 3:5.

LIVE, (1) have life; (2) conduct life.
tree of life, and *l.*, Gen. 3:22.
no man see me and *l.*, Ex. 33:20.
if man die, shall he *l.*?, Job 14:14.
heart shall *l.* forever, Ps. 22:26.
shall not die but *l.*, Ps. 118:17.
man *l.* many years, Eccles. 6:3.
can these bones *l.*?, Ezek. 37:3.
better to die than *l.*, Jonah 4:3.
dead, yet he shall *l.*, John 11:25.
in him we *l.* and move, Acts 17:28.
l. peaceably with all, Rom. 12:18.
I *l.*, yet not I, but, Gal. 2:20.
just shall *l.* by faith, Heb. 10:38.
l. to righteousness, I Pet. 2:24.

LIVELY, living, active.
Hebrew women are *l.*, Ex. 1:19.
received *l.* oracles, Acts 7:38.
again to a *l.* hope, I Pet. 1:3.
ye, as *l.* stones, are, I Pet. 2:5.

LIVES, *see* LIFE, LIVE.

LIVING, having life. *See* LIFE.
dominion over every *l.*, Gen. 1:28.
Eve, mother of all *l.*, Gen. 3:20.
in the land of the *l.*, Ps. 116:9.
God of the *l.*, Matt. 22:32.
why seek *l.* among dead, Luke 24:5.
bodies a *l.* sacrifice, Rom. 12:1.

LIZARD, lizards were ceremonially unclean among the Jews (Lev. 11:30).

LOAD, to heap on (Ps. 68:19).

LOAF, the Hebrews baked their bread in round cakes or loaves (Matt. 14:17).

LO-AMMI, (not my people), Hosea's second son whose name symbolized God's rejection of Israel (Hos. 1:9–10).

LOAN, the ancient Hebrews had no commercial credit systems for the raising of capital. Loans were allowed, even enjoined, for cases of necessity (Ex. 22:25; Lev. 25:35). In these interest was forbidden, but later interest was taken, especially from foreigners (Ezek. 18:13; 22:12). Nehemiah corrected wrongs in the loan system of his day (Neh. 5:1–13). Pledges were to be governed by laws in Deut. 15:9; 24:6, 17). The moneychangers profited from exchanging coin with those who came to pay the half-shekel (Mark 11:15).

LOATHE, abhor, detest.
hath soul *l.* Zion?, Jer. 14:19.

LOAVES, rolls of bread.
took five *l.* and two, Matt. 14:19.
seven *l.* and fishes, Mark 8:6.

LOCK, *see* KEY.

LOCUST, CANKERWORM, CATER-PILLAR, CRICKET, well-known winged insect of the grasshopper family. It commits ravages on vegetation in the countries it visits. Its huge swarms darken the sky (Ex. 10:15) and are noisily voracious (Joel 2:2–9), traveling only in the day (Nahum 3:17). With locusts God plagued Egypt (Ex. 10:6–6). They were food for John the Baptist (Matt. 3:4).

LOD, an ancient name for the city of Lydda (I Chr. 8:12; Neh. 7:37; 11:35).

LO-DEBAR, (no pasture), a city in Gilead (II Sam. 9:4), probably identical with **Debir** (Josh. 13:26).

LODGE, (1) a hut for a garden watchman (Is. 1-8); (2) to spend the night (Josh. 4:3, Ruth 1:16).
birds come and *l.* in, Mark 4:32.
called them and *l.* them, Acts 10:23.
prepare me a *l.*, Philem. 22.

LOFTY, high, exalted, proud.
nor mine eyes *l.*, Ps. 131:1.
on a *l.* mountain, Is. 57:7.

LOG, a liquid measure about the same as the pint (Lev. 14:10, 12, 15).

LOINS, part of the body between the ribs and the hipbone.
girdle about his *l.*, I Kin. 2:5.
let your *l.* be girded, Luke 12:35.
your *l.* girt about, Eph. 6:14.

LOIS, Timothy's grandmother (II Tim. 1:5).

LONG, desire greatly.
fed me all life *l.*, Gen. 48:15.
make *l.* prayers, Mark 12:40.
I *l.* to see you, Rom. 1:11.
if I tarry *l.* that, I Tim. 3:15.
judgment of *l.* time, II Pet. 2:3.

LONGIMANUS ARTAXERXES, *see* ARTAXERXES.

LOOK, to see, to seek.
l. to heaven and tell, Gen. 15:5.
fair to *l.* upon, Esther 1:11.
l. down from heaven, Is. 63:15.
do we *l.* for another, Matt. 11:3.
search and *l.*; for out, John 7:52.
l. ye out seven men, Acts 6:3.
we *l.* for new heavens, II Pet. 3:13.

LOOKINGGLASS, *see* MIRROR.

LOOSE, untie, set free.
l. thy shoe from off, Deut. 25:9.
what ye *l.* on earth, Matt. 18:18.
I am not worthy to *l.*, Acts 13:25.
worthy to *l.* the seals, Rev. 5:2.

LORD, basically designating the authority of ownership, the word Lord is used of: (1) a husband (Gen. 18:12); (2) an owner of slaves (Gen. 24:18; 32:5); (3) God as Lord of whole earth (Ex. 23:13; Ps. 114:7). In the King James Version it is used to translate the divine name YHWH. In the New Testament the word translated Lord is used in the sense of "sir" at times (Matt. 21:30), but usually suggests the idea of "master" (Mark 13:35), and in this sense it is used of Jesus in the Gospels (Matt. 8:25). Later the word proclaims the deity of Jesus (Acts 10:36; Rom. 14:8; I Cor. 7:22; Phil. 2:9–11). God is also called "Lord" and sometimes "Lord of heaven and earth" (Matt. 5:33; 11:25).

the *L.* he is God, Deut. 4:35.
L. do so to me and more, Ruth 1:17.
whose God is the *L.*, Ps. 33:12.
The *L.* our Righteousness, Jer. 23:6.
saying, Know the *L.*, Jer. 31:34.
L. if thou wilt, thou, Matt. 8:2.
David call him *L.?*, Mark 12:37.
why call me *L. L.* and?, Luke 6:46.
made both *L.* and Christ, Acts 2:36.
one *L.*, one faith, one, Eph. 4:5.
kingdoms of our *L.*, Rev. 11:15.
he is *L.* of lords, Rev. 17:14.

LORD, BRETHREN OF THE, *see*
BRETHREN OF THE LORD.

LORD OF HOSTS, a title of God used
often in the Old Testament. It emphasizes God's dominion over all forces
(Gen. 2:1; Is. 1:9; 45:12).

LORD'S DAY, (Rev. 1:10). This is believed to be the first day of the week, a
day on which the early Christians worshipped (Acts 20:7); it was the day of the
week that Christ was raised (Luke 24:1).

LORDSHIP, authority. *See* **LORD.**

LORD'S PRAYER, popular name for the
prayer Jesus taught his disciples (Matt.
6:8–13; Luke 11:2–4).

LORD'S SUPPER, LAST SUPPER, the
memorial meal established by Christ
(Matt. 26:26–29; Mark 14:22–25; Luke
22:19) and practiced by the early church
(I Cor. 11:24–26) the first day of the
week (Acts 20:7). It is also called the
"Communion" (I Cor. 10:16) and the
"Lord's Table." It commemorates
Christ's death for sin, celebrates communion and fellowship with the living
Lord, and prophesies His Second Coming (I Cor. 11:26). All Christians should
partake of this feast regularly (Acts 20:7)
and reverently (I Cor. 11:27–29).

LO-RUHAMAH, the name divinely given
to Hosea's daughter to show that God
will no longer have pity on rebellious
Israel (Hos. 1:6).

LOSE, to be deprived of.
caused owners to *l.* life, Job 31:39.
a time to *l.*, Eccles. 3:6.
finds life shall *l.* it, Matt. 10:39.

LOSS, deprivation.

pay for *l.* of time, Ex. 21:19.
shall suffer *l.*, I Cor. 3:15.
counted *l.* for Christ, Phil. 3:7.

LOST, was deprived of.
salt have *l.* savour, Matt. 5:13.
sheep which was *l.*, Luke 15:6.
my son was *l.*, Luke 15:24.
come to save the *l.*, Luke 19:10.

LOT, (1) casting lots (markers) was used
to decide a matter by chance (I Sam.
14:41; Num. 26:55; Acts 1:26). (2) Portion determined by casting lots (Deut.
32:9; Josh. 15:1; Is. 17:14).

LOT, Abraham's nephew who accompanied him to Canaan (Gen. 12:4) and
chose to settle at Sodom (Gen. 13:5)
from which wicked city he later barely
escaped (Gen. 19:1–30).

LOTAN, a prince of Idumaea (Gen. 36:
20).

LOUD, noisy.
l. instruments to, II Chr. 30:21.
cried with *l.* cry, Rev. 14:18.

LOVE, (1) signal attribute of God (I John
4:8). God's actions show His love for
men (John 3:16); love is the reason for
God's work in man's behalf. (2) The pre-
eminent virtue in the Christian life (I Cor.
13:13). It is learned from God (I John
4:19) and is the highest motive for moral
goodness. Love is a test of discipleship
(John 13:35); obedience is a test of love
(John 14:15). Love was the greatest
command in the Law (Matt. 22:37–39)
and is a primary command of Christ
(John 15:12).
l. Lord thy God, Deut. 6:5.
passing *l.* of women, II Sam. 1:26.
banner was *l.*, Song 2:4.
l. strong as death, Song 8:6.
Lord's *l.* to Israel, Hos. 3:1.
l. shall wax cold, Matt. 24:12.
L. your enemies, Luke 6:27.
l. of Christ, II Cor. 5:14.
faith works by *l.*, Gal. 5:6.
l. of money is root, I Tim. 6:10.
labour of *l.*, Heb. 6:10.
left thy first *l.*, Rev. 2:4.

LOVE FEAST, *see* **AGAPE.**

LOVELY, beautiful.
as a *l.* song, Ezek. 33:32.

whatever things are *l.*, Phil. 4:8.

LOVER, one who loves.
l. of pleasures more, II Tim. 3:4.
l. of hospitality, Titus 1:8.

LOVINGKINDNESS, steadfast love.
thy marvellous *l.*, Ps. 17:7.
multitude of *l.*, Is. 63:7.
shows *l.* to thousands, Jer. 32:18.
betroth thee to me in *l.*, Hos. 2:19.

LOW, to be humbled.
come down very *l.*, Deut. 28:43.
much cattle in *l.*, II Chr. 26:10.
regarded *l.* estate, Luke 1:48.

LOWER, less in elevation or rank.
Shout, ye *l.* parts, Is. 44:23.
little *l.* than angels, Heb. 2:7.

LOWEST, least in elevation or rank.
burn to *l.* hell, Deut. 32:22.
shame to take *l.* room, Luke 14:9.

LOWLAND, the western part of Palestine is a lowland (II Chr. 26:10).

LOWLINESS, humility (Eph. 4:2; Phil. 2:3).

LOWLY, humble.
hath respect to *l.*, Ps. 138:6.
I am meek and *l.*, Matt. 11:29.

LUBIM, an African race, the primitive Libyans (Nah. 3:9; II Chr. 12:3; 16:8; Dan. 11:43) who lived on the north coast of Africa, west of Egypt.

LUCAS, *see* LUKE.

LUCIFER, in Is. 14:12 this word refers to the king of Babylon, not to Satan.

LUCIUS, (1) a kinsman of Paul (Rom. 16:21); (2) a leader in the church at Antioch (Acts 13:1).

LUCRE, dishonest gain.
greedy of filthy *l.*, I Tim. 3:8.

LUD, LUDIM, descendants of Shem (Gen. 10:22). Another group by this name descended from Ham (Gen. 10:13), and a third group supplied mercenaries for Egypt. Probably the second of these is meant by the prophets (Jer. 46:9; Ezek. 30:5) in their denunciations.

LUHITH, a Moabite town to which some Israelites fled (Is. 15:5; Jer. 48:5).

LUKE, LUCAS, the evangelist author of Luke and Acts. A Gentile, he was a medical doctor who accompanied Paul and labored faithfully with him (Col. 4:11, 14; Philem. 24; II Tim. 4:11).

LUKE, GOSPEL OF, this third Gospel was intended first for the mind of the cultured Greek, and thus this book sets in precise order the facts of Christ to emphasize their certainty (Luke 1:1–4). The theme of this Gospel is the humanity of Christ: Christ is Son of Man come to seek the lost (Luke 19:10). Luke gives five outbursts of praise recorded by no other Gospel (Luke 1:42–55; 68–79; 2:14; 29–32). Luke gives the most detailed account of Christ's infancy and childhood. With its logical arrangement and flowing narration of the good news of Christ, this Gospel has been called "the most beautiful book that has ever been written."

LUKEWARM, (Rev. 3:16) insipidly and nauseatingly indifferent.

LUNATICK, (Matt. 4:24; 17:15), a diseased person, perhaps epileptic.

LUST, illegal desire.
not fulfill *l.* of flesh, Gal. 5:16.
drawn of his own *l.*, James 1:14.
l. of the flesh, *l.*, I John 2:16.

LUTE, *see* PSALTERY.

LUTHERAN BIBLE, *see* VERSIONS.

LUZ, (almond tree), (1) ancient name of Bethel (Gen. 28:19; 35:6); (2) a Hittite town destroyed by Benjamin (Judg. 1:23–26).

LYCAONIA, a small Roman province in Asia Minor; its people spoke corrupt Greek mixed with Assyrian (Acts 13:51–14:23). Chief cities of Lycaonia were Derbe, Iconium and Lystra.

LYCIA, a Roman province in Asia Minor (Acts 21:2; 27:5).

LYDDA, a town southeast of Joppa, formerly called Lod (I Chr. 8:12).

LYDIA, a Thyatiran lady who was a dealer in dyes dwelt in Philippi where she was converted to Christ by Paul (Acts 16:14, 40).

LYDIA, LYDIANS, (Ezek. 30:5; Jer. 46:9), *see* LUD, LUDIM.

LYING, telling intentional falsehoods. swearing, *l.*, killing, Hos. 4:2. put away *l.*, Eph. 4:25.

LYING, reclining, resting. path and *l.* down, Ps. 139:3. sick of palsy *l.*, Matt. 9:2.

LYSANIAS, governor of **Abilene** in the time of John the Baptist (Luke 3:1).

LYSIAS, CLAUDIAS, a Roman officer who rescued Paul and sent him to the procurator Felix (Acts 21:31; 23:17–30).

LYSTRA, a town of **Lycaonia** where Paul was first almost worshipped, but later almost killed (Acts 14:8–19).

M

MAACAH, MAACHAH, (1) child of Nahor and Reumah (Gen. 22:24), (2) David's wife and mother of Absalom (II Sam. 3:3), (3) Syrian city-state near Mount Hermon (Josh. 13:13), (4) father of Achish, king of Gath (I Kin. 2:39), (5) mother of King Abijam (I Kin. 15:2), (6) concubine of Caleb (I Chr. 2:48), (7) wife of Machir (I Chr. 7:15), (8) mother of Gibeon (I Chr. 8:29), (9) father of Hanan (I Chr. 11:43), (10) father of Shephatiah (I Chr. 27:16).

MAACHATHITES, MAACATHITE, MAACHATHI, inhabitants of Maachah.

MAACHIAH, *see* MAACAH.

MAADAI, one who had taken a foreign wife (Ezra 10:34).

MAADIAH, MOADIAH, a priest who returned from Babylon (Neh. 12:5).

MAAI, a priest after the exile (Neh. 12: 36).

MAALEH-ACRABBIM, a steep ascent in Southeast Palestine (Josh. 15:3).

MAARATH, a city of Judah (Josh. 15:59).

MAAREH-GEBA, in the Revised Standard Version for a place that is called "meadows of Gibeah" in the Authorized Version (Judg. 20:33).

MAASAI, *see* MAASIAI.

MAASEIAH, MAHSEIAH, a Levite and musician at the bringing up of the ark from Obed-edom, (I Chr. 15:18), (2) a captain of hundreds in Joash's reign (II Chr. 23:1), (3) a steward under King Uzziah (II Chr. 26:11), (4) an unknown person of royal blood slain in the Ephraimite invasion (II Chr. 28:7), (5) a "governor of the city" (II Chr. 34:8; Jer. 32:12), (6) priest who divorced his foreign wife (Ezra 10:18), (7) another priest doing the same (Ezra 10:21), (8) a priest of the sons of Pashur who divorced his Gentile wife (Ezra 10:22), (9) an Israelite who put away his Gentile wife (Ezra 10:30), (10) the father of Azariah (Neh. 3:23), (11) assistant to Ezra (Neh. 8:4), (12) a priest who expounded the law as it was read by Ezra (Neh. 8:7), (13) one of the covenanters with Nehemiah (Neh. 10:25), (14) son of Baruch (Neh. 11:5), (15) a son of Ithiel (Neh. 11:7), (16) a priest mentioned in Jer. 21:1, and (17) son of Shallum and keeper of the door of the temple (Jer. 35:4). (18) Grandfather of Baruch and Seraiah (Jer. 32:12; 51:59). (19) Father of Zedekiah, the false prophet (Jer. 29: 21). (20) A priest at the dedication of the wall in Jerusalem (Neh. 12:41). (21) Another priest at the dedication (Neh. 12:42).

MAASIAI, MAASAI, an Aaronite living in Jerusalem after the exile (I Chr. 9:12).

MAATH, unknown person (Luke 3:26).

MAAZ, first son of Ram (I Chr. 2:27).

MAAZIAH, (1) the head of the last course of priests arranged by David (I Chr. 24:18). (2) A priest who sealed the covenant (Neh. 10:8).

MACCABEAN, pertaining to the Maccabees.

MACCABEAN FESTIVAL, *see* DEDICATION, FEAST OF.

MACCABEES, a family of patriotic Jews who revolted against the Syrians. They were also known as the Hasmonaeans. The sacrilegious act of Antiochus Epiphanes (175–163 B.C.) had outraged the Jews. Mattathias, of priestly descent, and his five sons led the revolt. The Maccabean era lasted from 167 to 63 B.C., when the Romans defeated them. Maccabee means "the hammerer," and was the name given to Judas, one of Mattathias' five sons.

MACEDONIA, a country which lies north of Greece. Its chief cities were Amphipolis, Apollonia, Beria, Neapolis, Philippi, and Thessalonica. Under Alexander the Great it rose to its greatest power. Paul was called to Macedonia by a vision (Acts 16:9; 20:1). Acts 16:10–17: 15 gives an account of his trip through that area. Later he passed through this province again (Acts 20:1-6), and even a third time (Phil. 2:24; I Tim. 1:3).

MACHBANAI, a Gadite warrior at Ziklag (I Chr. 12:13):

MACHBENA, MACHBENAH, the son of Sheva (I Chr. 2:49).

MACHI, Gadite father of a spy (Num. 13:15).

MACHIR, (1) son of Manasseh who inhabited Gilead (Deut. 3:15). (2) Another Manassite (II Sam. 9:4).

MACHIRITES, of the family of Machir (Ezra 10:30).

MACHNADEBAI, a Jew who had a foreign wife in the captivity (Ezra 10:40).

MACHPELAH, a field which contained a cave, and which Abraham bought for a burying place (Gen. 23:9, 17). Those buried there were Abraham, Sarah, Isaac, Rebekah, Leah, and Jacob (Gen. 25:9; 49:29-32). The cave was in Hebron, and is now marked by a Mohammedan mosque.

MAD, insane, raving, furious.
feigned himself *m.*, I Sam. 21:13.
I am not *m.*, most, Acts 26:25.
that ye are *m.*, I Cor. 14:23.

MADAI, third son of Japheth and father of the Medes (Gen. 10:2).

MADE, caused to exist, created, formed.
day Lord hath *m.*, Ps. 118:24.
m. every thing, Eccles. 3:11.
all things *m.* by him, John 1:3.
m. nigh by blood, Eph. 2:13.
m. like brethren, Heb. 2:17.
m. an high priest, Heb. 6:20.
m. head of corner, I Pet. 2:7.

MADIAN, see **MIDIAN.**

MADMANNAH, a town south of Jerusalem, assigned to Simeon (Josh. 15: 31).

MADMEN, a city of Moab whose destruction was foretold in Jer. 48:2.

MADMENAH, a town north of Jerusalem, between Nob and Gibeah (Is. 10: 31).

MADON, Canaanite city of North Palestine (Josh. 11:1).

MAGADAN, see **MAGDALA.**

MAGBISH, one who returned with Zerubbabel (Ezra 2:30).

MAGDALA, small Galilean town between Capernaum and Tiberias on the sea of Galilee (Matt. 15:39). Also called Dalmanutha (Mark 8:10).

MAGDALENE, the surname of a Mary. *See* **MARY.**

MAGDIEL, duke of Edom (Gen. 36:43).

MAGI, sorcerers, the plural form of magus (Acts 13:6). It was a term used for priests and wise men among the Medes and Persians. Their religion consisted of astrology, exorcism, soothsaying, magic, and divination. The designation "Rab-Mag," in Jer. 39:3, 13, is thought to mean "the chief of wise men." Simon Magus and Elymas were thought of in this way (Acts 8:9; 13:8). The men from "the east" (Matt. 8:11; 24:27; Luke 13:29) perhaps were from Persia or Babylonia.

MAGIC, MAGICIAN, magic is the art of working wonders which go beyond ability and power. In ancient times magic was practiced extensively. In Egypt diviners worshipped the god Thot. In Chaldea divination became a science of necromancers, astrologers, and soothsayers. The earliest account of magic in the Bible is in the history of Rachel (Gen. 31:19; 30, 32–35). Jacob was accused of divining the cup he placed in Benjamin's sack (Gen. 44:5). In the time of Moses magicians were a class of people (Ex. 7: 11). Balaam, in Num. 22:6, used incantations. Saul consulted with one who claimed to be able to call up the dead. The prophets continually condemned the practices; soothsayers (Is. 2:6), diviners (Mic. 3:5–7), and false prophets (Jer. 14:14; 23:25). Ezekiel teaches us that fetishism was among the idolatrous practices of the Hebrews (8:7–12). Daniel was instructed in the learning of the Chaldeans (Dan. 2:18).

In the New Testament we read very little about magic. Simon Magus (Acts 8:9) and Elymas (Acts 13:6–12) were magicians. Paul cast a "spirit of divination" (Acts 16:16–18).

MAGISTRATE, see **RULER.**
set *m.* and judges, Ezra 7:25.
adversary to the *m.,* Luke 12:11.
them to the *m.,* Acts 16:20.
to obey *m.,* to be ready, Titus 3:1.

MAGNIFICAL, to make great, found only in I Chr. 22:5.

MAGNIFY, to make or become great.
thy name be *m.* for, II Sam. 7:26.
Lord will be *m.,* Mal. 1:5.
soul doth *m.* the Lord, Luke 1:46.
tongues, and *m.* God, Acts 10:46.

MAGOG, mentioned in Gen. 10:2 and I Chr. 1:5 as the son of Japhet, but considered by some to be the name of a people. Ezekiel places this great tribe in the north (39:2), near Togarmah. They were once a mighty people. They took Sardis in 629 B.C., and overran the country as far as Egypt. By the word Magog we understand "the land of Gog."

MAGOR-MISSABIB, name given to Pashur by Jeremiah (Jer. 20:3–6).

MACPIASH, chief Israelite who joined the covenant of Nehemiah (Neh. 10:20).

MAGUS, SIMON, see **SIMON.**

MAHALAH, see **MAHLAH.**

MAHALALEEL, (1) son of Cainan (Gen. 5:12; Luke 3:37). (2) A descendant of Perez (Neh. 11:4).

MAHALATH, (1) daughter of Ishmael (Gen. 28:9). (2) Wife of Rehoboam (II Chr. 11:18). (3) A musical chorus (Ps. 53 "Title").

MAHANAIM, town east of Jordan (Gen. 32:2).

MAHANEH DAN, place of Judah (Judg. 18:12).

MAHARAI, David's warrior (I Chr. 11: 30).

MAHATH, (1) descendant of Kohath (I Chr. 6:35). (2) Levite over the dedicated things, under Hezekiah (II Chr. 31:13).

MAHAVITE, family of Eliel (I Chr. 11:46).

MAHAZIOTH, means "visions." It is one of the names in the peculiar verse (I Chr. 25:4), later taken as the name of an individual (I Chr. 25:30).

MAHER-SHALAL-HASH-BAZ, the symbolic name given to one of the sons of Isaiah, the prophet (Is. 8:1). The name means "the booty hastens, the spoil speeds." It was indicative of the impending doom of Damascus and Samaria. This name is the longest word in the Bible.

MAHLAH, MAHALAH, (1) daughter of Zelophehad (Josh. 17:3). (2) Child of Hamoleketh (I Chr. 7:18).

MAHLI, MAHALI, (1) eldest son of Merari (Ex. 6:19). (2) Son of Mushi (I Chr. 23:23).

MAHLITE, descendant of Mahli (Num. 3:33).

MAHLON, son of Elimelech and husband of Ruth (Ruth 1:2).

MAHOL, father of Heman (I Kin. 4:31)

MAHSEIAH, see **MAASEIAH.**

MAID, unmarried woman.
a maidservant, Gen. 30:3.
a virgin, Ex. 2:8.
female child, II Kin. 5:2.

MAIDEN, damsel, young woman.
m. walked by river, Ex. 2:5.
young men and *m.*, Ps. 148:12.
got servants and *m.*, Eccles. 2:7.

MAIL, defensive armor (I Sam. 17:5). *See* ARMOUR.

MAIM, deprived of a limb, amputation.
broken, or *m.*, or, Lev. 22:22.
enter into life *m.*, Mark 9:43.
poor, the *m.*, the lame, Luke 14:13.

MAINTAIN, to continue, keep, retain.
he *m.* the cause of, I Kin. 8:59.
I will *m.* mine own, Job 13:15.
thou *m.* my lot, Ps. 16:5.
to *m.* good works, Titus 3:8.

MAINTENANCE, support, assistance, upkeep (Prov. 27:27; Ezra 4:14).

MAKAZ, district of Judah, location unknown (I Kin. 4:9).

MAKER, one who makes, creates, builds.
and the *m.* of it as, Is. 1:31.
striveth with his *m.*, Is. 45:9.
the *m.* of his work trust-, Hab. 2:18.
whose builder and *m.* is, Heb. 11:10.

MAKHELOTH, twenty-sixth station of Israel in the wilderness (Num. 33:25).

MAKKEDAH, a city southwest of Jerusalem (Josh. 10:10).

MAKTESTH, district near Jerusalem (Zeph. 1:11).

MALACHI, the last of the minor prophets and the last prophet of the Old Testament. (Mal. 1:1). Details of his life are unknown.

MALACHI, BOOK OF, the last book in the Old Testament, written about the same time as Ezra and Nehemiah. It deals with the problems of the nation as it tries to restore the pure worship of the Lord, and as the leaders try to keep the adulterous marriages with heathen women from corrupting the nation. The prophet condemned this as an abomination, because the men were divorcing the wives of their own nation before marrying the heathen. Malachi was afraid that this practice would lead the Jews to paganism rather than convert the heathen women to Judaism. They were therefore exhorted to set aside their foreign wives (Ez. 10:10–12).

MALCHAM, (their king), (1) a son of Shaharaim (I Chr. 8:9). (2) An idol of the Ammonites (Zeph. 1:5). *See* MOLOCH.

MALCHIAH, *see* MALCHIJAH.

MALCHIEL, son of Beriah (Gen. 46:17).

MALCHIELITES, descendants of Malchiel (Num. 26:45).

MALCHIJAH, MALCHIAH, MELCHIAH, (1) a Gershonite Levite (I Chr. 6:40). (2) The father of Pashur, and a priest (I Chr. 9:12; Jer. 38:1). (3) The head of the fifth division of priests in the time of David (I Chr. 24:9). (4) Two sons of Parosh, husbands who put away their foreign wives (Ezra 10:25). (5) A Jew of Harim who put away his gentile wife (Ezra 10:31). (6) Son of Rechab who repaired the gate in the time of Nehemiah (Neh. 3:14). (7) One who assisted in repairing the walls (Neh. 3:31). (8) One who was with Ezra when he read the book of the law (Neh. 8:4). (9) One of those who sealed the covenant in the time of Nehemiah (Neh. 10:3). (10) One of the singers selected for the dedication of the walls (Neh. 12:42).

MALCHIRAM, son of Jeconiah (I Chr. 3:18).

MALCHISHUA, MELCHISHUA, son of Saul (I Sam. 14:49).

MALCHUS, the servant of the high priest whose right ear Peter cut off when Jesus was arrested (John 18:10).

MALEFACTOR, rebels, insurgents.
two *m.* led with, Luke 23:32.
crucified him, and *m.*, Luke 23:33.
it not a *m.*, John 18:30.

MALELEEL, *see* MAHALALEEL.

MALICE, ill-will, spite.

not leaven of *m.*, I Cor. 5:8.
put away all *m.*, Eph. 4:31.
laying aside all *m.*, I Pet. 2:1.

MALICIOUSNESS, extreme malice.
filled with *m.*; full, Rom. 1:29.
for cloke of *m.*, I Pet. 2:16.

MALLOTHI, son of Heman (I Chr. 25:4).

MALLOWS, translated in the Authorized Version for "saltwort" (Job 30:4).

MALLUCH, MALLUCHI, MELICU, (1) Merarian Levite (I Chr. 6:44), (2) one who divorced his Gentile wife (Ezra 10:29), (3) another like (2), (Ezra 10:32), (4) priest of Nehemiah's day who returned with Zerubbabel (Neh. 12:2), (5) subscriber to the covenant of Nehemiah (Neh. 10:27).

MAMMON, wealth or riches.
serve God and *M.*, Matt. 6:24.
friends of the *m.*, Luke 16:9.
the unrighteous *m.*, Luke 16:11.

MAMRE, (1) an Amorite who, with his brothers, was a confederate of Abraham (Gen. 14:13, 24). (2) The dwelling place of Abraham, near Hebron (Gen. 23:17, 19; 35:27). Here Abraham was promised a son (Gen. 18:1, 10, 14). The cave of Machpelah lay before it (Gen. 23:17, 19; 25:9; 49:30).

MAN, as an individual, one of the male sex, and man as containing specific characteristics, such as strength and ownership. *See* **ADAM.**
m. in our image, Gen. 1:26.
wiser than all *m.*, I Kin. 4:31.
God dwell with *m.*, II Chr. 6:18.
m. . . is of few days, Job 14:1.
had likeness of *m.*, Ezek. 1:5.
will a *m.* rob God?, Mal. 3:8.
fishers of *m.*, Mark 1:17.
life . . light of *m.*, John 1:4.
by *m.* came death, I Cor. 15:21

MANAEN, early Christian prophet was a teacher in Antioch (Acts 13:1).

MANAHATH, (1) son of Shobal (Gen. 36:23). (2) Place where certain Benjamites were carried captive (I Chr. 8:6).

MANAHETHITES, the descendants or the inhabitants of Manahath (I Chr. 2:54).

MANASSEH, MANASSES, (1) the older son of Joseph by his Egyptian wife, Asenath, and father of the tribe of the same name. When Jacob blessed the sons of Joseph, he placed his right hand on Ephraim and his left hand on Manasseh. Joseph protested, because Ephraim was the second-born. But the blessing could not be changed (Gen. 48:1, 2, 8–20).
(2) The tribe of Manasseh. In some places it seems that Moses allotted the territory east of the Jordan to Reuben and Gad only (Num. 32:1, 2, 16–32). At times it seems that a half-tribe of Manasseh settled east of the Jordan (Num. 32: 33). This perhaps can be explained by saying that only later the Manassite families were raised to the status of a half-tribe. After they captured a few cities in the East (Num. 32:39, 41, 42), more moved into that area. They were bounded on the west by the Jordan, on the south by Gad, and on the east by Ammon.
(3) Son of Hezekiah and king of Judah for 55 years (II Kin. 21:1). He rebuilt the high places (II Kin. 21:3), and let his sons pass through the fire (II Kin. 21:6). (4) A change in the Hebrew text of the name of Moses (Judg. 18:30). (5) A son of Pahath-Moab (Ezra 10:30). (6) A son of Hashum (Ezra 10:33).

MANASSES, PRAYER OF, *see* **PRAYER OF MANASSES.**

MANASSITES, descendants of Manasseh, son of Joseph (Deut. 4:43).

MANDRAKES, a narcotic plant esteemed by ancients as a love potion (Gen. 30: 14).

MANEH, the pound weight (Ezek. 45: 12).

MANGER, a crib or trough where cattle are fed (Luke 2:7).

MANIFEST, evident, apparent, obvious
m. to all them that, Acts 4:16.
m. that he is except-, I Cor. 15:27.
folly shall be *m.*, II Tim. 3:9.

MANIFESTATION, uncovering.
But the *m.* of the, I Cor. 12:7.

by *m.* of the truth, II Cor. 4:2.

MANIFOLD, many, multiplied.
how *m.* are thy works, Ps. 104:24.
church the *m.* wisdom, Eph. 3:10.

MANNA, a food given miraculously to the
Israelites while they were in the wilderness (Ex. 16:35). It was given each day
except on the Sabbath. It appeared on
the ground as small as hoarfrost, and
as white as coriander seed. It tasted
like fresh oil or of wafers made of
honey.
Aaron puts in ark, Ex., 16:33.
Ceased at Jericho, Josh. 5:10–12.
Bread from heaven, John 6:31.
Kept in the Golden pot, Heb. 9:4.
Hidden manna, Rev. 2:17.

MANNER, custom, habit, way or method.
the *m.* of women, Gen. 18:11.
king's *m.* toward all, Esther 1:13.
the *m.* of the Romans, Acts 25:16.
as the *m.* of some is, Heb. 10:25.

MANOAH, father of Samson (Judg. 13:
2).

MANSERVANT, male servant.
and *m.,* and maid ser-, Gen. 12:16.
beat the *m.* and maidens, Luke 12:45.

MANSION, abode, dwelling place. Used
only in John 14:2.

MANSLAYER, murderer (Num. 35:6),
see **MURDER, CITIES OF REFUGE.**

MANTLE, CLOAK, an almost square
garment, similar to a blanket, worn over
the shoulders in fair weather and around
the body in bad weather for protection.
It was used by the poor as a covering at
night. *See* CLOTHING.
covered with a *m.,* I Sam. 28:14.
his face in his *m.,* I Kin. 19:13.
my garment and my *m.,* Ezra 9:3
apparel, and the *m.,* Is. 3:22.

MAOCH, father of Achish, king of Gath
(I Sam. 27:2).

MAON, (1) son of Shammai, (I Chr. 2:
45). (2) Elevated town of David's hiding from Saul (I Sam. 23:24).

MAONITES, an unknown tribe that oppressed Israel (Judg. 10:12).

MAR, damage, hurt, disrupt.
m. the corners of my, Lev. 19:27.
m. mine own inheritance, Ruth 4:6.
m. every good piece, II Kin. 3:19.
will I *m.* the pride, Jer. 13:9.

MARA, a designation meaning "bitter"
assumed by Naomi (Ruth 1:20).

MARAH, first station of Israel in the
wilderness (Ex. 15:23).

MARALAH, city of Zebulun (Josh. 19:
11).

MARANATHA, meaning "Our Lord
come (has come)" (I Cor. 16:22).

MARBLE, limestone or other fine-
grained mineral which takes a high
polish.
and pillars of *m.,* Esther 1:6.
and iron, and *m.,* Rev. 18:12.

MARCUS, *see* **MARK, JOHN.**

MARESHAH, (1) fortified Judean city
(Mic. 1:15), (2) father of Hebron (I
Chr. 2:42), (3) son of Laadah (I Chr.
4:21).

MARISHES, swamp or bog (Ezek. 47:
11).

MARK, *see* **MARK, JOHN.**

MARK, sign, stamp, token.
set . . *m.* upon Cain, Gen. 4:15.
m. . . . perfect man, Ps. 37:37.
m. them which cause, Rom. 16:17.
press toward *m.,* Phil. 3:14.
m. in right hand, Rev. 13:16.

MARK, GOSPEL OF, it is the second
book in the New Testament, and was
written between 56 and 65 A.D. Mark
primarily portrays the action of Jesus
and not his discourses. It is supposed by
many that the author is the same as
"Marcus" in I Pet. 5:13, but whether
he is the same as John Mark (Acts 15:
37–39; Col. 4:10; II Tim. 4: 11), is not certain. The old tradition states that Mark
wrote this Gospel at Peter's request or
dictation (Papias, Irenaeus). The Gospel
may have been written in Rome, due to a
few Latinisms in the book. He explains
the Jewish phrase "defiled hands" by

saying, "that is, unwashen hands." However, it seems clear that the author was a Jewish Christian, for he was familiar with Jewish customs and he knew Aramaic. The material of the narrative is arranged in an order which not only follows the recognized general development of Jesus' ministry, but is quite chronological in its sequence of individual events.

MARK, JOHN, MARCUS, son of Mary, a lady of Jerusalem, and companion of Paul and Barnabas. He was also the author of the second Gospel (Acts 12:12, 25; 13:13). It is generally agreed that he is identical with the Mark mentioned in the epistles. John Mark is remembered for leaving the missionary party at Perga. This caused Paul and Barnabas to separate on the second missionary trip, because Barnabas wanted John Mark as a companion and Paul did not (Acts 15:36–40). Later Paul commended Mark to the church at Colosse, saying that Mark had been a comfort to him (Col. 4:10, 11). Peter calls him "Marcus, my son" (I Pet. 5:13).

MARKETPLACE, MARKET, in the Old Testament, the Revised Version correctly translates "market" as "merchandise" (Ezek. 27:13, 17, 19, 25). In the New Testament it is a place of assembly, a place where business was carried on (Matt. 20:3, 4), trials were held (Acts 16: 19: 17: 17), and where children played (Matt. 11:16).

MARKET, SHEEP, see **SHEEP GATE.**

MARKS, see **MARK.**

MAROTH, a city in the northern part of Judah (Mic. 1:12).

MARRED, see **MAR.**

MARRIAGE, the union of man and woman as husband and wife, or, abstractly, the union or relationship viewed as an institution. One type of marriage in early times is illustrated by Samson, who left his tribe and married a Philistine woman (Judg. 14:1–4; 15:1, 2), and travelled back and forth between the tribes. Another form of marriage was the levirate form in which the Law of Moses required the brother of a deceased man to marry the widow, thus raising up his

brother's children to carry on the family name (Deut. 25:5–10). This is shown by the story of Tamar (Gen. 38:6–11). Although the Old Testament ideal was monogamy, polygamy was quite common. Marriage was divinely instituted in the Garden of Eden in the form of monogamy (Gen. 2:24). Noah, who could be described as the second founder of the race, had only one wife (Gen. 7:7). The mistakes of David could be attributed to his plural marriages (II Sam. 5:13; I Kin. 11:1–8). When the prophets looked for a way to describe the covenant relationship between God and man, they described a monogamous marriage relationship (Is. 50:1; Hos. 2).

The New Testament approves only monogamy. This is shown in Jesus' remarks (Matt. 19:3–9) and Paul's statement (Eph. 5:31). In Eph. 5:22–29, Paul tells the husbands to love their wives, and wives to obey their husbands. In New Testament times the ceremony consisted of a procession (Matt. 25:1–13), and a marriage supper which sometimes lasted seven days (Gen. 29:22). It was an insult to refuse an invitation (Matt. 22:1–10).
her duty of *m.*, Ex. 21:10.
and disciples to *m.*, John 2:2.
in *m.* doeth well, I Cor. 7:38.
m. is honourable, Heb. 13:4.
m. of the lamb, Rev. 19:7.

MARROW, inner substance of bones.
and *m.* to thy bones, Prov. 3:8.
of the joints and *m.*, Heb. 4:12.

MARRY, the act of contracting marriage.
odious woman *m.*, Prov. 30:23.
m. her that is, Matt. 5:32.
have *m.* a wife, Luke 14:20.
better *m.* than burn, I Cor. 7:9.
forbidding to *m.*, I Tim. 4:3.
younger women *m.*, I Tim. 5:14.

MARSENA, prince of Persia (Esther 1: 14).

MAR'S HILL, see **AREOPAGUS.**

MARTHA, the sister of Mary and Lazarus (John 11:1, 5, 19–28, 39). Martha appears to have been the head of the household, for she served when Jesus came (Luke 10:38–42; John 12:2). Once when Jesus was there, she complained to Jesus that Mary was not helping her. Jesus rebuked her because Mary had chosen to sit and listen to Jesus, and Martha was "anxious and troubled" about things that were not needful. She is sometimes identified with the women in the story of Simon the leper (Matt. 26:7; Mark 14:3).

MARTYR, witness, one who dies for his faith.
blood of the *m.*, Acts 22:20.
my faithful *m.*, who, Rev. 2:13.

MARVEL, something great, causing wonder or amazement (II Cor. 11:14).

MARVEL, to wonder, to be awed.
and all men did *m.*, Mark 5:20..
I *m.* that ye are so, Gal. 1:6.
m. not if the world, I John 3:13.

MARVELOUS, wonderful.
his *m.* works among, I Chr. 16:24.
and it is *m.* in our, Matt. 21:42.
into his *m.* light, I Pet. 2:9.

MARY, the mother of Jesus (Matt. 1, 2; Luke 1:26–56; 2:1–40; 3:23–38), and a descendant of David (Luke 1:27; Rom. 1:3). Mary presented herself to the temple for her purification (Lev. 12:2–4). She later visited the temple when Jesus was twelve years old (Luke 2:41–52). She appeared at the wedding feast at Cana (John 2:1–11). She also is mentioned when she and her other children wanted to see Jesus (Mark 3:31–35), at the cross (John 19:25–27), and after the Ascension (Acts 1:14).

MARY, the name for six women in the New Testament. (1) One greeted by Paul in the Roman letter (16:6). (2) The mother of John Mark (Acts 12:12). The disciples often met at her house for prayer. (3) The wife of Cleophas (John 19:25). She is generally identified with Mary the mother of James and Joses (Matt. 27:56), and with the "other Mary" of Matt. 27:61 and 28:11. It is believed by many that, according to John 19:25, the wife of Cleophas was the sister of Mary, the mother of Jesus. (4) Mary Magdalene, from whom Jesus cast seven demons. She was one of the women who was at the sepulchre (Matt. 27:55; Mark 15:47; John 19:25). She was the first to see Jesus after he arose (Mark 16:9). (5) Mary, the sister of Martha and Lazarus. She is the one who listened to Jesus as her sister served (Luke 10:38–42). She fell at Jesus' feet when he came to Bethany after Lazarus' death (John 11:22–32).

MASCHIL, a word in the titles of some Psalms (Ps. 32, 42, 44, 52–55, 74, 78, 88, 89, 142). The meaning of the word is uncertain; it may denote a contemplative poem.

MASH, son of Aram (Gen. 10:23).

MASHAL, Levitical city of Asher (I Chr. 6:74).

MASON, hewer and worker of stone.
to *m.*, and hewers of, II Kin. 12:12.
m. to hew wrought, I Chr. 22:2.

MASREKAH, city of Edom (I Chr. 1:47).

MASSA, son of Ishmael (Gen. 25:14).

MASSAH, *see* **MERIBAH.**

MASTER, one in authority.
of Abraham his *m.*, Gen. 24:9.
blessed my *m.* greatly, Gen. 24:35.
m. of the house shall, Ex. 22:8.
the ship *m.* came to, Jonah 1:6.

MATHUSALA, *see* **METHUSELAH.**

MATRED, mother of Mehetabel (Gen. 36:39).

MATRI, MATRITES, head of a Benjamite family (I Sam. 10:21).

MATTAN, (1) priest of Baal (II Kin. 11:18). (2) Father of Shephatiah (Jer. 38:1).

MATTANAH, station of Israel, across the Jordan (Num. 21:18).

MATTANIAH, (1) brother of Jehoiakim (II Kin. 24:17). (2) A Levite of Asaph (Neh. 11:17). (3) Son of Heman (I Chr. 25:4). (4) Descendant of Asaph (II Chr. 29:13). (5) Elamite who had a strange wife (Ezra 10:26). (6) Son of Zattu (Ezra 10:27). (7) One of the family of Pahath-Moab who took a foreign wife (Ezra 10:30). (8) Son of Bani (Ezra 10:37). (9) Grandfather of Hanan (Neh. 13:13).

MATTATHA, ancestor of Jesus (Luke 3:31).

MATTATHAH, a Hashumite that took a foreign wife (Ezra 10:33).

MATTATHIAS, ancestors of Jesus. (1) son of Amos (Luke 3:25), and (2) father of Maath (Luke 3:26).

MATTENAI, brother of Mattathah (Ezra 10:33). (2) Son of Bani, who took a foreign wife (Ezra 10:37). (3) A priest, son of Jeshua (Neh. 12:19).

MATTER, thing of consequence.
small *m.* that thou, Gen. 30:15.
of the same *m.*, Mark 10:10.
be ready as a *m.*, II Cor. 9:5.

MATHAN, son of Eleazar (Matt. 1:15).

MATHAT, ancestors of Jesus: (1) son of Levi (Luke 3:24), and (2) father of Jorim (Luke 3:29).

MATTHEW, an apostle and an evangelist; he was the same as Levi the son of Alphaeus. His call to be an apostle is found in Matt. 9:9; Mark 2:14, and Luke 5:27. He was a tax-collector. He wrote the Gospel which bears his name.

MATTHEW, GOSPEL OF, one of the major characteristics of this book is its constant quotations from the Old Testament (about 65). It was written to Jewish converts to show that Jesus of Nazareth is the Messiah to which the Old Testament looked forward. It relates Jesus ministry in its beginning (1–4), and gives us the great Sermon on the Mount (5–7). It tells of his wonderful works (8–9), and also tells of those who doubted him (11–12). It describes the Kingdom in parables (13), his instructions to his disciples (16:13; 18:35), and his Passion and Resurrection (26–28). The Gospel was no doubt written by the Apostle of the same name.

MATTHIAS, apostle chosen by lot to take the place of Judas (Acts 1:23).

MATTITHIAH, (1) Kohathite in the temple (I Chr. 9:31). (2) Levite singer (I Chr. 15:18). (3) Son of Jeduthun (I Chr. 25:3). (4) One with a foreign wife (Ezra 10:43). (5) Levite with Ezra at the reading of the law (Neh. 8:4).

MATTOCK, pickax for farming (Is. 7:25).

MAUL, club or axe (Prov. 25: 18).

MAW, stomach (Deut. 18:3).

MAY, be able, possible.
m. not eat bread, Gen. 43:32.
cup *m.* not pass, Matt. 26:42.
ye *m.* understand, Eph. 3:4.

MAZAROTH, signs of the zodiac (Job 38:32). Abolished by Josiah (II Kin. 23:5).

MEADOW, (1) the translation of a Hebrew word believed to mean reed grass, thus pasture land (Gen. 41:2, 18). (2) A word which probably means caves. It is used in connection with Gibeah of Benjamin (Judg. 20:33). *See* MAAREH-GEBA.

MEAH, tower of the wall of Jerusalem, near the sheep gate (Neh. 3:1).

MEAL OFFERING, *see* OFFERING and SACRIFICE.

MEALS, there were two regular meals in the Hebrew day: one was eaten about noon-time and one in the evening (Ex. 16:12; I Kin. 17:6). Complete meals eaten in the morning were considered to be signs of moral decay (Eccles. 10:16). However, it was permissible, especially for the labourers, to eat a light meal before noon (John 21:4–12). The evening meal was the chief meal. This was the meal that Martha served Jesus (John 12:2). The evening meal was used for banquets on special occasions, as marriages and birthdays (Mark 6:21; Luke 14:16–24; Rev. 19:9, 17). *See* BANQUET.

MEAN, to intend, to signify.
what *m.* ye by this, Ex. 12:26.
what *m.* by stones? Josh. 4:6.
rising should *m.*, Mark 9:10.
what vision *m.*, Acts 10:17.
what *m.* ye to weep, Acts 21:13.

MEAN, evil, wicked, obscure, base.
m. man boweth, Is. 2:9.
m. man be brought, Is. 5:15.
not of *m.* man, Is. 31:8.
of no *m.* city, Acts 21:39.

MEANS, ways, agency, power.
doth he devise *m.*, II Sam. 14:14.

by any *m.* redeem, Ps. 49:7.
by no *m.* come, Matt. 5:26.
by what *m.* whole, Acts 4:9.
by all *m.* save, I Cor. 9:22.

MEARAH, place near Sidon (Josh. 13:4).

MEASURE, standard, limit, judgment.
m. of my days, Ps. 39:4.
water by *m.*, Ezek. 4:11.
m. ye mete it, Matt. 7:2.
three *m.* of meal, Matt. 13:33.
amazed beyond *m.*, Mark 6:51.
stripes above *m.*, II Cor. 11:23.
m. of the gift of, Eph. 4:7.
m. of a man, Rev. 21:17.

MEAT, used only in Gen. 27:4 and Gen. 45:23 to mean animal flesh. Usually meant "food" as in the Meat Offering, which consisted of flour and oil.
m. offering, and of, Lev. 6:15.
soul abhorreth dainty *m*, Job 33:20.
giveth *m.* to her, Prov. 31:15.
milk, and not with *m.*, I Cor. 3:2.
abstain from *m.*, I Tim. 4:3.

MEAT OFFERING, *see* **OFFERING** and **SACRIFICE.**

MEBUNNAI, warrior of Judah (II Sam. 23:27).

MECHERATHITE, family of Hepher (I Chr. 11:36).

MECONAH, *see* **MEKONAH.**

MEDAD, an elder with Eldad who helped Moses (Num. 11:26).

MEDAN, son of Abraham (Gen. 25:2).

MEDDLE, intervene, encroach.
m. not with them, Deut. 2:5.
fool will be *m.*, Prov. 20:3.
m. with strife, Prov. 26:17.

MEDEBA, a city of Moab (Num. 21:30).

MEDES, inhabitants of Media, a people of Aryan stock (Gen. 10:2). After the Fall of Samaria, Sargon took many Hebrew captives to the cities of the Medes (II Kin. 17:6; 18:11). The law of the Medes and Persians was considered unalterable (Esther 1:19; Dan. 6:8). There were some Medes present at Pentecost (Acts 2:9).

MEDIA, an ancient land bounded on the north by the Caspian Sea, on the east by a great desert, on the south by Persia, and on the west by Assyria and Armenia. Shalmaneser of Assyria invaded it, Tiglathpileser III annexed part of its territory, and Sargon carried many of the people of the Northern Kingdom to the cities of Media (II Kin. 17:6; 18:11). Other than these indirect relationships, the Hebrews had no known dealings with the Medes. Dan. 5:31 contains the statement that "Darius the Mede received the kingdom." The two-horned ram of Daniel's vision symbolized the kings of Media and Persia (Dan. 8:20).

MEDIAN, *see* **MEDE.** (Dan. 5:31).

MEDIATOR, intercessor.
in the hands of a *m.*, Gal. 3:19.
one *m.* between God, I Tim. 2:5.
m. of a better covenant, Heb. 8:6.
to Jesus the *m.* of a, Heb. 12:24.

MEDICINE, ancient Egypt was renowned for its knowledge and skill of medicine. According to Herodotus (iii. 1, 129), Cyrus of Persia sent to Egypt for an oculist, and Darius had Egyptian physicians at Susa. They embalmed (Gen. 50:2), women practiced midwifery (Ex. 1:15), and they had many medicines (Jer. 46: 11). There is frequent medical allusions concerning difficult cases of midwifery (Gen. 25:24–26; 35:16–19). Mandrakes were prescribed for barrenness (Gen. 30: 14–16). Elisha prescribed antidotes for poisons (II Kin. 2:21; 4:39–41). Two other remedies were eye salve for partial blindness (Rev. 3:18) and a poultice of figs for boils (Is. 38:21).

MEDITATE, to contemplate, think.
shalt *m.* thereon day, Josh. 1:8.
law doth he *m.* day and, Ps. 1:2.
m. upon these things, I Tim. 4:15.

MEDITERRANEAN, the inland sea lying between Europe, Western Asia, and Africa. It is 2,320 miles long and 100 to 600 miles wide. It is known in the Scripture as the "Great Sea" (Num. 34:6; Josh. 1:4; Ezek. 47:10) and "Hinder," or "Western Sea" (Deut. 11:24; Joel 2: 20; Zech. 14:8).

MEEK, gentle, kind, mild.
m. shall eat and be, Ps. 22:26.

equity for the *m*. of, Is. 11:4.
Blessed are the *m*. for, Matt. 5:5.
a *m*. and quiet spirit, I Pet. 3:4.

MEEKNESS, quietness, gentleness.
of truth, and *m*., Ps. 45:4.
righteousness, and *m*., Zeph. 2:3.
receive with *m*. the, James 1:21.
his works with *m*., James 3:13.

MEET, fit or suitable for use.
fruits *m*. for repent-, Matt. 3:8.
it be *m*. that I go, I Cor. 16:4.
m. to be called an, I Cor. 15:9.
I think it *m*., as, II Pet. 1:13.

MEET, come together, assemble.
went out to *m*. him, Gen. 14:17.
go ye out to *m*., Matt. 25:6.
to *m*. the Lord in, I Thess. 4:17.

MEGIDDO, MEGIDDON, an ancient
Canaanite stronghold (Josh. 12:21). It
was captured by Thotmes III (1483 B.C.),
and was mentioned in the Tell el-Amarna
tablets (1400–1360 B.C.), as well as in
Assyrian inscriptions of the 8th century.
It was given to Manasseh, but remained
in possession of the Canaanites (Josh.
17:11–13; Judg. 1:27, 28). It was at the
pass of Megiddo that king Josiah was
slain (II Kin. 23:29, 30; II Chr. 35:22–
34). Stables have been found at Megiddo,
perhaps built by Solomon (I Kin. 4:26;
9:19), with the capacity for about 300
horses.

MEHETABEL, MEHETABEEL, (1) wife
of Hadad (Gen. 36:39), and (2) father of
Delaiah (Neh. 6:10).

MEHIDA, man whose descendants returned with Zerubbabel (Neh. 7:54).

MEHIR, son of Chelub (I Chr. 4:11).

MEHOLATHITE, inhabitant of a city in
Issachar (I Sam. 18:19).

MEHUJAEL, father of Methuselah,
(Gen. 4:18).

MEHUMAN, chamberlain of Ahasuerus
of Persia (Esther 1:10).

MEHUNIM, a Nethinim whose descendants returned with Zerubbabel (Ezra
2:50).

MEJARKON, city in Dan (Josh. 19:46).

MEKONAH, MECONAH, city in Judah (Neh. 11:28).

MELATIAH, Gibeonite who helped repair the wall (Neh. 3:7).

MELCHI, (1) ancestor of Jesus through
Mary (Luke 3:24), and (2) another ancestor of Jesus (Luke 3:28).

MELCHISEDEC, *see* **MELCHIZEDEK.**

MELCHISHUA, MALCHISHUA, third
son of King Saul (I Sam. 14:49).

MELCHIZEDEK, MELCHISEDEC,
means "king of righteousness." He appears suddenly in Gen. 14:18 as "priest
of the Most High God," and "king of
Salem" (Jerusalem). Such a person com-
bining both the priestly and kingly offices was afterward seen in the ideal king
of Israel. To this ideal king a priesthood
"after the order of Melchizedek" was
ascribed (Ps. 110:4). This unique priesthood was later applied to Christ (Heb.
5:6, 7).

MELEA, son of Menan (Luke 3:31).

MELEK, son of Micah (I Chr. 8:35).

MELICU, priest in Jerusalem (Neh.
12:14).

MELITA, the island of Malta in the Adriatic where Paul was shipwrecked (Acts
28:1).

MELODY, music, a tune.
and the voice of *m*., Is. 51:3.
the *m*. of thy viols, Amos 5:23.
m. in your hearts to, Eph. 5:19.

MELON, a temperate and tropical climate vegetable of the varieties of
watermelons and cantaloupes. (Num.
11:5).

MELT, to dissolve, soften.
multitude *m*. away, I Sam. 14:16.
m. away as waters, Ps. 58:7.
soul *m*. for heaviness, Ps. 119:28.
shall *m*. with fer-, II Pet. 3:12.

MELZAR, officer of the Babylonian court
(Dan. 1:11).

MEMBER, part of the body.
and all my *m.* as, Job 17:7.
one of my *m.* should, Matt. 5:29.
m. one of another, Eph. 4:25.
war in your *m.*, James 4:1.

MEMORY, MEMORIAL, remembrance.
burn the *m.* of it, Lev. 2:2.
the *m.* of them perish, Esther 9:28.
cut off the *m.* of them, Ps. 109:15.
the *m.* of the just, Prov. 10:7.
for the *m.* of them, Eccles. 9:5.
a *m.* before God, Acts 10:4.

MEMPHIS, an important ancient Egyptian capital on the west bank of the Nile about ten miles north of Cairo. Built by Menes (2900 B.C.) it lost importance after the founding of Alexandria, but continued until the Middle Ages when its ruins were carried away to build Cairo. The Hebrews knew Memphis as Noph (Is. 19:13). The prophets denounced this city (Jer. 46:19; Ezek. 30: 13; Hos. 9:6). After Judah's fall, some Jews settled at Memphis (Jer. 44:1).

MEMUCAN, prince of Persia (Esther 1:14).

MEN, *see* **MAN.**
he knows vain *m.*, Job 11:11.
m. with *m.* work that, Rom. 1:27.
speak after manner of *m.*, Rom. 6:19.
quit you like *m.*, I Cor. 16:13.
all *m.* to be saved, I Tim. 2:4.

MENAHEM, son of Gadi, he murdered the usurper Shallum and became King of Israel, reigning ten years. Menahem avoided Assyrian invasion by paying tribute to Tiglath-Pileser III (Pul) (II Kin. 15:14–22).

MENAN, MENNA, an ancestor of Jesus (Luke 3:31).

MENE, MENE, TEKEL, UPHARSIN, the words of the miraculous handwriting on a palace wall during Belshazzar's feast. The Aramaic words mean, respectively, "numbered," "weighed," and "divided," thus "destroyed." Daniel interpreted the words to spell Babylon's doom (Dan. 5:25).

MEN OF THE EAST, *see* **EAST, CHILDREN** or **MEN OF THE.**

MENTION, to speak, discuss.
will not make *m.* of, Jer. 20:9.
make *m.* of the name, Amos 6:10.
m. of you always in, Rom. 1:9.
when died made *m.*, Heb. 11:22.

MENUHOTH, *see* **MANAHETHITES.**

MEONENIM, site in Ephraim (Judg. 9:37).

MEONOTHAI, father of Ophrah (I Chr. 4:14).

MEPHAATH, a Levitical city of Reuben (I Chr. 6:79).

MEPHIBOSHETH, (1) son of Saul (II Sam. 21:8), (2) son of Jonathan (II Sam. 4:4).

MERAB, daughter of Saul (I Sam. 14:49).

MERAIAH, priest in Jerusalem during Joiakim's reign (Neh. 12:12).

MERAIOTH, (1) ancestor of Azariah, I Chr. 6:6. (2) Another of the same line, Neh. 11:11. (3) Priest at the close of the exile, Neh. 12:15.

MERARI, third son of Levi (Gen. 46:11).

MERARITES, descendants of Merari (Num. 26:57), these formed one of the three Levitical divisions. This group tended to part of the tabernacle (Num. 3:35–37; 4:29–33; 7:8). In David's day all of the divisions assisted with the temple music (I Chr. 6:31–47).
Mentioned after exile, I Chr. 9:14.
Divided into courses, I Chr. 23:6.
Helped in reform, II Chr. 29:12–15.

MERATHAIM, symbolic name for Babylon (Jer. 50:21).

MERCHANDISE, trade, business, barter.
the *m.* of silver, Prov. 3:14.
thy *m.*, thy mariners, Ezek. 27:27.
another to his *m.*, Matt. 22:5.
an house of *m.*, John 2:16.

MERCHANT, trader, seller, dealer.
king's *m.* received, I Kin. 10:28.
unto a *m.* man seek-, Matt. 13:45.
m. of earth waxed, Rev. 18:3.

MERCIFUL, compassionate, pitying.
God, *m.* and gracious, Ex. 34:6.

redeem me, be *m.*, Ps. 26:11.
I am *m.*, saith Lord, Jer. 3:12.
Blessed are *m.*, for, Matt. 5:7.
Be *m.* as Father is *m.*, Luke 6:36.
m. to me, a sinner, Luke 18:13.
m. and faithful priest, Heb. 2:17.

MERCURY, MERCURIUS, Roman god of commerce. He was also the patron god of oratory, which probably explains why the people of Lystra identified the eloquent Paul with this false deity (Acts14:12).

MERCY, kindness.
magnified thy *m.*, which, Gen. 19:19.
covenant and *m.* for, Neh. 9:32.
save me for *m.* sake, Ps. 6:4.
goodness, *m.* follow me, Ps. 23:6.
his *m.* endureth forever, Ps. 106:1.
do justly and love *m.*, Mic. 6:8.
will have *m.* and not, Matt. 9:13.
Lord have *m.* on son, Matt. 17:15.
Father of *m.*, and God, II Cor. 1:3.
God, rich in *m.*, Eph. 2:4.
grace, *m.* and peace, I Tim. 1:2.
that we may obtain *m.*, Heb. 4:16.
died without *m.* under, Heb. 10:28.
had not obtained *m.*, I Pet. 2:10.

MERCY SEAT, the golden top of the ark of the covenant in the Holy of Holies. Here God manifested his glory and communed with Israel (Num. 7:89). Measuring about 22 inches by 40 inches, the mercy seat had on its two ends kneeling golden cherubim facing each other with wingtips meeting above the center of the seat (Ex. 25:17–22). On the annual Day of Atonement sprinkled blood of a bull and goat on the seat as offering for sins (Lev. 16:2, 13–17).

MERED, son of Ezra (I Chr. 4:17).

MEREMOTH, (1) son of Uriah the priest (Ezra 8:33), (2) one of the family of Bani who had a foreign wife (Ezra 10: 36), and (3) a priest who sealed the covenant (Neh. 10:5).

MERES, prince of Persia and Media under Ahasuerus (Esther 1:14).

MERIBAH, MASSAH, MERIBAH-KA-DESH, place where the Israelites murmured for want of water. (Ex. 17:7). (2) Place near Kadesh where Moses smote the rock and offended God by his disobedience (Num. 20:10–12).

MERIBATH-KADESH, *see* **MERIBAH.**

MERIBBAAL, son of Jonathan (I Chr. 8:34).

MERODACH, Babylonian god of war (Jer. 50:2).

MERODACH-BALADAN, BERODACH-BALADAN, king of Babylon, contemporary with Hezekiah, king of Judah (Is. 39:1). First an important tribal chief, he seized chance in 722 B.C. to capture southern Babylon, and ruled from 721 to 710 when Sargon overthrew him. In 702 Merodach again seized the throne, ruling briefly before being chased by Sennacherib. About 702 Merodach tried to get Hezekiah's aid against Assyria under pretense of a goodwill embassy, it seems (II Kin. 20:12–19; Is.`39).

MEROM, a small lake on the Jordan River in upper Palestine (Josh. 11:5).

MERONOTHITE, inhabitant of a district of Zebulum (I Chr. 27:30).

MEROZ, place north of Mount Tabor near Lake Merom (Judg. 5:23).

MERRY, cheerful, jovial, joyous.
m. heart maketh, Prov. 15:13.
m. heart doeth good, Prov. 17:22.
drink and be *m.*, Eccles. 8:15.
them that make *m.*, Jer. 30:19.
eat, drink, be *m.*, Luke 12:19.
m. let him sing, James 5:13.

MESECH, *see* **MESHECH.**

MESHA, (1) an unidentified area in the region occupied by the descendants of Joktan (Gen. 10:30). (2) A Benjamite, son of Shahariam (I Chr. 8:8, 9). (3) A man of Judah, of the house of Caleb. (I Chr. 2:42). (4) A king of Moab (about 850 B.C.), and son of Chemoshmelech. He paid tribute to king Ahab (II Kin. 3:4). (II Kin. 3:4–9, 24–27). There is an account of this story on the Moabite Stone.

MESHACH, Babylonian name of Michael, Daniel's companion (Dan. 1:7).

MESHECH, MESECH, (1) son of Japheth (Gen. 10:2), (2) son of Shem (I Chr. 1:17), (3) tribe joined with Kedar (Ps. 120:5), and (4) descendants of Japheth (MOSOCHI) (Ezek. 27:13; 32:26).

MESHELEMIAH, Levite, son of Kore (I Chr. 9:21).

MESHEZABEEL, MESHEZABEL, grandfather of Meshullam, repairer of the wall (Neh. 10:21).

MESHILLEMITH, son of Immer (Neh. 11:13), (2) father of Berechiah (II Chr. 28:12).

MESHOBAB, a Simeonite prince (I Chr. 4:34).

MESHULLAM, (1) grandfather of Shaphan (II Kin. 22:3), (2) eldest child of Zerubbabel (I Chr. 3:19), (3) a Gadite (I Chr. 5:13), (4) a Benjamite (I Chr. 9:7; Neh. 11:7), (5) father of Sallu (Neh. 11:7), (6) son of Shephathiah (I Chr. 9:8), (7) priest, son of Zadok (Neh. 11:11), (8) son of Meshillemith (I Chr. 9:12), (9) Kohathite overseer (II Chr. 34:12), (10) chief man sent by Ezra to Iddo (Ezra 8:16), (11) Levite temple porter (Neh. 12:25), (12) son of Bani (Ezra 10:29). (13) son of Berechiah (Neh. 3:4), (14) repairer of old gate (Neh. 3:6), (15) Israelite who subscribed the law (Neh. 10:20), (16) covenant signer (Neh. 10:7), (17) son of Jeshua (Neh. 12:13).

MESHULLEMETH, wife of Manasseh and mother of Amon (II Kin. 21:19).

MESOBAITE, MEZOBAITE, hero of David (I Chr. 11:47).

MESOPOTAMIA, the Greek name for the area which once included the land between the Tigris and Euphrates rivers. The name in the Bible is equivalent to Aram-naharaim, an indefinite region restricted to the northern part of this general area. Haran was its chief city. Terah, Abraham, Sarah, and Lot came to this area from Ur of the Chaldees (Gen. 11:31, 32).

MESOPOTAMIAN, pertaining to Mesopotamia.

MESSAGE, communication.
have a *m.* from God, Judg. 3:20.
in the Lord's *m.* unto, Hag. 1:13.
sent a *m.* after him, Luke 19:14.
m. that ye heard, I John 3:11.

MESSENGER, bearer of a message.

Jacob sent *m.* before, Gen. 32:3.
m. an interpreter, Job 33:23.
m. of the covenant, Mal. 3:1.
send my *m.* before thy, Matt. 11:10.
m. of Satan to buffet, II Cor. 12:7.

MESSIAH, a Hebrew word meaning "anointed one," to which the Greek word *Christos* answers. It applied to anyone anointed with oil (Lev. 4:3; I Sam. 12:3; II Sam. 1:14, 16). The title was given to Abraham and Isaac (Ps. 105:15), and Cyrus, king of Persia (Is. 45:1). The title later became to denote the representative of the royal line of David (Ps. 2:2; 18:50; 84:9; 89:38, 51; 132:10, 17; Lam. 4:20; Hab. 3:13). This title ultimately became a designation for the coming one, being as common as "son of David" (John 1:41; 4:25).
M., the prince, Dan. 9:25.
shall *M.* be cut off, Dan. 9:26.
we have found the *M.,* John 1:41.
that *M.* cometh, John 4:25.

MESSIAHSHIP, the office and authority of the Messiah.

MESSIANIC, pertaining to the Messiah.

METAL, the metals in ancient times were gold, silver, iron, copper, lead, and tin (Num. 31:22).

METHEG-AMMAH, chief city of the Philistines, probably Gath (II Sam. 8:1).

METHUSAEL, METHUSHAEL, fifth in the line from Adam (Gen. 4:18).

METHUSELAH, MATHUSALA, the son of Enoch and father of Lamech (Gen. 5:21–27). He lived to the age of 969 years, the oldest recorded in the Bible.

METHUSHAEL, *see* **MAETHUSAEL.**

MEUNIM, MEHUNIM, a people who inhabited Mount Seir (II Chr. 10:1). Some of them were killed by the Simeonites near Gedor (I Chr. 4:39–41). They were mentioned in connection with the Philistines and Arabians (II Chr. 26:7).

MEZAHAB, father of Matred (Gen. 36:39).

MEZOBAITE, *see* **MESOBAITE.**

MIAMIN, (1) one who had taken a foreign wife (Ezra 10:25). (2) priest who returned with Zerubbabel (Neh. 12:5).

MIBHAR, son of Haggeri (I Chr. 11:38).

MIBSAM, (1) son of Ishmael (Gen. 25: 13), (2) son of Simeon (I Chr. 4:25).

MIBZAR, a chief of Edom (Gen. 36:42).

MICAH, MICA, MICAIAH, MICHAIAH, MICHA, MICHAH, (1) son of Mephibosheth (II Sam. 9:12; I. Chr. 8:34). (2) A Reubenite (I Chr. 5:5). (3) A Kohathite Levite (I Chr. 23:20; 24:24, 25). (4) Wife of Rehoboam and mother of Abijah (II Chr. 11:20). (5) One of those sent by Jehoshaphat to teach the cities of Judah (II Chr. 17:7). (6) A prophet, son of Imlah (I Kin. 22:8–28; II Chr. 18:7–27). (7) Father of Abdon (II Kin. 22:12; II Chr. 34:20). (8) An Asaphite Levite (I Chr. 9:15; Neh. 11:17, 22; 12:35). (9) One of the Levites who sealed the covenant (Neh. 10:11). (10) One of the priests at the dedication of the walls (Neh. 12:41). (11) Son of Gemariah (Jer. 36:11–13). (12) An Ephraimite who stole 1100 shekels of silver from his mother and made a graven and a molten image. (Judg. 17, 18). (13) The Morashite, who lived in the time of Isaiah, and prophesied during the reigns of Jotham, Ahaz, and Hezekiah (Mic. 1:1; Jer. 26:18). There is not much known about his call and history. He spoke against Samaria and Jerusalem, both the northern and the southern kingdoms. He denounced the social injustice of the kingdoms (Mic. 2: 1–3; 3:1–4, 11).

MICAH, BOOK OF, a prophetic book by the prophet of the same name. The first section is about the judgment of the Lord upon Samaria and Jerusalem (1:1–9). The judgment is based on the violence and greed of the wealthy, who do not care for the poor (2:1–13). The second section (3–5) continues to charge the guilty. Zion is to be "plowed as a field" (3:1–12). But the prophet also has hope for his chastised people (4:1–5:1). He looks to the Deliverer (5:2–15). In the last section he exhorts to repentance.

MICAIAH, prophet, son of Imlah (I Kin. 22:8).

MICE, small rodents (I Sam. 6:4).

MICHA, see **MICAH.**

MICHAEL, one of Moses' twelve spies, an Asherite (Num. 13:13). (2) A Gadite (I Chr. 5:13). (3) Another Gadite (I Chr. 5:14). (4) Messenger of God who came to Daniel (Dan. 10:21). (5) A Gershonite Levite (I Chr. 6-40). (6) Son of Izraiah (I Chr. 7:3). (7) A Benjamite (I Chr. 8:16). (8) Captain of Manasseh (I Chr. 12:20). (9) Father of Omri (I Chr. 27:18). (10) Son of Jehoshaphat (II Chr. 21:2–4) and (11) son of Shephatiah (Ezra 8:8).

MICHAIAH, MICAIAH, see **MICAH.**

MICHAL, Saul's daughter and David's wife (I Sam. 25:44).

MICHMASH, MICHMAS, Benjamite town between Bethel and Jerusalem (Ezra 2:27; I Sam. 13:1).

MICHMETHAH, MICHMETHATH, city between Ephraim and Manasseh (Josh. 16:6).

MICHRI, ancestor of Elah (I Chr. 9:8).

MICHTAM, "golden" Psalm, title to Ps. 16, 56–60.

MIDDIN, city in the desert (Josh. 15:61).

MIDDLE, MIDST, half-way, middle.
garments in the *m.*, II Sam. 10:4.
borders are in the *m.*, Ezek. 27:4.
in the *m.* of the week, Dan. 9:27.
through the *m.* of Sam-, Luke 17:11.
was rent in the *m.*, Luke 23:45.

MIDDLE WALL OF PARTITION, see **PARTITION, MIDDLE WALL OF.**

MIDIAN, MADIAN, (1) son of Abraham, Gen. 25:2, (2) his descendants and their land (Ex. 2:15; Is. 60:6).

MIDIANITES, a people of the desert (Gen. 25:2, 6; Num. 10:29–31; Is. 60:6). Midian merchants, who were with the caravan of Ishmaelites coming from Gilead, bought Joseph and took him to Egypt (Gen. 37:25, 28). The father-in-law of Moses was a Midianite (Ex. 3:1). After the Midianites joined the Moabites against the Israelites, the Israelites killed five Midian kings with all the male population and the married women (Num. 31). They came into Canaan with the Amalekites.

MIDIANITISH, of Midian.
brethren a *M.* woman, Num. 25:6.
name of the *M.* woman, Num. 25:15.

MIDNIGHT, middle of the night.
at *m.* there was a cry, Matt. 25:6.
at even, or at *m.*, Mark 13:35.
his speech until *m.*, Acts 20:7.

MIDST, central part, middle.
Lord in *m.* of earth, Ex. 8:22.
lieth in *m.* of sea, Prov. 23:34.
there am I in *m.*, Matt. 18:20.
Jesus stood in *m.*, Luke 24:36.
m. of crooked nation, Phil. 2:15.

MIGDALEL, city of Naphtali (Josh. 19: 38).

MIGDALGAD, city of Judah (Josh. 15:37).

MIGDOL, (1) a place west of the Red Sea (Ex. 14:2). (2) A city of northeast Egypt (Jer. 44:1).

MIGHT, perchance, if perhaps.
Egyptians *m.* not eat, Gen. 43:32.
what *m.* this parable, Luke 8:9.
m. be a merciful Priest, Heb. 2:17.
and hope *m.* be in God, I Pet. 1:21.

MIGHTIER, more mighty.
Israel *m.* than we, Ex. 1:9.
Lord *m.* than noise, Ps. 93:4.
one *m.* than I, Luke 3:16.

MIGHTY, strong, great, powerful.
m. hunter before Lord, Gen. 10:9.
wherefore wicked *m.*, Job 21:7.
Lord strong and *m.*, Ps. 24:8.
m. one of Israel, Is. 1:24.
righteousness *m.*, Is. 63:1.
rushing *m.* wind, Acts 2:2.
m. in . . scriptures, Acts 18:24.
of his *m.* power, Eph. 1:19.

MIGRON, (1) a place on the route of the invading Assyrian army, near Michmash (Is. 10:28). (2) A place where Saul's army encamped (I Sam. 14:2).

MIJAMIN, MIAMIN, (1) son of Parosh who married a heathen wife (Ezra 10:

25). (2) A priest who returned with Zerubbabel (Neh. 12:5). (3) Head of the sixth division of priests (I Chr. 24:9). (4) One of the priests who sealed the covenant with Nehemiah (Neh. 10:7).

MIKLOTH, (1) a Benjamite (I Chr. 8: 32). (2) Ruler of David's second division of guards (I Chr. 27:4).

MIKNEIAH, a Levite musician (I Chr. 15:21).

MILALAI, priest at the purification of the wall (Neh. 12:36).

MILCAH, (1) daughter of Haran (Gen. 11:29). (2) Daughter of Zelophehad, a Manassehite (Num. 26:33).

MILCOM, *see* **MOLOCH.**

MILE, a thousand paces (Matt. 5:41). Here it stands for the Roman mile, containing 1000 paces of 5 Roman feet each, and equivalent to about 12/13 of an English mile.

MILK, a basic food of the East. The milk of cows (II Sam. 17:29; Is. 7:22), sheep (Deut. 32:14), goats (Prov. 27:27), and camels (Gen. 32:15). Camel's milk was very strong, and not so sweet. Goat's milk is the favorite. Milk was also curdled and eaten in a solid state. Cheese was also made (Deut. 32:14; Judg. 5:25). Milk was kept in skin bottles, and served in dishes (Judg. 4:19; 5:25). Symbolically, it refers to abundance, as in the term "milk and honey" (Ex. 3:8; Josh. 5:6).

MILL, MILLSTONE, in ancient times it was an indispensable household utensil. It was a hand-operated stone grinding instrument used for making flour (Jer. 25:10; Eccles. 12:4). The mill consisted of two heavy basalt stones. The lower stone was extra hard and had a convex top. In the middle of it was a wooden peg. The upper stone was concave on the under side. It had a funnel-shaped hole which fitted loosely over the wooden peg. The grinding was usually done by female slaves (Ex. 11:5; Is. 47:2). Larger millstones were run with donkeys. Samson was compelled to work a millstone (Judg. 16:21). The millstone was used daily in the household, hence the Mosaic law prohibited the taking of the mill-

stones as a pledge of debt (Deut. 24:6).
ground it in *m.*, or, Num. 11:8.
take the *m.* and grind, Is. 47:2.
that a *m.* were hanged, Matt. 18:6.

MILLET, a type of very small grain, used for food (Ezek. 4:9).

MILLO, two fortifications, (1) near She-chem (Judg. 9:6) and (2) near Jerusalem where Joash was slain (II Sam. 5:9; II Kin. 12:20).

MIND, imagination, thought.
set not thy *m.* on, I Sam. 9:20.
desire of . . . *m.*, Eph. 2:3.
with one *m.* striving, Phil. 1:27.
my laws into their *m.*, Heb. 8:10.
I stir up pure *m.*, II Peter 3:1.

MINDFUL, to remember, be aware of.
Be ye *m.* always, I Chr. 16:15.
not been *m.* of the, Is. 17:10.
that thou art *m.* of, Heb. 2:6.
that ye may be *m.*, II Pet. 3:2.

MINGLE, mixed, of two or more kinds.
offering *m.* with oil, Lev. 7:10.
field with *m.* seed, Lev. 19:19.
all the *m.* people, Jer. 25:20.
vinegar to drink *m.*, Matt. 27:34.
hail and fire *m.*, Rev. 8:7.

MINIAMIN, (1) Levite who distributed the tithes and oblations (II Chr. 31:15), (2) priest with Zerubbabel (Neh. 12:7).

MINISTER, a personal or public attend-ant and helper. Joseph ministered in his master's household (Gen. 39:4). Joshua attended Moses (Ex. 24:13). Elisha served Elijah (I Kin. 19:21). The priests and the Levites ministered in the sanc-tuary (Ex. 28:43). Christ, as our high priest, ministers unto us (Heb. 8:2). Pub-lic officials minister (Rom. 13:6). The angels of heaven minister (Ps. 103:21; 104:4). In the New Testament there are several words used for the idea, *diakonos* being the most used. The magistrate was God's representative and minister (Rom. 13:4). It was especially used for God's servants in the Gospel, for Timothy (I Thess. 3:2), Paul and Apollas (I Cor. 3:5), Tychicus (Eph. 6:21), and Epaphras (Col. 1:7). The term *diakonos* was also used in a restricted sense for deacon, a church officer with special duties.
the Lord's *m.*, Joel 1:9.

let him be your *m.*, Matt. 20:26.
as *m.* of Christ, I Cor. 4:1.
m. of new testament, II Cor. 3:6.
m. of righteousness, II Cor. 11:15.
m. of Jesus Christ, I Tim. 4:6.

MINISTER, to serve, cause, inaugurate.
angels came and *m.*, Matt. 4:11.
and she *m.* unto them, Mark 1:31.
which *m.* questions, I Tim. 1:4.
If any man *m.*, let, I Pet. 4:11.

MINISTERING, MINISTRATION, act of serving, the service itself.
charge of the *m.* ves-, I Chr. 9:28.
days of his *m.*, Luke 1:23.
if the *m.* of death, II Cor. 3:7.
fellowship of the *m.*, II Cor. 8:4.

MINISTRY, ministration, service.
the *m.* of the word, Acts 6:4.
m. I received, Acts 20:24.
m. of reconciliation, II Cor. 5:18.
work of the *m.*, Eph. 4:12.
proof of thy *m.*, II Tim. 4:5.

MINNI, the district of Manavas, near Ararat, in later Armenia (Jer. 51:27).

MINNITH, Ammonite city, east of Jor-dan, noted for its wheat (Ezek. 27:17).

MINSTREL, music maker, player on an instrument (II Kin. 3:15; Matt. 9: 23).

MINT, a garden herb mentioned by Jesus as one of the herbs which the Jews scru-pulously tithed (Matt. 23:23; Luke 11:42).

MIPHKAD, gate of Jerusalem, exact loca-tion unknown (Neh. 3:31).

MIRACLE, a special manifestation of God, a sign of God's power. A miracle is much more than a supernatural event, for it is a special sign also. For example, a miracle is like the plagues of Egypt or the manna sent to feed the Israelites. A character of a miracle rests upon a pre-diction, such as God's promise to send them "bread from heaven" (Ex. 16:4). The miracles of the Lord were preceded by a gesture which showed that it was about to take place. The miracles were not used merely to display divine power, but they fulfilled a specific need. Jesus criticized those who would only believe

if some great sign were performed (John 4:48). Jesus wanted people to really believe in him, faith that needed no "great sign." There are four great periods of miracles: the time of Moses and Joshua, the time of Elijah and Elisha, the time of Daniel, and the days of Christ and his disciples.
have seen great *m.*, Deut. 29:3.
no man shall do *m.*, Mark 9:39.
hoped some *m.*, Luke 23:8.
followed saw *m.*, John 6:2.
John did no *m.*, John 10:41.
Stephen did *m.*, Acts 6:8.
God wrought special *m.*, Acts 19:11.
worketh *m.* among, Gal. 3:5.
by means of *m.*, Rev. 13:14.

MIRE, soft ground, mud, filth.
grow up without *m.*? Job 8:11.
waters cast up *m.* and, Is. 57:20.
sunk in the *m.*, Jer. 38:22.
wallowing in the *m.*, II Pet. 2:22.

MIRIAM, sister of Aaron and Moses.
and *M.*, the prophetess, Ex. 15:20.
M. and Aaron spake, Num. 12:1.
And *M.* was shut out, Num. 12:15.

MIRIAM, daughter of Ezra (I Chr. 4: 17).

MIRMA, MIRMAH, a Benjamite (I Chr. 8:10).

MIRROR, a polished surface for the purpose of reflecting objects. Ancient mirrors were made of brass or another alloy of copper (Ex. 38:8; Job. 37:18). They were imperfect, and the image in them was less clear and true (I Cor. 13:12).

MIRTH, rejoicing, happiness, joy.
thee away with *m.*, Gen. 31:27.
m., what doeth it? Eccles. 2:2.
prove thee with *m.*, Eccles. 2:1.
we then make *m.*? Ezek. 21:10.

MISCHIEF, a mishap, evil, harm.
will ye imagine *m.*, Ps. 62:3.
conceive *m.* and bring, Is. 59:4.
m. shall come upon, Ezek. 7:26.
men that devise *m.*, Ezek. 11:2.

MISCHIEVOUS, given to mischief.
speak *m.* things, Ps. 38:12.
shall be called *m.*, Prov. 24:8.
uttereth his *m.* desire, Mic. 7:3.

MISERABLE, unhappy, dejected.
of all men most *m.*, I Cor. 15:19.
wretched, and *m.*, and, Rev. 3:17.

MISERY, unhappiness, wretchedness.
for the *m.* of Israel, Judg. 10:16.
his *m.*, the wormwood, Lam. 3:19.
Destruction and *m.* are, Rom. 3:16.
howl for your *m.* that, James 5:1.

MISGAB, the capital or the country of Moab (Jer. 48:1).

MISHAEL, (1) son of Uzziel, a Kohathite (Ex. 6:22). (2) One who stood by Ezra as he read the Law (Neh. 8:4), and (3) Daniel's companion, also called, Meshek (Dan. 1:6).

MISHAL, MISHEAL, city of Asher, location uncertain (Josh. 19:26; 21:30).

MISHAM, son of Elpaal (I Chr. 8:12).

MISHEAL, *see* **MISHAL.**

MISHMA, son of Ishmael (Gen. 25:14; I Chr. 1:30). (2) A Simeonite (I Chr. 4: 25, 26).

MISHMANNAH, a Gadite friend of David (I Chr. 12:10).

MISHRAITES, family of Kirjath-jearim (I Chr. 2:53).

MISPAR, *see* **MIZPAR.**

MISPERETH, one of those returning with Zerubbabel from Babylon (Neh. 7: 7). Also called **Mizpar** in Ezra 2:2.

MISREPHOTH-MAIM, city of East Sidon (Josh. 11:8).

MISS, to err, fail to attain.
hair . . . and not *m.*, Judg. 20:16.
father at all *m.*, I Sam. 20:6.
neither *m.* we any-, I Sam. 25:15.

MITE, one-half a farthing, or 1.9 mills thus being the smallest coin of Bible days (Mark 12:42; Luke 12:59).

MITHCAH, MITHKAH, the 24th station of Israel in wilderness (Num. 33:28).

MITH-NITE, family name of Joshaphat (I Chr. 11:43).

MITHREDATH, (1) treasurer of King Cyrus of Persia (Ezra 1:8). (2) An enemy of the Jews during the reign of Artaxerxes, king of Persia (Ezra 4:7).

MITRE, turban or headdress.
coat, a *m.*, and a gir-, Ex. 28:4.
m. upon his head; also, Lev. 8:9.
set a fair *m.* upon, Zech. 3:5.

MITYLENE, capital city of Lesbos, of the Aegean Sea (Acts 20:14).

MIXED, intermingled.
m. multitude went up, Ex. 12:38.
thy wine *m.* with, Is. 1:22.
iron *m.* with miry clay, Dan. 2:41.
being *m.* with faith in, Heb. 4:2.

MIZAR, a hill near Hermon (Ps. 42:6).

MIZPAH, *see* MIZPEH.

MIZPAR, *see* MISPERETH.

MIZPEH, MIZPAH, (1) a heap of stones north of the Jabbok, called Galeed or heap of witness, to indicate that God is the watcher between the covenanting parties (Gen. 31:44-49). (2) A town in Gilead, east of the Jordan (Judg. 10:17; 9:11). It may be identical with Ramoth-Gilead (Deut. 4:43; I Kin. 4:13) and Ramah (II Kin. 8:28, 29). (3) An unidentified place at the foot of Mount Hermon (Josh. 9:3). (4) A village in or near the lowland of Judah (Josh. 15:38). (5) A town of Benjamin (Josh. 18:26), not far from Ramah (I Kin. 15:22). The Babylonian governor fixed his residence here (II Kin. 25:23-25; Jer. 40:6-16). (6) An unidentified place in Moab (I Sam. 22:3). (7) A valley, one of the places to which Joshua pursued the Canaanites (Josh. 11:8).

MIZRAIM, the Semitic name of Egypt, the dual form points to the two countries of Upper and Lower Egypt, settled by the descendants of Ham (Gen. 10:6).

MIZZAH, descendant of Esau, duke of Edom (Gen. 36:17).

MNASON, a native of Cyprus with whom Paul stayed (Acts 21:16).

MOAB, MOABITES, a Semitic people who lived just east of the Dead Sea. On the south was Edom, on the east was the Arabian desert, and on the north was a changeable border. It was a tableland of about 60 by 30 miles. Its first known name was Lotan or Lot. Its inhabitants were descendants of Lot (Gen. 19:30, 37). The Moabites were banned from the "congregation of the Lord" because of their hostility toward Israel (Deut. 23:3-6; Neh. 13:1). King Eglon, who fought Israel for eighteen years, was killed by Ehud, the judge (Judg. 3:12-30). Saul fought them, David fought them, and Solomon married their women and built a shrine to their god, Chemosh (I Sam. 14:47; I Kin. 11:1, 7). The story of king Mesh is found in II Kin. 3:4-27 and on the Moabite Stone. Ruth was a Moabitess (Ruth 1:1-4). The prophets spoke against them (Is. 15, 16; Jer. 48; Ezek. 25:8-11; Amos 2:1-3; Zeph. 2:8-11).

MOABITESS, a female Moabite (Ruth 1:22; I Kin. 11:1; II Chr. 24:26).

MOABITE STONE, a memorial pillar of black basalt, erected by Mesha. It gives the events of his reign. It was found in 1868 by F. A. Klein, a Prussian missionary. It contains the victories of Mesha, especially over Israel, thus confirming II Kin. 3:4-27.

MOABITISH, pertaining to **Moab.**

MOAB, KIR OF, *see* KIR OF MOAB.

MOADIAH, *see* MAADIAH.

MOCK, to deride or jeer.
Hebrew to *m.* us, Gen. 39:14.
scorn, and *m.* them, II Chr. 30:10.
wine is a *m.*, strong, Prov. 20:1.
to *m.*, and to scourge, Matt. 20:19.
God is not *m.*, for, Gal. 6:7.
had trial of . . . *m.* and, Heb. 11:36.

MOCKER, deceiver, impostor, scorner.
hypocritical *m.*, Ps. 35:16.
be ye not *m.* lest, Is. 28:22.
assembly of *m.*, Jer. 15:17.
m. in the last time, Jude 18.

MODERATION, fair, gentle, patient (I Tim. 3:3; Phil. 4:5).

MODEST, becoming (I Tim. 2:9).

MOISTURE, freshness, dampness.
my *m.* is turned into, Ps. 32:4.
because it lacked *m.*, Luke 8:6.

MOLADAH, city of South Judah (Josh. 15:26).

MOLE, some type of burrowing animal, as mice or rats (Is. 2:20; Lev. 11:30).

MOLECH, *see* **MOLOCH.**

MOLID, a descendant of Jerahmeel (I Chr. 2:29).

MOLOCH, MOLECH, MILCOM, MALCAM, MALCHAM, a group of names designating a signal deity, the abomination of the Ammonites (I Kin. 11:5, 7). Child sacrifice was part of his worship (II Kin. 23:10).

MOLTEN, melted, cast of metal.
made a *m.* sea, ten, I Kin. 7:23.
and brass is *m.* out, Job 28:2.
mountains shall be *m.*, Mic. 1:4.

MOLTEN SEA, BRASEN SEA, a large bowl-shaped basin which was in the court of Solomon's Temple. It was built upon twelve bronze oxen, and it held about 16,000 gallons. It was the washing-place of the priests (I Kin. 7:23–26, 29).

MOMENT, instant, twinkling.
and in a *m.* go down, Job 21:13.
tremble at every *m.*, Ezek. 32:10.
of the world in a *m.*, Luke 4:5.
in a *m.*, in the, I Cor. 15:52.

MONEY, coined or weighed metal used for exchange. Gold, silver, and sometimes bronze were used. Coined money was introduced into Palestine after the exile.
time to receive *m.*, II Kin. 5:26.
m. is a defence, Eccles. 7:12.
redeemed without *m.*, Is. 52:3.
hid his Lord's *m.*, Matt. 25:18.
changers of *m.*, John 2:14.
thy *m.* perish, Acts 8:20.
love of *m.* root, I Tim. 6:10.

MONEY CHANGER, EXCHANGER, BANKER, one who exchanges money for a fee. When the census was taken, everyone who had reached the age of twenty had to pay half a shekel to the temple treasury (Ex. 30:13–15). This money had to be in native coin, and since, at the time of Jesus, there were many different coins in circulation, the business of money changing sprang up. The premium paid for a half shekel, according to the Talmud, was equal to about twelve grains of silver, worth about three cents. The money changers were often dishonest. Jesus denounced them, turned their tables over, and ran them out of the temple (Matt. 21:12; Mark 11:15–17; John 2:13–16).

MONTH, a period of time corresponding to the lunar month, or when the moon was visible to the naked eye. The month is thus called a "new moon" in the Bible
second *m.*, the seven-, Gen. 7:11.
about three *m.*, after, Gen. 38:24.
hid herself five *m.*, Luke 1:24.
three years and six *m.*, James 5:17.

MOON, the heavenly body, visible usually at night, created by God to rule the night (Gen. 1:16) and for signs, seasons, and days and years (Gen. 1:14). "Religious seasons" may be meant in Ps. 104:19. The moon was an object of worship by neighboring nations of Israel (Job. 31:26; Deut. 4:19; II Kin. 23:5; II Kin. 21:3, 5).
the sun, and the *m.*, Gen. 37:9.
m., in the valley of, Josh. 10:12.
m. shall not give her, Matt. 24:29.
m. into blood, before, Acts 2:20.
holy day, or new *m.*, Col. 2:16.

MORASHTITE, MORASTHITE, one from Morastheth-Gath, and applied to Micah the prophet, to distinguish him from the elder prophet Micah (Jer. 26:18).

MORDECAI, (1) one of those who returned with Zerubbabel from Babylon (Ezra 2:2; Neh. 7:7). (2) A close relative of Esther, who squelched Haman's plot against the Jews (Esther 2:5–7; 3–8).

MORESHETH-GATH, city of West Judah and home of the prophet, Micah (Mic. 1:14).

MORIAH, (1) the land where Abraham offered up Isaac in response to God's command (Gen. 22:2). (2) The Mount where Solomon built the temple once occupied by the threshing floor of Onan, the Jebusite (II Sam. 24:18).

MORROW, next morning, next day.
leave none . . until . . *m.*, Lev. 22:30.
manna ceased on the *m.*, Josh. 5:12.
no thought for the *m.*, Matt. 6:34.
depart on the *m.*, Acts 20:7.
the *m.*, when Agrippa, Acts 25:23.

MORSEL, a bit, small portion.
fetch a *m.* of bread, and, Gen. 18:5.
eaten my *m.* alone, Job 31:17.
dry *m.*, and quietness, Prov. 17:1.
m. of meat sold his, Heb. 12:16.

MORTAL, having human characteristics.
that *m.* man should be, Job 4:17.
reign in your *m.* bodies, Rom. 6:12.
quicken your *m.* bodies, Rom. 8:11.
m. must put on immor-, I Cor. 15:53.
manifest in our *m.*, II Cor. 4:11.

MORTAR, (1) a hollowed-out vessel of wood or stone used to pulverize grain. (In later years, pottery was used as a mortar.) Israelites used it to grind the manna (Num. 11:8). Used figuratively in Prov. 27:22. (2) A glue-like substance made of slime, mud, or clay to bind building blocks together in construction.
slime had they for *m.*, Gen. 11:3.
hard bondage, in *m.*, and, Ex. 1:14.
take other *m.*, and, Lev. 14:42.
and tread the *m.*, make, Nahum 3:14.

MORTGAGE, pledge of security for payment (Neh. 5:3).

MORTIFY, put to death.
Spirit do *m.* the deeds, Rom. 8:13.
M. therefore your mem-, Col. 3:5.

MOSAIC, pertaining to Moses.

MOSAIC CODE, the body of law promulgated by Moses.

MOSERAH, MOSERA, place where Aaron died and was buried (Deut. 10:6).

MOSEROTH, 26th station of the Israelites in the wilderness (Num. 33:30).

MOSES, an Israelite, son of Amram and Jochebed, younger brother of Aaron and Miriam, born during the decree that all male Hebrew children should be put to death. Put into a basket by his mother,

found by Pharaoh's daughter, accepted and reared by her in all the wisdom of the Egyptians. He revolted against Egyptian tyranny, fled to Midian, married there, returned after 40 years to obey God's command and led the children of Israel out of captivity. Aaron was his spokesman. By the Spirit of God, he did many mighty works and intervened for the Israelites with God on many occasions. He was given the Law at Mount Sinai by God written on tablets of stone. He brought forth water from a rock at Meribah (Num. 20:7) by smiting the rock, which disobedience God called unbelief (Num. 20:12), and for which Moses did not enter into Canaan. He was a prophet of God (Deut. 18:15), and a type of Christ (Acts 7:37). He died at the age of one hundred and twenty years. The covenant given by God at Sinai is often called the Law of Moses and Jesus refers to those laws as those "commanded you by Moses". He, with Jesus and Elijah, was at the transfiguration of Jesus (Matt. 17:5).
she called his name, *M.*, Ex. 2:10.
gave *M.* Zipporah his, Ex. 2:21.
M. and Aaron went in, Ex. 7:10.
M. stretched out his hand, Ex. 14:21.
M. took the anointing, Lev. 8:10.
M. brought Aaron's sons, Lev. 8:13.
M. did as the Lord, Num. 17:11.
M. was an hundred and, Deut. 34:7.
Israel like unto *M.*, Deut. 34:10.
M., my servant, is dead, Josh. 1:2.
unto Caleb, as *M.* said, Judg. 1:20.
in the law of *M.*, I Kin. 2:3.
sons of *M.* were, I Chr. 23:15.
two tables which *M.*, II Chr. 5:10.
book of the law of *M.*, Neh. 8:1.
by the right hand of *M.*, Is. 63:12.
the law of *M.*, my, Mal. 4:4.
gift that *M.* comm-, Matt. 8:4.
and one for *M.*, and, Matt. 17:4.
law was given by *M.*, John 1:17.
had ye believed *M.*, John 5:46.
that the law of *M.*, John 7:23.
not justified by law of *M.*, Acts 13:39.
baptized unto *M.* in, I Cor. 10:2.
of more glory than *M.*, Heb. 3:3.
sing the song of *M.*, Rev. 15:3.

MOTE, splinter, speck.
beholdest thou the *m.*, Matt. 7:3.
pull out the *m.* that, Matt. 7:4.

MOTH, any one of several species of in-

sects which infests woolen goods and furs and damage them almost unnoticed.
crushed before the *m.*, Job 4:19.
consume . . . like a *m.*, Ps. 39:11.
m. and rust doth cor-, Matt. 6:19.
where neither *m.* nor, Matt. 6:20.

MOTHER, female parent.
m. of all living, Gen. 3:20.
obeyed his father and *m.*, Gen. 28:7.
Honor thy . . thy *m.*, Ex. 20:12.
nakedness of thy *m.*, Lev. 18:7.
young child and his *m.*, Matt. 2:13.
Behold, my *m.* and my, Matt. 12:49.
Jerusalem . . . *m.* of us all, Gal. 4:26.
elder women as *m.*; the, I Tim. 5:2.

MOTHER IN LAW, Jesus healed Peter's mother in law (Luke 4:38).
lieth with his *m.*, Deut. 27:23.
Orpah kissed her *m.*, Ruth 1:14.
daughter . . . against her *m.*, Mic. 7:6.
m. against her daughter, Luke 12:53.

MOUNT, to climb, rise, go up, ascend.
eagle *m.* up at thy, Job 39:27 .
shall *m.* up with wings, Is. 40:31.
Babylon should *m.* up, Jer. 51:53.

MOUNTAINS, MOUNT, an elevated mass of land. They were used for shrines and "high places." Some of the more important mountains were Carmel, Ebal, Gerizim, Gilboa, Hermon, Seir, and Sinai.
saw *m.* smoking, Ex. 20:18.
m. shall bring peace, Ps. 72:3.
m. . . . about Jerusalem, Ps. 125:2.
m. of Lord's house, Is. 2:2.
m. might flow down, Is. 64:1.
hunt from every *m.*, Jer. 16:16.
O *m.* of holiness, Jer. 31:23.
say unto this *m.*, Matt. 17:20.
could remove *m.*, I Cor. 13:2.

MOUNT OF CONGREGATION, location unknown, thought by many to be Mount Moriah (Is. 14:13).

MOUNT OF CORRUPTION, see **CORRUPTION, MOUNT OF.**

MOUNT OF OLIVES, see **OLIVES, MOUNT OF.**

MOURN, to lament, grieve.
and *m.* for his son, Gen. 37:34.
king weepeth and *m.*, II Sam. 19:1.

Blessed are . . . *m.*, Matt. 5:4.
tribes of the earth *m.*, Matt. 24:30.
have not rather *m.*, I Cor. 5:2.
Be afflicted, and *m.*, James 4:9.

MOURNER, one who mourns either in his own grief or for payment by another.
thyself to be a *m.*, II Sam. 14:2.
m. go about the, Eccles. 12:5.
as bread of *m.*, Hos. 9:4.

MOURNFULLY, in sadness (Mal. 3:14).

MOURNING, a show of grief at a time of calamity. It was usually accompanied by rending of clothes, wearing of sackcloth, tearing out the hair of the head, and sprinkling the head with ashes.
m. into dancing, Ps. 30:11.
oil of joy for *m.*, Is. 61:3.
their *m.* into joy, Jer. 31:13.
our Dance into *m.*, Lam. 5:15.
laughter be *m.*, James 4:9.

MOUSE, a rodent of about 40 varieties in Palestine. Lev. 11:29 probably refers to all mice. See Is. 66:17.

MOUTH, the organ of speech.
in her *m.* was an olive, Gen. 8:11.
will speak *m.* to *m.*, Num. 12:8.
lay . . hand upon thy *m.*, Judg. 18:19.
proceedeth out of the *m.*, Matt. 4:4.
confess with thy *m.*, Rom. 10:9.
Out of the same *m.*, James 3:10.

MOVE, to change, to influence, arouse, cause to act.
that *m.* in the waters, Lev. 11:10.
Spirit of the Lord . . *m.*, Judg. 13:25.
all the city was *m.*, Ruth 1:19.
patriarchs, *m.* with envy, Acts 7:9.
Noah *m.* with fear, Heb. 11:7.
they speak as *m.* by, II Pet. 1:21.

MOZA, (1) son of Caleb (I Chr. 2:46).
(2) A Benjamite descendant of Saul (I Chr. 8:36).

MOZAH, city in Benjamin (Josh. 18:26).

MUCH, in large degree, abundant.
eat little or *m.*, Eccles. 5:12.
for she loved *m.*, Luke 7:47.
m. is given of him, Luke 12:48.
faithful, also in *m.*, Luke 16:10.
m. in every way, Rom. 3:2.

MUFFLERS, a long, expensive, fluttering veil (Is. 3:19).

MULBERRY TREE, tree of unknown variety (II Sam. 5:23; I Chr. 14:14)

MULE, a hybrid between a horse and an ass. It was used along with horses (Ps. 32:9; II Sam. 13:29). The Tyrians obtained mules in Armenia (Ezek. 27:14). In the Authorized Version of Gen. 36:24 a word is translated mules that should be translated hot springs.
to ride on my *m.*, I Kin. 1:33.
grass to save the *m.*, I Kin. 18:5.
by riders on *m.*, Esther 8:10.

MULTIPLY, increase.
Be fruitful, and *m.*, Gen. 1:22.
number of disciples *m.*, Acts 6:7.
Word of God . . . and *m.*, Acts 12:24.
m. your seed, II Cor. 9:10.
grace and peace be *m.*, II Pet. 1:2.

MULTITUDE, a great company.
not numbered for *m.*, Gen. 16:10.
a mixed *m.* went up also, Ex. 12:38.
he feared the *m.*, Matt. 14:5.
m. that believeth were, Acts 4:32.
m. must needs come to-, Acts 21:22.
cover the *m.* of sins. I Pet. 4:8.

MUPPIM, SHUPHAM, SHEPHUPHAM, son of Benjamin, and one of the original colony in Egypt (Gen. 46:21).

MURDER, (1) the causing of the death of a person through willful intent, hate, neglect (as with allowing an animal to kill a person). The basic law of God is "Thou shalt not kill" (Ex. 20:13). Exception is made for the unintentional murder although being an accident does not fully excuse him (Ex. 21:13; Lev. 24:17). (2) Spiritually applied by Christ to any cruelty in thought, word, or deed (Matt. 19:18). *See* **AVENGER OF BLOOD.**
ye steal, *m.*, and commit, Jer. 7:9.
shalt do no *m.*, Matt. 19:18.
full of envy, *m.* and de-, Rom. 1:29.

MURMUR, talk against, censure.
hath heard your *m.*, Ex. 16:9.
and they *m.* against, Mark 14:5.
a *m.* of the Grecians, Acts 6:1.
things without *m.* and, Phil. 2:14.

MURRAIN, a type of pestilence or plague of unknown character, the fifth plague of God upon the Egyptians (Ex. 9:3) which affected the domestic animals.

MUSE, to meditate, reason.
I meditate . . . *m.* on the, Ps. 143:5.
all men *m.* in their, Luke 3:15.

MUSHI, son of Merari and father of the Mushites (Ex. 6:19; Num. 3:33).

MUSHITES, descendents of Mushi (Num. 3:33; 26:58).

MUSIC, MUSICK, it was not until the time of David that Hebrew music was used in the formal worship. In times of joy, singing, dancing, and playing on instruments were part of the festivity (Gen. 31:27; Ex. 32:18; Judg. 11:34). Music was sometimes used as an aid to prophetic ecstasy (II Kin. 3:15). It is mentioned in religious ceremony (II Chr. 5:1, 12, 13; 15:10; 23:9; 29:20; 35:15, 16).
daughters of *m.*, Eccles. 12:4.
instruments of *m.*, Amos 6:5.
m. and dancing, Luke 15:25.

MUSTARD, a well-known herb of Palestine, and is proverbial because of its small seeds. It sometimes grows to be ten or twelve feet high, and is classified as a tree (Matt. 13:31, 32; Mark 4:31, 32; Luke 13:19).

MUTH-LABBEN, death of Ben, or of the son (to be chanted by boys in the soprano), title to Ps. 9.

MUTTER, to whisper, mumble.
peep and that *m.*, Is. 8:19.
your tongue hath *m.*, Is. 59:3.

MUZZLE, to hinder, stop the mouth.
Thou shalt not *m.* the, Deut. 25:4.
not *m.* the mouth of, I Cor. 9:9.
shalt not *m.* the ox, I Tim. 5:18.

MYRA, one of the chief cities of Lycia, visited by Paul, while sailing to Rome (Acts 27:5).

MYRRH, well-known gum resin from the Nees tree, used as a perfume, and for embalming. Also, it was an ingredient of the anointing oil.
of pure *m.* five hundred, Ex. 30:23.

with oil of *m*., and, Esther 2:12.
perfumed with *m*., and, Song 3:6.
frankincense, and *m*., Matt. 2:11.
mixture of *m*. and aloes, John 19:39.

MYRTLE, evergreen shrub common to Palestine (Neh. 8:15).

MYSIA, province of Asia Minor. Troas is its chief port (Acts 16:7, 8).

MYSTERY, a word which was borrowed from the heathen religion, in which mystery was a secret that separated one religion from another, and found outward expression in rites and ceremonies. The word, in the biblical sense, does not imply that the mystery is incomprehensible. In the Old Testament the meaning of the symbolism was not a secret of the priesthood, but it was the common possession of the people. In the New Testament, the word mystery denotes a secret hidden from the world until the appointed time (Rom. 16:25), or until man is able to receive it (Mark 4:11). Something known to God is unknowable to man until God chooses to reveal it (Luke 8:10). Paul was able to disclose mysteries (Rom. 16:25; I Cor. 2:7). The institution of marriage as a prophetic representation of Christ and the Church is a mystery now made known (Eph. 5:31, 32).
m. of kingdom, Matt. 13:11.
understand all *m*., I Cor. 13:2.
m. of gospel, Eph. 6:19.
m. of God, Col. 2:2.
m. of iniquity, II Thess. 2:7.
m. of Godliness, I Tim. 3:16.
m. of God finished, Rev. 10:7.
m., Babylon the Great, Rev. 17:5.

N

NAAM, son of Caleb (I Chr. 4:15).

NAAMAH, (1) daughter of Lamech and Zillah (Gen. 4:22). (2) An Ammonitish woman whom Solomon married (I Kin. 14:21). (3) A city in the plain of Judah (Josh. 15:41).

NAAMAN, (1) a successful Syrian general. However, he was a leper. As informed by the Hebrew slave-maid in his home of an Israelite prophet, he went to Israel and obtained cleansing when he bathed himself seven times in the Jordan according to the word of Elisha (II Kin. 5:1–21; Luke 4:27). (2) A son of Benjamin (Gen. 46:21; Num. 26:40).

NAAMATHITE, an epithet of Zophar, one of Job's friends (Job 2:11; 42:9).

NAAMITE, a family which traced its descent from Naaman (Num. 26:40).

NAARAH, one of the two wives of Ashhur, father of Tekoa (I Chr. 4:5).

NAARAI, PAARAI, son of Ezbai, one of David's heroes. In II Sam. 23:35 he is called "Paarai the Arbite" (I Chr. 11:37).

NAARAN, NAARAH, NAARATH, a town in the territory of Ephraim.
to *N*. and came, Josh. 16:7.
eastward *N*., I Chr. 7:28.

NAASHON, NAASON, *see* **NAHSHON.**

NABAL, a wealthy man of Maon in the highlands of Judah, owner of many sheep and goats. He was wicked and refused to give any assistance to David when David's ten young men were sent to him at the time of sheep-shearing.
name of the man was *N*., I Sam. 25:3.
N. answered Daniel's, I Sam. 25:10.
N. is his name, I Sam. 25:25.
Lord smote *N*., I Sam. 25:38.
Abigail *N*. wife, II Sam. 2:2.

NABOTH, the owner of a vineyard contiguous to the palace of King Ahab. The king desired to add the vineyard to his own grounds. Since Naboth refused to part with his paternal inheritance, Jezebel, the king's wife, caused him to be stoned to death.
N. the Jezreelite, I Kin. 21:1.
the vineyard of *N*., I Kin. 21:7.
N. was stoned, I Kin. 21:15.
the blood of *N*., II Kin. 9:26.

NACHON, NACON, *see* **CHIDON.**

NACHOR, NAHOR, (1) the brother of Abraham (Josh. 24:2). (2) The grandfather of Abraham (Luke 3:34).

NACON, *see* **CHIDON.**

NADAB, (1) the eldest son of Aaron. Along with Abihu he was guilty of offering "strange fire", and both died before Jehovah (Ex. 6:23; 24:9; Num. 3:4). (2) Son of Jeroboam I and after him—for two years king of Israel (I Kin. 14:20; 15:27). (3) A son of Shammai (I Chr. 2:28). (4) A Gibeonite (I Chr. 8:30).

NAGGE, NAGGAI, an ancestor of Jesus, the son of Maath (Luke 3:25).

NAHALAL, NAHALOL, NAHALLAL, a city in the territory of Zebulun assigned to the Merarite Levites, out of which the Canaanite inhabitants were not driven.
N. with her suburbs, Josh. 21:35.
Kattath and *N.,* Josh. 19:15.
the inhabitants of *N.,* Judg. 1:30.

NAHALIEL, one of the encampments of Israel in the wilderness (Num. 21:19).

NAHALLAL, NAHALOL, *see* NAHA-LAL.

NAHAM, a Judahite chieftain, father of Keilah the Garmite (I Chr. 4:19).

NAHAMANI, one of the twelve heads who returned with Zerubbabel (Neh. 7:7).

NAHARAI, NAHARI, one of David's heroes, Joab's armor-bearer.
N, the Beerothite, II Sam. 23:37.
the Ammonite, *N.,* I Chr. 11:39.

NAHASH, (1) "Nahash the Ammonite," king of Ammon at the time of Saul in Israel (I Sam. 11:1; 12:12). (2) A resident of Rabbath-ammon (II Sam. 17:27). (3) The father of Abigail and Zeruiah (II Sam. 17:25).

NAHATH, (1) a grandson of Esau, sons of Reuel (Gen. 36:13; I Chr. 1:37). (2) A descendant of Levi and ancestor of Samuel (I Chr. 6:26). (3) A Levite who assisted in the oversight of the sacred offerings in the temple (II Chr. 31:13).

NAHBI, the representative of Naphtali among the 12 spies (Num. 13:14).

NAHOR, NACHOR, (1) son of Serug and grandfather of Abraham (Gen. 11:25). (2) Son of Terah and brother of Abraham (Gen. 11:27).

NAHSHON, NAASHON, NAASSON, a descendant of Judah and of Christ (Num. 1:7; Ruth 4:20; Luke 3:32).

NAHUM, the seventh of the minor prophets. He was an inhabitant of Elkosh (Nahum 1:1).

NAHUM, BOOK OF, one of the books of the Minor Prophets. Nahum's ministry was between the time of Assyria's capture of Thebes 664–3 B.C. under Assurbanipal, and the destruction of Nineveh itself in 612 B.C. Nahum's subject is the downfall of Nineveh, the bloody city. He begins in Chapter 1 with an introductory psalm, and in vivid language he describes in chapter 2 the siege of Nineveh and her destruction, and in chapter 3, the reasons for the city's downfall. Nahum is the author of the entire book.

NAIL, (1) the finger-nail, (2) pin or peg, (3) figuratively, the hard point of a stylus or engraving tool (Jer. 17:1).
pare her *n.,* Deut. 21:12.
n. of the tent, Judg. 4:21.
the print of the *n.,* John 20:25.

NAILING, fastening with nails.
n. it to the cross, Col. 2:14.

NAIN, the city at the gate of which Jesus raised the widow's son to life (Luke 7:11).

NAIOTH, the place in which David took refuge after his escape from Saul.
David is at *N.,* I Sam. 19:19.
dwelt in *N.,* I Sam. 19:18.

NAKED, NAKEDNESS, lightly clad, or without proper clothing.
n. of the land, Gen. 42:9.
people were *n.,* Ex. 32:25.
he was *n.,* John 21:7.
are in *n.,* I Cor. 4:11.
shame of thy *n.,* Rev. 3:18.

NAME, most Biblical names had a definite significance at once noted when the name was heard. Personal names might suggest plants or animals, such as Tamar (palm), Susanna (lily) or Rachel (ewe). They might reflect family relationship, vocation, some circumstance of birth, etc. Often names of prophets' children bore a message (Is. 8:3; Hos. 1:4, 6, 9). A

child was generally named by the parents, but sometimes kinsmen or friends would suggest a name (Ruth 4:17; Luke 1:59). Not seldom the name given at birth was changed after some momentous crisis, as was the case with Abram, Jacob, Peter and Paul (Gen. 17:5; 35:9-13; Matt. 16:17-19; Acts 13:9). Very many names contained in them mention of God, such as Jezreel, Nathaneel or Abijah. Population increase brought surnames, such as compounds with *bar* (son of) or second names like Mark in John Mark. Place names were usually derived from names of gods or physical features. El (God), Beth (house), Beer (well), Abel (meadow), Jearim (woods) and Gibeah, Ramah, or Ramoth (hill) in names are examples. The word "name" often signifies the nature of the being named (Ex. 34:5; John 17:6) or his authority (Matt. 28:19; Acts 3:6).
n. of the first, Gen. 2:11.
his wife's *n.*, Gen. 3:20.
called their *n.* Adam, Gen. 5:2.
the *n.* of the Lord, Gen. 12:8.
n. of a prophet, Matt. 10:41.
call his *n.* Jesus, Luke 1:31.
ask in my *n.*, John 14:13.
manifested thy *n.*, John 17:6.

NAOMI, wife of Elimelech and mother-in-law of Ruth (Ruth 1:2, 20; 2:22).

NAPHISH, NEPHISH, the eleventh son of Ishmael (Gen. 25:15; I Chr. 1:31).

NAPHTALI, NEPHTHALIM, the sixth son of Jacob (Gen. 30:8; Num. 1:15).

NAPHTALI, MOUNT, the mountainous district which formed the main part of the territory of Naphtali (Josh. 20:7).

NAPHTALI, TRIBE OF, four sons of Naphtali went to Egypt with Jacob (Gen. 46:24). The census at Sinai showed 53,400 fighters and the second census showed 45,400 at Moab (Num. 1:43, 26:50). On the wilderness march Naphtali took position north of the tabernacle with Dan and Asher (Num. 2:25-30). The tribe was given some of the best land in the apportionment. Its north limit was the limit of Israel; on the east, the Jordan, and on the west and south Asher, Zebulun and Issachar were the boundaries (Josh. 19:32-39). This was the first tribe

captured by the Assyrians (II Kin. 15:29). The area was a part of Galilee in Christ's day, and included Chorazin, Capernaum and Tiberias.

NAPHTALITE, descendant of Naphtali.

NAPHTUHIM, a Mizraite nation or tribe, mentioned only as descendants of Noah.
Lehabim, and *N.*, Gen. 10:13.
Anamim, . . . *N.*, I Chr. 1:11.

NAPKIN, *see* **HANDKERCHIEF.**

NARCISSUS, a Christian at Rome to whose household Paul sent greetings (Rom. 16:11).

NARD, *see* **SPIKENARD.**

NARROW, not wide, restricted.
Lord stood in *n.* way, Num. 22:26.
woman is *n.* pit, Prov. 23:27.
n. is the way which, Matt. 7:14.

NATHAN, (1) the Hebrew prophet in David's reign and a supporter of Solomon at his accession.
N. the prophet, II Sam. 7:2.
N. said unto David, II Sam. 12:13.
N. spake unto, I Kin. 1:11.
(2) A son of David (II Sam. 5:14). (3) father of Igal, one of David's heroes (II Sam. 23:36). (4) A descendant of Judah, being the son of Attai and father of Zabad (I Chr. 2:36). (5) A companion of Ezra from Babylon (Ezra 8:16).

NATHANAEL, a disciple of Jesus Christ, whom Philip brought to Jesus and, of whom Christ said, "an Israelite indeed in whom was no guile."
Philip findeth *N.*, John 1:45.
N. of Cana in, John 21:2.

NATHAN-MELECH, a Judaean official, to whose chamber King Josiah removed "the horses of the sun," (II Kin. 23:11).

NATION, race, people, country.
make of thee a great *n.*, Num. 14:12.
bring *n.* against thee, Deut. 28:49.
blessed is *n.* whose God, Ps. 33:12.
against hypocritical *n.*, Is. 10:6.
Israel, rebellious *n.*, Ezek. 2:3.
n. rise against *n.*, Mark 13:8.
men out of every *n.*, Acts 2:5.
crooked and perverse *n.*, Phil. 2:15.

redeemed out of every *n.*, Rev. 5:9.

NATIVITY, birth, esp. the birth of Christ.
the land of thy *n.*, Ruth 2:11.
land of our *n.*, Jer. 46:16.

NATURAL, according to nature.
his *n.* force, Deut. 34:7.
the *n.* use into, Rom. 1:26.
the *n.* man, I Cor. 2:14.
n. itself teach you, I Cor. 11:14.
Jews by *n.*, Gal. 2:15.
of the divine *n.*, II Pet. 1:4.

NATURE, law of moral world.
do by *n.* the law, Rom. 2:14.
which is wild by *n.*, Rom. 11:24.
on fire the course of *n.*, James 3:6.
partakers of divine *n.*, II Pet. 1:4.

NAUGHT, NOUGHTY, bad, worthless.
the *n.* of thine heart, I Sam. 17:28.
water is *n.*, II Kin. 2:19.
to a *n.* tongue, Prov. 17:4.
superfluity of *n.*, James 1:21.

NAUGHTINESS, evil, wickedness.
taken in their *n.*, Prov. 11:6.
superfluity of *n.*, James 1:21.

NAUM, ancestor of Jesus (Luke 3:25).

NAVY, is used in the sense of fleet.
made a *n.* of ships, I Kin. 9:26.
Solomon made a *n.*, I Kin. 9:28.
n. of Hiram, I Kin. 10:22.

NAZARENE, NAZARENES, an inhabitant of Nazareth (Matt. 2:23; 21:11).

NAZARETH, a town in Galilee, the home of Joseph and Mary (Matt. 2:23; Mark 1:9; Luke 2:39, 51).

NAZARITE, NAZIRITE, a man or woman consecrated to God's service by a special type of vow (Num. 6:1–22). This vow lasted for a fixed period (Num. 6) and sometimes for life, as was the case with Samson, Samuel and John the Baptist (Judg. 13:5; I Sam. 1:11; Luke 1:15). The vow required abstinence from wine, avoidance of the unclean, and uncut hair and beard. Stipulations for accidental breaking of the law were given. Nazarites were not hermits, but consecrated citizens (Amos 2:11–12).

NEAH, a town of Zebulun, on the southern border of Rimmon (Josh. 19:13).

NEAPOLIS, a place in northern Greece and seaport town of Philippi, where Paul first landed in Europe (Acts 16:11).

NEAR, not far distant, close.
thou art *n.* O Lord, Ps. 119:151.
salvation is *n.*, Is. 56:1.
day of the Lord is *n.*, Zech. 14:1.
know that it is *n.*, Matt. 24:33.

NEARIAH, (1) a descendant of David (I Chr. 3:22), (2) a descendant of Simeon (I Chr. 4:42).

NEBAI, NOBAI, a family of the heads of the people who signed the covenant with Nehemiah (Neh. 10:19).

NEBAIOTH, NEBAJOTH, (1) the eldest son of Ishmael (Gen. 25:13; I Chr. 1:29). (2) An Arabian tribe descended from Ishmael (Is. 60:7).

NEBALLAT, a place occupied by the Benjamites after the captivity (Neh. 11:34).

NEBAT, the father of Jeroboam I (I Kin. 11:26).

NEBO, (1) a town east of Jordan and occupied by Reuben (Num. 32:3, 38). (2) The mountain from which Moses saw the promised land (Deut. 34:1, 32:49). (3) A man whose descendants, to the number of fifty-two, returned from Babylon with Zerubbabel (Ezra 2:29; 7:33). (4) A Babylonian god (Is. 46:1; 48:1).

NEBUCHADNEZZAR, NEBUCHADREZZAR, the King of Babylon who conquered Judah, destroyed Jerusalem, and carried the Jews captive to Babylon (II Kin. 24–25). When his father was king, Nebuchadrezzar distinguished himself militarily, soundly defeating the ambitious Pharaoh Necho of Egypt at Carchemish in 605 B.C. and thus establishing the power of Babylon. In 604 B.C. Nebuchadrezzar became king, and a few years later crushed the rebellious Judah. According to his own records, Nebuchadrezzar was more interested in beautifying Babylon and glorifying its gods than in military affairs (Dan. 4:30).

NEBUSHASBAN, NEBUSHAZBAN, one of the officers of Nebuchadnezzar at the time of the capture of Jerusalem (Jer. 39:13).

NEBUZARADAN, Nebuchadnezzar's general at the siege of Jerusalem (II Kin. 25:8; 11, 20; Jer. 52:12, 15 etc.).

NECESSARY, essential, indispensable.
words more than *n.*, Job 23:12.
seem feeble are *n.*, I Cor. 12:22.
good works for *n.* uses, Tit. 3:14.
n. patterns should be, Heb. 9:23.

NECESSITY, pressing need (I Cor. 9:16); (2) a requisite (Heb. 9:16).
of *n.* he must release, Luke 23:17.
sent to my *n.*, Phil. 4:16.
made of *n.* a change, Heb. 7:12.

NECHO, *see* **PHARAOH-NECHOH.**

NECK.
fell on his *n.*, Gen. 33:4.
feet upon the *n.*, Josh. 10:24.
their *n.* to the work, Neh. 3:5.
with a stiff *n.*, Ps. 75:5.
laid down . . . *n.*, Rom. 16:4

NECO, *see* **PHARAOH-NECHOH.**

NECROMANCY, a type of magic, the adherents of which claim the power to call up the dead for consultation as a way to know present or future mysteries. The most famous case in Scripture concerned Saul and the medium of Endor (I Sam. 28:1–25), who seemed horrified at the success of her work. Moses' Law forbade consulting necromancers (Deut. 18:11). *See* **DIVINATION, SORCERY.**

NEDABIAH, the last named son of Jeconiah (I Chr. 3:18).

NEED, destitution, lack, want
n. to be baptized, Matt. 3:14.
whole *n.* not physician, Mark 2:17
Lord hath *n.* of them, Luke 19:31.
as every man had *n.*, Acts 2:45.
abound and to suffer *n.*, Phil. 4:12
have *n.* of patience, Heb. 10:36.
no *n.* of sun or moon, Rev. 21:23

NEED, to lack, require.
n. not any testify, John 2:25.
though he *n.* any thing, Acts 17:25
n. not be ashamed, II Tim. 2:15.

n. no candle, neither, Rev. 22:5.

NEEDFUL, necessary, requisite.
n. for house of God, Ezra 7:20.
one thing is *n.*, Luke 10:42.
things which are *n.*, James 2:16.
was *n.* for me to write, Jude 3.

NEEDLE, a proverb, "it is easier for a camel . . . eye of a needle," (Matt. 19:24; Mark 10:25; Luke 18:25).

NEEDLEWORK, *see* **EMBROIDERY** and **NEEDLEWORK.**

NEEDY, poverty-stricken, very poor.
open hand to *n.*, Deut. 15:11.
I am poor and *n.*, Ps. 40:17.
let *n.* praise thy name, Ps. 74:21.
cause of poor and *n.*, Jer. 22:16.
oppressed poor and *n.*, Ezek. 18:12.
buy *n.* for pair of shoes, Amos 8:6.

NEESING, obsolete for sneezing.
by his *n.* a light, Job 41:18.

NEGINAH, NEGINOTH, appears in the titles of Ps. 4, 6, 54, 67, 76, and means stringed instruments.

NEGLECT, disregard, slight.
if he *n.* to hear, Matt. 18:17.
widows were *n.*, Acts 6:1.
n. not the gift that, I Tim. 4:14.
how escape, if *n.*, Heb. 2:3.

NEGLIGENT, careless, indifferent.
sons, be not now *n.*, II Chr. 29:11.
not *n.* to put you in, II Pet. 1:12.

NEHELAMITE, the designation of Shemaiah, a false prophet who opposed Jeremiah (Jer. 29:24, 31, 32).

NEHEMIAH, (1) the second named of "the children of the province . . . whom Nebuchadnezzar had carried away," (Ezra 2:2; Neh. 7:7). (2) The son of Azbuk, ruler of Beth-zur, and one who was prominent in rebuilding the wall of Jerusalem (Neh. 3:16), (3) governor of the Jews, who was the son of Hachaliah, and brother of Hanani (Neh. 1:1; 7:2). He was a cup-bearer to King Artaxerxes. This position of close intimacy with the King enabled him to obtain his commission as governor of Judea and the letters and edicts which enabled him to restore the walls of Jerusalem. He instituted a number of social reforms also.

NEHEMIAH, BOOK OF, a post-exilic book taking its name from its main character and traditional author, Nehemiah. The book occurs in the third section of the Hebrew canon. It is closely linked with Ezra and shows God's faithfulness in the restoration of His exiled people to their own land. God's purpose is seen to work through great monarchs of the Persian Empire such as Cyrus, Darius and Artaxerxes, and also through the agency of His own servants, such as Ezra, Nehemiah, Zerubbabel. The book narrates the rebuilding of the walls of Jerusalem and the establishment of civil authority under Nehemiah as governor. The book was written by Nehemiah in the latter half of the fifth century B.C. (Neh. 1:1; 7:5).

NEHILOTH, title of Ps. 5, means wind instruments.

NEHUM, see **REHUM.**

NEHUSHTA, mother of King Jehoiachin (II Kin. 24:8).

NEHUSHTAN, the name given by King Hezekiah to the "brazen serpent," when he broke it into pieces because the people had made it an object of worship (II Kin. 18:4).

NEIEL, a town on the boundary between Zebulun and Asher (Josh. 19:27).

NEIGHBOR, a fellow creature.
against thy *n.*, Ex. 20:16.
love thy *n.*, Matt. 5:43.
who is my *n.*, Luke 10:29.
every man his *n.*, Heb. 8:11.

NEKEB, a town on the border of Naphtali (Josh. 19:33).

NEKODA, (1) one of the Nethinim whose descendants returned to Jerusalem after the captivity (Ezra 2:48), (2) head of a family which failed to prove its Israelitish descent (Ezra 2:60).

NEMUEL, (1) a Reubenite, brother of Dathan and Abiram (Num. 26:9). (2) The eldest son of Simeon (Num. 26:12).

NEMUELITES, descendants of Nemuel.

NEPHEG, (1) one of the sons of Izhar. (Ex. 6:21). (2) One of David's sons (II Sam. 5:15).

NEPHEW, the rendering of Hebrew *ben*, normally son (Judg. 12:14); offspring (Job 18:19; I Tim. 5:4); in the old English sense of grandson, or descendant.

NEPHILIM, see **GIANT.**

NEPHISH, see **NAPHISH.**

NEPHISHESIM, NEPHISIM, see **NEPHUSIM.**

NEPHTHAIIM, see **NAPHTALI.**

NEPHTHALIM, see **NAPHTALI.**

NEPHTOAH, THE WATER OF, the spring or source of the water or waters of Nephtoah.
of the waters of *N.*, Josh. 15:9.
to the well . . . *N.*, Josh. 18:15.

NEPHUSIM, NEPHISHESIM, NEPHISIM, NEPHUSHESIM, the head of a family of Nethini, who returned with Zerubbabel from Babylon (Ezra 2:50).

NER, a Benjamite, father of Kish and Abner (I Sam. 14:50; I Chr. 8:33).

NEREUS, the name of a Roman Christian to whom with his sister Paul sends greetings (Rom. 16:15).

NERGAL, one of the chief Assyrian deities (II Kin. 17:30).

NERGAL-SHAREZER, the name of two princes, the one Assyrian, the other Babylonian. Sharezer in Is. 37:38 is the latter part of the name Nergal-Sharezer.
gate, even *N.*, Jer. 39:3.
N., Rab-mag, and, Jer. 39:13.

NERI, the son of Melchi, and father of Salathiel (Luke 3:27).

NERIAH, the son of Maaseiah and father of Baruch, the amanuensis of Jeremiah.
Baruch the son of *N.*, Jer. 32:12.
the son of *N.* took, Jer. 36:14.

NERO, the fifth Roman emperor, born at Antium December 15, 37 A.D., began to reign October 13, 54, died June 9, 68. He ranks with Gaius for folly and vice and he was licentious. His cruelty made the latter part of his reign detestable. In A.D. 64 a dreadful conflagration raged in Rome, said to have been started by Nero, who watched the progress of the flames from the top of a tower, playing on his lyre. It was during Nero's reign that the war commenced between the Jews and Romans which terminated in the destruction of Jerusalem. Nero was the emperor before whom Paul was brought on his first imprisonment at Rome; and in the persecution of the Christians by Nero, Paul and Peter are supposed to have suffered martyrdom.

NEST, where birds lay eggs.
if a bird's *n.*, Deut. 22:6.
make her *n.* on, Job 39:27.
her *n.* in, Jer. 48:28.

NET, the Hebrews used seines and casting nets in fishing. Bird nets were traps made of netting and light wooden frames with a baited trigger underneath the collapsible structure. Large nets on poles and small nets for stopping gaps were used in hunting (John 21:6; Job 19:6; Ps. 140:5).
in the *n.* which, Ps. 9:15.
bull in a *n.*, Is. 51:20.
a *n.* for my feet, Lam. 1:13.
my *n.* also will, Ezek. 12:13.
brother with a *n.*, Mic. 7:2.

NETAIM, a place of residence used by royal aides (I Chr. 4:23).

NETHANEL, NETHANEEL, (1) a chief or prince of Issachar (Num. 1:8). (2) The fourth son of Jesse (I Chr. 2:14). (3) One of the trumpet-blowers before the ark (I Chr. 15:24). (4) A Levite scribe (I Chr. 24:6). (5) The fifth son of Obed-edom (I Chr. 26:4). (6) One of the princes whom Jehoshaphat sent to teach in the cities of Judah (II Chr. 17:7). (7) A Levite who gave cattle for Josiah's Passover (II Chr. 35:9). (8) One of the priests who had married foreign wives (Ezra 10:22). (9) A priest registered under the high priest Joiakim (Neh. 12:21). (10) A Levite musician who assisted at the dedication of the walls (Neh. 12:36).

NETHANIAH, (1) an Asaphite musician

(I Chr. 25:2). (2) A Levite who accompanied the princes sent by Jehoshaphat to teach in the cities of Judah (II Chr. 17:8). (3) The father of Jehudi (Jer. 36:14). (4) The father of Ishmael (Jer. 40:8).

NETHINIM, menial servants of the Levites in the temple. The depleted numbers of the Gibeonite menials (Josh. 9:21; I Sam. 22:1–19) led David to establish the group which was probably made up of naturalized prisoners and other strangers (Ezra 8:20; I Chr. 9:2; Neh. 7:46). Returning from exile, Nethinim sealed Nehemiah's covenant (Neh. 10:28) and lived in Ophel (Neh. 3:26) immune from taxes (Ezra 7:24).
Levites and the *N.*, I Chr. 9:2.
all the *N.* and the, Ezra 2:43.
N. or the ministers of, Ezra 7:24.
the singers and the *N.*, Neh. 10:28.
the *N.* and the children, Neh. 7:46.

NETOPHAH, a place in Judah, near Bethlehem.
the Ahohite, . . . the *N.*, II Sam. 23:28.
the men of *N.*, fifty, Ezra 2:2.

NETOPHATHITES, NETOPHATHI, inhabitants of Netopha.
Bethlehem and the *N.*, I Chr. 2:54.
the village of the *N.*, I Chr. 9:16.

NETTLES, thorns, wild brushwood.
under the *n.* they, Job 30:7.
n. and brambles, Is. 34:13.

NEVER, not ever, at no time.
shall *n.* be moved, Ps. 15:5.
shall *n.* see light, Ps. 49:19.
I give, shall *n.* thirst, John 4:14.
charity *n.* faileth, I Cor. 13:8.
I will *n.* leave thee, Heb. 13:5.

NEW, NEWNESS, bright, fresh, new
a *n.* king over, Ex. 1:8.
a *n.* covenant, Jer. 31:31.
the *n.* testament, Matt. 26:28.
with *n.* tongue, Mark 16:17.
n. commandment, John 13:34.
n. creature, II Cor. 5:17.
n. name, Rev. 2:17.
a *n.* heaven, Rev. 21:1.

NEW BIRTH, the technical expression frequently used for regeneration, which is the spiritual change wrought in man as a result of having been born of water and of the Spirit (John 3:3–5; I Pet. 1:23;

Eph. 5:26; John 1:12 etc.). *See* REGEN-ERATION.

NEW JERUSALEM, the name occurs in Rev. 21:2. It is not descriptive of any actual locality on earth, but allegorically depicts the final state of the Church, "the bride," "the wife of the Lamb," when the new heaven and the new earth shall have come into being.

NEWLY, lately, recently.
gods that came *n*. up, Deut. 32:17.
but *n*. set the watch, Judg. 7:19.

NEW MOON, FEAST OF THE, (Heb. beginning of month, Num. 10:10; 28:11). The ordinary New Moons, i.e., all except the seventh, were raised out of the rank of ordinary days, but not to that of festivals. They may be called demi-feast days. Many nations of antiquity celebrated the returning light of the moon with festivities, sacrifices, and prayers. For the Jews there was a deeper meaning in this observance. The New Moon stood as the representative of the month.

NEWNESS, freshness.
walk in *n*. of life, Rom. 6:4.
serve in *n*. of spirit, Rom. 7:6.

NEWS, report, tidings.
good *n*. from far, Prov. 25:25.

NEW TESTAMENT, *see* BIBLE, CANON.

NEZIAH, the head of a family of Nethinim (Ezra 2:54).

NEZIB, a town in the lowland of Judah (Josh. 15:43).

NIBHAZ, an Avite deity (II Kin. 17:31).

NIBSHAN, a town in the wilderness of Judah (Josh. 15:62).

NICANOR, one of the seven in the church at Jerusalem (Acts 6:5).

NICODEMUS, a Pharisee and a ruler of the Jews. He interviewed Christ at Jerusalem and was taught by Him the doctrine of the New Birth, defended Him before the Sanhedrin, and assisted at His burial.
named *N*., John 3:1.

N. saith unto them, John 7:50.
came also *N*., John 19:39.

NICOLAITANS, NICOLAITANES, a first century heretical sect condemned by Jesus (Rev. 2:6, 15). They were said to hold "the teaching of Balaam." Tradition says they denied God as creator and practiced idolatry and licentiousness. The identity of Nicolas, founder of the sect, is unknown, nothing linking him with the early deacon (Acts 6:5).

NICOLAUS, NICOLAS, one of the seven chosen to have the oversight of the daily ministration to the poor of the church. He is called a proselyte of Antioch (Acts 6:5).

NICOPOLIS, a city to which Paul refers (Tit. 3:12), as the place where he intended to pass the following winter.

NIGER, one of the teachers and prophets in the church at Antioch (Acts 13:1).

NIGHT, the time from sunset to sunrise. The night was divided into watches, three in the Old Testament, four in the New Testament (Judg. 7:19; Matt. 14:25). Figuratively, the word indicates distress (Is. 21:12), death (John 9:4), ignorance (Mic. 3:6) and evil (I Thess. 5:5).
songs in the *n*., Job 35:10.
watch in the *n*., Ps. 90:4.
the *n*. cometh, John 9:4.
the *n*. is far spent, Rom. 13:12.
as thief in the *n*., II Pet. 3:10.
shall be no *n*. there, Rev. 21:25.

NIGHT-HAWK, any member of the eagle, vulture, owl, or hawk families. The bird is mentioned in the list of abominations (Lev. 11:16).

NIGHT-MONSTER, *see* SCREECH OWL.

NILE, the one great river of Egypt navigable for larger craft for 2900 miles into the interior of Africa from the Mediterranean. The term does not occur in the Bible, but is referred to as "river" (Ex. 2:3; 7:20; etc.)

NIMRAH, *see* BETH-NIMRAH.

NIMRIM, a very fertile tract in Moab, southeast of the Dead Sea (Is. 15:6).

NIMROD, the son of Cush and the founder of the kingdom of Babylon (Gen. 10:8, 9).

NIMSHI, the grandfather of Jehu (II Kin. 9:2, 14).

NINEVEH, NINEVE, this famous ancient city on the eastern bank of the Tigris River was founded by Nimrod (Gen. 10:8–10) and became the capital of the Assyrian Empire, reaching its greatest glory under Sennacherib (704–681 B.C.) and his successors Esarhaddon (681–669 B.C.) and Ashurbanipal (669–626 B.C.). Earlier Nineveh had repented when warned by Jonah (Jonah 3:5). Nahum and Zephaniah predicted the fall of the "bloody and cruel" city (Nah. 2:1–3:19; Zeph. 2:13–15). Accordingly, in 612 B.C. this four-mile square city was so devastated by an alliance of Medes, Babylonians and Scythians that it became like a myth until its discovery by Sir Austen Layard and others in the 19th century.

NINEVITE, a man of Nineveh (Luke 11:30).

NISAN, *see* **ABIB.**

NISROCH, an Assyrian god (II Kin. 19:37; Is. 37:38).

NITRE, an alkali used in washing clothing, probably means sodium carbonite as the word is used in the Bible (Prov. 25:20; Jer. 2:22).

NO, NO-AMON, the name of the ancient Thebes, the chief seat of the worship of the god Ammon, denounced by Jeremiah (Jer. 46:25).

NOADIAH, (1) one of the Levites to whom Ezra intrusted the gold and silver and sacred vessels (Ezra 8:33). (2) A prophetess associated with Tobiah and Sanballat (Neh. 6:14).

NOAH, NOE, (1) the son of Lamech, and tenth in descent from Adam. In his 600th year the degenerate races of mankind were cut off by the Deluge, but Noah was saved by means of the ark, constructed according to divine direction. He was a just man and perfect in his generation, and he walked with God

(Gen. 5:28, 29, 32; chs. 6–9; Ez. 14:14; Is. 54:9; I Pet. 3:20; II Pet. 2:5).

(2) one of the daughters of Zelophehad (Num. 26:33).

NO-AMON, *see* **NO.**

NOB, an ancient priestly town to which David came on his way when he fled from Saul at Gibeah.
came David to *N.*, I Sam. 21:1.
N. the city of the, I Sam. 22:19.

NOBAH, (1) an Israelite, whose family is not named (Num. 32:42), (2) a city which marked the course of Gideon's pursuit of the Midianites (Jud. 8:11).

NOBAI, *see* **NEBAI.**

NOBLE, of high birth; illustrious.
n. of the people, Num. 21:18.
king's most *n.* princes, Esther 6:9.
Bereans more *n.* than, Acts 17:11.
that not many *n.*, I Cor. 1:26.

NOD, the land of Eden, to which Cain migrated (Gen. 4:16).

NODAB, the name of a Bedouin tribe mentioned in I Chr. 5:19.

NOE, *see* **NOAH.**

NOGAH, a son of David born at Jerusalem (I Chr. 3:7).

NOHAH, the fourth son of Benjamin (I Chr. 8:2).

NOISE, loud sound, clamor.
what meaneth the *n.*, I Sam. 4:6.
make a joyful *n.*, Ps. 100:1.
take from me the *n.*, Amos 5:23.
this was *n.* abroad, Acts 2:6.
pass with great *n.*, II Pet. 3:10.
as it were the *n.*, Rev. 6:1.

NOISOME, harmful, offensive.
the *n.* pestilence, Ps. 91:3.
fell a *n.* and grievous, Rev. 16:2.

NON, NUN, the father of Joshua (Ex. 33:11; I Chr. 7:27).

NOPH, *see* **MEMPHIS.**

NOPHAH, a city mentioned in Num. 21:30.

NOSE JEWEL, a ring worn on the nose as an adornment (Is. 3:21).

NOTHING, a nonentity, not anything.
n. will be restrained, Gen. 11:6.
Lord will do n., Amos 3:7.
n. shall be impossible, Matt. 17:20.
it profiteth me n., I Cor. 13:3.
law made n. perfect, Heb. 7:19.

NOUGHT, see NAUGHT.

NOURISH, feed or maintain; instruct.
will I n. thee, Gen. 45:11.
n. his flesh, as Lord, Col. 2:19.
n. in words of faith, I Tim. 4:6.

NOW, at the present time.
let him n. come down, Matt. 27:42.
true light n. shineth, I John 2:8.
n. are we sons of God, I John 3:2.

NUMBER, the Hebrews used letters for figures is evident from Maccabean coins in which aleph, the first letter of the alphabet, means one, beth, the second letter, means two, etc. In all existing copies of the Hebrew Old Testament the numbers are spelled out, but some believe that some shorter mode of writing was originally used. The Bible often uses round numbers instead of exact figures (Ex. 24:18; I Kin. 19:8). Many attach symbolic meaning to various numbers, such as seven (sacred completeness) or ten (wholeness). Gematria (Using the sum of the numerical values of the letters in a word to represent the word) is probably the key to the mysterious 666 of Rev. 13:18, but the name intended is uncertain now. It is computed by some as Nero Caesar.
lamb according to n., Ex. 12:4.
n. of those slain, Esther 9:11.
a great n. believed and, Acts 11:21.
n. of them was 10,000, Rev. 5:11.

NUMBER, to count.
if a man can n. dust, Gen. 13:16.
who can n. clouds?, Job 38:37.
hairs of head are n., Luke 12:7.
which no man could n., Rev. 7:9.

NUMBERS, BOOK OF, the fourth book of the Pentateuch, which was written by Moses (Num. 33:1, 2). The book is so designated because it makes a double reference to taking a census of the Jewish people—chs. 1–3 and ch. 26. The book

of Numbers follows legislation of Leviticus. It first relates the preparations which were made for the departure from Sinai (chs. 1:1–10:10), then the departure of Israelites from Sinai until finally they come to the plains of Moab (10:11–21:35), and the events in the plains of Moab (22:1–36:13).

NUN, see NON.

NURSE, (1) a woman who suckles the child of another (Ex. 2:7–9); (2) a female attendant (II Sam. 4:4); (3) a male attendant, called a nursing father (Is. 49:23).

NURSING, see NURSE.

NURTURE, the whole training and correction of children (Eph. 6:4).

NUTS, the nuts of Gen. 43:11 were pistachios, delicious and expensive. Walnuts were cultivated and highly esteemed in Bible lands (Song 6:11).

NYMPHAS, a prominent Christian at Laodicea (Col. 4:15).

O

OAK, a tree used often in ancient worship. Oak groves in early times were used as places of religious services; altars were set up in them (Josh. 24:26). Jacob buried some idols under an oak (Gen. 35:14), and idolatry was practiced under oaks (Is. 1:29; Ezek. 6:13).

OATH, an appeal to Divine authority to uphold the truth of a statement. They were used much in the O.T. (Ruth 1:17; I Sam. 2:17). Jesus was asked by the high-priest to swear, "By the living God," to what he was teaching (Matt. 26:63). It is believed that Jesus prohibited careless and profane swearing; he gave testimony on oath to the high-priest, and Paul did not teach against it (Gal. 1:20; I Cor. 15:31; II Cor. 1:23). However, the Bible teaches that it is best not to swear at all (James 5:12).
Joseph took an o., Gen. 50:25.
and love no false o., Zech. 8:17.
unto the Lord thine o., Matt. 5:33.
God had sworn an o., Acts 2:30.
neither by any other o., James 5:12.

OBADIAH, (1) an officer of high rank in the court of Ahab (I Kin. 18:3). (2) An obscure person referred to in I Chr. 3:21. (3) One of the sons of Izrahiah (I Chr. 7:3). (4) A son of Azel, a descendant of Saul (I Chr. 8:38). (5) A son of Shemaiah (I Chr. 9:16). (6) A captain in David's army (I Chr. 12:9). (7) The father of Ishmaiah (I Chr. 27: 19). (8) A prince during Jehoshaphat's reign (II Chr. 17:7). (9) A Levite who helped repair the temple during Josiah's reign (II Chr. 34:12). (10) The son of Jehiel (Ezra 8:9). (11) One of the priests who signed the covenant with Nehemiah (Neh. 10:5). (12) One of the twelve prophets; there is nothing certain known about his life.

OBADIAH, THE BOOK OF, a prophecy of the O.T. which starts with the proclamation of the destruction to come upon the Edomites, and the divine judgment which this nation would receive (Obad. 1–14). This will be followed by the victories of Judah (Obad. 17–21).

OBAL, a son of Joktan, and a founder of an Arabian tribe (Gen. 10:28).

OBED, (1) the son of Boaz and Ruth, and the father of Jesse (Ruth 4:17; I Chr. 2:12). (2) A descendant of Jarha (I Chr. 2:37). (3) One of David's mighty men (I Chr. 11:47). (4) A gatekeeper at the temple (I Chr. 26:7). (5) The father of Azariah (II Chr. 23:1).

OBED-EDOM, (1) a Levite of the family of Korhites, and a doorkeeper (I Chr. 15:18). (2) The son of Jeduthun, and one of the temple doorkeepers (I Chr. 16:38). (3) The treasurer of the temple in the reign of Amaziah (II Chr. 25:24).

OBEDIENCE, to submit, obey.
o. to faith among all, Rom. 1:5.
by *o.* of one shall many, Rom. 5:19.
women to be under *o.*, I Cor. 14:34.
o. by things suffered, Heb. 5:8.
sanctification unto *o.*, I Pet. 1:2.

OBEDIENT, to obey, to hearken.
if thou shalt be *o.*, Deut. 4:30.
if ye be willing and *o.*, Is. 1:19.
the priests were *o.*, Acts 6:7.
to make the Gentiles *o.*, Rom. 15:18.
servants be *o.* to them, Eph. 6:5.
o. to their own husbands, Titus 2:5.

OBEISANCE, obedience, humble service.
stars, made *o.*, Gen. 37:9.
Moses . . . did obeisance, Ex. 18:7.
Bath-sheba . . . did *o.*, I Kin. 1:16.

OBEY, to hearken, to be submissive.
Jacob *o.* father, Gen. 22:18.
to *o.* is better than, I Sam. 15:22.
o. words of the Lord, II Chr. 11:4.
even winds and sea *o.*, Matt. 8:27.
spirits . . . *o.* him, Mark 1:27.
o. God rather than man, Acts 5:29.
o. your parents, Eph. 6:1.
o. your masters, Col. 3:22.
o. not the gospel, II Thess. 1:8.

OBIL, an Ishmaelite who was a keeper of the herds of camels (I Chr. 27:30).

OBJECT, to be against, to speak against.
o., if they had ought, Acts 24:19.

OBLATION, *see* **OFFERING AND SACRIFICE.**

OBOTH, one of the encampments of the Israelites (Num. 21:10, 11; 33:43).

OBSCURE, OBSCURITY, dimness, dark.
lamp . . . put out in *o.*, Prov. 20:20.
eyes . . . see out of *o.*, Is. 29:18.

OBSERVATION, that which may be seen; having outward show. In the expression "The kingdom of God cometh not with observation" (Luke 17:20), it means that the kingdom has no outward demonstration.

OBSERVE, watch, heed, keep.
o. my statutes, Lev. 19:37.
hear, O Israel, and *o.*, Deut. 6:3.
teaching to *o.* all, Matt. 28:20.
ye *o.* days and months, Gal. 4:10.

OBSERVER, one who observes.
observers of times, Deut. 18:14.

OBSTINATE, hard, sharp.
God made his heart *o.*, Deut. 2:30.
I know . . . thou art *o.*, Is. 48:4.

OBTAIN, to reach, to attain, to acquire.
o. children by her, Gen. 16:2.
o. leave of the king, Neh. 13:6.
o. favour of the Lord, Prov. 8:35.
so run, that ye may *o.*, I Cor. 9:24.
that we may *o.* mercy, Heb. 4:16.

OCCASION, an event, an opportunity.

Oil

thou shalt find *o.*, Judg. 9:33.
taking *o.* by command, Rom. 7:8.
give none occasion, I Tim. 5:14.

OCCUPATION, work, trade.
what is your *o.*? Gen. 46:33.
o. were tentmakers, Acts 18:3.

OCCUPY, fill, possess, use.
said unto them, *o.*, Luke 19:13.
he that *o.* the room, I Cor. 14:16.

OCRAN, OCHRAN, the father of Pagiel, who helped Moses number the people (Num. 1:13; 2:27; 7:72; 10:26).

ODOUR, (1) referring to incense in Dan. 2:46. (2) Used generally for spices (II Chr. 16:14; Esther 2:2; Jer. 34:5; John 12:3).

OFFENCE, stumbling block.
rock of *o.* to Israel, Is. 8:14.
o. of cross ceased, Gal. 5:11.
a rock of *o.*, I Pet. 2:8.

OFFEND, transgress, sin.
have *o.* against Lord, II Chr. 28:13.
Edom hath greatly *o.*, Ezek. 25:12.
Caesar have I *o.*, Acts 25:8.

OFFENDER, sinner.
for if I be an *o.*, Acts 25:11.

OFFER, to draw nigh, to go up toward.
o. burnt offering, Gen. 8:20.
that *o.* an oblation, Is. 66:3.
ye *o.* polluted bread, Mal. 1:7.
things *o.* to idols, I Cor. 8:1.
o. spiritual sacrifices, I Pet. 2:5.

OFFERING, *see* **OFFERING AND SAC-RIFICE**.
Cain brought an *o.*, Gen. 4:3.
o. of the house of, Ezra 8:25.
offering and incense, Jer. 41:5.
offering of Gentiles, Rom. 15:16.
there is no more *o.*, Heb. 10:18.

OFFERING AND SACRIFICE, the first recorded offerings were those of Cain and Abel (Gen. 8:20). The sacrifice of Isaac was the only instance of human sacrifice mentioned in the Bible as a command of God (Gen. 22:1–13). The burnt-offerings of Job (Job 1:5) were accompanied by repentance and prayer. The law prescribed five kinds of sacrifices: the burnt-offering, the meat-offering, the peace offering, the sin-offering, and the trespass-offering. The regular temple sacrifices were burnt-offerings. There were also meat-offerings offered daily with the burnt-offerings. At the great feasts, there were even more offerings made of each kind. A sin-offering was offered each new moon, and at the Passover, Pentecost, Feast of Trumpets, and Feast of Tabernacles. There were also the individual offerings of the people.

The New Testament, especially the book of Hebrews, shows that the old sacrificial system is a type of the Christian order. Christ is the "Lamb without blemish and without spot" (I Pet. 1:19, 20). The Levitical offerings were imperfect; Christ was the perfect sacrifice. Jesus Christ, the great High Priest and the Lamb of God, offered himself once for all. Prayer and thanksgiving are offerings "well pleasing in his sight" (Heb. 13:15).

OFFICE, position, charge, oversight.
executed the priest's *o.*, Luke 1:8.
the *o.* of a bishop, I Tim. 3:1.
the *o.* of a deacon, I Tim. 3:10.

OFFSCOURING, a figurative term for something vile (I Cor. 4:13).

OFT, OFTEN, OFTENER, many a time.
spake *o.* one to another, Mal. 3:16.
sent for him the *o.*, Acts 24:26.
I punish them *o.*, Acts 26:11.

OG, an Amorite, king of Bashan (Num. 21:33), who ruled over sixty cities (Josh. 13:30). He was a giant of the race of Rephaim.

OHAD, the son of Simeon (Gen. 46:10).

OHEL, son of Zerubbabel (I Chr. 3:20).

OIL, usually olive oil. In Esther 2:12 it refers to myrrh, but everywhere else it refers to olive oil. Olive oil was used for food, similar to the way we use butter (I Kin. 17:12), a cosmetic (Is. 61:3), a lamp fuel (Ex. 25:6), and a healing agent (Is. 1:6; Mark 6:13). It was used for an ingredient for the meal offering also (Lev. 2:1). Oil was an important object of commerce (Ezek. 27:17; Hos. 12:1). After the olives were shaken from the trees (Deut. 24:20; Is. 17:6), they were pressed. To get a high quality oil, they pounded it in a mortar and strained it through a wicker sieve.

OIL OFFERING, *see* **OFFERING AND SACRIFICE.**

OINTMENT, a general term for perfumes, cosmetics, medicine, and oils. They were used in consecration (Ex. 30:23). This particular ointment was made of myrrh, cassia, sweet cinnamon, sweet calamus, and olive oil. A type of ointment was used for medicinal purposes (Is. 1:6).

OLD AGE, to be old.
in a good old age, Gen. 15:15.
nourisher of . . . old age, Ruth 4:15.
old age, full of days, I Chr. 29:28.
forth fruit in *o.*, Ps. 92:14.

OLD TESTAMENT, *see* **BIBLE, CANON.**

OLIVE, a tree, with dull green leaves, which is grown around the Bible lands. Its beauty and usefulness are alluded to many times in the Bible. Even now its fruit is important in commerce. It is preserved by pickling, but the primary use is found in the rich oil which it produces. This oil is used in salads, in soap, and is used much for frying.

OLIVES, MOUNT OF, OLIVET, it is called "Mount of Olives" only in Zech. 14:4. It is also called "Olivet" (II Sam. 15:30), "the hill that is before Jerusalem" (I Kin. 11:7), and simply "the mount" (Neh. 8:15). The mount is a limestone ridge, about a mile long. It runs north and south on the eastern side of the city of Jerusalem. The mount is mentioned in connection with the flight of David from Absalom (II Sam. 15:30); with the building of high places by Solomon (II Kin. 23:13); with the vision of the Lord's departure from Jerusalem (Ezek. 10:4). In the New Testament, the mount marks four great scenes: the triumphal entry (Matt. 21:1); the prediction of Jerusalem's overthrow (Mark 13:1); Gethsemane (John 18:1); the Ascension.

OLYMPAS, a Roman Christian (Rom. 16:15).

OMAR, the son of Eliphaz (Gen. 36:11, 15).

OMEGA, the last letter in the Greek alphabet (Rev. 1:8, 11).

OMER, an ancient Hebrew dry measure. Its relative value was the one tenth ephah (Ex. 16:36), approximately 7 pints.

OMITTED, left undone.
o. the weightier, Matt. 23:23.

OMRI, the seventh king of Israel, who was originally commander of the armies of Elah, king of Israel. After a four year civil war, Omri defeated Zimri (I Kin. 16:21,22). There were several other men named Omri: one of the sons of Becher (I Chr. 7:8), a descendant of Pharez (I Chr. 9:4), and a son of Michael, during the reign of David (I Chr. 27:18).

ON, (1) the son of Peleth, and one of the chiefs of the tribe of Reuben who took part with Korah, Dathan, and Abiram in their revolt against Moses (Num. 16:1). (2) A city of Egypt, the home of Asenath, Joseph's wife (Gen. 41:45).

ONAM, (1) son of Shobal (Gen. 36:23). (2) Son of Jerahmeel (I Chr. 2:26).

ONAN, the son of Judah (Gen. 38:4), *see* **SEED.**

ONE AND ANOTHER, both, each, individually (Jer. 36:16).

ONESIMUS, the servant in whose behalf wrote the Epistle to Philemon. Paul mentioned his name in the Colossian letter (4:9). While in Rome, Onesimus accepted the Gospel (Philem. 10). Onesimus and Tychicus returned to Asia carrying the letter to Philemon and the letter to the Colossians.

ONESIPHORUS, a Christian of Ephesus who ministered to Paul there (II Tim. 1:18).

ONIONS, mentioned in connection with the longing of the Israelites in the desert for the good things of Egypt (Num. 11:5).

ONO, a city in Benjamin, built by the sons of Elpaal (I Chr. 8:12).

ONYCHA, an ingredient of the sacred perfume (Ex. 30:34).

ONYX, an agate color (Ex. 28:20).

OPEN, uncovered.
shall see heaven *o.*, John 1:51.
put him to *o.* shame, Heb. 6:6.

OPERATION, work, working.
through faith of the *o.*, Col. 2:12.

OPHEL, a part of ancient Jerusalem, east of Zion (II Chr. 27:3).

OPHIR, (1) a son of Joktan (Gen. 10:29). (2) A place in Arabia (I Kin. 9:28).

OPHNI, a place in Benjamin (Josh. 18:24).

OPHRAH, (1) a city in Benjamin (Josh. 18:23). (2) A city in Manasseh (Judg. 6:11). (3) Son of Meonothai (I Chr. 4:14).

OPINION, knowledge, conclusion.
halt between two *o.*, I Kin. 18:21.

OPPORTUNITY, suitable time.
but ye lack *o.*, Phil. 4:10.

OPPOSE, put against.
o. and exalt thyself, II Thess. 2:4.

OPPRESS, crush, put down, burden.
Egyptians *o.* them, Ex. 3:9.
healing that were *o.*, Acts 10:38.
do not rich men *o.*, James 2:6.

OPPRESSION, unjust hardship.
delivered poor in *o.*, Job 36:15.
shalt be far from *o.*, Is. 54:14.

ORACLE, speaking.
received *o.* to give, Acts 7:38.
speak as the *o.*, I Pet. 4:11.

ORATOR, speaker.
o. named Tertullus, Acts 24:1.

ORCHARD, field of fruit.
as *o.* of pomegranate, Song 4:13.

ORDAIN, ORDAINED, appoint.
o. to eternal life, Acts 13:48.
ordained elders, Titus 1:5.

ORDER, ORDERED, arrangement.
set words in *o.*, Job 33:5.
all be done in *o.*, I Cor. 14:40.
order of Aaron, Heb. 7:11.

ORDINANCE, decree.

a statute and *o.*, Ex. 15:25.
o. of the Lord, Luke 1:6.
o. of divine service, Heb. 9:1.

OREB, (1) a prince of Midian (Judg. 7:25). (2) A rock east of the Jordan (Judg. 7:25).

OREN, a son of Jerahmeel (I Chr. 2:25).

ORGAN, flute, lute.
as handle the .. *o.*, Gen. 4:21.

ORION, a southern constellation seen in November. (Job 9:9; 38:31; Amos 5:8).

ORNAMENT, adornment.
o. of molten images, Is. 30:22.
o. of meek .. spirit, I Pet. 3:4.

ORNAN, *see* **ARAUNAH.**

ORPAH, daughter-in-law of Naomi (Ruth 1:4).

ORPHANS, fatherless child.
o. and fatherless, Lam. 5:3.

OSEE, variant of Hosea (Rom. 9:25).

OSHEA, *see* **HOSHEA, JOSHUA.**

OSPRAY, an unclean bird.
ossifrage, and the *o.*, Lev. 11:13.

OSSIFRAGE, an eagle.
the eagle, and the *o.*, Lev. 11:13.

OSTRICH, stork.
o. in the wilderness, Lam. 4:3.

OTHNI, a son of Shemaiah (I Chr. 26:7).

OTHNIEL, (1) a son of Kenaz, brother of Caleb (Josh. 15:17). (2) Perhaps the same as the preceding (I Chr. 27:15).

OUGHT, owe it, behooveth.
o. ye have done, Matt. 23:23.
men *o.* to worship, John 4:20.
how ye *o.* to answer, Col. 4:6.

OURS, belonging to us.
the water is *o.*, Gen. 26:20.
inheritance be *o.*, Mark 12:7.
o. in day of Lord, II Cor. 1:14.
not for *o.* only, I John 2:2.

OUTLANDISH, strange.

o. women caused Sol., Neh. 13:26.

OUTRAGEOUS, overwhelming.
anger is outrageous, Prov. 27:4.

OUTSIDE, without.
to *o.* of camp, Judg. 7:17.
clean *o.* of cup, Matt. 23:25.

OUTSTRETCHED, stretched out.
and with *o.* arm, Deut. 26:8.

OUTWARD, without.
our *o.* man perish, II Cor. 4:16.

OVEN, furnace.
shall burn as an *o.*, Mal. 4:1.
cast into an oven, Matt. 6:30.

OVERCHARGE, overload.
I may not *o.* you., II Cor. 2:5.

OVERCOME, gain victory.
stronger shall *o.*, Luke 11:22.
o. evil with good, Rom. 12:21.
that *o.* the world, I John 5:5.

OVERMUCH, too much.
be not righteous *o.*, Eccles. 7:16.
with *o.* sorrow, II Cor. 2:7.

OVERPASS, to pass over.
o. deeds of wicked, Jer. 5:28.

OVERPLUS, too much.
restore *o.* unto the man, Lev. 25:27.

OVERSEER, overlooker.
hath made you *o.*, Acts 20:28.

OVERSHADOW, protect.
Highest shall *o.* them, Luke 1:35.

OVERSIGHT, error, or charge.
it was an *o.*, Gen. 43:12.
taking the *o.* thereof, I Pet. 5:2.

OVERTAKE, catch up.
curses shall *o.* thee, Deut. 28:15.
if a man be *o.*, Gal. 6:1.
o. you as a thief, I Thess. 5:4.

OVERTHROW, overturn, breakdown.
Lord *o.* the Egyptians, Ex. 14:27.
Nineveh shall be *o.*, Jonah 3:4.
o. the faith of some, II Tim. 2:18.

OVERTURN, to turn over.
they *o.* the earth, Job 12:15.

OVERWHELM, cover over.
horror hath *o.* me, Ps. 55:5.
my spirit was *o.*, Ps. 77:3.

OWE, to be indebted.
o. no man anything, Rom. 13:8.

OWL, an unclean animal. It feeds on its prey at night. The word "owl" has been misused for other birds in the Bible. The owl of Ps. 102:6, the little owl of Lev. 11:17; Deut. 14:16 and the owl of Is. 34:15 were probably true owls. It may possibly be better rendered "ibis." The Revised Version translates "screech owl" as "night monster" (Is. 34:14). In many passages (Lev. 11:16; Deut. 14:15; Jer. 50:39) the bird is intended to be the ostrich. All of them were regarded as birds of evil omen.

OWNER, one who owns.
the ox knoweth his *o.*, Is. 1:3.

OX, OXEN, BULL, BULLOCK, these are valuable beasts of burden (II Sam. 6:6; I Kin. 19:19), and were used for treading out grain (Deut. 25:4), for food (I Kin. 1:25), and for sacrifices. "Shon" is a broad name for any kind of bovine (Gen. 32:5; I Sam. 22:19). See Cattle. "Par" and the feminine "parah" (Ps. 22:12) designate bulls and heifers intended for sacrifice. "Teo" was probably an antelope, instead of an ox. The Revised Version uses antelope (Deut. 14:5; Is. 51:20). The antelope here referred to was probably a species characterized by variegated colours of white and yellowish-brown and horns some three feet in length.

OZEM, (1) son of Jesse (I Chr. 2:15). (2) Son of Jerahmeel (I Chr. 2:25).

OZIAS, (1) son of Micha (Judg. 6:15). (2) Uzziah, king of Judah (Matt. 1:8,9).

OZNI, son of Gad (Num. 26:16).

OZNITES, descendants of Ozni (Num. 26:16).

P

PAARAI, one of the valiant men of David (II Sam. 23:35). He is called Naarai in I Chr. 11:37.

PACE, a step in walking.
had gone six *p.*, II Sam. 6:13.

PACIFY, to cover up, cause to rest.
wise man will *p.* it, Prov. 16:14.
a gift . . *p.* anger, Prov. 21:14.
for yielding *p.*, Eccles. 10:4.

PADAN, PADDAN same as **Padanaram.**

PADANARAM, PADDANRAM, the plains of Mesopotamia, or the land between the Tigris and Euphrates. It was the place from whence Isaac and Jacob took their wives (Gen. 25:20; 28:5).

PADDLE, (Deut. 23:13), some type lock or pin which is placed upon a weapon of the Hebrews.

PADON, the head of one of the Nethinim families who returned with Zerubbabel to Palestine around 536 B.C. (Neh. 7:47).

PAGIEL, the son of Ocran and head of the tribe of Asher. He was chosen to number the people (Num. 1:13).

PAHATHMOAB, the head of a family whose members returned to Jerusalem with Zerubbabel (Ezra 2:6; Neh. 7:11).

PAI, PAU, a town in Edom where Hadad, the last of the early kings, was born or reigned (I Chr. 1:50). It is called Pau in Gen. 36:39.

PAIN, PAINED, suffering.
My heart is . . *p.* within, Ps. 55:4.
sorely *p.* at the report, Is. 23:5.
p. at my very heart, Jer. 4:19.

PAINT, the Egyptians used a paint made from almond shells, or resin, in decorating the eyes. Various dyes were used in darkening the eyebrows. The Hebrews looked disfavorably upon this practice (II Kin. 9:30; Jer. 4:30; Ezek. 23:40).

PALACE, the living quarters for the sovereign. David built such a palace in Jerusalem (II Sam. 5:9; 7:1,2). Solomon, David's son, built a tremendous palace which took thirteen years to complete. It contained a hall which was 150 feet long, called "the house of the forest of Lebanon" (I Kin. 7:2).
p. of the king's house, I Kin. 16:18.
God . . known in her *p.*, Ps. 48:3.

the *p.* shall be forsaken, Is. 32:14.
consume . . *p.* of Benhadad, Jer. 49:27.
Peter was . . in the *p.*, Mark 14:66.

PALAL, the son of Uzzai who helped repair the wall of Jerusalem after Nehemiah's return to the city (Neh. 3:25).

PALE, bleached, white, pallid.
neither . . face wax *p.*, Is. 29:22.
behold a *p.* horse, Rev. 6:8.

PALESTINE, PALESTINA, the name used in the Old Testament for the land of the Philistines. It is called Canaan by the Hebrews to distinguish it from Gilead, east of the Jordan. The land of the Jews is only once called Palestine (Joel 3:4). When the area occupied by the Philistines was taken by Joshua it became known as Israel (I Sam. 13:19; Matt. 2:20). It is referred to as the land of promise (Heb. 11:9) and as the holy land (Zech. 2:12). When fully settled by the Hebrews the territory extended from Mount Hermon on the north to Kadeshbarnea on the south and from the Mediterranean on the west to the region occupied by Reuben and Gad, and half-tribe of Manasseh east of the Jordan.
the inhabitants of *P.*, Ex. 15:14.
Rejoice not thou . . *P.*, Is. 14:29.
and all the coasts of *P.*, Joel 3:4.

PALESTINIAN, pertaining to **Palestine.**

PALLU, PHALLU, the second son of Reuben and head of a tribal family (Ex. 6:14; Num. 26:5).

PALLUITES, descendants of Pallu (Num. 26:5).

PALM, a tall, straight tree (Song 7:7, 8; Jer. 10:5). Its wood was used in various portions of the Temple (I Kin. 6:29, 32, 35). A palm leaf was the symbol for both peace and victory (John 12:13; Rev. 7:9). Elim was noted for its palms (Ex. 15:27).

PALMERWORM, destructive insect which eats trees, vines, vegetables and cereals (Joel 1:4; 2:25; Amos 4:9).

PALM OF HAND, the palm of the hand is the inner surface which extends from the wrist to the bases of the fingers.

p. of hands cut off, I Sam. 5:4.

PALSY, a paralysis which is caused by a disease of the brain or spinal cord (Mark 2:3, 9–12; Acts 9:33–35).

PALTI, PHALTI, (1) a chief Benjamite who was chosen to spy out the land of promise (Num. 13:9). (2) The name of the man to whom Saul, Israel's first king, gave his daughter, Michal, the wife of David, to wed (I Sam. 25:44; II Sam. 3:3, 15).

PALTIEL, PHALTIEL, a chief of Issachar who was chosen to divide the land west of the Jordan (Num. 34:26).

PALTITE, a Patronymic of Helez and a native of Bethpelet (II Sam. 23:26).

PAMPHYLIA, a coastal region in southern Asia Minor (Acts 13:13; 14:24; 15:38).

PAN, FIRE, *see* **FIRE PAN.**

PANNAG, a place on the road from Damascus to Baalbeck (Ezek. 27:17).

PANT, to long with breathless eagerness.
p. after the water brooks, Ps. 42:1.
My heart *p.*, Is. 21:4.
p. after the dust, Amos 2:7.

PAPER, *see* **PAPYRUS.**

PAPER REED, a word of uncertain meaning in Is. 19:7. The Revised Version renders the word *meadow.*

PAPHOS, the capital of Cyprus and station of a Roman pro-consul. It was here that Paul caused Elymas to be blinded, thus converting Sergius Paulus (Acts 13:6–13). It was near a temple of Venus.

PAPYRUS, a variety of solid-stemmed grass which is native of the Nile region. It may have been used for writing paper as early as Jeremiah (Jer. 36:23). It is probably the plant referred to as bulrush in Ex. 2:3 and rush in Job 8:11.

PARABLE, a story or fable used to illustrate a religious or moral truth. Jesus made use of the parable to a great extent. All the gospel stories record many of his parables except the account of John. In the parable on the Good Shepherd the word parable is used (John 10:6), but it is not the word used generally for parable in the Synoptic Gospels. Jesus used parables in order to make the preaching of the kingdom more intelligible and impressive to the masses.
he took up his *p.*, Num. 23:7.
incline . . ear to a *p.*, Ps. 49:4.
take . . a *p.* against you, Mic. 2:4.
Why speakest . . in *p.*, Matt. 13:10.
open my mouth in *p.*, Matt. 13:35.
taught them . . by *p.*, Mark 4:2.
he spake by a *p.*, Luke 8:4.
but to others in *p.*, Luke 8:10.
he put forth a *p.*, Luke 14:7.
This *p.* spake Jesus, John 10:6.

PARACLETE, *see* **ADVOCATE.**

PARADISE, a word which denotes a place of rest. It is a place for the righteous and the just (Luke 23:43; II Cor. 12:4; Rev. 2:7). It is referred to as Abraham's bosom in Luke 16:22, 23.

PARAH, a town in Benjamin which was near Avim and Ophrah (Josh. 18:23).

PARAN, a wilderness between Sinai and Canaan (Num. 10:12; 12:16).
the wilderness of *P.*, Gen. 21:21.
unto the wilderness of *P.*, Num. 13:26.
shined..from mount *P.*, Deut. 33:2.
took men..out of *P.*, I Kin. 11:18.

PARBAR, a section on the west side of the Temple court (II Kin. 23:11; I Chr. 26:18) which is surrounded by a wall.

PARCEL, a part or portion of.
a *p.* of a field, Gen. 33:19.
a *p.* of ground, Josh. 24:32.
the midst of that *p.*, I Chr. 11:14.

PARCHMENT, the skin of a sheep or goat which may be used as material for writing (II Tim. 4:13). The name is derived from Pergumum because it was used there from early in the second century B.C. as a substitute for papyrus. It was not tanned like leather. Lines were made with a blunt instrument, and the page was divided into two or three columns. A finer writing material, called vellum, was made of calf and antelope skins, and was sometimes dyed purple. Unlike papyrus, parchment could be made into a book. Paul asked Timothy to bring such parchments to him (II Tim. 4:13).

PARDON, spare, forgive, excuse.
p. our iniquity, Ex. 34:9.
p., I beseech thee, Num. 14:19.
he will abundantly *p.,* Is. 55:7.
God, that *p.* iniquity, Mic. 7:18.

PARENTS, the fifth commandment sets forth the duty of the children to the parents, but the duties of the parents to the children are also strongly emphasized in the Scriptures. They must train the child to fear and respect the Lord, and must refrain from provoking the child to unnecessary anger in order that the child be not discouraged (Deut. 6:7; Eph. 6:1–4).
children..rise..against *p.,* Matt. 10:21.
this man, or .. *p.,* John 9:2.
disobedient to *p.,* Rom. 1:30.
obey your *p.,* Col. 3:20.
to requite their *p.,* I Tim. 5:4.
three months of his *p.,* Heb. 11:23.

PARLOR, PARLOUR, a cool room built upon the top of a house, as in the case of the parlor of Eglon (Judg. 3:20). It is also a receiving room for guests (I Sam. 9:22).

PARMASHTA, a son of Haman (Esther 9:9).

PARMENAS, one of the seven disciples chosen to serve tables (Acts 6:5).

PARNACH, father of Elizaphan who was chosen to divide the land west of the Jordan (Num. 34:25).

PAROSH, PHAROSH, a man who signed the covenant with Nehemiah after returning from captivity (Neh. 10:14).

PARSHANDATHA, the eldest of the ten sons of Haman (Esther 9:7).

PART, a portion or division of a whole.
have any *p.* among them, Num. 18:20.
on a *p.* of the field, Ruth 2:3.
will not conceal his *p.,* Job 41:12.
the toes .. *p.* of iron, Dan. 2:42.
into the *p.* of Galilee, Matt. 2:22.
blindness in *p.,* Rom. 11:25.
first into the lower *p.,* Eph. 4:9.

PARTAKE, to take or have a part.
p. with adulterers, Ps. 50:18.
made *p.* of their spirit, Rom. 15:27.

p. of the Lord's table, I Cor. 10:21.
p. of his promise, Eph. 3:6.
p. of his divine nature, II Pet. 1:4.

PARTHIANS, inhabitants of Parthia.

PARTIAL, respect of person.
been *p.* in the law, Mal. 2:9.
are ye not *p.?* James 2:4.

PARTIALITY, liking for.
doing nothing by *p.,* I Tim. 5:21.
without *p.,* and .. hypocrisy, James 3:17.

PARTICULAR, exact, especial.
in members in *p.,* I Cor. 12:27.
and everyone in *p.,* Eph. 5:33.

PARTITION, fence, division, wall.
made *p.* by chains, I Kin. 6:21.
broken down wall of *p.,* Eph. 2:14.

PARTITION, MIDDLE WALL OF, the symbolic wall which divided the Gentiles and Jews (Eph. 2:14). The law of Moses made the wall possible. Paul said Jesus took away the law of commandments contained in ordinances which allowed the enmity to exist. This was done when Jesus died on the cross. Once the wall of partition was gone both Jew and Gentile could be reconciled to God in Christ.

PARTNER, companion, associate.
p. with a thief, Prov. 29:24.
he is my *p.* and, II Cor. 8:23.
count me a *p.,* Philem. 17.

PARTRIDGE, two species of birds found in the Holy Land, which are hunted for food (I Sam. 26:20). Jeremiah compares a man with ill-gotten wealth to a partridge sitting of eggs that do not hatch (Jer. 17:11).

PARUAH, the father of Jehoshaphat. (I Kin. 4:17).

PARVAIM, the name of a place noted for having much gold. Its exact location is not known, but some feel it was in the vicinity of Ophir (II Chr. 3:6).

PASACH, a son of Japhlet of Asher (I Chr. 7:33).

PASDAMMIM, a place in western Judah, between Shocho and Azekah. It is called Ephes-dammim in I Sam. 17:1.

PASEAH, PHASEAH, (1) a son of Eshton of Judah (I Chr. 4:12). (2) An ancestor of Nethinim who returned from captivity (Ezra 2:49). (3) An ancestor of the Jehoiada (Neh. 3:6).

PASHUR, PASHHUR, (1) son of Immer, a priest (Jer. 20:1-6). (2) The son of Melchiah and militant enemy of Jeremiah (Jer. 21:1; 38:1, 4). (3) The father of Gedaliah wore this name also. He was an enemy of Jeremiah (Jer. 38:1). (4) A priest who sealed the covenant with Nehemiah (Neh. 10:3). (5) A head of a priestly family (Ezra 2:38; Neh. 7:41).

PASS, to go, move, proceed. Also **Passed.**
when see blood, will *p.*, Ex. 12:13.
heaven and earth *p.*, Matt. 5:18.
let this cup *p.*, Matt. 26:39.
p. from death to life, John 5:24.
as grass *p.* away, James 1:10.

PASSION, feeling, suffering.
alive after his *p.*, Acts 1:3.
men of like *p.*, Acts 14:15.
subject to like *p.*, James 5:17.

PASSION WEEK, *see* **HOLY WEEK.**

PASSOVER, the first of the three annual Jewish festivals at which all the men must appear at the sanctuary (Ex. 12:43; 13: 3-10; Deut. 16:1). The feast of the passover was instituted to commemorate the passing over or sparing of the Hebrews in Egypt when God killed the first born of the Egyptians (Ex. 12), but used in the general sense of the Feast of Unleavened Bread (Lev. 23:5-6) in commemoration of the deliverance from Egypt. The festival began on the eve of the 15th day of Nisan and originally lasted seven days. During this time no leaven was to be found in the Jewish houses. In Deut. 16: 1-8, the command is given to keep the passover in Jerusalem. A lamb was roasted whole, not having a bone broken, and eaten entirely. If all were not eaten, the rest was to be burned. The lamb's blood was to be posted on the door-post.

In the New Testament era the Passover lamb was taken by a representative of the family to the temple to be slain by the priests. After offered, the dressed lamb was taken back home and eaten. It was served with four cups of wine. The blessing of the first cup appears to be reflected in Jesus' blessing the first cup at the Lord's Supper (Luke 22:17). Paul said that Christ was our Passover, sacrificed for us (I Cor. 5:7).
it is the Lord's *p.*, Ex. 12:11.
a lamb was sacrificed, Ex. 12:21.
sacrifice the *p.*, Deut. 16:2.
the killing of the *p.*, II Chr. 30:17.
a feast of seven days, Ezek. 45:21.
make ready the *p.*, Mark 14:16.
eat . . *p.* with . . disciples, Luke 22:11.
p., a feast of . . Jews, John 6:4.
a prisoner was released, John 18:39.
Christ our *p.* . . . sacrificed, I Cor. 5:7.

PAST, aforetime, elapsed.
bitterness is *p.*, I Sam. 15:32.
my days are *p.*, Job 17:11.
winter is *p.* the, Song 2:11.
the harvest is *p.*, Jer. 8:20.
ways *p.* finding out, Rom. 11:33.

PASTOR, *see* **ELDER, BISHOP.**
I will give you *p.*, Jer. 3:15.
eat up all thy *p.*, Jer. 22:22.
Woe . . unto the *p.*, Jer. 23:1.
the *p.* that feed . . people, Jer. 23:2.
evangelists . . *p.* . . . teachers, Eph. 4:11.

PASTURE, feeding, herbage.
lie down in green *p.*, Ps. 23:2.
p. of wilderness, Ps. 65:12.
sheep of thy *p.*, Ps. 74:1.
p. of flocks, Is. 32:14.
feed in good *p.*, Ezek. 34:14.

PATARA, a city on the coast of Lycia in Asia Minor. It is the site of an oracle of Apollo (Acts 21:1).

PATH, way, road, going.
be an adder in *p.*, Gen. 49:17.
angel . . stood in *p.*, Num. 22:24.
shew me the *p.*, Ps. 16:11.
Lord, teach me thy *p.*, Ps. 25:4.
ask for the old *p.*, Jer. 6:16.
made my *p.* crooked, Lam. 3:9.
make his *p.* straight, Matt. 3:3.

PATHROS, the name of upper Egypt as distinguished from Matsor, or lower Egypt (Is. 11:11; Jer. 44:1, 15; Ezek. 30: 14).

PATHRUSIM, a people descended from Mizraim, the son of Ham (Gen. 10:14).

PATIENCE, forbearance, endurance.
Lord, have *p.*, and, Matt. 18:26.
tribulation worketh *p.*, Rom. 5:3.

now the God of *p.*, Rom. 15:5.
minister in *p.*, II Cor. 6:4.
your *p.* and faith, II Thess. 1:4.
faith, charity, *p.*, Titus 2:2.
run with *p.* the race, Heb. 12:1.
suffering and *p.*, James 5:10.
and to temperance *p.*, II Pet. 1:6.
thy works and *p.*, Rev. 2:2.

PATIENTLY, with calmness.
I waited *p.* for, Ps. 40:1.
after *p.* endured, Heb. 6:15.
ye take it *p.*, I Pet. 2:20.

PATMOS, an island in the Aegean Sea
which measures about thirty miles in cir-
cumference. It was here that John was
exiled by Domitian around 93–95 A.D.
He received a revelation from God while
here (Rev. 1:9).

PATRIARCH, a head of a family or tribe
(Acts 7:8; Heb. 7:4).
Jacob begat . . twelve *p.*, Acts 7:8.
the *p.* Abraham, Heb. 7:4.

PATRIMONY, paternal inheritance.
of sale of his *p.*, Deut. 18:8.

PATROBAS, a believer in Rome to whom
Paul sent a greeting (Rom. 16:4).

PATTERN, shape, type, example.
Jesus Christ a *p.*, I Tim. 1:16.
thyself *p.* of good, Titus 2:7.
p. shewed to thee in, Heb. 8:5.
p. of things in heavens, Heb. 9:23.

PAU, a city in Edom and capital of
Hadar (Gen. 36:39).

PAUL, PAULOS, the great apostle to
the gentiles. His name was Saul before he
became a follower of Jesus. Paul means
"little one." Paul was born of Jewish parents who were Roman citizens in Tarsus,
the chief city of Cilicia. He was born of
the tribe of Benjamin and was from the
beginning a child of the law. He was circumcised on the eighth day and later was
taught the Jewish law at the feet of
Gamaliel, the great doctor of the law of
Moses. He had a fine background in
Hellenism. He spoke vernacular Greek
and was acquainted with the Greek poets.
After the Christian movement was under
way he strongly opposed it, consenting
to the stoning of Stephen and seeking out
Christians to bring them into the judg-

ment seat. After his conversion in about
34 A.D., he began preaching Christ.
He began a series of three missionary
journeys about 47 A.D. He visited Jerusalem to discuss the Jewish-Gentile question about 49 A.D. and wrote his first
letter, I Thessalonians, around this date
also. He came to Jerusalem around 57
A.D., was taken captive, spent about two
years as a prisoner in Caesarea, and then
in Rome around 61 A.D. He wrote several of his thirteen letters while in Rome.
He was released from Rome, preached
for a period, and then taken prisoner
again. It is believed that he was beheaded
around 64 or 67 A.D. in Rome.
Saul . . also . . called *P.*, Acts 13:9.
a companion of Barnabas, Acts 13:46.
he was stoned, Acts 14:19.
a companion of Silas, Acts 16:25.
spent time in Athens, Acts 17:16.
he took *P.* girdle, Acts 21:11.
they left beating of *P.*, Acts 21:32.
left *P.* bound, Acts 24:27.
came before Agrippa, Acts 26:1.
P., a servant of Jesus, Rom. 1:1.
was an apostle, II Cor. 1:1.
P., . . prisoner of Jesus, Eph. 3:1.
beloved brother *P.*, II Pet. 3:15.

PAULUS, SERGIUS, *see* **SERGIUS
PAULUS.**

PAVEMENT, *see* **GABBATHA.**

PAVILION, an awning or tent.
drunk in the *p.*, I Kin. 20:16.
hide me in . . *p.*, Ps. 27:5.
secretly in a *p.*, Ps. 31:20.

PAY, render, make complete.
let him *p.* double, Ex. 22:7.
go *p.* my vow, II Sam. 15:7.
wicked *p.* not, Ps. 37:21.
defer not to *p.* it, Eccles. 5:4.
master *p.* tribute, Matt. 17:24.
I will *p.* thee all, Matt. 18:26.
p. tithe of mint, Matt. 23:23.

PEACE, a state of security and tranquil-
ity, a state in contrast to war.
Lord give thee *p.*, Num. 6:26.
p. to thine house, I Sam. 25:6.
lay me down in *p.*, Ps. 4:8.
keep in perfect *p.*, Is. 26:3.
thy *p.* as a river, Is. 48:18.
p., *p.* when is no *p.*, Jer. 6:14.
p. multiplied, Dan. 4:1.
p. one with another, Mark 9:50

on earth *p.*, good will, Luke 2:14.
we have *p.* with God, Rom. 5:1.
the gospel of *p.*, Rom. 10:15.
God author of *p.*, I Cor. 14:33.
spirit in bond of *p.*, Eph. 4:3.
be at *p.* among, I Thess. 5:13.
depart in *p.*, be ye, James 2:16.

PEACEABLE, quiet, at ease.
in *p.* habitation, Is. 32:18.
live *p.* with all, Rom. 12:18.
quiet and *p.* life, I Tim. 2:2.
pure, *p.*, gentle, James 3:17.

PEACE OFFERING, *see* **OFFERING AND SACRIFICE.**

PEACOCK, a bird which is native of the land of India (I Kin. 10:22; II Chr. 9:21). They were imported by ship by King Solomon along with ivory and apes.

PEARL, a precious substance which is found inside the shell of mollusks. Jesus and his message is called "the pearl of great price" (Matt. 13:46), showing its great value to man.
made of coral, or of *p.*, Job 28:18.
cast . . *p.* before swine, Matt. 7:6.
used to adorn women, I Tim. 2:9.
adorns New Jerusalem, Rev. 21:21.

PECULIAR, belonging exclusively to one person or thing.
Israel . . his *p.* treasure, Ps. 135:4.
p. treasure of kings, Eccles. 2:8.
purify . . a *p.* people, Titus 2:14.
ye are . . a *p.* people, I Pet. 2:9.

PEDAHEL, the chief of Naphtali who was chosen to divide the land west of the Jordan (Num. 34:28).

PEDAHZUR, the father of Gamaliel (Num. 1:10; 2:20; 7:54; 10:23).

PEDAIAH, (1) the grandfather of king Josiah (II Kin. 23:36). (2) The son or grandson of Jeconiah, son of king Jehoiakim, and father of Zerubbabel (I Chr. 3:18; 3:19). (3) The father of Joel, the ruler of Manasseh west of the Jordan in the days of David (I Chr. 27:20). (4) The sons of Parosh who helped repair the wall after the return of Nehemiah (Neh. 3:25). (5) A priest, prince or Levite (Neh. 8:4). (6) The Benjamite whose great grandson, Sallu, dwelt in Jerusalem (Neh. 11:7).

PEKAH, the son of Ramaliah and king of Israel. He was originally captain of the army of king Pekahiah, but became king himself by killing the king (II Kin. 15: 25–28).

PEKAHIAH, the son of Menahem, king of Israel. He was killed by Pekah and his murderer reigned in his stead. His reign lasted but two years (11 Kin. 15:22–26).

PEKOD, a symbolic name given to Chaldea (Jer. 50:21; Ezek. 23:33).

PELAIAH, (1) a son of Elivenai, of the family of David (I Chr. 3:24). (2) A priest who explained the law when Ezra read it (Neh. 8:7). (3) A Levite who, with Nehemiah, sealed the covenant (Neh. 10:10).

PELALIAH, a priest who was a descendant of Malchijah (Neh. 11:12).

PELATIAH, (1) the son of Benaiah. Ezekiel, in a vision, saw him die (Ezek. 11:1–13). (2) The name of a captain from Simeon who took part in the war with the Amalekites (I Chr. 4:42). (3) Son of Hananiah, a descendant of Salathiel wore this name (I Chr. 3:21). (4) A chief of the people who signed the covenant after the return to Jerusalem (Neh. 10:22).

PELEG, PHALEC, a son of Eber (Gen. 10:25; 11:16).

PELET, (1) a son of Jahdai (I Chr. 2:47). (2) A son of Azmaveth (I Chr. 12:3).

PELETH, a Reubenite and father of On (Num. 16:1). (2) A descendant of Jerahmeel (I Chr. 2:33).

PELETHITES, the faithful men who belonged to David's bodyguard (II Sam. 15:18–22; 20:7).

PELICAN, a bird which to the Jews was ceremonially unclean (Lev. 11:18). *See* **CORMORANT.**

PELONITE, the name for David's warriors, Helez and Ahijah (I Chr. 11:27,36).

PEN, an instrument used for writing on papyrus with ink (II John 12; III John 13). It was made from a reed. A pen was also a graving tool which was used to cut letters in stone (Job 19:24; Ps. 45:1; Jer. 8:8; 17:1).

PENIEL, *see* **PENUEL.**

PENINNAH, a wife of Elkanah, the father of Samuel the prophet (I Sam. 1:4).

PEN KNIFE, a scribe's knife which was used in sharpening the reed used for writing. Jehoiakim used it to cut up the scroll of Jeremiah's utterances (Jer. 36:23).

PENNY, the rendering of the Greek *denarion,* a silver coin used by the Romans. Its value during the time of Jesus was approximately seventeen cents (Matt. 18:28; 22:19-21). A pence is the same as a penny (Luke 10:35).
for a *p.* a day, Matt. 20:2.
brought .. him a *p.,* Matt. 22:19.
Show me a *p.,* Luke 20:24.
p. worth of bread, John 6:7.

PENTATEUCH, the first five books of the Old Testament, Genesis, Exodus, Leviticus, Numbers, and Deuteronomy.

PENTECOST, one of the three great annual festivals. It is called Pentecost because it falls fifty days after the first day of the Passover. It is also called the Feast of Weeks (Ex. 34:22; Deut. 16:10) since it falls seven weeks after the waving of the barley sheaf on the second day of the Passover. It is also called the Feast of Harvest (Ex. 23:16) and the day of first fruits (Num. 28:26). Leviticus gives the detail of the ritual and sacrifice (23:15-21). The outpouring of the Holy Spirit upon the early church was on Pentecost (Acts 2:1-4).

PENUEL, PENIEL, (1) the place where Jacob wrestled. It is also called Peniel (Gen. 32:30). (2) The name of the chief or father of Gedar (I Chr. 4:4) and a Benjamite mentioned in I Chr. 8:25. He was a son of Shashak.

PENURY, extreme poverty (Luke 21:4); dearth or insufficiency (Prov. 14:23).
talk .. tendeth .. to *p.,* Prov. 14:23.
of her *p.* ... cast in all, Luke 21:4.

PEOPLE, race, tribe, nation.
take you for a *p.,* Ex. 6:7.
a stiffnecked *p.,* Ex. 33:3.
reproach to any *p.,* Prov. 14:34.

p. laden with iniquity, Is. 1:4.
like *p.* like priest, Hos. 4:9.
save his *p.* from sins, Matt. 1:21.
purify a peculiar *p.,* Tit. 2:14.
p. of God, I Pet. 2:10.

PEOR, (1) the god of uncleanness which was worshipped by the Moabites in Mount Peor, sometimes called Baal-Peor (Num. 25:18). (2) A mountain in Moab is called by this name (Num. 23:28; 24:2).

PERAZIM, *see* **BAAL-PERAZIM.**

PERCEIVE, *see* **KNOW.**
p. Lord among, Josh. 22:31.
I cannot *p.* him, Job 23:8.
see ye but *p.* not, Is. 6:9.
p. their wickedness, Matt. 22:18.
p. their thoughts, Luke 5:22.
p. their craftiness, Luke 20:23.
p. thou prophet, John 4:19.
p. we the love of, I John 3:16.

PERDITION, damnation; loss; destruction. The "son of perdition" (II Thess. 2:3) means "the child of appalling destruction and calamity."
but the son of *p.,* John 17:12.
token of *p.,* Phil. 1:28.
in destruction and *p.,* I Tim. 6:9.
draw back into *p.,* Heb. 10:39.

PEREAN, pertaining to Perea.

PERES, *see* **MENE.**

PERESH, a son of Machir, son of Manasseh (I Chr. 7:16).

PEREZ, PHARES, PHAREZ, an ancestor of Jashobeam (Gen. 38:29).

PEREZITES, descendants of Perez.

PEREZ-UZZA, PEREZ-UZZAH, the place where Uzzah died (II Sam. 6:8).

PERFECT, complete, faultless, mature.
p. and just weight, Deut. 25:15.
with a *p.* heart, II Kin. 20:3.
Mark the *p.* man, Ps. 37:37
p. understanding, Luke 1:3.
having .. *p.* knowledge, Acts 24:22
yourselves know *p.,* I Thess. 5:2.
the man .. may be *p.,* II Tim. 3:17.
p. in good works, Heb. 13:21.
that ye may be *p.,* James 1:4.

p. love casteth . . fear, I John·4:18 .
not found thy works *p.*, Rev. 3:2.

PERFECTION, completeness.
find Almighty unto *p.*, Job 11:7.
Zion, *p.* of beauty, Ps. 50:2.
an end of all *p.*, Ps. 119:96.
no fruit to *p.*, Luke 8:14.
let us go on unto *p.*, Heb. 6:1 .

PERFECTLY, completely.
shall consider it *p.*, Jer. 23:20.
made *p.* whole, Matt. 14:36.
expound way . . *p.*, Acts 18:26.
p. joined together, I Cor. 1:10.

PERFORM, do, confirm, fulfill, establish.
I will *p.* the oath, Gen. 26:3.
enter to *p.* service, Num. 4:23 .
I *p.* my word, I Kin. 6:12.
p. not this promise, Neh. 5:13 .
p. thing appointed, Job. 23:14 .
daily *p.* my vows, Ps. 61:8 .
vow a vow and *p.* it, Is. 19:21 .
when I have *p.* this, Rom. 15:28 .
p. it till day of, Phil. 1:6.

PERFORMANCE, completion.
p. of those things, Luke 1:45 .
may be a *p.* also, II Cor. 8:11 .

PERFUME, sweet-smelling compounds
used by the Orientals (Prov. 27:9). The
material used in making it were cassia,
aloes, myrrh, cinnamon, frankincense,
and spikenard. Perfume was used as incense in the sanctuary (Ex. 30:22–38). It
was applied to clothing, person, and
furniture (Ps. 45:8; Prov. 7:17; Song
4:11). *See* INCENSE, OINTMENT.

PERFUMER, a translation in the Revised
Version for apothecary (Ex. 30:35).

PERGA, the capital city of Pamphylia,
located on the river Cestrus. It housed a
temple of Diana or Artemis (Acts 13:13,
14; 14:25). Paul preached there and here
John Mark turned back.

PERGAMOS, PERGAUM, a famous city
of Mysia, located on the river Caicus.
Parchment was first perfected here and a
great library came into existence, containing 200,000 volumes. One of the
seven churches of Asia was in Pergamos
(Rev. 1:11; 2:12).

PERIDA, PERUDA, ancestor of the chil-

dren of the servants of Solomon who
returned from captivity in Babylon (Neh.
7:57).

PERIL, exposure to danger.
nakedness, . . *p.*, or sword, Rom. 8:35.
p. of robbers, II Cor. 11:26.
p. in the wilderness, II Cor. 11:26.
p. among false, II Cor. 11:26.

PERISH, pass away, die.
let the day *p.* wherein, Job 3:3.
Lord, save us, we *p.*, Matt. 8:25 .
whoso believeth not *p.*, John 3:16.
money *p.* with thee, Acts 8:20 .
are to *p.* with using, Col. 2:22 .
not willing that any *p.*, II Pet. 3:9.

PERIZZITE, a tribe in the land of Palestine which was there when the Hebrews
arrived following their exodus. They were
dwellers in the land which was settled by
Abraham and Lot (Gen. 13:7).
the *P.* dwelt then in . . land, Gen. 13:7.
the Canaanites and the *P.*, Gen. 34:30.
I will drive out . . the *P.*, Ex. 33:2.
utterly destroy . . the *P.*, Deut. 20:17.
and they slew . . the *P.*, Judg. 1:5.
to give the land of the . . *P.*, Neh. 9:8.

PERMISSION, concession, liberty.
I speak this by *p.*, I Cor. 7:6 .

PERMIT, allow, suffer, consent to.
tarry if the Lord *p.*, I Cor. 16:7.
we do, if God *p.*, Heb. 6:3 .

PERNICIOUS, destructive.
follow their *p.* ways, II Pet. 2:2.

PERPETUAL, continuing or enduring.
p. statute, Lev. 3:17.
by a *p.* decree, Jer. 5:22.
Why is my pain *p.*, Jer. 15:18.
p. shame, Jer. 23:40.
sleep a *p.* sleep, Jer. 51:39.
a *p.* desolation, Zeph. 2:9.

PERPLEXED, worried, confused.
city of Shushan was *p.*, Esther 3:15.
herds of cattle are *p.*, Joel 1:18.
and he was *p.*, Luke 9:7.

PERPLEXITY, tangled, or confused.
now shall be their *p.*, Mic. 7:4.
distress . . with *p.*, Luke 21:25.

PERSECUTE, to pursue with harassing.
angel of . . Lord *p.*, Ps. 35:6.

p. them with the sword, Jer. 29:18 .
P. and destroy them, Lam. 3:66.
they which are *p*., Matt. 5:10.
the Jews *p*. Jesus, John 5:16.
P., but not forsaken, II Cor. 4:9.
have *p*. us, I Thess. 2:15.

PERSECUTION, act of persecuting or
the state of being persecuted.
there was a great *p*., Acts 8:1.
scattered . . upon the *p*., Acts 11:19.
raised *p*. against Paul, Acts 13:50.
tribulation . . distress . . *p*., Rom. 8:35.
take pleasure . . in *p*., II Cor. 12:10.
faith in . . your *p*., II Thess. 1:4.
what *p*. I endured, II Tim. 3:11.
live godly . . suffer *p*., II Tim. 3:12.

PERSECUTOR, one who persecutes.
deliver me from . . *p*., Ps. 142:6.
revenge me of . . *p*., Jer. 15:15.
my *p*. shall stumble, Jer. 20:11.
p. overtook her, Lam. 1:3.
p . . . swifter than eagles, Lam. 4:19.
Who was before . . a *p*., I Tim. 1:13.

PERSIA, a land bordered on the north by
Media, on the south by the Persian Gulf,
on the west by Elam, and on the east by
Carmania. It was the second world empire, the first being Babylon. Persia,
under Cyrus, defeated Babylon in 539
B.C. After the conquest, Cyrus allowed
the Jews to return home (Ezra 1:1–3).
The royal palace was at Susa or Shushan
(Neh. 1:1, Esther 1:2). Other Persian
rulers who are prominent in the Bible
are Xerxes, called Ahasuerus (Esther 2:
16, 21), and Artaxerxes. Nehemiah was
the latter's cupbearer (Neh. 2:1–8).

PERSIAN, an inhabitant of Persia.
reign of Darius the *P*., Neh. 12:22.
the laws of the *P*., Esther 1:19.
given to the Medes and *P*., Dan. 5:28.

PERSIS, a female disciple in Rome to
whom Paul sends greeting (Rom. 16:12).

PERSON, man, face, being, individual.
regardeth not *p*., Deut. 10:17.
vile *p*. is contemned, Ps. 15:4.
stand up vile *p*., Dan. 11:21.
p. of Christ, II Cor. 2:10.
express image of his *p*., Heb. 1:3.
ye have respect of *p*., James 2:9.

PERSUADE, move, sway, convince.
who shall *p*. Ahab, I Kin. 22:20.

priests *p*. the, Matt. 27:20.
p. them to continue, Acts 13:43.
almost thou *p*. me, Acts 26:28.
I *p*. men or God? Gal. 1:10.
I am *p*. that in thee, II Tim. 1:5.
p. better things, Heb. 6:9.

PERTAIN, to belong; appropriate.
p. unto the kings, I Sam. 27:6.
given . . all that *p*., II Sam. 9:9.
things which *p*. to God, Rom. 15:17.

PERUDA, *see* **PERIDA**.

PERVERSE, perverted or turned about.
thy way is *p*., Num. 22:32.
p. and crooked generation, Deut. 32:5.
he that is *p*., Prov. 14:2.
that hath a *p*. tongue, Prov. 17:20.
mingled a *p*. spirit, Is. 19:14.
speaking *p*. things, Acts 20:30.

PERVERT, divert, misdirect, corrupt.
doth God *p*. judgment? Job 8:3.
foolishness of man *p*., Prov. 19:3.
have *p*. their way, Jer. 3:21.
would *p*. the gospel, Gal. 1:7.

PESTILENCE, plague, epidemic.
lest fall upon us with *p*., Ex. 5:3.
three days *p*., II Sam. 24:13.
for the *p*. that walketh, Ps. 91:6.
before him went *p*., Hab. 3:5.

PESTILENT, pernicious, noxious.
this a *p*. fellow, Acts 24:5.

PESTLE, a blunt instrument used for
crushing grain (Prov. 27:22).

PETER, the surname of Simon, one of the
twelve disciples of Jesus. Jesus gave him
the name of Cephas. He was a fisherman
from Bethsaida. His father was Jona and
his brother was Andrew, the one who
brought him to Jesus. He was noted for
impulsive actions (Matt. 16:22; 26:33).
After his denial of Christ he became a
great stalwart in the Christ's Church
(John 21:15,17; Acts 2–11). It was he
who preached the great sermon on the
day of Pentecost (Acts 2) and he who
converted the first Gentile (Acts 10).
Simon called *P*., Matt. 4:18.
Mother-in-law sick, Matt. 8:14.
Confesses Christ, Matt. 16:16.
Rebukes Christ, Matt. 16:22.
Follows afar, Matt. 26:58.
Hears cock crow, Matt. 26:75.

Rebuked by Jesus, Mark 8:33.
At the transfiguration, Mark 9:2.
At the trial of Jesus, Mark 14:66.
Cuts off ear, John 18:10.
P. stood at the door, John 18:16.
Preaches Repentance, Acts 2:38.
Preaches in Samaria, Acts 8:14.
Conversion of Cornelius, Acts 10:19.
Visited by Paul, Gal. 1:18.
Author of an Epistle, I Pet. 1:1.

PETER, EPISTLES OF, these two general letters by the energetic apostle Peter have as their respective themes "hope" and "knowledge."

I Peter stresses the reality of Christian hope in the face of suffering and testing of faith. The Christian is sustained in persecution by his confident hope of future glory. His example in suffering for right is the Master Himself (1:11; 2:21; 4:1; 5:1).

The keynote of II Peter is knowledge as a defense against misleading false teaching (1:12–21; 2:1; 3:1). Peter urges to Christian growth (1:5–11).

PETHAHIAH, (1) a priest in the days of David (I Chr. 24:16). (2) A Levite who had taken a strange wife (Ezra 10:23). (3) A Levite who regulated the devotions of the people following the reading of the law by Ezra (Neh. 9:5). (4) A man of the family of Zerah of Judah, in the service of Artaxerxes, king of Persia (Neh. 11:24).

PETHOR, a city of Mesopotamia near the Euphrates (Num. 22:5).

PETHUEL, the father of Joel the prophet. (Joel 1:1).

PETITION, a request, entreaty.
grant thee thy p., I Sam. 1:17.
now I ask one p., I Kin. 2:16.
What is thy p., Esther 5:6.
Lord fulfil all thy p., Ps. 20:5.
maketh . . p. three times, Dan. 6:13.

PEULTHAI, PEULLETHAI, a Kohathite, son of Obed-edom (I Chr. 26:5).

PHALEC, the father of Ragau, an ancestor of Jesus (Luke 3:35).

PHALLU, see **PALLU.**

PHALTI, a Benjamite to whom Saul,

king of Israel, gave his daughter, Michal.

PHALTIEL, see **PALTIEL.**

PHANUEL, the father of Anna, the prophetess (Luke 2:36).

PHARAOH, (1) the earliest mentioned is the one during the time of Abraham (Gen. 12:10–20). (2) The Pharaoh of Joseph (Gen. 37:36). (3) The Pharaoh of the oppression "who knew not Joseph," who perhaps was Thutmose III (1479–1447 B.C.). (4) The Pharaoh of the exodus, who was perhaps Rameses II (Ex. 5–14) or his son Amenhotep II. (5) The father-in-law of Solomon (I Kin. 3:1; 9:16; 11:1). (6) The father-in-law of Hadad (I Kin. 11:18). (7) The father-in-law of Mered (I Chr. 4:18). (8) Pharaoh, the ally of the Jews against Sennacherib (Is. 36:6). (9) Pharaoh-Nechoh (Jer. 46:2). (10) The Pharaoh of Jer. 37:5 and Ezek. 29:2, probably Pharaoh-Hophra.

PHARAOH-HOPHRA, the grandson of Pharoh-Necho, and ruler of Egypt from 588 to 569 or 566 B.C. He was an ally of Zedekiah at the time Nebuchadnezzar destroyed Jerusalem and the temple. Jeremiah predicted his overthrow (Jer. 44:30). See **PHARAOH.**

PHARAOH-NECHOH, PHARAOH-NECOH, PHARAOH-NECHO, PHARAOH-NECO, NECHO, NECO, the second king of the 26th dynasty of Egyptian kings. He reigned about 609–593 B.C. Pharaoh-Nechoh defeated Josiah and the Jewish army at the Battle of Megiddo (II Kin. 23:29; II Chr. 35:20–24). He dethroned Jehoahaz, Josiah's successor, and placed Jehoiakim on the throne (II Kin. 23:30–37; II Chr. 36:1–4). Nebuchadnezzar defeated Pharaoh-Nechoh at the Battle of Carchemish (Jer. 46:2).

PHARES, see **PHAREZ.**

PHAREZ, PEREZ, the elder son of Judah by Tamar, his daughter-in-law (Gen. 38:29).

PHARISEE, the name is derived in the separation of the group from the main body of the Israelites. They insisted upon following the traditions of the elders, characterized by Paul as the "most straitest sect of our religion" (Acts 26:5). They were not known as the Pharisees until the time of John Hyrcanus (135–105 B.C.). They should not be thought of as a political "party." They were not like the Herodians who welcomed Roman rule; they were for national independence. However, they did not act fanatical as did the Zealots, and they did not act conciliatory, like the Sadducees. Their main purpose was to preserve traditional Judaism. They believed in spirits, angels, and in the resurrection (Acts 23:8). They insisted upon the literal interpretation of the Law. John the Baptist denounced them as a "generation of vipers" (Matt. 3:7). Jesus describes them as "hypocrites" (Matt. 23:27).

righteousness of the .. *P.*, Matt. 5:20.
came .. scribes and *P.*, Matt. 15:1.
chief priests and *P.*, Matt. 21:45.
P. sit in Moses' seat, Matt. 23:2.
woe unto you .. *P.*, Matt. 23:13.
the disciples of the *P.*, Luke 5:33.
P. besought him to dine, Luke 11:37.
the *P.*, named Nicodemus, John 3:1.
the sect of the *P.*, Acts 15:5.
Paul was a member, Acts 23:6.

PHAROSH, *see* **PAROSH.**

PHARPAR, a river in Damascus (II Kin. 5:12).

PHARZITES, PEREZITES, the family of Pharez, the son of Judah (Num. 26:20).

PHASEAH, *see* **PASEAH.**

PHEBE, PHOEBE, a female servant in the church at Cenchrea (Rom. 16:1).

PHENICE, a harbor on the south of Crete (Acts 27:12).

PHENICIA, *see* **PHOENICIA.**

PHICHOL, a chief captain of Abimelech, king of the Philistines, in the days of Abraham (Gen. 21:22; 26:26).

PHILADELPHIA, means brotherly love. It was a city of Lydia in Asia Minor. It was one of the seven churches to which John's *Revelation* was written (Rev. 1:11; 3:7-13).

PHILEMON, a Christian in Colosse to whom Paul wrote a letter (Philem. 1).

PHILEMON, EPISTLE TO, in this brief but moving letter Paul pleads with Philemon, a Christian slave-owner, to receive kindly his returning slave, Onesimus. Onesimus had previously wronged his master (vs. 18) and run away. Coming to Rome, he was brought into contact with Paul who converted him to Christ. The new Onesimus became very useful to Paul, but Onesimus' duty to return to Philemon was evident.

PHILETUS, one of two persons condemned by Paul for being in error regarding the resurrection (II Tim. 2:17).

PHILIP, (1) a member of the twelve disciples of Jesus. A native of Bethsaida, he was responsible for bringing Nathaniel to Jesus (John 1:43–48). (2) Philip the Evangelist, one of the seven men chosen to serve tables (Acts 6:5). When the disciples were dispersed, he preached in Samaria (Acts 8:4–8). He had four daughters who were able to prophesy (Acts 21:8, 9). (3) The son of Herod the Great (Matt. 14:3; Luke 3:1). *See* **HEROD.** (4) The name of the tetrarch of Iturea (Luke 3:1). *See* **HEROD.**

PHILIPPI, a chief city on the border of Macedonia (Acts 16:12; 20:6), located about seventy miles northeast of Thessalonica. It was the home of Lydia. Paul visited the city while on his mission travels (Acts 16:12), established a church there and later addressed the letter of Philippians to it.

PHILIPPI, CAESAREA, *see* **CAESAREA PHILIPPI.**

PHILIPPIANS, EPISTLE TO, written by Paul (1:1) to the Philippian church he had established (Acts 16:9–40), this letter exhorts to consistency of Christian living. The theme of the book is joy in Christ (4:4). Paul found cause for rejoicing despite his imprisonment (1:3–30). The believer's example of humble and loyal service is Christ (2:1–30), and disciples should share His attitude (2:5). The source of true joy is Christ in whom men may realize true righteousness (3:1, 9) which cannot be found in Judaism.

PHILISTIA, *see* **PALESTINE.**

PHILISTIAN, belonging to Philistia.

PHILISTINES, PHILISTIM, a powerful nation southwest of the land of Israel. The nation came out of Casluhim (Gen. 10:14). The Caphtorim are identified with the Philistines (Deut. 2:23). They are sometimes connected with Crete (I Sam. 30:14; Ezek. 25:16; Zeph. 2:5). They are not mentioned in the New Testament. Samson fought them single-handedly (Judg. 14:16). They captured the ark, but returned it at the outbreak of a plague (I Sam. 4–6). A famous stone, called Ebenezer was sent up to them by Samuel in commemoration of a victory over them (I Sam. 7:11, 12). Jonathan defeated them at Geba and Michmash (I Sam. 13:1–3; 14:1–23). They defeated Saul at Mount Gilboa (I Sam. 31). David then made war with them (II Sam. 5:2–25) although he had sought refuge among them earlier (I Sam. 21:10–15). Hezekiah and Uzziah were successful against them (II Kin. 18:8; II Chr. 26:6). Their chief god was Dagon (I Sam. 5:2–5).

PHILOLOGUS, a disciple in Rome to whom Paul sent greeting (Rom. 16:15).

PHILOSOPHY, see **STOIC, EPICUREAN.**

PHINEAS, PHINEHAS, (1) a son of Eleazar (Ex. 6:25). (2) The younger son of Eli (I Sam. 1:3; 2:34; 4:11, 19–22). (3) The father of a certain Eleazar (Ezra 8:33).

PHLEGON, a disciple at the church in Rome (Rom. 16:14).

PHOEBE, see **PHEBE.**

PHOENICIA, PHENICIA, PHENICE, an area on the Mediterranean coastland, about 150 miles long and lying north of Galilee. Their ancestors were called Zidonians (Sidonians) from Sidon, and were of the same people as the ancient Canaanites. Their geographical boundaries made them sea-faring people. They first colonized Carthage, and came close to defeating Rome. Tyre (Ezek. 27, 28) was its most important commercial city. It was from Tyre that David and Solomon received expert help and materials for the construction of the temple. King Hiram sent cedars and craftsmen (II Sam. 5:11; I Kin. 5:1–10). Jezebel was a Phoenician (I Kin. 16:31). Christians fled

to this area after the death of Stephen (Acts 11:19). Paul passed through this area as mentioned in Acts 15:3.

PHOENICIAN, pertaining to **Phoenicia.**

PHOENIX, PHENICE, a harbor in which Paul's ship wintered. It was on the southern coast of Crete (Acts 27:12).

PHRYGIA, an inland province of Asia Minor which was under Roman control in the days of the apostles. Paul traveled throughout the province in his preaching (Acts 16:6). The leading cities were: Laodicea, Hierapolis, Colossae and Antioch of Pisidia.

PHURAH, PURAH, a servant of Gideon (Judg. 7:10).

PHUT, see **PUT.**

PHUVAH, PUA, PUAH, (1) the second son of Issachar (Gen. 46:13; Num. 26:23; I Chr. 7:1). (2) The father of Tola, who judged Israel after the death of Abimelech (Judg. 10:1).

PHYGELLUS, PHYGELUS, a disciple of Asia who turned away from Paul (II Tim. 1:15).

PHYLACTERY, FRONTLET, a small case made of leather worn by some of the Jewish leaders in the days of Jesus. The case was worn on the forehead and left arm and contained compartments in which scriptural quotations were placed (Ex. 13:1–10; Deut. 6:4–9; 11:13–21). Jesus rebuked the Pharisees for ostentatiously wearing excessively large phylacteries (Matt. 23:5).

PHYSICIAN, doctor. See **MEDICINE.**
no *p.* in Gilead?, Jer. 8:22.
whole need not a *p.*, Matt. 9:12.
had suffered much of *p.*, Mark 5:26.
p. heal thyself, Luke 4:23.
Luke the *p.*, Col. 4:14.

PIBESETH, a town in lower Egypt which is about forty-five miles northeast of Cairo (Ezek. 30:17).

PICTURE, likeness, setting, painting.
apples of gold in *p.*, Prov. 25:11.
on all pleasant *p.*, Is. 2:16.

PIECE, part, fragment; a coin.

rent clothes in two *p.*, II Kin. 2:12.
tear you in *p.*, Ps. 50:22 .
thirty *p.* of silver, Matt. 27:3.
found *p.* I lost, Luke 15:9.

PIERCE, stab, penetrate.
p. my hands and feet, Ps. 22:16.
soldiers *p.* his side, John 19:34.
Word is quick, *p.*, Heb. 4:12.

PIETY, reverence for God.
shew *p.* at home, I Tim. 5:4.

PIGEON, *see* **DOVE.**

PIHAHIROTH, the last place in Egypt
where the Hebrews stopped before going
through the Red Sea (Ex. 14:2,9; Num.
33:7,8).

PILATE, PONTIUS, the fifth Roman
procurator of Judea, Samaria, and Idumea (26–36 A.D.). He was unwilling to
condemn Jesus as a malefactor (John
18:30, 38), and when he found out that
Jesus was a Galilean, he tried to turn the
case over to Herod Antipas, tetrarch of
Galilee, who was in Jerusalem at that
time (Luke 23:6–11). It was practice to
release a prisoner on the Passover, and
Pilate suggested that Jesus be the one.
The Jews refused (John 18:39, 40). Pilate
then washed his hands as a sign that he
was not taking the responsibility, although he continually allowed his soldiers to strip and mock him (Matt. 27:
24–31). It was probably because he was
an opportunist that he delivered Jesus over
to be crucified (John 19:6–16). He was later
summoned to Rome to answer charges
against his administration, but Emperor
Tiberius died before Pilate arrived.
delivered him to . . *P.*, Matt. 27:2.
P. commanded the body, Matt. 27:58
P. . . . released Barabbas, Mark 15:15.
was governor of Judea, Luke 3:1.
P. . . . Am I a Jew, John 18:35.

PILDASH, the sixth son of Nahor, the
brother of Abraham (Gen. 22:22).

PILEHA, PILHA, a man or family who
sealed the covenant (Neh. 10:24).

PILGRIMS, wanderers, travellers.
strangers and *p.*, Heb. 11:13.
as *p.* abstain from, 1 Pet. 2:11 .

PILHA, *see* **PILEHA.**

PILL, to peel off, rind (Gen. 30:38).

PILLAR, (1) the support for roofs and the
upper structure of buildings, especially
large ones. (2) The column of cloud and
the column of fire which guided and protected the Hebrews (Ex. 13:21; Judg.
16:26). (3) A stone set up in memory of a
great event was called a pillar. The
memorial at Gilgal (Josh. 4:5–9), the
Ebenezer of Samuel (I Sam. 7:12), and
the pillar of Absalom (II Sam. 18:18) are
a few examples.

PILLOW, anything placed under the head
while reclining.
even a *p.* of stone, Gen. 35:14.
by day . . *p.* of a cloud, Ex. 13:21.
by night . . *p.* of fire, Ex. 13:21 .
p. of shittim wood, Ex. 26:37.
cloudy *p.* descended, Ex. 33:9.

PILOT, guide, director.
wise men were thy *p.*, Ezek. 27:8.
p. of the sea shall, Ezek. 27:29.

PILTAI, a priest of Jerusalem (Neh.
12:7).

PINE, several varieties of pine grew upon
Mt. Lebanon. Some think that each
variety may not have been a conifer. One
variety may have been an elm.
the *p.*, and . . box tree, Is. 41:19.
p. . . . and myrtle branches, Neh. 8:15.

PINE, dry up; be consumed.
you shall *p.* away, Lev. 26:39.
and we *p.* away, Ezek. 33:10.
teeth, and *p.* away, Mark 9:18.

PINNACLE, a high point of the temple to
which Satan took Jesus and offered him
the land in sight in return for the homage
which he desired Jesus to pay him (Matt.
4:5; Luke 4:9).

PINON, an Edomite duke of the family of
Esau (Gen. 36:41; I Chr. 1:52).

PIPE, a wind instrument which might
consist of one reed which was blown with
the breath or two reeds played with both
hands. Several notes could be rendered
from it (I Sam. 10:5; I Kin. 1:40).
heart . . sound like *p.*, Jer. 48:36.
whether *p.* or harp, I Cor. 14:7.

PIRAM, a king of the Amorites or Canaanites (Josh. 10:3).

PIRATHON, a hill of the Amalekites in Ephraim (Judg. 12:13–15).

PIRATHONITE, an inhabitant of **Pirathon** (Judg. 12:13; II Sam. 23:30).

PISGAH, a ridge of the Abarim mountains, of which Nebo is the highest peak. Sihon took the area from Moab. The ridge overlooks the northeastern end of the Dead Sea (Deut. 3:17; 32:49; 34:1). Here Moses viewed the promised land and died (Deut. 3:27; 34:1–5).

PISHON, see **PISON.**

PISIDIA, a province of Asia Minor through which Paul and Barnabas passed (Acts 13:14; 14:24).

PISON, PISHON, one of the four rivers of Eden (Gen. 2:11).

PISPAH, an Asherite, a son of Jether (I Chr. 7:38).

PIT, well, opening, deep hole.
and cast him in *p.*, Gen. 37:20.
p. wherein is water, Lev. 11:36.
hid in some *p.*, II Sam. 17:9.
shall go down to *p.*, Job 17:16.
shall fall into *p.*, Jer. 48:44.
have ox fall into *p.*, Luke 14:5.

PITCH, see **BITUMEN.**

PITCHER, an earthenware jar with one or two handles.
let down thy *p.*, Gen. 24:14.
with empty *p.*, Judg. 7:16.
man bearing *p.*, Luke 22:10.

PITHOM, a city built by the Hebrews for Pharaoh while held captives in Egypt (Ex. 1:11).

PITHON, a descendant of Saul through Jonathan (I Chr. 8:35, 9:41).

PITY, have compassion, sympathy.
have *p.* upon me, Job 19:21.
hath *p.* upon poor, Prov. 19:17.
I will not *p.* nor, Jer. 13:14.
Lord *p.* his people, Joel 2:18.
p. on the gourd, Jonah 4:10.
I had *p.* on thee, Matt. 18:33.

PLACE, site, seat, spot.
p. whereon standest, Ex. 3:5.
p. of understanding, Job 28:12.
thou art my hiding *p.*, Ps. 32:7.
where *p.* of my rest? Is. 66:1.
p. where Lord lay, Matt. 28:6.
my word hath no *p.*, John 8:37.
Judas knew the *p.*, John 18:2.
p. unto wrath, Rom. 12:19.
neither *p.* to devil, Eph. 4:27.

PLACE, HIGH, see **HIGH PLACE.**

PLACE, HOLY, see **TABERNACLE, TEMPLE.**

PLAGUE, an affliction, stroke, smiting, scourging, or stroke used generally to punish sinful people. It might take several forms. A plague was first used in connection with Pharaoh and Abraham and Sarah (Gen. 12:17). The outstanding plagues were the ten which smote Egypt in the days of Moses and Aaron (Ex. 7:8–12:31). David's act of numbering the people of Israel was followed by a plague (Chr. 21). In the New Testament the word is used for specific diseases, as the issue of blood (Mark 3:10; 5:29; Luke 7:21).

PLAIN, see **ARABAH, LOWLAND.**

PLAIN, straight, clear, simple.
lead me in a *p.* path, Ps. 27:11.
way of righteous *p.*, Prov. 15:19.
rough places *p.*, Is. 40:4.
loosed, spake *p.*, Mark 7:35.

PLAIN, CITIES OF THE, see **CITIES OF THE PLAIN.**

PLAINLY, clearly, distinctly.
write law *p.*, Deut. 27:8.
letter . . *p.* read, Ezra 4:18.
stammerers speak *p.*, Is. 32:4.
I will show you *p.*, John 16:25.
such things declare *p.*, Heb. 11:14.

PLAIN, SEA OF THE, see **DEAD SEA.**

PLAISTER, PLASTER, a kind of cement (Dan. 5:5). It was also a medication composed of figs which was applied to boils (Is. 38:21).

PLANE-TREE, CHESTNUT, CHESNUT, a tree which has leaves similar to a sycamore (Gen. 30:37; Ezek. 31:8).

PLANT, shrub, shoot, young tree.
God made every *p.*, Gen. 2:5.
sons may be as *p.*, Ps. 144:12.
p., my Father hath not, Matt. 15:13.

PLASTER, *see* MORTAR.

PLATE, flat piece of metal.
p. or pure gold, Ex. 28:36.

PLATTER, flat shallow dish.
outside of cup and *p.*, Matt. 23:25.
clean outside of *p.*, Luke 11:39.

PLAY, perform, act a part, deride.
people rose up to *p.*, Ex. 32:6.
let men arise and *p.*, II Sam. 2:14.
when the minstrel *p.*, II Kin. 3:15.
p. skilfully with a, Ps. 33:3.
p. well on instrument, Ezek. 33:32.

PLEA, cause, defense, argument.
between *p.* and *p.*, Deut. 17:8.

PLEAD, strive, urge, defend, reason.
will ye *p.* for Baal? Judg. 6:31.
Lord *p.* my cause, I Sam. 24:15.
p. my cause, O Lord, Ps. 35:1.
p. with your mother, Hos. 2:2.

PLEASANT, desirable, grateful.
how good and how *p.*, Ps. 133:1.
words of . . pure are *p.*, Prov. 15:26.
I ate no *p.* bread, Dan. 10:3.
their *p.* houses, Mic. 2:9.
shall offering be *p.*, Mal. 3:4.

PLEASE, delight, make glad, gratify.
Balaam saw it *p.* Lord, Num. 24:1.
speech *p.* the Lord, I Kin. 3:10.
Lord is well *p.*, Is. 42:21.
p. with thousands, Mic. 6:7.
in whom I am well *p.*, Matt. 3:17.
flesh cannot *p.* God, Rom. 8:8.

PLEASURE, delight, good.
p. in uprightness, I Chr. 29:17.
he that loveth *p.*, Prov. 21:17.
I have no *p.* in them, Eccles. 12:1.
p. of the Lord prosper, Is. 53:10.
Father's *p.* to give, Luke 12:32.
p. in infirmities, II Cor. 12:10.
according to good *p.*, Eph. 1:5.
she that liveth in *p.*, I Tim. 5:6.
lovers of *p.* more, II Tim. 3:4.
soul shall have no *p.*, Heb. 10:38.
enjoy *p.* of sin, Heb. 11:25.

PLEDGE, surety. *See* LOAN.

raiment to *p.*, Ex. 22:26.
millstone to *p.*, Deut. 24:6.
take a *p.* of the poor, Job 24:9.
debtor his *p.*, Ezek. 18:7.
if wicked restore *p.*, Ezek. 33:15.
clothes laid to *p.*, Amos 2:8.

PLEIADES, a brilliant constellation of
seven stars. They appear in the constellation Taurus. Its appearance was
a sign of spring (Job 9:9; 38:31; Amos
5:8).

PLENTEOUS, fat, abundant, ample.
fifth part in *p.* years, Gen. 41:34.
Lord, *p.* in mercy, Ps. 86:5.
shall fat and *p.*, Is. 30:23.
harvest truly is *p.*, Matt. 9:37.

PLENTIFUL, fruitful, copious.
God didst send a *p.*, Ps. 68:9.
joy out of *p.* field, Is. 16:10.
into *p.* country, Jer. 2:7.

PLENTY, abundance, enough, sufficient.
seven years of *p.*, Gen. 41:29.
in power and *p.*, Job 37:23.
barns filled with *p.*, Prov. 3:10.
eat in *p.* and praise, Joel 2:26.

PLOW, PLOUGH, a farming implement
which consisted of a pole attached to a
yoke, the plowshare being a piece of
wood driven through the end (Is. 28:24).
It was pulled by an ox and manipulated
by the hands. It could make but a very
shallow furrow (Job 1:14; Luke 9:62).
It was illegal to plow with an ox and an
ass hitched together (Deut. 22:10). The
twelve oxen associated with Elisha's
plowing were doubtless hitched to several
plows, each with its plowman (I Kin.
19:19, 20).

PLUCK, pull, snatch, pick, draw.
p. down high places, Num. 33:52.
mayest *p.* ears, Deut. 23:25.
p. out of dwelling, Ps. 52:5.
time to *p.* up, Eccles. 3:2.
a brand *p.* out, Zech. 3:2.
eye offend *p.* it out, Matt. 5:29.
and *p.* ears of corn, Luke 6:1.
would *p.* out own eyes, Gal. 4:15.

POCHERETH, *see* POCHERETH-
HAZZEBAIM.

POCHERETH-HAZZEBAIM, some of
Solomon's servants who returned from

exile with Zerubbabel (Ezra 2:57; Neh. 7:59).

POETRY, the New Testament is written in prose; the Old Testament has at least six whole books and parts of some parts of the others which are poetry. Psalms, Proverbs, Song of Solomon, Lamentations, and Job are, except for a few verses, entirely poetry. Among the earliest Biblical poems are the songs of Moses and Deborah (Deut. 32:1–43; Judg. 5).

POINT, sharp end, instant.
with *p.* of diamond, Jer. 17:1.
p. of sword against, Ezek. 21:15.
in all *p.* tempted, Heb. 4:15.

POISON, harmful, deadly (Ps.140:3).
the *p.* of serpents, Deut. 32:24.
the *p.* of dragons, Deut. 32:33.
p. is under their lips, Ps. 140:3.
the *p.* of asps, Rom. 3:13.
full of deadly *p.*, James 3:8.

POLICY, skill, cunning, wisdom.
p. cause craft to, Dan. 8:25.

POLISH, to buff, smooth.
p. after similitude, Ps. 144:12.
in color to *p.* brass, Dan. 10:6.

POLL, a person in a number or list.
every man by their *p.*, Num. 1:2.
the names, by their *p.*, Num. 1:20.
he *p.* his head, II Sam. 14:26.
only *p.* their heads, Ezek. 44:20.

POLLUX, *see* CASTOR.

POMEGRANATE, a fruit tree usually standing between ten and twelve feet high. Its fruit has a red rind and pulp. It has many seeds in the pulp (Num. 13:23; Deut. 8:8; Song 4:3,13; Joel 1:12).
make *p.* of blue, Ex. 28:33.
fig trees, and *p.*, Deut. 8:8.
two rows of *p.*, II Chr. 4:13.
ninety and six *p.*, Jer. 52:23.
p., and the olive tree, Hag. 2:19.

POMMEL, a bowl or oil vessel. They were used as ornaments of the chapiter of a column (II Chr. 4:12,13).

POMP, pride, display, show.
p. is brought to grave, Is. 14:11.

make *p.* to cease, Ezek. 7:24.
p. of Egypt, Ezek. 32:12.

PONDER, consider, think, deliberate.
p. path of thy feet, Prov. 4:26.
p. all his goings, Prov. 5:21.
Lord *p.* the hearts, Prov. 21:2.
Mary *p.* them in heart, Luke 2:19.

PONTIUS, PILATE, *see* PILATE, PONTIUS.

PONTUS, a Roman province in northeastern Asia Minor. It was the home of Aquila, the disciple at Corinth (Acts 18:2). When Peter preached the great Pentecostal sermon, Jews from Pontus were there to hear (Acts 2:9).

POOL, a rather small body of water which obtained its supply from the springs or from the rain, although it is sometimes a stagnant body of water. It is occasionally translated "pond" (Ex. 7:19; 8:5). Among the artificial ponds were the pools of Gibeon, Hebron, Samaria, Bethesda, and Siloam (II Sam. 2:13; 4:12; I Kin. 22:38; John 5:2; 9:7). King Hezekiah constructed a pool, with an aqueduct leading to Jerusalem (II Kin. 20:20).

POOR, those in poverty. The law of Moses protected these persons (Deut. 15:7–11). In the first place, the considerable debts of the poor were waived in the years of Jubilee (Lev. 25, 27:14–25). Also, a poor person, if hungry, was permitted to eat in the field or vineyard of another (Deut. 23:24,25). After the reapers cut the grain in the field the poor were allowed to glean after them. They could also gather fruit which harvesters left on the tree (Lev. 19:9,10; 23:22; Deut. 24:19–21). The prophets denounced the people of means because the poor had been neglected or mistreated (Is. 1:23; 10:2; Ezek. 22:7,29; Mal. 3:5). In the New Testament there are similar injunctions (Luke 3:11; 14:13; Acts 6:1; Gal. 2:10).
that the *p.* . . . may eat, Ex. 23:11.
But he saveth the *p.*, Job 5:15.
He raised up the *p.*, Ps. 113:7.
first born of the *p.*, Is. 14:30.
the *p.* of the land, Jer. 52:16.
the *p.* in spirit, Matt. 5:3.
give to the *p.*, Mark 10:21.
should remember the *p.*, Gal. 2:10.
ye have despised the *p.*, James 2:6.

POPLAR, a tree common to Palestine (Hos. 4:13).

PORATHA, one of the ten sons of Haman the Agagite (Esther 9:8).

PORCH, see **SOLOMON'S PORCH.**
p. before the temple, I Kin. 6:3.
the pattern of the *p.*, I Chr. 28:11.
the *p.* of the gate, Ezek. 40:7.
between . . *p.* and . . altar, Joel 2:17.
out into the *p.*, Mark 14:68.
pool . . having five *p.*, John 5:2.
the *p.* . . . called Solomon's, Acts 3:11.

PORCIUS, the procurator of the Jews who followed Felix in A.D. 60. He sent Paul to Rome. See **FESTUS PORCIUS.**

PORPOISE, see **BADGERS' SKINS.**

PORTER, one stationed at a gate or at a door, a watchman. They were at the city gates (II Sam. 18:26; II Kin. 7:10), at a private house (Mark 13:34), at the tabernacle (I Chr. 9:22), and at the sheepfolds (John 10:3). David divided the porters into courses or divisions (I Chr. 23:5).

PORTION, share, part, allotment.
given it for *p.*, Lev. 6:17.
double *p.* of spirit, II Kin. 2:9.
p. of wicked, Job 20:29.
Lord is the *p.*, Ps. 16:5.
God my *p.* for ever, Ps. 73:26.
divide *p.* with great, Is. 53:12.
p. of king's meat, Dan. 1:8.
their *p.* in season, Luke 12:42.
p. with unbelievers, Luke 12:46.

POSSESS, acquire, own, control.
seed . . *p.* the gate, Gen. 22:17.
let us go up and *p.*, Num. 13:30.
Israel *p.* all land, Judg. 11:21.
p. the kingdom forever, Dan. 7:18.
nettles shall *p.*, Hos. 9:6.
tithes of all I *p.*, Luke 18:12.
nothing, yet *p.* all, II Cor. 6:10.

POSSESSION, holding.
Canaan I give for *p.*, Lev. 14:34.
to land of your *p.*, Josh. 1:15.
Levites left their *p.*, II Chr. 11:14.
houses of God in *p.*, Ps. 83:12.
give no *p.* in Israel, Ezek. 44:28.

POSSIBLE, able, likely, capable.
all things are *p.*, Matt. 19:26.

p. to him that, Mark 9:23.
if *p.*, as much as, Rom. 12:18.
not *p.* that blood of, Heb. 10:4.

POST, (1) the upright timber to the side of a door (Ex. 21:6; Deut. 15:17). (2) A messenger or a bringer of news (II Chr. 30:6; Esther 3:13, 15).

POSTERITY, succeeding generations.
preserve you a *p.*, Gen. 45:7.
you or of your *p.*, Num. 9:10.
take away thy *p.*, I Kin. 21:21.
his *p.* be cut off, Ps. 109:13.

POT, pans and kettles.
sat by the flesh *p.*, Ex. 16:3.
in a brasen *p.*, Lev. 6:28.
put . . broth in a *p.*, Judg. 6:19.
p. full of wine, Jer. 35:5.
p. in the Lord's house, Zech. 14:20.
the washing of . . *p.*, Mark 7:4.
golden. *p* that had manna, Heb. 9:4.

POTENTATE, one that is able, potent, or powerful. Jesus is called by this title (I Tim. 6:15).

POTIPHAR, Pharaoh's captain of the guard, to whom Joseph was sold by the Midianites (Gen. 37:36).

POTIPHERA, POTIPHERAH, a priest of On (or Heliopolis). He was the father of Asenath, Joseph's wife (Gen. 41:45).

POTSHERD, earthenware. It may denote anything mean and contemptible, or very dry (Is. 30:14; 45:9; Job 2:8).

POTTER, a maker of earthenware. Clay was mixed with water and made soft. It was then put on a spinning wheel, operated by the foot, and molded into form with the hands (Is. 41:25). After it is molded it is baked (Jer. 18:3,4). The figure of the potter molding the clay is used in the Bible to show that God is able to control human affairs. Sometimes the clay is willing and sometimes unyielding (Is. 45:9; Jer. 18:5–12; Rom. 9:20–25).
as the *p.* clay, Is. 29:16.
the *p.* treadeth clay, Is. 41:25.
I do with you as this *p.*, Jer. 18:6.
Cast it unto the *p.*, Zech. 11:13.
and bought . . the *p.* field, Matt. 27:7.
the vessels of a *p.*, Rev. 2:27.

POTTER'S FIELD, *see* **AKELDAMA.**

POUND, (1) a unit of weight which was probably about three times heavier than the modern pound (I Kin. 10:17; Ezra 2:69; Neh. 7:71,72). (2) A sum of money which had a value of a little less than twenty dollars (Luke 19:13–25).

POUR, make flow.
wrath *p.* upon us, II Chr. 34:21.
p. me as milk, Job 10:10.
grace *p.* into lips, Ps. 45:2.
p. out your heart, Ps. 62:8.
p. out my spirit, Prov. 1:23.
p. out soul unto, Is. 53:12.
ointment *p.* on head, Matt. 26:7.
p. out the money, John 2:15.

POVERTY, lack, need, want.
lest thou come to *p.,* Gen. 45:11.
it tendeth to *p.,* Prov. 11:24.
neither *p.* nor riches, Prov. 30:8.
deep *p.* abounded, II Cor. 8:2.
thy works and *p.,* Rev. 2:9.

POWDER, fine crushed dust.
Moses ground it to *p.,* Ex. 32:20.
make rain of land *p.,* Deut. 28:24.
stamped . . grove to *p.,* II Kin. 23:6.
grind him to *p.,* Matt. 21:44.

POWER, might, strength, authority.
p. to get wealth, Deut. 8:18.
God is my *p.,* II Sam. 22:33.
p. of the grave, Ps. 49:15.
p. of thine anger, Ps. 90:11.
p. of the tongue, Prov. 18:21.
p. on earth to forgive, Matt. 9:6.
his word was with *p.,* Luke 4:32.
the *p.* of darkness, Luke 22:53.
p. to become sons of, John 1:12.
p. to lay it down, John 10:18.
receive *p.* after Holy, Acts 1:8.
his eternal *p.* and, Rom. 1:20.
p. of his resurrection, Phil. 3:10.
had *p.* of death, Heb. 2:14.
p. of . . endless like, Heb. 7:16.

POWERFUL, strong, effective, mighty.
voice of the Lord is *p.,* Ps. 29:4.
his letters are *p.,* II Cor. 10:10.
word of God is quick, *p.,* Heb. 4:12.

PRAETOR, a Roman magistrate, next in rank to the consul. After 367 B.C. the number of praetors was increased from one to sixteen. Their duties were originally judicial. However, in the New Testament they were more like governors (Acts 16:20, 35, 38).

PRAETORIAN GUARD, *see* **PRAETORIUM.**

PRAETORIUM, the official headquarters of a Roman procurator. The palace of Pontius Pilate, in Jerusalem, was called by this name (Matt. 27:27; Mark 15:16). Jesus was led to this place by the soldiers, after he was scourged. This translation appears only once in the Authorized Version (Mark 15:16) and several times in the Revised Version (Matt. 27:27; John 18:28; 19:9), being once translated Praetorian Guard (Phil. 1:13).

PRAISE, homage, thanksgiving.
who is like thee in *p.,* Ex. 15:11.
sing *p.* to thy name, II Sam. 22:50.
exalted above *p.,* Neh. 9:5.
earth . . full of his *p.,* Hab. 3:3.
give God the *p.,* John 9:24.
Paul, Silas sang *p.,* Acts 16:25.
p. is in gospel, II Cor. 8:18.
found unto *p.* and honor, I Pet. 1:7.

PRAISE, to extol, give thanks.
brethren shall *p.,* Gen. 49:8.
fear Lord, *p.* him, Ps. 22:23.
I shall yet *p.* him, Ps. 42:5.
dead *p.* not Lord, Ps. 115:17.
another man *p.* thee, Prov. 27:2.
living shall *p.,* Is. 38:19.
disciples began *p.,* Luke 19:37.

PRATE, PRATING, to talk about one with no constructive motive in mind. It may be prompted by malice (III John 10) or by stupidity or ignorance (Prov. 10:8).

PRAY, petition, entreat, implore, ask.
sin in ceasing to *p.,* I Sam. 12:23.
p. for life of king, Ezra 6:10.
p. for the peace of, Ps. 122:6.
p. to Father which is, Matt. 6:6.
Lord teach us to *p.,* Luke 11:1.
I will *p.* the Father, John 14:16.
p. God, if perhaps, Acts 8:22.
p. without ceasing, I Thess. 5:17.
p. one for another, James 5:16.

PRAYER, man's communion with his creator, the highest expression of man's religious nature. From the beginning of the Bible to the end, prayer plays a major role. In Gen. 4:26 "men began to call upon the name of the Lord." In Gen.

12:8, 13:4 Abram prayed to the Lord. He prayed for his son (Gen. 15:2, 3) and for Ishmael (Gen. 17:18). He prayed for Sodom (Gen. 18:23–32) and for Abimelech's fruitfulness (Gen. 20:17, 18).

Some of the great prayers of the Old Testament are Moses' prayer for Israel (Ex. 32:11–13), Joshua's prayer after the defeat at Ai (Josh. 7:7–9), Samuel's prayer for help (Judg. 16:28), Hannah's prayer for a son (I Sam. 1:10, 11), and many of the Psalms. Solomon prayed for wisdom (I Kin. 3:6–9).

The New Testament teaches us how to pray. We must not pray to be seen of men, but should pray in private for the things we need, knowing that God is aware of our needs even before we ask (Matt. 6:5–8). Jesus taught his disciples how to pray (Matt. 6:9–13). As Jesus died on the cross he prayed for murderers (Luke 23:34). The last prayer in the Bible is for Jesus to return quickly (Rev. 22:20).

my *p*. is pure, Job 16:17.
give ear unto my *p*., Ps. 17:1.
poured out a *p*., Is. 26:16.
A *p*. of Habakkuk, Hab. 3:1.
sanctified by .. *p*., I Tim. 4:5.
the *p*. of faith, James 5:15.
watch unto *p*., I Pet. 4:7.
the *p*. of saints, Rev. 5:8.

PRAYER OF MANASSES, one of the books of the Apocrypha.

PREACH, herald, proclaim.
I have *p*. righteousness, Ps. 40:9.
p. good tidings unto, Is. 61:1.
Jesus began to *p*., Matt. 4:17.
p. kingdom of God, Luke 9:60.
p. Christ unto them, Acts 8:5.
p. in synagogue, Acts 9:20.
p. except be sent? Rom. 10:15.
p. Christ crucified, I Cor. 1:23.
other gospel than we *p*., Gal. 1:8.
Christ is *p*., I rejoice, Phil. 1:18.
p. unto Gentiles, I Tim. 3:16.
p. unto spirits in, I Pet. 3:19.

PREACHER, herald, one who proclaims.
vanity .., saith *p*., Eccles. 1:2.
how hear without *p*., Rom. 10:14.
I am ordained a *p*., I Tim. 2:7.
p. of righteousness, II Pet. 2:5.

PREACHES, PREACHING, *see* PREACH.

PRECEPT, a charge, doctrine.
commandedst them *p*., Neh. 9:14.
to keep thy *p*., Ps. 119:4.
never forget thy *p*., Ps. 119:93.
I have chosen thy *p*., Ps. 119:173.
p. .. upon *p*., Is. 28:10.
Moses had spoken .. *p*., Heb. 9:19.

PRECIOUS, rare, costly, very valuable.
p. things of heaven, Deut. 33:13.
word of Lord .. *p*., I Sam. 3:1.
redemption .. is *p*., Ps. 49:8.
more *p*. than gold, Is. 13:12.
p. sons of Zion, Lam. 4:2.
waiteth for the *p*. fruit, James 5:7.
exceeding *p*. promises, II Pet. 1:4.
gold and *p*. stones, Rev. 17:4.

PREDESTINATE, mark off, foreordain.
p. to be conformed, Rom. 8:29.
whom he did *p*., Rom. 8:30.
Having *p*. us, Eph. 1:5.
p. according to the, Eph. 1:11.

PRE-EMINENCE, first and foremost.
he might have the *p*., Col. 1:18.
loveth to have the *p*., III John 9.

PREFER, give precedence, select.
p. her and her maids, Esther 2:9.
p. not Jerusalem, Ps. 137:6.
after me *p*. before, John 1:15.
in honour *p*. one, Rom. 12:10.

PREMEDITATE, concern, consider.
neither *p*., but, Mark 13:11.

PREPARATION, the name of the Jewish day just before the Sabbath, Passover, or other religious festivals.
the day of the *p*., Matt. 27:62.
because it was the *p*., Mark 15:42.
the *p*. of the passover, John 19:14.
the Jews' *p*. day, John 19:42.

PREPARE, make ready, equip, arrange.
p. hearts unto the Lord, I Sam. 7:3.
p. city for habitation, Ps. 107:36.
p. ye way of Lord, Is. 40:3.
p. to meet thy God, Amos 4:12.
Lord *p*. great fish, Jonah 1:17.
fire *p*. for devil, Matt. 25:41.
go to *p*. a place for, John 14:2.
Noah *p*. an ark, Heb. 11:7.

PRESBYTERY, a body of elders in the church (I Tim. 4:14). The presbytery laid hands on Timothy, the young preacher. *See* ELDER, BISHOP.

PRESENCE, face, before, nearness.
from *p.* of the Lord, Gen. 3:8.
cut off from my *p.*, Lev. 22:3.
his *p.* with singing, Ps. 100:2.
angel of his *p.*, Is. 63:9.

PRESENT, to offer, to give.
Joseph *p.* himself, Gen. 46:29.
p. to the priest, Lev. 2:8.
Satan came to *p.*, Job 2:1.
p. your bodies a, Rom. 12:1.
p. glorious church, Eph. 5:27.

PRESENT, at hand, now, not absent.
p. help in trouble, Ps. 46:1.
evil is *p.* with me, Rom. 7:21.
p. with the Lord, II Cor. 5:8.
loved *p.* world, II Tim. 4:10.
chastening for *p.*, Heb. 12:11.

PRESENTLY, now, immediately.
fool's wrath is *p.*, Prov. 12:16.
p. fig tree withered, Matt. 21:19.
p. give me more, Matt. 26:53.

PRESERVE, save, keep, defend.
we may *p.* seed, Gen. 19:32.
might *p.* us alive, Deut. 6:24.
Lord *p.* the faithful, Ps. 31:23.
lose . . life shall *p.*, Luke 17:33.
p. blameless unto, I Thess. 5:23.

PRESS, to crowd, to bear down upon.
p. him with words, Judg. 16:16.
Paul . . *p.* in spirit, Acts 18:5.
I *p.* toward mark, Phil. 3:14.

PRESUME, dare, venture.
they *p.* to go up, Num. 14:44.
which *p.* to speak, Deut. 18:20.
durst *p.* in his heart, Esther 7:5.

PRESUMPTUOUS, proud, rash, daring.
prophet spoken *p.*, Deut. 18:22. ·
keep . . from *p.* sins, Ps. 19:13.
p. are they, II Pet. 2:10.

PRETENCE, pretext, show.
p. make long prayers, Mark 12:40.
in *p.* or in truth, Phil. 1:18.

PREVAIL, persuade, triumph, force.
did waters *p.*, Gen. 7:20.
let not man *p.*, Ps. 9:19.
could not *p.* against it, Is. 7:1.
gates of hell not *p.*, Matt. 16:18.
grew word and *p.*, Acts 19:20.

PREVENT, come before, stop.

snares of death *p.*, II Sam. 22:6.
God of mercy shall *p.*, Ps. 59:10.
evil shall not *p.*, Amos 9:10.
Lord shall not *p.*, I Thess 4:15.

PREY, seized food, booty, spoil.
earrings of his *p.*, Judg. 8:24.
lions roar after *p.*, Ps. 104:21.
shall *p.* be taken, Is. 49:24.
lion roar when no *p.*, Amos 3:4.

PRICE, value, hire, worth, wage.
not . . *p.* of dog, Deut. 23:18.
p. of wisdom above, Job 28:18.
wine, milk without *p.*, Is. 55:1.
pearl of great *p.*, Matt. 13:46.
p. of blood, Matt. 27:6.
bought with a *p.*, I Cor. 6:20.
meek spirit . . great *p.*, I Pet. 3:4.

PRICK, a long stick which was approximately nine feet long. It was used to stick cattle in order to move them along. When the cattle would kick at the antagonizers, only the pricks would be touched (Acts 9:5).

PRIDE, arrogance, vanity.
p. shall bring him low, Prov. 29:23.
the *p.* of Moab, Is. 16:6.
Woe to the crown of *p.*, Is. 28:1.
the *p.* of her power, Ezek. 30:6.
p. of thine heart, Obad. 3.
p., foolishness, Mark 7:22.
the *p.* of life, I John 2:16.

PRIEST, a representative of the people to God. He must offer up prayers, thanksgivings, and sacrifices. Before the time of Moses, the father of the family acted as priest (Job 1:5), or the head of the tribe filled this office (Gen. 12:7; 13:18; 26:25; 33:20). At Sinai the tribe of Levi was set apart for the conducting of religious functions. The priesthood became hereditary and in the family of Aaron (Ex. 28:1; 40:12–15; I Kin. 8:4; Ezra 2:36). After Aaron came Eleazar (Num. 20:25–28). Samuel was never called a priest, although he performed the duties of one (I Sam. 9:13). The kings of Israel also performed the priestly duties (II Sam. 6:14–19; I Kin. 8:22; 12:33). David appointed Zadok and Abiathar as priests when he established the priesthood at Jerusalem (II Sam. 20:25). The duties of the priesthood are given in Deut. 33: 8–10.

The priests were sometimes called Levites (Deut. 18:1; Ezek. 44:15). The name Levite is a general term, and some did not perform the particular duties of the priesthood. The Old Testament attaches a great importance to the high priest as a lineal descendant of Aaron (Num. 20:25-29; 25:10-13). Not much is known about the priesthood between the time of Nehemiah and the Maccabean revolt. In the New Testament times the high priest was chosen from the party of the Sadducees. The Jewish priesthood ended in 70 A.D. with the destruction of Jerusalem.

Jesus is called a high priest, even though he was not a Levite. He was of the order of Melchizedek (Heb. 7:11-17).
p. of . . most high God, Gen. 14:18.
the *p.* of Midian, Ex. 2:16.
the *p.*, Aaron's sons, Lev. 1:5.
p. shall wash . . clothes, Num. 19:7.
Eleazar the *p.*, Josh. 14:1.
Eli the *p.* sat, I Sam. 1:9.
the elders of the *p.*, II Kin. 19:2.
the *p.* of Baal, II Chr. 23:17.
p. praised the Lord, II Chr. 30:21.
the children of the *p.*, Ezra 2:61.
p. . . Levites, and . . people, Neh. 10:34.
both prophet and *p.*, Jer. 23:11.
p. . . take of the blood, Ezek. 45:19.
Thou . . a *p.* for ever, Heb. 5:6.
shall be *p.* of God, Rev. 20:6.

PRIESTHOOD, priest's office.
an everlasting *p.*, Ex. 40:15.
p. of Lord their, Josh. 18:7.
hath an unchangeable *p.*, Heb. 7:24.
house, an holy *p.*, I Pet. 2:5.

PRIEST, COURSE OF LEVITES AND, *see* **COURSE OF PRIESTS AND LEVITES.**

PRINCE, one in authority.
twelve *p.* shall he beget, Gen. 17:20.
a *p.* of Midian, Num. 25:18.
p. walking as servants, Eccles. 10:7.
p. of Judah, Jer. 24:1.
p. of the eunuchs, Dan. 1:7.
I will punish the *p.*, Zeph. 1:8.
the *p.* of the devils, Matt. 12:24.
the *p.* of the power, Eph. 2:2.
the *p.* of the kings, Rev. 1:5.

PRINCIPAL, chief, main part, highest.
wisdom is *p.* thing, Prov. 4:7.
p. of flock escape, Jer. 25:35.

against him *p.* men, Mic. 5:5.
p. of the city, Acts 25:23.

PRINCIPALITY, the dominion of a prince or ruler (Jer. 13:18).
your *p.* shall come down, Jer. 13:18.
p., nor powers, nor, Rom. 8:38.
Far above all *p.*, Eph. 1:21.
but against *p.* . . powers, Eph. 6:12.
having spoiled *p.*, Col. 2:15.

PRINT, a stroke, mark or type.
see in . . hands the *p.*, John 20:25.
put . . finger into the *p.*, John 20:25.

PRISCILLA, PRISCA, the wife of Aquila of Pontus. She and her husband came to Corinth when Claudius drove all the Jews out of Rome (49 A.D.). They were close associates of Paul (Acts 18:18).

PRISON, a place of confinement for criminals. The ancient Hebrews did not use prisons in the popular conception of the term. The Egyptians and Philistines did use them (Gen. 39:20,23; 40:3,5; Judg. 16:21,25). In the days of Jeremiah, dungeons and pits were used to hold criminals (Jer. 37:16; 38:6; Zech. 9:11). The Hebrews did use prisons in Jesus' day, but they were patterned after the Roman model. Prison rooms were in Herod's palace (Acts 12:6,10) and in the palace at Caesarea (Acts 26:10).

PRISONER, one bound, confined.
p. rest together, Job 3:18.
despiseth not his *p.*, Ps. 69:33.
released unto them *p.*, Mark 15:6.
and my fellow *p.*, Rom. 16:7.
Paul, *p.* of Jesus Christ, Eph. 3:1.

PRIVATE, one's own, secret.
of *p.* interpretation, II Pet. 1:20.

PRIVATELY, alone, by self, secretly.
disciples came *p.*, Matt. 24:3.
departed by ship *p.*, Mark 6:32.
went *p.* into deserted, Luke 9:10.
with him aside *p.*, Acts 23:19.

PRIVILY, secret, deceit.
sent messengers . . *p.*, Judg. 9:31.
cut off . . skirt . . *p.*, I Sam. 24:4.
Whoso *p.* slandereth, Ps. 101:5.
to put her away *p.*, Matt. 1:19.
they thrust us out *p.*, Acts 16:37.

PRIZE, reward, crown.

one receiveth the *p.*, I Cor. 9:24.
toward mark for *p.*, Phil. 3:14.

PROCEED, go on, go out.
p. out of candle, Ex. 25:35.
p. out of mouth, Deut. 8:3.
law shall *p.* from me, Is. 51:4.
p. from evil to evil, Jer. 9:3.
which *p.* from Father, John 15:26.
corrupt communication *p.*, Eph. 4:29.

PROCHORUS, one of the seven ministers chosen to serve tables in the Jerusalem church (Acts 6:5).

PROCLAIM, call, herald, publish.
p. name of Lord, Ex. 33:19.
p. liberty throughout, Lev. 25:10.
p. a fast, set, I Kin. 21:9.
p. own goodness, Prov. 20:6.
go *p.* these words, Jer. 3:12.
p. upon housetops, Luke 12:3.

PROCONSUL, the governor of a Roman province, translated "deputy" in the Authorized Version (Acts 13:7; 18:12; 19:38).

PROCURATOR, *see* **GOVERNOR.**

PROCURE, to obtain, get.
He that . . seeketh . . *p.*, Prov. 11:27.
Hast thou not *p.* this, Jer. 2:17.
thy doings have *p.*, Jer. 4:18.
we *p.* great evil against, Jer. 26:19.

PRODIGAL SON, the popular designation of one of Jesus' parables (Luke 15:11–32).

PRODUCE, bring forth.
p. your cause saith, Is. 41:21.

PROFANE, desecrate.
a wife that is . . *p.*, Lev. 21:7.
divorced woman, or *p.*, Lev. 21:14.
for the . . unholy and *p.*, I Tim. 1:9.
p. and vain babblings, I Tim. 6:20.
p. person, as Esau, Heb. 12:16.

PROFESS, promise, confess, claim.
I *p.* this day unto, Deut. 26:3.
I *p.* I never knew, Matt. 7:23.
p. themselves wise, Rom. 1:22.
some *p.* have erred, I Tim. 6:21.
p. they know God, Titus 1:16.

PROFIT, gain, benefit.
p. if slay our brother, Gen. 37:26.
what *p.* if we pray, Job 21:15.

in labour there is *p.*, Prov. 14:23.
no *p.* under sun, Eccles. 2:11.
teacheth thee to *p.*, Is. 48:17.
what is a man *p.*, Matt. 16:26.
not seeking own *p.*, I Cor. 10:33.
Christ *p.* you nothing, Gal. 5:2.
words to no *p.*, II Tim. 2:14.

PROFITABLE, that which profits, useful.
can man be *p.* to God, Job 22:2.
image *p.* for nothing, Is. 44:10.
godliness *p.* unto all, I Tim. 4:8.
scripture *p.* for, II Tim. 3:16.
p. to thee and me, Philem. 11.

PROLONG, make long, extend.
p. king's life, Ps. 61:6.
hateth covetousness *p.*, Prov. 28:16.
word no more *p.*, Ezek. 12:25.
lives *p.* a time, Dan. 7:12.

PROMISE, assurance, word, hope.
bless you as he *p.*, Deut. 1:11.
his *p.* fail evermore? Ps. 77:8.
p. of my Father, Luke 24:49.
p. of none effect, Rom. 4:14.
receive *p.* of Spirit, Gal. 3:14.
heirs according to *p.*, Gal. 3:29.
p. of life now, I Tim. 4:8.
p. of eternal life, Heb. 9:15.

PROMISED LAND, LAND OF PROMISE, names for Canaan, so-called because God promised it to Abraham (Gen. 15:18; 17:8).

PROMOTE, make high, advance, exalt.
p. thee unto honour, Num. 22:17.
exalt her *p.* thee, Prov. 4:8.
king *p.* Shadrach, Dan. 3:30.

PROMOTION, making high.
p. neither from east, Ps. 75:6.
shame *p.* of fools, Prov. 3:35.

PRONOUNCE, speak, utter, declare.
man *p.* with oath, Lev. 5:4.
p. clean or unclean, Lev. 13:59.

PROOF, trial, test, evidence.
alive by many *p.*, Acts 1:3.
p. of your love, II Cor. 8:24.
make full *p.* of, II Tim. 4:5.

PROPER, suitable, particular.
p. gift of God, I Cor. 7:7.

saw was *p*. child, Heb. 11:23.

PROPHECY, message, prediction.
he pronounced this *p*., Neh. 6:12.
in them fulfilled *p*., Matt. 13:14.
have gift of *p*., I Cor. 13:2.
sure word of *p*., II Pet. 1:19.
take from *p*. of, Rev. 22:19.

PROPHESY, foretell, expound, interpret.
prophets *p*. falsely, Jer. 5:31.
p. of peace when, Jer. 28:9.
sons shall *p*., Joel 2:28.
well did Esaias *p*., Matt. 15:7.
p. unto us, Christ, Matt. 26:68.
we *p*. in part, I Cor. 13:9.

PROPHET, God's spokesman, the divinely called minister who announced the will of God to his people. Some were called prophets even before the great day of prophecy: Abraham (Gen. 20:7), Aaron was Moses' prophet (Ex. 7:1), and Moses (Deut. 18:15). Samuel was the first of a long line of prophets, and he prophesied about Christ (Acts 3:24).

The prophet was God's representative, and he received his call directly from God (Amos 7:15). The first prophet to write was Amos in the early or middle part of the eighth century B.C. The last was Malachi in the late fifth century B.C. Many utterances of the prophets are repeated in the New Testament and are said to be fulfilled (Matt. 1:23; 8:17; Mark 8:18; Luke 22:20; Rom. 1:17).

Prophecy did not cease with the establishing of the Old Testament Canon. Zacharias, father of John the Baptist, prophesied (Luke 1:67–79); and Simeon (Luke 2:25–35) and Anna (Luke 2:36–38) prophesied. Several at the church at Antioch were called "prophets and teachers" (Acts 13:1). Paul describes prophets as being second to apostles (I Cor. 12:28). Jesus himself was a prophet (Matt. 13:57; 21:11; Luke 13:33).
Aaron . . shall be . . *p*., Ex. 7:1.
God will raise up . . a *p*., Deut. 18:15.
arose not a *p*. since, Deut. 34:10.
p. . . beforetime called a seer, I Sam. 9:9.
the sons of the *p*., I Kin. 20:35.
by his servants the *p*., II Kin. 21:10.
I am against . . *p*., Jer. 23:30.
the word . . came to . . the *p*., Dan. 9:2.
I raised . . sons for *p*., Amos 2:11.
by the former *p*., Zech. 7:7.
send . . Elijah the *p*. before, Mal. 4:5.
the sign of the *p*., Matt. 12:39.

counted John . . a *p*., Mark 11:32.
Art thou that *p*., John 1:21.
have killed thy *p*., Rom. 11:3.
God . . spake . . by the *p*., Heb. 1:1.
mouth of the false *p*., Rev. 16:13.

PROPHETESS, in most cases it means a female prophet.

PROPITIATION, that which appeases or makes atonement, *see* **ATONEMENT**.
a *p*. through faith, Rom. 3:25.
he is the *p*. for . . sins, I John 2:2.
his Son to be the *p*., I John 4:10.

PROPORTION, divisions.
p. of every one, I Kin. 7:36.
p. of faith, Rom. 12:6.

PROSELYTE, a New Testament term which designated a Greek who had been converted to the Hebrew religion (Acts 6:5; 8:27). It seems that the Jews were zealous in propagating their religion (Matt. 23:15). When a Gentile accepted the Jewish religion he had to renounce his previous religious allegiance, submit to circumcision, submit to ceremonial washing, and present a gift before the altar.
Jews and *p*., Acts 2:10.
p. followed Paul, Acts 13:43.

PROSPER, thrive, succeed, increase.
go up and *p*., I Kin. 22:12.
work *p*. in their hands, Ezra 5:8.
God will *p*. us, Neh. 2:20.
he doeth shall *p*., Ps. 1:3.
king reign and *p*., Jer. 23:5.
as God hath *p*., I Cor. 16:2.

PROSPERITY, well-being, success.
not seek their *p*., Deut. 23:6.
p. within palaces, Ps. 122:7.
day of *p*. be joyful, Eccles. 7:14.

PROSPEROUS, made to prosper.
he a *p*. man, Gen. 39:2.
make thy way *p*., Josh. 1:8.
righteousness *p*., Job 8:6.
have *p*. journey, Rom. 1:10.

PROTECTION, defense, hiding, guard.
and be your *p*., Deut. 32:38.

PROTEST, testify, express opposition.
I *p*. unto thee, I Kin. 2:42.
I earnestly *p*., Jer. 11:7.
angel *p*. unto Joshua, Zech. 3:6.

p. by your rejoicing, I Cor. 15:31.

PROUD, full of pride, presumptuous.
respecteth not the *p.*, Ps. 40:4.
rebuked the *p.*, Ps. 119:21.
high look, *p.* heart, Prov. 21:4.
patient better than *p.*, Eccles. 7:8.
God resisteth the *p.*, James 4:6.

PROUDLY, boastfully, haughtily.
talk no more so *p.*, I Sam. 2:3.
mouth speak *p.*, Ps. 17:10.
have spoken *p.*, Obad. 12.

PROVE, verify, demonstrate.
let me *p.* thee this, Judg. 6:39.
examine me, and *p.*, Ps. 26:2.
every man *p.* his work, Gal. 6:4.
p. all things, I Thess. 5:21.

PROVERB, a proverb is an axiom noted for its terseness or conciseness as well as its provocativeness. We are told in I Kin. 4:32 that Solomon was the author of three thousand proverbs.

PROVERBS, BOOK OF, "the proverbs of Solomon the son of David, king of Israel" (1:1) are concise sayings setting forth practical wisdom. In the strictest sense the word means a "repetition or comparison." In addition to its many terse truths, the Book of Proverbs contains didactic poems of longer length. The first nine chapters speak of Wisdom's call (1) and rewards (2–7), and the excellency of Wisdom (8–9). Chapters 10–24 contain various sayings (10:1–22:16) and words to the wise (22:17–24:34); Chapters 25–29 contain Solomon's proverbs set down by Hezekiah's scribes. The book concludes with the words of Agur (30), the words of Lemuel (31:1–9) and a poem in praise of the virtuous wife (31:10–31). The Book of Proverbs exhorts to piety and wisdom.

PROVIDE, prepare, furnish, supply.
God will *p.* lamb, Gen. 22:8.
p. neither gold nor, Matt. 10:9.
p. things honest in, Rom. 12:17.
p. not for house, I Tim. 5:8.

PROVIDENCE, forethought.
done . . by thy *p.*, Acts 24:2.

PROVINCE, an administrative district of a nation. The province of the Bible usually belongs either to Babylonia, Persia or Rome. The term may also be applied to the divisions of the Babylonian or Persian empires (Ezra 2:1; Neh. 7:6; Esther 1:1; 2:3; Dan. 2:49; 3:1, 30).
the *p.* of Judah, Ezra 5:8.
all the king's *p.*, Esther 1:22.
justice in a *p.*, Eccles. 5:8.
in the *p.* of Elam, Dan. 8:2.
of what *p.* he was, Acts 23:34.
Festus . . come into . . *p.*, Acts 25:1.

PROVISION, preparation, supply.
p. for way, Gen. 42:25.
each month made *p.*, I Kin. 4:7.
not *p.* for flesh, Rom. 13:14.

PROVOCATION, angers or irritates.
all the *p.*, II Kin. 23:26.
wrought great *p.*, Neh. 9:18.
Harden . . heart, as in . . *p.*, Ps. 95:8.
presented the *p.*, Ezek. 20:28.

PROVOKE, make angry, irritate, arouse.
obey, *p.* him not, Ex. 23:21.
how oft did they *p.*, Ps. 78:40.
p. to jealousy, Rom. 10:19.
p. not your children. Eph. 6:4.

PRUDENT, have understanding.
p. in matters, I Sam. 16:18.
regardeth reproof . . *p.*, Prov. 15:5.
Woe unto them that are *p.*, Is. 5:21.
for I am *p.*, Is. 10:13.
Who is . . *p.*, Hos. 14:9.

PSALMS, BOOK OF, collection of devotional material spans history from Moses to the exile, and the human spirit from the depths of despair to the heights of triumph. This book is also a prayerbook, for it contains penitent confessions, petitions for aid against afflictions or enemies, ringing affirmations of assurance and trust, thanksgiving for God's lovingkindness, and praise of His power and majesty. Some Psalms give moral instructions; others convey correct attitudes toward life. Ps. 119 praises the Word of God. Although the Psalms are largely devotional or didactic, many of them are also prophetic, and thus are often quoted in the New Testament. Messianic Psalms picture Christ's life, his death and resurrection, his ascension and glorious kingship (Ps. 2, 16, 22, 40, 45, 110, 118). The 23rd Psalm is perhaps the best known chapter of the Bible.

PSALTERY, a stringed instrument.

prophesy with . . *p.*, I Chr. 25:1.
singing with . . *p.*, Neh. 12:27.
awake, *p.* and, Ps. 57:8.
with the *p.* and harp, Ps. 150:3.

PTOLEMAIS, a seaport in Asher between Carmel and Tyre. It is also called Accho. Paul visited the town (Acts 21:7).

PUAH, PUVAH, PHUVAH, PUA, (1) the son of Issachar and founder of the family of the Punites (Gen. 46:13; Num. 26:23; I Chr. 7:1). (2) The father of Tola (Judg. 10:1). (3) A Hebrew midwife (Ex. 1:15).

PUBLICAN, a member of a group of Jews which collected customs for the Romans. They received the right to collect the customs by auction, when they gave security for the amount the government should receive. They were then known to collect more than the required custom for their own profit. They also sold to others certain portions of the revenue. The Jewish publican was a social outcast. Zacchaeus and Matthew were publicans (Luke 19:1,2; Matt. 9:9; Mark 2:14; Luke 5:27).
many *p.* and sinners, Matt. 9:10.
and Matthew the *p.*, Matt. 10:3.
came . . *p.* to be baptized, Luke 3:12.
a great company of *p.*, Luke 5:29.
p., justified God, Luke 7:29.
chief among the *p.*, Luke 19:2.

PUBLISH, proclaim, tell.
p. it not in . . streets, II Sam. 1:20.
should *p.* and proclaim, Neh. 8:15.
and *p.* in Jerusalem, Jer. 4:5.
p. through Nineveh, Jonah 3:7.
p. throughout the . . city, Luke 8:39.

PUBLIUS, the chief man of the island of Melita when Paul was shipwrecked (Acts 28:7,8).

PUDENS, a Christian at Rome who sent greetings by Paul to Timothy (II Tim. 4:21).

PUHITES, PUTHITES, a family in Kirjath-jearim which descended from Caleb, the son of Hur (I Chr. 2:53).

PUL, (1) a king of Assyria who invaded Israel in B.C. 771, but was bribed off. He is identified with Tiglath-Pileser III. *See* **TIGLATH-PILESER.** (2) The name of a place or tribe in Africa (Is. 66:19).

PULL, draw toward one.
sent to *p.* down and, Jer. 1:10.
Let me *p.* out mote, Matt. 7:4.
will *p.* down my barns, Luke 12:18.
might to *p.* down of, II Cor. 10:4.
save with fear, *p.*, Jude 23.

PULSE, seed of a plant resembling the bean or the pea. Daniel and his three companions used it for food while in Babylon (Dan. 1:12,16).

PUNISH, chastise, restrain.
p. the just not good, Prov. 17:26.
p. you according to, Jer. 21:14.
p. them for their ways, Hos. 4:9.
how they might *p.*, Acts 4:21.

PUNISHMENT, the act of chastisement upon an offender. There are various methods of punishment mentioned in the Bible. *See* **HANGING, CRUCIFIXION, GALLOWS, PRISON, SCOURGE, STONING.**
my *p.* greater than, Gen. 4:13.
of wrath suffer *p.*, Prov. 19:19.
into everlasting *p.*, Matt. 25:46.
sufficient is this *p.*, II Cor. 2:6.

PUNITES, the family of Pua, son of Issachar (Num. 26:33).

PUNON, a stopping place for the Hebrews just before they entered the land of Moab (Num. 33:42,43).

PUR, *see* **PURIM.**

PURAH, PHURAH, a servant of Gideon (Judg. 7:10,11).

PURCHASE, to buy, to acquire.
p. a field with, Acts 1:18.
gift of God may be *p.*, Acts 8:20.
p. with . . own blood, Acts 20:28.
redemption of *p.*, Eph. 1:14.

PURE, genuine, true, simple.
bring thee *p.* oil, Ex. 27:20.
mercy seat of *p.* gold, Ex. 37:6.
My doctrine is *p.*, Job 11:4.
words of . . Lord . . *p.*, Ps. 12:6.
p. in their own eyes, Prov. 30:12.
Blessed . . the *p.* in heart, Matt. 5:8.
keep thyself *p.*, I Tim. 5:22.
Unto the *p.* all things, Titus 1:15.

p. religion and, James 1:27.
wisdom . . is first *p.*, James 3:17.
the city was *p.* gold, Rev. 21:18.

PURENESS, purity, cleanness.
p. of hands, Job 22:30.
p. of heart, Prov. 22:11.
by *p.*, by knowledge, II Cor. 6:6.

PURER, more pure.
Nazarites *p.* than snow, Lam. 4:7.
of *p.* eyes than, Hab. 1:13.

PURGE, purify, cleanse from guilt.
p. me with hyssop, Ps. 51:7.
p. away our sins, Ps. 79:9.
cleanse and *p.* it, Ezek. 43:20.
p. them as gold, Mal. 3:3.
p. old leaven, I Cor. 5:7.
had *p.* our sins, Heb. 1:3.
p. dead works, Heb. 9:14.

PURIFICATION, the cleansing of the
ceremonially unclean person. Cleanliness was considered desirable in Bible
lands as elsewhere. But cleanliness was
more than mere bodily cleanness; it
meant acceptability before God. The
Mosaic law made elaborate provision for
the purification of unclean persons, particularly those defiled by contact with
issues or discharges, by childbirth, and
by leprosy. Contact with dead bodies
(Num. 19:11–22) and things touched by
unclean persons (Lev. 15:9) made one
unclean. Also certain animals were unclean (Lev. 11:2–24; Deut. 14:2–21).
Eating the flesh of torn or unnaturally
slain animals was a source of uncleanness (Ex. 22:31; Lev. 17:15).

Purification was secured in various
ways. Simple purification was secured by
bathing the body and clothes of the person purified (Lev. 15:8, 10, 11). Uncleanness due to an issue lasted seven days
(Lev. 15:19). At the end of this time the
person was bathed in running water; on
the eighth day the person appeared before
the priest with two turtledoves or young
pigeons and offered one as a sin-offering
and one as a burnt offering. In the case of
leprosy, the purification lasted seven
days. The person healed came with two
birds. The priest killed one bird and put
its blood into a bowl of water. He then
sprinkled hyssop into it and then sprinkled the person. Next he released the
other bird. The person then washed and
spent seven days in preparation, washing

again at this time. On the eighth day he
appeared before the priest with two male
lambs and a female one. After the priest
poured oil on him, he was completely
pure (Lev. 14). For uncleanness due to
touching a corpse, a red heifer without
blemish had to be sacrificed, her body
being burned with cedar wood and hyssop and scarlet, and the blood sprinkled
toward the sanctuary. It was also sprinkled on the person defiled, on the third
and seventh day (Num. 19). There were
additional laws for the cleansing of a
Nazarite (Num. 6:9–12). The uncleanness because of childbirth involved a
week of separation if a boy, and two if a
girl. This was followed by days of purification, 33 if a boy and 66 if a girl. After
these days the mother brought the required offering to the sanctuary (Lev.
12). Mary, the mother of Jesus, being
poor, brought a pair of turtledoves and
two young pigeons (Luke 2:21–24).

PURIFY, cleanse, make pure.
as silver *p.*, Ps. 12:6.
p. thyself with them, Acts 21:24.
p. peculiar people, Titus 2:14.
ye *p.* your souls, I Pet. 1:22.
this hope *p.* himself, I John 3:3.

PURIM, an annual feast celebrated on the
14th of the month of Adar. It is in memory of Esther and the deliverance of the
Jews in Persia from the destruction
planned by Haman. Instead of Haman's
killing the Jews, the Jews revolted and
killed their enemies, including Haman
and his ten sons. On the next day (14th
of Adar) they rested and feasted (Esther 9:17). The name Purim comes from
"pur," meaning "lot" (Esther 3:7; 9:24,
26). The feast of Purim through the years
has been characterized as a time of reading the book of Esther, praising her and
cursing Haman, and giving gifts to the
poor.

PURITY, state of being pure.
example in *p.*, I Tim. 4:12.
as sisters, with all *p.*, I Tim. 5:2.

PURLOIN, to take dishonestly or steal.
Not *p.*, but good fidelity, Titus 2:10.

PURPLE, a color created from blending
blue and red. Because of its scarcity it
was costly. It is natural, therefore, that
only the rich were able to buy and wear

purple (Luke 16:19). It was also worn by those in high official positions (Esther 8:15). Purple was placed upon Jesus in mockery (Mark 15:17).
blue . . *p*. and scarlet, Ex. 25:4.
shall take gold, and . . *p*., Ex. 28:5.
spread a *p*. cloth, Num. 4:13.
hair . . like *p*., Song 7:5.
Lydia, a seller of *p*., Acts 16:14.
woman . . arrayed in *p*., Rev. 17:4.

PURPOSE, intent, desire, design.
a time to every *p*., Eccles. 3:1.
with *p*. of heart, Acts 11:23.
the *p*. of God stand, Rom. 9:11.
every man as he *p*., II Cor. 9:7.
according to eternal *p*., Eph. 3:11.

PURSE, a bag or pouch.
all have one *p*., Prov. 1:14.
nor brass in your *p*., Matt. 10:9.
Carry neither *p*., Luke 10:4.
he that hath a *p*., Luke 22:36.

PURSUE, follow, chase, seek.
p. them to Hobah, Gen. 14:15.
seek peace and *p*. it, Ps. 34:14.
p. evil, *p*. it to his, Prov. 11:19.
sword shall *p*. thee, Jer. 48:2.

PUSH, thrust, shove, press with force.
ox were wont to *p*., Ex. 21:29.
thou shalt *p*. Syrians, I Kin. 22:11.
we *p*. down our enemies, Ps. 44:5.
ram *p*. westward, Dan. 8:4.

PUT, *see* **PHUT**.

PUTEOLI, a seaport in Italy which Paul passed through around A.D. 60 when he was en route to Rome. He was received and treated kindly by the disciples in this place (Acts 28:13).

PUTHITES, *see* **PUHITES**.

PUTIEL, the father-in-law of Eleazar, the son of Aaron (Ex. 6:25).

PUTRIFYING, decaying, corrupt.
bruises and *p*. sores, Is. 1:6.

PUVAH, *see* **PUAH**.

PYGARG, an animal which was ceremonially clean (Deut. 14:5). It is believed to be the white antelope.

PYRRHUS, the father of Sopater (Acts 20:4).

Q

QUAIL, a class of small birds related to the pheasant family. With these birds God fed the wandering Israelites (Ex. 16:13; Num. 11:31; Ps. 105).

QUAKE, to shake, vibrate or quiver.
earth did *q*. and rocks, Matt. 27:51.
I fear and *q*., Heb. 12:21.

QUARREL, angry contention.
Herodias had *q*. against, Mark 6:19.
if any have a *q*., Col. 3:13.

QUARTER, fourth part; area, region.
people from every *q*., Gen. 19:4.
to him from every *q*., Mark 1:45.

QUARTUS, a Corinthian Christian who sent greetings to Rome (Rom. 16:23).

QUATERNION, a guard consisting of four soldiers (Acts 12:4).

QUEEN, the Hebrews had no equivalent for our word "queen"; the wives of the kings had not the sovereignty or the dignity we usually associate with the term. The Bible uses the term to speak of: (1) a reigning queen (I Kin. 10:1); (2) a queen consort or chief wife (Esther 1:9; 7:1); (3) a wife of the first rank (Ps. 45:9; Dan. 5:2; Neh. 2:6). Sometimes queens had much influence, as did Jezebel (II Kin. 10:13), but the only reigning queen in Israel or Judah was the usurper Athaliah (II Kin. 11:1).

QUENCH, extinguish; put out a fire.
waters cannot *q*. love, Song 8:7.
q. the fiery darts, Eph. 6:16.
q. not Spirit, I Thess. 5:19.

QUESTION, (1) interrogation; (2) to ask.
lawyer asked a *q*., Matt. 22:35.
apostles about this *q*., Acts 15:2.
unlearned *q*. avoid, Titus 3:9.

QUICK, (1) speedy; (2) living.
down *q*. into the pit, Num. 16:30.
judge the *q*. and dead, II Tim. 4:1.
word of God is *q*., Heb 4:12.

QUICKEN, revive, bring to life again.

thou shalt *q.* me again, Ps. 71:20.
shall also *q.* your, Rom. 8:11.

QUICKLY, speedily.
with thy adversary *q.*, Matt. 5:25.
behold, I come *q.*, Rev. 22:12.

QUIET, free from noise, calm, still.
wise men heard in *q.*, Eccles. 9:17.
study to be *q.*, I Thess. 4:11.
a meek and *q.* spirit, I Pet. 3:4.

QUIETLY, calmly, in a quiet manner.
q. wait for salvation, Lam. 3:26.

QUIETNESS, calmness. *See* **QUIET**.
a handful with *q.*, Eccles. 4:6.
we enjoy great *q.*, Acts 24:2.
exhort that with *q.*, II Thess. 3:12.

QUIRINIUS, CYRENIUS, governor of
Syria from A.D. 6–10. Luke 2:2 declares
that this man ordered a census at the time
of Christ's birth (4 B.C.—*See* **JESUS
CHRIST**). The date disagreement here
seems to be solved by the probability
that Cyrenius was twice governor of
Syria, from B.C. 4–A.D. 1 and from A.D.
6–10.

QUIT, (1) free or clear (Ex. 21:19; Josh.
2:20). (2) Conduct (I Sam. 4:9).
q. ye like men, I Cor. 16:13.

QUITE, entirely, wholly, completely.
q. devoured also our, Gen. 31:15.
bow was made *q.* naked, Hab. 3:9.

QUIVER, a sheath for arrows, Gen. 27:3.
Used figuratively for: (1) a group (Ps.
127:5); (2) a protected place (Is. 49:2);
(3) a grave (Lam. 3:13).

R

RAAMAH, RAAMA, a descendant of Ham
through Cush (Gen. 10:7; I Chr. 1:9).

RAAMIAH, REELAIAH, one of the exiles who returned with Zerubbabel (Ezra
2:2; Neh. 7:7).

RAAMSES, RAMESES, RAMSES, (1)
a king of Egypt. *See* **PHARAOH**. (2) A
region in Egypt which Joseph gave to
his father and brothers (Gen. 47:11).
(3) One of the Egyptian treasure cities

built by the Hebrews under forced labor
(Ex. 1:11; 12:37; Num. 33:3, 5).

RABBAH, RABBATH, the capital city of
Ammon situated east of the Jordan near
the territory of Gad. It was besieged by
the Israelites during David's reign (II
Sam. 11:1; 12:26ff). The destruction of
this city, as representative of the destruction of the Ammonites, is foretold in the
Hebrew prophets (Amos 1:14; Jer. 49:2,
3; Ezek. 21:20).

RABBI, RABBONI, a Jewish title of respect given to recognized teachers and
learned men. It was addressed to Jesus
by his disciples (John 1:38, 49; 3:2; 6:25)
and once to John the Baptist (3:26).
There were three forms of this title used
with different degrees of honor: Rab,
master; Rabbi, my master; and Rabboni,
my Lord, master (John 20:16).

RABBITH, one of the cities of Canaan
allotted to Issachar (Josh. 19:20).

RABBONI, *see* **RABBI**.

RAB-MAG, a title borne by Nergalsha-
rezer, a Babylonian prince, which means
"the deeply wise prince" and may signify
the chief of the magi (Jer. 39:3, 13).

RABSARIS, RAB-SARIS, an Assyrian
official title, perhaps a chief of the eunuchs (II Kin. 18:17; Jer. 39:3, 13).

RAB-SHAKEH, an Assyrian official title.
It has been taken to refer to "the chief of
the cupbearers" but this interpretation is
doubtful. Possibly it refers to an army
officer. One of these, with two other officers, was sent by Sennacharib to demand Hezekiah's surrender (II Kin. 18:
17).

RACA, a Jewish term of contempt. The
basal meaning of the word is "empty."
It was used by the Rabbis to designate a
person of low education and morals
(Matt. 5:22).

RACAL, RACHAL, (trade), a town of
Judah to which David sent some of the
spoils taken from the Amalekites after
the raid on Ziklag (I Sam. 30:29).

RACHAB, *see* **RAHAB**.

RACHAL, *see* **RACAL**.

RACHEL, RAHEL, (ewe), the younger daughter of Laban, Jacob's uncle on his mother's side. Jacob labored for Laban seven years to pay the bridal price for Rachel, but was tricked into marrying Leah, the older daughter. He then labored another seven years to receive the woman he loved, and after receiving her, remained still another seven years. Rachel was barren at first but later gave birth to Joseph (Gen. 29:9–30:24). Rachel died in Canaan at the birth of her second son, Benjamin, and was buried near Bethlehem (Gen. 35:16–20).

RADDAI, the fifth son of Jesse; one of David's brothers (I Chr. 2:14).

RADIO, one of the most fruitful means of spreading the Gospel in this atomic age has been the radio. The Psalmist David declared that "their line is gone out through all the earth and their words to the end of the world" (Ps. 19:3, 4). In descriptive language similar to a Gospel broadcast, Paul depicted the spread of the Gospel by saying, "their sound went into all the earth and their words unto the ends of the world" (Rom. 10:18). Radio, even with the increase of Television, is playing an ever-increasing role in carrying out the Great Commission (Matt. 28: 19–20; Mark 16:15–16).

RAGAU, *see* **REU**.

RAGE, violent anger.
turned away in a *r.*, II Kin. 5:12.
Asa in a *r.*, II Chr. 16:10.
why do the heathen *r.*, Ps. 2:1.
jealousy is *r.* of man, Prov. 6:34.
fool *r.* and is, Prov. 14:16.

RAGING, storming.
rulest *r.* of sea, Ps. 89:9.
strong drink a *r.*, Prov. 20:1.
rebuked *r.* water, Luke 8:24.

RAGS, tattered clothing.
clothe a man with *r.*, Prov. 23:21.
righteousness filthy *r.*, Is. 64:6.
took old rotten *r.*, Jer. 38:11.

RAGUEL, *see* **REUEL**.

RAHAB, RACHAB, a prostitute living in Jericho when the Israelites invaded Ca-naan. She helped two Hebrew spies escape the city and in return was spared with her family in the ensuing siege of the city (Josh. 2:1–22, 6:22–25; Heb. 11: 31). Her name appears in Matthew's genealogy of Jesus (Matt. 1:5).

RAHAB, a symbolic name for Egypt suggesting the character of a sea-monster (Ps. 87:4, 89:10; Is. 51:9).

RAHAM, a descendant of Caleb (I Chr. 2:44).

RAHEL, *see* **RACHEL**.

RAILER, one who rails, scoffs.
not company with *r.*, I Cor. 5:11.

RAIMENT, clothing, garments.
r., not diminished, Ex. 21:10.
r. waxed not old, Deut. 8:4.
r. of camel's hair, Matt. 3:4.
body than *r.*, Matt. 6:25.
parted his *r.*, Luke 23:34.
clothed in white *r.*, Rev. 3:5.

RAIN, precipitation.
r. was upon the earth, Gen. 7:12.
r. in due season, Lev. 26:4.
doctrine drop as *r.*, Deut. 32:2.
abundance of *r.*, I Kin. 18:41.
hath *r.* a father? Job 38:28.
clouds after the *r.*, Eccles. 12:2.
r. on just and unjust, Matt. 5:45.

RAINBOW, the sign which God gave to Noah in His covenant with him that the earth would not again be destroyed by water (Gen. 9:12–17).

RAISE, elevate.
r. poor out of dust, I Sam. 2:8.
third day will *r.*, Hos. 6:2.
r. the dead, Matt. 10:8.
three days I will *r.*, John 2:19.
Father *r.* up dead, John 5:21.
r. for justification, Rom. 4:25.
r. up Christ, I Cor. 15:15.

RAISIN, a grape preserved by drying.
clusters of *r.*, I Sam. 25:18.
bunches of *r.*, II Sam. 16:1.

RAKEM, *see* **REKEM**.

RAKKATH, a fortified city allotted to the tribe of Naphtali in the division of Canaan (Josh. 19:35).

RAKKON, a town allotted to Dan in the division of Canaan (Josh. 19:46).

RAM, (1) an ancestor of David and member of the Messianic line (Ruth 4:19; Matt. 1:3, 4; Luke 3:33). (2) A son of Jerahmeel (I Chr. 2:25–27). (3) A relative of Elihu (Job 32:2).

RAM, a male sheep. Often used in sacrificial offerings (Gen. 22:13; Lev. 1:10).

RAM, an instrument of war. *See* BATTERING RAM.

RAMA, *see* RAMAH.

RAMAH, (1) a town allotted to Asher in the division of Canaan (Josh. 19:29). (2) A town in Benjamin north of Jerusalem. (Josh. 18:25; Judg. 4:5). (3) A city in Ephraim where Samuel lived (I Sam. 1:1). Also called, **Ramathaim-Zophim.** (4) A city allotted to Naphtali in the division of Canaan (Josh. 19:36). (5) A town in Simeon to which David sent some of the spoils taken from the Amalekites after the raid on Ziklag (I Sam. 30:27). (6) Another name for Ramoth-Gilead (II Kin. 8:29; II Chr. 22:6). *See* RAMOTH-GILEAD. (7) Ramah of the South. *See* RAMATH-NEGEB.

RAMATH, *see* RAMAH.

RAMATHAIM-ZOPHIM, *see* RAMAH.

RAMATHITE, a native of Ramah.

RAMATH-LEHI, a variant of Lehi.

RAMATH-MIZPEH, a city east of the Jordan in Gilead allotted to the tribe of Gad (Josh. 13:26).

RAMESES, *see* RAAMSES.

RAMIAH, one of the returned exiles who had married a foreign woman (Ezra 10:25).

RAMOTH, (1) a returned exile who had married a foreign woman (Ezra 10:29). (2) A city of Issachar. *See* JARMUTH. (3) A city of Gad in Gilead. *See* RAMOTH-GILEAD. (4) A town in Simeon. *See* RAMAH.

RAMOTH-GILEAD, RAMOTH, RAM-

AH, one of the cities of refuge located east of Jordan in the territory of Gad (Deut. 4:43; Josh. 20:8, 21:38).

RAMSES, *see* RAAMSES.

RANKS, row, line; orderly arrangement.
50,000 should keep *r.*, I Chr. 12:33.
that could keep *r.*, I Chr. 12:38.
not break their *r.*, Joel 2:7.

RANSOM, payment for the release.
a *r.* for his soul, Ex. 30:12.
to God a *r.* for him, Ps. 49:7.
to give his life a *r.*, Matt. 20:28.
who gave himself a *r.*, I Tim. 2:6.

RAPHA, RAPHAH, (1) the fifth son of Benjamin (I Chr. 8:2). (2) A descendant of Saul through Jonathan (I Chr. 8:37), also called Rephaiah (I Chr. 9:43).

RAPHU, father of one of the twelve spies sent into Canaan by Joshua (Num. 13:9).

RARE, infrequent, uncommon.
a *r.* thing that the king, Dan. 2:11.

RASH, without deliberation.
not *r.* with mouth, Eccles. 5:2.
do nothing *r.* Acts 19:36.

RATHER, on the other hand, instead.
death *r.* than life, Job 7:15.
r. be a doorkeeper, Ps. 84:10.
r. to the lost sheep, Matt. 10:6.
r. release Barabbas, Mark 15:11.
darkness *r.* than light, John 3:19.
obey God *r.* than men, Acts 5:29.
steal no more, but *r.*, Eph. 4:28.
thyself *r.* to godliness, I Tim. 4:7.
r. give diligence to, II Pet. 1:10.

RAVEN, a bird of the crow species but larger and more cunning than a crow. It is listed along with other scavenger birds as unclean (Lev. 11:15).

RAVENING, devouring, rapacious.
a roaring lion *r.*, Ezek. 22:25.
they are *r.* wolves, Matt. 7:15.
as a *r.* lion, I Pet. 5:8.

RAVENOUS, voracious, gluttonous.
r. beast shall go up, Is. 35:9.
calling a *r.* bird, Is. 46:11.
give thee to *r.* birds, Ezek. 39:4.

Ravish

RAVISH, fill with emotion; rape.
be *r.* with a strange, Prov. 5:20.
hast *r.* my heart, Song 4:9.
their wives *r.*, Is. 13:16.
r. women in Zion, Lam. 5:11.

RAZOR, a knife for cutting hair on the face and head. Ezekiel speaks of a barber's razor (Ezek. 5:1).

REACH, extend, stretch out.
tower whose top may *r.*, Gen. 11:4.
head *r.* unto clouds, Job 20:6.
r. hither thy finger, John 20:27.
Babylon's sins have *r.*, Rev. 18:5.

READ, to peruse.
book of the Lord and *r.*, Is. 34:16.
hear him *r.* Esaias, Acts 8:30.
worthy to *r.* the book, Rev. 5:4.

READINESS, preparedness, willingness.
received word with *r.*, Acts 17:11.
a *r.* to will, II Cor. 8:11.
a *r.* to revenge all, II Cor. 10:6.

READING, READS, *see* **READ.**

READY, prepared, willing, prompt.
almost *r.* to stone me, Ex. 17:4.
Ezra a *r.* scribe, Ezra 7:6.
a God *r.* to pardon, Neh. 9:17.
good, and *r.* to forgive, Ps. 86:5.
Lord *r.* to save me, Is. 38:20.
spirit is *r.* but flesh, Mark 14:38.
Lord, I am *r.* to go, Luke 22:33.
r. to preach the gospel, Rom. 1:15.
r. always to give an, I Pet. 3:15.
but of a *r.* mind, I Pet. 5:2.
woman which was *r.*, Rev. 12:4.

REAIAH, REAIA, (the Lord has seen), (1) a near descendant of Judah (I Chr. 4:2). (2) Head of one of the families, the Nethinims, that returned from exile with Zerubbabel (Ezra 2:47; Neh. 7:50). (3) A descendant of Reuben (I Chr. 5:5).

REAP, gather in harvest.
wickedness, *r.* the same, Job 4:8.
iniquity, *r.* vanity, Prov. 22:8.
shall *r.* the whirlwind, Hos. 8:7.
fowls of the air *r.* not, Matt. 6:26.
sparingly *r.* sparingly, II Cor. 9:6.
soweth, that shall he *r.*, Gal. 6:7.

REASON, proof, confer.
desire to *r.* with God, Job 13:3.

Recah, Rechah

and let us *r.* together, Is. 1:18.
he *r.* in the synagogue, Acts 18:4.
he *r.* of righteousness, Acts 24:25.
asketh you a *r.* of, I Pet. 3:15.

REASONABLE, rational, just.
your *r.* service, Rom. 12:1.

REBA, a Midianite king slain by the Israelites (Num. 31:8).

REBEKAH, REBECCA, the daughter of Bethuel, the son of Abraham's brother, Nahor. Abraham sent his servant into his own country to take a wife for Isaac from his kinsmen. Under Divine guidance Rebekah was selected and brought back to be Isaac's wife. (Gen. 24). She gave birth to twins, Jacob and Esau (Gen. 25:19–26). She favored Jacob and assisted him in deceiving Isaac into giving him the rights of the first born, which belonged rightfully to Esau (Gen. 27:1–29). Upon her death she was buried in the cave of Machpelah (Gen. 49:31).

REBEL, revolt, resist authority.
r. not against the Lord, Num. 14:9.
r. against the king? Neh. 2:19.
the Jews think to *r.*, Neh. 6:6.
r. against the light, Job 24:13.
a nation that hath *r.*, Ezek. 2:3.

REBELLION, revolt, insurrection.
thy *r.* and thy stiff, Deut. 31:27.
r. is as the sin, I Sam. 15:23.
addeth *r.* unto his sin, Job 34:37.
evil man seeketh *r.*, Prov. 17:11.

REBELLIOUS, insubordinate, seditious.
r. against Lord, Deut. 9:7.
r. dwell in a dry land, Ps. 68:6.
this is a *r.* people, Is. 30:9.
spread my hands to a *r.*, Is. 65:2.
send thee to a *r.* nation, Ezek. 2:3.

REBUKE, reproof; reprove, reprimand.
wise *r.* thy neighbor, Lev. 19:17.
O Lord, *r.* me not, Ps. 6:1.
r. a wise man, and he, Prov. 9:8.
shall *r.* many nations, Is. 2:4.
brother trespass, *r.* him, Luke 17:3.
r. not an elder, I Tim. 5:1.
them that sin, *r.*, I Tim. 5:20.
as many as I love, I *r.*, Rev. 3:19.

RECAH, RECHAH, an unidentified town of Judah (I Chr. 4:12).

349

RECALL, to remember, to call back.
this I r. to mind, Lam. 3:21.

RECEIPT, place of receiving.
at r. of custom, Matt. 9:9.

RECEIVE, to lay hold of.
will r. my prayer, Ps. 6:9.
r. blessing from Lord, Ps. 24:5.
r. little child r., Matt. 18:5.
believing ye shall r., Matt. 21:22.
r. not honour, John 5:41.
and ye shall r., John 16:24.
r. my spirit, Acts 7:59.
r. not grace of, II Cor. 6:1.
called might r., Heb. 9:15.

RECEIVED, to be accepted.
have I r. bribe? I Sam. 12:3.
r. no correction, Jer. 2:30.
freely r., freely, Matt. 10:8.
r. into heaven, Mark 16:19.
Martha r. him, Luke 10:38.
cloud r. him out, Acts 1:9.
I r. of Lord, I Cor. 11:23.
r. forty stripes, II Cor. 11:24.
I r. of Father, Rev. 2:27.

RECHAB, (1) one of the two sons of Rimmon who slew Ishbosheth (II Sam. 4:2–12). (2) The father of Jehonadab, who assisted Jehu in destroying the worshipers of Baal (II Kin. 10:15–28). (3) The father of Malchiah (Neh. 3:14).

RECHABITES, descendants of Jehonadab, the son of Rechab (I Chr. 2:55; II Kin. 10:15, 23).

RECHAH, see RECAH.

RECKON, to number, to account.
not r. among nations, Num. 23:9.
r. seven days, Ezek. 44:26.
not r. of grace, Rom. 4:4.
r. for righteousness, Rom. 4:9.

RECOMMENDED, to commend.
they had been r., Acts 14:26.
r. by the brethren, Acts 15:40.

RECOMPENCE, RECOMPENSE, to reward.
in r. for the life, II Sam. 14:7.
and r. them with all, Is. 57:18.
so I will r. them, Is. 61:8.
a r. be made, Luke 14:12.
a r. of reward, Heb. 2:2.

RECONCILE, to cover, to restore.
blood brought to r., Lev. 6:30.
so r. the house, Ezek. 45:20.
r. all unto himself, Col. 1:20.

RECONCILIATION, the bringing together of God and man in a union of peace. This reconciliation was brought about by the work of Jesus in the flesh. God, in taking the initiative, reconciled the world. Man, in turn, being reconciled through his death, is saved by the life of Jesus (Rom. 5:1, 10). The act of God through Christ is effective for all who will accept the divine pronouncement through Christ. The word is closely connected with the word "atonement," which means to make to people or parties "at one."

RECORD, to testify, to witness, to write.
I r. my name, Ex. 20:24.
John bare r., John 1:32.
bearest r. of thyself, John 8:13.
I bear him r., Col. 4:13.
bare r. of the word, Rev. 1:2.

RECORDER, one who kept the annals or chronicles of the kings. He was considered to be a high official in the king's court (II Sam. 8:16; I Chr. 18:15; Is. 36:3, 22). His exact function is not clear.

RECOUNT, to remember.
shall r. his worthies, Nahum 2:5.

RECOVER, revive, acquire, cure.
did ye not r. them, Judg. 11:26.
r. stones from the, Neh. 4:2.
lips are lilies r., Song 5:13.
they shall r., Mark 16:18.

REDEEM, to free, to purchase.
r. to be a people, II Sam. 7:23.
for I r. you, Is. 43:1.
Eternal has r., Is. 44:23.
I who r. them, Hos. 7:13.
to r. us from, Titus 2:14.

REDEEMER, one who frees.
know my r. liveth, Job 19:25.
their r. is mighty, Prov. 23:11.
r., the holy one, Is. 41:14.
the r. shall come, Is. 59:20.
their r. is strong, Jer. 50:34.

REDEMPTION, REDEEMER, redemption means the loosing of someone by the paying of a price. It is used to express God's work in the salvation of man. In

the Old Testament the people were redeemed through the firstborn for five
shekels (Num. 18:16). In the New Testament Christ is compared to a redeemer
divinely sent. He reveals the love of God
for his people (Rom. 3:24; Gal. 3:13;
Eph. 1:7; I Pet. 1:18; I Cor. 1:30). The
redemption of man means that man was
under bondage to sin (Gal. 3:13; I Cor.
15:56) and the power of Satan and death
(Acts 26:18; Heb. 2:14, 15). Christ, in his
death, redeemed us from the curse of sin.
And now, as followers of Christ, we can
look for the redemption of the body
(Heb. 2:9; Acts 3:19; II Tim. 2:26; I Cor.
15:55-57).
r. for land, Lev. 25:24.
r. of soul, Ps. 49:8.
r. that is in Christ, Rom. 3:24.
sanctification and r., I Cor. 1:30.
obtained eternal r., Heb. 9:12.

REDOUND, to be over and above.
r. to the glory of, II Cor. 4:15.

RED SEA, the gulf lying between Egypt
and Arabia. For some unknown reason
it became known as the Red Sea when
actually the Hebrew says "Reed Sea."
The Greeks included the Persian Gulf
and the Indian Ocean in this name. Because of the depth of the now known
Red Sea, and because of its lack of
"reeds," it is probable that the Red Sea
in the time of Moses extended to Lake
Timsah to the north. In the time of Solomon Israel had a harbor on the Gulf of
Akabah at Ezion-Geber (I Kin. 9:26-28).

REED, CANE, a tall, broad-leaved plant
found in the lowlands of the Jordan
valley and in Egypt. It symbolized insta-
bility (II Kin. 18:21) and weakness (Is.
42:3). It was used as a measuring rod
(Ezek. 40:3; Rev. 11:1). The Roman
soldiers placed a reed in Christ's hand as
a scepter, and later struck him with it.
The sour sponge which they offered
Christ was attached to a reed (Matt. 27:
29, 30, 48).

REED GRASS, a translation in the Revised Standard Version for "meadow."
It probably refers to marshy places, as in
the Nile (Gen. 41:2, 18).

REELAIAH, see **RAAMIAH.**

REFINE, to try, to purify.

I have r. thee, Is. 48:10.
r. them as silver, Zech. 13:9.

REFINER, one who purified metals, separating the dross from the pure ore. His
tools were a furnace and a bellows. The
word is used figuratively concerning
God's purifying of his people (Zech. 13:
9; Mal. 3:2, 3).

REFORMATION, reform.
until the time of r., Heb. 9:10.

REFORMED, to be restored.
if ye will not be r., Lev. 26:23.

REFRAIN, to withhold, keep back.
Joseph could not r., Gen. 45:1.
will not r. my mouth, Job 7:11.
r. voice from weeping, Jer. 31:16.
say unto you, r. from, Acts 5:38.
r. tongue from evil, I Pet. 3:10.

REFRESH, to support, to cool, to revive.
rested, was r., Ex. 31:17.
speak, be r., Job 32:20.
they r. my spirit, I Cor. 16:18.
saints are r. by, Philem. 7.

REFUGE, place of flight, asylum. *See*
CITIES OF REFUGE.
r. for oppressed, Ps. 9:9.
God is our r., Ps. 46:1.
my strong r., Ps. 71:7.
have a place of r., Prov. 14:26.
fled for r., Heb. 6:18.

REFUSE, to loathe, to despise.
r. to do judgment, Prov. 21:7.
r. to hear my, Jer. 13:10.
that you r. not, Heb. 12:25.

REGARD, to consider, to esteem.
r. not works of, Ps. 28:5.
if I r. iniquity, Ps. 66:18.
not r. any ransom, Prov. 6:35.
fear not God, nor r., Luke 18:4.
Lord he doth not r., Rom. 14:6.

REGEM, a son of Jahdai, of the family of
Caleb (I Chr. 2:47).

REGEM-MELECH, one who was sent
into the temple to pray and to consult the
priests and prophets concerning the continuation of weeping and fasting (Zech.
7:1-3).

REGENERATION, the change wrought

in the thought, feeling, and will of man, in his relation to God and the world. In the Old Testament, the fact that God demanded obedience rather than sacrifice shows that God dealt with the heart of man (I Sam. 15:22; Hos. 6:6; Mic. 6:7). The tension found in the morality of the Old Testament was resolved in the New in the idea of regeneration, being "born again." The instrument which God uses to bring regeneration is his word (I Thess. 2:13). This "new birth" is outwardly symbolized by baptism (John 3:5; Acts 2:38; Rom. 6:4).

REHABIAH, the ancestor of a number of Levitical families (I Chr. 23:17; 24:21; 26:25).

REHEARSE, declare, give forth.
r. in ears of Joshua, Ex. 17:14.
r. acts of Lord, Judg. 5:11.
Peter r. the matter, Acts 11:4.

REHOB, (1) the father of Hadadezer, king of Zebah, whom David fought (II Sam. 8:3). (2) A Levite who sealed the covenant with Nehemiah (Neh. 10:11). (3) A city on the northern border of Palestine (Num. 13:21). (4) A town given to Asher (Josh. 19:28). (5) Another town in Asher (Josh. 19:30).

REHOBOAM, ROBOAM, a son of Solomon and Naamah (I Kin. 14:21). When the people met to make him king, they asked him to lighten the load of taxation which his father Solomon had exacted for his heavy building program (I Kin. 12:1; II Chr. 10:1). He took the counsel of the younger men rather than the older. The result was that Jeroboam, son of Nebat, led all the tribes but Judah and Benjamin in secession (I Kin. 12:20, 21). There were two reasons why Rehoboam could not retaliate: the people accepted the words of Shemaiah, the prophet, as from the Lord, and these words forbade him to fight; also, Shishak invaded the land, and stripped the temple of the treasures of Solomon. He was succeeded by his son Abijam (I Kin. 14:31–15:6) and was an ancestor of the family of Jesus (Matt. 1:7).

REHOBOTH, (1) a well dug by Isaac (Gen. 26:22). (2) One of four cities founded by Asshur (Gen. 10:11, 12). The others were Nineveh, Caleh, and Resen.

The name of Rahabeh is still attached to two places in the area of ancient Mesopotamia; one lies on the western bank and one on the eastern bank of the Euphrates. The identification is not clear.

REHOBOTH-IR, *see* **REHOBOTH.**

REHUM, (1) a leader in the exile who returned with Zerubbabel (Ezra 2:2; Neh. 7:7). (2) A Persian official during the time of Artaxerxes (Ezra 4:8). (3) A Levite who helped to repair the wall (Neh. 3:17). (4) One who sealed the covenant (Neh. 10:25). (5) A priestly clan which returned with Zerubbabel (Neh. 12:3).

REI, one of the men in David's court. He remained loyal when Adonijah attempted to become king (I Kin. 1:8).

REIGN, to act as king.
a king shall r., I Sam. 12:12.
r. in righteousness, Is. 32:1.
so might grace r., Rom. 5:21.
we shall r. with, II Tim. 2:12.
he shall r. forever, Rev. 11:15.
r. . . 1000 years, Rev. 20:6.

REINS, the kidneys, seat of emotions.
God trieth the r., Ps. 7:9.
my r. instruct me, Ps. 16:7.
my r. rejoice, Prov. 23:16.
searcheth the r., Rev. 2:23.

REJECT, to loathe, put away.
r. his statutes, II Kin. 17:15.
despised, r. of men, Is. 53:3.
r. word of the Lord, Jer. 8:9.
stone, builders r., Matt. 21:42.
r. of this generation, Luke 17:25.

REJOICE, to be joyful, to exult.
r. in every good, Deut. 26:11.
r. with trembling, Ps. 2:11.
righteous shall r., Ps. 58:10.
who r. to do evil, Prov. 2:14.
r. and do good in, Eccles. 3:12.
r. not against me, Mic. 7:8.
Jesus r. in Spirit, Luke 10:21.
r. with them that, Rom. 12:15.
r. not in iniquity, I Cor. 13:6.
r. evermore, I Thess. 5:16.

REJOICING, exulting, expressing joy.
r. always before, Prov. 8:30.
went on their way r., Acts 8:39.
r. in hope, patient, Rom. 12:12.
r. more abundant, Phil. 1:26.

all such *r.* is evil, James 4:16.

REKEM, RAKEM, (1) a prince of Midian, slain by Phinehas when in the plains of Moab (Num. 31:8). (2) A son of Hebron, and the father of Shammai (I Chr. 2:43). (3) A city in Benjamin, now called Ain-Karim (Josh. 18:27).

RELEASE, to let go, to free.
r. a prisoner, Matt. 27:15.
rather *r.* Barabbas, Mark 15:11.
power to *r.*, John 19:10.

RELIEVE, to cause to stand, to support.
r. fatherless widow, Ps. 146:9.
r. the oppressed, Is. 1:17.
have *r.* afflicted, I Tim. 5:10.
widows, let them *r.*, I Tim. 5:16.

RELIGION, system of faith.
straitest sect of our *r.*, Acts 26:5.
this man's *r.* is vain, James 1:26.
pure *r.* and, James 1:27.

RELIGIOUS, pious, devout.
r. proselytes followed, Acts 13:43.
if any seem to be *r.*, James 1:26.

RELY, to lean upon, to trust.
thou didst *r.* on Lord, II Chr. 16:8.

REMAIN, to be left, to wait, to continue.
r. until morning, Ex. 12:10.
Dan *r.* in ships, Judg. 5:17.
r. in wilderness, Ps. 55:7.
city *r.* forever, Jer. 17:25.
fragments that *r.*, John 6:12.
not *r.* upon cross, John 19:31.
let *r.* unmarried, I Cor. 7:11.
r. a rest to, Heb. 4:9.
r. no more sacrifice, Heb. 10:26.

REMALIAH, the father of Pekah who slew Pekahiah and reigned in his stead (II Kin. 15:25-37; II Chr. 28:6; Is. 7:1-9; 8:6).

REMEDY, healing.
wrath, was no *r.*, II Chr. 36:16.
destroyed without *r.*, Prov. 29:1.

REMEMBER, to recall.
r. the Sabbath Day, Ex. 20:8.
r. days of old. Deut. 32:7.
r. me O God, Neh. 13:14.
r. now thy creator, Eccles. 12:1.

we will *r.* thy love, Song 1:4.
r. Lot's wife, Luke 17:32.
r. words of Lord, Acts 20:35.
r. words spoken, Jude 17.

REMEMBRANCE, memory.
I will put out the *r.*, Ex. 17:14.
bringing iniquity to *r.*, Num. 5:15.
keep my name in *r.*, II Sam. 18:18.
in death is no *r.* of thee, Ps. 6:5.
at *r.* of his holiness, Ps. 30:4.
in everlasting *r.*, Ps. 112:6.
no *r.* of former, Eccles. 1:11.
this do in *r.* of me, Luke 22:19.
all things to your *r.*, John 14:26.
drink it, in *r.* of me, I Cor. 11:25.
put them in *r.*, II Tim. 2:14.
there is a *r.* of sins, Heb. 10:3.
put you in *r.*, II Pet. 1:12.
putting you in *r.*, II Pet. 1:13.
Babylon came in *r.*, Rev. 16:19.

REMETH, *see* JARMUTH.

REMISSION, pardon, forgiveness.
for the *r.* of sins, Matt. 26:28.
repentance for *r.*, Mark 1:4.
baptized for *r.*, Acts 2:38.
believeth receive *r.*, Acts 10:43.
blood is no *r.*, Heb. 9:22.
where *r.* is, no more, Heb. 10:18.

REMIT, forgive, pardon.
sins ye *r.* are *r.*, John 20:23.

REMMON, *see* RIMMON.

REMMON-METHOAR, *see* RIMMON.

REMNANT, remaining portion.
r. be the priest's, Lev. 5:13.
a *r.* to escape, Ezra 9:8.
left us a small *r.*, Is. 1:9.
cut from Babylon the *r.*, Is. 14:22.
glean *r.* of Israel, Jer. 6:9.
word of the Lord, ye *r.*, Jer. 42:15.
I leave a *r.* that ye, Ezek. 6:8.
Esaias crieth, a *r.*, Rom. 9:27.
make war with the *r.*, Rev. 12:17.

REMOVE, take away, put out, banish.
not *r.* neighbor's land, Deut. 19:14.
some *r.* the landmarks, Job 24:2.
not *r.* mine integrity, Job 27:5.
r. not ancient landmark, Prov. 22:28.
r. violence and spoil, Ezek. 45:9.
I will *r.* the northern, Joel 2:20.
I will *r.* iniquity, Zech. 3:9.

half the mountain r., Zech. 14:4.
r. hence, and it r., Matt. 17:20.
r. this cup from me, Luke 22:42.
I r. thy candlestick, Rev. 2:5.

REMPHAN, REPHAN, a god which the
Israelites worshipped in the wilderness
(Acts 7:43).

REND, tear, rip, burst.
neither r. your clothes, Lev. 10:6.
surely r. the kingdom, I Kin. 11:11.
r. your heart, not, Joel 2:13.
turn and r. you, Matt. 7:6.

RENDER, give, impart, restore.
every offering they r., Num. 18:9.
I will r. vengeance, Deut. 32:41.
he will r. unto man, Job 33:26.
r. to them their desert, Ps. 28:4.
I will r. praises, Ps. 56:12.
r. unto Caesar, Matt. 22:21.
husband r. to wife, I Cor. 7:3.
none r. evil for, I Thess. 5:15.
not r. evil for evil, I Pet. 3:9.

RENDING, tearing, tearing apart.
tear my soul, r., Ps. 7:2.

RENEW, renovate, refresh, restore.
r. the kingdom there, I Sam. 11:14.
and r. a right spirit, Ps. 51:10.
thy youth is r., Ps. 103:5.
inward man is r., II Cor. 4:16.
be r. in the spirit, Eph. 4:23.
new man, which is r., Col. 3:10.
fall away, to r., Heb. 6:6.

RENOUNCE, reject, spurn, abandon.
have r. the hidden, II Cor. 4:2.

RENOWN, RENOWNED, well known.
giants of old, men of r., Gen. 6:4.
evildoers never be r., Is. 14:20.
thy r. went forth, Ezek. 16:14.
the r. city, Ezek. 26:17.
hast gotten thee r., Dan. 9:15.

RENT, torn, broken, ripped.
Joseph is r. in pieces, Gen. 37:33.
Samson r. the lion, Judg. 14:6.
Lord r. the kingdom, I Sam. 15:28.
he r. Israel from the, II Kin. 17:21.
r. is made worse, Matt. 9:16.
veil of temple r., Matt. 27:51.

REPAID, compensated, recompensed.
righteous, good be r., Prov. 13:21.

REPAIR, mend, rebuild.
priests r. breaches, II Kin. 12:5.
reviving to r. house, Ezra 9:9.
shall r. waste cities, Is. 61:4.

REPAIRER, one who mends, rebuilder.
shalt be called the r., Is. 58:12.

REPAY, recompense, compensate.
r. him to his face, Deut. 7:10.
he will r. fury, Is. 59:18.
is mine, I will r., Rom. 12:19.

REPEAT, do or say again, reiterate.
he that r. a matter, Prov. 17:9.

REPENT, think twice, change mind.
lest the people r., Ex. 13:17.
Lord shall r., Deut. 32:36.
not a man, that he r., I Sam. 15:29.
they r. in captivity, I Kin. 8:47.
R., the kingdom of heaven, Matt. 3:2.
afterward he r., Matt. 21:29.
except ye r. ye shall, Luke 13:3.
brother r. forgive him, Luke 17:3.
r. and be baptized, Acts 2:38.
commandeth all to r., Acts 17:30.
neither r. of murders, Rev. 9:21.

REPENTANCE, turn around, about face.
fruits meet for r., Matt. 3:8.
with water unto r., Matt. 3:11.
call sinners to r., Matt. 9:13.
r. and remission, Luke 24:47.
Gentiles granted r., Acts 11:18.
God leadeth to r., Rom. 2:4.
godly sorrow worketh r., II Cor. 7:10.
will give them r., II Tim. 2:25.
foundation of r., Heb. 6:1.
renew them to r., Heb. 6:6.
no place of r., Heb. 12:17.

REPETITIONS, repeatings, reiterations.
vain r. as heathen, Matt. 6:7.

REPHAEL, (God heals), son of Shemaiah, a descendant of Levi (I Chr. 26:7).

REPHAH, an Ephraimite and ancestor of
Joshua (I Chr. 7:25).

REPHAIAH, (1) a descendant of Saul
and Jonathan (I Chr. 9:43), also called
Rapha (I Chr. 8:37). (2) A descendant
of Issachar (I Chr. 7:2). (3) A Simionite
captain who helped destroy a colony of
Amalakites and seize their land (I Chr.
4:42, 43). (4) A descendant of David

through Zerubbabel (I Chr. 3:21). (5) A son of Hur (Neh. 3:9).

REPHAIM, REPHAIMS, (strong), (1) a people living in Palestine before Abraham (Gen. 14:5; Deut. 2:11, 20, 3:11; Josh. 17:15). (2) A valley in Palestine noted for its fertility (Josh. 15:8, 18:16; Is. 17:5).

REPHAN, *see* **REMPHAN.**

REPHIDIM, a location between the wilderness of Sin and Sinai, where the Israelites encamped during the journey to Canaan (Ex. 17:1; Num. 33:12, 15).

REPLENISH, fill, make plentiful.
and *r.* the earth, Gen. 1:28.
r. every sorrowful soul, Jer. 31:25.
r., now laid waste, Ezek. 26:2.

REPLIEST, answers.
that *r.* against God? Rom. 9:20.

REPROACH, dishonor, disgrace; scorn.
r. broken heart, Ps. 69:20.
sin is a *r.* to any, Prov. 14:34.
word of Lord made a *r.,* Jer. 20:8.
a *r.* among the heathens, Joel 2:19.
bear *r.* of my people, Mic. 6:16.
men shall *r.* you, Luke 6:22.
the *r.* of Christ, Heb. 11:26.

REPROACHFULLY, scornfully.
on the cheek *r.,* Job 16:10.
occasion to speak *r.,* I Tim. 5:14.

REPROBATE, wicked, corrupt.
over to a *r.* mind, Rom. 1:28.
except ye be *r.,* II Cor. 13:5.
r. concerning the faith, II Tim. 3:8.

REPROOF, rebuke, reprimand.
astonished at his *r.,* Job 26:11.
despised my *r.,* Prov. 1:30.
regardeth *r.* is prudent, Prov. 15:5.
rod and *r.* give wisdom, Prov. 29:15.
profitable for *r.,* II Tim. 3:16.

REPROVE, to reprimand, rebuke.
doth your arguing *r.*?, Job 6:25.
often *r.* hardeneth, Prov. 29:1.
backslidings shall *r.,* Jer. 2:19.
r., rebuke, exhort, II Tim. 4:2.

REPUTATION, estimation.
in *r.* for wisdom, Eccles. 10:1.
Gamaliel had in *r.,* Acts 5:34.

made himself of no *r.,* Phil. 2:7.

REQUEST, petition, entreaty, appeal.
O that I might have my *r.,* Job 6:8.
gave them their *r.* but, Ps. 106:15.
your *r.* be made known, Phil. 4:6.

REQUEST, to ask, petition, entreat.
Elijah *r.* that he, I Kin. 19:4.
Daniel *r.* of the king, Dan. 2:49.

REQUIRE, demand, prescribe.
I *r.* the life of man, Gen. 9:5.
what doth the Lord *r.*? Deut. 10:12.
I will *r.* it of him, Deut. 18:19.
his blood will I *r.,* Ezek. 3:18.
the Jews *r.* a sign, I Cor. 1:22.

REQUITE, repay, compensate, reward.
r. me evil for good, I Sam. 25:21.
God shall surely *r.,* Jer. 51:56.
let them learn to *r.,* I Tim. 5:4.

RESCUE, deliver, redeem, liberate.
r. my soul from, Ps. 35:17.
none shall *r.* him, Hos. 5:14.
an army, and *r.* him, Acts 23:27.

RESEMBLANCE, likeness, similarity.
this is their *r.,* Zech. 5:6.

RESEMBLE, be similar to, be like.
each *r.* the children, Judg. 8:18.
I *r.* kingdom of God?, Luke 13:18.

RESEN, a city near Nineveh (Gen. 10:11, 12).

RESERVE, hold, keep back, retain.
inheritance *r.* in heaven, I Pet. 1:4.
r. the unjust to the, II Pet. 2:9.
r. in everlasting chains, Jude 6.

RESHEPH, (a flame), an Ephraimite (I Chr. 7:25).

RESIDUE, remains, leavings, remnant.
locusts eat the *r.,* Ex. 10:5.
Lord a diadem to *r.,* Is. 28:5.
a derision to the *r.,* Ezek. 36:4.
that the *r.* might seek, Acts 15:17.

RESIST, oppose, withstand, hinder.
that ye *r.* not evil, Matt. 5:39.
not able to *r.* spirit, Acts 6:10.
who hath *r.* his will?, Rom. 9:19.
whosoever *r.* the power, Rom. 13:2.
have not *r.* yet unto, Heb. 12:4.

r. the devil and he, James 4:7.
he doth not *r.* you, James 5:6.

RESORT, go or apply for help.
r. ye thither to us, Neh. 4:20.
I may continually *r.,* Ps. 71:3.
people *r.* to him, Mark 10:1.
whither Jews always *r.,* John 18:20

RESPECT, regard, esteem, admire.
Lord had *r.* to Abel, Gen. 4:4.
not *r.* persons in, Deut. 1:17.
nor *r.* of persons with, II Chr. 19:7.
r. to the Holy One, Is. 17:7.
faith with *r.* of persons, James 2:1.
without *r.* of persons, I Pet. 1:17.

RESPITE, interval of rest.
saw there was *r.,* Ex. 8:15.
Give us seven days' *r.,* I Sam. 11:3.

REST, repose, place of rest, remainder.
tomorrow the *r.* of holy, Ex. 16:23.
is the sabbath of *r.,* Ex. 31:15.
God given thee *r.,* Deut. 25:19.
land had *r.* from war, Josh. 14:15.
there the weary be at *r.,* Job 3:17.
my flesh *r.* in hope, Ps. 16:9..
r. in the Lord and, Ps. 37:7.
wisdom *r.* in heart, Prov. 14:33.
find *r.* for souls, Jer. 6:16.
will *r.* in love, Zeph. 3:17.
I will give you *r.,* Matt. 11:28.
Christ may *r.* on me, II Cor. 12:9.
not enter my *r.,* Heb. 3:11.
r. not day and night, Rev. 4:8.
r. that were not killed, Rev. 9:20.
r. of dead lived not, Rev. 20:5.

RESTORE, replace, refund.
r. the man his wife, Gen. 20:7.
he shall *r.* double, Ex. 22:4.
he *r.* my soul, Ps. 23:3.
r. to me the joy, Ps. 51:12.
lead and *r.* comforts, Is. 57:18.
r. health to thee, Jer. 30:17.
his sight was *r.,* Mark 8:25.
wilt thou *r.* kingdom?, Acts 1:6.
r. such an one in, Gal. 6:1.

RESTRAIN, suppress, hold back, inhibit.
rain from heaven *r.,* Gen. 8:2.
r. prayer before God, Job 15:4.
dost thou *r.* wisdom?, Job 15:8.
wrath shalt thou *r.,* Ps. 76:10.

RESURRECTION. The event at which life and personality are restored to a body.

There is no clear reference in the early books of the Old Testament to a resurrection. There is a reference to the continued existence of a person after death in the instance of the recall of Samuel by the witch of Endor in I Sam. 28:8–14. Mention of a resurrection is met in Ps. 49:14, 15; Is. 26:19; and Ezek. 37. The concept of a resurrection of all men with an accompanying judgment is explicitly stated in Dan. 12:2.

In the time of Jesus the doctrine of a resurrection was well established among the Jews, though it was denied by the Sadducees (Matt. 22:23–32; Luke 20:27–38; John 11:24; Acts 23:6–8). Jesus taught the resurrection of the dead (Mark 12:24–27), and a judgment upon men for the life they lived (Matt. 11:22–24; 12:41, 42).

Jesus' own resurrection from the dead, along with the redemptive nature of his death, became the foundation of the Christian community. It was the substance of the Gospel and the guarantee to Christians of their own resurrection (I Cor. 15:12–24).

The resurrection, with a subsequent judgment, is a fundamental theme in Apostolic writings (I Thess. 4:13–17; I Cor. 15). The idea of judgment necessarily implies the survival of personality and personal identity as does also the idea of a resurrection body which is also clearly taught (Phil. 3:20, 21; I Cor. 15:42–50).

Some passages are interpreted as implying a resurrection of the just and another of the unjust (Luke 14:14; I Thess. 4:13–17; Rev. 20:46). It should be observed, however, that Christ's statement in Luke does not necessarily imply a resurrection of the just as distinguished from a resurrection of the unjust; and in I Thess. 4 the contrast is not between the "dead in Christ" and those not in Christ, but between the "dead in Christ" and the "living in Christ." How one will understand Rev. 20 will depend on whether he takes "dead" to refer to the physically dead or to the spiritually dead.

RETAIN, to lay hold of.
r. thine integrity, Job 2:9.
strong men *r.* riches, Prov. 11:16.
whose sins ye *r.,* John 20:23.
not like to *r.* God, Rom. 1:28.

RETIRE, to turn back, to scatter.

Israel *r.* in battle, Judg. 20:39.
r., stay not, Jer. 4:6.

RETURN, to turn back, repay.
unto dust shall *r.*, Gen. 3:19.
naked shall I *r.*, Job 1:21.
r. we beseech thee, Ps. 80:14.
spirit *r.* unto God, Eccles. 12:7.
r. unto me, I have, Is. 44:22.
r. every one from, Jer. 18:11.
r. unto me and I will, Mal. 3:7.
will *r.* into my, Matt. 12:44.

REU, RAGAU, the son of Peleg and the father of Serug (Gen. 11:18–21; I Chr. 1:25). He is called Ragau in Luke 3:35.

REUBEN, (1) the first-born of Jacob and Leah, and one of the twelve patriarchs (Gen. 29:32). Jacob said that Reuben was unstable and that he would not succeed (Gen. 35:22). (2) The tribe of Reuben, to whom the birthright belonged, played an unimportant role in the history of Israel. When they came to Canaan, Reuben and Gad were permitted to settle on the eastern side of Jordan provided they help take the land on the western side (Num. 32:1–32). Its territory lay north of Moab. It was rebuked in the Song of Deborah because it refused to fight in the war against Sisera (Judg. 5:15–16).

REUBENITE, a descendant of Reuben.

REUEL, (1) the son of Esau by his wife Bashemath (Gen. 36:4, 10, 35). (2) A priest of Midian who received Moses when he escaped from Egypt (Ex. 2:8). (3) The father of Eliasaph, the captain of the host of Gad (Num. 2:14). (4) The son of Ibnijah and the father of Shephatiah (I Chr. 9:8).

REUMAH, the concubine of Nahor (Gen. 22:24).

REVEAL, uncover, disclose.
heaven shall *r.*, Job 20:27.
arm of Lord *r.*, Is. 53:1.
r. unto babes, Matt. 11:25.
be *r.* by fire, I Cor. 3:13.
r. his son in me, Gal. 1:16.
man of sin be *r.*, II Thess. 2:3.

REVELATION, means uncovering or unveiling, and expresses the idea that God

has made known to men truths and realities which men could not discover for themselves. Usually distinction is made between general and special revelation. General revelation is that which is given to all men, in nature and history, and in the nature of man himself (Ps. 19:1; Rom. 1:19, 20; 2:14; Acts 17:25). Special revelation is given to us by Christ and His Apostles in the Holy Scriptures, which are the final and ultimate revelation of God (Heb. 1:1–2; II Pet. 1:19; Jude 1:3).
the *r.* of the mystery, Rom. 16:25.
by the *r.* of Jesus, Gal. 1:12.
spirit of wisdom and *r.*, Eph. 1:17.
r. of Jesus Christ, I Pet. 1:13.
the *r.* of Jesus Christ, Rev. 1:1.

REVELATION, THE BOOK OF, the last book of the New Testament and the consummation of Biblical prophecy and revelation. It is a record of prophetic visions given by Jesus Christ to John the Apostle, while the latter was a prisoner for the cause of Jesus in Patmos, a small island in the Aegean (Rev. 1:1, 9). John wrote it by express command of Christ (1:10–13) about 95 or 96 A.D. and it was addressed to the seven churches of Asia (1:10, 11). The Book relates to "things which must shortly come to pass" (1:1), and a distinct blessing is vouchsafed to the person that reads and to those who hear the words of this prophecy (1:3). The Book is highly symbolical. The theme of it is the conflict of Christ and His church with anti-Christian powers (the devil, the beast, the false prophet, Ch. 16:13), and the ultimate and decisive defeat of the latter. This theme is expressed in these words: "The kingdom of the world is become the kingdom of Our Lord, and of His Christ: and he shall reign forever and ever" (11:15). Its keynote is in the words, "Come, Lord Jesus" (22:20, cf 1:7). The Book refers chiefly to events contemporary to that day, and is intended to comfort the then-persecuted church.

REVELLINGS, lustful indulgence.
drunkenness, *r.*, Gal. 5:21.
r. banquetings, I Pet. 4:3.

REVENGE, REVENGER, indicates to avenge a wrong or the one who brings punishment. *See* **AVENGER OF BLOOD.**

the r. of blood, Num. 35:19.
r. me of my persecutors, Jer. 15:15.
take r. on him, Jer. 20:10.
a r. to execute, Rom. 13:4.
what r., II Cor. 7:11.
r. all disobedience, II Cor. 10:6.

REVENUE, income or revenue, increase.
the r. of the king, Ezra 4:13.
the r. of the wicked, Prov. 15:6.
great r. without right, Prov. 16:8.
her r., Is. 23:3.

REVERENCE, respect, honour.
r. my sanctuary, Lev. 19:30.
fell on his face and did r., II Sam. 9:6.
did r., to the king, I Kings 1:31.
r. of all them, Ps. 89:7.
she r. her husband, Eph. 5:33.
gave them r., Heb. 12:9.

REVEREND, to be feared, honoured.
holy and r. is . . name, Ps. 111:9.

REVERSE, to cause to turn back.
I cannot r. it, Num. 23:20.
to r. the letters, Esther 8:5.

REVILE, REVILER, to make light of.
thou shalt not r., Ex. 22:28.
afraid of their r., Is. 51:7.
the r. of the children, Zeph. 2:8.
men shall r. you, Matt. 5:11.
passed by r., Matt. 27:39.
nor r., I Cor. 6:10.

REVISED STANDARD VERSION, see
VERSIONS.

REVISED VERSION, see VERSIONS.

REVIVE, REVIVING, cause to live.
Jacob their father r., Gen. 45:27.
he r., Judges, 15:19.
thou wilt r., Ps. 138:7.
r. thy work, Hab. 3:2.
rose and r., Rom. 14:9.

REVOLT, insurrection, transgression.
from whom Israel r., Is. 31:6.
oppression and r., Is. 59:13.
this people are r., Jer. 5:23.

REWARD, to recompense, wages.
the r. of the wicked, Ps. 91:8.
victuals and a r., Jer. 40:5.
asketh for a r., Mic. 7:3.
your r. in heaven, Matt. 5:12.
worthy of his r., I Tim. 5:18.

great recompense of the r., Heb. 10:35.
r. of them, Heb. 11:6.
my r. is with me, Rev. 22:12.

REZEPH, a stronghold near Haran, taken
by the Assyrians (II Kin. 19:12; Is. 37:
12).

REZIA, one of the sons of Ulla, of the
tribe of Asher (I Chr. 7:39).

REZIN, (1) the last of the kings of Syria,
who was contemporary with Pekah in
Israel and with Jotham and Ahaz in
Judah (II Kin. 15:37; 16:5). (2) One of
the families of the Nethinims (Ezra
2:48; Neh. 7:50).

REZON, the son of Eliadah, and a subject of Hadadezer (I Kin. 11:23).

RHEGIUM, a town on the southwest
coast of Italy, at the southern entrance of
the Strait of Messina. It is now called
Reggio (Acts 28:13).

RHESA, a son of Zerubbabel in the genealogy of Jesus (Luke 3:27).

RHODA, the maiden who announced the
arrival of Peter at the door of Mary's
house after his release from the prison by
the angel (Acts 12:13).

RHODES, an island in the Mediterranean
Sea, near the coast of Asia Minor. The
Colossus, one of the wonders of the
world, was erected at its harbor (Acts
21:1).

RIBAI, a Benjamite of Gibeah, whose son
Ittai was one of David's mighty men (II
Sam. 23:29; I Chr. 11:31).

RIBLAH, (1) a landmark on the eastern
boundary of Israel, as given by Moses
(Num. 34:11). (2) A town of Hamath,
the camping ground of the kings of
Babylon, from which they directed oper-
ations against Palestine and Phoenicia
(II Kin. 23:33; 25:6).

RICHES, wealth.
the r. of his goodness, Rom. 2:4.
r. of his grace, Eph. 1:7.
r. of Christ, Eph. 3:8.
his r. in glory, Phil. 4:19.

RICHLY, abundantly, greatly.

word dwell in you *r.*, Col. 3:16.
God, who giveth *r.*, 1 Tim. 6:17.

RID, RIDDANCE, remove or clean out.
r. him out of, Gen. 37:22.
r. evil beasts, Lev. 26:6.
a speedy *r.*, Zeph. 1:18.

RIDDLE, a hard question or dark saying.
put forth a *r.*, Judg. 14:12.
put forth a *r.*, Ezek. 17:2.

RIDE, to be carried.
r. upon Heaven, Deut. 33:26.
to *r.* upon it, Job 30:22.
that *r.* upon Heavens, Ps. 68:4.
Lord *r.* upon a cloud, Is. 19:1.

RIDER, one who rides.
this *r.*, Gen. 49:17.
horse and his *r.*, Ex. 15:21.
the horse and his *r.*, Job 39:18.

RIE, *see* **FITCHES.**

RIGHT, straight, direct, just, upright.
which is *r.*, Ex. 15:26.
are *r.* words, Job 6:25.
know not to do *r.*, Amos 3:10.
thy heart is not *r.*, Acts 8:21.

RIGHTEOUSLY, rightly, justly.
judge *r.* between, Deut. 1:16.
judge the people *r.*, Ps. 67:4.
Lord .. judgest *r.*, Jer. 11:20.
live soberly, *r.*, Titus 2:12.

RIGHTEOUSNESS, purity of heart and
rectitude of life; the being and doing
right. The righteousness of God is the
divine holiness applied in moral government and the domain of law. The righteousness of the law is that obedience
which the law requires (Rom. 3:10). The
righteousness of faith is the justification
which is received by faith in Christ (Rom.
3:21–28; 5:1–11; I Cor. 1:30).
to him for *r.*, Gen. 15:6.
my *r.* I hold fast, Job 27:6.
r. as a mighty stream, Amos 5:24.
r. of God, Rom. 1:17.
counted for *r.*, Rom. 4:5.
hope of *r.* by faith, Gal. 5:5.
follow after *r.*, I Tim. 6:11.
r. and truth, Eph. 5:9.

RIGHTLY, correctly.
hast *r.* judged, Luke 7:43.

thou teachest *r.*, Luke 20:21.
r. dividing the word, II Tim. 2:15.

RIGOUR, severity, strictness.
to serve with *r.*, Ex. 1:13.
not rule .. with *r.*, Lev. 25:43.

RIMMON, REMMON, RIMMONO,
(1) a Benjamite, whose sons, Baanah and
Rechab, murdered Ish-bosheth (II Sam.
4:2–9). (2) A Syrian deity worshipped in
Damascus (II Kin. 5:18). (3) A town in
the south of Judah allotted to Simeon
(Josh. 15:32). (4) A city of Zebulon
(I Chr. 6:77).

RIMMON-METHOAR, one of the landmarks of the eastern boundary of Zebulun, probably identical with Rimmon
(Josh. 19:13).

RIMMON-PAREZ, RIMMON-PEREZ,
one of the seventeen camping grounds of
the Israelites during their thirty-seven
years of wandering about in the desert
after leaving Kadesh (Num. 33:19, 20).

RING, was at a very ancient date a symbol of authority and dignity. Pharaoh
gave his ring to Joseph as a token that he
transferred to him the exercise of the
royal authority. Such a transfer is twice
related of Ahasuerus (Esther 3:8–10;
8:2). In the New Testament the ring is a
symbol of honor and dignity (Luke 15:
22).
Pharaoh took off his *r.*, Gen. 41:42.
with the king's *r.*, Esther 3:12.
put a *r.* on, Luke 15:22.
man with a gold *r.*, James 2:2.

RINNAH, a son of Simeon, of the tribe of
Judah (I Chr. 4:20).

RIOT, unrestrained behaviour.
not in *r.*, Rom. 13:13.
not accused of *r.*, Titus 1:6.
excess of *r.*, I Pet. 4:4.
to *r.* in the day, II Pet. 2:13.

RIPE, mature, full grown.
first of *r.* fruits, Ex. 22:29.
sickle, harvest is *r.*, Joel 3:13.
harvest of earth *r.*, Rev. 14:15.

RIPHATH, DIPHATH, the second son
of Gomer, and grandson of Japheth,
(Gen. 10:3; I Chr. 1:6).

RISE, to get up, to arise.
war r. against me, Ps. 27:3.
maketh sun to r., Matt. 5:45.
third day he shall r., Matt. 20:19.
r., take thy bed, John 5:8.
if dead r. not, I Cor. 15:15.

RISSAH, one of the stations of Israel in the wilderness, thought to be identical with Rasa, thirty-two Roman miles from Ailah (Num. 33:21, 22).

RITHMAH, a desert camp of the Israelites (Num. 33:18, 19).

RIVER, a flowing stream of water. It might be a canal, brook or muddy wadi. The largest rivers mentioned in the Bible are the Tigris, Euphrates, Nile, Jordan, Pharpar, and Abana. The most important river in the Bible is the River Jordan. Frequently "rivers" and "waters" are used in the Bible to symbolize abundance, as grace of God, of peace, of good things of life, or of the prosperity of God's children.
he stood by the r., Gen. 41:1.
cast into the r., Ex. 1:22.
the great r., Josh. 1:4.
r. of thy pleasures, Ps. 36:8.
r. of waters, Prov. 5:16.
peace, like a r., Is. 66:12.
with thy r., Ezek. 32:2.

RIZIA, an Asherite (I Chr. 7:39).

RIZPAH, a concubine of King Saul. In II Sam. 3:7 the subject of a coarse slander. II Sam. 21 contains the pathetic story of Rizpah's faithful watch over the bodies of her dead sons, Mephibosheth and Armoni.

ROAD, (1) raid, invasion. Occurs in the King James Version only in I Sam. 27:10. (2) Way, a means of communication. Five roads in Palestine are worthy of mention: (a) the one from Ptolemais, on the coast of the Mediterranean, to Damascus. (b) the one passing along the Mediterranean coast southward to Egypt. (c) the third connected Galilee with Judea, running through Samaria. (d) one running from Jerusalem to Mt. Olives. (e) Another running from Jerusalem to Joppa.
by the king's high w., Num. 20:17.
the w. that goeth, Acts 8:26.

ROAR, ROARING, a loud deep sound.
the sea r. and the, Ps. 46:3.
thine enemies r., Ps. 74:4.
young lions r. like, Ps. 104:21.
the Lord will r., Amos 1:2.

ROAST, cook meat. Prepare by fire.
r. with fire, Ex. 12:8.
r. and eat it in the, Deut. 16:7.
r. the passover with, II Chr. 35:13.
I have r. flesh, Is. 44:19.

ROB, ROBBERY, theft and plunder, systematically organized. Robbery was forbidden in the Mosaic law (Lev. 19:13), in the Proverbs (22:22) and in the Prophets (Is. 10:2; Ezek. 22:29; Hos. 6:9).
r. their treasures, Is. 10:13.
I hate r. for, Is. 61:8.
ye have r. me, Mal. 3:8.
I r. other churches, II Cor. 11:8.
not r. to be equal, Phil. 2:6.

ROBBER, see THIEF.
r. swalloweth up, Job 5:5.
full of lies and r., Nahum 3:1.
a thief and a r., John 10:1.
neither r. of churches, Acts 19:37.
in perils of r., II Cor. 11:26.

ROBBERS OF CHURCHES, a term used by the town clerk of Ephesus. The temple of Diana at Ephesus had a great treasure-chamber (Acts 19:37).

ROBE, attire, clothes, raiment, garments, etc. See CLOTHING.
Saul's r. privily, I Sam. 24:4.
the best r., Luke 15:22.
walk in long r., Luke 20:46.
a purple r., John 19:2.
White r., Rev. 6:11.

ROBOAM, the Greek form of King Rehoboam (Matt. 1:7).

ROCK, FIGURATIVE, (1) illustrative of God, as the Creator of His people, as the strength of His people, as their refuge and salvation.
He is the R., Deut. 32:4.
the r. that begat, Deut. 32:18.
my strong r., Ps. 31:2.
the r. of my salvation, Ps. 89:26.
   (2) rocks are a refuge both figuratively and literally.
a r. for the conies, Ps. 104:18.

a *r.* of offence, Is. 8:14.
dwell in the *r.*, Jer. 48:28.
　(3) a symbol of hardness and of that which endures.
in the *r.* for ever, Job 19:24.
harder than a *r.*, Jer. 5:3.
that breaketh the *r.*, Jer. 23:29.

ROCK BADGER, *see* **CONEY.**

ROD, (1) a stick; a shepherd's staff. *See* **AARON'S ROD.**
with the *r.* of men, II Sam. 7:14.
spareth his *r.*, Prov. 13:24.
under the *r.*, Ezek. 20:37.
with thy *r.*, Mic. 7:14.
with a *r.*, I Cor. 4:21.
beaten with *r.*, II Cor. 11:25.

RODANIM, variant of Dodanim and are generally identified as inhabitants of the island of Rhodes. (Gen. 10:4; I Chr. 1:7).

ROE, ROEBUCK, a kind of deer or hart.
as the *r.* and the, Deut. 15:22.
and pleasant *r.*, Prov. 5:19.
as a *r.* from the, Prov. 6:5.

ROGELIM, the place whence came Barzillai the Gileadite to succor David in his flight from Absalom (II Sam. 17:27; 19:31).

ROHGAH, the second son of Shamer, of the tribe of Asher, and fifth in descent from that patriarch (I Chr. 7:34).

ROIMUS, REHUM, one of the leaders with Zerubbabel in the return (Ezra 2:2).

ROLL, SCROLL, the usual form of book in Bible times. It had been in use in Egypt for perhaps 2,000 years at the time when, according to Pentateuch, the earliest Bible books were written in this form. It was made of papyrus or parchment. *See* **DEAD SEA SCROLLS.**
a great *r.* and write, Is. 8:1.
a *r.* of a book, Jer. 36:2.
a *r.* of a book was, Ezek. 2:9.
eat this *r.* and go, Ezek. 3:1.

ROLL, to move by turning over.
r. great stones upon, Josh. 10:18.
he that *r.* a stone, Prov. 26:27.
r. back the stone, Matt. 28:2.
found . . stone *r.* away, Luke 24:2.

scroll when it is *r.*, Rev. 6:14.

ROMAMTI-EZER, son of Heman appointed chief of the 24th division of singers in David's time (I Chr. 25:4, 31).

ROMAN, a citizen of the Roman empire.
R. shall come, John 11:48.
strangers of *R.*, Acts 2:10.
man that is a *R.*, Acts 22:25.
the hands of the *R.*, Acts 28:17.

ROMAN EMPIRE, the government of the Romans under the emperors, beginning with Augustus. By the victory of Actium, Octavianus became the undisputed master of the Roman world. He did not take the name of king, but had taken the title of Caesar, and now allowed himself to be called Augustus, retaining the old official title of imperator. The emperor was nominally elected, but practically it passed by adoption and till Nero's time a sort of hereditary right seemed to be recognized. Before the conquests of Pompey and Caesar the Roman empire was confined to a narrow strip encircling the Mediterranean Sea. Pompey added Asia Minor and Syria; Caesar added Gaul. The subsequent conquests made it a large empire. The population of the empire at the time of Augustus has been calculated at eighty-five million. The usual fate of a country conquered by Rome was to become a subject province, governed by officers sent from Rome. The provinces were heavily taxed for the benefit of the empire. The chief prophetic notices of the empire are found in Daniel and Revelation.

ROMANS, EPISTLE TO, the greatest of Paul's epistles, and considered by many as the greatest book in the New Testament. Galatians has been called the "Magna Charta" of Christian liberty and the Roman epistle has been called the "Constitution" of Christianity. The greatness of the Epistle is seen in the importance of its subject matter, the comprehensiveness of its grasp, the acuteness of its reasoning, the breadth of its outlook, and the vigor of its style.
　The letter was written to the Church at Rome by Paul (Rom. 1:1) about 56 A.D. It was written in Corinth during Paul's three months' visit in Greece (Acts 20:2, 3). The Epistle appears to have been occasioned by Paul's interest in the

Church at Rome and his purpose to visit it in the near future and by the opportunity presented by the going of Phoebe to Rome to send a letter to the saints in that city (Rom. 1:13; 15:22-24; 28, 29; 16:1, 2). Judging from the contents of the Epistle, the Apostle's purpose seems to be to teach the believers at Rome the fundamental doctrines of salvation and justification (Chs. 1-8), to explain the unbelief of Israel and to indicate its extent and duration (Chs. 9-11) and to exhort his readers about practical Christian life (Chs. 12-16). The theme of the Book is the Gospel, God's power unto salvation (Rom. 1:16).

ROME, one of the most famous cities of the world. The foundation of Rome dates from 753 B.C. It takes its name from the name of its founder, Romulus. It was located upon marshy ground by the river Tiber, in Italy. It was situated on seven hills. The monarchical government existed under seven princes like Romulus, Numa, etc. The abolition of monarchy was followed by a period of government under the consuls. With the battle of Actium Octavianus was invested with the title of Augustus, to which was added the title "Imperator," or emperor. In the reign of Augustus Christ was born and in the reign of Tiberius Christ was crucified on Calvary. The successive emperors were among the worst of mankind. The history of Rome, politically and morally, from Tiberius, in 37 A.D., to the reign of Constantine, in 313 A.D., when the edict in favor of Christianity was issued, was lamentably bad.
strangers of R., Acts 2:10.
depart from R., Acts 18:2.
must also see R., Acts 19:21.
witness also at R., Acts 23:11.
went toward R., Acts 28:14.
came to R., Acts 28:16.
that be in R., Rom. 1:7.

ROOF, the top-covering of a house.
shadow of my r., Gen. 19:8.
the r. of the house, Josh. 2:6.
upon whose r., Jer. 19:13.
r. of one little, Ezek. 40:13.
uncovered the r., Mark 2:4.
enter under my r., Luke 7:6.

ROOM, an apartment of a house.
his r. over the, I Kin. 2:35.
in the r. of David, I Kin. 8:20.

reigned in his r., II Kin. 15:25.
in a large r., Ps. 31:8.
preparedst r., Ps. 80:9.
gift maketh r., Prov. 18:16.

ROOT, part of a plant.
taking r., Job 5:3.
r. thee out of, Ps. 52:5.
take deep r., Ps. 80:9.
r. of the righteous, Prov. 12:3.
a r. of Jesse, Is. 11:10.
out of the serpent's r., Is. 14:29.
to take r., Is. 27:6.
plucked up by the r., Luke 17:6.
being r. and, Eph. 3:17.
the r. of all evil, I Tim. 6:10.
any r. of bitterness, Heb. 12:15.
r. of David, Rev. 5:5.

ROSE, a flower, a lily.
the r. of Sharon, Song. 2:1.
blossom as the r., Is. 35:1.

ROSE, got up, ascended.
Cain r. up against, Gen. 4:8.
though one r. from, Luke 16:31.
Christ died and r., Rom. 14:9.

ROSH, (1) a son of Benjamin (Gen. 46:21). (2) In the Revised Version of Ezek. 38:2, 3; 39:1, it is translated as a name. In the Authorized Version it is translated "chief prince."

ROT, ROTTEN, ROTTENNESS, symbol of gradual decay, and of weakness.
as a r. thing, Job 13:28.
as r. wood, Job 41:27.
wicked shall r., Prov. 10:7.
as r. in his bones, Prov. 12:4.
r. of the bones, Prov. 14:30.
r. entered into, Hab. 3:16.

ROUGH, harsh, hairy, sharp.
into an r. valley, Deut. 21:4.
the r. places plain, Is. 40:4.
and the r. goat, Dan. 8:21.
wear a r. garment, Zech. 13:4.
r. ways made smooth, Luke 3:5.

ROUGHLY, harshly, sharply.
spake r. unto them, Gen. 42:7.
answer thee r., I Sam. 20:10.
king answered . . r., II Chr. 10:13.

ROW, ROWING, move by oars.
thy r. have, Ezek. 27:26.
men r. hard, Jonah 1:13.
toiling in r., Mark 6:48.

they had *r*. about, John 6:19.

ROYAL, fit for a king, majesty.
he shall yield *r*., Gen. 49:20.
one of the *r*. cities, Josh. 10:2.
such *r*. majesty, I Chr. 29:25.
seed *r*. of the house, II Chr. 22:10.
in *r*. apparel, Acts 12:21.
the *r*. law, James 2:8.

RUBIES, RUBY, red precious stones.
wisdom is above *r*., Job 28:18.
precious than *r*., Prov. 3:15.
a multitude of *r*., Prov. 20:15.

RUDDY, red in color.
he was *r*. and, I Sam. 16:12.
a youth and *r*., I Sam. 17:42.
is white and *r*., Song. 5:10.
r. in body than rubies, Lam. 4:7.

RUDE, untrained, ignorant, unlearned.
be *r*. in speech, II Cor. 11:6.

RUDIMENTS, the first principles. In II
Pet. 3:10 it is rendered "elements" and
in Heb. 5:12, "the first principles."
the *r*. of the world, Col. 2:8.
from the *r*. of the, Col. 2:20.

RUE, a small plant growing 2 to 4 ft. high
with a heavy odor, and is mentioned in
Luke 11:42 as subject to tithe.

RUFUS, (1) brother of Alexander, and
son of Simon the Cyrenian, whom the
Jews compelled to bear the cross of Jesus
(Mark 15:21). (2) One included by Paul
among those in Rome to whom he sends
greetings (Rom. 16:13).

RUHAMAH, a figurative title applied to
the daughter of the prophet Hosea, signifying that God would restore Israel to
favor provided they repent (Hos. 2:1).

RUIN, breakage or desolation.
strongholds to *r*., Ps. 89:40.
brought it to *r*., Is. 23:13.
defenced city a *r*., Is. 25:2.
day of thy *r*., Ezek. 27:27.
r. of that house, Luke 6:49.
build again the *r*., Acts 15:16.

RULE, to have dominion, to have power.
light *r*. the day, Gen. 1:16.
by me princes *r*., Prov. 8:16.
r. in judgment, Is. 32:1.
put down all *r*., I Cor. 15:24.

peace of God *r*., Col. 3:15.
elders that *r*. well, I Tim. 5:17.
r. with rod of iron, Rev. 2:27.

RULER, kings, stewards, high priests, etc.
r. throughout the, Gen. 45:8.
r. over my cattle, Gen. 47:6.
appointed thee *r*., I Sam. 25:30.
r. over the people of, II Sam. 6:21.
chief *r*. about David, II Sam. 20:26.
r. over all the charge, I Kin. 11:28.
r. of the house of God, I Chr. 9:11.
r. of the treasures, I Chr. 26:24.
r. of the half part, Neh. 3:9.
r. over his household, Matt. 24:45.

RUMAH, *see* ARUMAH.

RUMOUR, RUMOURS, reports.
shall hear a *r*., II Kin. 19:7.
a *r*. from the, Jer. 49:14.
r. of wars, Matt. 24:6.
r. of him went, Luke 7:17.

RUN, to go, to rush.
strong . . to *r*. race, Ps. 19:5.
rivers *r*. into sea, Eccles. 1:7.
nations *r*. unto thee, Is. 55:5.
eyes of the Lord *r*., Zech. 4:10.
had *r*. in vain, Gal. 2:2.
r. with patience, Heb. 12:1.

RUSH, a plant with a long flat leaf which
grows in the marshy lowlands of Palestine and Egypt. It is translated from two
different words: one meaning papyrus
(Job 8:11; Is. 53:7), and one meaning
bulrush (Is. 58:5) and hook (Job 41:2).

RUSH, to move rapidly.
r. forward, and stood, Judg. 9:44.
nations shall *r*. like, Is. 17:13.
they *r*. with one accord, Acts 19:29.

RUST, the red oxide of iron formed by
the corrosion of metal.
r. doth corrupt, Matt. 6:19.
neither moth nor *r*., Matt. 6:20.
the *r*. of them, James 5:3.

RUTH, a Moabitess, first the wife of
Mahlon, and then of Boaz, and an ancestress of David and of Christ. She was
first married to Mahlon, the son of
Elimelech and Naomi, who emigrated
to the land of Moab. When Naomi resolved to return to her own country,
Bethlehem, after the death of her two
sons, Ruth determined to accompany

her in spite of her mother-in-law's entreaty that she should return to her own people and god. They arrived at Bethlehem just at the beginning of the barley harvest. Ruth went out to glean for the purpose of procuring support for herself and Naomi and in gleaning came by chance upon Boaz, a kinsman of Naomi, who later married Ruth according to the right of a nearer redeemer. In process of time Ruth became the mother of Obed, the father of Jesse and grandfather of David, an ancestor of Christ.

name of the other *R.*, Ruth 1:4.
R. clave unto her, Ruth 1:14.
R. the Moabitess, Ruth 1:22.
R. hearest, Ruth 2:8.
R. thine handmaid, Ruth 3:9.
Boaz took *R.*, Ruth 4:13.
begat Obed of *R.*, Matt. 1:5.

RUTH, BOOK OF, in the Hebrew canon the Book is one of the five Rolls, which were ordered to be read in the synagogue on five special occasions or festivals during the year. The Book is written without name of author, and there is no direct indication of its date. However, according to the language and style and the contents of the Book it seems likely that it was composed at some time during the reign of David. The Book records an event of interest and importance in the family history of David, and incidentally illustrates ancient custom and marriage law. The ethical value of the Book of Ruth is considerable, as setting forth an example of stedfast filial piety. The action of Ruth in refusing to desert her mother-in-law and persevering in accompanying her to her own land meets with its due reward in the prosperity and happiness which become hers, and in the honor which she receives as ancestress of the royal house of David. The Book shows that the true religion is supernatural, and not confined to the bounds of any one people.

S

SABACHTHANI, "thou hast forsaken me." (Matt. 27:46). *See* ELOI, ELOI, LAMA SABACHTHANAI.

SABAOTH, *see* GOD.
except the Lord of *S.*, Rom. 9:29

ears of the Lord of *S.*, James 5:4.

SABBATH, the Jewish day on which labor ceased and rest prevailed. God created the world in six days and on the seventh day he rested from his labors (Gen. 2:1–3). God set apart the day as a day of rest (Gen. 2:3). The observing of the Sabbath was peculiar to the Jews and was one of the ways to distinguish them from foreigners (Neh. 10:31; 13:15). The Israelites first observed the Sabbath in the wilderness when God told them to gather enough manna to last for two days (Ex. 16:23). In the fourth commandment, Moses received instruction to remember the Sabbath, and to keep it holy, as the day sanctified by God in the days of Creation (Ex. 20:8–11; 31:16–18; Deut. 5:15). Two lambs instead of one were offered on the Sabbath. And anyone who worked on the Sabbath was put to death (Lev. 23:3; Num. 15:36; 28:9). The Jews, before the exile in Babylon, were accused of profaning and neglecting the Sabbath (Jer. 17:27). After the return to Jerusalem the Jews covenanted to keep the Sabbath. Nehemiah refused to allow traders from Tyre to trade in Jerusalem on the Sabbath (Neh. 10:31; 13:15–22). In New Testament times the Pharisees enforced observance of the Sabbath upon the people in such a way as to make man a slave to it. Jesus said the Sabbath was made for man, and not man for the Sabbath (Mark 2:27). Paul and companions used that day for teaching the Jews in their synagogues (Acts 13:14; 17:2). The first day of the week was the day of worship for the disciples of Christ (Acts 20:7; I Cor. 16:2; Rev. 1:10).

Remember the *s.* day, Ex. 20:8.
seventh day is the *s.*, Ex. 20:10.
shalt number seven *s.*, Lev. 25:8.
it was made for man, Mark 2:27.
lawful to do good on . . *s.*, Mark 3:4.
new moon, or of the *s.*, Col. 2:16.

SABBATICAL YEAR, Moses' Law ordered the keeping of a year long Sabbath each seventh year (Ex. 23:10; Lev. 25: 2–7; Deut. 15:1–11; 31:10–13). Regulations of this year were: (1) No cultivation of the land; (2) Freeing of slaves; (3) Cancellation of all debts; and (4) Public reading of the Law at the Feast of Tabernacles. The first day of Tisri marked the start of the year. Refusal to keep this year of spiritual emphasis was one cause of the Captivity (II Chr. 36:21).

SABEANS, the descendants of Seba (Job 1:15; Joel 3:8).

SABTAH, SABTA, the third son of Cush (Gen. 10:7; I Chr. 1:9).

SABTECHA, SABTECHAH, SABTECA, the fifth son of Cush and grandson of Ham (Gen. 10:7; I Chr. 1:9).

SACAR, (1) the father of Ahiham, one of the valiant men of king David (I Chr. 11:35). (2) A Kohathite, the son of Obed-edom, who was a gatekeeper of the tabernacle (I Chr. 26:4).

SACK, bag.
put silver cup in *s.*, Gen. 44:2.
or *s.* of unclean must, Lev. 11:32.

SACKBUT, a wind instrument, resembling a trombone, which had a slide to regulate the pitch (Dan. 3:5).

SACKCLOTH, a coarse dark cloth made of goat's hair (Is. 50:3; Rev. 6:12). It was known as the garment worn in mourning (II Sam. 3:31; II Kin. 19:1, 2), sometimes of a prophet (Is. 20:2).
put *s.* upon his loins, Gen. 37:34.
and lay in *s.*, I Kin. 21:27.
put on *s.* with ashes, Esther 4:1.
sewed *s.* upon my skin, Job 16:15.
loose the *s.*, Is. 20:2.
spread *s.* and ashes, Is. 58:5.
repented long ago in *s.*, Matt. 11:21.
sun became black as *s.*, Rev. 6:12.

SACRIFICE, *see* **OFFERING AND SAC-RIFICE.**
let us go and *s.*, Ex. 3:18.
they *s.* on the tops of, Hos. 4:13.
desired mercy and not *s.*, Hos. 6:6.
offer blind for *s.*, Mal. 1:8.
offer a *s.* according, Luke 2:24.
bodies a living *s.*, Rom. 12:1.
a *s.* to God for sweet, Eph. 5:2.
a *s.* acceptable, Phil. 4:18.
put away sin by *s.*, Heb. 9:26.
remaineth no more *s.*, Heb. 10:26.
offer *s.* of praise, Heb. 13:15.

SACRILEGE, to profane a holy thing. This is forbidden the Jews (Lev. 19:8). In the New Testament it means "to rob temples" (Rom. 2:22).

SAD, dejected.
why is thy spirit *s.*?, I Kin. 21:5.
as hypocrites of a *s.*, Matt. 6:16.
was *s.* at that saying, Matt. 10:22.

SADDLE, to cover a riding animal's back to prevent chafing; also, the covering.
early, and *s.* his ass, Gen. 22:3.
Balaam *s.* his ass, Num. 22:21.

SADDUCEES, one of the three or four religious Jewish sects which was in existence in the day of Jesus and the apostles. They were of the social elite and denied the doctrine of the resurrection (Acts 23:7, 8), as well as the existence of angels and the possibility of life after death. They were strongly rebuked by John the Baptist (Matt. 3:7–9). They severely opposed and persecuted the apostles (Acts 4:1–3; 5:17–33). Politically, they favored Rome. They were the ones who controlled the priesthood for about 200 years prior to the destruction of Jerusalem (A.D. 70).
S. come to his baptism, Matt. 3:7.
Pharisees with the *S.*, Matt. 16:1.
the leaven . . of the *S.*, Matt. 16:6, 11.
the doctrine . . of the *S.*, Matt. 16:12.
the priest . . and the *S.*, Acts 4:1.
which is the sect of . . *S.*, Acts 5:17.
S. say . . no resurrection, Acts 23:8.

SADOC, an ancestor of Jesus who lived in the post-exilic period (Matt. 1:14).

SAFE, secure, free from harm.
and ye dwelled *s.*, I Sam. 12:11.
man Absalom *s.*?, II Sam. 18:29.
had received him *s.*, Luke 15:27.
for you it is *s.*, Phil. 3:1.

SAFELY, securely, without danger.
to me shall dwell *s.*, Prov. 1:33.
make to lie down *s.*, Hos. 2:18.
jailor to keep them *s.*, Acts 16:23.

SAFETY, freedom from harm or danger.
I was not in *s.*, Job 3:26.
I will set him in *s.*, Ps. 12:5.
say, Peace and *s.*, I Thess. 5:3.

SAFFRON, a variety of sweet-scented crocus (Song 4:14).

SAIL, part of wind-propelled ship.
could not spread *s.*, Is. 33:23.
spreadest to be thy *s.*, Ezek. 27:7.

SAIL, be propelled by wind on sails.
as he was about to s., Acts 20:3.
we should s. into Italy, Acts 27:1.

SAINT, in the Old Testament, the term applies to the "kind" or "pious" souls of the Hebrews. In the New Testament, one reference is made to the dead saints who arose when Jesus died (Matt. 27:52). Elsewhere in the New Testament the term is used exclusively for the disciples or Christians.
his s. are in thy hand, Deut. 33:3.
the feet of his s., I Sam. 2:9.
forsaketh not his s., Ps. 37:28.
the flesh of thy s., Ps. 79:2.
s. of the most High, Dan. 7:18.
bodies of the s., Matt. 27:52.
intercessions for the s., Rom. 8:27.
called to be s., I Cor. 1:2.
ministering to the s., II Cor. 8:4.
supplication for all s., Eph. 6:18.
the s. in Christ Jesus, Phil. 1:1.

SAKE, objective or end; benefit.
cursed ground for thy s., Gen. 3:17.
for his name's s., Ps. 23:3.
for thy mercies' s., Ps. 44:26.
for righteousness s., Matt. 5:10.
for my name's s., Matt. 10:22.
kingdom of heaven's s., Matt. 19:12.
for conscience s., Rom. 13:5.
wine for stomach's s., I Tim. 5:23.

SALA, SALAH, see **SHELA.**

SALAMIS, a city in the southeastern part of Cyprus (Acts 13:4, 5).

SALATHIEL, SHEALTIEL, a son or grandson of Jeconiah, the son of Jehoiakim, king of Judah before the Babylonian exile (I Chr. 3:17; Neh. 12:1; Hag. 1:1).

SALCHAN, SALCAH, SALECAH, a town of Gad in the northeast of Bashan (Deut. 3:10; Josh. 12:5; I Chr. 5:11).

SALEM, means "peaceful." It was the city of Melchisedec, the priest to whom Abraham paid tithes (Heb. 7:2). Some think it is used as an abbreviation for Jerusalem (Ps. 76:2).

SALIM, a city near Aenon where John the Baptist preached repentance and baptized (John 3:23).

SALLAI, (1) a leading Benjamite, the son of Meshullam, dwelling in Jerusalem in the post-exilic period (Neh. 11:8). (2) A priest who returned to Jerusalem with Zerubbabel (Neh. 12:20).

SALLU, a priest who returned with Zerubbabel from captivity (Neh. 12:7). He is thought to have been the same as Sallai (Neh. 12:20).

SALMA, a son of Caleb, the son of Hur, and father of Bethlehem (I Chr. 2:51).

SALIM, see **SHALMAI.**

SALMON, SALMA, (1) the father of Boaz, the husband of Ruth and great-grandfather of Jesse (Ruth 4:21; Matt. 1:5; Luke 3:32). (2) A wooded mount near Shechem in Samaria (Ps. 68:14).

SALMONE, a point in the eastern section of Crete. It is mentioned in connection with Paul's trip, by sea, to Rome (Acts 27:7).

SALOME, (1) the daughter of Herodias and Philip. Herodias married Philip's brother, Herod Antipas, and lived with him in open adultery. John condemned the unholy union and was put into prison. When Salome danced before Herod he was pleased and promised to give her anything she desired to have. She, persuaded by her mother, requested the head of John the Baptist on a charger (Matt. 14:6). Her wish was granted. (2) The wife of Zebedee and mother of James and John (Matt. 27:56; Mark 15:40; 16:1).

SALT, a mineral used as a condiment and preservative for food (Job 6:6). It could be easily scraped up on the edge of the Dead Sea. Under the law, it was presented with all kinds of offerings (Lev. 2:13; Ezek. 43:24). Since salt was destructive to plants, sometimes the last step in destroying a city would be to sow it with salt. Abimelech did this to Shechem (Judg. 9:45). Lot's wife turned to a pillar of salt (Gen. 19:26). Jesus called his disciples the "salt of the earth" (Matt. 5:13).
became a pillar of s., Gen. 19:26.
coast of the s. sea, Num. 34:3.
the valley of s., II Kin. 14:7.
in a s. land, Jer. 17:6.
Ye are . . . s. of . . earth, Matt. 5:13.

seasoned with *s.*, Col. 4:6.
yield *s.* water and fresh, James 3:12.

SALT, CITY OF, (Josh. 15:62) a city in the wilderness of Judah, probably at the lower end of the Dead Sea.

SALT SEA, *see* **DEAD SEA.**

SALT, VALLEY OF, a ravine south of the Dead Sea, on the border between Judah and Edom (II Sam. 8:13; II Kin. 14:7).

SALT-WORT, a sour, salty plant used by the poor as food. It grows on the shores of the Dead Sea (Job 30:4).

SALU, a Simeonite, the father of Zimri (Num. 25:14).

SALUTATION, the Hebrews greeted each other with various expressions of blessing (Gen. 43:29; Ruth 3:10; I Sam. 15:13) and parted with like blessings or "Go in Peace" (I Sam. 1:17; Mark 5:34). A common greeting in New Testament times was "Hail" (Matt. 26:49; 27:29). Letters began and ended with salutations, either extended (Rom. 1:1–7) or brief (I Thess. 1:1; 5:26–28).
scribes love *s.* in, Mark 12:38.
what manner of *s.*, Luke 1:29.
s. of me, Paul, I Cor. 16:21.

SALUTE, to greet.
if *s.* brethren only, Matt. 5:47.
began to *s.* him, Mark 15:18.
all saints *s.* you, II Cor. 13:13.
our friends *s.* thee, III John 14.

SALVATION, a word which is the rendering of various Hebrew and Greek words which carry the general idea of "safety, deliverance, state of security, saved, rescued, or forgiveness of sins." In the Old Testament the idea given by it is usually that deliverance from foes or from the devices and traps of the wicked (Ps. 37: 40; 59:2; 106:4). Sometimes, however, it denotes the forgiveness of sins (Ps. 51:12; 69:13; 79:9). The prophets spoke of one who would come and bring spiritual deliverance or salvation. The sending of the Messiah to bring about salvation was a sign of God's love (John 3:16). The gospel of Christ is the power of God which brings about salvation only to those who believe (Rom. 1:16).

waited for thy *s.*, Gen. 49:18.
I rejoice in thy *s.*, I Sam. 2:1.
the *s.* of Israel, Ps. 14:7.
from him cometh . . *s.*, Ps. 62:1.
working *s.* in . . the earth, Ps. 74:12.
Lord God of my *s.*, Ps. 88:1.
hoped for thy *s.*, Ps. 119:166.
and strength of *s.*, Is. 33:6.
S. is of the Lord, Jonah 2:9.
an horn of *s.*, Luke 1:69.
eyes have seen . . *s.*, Luke 2:30.
power of God unto *s.*, Rom. 1:16.
the gospel of your *s.*, Eph. 1:13.
the helmet of *s.*, Eph. 6:17.
grace of God bringeth *s.*, Titus 2:11.
neglect so great *s.*, Heb. 2:3.
Now is come *s.*, Rev. 12:10.

SAMARIA, (1) the capital city of the northern kingdom of Israel. It was located on a hill about three hundred feet high. To the west it looked upon the Mediterranean. Omri and Ahab erected fine buildings and fortifications there (I Kin. 22:39). It was. the "crown and pride" of Israel (Is. 28:1). During the reign of Ahab and Jezebel, a temple to Baal was erected there. The prophets quickly tried to destroy this idolatry (II Kin. 10:7, 14, 25). Later the prophets brought divine judgment upon the city and the nation (Is. 28:1–4; Hos. 8:3; Amos 3:11). In 722 B.C. Samaria fell to the Assyrians, and foreigners settled in the land (II Kin. 17:3–6, 24). The city continued to exist, and in the time of Jesus it was filled with pagan temples. It was also the center of Herod the Great's splendor. (2) The whole northern kingdom is sometimes called by this name (I Kin. 21:1; II Kin. 17:24; Jer. 31:5). (3) The district of Samaria (Neh. 4:2). In the time of Christ it was joined along with Idumea to make up the province of Judah.
bought the hill *S.*, I Kin. 16:24.
house of Baal . . in *S.*, I Kin. 16:32.
buried the king in *S.*, I Kin. 22:37.
Ben-hadad . . besieged *S.*, II Kin. 6:24.
Jehu reigned . . in *S.*, II Kin. 10:36.
Assyria took *S.*, II Kin. 17:6.
Shalmaneser against *S.*, II Kin. 18:9.
cometh . . to a city of *S.*, John 4:5.
scattered . . throughout *S.*, Acts 8:1.
Philip . . to . . city of *S.*, Acts 8:5.

SAMARITAN, only time used in the Old Testament (II Kin. 17:29). It means an individual belonging to the old kingdom of northern Israel. They became a mixed race after the destruction of Samaria in 722 B.C. There was a social repugnance on the part of most Jews to the association with the Samaritans (Ezra 4:3; Luke 9:52, 53; John 4:9). There remained a group of Samaritans who lived in the area between Judea and Galilee. They accepted only the books of the Pentateuch as proper Jewish scripture. They did not have Christ preached unto them until the persecution in Jerusalem (Acts 8:1). Philip came and preached the gospel in the city of Samaria (Acts 8:5).

SAME, identical, not different.
thou art the *s.,* Ps. 102:27.
Jesus Christ the *s.,* Heb. 13:8.

SAMGAR NEBO, a prince of the king of Babylon (Jer. 39:3).

SAMLAH, the fifth in the line of the ancient kings of Edom (Gen. 36:36, 37).

SAMOS, an island in the Aegean Sea, about nine miles off the coast of Lydia (Acts 20:15).

SAMOTHRACE, SAMOTHRACIA, an island off the coast of Thrace (Acts 16: 11).

SAMSON, a Danite, the son of Manoah. He was to be a Nazarite from birth (Judg. 13:1–24), and was to be a strong man because of his hair. He judged Israel for twenty years, opposing the Philistines during this time. He loved a Philistine woman whom he, at length, told the secret of his strength. As he slept, she cut his hair, reducing him to impotence. He, being unable to resist, was taken prisoner by the Philistines and blinded (Judg. 16: 16–30). When the princes of the Philistines were making sport of him in the house of Dagon, God gave him power to push down the pillars and cause the house to fall in, killing him and a multitude of Philistines.
and called his name *S.,* Judg. 13:24.
he caught 300 foxes, Judg. 15:4.
S. lay till midnight, Judg. 16:3.
Delilah said to *S.,* Judg. 16:6.
for *S* . . . make . . sport, Judg. 16:25.
S. called . . the Lord, Judg. 16:28.
died with Philistines, Judg. 16:30.
to tell of Gideon . . *S.,* Heb. 11:32.

SAMUEL, SHEMUEL, the son of Elkanah and Hannah, a Levite family of Kohath· (I Sam. 1:1; I Chr. 6:26, 35). Hannah was barren and prayed to God for a child. She promised him to God after he was weaned and God replied by giving her Samuel. He lived in the temple with Eli, the judge and religious leader of Israel. After the death of Eli, Samuel became the religious leader of the people. It was he who picked out Saul, rebuked Saul, and anointed David.
judged Israel, I Sam. 7:6.
anointed Saul king, I Sam. 10:1.
rebuked Saul severely, I Sam. 15:22.
anointed David king, I Sam. 16:13.
the sons of *S.,* I Chr. 6:28.
and *S.* the seer, I Chr. 9:22.
the prophets from *S.,* Acts 3:24.
David also, and *S.,* Heb. 11:32.

SAMUEL, BOOKS OF, these books cover the last days of the Judges, the days of Samuel, and the beginnings of the days of the kings, the days of Saul and David. The books begin with the story of the birth of Samuel, his call as a prophet, and the clamor of the people for a king (I Sam. 1–8). Then came Saul, a Benjamite. He was a tall man, kingly in appearance. But soon his jealousy revealed itself; he did not show much concern for the divine institutions. When Samuel told him that he would have to yield the throne, he refused to accept it. After Saul died, David became king. He was of Judah, from whom it was promised, "the sceptre shall not depart" (Gen. 49:10).

SANBALLAT, a native of Beth-horon in Ephraim. When Nehemiah came back to Jerusalem to rebuild the walls, Sanballat and his cohorts were his bitterest enemies (Neh. 2:10). Sanballat had a large group behind him, including a priest named Eliashib (Neh. 13:28). These men first ridiculed Nehemiah, then they attacked him with physical force, and they tried to assassinate him (Neh. 4:7; 6:1–4). However, Nehemiah finished his task in spite of them.

SANCTIFICATION, to set apart. Under the Mosaic Law the priests and the Levites were set apart for special service. Objects of use in the tabernacle were also sanctified, and days were set apart for special use. In the New Testament it

means to be made inwardly whole. The agent of this sanctification is the Holy Spirit (Rom. 15:16). It is the indwelling of Christ himself. Believers are referred to as "saints" (Rom. 12:13; II Cor. 1:1; Eph. 1:1).
salvation through *s.*, II Thess. 2:13.
s. of the spirit, I Pet. 1:2.

SANCTIFY, to dedicate, make holy.
s. unto me the firstborn, Ex. 13:2.
shalt *s.* the breast, Ex. 29:27.
s. the tabernacle, Ex. 29:44.
shall *s.* yourselves, Lev. 11:44.
the Lord do *s.*, Lev. 21:15.
s. the congregation, Joel 2:16.
s. through thy word, John 17:17.
God of peace *s.*, I Thess. 5:23.
s. the Lord God in, I Pet. 3:15.

SANCTUARY, the holy of holies in the tabernacle (Heb. 9:2) and in the temple (Lam. 2:7, 20; Ezek. 42:20).
make me a *s.*, Ex. 25:8.
the service of the *s.*, Ex. 36:1.
the charge of the *s.*, Num. 3:32.
the border of his *s.*, Ps. 102:19.
Praise God in his *s.*, Ps. 150:1.
minister of the *s.*, Heb. 8:2.

SAND, a symbol of uncounted multitudes.
thy seed as the *s.*, Gen. 22:17.
treasures hid in *s.*, Deut. 33:19.
Israel gathered as *s.*, II Sam. 17:11.
heavy *s.* weighty, Prov. 27:3.
captivity as the *s.*, Hab. 1:9.
built house on *s.*, Matt. 7:26.
number as the *s.*, Rev. 20:8.

SANDAL, *see* SHOE.

SANHEDRIN, SANHEDRIM, *see* COUNCIL.

SANSANNAH, a city in southern Judah, near Madmannah (Josh. 15:31).

SAPH, SIPPAI, a giant of the Philistines (II Sam. 21:18; I Chr. 20:4).

SAPHIR, SHAPHIR, a city in Ephraim or Judah (Mic. 1:11).

SAPPHIRA, the wife of Ananias (Acts 5:1–10). She and her husband sold a plot of land and presented a portion of the profit to Peter and the disciples in Jerusalem, telling them the amount given was the entire amount received for the land. Because they lied to God, they were both struck dead (Acts 5:1–11).

SAPPHIRE, a precious stone which is blue in color and transparent. It is found in Ethiopia and India. It was found in the breastplate of the high priest. In John's vision of the New Jerusalem, it was found in the city's foundation (Ex. 28:18; Song 5:14; Is. 54:11; Rev. 21:19).

SARAH, SARAI, SARA, (1) the wife of Abram, who bare Isaac at the age of ninety years. She died at the age of 127 and was buried at Machpelah (Gen. 17:1–19; 17:15–22; 20:12; Heb. 11:11, 12). Sarah means "princess." (2) A daughter of Asher (Num. 26:46).
S. shall have a son, Gen. 17:19.
Abraham and *S.* were old, Gen. 18:11.
Abimelech .. sent .. took *S.*, Gen. 20:2.
the Lord visited *S.*, Gen. 21:1.
Abraham came to mourn...*S.*, Gen.23:2
in cave of Machpelah, Gen. 23:19.
as *S.* obeyed Abraham, I Pet. 3:6.

SARAPH, a descendant of Shelah (I Chr. 4:22).

SARDINE, SARDIUS, a precious stone which was found near Sardis. In John's vision of the New Jerusalem, it garnished the sixth foundation of the city (Rev. 21:20). The stone adorned the breastplate of the high priest (Ex. 28:17).

SARDIS, a city of Asia Minor at the foot of Mount Tmolus. It was the home of one of the seven churches to whom John's Revelation was addressed (Rev. 1:11).

SARDITES, the family of Sered, a son of Zebulun (Num. 26:26).

SARDIUS, *see* SARDINE.

SARDONYX, a variety of chalcedony (Rev. 21:20). It garnished the fifth foundation of the wall of the New Jerusalem in the vision of John.

SAREPTA, *see* ZAREPHATH.

SARGON, a king of Assyria, mentioned by name in only one place in the Scripture (Is. 20:1). He was the successor of the last Shalmaneser. He was on the throne soon after the fall of Samaria (722 B.C.). His first years were spent in trying to unite Assyria. He had to crush many revolts, one of them being the occasion of one of Israel's oracles against Egypt (Is. 20:2–6). He soon conquered Armenia and Babylonia, and was free to build his great palace. He died in 705, leaving the throne to his son, Sennacherib.

SARID, a village in Zebulun or Issachar (Josh. 19:10, 12).

SARON, the sea coast between Joppa and Caesarea (Acts 9:35).

SARSECHIM, a prince of Nebuchadrezzar (Jer. 39:3).

SARUCH, the father of Nachor and an ancestor of Jesus (Luke 3:35).

SAT, occupied a seat, reposed.
Moses *s*. to judge, Ex. 18:13.
people *s*. in darkness, Matt. 4:16.
cloven tongues *s*. upon, Acts 2:3.
s. down on right hand, Heb. 1:3.
he that *s*. on throne, Rev. 4:3.

SATAN, the term meaning "adversary." It is used generically in I Kin. 11:14, "The Lord stirred up an adversary." He is specifically mentioned by name first in Job 1:6–12; 2:1. Christ also called him by name (Matt. 4:10) when he tried to prevail over the savior in the temptation after Jesus' period of fasting. He is hostile to both man and God (Job 2:3; Luke 22:3) in his attempt to destroy the work of God (Mark 4:15). His initial appearance in Biblical history was to Eve in the Garden of Eden (Gen. 3:1–3; II Cor. 11:3; Rev. 12:9). It was Satan, who was a murderer from the beginning (John 8:44), who persuaded Judas to betray the Lord (Luke 22:3; John 13:27).

In the New Testament, he is pictured as a real, vital power. He is a ruler of a kingdom which has powers. He rules over demons (Matt. 12:24; Luke 11:18; Rev. 12:7). He is the god and prince of this world (the world which opposes God) and goes about seeking to devour and enslave men (Luke 22:3; Acts 26:18; II Cor. 4:4; II Thess. 2:9; Rev. 12:9). *See* **DEVIL**.
and *S*. came also along, Job 1:6.
S. . . at his right hand, Zech. 3:1.
Jesus. Get hence, *S*., Matt. 4:10.
How can *S*. cast out *S*., Mark 3:23.
If *S*. . . be divided, Luke 11:18.

S. entered into him, John 13:27.
that *S*. tempt you not, I Cor. 7:5.
the messenger of *S*., II Cor. 12:7.
the working of *S*., II Thess. 2:9.
hold on the dragon . . *S*., Rev. 20:2.

SATIATE, to fill or satisfy. It may often denote satisfying with an excess, such as in (Jer. 31:14; 46:10).

SATISFIED, fully gratified.
meek eat and be *s*., Ps. 22:26.
eye is not *s*. with, Eccles. 1:8.
eat and not be *s*., Is. 9:20.
people shall be *s*., Jer. 31:14.

SATISFY, to gratify fully.
s. us early with thy, Ps. 90:14.
her breasts *s*. thee, Prov. 5:19.
whence can a man *s*., Mark 8:4.

SATRAP, a Persian official in control of a province (Ezra 8:36; Esther 3:12).

SATYR, a Greek and Roman god which had the appearance of a hairy goat. It was the image of lust and immorality. It may denote an idol in the form of the male goat (II Chr. 11:15).

SAUL, SHAUL, (1) the sixth of the ancient kings of Edom is the first character in the Bible who wears this name (Gen. 36:37).

(2) The first king of Israel. He was a Benjamite, the son of Kish. At first he was a loyal worshipper of Jehovah and a great military leader. After disobeying God in connection with the destruction of the Amalekites (I Sam. 15), he began to decrease and David began increasing. He finally took his life when his Hebrew army was defeated by the Philistines (I Sam. 31:1–10).

(2) the name of the Apostle Paul before his conversion (Acts 7:58). *See* **PAUL**.
S. of Rehoboth . . reigned, Gen. 36:37.
Kish, *S*. father, I Sam. 9:3.
S. did eat with Samuel, I Sam. 9:24.
Spirit of God . . upon *S*., I Sam. 11:6.
Jonathan, *S*. son, I Sam. 23:16.
battle . . against *S*., I Chr. 10:3.
Barnabas and *S*. returned, Acts 12:25.
Separate . . Barnabas and *S*., Acts 13:2.
S., *S*., why persecutest, Acts 26:14.

SAVE, deliver, rescue, preserve.
God sent me to *s*., Gen. 45:7.
he shall *s*. them, Ps. 37:40.

a god that cannot *s*., Is. 45:20.
s. them by Lord God, Hos. 1:7.
shall *s*. his people, Matt. 1:21.
whoever will *s*. life, Matt. 16:25.
himself he cannot *s*., Matt. 27:42.
but to *s*. the world, John 12:47.
s. yourselves from this, Acts 2:40.
can faith *s*. him?, James 2:14.
others *s*. with fear, Jude 23.

SAVIOR, one who performs the act of saving or delivering. In the Old Testament, Jehovah God is the savior of his people (Ps. 106:21; Is. 43:3, 11; 45:15, 21; 63:8; Jer. 14:8; Hos. 13:4). The deliverance is physical deliverance in the Old Testament. In the New Testament, Jesus is the savior *par excellence* (Luke 2:11). He saves one from sin and condemnation, therefore, his saving act is spiritual (Phil. 3:30; II Pet. 2:20; I John 4:14). *See* **SALVATION.**
God of Israel, the *s*., Is. 45:15.
I the Lord am . . *s*., Is. 60:16.
in God my *s*., Luke 1:47.
unto Israel a *s*., Acts 13:23.
the *s*. of the body, Eph. 5:23.
Lord Jesus Christ . . *s*., Titus 1:4.
of God and our *s*., II Pet. 1:1.
our Lord and *s*. Jesus, II Pet. 1:11.
sent . . Son to be . . *s*., I John 4:14.

SAVOUR, a smell or fragrance.
smelled a sweet *s*., Gen. 8:21.
by fire . . a sweet *s*., Lev. 3:16.
sweet *s*. unto the Lord, Num. 15:10.
we are . . sweet *s*., II Cor. 2:15.

SAVOURY, tasteful or tasty.
make me *s*. meat, Gen. 27:4.

SAW, ancient saws were very crude. One was made by fitting a long flint knife with jagged edges into a wooden frame. Later they were made of bronze. Saws were used in the cutting of stone (I Kin. 7:9). Tradition taught that the prophet Isaiah was cut to pieces by a wooden saw.
put them under *s*., II Sam. 12:31.
cut them with *s*., I Chr. 20:3.
shall . . *s*. magnify itself, Is. 10:15.
they were *s*. asunder, Heb. 11:37.

SAW, perceived.
woman *s*. tree was good, Gen. 3:6.
Jesus *s*. their faith, Mark 2:5.
Cornelius *s*. a vision, Acts 10:3.
fathers *s*. my works, Heb. 3:9.

SAY, speak, relate
think not to *s*., Matt. 3:9.
Whom do men *s*.?, Matt. 16:13.
they *s*. and do not, Matt. 23:3.
we may boldly *s*., Lord, Heb. 13:6.

SAYING, expression, proverb, speaking.
father observed *s*., Gen. 37:11.
s. pleased the king, Esther 1:21.
they heard this *s*., Matt. 15:12.
sad at that *s*., Mark 10:22.
this is a hard *s*., John 6:60.
this is a faithful *s*., I Tim. 1:15.

SCANT, meager.
s. measure abominable, Mic. 6:10.

SCAPE GOAT, a goat used for sending away. The Lord commanded that on the day of atonement Aaron would take two goats. He would kill one for a sin offering. On the live one Aaron would place both hands and confess over him all the sins of the Israelites (Lev. 16:21). The sins of the people would be placed upon the goat and he would be sent out into the wilderness (Lev. 16:22). *See* **ATONEMENT, AZAZEL.**

SCARCELY, hardly, barely.
s. for a righteous, Rom. 5:7.
righteous *s*. saved, I Pet. 4:18.

SCARLET, brilliant crimson. The dye was made from the bodies of insects called Kermez by the Arabs and found on holm oaks. This color was used in priestly garments, tabernacle hangings and some ceremonies (Lev. 14:4; Num. 19:6).

SCATTER, strew, spread, disperse.
s. them by thy power, Ps. 59:11.
I will *s*. your bones, Ezek. 6:5.
were *s*. as sheep, Matt. 9:36.
tribes *s*. abroad, James 1:1.

SCENT, odor, smell.
s. is not changed, Jer. 48:11.
s. thereof be the wine, Hos. 14:7.

SCEPTRE, a rod or reed which served as a symbol of authority, especially for a royal personage (Ps. 45:6; Amos 1:5; Heb. 1:8).
the *s*. shall not depart, Gen. 49:10.
the *s*. of thy kingdom, Ps. 45:6.
s. of righteousness, Heb. 1:8.

SCEVA, a Jewish priest in Ephesus, he

was the father of seven sons (Acts 19: 14–16). His sons tried to cast out a demon in the name of Jesus, but were wounded by it and were forced to flee.

SCHISM, a renting, separating, hence a dividing. Paul admonished Christians to have no schism in the church (I Cor. 12:25).

SCHOLAR, one who is being taught.
teacher as the *s.*, I Chr. 25:8.
Lord will cut off . . *s.*, Mal. 2:12.

SCHOOL, after the exile, the Jews became interested in education in a public way. Parents were responsible according to the Law (Ex. 12:26, 27; 13:8–10; Deut. 6:7; Prov. 1:8). Some prophets gathered students around them (Is. 8:16). Under the influence of Ezra, the Jews made an effort to teach everyone the Law. The synagogue was for young and old. Even small villages had their teachers (Luke 5:17). Instruction in every Jewish boy was made compulsory in 75 B.C. Before he enters school, his parents taught him the important points of the Law. He then is taught to read and write. A few continued on in higher learning. Paul sat at the feet of Gamaliel (Acts 22:3).

SCHOOLMASTER, the rendering of the Greek *paidagogos*, a child leader, tutor (I Cor. 4:15), or pedagogue (Gal. 3:24, 25). A *paidagogos* was a sort of "child-keeper" who protected the child from danger and directed him to and from school. The term is used figuratively by Paul. He says the law was our *paidagogos* to bring us to Christ (Gal. 3:24).
the law was our *s.*, Gal. 3:24.
no longer under the *s.*, Gal. 3:25.

SCIENCE, the rendering of the Hebrew and Greek words which really mean "knowledge" (Dan. 1:4; I Tim. 6:20). The words do not denote the same idea as "science" does in modern times.
understanding *s.*, Dan. 1:4.
and oppositions of *s.*, I Tim. 6:20.

SCOFFERS, mockers.
in last days *s.*, II Pet. 3:3.

SCORN, disdain, contempt; to despise.
princes shall be a *s.*, Hab. 1:10.

SCORNER, scoffer, derider, mocker.
reprove not a *s.*, Prov. 9:8.
judgments for *s.*, Prov. 19:29.
the *s.* is consumed, Is. 29:20.

SCORPION, a specie of the spider class, this animal has a sting in its tail (Rev. 9:5, 10). It was quite common in the wilderness of wandering (Deut. 8:15) and in Palestine proper. It could be used to punish a wrongdoer (I Kin. 12:11).

SCOURGE, an instrument used for severe punishment. It was not used by the Mosaic Law. However, it may be alluded to in I Kin. 12:11, 14. It was recognized as a legal penalty by the Jews, for disobedience of the orders of the sanhedrin and for heresy. Rods were used for beating (II Cor. 11:25), and a whip was used for scourging. The number of strikes varied from a few to thirty-nine. The Romans used a scourge of thongs, made more painful because of the use of metal pieces or bones.
he had *s.* Jesus, Matt. 27:26.
Pilate took Jesus and *s.*, John 19:1.
is it lawful . . to *s.*, Acts 22:25.
and *s.* every son, Heb. 12:6.

SCREECH OWL (Is. 34:14) The American Revised Version renders the word "night monster;" the Revised Standard gives "night hag." The precise animal or bird intended is uncertain.

SCRIBE, one that writes or numbers. Jeremiah had a scribe who copied down the prophets' utterances. He was called Baruch (Jer. 36:4.18). A scribe might also have been a governmental clerk (II Kin. 12:10; Ezra 4:8). As one who copied the scriptures, Ezra was the most famous of the Old Testament scribes (Ezra 7:6, 10). In the New Testament, the scribes are pictured as those who copied, studied and taught the law. They were the scholars, having the respect of the people. Scribes were members of the Jewish Sanhedrin (Matt. 16:21; 26:3). They were bitter enemies of Jesus and his preaching (Matt. 21:15) and came in for a share in a bitter denunciation by Jesus (Luke 11:44).
Sheva was *s.*, II Sam. 20:25.
families of the *s.*, I Chr. 2:55.
s. of the law of . . God, Ezra 7:12.
to Baruch the *s.*, Jer. 36:32.

s. and . . the Pharisees, Matt. 12:38.
W. unto you, *s.*, Matt. 23:14.
he taught . . not as the *s.*, Mark 1:22.
the *s.* . . . of the Pharisees, Acts 23:9.
where is the *s.*, I Cor. 1:20.

SCRIP, a bag made of leather.
put them . . in a *s.*, I Sam. 17:40.
s. for your journey, Matt. 10:10.
I sent you without . . . *s.*, Luke 22:35.
let him take . . his *s.*, Luke 22:36.

SCRIPTURE, anything written; literature. In the technical sense, it refers to
the Bible or portion of the Bible, usually
the Old Testament. When regarded in
the collective sense the word is used in the
plural (Matt. 21:42; Luke 24:27; John
5:39; Rom. 1:2; II Tim. 3:15). Specific
portions are indicated by the singular
(Mark 12:10; Luke 4:21; John 19:37).
See BIBLE, CANON.
is noted in the *s.*, Dan. 10:21.
Did ye . . read in the *s.*, Matt. 21:42.
is this *s.* fulfilled, Luke 4:21.
The place of the *s.*, Acts 8:32.
in the holy *s.*, Rom. 1:2.
died . . according to . . . *s.*, I Cor. 15:3.
hast known the Holy *S.*, II Tim. 3:15.
no prophecy of the *s.*, II Pet. 1:20.

SCROLL, the word in Greek is the one
from which we get the word "Bible." A
scroll was an ancient book. It was leather
or papyrus rolled into a cylinder after
having been written upon.
heavens . . rolled . . as a *s.*, Is. 34:4.
heaven departed as . . . *s.*, Rev. 6:14.

SCYTHIA, *see* SCYTHIAN.

SCYTHIAN, a native of Scythia, the
area north of the Black Sea (Col. 3:11).

SEA, (1) waters in general, the ocean
(Deut. 30:13; I Kin. 10:22; Ps. 24:2).
roaring of the *s.*, Is. 5:30.
as waters cover the *s.*, Is. 11:9.
and rebuked the *s.*, Matt. 8:26.
like a wave of the *s.*, James 1:6.

SEA, BRASEN, an immense copper laver
in Solomon's Temple, used for priestly
washings (I Kin. 7:39; Jer. 52:17).

SEAL, a signet, impression or inscription.
A signet ring was used by kings to make
official sealings. The seal, which leaves
an impression in wax or clay, was used

to fasten documents and letters. If ·the
seal was unbroken, it was a sign that the
document or letter had not been opened.
The seal could also be used as a signa-
ture for an illiterate person (I Kin. 21:8;
Neh. 10:1; Dan. 12:4; Rev. 5:1).
sealed . . with his *s.*, I Kin. 21:8.
turned as clay to the *s.*, Job 38:14.
set me as . . . *s.* upon . . heart, Song 8:6.
a *s.* of the righteousness, Rom. 4:11.
open . . book . . to loose . . . *s.*, Rev. 5:2.
Lamb opened one of . . . *s.*, Rev. 6:1.
the *s.* of the living God, Rev. 7:2.

SEAL, to affix a seal, fasten securely.
shut up words, *s.*, Dan. 12:4.
book *s.* with seven *s.*, Rev. 5:1.
s. not sayings of the, Rev. 22:10.

SEALSKIN, rendering in American Revised Version for a word rendered "badgers' skin" and "goats' skin" in the other
versions (Ex. 35:7; Num. 4:25).

SEA MEW, a ceremonially unclean bird
to the Hebrews (Lev. 11:16; Deut. 14:
15). *See* CUCKOW.

SEA-MONSTER, *see* WHALE.

SEA OF THE PLAIN, *see* DEAD SEA.

SEARCH, seek, inquire after.
s. me, O God, and know, Ps. 139:23.
I *s.* the heart, Jer. 17:10.
s. the Scriptures, John 5:39.
s. scriptures daily, Acts 17:11.

SEARED, branded or burned with an
iron. It may be used symbolically of
the conscience to show that it may become calloused after the searing. (I Tim.
4:2).

SEASON, appointed period of time.
bare a son at that *s.*, II Kin. 4:17.
corn cometh in his *s.*, Job 5:26.
bringeth fruit in his *s.* Ps. I:3.
word spoken in *s.*, Prov. 15:23.
every thing is a *s.*, Eccles. 3:1.
devil departed a *s.* Luke 4:13.
have a convenient *s.*, Acts 24:25.
instant in *s.*, II Tim. 4:2.
rest for a *s.*, Rev. 6:11.

SEAT, chair, post of authority.
Haman's *s.* above all, Esther 3:1.
s. of the scornful, Ps. 1:1.
Pharisees in Moses' *s.*, Matt. 23:2.

where Satan's *s.* is, Rev. 2:13.

SEBA, the name given to the eldest son of Cush, the son of Ham. Later the name was given to the place where his descendants settled (Gen. 10:7; Is. 43:3).

SEBAM, *see* **SIBMAH.**

SEBAT, SHEBAT, the eleventh month of the Jewish year, beginning with the new moon in February (Zech. 1:7).

SECACAH, a town in the Judean wilderness (Josh. 15:61), near Middin.

SECHU, SECU, a city in Benjamin, near Ramah (I Sam. 19:22).

SECOND COMING, throughout modern history men have tried to figure the date of Christ's second coming from numbers in Daniel and elsewhere. Scripture plainly shows the futility of such efforts (Matt. 24:36; II Pet. 3:10).

SECRET, hidden, concealed, private.
heard the *s.* of God?, Job 15:8.
bread eaten in *s.*, Prov. 9:17.
reveals *s.* to prophets, Amos 3:7.
alms be in *s.*, Matt. 6:4.
pray to Father in *s.*, Matt. 6:6.

SECRETLY, privately, in secret manner.
hath been *s.* enticed, Job. 31:27.
called Mary *s.*, John 11:28.
a disciple, but *s.*, John 19:38.

SECT, a party or denomination. Examples of religious sects were the Pharisees (Acts 15:5) and the Sadducees (Acts 5:17).
the *s.* of the Nazarenes, Acts 24:5.
the most straitest *s.*, Acts 26:5.
as concerning this *s.*, Acts 28:22.

SECU, *see* **SECHU.**

SECUNDUS, a believer of Thessalonica, and companion of Paul (Acts 20:4).

SECURE, not exposed to danger, safe.
come to a people *s.*, Judg. 18:10.
thou shalt be *s.*, Job 11:18.

SEDITION, rebellious disorder.
rebellion and *s.*, Ezra 4:19.
released him that for *s.*, Luke 23:25.
mover of *s.*, Acts 24:5.
emulation, wrath, .. *s.*, Gal. 5:20.

SEDUCE, to lead astray, deceive.
they have *s.* my people, Ezek. 13:10.
concerning them that *s.*, I John 2:26.
s. my servants to commit, Rev. 2:20.

SEE, perceive by the eye, experience.
s. salvation of Lord, Ex. 14:13.
no man *s.* me and live, Ex. 33:20.
lest they *s.* with eyes, Is. 6:10.
they shall *s.* God, Matt. 5:8.
we *s.* Jesus who was, Heb. 2:9.
we shall *s.* him as, I John 3:2.

SEED, progeny, descendants. To bear seed was a sacred duty for the Jews. Every Jewish woman longed to bear her husband a male heir. When a man died without an heir it was the duty of his brother to bear an heir for his name (Deut. 25:5-10; Matt. 22:23-33). Onan, the brother of Er was desirous of the physical relationship between Er's wife, Shua, but refused to accept the responsibility of raising up an heir for Er and therefore spilled his seed on the ground (Gen. 38:1-11).
like coriander *s.*, Ex. 16:31.
s. of the blessed, Is. 65:23.
the *s.* is word, Luke 8:11.
till *s.* should come, Gal. 3:19.
not corruptible *s.*, I Pet. 1:23.
remnant of her *s.*, Rev. 12:17.

SEEK, search for.
s. him with all thy, Deut. 4:29.
s. peace and pursue it, Ps. 34:14.
heart to *s.* wisdom, Eccles. 1:13.
s. first the kingdom, Matt. 6:33.
s. and ye shall find, Matt. 7:7.
s. and save the lost, Luke 19:10.
s. living among dead?, Luke 24:5.
s. those things above, Col. 3:1.
s. city to come, Heb. 13:14.

SEEM, to appear.
s. evil to serve, Josh. 24:15.
s. a setter forth of, Acts 17:18.
no chastening *s.* to, Heb. 12:11.
any *s.* to be religious, James 1:26.

SEEMLY, comely or fitting.
not *s.* for fool, Prov. 19:10.
honour .. not *s.* for .. fool, Prov. 26:1.

SEEN, perceived by the eye.
hath *s.* perverseness, Num. 23:21.
eyes have *s.* Lord, Is. 6:5.
no man hath *s.* God, John 1:18.
Galileans had *s.* all, John 4:45.

eye hath not *s.*, I Cor. 2:9.
things thou hast *s.*, Rev. 1:19.

SEER, *see* **PROPHET.**

SEETHE, to boil or stew.
not *s.* kid in mother's, Ex. 23:19.
I see a *s.* pot, Jer. 1:13.

SEGUB, (1) the younger son of Hiel, the
Bethelite who rebuilt the city of Jericho
in the days of king Ahab (I Kin. 16:34).
When Hiel set up the gates of the city,
Segub, his younger, died (Josh. 6:26). (2)
A son of Hezron, the grandson of Judah
(I Chr. 2:21).

SEIR, (1) a mountain range of Edom
which ran south from the Dead Sea
(Gen. 36:21; Num. 24:18). The area was
once settled by the Horites (Gen. 14:6),
but was taken and settled later by the
descendants of Essau (Gen. 32:3; Josh.
24:4). (2) The grandfather of the Hori,
ancestor of the Horites (Gen. 36:20, 21;
I Chr. 1:38).

SEIRATH, SEIRAH, a town in Ephraim,
near Gilgal. Ehud, the judge, slew king
Edlon at Jericho and then fled to Seirath
(Judg. 3:26, 27).

SEIZE, take suddenly, grasp.
rise up and *s.* city, Josh. 8:7.
night, let darkness *s.*, Job 3:6.
death *s.* upon them, Ps. 55:15.
let us kill and *s.*, Matt. 21:38.

SELA HAMMAHLEKOTH, a hill in the
wilderness of Maon, south of Judah. It
was here that David escaped from Saul
(I Sam. 23:28).

SELA, SELAH, the capital of Edom,
later called Petra. It was taken by Amaziah of Judah who changed its name to
Joktheel (II Kin. 14:7).

SELAH, (1) a word which appears in the
Psalms seventy-one times. It is probably
a musical note or a pause (Ps. 3:2, 4). (2)
See SELA.

SELED, a descendant of Jerahmeel, the
grandson of Pharez, the son of Judah by
Tamar (I Chr. 2:30).

SELEUCIA, a city on the coast of Syria.
It was from this point that Paul and

Barnabas sailed for Cyprus (Acts 13:4).

SELFWILLED, obstinate.
bishop not be *s.*, Tit. 1:7.
presumptuous, *s.*, II Pet. 2:10.

SELL, exchange, bargain.
s. thy birthright, Gen. 25:31.
s. him to Ishmaelites, Gen. 37:27.
buy truth, *s.* it not, Prov. 23:23.
buy, *s.*, get gain, James 4:13.

SEM, *see* **SHEM.**

SEMACHIAH, the son of Shemiah, son
of Obed-edom, a gatekeeper of the
tabernacle in the days of David (I Chr.
26:7).

SEMEI, SEMEIN, the father of Mattathias, an ancestor of Christ (Luke 3:26).

SENAAH, a city of Judah. Some of her
inhabitants returned there with Zerubbabel from exile (Ezra 2:35; Neh. 7:38).

SENATORS, elders, chief men.
teach his *s.* wisdom, Ps. 105:22.

SEND, transmit, dispatch.
shall *s.* a Savior, Is. 19:20.
s. forth labourers, Matt. 9:38.
shall *s.* forth angels, Matt. 13:41.
whom Father will *s.*, John 14:26.
shall *s.* delusion, II Thess. 2:11.

SENEH, a rock at the pass of Michmash
where the Philistines had a garrison in
the days of king Saul (I Sam. 14:4).

SENIR, SHENIR, a mountain northeast
of Jordan. It may be between Amanah
and Hermon. It is possible that it is the
Ammonite name for Mount Hermon
(Deut. 3:9).

SENNACHERIB, the son of Sargon and
king of Assyria. He began to rule in B.C.
705. About 701 B.C. he invaded Judah
and "caged up" Hezekiah in Jerusalem.
During the campaign he took forty-six
cities and 200,000 captives. His army
drew up outside Jerusalem and prepared
for an attack, being 185,000 strong. But
the Lord smote the army of the Assyrians
that night. Morning found all the soldiers
dead (Is. 37:36). After this calamity
Sennacherib left and went back to Nineveh. As he was worshipping in the house

of his god, Nisroch, his two sons killed him with the sword (Is. 37:37, 38). This took place in about 680 B.C.

SENSUAL, animalistic; carnal.
This wisdom .. is .. s., James 3:15.
These be they .. s., Jude 19.

SENT, dispatched, caused to go.
him that s. me, Matt. 10:40.
Father who s. me, John 5:23.
Father s. the Son, I John 4:14.

SENTENCE, statement, decision.
let s. come forth, Ps. 17:2.
Pilate gave s. that, Luke 23:24.
we had s. of death, II Cor. 1:9.

SENUAH, see HASSENUAH.

SEORIM, a descendant of Aaron, he was given by lot the fourth charge of the sanctuary during the days of David (I Chr. 24:1, 6, 8).

SEPARATE, cause to part, divide.
s. themselves to vow, Num. 6:2.
s. as a shepherd, Matt. 25:32.
who shall s. us from, Rom. 8:35.
and be ye s., II Cor. 6:17.

SEPARATION, WATER OF, see PURIFICATION.

SEPHAR, probably a mount in southern Arabia, on the boundary of the land of the descendants of Joktan (Gen. 10:30).

SEPHARAD, a place to which some captives of Judah were taken (Obad. 20).

SEPHARVAIM, a city under the rule o Assyria. Inhabitants of the city were brought in to settle Samaria after the Jews of the northern kingdom, Israel, were taken away into Assyrian captivity (II Kin. 17:24, 31).

SEPHARVITES, inhabitants of Sepharvaim. It is believed that they sacrificed their children by fire (II Kin. 17:31).

SEPTUAGINT, see VERSIONS.

SEPULCHRE, TOMB, natural or artificial caves or caverns were used by the Hebrews as places of burial for their dead (Gen. 23:9; Is. 22:16; John 11:38). To protect the bodies of the dead and to insure sanitation, a stone was placed against the entrance of the tomb (Matt. 27:60). They were generally placed outside a city and whitewashed so that they could be clearly seen and not contacted. Contact with a sepulchre made one ceremonially unclean. Family burial places were common (Gen. 49:29–31; II Sam. 2:32; I Kin. 13:22). Public burial grounds were provided for the poor and for strangers (II Kin. 23:6; Jer. 26:23; Matt. 27:7).
by Rachel's s., I Sam. 10:2.
s. of the kings, II Chr. 21:20.
like unto whited s., Matt. 23:27.
a stone .. of the s., Mark 15:46.
s. of the prophets, Luke 11:47.
Peter .. ran unto the s., Luke 24:12.
taken .. Lord out of .. s., John 20:2.
and laid him in a s., Acts 13:29.
throat is .. open s., Rom. 3:13.

SERAH, SARAH, a daughter of Asher (Gen. 46:17; I Chr. 7:30).

SERAIAH, (1) the name of David's scribe (II Sam. 8:17). (2) The son of Azariah who was chief priest in Jerusalem when it fell to Nebuchadrezzar in 586–8 B.C. (II Kin. 25:18; Jer. 52:24). (3) The son of Tanhumeth, whom Gedaliah advised to submit to the Babylonians in the invasion of 586–8 B.C. (II Kin. 25:23; Jer. 40:8). (4) A son of Kenaz also wore this name. He was also the father of Joab (I Chr. 4:13, 14). (5) A Simeonite who was the son of Asiel also wore this name (I Chr. 4:35). (6) A priest who returned to Jerusalem with Zerubbabel (Ezra 2:2; Neh. 10:2). (7) A priest, the son of Hilkiah, who dwelt in Jerusalem after the exile and was called "ruler of the house of God" was known by this name also. (8) A man sent by Jehoiakim to take Jeremiah and Baruch was called Seraiah (Jer. 36:26). (9) A prince of Judah who was carried away into Babylonian exile along with Zedekiah (Jer. 51:59; 51:61).

SERAPHIM, beings seen in the vision of God by Isaiah. They were before the throne of God. He described them as having six wings (Is. 6:2–7). They declare the glory and holiness of God in heaven and that "the whole earth is full of his glory."

SERED, a son of Zebulun, (Gen. 46:14; Num. 26:26).

SERGIUS PAULUS, the Roman proconsul of Cyprus (Acts 13:7-12).

SERMON ON THE MOUNT, a name
given to the words in Matt. 5, 6, 7. As is
here used, the mountain may mean a
high plateau region in contrast to the
lowlands around the Sea of Galilee. The
mountain may have been the twin peaks
west of the Sea. There is much of the
same material recorded in Luke 6:17-19,
although Jesus is described as having
"stood on the plain."

SERPENT, a snake. Satan used the serpent as a disguise when he tempted the
first man (Gen. 3:1-5). In Rev. he is
called "that old serpent" (Rev. 12:9; 20:
2). When the Israelites murmured in the
wilderness, fiery serpents were sent to
punish them (Num. 21:6). Jesus instructed his apostles to be as wise as serpents
(Matt. 10:16).
the *s.* was more subtle, Gen. 3:1.
his rod . . became a *s.*, Ex. 7:10.
made a *s.* of brass, Num. 21:9.
the *s.* will bite, Eccles. 10:11.
and fiery flying *s.*, Is. 30:6.
voice . . like a *s.*, Jer. 46:22.
be . . wise as *s.*, Matt. 10:16.
power to tread on *s.*, Luke 10:19.
the *s.* beguiled Eve, II Cor. 11:3.
s., which is the Devil, Rev. 20:2.

SERUG, SARUCH, the grandson of Peleg,
and father of Nahor, the father of Terah,
the father of Abraham. He was an ancestor of Jesus (Gen. 11:20; I Chr. 1:26;
Luke 3:35).

SERVANT, minister, helper, slave. *See*
SERVANT OF GOD.
Canaan, a *s.* of *s.*, Gen. 9:25.
wast a *s.* in Egypt, Deut 5:15.
was sold for a *s.*, Ps. 105:17.
fool shall be *s.* to, Prov. 11:29.
Israel a *s.*, Jer. 2:14.
s. honoureth his master, Mal. 1:6.
wicked and slothful *s.*, Matt. 25:26.
be your *s.*, Mark 10:44..
Peter struck a *s.*, Mark 14:47.
sin, is the *s.* of sin, John 8:34.
Paul a *s.* of Jesus Christ, Rom. 1:1.
took form of a *s.*, Phil. 2:7.
Simon Peter, a *s.*, II Pet. 1:1.

SERVANT OF GOD, anyone who believes in God and/or does his will. Some
men who were voluntary servants of God
were Moses (Ps. 105:26), David (Ps. 132:
10), and Abraham (Ps. 105:6). In Is. 52:
13-53:12, a servant of Jehovah is depicted as having suffered affliction and
death to atone for the sins of men. In the
New Testament (Acts 8:35), one learns
that the suffering servant is Jesus.
seed of Abraham his *s.*, Ps. 105:6.
for thy *s.* David's sake, Ps. 132:10.
Israel . . my *s.*, Is. 41:8.
my *s.* shall sing, Is. 65:14.
O Daniel, *s.* of . . God, Dan. 6:20.
s. of Lord not strive, II Tim. 2:24.

SERVANTS, SOLOMON'S, *see* **SOL-
OMON'S SERVANTS.**

SERVE, minister to, obey.
shall *s.* them 400 years, Gen. 15:13.
elder shall *s.* younger, Gen. 25:23.
ye shall *s.* strangers, Jer. 5:19.
cannot *s.* two masters, Matt. 6:24.
should not *s.* sin, Rom. 6:6.
s. the Lord Christ, Col. 3:24.
his servants shall *s.*, Rev. 22:3.

SERVICE, ministry, obedience.
think doeth God *s.*, John 16:2.
your reasonable *s.*, Rom. 12:1.
doing *s.* as to Lord, Eph. 6:7.

SERVILE, slavish.
shall do no *s.* work, Lev. 23:7.

SET, to place, fix in position.
s. stars in firmament, Gen. 1:17.
s. his love on me, Ps. 91:14.
s. at liberty them, Luke 4:18.
s. your affection on, Col. 3:2.
have *s.* an open door, Rev. 3:8.

SETH, SHETH, the third son of Adam
and Eve. He was the head of the gene-
alogical line which produced Jesus, the
Christ (Luke 3:38).

SETHUR, the son of Michael, he was a
spy, representing Asher, sent to Canaan
by Moses from Kadesh-barnea (Num.
13:13).

SETTLE, fix, establish.
he *s.* his countenance, II Kin. 8:11.
Lord, thy word is *s.*, Ps. 119:89.
are *s.* on the lees, Zeph. 1:12.
in faith grounded and *s.*, Col. 1:23.

SEVENEH, *see* **SYENE.**

SEVENS, many groups of seven occur in Scripture, such as seven things God hates (Prov. 6:16–19), seven years' work for a wife (Gen. 29:20), seven women after one man (Is. 4:1).

SEVENTY, ten multiplied by seven.
of Jacob were *s.* souls, Ex. 1:5.
s. weeks determined, Dan. 9:24.
forgive *s.* times seven, Matt. 18:22.
appointed other *s.*, Luke 10:1.

SEVER, to separate or part.
s. you from other people, Lev. 20:26.
they shall *s.* out men, Ezek. 39:14.
and *s.* the wicked, Matt. 13:49.

SEVERITY, austerity, extreme strictness,
goodness and *s.* of God, Rom. 11:22.

SEW, to fasten with stitches.
s. fig leaves, Gen. 3:7.
I *s.* sackcloth upon, Job 16:15.
time to rend, to *s.*, Eccles. 3:7.
s. new cloth on old, Mark 2:21.

SHAALBIM, SHAALABBIN, an Amorite city in the territory of Dan (Judg. 1:35; I Kin. 4:9).

SHAALBONITE, patronymic of Eliahba, a native of Shaalabbin (II Sam. 23:32; I Chr. 11:33).

SHAALIM, *see* **SHALIM.**

SHAAPH, (1) a son of Jahdai, the son of Caleb, by his concubine Ephah (I Chr. 2: 47). (2) The son of Caleb, the son of Hezron, by his concubine Maachah (I Chr. 2:49).

SHAARAIM, SHARAIM, SHARUHEN, SHILHIM, a town in Judah or Simeon, near Adithaim and Bethbirei (Josh. 15: 36; I Sam. 17:52; I Chr. 4:31).

SHAASHGAZ, a eunuch or chamberlain in court of Ahasuerus, king of Persia and husband of Esther (Esther 2:14).

SHABBETHAI, a leading Levite of Jerusalem after the return from exile. He was overseer of the temple and interpreter of the law to the people. He, however, opposed Ezra in the matter of divorcing strange wives (Ezra 10:15; Neh. 8:7; 11: 16).

SHACHIA, a son of Shaharaim, the Benjamite (I Chr. 8:10).

SHADDAI, *see* **GOD.**

SHADE, cover, protection.
Lord is thy *s.* upon, Ps. 121:5.

SHADOW, shelter, shade; sample.
hide me under *s.*, Ps. 17:8.
days are as a *s.*, Eccles. 8:13.
under elms, because *s.*, Hos. 4:13.
s. of things to come, Col. 2:17.
s. of heavenly things, Heb. 8:5.

SHADRACH, the name given to Hananiah, one of Daniel's three companions, by the Babylon eunuch (Dan. 1:7; 3: 12–30).

SHAFT, pole, stalk.
his *s.* and branches, Ex. 25:31.
make a polished *s.*, Is. 49:2.

SHAGE, SHAGEE the father of Jonathan the Hararite (I Chr. 11:34).

SHAHAR, *see* **AIJELETH SHAHAR.**

SHAHARAIM, a Benjamite who went to Moab and begat children of two women there (I Chr. 8:8).

SHAHAZIMAH, SHAHAZUMAH, a city in Issachar, between Tabor and Beth-shemesh (Josh. 19:22).

SHALEM, a town in Ephraim near Shechem (Gen. 33:18).

SHALIM, SHAALIM, a region in Dan, between Philistia and Ophrah (I Sam. 9:4).

SHALISHAH, SHALISHA, a region, probably in Ephraim, where Saul, the son of Kish, searched for his father asses (I Sam. 9:4).

SHALLECHETH, the west gate of the first Jewish temple, built by Solomon (I Chr. 26:16).

SHALLUM, (1) the son of Naphtali (I Chr. 7:13). He is called Shillem in Gen.

46:24. (2) The son of Shaul, the grandson of Simeon (I Chr. 4:25). (3) The father of Jehizkiah (II Chr. 28:12). (4) A son of Tikvah, the husband of the prophetess, Huldah (II Kin. 22:14; II Chr. 34:22). (5) The son of Zadok, the high priest and father of Hilkiah and ancestor of Ezra, the scribe and priest (I Chr. 6:12, 13; Ezra 7:2). He is called Meshullam in I Chr. 9:11. (6) The son of king Josiah of Judah. His other name was Jehoahaz (II Kin. 23:30–34). (7) The uncle of Jeremiah wore this name (Jer. 32:7, 8). (8) The son of Sisamai and descendant of Judah (I Chr. 2:40, 41). (9) A descendant of Kore and a porter of the sanctuary during the reign of David (I Chr. 9:17, 18). (10) A son of Hallohesh wore this name. He ruled half of Jerusalem and labored with his daughters on the city's walls (Neh. 3:12). (11) A son of Bani, who renounced his Gentile wife (Ezra 10:42). (12) The king of Israel, the son of Jabesh, who killed Zechariah, son of Jeroboam II and the last king of the fifth dynasty (II Kin. 10:30).

SHALLUN, the son of Colhozeh (Neh. 3:15).

SHALMAI, SALMAI, SHAMLAI, a Nethinim whose descendants returned with Zerubbabel (Ezra 2:46; Neh. 7: 48).

SHALMAN, an Assyrian king who laid waste Beth-Arbel (Hos. 10:14). Some think the name is an abbreviation of Shalmaneser, but others think he was the predecessor of Pul (Tiglath-Pileser III).

SHALMANESER, the king who followed Tiglath-Pileser III to the Assyrian throne. He carried off Hoshea and the ten northern tribes of Israel to Assyria (B.C. 730–716).

SHAMA, one of the valiant men of king David (I Chr. 11:44).

SHAMARIAH, see **SHEMARIAH.**

SHAME, dishonor, disgrace.
turn my glory into s.?, Ps. 4:2.
not be put to s., Is. 54:4.
worthy to suffer s., Acts 5:41.
despising the s., Heb. 12:2.

SHAMED, SHEMED, the third son of Elpaal (I Chr. 8:12).

SHAMER, see **SHEMER.**

SHAMGAR, a judge of Israel, he was the son of Anath. He, as Israel's third judge, delivered them from the Philistines when he killed 600 of them with an oxgoad (Judg. 3:31; 5:6).

SHAMHUTH, an Izrahite, he was a captain of David's army (I Chr. 27:8).

SHAMIR, (1) a city in the hill country of Judah (Josh. 15:48). (2) A town near Ephraim, the residence and burial place of Tola, a judge of Israel (Judg. 10:1, 2). (3) The name of the son of Micah, a Levite (I Chr. 24:24).

SHAMLAI, see **SHALMAI.**

SHAMMA, a son of Zophah, an Asherite. (I Chr. 7:37).

SHAMMAH, (1) a son of Reuel, the son of Essau wore this name (Gen. 36:3, 4, 13, 17). (2) The brother of David, the son of Jesse (I Sam. 16:9; 17:13). He is the same as Shimea (I Chr. 20:7). (3) The name of a son of Agee, a captain of David (II Sam. 23:11). (4) A warrior of David (II Sam. 23:25). (5) A Harodite, he was also called Shammoth and Shamhuth (I Chr. 11:27; 27:8).

SHAMMAI, (1) a son of Onam of Judah (I Chr. 2:28). (2) The son of Rekem of Judah (I Chr. 2:44). (3) The son or grandson of Ezra, of the family of Caleb, the son of Jephunneh (I Chr. 4:17).

SHAMMOTH, a Harorite, one of David's valiant men (I Chr. 11:27).

SHAMMUA, SHAMMUAH, (1) a Reubenite, the son of Zaccur, who was sent by Moses to spy out the land of Canaan (Num. 13:4). (2) A son of David by Bathsheba (II Sam. 5:14; I Chr. 3:5). (3) A priest of the family of Bilgah in the days of the high priest, Hoiakim (Neh. 12: 18). (4) The father of Abda (Neh. 11:17).

SHAMSHERAI, a son of Jeroham, a Benjamite (I Chr. 8:26).

SHAPE, form.

descended in bodily s., Luke 3:22.
nor seen his s., John 5:37.

SHAPHAM, second in rank among the Gadites (I Chr. 5:12).

SHAPHAN, the scribe and secretary of Josiah, king of Judah (II Kin. 22:8-14; Jer. 26:24; 39:14).

SHAPHAT, (1) a Simeonite, the son of Hori, sent by Moses to spy out the land of Canaan (Num. 13:5). (2) The father of the prophet Elisha (I Kin. 19:16, 19). (3) A grandson of Shechaniah, of the family of David (I Chr. 3:22). (4) A chief man of Gad, who lived in Bashan (I Chr. 5:12). (5) The son of Adlai. He was put in charge of David's herds in the valleys (I Chr. 27:29).

SHAPHER, see **SHEPHER**.

SHAPHIR, see **SAPHIR**.

SHARAI, a son of Bani who had married a strange wife in exile (Ezra 10:40).

SHARAIM, see **SHAARAIM**.

SHARAR, one of David's valiant men (II Sam. 23:33).

SHAREZER, SHEREZER, (1) one of the sons of Sennacherib, king of Assyria. He and his brother murdered their father (II Kin. 19:37; Is. 37:38). (2) A man of Bethel (Zech. 7:2). He was sent to consult the priests and prophets in the temple as to a day of humiliation (Zech. 7:2).

SHARON, SARON, (1) a plain, pasture or city east of the Jordan (I Chr. 5:16), probably in Gad. (2) The plain on the seacoast between Carmel and Joppa. It was a great pasture region (I Chr. 27:29; Is. 35:2; 65:10).

SHARONITE, a patronymic of Shitrai who was over the king's herds in Sharon (I Chr. 27:29).

SHARP, keen, cutting, severe.
make thee s. knives, Josh. 5:2.
tongue like s. razor, Ps. 52:2.
contention was so s., Acts 15:39.

SHARUHEN, a village of Simeon (Josh.

19:6). It is also called Shilhim and Shaaraim (Josh. 15:32; I Chr. 4:31).

SHASHAI, one of the sons of Bani (Ezra 10:40).

SHASHAK, a son of Elpal, a Benjamite (I Chr. 8:14).

SHAUL, (1) a son of Simeon, the second son of Jacob, by a Canaanitish woman (Gen. 46:10; Ex. 6:15). (2) Ancient kings of Edom (I Chr. 1:48, 49). (3) A Levite descended from Korah (I Chr. 6:24).

SHAULITES, descendants of Shaul, the son of Simeon (Num. 26:13).

SHAVE, pare with razor.
to s. off seven locks, Judg. 16:19.
Lord s. with a razor, Is. 7:20.
they s. their heads, Acts 21:24.

SHAVEH, a valley in Salem or Salim, near Aenon (Gen. 14;17). It is also called the "king's dale", and is near Jerusalem (II Sam. 18:18).

SHAVEH KIRIATHAIM, a plain in Moab which is near the city of Kiriathaim (Gen. 14:5; Josh. 13:19).

SHAVSHA, see **SHEVA**.

SHEAF, see **SHEAVES**.

SHEAL, one of the sons of Bani who had married a Gentile woman during the Babylonian exile (Ezra 10:29).

SHEALTIEL, SALATHIEL, the father of Zerubbabel, who led the Hebrews back to the city of Jerusalem after the Babylonian exile (Ezra 3:2, 8; Neh. 12:1). He was in the ancestral line of Jesus (Matt. 1:12; Luke 3:27).

SHEARER, one who shears sheep.
sheep before s., Is. 53:7.
lamb dumb before his s., Acts 8:32.

SHEARIAH, a son of Azel, of the family of Saul (I Chr. 8:38; 9:44).

SHEARING HOUSE, a place between Jezreel and Samaria where Jehu killed forty-two men of the royal house of Judah (II Kin. 10:12-14).

SHEAR JASHUB, a son of Isaiah the prophet. The name means "a remnant shall return." The name worn by his son helped the prophet to keep his message before the eyes of the people continually. The name signified hope (Is. 7:3).

SHEATH, a scabbard.
drew it out of the *s.*, I Sam. 17:51.
put .. sword .. into .. *s.*, I Chr. 21:27.
put .. sword into .. *s.*, John 18:11.

SHEAVES, bundles of grain.
let gather among the *s.*, Ruth 2:7.
shall come bringing *s.*, Ps. 126:6.

SHEBA, (1) the son of Raamah, the son of Cush, the son of Nam, wore this name. He dwelt in Ethiopia (Gen. 10:7; I Chr. 1:9). (2) The son of Yoktan, of the family of Shem, the son of Noah (Gen. 10:28; I Chr. 1:22). (3) A son of Yokshan, the son of Abraham by Keturah, in Edom (Gen. 25:3; I Chr. 1:32).

(4) The land in southwestern Arabia, or in Africa near the Straits of Babel-mandeb. The people there were commercial. When the Queen of Sheba heard of the fame of king Solomon, she came to Jerusalem to see for herself. To test him, she asked him riddles which Solomon solves with no trouble at all (I Kin. 10: 1–13; II Chr. 9:1–12).

(5) A city in Simeon, near Beersheba and Moladah. It might be the same as Beersheba (Josh. 19:2). (6) A son of Bichri, a Benjamite who rebelled against king David after the death of Absalom. He was beheaded by the people of Abel (II Sam. 20:1; 20:21; 20:22). (7) A chief Gadite also wore this name (I Chr. 5:13).

SHEBAH, SHIBAH, a well dug by the servants of Isaac near Beersheba in Judah (Gen. 26:33).

SHEBAM, a city in Reuben which once belonged to Moab, then to the Amorites (Num. 32:3).

SHEBANIAH, (1) the Levite who blew the trumpet when the ark was brought to Jerusalem by David (I Chr. 15:24). (2) A Levite who sealed the covenant and prayed at the feast of tabernacles after the return from Babylonian exile (Neh. 9:4, 5; 10:10). (3) A priest who sealed the covenant with Nehemiah (Neh. 10:4;

12:14). (4) A Levite who sealed the covenant after the return from exile (Neh. 10:12).

SHEBARIM, a place in Benjamin. It was north of Jericho, near Ai (Josh. 7:5).

SHEBAT, *see* SIBMAH.

SHEBER, a son of Caleb by his concubine Maachah (I Chr. 2:48).

SHEBNA, SHEBNAH, an official in the court of king Hezekiah of Judah in the days of Isaiah. He was the minister of the household (Is. 22:15). Later he was demoted to a secretarial position, and his old position was taken by Eliakim (II Kin. 18:18, 26, 37; 19:2; Is. 36:3; 37:2).

SHEBUEL, SHUBAEL, (1) a son of Gershom, the son of Levi (I Chr. 23:16; 26:24). (2) The son of Haman, the chief singer of the sanctuary, in the days of king David (I Chr. 25:4). He is called Shubael in I Chr. 25:20.

SHECANIAH, (1) the name of a priest in the days of David (I Chr. 24:11). (2) A priest in the days of Hezekiah, king of Judah (II Chr. 31:15).

SHECHANIAH, (1) a head of a family of the house of David after the return of the Hebrews from Babylonian exile (I Chr. 3:21, 22). (2) A man whose descendants returned to Palestine with Ezra in the days of Artaxerxes (Ezra 8:3). (3) A man whose descendants did the same (Ezra 8:5). (4) A son of Jehiel who first confessed the sin of taking a strange (Gentile) wife while in exile (Ezra 10:2). (5) The father of Shemaiah, who helped repair the wall of Jerusalem (Neh. 3:29). (6) The father-in-law of Tobiah, the Ammonite who oppressed and opposed Nehemiah (Neh. 6:18). (7) A priest who returned from exile with Zerubbabel (Neh. 12:3).

SHECHEM, SICHEM, SYCHEM, (1) the son of Hamor, the Hivite. He seduced Dinah, Jacob's daughter and then desired her as his wife. His act was avenged by Simeon and Levi, Dinah's brothers when they slew the Shechemites with the sword (Gen. 34:1–31; Acts 7:16). (2) The son of Gilead and head of a tribal family (Num. 26:31; John 17:2). (3) A son of

Shemidah of Manasseh (I ´ Chr. 7:19). (4) A town of Palestine in Ephraim. Abraham camped there on his way to the land of Canaan (Gen. 12:6; 34:20; Josh. 20:7).

SHECHEMITE, the family of Shechem, son of Gilead (Num. 26:31).

SHED, to pour forth, to cause to flow.
blood s. for many for, Matt. 26:28.
Holy Ghost hath s., Acts 2:33.
love of God s. abroad, Rom. 5:5.
s. on us abundantly, Tit. 3:6.

SHEDEUR, a Reubenite, the father of Elizur who was chosen to assist in numbering the people in the days of Moses (Num. 1:5; 2:10).

SHEEP, an animal which was common to the region of Palestine. It was raised for its wool, skin, meat, and milk. It was a ceremonially clean animal (Lev. 1:10; 4:32; 5:15; 22:21) and was used for sacrificing.
Abel . . a keeper of s., Gen. 4:2.
shall take . . from the s., Ex. 12:5.
five s. ready dressed, I Sam. 25:18.
six choice s., Neh. 5:18.
the fleece of my s., Job 31:20.
all we like s., Is. 53:6.
in s. clothing, Matt. 7:15.
as s. going astray, I Pet. 2:25.

SHEEP COTE, SHEEP FOLD, an enclosure in which sheep are gathered for the night (Num. 32:16; Ezek. 34:14). A door or gate allowed the sheep to enter and go out (John 10:1, 2). The guardian of the flock sometimes used a watchtower which stood close by (II Kin. 17:9; II Chr. 26:10; Mic. 4:8).
abodest . . among the s. f., Judg. 5:16.202
thee from the s. c., II Sam. 7:8 .
the door of the s. f., John 10:1.

SHEEP MARKET, a term rendered "sheep gate" in the Revised Standard Version. In John 5:2 it is generally agreed that a gate, not a market, is intended.

SHEHARIAH, a son of Jeroham, a Benjamite (I Chr. 8:26).

SHEKEL, an ancient weight and money unit introduced to the Hebrews from Babylonia. The weight of it was equal to about one half an ounce. The mone-

tary value varied according to the material of which it was made. Silver was the most common material used to make the "shekel."
land is worth . . s., Gen. 23:15.
s. of silver, Gen. 23:16.
and for . . female ten s., Lev. 27:5.
fifty s. of silver, II Kin. 15:20.
s. of gold, I Chr. 21:25 .
twenty s. a day, Ezek. 4:10.

SHELAH, (1) the youngest son of Judah, the fourth son of Jacob, by the daughter of Shua, the Canaanite (Gen. 38:2, 5, 11, 14, 26; Num. 26:20). (2) A son of Arphaxad (Gen. 10:24; 11:12–15; I Chr. 1:18). He was an ancestor both to Abraham and to Christ (Luke 3:35, 36).

SHELANITES, the family of Shelah, the youngest son of Judah (Num. 26:20).

SHELEMIAH, (1) a Levite who was a gatekeeper of the tabernacle in the days of king David (I Chr. 26:14). (2) One of the sons of Bani who had married a Gentile during the Babylonian exile was named Shelemiah. (3) A man of the same family who had done the same thing (Ezra 10:39, 41). (4) The father of Hananiah who helped repair the Jerusalem wall after the return from exile. (Neh. 3:30). (5) A priest set over the treasures by Nehemiah (Neh. 13:13). (6) The son of Cushi who was sent by the princes of Judah to bring Baruch the scribe and Jeremiah the prophet to them (Jer. 36:14). (7) The son of Abdeel. He was ordered, by king Jehoiakim, to bring Baruch the scribe and Jeremiah the prophet to him (Jer. 36:26). (8) the father of Jehucal, who was sent by Zedekiah to ask the prayers of Jeremiah the prophet (Jer. 37:3; 38:1). (9) The father of Irijah, captain of the guard at the gate of Benjamin. He took Jeremiah into custody when the prophet was about to leave Jerusalem, thinking the man of God was deserting to the Babylonians (Jer. 37:13).

SHELEPH, a son of Joktan of the family of Shem (Gen. 10:26; I Chr. 1:20).

SHELESH, a son of Helem, the grandson of Beriah (I Chr. 7:35).

SHELOMI, the father of Ahihud, a chief of Asher (Num. 34:27).

SHELOMITH, (1) the daughter of Dibri and mother of the person stoned for blaspheming the name of the Lord in the wilderness, in the days of Moses (Lev. 24:11). (2) The daughter of Zerubbabel, grandson of Jeconiah, the son of king Jehoiakim of Judah (I Chr. 3:19). (3) A son of Shimei, and descendant of Gershon, the son of Levi, in the days of king David (I Chr. 23:9). (4) A son of Izhar, a Kohathite (I Chr. 23:18). (5) A descendant of Eliezer, the son of Moses, put over the treasures dedicated in the days of David (I Chr. 26:25, 26, 28). (6) A son or daughter of king Rehoboam, the son of Solomon (II Chr. 11:20). (7) An ancestor of a family which returned with Ezra to Palestine after the Babylonian exile (Ezra 8:10).

SHELOMOTH, a descendant of Izhar (I Chr. 24:22). See **SHELOMITH.**

SHELTER, refuge, retreat, covering.
for want of a *s.*, Job 24:8 .
thou hast been *s.*, Ps. 61:3 .

SHELUMIEL, the son of Zurishaddai, he was a prince of Simeon who helped Moses in numbering the Hebrews in the wilderness (Num. 1:6; 2:12; 7:41).

SHEM, SEM, (1) a son of Noah, perhaps the eldest of the three (Gen. 5:32). Shem, at the age of 100, entered the ark, taking his wife with him (Gen. 7:7; I Pet. 3:20). He received a blessing from Noah because he refused to look upon his father's nakedness (Gen. 9:23-37). He, the father of Arphaxad, was in the ancestral line of Jesus Christ (Luke 3:36).

SHEMA, (1) the son of Hebron of Judah (I Chr. 2:43, 44). (2) A son of Elpaal, a Benjamite, and head of the house in Aijalon (I Chr. 8:13). (3) The son of Joel the Reubenite (I Chr. 5:8). (4) The man who assisted Ezra when the scribe read the law to those who returned from exile to Jerusalem (Neh. 8:4). (5) A town in southern Judah (Josh. 15:26), called Sheba in Josh. 19:2.

SHEMAAH, a man of Gibeah who was an ally of king David at Ziklag (I Chr. 12:3).

SHEMIAH, (1) a prophet which God sent to prevent Rehoboam from warring against Israel (I Kin. 12:22; II Chr. 12:7). (2) Son of Shechaniah, and father of Hattush, a descendant of David through Jehoiakim (I Chr. 3:22). (3) The father of Shimri, and head of a Simeonite family (I Chr. 4:37). (4) The son of Joel the Reubenite (I Chr. 5:4). (5) A Merarite which returned from exile (I Chr. 9:14; Neh. 11:15).

(6) A Levite who was the father of Obadiah (I Chr. 9:16). (7) A Kohathite whom David summoned to assist in bringing the ark from the house of Obededom (I Chr. 15:8). (8) A Levite who recorded the allotment of the priestly offices in the days of David (I Chr. 24:6). (9) A Kohathite who was a gatekeeper for the tabernacle in the days of David (I Chr. 26:4). (10) A Levite who was sent by Jehoshaphat to teach the people in the cities of Judah (II Chr. 17:8).

(11) A son of Jeduthun who assisted in the cleansing of the temple in the days of Hezekiah (II Chr. 29:14). (12) A Levite in the days of king Hezekiah who distributed a freewill offering in the Levite cities (II Chr. 31:15).

(13) A chief Levite in the days of king Josiah (II Chr. 35:9). (14) A son of Adonikam who returned with Ezra in the days of Artaxerxes (Ezra 8:13). (15) A person whom Ezra sent to Iddo to ask for ministers (Ezra 8:16). (16) A priest who married a Gentile during the Babylonian exile (Ezra 10:21).

(17) Another by this name was guilty of doing the same thing (Ezra 10:31). (18) A person who helped repair the wall of Jerusalem following the return from exile (Neh. 3:29). (19) Another by this name tried to intimidate Nehemiah (Neh. 6:10). (20) A priest that, with Nehemiah, sealed the covenant (Neh. 10:8; 12:18; 12:34, 35). (21) The one who took part in the purification of the wall of Jerusalem (Neh. 12:36).

(22) The one who gave thanks at the dedication of the wall (Neh. 12:42). (23) The father of Uriah who was killed by Jehoiakim because he prophesied against Jerusalem and Judah during the days of Jeremiah (Jer. 26:20). (24) A Nehelamite who wrote from Babylon to the priests in Jerusalem to instruct them to reprove the prophet Jeremiah (Jer. 29:24, 31, 32). (25) The father of Delaiah, a prince of the Jews to whom Baruch read the scroll which he had written from the mouth of Jeremiah (Jer. 36:12).

SHEMARIAH, SHAMARIAH, (1) a mighty man who joined David at Ziklag (I Chr. 12:5). (2) A son of Rehoboam, the son of king Solomon, by Abihail (II Chr. 11:19). (3) A son of Harim in the days of Ezra. He renounced his Gentile wife (Ezra 10:32). (4) The name of one of the sons of Bani who put away the Gentile wife he had taken while in Babylonian exile (Ezra 10:41).

SHEMEBER, king of Zeboim in the days of Abraham (Gen. 14:2).

SHEMED, *see* **SHAMED.**

SHEMER, the owner of a hill which was bought by Omri. Samaria was built by him on it (I Kin. 16:24).

SHEMIDAH, SHEMIDA, the son of Gilead (Num. 26:32; Josh. 17:2; I Chr. 7:19).

SHEMIDAITES, family of Shemidah (Num. 26:32).

SHEMINITH, a musical term; an octave (I Chr. 15:31; Ps. 12:title).
with harps on the *s.*, I Chr. 15:21.
Neginoth upon *s.*, Ps. 6:title.
Musician upon *s.*, Ps. 12:title.

SHEMIRAMOTH, (1) a Levite singer who lived in the days of king David (I Chr. 15:18, 20). (2) A Levite whom Jehoshaphat appointed to teach the people (II Chr. 17:8).

SHEMUEL, (1) a chief Simeonite who was chosen to help in dividing the land west of the Jordan (Num. 34:20). (2) Samuel the prophet, the father of Joel (I Chr. 6:33). (3) The head of a family in Issachar (I Chr. 7:2).

SHEN, a place near the spot where Samuel set up the stone called Ebenezer (I Sam. 7:12).

SHENAZAR, SHENAZZAR, the son or grandson of Jeconiah, (I Chr. 3:18).

SHENIR, SENIR, the mountain between Amanah and Hermon, at the northeast of Jordan (Deut. 3:9; Song 4:8; Ezek. 27:5).

SHEOL, *see* **HELL.**

SHEPHAM, an unidentified place in Canaan (Num. 34:10, 11).

SHEPHATIAH, SHEPHATHIAH, (1) the fifth son of king David (I Chr. 3:3) by Abital. (2) A Benjamite, the father of Meshullam who dwelt in Jerusalem after the Babylonian exile (I Chr. 9:8). (3) One of the valiant men of David who joined him at Ziklag (I Chr. 12:5). (4) A prince of Simeon in the days of David (I Chr. 27:16). (5) A son of king Jehoshaphat (II Chr. 21:2). (6) A person whose descendants returned to Jerusalem after the Babylonian exile (Ezra 2:4; Neh. 7:9). (7) One of the servants of king Solomon whose descendants also returned to Jerusalem with Zerubbabel after the Babylonian exile (Ezra 2:57; Neh. 7:59). (8) One whose descendant, Zebadiah, and eighty males returned to Jerusalem with Ezra after the Babylonian exile (Ezra 8:8). (9) A descendant of Pharez, some of whose descendants dwelt in Jerusalem (Neh. 11:4). (15) The son of Mattan, a prince of Judah (Jer. 38:1).

SHEPHER, *see* **SHAPHAR.**

SHEPHERD, one that herds and cares for a flock or flocks of sheep. He led the sheep to pasture, to places of water, and at night to the fold. His was the responsibility of protecting the flock from wild beasts (I Sam. 17:34–36). Patriarchs of Israel were shepherds (Gen. 13:6). It appears that the kings and/or the rulers and princes of the land are called shepherds of the people in Ezek. 34:1–19. They were rebuked for neglecting the flock. In the New Testament, Jesus called himself the good shepherd (John 10:14) and his believers the flock (John 21:15–17).
the men are *s.*, Gen. 46:32.
from thence is the *s.*, Gen. 49:24.
sheep that have no *s.*, II Chr. 18:16.
Lord is my *s.*, Ps. 23:1.
will set up *s.*, Jer. 23:4.
smite the *s.*, Zech. 13:7.
scattered . . having no *s.*, Matt. 9:36.
in the . . country *s.*, Luke 2:8.
I am the good *s.*, John 10:11.
returned unto the *s.*, I Pet. 2:25.

SHEPHO, SHEPHI, a son of Shobal (Gen. 36:23; I Chr. 1:40).

SHEPHUPHAN, SHEPHUPHAN, *see* **MUPPIM.**

SHERAH, SHEEAH, the daughter of Beriah, the son of Ephraim, or the daughter of Ephraim sister of Beriah (I Chr. 7:24).

SHERD, see **POTSHERD.**

SHEREBIAH, (1) a priest who had eighteen sons who were brought to Ezra to return to Jerusalem after the exile (Ezra 8:18; Neh. 8:7). (2) A Levite who, with Nehemiah, sealed the covenant after the return from exile (Neh. 10:12; 12:8).

SHERESH, the son of Machir, the son of Manasseh (I Chr. 7:16).

SHEREZER, see **SHAREZER.**

SHESHACH, a symbolic name for Babylon (Jer. 25:26; 51:41).

SHESHAI, a son of Anak (Num. 13 22; Josh. 15:14; Judg. 1:10).

SHESHAN, a descendant of Jerahmeel, the grandson of Pharez, the son of Judah by Tamar (I Chr. 2:31).

SHESHBAZZAR, the governor whom Cyrus, king of Persia, set over Judah. He is believed to be the same as Zerubbabel (Ezra 1:8:11; 5:14–16). He helped lay the foundation for the second Temple.

SHETH, a Moabite chief or tribe (Num. 24:17).

SHETHAR, an official or a prince under the king of Persia who saw the king's face at pleasure (Esther 1:14).

SHETHAR BOZNAI, SHETHAR-BOZ-ENAI, a Persian official during the reign of Darius. (Ezra 5:3, 6; 6:6).

SHEVA, (1) a man of Judah of the house of Caleb (I Chr. 2:49). (2) It was the name of David's secretary (II Sam. 20:25).

SHEW BREAD, SHOWBREAD, the word denotes "bread of the presence." It was placed on the table in the holy place of the sanctuary in two rows, six loaves in each. The bread was changed on the Sabbath and was eaten only by the priests (Ex. 25:30; Lev. 24:5–9; Matt. 12:4). The twelve loaves represented the twelve tribes of Israel (Lev. 24:7). Jo-

sephus records that the bread was unleavened.

thou shalt set . . s. b., Ex. 25:30.
upon the table of s. b., Num. 4:7.
the tables of s. b., I Chr. 28:16.
did eat the s. b., Matt. 12:4.
eaten only by priests, Mark 2:26.
take and eat the s. b., Luke 6:4.

SHIBAH, see **SHEBAH.**

SHIBBOLETH, the word used as a test by the Gileadites to the defeated men of Ephraim at the fords of the Jordan. Those who tried to cross the river were asked to pronounce the name. If they pronounced it Sibboleth, they were recognized as Ephraimites and were slain (Judg. 12:5, 6).

SHIBMAH, see **SIBMAH.**

SHICRON, see **SHIKKERON.**

SHIELD, see **ARMOR.**
I am thy s., Gen. 15:1.
s. of beaten gold, I Kin. 10:17.
spear and the s., Job 39:23.
there brake . . the . . s., Ps. 76:3.
the s. and the bucklers, Ezek. 39:9.
s. of his mighty men, Nahum 2:3.
the s. of faith, Eph. 6:16.

SHIGGAION, SHIGIONOTH, a musical term which perhaps denotes enthusiasm in the singing of it (Ps. 7:title).

SHIHON, SHION, a town in Issachar which was near Haphraim and north of Tabor (Josh. 19:19).

SHIHOR, SIHOR, a name which was given to the Nile (Is. 23:3; Jer. 2:18).

SHIHOR-LIBNATH, a small river in south Asher near Carmel (Josh. 19:26).

SHIKKERON, SHICRON, a city on the northern border of Judah (Josh. 15:11).

SHILHI, the father of Azubah (I Kin. 22:42).

SHILHIM, a city in southern Judah near Lebaoth (Josh. 15:32).

SHILLEM, the fourth son of Naphtali

(Gen. 46:24; Num. 26:49). He is called Shallum in I Chr. 7:13.

SHILLEMITES, the family of Shillem (Num. 26:49).

SHILOAH, *see* SILOAM.

SHILOH, a town in Ephraim which was north of Bethel. In the days of Eli, the judge of Israel, the tabernacle was set up here and it was the center of religious activity. Eli died after the ark was captured by the Philistines (Josh. 18:1; I Sam. 4:12-18). The loss of the ark of the covenant signified that God had forsaken Shiloh (Ps. 78:60; Jer. 7:12, 14; 26:6, 9).

The word was also used by Jacob when blessing Judah (Gen. 49:10). The term is generally taken to signify the coming of the Messiah.

depart until *S.* come, Gen. 49:10.
Israel assembled .. at *S.*, Josh. 18:1.
divided .. by lot in *S.*, Josh. 19:51.
daughters of *S.* .. dance, Judg. 21:21.
house of .. Lord in *S.*, I Sam. 1:24.
Lord appeared .. in *S.*, I Sam. 3:21.
the Lord's priest in *S.*, I Sam. 14:3.
the tabernacle of *S.*, Ps. 78:60.

SHILONI, the father of Zechariah, of the sons of Pharex (Neh. 11:5).

SHILONITE, an inhabitant of Shiloh.
Ahijah the *S.*, I Kin. 11:29.
and of the *S.*, I Chr. 9:5.
the hand of .. the *S.*, II Chr. 10:15.

SHILSHAH, the ninth son of an Asherite by the name of Zophah (I Chr. 7:37).

SHIMEA, SHIMEAH, (1) a Levite of the family of Gershom (I Chr. 6:39, 43). (2) The son of Uzza, a Levite of the family of Merari (I Chr. 6:30). (3) The son of David by Bath-sheba (I Chr. 3:5). This one is also called Shammua in II Sam. 5:14 and I Chr. 14:4. (4) One of the brothers of David (I Chr. 20:7). He is also called Shimma in I Chr. 2:13.

SHIMEAM, *see* SHIMEAH.

SHIMEATH, an Ammonitess who was the mother of Jozachar, who slew Jehoash, the king of Judah (II Kin. 12:21).

SHIMEATHITES, a family of scribes who lived in Jabez (I Chr. 2:55).

SHIMEI, SHIMI SHIMHI, (1) a son of Gershom, son of Levi (Ex. 6:17). (2) A Benjamite who was the son of Gera. He cursed king David when fleeing from Absalom (II Sam. 16:5; I Kin. 2:8). (3) An officer of David who remained steadfast when Adonijah usurped the throne (I Kin. 1:8). (4) A son of Elah, one of the twelve purveyors of Solomon in Benjamin (I Kin. 4:18). (5) A grandson of Jeconiah, the son of king Jehoiakim of Judah (I Chr. 3:19). (6) A son of Zacchar, a Benjamite with sixteen sons and six daughters (I Chr. 4:26, 27). (7) The son of Gog, a Reubenite (I Chr. 5:4). (8) A son of Libni, a Merarite (I Chr. 6:29). (9) The father of an important family of Judah (I Chr. 8:21). (10) A Levite of the family of Laadan (I Chr. 23:9). (11) A Levite to whom the tenth lot fell in the service of song in the sanctuary in the days of David (I Chr. 25:17). (12) A Ramathite who was over the vineyards in the days of king David (I Chr. 27:27). (13) A descendant of Heman who assisted in cleansing the Temple in the days of king Hezekiah and Isaiah the prophet (II Chr. 29:14). (14) A Levite put in charge of the offerings in the days of king Hezekiah of Judah (II Chr. 31:12, 13). (15) A Levite who had married a Gentile wife while living during the Babylonian exile (Ezra 10:23). (16) One of the family of Hashum who had done the same thing (Ezra 10:33). (17) One of the sons of Bani who had done the same (Ezra 10:38). (18) A Benjamite, the grandfather of Mordecai who brought up Esther (Esther 2:5). (19) The name of the simple representative of the Gershomites (Zech. 12:13).

SHIMEITES, *see* SHIMITES.

SHIMEON, a son of Harim who divorced his Gentile wife after the Babylonian exile (Ezra 10:31).

SHIMHI, *see* SHIMEI.

SHIMITES, SHIMETES, Levites descended from Shimei (Num. 3:21).

SHIMMA, *see* SHIMEA.

SHIMON, a descendant of Caleb, the son of Jephunneh (I Chr. 4:20).

SHIMRATH, son of Shimei the Benjamite (I Chr. 8:21).

SHIMRI, SIMRI, (1) the son of Shemaiah of Simeon (I Chr. 4:37). (2) The son of Hosah, a Levite of Merari (I Chr. 26:10). (3) The father of Jediael, a warrior of king David (I Chr. 11:45). (4) The son of Elizaphan (II Chr. 29:13).

SHIMRITH, a Moabitess who was the mother of one of the killers of king Joash of Judah (II Chr. 24:26). She is called Shomer in II Kin. 12:21.

SHIMROM SHIMRON, the name of Issachar's fourth son and head of a tribal family (Gen. 46:13; Num. 26:24). (2) The name of a town on the Zebulun border (Josh. 11:1; 19:15).

SHIMRONITES, the family of Shimron, the son of Issachar (Num. 26:24).

SHIMRON-MERON, a town which Joshua conquered which belonged to the Canaanites (Josh. 12:20).

SHIMSHAI, a scribe who wrote, with others, to the king of Persia in order to prevent Nehemiah from rebuilding the city of Jerusalem after the Babylonian exile (Ezra 4:8).

SHINAB, the king of Admah (Gen. 14:2, 8, 10). He lived in the days of Abraham.

SHINAR, Babylonia in its fullest extent. Some refer to it as the "plain of Babylon" (Gen. 10:10; 11:2; Dan. 1:2).

SHINE, give light, steady radiance.
make his face s., Num. 6:25.
s. on counsel of wicked, Job 10:3.
face to s. on us, Ps. 67:1.
are waxen fat, they s., Jer. 5:28.
let your light s., Matt. 5:16.
gospel should s., II Cor. 4:4.
sun nor moon s. in it, Rev. 21:23.

SHION, see SHIHON.

SHIP, a craft used for water transportation. It was propelled by oars and by sails. The first ship, loosely speaking, was the ark of Noah (Gen. 6:13-22). The Hebrews had little to do with ship-ping and commerce. The trade along the Mediterranean coast in the ancient days was done by the Phoenicians and the Philistines. Solomon, nevertheless, owned a navy made up of Phoenician sailors. He traded with Ophir. His port was Ezion-geber on the Red Sea (I Kin. 9:26-28). In the New Testament, ships are in common use by the Jews, especially for the purpose of fishing (Matt. 4:21, 22). Paul made a trip to Rome by ship (Acts 27:41).
an haven for s., Gen. 49:13.
the king's s., II Chr. 9:21.
the sides of the s., Jonah 1:5.
in a s. with Zebedee, Matt. 4:21.
departed thence by s., Matt. 14:13.
taught . . out of the s., Luke 5:3.
ran the s. aground, Acts 27:41.
behold also the s., James 3:4.

SHIPHI, the father of Ziza, a leading Simeonite (I Chr. 4:37).

SHIPHRAH, a Hebrew midwife during the time of the birth of Moses (Ex. 1:15).

SHIPHTAN, the father of Kemuel of Ephraim (Num. 34:24).

SHIPWRECK, failure, destruction, loss.
thrice suffered s., II Cor. 11:25.
faith made s., I Tim. 1:19.

SHISHA, the father of Elihoreph and Ahiah, two of Solomon's scribes (I Kin. 4:3).

SHISHAK, one of the Egyptian Pharaoh's. He was Sesconchis I, king of the twenty-second Bubastic dynasty. He protected Jeroboam against Solomon (I Kin. 11:40), invaded Judah under Rehoboam (I Kin. 14:25), took fenced cities, and plundered Jerusalem.

SHITRAI, the Sharonite who was in charge of the herds of David (I Chr. 27:29).

SHITTAH, a tree and its wood, from which the ark and other objects in the tabernacle were made (Ex. 25:5, 10, Deut. 10:3). It is a kind of Acacia wood, hard and resistent to insects.

SHITTIM, (1) see SHITTAH. (2) A place

in Moab, about seven miles east of the Jordan. It was the last encampment of the (Num. 33:49). From here Joshua sent out two spies (Josh. 2:1). It was here that Israel was seduced by Baal-peor, and the anger of the Lord was kindled (Num. 25:3). (3) The valley of Shittim, probably the lower Kidron Valley (Joel 3:18). From this point Joshua sent spies to spy out the city of Jericho (Josh. 2:1). It was also the name given to a barren valley near Jerusalem and the Dead Sea (Joel 3:18).

Israel abode in S., Num. 25:1.
sent out of S. . . to spy, Josh. 2:1.
they removed from S., Josh. 3:1.
water the valley of S., Joel 3:18.
answered him from S., Mic. 6:5.

SHIZA, a man of Reuben and father of Adina (I Chr. 11:42).

SHOA, a tribe of people mentioned along with the Chaldeans and Pekod as an enemy of Israel (Ezek. 23:23).

SHOBAB, (1) a son which was born to David after he had become king (II Sam. 5:14). (2) A son of Caleb, son of Hezron of Judah (I Chr. 2:18).

SHOBACH, SHOPACH, the general of Hadarezer, king of Zobah (II Sam. 10:16). He was defeated and killed by Joab, David's captain (II Sam. 10:18).

SHOBAI, a gatekeeper of the tabernacle whose descendants returned from Babylonian exile with Zerubbabel (Ezra 2:42; Neh. 7:45).

SHOBAL, (1) a son of Seir and one of the Horite dukes (Gen. 36:20, 29). (2) A son of Caleb, the son of Hur (I Chr. 2:50, 52). (3) A son of Judah and father of Reaiah (I Chr. 4:1, 2).

SHOBEK, a man or family who sealed the covenant with Nehemiah (Neh. 10:24).

SHOBI, an Ammonite, a son of Nahash of Rabbah who received David when he fled from Absalom (II Sam. 17:27).

SHOCO, SHOCHO, SHOCHOH, see SOCHO.

SHOES, a sandal which was strapped to the foot by latchets. They were always removed when one was about to enter someone's house (Mark 1:7). They were also removed when one stood on holy ground (Ex. 3:5; Josh. 5:15). It may be that the absence of shoes in the list of priests' garments may mean that they performed their duties barefooted. The shoe was often given to the partner in an agreement as a kind of confirmation for the transaction (Ruth 4:7, 8). To cast a shoe into a place symbolized taking possession of it (Ps. 60:8).

put off thy s., Ex. 3:5.
s. is not waxen old, Deut. 29:5.
plucked off his s., Ruth 4:7.
how beautiful . . with s., Song 7:1.
latchet of their s. Is. 5:27.
s. I am not worthy, Matt. 3:11.
neither two coats . . s., Matt. 10:10.
latchet of whose s., Mark 1:7.
without purse . . and s., Luke 22:35.

SHOHAM, the son of Jaaziah, a Merarite (I Chr. 24:27).

SHOMER, (1) son of Heber the Asherite (I Chr. 7:32). (2) A Moabitess, mother of Jehozabad, one of those who killed king Jehoash of Judah (II Kin. 12:21). See SHIMRITH.

SHOPHACH, see SHOBACH.

SHOPHAN, a city in Gad; or a denominative of the city Atroth (Num. 32:35).

SHORT, brief, limited, deficient.
Lord's hand waxed s.?, Num. 11:23.
light is s. because, Job 17:12.
triumph of wicked s., Job 20:5.
come s. of God's glory, Rom. 3:23.
the time is s., I Cor. 7:29.
hath but a s. time, Rev. 12:12.

SHORTLY, in brief time, soon.
bruise Satan s., Rom. 16:20.
will come to you s., I Cor. 4:19.
s. I must put off, II Pet. 1:14.
things that must s. come, Rev. 1:1.

SHOSHANNIM, SHOSHANNIM-EDUTH, SHUSHAN-EDUTH, a word in the Psalms which was a musical term which probably signified the air to which the psalm was to be sung (Ps. 45: title; 60: title; 69: title; 80: title).

SHOUT, an outcry, yell.
shouted with great s., Josh. 6:5.

lift *s.* against Babylon, Jer. 51:14.
gave *s.*, saying voice, Acts 12:22.
Lord descend with *s.*, I Thess. 4:16.

SHOUT, to yell, make sudden, loud cry.
s. when bidded, Josh. 6:10.
people *s.* aloud for joy, Ezra 3:12.
mighty man that *s.*, Ps. 78:65.
s. O Israel, be glad, Zeph. 3:14.

SHOWBREAD, *see* **SHEWBREAD.**

SHOWERS, bursts of rain; full supply.
distil as *s.* on grass, Deut. 32:2.
shall come down as *s.*, Ps. 72:6.
can heavens give *s.*?, Jer. 14:22.
be *s.* of blessing, Ezek. 34:26.
Lord shall give *s.*, Zech. 10:1.

SHRINE, an idolatrous symbol of the Temple of Diana in Ephesus (Acts 19:24).

SHUA, SHUAH, SHUHAH, (1) a daughter of Heber the Asherite (I Chr. 7:32). (2) A Canaanite of Adullam, whose daughter was chosen as the wife of Judah (Gen. 38:2; I Chr. 2:3). (3) The brother of Chelub, a descendant of Caleb (I Chr. 4:11).

SHUAL, (1) a district near Bethel which was invaded by the Philistines (I Sam. 13:17). (2) The son of Zophah of Asher (I Chr. 7:36).

SHUBAEL, (1) a son or descendant of Amram, a grandson of Levi (I Chr. 24; 20). (2) A singer in the sanctuary in the days of David. He may be the same as Shebuel in I Chr. 25:4.

SHUHAH, *see* **SHUA.**

SHUHAM, *see* **HUSHIM.**

SHUHAMITES, the family of Shuham (Num. 26:42).

SHUHITE, a descendant of Shuah, the son of Keturah, Abraham's concubine (Job 2:11; 8:1; 18:1; 42:9).

SHULAMITE, SHULAMMITE, the designation for the young woman who was the lover of the shepherd in the Song of Solomon (Song 6:13).

SHUMATHITES, a family in Kirjathjearim which descended from Shobal, Hur's son (I Chr. 2:53).

SHUN, avoid.
not *s.* to declare, Acts 20:27.
s. profane babblings, II Tim. 2:16.

SHUNAMMITE, a native of Shunem. Two Shunammite women mentioned are Abishag, a beautiful woman who was brought to David (I Kin. 1:3; 2:17, 21), and the woman whose child Elisha brought back to life (II Kin. 4:8, 12; 8:1).

SHUNEM, (1) a city on the border of Issachar where the Philistines camped before the great victory they won over Saul (I Sam. 28:4). It was about sixteen miles southwest of the Sea of Galilee (Josh. 19:18). (2) The home of the woman whose son Elisha restored to live (II Kin. 4:8, 12) and of the maiden of the Song of Solomon (Song 6:13).

SHUNI, a son of Gad and head of a tribal family (Gen. 46:16; Num. 26:15).

SHUNITES, the family of Shuni, (Num. 26:15).

SHUPHAM, *see* **MUPPIM.**

SHUPHAMITES, the family of Shupham (Num. 26:39).

SHUPPIM, (1) a certain man of Benjamin (I Chr. 7:12, 15). (2) *See* **MUPPIM.**

SHUR, a large desert which reached from the east border of Egypt, in Africa, as far as the land of Amalek and Ishmael (Gen. 16:7; 20:1; 25:18).

SHUSHAN, SUSA, a city in Elam which was the Persian capital.
as I was in *S.*, Neh. 1:1.
young virgins unto *S.*, Esther 2:3.
were slain in *S.*, Esther 9:11.
I was at *S.*, Dan. 8:2.

SHUSHANCHITES, SUSANCHITES, people from Shushan (Susa) whom the Assyrians settled in Samaria (Ezra 4:9).

SHUSHAN-EDUTH, a temple music choir (Ps. 60: title).

SHUT, close, confine, lock.
s. their eyes, lest, Is. 6:10.
s. up John in prison, Luke 3:20.
s. and no man openeth, Rev. 3:7.
power to *s.* heaven, Rev. 11:6.
s. up the devil, Rev. 20:3.

SHUTHALHITES, the family of Shuthelah (Num. 26:35).

SHUTHELAH, (1) a son of Ephraim and head of a tribal family (Num. 26:35, 36). (2) The son of Zabad of the family of Ephraim (I Chr. 7:21).

SIA, SIAHA, one of the Nethinim whose descendants returned with Zerubbabel to Jerusalem after the Babylonian exile (Ezra 2:44; Neh. 7:47).

SIBBECAI, SIBBECHAI, *see* **MEBUNNAH.**

SIBBOLETH, *see* **SHIBBOLETH.**

SIBMAH, SHIBMAH, SEBAM, SHEBAM, a city in Reuben which was east of the Jordan (Josh. 13:19).
and the vine of *S.,* Is. 16:8.
bewail . . the vine of *S.,* Is. 16:9.
O vine of *S.,* Jer. 48:32.

SIBRAIM, a city of Syria which was probably between Hamath and Damascus (Ezek. 47:16).

SICHEM, a place in the plain of Moreh in mount Ephraim (Gen. 12:6).

SICK, ill, diseased.
maketh heart *s.,* Prov. 13:12.
I am *s.* of love, Song 2:5.
healed all the *s.,* Matt. 8:16.
I was *s.,* ye visited, Matt. 25:36.
is any *s.* let him call, James 5:14.

SICKNESS, malady, illness, disease.
will take *s.* away, Ex. 23:25.
Ephraim saw his *s.,* Hos. 5:13.
healing all *s.,* Matt. 4:23.
s. not unto death. John 11:4.

SIDDIM, a valley in the region of the Dead Sea (Gen. 14:3, 8).

SIDON, ZIDON, (1) the eldest son of Canaan (Gen. 10:15). (2). *See* **ZIDON.**

SIDONIANS, the inhabitants of Sidon (Deut. 3:9; Josh. 13:6; I Kin. 5:6).

SIEGE, *see* **WAR.**

SIFT, analyze, test, prove.
Satan desires to *s.* you, Luke 22:31.

SIGH, to groan.
children of Israel *s.,* Ex. 2:23.
men . . *s.* and . . cry, Ezek. 9:4.
with bitterness *s.,* Ezek. 21:6.
he *s.,* and saith unto him, Mark 7:34.
s. deeply in . . spirit, Mark 8:12.

SIGN, token, omen, symbol.
let them be for *s.,* Gen. 1:14.
Lord shall give a *s.,* Is. 7:14.
what *s.* of thy coming?, Matt. 24:3.
other *s.* did Jesus, John 20:30.
bearing witness with *s.,* Heb. 2:4.

SIGNET, *see* **SEAL.**

SIGNIFY, indicate, manifest.
s. by what death he, John 12:33.
the Holy Ghost this *s.,* Heb. 9:8.
s. removing of those, Heb. 12:27.

SIHON, an Amorite king in Heshbon who refused the Israelites passage through his land (Num. 21:21–32).
he had slain *S.,* Deut. 1:4.
shall do . . as . . to *S.,* Deut. 31:4.
the Lord . . delivered *S.,* Judg. 11:21.
from the midst of *S.,* Jer. 48:45.

SIHOR, *see* **SHIHOR.**

SILAS, SILVANUS, a shortened form of Silvanus who was a member of the church in Jerusalem (Acts 15:22). He went with Paul on what is called the second missionary journey. He was imprisoned with the apostle at Philippi (Acts 16:19, 25). Paul calls him Silvanus in his epistles (I Thess. 1:1; II Thess. 1:1).

SILENCE, (1) quiet; (2) ruin, nought. (Is. 15:1); (3) The grave (Ps. 94:17).
before me, there was *s.,* Job 4:16.
put Sadducees to *s.,* Matt. 22:34.
woman learn in *s.,* I Tim. 2:11.
was *s.* in heaven, Rev. 8:1.

SILENT, still, quiet. *See* **SILENCE.**
wicked shall be *s.,* I Sam. 2:9.
be *s.* in the grave, Ps. 31:17.

let us be *s.* there, Jer. 8:14.

SILK, see **CLOTHING.**
her clothing is *s.*, Prov. 31:22.
I covered thee with *s.*, Ezek. 16:10.
fine linen, and *s.*, Ezek. 16:13.
linen . . purple, and *s.*, Rev. 18:12.

SILLA, a place near or in Jerusalem near the house of Millo (II Kin. 12:20).

SILOAM, SILOAH, SHILOAH, SHE-LAH, (sent) a famous pool located in Jerusalem west of the Kidron valley. Perhaps it is to be identified with the King's Pool mentioned in Neh. 2:14. Hezekiah constructed an underground aquaduct to connect this pool with the Gibon in preparation for the siege of Sennacherib. Jesus sent a blind man to wash in this pool after he had anointed his eyes with clay to heal him. (John 9:6, 7).

SILVANUS, see **SILAS.**

SILVER, the ore was common in Tarshish (Jer. 10:9; Ezek. 27:12) and in Arabia (II Chr. 9:14). The ore was put into a furnace and the real silver was separated from the slag or dross (Ps. 12:6; Prov. 17:3; Ezek. 22:22). It was used very early for money, its value being determined according to weight (Is. 46:6). It had uses other than money. It was used for making cups (Gen. 44:2), instruments of music (Num. 10:2), ornaments (Ex. 3:22), crowns (Zech. 6:11), and shrines (Acts 19:24). See **MONEY.**
Abram was . . rich . . in *s.*, Gen. 13:2.
not make . . gods of *s.*, Ex. 20:23.
all the *s.* vessels, Num. 7:85.
a talent of *s.*, II Kin. 5:22.
fifty talents of *s.*, Ezra 8:26.
buy the poor for *s.*, Amos 8:6.
for thirty pieces of *s.*, Matt. 26:15.
S. and gold have I none, Acts 3:6.
which made *s.* shrines, Acts 19:24.

SILVERSMITH, one who works in silver. Demetrius, a craftsman of Ephesus, was such a worker. He, as well as others in the city, made and sold silver shrines of Diana (Acts 19:24).

SIMEON, SYMEON, (1) the second son of Jacob by Leah. It was he, along with Levi, who took vengeance upon the Shechemites in connection with the de-

filing of Dinah (Gen. 29:33; 34:25). (2) The posterity of Simeon and the land which they possessed was also called by this name (Num. 1:6; Deut. 27:12; Josh. 19:1; II Chr. 34:6). (3) A devout man in Jerusalem who waited for the consolation of Israel. When he saw Jesus in the Temple he blessed him(Luke 2:25, 34). (4) An ancestor of Jesus (Luke 3:30). (5) A disciple and prophet at Antioch who was surnamed Niger (Acts 13:1). (6) The Apostle Peter (Act 15:14). See **PETER.**

SIMEON, TRIBE OF, this tribe received its portion of the Holy Land out of what had been allotted to the tribe of Judah (Josh. 19:1, 9). It lay on the southern frontier of Judah. As a political entity it was later absorbed by Judah. Ezekiel recognizes it as a tribe (Ezek. 48:24) and it is mentioned along with the others in the vision in Rev. 7:7.

SIMEONITES, the descendants of Simeon (Num. 25:14; Deut. 4:12).

SIMILITUDE, likeness, resemblance.
the *s.* of the Lord, Num. 12:8.
the *s.* of oxen, II Chr. 4:3.
s. of . . sons of men, Dan. 10:16.
after the *s.* of Adam, Rom. 5:14.
the *s.* of Melchisedek, Heb. 7:15.

SIMON, several in the Bible wear this name. (1) Foremost was the great apostle of Jesus who was surnamed Peter (or Cephas). See **PETER.** (2) One of the twelve disciples of Jesus. He was called the *Canaanite* because he was from Cana of Galilee, or rather because he was a Zealot (*cana* in Hebrew meaning *zealous*) (Matt. 10:4; Mark 3:18; Luke 6:15). (3) One of the brethren of Jesus (Matt. 13:55; Mark 6:3). (4) A leper of Bethany in whose house Jesus' head was anointed with oil (Matt. 26:6; Mark 14:3). (5) A man of Cyrene who was compelled to carry the cross of Jesus (Matt. 27:32; Luke 23:26). (6) A Pharisee in whose house the feet of Jesus were washed with tears and anointed with an ointment (Luke 7:40, 43, 44). (7) The father of Judas Iscariot (John 6:71; 12:4; 13:26), the disciple who betrayed Jesus. Another was a sorcerer in Samaria who, after believing and being baptized, asked to buy the power of laying on hands from the apostles Peter and John (Acts 8:9, 13, 18, 24). Finally, it was the name of a tanner in Joppa with whom Peter lodged (Acts 10:6, 17, 32).

SIMON BAR-JONA, SIMON PETER, *see* PETER.

SIMPLE, (1) undesigning (Rom. 16:19); (2) ignorant, yet teachable (Prov. 9:4); (3) silly, foolish (Prov. 14:15).

SIMRI, *see* SHIMRI.

SIN, the simple definition is "transgression of the law" (I John 3:4). Sin may be viewed as a single act of transgressing or it may be viewed as a state in which all men are or have been (Rom. 3:23; I John 1:8). The consequences of sin are physical death (Gen. 2:17; Rom. 5:12). The wages of sin, under the age of the reign of Christ, is spiritual death (Rom. 6:23). The seat of all sin is the heart (Matt. 15:19), because out of it come all things one says or does. Because man was in sin, God loved man and sent Jesus to save men from sin (John 3:16; Acts 10:43). The unpardonable sin seems to be the denial of the power of God which is invested in Jesus Christ (Matt. 12:31).
s. lieth at the door, Gen. 4:7.
do not *s.* against . . child, Gen. 42:22.
God shall bear his *s.*, Lev. 24:15.
consumed in . . their *s.*, Num. 16:26.
s. will find you out, Num. 32:23.
Lord . . put away thy *s.*, II Sam. 12:13.
forgive *s.* of servants, II Chr. 6:27.
shall die in his *s.*, Ezek. 3:20.
save . . people from . . *s.*, Matt. 1:21.
brother *s.* against me, Matt. 18:21.
baptized . . confessing . . *s.*, Mark 1:5.
I . . *s.* against heaven, Luke 15:18.
Lord, lay not . . *s.*, Acts 7:60.
forgiveness of *s.*, Acts 13:38.
the body of *s.*, Rom. 6:6.
died for our *s.*, I Cor. 15:3.
be . . angry . . *s.* not, Eph. 4:26.
if any man *s.*, I John 2:1.

SINA, SINAI, the mount upon which God met Moses and gave to him and to the Hebrews the Ten Commandments (Ex. 19). The mount is in a peninsula east of the Red Sea.
between Elim and *S.*, Ex. 16:1.
to the desert of *S.*, Ex. 19:2.
Lord . . down upon . . *S.*, Ex. 19:20.
Lord abode upon . . *S.*, Ex. 24:16.
Lord commanded . . in . . *S.*, Lev. 7:38.
the wilderness of *S.*, Num. 3:14.

Agar is mount *S.*, Gal. 4:25.

SINAITIC, pertaining to Sinai.

SINCERE, purely honest, true.
s. till day of, Phil. 1:10.
desire *s.* milk of word, I Pet. 2:2.

SINCERITY, honesty of mind.
serve Lord in *s.* and, Josh. 24:14.
in godly *s.* we, II Cor. 1:12.
prove *s.* of your love, II Cor. 8:8.
doctrine showing *s.*, Tit. 2:7.

SINEW, a tendon, muscle.
eat not of the *s.*, Gen. 32:32.
Jacob's thigh in the *s.*, Gen. 32:32.
with bones and *s.*, Job 10:11.
neck is an iron *s.*, Is. 48:4.
lay *s.* upon you, Ezek. 37:6.

SINFUL, wicked, characterized by Sin.
ah *s.* nation, a people, Is. 1:4.
ashamed in *s.* generation, Mark 8:38.
I am a *s.* man, O Lord, Luke 5:8.
sin become exceeding *s.*, Rom. 7:13.
in likeness of *s.* flesh, Rom. 8:3.

SING, produce music with the voice.
s. unto him a new song, Is. 42:10.
s. of righteousness, Ps. 51:14.
s. aloud to God, Ps. 81:1.
shall *s.* as in days, Hos. 2:15.
for this cause I *s.*, Rom. 15:9.
s. with spirit and, I Cor. 14:15.
s. in heart to Lord, Eph. 5:19.
merry? let him *s.*, James 5:13.
s. the song of Moses, Rev. 15:3.

SINGLE, sound, healthy, free of defect.
if thine eye be *s.*, Matt. 6:22.

SINGLENESS, sincerity.
gladness and *s.* of heart, Acts 2:46.
be obedient, in *s.* of, Eph. 6:5.

SINIM, a distant land from which exiles should return (Is. 49:12).

SINITE, a tribe of Canaanites which probably lived in the north of Lebanon (Gen. 10:17).

SINK, fall below surface.
I *s.* in deep mire, Ps. 69:2.
thus shall Babylon *s.*, Jer. 51:64.
beginning to *s.*, cried, Matt. 14:30.
let sayings *s.* down, Luke 9:44.

SINNER, (1) one who falls short; (2) rebellious wicked person. See SIN.
standeth in way of *s.*, Ps. 1:1.
if *s.* entice thee, Prov. 1:10.
one *s.* destroyeth, Eccles. 9:18.
call *s.* to repentance, Matt. 9:13.
friend of publicans, *s.* Matt. 11:19.
joy in heaven over *s.*, Luke 15:7.
how can *s.* do such?, John 9:16.
while yet *s.*, Christ died, Rom. 5:8.
we are found *s.*, Gal. 2:17.
cleanse hands ye *s.*, James 4:8.
where ungodly and *s.*?, I Pet. 4:18.

SIN OFFERING, *see* **OFFERING AND SACRIFICE.**

SIN, WILDERNESS OF, a large plain on the eastern shore of the Red Sea. Here the encamped Israelites murmured (Num. 33:11) and miraculously received the quails and manna (Ex. 16:13–20).

SION, the peak of mount Hermon; called Sirion by the Sidonians and Shenir by the Amorites (Deut. 4:48). It was also the name given to Jerusalem, the city of Zion (Matt. 21:5; Rom. 9:33; Heb. 12: 22). *See* ZION.

SIPHMOTH, a city in Judah where David took refuge from Saul (I Sam. 30:28).

SIPPAI, *see* **SAPH.**

SIRAH, a well, pit or cistern near Hebron where the messengers of Joab found Abner (II Sam. 3:26).

SIRION, the name by which mount Hermon was known to the Sidonians (Deut. 3:9; Ps. 29:6).

SISAMAI, SISMAI, son of Eleasah, and father of Shallum, (I Chr. 2:40).

SISERA, (1) captain of Jabin's Canaanite army which was defeated by the Israelite host which was led by Barak and Deborah. He fled and hid in the home of a Kenite named Heber. Jael, Heber's wife, drove a nail through his head as he slept (Judg. 4:2–22; 5:20–30; I Sam. 12:9; Ps. 83:9). (2) An ancestor of Nethinim (Ezra 2:53; Neh. 7:55) who returned to Jerusalem with Zerubbabel after the Babylonian exile.

SISMAI, *see* **SISAMAI.**

SISTER, the title was used quite broadly by the Hebrews and Christians. It may denote a full or half-sister, as in the case of Sarah and Abraham, (Gen. 20:12; Deut. 27:22). It may also denote a female of the same tribe or religion (Num. 25: 18; Rom. 16:1; James 2:15). Used of Christian women (Rom. 16:1).
Rachel envied her *s.*, Gen. 30:1.
the nakedness of . . *s.*, Lev. 18:9.
and Miriam their *s.*, Num. 26:59.
treacherous *s.* Judah, Jer. 3:7.
my brother, and *s.*, Matt. 12:50.
lead about a *s.*, I Cor. 9:5.
thy elect *s.* greet, II John 13.

SIT, occupy a seat; abide.
s. still, my daughter, Ruth 3:18.
s. at receipt of custom, Matt. 9:9.
two blind men *s.*, Matt. 20:30.
changers of money *s.*, John 2:14.
Christ *s.* on right hand, Col. 3:1.
he, as God, *s.* in, II Thess. 2:4.

SITHRI, *see* **ZITHRI.**

SITNAH, the name given to a well which the servants of Isaac dug in the Philistine country near Gerar (Gen. 26: 21).

SITUATION, position, location.
s. of the city, II Kin. 2:19.
beautiful for *s.* the joy, Ps. 48:2.

SIVAN, the third Hebrew month, from the new moon of June to that of July (Esther 8:9). It was the ninth month of the civil year.

SKILLFUL, expert.
every willing *s.* man, I Chr. 28:21.
men *s.* to destroy, Ezek. 21:31.
s. in all wisdom, Dan. 1:4.

SKILL, expert ability.
favor to men of *s.*, Eccles. 9:11.
God gave knowledge, *s.*, Dan. 1:17.

SKIN, hide of body. *See* **BADGERS' SKINS.**
s. of his face shone, Ex. 34:29.
my *s.* is broken, Job 7:5.
bones cleave to my *s.*, Ps. 102:5.
John had girdle of *s.*, Mark 1:6.

SKIP, bound, spring, leap.

s. like a calf, Ps. 29:6.
mountains *s.* like rams, Ps. 114:4.

SLACK, slow, sluggish, remiss.
deal with a *s.* hand, Prov. 10:4.
law is *s.,* judgment, Hab. 1:4.
Lord is not *s.,* II Pet. 3:9.

SLAIN, violently killed.
for I have *s.* a man, Gen. 4:23.
I weep for *s.* of, Jer. 9:1.
having *s.* enmity, Eph. 2:16.
Lamb as had been *s.,* Rev. 5:6.

SLANDER, malicious false report.
s. own mother's son, Ps. 50:20.
neighbor walk with *s.,* Jer. 9:4.

SLANDEROUSLY, falsely and maliciously.
as we be *s.* reported, Rom. 3:8.

SLAUGHTER, butchery, murder.
as sheep for the *s.,* Ps. 44:22.
brought as lamb to *s.,* Is. 53:7.
led as sheep to the *s.,* Acts 8:32.
Saul yet breathing out *s.,* Acts 9:1.

SLAVE, slavery was practiced widely in the ancient world. A slave might be purchased (Gen. 37:28, 36; Ezek. 27:13). It was common to enslave a debtor and his family due to the inability to pay a debt, but this practice was forbade by the Mosaic law (Ex. 22:3; II Kin. 4:1; Amos 2:6). A common way of obtaining slaves was the taking of captives of war (Num. 31:9; II Kin. 5:2). One might sell himself, or a child into slavery (Ex. 21: 2, 7; Lev. 25:39, 47). The Jews had laws to protect the Hebrew slaves. After six years of servitude a slave could have his freedom, and in the year of Jubilee all Hebrew slaves were released (Lev. 25:40). In the New Testament, neither Jesus nor his apostles commend or denounce the system of slavery in Palestine. The writers of the New Testament enjoin the slaves to give dutiful, conscientious service to their masters (Eph. 6:5–8; Col. 3:22–25). The master of slaves is admonished to recognize the rights and dignity of the slave (Eph. 6:9; Col. 4:1).
is Israel a *s.,* Jer. 2:14.
horses . . chariots . . .*s.,* Rev. 18:13.

SLAY, kill, murder.
find me shall *s.* me, Gen. 4:14.
sought to *s.* Moses, Ex. 2:15.

s. children in valleys, Is. 57:5.
sought to *s.* Jesus, John 5:16.
went about to *s.* him, Acts 9:29.

SLEEP, (1) slumber; (2) indolence of soul (Rom. 13:11); (3) figurative for death (John 11:11).
God caused a deep *s.,* Gen. 2:21.
lest I *s.* the *s.* of death, Ps. 13:3.
a little *s.,* slumber, Prov. 24:33.
s. of laboring man, Eccles. 5:12.
being raised from *s.,* Matt. 1:24.
were heavy with *s.,* Luke 9:32.
our friend Lazarus *s.,* John 11:11.
many among you *s.,* I Cor. 11:30.
we shall not all *s.,* I Cor. 15:51.
awake, thou that *s.* and, Eph. 5:14.
them who *s.* in Jesus, I Thess. 4:14.

SLEIGHT, artful trick.
by *s.* of men, Eph. 4:14.

SLEW, killed.
Saul *s.* his thousands, I Sam. 29:5.
s. and hanged on tree, Acts 5:30.
and by it *s.* me, Rom. 7:11.

SLIDE, slip, fall.
their foot shall *s.,* Deut. 32:35.
people of Jerusalem *s.,* Jer. 8:5.
Israel *s.* back as a, Hos. 4:16.

SLIGHTLY, lightly, imperfectly.
healed hurt of people *s.,* Jer. 6:14.

SLIME, *see* BITUMEN.
had brick . . and *s.,* Gen. 11:3.
Siddim . . full of *s.* pits, Gen. 14:10.
daubed it with *s.,* Ex. 2:3.

SLING, an offensive weapon of battle. It consisted of a leather thong which was wider in the middle than at the two ends. A stone was placed in the middle, and the sling was spun around the head. When one end of the thong was released the stone was hurled toward the mark. The sling was used by David to kill the giant Goliath (I Sam. 17:50).

SLIP, fall into error.
my feet did not *s.,* II Sam. 22:37.
he that is ready to *s.,* Job 12:5.
lest we let them *s.,* Heb. 2:1.

SLOTHFUL, lazy, indolent.
be not *s.* to go, Judg. 18:9.
the way of . . .*s.* man, Prov. 15:19.
the *s.* hideth . . hand, Prov. 26:15.

wicked . . s. servant, Matt. 25:26.
not s. in business, Rom. 12:11.

SLOW, not quick; dull.
s. of speech and tongue, Ex. 4:10.
God s. to anger, Neh. 9:17.
fools and s. of heart, Luke 24:25.
man be s. to speak, James 1:19.

SLUGGARD, lazy person, slothful.
go to the ant, thou s., Prov. 6:6.
how long sleep, O s., Prov. 6:9.
s. wiser in conceit, Prov. 26:16.

SLUMBER, sleep.
keepeth thee will not s., Ps. 121:3.
lying down, loving to s., Is. 56:10.
given them spirit of s., Rom. 11:8.
damnation s. not, II Pet. 2:3.

SMALL, not large; trivial, petty.
is it a s. thing, Num. 16:13.
thy strength is s., Prov. 24:10.
left us a s. remnant, Is. 1:9.
had no s. dissension, Acts 15:2.
turned with very s. helm, James 3:4.

SMART, feel sharp, stinging pain.
stranger s. for it, Prov. 11:15.

SMELL, give off odor; receive scent.
s. battle afar off, Job 39:25.
garments s. of myrrh, Ps. 45:8.

SMITE, strike; put to death.
s. this people with, II Kin. 6:18.
sun shall not s., Ps. 121:6.
s. a scorner and, Prov. 19:25.
s. thee with a rod, Is. 10:24.
s. thee on cheek, Matt. 5:39.
Lord, shall we s.?, Luke 22:49.

SMITH, a metalworker. These learned
smelting and hammering, and made
weapons, tools, ornaments, and larger
implements (I Chr. 23:2; Judg. 17:4).
Tubal-Cain the first s., Gen. 4:22.
Hiram, Solomon's s., I Kin. 7:13–51.
s. taken to Babylon, II Kin. 24:14.
God created the s., Is. 54:16.

SMITTEN, struck, killed, afflicted.
Lord had s. the river, Ex. 7:25.
my heart is s., Ps. 102:4.
in vain have I s., Jer. 2:30.
command me to be s., Acts 23:3.

SMOKE, vapor from fire.
s. of country went up, Gen. 19:28.

as s. to the eyes, Prov. 10:26.
fire and pillars of s., Joel 2:30.
blood, fire, vapour s., Acts 2:19.
s. of their torment, Rev. 14:11.

SMOOTH, not rough, even.
and I am a s. man, Gen. 27:11.
chose five s. stones, I Sam. 17:40.
speak to us s. things, Is. 30:10.
rough ways be made s., Luke 3:5.

SMOTE, killed.
Lord s. all firstborn, Ex. 12:29.
Moses s. the rock, Num. 20:11.
Peter drew sword, s., Matt. 26:51.
prophesy who s. thee, Luke 22:64.

SMYRNA, a city of Ionia in Asia Minor.
It was the city which housed one of
the seven churches to whom the Revelation of John was addressed (Rev.
1:11).

SNAIL, (1) common in Bible lands, this
slow-creeping mollusk has a shell. The
slimy trail left by snails is probably
meant by "melting" in Ps. 58:8. (2) Sand
lizard (Lev. 11:30).

SNARE, a trap set for prey (Ps. 91:3;
Amos 3:5). In Job 11:24 it denotes a
noose used for catching birds.
that will be a s., Deut. 7:16.
the s. is laid, Job 18:10.
of laying s. privily, Ps. 64:5.
the s. of his soul, Prov. 18:7.
fall into reproach and s., I Tim. 3:7.

SNOW, the many references to snow in
the Old Testament show that snowfall
was an ordinary occurrence in Palestine
(II Sam. 23:20; I Chr. 11:22). The highest ridge of Lebanon and the summit of
Hermon are snow-capped all year long.
Figuratively, snow pictures brilliancy
(Matt. 28:3), purity (Is. 1:18), whiteness
(Ex. 4:6), fleeting character (Job 24:19),
etc.
leprous, white as s., Num. 12:10.
shall be whiter than s., Ps. 51:7.
as the s. from heaven, Is. 55:10.
will man leave the s., Jer. 18:14.
garment white as s., Dan. 7:9.
hairs as white as s., Rev. 1:14.

SO, the king of Egypt to whom Hoshea,
king of Israel, sent letters (II Kin. 17:4).
Hoshea hoped for an alliance against
Assyria.

SOAP, SOPE, a cleansing agent usually made by the action of alkali on oil or fatty acid. Certain vegetables and their ashes were used for cleansing linen.
and take thee much *s.*, Jer. 2:22.
and like fullers' *s.*, Mal. 3:2.

SOBER, calm, temperate, sound-minded.
let watch, be *s.*, I Thess. 5:6.
bishop must be *s.*, I Tim. 3:2.
aged men be *s.*, grave, Tit. 2:2.
young women to be *s.*, Tit. 2:4.

SOCHO, SHOCO, SHOCHO, (1) a son of Heber (I Chr. 4:18). (2) A city in Judah which was rebuilt by Rehoboam (II Chr. 11:7; 28:18).

SOCOH, SHOCHOH, SOCHOH, (1) a city in the hill country of Judah (Josh. 15:48), located near Jattir. (2) The name of city in the northwest plain of Judah (Josh. 15:35; I Sam. 17:1), located near Adullam or Azekah.

SODDEN, boiled.
eat not of it raw, *s.*, Ex. 12:9.
women have *s.* their, Lam. 4:10.

SODI, the father of the spy sent out from the tribe of Zebulun to spy out the land of Canaan (Num. 13:10).

SODOM, SODOMA, one of the five cities of the plain of the Jordan, near the Salt Sea (Gen. 13:10). It was noted for its wickedness (Gen. 13:13; 18:20; Is. 3:9; Lam. 4:6). It was destroyed because it was full of sin, but Lot, Abraham's nephew, was given time to leave the city before its destruction began. Lot's wife, however, looked back at the city and was turned into a pillar of salt (Gen. 19:1-26).
Lord destroyed *S.*, Gen. 13:10.
Lot . . dwelt in *S.*, Gen. 14:12.
came two angels to *S.*, Gen. 19:1.
Moab shall be as *S.*, Zeph. 2:9.
more tolerable . . for *S.*, Luke 10:12.
spiritually . . called *S.*, Rev. 11:8.

SODOMITE, he was not only an inhabitant of Sodom (I Kin. 14:24; 22:46) but rather anyone committed to the unnatural sexual vice of Sodom (Gen. 19:5).
no *s.* of the sons, Deut. 23:17.
also . . *s.* in the land, I Kin. 14:24.
remnant of the *s.*, I Kin. 22:46.

houses of the *s.*, II Kin. 23:7.

SODOM, VINE OF, *see* **VINE OF SODOM.**

SOFT, tender, melted, smooth.
God maketh my heart *s.*, Job 23:16.
a *s.* answer turneth, Prov. 15:1.
a *s.* tongue breaketh, Prov. 25:15.
that wear *s.* clothing, Luke 7:25.

SOIL, earth, ground (Ezek. 17:8).

SOJOURN, dwell temporarily.
down into Egypt to *s.*, Gen. 12:10.
Elimelech went to *s.*, Ruth 1:1.
his seed should *s.*, Acts 7:6.
by faith he *s.* in land, Heb. 11:9.

SOJOURNER, *see* **STRANGER.**
I am a *s.* with you, Gen. 23:4.
cities of refuge for *s.*, Num. 35:15.

SOLD, made sale of, bargained.
Esau *s.* his birthright, Gen. 25:33.
Midianites *s.* him into, Gen. 37:36.
land shall not be *s.*, Lev. 25:23.
if brother be *s.*, Deut. 15:12.
are not sparrows *s.*?, Matt. 10:29.
went, *s.* all he had, Matt. 13:46.
s. possessions and goods, Acts 4:34.
I carnal, *s.* under sin, Rom. 7:14.

SOLDIER, man of war, warrior.
to every *s.* a part, John 19:23.
sleeping between two *s.*, Acts 12:6.
make ready 200 *s.*, Acts 23:23.
endure as a good *s.*, II Tim. 2:3.

SOLE, bottom of foot.
not set *s.* of foot, Deut. 28:56.
smote Job from *s.* to, Job 2:7.

SOLEMN, appointed, set, reverential.
in your *s.* days ye, Num. 10:10.
what do in *s.* day?, Hos. 9:5.

SOLEMNITY, appointed ceremony.
in the *s.* of the year, Deut. 31:10.
song as when holy *s.* is, Is. 30:29.

SOLEMNLY, with testimony, gravely.
man did *s.* protest, Gen. 43:3.
yet protest *s.* to them, I Sam. 8:9.

SOLITARY, separate, lonely.
that night be *s.*, let no, Job 3:7.
setteth *s.* in families, Ps. 68:6.
wilderness, *s.* place, Is. 35:1.

how doth city sit *s.*, Lam. 1:1.

SOLOMON, the tenth son of David, and second by Bath-sheba, and the third king of Israel. As king he sent the nation to its peak in power and glory. Under his rule Jerusalem was embellished with several royal buildings and the Temple of God (I Kin. 9:15, 24; 11:27). He had a great army and navy (I Kin. 4:26; 10:26). He, according to the Scriptures, had 700 wives and 300 concubines and reigned in luxury and extravagance (I Kin. 11:3). He was a man noted for his wisdom (I Kin. 3:3–14). He was the author of 3000 proverbs and 1005 songs (I Kin. 4:32). Later he lapsed into idolatry, being influenced by his foreign wives (I Kin. 11:4), and even built an altar to Chemosh, the Moabite god of child sacrifice. He ruled for a forty year period and then was succeeded, after his death, by his son, Rehoboam (I Kin. 11: 42, 43).
he called his name *S.*, II Sam. 12:24.
but *S.* thy servant, I Kin. 1:19.
Zadok . . anointed *S.*, I Kin. 1:39.
Bath-sheba went unto *S.*, I Kin. 2:19.
S. loved the Lord, I Kin. 3:3.
Lord gave *S.* wisdom, I Kin. 5:12.
so *S.* built the house, I Kin. 6:14 .
S. offered a sacrifice, I Kin. 8:63.
father of Rehoboam, I Kin. 14:21.
S. build house of Lord, II Chr. 3:1.
to hear . . . wisdom of *S.*, Matt. 12:42 .
greater than *S.* is here, Luke 11:31.
temple in *S.* porch, John 10:23 .
S. built an house, Acts 7:47.

SOLOMON'S PORCH, the outer corridor or foyer on the east side of Herod's temple (John 10:23; Acts 3:11).
the temple in *S. p.*, John 10:23.
the *p.* that is called *S.*, Acts 3:11.
were all . . in *S. p.*, Acts 5:12.

SOLOMON'S SERVANTS, a class of servants probably descended from Canaanite slaves used by Solomon in quarry and temple work (II Chr. 8:7, 8; Ezra 2:58; Neh. 7:57). *See* SLAVE.

SOLOMON'S TEMPLE, *see* TEMPLE.

SOLOMON, WISDOM OF, one of the books of the Apocrypha.

SOME, indefinite quantity.

s. trust chariots, *s.*, Ps. 20:7.
s. to everlasting life, Dan. 12:2.
s. say thou art, Matt. 16:14.
s. doubted, Matt. 28:17.

SOMETIME, once, at a previous time.
who were *s.* afar off, Eph. 2:13.
also were *s.* foolish, Tit. 3:3.
s. were disobedient, I Pet. 3:20.

SON, (1) male child (Gen. 17:16); (2) grandson (Gen. 29:5) or more distant descendant (Num. 2:14, 18); (3) foster son (Ex. 2:10); (4) figuratively used for subject or disciple (I Kin. 20:35; I Sam. 3:6), production of (Lam. 3:13), deserving of (Deut. 25:3). The word is used of the sonship of Christ (Mark 1:1) and of Christians (John 1:12).
wise *s.* makes glad, Prov. 10:1.
unto us *s.* is given, Is. 9:6.
my beloved *s.*, Matt. 3:17.
Christ, *S.* of God, Matt. 16:16.
s. abideth ever, John 8:35.
Gospel of his *S.*, Rom. 1:9.
spared not his own *S.*, Rom. 8:32.
sent forth his *S.*, Gal. 4:4.
be to me a *S.*, Heb. 1:5.
whosoever denieth *S.*, I John 2:23.
S. hath life, I John 5:12.

SON OF GOD, an expression which identified Jesus of Nazareth as the being who has had an eternal relationship to the Father (Ps. 2:7). Christ claimed to be the only begotten son of the Father (Matt. 4:3; 8:29; 27:54). This placed Jesus on the level with God (John 5:18), at least in the qualitative sense. The term appears in the New Testament almost fifty times. God confessed that he was his son at his baptism and at the transfiguration (Matt. 3:16, 17; 17: 5). Because he said he was the son of God, the Jewish Sanhedrin condemned him for blasphemy (Matt. 26:63–66; Mark 14:61).
if thou be . . *S. o. G.*, Matt. 4:3 .
gospel of . . the *S. o. G.*, Mark.1:1.
S. o. G. most high, Luke 8:28 .
Jesus . . the *S. o. G.*, John 20:31.
the *S. o. G.*, Jesus, II Cor. 1:19.
S. . . . the propitiation, I John 4:10.
Jesus is . . *S. o. G.*, I John 4:15.
saith the *S. o. G.*, Rev. 2:18.

SON OF MAN, a term which appears numerous times in Ezekiel (Ezek. 25: 2; 26:2; 27:2; 28:2, 12, 21; 29:2, 18) to signify that Ezekiel (called "son of men" by Jehovah) was just human. God was not poking fun at the prophet. Just why he kept repeating the term can not be known for sure. Jesus is eighty times called the son of man in the New Testament. It was probably used to signify Jesus and his humiliation (John 1:51). In the Jewish religious writings which were written between the Testaments, the term appears in connection with the Messiah who was to come and bring deliverance and the kingdom.

S. o. m., set thy face, Ezek. 25:2.
S. o. m., prophesy, Ezek. 30:2.
he said .. *S. o. m.*, Ezek. 37:3.
one like the *S. o. m.*, Dan. 7:13.
S. o. m. be three days, Matt. 12:40.
S. o. m. .. send .. angels, Matt. .13:41
S. o. m. is betrayed, Matt. 26:2.
they see the *S. o. m.*, Mark 13:26.
shall .. *S. o. m.* .. confess, Luke 12:8.
S. o. m. is revealed, Luke 17:30.
the *S. o. m.* be lifted up, John 3:14.
see .. *S. o. m.* ascend, John 6:62.
on right hand of God, Acts 7:56.

SONG, ode. *See* **DEGREES, SONG OF.**
Lord is strength and *s.*, Ex. 15:2.
put a new *s.* in my, Ps. 40:3.
praise God with *s.*, Ps. 69:30.
s. of my beloved, Is. 5:1.
psalms, spiritual *s.*, Eph. 5:19.
sing *s.* of Moses, Lamb, Rev. 15:3.

SONG OF SOLOMON, SONG OF SONGS, CANTICLES, this book has been understood literally, as an exalted picture of pure human love; allegorically, as an analogy of God's love for Israel, Christ's love for the church, or divine love for the soul of man; and typically, as a narrative of Solomon's love which prefigures (typifies) love of Christ for the church. Whether the Song is understood literally or figuratively, its story may be outlined as follows: (1) The maiden's longing and satisfaction (1:1–2:7); (2) the beloved's visit and the maiden's dream (2:8–3:5); (3) Solomon's procession and songs (3:6–5:1); (4) the maiden's tardy welcome and prolonged search (5:2–8:3); and (5) conversation of the maiden and the beloved (8:4–14).

Some distinguish between Solomon and the maiden's beloved, and thus picture the maiden as continuing faithful to her beloved and longing for him despite Solomon's earnest wooing.

SONG OF THE THREE HOLY CHILDREN, a book of the Apocrypha.

SONS OF GOD, (1) angelic beings (Job 1:6; 2:1); (2) scholars are disagreed whether Gen. 6:2, 4 refers also to angelic beings or, instead, to righteous worshippers of God in contrast to worldly men.

SOON, quickly, without delay.
that is *s.* angry, Prov. 14:17.
marvel that are so *s.*, Gal. 1:6.
ye be not *s.* shaken, II Thess. 2:2.
not *s.* angry, Tit. 1:7.

SOOTHSAYER, one who claimed to have the power to foresee the future (Josh. 13:22; Jer. 27:9), interpret dreams and utterances (Dan. 4:7, 9; 5:11, 12), and bring to light secrets (Dan. 2:27). Paul and Silas encountered one of these at Philippi (Acts 16:16). *See* **MAGIC.**
s. like the Philistines, Is. 2:6.
astrologers magicians *s.*, Dan. 2:27.
to bring the *s.*, Dan. 5:7.
Chaldeans, and *s.*, Dan. 5:11.
have no more *s.*, Mic. 5:12.
one followed Paul, Acts 16:16.

SOP, a piece of bread dipped into sauce (John 13:26–30).

SOPATER, a Christian of Berea who went with Paul, during the apostle's third journey, from Philippi to Asia (Acts 20:4). His father was Pyrrhus.

SOPE, *see* **SOAP.**

SOPHERETH, HASSOPHERETH, a servant of king Solomon whose descendants returned to Jerusalem with Zerubbabel after the exile (Neh. 7:57) in Babylonia.

SORCERY, the practice of magic by using oracular formulas, incantations and mystic mutterings (Ex. 7:11; Dan. 2:2; Rev. 21:8; 22:15). One form of sorcery was **Necromancy.** The New Testament mentions Simon Magus and Bar-Jesus as sorcerers (Acts 8:9; 13:6). Sorcery is also called witchcraft (Ex. 22:18; Deut. 18:10; II Chr. 33:6). *See* **DIVINATION, MAGIC, NECROMANCY, WIZARD.**

SORE, painful, grievous; a pain.
famine *s.* in land, Gen. 41:56.
smote Job with *s.* boils, Job 2:7.

s. evil I have seen, Eccles. 5:13.
king *s.* displeased, Dan. 6:14.

SOREK, a valley west of Jerusalem through which the ark was taken to Bethshemesh (I Sam. 6:7–13).

SORROW, grief, affliction, mourning.
multiply thy *s.*, Gen. 3:16.
with *s.* to the grave, Gen. 42:38.
I know their *s.*, Ex. 3:7.
s. turned into joy, Job 41:22.
a man of *s.*, Is. 53:3.
beginning of *s.*, Matt. 24:8.
s. filled your heart, John 16:6.
I have continual *s.*, Rom. 9:2.
s. works repentance, II Cor. 7:10.
no death, neither *s.*, Rev. 21:4.

SORROWFUL, distressed, sad, grieved.
he went away *s.*, Matt. 19:22.
he began to be *s.*, Matt. 26:37.
s. yet rejoicing, II Cor. 6:10.

SORRY, grieved, sad.
be *s.* for my sin, Ps. 38:18.
and the king was *s.*, Matt. 14:9.

SORT, kind, species, manner.
two of every *s.* to ark, Gen. 6:19.
fellows of baser *s.*, Acts 17:5.

SOSIPATER, a kinsman of Paul who sent salutation, by Paul's letter, to the church at Rome (Rom. 16:21).

SOSTHENES, the ruler of the synagogue in Corinth who was beaten by the Greeks following a riot over Paul's preaching (Acts 18:17). A man by this name united with Paul in addressing the church in Corinth (I Cor. 1:1).

SOTAI, a servant of Solomon whose descendants returned to Jerusalem with Zerubbabel after the Babylonian exile (Ezra 2:55; Neh. 7:57).

SOUGHT, did seek, searched for.
s. Lord and he heard, Ps. 34:4.
s. child's life, Matt. 2:20.
s. opportunity to betray, Matt. 26:16.
Jews *s.* to slay him, John 5:16.
s. it not by faith, Rom. 9:32.
he *s.* it carefully with, Heb. 12:17.

SOUL, a living being, a person (Gen. 2: 7; Acts 7:14, 27:37; I Pet. 3:20). The life principle (Mark 3:4; Matt. 2:20; Acts

20:10. In these passages the word ordinarily translated "soul" is translated "life"). The seat of the affections and the will (Acts 2:43; Rom. 2:9; 2 Pet. 2:8; John 12:27). The term is used sometimes as synonymous with "spirit" (Isa. 26:9; Luke 1:46, 47; Phil. 1:27) while at other times as distinct from the spirit (Heb. 4:12; I Thess. 5:23). One aspect of this distinction is that "spirit" is used with reference to man's relation to God, while "soul" infers the individuality of man, i.e., man as apart from God.
man became . . living *s.*, Gen. 2:7.
my *s.* shall live, Gen. 12:13.
were seventy *s.*, Ex. 1:5.
s. of thine enemies, I Sam. 25:29.
the bitterness of *s.*, Job 10:1.
say ye to my *s.*, Ps. 11:1.
deliver . . *s.* from sword, Ps. 22:20.
s. shall make her boast, Ps. 34:2.
an idle *s.* hunger, Prov. 19:15.
their *s.* delighted, Is. 66:3.
save the *s.* alive, Ezek. 13:19.
able to kill the *s.*, Matt. 10:28.
one heart and . . *s.*, Acts 4:32.
and fifteen *s.*, Acts 7:14.
dividing . . soul and spirit, Heb. 4:12.
fruits of thy *s.*, Rev. 18:14.

SOUND, voice, noise.
his *s.* shall be heard, Ex. 28:35.
hearest *s.*, cannot tell, John 3:8.
there came *s.* from heaven, Acts 2:2.
s. went into all earth, Rom. 10:18.
not come to *s.* of trumpet, Heb. 12:19.
as *s.* of many waters, Rev. 1:15.

SOUND, healthy, perfect.
received safe and *s.*, Luke 15:27.
contrary to *s.* doctrine, I Tim. 1:10.
God has given *s.* minds, II Tim. 1:7.
aged men be *s.* in faith, Tit. 2:2.

SOUR, acidic.
fathers ate *s.* grapes, Ezek. 18:2.
Their drink is *s.*, Hos. 4:18.

SOUTH, opposite north.
Abraham went into *s.*, Gen. 13:1.
out of *s.* whirlwind, Job 37:9.
tree fall toward *s.*, Eccles. 11:3.
queen of the *s.*, Matt. 12:42.
come from *s.* and sit, Luke 13:29.

SOUTH, THE. South of Palestine lay the vast wasteland known as the Negeb, suitable only for grazing (Gen. 20:1, 14). It was this area that prevented the Israelites

from entering Canaan in direct line from Egypt. Beer-sheba, Ziklag and Kadesh-Barnea were notable towns of the Negeb.
Abraham wanders in *S.*, Gen. 12:9.
Isaac dwells in *S.*, Gen. 24:62.
Spies pass through *S.*, Num. 13:17.

SOW, adult female pig (II Pet. 2:22).

SOW, scatter seeds on earth.
not *s.* mingled seed, Lev. 19:19.
s. wickedness, reap, Job 4:8.
s. in tears, reap in joy, Ps. 126:5.
they *s.* not nor reap, Matt. 6:26.
sower *s.* the word, Mark 4:14.

SOWER, one who scatters seeds. Sowing in Bible times was done by hand.
seed to the *s.*, Is. 55:10.
parable of the *s.*, Matt. 13:18.
s. soweth the word, Mark 4:14.

SPAIN, the territory which is now called Spain and Portugal. Paul, in the letter to Rome, expressed the desire to go to Spain with the gospel (Rom. 15:24, 28).

SPAKE, spoke, uttered words.
s. against God, Ps. 78:19.
never man *s.* like this, John 7:46.
I *s.* as a child, I Cor. 13:11.
God who *s.* in past by, Heb. 1:1.

SPAN, about nine inches.
s. shall be length, Ex. 28:16.
six cubits and a *s.*, I Sam. 17:4.
meted out heaven with *s.*, Is. 40:12.

SPARE, withhold punishment, use mercy.
s. the poor and needy, Ps. 72:13.
that *s.* rod hates son, Prov. 13:24.
s. not his own Son, Rom. 8:32.
to *s.* you I came not, II Cor. 1:23.
if God *s.* not angels, II Pet. 2:4.

SPARKS, fiery particles.
trouble, as *s.* fly up, Job 5:7.
maker of it as a *s.*, Is. 1:31.

SPARROW, the Greek *strouthion* means any small bird of the sparrow family. They were sold for food (Matt. 10:29).
the *s.* found an house, Ps. 84:3.
as a *s.* alone, Ps. 102:7.
two *s.* sold for a, Matt. 10:29.
more value than *s.*, Luke 12:7.

SPEAK, talk, utter words, say.
know he can *s.* well, Ex. 4:14.
and a time to *s.*, Eccles. 3:7.
s. unto us smooth, Is. 30:10.
what ye shall *s.*, Matt. 10:19.
men *s.* well of you, Luke 6:26.
s. a word against Son, Luke 12:10.
slow to *s.*, James 1:19.
so *s.* ye and so do, James 2:12.

SPEAR, LANCET, a weapon consisting of a wooden shaft tipped with a metal or flint point (II Sam. 2:23; Neh. 4:13).
beat *s.* into pruninghooks, Is. 2:4.
Pruninghooks into *s.*, Joel 3:10.
sword and glittering *s.*, Nah. 3:3.
with *s.* pierced side, John 19:34.

SPECIAL, particular, singular.
chosen a *s.* people, Deut. 7:6.
God wrought *s.* miracles, Acts 19:11.

SPECKLED BIRD, Jeremiah likens sinful Israel to a speckled bird which is attacked by other birds because of its unfamiliar plumage (Jer. 12:9).

SPECTACLE, show, public display.
are made *s.* to world, I Cor. 4:9.

SPEECH, talk, language.
whole earth of one *s.*, Gen. 11:1.
Moses slow of *s.*, Ex. 4:10.
s. shall distill as dew, Deut. 32:2.
day to day uttereth *s.*, Ps. 19:2.
thy *s.* betrayeth thee, Matt. 26:73.
Let *s.* be with grace, Col. 4:6.

SPEECHLESS, silent, mute, dumb.
Zacharias remained *s.*, Luke 1:22.
men stood *s.*, Acts 9:7.

SPEED, haste, progress.
come with all *s.*, Acts 17:15.
neither bid God *s.*, II John 10.

SPEEDILY, quickly.
deliver me *s.*, Ps. 31:2.
go *s.* and pray, Zech. 8:21.
will avenge them *s.*, Luke 18:8.

SPELT, *see* **FITCHES.**

SPEND, pay out, pass, exhaust.
will *s.* my arrows, Deut. 32:23.
s. days in wealth, Job 21:13.
will gladly *s.* for, II Cor. 12:15.

SPENT, paid out, exhausted.
strength *s.* in vain, Lev. 26:20.
days *s.* without hope, Job 7:6.
s. all that she had, Mark 5:26.
he had *s.* all, Luke 15:14.
night is far *s.*, Rom. 13:12.

SPICE, vegetable substances with aromatic qualities. Southern Arabia was particularly noted for spices (I Kin. 10: 2; Ezek. 27:22). Spice was used in making both ointment and perfume. Some spices named were myrrh, cinnamon, calamus, cassia, onycha, galbanum, and stacte (Ex. 30:23, 24, 34). Two spices, myrrh and aloes, were used on the body of Jesus after his death (John 19:39, 40).
s. for anointing oil, Ex. 25:6.
take . . thee sweet *s.*, Ex. 30:34.
such abundance of *s.*, I Kin. 10:10.
oil . . frankincense . . *s.*, I Chr. 9:29.
to the beds of *s.*, Song 6:2.
the *s.*, and . . ointment, Is. 39:2.
had bought sweet *s.*, Mark 16:1.
and prepared *s.*, Luke 23:56.

SPIDER, (1) the frailty of a spider's web is used figuratively for evil's worthlessness (Job 8:14; Is. 59:5). (2) Better rendered **Lizard** (Prov. 30:28).

SPIED, *see* **SPY**.

SPIES, watchers, secret agents.
watched, sent forth *s.*, Luke 20:20.
Rahab received *s.*, Heb. 11:31.

SPIKENARD, a sweet plant which grows in regions of high elevation. An ointment is made from it (Song 4:13, 14).
s. sendeth forth . . smell, Song 1:12.
s. and saffron; calamus, Song 4:14.
box of ointment of *s.*, Mark 14:3.
a pound of . . *s.*, John 12:3.

SPIN, to draw out and twist into thread.
women did *s.*, Ex. 35:25.
toil not, neither *s.*, Matt. 6:28.

SPINNING, this common craft of Bible times is mentioned by name only in Ex. 35:25, Matt. 6:28, Luke 12:27. Flax, cotton, wool and goats' hair were the chief materials spun. Women did this work in Palestine by means of a distaff and spindle (Prov. 31:19).

SPIRIT, *see* **SOUL, HOLY SPIRIT,**

DEMON, FAMILIAR SPIRIT.
S. of God moved on waters, Gen. 1:2.
my *s.* not always strive, Gen. 6:3.
Lord stirred *s.* of Cyrus, Ezra 1:1.
I commit my *s.*, Ps. 31:5.
renew a right *s.*, Ps. 51:10.
s. return to God, Eccles. 12:7.
S. of Lord God upon me, Is. 61:1.
a new *s.* within, Ezek. 11:19.
s. indeed is willing, Matt. 26:41.
S. like a dove, Mark 1:10.
except be born of *S.*, John 3:5.
God is a *s.*, John 4:24.
even the *S.* of truth, John 14:17.
speak as *S.* gave, Acts 2:4.
Lord, receive my *s.*, Acts 7:59.
walk in the *S.*, Gal. 5:16.
keep unity of *S.*, Eph. 4:3.
quench not the *S.*, I Thess. 5:19.
unto Father of *s.*, Heb. 12:9.
believe not every *s.*, I John 4:1.

SPIRITUAL, pertaining to the Spirit.
the *s.* man is mad, Hos. 9:7.
he that is *s.*, I Cor. 2:15.
sown unto you *s.* things, I Cor. 9:11.
eat the same *s.* meat, I Cor. 10:3.
think himself . . *s.*, I Cor. 14:37.
ye which are *s.*, Gal. 6:1.
hymns and *s.* songs, Col. 3:16.
built up a *s.* house, I Pet. 2:5.
offer up *s.* sacrifices, I Pet. 2:5.

SPIRITUALLY, incorporeally, purely.
s. minded is life, Rom. 8:6.
they are *s.* discerned, I Cor. 2:14.
s. called Sodom, Rev. 11:8.

SPITE, malice, hatred.
s. to requite it, Ps. 10:14.
entreated them *s.*, Matt. 22:6.
be *s.* entreated, Luke 18:32.

SPOIL, plunder, booty.
shall divide *s.*, Gen. 49:27.
one findeth great *s.*, Ps. 119:162.
no need of *s.*, Prov. 31:11.
s. shall be divided, Zech. 14:1.

SPOIL, to plunder, despoil, strip.
shall *s.* the Egyptians, Ex. 3:22.
pass by the way *s.* him, Ps. 89:41.
s. not his resting, Prov. 24:15.
evenings shall *s.* them, Jer. 5:6.
beware lest man *s.*, Col. 2:8.

SPOKEN, talked, uttered words.
as ye have *s.* so, Num. 14:28.
God hath *s.* once, Ps. 62:11.

cannot be *s.* of, I Cor. 10:30.
truth be evil *s.* of, II Pet. 2:2.

SPORT, mockery, derision, trifling.
Samson made *s.*, Judg. 16:25.
Am not I in *s.*, Prov. 26:19.

SPOT, stain, fault, reproach, blemish.
heifer without *s.*, Num. 19:2.
not having *s.*, Eph. 5:27.
without *s.* to God, Heb. 9:14.
lamb without *s.*, I Pet. 1:19.
found without *s.*, II Pet. 3:14.

SPOUSE, husband or wife.
thy lips, O my *s.*, Song 4:11.
your *s.* shall commit, Hos. 4:13.

SPREAD, distribute, extend, open, furl.
s. out my hands, Ezra 9:5.
s. it before me, Ezek. 2:10.
it *s.* no further, Acts 4:17.

SPRING, *see* FOUNTAIN.
truth shall *s.*, Ps. 85:11.
righteousness *s.* up, Is. 45:8.

SPRINKLE, to scatter in drops.
s. many nations, Is. 52:15.
s. clean water, Ezek. 36:25.
hearts *s.* from, Heb. 10:22.

SPROUT, to germinate, grow like a plant.
tree that it will *s.*, Job 14:7.

SPUE, cast forth, eject, vomit.
land *s.* not out, Lev. 18:28.
drink, *s.* and, Jer. 25:27.
will *s.* thee out, Rev. 3:16.

SPUNGE, piece of porous material.
took *s.*, vinegar, Matt. 27:48.
filled *s.* with vinegar, John 19:29.

SPY, search out secretly, traverse.
Moses sent to *s.* out, Num. 21:32.
sent men to *s.*, Josh. 2:1.
s. out our liberty, Gal. 2:4.

STABILITY, firmness, solidity.
knowledge *s.* of thy times, Is. 33:6.

STABLE, (1) lodging (Ezek. 25:5); (2) established, firm (I Chr. 16:30).

STACHYS, a disciple in the church of Rome to whom Paul sent personal greetings (Rom. 16:9).

STACTE, an aromatic gum used in making incense (Ex. 30:34).

STAFF, bar, rod, stave, sceptre.
with your *s.* in hand, Ex. 12:11.
put forth end of *s.*, Judg. 6:21.
thy rod and *s.* comfort, Ps. 23:4.
how is strong *s.* broken, Jer. 48:17.
have been *s.* to Israel, Ezek. 29:6.
take nothing, save *s.*, Mark 6:8.
leaning on his *s.*, Heb. 11:21.

STAGGER, reel, waver.
s. like drunken man, Job 12:25.
reel to and fro and *s.*, Ps. 107:27.
s. not at God's promise, Rom. 4:20.

STAIN, pollute, soil, claim.
shadow of death *s.* it, Job 3:5.
s. pride of all glory, Is. 23:9.

STAKE, pin, nail, stay.
not one of *s.* removed, Is. 33:20.
strengthen thy *s.*, Is. 54:2.

STAMMERING, indistinct, strange.
s. lips, another tongue, Is. 28:11.
people of *s.* tongue, Is. 33:19.

STAMP, tread down, strike with foot.
did *s.* as mire, II Sam. 22:43.
s. it to powder, II Kin. 23:6.

STAND, remain erect, be firm.
s. still and see, Ex. 14:13.
nor *s.* in way of sinners, Ps. 1:1.
it shall not *s.*, Is. 7:7.
who shall *s.* when, Mal. 3:2.
house divided not *s.*, Matt. 12:25.
why *s.* ye here all, Matt. 20:6.
I *s.* in doubt, Gal. 4:20.
having done all, to *s.*, Eph. 6:13.
s. fast in the Lord, Phil. 4:1.
I *s.* at door and knock, Rev. 3:20.
who shall be able to *s.*, Rev. 6:17.

STANDARD, banner, ensign, sail.
every man by own *s.*, Num. 1:52.
set up the *s.* toward Zion, Jer. 4:6.

STAR, any heavenly body, with the exception of the sun and moon, was a star to the Hebrews. They recognized the stars to be the handiwork of God (Ps. 8:3). The constellations attracted the attention of the ancients (Gen. 22:17; Is. 13:10). In Job there is reference to Orion, Pleiades, the Bear, Mazzaroth (Job 9:9; 38:31, 32). The star in the East guided

the Magi to the child in Bethlehem
(Matt. 2:1–12). Jesus is called the
"bright and morning star" (Rev. 22:
16).
God made .. the *s.* also, Gen. 1:16.
thy seed as the *s.*, Gen. 22:17.
s. of the twilight, Job 3:9.
maketh the seven *s.*, Amos 5:8.
his *s.* in the east, Matt. 2:2.
s. of heaven shall fall, Mark 13:25.
wandering *s.*, Jude 13.
and the .. morning *s.*, Rev. 22:16.

STATE, station, condition, circumstance.
last *s.* worse than, Matt. 12:45.
care for your *s.*, Phil. 2:20.
whatsoever *s.* I am in, Phil. 4:11.

STATER, a silver coin, valued by some
at about 75 cents (Matt. 17:27).

STATURE, the measurement of one's
height (I Sam. 16:7; Luke 19:3). In certain connections, it seems to denote
greatness (Is. 45:14; Matt. 6:27).
on the height of .. *s.*, I Sam. 16:7.
a man of great *s.*, II Sam. 21:20.
Sabeans, men of *s.*, Is. 45:14.
vine of low *s.*, Ezek. 17:6.
can add .. unto his *s.*, Matt. 6:27.
Jesus increased in .. *s.*, Luke 2:52.
he was little in *s.*, Luke 19:3.

STATUTE, decree, law.
keep all his *s.*, Ex. 15:26.
s. of Lord are right, Ps. 19:8.
delight in thy *s.*, Ps. 119:16.
afflicted, learn *s.*, Ps. 119:71.

STAVES, bars, rods, staffs.
did strike with his *s.*, Hab. 3:14.
provide shoes nor *s.*, Matt. 10:10.
comes multitude with *s.*, Mark 14:43.

STAY, a support.
Lord was my *s.*, II Sam. 22:19.
take away *s.* of bread, Is. 3:1.

STAY, stand, support, cease, delay.
the plague was *s.*, Num. 16:50.
let no man *s.*, Prov. 28:17.
whose mind is *s.* on thee, Is. 26:3.
heaven is *s.* from dew, Hag. 1:10.

STEAD, in place of another.
ram in *s.* of his son, Gen. 22:13.
pray in Christ's *s.*, II Cor. 5:20.

STEAL, (1) rob, pilfer; (2) go furtively

thou shalt not *s.*, Ex. 20:15.
will ye *s.*, commit?, Jer. 7:9.
break through and *s.*, Matt. 6:19.
commandments, do not *s.*, Mark 10:19.
dost thou *s.*?, Rom. 2:21.
stole *s.* no more, Eph. 4:28.

STEALING, robbing, thieving.
if man be found *s.*, Deut. 24:7.
only swearing and *s.*, Hos. 4:2.

STEALTH, furtive action.
got them by *s.* into, II Sam. 19:3.

STEADFAST, firm, steady.
thou shalt be *s.*, Job 11:15.
living God, *s.* forever, Dan. 6:26.
be *s.*, unmovable, I Cor. 15:58.
anchor sure and *s.*, Heb. 6:19.
s. in faith, I Pet. 5:9.

STEEL, a word which probably refers to
tempered bronze, a material made of tin
and copper (II Sam. 22:35; Ps. 18:34;
Jer. 15:12).
a bow of *s.* is broken, II Sam. 22:35.
bow of *s.* shall strike, Job 20:24.

STEEP, precipitous, extremely inclined.
waters pour down *s.* place, Mic. 1:4..684
swine down *s.* place, Matt. 8:32.

STEP, stride, going, stair.
numbers my *s.*, Job 14:16.
order my *s.* in thy, Ps. 119:133.
Lord directs his *s.*, Prov. 16:9.
walk in *s.* of faith, Rom. 4:12.
walked not in *s.*?, II Cor. 12:18.
ye follow his *s.*, I Pet. 2:21.

STEPHANAS, a man of Corinth who believed in the Lord with his household
and became the first converts of Paul in
Achaiah (I Cor. 16:15). He was with
Paul when he wrote the first epistle to
the Corinthians (I Cor. 1:16; 16:17).

STEPHEN, one of the seven ministers
chosen to serve tables in Jerusalem
(Acts 6:5). He became the first martyr of
the faith when he was stoned to death
by the Jews after preaching Christ to
them (Acts 7:59).

STEWARD, head servant, chief.
faithful and wise *s.*, Luke 12:42.
s. of mysteries, I Cor. 4:1.
as *s.* of God, Tit. 1:7.
s. of grace of God, I Pet. 4:10.

STIFFNECKED, hardened, stubborn.
this is a *s.* people, Ex. 32:9.
speak not with *s.*, Ps. 75:5.
ye *s.* and uncircumcised, Acts 7:51.

STILL, quiet, calm, serene.
sit *s.* daughter, Ruth 3:18.
a *s.* small voice, I Kin. 19:12.
leadeth beside *s.* waters, Ps. 23:2.
be *s.* and know that I, Ps. 46:10.
strength to sit *s.*, Is. 30:7.
unto sea, Peace be *s.*, Mark 4:39.

STILL, yet.
s. holdeth integrity, Job 2:3.
s. praising thee, Ps. 84:4.
arm stretched out *s.*, Is. 5:25.
not *s.* in unbelief, Rom. 11:23.
unjust *s.*, righteous *s.*, Rev. 22:11.

STING, bite, smart, cut.
s. like an adder, Prov. 23:32.
O death, where thy *s.*, I Cor. 15:55.

STINK, foul smell; smell offensively.
fish die, river *s.*, Ex. 7:18.
his *s.* shall come up, Joel 2:20.
by this time he *s.*, John 11:39.

STIR, turn, move, rouse, excite tumult.
grievous words *s.* anger, Prov. 15:1.
caused no small *s.*, Acts 12:18.
s. up gift of God, II Tim. 1:6.
I *s.* up your minds, II Pet. 3:1.

STOCK, root, stem, race, lineage.
s. die in ground, Job. 14:8.
s. of Abraham, Acts 13:26.
of *s.* of Israel, Phil. 3:5.

STOCKS, a wooden frame in which hands, feet and neck were firmly held. The body was kept in a bend position. This was quite painful and uncomfortable and was used only as a mode of punishment for lawbreakers (Job 13:27; 33:11; Acts 16:24).

STOICS, a sect of Greek philosophers who sprung from the teaching and manner of living of Zeno, born in Cyprus in 357 B.C. The Stoics were lofty pantheists and showed indifference to life in all circumstances. Temperance and moderation were practiced and taught. Paul came into contact with some in Athens (Acts 17:18).

STOLE, did steal, robbed

disciples *s.* him, Matt. 28:13.
him that *s.* steal no, Eph. 4:28.

STOLEN, taken by thievery.
hast *s.* my gods, Gen. 31:30.
s. waters sweet, Prov. 9:17.

STOMACH, belly.
wine for *s.* sake, I Tim. 5:23.

STOMACHER, an article of female clothing worn over the stomach or breast, probably a wide girdle (Is. 3:24).

STONE, rock. Stones were used: (1) As building material (I Kin. 5:18; Mark 13:1); (2) to seal burial caves (Matt. 27:60); (3) as missiles of war (I Sam. 17:40; II Chr. 26:14); (4) as boundary markers (Deut. 19:14); and (5) as memorials (Gen. 28:18; Josh. 4:9. The Messiah is likened to a rejected building stone (Ps. 118:22; Matt. 21:42; Acts 4:11). *See* STONING.
sank as a *s.*, Ex. 15:16.
wrote on tables of *s.*, Deut. 4:13.
for a *s.* of stumbling, Is. 8:14.
God is able of *s.*, Matt. 3:9.
bread, will give *s.?*, Matt. 7:9.
without sin, cast *s.*, John 8:7.
law engraved on *s.*, II Cor. 3:7.
lay in Zion corner *s.*, I Pet. 2:6.

STONING, the most common mode of capital punishment among the Hebrews. Those who witnessed against the condemned person had to place their hands upon him to signify he was the bearer of his guilt (Lev. 24:14). The witnesses also were the ones who threw the first stones (Deut. 13:9) Eighteen different crimes were punishable by stoning (Lev. 20:27; 24:16; Num. 15:32–36; Deut. 17:2–5). Paul was stoned at Lystra (Acts 14:19).
will they not *s.* us, Ex. 8:26.
he shall . . be *s.*, Ex. 19:13.
and let all . . . *s.* him, Lev. 24:14.
congregation bade *s.* him, Num. 14:10.
after they . . . *s.* him, Josh. 7:25.
saying, Naboth is *s.*, I Kin. 21:14.
people will *s.* us, Luke 20:6.
Jews took . . stones . . to *s.*, John 10:31
they *s.* Stephen, Acts 7:59.
having *s.* Paul, Acts 14:19.
once was I *s.*, II Cor. 11:25.

STONY, like stone, rugged, hardened

will take out *s.* heart, Ezek. 11:19.
some upon *s.* places, Matt. 13:5.

STOOP, bend, bow, submit.
Bel bows, Nebo *s.*, Is. 46:1.
I am not worthy to *s.*, Mark 1:7.

STOP, cease, restrain, shut.
s. their ears, ran upon, Acts 7:57.
that every mouth be *s.*, Rom. 3:19.
s. mouths of lions, Heb. 11:33.

STORE, deposit, reserve.
food shall be for *s.*, Gen. 41:36.
every one lay in *s.*, I Cor. 16:2.

STORK, a bird common to Palestine. It
was ceremonially unclean (Lev. 11:19;
Deut. 14:18). It nested in the trees,
chimneys and ruins (Ps. 104:17).

STORM, tempest, whirlwind.
been refuge from *s.*, Is. 25:4.
there arose a great *s.*, Mark 4:37.
there came *s.* of wind, Luke 8:23.

STOUT, strong, brave.
hearken, ye *s.* hearted, Is. 46:12.
words *s.* against me, Mal. 3:13.

STRAIGHT, direct, plain.
make crooked things *s.*, Is. 42:16.
make his paths *s.*, Matt. 3:3.
street called *S.*, Acts 9:11.
make *s.* paths for feet, Heb. 12:13.

STRAIGHTWAY, immediately.
they *s.* left their nets, Matt. 4:20.
s. damsel arose and, Mark 5:42.
God shall *s.* glorify, John 13:32.
s. forget what manner, James 1:24.

STRAIN, filter.
guides which *s.* gnat, Matt. 23:24.

STRAIT, (1) restricted; (2) distress.
enter at *s.* gate, Matt. 7:13.
I am in *s.* between two, Phil. 1:23.

STRAITLY, strictly.
Jericho *s.* shut up, Josh. 6:1.
he *s.* charged him, Mark 1:43.
let us *s.* threaten them, Acts 4:17.

STRANGE, unfamiliar, foreign.
offered *s.* fire, Lev. 10:1.
have seen *s.* things, Luke 5:26.
sojourn in *s.* country, Heb. 11:9.
they think it *s.* ye, I Pet. 4:4.

STRANGER, one who was not a Hebrew
by birth, but who still lived among
them. A visitor of the land would be
called a stranger also (Lev. 16:29; 17:8;
II Sam. 1:13). While in the land of the
Hebrews he was guaranteed safety and
kind treatment (Deut. 10:18, 19; Ex. 22:
21; 23:9). He had to observe laws of the
sanctity of the Sabbath but was not required to perform the religious duties
which Hebrews did (Ex. 12:43–46).
wherein thou art a *s.*, Gen. 17:8.
his father was a *s.*, Gen. 37:1.
only a *s.* in Jerusalem, Luke 24:18.
if she have lodged *s.*, I Tim. 5:10.
to entertain *s.*, Heb. 13:2.

STRANGLED, choked, suffocated.
lion did tear and *s.*, Nah. 2:12.
abstain from things *s.*, Acts 15:20.

STRAW, grain stalks. Straw was used as
fodder for domestic animals (Gen. 24:
25; I Kin. 4:28; Is. 11:7) and as an ad-
hesive in brickmaking (Ex. 5:7, 16).

STREAM, flowing brook, river.
brought *s.* out of rock, Ps. 78:16.
living waters *s.* from, Song 4:15.
righteousness as *s.*, Amos 5:24.
s. beat vehemently on, Luke 6:48.

STREET, most Biblical streets were narrow, crooked, filthy alleys. The beautiful
street called Straight was a notable exception (Acts 9:11). Often men of the
same craft lived on one street (Jer. 37:21).
cast out as dirt in *s.*, Ps. 18:42.
utters her voice in *s.*, Prov. 1:20.
doors be shut in *s.*, Eccles. 12:4.
praying in corner of *s.*, Matt. 6:5.
dead bodies lie in *s.*, Rev. 11:8.
s. was of pure gold, Rev. 21:21.

STRENGTH, might, power, security.
Lord is my *s.*, Ex. 15:2.
God is refuge and *s.*, Ps. 46:1.
God, *s.* of my heart, Ps. 73:26.
go from *s.* to *s.*, Ps. 84:7.
wisdom better than *s.*, Eccles. 9:16.
showed *s.* with his, Luke 1:51.
were yet without *s.*, Rom. 5:6.
s. of sin is the law, I Cor. 15:56.

STRENGTHEN, make strong.
O God, *s.* my hands, Neh. 6:9.
s. with might by Spirit, Eph. 3:16.
S. with all might, Col. 1:11.
Christ with *s.* me, Phil. 4:13.

s. things that remain, Rev. 3:2.

STRETCH, spread out, extend.
s. out hand against God, Job 15:25.
all day *s.* my hands, Rom. 10:21.
we *s.* not ourselves, II Cor. 10:14.

STRIFE, contention, quarreling.
let there be no *s.*, Gen. 13:8.
wrathful stir up *s.*, Prov. 15:18.
walk honest, not is *s.*, Rom. 13:13.
is among you *s.*, I Cor. 3:3.
wrath, *s.*, seditions, Gal. 5:20.
nothing done through *s.*, Phil. 2:3.

STRIKE, smite, beat, afflict.
s. it on side posts, Ex. 12:7.
Lord *s.* through kings, Ps. 110:5.
did *s.* him with hands, Mark 14:65.

STRIKE, loose, let go (Acts 27:17).

STRIPES, marks of whip. *See*
  SCOURGE.
for wound, *s.* for *s.*, Ex. 21:25.
forty *s.* he may give, Deut. 25:3.
s. prepared for fools, Prov. 19:29.
washed *s.*, was baptized, Acts 16:33.
by whose *s.* ye were, I Pet. 2:24.

STRIVE, contend, endeavor.
Spirit not always *s.*, Gen. 6:3.
s. not without cause, Prov. 3:30.
s. against the Lord, Jer. 50:24.
I *s.* to preach gospel, Rom. 15:20.
Lord's servant not *s.*, II Tim. 2:24.

STRONG, mighty, hard, robust.
out of *s.* came sweet, Judg. 14:14.
battle not to *s.*, Eccles. 9:11.
how enter *s.* man's, Matt. 12:29.
child grew, waxed *s.*, Luke 1:80.
send *s.* delusion, II Thess. 2:11.

STRONG DRINK, any intoxicating beverage. Wine (*yayin*) was fermented grape
juice whereas strong drink (*shekar*) included all kinds of intoxicating drinks
(I Sam. 1:15; Prov. 20:1; Is. 29:9).
Priests were forbidden to partake of
strong drink when about to engage in
sacred duties (Lev. 10:9). Princes and
kings were warned against their use lest
the administration of justice be perverted
(Prov. 31:4, 5). The Nazarites vow committed the men to total abstinence from
strong drink (Num. 6:3) and even the
eating of grapes (Judg. 1 13:4; Luke
1:15). Unfermented grape juice is called

new wine (Neh. 13:5; Prov. 3:10; Is.
65:8; Zech. 9:17; Acts 2:13). The new
wine put into old wine skins was unfermented and when it fermented would
burst the old skins (Matt. 9:17).
do not drink . . *s. d.*, Lev. 10:9.
separate himself from *s.d.*, Num. 6:3.
beware . . drink not . . *s.d.*, Judg. 13:4.
s.d. is raging, Prov. 20:1.
men to mingle *s.d.*, Is. 5:22.
erred through *s.d.*, Is. 28:7.
prophesy *s.d.*, Mic. 2:11.
wine or *s.d.*, Luke 1:15.

STUBBLE, grain stalks left at harvest.
make them as *s.*, Ps. 83:13.
scatter them as *s.*, Jer. 13:24.
wicked shall be *s.*, Mal. 4:1.
on foundation, hay, *s.*, I Cor. 3:12.

STUBBORN, obstinate.
if man have a *s.* son, Deut. 21:18.
she is loud and *s.*, Prov. 7:11.

STUDY, apply mind.
much *s.* is weariness, Eccles. 12:12.
S. to show approved, II Tim. 2:15.

STUMBLE, trip, be overthrown.
proud *s.* and fall, Jer. 50:32.
s. at that *s.* stone, Rom. 9:32.
unto Jews a *s.* block, I Cor. 1:23.
stone of *s.*, rock, I Pet. 2:8.

SUAH, son of Zophah and head of the
  tribe of Asher (I Chr. 7:36).

SUBDUE, put down, humble, conquer.
replenish earth, *s.* it, Gen. 1:28.
to *s.* nations before him, Is. 45:1.
able to *s.* all things, Phil. 3:21.

SUBJECT, under authority; place under.
even devils are *s.*, Luke 10:17.
be *s.* to higher powers, Rom. 13:1.
church *s.* to Christ, Eph. 5:24.
lifetime *s.* to bondage, Heb. 2:15.
be *s.* to your masters, I Pet. 2:18.

SUBMIT, yield, be subject.
enemies *s.* to thee, Ps. 66:3.
S. yourselves, one to, Eph. 5:21.
wives, *s.* to husbands, Col. 3:18.
S. to every ordinance, I Pet. 2:13.

SUBSCRIBE, write, sign.
s. unto the Lord, Is. 44:5.
I *s.* the evidence and, Jer. 32:10.

SUBSTANCE, material, thing, goods.
destroy every living s., Gen. 7:4.
leave their s. to babes, Ps. 17:14.
wasted his s. with, Luke 15:13.
faith is s. of things, Heb. 11:1.

SUBTIL, wise, crafty, wily, shrewd.
serpent more s. than, Gen. 3:1.
harlot, and s. of heart, Prov. 7:10.

SUBTILTY, deceit, guile, cunning.
brother came with s., Gen. 27:35.
give s. to the simple, Prov. 1:4.
O full of s. and, Acts 13:10.

SUBVERT, overturn, pervert.
s. souls saying, ye, Acts 15:24.
s. whole houses, Titus 1:11.
is s. and sinneth, Titus 3:11.

SUCATHITES, SUCHATHITES, a
family of scribes living at Jabez (I Chr.
2:55).

SUCCESS, prosperous result.
thou shalt have s., Josh. 1:7.

SUCCOTH, (1) a place east of the Jordan
where Jacob went after Essau had departed from him (Gen. 33:17). (2) The
first station of Israel after leaving
Rameses in Egypt (Ex. 12:37; Num. 33:
5). (3) A place in Gad which could have
been the same as the first one mentioned
(Josh. 13:17; Judg. 8:5, 6, 8, 14). (4) A
city in Ephraim, near Zarthan (I Kin.
7:46; II Chr. 4:17; Ps. 60:6).

SUCCOTH-BENOTH, an idol set up in
Samaria. It was worshipped by the set-
tlers who poured in from Babylon (II
Kin. 17:30, 31).

SUCHATHITES, see SUCATHITES.

SUCK, draw with mouth, drain.
shall s. poison, Job 20:16.
s. milk of Gentiles, Is. 60:16.
blessed paps thou s., Luke 11:27.

SUDDEN, quick, abrupt.
s. fear troubleth, Job 22:10.
s. destruction comes, I Thess. 5:3.

SUFFER, permit, endure, undergo pain.
not s. a witch to live, Ex. 22:18.
s. Holy One to see, Ps. 16:10.
s. not thy mouth to, Eccles. 5:6.
S. little children, Matt. 19:14.

s. not devils to speak, Mark 1:34.
must needs have s., Acts 17:3.
if we s. with him, Rom. 8:17.
sufferings which we s., II Cor. 1:6.
ye s. in vain?, Gal. 3:4.
to believe and s., Phil. 1:29.
s. vengeance of, Jude 7.

SUFFICE, be enough.
she did eat, was s., Ruth 2:14.
show us Father, it s., John 14:8.
for time past may s., I Pet. 4:3.

SUFFICIENCY, enough, adequacy.
fulness of his s., Job 20:22.
our s. is of God, II Cor. 3:5.

SUFFICIENT, adequate, enough.
s. unto day is evil, Matt. 6:34.
bread is not s. for, John 6:7.
grace is s. for thee, II Cor. 12:9.

SUKKIM, SUKKIMS, a race of Africans
(II Chr. 12:3).

SUM, total, amount.
with great s. obtained, Acts 22:28.
spoken this is the s., Heb. 8:1.

SUMMER, hot season of the year.
harvest past, s. ended, Jer. 8:20 .
basket of s. fruit, Amos 8:2.
know s. is nigh, Matt. 24:32.

SUMPTUOUSLY, splendidly.
rich man fared s., Luke 16:19.

SUN, the heavenly body, made by God,
which is called "the greater light to rule
the day" (Gen. 1:16). To the Hebrew
mind, the sun rose and set and moved
about (II Kin. 20:11; Ps. 19:4–6; Hab.
3:11). The sun was stayed while Joshua
defeated the Amorites (Josh. 10:12; 13).
The Egyptians, Phoenicians, and Assyrians were known to worship gods of the
sun. In Mal. 4:2, it seems that the coming
Messiah was called the "sun of righteousness."
the s. was going down, Gen. 15:12.
the s. rose upon, Gen. 32:31.
S., stand . . still, Josh. 10:12.
praise ye him, s., Ps. 148:3.
he maketh . '. s. to rise, Matt. 5:45.
s. . . . turned into darkness, Acts 2:20.
countenance was as the s., Rev. 1:16.

SUN DIAL, see DIAL.

SUP, sip up, take supper.
when he had *s.*, I Cor. 11:25.
I will *s.* with him, Rev. 3:20.

SUPERFLUITY, overflowing.
s. of naughtiness, James 1:21.

SUPERSTITION, religion, false religion.
questions of their *s.*, Acts 25:19.

SUPH, (reeds), found in the American Revised Version, this is doubtless an abbreviation of Yam-Suph, the name of the Red (Reed) Sea (Deut. 1:1).

SUPHAH, Found in the American Revised Version, this term seems to refer to some area east of Jordan (Num. 21:14).

SUPPER, *see* **MEAL.**

SUPPLICATION, entreaty, petition.
Lord heard my *s.*, Ps. 6:9.
in prayer and *s.*, Acts 1:14.
in everything by *s.*, Phil. 4:6.
s. be made for all, I Tim. 2:1.

SUPPLY, furnish, provide.
s. want of saints, II Cor. 9:12.
that every joint *s.*, Eph. 4:16.
s. lack of service, Phil. 2:30.

SUPPORT, help, hold up, aid.
ought to *s.* the weak, Acts 20:35.

SUPREME, authoritative, placed over.
to the king as *s.*, I Pet. 2:13.

SUR, a gate of Solomon's Temple which was called "the gate of the foundation" (II Kin. 11:6; II Chr. 23:5).

SURE, firm, secure, certain.
be *s.* sin find you out, Num. 32:23.
build thee a *s.* house, I Kin. 11:38.
make a *s.* covenant, Neh. 9:38.
Lord's testimony *s.*, Ps. 19:7.
sepulchre be made *s.*, Matt. 27:64.
we believe, are *s.*, John 6:69.
s. mercies of David, Acts 13:34.
both *s.* and stedfast, Heb. 6:19.
calling, election *s.*, II Pet. 1:10.

SURETISHIP, pledge. *See* **SURETY.**
hateth *s.* is sure, Prov. 11:15.

SURETY, a person who assumed the responsibility for the financial obligations of another. The one who acted as surety would give his hand to the creditor in the presence of witness to show that he was promising the debt would be paid if the debtor failed to meet his obligation (Prov. 6:1, 2; 17:18). Jesus is the Christians *surety* (guarantee) of a better covenant (Heb. 7:22).
I will be *s.* for him, Gen. 43:9.
s. for a stranger, Prov. 11:15.

SURFEITING, drunken giddiness.
overcharged with *s.*, Luke 21:34.

SURPRISED, caught suddenly, unawares.
fearfulness *s.* hypocrites, Is. 33:14.
the strongholds are *s.*, Jer. 48:41.

SUSA, *see* **SHUSHAN.**

SUSANCHITES, *see* **SHUSHAN-CHITES.**

SUSANNA, a female who followed and ministered to Jesus (Luke 8:3).

SUSANNA, HISTORY OF, a book of the Apocrypha.

SUSI, the father of Gaddi, the man who represented the tribe of Manasseh when Moses sent spies to spy out the land of Canaan (Num. 13:11).

SUSTAIN, support, uphold.
with corn I have *s.*, Gen. 27:37.
spirit of man *s.*, Prov. 18:14.
righteousness *s.* him, Is. 59:16.

SWADDLING BAND, SWADDLING CLOTHES, a cloth in which newborn Oriental babies were wrapped (Job 38:9; Luke 2:7, 12).
darkness a *s. b.*, Job 38:9.
wrapped him in *s. c.*, Luke 2:7.
babe wrapped in *s. c.*, Luke 2:12.

SWALLOW, this small non-migratory bird is noted for its long wings and tireless (Ps. 84:3). The King James Version sometimes incorrectly renders "crane" (Is. 38:14; Jer. 8:7).

SWALLOW, devour, engulf.
earth opened, *s.* them, Num. 16:30.
fish *s.* Jonah, Jonah 1:17.
at gnat, *s.* a camel, Matt. 23:24.
death *s.* in victory, I Cor. 15:54.

SWAN, mistranslation for an unclean bird, probably the ibis or the horned owl (Lev. 11:18; Deut. 14:16).

SWEAR, affirm by oath.
s. to own hurt and, Ps. 15:4.
nor *s.* As Lord lives, Hos. 4:15.
S. not at all, Matt. 5:34.
s. by no greater, Heb. 6:13.
s. not, neither by, James 5:12.

SWEAT, Luke 22:44 may refer to merely a profuse sweat or, as is medically possible, actual bloody sweat caused by extreme emotional stress.
in *s.* of face eat bread, Gen. 3:19.
anything causing *s.*, Ezek. 44:18.

SWEET, of pleasing taste.
Lord smelled *s.* savour, Gen. 8:21.
David, *s.* psalmist, II Sam. 23:1.
stolen waters are *s.*, Prov. 9:17.
labourer's sleep *s.*, Eccles. 5:12.
odor of a *s.* smell, Phil. 4:18.
s. waters and bitter?, James 3:11.

SWELLING, rising, puffing up.
breach *s.* in a wall, Is. 30:13.
lest there be *s.*, II Cor. 12:20.
they speak *s.* words, II Pet. 2:18.

SWIFT, speedy, rapid, quick.
run *s.* to mischief, Prov. 6:18.
race not to *s.*, Eccles. 9:11.
be *s.* to hear, James 1:19.
s. destruction, II Pet. 2:1.

SWIM, float, progress on water.
and iron did *s.*, II Kin. 6:6.
make my bed to *s.*, Ps. 6:6.
lest any *s.* out, Acts 27:42.

SWINE, a word usually used in the collective sense to denote domestic hogs. A hog was ceremonially unclean to the Hebrews (Lev. 11:7; Deut. 14:8). The Jews regarded the hog as the very epitome of filth (Matt. 7:6; II Pet. 2:22). The lowest state the prodigal son reached was that of attending swine (Luke 15:15).

SWOLLEN, swelled, puffed up.
when should have *s.*, Acts 28:6.

SWOON, faint.
children *s.*, in street, Lam. 2:11.

SWORD, an offensive weapon with an iron or bronze blade. It was especially lethal when it was two-edged. It was worn by the side in a scabbard (II Sam. 20:8; Ezek. 32:27). The sword was symbolic of war (Is. 2:4).
a flaming *s.*, Gen. 3:24.
I whet my .. *s.*, Deut. 32:41.
gird thy *s.* upon .. thigh, Ps. 45:3.
did pursue .. with the *s.*, Amos 1:11.
he that hath no *s.*, Luke 22:36.
sharper than .. two edged *s.*, Heb. 4:12.
remnant .. slain with .. *s.*, Rev. 19:21.

SYCAMINE TREE, a black mulberry tree. It grows about twenty-five feet high (Luke 17:6).

SYCHAR, a city of Samaria which was near Jacob's well (John 4:5). It was here that Jesus conversed with the Samaritan woman.

SYCHEM, *see* **SHECHEM.**

SYCOMORE, a massive type of fig tree, it provided lumber, shade, fruit, and fuel (Ps. 78:47; Is. 9:10) and was once abundant in Palestine (I Kin. 10:27; II Chr. 1:15). Amos gathered sycomore figs (Amos 7:14) and from a sycomore Zacchaeus saw Jesus (Luke 19:4). This tree is not the same as the American sycamore.

SYENE, a town in the south of Egypt towards Ethiopia (Ezek. 29:10; 30:6).
from the tower of *S.*, Ezek. 29:10.
tower of *S.* shall they, Ezek. 30:6.

SYMEON, *see* **SIMEON.**

SYNAGOGUE, an assembly of Jews which was organized for the purpose of worship and teaching the Law. The word appears only once in the Old Testament (Ps. 74:8), but several times in the New Testament. The synagogue was instituted after the exile for the religious purpose of teaching the law and the prophets. Some trace it back to gatherings in Babylon (Ezek. 8:1).

The furniture of the synagogue consisted of a chest in which the sacred rolls were kept. In front of the chest a lamp burned continually. Also there was a readers desk and some benches for the listeners. Matt. 23:6 mentions some "chief seats" which the Pharisees gloried in.

The service was in four parts: (1) a brief reading from the Law, (2) prayer,

(3) a reading from the Law and the Prophets, (4) a priestly benediction. Visitors sometimes spoke in the assembly (Acts 13:14, 15). The ruler of the synagogue was the chief officer (Luke 8:41; 13:14). Jesus was once asked to read (Luke 4:16, 17).

The Great Synagogue of Ezra was established for the purpose of re-establishing the Mosaic institutions. It was started by Ezra and Nehemiah. It is also held that they established the canon of the Old Testament. *See* CANON.
burnt . . all the *s*., Ps. 74:8.
teaching in their *s*., Matt. 4:23.
to pray . . in the *s*., Matt. 6:5.
scourge in your *s*., Matt. 23:34.
loveth . . and . . built . . *s*., Luke 7:5.
highest seats in . . *s*., Luke 20:46.
preached . . in the *s*., Acts 13:5.
disputed . . in the *s*., Acts 17:17.
the *s*. of Satan, Rev. 2:9.

SYNOPTIC, affording the same or a common view. This is used of the first three Gospels to distinguish them from the Gospel of John.

SYNTYCHE, a female disciple of Philippi who seemed to be at variance with another woman. Paul admonished them to reach a state of harmony (Phil. 4:2).

SYRACUSE, an important town on the east coast of Sicily. Paul touched it on his sea voyage to Rome (Acts 28:12).

SYRIA, a region which had somewhat indefinite boundaries. In general, it was bounded by the Taurus Mountains, the Euphrates River, the Syrian and Arabian deserts, northern Palestine and the Mediterranean (II Sam. 8:6; 15:8; Luke 2:2; Acts 15:23, 41).
the gods of *S*., Judg. 10:6.
Ben-hadad king of *S*., II Kin. 6:24.
Cyrenius . . governor of *S*., Luke 2:2.
in Antioch and *S*., Acts 15:23.
into the regions of *S*., Gal. 1:21.

SYRIAC, SYRIAN, an inhabitant of Syria (Gen. 28:5). It was also the language of the people of Syria (II Kin. 18:26; Ezra 4:7; Is. 36:11; Dan. 2:4).

SYRIAC VERSIONS, *see* VERSIONS.

SYRIA-MAACHAH, *see* MAACAH.

SYRIAN, pertaining to Syria, or, an inhabitant of Syria. In the Old Testament the word means a native of Aram.

SYROPHENICIAN, belonging to Phenicia in Syria. It was used as a racial designation of a woman whose daughter was cured by Jesus (Mark 7:26).

T

TAANACH, TANACH, an ancient Levitical city on the western side of the Jordan in Manasseh or Isaachar. It was the headquarters of the army of Deborah and Barak, and Sisera's host was encamped between it and Megiddo (Judg. 5:19).

TAANATH-SHILOH, a city on the borders of Ephraim and Benjamin (Josh. 16:6).

TABBAOTH, one of the family of Nethinim whose descendants returned with Zerubbabel (Ezra 2:43; Neh. 7:46).

TABBATH, a city in the Jordan valley not far from Bethshean (Judg. 7:22).

TABEAL, TABEEL, means "God is good." (1) Father of one whom Syria and Ephraim sought to make king in Judah instead of Ahaz (Is. 7:6). (2) An officer of the Persian government (Ezra 4:7).

TABER, to beat.
t. upon their breasts, Nahum 2:7.

TABERAH, a place near Sinia, but not identified (Num. 11:3; Deut. 9:22).

TABERNACLE, a tent-like structure, adapted to the roving life of the desert. It was the dwelling-place of God's glory (Ex. 40:34, 35). It was a sacred tent (Ex. 26:9), a sanctuary (Ex. 25:8), a place of meeting (Ex. 29:42), a temple (II Kin. 24:13), and a tent of testimony (Num. 17:7). In the Old Testament there were three tabernacles: a provisional one which was established after the sin of the golden calf (Ex. 33:7); the Sinaitic tabernacle which the Lord directed Moses to erect; and the Davidic tabernacle which David built in Jerusalem to house the ark (II Sam. 6:12). The tabernacle which Moses erected was made to be the center of the religious life of Israel. The various tribes encamped around it. In all special facts connected with the tabernacle, the idea of a "meeting place" is the central one. It was moved from its place in the Wilderness and in Canaan until the Temple was built, or rather until it lost its glory, when the ark was captured by the Philistines (I Sam. 4:22; Ps. 78:60). The form and size of the tent were symbolic; it was peculiarly sacred because of its peculiar structure. On its altar of incense no strange fire must ever be used.

TABERNACLES, FEAST OF, it was the last of the appointed feasts under the old covenant, beginning on the 15th of the 7th month, and lasting seven days. The real name is "booths;" they are built from sticks and leaves. Its object was to keep in memory the sojourn in the Wilderness; a perpetual renewing of their religious youth, in remembering the covenant.

TABITHA *see* **DORCAS.**

TABLE, used especially of the tablets of stone on which the Ten Commandments were written (Ex. 24:12). Also used for a table spread for food (Ex. 25:23). In Matt. 9:2, 6 it is used as a couch for reclining during meals.

TABLET, an inaccurate rendering of two Hebrew words. In Ex. 35:22 and Num. 31:50, it means drops of gold worn about the neck. In Is. 3:20, it means perfume bottle.

TABOR, MOUNT, it is a conical shaped mound of limestone on the northeastern part of the plain of Esdraelon. It is in Zebulun and Issachar in the middle of Galilee (Josh. 19:22; Ps. 89:12).

TABOR, PLAIN OF, it is a place or plain in Benjamin south of Bethel (I Sam. 10:3).

TABRET, TIMBREL, a tambourine, held in one hand and beat with the other, accompanied generally with dancing, and used on festal occasions.

TABRIMON, TABRIMMON, the father of Benhadad I., king of Syria in the reign of Asa (I Kin. 15:18).

TACHES, one of the knobs upon which were hung the curtains of the tabernacle (Ex. 26:6).

TACHMONITE, chief among David's captains (II Sam. 23:8).

TADMOR, a city built by Solomon in the wilderness (II Chr. 8:4). The Greeks and Romans called it Palmyra. It was perhaps on the southern border of Palestine (Ezek. 47:19).

TAHAN, (1) head of one of the families of the tribe of Ephraim at the end of the Exodus (Num. 26:35). (2) The son of Telah and the father of Laadan (I Chr. 7:25).

TAHANITES, the descendants of Tahan (Num. 26:35).

TAHAPANES, *see* **TAHPHANHES.**

TAHASH, *see* **THAHASH.**

TAHATH, (1) a Levite, son of Assir and father of Uriel (I Chr. 6:24, 37). (2) An Ephraimite, son of Bered and father of Eladah (I Chr. 7:20). (3) Son of Eladah (I Chr. 7:20). (4) A desert place between Makheloth and Tarah (Num. 33:26).

TAH-CHEMONITE, *see* **TACHMONITE.**

TAHPANHES, TAHAPANES, TEHAPHNEHES, an important city in the time of Jeremiah and Ezekiel. It is located in Lower Egypt, in the land of Goshen, near Pelusium (Jer. 43:7).

TAHPENES, an Egyptian queen, wife of Pharaoh (I Kin. 11:18–20).

TAHREA, TAREA, the son of Micah (I Chr. 9:41).

TAHTIM-HODSHI, a land that is now lost (II Sam. 24:6).

TAKE, receive, capture.
Boaz *t.* Ruth, Ruth 4:13.
Asa .. *t.* all Judah, II Chr. 16:6.
t. up thy bed, Mark 2:9.
t. care of the church, I Tim. 3:5.
to *t.* away sins, I John 3:5.

TALE, a story, talk.

words seemed as a *t.*, Luke 24:11.

TALEBEARER, *see* **GOSSIPER.**

TALENT, the largest weight of the Hebrews; it was used for weighing metals (I Kin. 9:14; II Kin. 5:22; Zech. 5:7; Ex. 38:29). It was about the weight which a man could carry, about ninety-three or ninety-four pounds. In the New Testament the talent occurs in a parable (Matt. 25:15).

TALITHA CUMI, two Syriac words meaning "damsel arise." It is found in Mark 5:41.

TALK, speech.
t. tendeth to penury, Prov. 14:23.
lips *t.* of mischief, Prov. 24:2.
he *t.* with a woman, John 4:27.

TALL, high.
people great .. and *t.*, Deut. 1:28.

TALMAI, (1) son of Anak (Num. 13:22). (2) Son of Ammihud, and king of Gesher (II Sam. 3:3).

TALMON, one of the porters for the camps of the sons of Levi (I Chr. 9:17).

TALMUD, a work which contains the civil and canonical law of the Jews. It contains not merely religious laws, but philosophy, medicine, jurisprudence, history, and various branches of practical duty.

TAMAH, *see* **THAMAH.**

TAMAR, THAMAR, (1) wife of Er and Onan (Gen. 38:6–30). (2) Daughter of David, mother of Absalom (II Sam. 13:1–32). (3) Daughter of Absalom (II Sam. 14:27).

TAMAR, a city in the southern part of Hebron (Ezra Ezek. 19).

TAMARISK, a variety of trees which grows in Palestine.

TAME, subdue.
tongue can no man *t.*, James 3:8.

TAMMUZ, a Syrian idol, perhaps the same deity as the Phoenician Adonis,

which was supposed to symbolize the departure and return of the sun.
women weeping for *T.*, Ezek. 8:14.

TANACH, *see* **TAANACH.**

TANHUMETH, father of Seraiah (II Kin. 25:23).

TANNER, a dresser of hides.
house of Simon the *t.*, Acts 10:32.

TAPESTRY, a word of uncertain meaning; maybe a colored spread.

TAPHATH, daughter of Solomon (I Kin. 4:11).

TAPPUAH, (1) one of the sons of Hebron (I Chr. 2:43). (2) A city of Judah, twelve miles west of Jerusalem (Josh. 15:34). (3) A town in the tribe of Ephraim (Josh. 16:8).

TARAH, *see* **TERAH.**

TARALAH, a town in the western part of the territory of Benjamin (Josh. 18:27).

TARE, *see* **TEAR.**

TAREA, *see* **TAHREA.**

TARES, weeds.
enemy sowed tares, Matt. 13:25.

TARGET, a small, round shield (I Sam. 17:6).

TARGUM, *see* **VERSIONS.**

TARPELITES, a name which perhaps refers to the people of Tripolis. It is mentioned in Ezra 4:9.

TARRY, abide, stay.
tarry all night, Gen. 19:2.
the bridegroom *t.*, Matt. 25:5.
t. many days in Joppa, Acts 9:43.

TARSHISH, THARSHISH, (1) a son of Javan grandson of Noah (Gen. 10:4). (2) The mighty ships built for long voyages (I Kin. 10:22). (3) Son of Bilhan, the grandson of Benjamin (I Chr. 7:10). (4) A place, perhaps in Spain, or perhaps in Carthage or Ceylon.

(5) One of the seven princes of Persia (Esther 1:14).

TARSUS, the birthplace of Paul the Apostle (Acts 9:11). It was a great city in the time of the Greek kings. Alexander the Great conquered it. Augustus made it a free city. It was a seat of learning in the time of the Roman emperors.

TARTAK, a god worshipped by the Avites whom Shalmaneser removed to Samaria.

TARTAN, perhaps a proper name; perhaps a title or official designation, like Pharaoh. It is used in II Kin. 18:17 and Is. 20:1.

TASKMASTERS, persons appointed by Pharaoh to see that the Israelites were kept working (Ex. 1:11; 3:7; 5:6–14).

TASTE, palate.
t. of fresh oil, Num. 11:8.
fruit was sweet to t., Song 2:3.

TASTE, experience.
t. and see the Lord, Ps. 34:8.
touch not, t. not, Col. 2:21.
should taste death, Heb. 2:9.

TATNAI, TATTENAI, a satrap of the province west of the Euphrates in the time of Darius Hystaspis (Ezra 5:3, 6).

TATTLER, a person uttering and doing silly things, babbling (I Tim. 5:13).

TATTOOING, it was forbidden to tattoo the skin (Lev. 19:28).

TAUGHT, see **TEACH.**

TAUNT, reproach.
deliver them to be a t., Jer. 24:9.
a reproach and a t., Ezek. 5:15.

TAUNTING, reproving.
a t. proverb against, Hab. 2:6.

TAVERNS, THE THREE, see **THREE TAVERNS, THE.**

TAXATION, valuation.
according to his t., II Kin. 23:35.

TAXES, taxation was unknown to the Hebrews in the nomadic period before the captivity in Egypt. The chieftains re-

ceived voluntary presents from those who sought their protection (Gen. 32:13–21; 33:10). This was also the practice during the time of the "Judges"(Judg. 8:24; I Sam. 30:26). When Israel was subjected to foreign kings they were forced to work or pay tribute (Gen. 49:15–20; Judg. 3:15–18). Taxation for the support of the kingdom was started in the reign of Solomon. Saul and David had supported their government from the booty gained from battle (II Sam. 8:2–10) and from subject nations. Solomon's building program made it necessary to tax the people. He divided the nation into twelve districts, and each district had to support the royal household one month out of the year (I Kin. 4:7, 27). Taxation was one of the reasons that the kingdom divided (I Kin. 12:4).

Under the later kings, who had no income from trade or from foreign resources, taxes became very oppressive (I Sam. 8:11–13). At the time of Syrian domination large sums of money had to be sent to Damascus as "presents" (I Kin. 15:18f.; 20:1–6). Other nations also taxed the people (II Kin. 15:19f.; 16:8; 23:33–35).

After the Exile, the Jews were almost constantly under the heavy taxation of foreign powers. They also were expected to support the temple, which amounted to a half a shekel for each Jew over twenty. In the time of Nehemiah the oppression of some was causing them to mortgage their lands and enslave their children (Neh. 5:1–5).

Under the Greek kings, the right to collect taxes was sold to individuals. They were allowed to keep the profits. Under the Romans the same practice was adopted, and these men were called Publicans. There were taxes on salt, a special tax to furnish new crowns for the monarch (I Maccabees 10:29), and a poll tax on each individual (Matt. 9:9; 22:17). It is no surprise that the Jews considered the tax collectors to be oppressors. To make taxation easier the Romans periodically took a census of the people (Luke 2:1–3; Acts 5:37).

TAXING, registration for the purpose of taxation. Under the Roman emperor, Augustus, Mary and Joseph went to Bethlehem to be taxed. Soon afterward, Jesus was born (Luke 2:1–20). Another tax was so heavy that it led to a revolt

against the Romans by Judas of Galilee
(Acts 5:37).

TEACH, to cause to know.
t. you the good, I Sam. 12:23.
teach . . statutes, Ezra 7:10.
t. me thy way, O Lord, Ps. 27:11.
Holy Ghost shall *t.*, Luke 12:12.
doth not nature *t.*, I Cor. 11:14.
warning, . . and teaching, Col. 1:28.
shall be able to teach, II Tim. 2:2.

TEACHER, one who teaches.
eyes shall be thy *t.*, Is. 30:20.
pastors and teachers, Eph. 4:11.
t. of the Gentiles, I Tim. 2:7.
false *t.* among you, II Pet. 2:1.

TEACHING, instructing.
rising early and *t.*, Jer. 32:33.
apostles *t.* the people, Acts 5:25 .

TEAR, rip up, rend.
he *t.* . . in his anger, Job 18:4.
lest he *t.* my soul, Ps. 7:2.
his anger did tear, Amos 1:11.
unclean spirit . . *t.* him, Mark 1:26.

TEARS.
will wipe away tears, Is. 25:8.
eyes a fountain of *t.*, Jer. 9:1.
tears . . like a river, Lam. 2:18.
wash his feet with *t.*, Luke 7:38.
shall wipe away . . tears, Rev. 7:17.

TEBAH, the eldest son of Ḥahor (Gen.
22:24).

TEBALIAH, a son of Hosah, a Merarite
(I Chr. 26:11).

TEBETH, the tenth month of the Jewish
sacred year, from the new moon of
January to that of February (Esther
2:16).

TEETH, jaw, teeth.
jaw teeth as knives, Prov. 30:14.
cheek teeth of . . lion, Joel 1:6.

TEHAPHNEHES, *see* **TAHPANHES.**

TEHINNAH, a son of Eshton, a descendant of Judah and father Ir-na-hash (I
Chr. 4:12).

TEIL TREE, the lime-tree, or linden.

TEKEL, *see* **MENE.**

TEKOA, TEHOAH, a city in Judah,
southeast of Bethlehem, and twelve
miles south of Jerusalem. It was built by
Ashur (II Chr. 2:24). It was the home of
the wise woman (II Sam. 14:2) and the
home of Amos (Amos 1:1). It is the
modern Tekua.

TEKOITE, an inhabitant of the city of
Tekoa. Ira ben Ikkesh, one of David's
warriors, is called a Tekoite (II Sam.
23:26).

TELABIB, a hill on the river Chebar,
where Ezekiel stayed with the Jewish
exiles for a week (Ezek. 3:15).

TELAH, a descendant of Ephraim, and an
ancestor of Joshua (I Chr. 7:25).

TELAIM, a place in Judah, near Edom,
where Saul collected and numbered his
forces before his attack on Amalek (I
Sam. 15:4).

TELASSAR, THELASAR, a city and
district in Mesopotamia, inhabited by
the children of Eden. It is mentioned in
II Kin. 19:12 and Is. 37:12.

TELEM, (1) one of the temple porters
(Ezra 10:24). (2) A town in the southern
border of Judah (Josh. 15:24).

TELEPHONE. The mention of sending
"lightnings" which speak (Job 38:35)
is suggestive of this instrument.

**TELHARSHA, TELHARSA, TEL-
HARESHA**, one of the Babylonian
towns from which some Jews returned
to Judea with Zerubbabel (Ezra 2:
59).

TELL, say, speak, declare.
t. it not in Gath, II Sam. 1:20.
t. no man, but go, Matt. 8:4.
t. me, ye that desire, Gal. 4:21.

TELMELAH, a place probably near the
Persian Gulf, and from which the Jews
returned (Ezra 2:59).

TEMA, (1) a son of Ishmael and his
descendants at the Persian Gulf (Gen.
25:15). (2) A city north of Arabia, near
the desert of Syria (Job 6:19).

TEMAH, *see* **THAMAH.**

TEMAN, (1) the eldest son of Eliphaz, the son of Esau (Gen. 36:11). (2) The country of the Temanites, the southern part of Idumaea. (3) An Edomite chief (Gen. 36:42).

TEMANI, a descendant of Teman, or an inhabitant of the land (I Chr. 1:45).

TEMANITE, a descendant of Teman, or an inhabitant of the land.

TEMENI, a son of Ashur, and descendant of Caleb son of Hur (I Chr. 4:6).

TEMPERANCE, self-restraint.
reasoned of *t.*, Acts 24:25.
meekness, temperance, Gal. 5:23.

TEMPERATE, continent, sober.
striveth .. is *t.*, I Cor. 9:25.
just, holy, temperate, Titus 1:8.
aged men sober, *t.*, Titus 2:2.

TEMPEST, storm, whirlwind.
mighty *t.* in the sea, Jonah 1:4.
unto darkness and *t.*, Heb. 12:18.

TEMPESTUOUS, stormy.
t. around about, Ps. 50:3.
arose a *t.* wind, Acts 27:14.

TEMPLE, the place where God's glory dwells, as it did in the Tabernacle. Solomon's Temple took its plan from the Tabernacle. The Temple proper was 60 cubits long, 20 broad, and 30 high. The Holy of Holies was a cube of 20 cubits. The Holy Place was 40 cubits long, 20 wide, and 30 high (I Kings 6:17). There were two courts: the great court for Israel (II Chr. 4:9), and the inner or upper court of the priests (I Kings 6:36). This Temple was burned by Nebuzaradan, Nebuchadnezzar's general (II Kings 25:8). Zerubbabel's Temple was erected by the Jews under Zerubbabel on their return from captivity. It was less magnificent (Ezra 6:3) than Solomon's. Herod's Temple superseded Zerubbabel's. The area was larger than former dimensions. The Temple proper reproduced the old plan, except that the height was 40 instead of 30 cubits. The Holy of Holies was separated from the Holy Place by a veil (Matt. 27:51; Heb. 6:19) and was empty. A grand portal in the eastern wall was probably the Beautiful Gate (Acts 3:2).

TEMPORAL, for a limited time.
things seen are *t.*, II Cor. 4:18.

TEMPT, test, prove, try.
God did *t.* Abraham, Gen. 22:1.
shall not *t.* the Lord, Deut. 6:16.
Jesus led .. to be *t.*, Matt. 4:1.
lest thou also be *t.*, Gal. 6:1.
t. like as we are, Heb. 4:15.
neither *t.* he any man, James 1:13.

TEMPTATION, proof, trial.
lead us not into *t.*, Matt. 6:13.
ye enter not into *t.*, Matt. 26:41.
rich fall into *t.*, I Tim. 6:9.
deliver .. out of *t.*, II Pet. 2:9.

TEMPTING, *see* **TEMPT.**

TEN COMMANDMENTS, DECALOGUE, the basis of all the laws found in the Old Testament. These ten are found in Ex. 20:3–17 and Deut. 5:7–21. They were inscribed on both sides of two tables of stone (Ex. 31:18; 32:15). They may be divided into two parts: religious and moral. The first four commandments are religious; they deal with such things as the belief in one God, the prohibition of idolatry, and the keeping of the Sabbath. The other six are moral laws. Even though these were given to the Jews, the Christians also considered them to be authoritative (Matt. 5:19; Rom. 13:8–10). This is the reason the Christian Church has always used them as a basic rule of conduct.

TENDER, soft, merciful.
Leah was *t.* eyed, Gen. 29:17.
as *t.* grass springing, II Sam. 23:4.
t. mercy of our God, Luke 1:78.
kind .. *t.* hearted, Eph. 4:32.

TENONS, probably dowel pins at the end of planks of the Tabernacle (Ex. 26:17; 36:22).

TENT, a movable habitation, made of curtains extended upon poles. Dwelling in tents was very common in ancient times (Gen. 4:20). The Israelites who came out of Egypt lived in tents (Judg. 7:8). The house of God, and heaven, are spoken of in Scripture as the tent or tabernacle of the Lord (Ps. 15:1). The Apostle Paul occasionally worked in the trade of making tents (Acts 18:3).

TENTH, the tenth part of an ephah, probably the same as the Omer.
t. part of flour, Lev. 14:21.
the *t.* of your seed, I Sam. 8:15.
t. part of a bath, Ezek. 45:14.

TERAH, TARAH, THARA, son of Nahor, and father of Abram (Gen. 11:24–32). He lived to be two hundred and five years old, and he died in Haran (Gen. 11:31, 32).

TERAPHIM, household gods, probably in human form. The word is translated "images." Rachel stole her father's teraphim (Gen. 31:19). Laban calls them his gods (Gen. 31:30). They were objects of worship in Judges 17:5. Hosea named them as articles of false worship (Hos. 3:4).

TEREBINTH, a turpentine tree from which the people extracted the resin. It is a rather large tree, ordinarily about fifteen feet in height. Its fruit grows in a grape-like cluster, and its leaves are beautiful in color, changing with the seasons. It is sometimes used in connection with tombs and groves. The word does not appear in the Authorized Version, but is used in the Revised Version for Teil Tree (Hos. 4:13). *See* **OAK.**

TERESH, one of the two eunuchs whose plot to assassinate Ahasuerus was discovered by Mordecai (Esther 2:21).

TERRESTRIAL, earthly.
glory of *t.* is, I Cor. 15:40.

TERRIBLE, dreadful, fearful.
mighty God and *t.*, Deut. 7:21.
great and *t.* God, Neh. 1:5.
a people terrible, Is. 18:2.
the terrible famine, Lam. 5:10.

TERRIBLENESS, fear inspiring.
make name of *t.*, I Chr. 17:21.
thy *t.* hath deceived, Jer. 49:16.

TERRIFY, make afraid.
let blackness of day *t.*, Job 3:5.
wars, be not *t.*, Luke 21:19.
t. and affrighted, Luke 24:37.

TERROR, fear, dread, trouble.
terror of God, Gen. 35:5.
t. shall make afraid, Job 18:11.

be not afraid of *t.*, I Pet. 3:14.

TERTIUS, a disciple who assisted Paul (Rom. 16:22).

TERTULLUS, a Roman orator, whom the Jews employed to bring forward their accusation against Paul (Acts 24:1–2).

TESTAMENT, (1) a disposition.
my blood of the new *t.*, Matt. 26:28.
reading of the Old *T.*, II Cor. 3:14.
surety of a better *t.*, Heb. 7:22.

TESTATOR, the maker of the testament.

TESTIFY, to bear witness.
I testify against you, Deut. 8:19.
Lord *t.* against, II Kin. 17:13.
I will *t.* against thee, Ps. 50:7.
sins *t.* against us, Is. 59:12.
we have *t.* of God, I Cor. 15:15.
sent angel to *t.*, Rev. 22:16.

TESTIMONY, witness.
the ark of the *t.*, Ex. 25:22.
the veil of the *t.*, Lev. 24:3.
the tabernacle of *t.*, Num. 1:53.
the *t.* of the Lord, Ps. 19:7.
the *t.* of Christ, I Cor. 1:6.
the *t.* of . . conscience, II Cor. 1:12..

TETRARCH, one who governs over a fourth part of a country. Herod Antipas is called "Herod the tetrarch" (Matt. 14:1). Herod Philip II is called tetrarch of Iturea (Luke 3:1). Lysanias is called tetrarch of Abilene (Luke 3:1).

THADDAEUS, *see* **JUDAS.**

THAHASH, TAHASH, son of Nahor by his second wife, Reumah (Gen. 22:24).

THAMAH, TAMAH, TEMAH, ancestor of a family of Nethinim who returned from Babylonian Captivity (Ezra 2:53).

THAMAR, *see* **TAMAR.**

THANK, gratitude, blessing.
I give *t.* to thee, II Sam. 22:50.
prayed, and gave *t.*, Dan. 6:10.
Jesus . . gave thanks, Matt. 26:27.
he giveth God *t.*, Rom. 14:6.
cease not to give *t.*, Eph. 1:16.
give *t.* to God always, I Thess. 1:2.

THANK, to express gratitude, to bless.
to t. the Lord God, I Chr. 16:4.
I t. thee, O Father, Matt. 11:25.
I t. my God always, I Cor. 1:4.
bound to t. God, II Thess. 1:3.
I t. Christ Jesus, I Tim. 1:12.

THANK-OFFERING, see **OFFERING.**

THANKSGIVING, giving thanks.
to begin t. in prayer, Neh. 11:17.
enter . . gates with t., Ps. 100:4.
a sacrifice of t., Amos 4:5.
abounding . . with t., Col. 2:7.

THARA, see **TERAH.**

THARSHISH, see **TARSHISH.**

THEATER, (1) a place in which games and dramatic spectacles are held. The Greeks used the theater also as the forum (Acts 19:25, 31). (2) A public show; a "spectacle."

THEBES, see **NO.**

THEBEZ, a place near Shechem, now called Tubas. Abimelech was killed here by a piece of a millstone (II Sam. 11:21).

THELASAR, see **TELASSAR.**

THEOCRACY, the form of government among the early Israelites, in which Jehovah was recognized as their supreme civil ruler. Moses, Joshua, and the Judges were agents of Jehovah. The kings were anointed in his name, and the prophets were commissioned to speak for him.

THEOPHANY, an appearance of God to man.

THEOPHILUS, means "friend of God." (1) The person to whom Luke writes his Gospel and the Acts of the Apostles (Luke 1:3). (2) A Jewish high-priest; son of Annas.

THESSALONIANS, the people of Thessalonica.

THESSALONIANS, FIRST AND SECOND EPISTLES TO THE, two epistles written by Paul from Corinth; about 49 or 50 A.D. They are the earliest of Paul's books; they are perhaps the earliest New Testament products. One of the main subjects of these books is the second advent of Christ. The books teach that Christ is surely coming, and his advent will be visible and sudden.

THESSALONICA, once called Therma. It was named after the wife of Cassander, who rebuilt the city. Under the Roman's it was one of four divisions of Macedonia. Paul and Silas organized the church there (Acts 17:1-4). It is also mentioned in I Thess. 1:9; Acts 20:1-3; Phil. 4:16; and II Tim. 4:10. Being of the great road which connected Rome with the whole region north of the Aegean Sea, Thessalonica was an important center for the spread of the Gospel.

THEUDAS, an insurgent mentioned by Gamaliel in his speech before the Sanhedrin (Acts 5:35-39). He is not to be confounded with the Theudas of 44 A.D. mentioned by Josephus.

THICK, heavy, dense.
I come in a t. cloud, Ex. 19:9.

THICKET, thick growth.
a ram caught in a t., Gen. 22:13.
lion . . from his t., Jer. 4:7.

THIEF, one who unlawfully uses the property of another, such as a burglar (Matt. 6:20) or a pilferer (John 12:6). He is called a robber if he uses force or threats. The eighth of the Ten Commandments prohibited theft (Ex. 20:15). Thieves, who were caught, were required to pay double (Ex. 22:4). Evidently the thieves on the cross were actually robbers (Matt. 27:44).
murderer . . is as a t., Job 24:14.
as a t. is ashamed, Jer. 2:26.
where t. break through, Matt. 6:19.
t. shall not inherit, I Cor. 6:10.
day of Lord . . as t., I Thess. 5:2.
I will come as t., Rev. 3:3.

THIGH, leg.
gird sword upon t., Ps. 45:3.
I smote upon my t., Jer. 31:19.
belly and t. of brass, Dan. 2:32.

THIMNATHAH, a city near Elon in Dan (Josh. 19:43).

THINE, thy.
a beam is in t. . . . eye, Matt. 7:4.

not my will, but *t.*, Luke 22:42.
all mine are thine, John 17:10.
say not in *t.* heart, Rom. 10:6.

THING, object, matter, word.
who hath done this *t.*, Judg. 6:29.
people imagine a vain *t.*, Ps. 2:1.
these *t.* spake Jesus, Matt. 13:34.
sheweth Son all *t.*, John 5:20.
these *t.* ought not so, James 3:10.
I John saw these *t.*, Rev. 22:8.

THINK, reckon, consider, believe.
I *t.* to promote thee, Num. 24:11.
as he *t.* in his heart, Prov. 23:7.
what *t.* ye of Christ? Matt. 22:42.
I *t.* as a child, I Cor. 13:11.
wherein they *t.* strange, I Pet. 4:4.

THIRST, to thirst.
people *t.* . . for water, Ex. 17:3.
my soul *t.* for God, Ps. 42:2.
shall never thirst, John 4:14.
Jesus saith, I thirst, John 19:28.

THIRSTY, athirst.
give me water, I am *t.*, Judg. 4:19.
I was *t.*, ye gave me, Matt. 25:35.

THISTLE, *see* **THORN.**
t. shall it bring forth, Gen. 3:18.
t. grow instead of wheat, Job 31:40.
gather . . figs of *t.*? Matt. 7:16.

THOMAS, a native of Galilee. One of the
apostles also called Didymus (Matt.
10:3).
He was slow to believe, but he was ardently close to his Master. He was one of
the seven who saw Jesus at the Sea of
Galilee. Tradition says that he preached
in Parthia, was a martyr, and was buried
in Edessa.
an apostle, Matt. 10:3.
also called Didymus, John 11:16.
Thomas skeptical, John 20:25.
Thomas believes, John 20:28.

THORN, THISTLE. There are about
twenty words in the Hebrew for different
kinds of prickly or thorny shrubs. They
grow throughout Palestine, and reach
heights of fifteen feet. They are used as
food for goats and camels, and are also
used for fuel. The variety of thorns
which was used for the crown which
Jesus wore is not known.
t. shall it bring forth, Gen. 3:18.

shall rest upon *t.*, Is. 7:19.
some fell among *t.*, Mark 4:7.
crown of thorns, John 19:2.
a thorn in the flesh, II Cor. 12:7.

THOUGHT, a thinking, judgment, design.
imagination of the *t.*, Gen. 6:5.
knoweth the *t.* of man, Ps. 49:11.
t. of foolishness, Prov. 24:9.
shall thy vain *t.* lodge, Jer. 4:14.
take no *t.* beforehand, Mark 13:11.
Jesus perceived . . *t.*, Luke 5:22.
if *t.* of thy heart, Acts 8:22.

THREAD, string.
this line of scarlet *t.*, Josh. 2:18.
brake . . like a *t.*, Judg. 16:12.
thy lips like *t.*, Song 4:3.

THREATENING, menacing.
Lord, behold their *t.*, Acts 4:29.
Saul, . . breathing out *t.*, Acts 9:1.

THREE, a number regarded, both by the
Jews and other nations, as a specially
complete and mystic number.
Noah had *t.* sons, Gen. 6:10.
eat not . . *t.* days, Esther 4:16.
Job's three friends, Job 2:11.
there are *t.* things, Prov. 30:18.
t. berries in the top, Is. 17:6.
belly . . *t.* days, Jonah 1:17.
after *t.* days rise, Mark 8:31.

THREE TAVERNS, THE, a village
about ten miles from the Appii Forum, and about thirty-three miles from
Rome.

THRESH, tread down.
made like dust by *t.*, II Kin. 13:7.
Ornan was *t.* wheat, I Chr. 21:20.
shalt *t.* the mountains, Is. 41:15.
he that *t.* in hope, I Cor. 9:10.

THRESHING, threshing was sometimes
done by beating the sheaves with a flail or
stick (Ruth 2:17; Judg. 6:11). On a
larger scale, they used the threshing
floor. These threshing floors were built on
elevated ground so that the wind would
carry away the chaff (Hos. 13:3; Jer.
4:11). Threshing was done by oxen
driven over the grain to tread out the
kernels (Hos. 10:11), by threshing
sledges which were weighted with something heavy and dragged over the grain
(Is. 28:27; 41:15), or by small wagons

with low cylindrical wheels like saws. The final process was winnowing. The loosened grain and chaff were tossed high into the air, and the wind would carry the chaff away, allowing the grain to fall in heaps on the floor (Is. 30:24; Amos 9:9; Ps. 1:4).
t. floor of Atad, Gen. 50:10.
t. instruments of iron, Amos 1:3.

THREW, *see* **THROW.**

THROAT, gullet.
t. is open sepulchre, Ps. 5:9.
and took . . by the *t.*, Matt. 18:28.

THRONE, a seat for the king, judge, or priest. The Hebrew word applies to an elevated chair (I Kin. 10:19). The Lord's throne is described as "high and lifted up" (Is. 6:1).
upon the *t.* of David, I Kin. 2:12.
the *t.* of the governor, Neh. 3:7.
Lord's *t.* in heaven, Ps. 11:4.
Christ . . on his *t.*, Acts 2:30.

THRONG, squeeze together.
seest the multitude *t.*, Mark 5:31.
the multitude *t.* thee, Luke 8:42.

THROW, hurl, cast, cause to fall.
t. down their altars, Judg. 2:2.
they *t.* Jezebel down, II Kin. 9:33.
t. in two mites, Mark 12:42.

THRUST, cast, pierce, push.
God *t.* him down, Job 32:13.
t. . . . out of the city, Luke 4:29.
t. in thy sickle, Rev. 14:15.

THUMMIM, *see* **URIM** and **THUM-MIM.**

THUNDER, a sound produced by a flash of lightning. The word thunder was chosen by Samuel as a striking expression of the divine displeasure toward the Israelites. It is sometimes likened to the voice of God (Ps. 29; Rev. 6:1), and God dwelt behind the thundercloud (Ps. 81:7). It is mentioned with reference to the plague of hail in Egypt (Ex. 9:22–29) and the giving of the law (Ex. 19:16).
Lord *t.* from heaven, II Sam. 22:14.
people . . said that it *t.*, John 12:29.

THYATIRA, a city in Asia Minor, the seat of one of the seven churches (Rev. 1:11). It was situated in the area of Mysia

and Ionia, just south of the river Hyllus. It was one of the many cities built after Alexander defeated the Persians. Lydia (Acts 16:14) was from Thyatira, and worked in one of the city's important trades—dyeing. Thyatira seems to have been an international city.

THYINE WOOD, a fragrant, evergreen tree, which resembles a cedar. The wood was used in burning incense, and for elaborate wood-work (Rev. 18:12).

TIBERIAS, a city in the time of Christ, on the Sea of Galilee. Josephus says that it was built by Herod Antipas, and was named by him in honor of the emperor Tiberius. It was the capital of Galilee from the time of its origin until the reign of Herod Agrippa II, who changed it to Sepphoris. Tiberias had both Greeks and Romans (John 6:23).

TIBERIAS, THE SEA OF, another name for the Sea of Galilee (John 21:1). This was probably the name which those outside Palestine used for the sea.

TIBERIUS, *see* **CAESAR.**

TIBHATH, *see* **BETAH.**

TIBNI, the sixth king of Israel, and son of Ginath. Omri defeated and succeeded him (I Kin. 16:21, 22).

TIDAL, a king under Chedorlaomer, and called "a king of nations" (Gen. 14:1–16).

TIDINGS, news, report, information.
heard these evil *t.*, Ex. 33:4.
t. in his mouth, II Sam. 18:25.
shew thee glad *t.*, Luke 1:19.
declare glad *t.*, Acts 13:32.

TIGLATH-PILESER, TILGATH-PIL-NESER, PUL, king of Assyria (742–727 B.C.). He was invited by Ahaz, king of Judah, to assist him against the kings of Syria and Israel (II Kin. 16:7–10). He made Ahaz pay heavy tribute (II Chr. 28:20–21). He made captive many of the inhabitants of Israel (I Chr. 6:26), fulfilling the predictions of Is. 7:17, 8:4.

TIGRIS, *see* **HIDDEKEL.**

TIKVAH, TIKVATH, TOKHATH, (1)

father of Shallum (II Kin. 22:14; II Chr. 34:22). (2) Father of Jahaziah (Ezra 10:15).

TILING, perhaps the layer of sticks, brush, and clay which constitutes the ordinary flat roof of an oriental home, or building. It is mentioned in Luke 5:19.

TILGATH-PILNESER, *see* TIGLATH-PILESER.

TILL, to work, to cultivate.
not a man to *t*., Gen. 2:5.
servants shall *t*., II Sam. 9:10.
he that *t*. his land, Prov. 12:11.
desolate land . . *t*., Ezek. 36:34.

TILLAGE, working, cultivation.
work of field for *t*., I Chr. 27:26.
much food in the *t*., Prov. 13:23.

TILLER, worker.
Cain was *t*. of ground, Gen. 4:2.

TILON, the last named of the four sons of Shimon, of the tribe of Judah (I Chr. 4:20).

TIMAEUS, father of the blind beggar who was cured by Christ (Mark 10:46), the son being therefore called Bartimeus.

TIMBER, wood, beam, tree.
shall break down the *t*., Lev. 14:45.
t. is laid in . . walls, Ezra 5:8.
lay thy stones and *t*., Ezek. 26:12.
beam of *t*. shall answer, Hab. 2:11.
consume it with *t*., Zech. 5:4.

TIMBREL, *see* TABRET.

TIME, duration, period, season.
in process of time, Gen. 4:3.
ark was at that *t*., I Sam. 14:18.
bless at all times, Ps. 34:1.
a *t*. to be born, a *t*., Eccles. 3:2.
t. to seek the Lord, Hos. 10:12.
the *t*. is fulfilled, Mark 1:15.
the *t*. draweth near, Luke 21:8.
t. is not yet come, John 7:6.
now is . . accepted time, II Cor. 6:2.
redeeming the time, Col. 4:5.
t. and *t*. and half a *t*., Rev. 12:14.

TIMNAH, (1) a place which was one of the landmarks on the north boundary of Judah (Josh. 15:10). It is probably identical with the Thimnathah which belonged

to Dan (Josh. 19:43), and Timnath of Samson (Judg. 14:1). (2) A town in the mountain district of Judah (Josh. 15:57).

TIMNATH, *see* TIMNAH.

TIMNATH-HERES, *see* TIMNATH-SERAH.

TIMNATH-SERAH, TIMNATH-HERES, the name of the city which was presented to Joshua after the partition of the country (Josh. 19:50). He was also buried there (24:30). It was also called Timnath-Heres (Judg. 2:9).

TIMNITE, a designation of Samson's father-in-law, because of his residence in Timnah (Judg. 15:6).

TIMON, one of the seven to serve on the occasion of complaints of partiality being made by the Hellenistic Jews at Jerusalem (Acts 6:5).

TIMOTHEUS, the Greek form of Timothy. See TIMOTHY.

TIMOTHY, the convert of Paul. His mother was a Jewess and his father was a Greek (Acts 16:1–3). Paul tells how his mother and grandmother instructed him in the Scriptures (I Tim. 1:5; 3:15). Timothy appears to have been converted at Lystra when Paul made his first visit there (Acts 14:6; II Tim. 1:5). Seeing that Timothy was suitable for missionary work, Paul desired to have him as a companion. After being circumcised, Timothy was set apart as an evangelist by the laying on of hands (I Tim. 4:14; II Tim. 1:6; 4:5). With Luke and Silvanus, he journeyed to Phillippi (Acts 16:12), where he was left to care for a young church. He appears at Berea, later joining Paul at Athens. From Athens he is sent to Thessalonica (I Thess. 3:2). He returned to Athens, and his name appears with Paul's in the opening words of the letters from that city to the city of Thessalonica (I Thess. 1:1; II Thess. 1:1). He was also with Paul when he wrote the Epistles to the Philippians, to the Colossians, and to Philemon (Phil. 1:1; Col. 1:1; Philem. 1). Paul later left Timothy at Ephesus to care for the church there (II Tim. 1:4).
friend of Silas, Acts 17:14.
close friend of Paul, Rom. 16:21.

preached in Corinth, II Cor. 1:19.
Paul's son in faith, I Tim. 1:2.
sent to Ephesus, I Tim. 1:3.
trained in Scripture, II Tim. 1:5.
in Rome with Paul, II Tim. 4:9.

TIMOTHY, EPISTLE TO, personal letters written by Paul to Timothy, his son in the Gospel. They are called "Pastoral" because they are counsels for a pastor or shepherd of a spiritual flock. The first was written at Rome soon after the apostle's release from his first imprisonment, about A.D. 63. It was designed partly to instruct Timothy in the duties of the office with which he had been intrusted, partly to supply him with credentials to the churches, and partly to furnish through him guidance to the churches themselves. The second epistle was written at Rome before the second trial of Paul, about A.D. 64. Its design was to inform Timothy of the apostle's peril and to summon him to his side.

TIN, a white metal, easily melted. It was used very early (Num. 31:22), and was brought from Tarshish by the Tyrians (Zech. 27:12). It was used to make plummets (Zech. 4:10). It is not mined in Palestine.

TINGLE, to tingle, ring.
ears .. shall tingle, I Sam. 3:11.
his ears shall *t*., II Kin. 21:12.

TINKLE, sound, clang. Also **Tinkling**
a *t*. with their feet, Is. 3:16.
a tinkling cymbal, I Cor. 13:1.

TIPHSAH, the limit of Solomon's land toward the Euphrates (I Kin. 4:24). It was attacked by Menahem, king of Israel (II Kin. 15:16). Since many trade routes emerged there, it was of great importance.

TIRAS, the son of Japheth, the son of Noah (Gen. 10:2).

TIRATHITE, the name of one of the three families of scribes living at Jabez (I Chr. 2:55).

TIRE, (1) a headdress, perhaps an ornate turban, worn by the high priest, the bridegroom, and many ladies (Ex. 39:28; Is. 3:20; 61:10; Ezek. 24:17). (2) A pendant worn by women (Is. 3:18).

TIRHAKAH, an Ethiopian king from the south of Egypt, and an opponent of Sennacherib (II Kin. 19:9). The king of Assyria was fighting against Hezekiah, when he heard that Tirhakah was advancing against him.

TIRHANAH, the second son of Caleb the Hezronite by Maachah (I Chr. 2:48).

TIRIA, the third of four sons of Jehaleleel of the tribe of Judah (I Chr. 4:16).

TIRSHATHA, the title of the governor of Judea after the Persians (Ezra 2:63). It was also added after the name of Nehemiah (Neh. 8:9; 10:1). It perhaps denotes the prefect or governor of a province of less extent than a satrapy. It is used of Assyrians (II Kin. 18:24) and Babylonians (Jer. 51:57).

TIRZAH, (1) one of the five daughters of Zelophehad (Num. 26:33). This was the case that gave rise to the Levirate provision, that if a man had no male children his property passed to his daughters. (2) A Canaanitish city, whose king was one of the thirty-one kings overcome by Joshua of the west side of the Jordan (Josh. 12:24). It was the capital of Israel until the time of Omri (I Kin. 14:17). It was a beautiful city (Song 6:4).

TISHBITE, the title of Elijah, probably meaning a resident of some town of a similar name in Gilead (I Kin. 17:1; 21:17; II Kin. 1:3; 9:36). The name of the town is Tishbeh, Tishbi, or perhaps Tesheb. It ·is to be the same as the Thisbe of Tobit 1:2; however, it is uncertain.

TITHE, a tenth. In early times Abram presented tithes to Melchizedek (Gen. 14:20; Heb. 7:2, 6). Jacob promised a tenth of all his property to the Lord if the Lord allowed him to return home safely (Gen. 28:20; Heb. 7:6). Under the Mosaic Law, the tenth of all the produce, flocks, and cattle was pronounced sacred to the Lord. It was a kind of rent for the land which the Lord had given the Israelites and which the Lord owned. The tithe probably began with the voluntary offering of the firstfruits (Deut. 26:2, 10). The tithe, in kind or money value was taken to the priest. It provided for a sacrificial meal for the Levites (Deut.

14:22–27). Every third year the tithe was not sent to the sanctuary, but was used for charity (Deut. 14:28; 26:12–15). Of all the tithes the Levites gave a tenth, a tithe of the tithe (Num. 18:21, 26–28). At times the payment of tithes was neglected (II Chr. 31:4–12). Malachi taught that this was equivalent to robbing God (Mal. 3:8–11). The Mishna includes everything eatable that grows out of the earth for the tithe. The Pharisees, in the time of Jesus, included even the minutest kitchen herbs (Matt. 23:23).

gave Melchizedek *t.*, Gen. 14:20.
t. . . unto Levites, Neh. 10:37.
ye pay *t.* of mint, Matt. 23:23.
t. of all I possess, Luke 18:12..
take *t.* of the people, Heb. 7:5.

TITLE, inscription.
what *t.* is that I, II Kin. 23:17.
Pilate wrote a *t.*, John 19:19.

TITTLE, a little mark in Hebrew letters. *See* JOT.
jot or one *t.* shall, Matt. 5:18.
than one *t.* of . . law, Luke 16:17.

TITUS, one of Paul's fellow-workers. If the journey mentioned in Gal. 2:1 is the same as that recorded in Acts 15, then Titus was closely associated with Paul at Antioch, and was with him in Jerusalem. Paul was to meet Titus in Troas (II Cor. 2:13); however, he joined him in Macedonia (II Cor. 7:6). He was sent back to Corinth to take the second letter of Paul's to them. In the interval between Paul's first and second imprisonment at Rome, he and Titus visited Crete (Titus 1:5). Here Titus remained and received a letter from Paul. Titus was to take up where Paul had stopped, and he was to organize the Church throughout the island of Crete by appointing elders in every city. He is to look for the arrival of Artemas and Tychicus (Titus 3:12), and then to meet Paul in Nicopolis. Whether or not Titus did join Paul is not known.
sent to Corinth, II Cor. 8:6.
convert of Paul's, Titus 1:4.
went to Crete, Titus 1:5.

TITUS, EPISTLE TO, a personal letter written by Paul at Rome shortly after his release from his first imprisonment in the same place. It was written to Titus, who, by the apostle's appointment, was ministering to the Church in Crete. Its aim is to help him in his difficult work, giving him particular instruction concerning the qualifications of church officers and members. The epistle closely resembles the First Epistle to Timothy, and is called "Pastoral." It was written about A.D. 63.

TIZITE, the name of Joha, the brother of Jediael and son of Shimri, a hero of David's army (I Chr. 11:45).

TOAH, son of Zuph and father of Eliel, ancestor of Samuel and Heman (I Chr. 6:34. He is called Tohu (I Sam. 1:1) and Nahath (I Chr. 6:26).

TOB, ISH-TOP, a district in the northeast of Perea, on the border of Syria. It was here that Jephthah took refuge when he was sent from home by his half-brother (Judg. 11:3). It is mentioned in II Sam. 10:6.

TOB-ADONIJAH, one of the Levites which Jehoshaphat sent through the cities of Judah to teach the law to the people (II Chr. 17:8).

TOBIAH, (1) one of the families which returned with Zerubbabel, but could not prove that they were Israelites (Ezra 2:60). (2) One of the opponents to the rebuilding of Jerusalem under Nehemiah. He was perhaps a governor of the Ammonites (Neh. 2:10, 19). He and Sanballet were in league against the Jews.

TOBIJAH, (1) one of the Levites sent by Jehoshaphat to teach the law in the cities of Judah (II Chr. 17:8). (2) One of the captivity during the time of Zechariah (Zech. 6:10, 14).

TOBIT, the father of Tobias (Tobit 1:1).

TOBIT, THE BOOK OF, one of the Apocryphal books of the Greek Old Testament.

TOCHEN, a town in Simeon (I Chr. 4:32). It is probably the same as Telem (Josh. 15:24) or Telaim (I Sam. 15:4).

TOGARMAH, one of the sons of Gomer, and brother of Ashkenaz and Riphath (Gen. 10:3).

TOGETHER, with each other.
striving *t.* for . . faith, Phil. 1:27
eat and drink *t.*, Judg. 19:6.
that we may fight *t.*, I Sam. 17:10.
we took counsel *t.*, Ps. 55:14.
shall both burn *t.*, Is. 1:31.
both *t.* into . . synagogue, Acts 14:1.
be caught up *t.*, I Thess. 4:17.

TOHU, a Kohathite, ancestor of Samuel; the same as Nahath (I Chr. 5:26), or Toah (I Chr. 6:34).

TOI, TOU, a king of Hamath in the time of David. When David defeated Hadadezer, Toi sent his son Joram to congratulate him, and to make presents of gold, silver, and brass (II Sam. 8:9).

TOIL, to labor, also **Toiling.**
lilies, they *t.* not, Matt. 6:28.
saw them *t.* in rowing, Mark 6:48.
we have *t.* all . . night, Luke 5:5.

TOKEN, evidence, manifestation.
t. of the covenant, Gen. 9:12.
blood shed . . for a *t.*, Ex. 12:13.
are afraid at thy *t.*, Ps. 65:8.
t. of judgment, II Thess. 1:5.

TOKHATH, a marginal reading for the Tikvath (II Chr. 34:32).

TOLA, (1) the eldest son of Issachar (Gen. 46:13). (2) The son of Puah of the tribe of Issachar, and a judge of Israel. He succeeded Abimelech in the judgeship (Judg. 10:1, 2).

TOLAD, a town in Simeon in David's time (I Chr. 4:29). It is also given in its fuller form El-tolad (Josh. 15:30).

TOLAITES, the generation named after Tola, the son of Issachar (Num. 26:23).

TOMB, a natural cave or an artificial one was the standard type of sepulcher. The entrance was closed by a heavy stone door, or by a roller. Eleven of the kings of Judah were buried in the Sepulchre of the Kings, in the City of David (II Chr. 16:14; 32:33). This sepulchre was probably on Zion, but it has not yet been discovered. No tomb can be traced beyond the Roman era. *See* SEPULCHRE.

TONGUE, the organ of speech (Job 29:

10; Ps. 39:3; 71:24; James 3:6), or a particular language of any people (Dan. 1:4; Acts 1:19; 2:4). The Lord used the language of men both for evil (Gen. 11:1–9) and good (Acts 2:1–13). It is used figuratively for speech generally (I John 3:18; Prov. 25:15; Ps. 31:20).
slow of speech and *t.*, Ex. 4:10.
flatter with their *t.*, Ps. 5:9.
hold thy tongue, Amos 6:10.
t. should confess, Rom. 14:11.
t. is a little member, James 3:5.
out of every tongue, Rev. 5:9.

TONGUES, GIFT OF, the gift of tongues was the special work of the Holy Spirit on the Day of Pentecost. This gift was only for a short time. It appears from the record that the gift on the day of Pentecost fell on all alike (Acts 2: 2, 3). The same gift fell upon Cornelius and his household (Acts 10:44–46). In the list of spiritual endowments mentioned in I Cor. 12:8–10 are "divers kinds of tongues." Paul places tongues lower than prophecy as to its value; it tended to bring on confusion rather than understanding.

TOOL, weapon, vessel.
lift up thy *t.* upon it, Ex. 20:25.
nor ax nor any *t.*, I Kin. 6:7.

TOOTH.
eye for eye, and *t.*, Lev. 24:20.
hook of three *t.*, I Sam. 2:13.
t. of the young lions, Job 4:10.
with the skin of my *t.*, Job 19:20.
as vinegar to the *t.*, Prov. 10:26.
t. are set on edge, Jer. 31:29.
beast . . had great iron *t.*, Dan. 7:7.
weeping . . gnashing of *t.*, Matt. 8:12.
as the *t.* of lions, Rev. 9:8.

TOP, head, upper part, roof.
altar on *t.* cf rock, Judg. 6:26.
t. of mulberry trees, I Chr. 14:15.
from *t.* to bottom, Matt. 27:51.
woven from the *t.*, John 19:23.

TOPAZ, a precious stone which is wine yellow, of every degree of shade, from dark red, sometimes lilac, to pale grayish yellow. It was second in the breastplate of the high-priest (Ex. 28:17), and the ninth in the foundation of the heavenly Jerusalem (Rev. 21:20).

TOPHEL, appears to be a boundary of

the great Sinaitic desert of Paran (Deut. 1:1). It is at the southeast corner of the Dead Sea, and is now called Tufileh.

TOPHETH, TOPHET, a place southeast of Jerusalem, in the valley of Hinnom (Jer. 7:31; 19:2). It was a music-grove of the king, a royal garden. After the sacrifices to the idol Moloch, it became a place of abomination (Jer. 7:32).

TORCH, usually signifies a lamp. In Nahum 2:3 it describes the chariots as flaming torches. Zechariah uses it as a symbol of anger and destruction (12:6).

TORMENT, torture, anguish.
with disease and *t.*, Matt. 4:24.
lifted eyes, in *t.*, Luke 16:23.
as *t.* of scorpions, Rev. 9:5.

TORMENTOR, one who torments.
delivered him to *t.*, Matt. 18:34.

TORN, ripped, torn.
that which was *t.*, Gen. 31:39.
is *t.* in pieces, Ezek. 4:14.

TORTOISE, various fresh-water tortoises, land-tortoises, and sea-tortoises, are found in Palestine (Lev. 11:29).

TOSS, to shake, agitate.
vanity *t.* to and fro, Prov. 21:6.
violently turn and *t.*, Is. 22:18.
driven . . and *t.*, James 1:6.

TOUCH, come in contact. **Touched.**
neither shall ye *t.*, Gen. 3:3.
if a soul *t.* any, Lev. 5:2.
nor *t.* their died, Deut. 14:8.
the Lord *t.* my mouth, Jer. 1:9.
who touched me? Luke 8:45.
t. me not, John 20:17.

TOWER, these were erected on the outer walls of the cities (Judg. 9:47–49) and on the frontiers (Judg. 9:17). It was used as a place of refuge in time of invasion (Prov. 18:10). They were also used in vineyards and orchards to serve as posts for watchmen. The figure of the tower was used for God (Ps. 61:3) and for proud and powerful men (Is. 2:15).
t. of Edar, Gen. 35:21.
t. of Penuel, Judg. 8:17.
t. of Shechem, Judg. 9:46.
t. of Meah, Neh. 3:1.
t. of Hananeel, Neh. 3:1.

t. of David, Song 4:4.
t. of Lebanon, Song 7:4.
t. of the Flock, Mic. 4:8.

TOWN, neither the Old nor the New Testament makes a distinction between cities and towns. It is used in specifying small, dependent "towns" and "villages" (Josh. 15:45), used for any places of dwelling (Josh. 13:30), used for unwalled cities (Zech. 2:4), and small hamlets without walls.

TOWN CLERK, the city secretary, recorder, to whose office belonged the care of the archives, the drawing up of official decrees, and the reading of them in public assemblies of the people. One of these men appeased the mob at Ephesus (Acts 19:35).

TRACHONITIS, a district mentioned only in Luke 3:1. The region is also called Argob, Geshur, and now El-Lejah. It is south of Damascus on the west slope of Jebel Hauran. Josephus describes the inhabitants as cave-dwellers.

TRADE, *see* **COMMERCE** and **TRADE.**

TRADITION, a word particularly applied to the oral law of the Jews (Matt. 15:2; Mark 7:3; Col. 2:8). In Gal. 1:14 the "traditions of my fathers" are precepts received from the fathers, whether written or oral. Paul refers to the Christian teachings in the same way (II Thess. 3:6; I Cor. 11:12).

TRAIN, to instruct, to dedicate.
Abram armed *t.* servants, Gen. 14:14.
t. up a child, Prov. 22:6.

TRAITOR, one gives over, betrays.
Judas, . . also was the *t.*, Luke 6:16.
t. . . . high minded, II Tim. 3:4.

TRAMPLE, to tread upon.
dragon . . *t.* under feet, Ps. 91:13.
I will *t.* them, Is. 63:3.
lest they *t.* them, Matt. 7:6.

TRANCE, an ecstasy.
he fell into a trance, Acts 10:10.
in a *t.* I saw a vision, Acts 11:5.
I was in a trance, Acts 22:17.

TRANQUILLITY, security, ease.
lengthening of thy *t.*, Dan. 4:27.

TRANSFIGURATION, to change into another form. It is written (Matt. 17:2; Mark 9:2) that our Lord "was transfigured" before his disciples, Peter, James, and John. It took place eight days after the Lord told them of his suffering, death, and resurrection which were to come. Moses and Elias also appeared, and Peter suggested that three tents should be erected in honor of such glorious company. A voice from a bright cloud said to them, "This is my beloved Son, hear ye him." The same event is alluded to by Peter, in his later life, as one of the proofs of the Lord's majesty (II Pet. 1:18). John also mentions the event (John 1:14).

TRANSFIGURED, to be transformed.
was *t.* before them, Matt. 17:2.

TRANSFORM, to give a different form.
Satan himself is *t.*, II Cor. 11:14.
his ministers .. *t.*, II Cor. 11:15.

TRANSGRESS, to deceive, to step over.
not *t.* thy commandments, Deut. 26:13.
they .. *t.* my covenant, Josh. 7:11.
ye make .. people to *t.*, I Sam. 2:24.
ye have transgressed, I Sam. 14:33.
my mouth shall not *t.*, Ps. 17:3.
all Israel have *t.*, Dan. 9:11.
because they have *t.*, Hos. 7:13.
come to Bethel, and *t.*, Amos 4:4.
neither *t.* I, Luke 15:29.
whosoever *t.*, and abides, II John 9.

TRANSGRESSION, trespass, sin.
will not pardon .. *t.*, Ex. 23:21.
forgive people's *t.*, I Kin. 8:50.
wicked snared by *t.*, Prov. 12:13.
for three *t.* of, Amos 1:3.
no law is, is no *t.*, Rom. 4:15.
added because of *t.*, Gal. 3:19.
sin is *t.* of law, I John 3:4.

TRANSGRESSOR, one who steps over, one who trespasses.
t. shall be destroyed, Ps. 37:38.
t. are come to the full, Dan. 8:23.
but *t.* shall fall, Hos. 14:9.
numbered with the *t.*, Mark 15:28.
reckoned among *t.*, Luke 22:37.

TRANSLATE, putting over, transpose.
t. kingdom from Saul, II Sam. 3:10.
t. us into kingdom, Col. 1:13.
Enoch was *t.*, Heb. 11:5.

TRANSLATION, transposing.
before his *t.*, he had, Heb. 11:5.

TRAP, a snare, a destruction.
shall be snares and *t.*, Josh. 23:13.
wicked, they set a *t.*, Jer. 5:26.
table .. be made a *t.*, Rom. 11:9.

TRAVAIL, pain, toil, bringing.
in time of her *t.*, Gen. 38:27.
pain, as a woman in *t.*, Ps. 48:6.
t. hath God given, Eccles. 1:13.
remember our .. *t.*, I Thess. 2:9.

TRAVAIL, to bring forth, to be pained.
he *t.* with iniquity, Ps. 7:14.
t. in birth, and pained, Rev. 12:2.

TRAVEL, journeying, traveling.
Paul's companions in *t.*, Acts 19:29.

TRAVEL, to walk, to go, to journey.
poverty .. as one that *t.*, Prov. 6:11.
heaven .. as a man *t.*, Matt. 25:14.
t. as far as Phenice, Acts 11:19.
chosen to *t.*, II Cor. 8:19.

TRAVELLER, one who journeys, wayfarer.
opened .. doors to the *t.*, Job 31:32.
o ye *t.* companies, Is. 21:13.

TREACHEROUS, deceitful.
her *t.* sister Judah, Jer. 3:8.
her prophets are .. *t.*, Zeph. 3:4.

TREACHEROUSLY, deceitfully.
friends .. dealt *t.*, Lam. 1:2.
dealt *t.* against Lord, Hos. 5:7.
Judah hath dealt *t.*, Mal. 2:11.

TREAD, to trample, to proceed.
t. ... high places, Deut. 33:29.
thou hast *t.* down, Judg. 5:21.
let him *t.* down my life, Ps. 7:5.
t. the mortar, make, Nahum 3:14.
to *t.* on serpents, Luke 10:19.
not muzzle .. ox that *t.*, I Cor. 9:9.

TREASON, betrayal, conspiracy.
Zimri, and his *t.*, I Kin. 16:20.
and cried *t.*, *t.*, II Chr. 23:13.

TREASURE, that which is laid up, valuable, hidden away.
built Pharaoh *t.* cities, Ex. 1:11.
belly .. fillest with *t.*, Ps. 17:14.
lay not up *t.* on earth, Matt. 6:19.
where *t.* is, .. heart, Luke 12:34.

t. in . . vessels, II Cor. 4:7.
t. for the last day, James 5:3.

TREASURER, one who keeps the treasure.
Mithredath the *t.,* Ezra 1:8.
t. over the treasuries, Neh. 13:13.
go, . . unto this *t.,* Is. 22:15.

TREASURY, the place where the treasure
is kept.
Levites . . over the *t.,* I Chr. 9:26.
bringeth wind out of *t.,* Ps. 135:7.
sat over against *t.,* Mark 12:41.

TREE, wood, timber, tree.
t. of lign aloes, Num. 24:6.
cedar *t.* . . of Lebanon, II Chr. 2:8.
t. planted by river, Ps. 1:3.
t. that bringeth not, Matt. 3:10.
eat of the *t.* of life, Rev. 2:7.

TREMBLE, shake, to be afraid.
people in . . camp *t.,* Ex. 19:16.
nations should *t.,* Deut. 2:25.
pillars of heaven *t.,* Job 26:11.
devils believe and *t.,* James 2:19.

TRENCH, a rampart, a bulwark.
Saul lay in the *t.,* I Sam. 26:5.
shall cast a *t.* about, Luke 19:43.

TRESPASS, stepping aside, guilt.
soul committeth *t.,* Lev. 5:15.
for our *t.* is great, II Chr. 28:13.
forgive men their *t.,* Matt. 6:14.

TRESPASS, to transgress, err, sin.
ye *t.* against me, Deut. 32:51.
t. against my law, Hos. 8:1.
if a brother *t.,* rebuke, Luke 17:3.

TRESPASS OFFERING, *see* **OFFERING
AND SACRIFICES.**

TRIAL, the judicial procedure of the law.
The trial of Jesus Christ was for an offense
punishable by Roman law with death
(Luke 23:2, 14; John 19:12). Paul and
Stephen were tried before the high-priest
and rulers (Acts 5:27; 6:12).
in *t.* of affliction, II Cor. 8:2.
t. of your faith, I Pet. 1:7.

TRIBE, a race, a nation. (Ex. 31:2).
twelve *t.* of Israel, Gen. 49:28.
the chief of your *t.,* Deut. 1:15.
judging . . twelve *t.,* Luke 22:30.
twelve *t.* . . . scattered, James 1:1.
lion of *t.* of Judah, Rev. 5:5.

TRIBULATION, distress, affliction.
saved you out of *t.,* I Sam. 10:19.
those days, after *t.,* Mark 13:24.
we glory in *t.* also, Rom. 5:3.
ye faint not at my *t.,* Eph. 3:13.

TRIBUTARY, under tribute.
the people shall be *t.,* Deut. 20:11.
Canaanites became *t.,* Judg. 1:30.

TRIBUTE, a tax, a levy. In the Old Testament, particularly in the time of David
and Solomon, the word meant labor that
was forced, as that inforced upon the
Canaanites after the conquest (II Sam.
20:24). Later the Jews had to pay tribute
to foreign countries (II Kin. 23:33; Ezra
4:13). In the New Testament times tribute was paid to Caesar. Jesus and Paul
did not oppose this tribute, even though
it was unpopular (Luke 20:22–25; Rom.
13:6, 7). Everyone over twenty years of
age had to pay a half a shekel as tribute
for the maintenance of the temple (Matt.
17:24–27).
put . . Canaanites to *t.,* Josh. 17:13.
Ahasuerus laid a *t.,* Esther 10:1.
slothful . . under *t.,* Prov. 12:24.
t. to whom *t.,* Rom. 13:7.

TRIM, to make good, to do well.
t. his beard, II Sam. 19:24.
virgins arose, and *t.,* Matt. 25:7.

TRINITY, *see* **GOD.**

TRIUMPH, to overcome, rejoice, sing.
he hath *t.* gloriously, Ex. 15:1.
t. of wicked is short, Job 20:5.
made show of *t.* over, Col. 2:15.

TROAS, a city on the coast of Mysia,
opposite the southeast extremity of the
island of Tenedos, and near Troy. It was
in Troas that Paul received the divine
instruction that he was to carry the Gospel into Europe (Acts 16:8–11). On the
next missionary journey he waited there
in the expectation of meeting Titus (II
Cor. 2:12, 13). It was also the place where
years later he left a cloak, some books
and parchments in the house of Carpus
(II Tim. 4:13).

TROGYLLIUM, a town on the Ionian
coast, directly opposite Samos. Paul
sailed through the channel between these
cities on his way to Jerusalem at the end

of his third journey, spending the night in Trogyllium (Acts 20:15).

TROOP, group, band, company.
shall I pursue this *t.*, I Sam. 30:8.
o daughter of *t.*, Mic. 5:1.

TROPHIMUS, a companion of Paul, accompanying him in his third missionary journey when returning from Macedonia to Syria (Acts 20:4). In II Tim. 4:20 Paul writes that he had left Trophimus in ill health at Miletus.

TROUBLE, to disturb, to trouble.
all Israelites were *t.*, II Sam. 4:1.
king of Syria was *t.*, II Kin. 6:11.
isles in sea . . *t.*, Ezek. 26:18.
Herod was *t.*, Matt. 2:3.
let not . . heart be *t.*, John 14:1.
lest bitterness *t.* you, Heb. 12:15.

TRUCEBREAKERS, irreconcilable.
without . . affection, *t.*, II Tim. 3:3.

TRUE, sincere, real.
thy words be *t.*, II Sam. 7:28.
judgments of Lord are *t.*, Ps. 19:9.
let God be *t.*, Rom. 3:4.
whatsoever things are *t.*, Phil. 4:8.
this is the *t.* God, I John 5:20.

TRUMPET, there are two kinds of trumpets. The "shophar" is made of a ram's horn. It was not very musical, but its sound could be heard far away. It was primarily used to give signals in time of war (Judg. 3:27; II Sam. 18:16; Job 39:24), to sound the alarm (Jer. 6:1), or to announce a new king (I Kin. 1:34). It was used at the beginning of the year of Jubilee (Lev. 25:9). There was another trumpet made of metal. It was used primarily during the religious festivals. There were two of them in the tabernacle (Num. 10:2). At the dedication of the Temple, 120 were used (II Chr. 5:12). Christ's coming and the resurrection of the dead will be announced by a trumpet (Matt. 24:31; I Cor. 15:52). They were also used in Revelation to announce important events (Rev. 8:2).
priests . . blow with *t.*, Josh. 6:4.
Joab blew *t.*, II Sam. 2:28.
lift voice with *t.*, II Chr. 5:13.
blow the *t.* in Tekoa, Jer. 6:1.
voice, as of *t.*, Rev. 1:10.

TRUST, to believe, to be confident.

rock, in him I *t.*, II Sam. 22:3.
he *t.* in the Lord, II Kin. 18:5.
t., and not be afraid, Is. 12:2.
t. in name of Lord, Zeph. 3:12.
that *t.* in riches, Mark 10:24.
who first *t.* in Christ, Eph. 1:12.
t. in the living God, I Tim. 4:10.
I *t.* to come, II John 12.

TRUTH, reality, steadfastness.
serve him in *t.*, I Sam. 12:24.
walk before me in *t.*, I Kin. 2:4.
buy the *t.*, sell . . not, Prov. 23:23.
is no *t.*, nor mercy, Hos. 4:1.
told him all the *t.*, Mark 5:33.
grace and *t.* came, John 1:17.
I say *t.* in Christ, Rom. 9:1.
knowledge of *t.*, I Tim. 2:4.
dividing word of *t.*, II Tim. 2:15.
grace . ., in *t.*, II John 3.

TRY, test, prove.
word of Lord is *t.*, II Sam. 22:31.
hast *t.* my heart, Jer. 12:3.
t. them as gold, Zech. 13:9.
be *t.* with fire, I Pet. 1:7.
t. the spirits, I John 4:1.

TRYPHENA, a Christian woman of Rome to whom, in connection with Tryphosa, Paul sent a special salutation (Rom. 16:12).

TRYPHOSA, *see* **TRYPHENA.**

TUBAL, son of Japheth, who with his brothers Javan and Meshech, traded in slaves and vessels of brass (Gen. 10:2; I Chr. 1:5).

TUBAL-CAIN, the son of Lamech by his wife Zillah, who is described (Gen. 4:22) as "hammering all kinds of cutting things in brass and iron," the inventor of edge tools.

TUMULT, noise, roar, trouble.
enemies make a *t.*, Ps. 83:2.
noise of *t.* people, Is. 33:3.
Moab . . die with *t.*, Amos 2:2.
imprisonments, in *t.*, II Cor. 6:5.

TURBAN, *see* **DIADEM.**

TURN, alter, direct, turn.
t. from his anger, Josh. 7:26.
t., my daughters, Ruth 1:11.
soft answer *t.* away, Prov. 15:1.
all *t.* to dust again, Eccles. 3:20.

Ephraim . . a cake not *t.*, Hos. 7:8.
cheek, *t.* . . other, Matt. 5:39.
t. to God from idols, I Thess. 1:9.
laughter . . *t.* to sorrow, James 4:9.

TURTLE, TURTLEDOVE, one of the best-known birds of the Holy Land, a bird of the pigeon family. According to the Law of Moses they could be used for the burnt and sin offerings (Lev. 1:14). This was primarily for the poor, for the bird was abundant in Palestine. It comes in the Spring and goes South for the Winter. It is gentle, and therefore, is a suitable symbol for the innocent (Ps. 74:19).

TUTORS, guardians.
child is under *t.*, Gal. 4:1–2.

TWAIN, two.
with *t.* he covered, Is. 6:2.
go with him *t.*, Matt. 5:41.
they are no more *t.*, Mark 10:8.

TWELVE, *see* **APOSTLES.**

TWICE, two times.
appeared to him *t.*, I Kin. 11:9.
before . . cock, crow *t.*, Mark 14:30.
I fast *t.* in week, Luke 18:12.

TWINS, twofold, double.
fulfilled, behold *t.*, Gen. 25:24.
like roes that are *t.*, Song 4:5.

TYCHICUS, one of Paul's fellow-laborers. We first meet him as a companion of the apostle during a portion of his return journey from the third missionary tour (Acts 20:4). He was with the apostle again in Paul's first imprisonment (Col. 4:7, 8; Eph. 6:21, 22). In Titus 3:12 Paul says that he may send Tychicus to Crete as he goes to Nicopolis. Paul, in his second imprisonment, sends Tychicus to Ephesus (II Tim. 4:12).

TYRANNUS, the man in whose school Paul taught for two years while at Ephesus (Acts 19:9).

TYRE, TYRUS, an ancient Phoenician city which was located on the shore of the Mediterranean Sea, twenty-five miles from Sidon and about thirty-five miles north of Mount Carmel. It was a city in the 14th century B.C., and even then was a city of trade and commerce. After Canaan was captured by Israel, this territory was assigned to Asher (Josh. 19:29). However, it was probably not occupied. David formed an alliance with Tyre for trading purposes (II Sam. 5:11; I Kin. 5:1). King Hiram of Tyre aided the building projects of David and Solomon by sending them craftsmen and cedar (I Kin. 5:1–10). Tyre was repeatedly attacked by the Assyrian kings. Ezekiel predicted the downfall of Tyre because of her enormous sins (Ezek. 28). At the time of Joel (3:6–8) the Phoenicians sold Jewish children as slaves. In 332 B.C. Alexander the Great massacred and enslaved about 40,000 of their inhabitants. In 65 B.C. the Romans made Tyre a free city. Some of the citizens of Tyre heard Jesus preach in Galilee (Mark 3:8). Jesus himself visited that area (Mark 7:24). Paul landed at Tyre (Acts 21:3, 7).

U

UCAL, an unknown person mentioned with Ithiel in Prov. 30:1.

UEL, a son of Bani who had taken a foreign wife (Ezra 10:34).

ULAM, (1) a descendant of Gilead (I Chr. 7:17), (2) the first-born of Eshek, (I Chr. 8:39, 40).

ULLA, an Asherite and father of Arah (I Chr. 7:39).

UMMAH, a city in Asher (Josh. 19:30).

UNACCUSTOMED, exceptional, as a bullock "not trained" (Jer. 31:18).

UNADVISEDLY, without advice, lacking wisdom in action. (Ps. 106:33).

UNAWARES, without knowledge.
stole away *u.* to Laban, Gen. 31:20.
come upon you *u.*, Luke 21:34.
entertained angels *u.*, Heb. 13:2.

UNBELIEF, lack of faith, distrust.
because of *u.* they were, Rom. 11:20.
obtained mercy through *u.* Rom. 11:30
did ignorantly in *u.*, I Tim. 1:13.
because of *u.*, Heb. 3:19.

UNBLAMEABLE, not blameable.

present you holy, *u.*, Col. 1:22.

UNCERTAIN, not manifest, not sure.
so run, not as *u.*, I Cor. 9:26.
trust in *u.* riches, I Tim. 6:17.

UNCIRCUMCISED, not circumcised.
the *u.* man child, whose, Gen. 17:14.
daughters of the *u.*, II Sam. 1:20.
u. in heart and ears, Acts 7:51.
him not become *u.*, I Cor. 7:18.

UNCIRCUMCISION, the condition of
being uncircumcised.
u. is nothing, but the, I Cor. 7:19.
are called *u.* by that, Eph. 2:11.

UNCLE, the brother of one's father or
mother; also, any male relation.
sons of Uzziel, the *u.*, Lev. 10:4.
Saul's *u.* said to him, I Sam. 10:14.
man's *u.* shall take him, Amos 6:10.

UNCLEAN ANIMALS, according to the
Law of Moses, many animals were not
to be eaten because they were unclean.
Animals with cloven hoofs or those that
did not chew the cud were not to be eaten
(Lev. 11:3, 4). There were also unclean
birds (Lev. 11:13–19). Of all the insects,
only the locust was permitted to be eaten
(Lev. 11:21–23). As for sea foods, those
animals which did not have fins and scales
were not to be eaten (Lev. 11:9, 10).

UNCLEANNESS, *see* CLEAN AND UN-
CLEAN; PURIFICATION.

UNCLE'S WIFE, the wife of an uncle or
other male relative.
shall lie with his *u.*, Lev. 20:20.

UNCLOTHED, uncovered, made open.
we would be *u.*, but, II Cor. 5:4.

UNCONDEMNED, not judged guilty.
beaten us openly *u.*, Acts 16:37.
a Roman, and *u.*, Acts 22:25.

UNCORRUPTNESS, not corrupted.
doctrine showing *u.*, Titus, 2:7.

UNCOVER, to reveal, make bare.
nakedness shall be *u.*, Is. 47:3.
shall *u.* the cedar, Zeph. 2:14.
u. the roof where he, Mark 2:4.
pray unto God *u.*, I Cor. 11:13.

UNCTION, anointing. I John 2:20

UNDEFILED, perfect, whole, unpolluted.
my dove, my *u.*, Song 5:2.
holy, harmless, *u.*, Heb. 7:26.
pure religion and *u.*, James 1:27.
incorruptible, and *u.*, I Pet. 1:4.

UNDER, beneath, below, underneath.
smote him *u.*, the, II Sam. 2:23.
off the dust *u.* your, Mark 6:11.
who are *u.* the law, Rom. 3:19.
without mercy *u.* two, Heb. 10:28.

UNDERSTAND, comprehend.
u. all the imaginations, I Chr. 28:9.
they might not *u.*, Luke 8:10.
they *u.* not that he, John 8:27.
have not heard shall *u.*, Rom. 15:21.
through faith we *u.* that, Heb. 11:3.

UNDERSTANDING, wisdom.
taketh away the *u.*, Job 12:20.
astonished at his *u.*, Luke 2:47.
opened he their *u.*, Luke 24:45.
pray with *u.*, also, I Cor. 14:15.

UNDERTAKE, begin, start, inaugurate.
the Jews *u.* to do as, Esther 9:23.
I am oppressed, *u.* for, Is. 38:14.

UNDONE, result of the act of undoing.
thou art *u.*, O people, Num. 21:29.
Joshua left nothing *u.*, Josh. 11:15.
to leave the other *u.*, Matt. 23:23.

UNEQUAL, not equal, not on even par.
are not your ways *u.*, Ezek. 18:25.

UNFAITHFUL, not trustworthy.
back, and dealt *u.*, Ps. 78:57.
confidence in an *u.* man, Prov. 25:19.

UNFEIGNED, without hypocrisy.
Ghost, by love *u.*, II Cor. 6:6.
pure heart and faith *u.*, I Tim. 1:5.
unto *u.* love of the, I Pet. 1:22.

UNFRUITFUL, not bearing fruit.
understanding is *u.*, I Cor. 14:14.
no fellowship with *u.*, Eph. 5:11.
be barren nor *u.* in, II Pet. 1:8.

UNGODLINESS, lack of respect for God.
against all *u.* and un-, Rom. 1:18.
shall turn away *u.*, Rom. 11:26.
increase unto more *u.*, II Tim. 2:16.
denying *u.* and worldly, Titus 2:12.

UNGODLY, worthless, wicked.
floods of *u.* men made, II Sam. 22:5.

cause against an *u.*, Ps. 43:1.
Christ died for the *u.*, Rom. 5:6.
all that are *u.*, Jude 15.

UNHOLY, common, not holy, worthless.
between holy and *u.*, Lev. 10:10..
for *u.* and profane, for, I Tim. 1:9.
an *u.* thing, and hath, Heb. 10:29.

UNICORN, a horned, large animal of a
  fierce nature, probably some kind of
  wild ox or buffalo, not to be confused
  with the animal of Greek writings.
the strength of an *u.*, Num. 23:22.
from the horns of *u.*, Ps. 22:21.

UNITE, to bind together, attach.
be not thou *u.*, Gen. 49:6.
u. my heart to fear thy, Ps. 86:11.

UNITY, oneness, togetherness.
dwell together in *u.*, Ps. 133:1.
keep the *u.* of the, Eph. 4:3.
in the *u.* of the faith, Eph. 4:13.

UNJUST, perverse, unrighteous.
the deceitful and *u.*, Ps. 43:1.
an *u.* man is an abom-, Prov. 29:27.
to law before the *u.*, I Cor. 6:1.
to reserve the *u.* unto, II Pet. 2:9.

UNKNOWN, not revealed, concealed.
to the *u.* God, Acts 17:23.
speaketh in an *u.*, I Cor. 14:2.
as *u.* and yet well-, II Cor. 6:9.

UNLAWFUL, not lawful, illegal.
that it is an *u.*, Acts 10:28.
day with their *u.*, II Pet. 2:8.

UNLEARNED, uneducated, untaught.
that they were *u.*, Acts 4:13.
foolish and *u.* quest-, II Tim. 2:23.
they that are *u.* and, II Pet. 3:16.

UNLEAVENED, without leaven or yeast
did bake *u.* bread, and, Gen. 19:3.
Passover, and of *u.*, Mark 14:1.
the days of *u.* bread, Acts 12:3.
the days of *u.* bread, Acts 20:6.

UNLEAVENED BREAD, FEAST OF,
  see PASSOVER.

UNMARRIED, unwed, not married.
to *u.* and widows, I Cor. 7:8.
let her remain *u.*, I Cor. 7:11.

UNMERCIFUL, without kindness, **the**
  absence of mercy (Rom. 1:31).

UNMINDFUL, not aware of, to forget.
thou art *u.*, and, Deut. 32:18.

UNMOVEABLE, steadfast, staunch, firm.
and remained *u.*, Acts 27:41.
ye steadfast, *u.* al-, I Cor. 15:58.

UNNI, (1) one of the Levite doorkeepers
  of David (I Chr. 15:18). (2) Another
  Levite (Neh. 12:9).

UNNO, *see* UNNI.

UNPARDONABLE SIN, the sin against
  the Holy Spirit. The Pharisees charged
  that the miracles which Jesus did were
  of the power of Beelzebub, not of the
  Holy Spirit (Matt. 12:24, 31, 32; Mark
  3:22, 28, 29; Luke 12:10). Jesus, on this
  occasion, taught that this sin could never
  be forgiven. The reference of John to "the
  sin unto death" (I John 5:16) is thought
  to be the same as the unpardonable sin.

UNPERFECT, imperfect, not perfect.
yet being *u.*, Ps. 139:16.

UNPREPARED, not ready.
and find you *u.*, II Cor. 9:4.

UNPROFITABLE, useless, worthless.
reason with *u.* talk, Job 15:3.
cast ye the *u.* servant, Matt. 25:30.
we are *u.* servants, Luke 17:10.
for they are *u.* and, Titus 3:9.

UNPUNISHED, free, innocent.
shall not be *u.*, but, Prov. 11:21.
thee altogether *u.*, Jer. 30:11.

UNQUENCHABLE, used in the Bible for
  fire of God that cannot be put out (Matt.
  3:12).

UNREASONABLE, irrational.
me *u.* to send a, Acts 25:27.
delivered from *u.*, II Thess. 3:2.

UNREPROVABLE, blameless.
unblameable and *u.*, Col. 1:22.

UNRIGHTEOUS, evil, wicked.
them that decree *u.*, Is. 10:1.
the mammon of *u.*, Luke 16:9.
not that the *u.*, I Cor. 6:9.
all *u.* is sin, and, I John 5:17.

UNRULY, unrestrained, disobedient.
them that are *u.*, I Thess. 5:14.
accused or riot or *u.*, Titus 1:6.
many *u.* and vain talk-, Titus 1:10.

UNSAVORY, insipid, not desirable.
wilt show thyself *u.*, II Sam. 22:27.
that which is *u.* be, Job 6:6.

UNSEARCHABLE, not discernable.
great things and *u.*, Job 5:9.
heart of kings is *u.*, Prov. 25:3.
u. are his judgments, Rom. 1:27.
the *u.* riches of Christ, Eph. 3:8.

UNSEEMLY, improper, indecent.
that which is *u.*, Rom. 11:33.
behave itself *u.*, is, I Cor. 13:5.

UNSKILLFUL, not skillful or adept.
babe is *u.* in the word, Heb. 5:13.

UNSPEAKABLE, not able to be spoken.
to God for his *u.*, II Cor. 9:15.
heard *u.* words, which, II Cor. 12:4.
rejoice with joy *u.*, I Pet. 1:8.

UNSPOTTED, unstained, unmarred.
keep oneself *u.* from, James 1:27.

UNSTABLE, uncertain, fickle.
man is *u.* in his ways, James 1:8.
are unlearned and *u.*, II Pet. 3:16.

UNSTOPPED, opened, cleared.
the deaf shall be *u.*, Is. 35:5.

UNTHANKFUL, not thankful.
kind unto the *u.* and, Luke 6:35.
to parents, *u.*, un-, II Tim. 3:2.

UNTOWARD, crooked, perverse.
this crooked and *u.* gen-, Acts 2:40.

UNWASHEN, not washed.
eat with *u.* hands, de-, Matt. 15:20.
to say, with *u.* hands, Mark 7:2.

UNWISE, without understanding.
he is an *u.* son, he, Hos. 13:13.
wise and to the *u.*, Rom. 1:14.
not *u.* but understand-, Eph. 5:17.

UNWORTHY, not worthy.
ourselves *u.* of life, Acts 13:46.
u. to judge the small-, I Cor. 6:2.

UPBRAID, reproach, expose.
began he to *u.* the, Matt. 11:20.

all liberally and *u.*, James 1:5.

UPHARSIN, *see* MENE.

UPHAZ, (OPHIR), a place in South Arabia which was a source of gold (Jer. 10:9).

UPHOLD, sustain, support.
the Lord *u.* the right-, Ps. 37:17.
also that *u.* Egypt, Ezek. 30:6.
u. all things by the, Heb. 1:3.

UPPERMOST, highest of a comparison.
u. basket were all, Gen. 40:17.
love the *u.* rooms, Matt. 23:6.

UPRIGHT, erect, straight.
u. shall dwell in the, Prov. 2:21.
He that walketh *u.*, Prov. 10:9.
me, and set me *u.*, Dan. 8:18.
that speaketh *u.*, Amos 5:10.
stand *u.* on your, Acts 14:10.

UPRIGHTLY, upright way, honestly.
he that walketh *u.*, Ps. 15:2.
them that walk *u.*, Ps. 84:11.
he that walketh *u.*, Prov. 10:9.
he that speaketh *u.*, Is. 33:15.

UPRIGHTNESS, integrity.
pleasure in *u.*, I Chr. 29:17.
walketh in *u.*, Prov. 14:2.
way of just is *u.*, Is. 26:7.

UPROAR, turmoil, excitement.
city being in an *u.*, I Kin. 1:41.
an *u.* among the people, Matt. 26:5.
the *u.* was ceased, Paul, Acts 20:1.

UPWARD, toward the higher, the top.
Fifteen cubits *u.* did, Gen. 7:20.
years old and *u.*, Ex. 38:26.
from shoulders and *u.*, I Sam. 9:2.
God, and look *u.*, Is. 8:21.

UR, (1) a city of Lower Mesopotamia, halfway between Babylon and the Persian Gulf and about six miles from the Euphrates River. (Gen. 11:28; Neh. 9:7). (2) Father of Eliphal, one of David's valiant men (I Chr. 11:35).

URBANE; a believer in Rome to whom Paul sends greetings (Rom. 16:9).

URGE, encourage, press.
And he *u.* him, and, Gen. 33:11.
when they *u.* him, II Kin. 2:17.

Pharisees began to *u.*, Luke 11:53.

URGENT, important, necessary.
Egyptians were *u.*, Ex. 12:33.
commandment was *u.*, Dan. 3:22.

URI, (1) son of Hur and father cf Bezaleel (Ex. 38:22), and (2) father of Geber, one of Solomon's officers (I Kin. 4:19), (3) a gatekeeper that had taken a strange wife in Babylon (Ezra 10:24).

URIAH, URIJAH, (1) a Hittite, husband of Bathsheba, soldier of David. David desired Bathsheba, and ordered Joab to place Uriah in a dangerous position in battle. Uriah was killed, and the Lord reproached David through Nathan (II Sam. 12:9, 10, 15; I Kin. 15:5). He is called Urias in Matt. 1:6. (2) A priest who built an altar for Ahaz and who heard Isaiah s prophecies (II Kin. 16: 10–16; Is. 8:2). (3) A prophet of Kir-jath-Jearim who was slain by King Jehoiakim for predicting judgments on Judah (Jer. 26:20–23). (4) Father of Meremoth (Ezra 8:33; Neh. 3:4, 21). (5) One who was with Ezra when the law was read (Neh. 8:4).

URIAS, *see* **URIAH.**

URIEL, (1) a Kohathite Levite, son of Uzziah (I Chr. 6:24), (2) Chief of the Kohathites who assisted in bringing the ark from Obed-edom (I Chr. 15:5), (3) the father of Maachah, wife of Reho-boam, and mother of Abijah (II Chr. 13:2).

URISAH, *see* **URIAH.**

URIM AND THUMMIM, small sacred objects, probably stones, which the high priest wore on his breastplate (Ex. 28: 30; Lev. 8:8). The method of use is un-certain, but we do know that they were used to ascertain divine will (Num. 27: 21; I Sam. 14:37–42; 28:6). The exact nature of these sacred objects is not known. When the question of guilt was raised, the answer came by Urim; if innocence was asked, the answer came by Thummim. It may be that they cast a light or were shaken from their con-tainers when the questions were asked. At the time of the exile they fell into disuse (Ezra 2:63; Neh. 7:65).

USE, activity, purpose, work or serv-ice.
in any other *u.*, Lev. 7:24.
the *u.* of bow, II Sam. 1:18.
for the master's *u.*, II Tim. 2:21.
by *u.* have their senses, Heb. 5:14.

USE, USED, to employ, handle, speak, work.

USURER, one who practices usury; that is, loaning money for interest. *See* **USURY.** Used only once in Ex. 22:25.

USURP, to seize or hold in possession.
woman to *u.* authority, I Tim. 2:12.

USURY, *see* **LOAN.**
not lend upon *u.* to, Deut. 23:19.
ye exact *u.*, every, Neh. 5:7.
not received *u.* or in-, Ezek. 18:8.
mine own with *u.*, Matt. 25:27.

UTHAI, (1) son of Ammihud (I Chr. 9:4), (2) one of the sons of Bigvai, who returned in the second caravan with Ezra (Ezra 8:14).

UTTER, to say, speak, proclaim.
u. a parable unto the, Ezek. 24:3.
I will *u.* things which, Matt. 13:35.
hard to be *u.*, Heb. 5:11.

UTTERANCE, speech.
Spirit gave them *u.*, Acts 2:4.
in *u.* and knowledge, II Cor. 8:7.
that *u.* may be given, Eph. 6:19.
us a door of *u.*, Col. 4:3.

UTTERLY, entirely, surely, fully.
O forsake me not *u.*, Ps. 119:8.
I will *u.* forget, Jer. 23:39.
I will *u.* destroy, Jer. 25:9.
shall *u.* perish, II Pet. 2:12.

UTTERMOST, extremity, farthest, last.
paid *u.* farthing, Matt. 5:26.
know *u.* of matter, Acts 24:22.
wrath to *u.*, I Thess. 2:16.
to save to *u.*, Heb. 7:25.

UZ, HUZ, (1) son of Aram and a grand-son of Shem (Gen. 10:23), (2) a son of Nahor, by Milcah (Gen. 22:21), (3) a son of Dishan, and a grandson of Seir (Gen. 36:28) and (4) the land where Job did live (Job 1:1). Its location is not certain although Jeremiah lists it with

Egypt, Philistia, Edom, and Moab (in Jer. 25:20) and that the Edomites inhabited a portion of it (Lam. 4:21).

UZAI, the father of Palal, one of those who assisted in rebuilding the walls of Jerusalem (Neh. 3:25).

UZAL, the sixth of the sons of Joktan, a descendant of Shem (Gen. 10:27; I Chr. 1:21).

UZZA, UZZAH, (1) a son of Abinadab who died for touching the ark (II Sam. 6:3), (2) owner of a garden where Manasseh and Amon, kings of Judah, were buried (II Kin. 21:18), (3) son of Shimei, a Merarite (I Chr. 6:29), (4) a Benjamite, brother of Alihud (I Chr. 8:7), (5) ancestor of a family of the Nethinim that returned with Zerubbabel (Ezra 2:49).

UZZEN-SHERAH, UZZEN-SHER-RAH, a city in Ephraim, near the two Beth-horons (I Chr. 7:24).

UZZI, (1) a son of Bukki and a descendant of Aaron (I Chr. 6:5), (2) grandson of Issachar, and father of Izrahiah (I Chr. 7:2), (3) son of Bela, tribe of Benjamin (I Chr. 7:7), (4) father of Elah, a Benjamite, whose descendants dwelt in Jerusalem after the exile (I Chr. 9:8), (5) an overseer of the Levites in Jerusalem (Neh. 11:22), and (6) a priest of the family of Jedaiah (Neh. 12:19).

UZZIA, an Asherite, one of David's valiant men (I Chr. 11:44).

UZZIAH, (1) the tenth king of Judah, sometimes known as Azariah. Uzziah became king at the age of sixteen (II Kin. 14:21). He waged war against the Edomites, and he penetrated even to the city of Elath at the head of the Gulf of Akaba (II Kin. 14:22). He also fought against the Arabs and the Philistines with success. He never deserted the worship of the true God, and he was influenced by Zechariah (II Chr. 26:5). He was stricken with leprosy because he determined to burn incense on the altar of God (Ex. 30:7, 8). (2) A Kohathite Levite, and ancestor of Samuel (I Chr. 6:24). (3) Father of Jehonathan (I Chr. 27:25). (4) Father of Athaiah, who lived in Jerusalem after the exile (Neh. 11:4). (5) One

of the priests who took a foreign wife in the days of Ezra (Ezra 10:21).

UZZIEL, (1) a son of Kohath, a Levite. (Ex. 6:18; I Chr. 6:2), (2) a Simeonite who smote the Amalekites at Mt. Seir and dwelt there (I Chr. 4:42), (3) a son of Bela, son of Benjamin (I Chr. 7:7), (4) a son of Heman, who was over the service of song under David (I Chr. 25:4), (5) a Levite who helped cleanse the temple in the days of Hezekiah (II Chr. 29:14), and (6) son of Hashaiah, a goldsmith who repaired part of the wall of Jerusalem (Neh. 3:8).

UZZIELITES, the family of Uzziel, son of Kohath (Num. 3:27; I Chr. 26:23).

V

VAGABOND, a wanderer (Gen. 4:12; Ps. 109:10). In Acts 19:13 the term denotes wandering Jewish exorcists.

VAHEB, (Num. 21:14) an unidentifiable place in the region of the Arnon.

VAIL, VEIL, (1) a covering for the face (Gen. 24:65; II Cor. 3:15); (2) a curtain in the tabernacle (Ex. 26:31; 40:3); (3) figuratively for ignorance and hardness of heart (II Cor. 3:14–15).

VAIN, ineffectual, idle.
not take name in *v.*, Ex. 20:7.
people imagine a *v.* thing, Ps. 2:1.
days of his *v.* life, Eccles. 6:12.
use not *v.* repetitions, Matt. 6:7.
became *v.* in their, Rom. 1:21.

VAJEZATHA, VAIZATHA, one of the ten sons of Haman (Esther 9:9).

VALE, a valley. *See* **VALLEY.**

VALIANT, brave, courageous.
a mighty *v.* man, I Sam. 16:18.
waxed *v.* in fight, Heb. 11:34.

VALLEY, a lowland, usually with an outlet, between hills or along rivers (Gen. 14:17; Hos. 1:5; Luke 3:5).

VALOUR, courage (Judg. 3:29; 6:12).

VALUE, (1) worth; (2) estimate worth of.

physicians of no *v.*, Job 13:4.
more *v.* than sparrows, Matt. 10:31.
of Israel did *v.*, Matt. 27:9.

VANIAH, a son of Bani (Ez. 10:36).

VANISH, disappear.
heavens shall *v.* away, Is. 51:6.
knowledge, it shall *v.*, I Cor. 13:8.
is ready to *v.* away, Heb. 8:13.

VANITY, emptiness, falseness.
they followed *v.* and, II Kin. 17:15.
v. of vanities, all is, Eccles. 1:2.
Gentiles walk in *v.*, Eph. 4:17.
swelling words of *v.*, II Pet. 2:18.

VAPOUR, mist or fog; cloud.
earth, *v.* of smoke, Acts 2:19.
it is even a *v.*, James 4:14.

VARIABLENESS, changeableness (James 1:17).

VARIANCE, dissension, discord (Matt. 10:35; Gal. 5:20).

VASHNI, name of Samuel's oldest son in I Chr. 6:28; elsewhere this son is called Joel (I Sam. 8:2; I Chr. 6:33).

VASHTI, the queen of the Persian king Xerxes whom he divorced (Esther 1:9).

VAUNT, to boast, exalt self (Judg. 7:2).

VEDAN, a place which traded with Tyre (Ezek. 27:19).

VEHEMENT, with great force, very ardent (Song 8:6; Luke 6:48; 23:10).

VEIL, *see* **VAIL.**

VENGEANCE, revenge, retribution.
to me belongeth *v.*, Deut. 32:35.
the *v.* of the Lord, Jer. 50:15.
v. is mine, I will, Rom. 12:19.
fire, taking *v.*, II Thess. 1:8.
suffering the *v.*, Jude 7.

VENISON, meat from hunted game (Gen. 25:28; 27:3).

VERILY, truly.
v. I say unto you, Matt. 5:18.
John *v.* baptized with, Acts 19:4.
in him *v.* is the love, I John 2:5.

VERITY, truth (Ps. 111:7; I Tim. 2:7).

VERMILION, a bright red pigment used in fresco painting on walls (Jer. 22:14; Ezek. 23:14) and idols.

VERSIONS, the Old Testament was written in Hebrew with a few Aramaic sections; the New Testament was written in Greek. Versions are translations of all or parts of the Bible into languages other than the originals. Most people study the Bible in their own tongue by means of translations.

1. **The Septuagint.** This, the oldest extant version, was the Greek translation of the Old Testament made at Alexandria for Greek-speaking Jews. Begun about 280 B.C. and finished before the Christian era, this version was widely used by early Christians. It is quoted in the New Testament, and is still used, in revision, in the Greek Catholic Church. The name means "seventy" and seems to refer to the traditional writing of the version by about seventy scholars from Jerusalem.

2. **Minor Greek Versions.** In the 2nd century A.D. Jews, dissatisfied with the Septuagint, produced three versions. Aquila put forth a very literal translation; Theodosius revised the Septuagint; and Symmachus' work was an improvement on both of these.

3. **The Targums.** These translations of parts of the Old Testament into the Aramaic of Palestine were made for Jews who no longer read Hebrew.

4. **The Syriac Versions.** The most famous of the several versions made for Christians of Syria was the Peshito (common), a work of the early Christian centuries.

5. **The Old Latin Versions,** used in Africa in the early Christian centuries, were based in the Old Testament on the Septuagint, not the Hebrew.

6. **The Vulgate.** This great version is a monument to the work of the scholar Jerome who translated the Bible from the original languages into Latin near the end of the fourth century A.D. The Council of Trent (1546) declared this the standard Roman Catholic Version.

7. **The Coptic (Egyptian) Versions** were made in three different dialects. The Coptic Old Testament was translated from the Greek Septuagint.

8. **The Ethiopic (Abyssinian) Versions**

were finished by the seventh century and appear in various dialects.

9. **The Gothic Version** was made in the fourth century by Ulfilas, a missionary to the Goths.

10. **Ancient Versions** of lesser importance are the Arabic, the Armenian, the Georgian, and the Slavonic.

The English Bible

1. **Early English Versions.** The first real English translation was the fourteenth century work of Wyclif which inspired and influenced later English versions. It was based on the Vulgate. Tyndale's Version, based on the original languages, brought death to its author in 1536 A.D. Other versions include Coverdale's Bible, the first complete printed English Bible (1535), the Geneva Bible (1560) and the Bishops' Bible (1568).

2. **The Rheims or Douay Version** is a Roman Catholic translation of the Vulgate. The New Testament was printed at Rheims (1582), the Old Testament at Douay (1609). Various revisions have appeared.

3. **The King James Version** is called by some the "Authorized Version," but it was never officially authorized by King James. Begun in 1604 and printed in 1611, this famous translation is a thorough revision of the Bishops' Bible. Its indebtedness to its forerunners is seen in the fact that about ninety percent of its New Testament is almost identical to the work of Tyndale.

4. **The Revised Version.** The nineteenth century saw need to revise the King James Version to eliminate obsolete words and to take advantage of numerous Biblical manuscripts found which were older than and superior to those previously used. The New Testament appeared in 1881, the Old Testament in 1885.

5. **The American Standard Version** (abbreviated ASV). The Revised Version was re-edited by the Americans to incorporate the readings recommended by the American Advisory Committee.

6. **The Revised Standard Version** (abbreviated RSV), made for the purpose of bringing the English Bible closer to modern language usage, was completed in 1952, and has grown more popular each year.

7. **Modern Speech Versions.** Since the discovery that New Testament Greek was the common Greek of everyday speech, many have tried to render the New Testament into everyday English. Notable among such efforts are the works of Weymouth, Moffatt, Goodspeed and, more recently, Phillips.

8. **A Jewish Version** of the Old Testament according to the Masoretic text was published in 1916.

VESSEL, (1) utensil, dish.
I am like a broken *v.*, Ps. 31:12.
v. was marred, Jer. 18:4.
power to make one *v.*, Rom. 9:21.
possess *v.* in honor, I Thess. 4:4.
wife as weaker *v.*, I Pet. 3:7.

VESTURE, garments, clothing.
cast lots upon my *v.*, Ps. 22:18.
as *v.* fold them, Heb. 1:12.
a *v.* dipped in blood, Rev. 19:13.

VEX, disturb, provoke.
how long will ye *v.*?, Job 19:2.
Herod shall *v.* certain, Acts 12:1.

VEXATION, trouble, irritation, sorrow.
vanity and *v.* of, Eccles. 1:14.
howl for *v.* of spirit, Is. 65:14.

VIAL, small vessel for liquids, bowl.
took *v.* of oil, I Sam. 10:1.
pour out *v.* of wrath, Rev. 16:1.

VICTORY, triumph.
hath gotten him *v.*, Ps. 98:1.
swallow death in *v.*, Is. 25:8.
grave, where is *v.*?, I Cor. 15:55.
this is the *v.*, even, I John 5:4.
v. over the beast, Rev. 15:2.

VICTUALS, food.
bring *v.* on Sabbath, Neh. 10:31.
into villages to buy *v.*, Luke 9:12.

VIEW, see, inspect.
go *v.* the land, Josh. 2:1.
I *v.* walls of Jerusalem, Neh. 2:13.

VIGILANT, alert, watchful.
bishop must be *v.*, I Tim. 3:2.
be sober, be *v.*, I Pet. 5:8.

VILE, morally corrupt, base.
in whose eyes *v.* person, Ps. 15:4.
God gave them up to *v.*, Rom. 1:26.
change our *v.* body, Phil. 3:21.
poor man in *v.* raiment, James 2:2.

VILLAGE, a collection of houses less protected and less important than a Town or City (Ezek. 38:11; Luke 8:1).

VILLAINY, wickedness, folly.
vile speak *v.*, Is. 32:6.
v. in Israel, Jer. 29:23.

VINE, grapevines were cultivated from earliest times in Palestine, and their productivity was impressive (Num. 13:23). Figuratively, the vine symbolized the Israelite nation (Is. 5:7). Jesus applied the vine figure to himself (John 15:1–8).

VINEGAR, acidic, sour wine (Prov. 10: 26), sometimes artificially made.
Forbidden to Nazarites, Num. 6:3.
Bread eaten with *v.*, Ruth 2:14.
Offered to dying Jesus, Mark 15:36.

VINE OF SODOM, an unidentified plant bearing poor fruit (Deut. 32:32).

VINEYARD, cultivated plot of grapevines. The first is credited to Noah (Gen. 9:20). Vineyard preparation was the most costly and tedious type of husbandry, demanding: (1) hedging or fencing of the plot; (2) gathering of all large stones; (3) hewing of a rock wine press; and (4) building of a watchtower. Actual cultivation demanded repeated diggings and prunings of the choice vines (Is. 5:1–7). *See* **VINE**.
burnt up the *v.*, Judg. 15:5.
hire laborers into *v.*, Matt. 20:1.
who planteth a *v.*, I Cor. 9:7.

VINEYARDS, PLAIN OF THE, rendering for Abel-Cheramin in the King James Version.

VINTAGE, seasonal harvest of grapes.
v. of the wicked, Job 24:6.
the *v.* shall fail, Is. 32:10.
grapegleanings of the *v.*, Mic. 7:1.

VIOL, ancient guitar. *See* **PSALTERY**.
noise of thy *v.*, Is. 14:11.
melody of *v.*, Amos 5:23.

VIOLENCE, outrageous injury.
redeem soul from *v.*, Ps. 72:14.
I cried *v.* and spoil, Jer. 20:8.
kingdom suffereth *v.*, Matt. 11:12.
with *v.* shall Babylon, Rev. 18:21.

VIOLENT, vehement. fierce.

assemblies of *v.* men, Ps. 86:14.
v. take it by force, Matt. 11:12.

VIPER, poisonous snake (Job 20:16; Is. 30:6; 59:5). At Melita a deadly viper could not harm Paul (Acts 28:3–6). Jesus and John the Baptist used the term figuratively in denunciations (Matt. 3:7; 12:34; 23:33; Luke 3:7).

VIRGIN, a person, especially a woman, who has not had sexual intercourse.
v. shall conceive, Is. 7:14.
v. shall be with child, Matt. 1:23.
you as chaste *v.*, II Cor. 11:2.

VIRTUE, moral excellence, power.
if be any *v.*, think on, Phil. 4:8.
called us to *v.*, II Pet. 1:3.

VIRTUOUS, pure, chaste.
v. woman is crown, Prov. 12:4.
find a *v.* woman?, Prov. 31:10.

VISAGE, face, countenance.
his *v.* was marred more, Is. 52:14.
form of his *v.* changed, Dan. 3:19.

VISIBLE, apparent to sight (Col. 1:16).

VISION, a supernatural communication to the mind of a person. Through visions God directed his prophets (Is. 6; Ezek. 1; Dan. 7:2) and others (Gen. 46:2; Num. 12:6; 24:16). Some falsely claimed visions (Jer. 23:16). Paul had various visions (Acts 16:9; 26:19; II Cor. 12:1–4).

VISIT, avenge, requite; help. Also **Visiting, Visits**.
when I *v.* I will *v.*, Ex. 32:34.
v. on her the days, Hos. 2:13.
God at first did *v.*, Acts 15:14.
v. the fatherless, James 1:27.

VISITATION, inspection, special time.
in day of *v.*, Is. 10:3.
not the time of thy *v.*, Luke 19:44.
glorify in day of *v.*, I Pet. 2:12.

VOCATION, divine calling.
walk worthy of *v.*, Eph. 4:1.

VOICE, speech, sound, utterance.
v. of brother's blood, Gen. 4:10.
a still, small *v.*, I Kin. 19:12.
fool's *v.* is known, Eccles. 5:3.
v. of him that crieth, Is. 40:3.
a *v.* from heaven, Matt. 3:17.

came *v.* saying, Rise, Acts 10:13.
it is *v.* of a god, Acts 12:22.
v. then shook earth, Heb. 12:26.

VOID, empty, vain.
earth without form and *v.,* Gen. 1:2..
made *v.* thy law, Ps. 119:126.
word shall not return *v.,* Is. 55:11.
faith is made *v.,* Rom. 4:14.

VOLUME, scroll, book.
in *v.* of the book, Heb. 10:7.

VOLUNTARY, by free will or choice.
v. offering, Lev. 7:16.
in a *v.* humility, Col. 2:18.

VOLUNTARY OFFERING, *see* **OFFER-
ING AND SACRIFICE.**

VOMIT, eject from stomach, spew.
land *v.* out inhabitants, Lev. 18:25.
eaten shalt thou *v.* up, Prov. 23:8.

VOMIT, matter ejected from stomach.
dog returneth to *v.,* Prov. 26:11.
turned to his own *v.,* II Pet. 2:22.

VOPHSI, father of Nahbi, one of the ex-
plorers of Canaan (Num. 13:14).

VOTIVE OFFERING, *see* **OFFERING
AND SACRIFICE.**

VOW, a promise to God to act in a certain way, often conditioned on some return favor (Gen. 28:20–22; Judg. 11:30;
I Sam. 1:11). A Nazarite dedicated himself with a vow (Num. 6:1–21). Vows
were voluntarily undertaken, but still
regulated by laws which were: (1) once
made, vows were binding religious obligations (Deut. 23:21–3); (2) a woman's
vow could be voided by husband or father (Num. 30:3–16); (3) the firstborn,
already devoted, could not be vowed
(Lev. 27:26); (4) redemption was possible in some cases (Lev. 27).
when thou vowest a *v.,* Eccles. 5:4.
better not to *v.,* Eccles. 5:5.
Paul had a *v.,* Acts 18:18.

VOYAGE, a journey by water.
this *v.* will be, Acts 27:10.

VULGATE, *see* **VERSIONS.**

VULTURE, *see* **FALCON, KITE.**

W

WAG, to cause to move to and fro.
passeth by shall *w.* his, Jer. 18:16.
hiss and *w.* their head, Lam. 2:15.

WAGES, payment for labor or service.
The Mosaic Law required wages to be
paid every night (Lev. 19:13). In Jesus'
day the wage for a day's labor was equal
to about seventeen cents (Matt. 20:2).
what shall *w.* be, Gen. 29:15.
w. of hired not abide, Lev. 19:13.
hireling in his *w.,* Mal. 3:5.
content with your *w.,* Luke 3:14.
reapeth receiveth *w.,* John 4:36.
w. of sin is death, Rom. 6:23.
Balaam loved the *w.,* II Pet. 2:15.

WAGGING, *see* **WAG.**

WAGON, *see* **CART.**
w. out of Egypt, Gen. 45:19.
w. for two of the princes, Num. 7:3.
against thee with *w.,* Ezek. 23:24.

WAILING, lamentation.
decree came there was *w.,* Esther 4:3.
take up a *w.* for us, Jer. 9:18.
there shall be *w.,* Matt. 13:42.

WAIT, stay or remain.
if I *w.* the grave is, Job 17:13.
my soul *w.* upon God, Ps. 62:1.
I *w.* for the Lord, Ps. 130:5.
that *w.* upon the Lord, Is. 40:31.
w. for the kingdom, Mark 15:43.
w. for the promise, Acts 1:4.
w. for adoption, Rom. 8:23.
w. for his son, I Thess. 1:10.

WAKE, (1) to awake up or to stir up
(Is. 50:4; Zech. 4:1), (2) to be vigilant or
watchful (I Thess. 5:10).

WALK, advance by step.
Lord, before whom I *w.,* Gen. 24:40.
w. after other gods, Deut. 8:19.
w. in my statutes and, I Kin. 6:12.
w. through the valley, Ps. 23:4.
not *w.* in darkness but, John 8:12.
w. in newness of life, Rom. 6:4.
w. worthy of the vocation, Eph. 4:1.
w. in the light, I John 1:7.
nations *w.* in the light, Rev. 21:24.

WALKING, *see* **WALK.**
voice of Lord *w.* in garden, Gen. 3:8.
I see four men loose, *w.*, Dan. 3:25.
Jesus went to them *w.*, Matt. 14:25.
thy children *w.* in truth, II John 4.
w. after their own lusts, Jude 16.

WALL, defense.
fenced with high *w.*, Deut. 3:5.
make up this *w.*, Ezra 5:3.
I will be unto her a *w.*, Zech. 2:5.

WALLET, *see* **SCRIP.**

WALLOW, to roll about, tumble.
w. thyself in ashes, Jer. 6:26.
shall *w.* in his vomit, Jer. 48:26.
turn to *w.* in mire, II Pet. 2:22.

WANDER, stray, deviate.
while Israel *w.*, Josh. 14:10.
my sheep *w.*, Ezek. 34:6.
learn to be idle *w.*, I Tim. 5:13.

WANDERING, WILDERNESS OF THE,
see **WILDERNESS OF THE WAN-
DERING.**

WANT, behind, deficiency.
God caused me to *w.*, Gen. 20:13.
I shall not *w.*, Ps. 23:1.
die for *w.* of wisdom, Prov. 10:21.
ministereth to my *w.*, Phil. 2:25.

WANTON, to glance round, ogle, look
much (Is. 3:16).

WANTONNESS, lasciviousness.
chambering and *w.*, Rom. 13:13.

WAR, a conflict between armies. The
Israelites believed that God led their
armies, and they consulted with him
before they fought (Judg. 20:23; I Sam.
14:37; I Kin. 22:6). The heathen nations
did the same through divination (Ezek.
21:21). Wars were small in the early days
of Israel's history. Abraham fought with
318 men, and the Danites had about 600
men (Gen. 14:14; Judg. 18:11). The
faint-hearted were exempted from battle.
Those who had built a new house, but
not lived in it, planted a vineyard but not
enjoyed its fruit, betrothed a wife but not
married her (Deut. 20:2–9; II Chr. 20:14–
20), are exempted from battle. When the
battle began, a champion from each side
came out to fight (I Sam. 17). Then the
bugle was blown and the attack began

(Num. 10:9; Josh. 6:5; Judg. 7:20). After
the battle the victors pillaged the camp
of the enemy (Judg. 8:24–26; I Sam. 31:
9), and the prisoners were sometimes
killed (Josh. 8:23, 29; Judg. 1:6).
   The cities were attacked with battering-
rams, scaling-ladders, fire, and arrows.
The city defended itself by protecting its
water supply, and by throwing off the
attacks of the enemy by means of fire and
boulders (II Sam. 11:21, 24; II Chr. 26:
15). Victory was celebrated with song
and dance (Ex. 15:1–18; I Sam. 18:6).
before Lord to *w.*, Num. 32:20.
the *w.* of God, I Chr. 5:22.
w. was in his heart, Ps. 55:21.
grievousness of *w.*, Is. 21:15.
not *w.* after flesh, II Cor. 10:3.
was *w.* in heaven, Rev. 12:7.

WARFARE, engaged in war.
armies for *w.*, I Sam. 28:1.
weapons of our *w.*, II Cor. 10:4.
war a good *w.*, I Tim. 1:18.

WARM, to give heat to, to become warm.
flesh waxed *w.*, II Kin. 4:34.
thy garments are *w.*, Job 37:17.
Peter *w.* himself, Mark 14:67.
be *w.* and filled, James 2:16.

WARN, to give notice to, to admonish.
thy servant is *w.*, Ps. 19:11.
w. the wicked, Ezek. 3:19.
w. the unruly, I Thess. 5:14.

WARS OF THE LORD, BOOK OF, a
work of unknown authorship which
probably consisted of songs which celebrated the victories of Israel. It is quoted
in Num. 21:14ff and was probably written some time before the death of Moses.

WASH, to cleanse oneself
w. your feet and rest, Gen. 18:4..
let them *w.* the clothes, Ex. 19:10.
w. me from iniquity, Ps. 51:2.
w. away thy sins, Acts 22:16.

WASHINGS, *see* **BATH.**

WASTE, wild and uninhabited, desert.
meal shall not *w.*, I Kin. 17:14.
man dieth and *w.* away, Job 14:10.
why was this *w.*, Mark 14:4.
w. his substance, Luke 15:13.

WATCH, to guard.
morning *w.*, Ex. 14:24.

middle *w.*, Judg. 7:19.
ye have a *w.*, Matt. 27:65.
second *w.* or third, Luke 12:38.
w. and be sober, I Thess. 5:6.

WATER, due to its scarcity water was of special value in Palestine. There was heavy rain in the fall and light rain in the spring. During the rest of the year most of the streams dried up and the water supply was limited to those who had good wells. God's grace is described as a never-ending spring.
divide the *w.* from the *w.*, Gn. 1:6.
asked *w.*, she gave milk, Judg. 4:19.
he withholdeth the *w.*, Job 12:15.
leadeth beside still *w.*, Ps. 23:2.
fountain of loving *w.*, Jer. 2:13.
baptize you with *w.*, Matt. 3:11.
cup of cold *w.*, Matt. 10:42.
dip tip of finger in *w.*, Luke 16:24.
souls saved by *w.*, I Pet. 3:20.
w. of life freely, Rev. 22:17.

WATER OF SEPARATION, *see* **PURIFICATION.**

WATERPOT, a large earthenware vessel used to store water. The women filled these pots by carrying water in a jar from the village well (John 2:6–7).

WAVE, billow, breaker.
w. them for an offering, Ex. 29:24.
w. are gone over me, Ps. 42:7.
like a *w.* of the sea, James 1:6.

WAVE OFFERING, *see* **OFFERING AND SACRIFICE.**

WAVERING, unsettled.
hold faith without *w.*, Heb. 10:23.
ask in faith nothing *w.*, James 1:6.

WAX, increase, grow.
wrath shall *w.* hot, Ex. 22:24.
my heart is like *w.*, Ps. 22:14.

WAY, a road or journey, manner of life.
to lead them the *w.*, Ex. 13:21.
the *w.* of truth, Ps. 119:30.
where is the good *w.*, Jer. 6:16.
broad is the *w.*, Matt. 7:13.
stir about that *w.*, Acts 19:23.

WEAK, lacking physical strength.
I be *w.* as other men, Judg. 16:7.
O, Lord for I am *w.*, Ps. 6:2.

to the *w.* I became *w.*, I Cor. 9:22.
when *w.* then strong, II Cor. 12:10.

WEALTH, having many possessions, riches. In the Old Testament possession of wealth was regarded as an evidence of God's favor (Ps. 1:3). The New Testament does not condemn the possession of wealth but because of the great tendency to covetousness it is regarded as dangerous (I Tim. 6:9–10).
Jacob took all their *w.*, Gen. 34:29.
I will give riches, and *w.*, II Chr. 1:12.
this craft we have *w.*, Acts 19:25.
every man another's *w.*, I Cor. 10:24.

WEAPON, the offensive arms of a soldier.
wisdom better than *w.*, Eccles. 9:18.
turn back the *w.*, Jer. 21:4.
w. not carnal, II Cor. 10:4.

WEAR, to use up by wearing.
wilt surely *w.* away, Ex. 18:18.
that *w.* soft clothing, Matt. 11:8.

WEARINESS, the state of being weary.
much study is a *w.* of, Eccles. 12:12.
in *w.* and painfulness, II Cor. 11:27.

WEARY, lacking in strength, tired.
Rebekah said, I am *w.*, Gen. 27:46.
w. be at rest, Job 3:17.
lest he be *w.* of thee, Prov. 25:17.
not *w.* in well doing, Gal. 6:9.

WEASEL, an unclean animal listed in Lev. 11:29. The Hebrew word probably means mole.

WEATHER, condition of the atmosphere.
fair *w.* cometh out, Job 37:22.
fair *w.* for sky is red, Matt. 16:2.

WEAVING, the process of turning threads into fabric. The Israelites probably learned the art from the Egyptians while in bondage to them. For coarser materials such as tent cloth and cloaks camel hair and goat hair was used. The finer fabrics were made from wool and flax.
a binding of *w.* work, Ex. 28:32.
robe of the ephod *w.*, Ex. 39:22.

WEB, that woven.
pin of beam and *w.*, Judg. 16:14.
weave the spider's *w.*, Is. 59:5.

WEDDING, see **MARRIAGE.**
call them to a w., Matt. 22:3.
return from the w., Luke 12:36.
art bidden to a w., Luke 14:8.

WEDGE, a piece of wood or metal tapering to a thin edge.
a w. of gold, Josh. 7:21.

WEEK, a measure of time equal to seven days. See **HOLY WEEK.**
fulfill her w., Gen. 29:27.
fast twice in the w., Luke 18:12.
first day of the w., Acts 20:7.

WEEKS, FEAST OF, see **PENTECOST.**

WEEP, an expression of grief.
mourn and w. for Sarah, Gen. 23:2.
I might w. day and night, Jer. 9:1.
w. with them that w., Rom. 12:15.

WEEPING, to shed tears.
heard voice of my w., Ps. 6:8.
w. and gnashing of teeth, Matt. 8:12.
Jesus saw her w., John 11:33.

WEIGH, to estimate, balance.
Abraham w. silver, Gen. 23:16.
crown to w. a talent, I Chr. 20:2.
thou dost w. the path, Is. 26:7.
w. thirty pieces of silver, Zech. 11:12.

WEIGHT.
perfect and just w., Deut. 25:15.
lay aside every w., Heb. 12:1.
the w. of a talent, Rev. 16:21.

WELFARE, health or prosperity.
asked of their w., Gen. 43:27.
seeketh not the w., Jer. 38:4.

WELL, a shaft dug into the ground to reach water. The heat and the large flocks and herds made it necessary to have a supply of water (Judg. 1:15). The well involved among Eastern nations questions of property, of the highest importance, and sometimes gave rise to serious contention (Gen. 21: 30, 31).
To acquire wells which they had not themselves dug was one of the marks of favor foretold to the Hebrews on their entrance into Canaan (Deut. 6:11). To possess one is noticed as a mark of independence (Prov. 5:15), and to abstain from the use of wells belonging to others, a disclaimer of interference with their property (Num. 20:17, 19; 21:22).

Wells in Palestine were dug from the solid limestone rock, sometimes with steps to descend into them (Gen. 24:16). The brims were furnished with a curb or low wall of stone to avoid accidents (Gen. 29:2, 3). It was on a curb of this sort that Jesus sat when He conversed with the woman of Samaria (John 4:6), and it was this which the woman placed on the mouth of the well at Bahurim (II Sam. 17:19), which was at times dry.
The usual methods for raising water were: the rope and bucket, or water-skin (Gen. 24:14–20; John 4:11); or, shallow wells were furnished with steps leading to the water, which could be dipped directly with a pitcher (Gen. 24:16).
Wells are figuratives of: God as the source of salvation (Is. 12:3; Jer. 2:13; John 4:10); mouth of the righteous (Prov. 10:11); wisdom and understanding in a man (Prov. 16:22; 18:4); "drinking from one's own," domestic happiness (Prov. 5:15); "wells without water," of hypocrites (II Pet. 2:17).

WELL, whole, right.
if thou doest not w., Gen. 4:7.
it may be w. with me, Gen. 12:13.
it may go w. with thee, Deut. 4:40.
w. done, thou good and, Matt. 25:21.
thou hast w. said, Luke 20:39.
ye did run w. who did hinder, Gal. 5:7.

WENT, left, departed.
in the way I w., Gen. 35:3.
disciples w. back, John 6:66.
w. out from us, I John 2:19.

WEPT, the past tense of weep.
Hagar sat and w., Gen. 21:16.
man of God w., II Kin. 8:11.
Jesus w., John 11:35.

WET, damp, moist.
w. with showers, Job 24:8.
body w. with dew, Dan. 4:33.

WHALE, large seagoing mammals. The word translated whale in the Old Testament is at other times translated dragon, serpent or sea-monster. The "great fish" of Jonah 1:17 is called a whale in Matt.12:40.
created great w., Gen. 1:21.
am I a sea, or a w., Job 7:12.

WHEAT, the well-known cereal grain of our own day. Wheat of the bearded variety was widely grown in western

Palestine. Wheat harvest was from April to June and was considered as one of the seasons of the year (Ex. 34:22). The word corn in the King James Version refers to wheat or to one of the other grains of Palestine.
the w. and rye were, Ex. 9:32.
gather his w. into, Matt. 3:12.
Satan sift you as w., Luke 22:31.
except a grain of w. fall, John 12:24.

WHEEL, a circular body.
their chariot w., Ex. 14:25.
like a w., Ps. 83:13.
against thee with w., Ezek. 23:24.

WHET, to sharpen by rubbing.
I w. my sword, Deut. 32:41.
w. tongue like sword, Ps. 64:3.

WHIP, a lash.
chastised you with w., I Kin. 12:11.
a w. for a horse, Prov. 26:3.

WHIT, the smallest bit or particle.
told Samuel every w., I Sam. 3:18.
not a w. behind, II Cor. 11:5.

WHITE, of the color of pure snow.
made the w. appear, Gen. 30:37.
like coriander seed w., Ex. 16:31.
shall be as w. as snow, Is. 1:18.
raiment was w. as light, Matt. 17:2.
two in w. apparel, Acts 1:10.
a great w. throne, Rev. 20:11.

WHITED, made white.
like to w. sepulchres, Matt. 23:27.
thou w. wall, Acts 23:3.

WHITER, more white.
be w. than snow, Ps. 51:7.
Nazarites w. than milk, Lam. 4:7.

WHOLE, possessing soundness.
burn w. ram, Ex. 29:18.
w. duty of man, Eccles. 12:13.
hand was made w., Matt. 12:13.
w. armour of God, Eph. 6:11.
shall keep w. law, James 2:10.

WHOLESOME, pure, good.
a w. tongue is a tree, Prov. 15:4.
consent not to w. words, I Tim. 6:3.

WHORE, one who engages in illicit sexual relations, usually a female.
playing the w., Lev. 21:9.
hast played the w., Ezek. 16:28.

WICKED, sinful.
righteous with w., Gen. 18:23.
w. reserved to the day, Job 21:30.
w. will he destroy, Ps. 145:20.
w. hands have crucified, Acts 2:23.
fiery darts of w., Eph. 6:16.
w. be revealed, II Thess. 2:8.

WICKEDLY, contrary to law.
do not so w., Gen. 19:7.
God will not do w., Job 34:12.
wicked shall do w., Dan. 12:10.

WICKEDNESS, sinfulness.
inward full of w., Luke 11:39.
spiritual w. in heavenly places, Eph. 6:12.
world lieth in w., I John 5:19.

WIDE, broad, spacious.
the land was w., I Chr. 4:40.
open thy mouth w., Ps. 81:10.
w. is the gate that, Matt. 7:13.

WIDOW, in the Law of Moses special regard was paid to widows. No legal provision was made for their maintenance; but they were left dependent partly on the affection of relations, and more especially of the eldest son, whose birthright imposed such a duty upon him, and partly on the privileges accorded to other distressed classes, such as a participation in the triennial third tithe (Deut. 14:29; 26:12), in leasing (Deut. 24:19–20), and in religious feasts (Deut. 16:11, 14). God himself claimed a special interest in the widows, even calling himself their husband (Ps. 68:5; 146:9); and uttered the severest denunciations against such as defraud and oppress them (Ps. 94:6; Ezek. 22:7; Mal. 3:5). With regard to remarriage of widows, the Law had but one restriction and that had reference to the widow left childless, in which case the brother of the deceased husband had a right to marry the widow and raise up an heir (Deut. 25:5, 6; Matt. 22:23–30).

In the New Testament Church the widows were sustained at the public expense, the relief being daily administered (Acts 6:1–6). It was the duty of the Church to care for the widows (James 1:27). Specific directions are given by Paul as to the classes of widows entitled to support by the Church (I Tim. 5:3–16). The Christian widow could remarry "only in the Lord" (I Cor. 7:39).
I am a w. woman, II Sam. 14:5.

a *w.* be taken into, I Tim. 5:9.
w. in their affliction, James 1:27.

WIFE, *see* **MARRIAGE.**
not covet neighbour's *w.*, Ex. 20:17.
lie with neighbour's *w.*, Lev. 20:10.
whoso findeth a *w.*, Prov. 18:22.
render to the *w.*, I Cor. 7:3.
w. is bound as long as, I Cor. 7:39.
husband of one *w.*, I Tim. 3:2.
the bride, the Lamb's *w.*, Rev. 21:9.

WILDERNESS, (1) dry pasture land with
scanty grazing, (2) a dry, desolate, un-
fertile land, (3) cities and districts once
inhabited but now lying waste.
are entangled, the *w.*, Ex. 14:3.
waste howling *w.*, Deut. 32:10.
make the rivers a *w.*, Is. 50:2. .

WILDERNESS OF THE WANDERING,
that part of the Arabian desert in which
the children of Israel wandered for forty
years because of rebellion against God.
It is located in the peninsula of Sinai,
in the region between Egypt and Canaan.
died in this *w.*, Num. 14:2.
people through the *w.*, Ps. 136:16.

WILES, a trick or sly action, deceit.
the *w.* of the devil, Eph. 6:11.

WILFULLY, self-design or intentional
manner.
if we sin *w.* after, Heb. 10:26.

WILL, desire to do.
I *w.* be thou clean, Matt. 8:3.
not my *w.* but thine, Luke 22:42.
I *w.* return again, Acts 18:21.
power over his own *w.*, I Cor. 7:37.

WILLING, consenting.
if ye be *w.* ye shall, Is. 1:19.
the spirit is *w.* but, Matt. 26:41.
be first a *w.* mind, II Cor. 8:12.
not *w.* any perish, II Pet. 3:9.

WILLOW, a tree growing beside rivers
and streams. They are plentiful in Palestine and Babylon.
ye shall take *w.* of the, Lev. 23:40.
our harps upon the *w.*, Ps. 137:2.

WILLOWS, BROOK OF THE, a wady
located on the southern boundary of
Moab. It is mentioned by Isaiah (Is. 15:

7) and is generally known by the name
Wady-el-Aksa.

WILT, desire to do.
if thou *w.* thou canst, Matt. 8:2.
but as thou *w.*, Matt. 26:39.

WIMPLE, an old English word for hood
or veil which is found only in Is.
3:22.

WIN, obtain victory.
he that *w.* souls, Prov. 11:30.
that I might *w.* Christ, Phil. 3:8.

WIND, movements of air which were designated by four points of the compass.
The direction of the wind had great bearing upon the welfare of Palestine: cool
air from the north, moist air from the
west, warm air from the south and dry
sand-filled air from the east.
made a *w.* to pass, Gen. 8:1.
in the day of his east *w.*, Is. 27:8.
w. bloweth where it willeth, John 3:8.
about with every *w.*, Eph. 4:14.
shaken of a mighty *w.*, Rev. 6:13.

WINDOW, in Palestinian houses consisted of an opening high in the wall
which was covered by lattice work. They
usually opened into the inner court of the
house.
a *w.* shalt thou make, Gen. 6:16.
down through a *w.*, Josh. 2:15.
as doves to their *w.*, Is. 60:8.
through *w.* let down, II Cor. 11:33.

WINE, *see* **STRONG DRINK.**
eyes red with *w.*, Gen. 49:12.
w. is a mocker, Prov. 20:1.
not given to *w.*, I Tim. 3:3.
w. of his wrath, Rev. 16:19.

WINEPRESS, a mechanism used for ex-
tracting the juice from grapes. It consisted of two rock-hewn troughs at different levels with a connecting channel.
fullness of the *w.*, Num. 18:27.
digged a *w.* in it, Matt. 21:33.

WINGS.
bare you on eagles' *w.*, Ex. 19:4.
had *w.* like a dove, Ps. 55:6.
chickens under her *w.*, Matt. 23:37.

WINK, WINKED.
do thy eyes *w.* at, Job 15:12.
ignorance God *w.* at, Acts 17:30.

WINNOW, WINNOWING, WINNOW-ETH, *see* **THRESHING.**

WINTER, (1) In Palestine winter is a season of rain lasting from November to May. The Hebrew word means "to overflow." The lowest temperature is about 40. (2) A verb meaning to pass the winter.
flight be not in *w.*, Matt. 24:20.
abide and *w.* with you, Acts 27:12.

WIPE, WIPED, WIPING, to cleanse or to remove by rubbing over the surface.
I will *w.* Jerusalem, II Kin. 21:13.
began to *w.* them, John 13:5.

WISDOM, the ability to judge rightly. The wisdom literature takes up one part of the writings of the Old Testament. The law gave men the commandments of Jehovah; prophecy called for right conduct in view of the covenant with Jehovah; wisdom commented upon the reality of things by means of observation and reflection. However, this wisdom is seen as being from God, and the first rule of wisdom is to fear God (Ps. 111:10; Prov. 9:10; Eccles. 12:13). The book of Job wrestles with the problem of suffering. Ecclesiastes asks its readers to hold on to their faith in God and keep His commandments. The wisdom of Israel became one of the noblest expressions of their faith, and is one of the preparations for the revelation of God through Christ, who is the incarnation of the wisdom of God (I Cor. 1:24). The wisdom of which Paul spoke in the epistle to the Corinthians was the wisdom of the Greeks. He contrasted this wisdom with the foolishness of preaching (I Cor. 1:21).
w. is principal, Prov. 4:7.
in much *w.* is, Eccles. 1:18.
w. is justified, Matt. 11:19.
not with *w.* of, I Cor. 1:17.
be filled with *w.*, Col. 1:9.
if any lack *w.*, James 1:5.

WISDOM OF SOLOMON, a book of the Apocrypha which contrasts divine wisdom with the wisdom of the world setting forth the advantages of divine wisdom as they are revealed in the history of Israel. The book was probably written by an Egyptian Jew between 120 B.C. and 80 B.C.

WISE, guided by wisdom.

desired to make one *w.*, Gen. 3:6.
given thee *w.* heart, I Kin. 3:12.
making *w.* the simple, Ps. 19:7.
to God only *w.*, Rom. 16:27.
w. unto Salvation, II Tim. 3:15.

WISELY, prudently.
behaved himself *w.*, I Sam. 18:5.
handleth matter *w.*, Prov. 16:20.
he had done *w.*, Luke 16:8.

WISER.
for Solomon was *w.*, I Kin. 4:31.
foolishness of God *w.*, I Cor. 1:25.

WISH, WISHED, WISHING, desire.
Jonah *w.* to die, Jonah 4:8.
cast anchors and *w.*, Acts 27:29.
I could *w.* myself, Rom. 9:3.

WIT, to know, knowledge.
at their *w.* end, Ps. 107:27.

WITCH, *see* **MAGIC.**
not suffer a *w.* to live, Ex. 22:18.
not be among you a *w.*, Deut. 18:10.

WITCHCRAFT, *see* **MAGIC.**
as the sin of *w.*, I Sam. 15:23.
long as Jezebel's *w.*, II Kin. 9:22.
works of the flesh, *w.*, Gal. 5:20.

WITHDRAW, retract.
God not *w.* his anger, Job 9:13.
w. yourselves from, II Thess. 3:6.

WITHER, WITHERED, WITHERETH, to dry up.
leaf also shall not *w.*, Ps. 1:3.
which had his hand *w.*, Matt. 12:10.
had no roots, *w.*, Matt. 13:6.

WITHHOLD, to hold back, to refrain.
w. not good from them, Prov. 3:27.
you know what *w.*, II Thess. 2:6.

WITHIN, on the inside.
none of men was *w.*, Gen. 39:11.
law *w.* my heart, Ps. 40:8.
kingdom *w.* you, Luke 17:21.

WITHOUT, on the outside.
wisdom crieth *w.*, Prov. 1:20.
multitudes were praying *w.*, Luke 1:10.
no hope, *w.* God, Eph. 2:12.
w. father, *w.* mother, Heb. 7:3.

WITHSTAND, to stand against, to oppose.
went out to *w.* Balaam, Num. 22:32.

that I could *w.* God, Acts 11:17.

WITNESS, (1) a monument or object which serves as a reminder of an event, such as a covenant. A memorial of stone witnessed the covenant between Jacob and Laban (Gen. 31:44–52) and between Joshua and Israel (Josh. 24:27).

(2) A person who testifies for another person, such as in legal cases (Jer. 32:10; Ruth 4:9). In criminal cases the testimony of two witnesses had to agree. False witnessing was punishable by the same penalty as the accused would have received. In death penalties the witnesses had to cast the first stones (Deut. 17:6; Lev. 5:1; I Kin. 21:10).

(3) One who testifies for Christ (Luke 24:48; Heb. 12:1), one who remains steadfast in face of death; a martyr (Acts 22:20; Rev. 2:13). *See* **FALSE WITNESS.**

not bear false *w.*, Ex. 20:16.
my *w.* is in heaven, Job 16:19.
bear *w.* of the light, John 1:7.
conscience beareth *w.*, Rom. 2:15.
Spirit beareth *w.*, Rom. 8:16.
beheaded for *w.*, Rev. 20:4.

WITTY, one who possesses wit.
knowledge of *w.*, Prov. 8:12.

WIVES, plural of wife. *See* **MARRIAGE.**
Solomon had 700 *w.*, I Kin. 11:3.
w. give husbands honour, Esther 1:20.
w. submit to husbands, Eph. 5:22.
conversation of *w.*, I Pet. 3:1.

WIZARD, a person claiming to have contact with familiar spirits. The Jews were forbidden to consult them.
a *w.* shall surely be, Lev. 20:27.
Saul put *w.* out, I Sam. 28:3.
Seek unto *w.* that, Is. 8:19.
to idols and *w.*, Is. 19:3.

WOE, WOEFUL, miserable.
w. to thee, Moab, Num. 21:29.
desired the *w.* day, Jer. 17:16.

WOLF, a carnivorous animal, ferocious and wild (Is. 11:6; Hab. 1:8). It seeks its prey in the evening (Zeph. 3:3). Benjamin was compared to a wolf (Gen. 49:9, 27). Violent princes (Ezek. 22:27), false teachers (Matt. 7:15; Acts 22:29), and enemies of the flock of God (Matt. 10:16) were

compared to wolves in an unfavorable way.

WOMAN, the translation of several words for female or wife. The younger women tended the sheep (Gen. 29:6), worked in the harvest (Ruth 2:3, 8), brought in water (Gen. 24:13), ground the grain (Matt. 24:41), prepared the meals (Gen. 18:6), made clothing (I Sam. 2:19), and taught her children truths of religion (Prov. 1:8). She was exalted more highly among the people of Israel than in surrounding nations. She is exalted in the books of Ruth, Esther, and Songs of Solomon. She is praised in Prov. 31:10–31. Christ also ennobled woman in his attitude toward his mother, the sisters at Bethany, and the woman at the well (Luke 10:38–42; John 4:7–30; 19:25–27). Paul encouraged women to remain silent in the church, but he also said that in Christ there is neither male nor female (I Cor. 14:34; Gal. 3:28).
shall be called *w.*, Gen. 2:23.
virtuous *w.* crown, Prov. 12:4.
every wise *w.*, Prov. 14:1.
w. is the glory, I Cor. 11:7.
suffer not *w.*, I Tim. 2:12.

WOMB, the uterus of a woman.
sons in my *w.*, Ruth 1:11.
Lord called me from *w.*, Is. 49:1.
conceive in thy *w.*, Luke 1:31.
blessed *w.* never bare, Luke 23:29.

WOMEN, *see* **WOMAN.**

WONDER, miracle.
the prophets shall *w.*, Jer. 4:9.
signs and *w.* were, Acts 2:43.
appeared great *w.*, Rev. 12:1.

WONDERFUL, marvelous.
things too *w.* for me, Job 42:3.
called *W.* Counsellor, Is. 9:6.

WONDERFULLY, amazingly.
for I am *w.* made, Ps. 139:14.
shall destroy *w.*, Dan. 8:24.

WONDROUS, wonderful or marvelous.
God who doeth *w.*, Ps. 72:18.
had done *w.* works, Ps. 106:22.
according to his *w.*, Jer. 21:2.

WONDROUSLY, *see* **WONDERFULLY.**
angel did *w.*, Judg. 13:19.

Lord hath dealt *w.*, Joel 2:26.

WOOD, hard, fibrous part of a tree.
Abraham took *w.*, Gen. 22:6.
make ark of *w.*, Deut. 10:1.
w. of their image, Is. 45:20.
broken the yokes of *w.*, Jer. 28:13.
vessels of gold, *w.*, II Tim. 2:20.

WOOL, the fleece of animals, especially
sheep. Wool was a valuable article of
commerce (Ezek. 27:18). Undyed wool
was the symbol of dazzling whiteness
(Ps. 147:16; Is. 1:18; Rev. 1:14). Wool
was a valuable clothing material. The art
of weaving hair was known to the
Hebrews at an early period (Ex. 26:7;
35:6); the sackcloth used by mourners
was of wool. John the Baptist's robe was
of camel's hair, a sort of wool (Matt.
3:4). The weaving of garments made of
wool mingled with linen was forbidden
by the Law of Moses (Lev. 19:19; Deut.
22:11). The occupation of Lydia was "a
seller of purple" (Acts 16:14), which was
used to dye wool.

WORD, language, revelation of God.
let me speak a *w.*, Gen. 44:18.
speak of thy *w.*, Ps. 119:172.
beginning was the *w.*, John 1:1.
the *w.* became flesh and, John 1:14.

WORK, labor.
six days thou shalt *w.*, Ex. 34:21.
the Lord will *w.* for us, I Sam. 14:6.
people had a mind to *w.*, Neh. 4:6.
woe to them that *w.* evil, Mic. 2:1.
I will *w.* a work in your days, Hab. 1:5.
they that *w.* wickedness, Mal. 3:15.
son, go *w.* today, Matt. 21:28.
that we might *w.* the works, John 6:28.
we know that all things *w.*, Rom. 8:28.
w. out your own salvation, Phil. 2:12..
not *w.*, neither eat, II Thess. 3:10.
destroy *w.* of devil, I John 3:8.
their *w.* do follow, Rev. 14:13.

WORKMAN, one who does work.
w. melteth image, Is. 40:19.
the *w.* made it, Hos. 8:6.
w. not ashamed, II Tim. 2:15.

WORLD, creation, universe.
foundations of *w.*, II Sam. 22:16.
chased out of the *w.*, Job 18:18.
the face of the *w.*, Job 37:12.
w. is the Lord's, Ps. 24:1.
formed the *w.*, Ps. 90:2.

devil sheweth him the *w.*, Matt. 4:8.
ye are the light of the *w.*, Matt. 5:14.
gain the whole *w.* and lose, Mark 8:36.
taketh away the sin of *w.*, John 1:29.
God so loved the *w.*, John 3:16.
I am the light of the *w.*, John 8:12.
if *w.* hate you, John 15:18.
not take them out of the *w.*, John 17:15
turned the *w.* upside down, Acts 17:6.
God judge the *w.*, Rom. 3:6.
received not spirit of *w.*, I Cor. 2:6..
God reconciling the *w.*, II Cor. 5:19.
unspotted from the *w.*, James 1:27.
love not the *w.*, I John 2:15.
overcometh the *w.*, I John 5:4.

WORLDLY, pertaining to the world.
ungodliness and *w.*, Titus 2:12.
had *w.* sanctuary, Heb. 9:1.

WORM, in the Bible these refer to the
larvae stage of insects. It is mentioned as
destroying grapes and the gourd vine
(Deut. 28:39; Jonah 4:7). They can breed
over night in manna (Ex. 16:20), it con-
sumes the corpse (Is. 14:11), and it can
kill even the living (Acts 12:23). It is used
to signify man's low and feeble condition
(Ps. 22:6; Is. 41:14).

WORMWOOD, a plant having very bitter juice (Deut. 29:18), with a very disagreeable taste (Jer. 9:15; 23:15). It was
used figuratively for sorrow (Deut. 29:
18), affliction (Lam. 3:15), and injustice
(Amos 5:7). In Rev. 8:11 the fallen star
is called Wormwood.

WORSE, evil or bad.
last error shall be *w.*, Matt. 27:64.
are we the *w.*, I Cor. 8:8.
wax *w.* and, II Tim. 3:13.

WORSHIP, honor and respect shown to
a person (Luke 14:10). It came to mean
respect shown to God. Man is forbidden
to worship anyone but God alone (Ex.
34:14; Matt. 4:10; Acts 10:25). Cain and
Abel offered their first fruits of their
works (Gen. 4:3, 4). At the time of Enos,
men began to call upon the "name of the
Lord" (Gen. 4:26). The Israelites worship in the Tabernacle and then in the
Temple, but every man worshipped with
his family (Deut. 6).
w. Lord in holy, Is. 27:13.
fall down and *w.*, Matt. 4:9.
ye ignorantly *w.*, Acts 17:23.
w. and served, Rom. 1:25.

angels of God w., Heb. 1:6.
w. him that made, Rev. 14:7.

WORSHIPPED, WORSHIPPER, *see*
WORSHIP.

WORTH, value.
money as it is w., Gen. 23:9.
thou w. 10,000 of us, II Sam. 18:3.
w. of it in money, I Kin. 21:2.

WORTHY, worth, value.
I am not w. of, Gen. 32:10.
no more w. to be, Luke 15:19.
ye walk w. of the, Eph. 4:1.
world was not w., Heb. 11:38.
w. to receive glory, Rev. 4:11.

WOULD, desired.
I w. it might be, Gen. 30:34.
they w. not come, Matt. 22:3.

WOUND, an injury.
my w. is incurable, Job 34:6.
what are these w., Zech. 13:6.
ye w. their weak, I Cor. 8:12.
deadly w. was healed, Rev. 13:3.

WRAP, to cover by winding or folding.
he can w. himself in it, Is. 28:20.
w. in swaddling clothes, Luke 2:7.

WRATH, violent anger.
provokedst the Lord to w., Deut. 9:7.
a fool's w., Prov. 12:16.
answer turneth away w., Prov. 15:1.
flee from w. to come, Matt. 3:7.
not sun go down upon w., Eph. 4:26.
provoke not children to w., Eph. 6:4.
deliver us from w., I Thess. 1:10.
slow to speak, slow to w., James 1:19.
nations drink wine of w., Rev. 14:8.

WRATHFUL, full of wrath.
let thy w. anger take, Ps. 69:24.
a w. man stirreth up, Prov. 15:18.

WREST, to turn or twist.
they w. my words, Ps. 56:5.
that are unstable w., II Pet. 3:16.

WRESTLE, the wrestling match was a
favorite game of the Greeks and Romans.
Christians were often punished by having
to wrestle with wild beasts. The word is
also used of the Christian's struggle
against sin.

w. a man with him, Gen. 32:24.
we w. not against flesh, Eph. 6:12.

WRETCHED, dejected, miserable.
w. man that I am, Rom. 7:24.
knowest not art w., Rev. 3:17.

WRINKLE, blemish.
not having spot or w., Eph. 5:27.

WRITE, inscribe.
w. on these tablets, Ex. 34:1.
w. in the great roll, Is. 8:1.
we w. none other, II Cor. 1:13.

WRITING, the Bible states that the
Hebrews knew how to write (Ex. 17:14;
24:4; Num. 33:2). The art is very ancient,
and was practiced in Babylonia centuries
before Abraham left the Ur of the
Chaldees. The ancient inscriptions of
Babylonia were impressed on soft clay,
and then baked. They also engraved on
stone and metal. In Egypt paper-like
sheets were made from papyrus reeds.
When the Hebrews began to write, they
adopted the form used around Palestine
for many centuries. The same system
was taken by the Greeks and then passed
on down to modern times. The Hebrew
alphabet has 22 letters, and these were all
consonants. It was not until centuries later that men added the vowels for an aid
to study and reading. One of the most
important discoveries in modern times
is that there was writing in the ancient
world. Not too many years ago there
were some who claimed that Moses could
not have written the first five books of the
Bible. Now this has been proved erroneous.

WRONG, violation of right.
Sarai said, My w., Gen. 16:5.
I cry out of w., Job 19:7.
Friend, I do no w., Matt. 20:13.
why w. one to another, Acts 7:24.
rather take w., I Cor. 6:7.
w. receive for the w., Col. 3:25.

WRONGFULLY, unjustly.
mine enemies w., Ps. 35:19.
oppressed stranger w., Ezek. 22:29.
suffering w., I Pet. 2:19.

WROTE, to write. *See* **WRITING.**
Moses w. words of Lord, Ex. 24:4.
Lord w. Ten Commandments, Ex. 34:28.
John w. and testified, John 21:24.

I w. unto you, I Cor. 5:9.
I w. to the church, III John 9.

WROTH, full of wrath, angry.
Cain was very w., Gen. 4:5.
be always w., Is. 57:16.
Lord was w., Matt. 18:34.

WROUGHT, to do, to make.
What hath God w., Num. 23:23.
works my hands had w., Eccles. 2:11.
she hath w. a good work, Matt. 26:10.
God w. special miracles, Acts 19:11.
which he w. in Christ, Eph. 1:20.
false prophet that w., Rev. 19:20.

WRUNG, squeezed by twisting.
blood shall be w. out, Lev. 1:15.
waters are w. out, Ps. 73:10.

WYCLIFFE'S BIBLE, see **VERSIONS.**

X

XERXES, see **AHASUERUS.**

Y

YAH, YAHWEH, see **GOD.**

YARN, the yarn of Egypt was most likely
linen. In I Kin. 10:28 and II Chr. 1:16
the Hebrew word thus rendered is
problematical and may be a proper
name.

YEA, yes.
let communication be y., Matt. 5:37.
y. y. and nay, nay, II Cor. 1:17.
y. I count all things, Phil. 3:8.

YEAR, 365 days, period of time. See
SABBATICAL YEAR.
for days and y., Gen. 1:14.
y. should teach, Job 32:7.
y. have no end, Ps. 102:27.
observe times and y., Gal. 4:10.
went in once a y., Heb. 9:7.
bound a thousand y., Rev. 20:2.

YEARN, long for. Also Yearned.
his bowels did y., Gen. 43:30.
for her bowels y. upon, I Kin. 3:26.

YESTERDAY, a day ago, past time.
thousand years as y., Ps. 90:4.
the same y., today, and, Heb. 13:8.

YIELD, (1) produce; (2) give over.
land shall y. increase, Ps. 67:6.
vineyard y. one bath, Is. 5:10.
neither y. members to, Rom. 6:13.

YOKE, (1) wooden bar or frame joining
two work animals, such as oxen, for
drawing a load, pulling a plow, etc.
(2) A pair thus joined (I Kin. 19:19).
(3) Figuratively: Burden or oppression.
shalt break his y., Gen. 27:40.
Saul took y. of oxen, I Sam. 11:7.
neck under the y., Jer. 27:8.
take my y. upon you, Matt. 11:29.
not entangled with y., Gal. 5:1.

YOKED, joined as with yoke (II Cor.
6:14).

YOKEFELLOW, sharer of yoke (Phil.
4:3).

YONDER, at a distance, beyond.
meet the Lord y., Num. 23:15.
I go and pray y., Matt. 26:36.

YOUNG, (1) not very old; (2) progeny.
beloved like y. hart, Song 2:9.
whose y. daughter had, Mark 7:25.
when y. thou girdest, John 21:18.
may teach y. women, Tit. 2:4.

YOUNGER, of fewer years.
elder serve y., Rom. 9:12.
ye y. submit, I Pet. 5:5.

YOURS, belonging to you.
all things are y., I Cor. 3:21.
my spirit and y., I Cor. 16:18.

YOUTH, state of being young.
not the sins of my y., Ps. 25:7.
O young man in y., Eccles. 11:9.
kept from y. up, Matt. 19:20.
no man despise thy y., I Tim. 4:12.

YOUTHFUL, not yet mature, young.
Flee also y. lusts, II Tim. 2:22.

Z

ZAANAIM, a "plain" or more accurately
"the oak by Zaanaim," probably a sacred tree. It marked the spot near which
Heber the Kenite was encamped when
Sisera took refuge in his tent (Judg. 4:11).

ZAANAN, a place named by Micah in his

address to the towns of the Shephelah (Mic. 1:11).

ZAANANIM, only in Josh. 19:33 and the margin of Judg. 4:11, and probably the same as Zaanaim.

ZAAVAN, the son of Ezer and a Horite chief (Gen. 36:27; I Chr. 1:42).

ZABAD, six men in the Old Testament have this name.
son of Nathan, I Chr. 2:31-37.
son of Tahath, I Chr. 7:21.
son of Shimeath, II Chr. 24:26.
three sons of Zattu, Ezra 10:27-43.

ZABBAI, (1) a son of Bedai, who divorced his Gentile wife (Ezra 10:28), (2) father of the Baruch who assisted in rebuilding the walls of Jerusalem (Neh. 3:20).

ZABBUD, son of Bigvai who returned from Babylon with Ezra (Ezra 8:14).

ZABDI, (1) son of Zerah of the tribe of Judah (Josh. 7:1, 17), (2) son of Shimhi the Benjamite (I Chr. 8:19), (3) the Shiphmite and custodian of David's wine cellars (I Chr. 27:27), (4) son of Asap and grandfather of Mattaniah (Neh. 11:17).

ZABDIEL, (1) the father of Jashobeam who was the commander of the first division of David's army (I Chr. 27:2), (2) song of Haggedolim who was overseer of some of the returning captives (Neh. 11:14).

ZABUD, son of Nathan (I Kin. 4:5), a priest and "king's friend" in the court of Solomon.

ZABULON, Greek form of Zebulum.
borders of Z. and, Matt. 4:13.
tribe of Z. were sealed, Rev. 7:8.

ZACCAI, seven hundred and sixty sons of Zaccai returned with Zerubbabel from Babylon (Ezra 2:9; Neh. 7:14).

ZACCHAEUS, a chief publican (tax-collector) at Jericho. He was short of stature and climbed up into a sycamore tree in order to see Jesus. Jesus ate with Zacchaeus and Zacchaeus made the vow

to give half of his goods to the poor (Luke 19:1-10).

ZACCHUR, ZACCUR, (1) father of Shammua the Reubenite spy (Num. 13:4), (2) son of Hamuel and father of Shimei (I Chr. 4:26), (3) son of Merari by Jaaziah, a Levite (I Chr. 24:27), (4) son of Asaph (I Chr. 25:2; Neh. 12:35), (5) son of Imri (Neh. 3:2), (6) a Levite who signed the covenant with Nehemiah (Neh. 10:12), (7) a Levite (Neh. 13:13).

ZACHARIAH, another form of Zechariah. He was the son of Jeroboam II, the last of the house of Jehu, and fourteenth king of Israel. He reigned only six months, being slain by Shallum (II Kin. 15:8-10).

ZACHARIAS, (1) son of Barachias who was slain between the altar and the temple (Matt. 23:35; Luke 11:51). He was probably the son of Jehoiada (II Chr. 24:20, 21), (2) a priest of the course of Abijah and father of John the Baptist (Luke 1:5ff).

ZACHER, a son of Jehiel, the father of Gibeon (I Chr. 8:31; 9:37).

ZADOK, son of Ahitub (II Sam. 8:17) of the house of Eleazar, the son of Aaron (I Chr. 24:3). Early in David's reign he became joint high priest with Abiathar. Zadok remained faithful to David during the revolt led by Absalom. After the death of Absalom, Zadok and Abiathar persuaded the elders of Judah to invite David to return (II Sam. 19:11). David had Zadok to anoint Solomon king over Israel. Solomon deposed Abiathar and Zadok was the sole occupant of the office of the high priest (II Sam. 2:26, 27). Zadok's duty was to minister before the tabernacle at Gibeon (I Chr. 16:39).
Z., the son of Ahia-, II Sam. 8:17.
Z., carry back the, II Sam. 15:29.
Z., the priest, and Be-, I Kin. 1:8.
Z. begat Ahimaaz, I Chr. 6:8.
Shallum, the son of Z., Ezra 7:2.
the sons of Z. that, Ezek. 44:15.

ZADOK, (1) father of Jerusha (II Kin. 15:33). (2) Son of Ahitub (I Chr. 6:12). (3) A courageous young warrior who came to David at Hebron (I Chr. 12:28). (4) Son of Baana (Neh. 3:4). (5) A priest, son of Immer (Neh. 3:29). (6) Person

448

who sealed the covenant with Nehemiah (Neh. 10:21). (7) Son of Meraioth (Neh. 11:11). (8) Scribe in charge of the treasuries of the Lord's house under Nehemiah (Neh. 13:13).

ZAHAM, son of Rehoboam by Abihail (II Chr. 11:19).

ZAIR, an Edomite city, east of the Dead Sea, mentioned in II Kin. 8:21.

ZALAPH, father of Hanun (Neh. 3:30).

ZALMON, warrior of David of the Benjamite family of Ahoah (II Sam. 23:28).

ZALMON, MOUNT, wooded hill near Ebal or Shechem in Samaria (Judg. 9:48).

ZALMONAH, thirty-fourth station of Israel in the wilderness (Num. 33:41, 42).

ZALMUNA, one of the two kings of Midian, defeated and slain by Gideon. (Judg. 8:5; Ps. 83:11).

ZAMZUMMIM, a tribe of the Rephaim, a nation of giants, mentioned only in Deut. 2:20.

ZANOAH, (1) town in the low country in the western area of Judah (Josh. 15:34; Neh. 3:13), (2) city in the eastern hill country of Judah, near Hebron (Josh. 15:34), and (3) one of the family of Caleb (I Chr. 4:18).

ZAPHENATH-PAANEAH, name given to Joseph by Pharaoh, meaning "sustenance of the land is the living one" (Gen. 41:45.)

ZAPHON, city in the Jordan Valley just east of the Sea of Galilee (Josh. 13:27).

ZARA, ZARAH, see ZERAH.

ZAREAH, see ZORAH.

ZAREATHITE, see ZORATHITE.

ZARED, see ZERED.

ZAREPHATH, SAREPTA, city of the Phoenicians where Elijah lodged with a widow (I Kin. 17:9), called Sarepta in Luke 4:26.

ZARETHAN, ZARETAN, ZARTANAH, ZARTHAN, ZEREDATHAH, the city mentioned in the Israelites, crossing of the Jordan River (Josh. 3:16; I Kin. 4:12).

ZARETH-SHAHAR, ZERETH-SHAHAR, city of Reuben, south of Heshbon (Josh. 13:19).

ZARHITES, descendants of Zerah, son of Judah (Num. 26:20). (2) the descendants of Zerah (Num. 26:13).

ZARTANAH, see ZARETHAN.

ZARTHAN, see ZEREDATHAH.

ZATTU, ZATHU, ZATTHU, one whose descendants returned with Zerubbabel (Ezra 2:8).

ZAVAN, see ZAAVAN.

ZAZA, son of Jonathan (I Chr. 2:33).

ZEAL, ardent and active interest.
he was z. for my, Num. 25:11.
z. of thine house hath, Ps. 69:9.
they have a z. of, Rom. 10:2.
concerning z., persecu-, Phil. 3:6.
a peculiar people, z., Titus 2:14.

ZEALOT, ZELOTES, means "zealous one." It is a name given to Simon the Canaanite (Luke 6:15; Acts 1:13). The Zealots were the party organized by Judas of Gamala in opposition to the census under Quirinius, in 6 A.D. They were intensely nationalistic.

ZEALOUS, ardent, fervent.
z. for his God, Num. 25:13.
all z. for the law, Acts 21:20.
people z. of good, Titus 2:14.
be z. therefore, and, Rev. 3:19.

ZEALOUSLY, ardently, with eagerness.
they z. affect you, Gal. 4:17.

ZEBADIAH, (1) a Benjamite, son of Beriah (I Chr. 8:15). (2) Another Benjamite (I Chr. 8:17). (3) Son of Jeroham who joined David at Ziklag (I Chr. 2:7). (4) Son of Meshelemiah (I Chr. 26:2). (5) Son of Asahel, brother of Joab (I Chr. 27:7). (6) Levite in the time of Jehoshaphat, who taught the law to the cities of Judah (II Chr. 17:8). (7) Son of Ishmael, prince of the house of Judah (II

Chr. 19:11). (8) Son of Michael (Ezra 8:8). (9) Priest of the sons of Immer (Ezra 10:20).

ZEBAH, one of the two kings of Midian, overthrown by Gideon. They were overtaken, defeated, and slain by Gideon (Judg. 8:5–21).

ZEBAIM, unknown place, native home of the sons of Pochereth (Ezra 2:57).

ZEBEDEE, mentioned only once in the Bible at Matt. 4:21 (Mark 1:19, 20) where he is in his fishing boat with his sons, James and John.

ZEBIDAH, see **ZEBUDAH.**

ZEBINA, son of Nebo who took a foreign wife (Ezra 10:43).

ZEBOIM, ZEBOIIM, (1) one of the five cities of the plain of Siddim, destroyed with Sodom and Gomorrah (Gen. 10:19). (2) Name of a valley, ravine, or gorge, east of Michmash (I Sam. 13:18).

ZEBUDAH, ZEBIDAH, wife of Josiah and mother of Eliakim (Jehoiakim), kings of Judah (II Kin. 23:36).

ZEBUL, officer of Abimelech and governor of Shechem (Judg. 9:28).

ZEBULONITES, members of the tribe of Zebulun (Num. 26:27; Judg. 12:11).

ZEBULUN, ZABULON, (1) tenth son of Jacob, and sixth son of Leah (Gen. 30:19, 20). (2) A place on the eastern border of the tribe of Asher (Josh. 19:27).

ZEBULUN, TRIBE OF, descended from Zebulun, and numbered 57,400 in the wilderness (Num. 1:31). Their territory in Canaan lay between the Sea of Galilee and the Mediterranean Sea, north of the land of Benjamin. Nazareth and Cana were in Zebulun. It included part of the shore of the Sea of Galilee where Jesus did so many miracles, which fulfilled Isaiah's prophecy (Is. 9:1, 2; Matt. 4:12–16).

ZEBULUNITE, ZEBULONITE, a member of the tribe of Zebulun (Num. 26:27; Judg. 12:11, 12).

ZECHARIAH, (1) a chief of the Reubenites at the time of the captivity by Tiglath-pileser (I Chr. 5:7). (2) Son of Meshelemiah, or Shelemiah (I Chr. 9:21). (3) One of the sons of Jehiel (I Chr. 9:37). (4) A Levite of the second order in the temple band as arranged by David (I Chr. 15:18; 16:5). (5) One of the priests who, with trumpets, accompanied the ark from the house of Obed-edom (I Chr. 15:24). (6) Son of Isshiah, or Jesiah, a Kohathite Levite (I Chr. 24:25). (7) Fourth son of Hosah (I Chr. 26:11). (8) The father of Iddo, who was chief of his tribe (I Chr. 27:21). (9) One of the princes of Judah (II Chr. 17:7). (10) The son of Benaiah and father of Jahaziel (II Chr. 20:14). (11) One of the sons of King Jehoshaphat (II Chr. 21:2). (12) Son of the high priest Jehoiada in the reign of Joash, king of Judah (II Chr. 24:20). (13) A prophet in the reign of Uzziah (II Chr. 26:5). (14) The father of Abijah, or Abi (II Chr. 29:1). (15) A Levite who, in the reign of Hezekiah, assisted in the purification of the temple (II Chr. 29:13). (16) A Kohathite Levite and an overseer of the temple (II Chr. 34:12). (17) One of the rulers of the temple in the reign of Josiah (II Chr. 35:8). (18) The leader of the sons of Pharosh (Ezra 8:3). (19) The leader of the twenty-eight sons of Bebai (Ezra 8:11). (20) One of the chiefs of the people who Ezra summoned in council at the river Ahava. (Neh. 8:4). (21) One of the family of Elam (Ezra 10:26). (22) One of the ancestors of Athaiah (Neh. 11:4). (23) The son of Shiloni and father of Joiarib (Neh. 11:5). (24) A priest and ancestor of Adaiah (Neh. 11:12). (25) The representative of the priestly family of Iddo in the days of Joiakim (Neh. 12:16). (26) One of the priests who blew with the trumpets at the dedication of the city wall by Ezra and Nehemiah (Neh. 12:35, 41). (27) The son of Jeberechiah (Is. 8:2). (28) The eleventh of the twelve minor prophets. Zechariah was of priestly descent, a son of Berechiah and grandson of Iddo (Zech. 1:1, 7).

ZECHARIAH, BOOK OF, one of the post-exilic books of the Minor Prophets. The prophet commenced his ministry two months after his contemporary Haggai, in 520. Their combined prophecies or preaching eventuated in the finished temple in the latter part of 516 B.C.

Zechariah's last dated prophecy was marked 518 B.C. He prophesied during the high priesthood of Joshua and the governorship of Zerubbabel. He is the author of the entire prophecy bearing his name. The main theme of the book is "Return unto me and I will return unto you." Chs. 1–6 deal with the Visions of the Night, chs. 7–8, with the question of fasting and chs. 9–14 with the future of the world powers and of God's kingdom. Zechariah serves to encourage the nation in its divinely appointed task.

ZECHER, a form of **Zechariah.**

ZEDAD, a city on the northern boundary of Palestine (Num. 34:8; Ezek. 47:15).

ZEDEKIAH, (1) son of Chanaanah and the spokesman of the 400 prophets when consulted by Ahab as to the result of his proposed expedition to Ramoth-gilead (I Kin. 22:11, 24). (2) The last king of Judah (II Kin. 24:18; 23:31; 25:7; II Chr. 36:11, 12). (3) The son of Hananiah (Jer. 36:12). (4) The son of Maaseiah and a false prophet among the captives in Babylon (Jer. 29:21–23). (5) One of the officials who sealed the renewed covenant (Neh. 10:1).

ZEEB, prince of Midian, always associated with **Oreb,** defeated and slain by Gideon in a wine press which later bore his name (Judg. 7:24; Ps. 83:11).

ZELAH, ZELA, city in Benjamin where Saul and his sons were buried (II Sam. 21:14).

ZELEK, an Ammonite warrior (I Chr. 11:39).

ZELOPHEHAD, grandson of Gilead (Num. 26:33). He died without sons. His daughters claimed the inheritance and a new law became effective (Num. 27:1–11).

ZELOTES, surname for Simon, one of the twelve apostles (Luke 6:15).

ZELZAH, a place named only once (I Sam. 10:2) as on the boundary of Benjamin, near Rachel's tomb.

ZEMARAIM, (1) city in North Benja-

min, near Bethel (Josh. 18:22). (2) A mountain in Ephraim (II Chr. 13:4).

ZEMARITE, tribe of Canaanites, location uncertain (Gen. 10:18; I Chr. 1:16).

ZEMIRA, ZEMIRAH, son of Becher, a Benjamite (I Chr. 7:8).

ZENAN, ZAANAN, city in Judah, east of Askelon (Josh. 15:37; Mic. 1:11).

ZENAS, a Christian lawyer of Crete mentioned in Titus 3:13 with Apollos.

ZEPHANIAH, (1) a Kohathite Levite, ancestor of Samuel and Heman (I Chr. 6:36). (2) The son of Maaseiah, and second priest in the reign of Zedekiah (Jer. 21:1; 29:25, 26). (3) Father of Josiah (Zech. 6:10) and of Hen, according to the reading of the received text of Zech. 6:14. (4) The prophet, son of Cushi, who prophesied in the days of King Josiah (Zeph. 1:1).

ZEPHANIAH, BOOK OF, the prophecy was received by Zephaniah during the reign of Josiah, prior to the great reformation of 621 B.C. This is affirmed by the low moral condition of the people (1:4–9; 3:1–3). The ancestry of the prophet is traced back four generations to Hizkiah (1:1). The purpose of the book is to warn the nation of approaching doom. The prophet deals with the coming invasion of Nebuchadnezzar as a figure of the day of the Lord (1:1–2:3). He utters predictions of Judgment on certain peoples (2:4–15), and outlines the sin of Jerusalem and the future salvation (3:1–20). The book is one of the Minor Prophets, and Zephaniah is the author of the entire prophecy.

ZEPHATH, see **HORMAH.**

ZEPHATHAH, the place where Asa defeated the Ethiopians (II Chr. 14: 10).

ZEPHI, ZEPHO, a son of Eliphaz, son of Esau (Gen. 36:11; I Chr. 1:36).

ZEPHON, the first of the seven sons of Gad (Num. 26:15).

ZEPHONITES, see **ZEPHON.**

ZER, one of the fortified cities in Naphtali (Josh. 19:35).

ZERAH, ZARAH, (1) son of Reuel (Gen. 36:17), (2) twin son with his brother Pharez of Judah and Tamar (Gen. 38:30; Matt. 1:3), (3) sons of Simeon (Gen. 46:10; I Chr. 4:24; Zohar), (4) a Levite (I Chr. 6:21, 41), (5) the Ethiopian king (II Chr. 14:9).

ZERAHIAH, (1) a priest of the line of Eleazar (I Chr. 6:6, 51; Ezra 7:4), (2) a head of a family, returned with Ezra (Ezra 8:4).

ZERED, ZARED, a valley separating Moab from Edom (Deut. 2:13; Num. 21:12).

ZEREDA, a town in Mount Ephraim given as the birthplace of Jeroboam, the son of Nebat (I Kin. 11:26).

ZEREDATHAH, place of Solomon's brass foundry (II Chr. 4:17).

ZERERATH, place mentioned in Judg. 7: 22, about the route of flight of the Midianites.

ZERESH, wife of Haman the Agagite who advised the hanging of Mordecai (Esther 5:10).

ZERETH, son of Ashur, the founder of Tekoa (I Chr. 4:7).

ZERI, *see* IZRI.

ZEROR, Benjamite ancestor of Kish (I Sam. 9:1).

ZERUAH, mother of Jeroboam, wife of Nebat (I Kin. 11:26).

ZERUBBABEL, the son of Shealtiel (Ezra 3:2) or Pedaiah, an uncle, who may have married his brother's wife when the brother died childless (I Chr. 3:19). A prince of Judah in the captivity, he was given the office of governor in Babylon. He led the first colony of captives back to Jerusalem, restored the altar on its old site, and restored the daily sacrifices (Ezra 3:1–3). He laid the foundation for the temple amid solemnity and pomp but allowed the Samaritans to hamper the building of the temple for sixteen years.

He was not without blame as he and others built costly houses for themselves (Hag. 1:2–4). Upon exhortation of Haggai and Zechariah, he revived the work, completed the temple, arranged the courses of the priests and Levites, and provided for their maintenance according to the institutions of David (Ezra 6: 18; Neh. 12:47).

ZERUIAH, daughter of Jesse (I Sam. 26: 6; II Sam. 2:13, 23:18).
Abishai . . . son of Z., I Sam. 26:6.
Joab, the son of Z., II Sam. 2:13 .
you, ye sons of Z.? II Sam. 16:10 .
son of Z. was chief, II Sam. 23:18.

ZETHAM, a Gershonite Levite, and keeper of temple treasury (I Chr. 23:8; 26: 22).

ZETHAN, son of Bilhan (I Chr. 7:10).

ZETHAR, chamberlain of the King of Persia (Esther 1:10).

ZIA, a Gadite of Bashan (I Chr. 5:13).

ZIBA, former servant of Saul who, by trickery, obtained one-half of Saul's estate (II Sam. 9:2–12; 16:1–3).

ZIBEON, father of Anah (Gen. 36:2), maybe same one of Gen. 36:20.

ZIBIA, a Benjamite son of Shaharaim (I Chr. 8:9).

ZIBIAH, wife of Ahaziah and mother of Jehoash (Joash) king of Judah (II Kin. 12:1; II Chr. 24:1).

ZICHRI, (1) son of Izhar, grandson of Levi (Ex. 6:21). (2) Benjamite of family of Shimhi (I Chr. 8:19). (3) Benjamite son of Shishak (I Chr. 8:23). (4) Benjamite son of Jeroham (I Chr. 8:27). (5) Levite, son of Asaph (I Chr. 9:15). (6) Descendant of Eliezer (I Chr. 26:25). (7) Father of Eliezer, the Reubenite (I Chr. 27:16). (8) Father of Amaziah (II Chr. 17:16). (9) Father of Elishaphat, who helped inaugurate Joash (II Chr. 23:1). (10) Ephraimite warrior that slew Ahaz the king (II Chr. 28:7). (11) Father of Joel (Neh. 11:9). (12) Priest of the sons of Abijah (Neh. 12:17).

ZIDDIM, fenced city of Naphtali (Josh. 19:35).

ZIDKIJAH, *see* **ZEDEKIAH.**

ZIDON, SIDON, the most influential city of ancient Phoenicia. It was located twenty-five miles north of Tyre. It had an excellent harbor, but its reputation was often relegated to a status lower than Tyre. Zidon was the northern limit to Zebulun and Asher (Gen. 49:13; Josh. 19:28; Judg. 1:31). The importance of this city can be seen in the fact that the name Zidonians was given to all the Phoenicians. In the time of David and Solomon, the Zidonians influenced the religious life of the Israelites (I Kin. 11: 5). Jezebel, the wife of king Ahab, was a daughter of the king of the Zidonians (I Kin. 16:31-33). The city of Zidon furnished cedar for the building of the temple (Ezra 3:7). People from Sidon heard Jesus preach (Matt. 15:21; Mark 3:8). Paul visited Sidon (Acts 27:3).

ZIDONIANS, SIDONIANS, inhabitants of Zidon.

ZIF, ZIV, early name of the second Hebrew month (I Kin. 6:1, 37).

ZIHA, (1) one of the Nethinim whose descendants returned from the captivity (Ezra 2:43), and (2) ruler of the Nethinim after the return (Neh. 11: 21).

ZIKLAG, city of the south of Judah, assigned to Simeon, where David heard of Saul's death (II Sam. 1:1; 4:10).

ZILLAH, one of Lamech's wives (Gen. 4:19, 22).

ZILLETHAI, *see* **ZILTHAI.**

ZILPAH, Leah's slave and servant, given to Jacob as a concubine; mother of Gad and Asher (Gen. 30:9-13; 37:2).

ZILTHAI, ZILLETHAI, (1) Benjamite son of Shimhi, (I Chr. 8:20). (2) Captain of Manasseh with David at Ziklag (I Chr. 12:20).

ZIMMAH, (1) son of Jahath (I Chr. 6:20). (2) Ancestor of Joah (II Chr. 29:12).

ZIMRAN, son of Abraham by Keturah (Gen. 25:2).

ZIMRI, (1) a Simeonite prince slain by Phinehas (Num. 25:14), (2) the fifth king of Israel (I Kin. 16:8-20), (3) a Judahite son of Zerah (I Chr. 2:6), (4) a Benjamite, descendant of King Saul (I Chr. 8:36; 9:42).

ZIN, deserted, wilderness area south of Judah. (Not the Wilderness of Sin.)
the wilderness of *Z.,* Num. 13:21.
the desert of *Z.,* Num. 20:1.
the wilderness of *Z.,* Deut. 32:51.
passed along to *Z.,* Josh. 15:3.

ZINA, *see* **ZIZAH.**

ZION, historically, Zion was the rock outcropping between two valleys in Jerusalem. Later, the term came to mean the entire western ridge of early Jerusalem, and still later, to Jerusalem, itself (Ps. 126:1). This area was originally inhabited by the Jebusites (II Sam. 5:7), later becoming the City of David. Here David constructed his palace, acquired the threshing floor of Araunah, there erected an altar, and there Solomon built his temple. Spiritually, the term applies to the City of David (I Chr. 11:5), to the Church of God (Is. 2:3; Heb. 11:10; 12:22), and to the Heavenly City (Heb. 12:22-24).
the stronghold of *Z.,* II Sam. 5:7.
ark .. out of *Z.,* I Kin. 8:1.
Judah, the mount *Z.,* Ps. 78:68.
out of *Z.* shall go, Is. 2:3.
I lay in *Z.* . . . stone, a, Is. 28:16.
are at ease in *Z.,* Amos 6:1.
go forth out of *Z.,* Mic. 4:2.

ZIOR, town in the mountain district of Judah (Josh. 15:54).

ZIPH, (1) town in south of Judah (Josh. 15:24), (2) town in the desert, near Hebron (I Sam. 23:14; II Chr. 11: 8). (3) Son of Jehaleleel (I Chr. 4: 16).

ZIPHAH, second son of Jehaleleel and brother of Ziph (I Chr. 4:16).

ZIPHIMS, *see* **ZIPHITES.**

ZIPHION, *see* **ZIPHON.**

ZIPHITES, ZIPHIMS, inhabitants of Ziph (I Sam. 23:19).

ZIPHRON, place in north Palestine (Num. 34:9).

ZIPPOR, father of Balak, king of Moab (Num. 22:2).

ZIPPORAH, daughter of Reuel or Jethro, wife of Moses and mother of Gershom and Eliezer (Ex. 2:21; 4:25). She circumcised Gershom (Ex. 4:24–26).

ZITHRI, SITHRI, son of Uzziel (Ex. 6:22).

ZIZ, pass in wilderness leading from the Dead Sea to Tekoa (II Chr. 20:16).

ZIZA, ZINA, (1) son of Shiphi (I Chr. 4:37). (2) Son of Rehoboam by Maachah (II Chr. 11:20).

ZIZAH, son of Shimei (I Chr. 23:11).

ZOAN, ancient city on the Nile, seven years younger than Hebron, famed as a storehouse for Egypt. Its destruction was foretold by Ezekiel (30:14).

ZOAR, small city on the edge of the Dead Sea, one of the cities of the plain, spared destruction as a place of escape for Lot and his family (Gen. 14:2; 19:22).

ZOBA, see ZOBAH.

ZOBAH, district of Northern Syria, near Hamath, with which Saul, David, and Solomon struggled (I Sam. 14:47).

ZOBEBAH, child of Coz (I Chr. 4:8).

ZOHAR, father of Ephron (Gen. 23:8). (2) Son of Simeon (I Chr. 4:24).

ZOHELETH, the stone where Adonijah slew oxen and sheep (I Kin. 1:9).

ZOHETH, son of Ishi (I Chr. 4:20).

ZOPHAH, an Asherite, son of Helem (I Chr. 7:35).

ZOPHAI, Kohathite Levite, son of Elkanah (I Chr. 6:26).

ZOPHAR, a Namathite friend of Job (Job 2:11).

ZOPHIM, one of the high places on Pisgah to which Balak brought Balaam that he might see Israel (Num. 23:14). (2) A city on Mount Ephraim, the birthplace of Samuel, generally called RAMA (I Sam. 1:1).

ZORAH, ZAREAH, ZOREAH, town in Judah given to Dan, the birthplace and burial place of Samson (Judg. 13:2; 16:31).

ZORATHITES, inhabitants of Zorah (I Chr. 4:1, 2).

ZORITES, descendants of Salma (I Chr. 2:54).

ZOROBABEL, see ZERUBBABEL.

ZUAR, father of Nethaneel of the tribe of Issachar (Num. 1:8; 10:15).

ZUPH, ZOPHAI, (1) Levite of Kohath, father of Tohu (I Sam. 1:1). (2) District northwest of Jerusalem through which Saul and his servant passed. Location uncertain (I Sam. 9:5).

ZUR, (1) father of Cozbi (Num. 25:15) and one of the princes of Midian slain by the Israelites (Num. 31:8). (2) Son of Jehiel, founder of Gibeon (I Chr. 8:30).

ZURIEL, chief of the Merarite Levites at the Exodus, son of Abihail (Num. 3:35).

ZURISHADAI, father of Shelumiel (Num. 1:6; 2:12; 7:36, 41; 10:19).

ZUZIM, see ZAMZUMMIM. Mentioned only in Gen. 14:5. An ancient people dwelling in Ham.